D1258448

A Review of the Events of 1966

The 1967 World Book Year Book

The Annual Supplement to The World Book Encyclopedia

Field Enterprises Educational Corporation, Publishers
Merchandise Mart Plaza, Chicago, Illinois 60654
Chicago • London • Rome • Stockholm • Sydney • Toronto

Staff

Printed in the United States of America
Library of Congress Catalog Card Number: 62-4818

Preface

Fine printing and binding have been the hallmark of the World Book family of publications for 50 years. This is no accident. For while we editors and artists have been pursuing the elusive goal of editorial excellence, our manufacturing department has been engaged in its own endless quest: the search for new and improved ways of producing books. As with our editorial program, many of the changes are visible only to the most experienced eye. But together, they result in the finest printing and binding that skilled craftsmanship and modern technology can provide.

This 1967 World Book Year Book represents a major step forward in our manufacturing methods. It is one of the first publications to be printed on our new multimillion dollar web offset presses. Our two printers have installed three of these fast new presses to meet the ever-increasing demand for our World Book products. Each stands three stories high, is 110 feet long, and 13 feet wide. Yet, as immense as these presses are, they are capable of printing in perfect registration the thousands of tiny dots–each only .00833 of an inch in diameter–that make up a single picture in this book.

One of World Book's new printing presses

The paper is supplied to the presses in large rolls, each five feet wide and containing six and one-half miles of paper. But the presses run so fast that even this vast supply of paper lasts for only 25 minutes once the presses have reached full speed. The paper wends its way through the presses at 1,000 feet per minute, between plates that print as many as five colors on each side of the paper, through dryers and slitters and folders, finally emerging as 64-page sections of The Year Book.

The actual printing is, of course, only one step in the production process. Two years of preparation were required before these new presses could be put into operation. Before that, a decision had to be made as to whether web offset printing could provide the quality we demand. Then, various types of equipment were examined, production techniques reviewed and new paper stocks and inks tested. Finally, after using 86,000 pounds of paper in press tests, the presses were ready to roll.

Was all the time, money, and effort worth it? We think so, and for your consideration we submit this volume. For instance, look at the brilliant details in Dr. Paul Peck's imaginative paintings of the organs and systems of the human body. Or examine the stunning photographs that accompany "They Speak to No Strangers," a report of a Year Book mission into Africa to study the mysterious Beja tribe. We think you will find this quality unsurpassed in the publishing field today. Thus, it is with pride that we present this exciting record of 1966 to our World Book family.

A.R.H.

Contents

A chronology of the most important events of 1966 will be found on pages 8 to 12. A preview of 1967 will be found on pages 629 and 630.

Contributors

Anderson, Joseph P., M.S.S.A., Ph.B., LL.D.; Exec. Director, National Association of Social Workers.
Social Organizations

Andrews, James H., B.A., M.A.; Research Associate, Institute of Government and Public Affairs.
STATE GOVERNMENT

Baker, John C.; Public Information Officer, Bureau of the Census.
CENSUS

Baron, Samuel H., B.S., M.A., Ph.D.; Chairman, Department of History, University of California, San Diego.
TRANS-VISION®

Berkwitt, George J., B.S.J.; Senior Editor, *Modern Industry*.
MANUFACTURING

Bhote, Keki R., B.E., M.S.; Author; Lecturer. INDIA; PAKISTAN

Bingham, June, B.A.; Writer.
Special Report

Bradley, Van Allen, B.J.; Literary Editor, *Chicago Daily News*.
LITERATURE

Brown, Kenneth; Journalist.
Western Europe

Bryan, Leslie A., Ph.D., LL.B.; Dir., Institute of Aviation, University of Illinois. AVIATION

Burnet, Alastair, B.A.; Editor, *The Economist*. GREAT BRITAIN

Cain, Charles C., III, A.B.; Automotive Editor, Associated Press.
AUTOMOBILE

Carruth, Hayden, A.B., M.A.; Poet.
LITERATURE (Poetry)

Carpenter, M. Scott, B.S.; C.D.R., U.S.N., NASA Astronaut.
Special Report

Conley, Clare, B.A.; Managing Editor, *Field & Stream*.
HUNTING AND FISHING

Cook, Robert C.; President, Population Reference Bureau, Inc.
POPULATION

Crankshaw, Edward; Writer and Correspondent on Soviet Affairs, *The Observer*, London. Special Report

Csida, June Bundy; Former Radio-TV Editor, *Billboard* Magazine.
RADIO; TELEVISION

Dale, Edwin L., Jr., B.A.; Reporter, *New York Times*, Washington Bureau.
INTERNATIONAL TRADE AND FINANCE

Darby, Edwin W., B.S.J.; Financial Editor, *Chicago Sun-Times*.
Business Articles

Dewald, William G., Ph.D.; Associate Professor of Economics, Ohio State University. Finance Articles

Donahoe, Miriam C., B.S., M.S.L.S.; Assistant Librarian, Headquarters Library, American Library Association. LIBRARY

Dumouchel, J. Robert; Director of Public Affairs, National Association of Housing and Redevelopment Officials, Washington, D.C.
CITY AND REGIONAL PLANNING; HOUSING

Dunaway, James O., B.S.; Eastern Editor, *Track and Field News;* Author, *The Sports Illustrated Book of Track and Field*. Sports Articles

Elsbree, John J., B.A.; Assistant Editor, *Chemical and Engineering News*.
DRUGS

Farr, David M. L., M.A., D.Phil.; Dean of Arts, Carleton University, Ottawa. CANADA

Feare, Thomas E., B.A.; Editorial Assistant, *Chemical and Engineering News*.
CHEMICAL INDUSTRY

Feather, Leonard G.; Author, *Encyclopedia of Jazz*. Music Articles

Feinberg, Harold, B.A., M.A., Ph.D.; Assoc. Prof., University of Ill. School of Medicine. BIOCHEMISTRY; BIOLOGY

Fenner, Frank E., B.S., Fellow of the Photographic Society of America.
PHOTOGRAPHY

Freeman, Leslie G., Jr., Ph.D.; Assistant Professor, Department of Anthropology, University of Chicago.
ANTHROPOLOGY; ARCHAEOLOGY

French, Charles E., B.S., A.M., Ph.D.; Professor, Department of Agricultural Economics, Purdue University. AGRICULTURE

Freudenheim, Milt, A.B.; National/Foreign News Editor, *Chicago Daily News*. Director, Chicago Daily News Foreign Service.
DISARMAMENT; UNITED NATIONS

Gassner, John, L.H.D.; Sterling Professor of Playwriting and Dramatic Literature, Yale Univ. THEATER

Gayn, Mark, B.A., B.S.; Chief, Asia Bureau, *Toronto Star*.
CHINA; FORMOSA; PHILIPPINES

Goy, Robert W., B.S., Ph.D.; Senior Scientist, Oregon Regional Primate Research Center. PSYCHOLOGY

Griffin, Alice, M.A., Ph.D.; Associate Professor of English, Hunter College. THEATER, AMATEUR

Hanson, Donald D., M.A. (Arch.); Chairman, Dept. of Architecture, Chicago Circle Campus, University of Illinois. ARCHITECTURE

Harris, Allen, A.B., LL.B.; Associate Director, Institute of Judicial Administration, New York University.
SUPREME COURT

Hasson, Rachelle Joy, B.A.; Fashion Editor, *California Apparel News*.
FASHION

Havighurst, Robert J., Ph.D.; Prof. of Education, University of Chicago; Author, *Older People*. OLD AGE

Hechinger, Fred M., B.A., LL.D.; Education Editor, *The New York Times*. EDUCATION

Higgins, Elizabeth, A.S.; Reference Librarian, Massachusetts Horticultural Society. GARDEN AND LAWN

Holmes, Jay E., B.A.; Special Staff, Office of Manned Space Flight, NASA. SPACE EXPLORATION

Izenberg, Jerry, B.A.; Syndicated Sports Columnist, *Newark Star Ledger*. Special Report

Jessup, M. E., A.B.; News Editor, *Civil Engineering*.
Engineering Articles

Johnson, Robert I., A.B.; Director, Kansas City Museum of History and Science. ASTRONOMY

Joseph, Lou, B.A.; Asst. Director, Bureau of Public Information, American Dental Association.
DENTISTRY

Klein, Fannie J., LL.B., LL.M.; Research Associate Professor of Judicial Administration, New York University. COURTS AND LAWS

Knight, Arthur, B.A.; Professor, University of So. California Cinema Department. MOTION PICTURES

Koczy, F. F., Ph.D.; Chairman, Division of Physical Sciences, University of Miami. OCEAN

Koenig, Louis W., Ph.D., L.H.D.; Professor of Government, New York University. CIVIL RIGHTS

Lach, Alma; Diplome de Corden Bleu; Author. FOOD

Lake, John E., B.A.; Sports Editor, *Newsweek* Magazine. SPORTS

Lewis, Ralph H., A.B., M.A.; Chief, Museum Branch, National Park Service. MUSEUMS

Lief, Donald W., A.B., M.A.; Managing Editor, *Nation's Cities*. City Articles

Lohman, Joseph D., B.A., M.A.; Dean, School of Criminology, University of California. CRIME

MacFarland, Douglas C., Ph.D.; Chief, Division of Services to the Blind, Dept. of Health, Education, and Welfare. BLINDNESS

Maki, John M., B.A., M.A., Ph.D.; Chairman, Program of Asian Studies, University of Massachusetts. JAPAN

Malia, Thomas M., Ph.B.; Executive Editor, *Telecommunications Reports*. COMMUNICATIONS

Manchester, P. W.; Managing Editor, *Dance News;* New York Dance Critic, *Christian Science Monitor*. DANCING

Marsh, Robert C., A.M., Ed.D.; Music Critic, *Chicago Sun-Times*. MUSIC

Marty, Martin E., B.D., S.T.M., Ph.D.; Associate Editor, *The Christian Century*. PROTESTANT

Maxon, John, M.A., Ph.D.; Associate Director, The Art Institute of Chicago. PAINTING AND SCULPTURE

McCaul, Eugene B.; Director, Statistical Department, American Transit Association. TRANSIT

McGaffin, William, A.B., B.S.; Washington Correspondent, *Chicago Daily News*. U.S. Government Articles

Mencher, Melvin, B.A.; Assoc. Professor, Graduate School of Journalism, Columbia University. PUBLISHING

Mendel, Arthur P., B.A., M.A., Ph.D.; Professor of History, University of Michigan. TRANS-VISION®

Morse, Walter F., B.A.; Assistant City Editor, *Chicago Sun-Times*. Biographies

Morton, Elizabeth H., B.A.; Executive Director, Canadian Library Association. CANADIAN LITERATURE

Mullen, Frances A., Ph.D.; Consultant on Education of the Handicapped, U.S. Office of Education. CHILD GUIDANCE; CHILD WELFARE

Murray, Thomas, J., B.A., M.A.; Senior Editor, *Dun's Review*. MINES AND MINING; STEEL INDUSTRY

Newman, Andrew L., A.B., M.A.; Deputy Director of Information, U.S. Department of the Interior. Conservation Articles

Norman, Lloyd, B.S.; Military Affairs Correspondent, *Newsweek* Magazine. ARMED FORCES OF THE WORLD; ESPIONAGE; NATIONAL DEFENSE

O'Connor, James, J., E.E.; Executive Editor, *Power* Magazine. ELECTRIC POWER AND EQUIPMENT

O'Leary, Theodore M., A.B.; Special Correspondent, *Sports Illustrated* Magazine. HOBBIES; PETS

Patterson, William D., A.B.; Vice-President and Associate Publisher, *The Saturday Review*. TRAVEL

Pearre, James A., B.S.J.; Illinois Institute of Technology Research Institute News Supervisor. SCIENCE AND RESEARCH

Peck, Paul, B.S., M.A., Ph.D.; Medical Artist and Teacher. Special Report

Perkins, R. Marlin; Director, St. Louis Zoological Gardens. ZOOS AND AQUARIUMS

Pyle, Howard; President, National Safety Council. SAFETY

Rue, Eloise, M.A., B.A., in L.S.; Associate Professor of Library Science, University of Wisconsin, Milwaukee. LITERATURE FOR CHILDREN

Schaefle, Kenneth E., B.S., M.B.A.; Director, Management Programs Transportation Center at Northwestern University. TRANSPORTATION

Schmemann, The Rev. Alexander, S.T.D., LL.D.; Dean, St. Vladimir's Orthodox Theological Seminary. EASTERN ORTHODOX

Schubert, Helen C., B.S.; Administrative Director, The National Design Center. INTERIOR DESIGN

Shearer, Warren W., Ph.D.; Chairman, Department of Economics, Wabash College. Business Articles

Sheen, Fulton J., Ph.D., D.D., LL.D.; Bishop of the Rochester, N.Y., Diocese. ROMAN CATHOLIC

Silverman, David Wolf, Rabbi, M.A., M.H.L.; Director, Department of Special Education, Jewish Theological Seminary, N.Y. JEWS AND JUDAISM

Skilling, H. Gordon, B.A., M.A., Ph.D.; Professor of Political Science, University of Toronto. COMMUNISM; RUSSIA; East European Countries

Spencer, William, A.B., A.M., Ph.D.; Director, Institute of Non-Western Studies, The American University, Beirut. North Africa and Middle East Articles

Stalker, John N., B.A., M.A., Ph.D.; Director, Office for International Programs, University of Hawaii. ASIA; Asia Articles

Stern, James L., B.S., Ph.D.; Professor of Economics, University of Wisconsin. AUTOMATION; LABOR

Thomas, Benjamin E., M.A., M.S., Ph.D.; Professor of Geography, University of California. Africa Articles

Thompson, Carol L., A.B., M.A.; Editor, *Current History* Magazine. U.S. Government Articles

Treuting, Theodore F., B.S., M.D., F.A.C.P.; Professor of Medicine, Psychiatry, and Neurology, Tulane University School of Medicine. Health Articles

Ubell, Earl, B.S.; Science Editor, WCBS-TV News. Special Report

Uphaus, Robert A., B.S., M.S., Ph.D.; Chemist, Argonne National Laboratory. CHEMISTRY

Webster, Mary C., B.A.; Editor, *Noticias* Magazine. Latin America Articles

Weller, George, B.A.; Correspondent of *Chicago Daily News* for the Mediterranean, Africa, and the Middle East. Special Report

White, Ruth M., B.S. in Ed., B.S. in L.S., A.M.; Headquarters Librarian, American Library Assoc. AMERICAN LIBRARY ASSOCIATION

White, Thomas O., B.S., Ph.D.; Research Associate, Department of Physics, Northwestern University. PHYSICS

Chronology 1966

January

Sun	Mon	Tue	Wed	Thu	Fri	Sat
						1
2	3	4	5	6	7	8
9	10	11	12	13	14	15
16	17	18	19	20	21	22
23/30	24/31	25	26	27	28	29

1 **Central African Republic Revolt.** Army Chief of Staff Col. Jean-Bedel Bokassa deposes President David Dacko.

3 **Chile Outlaws Siesta** for government workers. Traditional two-hour lunch-nap break to end in business and industry later in 1966.

4 **Upper Volta Revolt.** Army Chief of Staff Lieut. Col. Sangoulé Lamizana deposes President Maurice Yameogo.

8 **France Inaugurates President.** Charles de Gaulle begins his second seven-year term.

10 **89th Congress of U.S. Opens** its second session in Washington, D.C.
Tashkent (Cease-Fire) Declaration on Kashmir Signed by India and Pakistan.

11 **Prime Minister of India Dies in Russia.** Lal Bahadur Shastri had signed the Kashmir cease-fire accord with Pakistan in Tashkent.

12 **President Johnson Delivers State of Union Message.** Pledges U.S. forces to stay in Vietnam until aggression is ended there.

13 **New York Transit Strike Ends.** City bus and subway service resumes after 12-day walkout.

15-17 **Revolt in Nigeria.** Army Commander Maj. Gen. Aguiyi-Ironsi takes power as chief of state.

18 **First U.S. Secretary of Housing and Urban Development.** Robert C. Weaver takes office as nation's first Negro Cabinet member.

24 **New Prime Minister in India.** Indira Nehru Gandhi takes office as successor to the late Lal Bahadur Shastri.

26 **New Prime Minister in Australia.** Harold E. Holt succeeds Sir Robert Menzies, retired.

31 **U.S. Resumes North Vietnam Air Raids** after 37-day world-wide peace offensive to end war.
Luna IX Launched to Moon by Russia.

February

Sun	Mon	Tue	Wed	Thu	Fri	Sat
		1	2	3	4	5
6	7	8	9	10	11	12
13	14	15	16	17	18	19
20	21	22	23	24	25	26
27	28					

3 **Luna IX Makes Soft Landing on Moon,** first in history.
ESSA I Launched at Cape Kennedy. First of TOS (Tiros Operational Satellite) system.

7-8 **Honolulu Conference.** President Johnson and Premier Nguyen Cao Ky outline U.S. and South Vietnamese political and military policies and social and economic programs.

10-23 **U.S. Peace Mission in Asia.** Vice-President Humphrey visits nine Asian Countries.

14 **Australia Institutes Decimal Monetary System.** Begins changeover from pound-shilling-pence system to dollars and cents.

17 **French Launch Diapason,** technical research satellite, at its Sahara base in Algeria.

21 **President De Gaulle Announces NATO Decision.** France to take control of all foreign military bases on its territory by April 4, 1969.

22 **Cosmos CX Launched with Two Dogs Aboard.** First spaceship to carry animals into Van Allen radiation belt.

22-24 **British Prime Minister in Moscow.** Harold Wilson confers with Russian Premier Aleksei N. Kosygin on Vietnam and other problems.

23-25 **Coup D'Etat in Syria.** Nur al-Din al-Atasi named Chief of State and Yusuf Zuayn as Premier.

24 **Ghanaian President Kwame Nkrumah Deposed** while in Asia on Vietnam peace mission. Maj. Gen. J. A. Ankrah heads National Liberation Council.

27 **Venus II Misses Planet Venus.** Russian satellite on space journey since Nov. 12, 1965.

28 **ESSA II Launched** at Cape Kennedy.

March

Sun	Mon	Tue	Wed	Thu	Fri	Sat
		1	2	3	4	5
6	7	8	9	10	11	12
13	14	15	16	17	18	19
20	21	22	23	24	25	26
27	28	29	30	31		

1 **Venus III Crashes on Planet Venus.** Russian spacecraft launched Nov. 16, 1965.
New U.S. Peace Corps Director. Jack Hood Vaughn succeeds R. Sargent Shriver.

10 **Netherlands Royal Wedding.** Crown Princess Beatrix and German commoner Claus von Amsberg married in West Church of Amsterdam. The former West German diplomat becomes Prince Claus of The Netherlands.
Buddhist Dismissed in South Vietnam from National Leadership Committee. Lieut. Gen. Nguyen Chanh Thi also relieved as commander of I Corps area in north.

11-12 **Indonesian Army Gives Sukarno Ultimatum** after days of anti-Communist demonstrations. Lieut. Gen. Suharto takes over government.

16 **Asian Bank Legislation Signed** by President Johnson. Authorizes U.S. participation.
Gemini VIII Flight. Civilian Neil A. Armstrong and Air Force Maj. David R. Scott make first docking in space.
Russian Space Dogs Return to Earth after 22 days aboard Cosmos CX.

19 **New Prime Minister in Belgium.** Paul Vanden Boeynants succeeds Pierre Harmel.

22 **Functions of Congo Parliament Abolished.** Joseph D. Mobutu assumes legislative powers.

23 **Anglican Primate at Vatican.** Archbishop of Canterbury Arthur Michael Ramsey visits Pope Paul VI, first official meeting of leaders of two churches since 1534.

28 **New President in Turkey.** Gen. Cevdet Sunay succeeds critically ill Gen. Cemal Gürsel.

28-29 **India's Prime Minister in Washington, D.C.** Indira Gandhi and President Johnson discuss India's food crisis and Asian peace.

29-30 **Military Junta Deposed in Ecuador.** Clemente Yerovi Indaburu is installed as interim president.

31 **British General Election.** Labour party wins majority of 97 seats in House of Commons. **Luna X Launched into Space** by Russia.

April

Sun	Mon	Tue	Wed	Thu	Fri	Sat
					1	2
3	4	5	6	7	8	9
10	11	12	13	14	15	16
17	18	19	20	21	22	23
24	25	26	27	28	29	30

5 **Canada Retains Death Penalty.** House of Commons rejects change in capital punishment law.

7 **U.S. Recovers Hydrogen Bomb,** lost off southeast coast of Spain for 13 weeks.

8 **OAO-I Launched** at Cape Kennedy, first Orbiting Astronomical Observatory.

9 **New Premier in Lebanon.** Abdullah Yafi completes new cabinet.

12 **Atlanta Opens $18,000,000 Civic Stadium.** The Braves, city's new National League baseball team, play the Pittsburgh Pirates.

14 **Elections in South Vietnam Promised** in three to five months by Premier Nguyen Cao Ky.

14-15 **President Johnson in Mexico City.** Unveils statue of Abraham Lincoln.

15 **Uganda Adopts New Constitution.** Prime Minister A. Milton Obote elected president.

16 **New York's Metropolitan Opera House Closes** with gala evening farewell, after 83 years. **New President in Iraq.** Maj. Gen. Abdul Rahman Arif succeeds his brother Abdul Salam Muhammad Arif, who was killed in a helicopter crash.

21 **British Parliament on Television** for first time as Queen Elizabeth II opens fourth Parliament of her reign.

22 **OV3-I Launched into Polar Orbit** at Vandenberg Air Force Base, California.

30 **Cultural Revolution in Communist China.** Premier Chou En-lai calls for struggle to wipe out bourgeois ideology.

May

Sun	Mon	Tue	Wed	Thu	Fri	Sat
1	2	3	4	5	6	7
8	9	10	11	12	13	14
15	16	17	18	19	20	21
22	23	24	25	26	27	28
29	30	31				

4 **International Agreement on Mekong River Development Signed** in Washington, D.C., for Nam Ngum hydroelectric project to be constructed in Laos.

5 **Unity Principles for Eventual Merger of Eight Major Protestant Churches Announced** by the Presbyterian, Protestant Episcopal, United Presbyterian, Evangelical United Brethren, Methodist, Disciples of Christ, African Methodist Episcopal, and the United Christian churches in the United States.

6 **New Congo Premier in Brazzaville.** Ambroise Noumazalay succeeds Pascal Lissouba.

7 **Algeria Nationalizes 11 Foreign-Owned Mines.** Also takes title to French factories, farms, and homes abandoned in 1962. **World Health Organization Dedicates New Headquarters** in Geneva, Switzerland. Site of $14,500,000 building gift of Geneva state government.

8 **Communist China Explodes Its Third Atomic Device,** "a nuclear explosion that contained thermonuclear materials."

9-13 **Queen Elizabeth II in Brussels.** First state visit by a British monarch since King George V visited Belgium in 1922.

12 **$26,000,000 Busch Memorial Stadium Opens** in Saint Louis (Mo.). Cardinals host to Atlanta Braves baseball team.

15 **Nimbus II Weather Satellite Launched** at Vandenberg Air Force Base, California.

17-26 **First General Elections in Gambia.** Prime Minister David Jawara's People's Progressive party wins 24 of 32 seats in Legislative Assembly.

18 **Atom Spy Harry Gold Released from Prison.** Served nearly 16 years of 30-year sentence. He was a key government witness at the Julius and Ethel Rosenberg trial (1951), after confessing his part in the case.

22-23 **Da Nang Taken by South Vietnamese Government Troops** after week battling Buddhists, rebel troops, and armed civilians.

23-27 **Uganda Crushes Separatist Movement in Buganda.** Deposes Kabaka Edward F. Mutesa II.

25 **Explorer XXXII Launched** at Cape Kennedy.

26 **British Guiana Proclaims Independence as Guyana.** Remains in British Commonwealth.

27 **Government Crisis Ends in Finland** with Rafael Paasio as Premier. Coalition cabinet includes Communists, first time since 1948.

30 **Surveyor I Launched on Way to Moon** at Cape Kennedy.

June

Sun	Mon	Tue	Wed	Thu	Fri	Sat
			1	2	3	4
5	6	7	8	9	10	11
12	13	14	15	16	17	18
19	20	21	22	23	24	25
26	27	28	29	30		

2 **Surveyor I Makes Perfect Soft Landing on Moon,** first such attempt by U.S. **Congo Hangs Four Former Cabinet Ministers.** Former Premier Evariste Kimba and three others executed as conspirators against President Joseph D. Mobutu.

3 **Malaysia and Philippines Resume Diplomatic Relations,** ending three-year break.

3-6 **Gemini IX Space Flight.** Air Force Lieut. Col. Thomas P. Stafford and Navy Lieut. Comdr. Eugene A. Cernan make 46-orbit journey.

6 **Supreme Court Reduces Power of Federal Judges** in criminal contempt cases. Terms of more than six months require trial by jury. **James H. Meredith Shot on Mississippi March.** Aubrey J. Norvell, a white man, arrested. **OGO III Launched** into space at Cape Kennedy, Orbiting Geophysical Observatory.

13 **Supreme Court Rules on Police Interrogation.** Must inform suspect of rights.

20 **French President in Moscow.** Gen. De Gaulle begins 12-day state visit to Russia.

21-22 **Saudi Arabian King Faisal in Washington, D.C.** Begins 10-day visit in U.S.

23 **Pageos I Launched** at Vandenberg Air Force Base, California. Passive Geodetic Earth Orbiting Satellite to map earth's surface.

25 **Yugoslavia Ends 14-Year Break with Vatican.** Signs accord for exchange of envoys.

26 **Mississippi Voter-Registration March Ends** in Jackson. Continued by others after James J. Meredith wounded at Hernando.

28-29 **Argentine President Deposed.** Arturo U. Illia replaced by Lieut. Gen. Juan Carlos Ongania.

29 **U.S. Bombs North Vietnam Oil Centers.** Ends policy of avoiding major cities there.

Australian Prime Minister in Washington, D.C. Harold E. Holt pledges to stay in Vietnam.

Union Suspends British Ship Strike for 12 months. Idled seamen and ships for 45 days.

30 **U.S. Armed Forces Leave France.** Begins withdrawal at Evreux Air Force Base.

July

Sun	Mon	Tue	Wed	Thu	Fri	Sat
					1	2
3	4	5	6	7	8	9
10	11	12	13	14	15	16
17	18	19	20	21	22	23
24/31	25	26	27	28	29	30

1 **France Withdraws Its Armed Forces from NATO** integrated command, but stays in alliance.

Yugoslavia Expels Vice-President Rankovic from Communist party executive and central committees, after microphones were found (June 9) in President Tito's residence.

U.S. Launches Medicare with some 17,000,000 older persons enrolled in program.

Guatemala Inaugurates President. Julio César Méndez Montenegro elected Mar. 6, 1966.

Dominican Republic Inaugurates President. Joaquín Balaguer elected June 1, 1966.

2 **France Explodes Atomic Bomb** at Mururoa, French Polynesia, nation's fifth such blast.

4 **President John F. Kennedy Memorial Dedicated** in Judean hills of Jerusalem, Israel.

5 **Indonesia Strips Sukarno of President for Life Title,** and of power to issue decrees.

Saturn I Launched at Cape Kennedy.

6 **Malawi Proclaimed Republic** in British Commonwealth, with Hastings K. Banda as President.

Proton III Launched by Russia.

8 **Machinists Union Strikes Five Major Airlines** in U.S., after breakdown in negotiations.

Crown Prince Seizes Power in Burundi. Ailing Mwami Mwambutsa IV in Switzerland.

12-15 **Negroes Riot on Chicago's West Side.** National Guardsmen patrol streets.

18 **Complaint Dismissed Against South Africa** on administration in South West Africa. International Court of Justice rules plaintiffs, Ethiopia and Liberia, had not established sufficient legal interest in subject.

18-21 **Gemini X Flight.** Navy Comdr. John W. Young and Air Force Maj. Michael Collins make perfect rendezvous and other "firsts."

18-23 **Negroes Riot in Cleveland Hough Area.** National Guardsmen patrol area.

21 **U.S.S. *Will Rogers* Launched** at Groton, Conn., nation's 41st and last Polaris submarine.

23 **Buddhist Decrees End to Suicide by Fire.** Thich Thien Hoa says too many such acts committed (10 in 1966) in South Vietnam.

25 **New Ruler in Indonesia.** Lieut. Gen. Suharto named chairman of Presidium in new cabinet.

27 **Paul-Henri Spaak Retires.** Belgian statesman in national and world affairs for 34 years.

29 **Nigerian Army Mutiny.** Moslem Hausa of Northern Region kidnap Maj. Gen. J. T. U. Aguiyi-Ironsi. Many others killed.

30 **U.S. Bombs Vietnam Demilitarized Zone** for first time. Long used by North Vietnamese.

August

Sun	Mon	Tue	Wed	Thu	Fri	Sat
	1	2	3	4	5	6
7	8	9	10	11	12	13
14	15	16	17	18	19	20
21	22	23	24	25	26	27
28	29	30	31			

1 **New Military Government in Nigeria.** Army Chief of Staff Lieut. Col. Yakubu Gowon, a Moslem Hausa of the North, assumes power.

3 **Nicaragua President Dies.** René Schick Gutiérrez suffers heart attack.

4 **New Premier in Sudan.** Sadiq el-Mahdi forms new cabinet.

6 **Europe's Longest Suspension Bridge Opens** near Lisbon, Portugal. *Ponte Salazar,* across River Tagus, is 7,472 feet from anchorage to anchorage. Main span 3,323 feet.

Bolivia Inaugurates President. Lieut. Gen. René Barrientos Ortuño elected July 3, 1966.

Johnson-Nugent Wedding. Luci Baines, younger daughter of President and Mrs. Lyndon B. Johnson, and Patrick J. Nugent of Waukegan, Ill., are married in Roman Catholic Shrine of the Immaculate Conception in Washington.

7 **Colombia Inaugurates President.** Carlos Lleras Restrepo elected May 1, 1966.

9 **New Premier in Iraq.** Naji Talib succeeds Abdul Rahman al-Bazzaz.

10 **Lunar Orbiter I Launched** at Cape Kennedy.

10-12 **Britain Enacts Prices and Incomes Law** for six-month freeze on increases, followed by six-month "severe restraint" period.

11 **Malaysia-Indonesia Confrontation Ends.** Peace accord signed in Djakarta.

14 **Lunar Orbiter I Orbits Moon,** first U.S. satellite to do so.

15 **New York *Herald Tribune* Closes.** Strike, now in 114th day and other problems, ends newspaper dating back to 1835.

16 **U.S. Banks Increase Lending Rates to 6 Per Cent,** highest since 1920. New York's First National City Bank first to raise rates.

17 **Pioneer VII Launched** at Cape Kennedy.

18 **Communist China Celebrates "Great Proletarian Cultural Revolution."** Defense Minister Lin Piao appears second to Chairman Mao Tse-tung.

19 **Airline Strike Ends in U.S.** Machinists union members accept three-year contract.

20 **Violent Demonstrations of Young Red Guards** in China spread from Peking to other areas.

21 **President Johnson in New Brunswick.** Confers with Canadian Prime Minister Pearson.

22 **Asian Development Bank in Force.** Canada's ratification gives required approval by 15 countries.

24 **Luna XI Launched into Orbit** by Russia.

25 **Disarmament Conference Recesses** after seven months of fruitless talks in Geneva, Switzerland.

25-26 **President Charles De Gaulle Starts World Tour** in French Somaliland. Rioting mobs demand total independence from France.

30 **Israel Dedicates New Parliament Building** in Jerusalem, first permanent home for Knesset.

September

Sun	Mon	Tue	Wed	Thu	Fri	Sat
				1	2	3
4	5	6	7	8	9	10
11	12	13	14	15	16	17
18	19	20	21	22	23	24
25	26	27	28	29	30	

1 **U Thant Announces Intent to Resign After First Term** at United Nations as Secretary-General.

1-2 **Canada Enacts Railway Legislation.** Ends week-long strike.

6 **South African Prime Minister Stabbed to Death** in Parliament at Capetown. Hendrik F. Verwoerd's assassin, Dimitri Tsafendas, a temporary parliamentary messenger.

8-9 **Burmese Chief of State in Washington, D.C.** Ne Win confers with President Johnson.

9 **Automobile Safety Legislation Signed** by President Johnson.

11 **South Vietnam Election.** About 80.8 per cent of registered voters cast ballots as Viet Cong continue terrorist attacks.
France Explodes Atom Bomb at Mururoa, French Polynesia, as President De Gaulle watches.

11-12 **140-Day Newspaper Strike Ends** in New York City. *World Journal Tribune* publishes its first edition. Replaces *World-Telegram and Sun*, *Journal-American*, and *Herald Tribune*.

12-15 **Gemini XI Flight.** Navy Comdr. Charles Conrad, Jr., and Lieut. Comdr. Richard F. Gordon perform four docking maneuvers during 45-orbit, 71-hour space journey.

12-16 **White Mob Attacks Negro Pupils in Grenada,** Miss. Federal judge orders officials to protect children at integrated schools.

13 **New Prime Minister in South Africa.** Balthazar J. Vorster, apartheid advocate.

14 **Ku Klux Klan Leader Convicted of Contempt of Congress.** Robert M. Shelton, Jr., refused Klan record to House Committee on Un-American Activities.

14-16 **Philippines President in Washington, D.C.** Ferdinand Marcos praises President Johnson's Vietnam and Asian policies.

16 **First British Polaris Submarine Launched.** H. M. S. *Resolution* at Barrow-in-Furness, Eng.

19 **Civil Rights Legislation for 1966 Shelved** in Senate. Fails to end filibuster.

20 **Six-Nation Inter-American Force Leaves Dominican Republic.** Ends peacekeeping action.
Surveyor II Sent to Moon at Cape Kennedy.
United Nations General Assembly Opens. Elects Abdul Rahman Pazhwah of Afghanistan President of 21st session. Admits Guyana as 118th member of organization.

23 **Minimum Wage Legislation Signed** by President Johnson, up to $1.60 an hour by 1968.

26 **Japan Orbits Satellite into Space,** its first.

27 **South Vietnam Inaugurates Constituent Assembly** to write a new constitution.

27-28 **Whitney Museum of American Art Opens** in New York City with "Art of the United States, 1670-1966" exhibit.

27-29 **Race Riots Erupt in San Francisco.** National Guardsmen patrol areas.

28 **Indonesia Returns to United Nations,** increasing its membership to 119 nations.
Senegal President in Washington, D.C. Léopold Senghor confers with President Johnson.

30 **Bechuanaland Proclaims Independence as Republic of Botswana.** Ends 81-year British rule.

October

Sun	Mon	Tue	Wed	Thu	Fri	Sat
						1
2	3	4	5	6	7	8
9	10	11	12	13	14	15
16	17	18	19	20	21	22
23/30	24/31	25	26	27	28	29

1 **Former High Nazis Leave Spandau Prison** in Berlin. Albert Speer and Baldur von Schirach complete 20-year sentences. Only Rudolf Hess, sentenced for life, now in Spandau.

2 **ESSA III Launched** at Vandenberg Air Force Base (California), a weather satellite.

3 **U.S. Attorney General Joins State Department.** Nicholas deB. Katzenbach succeeds George W. Ball as Undersecretary of State.
Brazilian Congress Elects President. War Minister Arthur Costa e Silva begins four-year term on Mar. 15, 1967.
Tunisia Severs Diplomatic Relations with United Arab Republic. Charges Cairo "waged a continued campaign of insults."

4 **Basutoland Proclaimed Kingdom of Lesotho** with Moshoeshoe II as monarch. Former British colony is located in South Africa.
France Ends Atomic Tests in Pacific, started at Mururoa on July 2.

5-9 **World Series Won by Baltimore Orioles.** Defeat Los Angeles Dodgers in four straight games.

6 **Britain's Prices and Incomes Freeze Now Mandatory** as voluntary support of act crumbles.

15 **U.S. Department of Transportation Authorized.** Bill signed by President Johnson adds a Secretary (12th) of Transportation to his Cabinet.

15-19 **Lebanese Bank Crisis.** Heavy withdrawals closes Intra Bank in Beirut. Private banks closed to prevent depositors run on them.

17 **United Nations Admits Botswana and Lesotho.** Organization's membership now 121 countries.
President Johnson Leaves for Pacific-Asian Trip and Manila Conference.

20 **Russia Launches Space Satellites:** the fourth *Molniya I* (all four designated *Molniya I*) and Cosmos CXXX.

22 **89th Congress of U.S. Adjourns** second session in Washington, D.C.
British Spy Escapes from West London Prison. George Blake sentenced to 42 years (1961) as spy for Russia.
Luna XII Launched by Russia.

24-25 **Manila Conference** attended by Australia, New Zealand, Philippines, South Korea, South Vietnam, Thailand, and United States.

25 **Subandrio Condemned to Death** in Indonesia for part in Communist plot (Oct. 1, 1965).

26 **Lani Bird Launched** at Cape Kennedy. Intelsat II (International Telecommunications Satellite Consortium) to open first such commercial communications across the Pacific.

27 **United Nations Revokes South Africa's Mandate in South West Africa.** General Assembly creates 14-state committee for territory.

Communist China Explodes Its Fourth Atomic Device in Sinkiang Province.

November

Sun	Mon	Tue	Wed	Thu	Fri	Sat
		1	2	3	4	5
6	7	8	9	10	11	12
13	14	15	16	17	18	19
20	21	22	23	24	25	26
27	28	29	30			

1 **India Creates 17th State.** Divides Punjab on language basis into Punjabi Subha (Sikhs) and Hariana (Hindi).

2 **President Johnson Returns to U.S.** from Pacific-Asian tour and Manila Conference.

4 **Russia Casts 104th Veto in United Nations Security Council.** Defeats resolution asking Israel and Syria to reduce border tensions.

Yantar Launched in October, Russia says. Spacecraft has ion-propulsion system.

$500,000 Space Transit Planetarium Opens in Miami, Fla., a part of the Museum of Science and Natural History.

6 **Alan S. Boyd First U.S. Secretary of Transportation,** former Undersecretary of Commerce.

Lunar Orbiter II Launched at Cape Kennedy.

8 **U.S. Elections.** Major gains for Republicans.

10 **John Lynch Prime Minister of Ireland.** Replaces Seán F. Lemass, who retired.

11 **United Nations Elects Security Council Nonpermanent Members:** Brazil, Canada, Denmark, Ethiopia, and India replace Uruguay, New Zealand, Uganda, The Netherlands, and Jordan for two-year terms.

11-15 **Gemini XII Space Flight Last in Series.** Navy Capt. James A. Lovell, Jr., and Air Force Maj. Edwin E. Aldrin, Jr., perform many tasks during 94 hrs. 36 min. in space.

16 **Israel Condemned in United Nations Security Council** for raid (Nov. 13) on Jordan by Britain, France, Russia, and United States.

Interim President in Ecuador. Constituent Assembly elects Otto Arosemena Gomez.

27 **Colombia Establishes Diplomatic Relations with East European Countries** (except Russia). Broke Communist ties in 1948.

Uruguay Ends Rule by Council. Oscar D. Gestido begins five-year term on March 1, 1967.

28 **United States Elevates Legations to Embassies** in Bulgaria and Hungary under mutual agreement with the two Communist countries.

Burundi Mwami Mioame Ntare V Deposed while on visit to Congo. Premier Michel Micombero takes title of President.

29 **Communist China Barred from United Nations** for 16th time. Sixteen black African states among the countries that are opposed to its admission.

Barbados Proclaims Independence. Caribbean island under British control since 1627.

December

Sun	Mon	Tue	Wed	Thu	Fri	Sat
				1	2	3
4	5	6	7	8	9	10
11	12	13	14	15	16	17
18	19	20	21	22	23	24
25	26	27	28	29	30	31

1 **New Chancellor in West Germany.** Bundestag (lower house of Parliament) elects Kurt Georg Kiesinger to replace Ludwig Erhard.

2 **U Thant Stays as United Nations Secretary-General.** Unanimously elected to second term.

Meatless Fridays End for Roman Catholics in U.S., except during Lent. First day of Lent, Ash Wednesday, also remains a meatless day.

3 **President Johnson in Mexico.** He and President Gustavo Díaz Ordaz celebrate U.S.-Mexican construction of Amistad Dam on Rio Grande.

9 **United Nations Admits Barbados** as its 122d member nation.

14 **New Spanish Constitution Approved** by 95.5 per cent of votes cast. Generalissimo Francisco Franco retains executive and legislative powers for life.

Biosatellite I Launched at Cape Kennedy, with plant and insect cargo.

15 **Walt Disney Dies** at 65, creator of Mickey Mouse, Donald Duck, and Snow White. Also the creator of Disneyland.

16 **Human Rights Covenants Approved** by United Nations General Assembly after 18 years.

United Nations Approves Mandatory Economic Bans on Rhodesia. First such action by the Security Council.

17 **Biosatellite I Lost in Space.** Capsule and cargo separate from spacecraft.

19 **Treaty Banning Arms in Space Approved** by United Nations General Assembly. Prohibits orbiting of nuclear weapons, and use of moon and other such bodies as military bases.

Asian Development Bank Inaugurated in Manila, Philippines, with Takeshi Watanabe of Japan as its first president.

20 **United Nations General Assembly** ends its 21st session.

21 **Luna XIII Launched to Moon** by Russia.

Florence Reopens Art Galleries and Museums. Only Church of Santa Croce museum remains closed following flood in Italy.

22 **New Premier in Greece.** Ioannis Paraskevopoulos heads interim government, after resignation of Stephanos C. Stephenopoulos.

24 **Luna XIII Makes Soft Landing on Moon,** second such success by Russia.

24-26 **Christmas Cease-Fire in Vietnam.** Shootings by Viet Congs called "incidents" by the United States.

27 **New U.S. Ambassador to Russia.** Llewellyn E. Thompson, Jr., succeeds Foy D. Kohler.

28 **Communist China Explodes Its Fifth Atomic Device** in Sinkiang Province.

31 **New Year's Truce in Vietnam Begins.** U.S. reports some 60 incidents of enemy attacks on first day of 48-hour cease-fire.

Section One

The Year Book Board of Editors analyzes the significant developments of 1966 and considers their impact upon contemporary affairs. The Related Articles list following each report directs the reader to THE YEAR BOOK's additional coverage of related subjects.

The Year in Focus

Paul-Henri Spaak: Focus on The World

The international situation did not improve in 1966; the two major problems were the war in Vietnam and the NATO crisis

History teaches us that international relations, when allowed to drift, have a tendency to get beyond control. Then, even with imagination and good will, events are difficult for men to master. This was exemplified in 1966 by the war in Vietnam. In Europe, there was the North Atlantic Treaty Organization (NATO) crisis due to French President Charles de Gaulle's determination to move his country on an independent course. The conflict between the Soviet Union and Communist China received increasing attention.

No improvement occurred in Southeast Asia in 1966. The situation there, in fact, grew worse. Nothing purposeful can be accomplished by statements, gestures of peace, or prayers, if the facts of the situation contradict good intentions.

United States attempts to restore peace in Vietnam encountered an uncompromising attitude from the Hanoi government of North Vietnam. This attitude was encouraged by Communist China. (Of all the world's governments, the Communist Chinese seemed the only one willing to go to war.) Peking apparently hoped that eventually the United States, worn out by longer and longer military efforts, would abandon the fight. Should this happen, it would result in a major loss of American prestige in Asia. It probably would also result in the triumph of Communism throughout that area.

U.S. attempts to restore peace in Vietnam were rebuffed by the powers in Hanoi

Meanwhile, as long as the war lasted, the United States and Russia could not continue to pursue a policy of "rapprochement," inaugurated by the Atomic Test-Ban Treaty of 1963.

To Peking, the Vietnamese war was an important instrument of blackmail against Moscow. The human tragedy did not seem to affect the Chinese. The situation in Vietnam enabled them, at least to some extent, to embarrass Moscow's relations with the U.S. and thus hold Russia in line.

Nonetheless, conditions for an honorable peace in Vietnam did exist. The U.S. clearly stated its readiness to discuss, with all parties concerned, every proposal which had been made.

U.S. statements were positive and reasonable, but every peace effort met with one seemingly insuperable obstacle. That was the demand by Hanoi for the withdrawal—before any discussions—of American troops from South Vietnam, without assurance from North Vietnam or the Viet Cong that they would refrain from taking advantage of such a withdrawal. To accept this demand would, from the American viewpoint, have been an admission of defeat and guilt. The demand was consequently regarded as unacceptable. Those who had insisted on it were perfectly conscious that this would be the case.

Thus, throughout 1966, the deadlock continued with its disadvantages and dangers. The United States, of course, could have won a military victory by using extreme measures. If it had employed its maximum military force, North Vietnam could have been very rapidly eliminated. But a real peace could not come out of such military success. More probably, a major conflict with Communist China would occur. An aggrevation of relations between the Soviet Union and the United States would be an inevitable result. In a large part of the world, the reputation of the U.S. would certainly have been deeply affected.

These were the most discouraging facts of 1966. It was easy to say what should not have been done, but infinitely more difficult to say what should have been done. Apparently Communist China, for a long time, will remain the only beneficiary of the situation. This will be true until the North Vietnam government frees itself from the pressures Peking exercises on it and seeks reasonable solutions in Vietnam; i.e., ones which are within its reach. The present danger is obvious. Hopefully the situation will not drift too long. If so, it might become necessary to do what could have been avoided.

After World War II, the Soviet Union, headed at that time by Joseph Stalin, ruptured the harmony which had assured the Allies victory over Germany and Japan. Russia adopted a policy designed to dominate Eastern Europe and soon succeeded in installing Communist governments throughout that area. In 1948, the free states of Western Europe, the United States, and Canada determined to halt Soviet imperialism. In April, 1949 they set up NATO. The importance of this move cannot be overemphasized.

The present danger is obvious; hopefully the situation will not drift too long

Seventeen years later, the once aggressive role of Communism in Europe had been stopped. A balance of power had been established. Of all the continents, Europe in 1966 was the quietest. German reunification remained the only problem. The problem was definitely an important one, but it did not appear to threaten war.

In a Europe fortunate enough to live in peace, and organized to maintain it, General De Gaulle's attitude toward NATO, however, introduced an element of anxiety. The French government, in deciding eventually to withdraw from NATO, and demanding that NATO troops be removed from French soil, imposed on France's erstwhile partners major political and military problems.

The anguish of Vietnam

This development occurred at a particularly ill-chosen moment. The United States was involved in Asian problems. Great Britain was trying to cope with internal and external difficulties which drew its attention away from Europe. Internally, the nation faced serious economic problems. The pound sterling was saved from further devaluation by stringent economic measures instituted by the government of Prime Minister Harold Wilson. Externally, of course, Britain had to cope with the volatile situation in Rhodesia. Germany was divided between its French and American friendship policies. The Greeks and the Turks were quarreling over Cyprus. Budgetary problems caused the smaller European states to hold down their military expenditures. Toward the end of 1966, natural disasters raised havoc in Italy. Unusually high tides, floods, and landslides resulted in extensive loss of life and massive property damage. The economic fabric of the country was seriously disrupted.

Amid this scene loomed the figure of General De Gaulle. Even if one does not agree with the general's attitude, one fears his wrath. His policies appear secret and mysterious. Their final objectives no one can seem to discern. The recent thrust of French policy has been essentially disruptive to the Atlantic community. It has weakened the European defense system and created doubt and dissensions at a time when settlement of major problems has called for unity.

The Atlantic Union has been shaken. It awaits a leader who can give it new impetus and restore its confidence. To resolve its problems, NATO must adapt to contemporary, military necessities. This, of course, involves the development of a common strategic policy. The future health of NATO depends on the judgment and faith of those who had always trusted it.

Though the war in Vietnam and the NATO crisis were probably the major events of 1966, perhaps the most important for the future was the growing conflict between the Soviet Union and Communist China. Which of these two powers will assume leadership of the Communist world? What is the trend of events in that important part of the world? Will there be peaceful coexistence? Or will there be a complete deterioration in the relations between the two nations until a devastating and decisive conflagration results?

The Sino-Soviet split has fanned the struggle for leadership in the Communist world

On Russia's Western flank, significant transformations have occurred in the economic dialogue between the Soviet Union and the European Communist countries. These countries will doubtless remain faithful to the collective appropriation of the means of production, but the adoption of certain so-called capitalistic principles (the importance of private profit, the laws of competition, etc.,) has become increasingly apparent. Political regimes have been somewhat liberalized and the desire for cooperation with the West is now obvious. The days of the Iron Curtain are over.

By 1966, the policy of peaceful coexistence was accepted. To Peking, this was unbearable. The Communist Chinese denounced this attitude with fury and violence. The Chinese were in favor of the most excessive, the most dangerous principles of rigid Communist doctrine. Agreements or compromises were neither possible nor desirable to those who did not think as Peking did. The Chinese felt that they alone held the key to the truth. Their major objective was victory by any means—even war—which, according to their doctrine, was inevitable.

The Sino-Soviet split kept alive the struggle for leadership in the Communist world. It augured further antagonism between two powers joined by a long, common frontier. The Russians felt more and more keenly their affinity with the West. They remembered their historic ties with Europe. They knew that good relations with the United States were necessary to the maintenance of world peace. And only under such conditions could they pursue their economic and social experiments.

A book published in 1966 bore the ironic title, *The Soviets in NATO*. The possibility implied by the title was not as ridiculous as it might seem. While Peking resorted to absurd demonstrations in its domestic politics, and to dangerous external activities, Moscow increasingly appeared to be the capital of a mature state, of a regime hostile to adventurous actions. Peking's policies were not successful. Within the Communist world, only Albania remained faithful to Red China. The other European Communist countries leaned more and more toward the direction of Moscow.

Elsewhere in Asia, Indonesia threw back domestic Communism with violence, and moved away from the Chinese. It also had a reconciliation with Malaysia and returned to the United Nations (UN). This constituted an important defeat for Peking. In Africa, despite great efforts and spectacular tours by Premier Chou En-lai, Chinese ambitions were, for the most part, thwarted.

Africa witnessed some remarkable coups d'état in 1966, but the fundamental patterns were consistent with developments of previous years. That is to say military regimes came increasingly into evidence.

General Joseph Mobutu seized power in the Democratic Republic of Congo, (Kinshasa, formerly Leopoldville). His coup put an end to the regime of President Joseph Kasavubu who had been head of state since independence in 1960. Premier Moishe Tshombe was in exile for the second time. Relations between Belgium and Congo deteriorated. Congo broke off diplomatic ties with Portugal. Such events pointed up the difficulties that the new African nations faced in searching to develop their resources and achieve political equilibrium. General Mobutu's action set an example to Dahomey, the Central African Republic, Upper Volta, and Ghana. In these countries, military leaders also seized power.

Europe, despite DeGaulle's actions, was relatively calm; but Africa was in deep ferment

Kwame Nkrumah's fall in Ghana was most unexpected. He appeared to be one of the most popular African leaders. His power seemed firmly established. Taking advantage of his visit to Communist China, however, his enemies overthrew his government with ease. Nobody defended him. The army, the police, and the people whose loyalty had seemed undoubted left him. It quickly became obvious that all the pomp which had surrounded him had meant nothing.

Nigeria, which had gained considerable world respect from the moderation and wisdom of its leaders, was torn by an internal tribal crisis. There was a succession of coups, and the unity of the country was quite obviously threatened.

French President
Charles de Gaulle

In addition to these problems, one could sense ominous clouds of tragedy forming in South Africa and Rhodesia. These countries are committed to racial policies which seem destined to lead to a bloody conclusion. These policies contradict resolutions voted in the United Nations, and no compromise is apparently possible between the white minority and the nonwhite majority of either country. The principle of the equality of races faces traditions and prejudices not easy to erase. Vested interests still attempt to counter the current of history. This was exemplified in South West Africa, long administered by South Africa under a mandate from the League of Nations. After much legal maneuvering, the UN voted in the fall of 1966 to terminate South Africa's mandate. But the government of that nation stoutly resisted the action. Subsequently, a UN committee was set up to study the case. It would probably reach a decision sometime in 1967. Whatever the outcome of that situation, and the particularly troublesome events in Rhodesia, the future of Africa created grave concern. At year's end, the Security Council of the UN, in an unprecedented action, voted economic sanctions against Rhodesia. But it was doubtful whether these could be totally enforced.

The boiling cauldron of relationships in the Middle East seemed increasingly dangerous. There was an outbreak of armed hostility between Israel and its Arab neighbors. Israel was censured by the UN for attacking a Jordanian village, but insisted that its action was justified by previous Arab provocation.

Even within the Arab world itself, there was dissension and upheaval. There was a deepening schism between Saudi Arabia and Jordan, on the one hand, and Syria and the United Arab Republic (UAR), on the other. There was civil war in Yemen. Lebanon underwent a financial crisis. Altogether, the picture was not encouraging.

In Latin America, there were no major new developments. Elections and coups continued. But progress and stability can only be achieved if economic and social reforms and democratic elections are introduced. Unfortunately, the prospects for such developments seem slight in the immediate years ahead.

Too many conflicts have arisen for which no settlement is in sight

Looking back on 1966, one could only feel a certain uneasiness at the deterioration of the international situation. Too many conflicts had arisen for which no reasonable settlement was in sight. Where would the solutions originate? Would they come from an agreement between the United States and the Soviet Union? Undoubtedly that would be an essential step. But to reach it, the war in Vietnam would have to be terminated. That would be the first important step.

Related Articles

For a complete report on international relations in the year 1966, see Section Two, The Most Impossible Job in the World, Russia: Fifty Years of Turmoil, and articles on the various nations in Section Three. In the same section, see also the following:

Africa
Asia
Communism
Democracy
Europe
Latin America
Middle East
North Atlantic Treaty Organization
United Nations

James B. Reston: Focus on The Nation

Despite immense economic and military power, there was a mood of questioning, doubt, and frustration in America

In 1966, the United States entered the last third of the 20th century in a curious mood. It was engaged in two wars: One was against military aggression in Vietnam and the other against poverty in its own cities. Immensely powerful, rich beyond the dreams of any other nation, America was finding that its power was not producing victory in Vietnam, and its wealth was not removing poverty or racial tension in its cities. The children born in 1966 would live much of their lives in the 21st century. The 1966 population of nearly 200,000,000 people would double by the year 2000, and most of those people would live in vast urban areas. By 1970, over half the population of the United States would be under 25.

In 1966, the nation's leaders worried about precisely these things: the problems of military power, political power, presidential power; the problems of the cities and the races; and the problems of youth struggling to adapt the old American Frontier values of life to the wholly different environment of congested, computerized, urban and suburban communities.

If Americans found no clear answers, they at least asked the right questions

This produced a mood of questioning, doubt, and frustration in America. Political institutions found themselves in a strange situation. Hundreds of separate local governments located around a single city had discovered that they could not deal with their problems except on a regional basis; yet they had not learned the art of cooperating with scores of other local governments to the benefit of all. The federal government began attacking poverty in the cities by grants of money, not through the state governments, as some observers might have expected, but directly to local officials and sometimes even to local poverty committees.

American big business was rapidly venturing into the world and running into resentment from foreign competitors and foreign governments. American universities were growing at a fantastic rate but not quite keeping up with the population growth. Even America's political parties were discovering that dogmas and policies of the past were inadequate to the new problems of this last third of the 20th century.

Nevertheless, if Americans found no clear answers in 1966, they were at least asking fundamental questions. Throughout the country, political, educational, religious, and business leaders were conscious of the need to adapt to a rapidly changing society. They were questioning their methods and their relevance. They were passing power to a new generation of younger managers and specialists. They were no longer scoffing at the educated man as a helpless theorist. They were seeking well-trained minds and putting them to work. A vast search was in process. The resourceful, pragmatic American mind was looking for new machinery and new programs to deal with urban transport, housing, unemployment, water and air pollution, education, retraining, and particularly rejected and poorly educated Negroes.

There have been three remarkable Congresses of the United States in this century–the 59th in Theodore Roosevelt's time, the 63rd under Woodrow Wilson, and the 73rd, which created the New Deal, under Franklin D. Roosevelt. But none of these, in terms of legislation enacted, surpassed or even equaled the remarkable record of the 89th which completed its two-year span in office during 1966.

The first 88 Congresses, for example, invested $5,800,000,000 of federal funds on education over a period of 174 years. Yet the 89th Congress, operating with the large majorities gained by President Lyndon B. Johnson in the presidential election of 1964, invested not $5,800,000,000, but $9,600,000,000 in that single session.

From 1798, when the U.S. Public Health Service was founded, until 1964, the federal government passed 17 major health measures–17, that is, in 165 years. Between 1963 and the end of 1966, by contrast, the Congress passed not 17, but 24 major health programs. The 89th Congress voted $8,200,000,000 for health. This included major medical care for the aged which had been the subject of lively debate for over a decade. This $8,200,000,000 was almost as much as federal health expenditures in more than the previous century-and-a-half. President Johnson summed up the record of the 89th in these words:

Never before had Congress passed so many laws affecting so many people

"The Cities Act, the Mass Transit Act, the act to clean up our dirty water and our dirty air begin a major battle to make American cities places where American people can live full and decent lives. Never in the history of any Congress has so much legislation been passed affecting so many people in so many cities of America."

Despite this, there were racial riots in the streets of Chicago, Los Angeles, San Francisco, Dayton, Ohio, and other cities. And for obvious reasons. It was not that the housing, sanitation, education, and employment of urban Negroes were worse in 1966 than in 1965. They were better; but they were still bad. The difference was that the Negro had been made more aware of his unequal situation. He had been told by his government and his own leaders that poor housing, inferior education, and unemployment were not inevitable, but correctable. Yet they were not corrected; at least not rapidly enough to meet rising Negro expectations. The government's promises of equality, opportunity, a War on Poverty leading to a Great Society, exceeded the performance. The Negro was made aware of his inequality without being relieved of it. Though he was better off than in 1965, "the full and equal life" the President talked about was now part of the Negro's expectation without being part of his reality.

The policies of the United States government beyond the geographic boundaries of the country complicated and in many ways distorted this problem. The national economy was not in dire trouble, though substantial problems had arisen. The Vietnam war was costing about $20,000,000,000 a year, unbalancing the budget and reducing funds for the War on Poverty. One result was that there were even a few echoes of the old American isolationist spirit in 1966. More importantly, Negro leaders asked why the United States should spend massive sums to fight a war in Vietnam and short-change the poor at home. Why "liberate" the South Vietnamese before people in American slums had been liberated? Even moderate Negro leaders were warning that Negro soldiers coming home from Vietnam might be in a savage mood if they returned to Negro urban ghettos where they still faced the prospect of rejection and unemployment.

By the end of 1966, in fact, Vice-President Hubert H. Humphrey, who had the difficult task of coordinating all the poverty programs for the President, talked ominously about seeing "a flicker of revolution" in American cities. For the first time, even those Negro leaders who had rather cautiously sought legal remedies for the economic, social, and educational problems of their people were challenged by young Negro militants threatening to use violence, or what they called Black Power, to bring about equal opportunities for Negroes.

Such development mirrored the most remarkable characteristic of the United States in 1966. The year was one of paradox. America had never been so prosperous nor heard more about poverty. It had never had more military power nor been more conscious of the limitations of military power. The government had never done more for the poor in a single year nor had more trouble with the poor. It had never spent more money on higher education nor met with more protests—and even defiance—on college and university campuses. It had never talked more about the importance of cooperation among the Western allies and received less cooperation. At no time in this century had the nation had a President who proposed and enacted so many popular measures or come to the end of a successful legislative program under such a cloud of criticism and even personal vilification.

The President ended a successful legislative program under a heavy cloud of criticism

Between the time when President Johnson announced his program for the War on Poverty and the time when, by remarkable exertions, he got it through the second session of the 89th Congress at the end of 1966, his rating had dropped dramatically in the popularity polls. More than any other President of the last generation, he had identified and dramatized the problems of the poor, but he nonetheless became increasingly unpopular.

Freedom marchers

There were a number of reasons why. The American people seemed to be in a highly skeptical mood. The true cost of the war in Vietnam was not clearly explained to the public, for fear that the Congress would cut the administration's domestic programs. The President's official statements were widely questioned in the press. The report of the Warren Commission on the assassination of President John F. Kennedy, presided over by the Chief Justice of the United States, was challenged in many parts of the world. Senator Robert F. Kennedy of New York, a former Attorney General, and J. Edgar Hoover, director of the Federal Bureau of Investigation (FBI), challenged one another as to who was tapping whose telephones in the United States. The government was caught, not only tapping telephones of foreign embassies in Washington, D.C., but even listening in on the telephone conversations of Negro leaders, including Martin Luther King. The year finally ended with a spectacular controversy over a book on the assassination of President Kennedy, with the Kennedy family accusing the author, William Manchester, of breaking his contract, and Manchester accusing the Kennedys of tampering with history.

While these events were taking place, the war in Vietnam did dramatize the immense power of the President. It was obvious that he alone really decided such questions as whether to bomb and where to bomb in North Vietnam, how many troops to send to Southeast Asia, whether to accept or reject the enemy's peace offers, whether to provide or withhold wheat for India, whether to call the military reserves or fight the war with conscripts. Such power in the command of a President who was losing the confidence of important segments of the American populace led to an appreciable rearrangement of political power in the mid-term elections of 1966.

After winning the presidency by the largest plurality in history in 1964, Mr. Johnson started 1966 with a Democratic majority of 295 to 140 in the House of Representatives and 67 to 33 in the Senate. In the election of November 8, 1966, however, the Republicans gained 47 seats in the House, and three in the Senate. More importantly, the Republicans increased their state governorships from 17 to 25 and went into 1967 in control of the state houses in five of the seven most populous states in the Union.

Republicans began to recover from the pessimism of 1966 and look forward to 1968

What was particularly interesting about the 1966 elections was the decline of Democratic strength in the cities, among organized labor, among the Negro communities, and among the colleges and universities. President Johnson, of course, retained all the power he had had in the field of foreign policy, and his party still had a majority in both the House and Senate. But a strong Republican opposition was restored. A coalition of conservative Republicans and Democrats was in a position to challenge the President's social and economic policies. Republicans began to recover from the pessimism of early 1966 and to think that they might even regain the presidency in 1968.

By the year's end, in fact, the political prophets had already identified the most likely presidential nominees. On the Democratic side, of course, it was generally assumed that President Johnson would stand for re-election. On the Republican side, the leading candidates seemed to be Governor George W. Romney of Michigan and former Vice-President Richard M. Nixon.

Governor Romney not only won a spectacular victory in his race for re-election, but proved to be popular among city voters and urban minority groups. He also helped elect a Republican to the U.S. Senate. This brought him the support of liberal Republican governors, such as Nelson A. Rockefeller of New York and the retiring governor of Pennsylvania, William W. Scranton. They immediately began organizing to put over a liberal candidate in 1968.

Nixon strengthened his position by campaigning vigorously and effectively for Republican candidates throughout the country. If Governor Romney should not do well in the primary elections of 1968, Nixon, and even Governor Rockefeller, might easily come into the race.

President Johnson

In both parties, there was an acute awareness that the last third of the century was going to force a transformation of thought, perhaps as great as the transformation which had been required in the first and second thirds. In the first third, America went through World War I and a vast economic depression. In the second third, it was embroiled in World War II, and made large-scale commitments in many parts of the globe. At the start of the last third of the century, the U.S. was confronted with new centers of power, new and more virulent forms of nationalism, new challenges at home, and new opportunities to end the Cold War. While nobody seemed to have a clear sense of national purpose, there was, at least, a realization that a new age was opening and that this would require new thought.

The striking thing about America in 1966 was that the "new thought" for "the new age" was not really coming from political leaders. America was, in fact, being changed by people outside of government.

The natural growth of the people–increasing by almost 3,000,000 persons each year–and the movement of people into cities and suburbs was one compelling factor in the process of change. This was particularly true of the movement of Negroes out of the rural South into the cities of the border states and the North. The District of Columbia, for example, had become almost 60 per cent Negro by the end of 1966, and public school children in the federal capital were 93 per cent Negro.

At the end of 1966, there was a realization that a new age was opening

The effects of science and technology on the nation were also increasingly significant. "What are you going to do when a computer takes your job?" was a frequent question. The federal government emphasized retraining for unskilled workers.

In 1950, the government's budget for research and development had been approximately $1,200,000,000. By 1963, it was over $12,000,000,000. By 1966, it was over $15,000,000,000. The government had thus become the major patron of science and technology in America. Whole industries and regions of the country existed primarily on government contracts.

"Today," Carnegie Institution President Caryl Hasking observed, "for every eight scientists who have ever existed, some seven are now living." It is this startling fact that is apt to have the greatest effect on the last third of the 20th century in the United States.

Related Articles

For a complete report on the year 1966 in national affairs, see also Section One, SYLVIA PORTER: FOCUS ON THE ECONOMY; and the following articles in Section Three:

Armed Forces of the World
City and Regional Planning
Civil Rights
Communications
Congress of the United States
Courts and Laws
Democratic Party
Economy, The
Elections
Governors of the States
Housing
Johnson, Lyndon B.
Labor
Manufacturing
Medicare
National Defense
Peace Corps
Poverty
President of the U.S.
Republican Party
State Government
Supreme Court
Taxation
Transportation

Sylvia Porter: Focus on The Economy

The United States had proved its ability to spur a healthy economy, but in 1966 it lacked the courage to control unhealthy inflation

In 1966, the problems of a prolonged, war-fueled prosperity smeared the magnificent economic boom of the United States. As 1967 began, the economy was still rising, though at a slower pace, and serious distortions had emerged to endanger the expansion's balance, health, quality, and duration.

Inflation, which had been kept under remarkable control since 1958 and which had been only a minor threat in 1965, became a reality in 1966. The result was a rise of more than 3½ per cent in the cost of living in a single year; the biggest increase since the Korean War.

Demands for credit for construction, modernization, and expansion —welcomed in the early 1960s as a signal of economic growth—became so enormous that the Federal Reserve System slammed on the credit brakes in a deliberate effort to force a cutback in borrowing and thus curtail inflation. The result was a spectacular upsurge in interest rates to the highest peaks in more than a generation. Mortgage money dried up, creating a slump in the vast housing industry. A credit squeeze was exerted on small business, and on states and cities.

The era of great business and consumer confidence and comparative labor peace ended

The extraordinarily skillful meshing of government fiscal and monetary policies with the policies of private business and organized labor, a key to our solid, noninflationary upswing from 1961 to 1966, fell apart. Tax policy did not dovetail with credit policy. Businessmen were not statesmanlike in their pricing actions. Labor leaders were not restrained in their wage demands.

The era of great business and consumer confidence and comparative labor peace ended. The result was a growing uneasiness about where the economy was heading. The stock market reflected the changed atmosphere by a price break which between February and November of 1966 wiped out 25 per cent of the value of stocks. With an all-time record of 22,500,000 Americans owning securities of this type, every city, town, and hamlet in the nation felt the depressing influence of the stock market plunge.

What happened? What went wrong?

What happened was the war in Vietnam.

What went wrong was that the U.S. failed to live up to the fundamental rules of the "New Economics" which demand restraints on the economy as soon as it starts surging upward too rapidly; just as they demand stimulants as soon as the economy becomes sluggish.

The United States had the insight and courage to spur a healthy boom between 1961 and mid-1965. Income and excise taxes were cut in the face of multibillion dollar budget deficits. Businessmen were given major incentives to invest in new plants and modern equipment. But in 1966, there was not the insight and courage to cool the boom as it developed obvious signs of becoming unhealthily inflationary. Only the Federal Reserve System acted aggressively. And the severe extent to which it tightened credit could be criticized as discriminatory and dangerous to the economy's balance.

Even under relatively simple conditions, the typical annual economists' forecasts of the nation's output of goods and services have previously missed the mark. Even when economists have been generally correct in predicting the direction of a significant change, they have consistently underestimated its extent.

This is an unfortunate record, but business forecasts are still essential for intelligent planning. And, under law, the President's chief economists must each January make official projections for 12 months ahead to help guide the White House on crucially important policy decisions.

In 1966, virtually all statistics had become obsolete within weeks after the economists had submitted their 306-page report to Congress in January. Accelerating spending in Vietnam, piled on top of record peacetime domestic expenditures, sent the U.S. economy soaring upward at a pace the economists had not dreamed possible. The peace-plus-war demand for goods expanded at an unsustainable rate. President Lyndon B. Johnson's economic advisers had anticipated price rises no larger in 1966 than in 1965. Instead, the familiar "demand-pull" type of inflation–in which excessive demands for goods and services "pull up" prices–was clearly emerging.

Economists urged that the economy be restrained, but the White House hesitated

Corporations responded to the market place's excessive demands by speeding up their spending for plant and equipment to a huge 16 per cent above 1965. They thereby put sources of capital which lend money under tremendous pressure. Manpower and materials shortages began to replace surpluses in many areas. Labor therefore saw an opportunity to increase demands for wage hikes. A year that was supposed to have seen comparative labor peace was instead marred by strikes and wage settlements which resulted in rising labor and other costs for businessmen. Thus, the threat of renewed "cost-push" inflation–in which rising costs "push up" prices–also emerged.

With our economy overheating as it strained at its resources of manpower and materials, New Economics policies of economic stimulation were distinctly *not* needed. What was distinctly needed were policies of restraint to cool the heat. Early 1966 was the time for meshing fiscal and monetary policies to slow the boom before a new price-wage spiral could get underway and unbalance our prosperity.

Picketing housewives

Leading economists had urged restraints. At the outset of 1966, Dr. Walter Heller, former chairman of the Council of Economic Advisers under both Presidents John F. Kennedy and Johnson and one of the architects of the New Economics, revealed the trend of informed thinking. He said flatly: "The New Economics must be a two-way street. We have always stood ready to reverse gears." This meant moderation of non-defense government spending, or, if this was deemed undesirable, increases in both corporation and individual income taxes to help balance the Federal budget and curtail the country's ability to spend. In addition to the economists' tax increase proposals, top business leaders asked for tax hikes which would have shrunk their own net profits. Their calls for a policy of restraint are a matter of record.

But the White House hesitated. Only insignificant requests for tax increases were initiated by the President in the first half of the year. It was not until fall that the President proposed, and Congress approved, a suspension until 1968 of the tax incentives which had fostered business' roaring spending for plant and equipment. This suspension, in addition to other forces, is slashing the rate of increase in business investment, but it came too late to have much effect in 1966. Congress continued in a free-spending mood—hardly appropriate to a feverish economy—and with Vietnam war spending skyrocketing from month to month, the federal budget sank billions into the red. This, remember, happened in a year in which the rules of the New Economics called for an anti-inflationary budget surplus.

The President's agony in asking for politically unpalatable across-the-board tax increases, and his worry over whether this would be too strong economic medicine, was understandable. Beginning in the spring of 1966, our economy moved into an "*Alice Through the Looking Glass*" phase. Every item of so-called bad news signaling a downtrend in an industry or occupation was hailed as good news because it gave the President grounds for putting off a decision on an income tax hike. The fact was that the administration's unwillingness to take appropriate steps early enough to cool the heat permitted much of 1966's inflation and credit squeeze.

A tight money policy boosted interest rates to the highest level since the 1920s

The Federal Reserve System, though, did take action. By a series of direct regulations, and through credit-shrinking actions in the nation's money markets, it cut the capacity of the banking system to make loans. Borrowers paid the steepest interest rates since the early 1920s.

The Federal Reserve's action was exceedingly discriminatory in its effects. While bank loan rates to the country's top corporation borrowers climbed to 6 per cent—or about 7 per cent after allowance for "fringes"—the hike did little more than annoy most large companies. Even a 7 per cent loan rate drops to a cost of only about 3½ per cent after taxes. But rates to smaller businessmen, home builders, home buyers, and consumers were even higher, and the chance for taking tax charge-offs less. The basic housing industry was forced into a nose-dive as buyers, sellers, and home builders found it impossible to get mortgage money. Even if they could get it, the rate was often more than they could afford. Small businessmen were hard-pressed. Many municipalities were compelled to shelve much-needed projects.

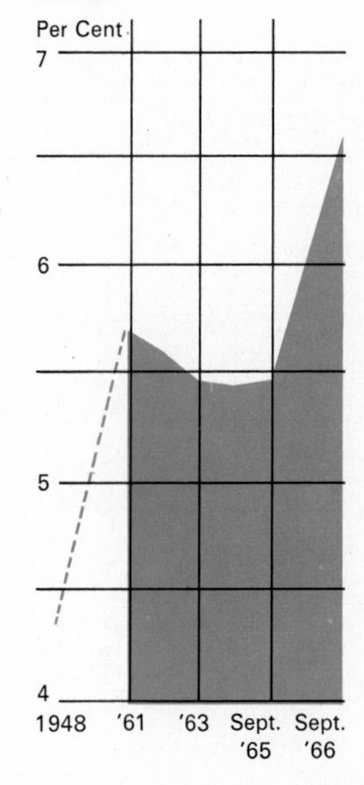

Ironically, the "tight-money" policy also helped to push up the cost of living. An extra dollar spent for mortgage and loan interest increases the cost of living and doing business, just as does an extra dollar spent for food, clothing, or machinery. The tight money policy furthermore helped to set off a convulsion in interest rates paid on savings, as well as a fiercely competitive war among financial institutions. High interest payments were used to pull in more savings funds which, in turn, were loaned out at even higher interest rates. This ballooned the cost of carrying the public debt—a burden shared by all taxpayers—to an all-time peak. At $12,000,000,000 a year, interest on the public debt is second only to defense spending in the federal budget.

The credit squeeze undoubtedly moderated spending, but it could not directly attack the cost-push type of inflation. The Federal Reserve admitted the inadequacies of its policy, but it did not start to ease the policy until the closing weeks of the year. Its reasoning was that without anti-inflation support from higher taxes or lower government spending, it could follow no other course.

Meanwhile, dwindling food surpluses, crop failures, and an ever-mounting demand for food for an expanding population gave the farmer a chance to regain some of his lost share of the income pie. The farmer grabbed the opportunity. His share of every $1 spent for food rose from a postwar low of 37¢ in 1964 to around 41¢, and the average cost of food at the retail counter climbed more than 5 per cent.

At the same time, the rising costs of doing business, an eagerness to protect profit margins, and record demands for goods and services, gave businessmen the background against which to mark up prices. There were "confrontations" between the administration and big business leaders in Washington, D.C., to curtail inflation, but in general business snubbed the administration's "voluntary" guidelines.

Businessmen, labor leaders, farmers, and consumers all contributed to 1966's inflation

The rise in living costs, added to a boost in Social Security taxes, resulted in a drop in the "real spendable earnings" of the typical U.S. factory worker. This financial reversal, plus growing labor shortages, and indisputable evidence of a rise in corporate profits provided labor leaders with a basis for demanding higher wages and salaries. Negotiated cash wage hikes during 1966 were the highest since the wage spiral that occurred during the mid-1950s.

Individual consumers would have helped themselves and the economy if they had voluntarily added to their savings and voluntarily curbed their spending, to encourage stabilization of prices. But with the exception of a small decline in a few areas of consumer goods, people kept on spending at an undiminished rate. A housewives' boycott of supermarkets at year's end was hullabalooed, but ended up as little more than a whimper.

And so the nation failed to meet the economic challenge of a peace boom fueled by war. It broke the rules of the New Economics when they dictated unpleasant restraint, instead of pleasant stimulation.

The Shrinking Purchasing Power Of the Dollar

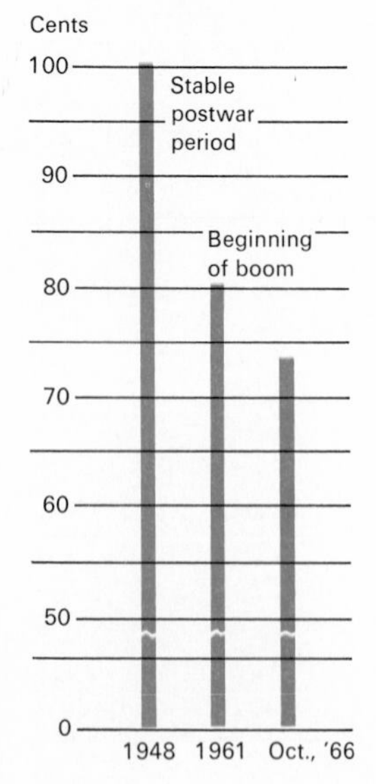

If expenditures for the war in Vietnam continued to rise as projected in late 1966, predictions were that the economy would keep on climbing to new peaks, but at a slower pace than in the past. The reduction in the pace of the rise was made a virtual certainty by the stated plans of businessmen to reduce drastically their spending for new plant and equipment. But assuming mounting war expenditures, anything more than a slowdown in the economy seemed unlikely.

Under any circumstances, the nation faced profound inflationary problems. Wage inflation was a clear and present danger as 1966 ended. With 107 major labor-management agreements affecting more than 2,000,000 workers due to expire during 1967, and with labor leaders making it obvious that they intended to seek liberal wage increases, the outlook for avoiding inflationary pressures appeared slim.

The most optimistic hope for price stability was that the pace of the inflationary rise would be smaller than in 1966. In certain key areas of living costs, however, relentless inflation was a certainty.

Even if the most optimistic hopes were realized in 1967, and the climb in the cost of living in the U.S. was *only* 2½ per cent to 3 per cent, this climb would reduce the dollar to a new all-time low in purchasing power. A 3 per cent erosion may seem small on the surface. But on the basis of a yearly 3 per cent rise in prices, the dollar which bought 100¢ in goods and services in 1966 would be worth only 74.4¢ 10 years hence; worth only 55.4¢ in 20 years, and only 22.8¢ in 50 years.

And inflation is just one economic problem. The nation needs to find ways to employ the skills and wisdom of older Americans and eliminate job discrimination on the basis of age. Solutions are needed regarding employment of Negroes, of young people, and the unskilled. Even with 1966's record employment and income levels, the Negro jobless rate was twice that of whites, and their average family income half that of whites.

The question was not what could be done, but what would be done and when

The United States has to develop a program under which the federal government will channel more funds to state and local governments to help them meet their staggering responsibilities in education, health, citizen protection, law enforcement, slum clearance, etc., and to intensify the fight against air and water pollution. States and cities cannot possibly finance their own expenditures. The only reasonable solution seems to be a more generous sharing of federal revenues with state and local governments.

Finally, there is the towering problem of sustaining and strengthening the aging economic upturn, if and when the Vietnam war ends. Actually, the United States has a great many anti-recession weapons to pull out of its arsenal. These include income and excise tax cuts, easy money to spur building and buying of houses, and other incentives to stimulate business investments.

The question is not what *can* be done when problems arise, but what *will* be done and, will the timing be right? These questions reflected the key challenge that was fumbled in 1966.

That challenge is to use our growing economic knowledge to master our economic, social, and physical environment and thereby create a richer, more rewarding life.

Related Articles

For a complete report on the 1966 year in economics, see Section One, James B. Reston: Focus on The Nation, and the following articles in Section Three:

Agriculture
Atomic Energy
Automobile
Aviation
Banks and Banking
Communications
Economy, The
Electric Power and Equipment
Housing
Insurance
International Trade and Finance
Labor
Manufacturing
Mines and Mining
Money
Petroleum and Gas
Poverty
Publishing
Retailing
Steel Industry
Stocks and Bonds
Taxation
Transportation

Harrison Brown: Focus on Science

A proper relationship between basic and applied research is essential if the U.S. is to reap maximum benefits from science

On Thursday morning, Oct. 13, 1966, Charles Brenton Huggins, director of the Ben May Laboratory for Cancer Research at the University of Chicago, awoke to learn that he had been named co-winner of the 1966 Nobel prize for physiology and medicine. Huggins was honored for his discovery that female sex hormones could be used to control cancer of the prostate in males. It is remarkable that the work recognized by the Nobel prize took place a quarter of a century ago. It is even more remarkable that the Huggins' treatment was based on diverse discoveries going back almost 200 years. And these were discoveries by scientists not engaged in cancer research.

The history of the treatment for cancer of the prostate gland is a classic example of the great importance of fundamental research. Our present knowledge of this cancer is based on work that began with John Hunter, a great 18th-century English physiologist. Hunter noted that the prostate of a castrated bull becomes small and flabby. In the mid-19th century, W. Gruber in Russia discovered that the prostates of castrated men suffer a similar fate. In 1889, J. Griffiths in England published a study of how the size of the prostate in the mole and hedgehog changes with the seasons. In 1926, Eugen Steinach and H. Kun in Paris demonstrated that injecting moles with female hormones, like castration, decreases the size and activity of the prostate gland.

Dr. Huggins' prizewinning work evolved from discoveries made 200 years ago

Meanwhile, in Germany, Paul Grosser and Joseph Husler discovered a substance called *phosphatase*, an enzyme in the lining of the human intestine. Subsequent investigations in Wales and Germany showed that there were two types of phosphatase, and that secretions from the human prostate is rich in one of them.

None of these people had been studying cancer. Then, in the United States in 1938, Alexander B. and Ethel B. Gutman discovered that the blood of patients with cancer of the prostate often contains surplus phosphatase. They showed that prostate cells, though malignant, continue to produce phosphatase and that they pour it into the blood stream in abnormal quantities.

While experimenting on dogs in 1940, Dr. Huggins found that the functioning of the prostate gland was dependent on the production of male sex hormones. In support of these studies, Huggins and his assistant engaged in a few Sunday morning roundups of elderly tumor-ridden dogs from a Chicago pound. From learning how to control the dogs' prostate tumors by manipulating their sex hormones, the scientists moved to devise a diagnosis and treatment for cancer of the prostate, a common, painful, and often fatal affliction of older men.

Huggins' great achievement was to fit together many isolated pieces of information and then build onto them. For having done this, he certainly deserves the Nobel prize. But we must not overlook the patient research of the scientists who produced the basic facts and insights Dr. Huggins needed. Dr. John R. Baker, a distinguished English zoologist asked two decades ago: "What central planner, interested in the cure of cancer, would have supported Griffiths in his studies of the seasonal cycle of the hedgehog, or Grosser and Husler in their biochemical work on the lining membrane of the intestine? How could anyone have connected phosphatase with cancer, when the existence of phosphatase was unknown? And while it was yet unknown, how could the man in charge of the cancer funds know to whom to give the money for research? How lucky it is for sufferers from cancer of the prostate that Griffiths and Grosser and Husler and the others were not doing cancer research!"

Ironically, at about the time the decision was being made in Sweden to honor Dr. Huggins for his achievement, President Lyndon B. Johnson was asking United States health agencies to determine if too much emphasis was being placed on basic research at the expense of immediate medical problems. On June 27, 1966, he stated: "Today I have met with Secretary Gardner, the surgeon general, and the top government team connected with medical research and health services. These men constitute my strategy council in the war against disease. We began a review of the targets and the timetable they have set for winning victories in this war. The National Institutes of Health are spending more than $800,000,000 a year on biomedical research. I am keenly interested to know not only what knowledge this buys but what are the payoffs in terms of healthy lives for our citizens."

Federal spending for R and D is now 20 times the amount that was spent prior to World War II

In light of these remarks, one cannot help but wonder how a "health strategy council" would have viewed Griffiths' work on the prostates of moles and hedgehogs. Or, for that matter, would such a council have encouraged the work of Wilhelm Roentgen, who discovered X rays, or Pierre and Marie Curie who contributed so much to our knowledge of radioactive substances? These people have helped cancer sufferers more than any individuals before or since, yet they were not engaged in cancer research.

President Johnson is not the only one in Washington questioning the size of federal expenditures for research and development (R and D). Congressmen are also asking just how large our R and D efforts ought to be. And they are beginning to question the distribution of funds. By 1966, federal R and D allocations had grown to more than $15,000,000,000 annually, which meant the federal government was footing over 70 per cent of the $21,000,000,000 total support–government and private–of R and D. This is a large sum of money. It represents about 2.3 per cent of our gross national product (GNP) and nearly 15 per cent of our annual federal budget.

Dr. Charles Huggins

In part, the new examination of our nation's R and D effort has been brought about by the financial pressures generated by the war in Vietnam. A major contributing factor, however, has been a lessening of a feeling of urgency. The Cold War has been cooling off. With the completion of the Minuteman and Polaris weapons systems, the missile gap no longer exists. The U.S. is at least holding its own with Russia in space, and in some space activities clearly excels. But perhaps the most important factor is simply that the total amount of money being made available for R and D has become so large. Congressmen feel compelled to ask whether this is in the national interest and whether their constituents are getting a reasonable share of the R and D pie.

Substantial government subsidization of research and development in the United States began over a century ago with the Morrill Act of 1862. The act provided for the creation and maintenance of colleges for agriculture and mechanical arts. Over the decades, federal and state investments in agricultural research have produced staggering results. Research has been largely responsible for the complete transformation of farming techniques and practices. Measured in monetary terms, government investment in agricultural research appears to have paid an average annual return on the investment of about 100 per cent—an achievement which any businessman would applaud enthusiastically.

The federal government did not subsidize other areas of science significantly until World War II. The tremendous technological successes brought about by the mobilization of scientists during that war resulted in a rapid postwar growth of federally sponsored R and D. Today, the government is spending 20 times the amount of money that it spent for R and D in 1939.

Technological innovation has become a major factor in national economic growth

Will federal research and development expenditures continue to rise? There is presently a leveling off of annual expenditures at about $15,000,000,000, partly because development on Minuteman and Polaris systems has been completed, and partly because expenditures for the space effort seem to be steadying. Other components of the total R and D budget, however, are continuing to grow.

For example, when one examines the major R and D needs in transportation and communication, pollution and waste disposal, resource utilization, health, and general urban problems, there can be little doubt that federal expenditures for R and D will rise again—and rise rapidly. Indeed, the point can be made that technological innovation is fully as important a factor in economic growth as any of the traditional factors such as land, labor, and capital.

The relationship between technological innovation and economic growth is extremely difficult to measure. It has been estimated that about 90 per cent of the rise in output per man-hour in the United States since 1900 is attributable to technological progress. But we cannot specify as yet just what our optimum investment in research and development should be. Thus, in the current debate on the size of the federal R and D budget, it is extremely difficult to decide who is right and who is wrong. Nevertheless, examination of the problems now confronting us indicates our national rate of expenditure may be too low.

Be that as it may, the United States ranks first among nations in gross R and D expenditures. The total of $21,000,000,000 greatly exceeds that spent by other nations. In proportion to GNP, our R and D expenditure of 3 per cent also stands at the top of the list. Similarly, our per capita expenditure of over $100 exceeds that of other nations. The United Kingdom comes close to the United States in R and D spending with about 2.5 per cent of its GNP. The percentage allocated by the Soviet Union is also probably near the 2.5 figure.

Study of hedgehogs contributed to cancer cure

Russia, the United Kingdom, and the United States rank high partly because of their large expenditures for military R and D. For civilian R and D expenditures alone, Japan, Sweden, the United Kingdom, and the United States spend about the same proportion of their GNP (1.5 per cent). France, The Netherlands, and West Germany spend only slightly less.

Recognizing that R and D properly handled can stimulate economic growth, many countries are making strenuous efforts to increase these expenditures. For example, Japan, whose economy is growing explosively, is developing a variety of science-based industries. It will probably soon be spending over 2 per cent of its GNP on civilian R and D.

By contrast, the less technologically advanced nations spend very little. Most of the nations of Africa, Asia, and Latin America spend less than .2 per cent of their GNP on R and D. It is not that these poorer countries do not need research and development. Problems of agriculture, health, resource evaluation, and industrial development beg to be solved. But the competing demands for limited funds often result in science being excluded from the development plans of such countries.

A proper ratio between basic and applied research must be maintained

Today, in the United States, about two-thirds of the federal R and D appropriations is used for development and one-third for research. The greater part of the research is *applied* in the sense that it is directed at specific practical objectives. Of the $15,000,000,000 spent in 1965 by the federal government for R and D, only about $2,000,000,000 was allocated for *basic* research. This term defines research that is carried out for its own sake without thought of immediate application. Roentgen's studies of X rays or Griffiths' studies of the seasonal cycle of the hedgehog would be considered basic research.

What fraction of R and D expenditures in the United States should be devoted to basic research? We should spend as much money as possible without substantially impeding R and D aimed at the solution of practical problems. Using this guideline, were we to allocate much less than 10 per cent of our total R and D expenditures to basic research, it would probably be too little. It is interesting that the current annual amount spent for basic research seems to be about right–approximately 10 per cent of the total R and D expenditure.

Federal Funds For Research And Development

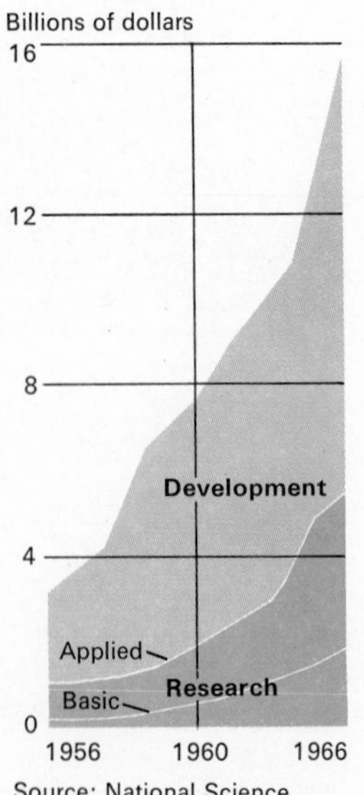

Source: National Science Foundation

The total money spent on basic research is one problem; the way it is spent is another. More than 90 per cent of the federal expenditures for all research is now channeled through government agencies, such as the Department of Defense (DOD) and its various agencies, which have concrete goals or missions. The greater part of the funds available to colleges and universities for basic research comes from these mission-oriented agencies. Not infrequently, these basic research programs are tailored to meet the needs of the agency, rather than the scientist's conception of what is important from a purely scientific point of view.

Another problem involving the distribution of basic research funds lies in the tendency for those academic institutions which are already large and competent to become more so, often at the expense of the smaller institutions. The 10 largest universities with Department of Defense contracts receive 70 per cent of the funds earmarked for university research. The 10 largest universities with National Aeronautics and Space Administration (NASA) contracts receive about 60 per cent of federal outlays for space research. As these institutions tend to be concentrated geographically—notably in Massachusetts and California—serious political problems arise.

Along with the political problems lies the deep-seated feeling of many members of Congress that to support research in universities is to support a giveaway program. Most Congressmen look upon space and nuclear research as a necessity. But the need of research for its own sake is less obvious. It is difficult for most people to appreciate that far from being a giveaway, sponsorship of such research is a most vital part of our entire national research fabric.

Can anything be done to assure that government money for fundamental research is distributed efficiently? One suggestion would be to channel more R and D funds through NSF. There is a growing feeling, particularly among scientists, that although government agencies with specific goals should sponsor research appropriate to their work, the greater part of basic research money should be handled by agencies like NSF which do not have specific goals.

How the funds are distributed, and who gets what, are two other problems facing the U.S.

The National Science Foundation itself is attacking the problem of uneven geographic distribution of funds to university research programs by helping smaller institutions to improve their research capacity and competence.

Whatever comes of presidential and congressional uneasiness about what we are getting for our basic research dollars, one hopes science will not always be required to deliver immediate payoffs. As in the case of the treatment of prostate cancer, it can take centuries to connect the problems of castrated bulls, seasonally affected hedgehogs, and tumor-ridden dogs. But how fortunate it is for mankind when an unfettered science is permitted to make those connections.

Related Articles

For a complete report on the 1966 year in science and in technology, see Section One, JOHN H. GLENN, JR.: FOCUS ON SPACE; Section Two, MAN OF TWO WORLDS, and OUR PILL-FILLED LIVES; and the following articles in Section Three:

Anthropology
Archaeology
Astronauts
Astronomy
Atomic Energy
Aviation
Awards and Prizes (Science and Industry)
Biochemistry
Biology
Botany
Chemistry
Communications
Computers
Dentistry
Electronics
Engine and Energy
Engineering
Geology
Health & Disease
Huggins, Charles
Insect
Invention
Kastler, Alfred
Medicine
Mental Health
Metallurgy
Mulliken, Robert S.
Nobel Prizes
Ocean
Physics
Psychology
Rous, Francis Peyton
Science and Research
Science Clubs of America
Space Travel
Weather
Zoology

Lawrence A. Cremin: Focus on Education

Despite a number of exciting events in education during 1966, the year will, perhaps, be best remembered as the 'Year of the Merger'

The educational headlines of 1966 were dramatic, yet familiar. Enrollments soared to an all-time high. The federal government contributed more to education than ever before and controversy flared over desegregation in the schools. Yet for all their drama, these developments may well have been less significant than a series of terse announcements buried amid the statistics of the financial pages. The announcements told of a succession of corporate mergers that promised to exert a profound influence on the character and content of school and college programs.

In January, 1966, for example, Random House announced its intention to merge its publishing business with the Radio Corporation of America (RCA). Bennett Cerf, chairman of Random House, said the agreement "reflects our conviction that publishing and electronics are natural partners in the incredible expansion immediately ahead for every phase of education in our country." David Sarnoff, chairman of RCA, indicated that while RCA had no interest in running a book business, publishing and electronics were inevitably converging. "They have the software, and we have the hardware," he explained.

Mergers between electronic and publishing firms will greatly affect U.S. education

Other mergers occurred in rapid succession. The Columbia Broadcasting System, Inc. (CBS) said it would acquire Creative Playthings, a producer of toys and educational materials for nursery schools and kindergartens. Raytheon, a manufacturer of communications equipment, bought D. C. Heath and Company, an old and respected publisher of textbooks. The Minnesota Mining and Manufacturing Company (3M) and *Newsweek* magazine reported a joint arrangement to produce and distribute current events materials to classrooms. And the Sylvania Company formed a study group with *Reader's Digest* magazine to develop electronic systems for schools.

These new enterprises took their places beside a number of other rapidly growing ventures; most of them resulting from corporate mergers or purchases only recently completed. The Xerox Corporation, for example, had entered the education market by buying the Wesleyan University Press; American Education Publications, producers of periodicals and books for children; Basic Systems, a manufacturer of teaching machines; and University Microfilms, a publisher of scholarly and scientific materials. Similarly, International Business Machines (IBM) had acquired Science Research Associates, a producer of test materials, science kits, and teaching machines and programs. And in the most dramatic action of all, General Electric and Time, Inc., had formed an entirely new company, General Learning Corporation. Former Commissioner of Education Francis Keppel was named chairman of the board.

What was significant about these ventures? Why had they been launched? What would be their influence?

At least part of the story goes back to the earliest days of the American school system. The fact is that the schools and colleges have always needed books and other materials for teaching programs, and from the beginning, private publishers and manufacturers have supplied them. In the 18th century, the most popular schoolbook was the *New England*

Primer, a text that began with the alphabet and proceeded through a series of graded exercises designed to teach children to read while they learned certain religious doctrines. Such books were produced in vast quantities. One scholar has estimated that as many as six to eight million copies were sold between 1680 and 1830.

In the 19th century, as public schooling became more widely available, the so-called education market rapidly expanded. During this period, the most popular schoolbooks were the McGuffey readers, a series of graded texts that started children on familiar stories and poems, such as *Mary Had A Little Lamb*, or *Twinkle, Twinkle Little Star*, and introduced them by the time they reached the *Sixth Reader* to works of Shakespeare, Milton, Tennyson, and Longfellow.

The dominance of the McGuffey readers should not, however, obscure the fact that there were other series on the market and that competition among publishers was spirited and often cutthroat. In a long and bitter contest between the McGuffey readers and the Appleton readers, as one publisher put it, "every device known to the agency managers of the houses was employed. . . . It was war." All the techniques of aggressive salesmanship were employed. The product itself—in this case the schoolbook—was packaged as attractively and written as inoffensively as possible. And prospective purchasers—superintendents, principals, and school board members—were visited, flattered, threatened, cajoled, wined, and dined. Practices of that day have, in some cases, persisted to our own time, at every level of the educational system.

The number of young Americans attending school has doubled since World War II

It should also be pointed out that textbooks represent only one of many products supplied to the education market. Aside from school buildings themselves, which in 1964 accounted for roughly 6 per cent of the total new construction in the United States, there are school furnishings, athletic equipment, laboratory and shop materials, lunchroom supplies, maps, encyclopedias, typewriters, projectors, uniforms, musical instruments, buses, and a host of other products. All of them are sold to schools by competing private concerns.

Francis Keppel

Thus the relationship between suppliers of educational materials and schools and colleges is in some ways as old as the schools themselves. What was new about that relationship that made 1966 the year of the merger in the education industry?

Essentially, it resulted from the convergence of three profound changes. There were skyrocketing enrollments, which dramatically increased the size of the education market. There were technological innovations which fundamentally altered the kinds of educational materials that were both possible and desirable to produce. Finally, there were federal funds which for the first time became available to private industry through direct grants.

Increased enrollments were the clearest and most obvious factor in the situation. The number of young Americans attending schools and colleges had exploded since World War II, and there was every indication that the increase would continue into the 1970s. Due to high birth rates, more children were entering the schools. Given the economic vitality of the society of the United States and the importance of education in the economy, these children were remaining for ever-longer periods of time. Thus, the number of consumers of educational materials was growing steadily.

Beyond that, there were radical changes in the nature of schooling itself. The American people were demanding more of the schools at every level. This created a market for better materials. Then, too, new knowledge was being developed at an unprecedented rate, and this occasioned fundamental changes in curricula. Most important, there were revolutionary changes in the technology of teaching itself, brought about by the development of teaching machines, programmed learning, and computer-based instruction.

Interest in teaching devices, first developed in the 1920s, has been revived

Teaching machines, the name given to various devices by which students can proceed step by step at their own pace through material to be learned, were initially conceived by Professor Sidney Pressey at Ohio State University in the 1920s. They were based on the psychological principle of reinforcement, which maintains that learners tend to make habitual those behaviors that are rewarded. Following this principle, Pressey developed simple devices which would question students on certain material, tell them when they had given the correct answers (thereby rewarding them), and indicate where accurate information might be found when they had given incorrect answers. Somehow, as has often happened in the history of technology, Pressey's ideas did not take hold.

Interest was revived in the 1950s, however, largely through the work of Professor B. F. Skinner at Harvard University. He suggested that simple teaching machines could be developed, which would not only test whether a student had learned information correctly, but which would actually present new information to the student.

Skinner's technique was to devise a series of questions that presented certain facts or ideas in a carefully graded sequence. The initial ones were relatively simple, and then subsequent ones became more complex. The learner answered each question by choosing from a series of responses. If he chose the correct answer, the machine permitted him to go on to the next question, thus rewarding him. If he chose the incorrect answer, the machine held the question in front of him until he did choose the correct answer.

The educational and business world quickly became fascinated with Skinner's devices. But, as Skinner and his associates soon became aware, the crucial educational problem lay not in the construction of machines, but rather in the development of sequences of questions—called programs—that would lead students, working on their own, through the information and concepts they needed to learn.

The machines themselves were easy to design. A number of companies put them into production rapidly and sold them in large quantities to schools and families. But good programs were another story. They took time to develop. They demanded rare pedagogical insight into both the nature of learning and the organization of various kinds of subject matter. They required testing, retesting, and still more retesting. As a result, they were exceedingly expensive. It is no surprise, therefore, that progress in the technology of the machines, or "hardware," as they are called, was far more rapid than progress in the quality of the educational content of the programs, or "software."

The next major development came in the early 1960s, when a number of companies began to cooperate with university behavioral scientists in developing computer-assisted teaching machines that would lead students through far more sophisticated programs in a far more sophisticated way.

Federal support for research and development programs became available for the first time

Professor Patrick Suppes of Stanford University, using computer-assisted typewriters (produced by IBM) that could be operated by either the computer or the student, attempted to devise instructional systems that would not only drill and tutor students through regular sequences of questions, but also initiate dialogues between students and the computer around such topics as "What was the role of the railroad in the economic development of the Mississippi Valley?" Suppes conceded the extraordinary difficulty of designing computer systems that could carry their share of such dialogues, but he did not think the problems were insurmountable. The key, of course, lay in anticipating the sorts of information the students would have and need, and in programming that information in such a systematic way that questions and answers from a particular student would elicit appropriate responses from the computer. It was this very problem that lay behind some of the corporate mergers designed to bring together specialists in computer technology and specialists in academic subjects.

The last factor that made 1966 the year of the merger was the availability for the first time of federal support for educational research and development under private commercial auspices. As the new U.S. Commissioner of Education, Harold Howe, said in a June address announcing the new program: "Technological advances can make their greatest contribution to educational improvement if we have a close give-and-take between the 'hardware' and the 'software' people, so that they share understandings and objectives. It is clear from the many weddings of publishers and electronics firms that industry is becoming increasingly aware of this need." Obviously, the prospect of give-and-take, assisted by federal research and development funds, had figured prominently in the rash of corporate mergers.

Learning from a machine

What, then, was the significance of the new ventures? It was clear from the outset that they would be controversial. There was, for instance, bitter disagreement within the teaching profession. Some educators saw computer-assisted instruction as the kind of revolutionary breakthrough that would finally permit schools really to individualize their programs; that is, to adjust the pace and character of teaching to the special needs and abilities of each student. Moreover, they added, by taking over the burden of drill, practice, and other humdrum activities, the machines would free teachers for more creative work.

Critics of computer-assisted instruction contended, on the other hand, that it was inordinately expensive and ultimately dehumanizing. Teaching machines, they argued, were based on reinforcement theories of learning. These theories, they contended, were grossly inadequate for explaining human mental processes. Real teaching, the critics insisted, involves a relationship between human beings.

It was with respect to the public control of education, however, that the most important questions were being raised. The new companies which had entered the field were well financed and well staffed. There was no question that they had already produced some materials that were better and more effective than anything previously available.

But whatever their accomplishments, there was no denying that the new companies were private, profit making concerns. Their ultimate responsibility was to their stockholders. This ultimate responsibility in no way needed to conflict with the public interest, but it clearly could. If it did, who was to represent the public interest?

How the direction and the content of American education will be determined is now at stake

A publication issued by the Ohio State University College of Education devoted an entire issue to "Commercial Pressures in the Schools," citing the way teachers, administrators, and board members across the country were being subjected to aggressive sales campaigns. As Dean Theodore Sizer of Harvard's Graduate School of Education observed in his annual report, "The new companies are . . . impatient . . . and we run the risk of having the schools inundated with quantities of technically exciting but intellectually inadequate materials."

It was easy enough to reply that teachers, administrators, and board members would simply have to be more prudent, wise, and discriminating than ever. But with the large amounts of money involved, the complexity of the decisions to be made, the growing tendency of companies to package whole courses or programs on an all-or-nothing basis, and the ever-present desire of stockholders, prudence, wisdom, and discrimination would be increasingly difficult to achieve.

Ultimately, what was at stake was the way in which the direction and content of American education would be determined. And in the development of new procedures, the whole delicately balanced system of public and professional control that had evolved over the years would be facing some of its severest and most critical tests.

Related Articles

For a complete report on the 1966 year in education, see the following articles in Section Three:

American Library Association
Blindness
Canadian Library Association
Canadian Literature
Child Guidance
Child Welfare
Communications
Congress of the United States
Education
Foundations
Handicapped, The
Library
Literature
Literature for Children
Parents and Teachers, National Congress of
Poverty
Publishing
State Government
Television

John H. Glenn, Jr.: Focus on Space

Despite the Gemini successes and the space probes to and around the moon, the year ended with a nagging problem still unresolved

In successfully completing the manned Gemini program and inaugurating remote controlled on-the-surface investigation of the moon, man has reached new dimensions of professionalism and accomplishment in his exploration of space. If 1964 was a year of building, and 1965 was a period of perfecting, then 1966 was "where the action was."

In manned investigation, five successful Gemini missions in 1966 concluded a brilliant effort that saw the United States launch a string of 10 manned flights in just 20 months. Highly trained astronauts effected the first docking with an orbiting spacecraft, established a new altitude record of 851 miles, and finally overcame the difficulties of extra vehicular activity. The United States not only moved solidly toward the goal of a manned lunar landing, it also enlarged and crystallized man's knowledge of the space surrounding his planet and greatly improved his ability to operate in that environment.

When the Gemini program ended with the splashdown of Gemini XII on Nov. 15, 1966, American astronauts had amassed more hours of space flight than the total flying hours—both training and combat—of many World War II pilots. And one of the astronauts, James Lovell, traveled more miles during his nearly 14 days in Gemini VII than any other man. His 431 hours took him more than 7,300,000 miles, far exceeding the distance traveled by even the most experienced airline pilot. As 1966 ended, the box score on manned space flight read:

Project Gemini has proved man's ability to perform complex maneuvers in outer space

	Manned Flights	Manned Earth Revolutions	Man-Hours
United States	16	684	1,993
Russia	8	293	507

The significance of Projects Mercury and Gemini, however, does not lie in the number of manned flights or the total hours spent in space, as impressive as these statistics may be. Rather it lies in the fact that the major objectives of learning the effects of extended weightlessness and developing space rendezvous and docking capabilities have both been adequately met. While the Gemini missions included a number of experiments in astronomy, biology, and other sciences, their major purpose was to develop the tools and techniques necessary to proceed with Project Apollo, the next stage in the U.S. lunar program.

The most lengthy Project Apollo mission will require approximately 14 days; the two-week flight of Gemini VII demonstrated that man can well withstand the rigors of weightless space flight for that period. The rendezvous and docking procedures required for the round trip to the moon are exacting and intricate maneuvers which had never been attempted before the Gemini flights of 1966. If there were previous doubts regarding man's ability to perform such highly complex maneuvering in space, they have now been erased. It has been dramatically proved that the procedures and plans for sending men to the moon's surface and returning them safely to earth are within the capabilities of U.S. personnel and technology.

Meanwhile successful tests of the three-man Apollo spacecraft and the huge new Saturn rocket series indicate that Project Apollo is moving ahead on schedule. On Feb. 26, 1966, the heat shield of the new Apollo capsule withstood the scorching heat of re-entry during a 5,000-mile unmanned ballistic flight. Then, on July 5, the 92-foot Saturn I lofted the heaviest payload (58,000 pounds) the U.S. has ever put into orbit. Even more significantly, the hydrogen-fueled rocket that will be the final stage atop the mighty Saturn V—the stage that will carry the astronauts to the moon—ignited successfully on command.

Project Apollo is expected to enter the manned flight stage early in 1967 when three astronauts are scheduled to fly an earth-orbital mission of up to 14 days' duration. Thus the objective of completing the first lunar exploration and return before the end of this decade still appears to be well within our reach. Manned space flight is now entering the third and final phase of this breathtaking adventure.

We learned more about the moon in 1966 than in all the history of lunar study

1966 was also a year of action in unmanned space exploration. Both Russia and the United States reached an information-return ratio never before approached in the Space Age. Both nations successfully soft-landed spacecraft on the moon for the first time and sent others at such a precise speed and direction that they were captured by the moon's gravity and became the first lunar satellites.

On Feb. 3, 1966, the Russian Luna IX gently lowered itself down to the Ocean of Storms just before the lunar dawn. The Russians had failed to "soft land" instruments on at least four previous occasions; this successful landing testified to both the difficulty of the feat and their determination. The Luna IX moon station sent back the first photographs taken from the surface of the moon. Two months later, on April 4, the Russians scored another dramatic first by placing Luna X in a great, sweeping orbit of the moon. The data collected as it circled the moon gave us the first indication of the extent of the radiation "tail" that trails behind the earth.

The United States unmanned moon program bounced back on June 2 when Surveyor I achieved a soft landing near the lunar equator on its first try. During its first 12 days on the moon, Surveyor's solar powered instruments responded to over 100,000 commands sent from earth. Then in August, Lunar Orbiter I was placed in orbit around the moon. This maneuverable satellite had among its assignments the photographing of possible Apollo landing sites.

Later in the year, both Russia and the United States sent additional spacecraft to the moon. Not only were navigation techniques further refined, but both countries independently established that lunar landing sites and surface characteristics appear safe for manned exploration. Surveyor and Lunar Orbiter gave geophysicists, selenographers, and astronomers a wealth of new basic material that will be under intensive study for months—and perhaps years—to come. I think it is safe to say that man learned more about the moon and its surface during 1966 than in all the previous history of lunar observation.

The most curious aspect of recent space exploration was the extended absence of Russian manned flights. Not since March 18, 1965, when Cosmonaut Aleksei Leonov "walked" in space for 11 minutes, had a

Soviet cosmonaut gone into orbit. Due to the deep snow over most of the Soviet Union, the Russians have never orbited a cosmonaut earlier than March 18 or later than October 12. However, they inexplicably allowed two summers to pass without attempting to extend their manned experience in such vital areas as maneuvering, docking, and extra vehicular activity. They claim to be neck and neck with the U.S. in unmanned lunar exploration which is a reasonably sure sign that they have not abandoned their often stated goal of being the first to land a man on the moon. They continued their experiments with communications satellites, especially the transmission of color television. They continued to launch their Cosmos satellites at a rate of more than one a month. And on March 1, 1966, their Venus III made man's first contact with another planet. But why were their cosmonauts grounded?

There was an inexplicable absence of Soviet manned space activity

A close veil of secrecy surrounds the Soviet space program—the Russians release only what they wish, when they wish. It was known, however, that the Soviets were testing new rockets in the Pacific and this is often a good indication of forthcoming flights. At least one report hinted at the development of a new spacecraft to succeed their Vostok and Voshkod, just as Apollo succeeds the Gemini and Mercury vehicles. The year 1967 is the 50th anniversary of the Russian revolution—an occasion that will cause great celebration in the Soviet Union. Some observers feel that during 1967 the Soviets will probably attempt to make up, in one or several strokes, what they may have previously lost in manned space flight experience.

Some slight cracks in the Russian veil of secrecy did occur in 1966. The most notable was that, concurrent with the visit of French President Charles de Gaulle, outsiders were permitted to witness a Russian unmanned space launching for the first time. This was followed by a joint Soviet-French agreement to conduct cooperative space shots in which French payloads will be lofted by Russian rockets. By the end of 1966, few details on how this cooperative program would be implemented had been revealed. More Soviet papers and technical reports, especially in the biomedical area, were presented at international conferences in 1966 than in previous years. While this hardly represented a thaw in their previous policies, the temperature may have risen a few degrees from the subzero "hard freeze" of past seasons.

Splashdown of Gemini XII

The United States space program, in contrast, maintained its open stance before the world. The Russian-French space agreement was obviously disappointing to the U.S. since the latter had worked closely with the French space program for several years. However, the agreement may have indicated a trend which will see smaller or less capable space-interested powers aligning themselves with larger efforts which are already underway.

Early in the fall of 1966, James E. Webb, administrator of the National Aeronautics and Space Administration (NASA), indicated the possibility of still greater foreign participation in the U.S. program, and did not rule out consideration of foreign astronaut candidates at some future date. This action was not just a reaction to the Russian

French agreement. The U.S. has followed a pattern of openness and cooperation from the very inception of its space program. In fact, Congress wrote it into the Space Act of 1958. In the years since then, the U.S. has developed working agreements with 71 countries, has included 17 scientific experiments for foreign scientists on its flights, and has launched seven boosters where the complete payload belonged to Canada, France, Italy, The Netherlands, and the United Kingdom. Still more such missions are planned, adding West Germany and the European Space Research Organization (ESRO) to the participants.

The esteem with which the U.S. space effort is regarded in other parts of the world was brought forcefully home to me once again in the spring of 1966. For five weeks, I visited with scientists and leaders of governments, universities, and technical organizations throughout Western Europe. Without exception, I found them extremely appreciative of the openness of the U.S. program and intensely interested in becoming more involved with its space activities.

The future direction of the U.S. space program must now be decided

The efforts of European nations to develop their own space organization ran into some serious difficulties in 1966. Both ESRO and European Launch Development Organization (ELDO) have had funding problems from the start, and these came to a head with the withdrawal of considerable financial support by some member nations. It is probably still too early to make an accurate forecast, but such financial difficulties might well produce a still closer alignment of European interests with the U.S. program.

As the basic tools of space exploration become more common, international effort and cooperation is almost certain to increase. Scientists the world over are vitally interested in such research and exploration, even though they do not have their own national programs. This past year saw a great increase in the activities of the liaison office which NASA maintains in Paris to coordinate U.S. efforts with Europe's governments and scientists.

But even as 1966 produced many reasons for optimism, it also ended with a nagging and persistent problem that had not been resolved. While Project Mercury determined that man could go safely into space, and Project Gemini built the know-how that enabled us to proceed to the lunar exploration of Project Apollo, there remained no clear-cut goal of what U.S. objectives should be beyond Apollo. This is a problem that not only played a predominant role in NASA considerations in 1966; it was also the subject of intensive study by presidential advisory groups and congressional committees. But such studies, though useful, do not constitute positive action. The capability to continue future large-scale space programs will go inexorably downhill with the passage of time unless concrete decisions are made.

Gemini XII edges up to Agena target vehicle

Research and engineering for space exploration require technical excellence of the highest order. These projects are large, complex, and without parallel. They require that planning be begun far in advance of the actual space event. For instance, planning was underway in 1961 for Project Apollo equipment that will not be tested until 1967 and will not actually be put into use until lunar landing and return perhaps in 1969. This long lead time creates large problems for personnel management in that the design and engineering team is mostly finished with its work many months or, in some cases, years before the actual testing and use of the hardware. In the course of making possible our dramatic space achievements, the U.S. has developed a very large, extremely capable research organization—an organization experienced in new areas of design where unprecedented power, speed, and complexity must work in a hostile environment. Yet this team now has no assignments because no clear-cut projects beyond Apollo have been selected.

There are literally thousands of projects which could utilize this vast talent. To get a mandate on the future direction of the space program is probably the single greatest problem facing NASA management. Determination of such objectives is not a simple matter, for there are not unlimited research dollars in the nation's economy. The purposes for which these dollars are to be expended must be weighed very carefully. There are always those who like to compare what could be done if these funds were spent for medicine, schools, or other worthy projects. I do not feel, however, that the U.S. has ignored other areas, or that the space program is being run at the expense of other programs. On the contrary, I think a quickened interest in science and research has probably benefited all other fields, and is in itself a beneficial fallout from the space program.

A historic treaty hopefully assures the peaceful use of outer space

Despite this lingering problem, 1966 ended on an optimistic note. The first international treaty governing space exploration was approved by the United Nations General Assembly in December, 1966. President Lyndon B. Johnson hailed the treaty as the "most important control development" since the 1963 treaty banning nuclear testing in the atmosphere, in space, and under water. The historic treaty prohibits the placing of nuclear arms and other weapons of mass destruction in orbit around the earth or installing such weapons on the moon or other celestial bodies. The treaty also provides for free access to space installations on celestial bodies. The intent of the treaty is perfectly clear: that our earthly conflicts not be extended into outer space. The treaty is open to all nations, both in and out of the United Nations. Hopefully, all nations would endorse the treaty and thus ensure the peaceful uses of outer space.

Related Articles

For a complete report on the 1966 year in space, see also Section One, Harrison Brown: Focus on Science, and the following articles in Section Three:

Astronauts
Astronomy
Communications
Electronics
France
Russia
Space Exploration
United Nations
Weather

Alistair Cooke: Focus on The Arts

The absence of proper urban and suburban planning is creating an environment devoid of essential aesthetic stimulation

Somewhere, I do not doubt, a neglected artist is living out his last days in a garret stocked with unsold canvases. Somewhere, a board of trustees is promising an American city a "cultural center." Somewhere, a jazz performer is planning to single out for glory a hitherto neglected instrument, as musicians did with the saxophone in the early 1900s and as the blues pianists did a year or more ago with the proud organ. Somewhere, a young playwright is about to dynamite the Theater of the Absurd, and a young film director, let us hope, is writing finis to *cinéma vérité* by riveting his camera, for a change, to the floor. And everywhere, network tycoons are wondering how to break out of television's "wasteland" or, preferably, how to make it more profitable.

But if there is now pending a radical rejection of Op and Pop, and Pinter plays, and obsessive sex films, and the Batman formula, it is all being done in secret. In painting, theater, movies, opera, television, and jazz—and in the manner of presenting these things within four walls—1966 will not, I fancy, go down as a revolutionary year.

Our burgeoning population is becoming more heavily centered around the city

For this reason, I would like to devote this annual report to a single theme and an art that none of us can escape from, however indifferent we may be to Tintoretto, Tchaikovsky, and Turner (Joseph Mallard, William, or Lana). In fact, it overwhelms us every day of our lives. I mean the art of architecture. In particular, the art, or nonart, of cities.

Every generation seems to take for granted that the cities it grew up in are the usual shell for living, just as all of us take for granted that the language we speak assumed its more or less final form in the years we were in high school. When I was in elementary school in England, we used to be asked, about once a year, to write an essay on the advantages and disadvantages of living in "town or country." It was a dismal chore, for the answers were known beforehand. The town, as I recall, had less oxygen but more zip, and the country was pretty but dull. None of us, sitting in a forest of grimy red brick under Manchester skies as dramatic as blotting paper, ever doubted that we were living in the only bearable sort of human community. All of us assumed that farm boys were clods who, on their privileged trips into town, were bowled over by the ingenious streetcars, the dense horizon of slums, and the sophisticated rumblings of the Halle Orchestra.

That was before radio and television; and long before the internal combustion engine, the five-day week, and the supermarket had combined to empty the old cities and pour their fugitives over the surrounding landscape to create the new "suburb."

I do not suppose any schoolboy is required today to make a simple contrast between town and country because, in spite of the still flourishing magazine of that name, the distinction is obsolete. A majority of Americans now live in neither, but in one or another of the regional variations of suburbia: the split-level mortgage tract on the freeway, a type of human community practically unknown before World War II. From 1950 to 1960, two-thirds of the 29,000,000 who increased the population landed in the new suburbs. Yet to this day, the figures of the Bureau of the Census and the Bureau of Agricultural Economics go on making a simple separation between "urban" and "rural" populations. The number of genuine countrymen, that is to say farmers, has declined from more than half of the population in 1870 to less than 8 per cent in 1964, the latest year for which statistics are available.

Come to think of it, it is astonishing that in all the writing and speechifying that goes on in this country about the arts, so little has been said, and even less done, about actually *creating* the 20th century city. Governors and mayors, boards of estimate, housing and public health commissioners, lately the police, and more recently still the politicians, have moaned about the decay of our cities and the flight to the suburbs. We have been involved for a decade or more in trying to patch up the downtown slums with something called "urban renewal," which in practice has come to mean everything from civic drives for cultural centers and brave little efforts to preserve an old city hall or a Civil War monument, to cosy deals between wrecking contractors and real estate boards. A subcommittee of the Senate has just ended a series of exhausting—and exhaustive—hearings into the so-called "crisis of the cities." It was an inquest long overdue, and the Ribicoff committee is to be honored for exposing the complexity of the city's social problems rising from the dust of its disintegration. One of these problems, and surely not the least, is how the old cities can be renewed in a modern form, and how the new suburbs are to be decently designed to meet human needs. How, in a word, can architecture be made to serve and at the same time please us?

Very little has been done about actually creating a truly 20th century city

A city, of course, does not spring from a drawing board. More than in most of the arts, its form is dictated by its function, and also by dubious functions that interested parties would like to wish on it. (Who asked *you* if you wanted eight motels, 10 secondhand car lots, and a drag-race strip on the way into town?)

It is an unfortunate fact, and also a law of life, that most cities of any great age are a bundle, or amalgam, of all the styles of architecture, and all the passing interests, of the people who have lived in them. If they retain a homogeneous character, it is usually because they were built, or flourished, in a single period, and then progress passed them. Williamsburg, Va., for example, could be restored without a drastic overhauling because when Richmond became a safer place from which to defend the Old Dominion during the Revolutionary War, Williamsburg was abandoned in its prime. It slumbered on as a colonial relic, despite some new building, until the 1920s, when John D. Rockefeller, Jr., recognized the ease of reviving it.

Paris enjoys the reputation of being the most beautiful of modern metropolises not because its citizens are, as they like to think, the most civilized of contemporary Westerners, but because long ago the city council decided to preserve the 17th century core of the city with a code of the strictest prohibitions which even the Nazis respected until the day they decided to blow it up. Thanks to the conscience of the occupation commander, this order was never given. And so Paris still remains. (When the commander, General Dietrich von Choltitz, died in November, 1966, his funeral was appropriately attended by an honor guard comprised of French, British, and also American officials.)

Florence is another example of a city that culture-vultures constantly compare, to our shame, with our own steel and cow capitals. But, as you can easily see by peering into the shops, and up at the modern buildings, the 20th century Florentine is as lumpish and tasteless as the rest of us; he is lucky that Florence has been more or less in a coma since it put the violent and beautiful visions of the Renaissance in paint and stone.

I have gone on about these old cities and the reasons for their elegant reputations, because there is a type of American who is just as crass as the Europeans who scold him for building formless and ugly cities, so unlike the ones they (i.e. their great-great-great-great grandfathers) built. It is a brutal and obvious truth, nevertheless not much remarked on, that the cities of Europe (and Asia) are beautiful only to the extent that they have retained their oldest parts. And the small country towns have kept the charm of a single style because their inhabitants have stayed too poor to change it. Once their crop is in demand, or somebody starts a bicycle factory, and the people begin to struggle toward the middle class, their towns take on the flashy store facades, the fluorescent strip lighting, the garish villadom of Newark or Streatham; their prosperous cities become as ghastly as Brussels, Berlin, Sheffield, Providence, or Gary, Indiana.

The modern city is a barnacled monstrosity, unfit for the decent life of its poeple

So most of our cities are disheveled and ugly, as are most of the commercial cities of Europe, because they are children of the mid-19th century. On the other hand, the late 18th and early 19th century New England house happily combined grace with utility, as few domestic forms before or since; so much so that to this day, like the Georgian house in England, it is every bit as liveable as the ranch-style, split-level box in which the tired commuter suppresses his children in the interests of privacy, work, or simply hearing his friends talk. But wherever manufacturing came to New England, or for that matter to the Midwest and the South, the Victorian factory and its dingy row houses and its brick Gothic church and its dismal schools came, too.

In short, the modern city is today in much the same plight on three or four continents. It is a barnacled monstrosity, run-down and inadequate for the decent life of most of its teeming people. From our point of view (which, I had better say, is that of high-minded students yearning for beauty in the places we live and move among, as well as on museum walls and television screens), the significant thing about it is that it was created, not by architects, but by builders and real estate men.

Entrance to suburbia

How about city planners? They are an admirable species, as architects are, but while they may have the vision of the good life, they do not have the power to create it. That lies with cement contractors, and construction men, and real estate boards, and their political buddies. The last effective city planners were the founders of the cities we go abroad to gape at: The enlightened monarchs who could hire their favorite architect and, when the notion occurred to them, command him to create a Salzburg or perhaps a Bath or a Vienna.

The great patrons of the arts, it has been said, have now been replaced by boards of well-meaning, and rich, foundations. Only partly. For if it takes $165,000,000 (so far) of Rockefeller money to turn two blocks of tenements into Lincoln Center, what would it take to build, or rebuild, a whole city?

The answer ought to be an enlightened minority of a state or city government that has the power to pass the job once again back to an architect, or a team of architects. But this is the kind of answer given by Plato and liberal professors of political science and is wildly impossible in any political oligarchy we know. There is this to be said for Plato: He was able to offer his bland and beautiful prescriptions of the ideal society because he presumed it would be run by a dictator. The liberal professors just have to hope that a bunch of idealistic statesmen will somehow float to the top of our power structure and that the money, the contractors, the voters, and the governor will miraculously lie down and do what they are told. In fact, no one in power in England was able to prevent the cleaned, and magnificent, facade of St. Paul's being partly obscured by a cube of cement and glass that would win the booby prize in any competition for a modern office building.

Our daily needs must be met by communities that have both style and space

Whether or not you like the prevailing international style of office or hotel building, the fact is that it evades the main problem, which is to create whole communities whose daily needs, by way of work, health, education, recreation, and "maintenance" are reasonably satisfied with style and space.

These rebuilt cities and handsome new suburbs, if they ever come to be, will not be put up, in defiance of the pressing needs of the citizen and the form that the economy is taking. This was the delusion so sweetly embodied in the City of the Future exhibit, at the New York World's Fair in 1939. It was, as artistic projections into the future usually are, a vague extension of the city planning style then in vogue. In the late 1930s, the Greenbelt plan was the big thing: decentralized cities, gobs of open countryside rearranged on a drawing board to allow about an acre of lawn for every humble worker, a riot of clover-leaf intersections leading to spacious (though two-lane) highways, hidden and smokeless factories, and a small drift of automobiles idling over the boundless landscape.

Marina City, Chicago

In the last 30 years, the Greenbelt plan has been obliterated by the harsh facts of a bulging population, 70,000,000 automobiles, unchecked industrial wastes and smog, leading to the unplanned freeway suburbs (at its characteristic worst in the grim 40-mile congested palisade that borders the Anaheim Freeway in Southern California) which fights with its burgeoning neighbors over fire and water districts, real estate divisions, school authorities, and the rest of it. The harassed residents are lucky to have three feet of space between their corner bedroom and the neighbor's bathroom. During those 30 years, the population of the United States has gone from 135,000,000 to nearly 200,000,000. Robert Moses, the revolutionary designer of

New York's first parkways and an American John Nash if ever there was one, has lately repented of his early concern to mate the country and the highway and declared that if it comes to a choice between a new park and a new freeway, a tree is a luxury that America today cannot afford.

So long as states, cities, and municipalities do not face the long range problem of recreating their whole environment, the solutions are bound to be improvisations left to the big real estate men, the contractors, and the few architects close enough to the politicians to command a hearing and a contract. One expedient is to provide more land for building by filling in the lakes and waterways, as they are doing with San Francisco's noble bay, where prospective buyers can already stake out a flag on a buoy which bears their name and marks the spot where one day they will have a suburban box with a harbor view. Another, and more radical, solution is that of Bertrand Goldberg's Marina City in Chicago, a vertical community on a supermarket base. This accepts the population explosion as an incurable fact of life and builds a tower of Babel capable of housing thousands of people in one apartment building (the assumption being that they won't all go onto the streets at once). We are already talking cheerfully about the coming exhaustion of our farmlands and the necessity of dredging the oceans for our food and even drafting the first underwater cities. Before this exciting horror, I pause.

Young architects and budding politicians must reshape our environment

If we had a vivid awareness of the kind of chaos we have made of the 20th century city, we would surely think about limiting the population, conserving the shrinking landscape, purging the air and the rivers and streams of their poisons, and planning new and whole communities with a spaciousness that would make the old Greenbelt suburbs look amateur, and with an architectural harmony that would bear comparison with Bath and Williamsburg.

I have stated some of the problems. I leave it to the young architects, and the budding politicians, to figure how they can contrive a quite new partnership of power and impose on "the pee-pul," for their own good a type of intelligent, worthy, and handsome 20th century city.

Related Articles

For a complete report on the 1966 year in the arts, see the following articles in Section Three:

Architecture
City
City and Regional Planning
Dancing
Education
Fashion
Interior Design
Library
Literature
Motion Pictures
Museums
Music
Painting and Sculpture
Photography
Publishing
Radio
Television
Theater

Red Smith: Focus On Sports

When Kansas City can look down its nose at New York City, a revolution has taken place in professional baseball

The New York Yankees hit bottom in the American League on Sept. 18, 1966, and a few days after that a defeat in Chicago made sure they would stay there. The newspapers reported that this was the first time the Yankees had finished last since 1912, but the papers were being charitable. In 1912, the Yankees wound up in eighth place; in the ten-club league of 1966, they were two notches below the low-water mark for all their 63 previous years.

Reliable witnesses to the decline and fall of the Roman Empire are so scarce these days that it is difficult to determine which collapse had the greater impact on its time. The comparison really is not important. When the Kansas City Athletics can look down their noses at the New York Yankees, little else seems important to the baseball fan.

For the knowledgeable buffs who read the box scores, there was no mystery about the failure of the Yankees. They did not have a regular player who could hit for an average of .300 or drive in 85 runs. They did not have a pitcher who could win 13 games. They did not have an accredited major league shortstop, and they were hurting at other positions. For the first time since the American League's Most Valuable Player Award was established, no Yankee was mentioned among the top 10 candidates.

The Yankees did not have a regular player who hit .300 or drove in 85 runs

Only the men in charge were bewildered. In 1965 when the team finished sixth, management had blamed it on the injury of key players like Mickey Mantle, Roger Maris, and Tony Kubek. Dispassionate observers had detected cracks in the masonry as early as 1963. When the 1966 season started sorrily, the brass went into panic. After 20 games—four victories and 16 defeats—they fired the manager, Johnny Keane, and reactivated Ralph Houk. He had managed three straight pennant winners and had then moved up to the front office in the position of general manager.

For a fortnight, the Yankees won under Houk, though there is no reason to believe they would not have won the same games by the same scores for Keane. Then they reverted to type.

The inability of the owners to understand what had happened is not difficult to explain. People at Columbia Broadcasting System, Inc. (CBS), which now owns the Yankees, do not read history. They regard July 21, 1931, as the dawn of civilization. On that date, CBS sent out its first television signal over station W2XAB.

A reader of baseball history—and he must go back farther than 1931—can easily recognize that the history of the Yankees' success and failure is the story of two men: Edward Grant Barrow and George Martin Weiss. Neither ever hit a major league pitch or threw one, but hitters and pitchers do not really write the history of baseball.

Superstars like Babe Ruth and Ty Cobb, Walter Johnson, Joe DiMaggio, and Sandy Koufax do have a major influence on the game while they are playing, but their influence is necessarily limited to the span of their activity on the field. Obviously Ruth, who closed out his career with the Yankees in 1934, played no part in winning four world championships in 1936, 1937, 1938, and 1939. DiMaggio, retired in 1952, obviously contributed nothing toward the winning of five pennants in a row during the years from 1960 through 1964.

When a single club, despite constantly changing personnel, dominates the game for 44 years, winning 29 championships and dropping out of the first division only once, there is only one place to look for the secret of its success. That search leads in this instance directly to Ed Barrow and George Weiss; the men who kept the supply of talent constant from the day of Ruth and Lou Gehrig to the triumphal reign of Mantle and Whitey Ford.

The Yankees, originally called the Highlanders, opened their initial season in 1903, but it was 1921 before they won their first pennant. It was no coincidence that the original pennant came at the end of Ed Barrow's initial year as general manager.

When Barrow moved to New York, he was 52 years old, a burly man whose black eyebrows could have concealed a covey of quail. He had played baseball as a youth, covered it as a reporter for the Des Moines *Leader*, managed teams on the field, operated clubs from the front office, and headed up minor leagues. He had sold oil pumps, and soap, and hot dogs, and served a hitch in the hotel business.

Ed Barrow and George Weiss are the men who kept the flow of talent constant

When he was managing Paterson, N.J., in the Atlantic League, a talent hunt took him to the Pittsburgh area. Outside Carnegie, Pa., he found a broad-shouldered, bowlegged kid wearing a derby hat heaving lumps of coal at tin cans along the railroad right of way. The boy was John Peter Wagner. Some men still live to argue that Honus Wagner was the greatest ballplayer of all.

In 1918, Barrow went to Boston as manager of the Red Sox. His first team there won the world championship, and the following spring he made a decision that would alter the face of baseball. He converted a young left-handed pitcher into an outfielder so that the young man could be in the batting order every day. The young man's name was George Herman Ruth.

Because the Red Sox owner, Harry Frazee, needed cash to finance his theatrical ventures, Ruth was sold to the Yankees for $100,000 (and a personal loan of $350,000 to Frazee from Colonel Jacob Ruppert of the Yankees). A year later Barrow himself went to New York.

Babe Ruth

This was the start of the Yankee dynasty, with Ruth and Barrow as the founding fathers. After the first pennant in 1921, there came another in 1922, then a third in succession and the first world championship. Within 10 years, two expressions became current in baseball.

One was "five o'clock lightning," describing a phenomenon that had become painfully familiar to seven teams in the American League. In that era, baseball was a game played by daylight. A contest started in mid-afternoon and sometimes the Yankees would be held in check for six or seven or even eight innings. Then, like as not, Ruth would walk up to the plate, or Gehrig, or Tony Lazzeri, or Bob Meusel, and thunderbolts would start bouncing off the walls.

The other cry heard 'round the league was, "Break up the Yankees!" They had not only won in 1921, 1922, and 1923; they also won in 1926, 1927, and 1928. And nobody who knew Ed Barrow doubted that they would continue to win again and again and again, probably forever.

Through the years of Yankee ascendancy, it was widely believed that their success resulted from the fact that they could buy all the best players and crowd all rivals aside by weight of wealth. This never was true. No poor man ever owned the Yankees, but there was never a time when there were not a dozen other owners—men named Phil Wrigley or Powel Crosley or Tom Yawkey or Phil Ball or Bob Carpenter or Walter Briggs or John Galbreath—who were just as wealthy as any owner of the Yankees.

The truth was that Ed Barrow knew more about his job, worked harder at it, and did it better than anybody else. He was a reasonable man who never asked an employee to give more to the job than he himself gladly gave, which was approximately 23 hours a day. Employing the best scouts and getting them there first, the Yankees got the best players. Then they began to grow their own.

The majority of Yankee stars came up through their farm system

Branch Rickey in St. Louis had been the first to see the possibilities of a minor league chain that would train young players for the parent club. Others were by no means sold on the farm system when a glib lawyer named Max Steuer talked Colonel Ruppert into buying the Newark club of the International League. Now the Yankees needed a man to work for them in Newark. Barrow knew the man.

He did not like him much. Barrow and George Weiss had clashed more than once over deals for players, but each had developed a grudging respect for the other. It was December, 1931 when Weiss joined the Yankee organization on Barrow's recommendation. He was hired to run the Newark club, but that job occupied only 12 hours a day. To fill the remaining 12, he set out to build a farm system that would dwarf Rickey's chain.

Nobody was better equipped for the job. Weiss's father, a grocer in New Haven, Conn., had urged young George to learn a trade, but as a high school freshman in 1912, the boy had found his métier. He became manager of the high school baseball team.

He reorganized the high school team into a semiprofessional club called the Colonials. They played on Sundays, which the law forbade professionals to do. Weiss recruited the most popular college athletes of the day. He brought in big league stars like Ty Cobb and Walter Johnson. During World War I, he persuaded many major league teams to play exhibition games with the Colonials.

Mickey Mantle

Unable to buck this competition, the Eastern League offered its New Haven franchise to Weiss for $5,000. He borrowed the money and took over in 1919. His club finished fifth that year. Never again, until he presented the newborn New York Mets to the world 43 years later, did a team of his finish in the second division. After 10 years in New Haven, Weiss took over as general manager of the Baltimore Orioles in the International League. Then the Yankees hired him.

The farm system he created for New York has never been surpassed. He had teams in Newark and Kansas City that could have beaten more than a few of those claiming major league stature. For years, the great majority of Yankee stars came up through that farm system. When the club got a player from outside the organization, Weiss usually had a hand in that, too.

Eventually Jacob Ruppert died, and, after World War II, the Yankees were bought by Dan Topping, Del Webb, and Larry MacPhail. MacPhail took active charge, and Barrow retired. Then in 1947 MacPhail sold out to his partners, and Weiss became general manager.

In the next 13 years, the Yankees won 10 pennants and eight world championships. Each season produced a handsome profit of $1,000,000 or more. Following his first summer in command, Weiss hired a new manager—Casey Stengel, whom he had admired in the past.

There is no record in baseball to match Stengel's. He was the first to manage five straight pennant winners. Except for a curious accident, it could have been 10 straight. The year the string was broken, 1954, the Yankees won 103 games for their best record under Stengel. That year, however, Cleveland won 111 games.

In 1965, the remnants of the last Weiss-Stengel team slid out of the first division

Even though his teams won monotonously, Weiss never stood pat. Every year there were new faces—kids named Ford or Mantle or Kubek or Maris or Gil McDougald or Bobby Richardson or Elston Howard.

Most of the players who won for the Yankees had been brought up as Yankees, but Weiss never was too proud to reach out for help in a pennant race. He would buy a Johnny Sain or Johnny Mize at any price, if it brought a pennant. Usually it did.

In the winter of 1960, after the Yankees had won another pennant but lost the World Series, Stengel and Weiss were fired. The brass said it was a youth movement. Stengel was 71, Weiss 66.

They had built so well, Weiss and Stengel, that the team they left behind won four more pennants, making it five in a row. But in 1965, the remnants of the last Weiss-Stengel team slid out of the first division. In 1966 came ruin. The architects of success were gone, but in the fall a fresh spark of hope glowed.

CBS hired a new general manager, Lee MacPhail, son of Weiss's old boss, Larry. Lee had worked under Weiss with the Yankees before going to Baltimore and putting together the team that won the World Series of 1966. Given time, he may bring the Yankees back. After all, George Weiss taught him the business.

Related Articles

For a complete report on the 1966 year in sports, see Section Two, The Other Face of Pro Sports; and the following articles in Section Three:

Automobile Racing
Baseball
Basketball
Boats and Boating
Bowling
Boxing
Football
Golf
Horse Racing
Ice Hockey
Ice Skating
Ryun, Jim
Skiing
Soccer
Sports
Swimming
Tennis
Track and Field
Wrestling

Section Two

Seven special articles and the exclusive YEAR BOOK Trans-Vision® bring special treatment to subjects chosen for their current importance and lasting interest.

Special Reports

A Year Book Special Report

By M. Scott Carpenter

Man of Two Worlds

The second American to circle the earth describes his descent into the ocean depths to explore the important new frontier that lies beneath the surface of the sea

For centuries man has feasted on the richness of the seas. Yet only now is he fully awakening to their scientific and commercial treasures. Excursions into the dense world beneath the waves, like explorations into outer space, are beginning to challenge man's inquisitiveness, technology, courage, and sense of adventure. I have had the unique privilege of exploring both these environments. My experience has been limited, but it has shown me that both worlds are significantly related and that both can eventually enrich life on earth.

Three years after my 1962 orbital flight in *Aurora 7*, I was privileged to be part of a navy team that lived and worked for many weeks 205 feet below the surface in Scripps Canyon, off the coastline of

California at La Jolla. The name of our underwater home and workshop was *Sealab II*, the successor to *Sealab I* in which four men had worked for 11 days off Bermuda at a depth of 192 feet. Sometime in 1967, *Sealab III* is expected to make its descent to the ocean depths. This improved vessel is scheduled to descend 430 feet into Wilson's Cove, about 75 miles to the west of Scripps Canyon.

The purpose of the Sealab experiments is to extend man's ability to explore and exploit the ocean floor to the limits of the world's continental shelves. The economic importance of such studies cannot be overstressed. The continental shelves, some scientists believe, can provide as much as 85 per cent of the edible protein needed by the world in the form of fish, shellfish, and marine plants. These areas also contain large, untapped supplies of petroleum, industrial metals, and minerals. And, in this day of missile-firing nuclear submarines, military interest in undersea capability is readily understandable. But even without these economic and military reasons for studying this new environment, I would find it just as intriguing to study man's performance in the underwater world as it is to examine his capability in outer space.

The author: Scott Carpenter is the only person to have explored both inner and outer space. He took a historic flight in the Mercury capsule, *Aurora 7,* on May 24, 1962. Three years later he spent weeks on the ocean floor in the navy's *Sealab II.*

Sea and space similarities

Man's exploration of the sea cannot yet be compared to manned spaceflights since the latter involve sophisticated equipment and advanced scientific techniques. Yet I have found that the problems of putting man beneath the surface of the sea are related in a number of ways to the task of making him effective in space. In the underwater program, for instance, we must select and train crews, design new types of capsules, devise special tools, provide a viable atmosphere, plan and conduct a schedule of unprecedented scientific experiments–requiring extensive extra vehicular activity–and conduct physiological and psychological tests on man outside his natural environment. Man leaves his natural environment not without some hazard, and a few surprises, since he has become conditioned to it through eons of existence in the earth's atmosphere.

There are obvious differences, however, between space and sea exploration. In space, I did not encounter other forms of life, but in *Sealab II* we had company constantly. Fish swarmed all over the place and peered in at us through our glass ports. We caught some and ate them. Others we tagged with metal and plastic disks so that their movements and habits could be studied over many days. Three of us were even painfully stung by scorpion fish. The poison is something like that of a cobra, but fortunately this type of scorpion fish injects only a small amount of venom.

We also worked, at times, with a highly trained and friendly bottlenosed dolphin we named Tuffy. It came down from the surface whenever we sounded an electric buzzer, just as you might whistle for a dog. We were testing Tuffy's ability to deliver messages and to respond to signals from a diver simulating distress. Between dives,

Sealab II, shown here moored to its support ships, descended 205 ft. into Scripps Canyon near La Jolla, Calif.

which sometimes took as long as four and a half minutes, Tuffy leaped and frolicked on the surface. It earned a meal of fish each time it correctly responded to our buzzer. Tuffy was not shy around divers, but nothing in its training–either with the navy at Point Magu, Calif., or at its original home in a California amusement park–had prepared it for the strange sights and sounds of our Sealab. Tuffy was so fearful of this big underwater object that it shied away if the diver who summoned it was too close to Sealab.

We were not bothered by sharks, though several years before a great white shark had come up out of the La Jolla undersea canyon and eaten a skin diver. *Sealab II* was deliberately positioned on the edge of this deep trench to provide for deepwater excursion dives. While none of us expected shark trouble, we had an outside cage for refuge, if necessary. The boxlike cage was attached to the underside of *Sealab II* where our hatch was located. We used it as a sort of underwater vestibule. Sometimes small fish–including the poisonous scorpion–swam through its Dutch door into the cage with us.

Our underwater capsule had to have a highly specialized atmosphere just as does a space capsule. But the pressure problems were

U.S.NAVY
SEALAB II
ONR-SP

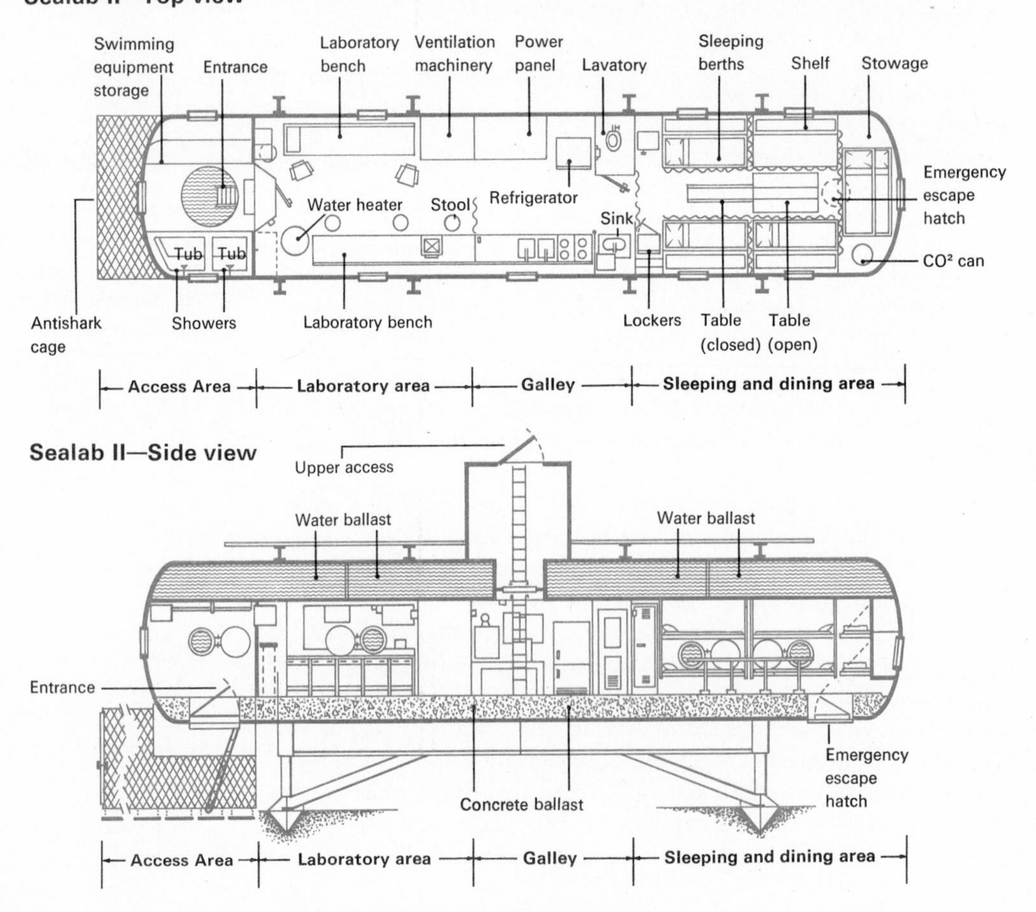
Sealab II—Top view
Swimming equipment storage
Entrance
Laboratory bench
Ventilation machinery
Power panel
Lavatory
Sleeping berths
Shelf
Stowage
Emergency escape hatch
Water heater
Stool
Refrigerator
Sink
Tub
Tub
CO² can
Antishark cage
Showers
Laboratory bench
Lockers
Table (closed)
Table (open)
Access Area
Laboratory area
Galley
Sleeping and dining area
Sealab II—Side view
Upper access
Water ballast
Water ballast
Entrance
Emergency escape hatch
Concrete ballast
Access Area
Laboratory area
Galley
Sleeping and dining area

Facts About The Sealabs

Sealab II, a 58-foot cylindrical craft weighing 200 tons, is designed to operate to depths of 400 feet. Its walls are made of steel one inch thick. This enables it to withstand pressure of 200 pounds per square inch.

The vessel is divided into four compartments: an access room, a laboratory, a galley, and a bunkroom. Atmospheric pressure inside *Sealab II* is maintained at approximately 94 pounds per square inch. This is sufficient to keep seawater from entering the access hatch.

A special mixture is needed for breathing at this pressure. It contains mostly helium (85 per cent). The carbon dioxide exhaled by the crew is continually removed from the breathing mixture.

The interior of *Sealab II* is kept at 91°F. by heating cables in the concrete floor. This high temperature is necessary because the aquanauts lose body heat more rapidly in a helium atmosphere than they do in ordinary air. Excess humidity is controlled by four electric dehumidifiers in the vessel.

Sealab III is similar to *Sealab II* in size and design. Modifications include adjustable legs that will enable the vessel to level itself on the ocean floor, an added ballast tank that will permit descents to greater depths, and an additional compartment at each end. One compartment will serve as the diving locker, the other will be equipped with special ports for underwater viewing.

Descents of Sealabs II and III

Sealab II was lowered 205 feet into Scripps Canyon on Aug. 28, 1965, and spent 45 days on the ocean bottom. Sometime in 1967, *Sealab III* is scheduled to descend 430 feet into Wilson's Cove. Below the map of the area, *right*, is a distorted view of the ocean's floor. It shows the comparative depths of the two descents. At bottom is the same area as it appears without distortion. The underwater capabilities derived from these experiments are expected to help tap the vast resources of the world's continental shelves.

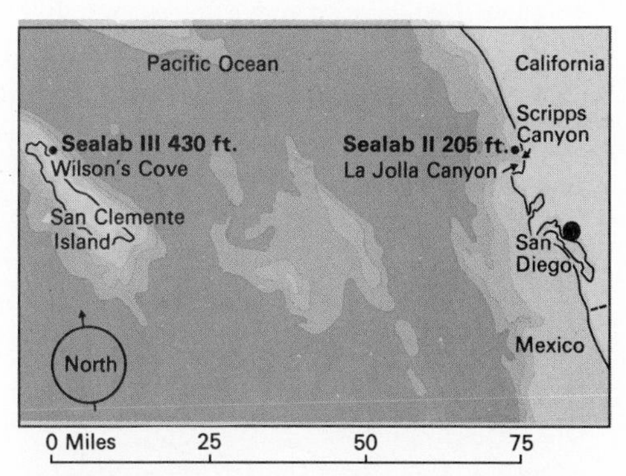

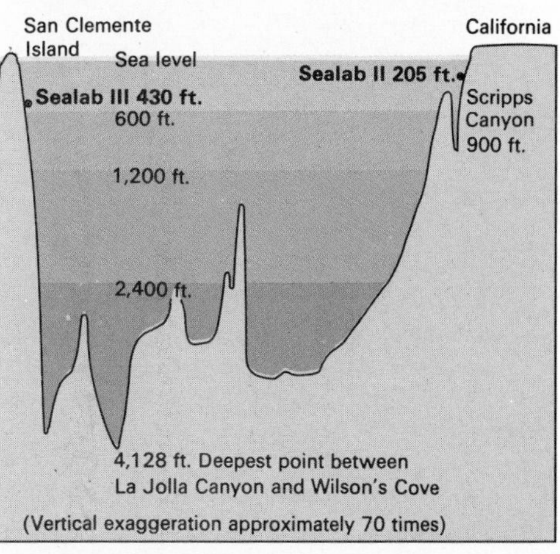

Sealab III

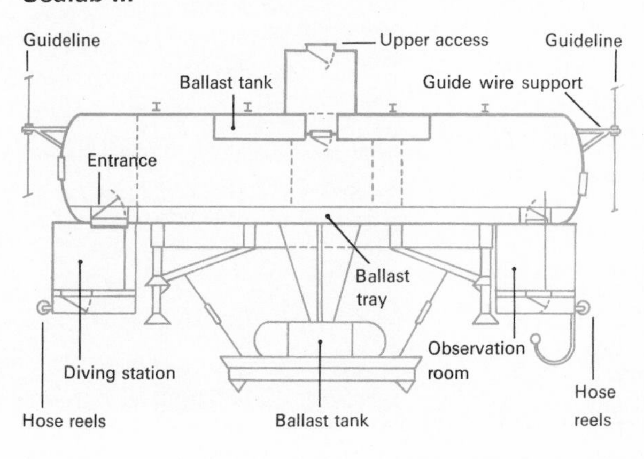

different. An astronaut is surrounded by an atmosphere of pure oxygen but at a pressure of only one-third as much as the pressure of the atmosphere on the earth's surface. In *Sealab II*, because of the tremendous pressure of the water at that depth, we had to maintain an atmospheric pressure seven times greater than that on land. The air we breathed consisted of a special mixture of inert gases: 85 per cent helium, 11 per cent nitrogen, and only 4 per cent oxygen. Oxygen cannot be used in normal quantities because it becomes toxic under too much pressure. We breathed roughly the same mixture from our scuba tanks when outside the vessel.

There were two good reasons why we maintained a high pressure in our undersea laboratory. *Sealab II*, a cylinder 58 feet long and 12 feet in diameter, had a 48-inch hatch in the floor at one end. Through this hatch, divers could quickly leave or enter directly from air to water or water to air. The high pressure was needed, first of all, to keep the water out. Secondly, it permitted far more effective use of the diver's work time. If a surface diver came down to our depth, the maximum amount of air mixture he could carry on his back would permit him only 20 minutes of work time at most. He would have to spend about 60 per cent of his available supply of air mixture just decompressing on the way up. But we Sealab divers, working out of, and returning to, an atmosphere at the same pressure, did not need to decompress. We could perform a day's work equal to that of about 50 surface divers.

A surface diver who spends too much time at too great a depth risks painful, and sometimes fatal, "bends" if he returns to the surface without decompressing. This is because the rapid change in pressure allows the inert gases in his body to expand faster than he can exhale them. The gases enter his blood stream and are carried to his joints, causing intense pain, or sometimes to his brain, causing convulsions, unconsciousness and, eventually, death. Deep-sea divers can avoid the bends by entering a sealed decompression chamber, where the air

The first of three 10-man teams of aquanauts, led by Carpenter, prepares to dive to the ocean floor where *Sealab II* awaits them. The first team surfaced after 15 days, and a second team took over. Carpenter, however, stayed below for 30 days.

14
14

pressure is gradually decreased, or by stopping at various depths on the way to the surface. Sealab divers must also be slowly decompressed, of course, but only when they are ready to return to the surface. This is true whether a Sealab diver remains below the surface for 36 hours —the amount of time required for so-called complete "saturation" in the undersea environment—or whether he stays under water for as long as 36 days. Decompression for Sealab divers is a process that takes 33 hours in a special chamber aboard the ship from which the Sealab project is directed.

The combination of pressure and the unique breathing mixture required at our depth of 205 feet caused some peculiar effects that may prove to be as troublesome in the future as the effect of pure oxygen is on long duration space flights. One of these is the odd effect on the human voice and on sound itself. The helium atmosphere distorts speech into a high-pitched quack so that everyone sounds like Donald Duck. When we first began to talk to one another in the new atmosphere, we collapsed with laughter. The sound was not only comical, but so many consonants in words were lost that it was very difficult to make yourself understood. "Paul" became "aul" and "jello" became "yello." We had to become adept at lip reading, or stand close together while talking. The cause of this effect needs further study, but it is related to the fact that the more helium is pressurized, the higher becomes the frequency of the human voice. The speed of sound increases in a helium atmosphere so that there is a loss of sound directionality. If I stood in the middle of Sealab and someone called my name, I could not tell from which direction the sound came. The accustomed time differential between the sound reception by the right ear and left ear was too short for the brain to measure.

As we go to greater depths, where greater helium pressures are required, the problem will become magnified. I doubt, for instance, that two men standing close together in a Sealab at a depth of 600 feet could make themselves understood. The navy, which is, of course, aware of the problem, is working on an electronic device called a helium voice unscrambler to solve it. But such equipment at present is crude and unsatisfactory for great depths.

Cooking presents problems

Food preparation and eating are specialized processes that require different techniques in outer and inner space. In a spacecraft, I had to learn to consume liquids and solid food from containers especially prepared for the weightless environment. In the more spacious Sealab, we had room for an electric stove, a refrigerator, and even a freezer. But in our atmosphere, matches did not burn, and water boiled at 330° F. (instead of the normal 212° F.). We had to be careful not to let our stew or coffee get too hot or they would burn. We saw peas turn brown in water that was not even simmering. We also could not fry anything, for this might contaminate our Sealab atmosphere. Fresh eggs were especially taboo since yolks give off toxic hydrogen

Commander Carpenter talks over the telephone with members of the overhead support ship. The aquanauts kept in constant contact with their mother ship.

Entering *Sealab II* through its open hatch are Carpenter, *right*, and fellow diver. The pressure in the capsule, equal to that of the ocean outside, keeps the water from rushing in.

sulfide, a gas difficult for our purifying equipment to scrub out of the air. Even though our atmosphere affected our sense of smell—dulling all odors—we were still delighted at the way food tasted. After coming in from that cold water, a peanut butter and jelly sandwich was absolutely delicious.

Proper garbage disposal was also a problem for those of us in the Sealab, as it is for those in spacecraft. We had to cut the bottoms out of cans and flatten them to reduce bulk. We tried to float garbage up to the surface in bags where it could be retrieved, but high pressure often ruptured the bags on ascent and the garbage would rain back on us. We never completely solved this problem. Perhaps it will be solved by the time *Sealab III* descends.

The human response to working, sleeping, and eating below the surface was, in general, very good. We knew that what we were doing was new and important. This, and our demanding work assignments, kept our moments of anxiety to a minimum. But like every new environment—even a new home or apartment—it took a while to become accustomed to things. Since we were on the edge of a deep canyon, the sea floor was not level, and the deck of our Sealab inclined to an angle of about 10 degrees. We had to get used to tying pots and pans to the canted stove, and we had to hold our plates to keep them from sliding off the table. Jay Skidmore, our photographer, called our home the "Tiltin' Hilton." We also had to get used to the constant hum of our fans, pumps, and motors.

Once, we were startled by a loud noise that sounded like a massive landslide. We thought for a moment that our anchor had given way and that we were all sliding into the canyon. The sound came, however, from the propellers of a surface ship.

Throughout the weeks, we conducted a total of 44 work and research assignments. Some seemed deceptively simple until we realized that we were trying to get answers to questions that had never been asked before. Other tasks, of course, were much more complex. Among them was the construction

Laboratory space in *Sealab II* was severely limited. But in spite of the many handicaps, the three teams were able to complete 44 different experiments inside and outside the capsule during the project. Note the curious fish peering in the porthole.

A porpoise named Tuffy, a popular member of the crew, was specially trained to respond to buzzer signals from divers deep beneath the ocean's surface.

of an underwater weather station which recorded temperature, pressure, salt content, and variations in the direction and velocity of the current. Another assignment was to cover a section of the ocean bed with an experimental gelatin mixture that solidified the sediment. We made extensive studies of underwater life that included the counting and tagging of fish, and we made excursion dives down to the 300 foot level into Scripps Canyon. We also successfully tried an experiment in underwater salvage, the raising of the fuselage of a navy fighter plane that had been lowered into the ocean for this purpose. We did this by pumping it full of polyurethane foam so that it would be buoyant and could be easily floated to the surface.

Visibility on the ocean bottom was sometimes limited to only five feet. Consequently, we had to lay yellow plastic guidelines to find our way to our work stations. We were responsible for such yard work and housekeeping functions as replacing fogged underwater TV cameras and burned out diving lights, bringing in supplies, and performing the myriad other tasks required to maintain a crew of 10 closely confined men.

All of our outside work, which can be compared to extra vehicular activity in space, was a new kind of scientific experiment. We needed to test man's ability to work efficiently in 47°F. water, measure his manual dexterity and endurance at extremes of depth and temperature, and evaluate the effects of this particular kind of environment on the human organism.

We usually attached 15 to 20 pounds of lead weights to our belts before we went outside *Sealab II*. The weights achieved what divers call neutral buoyancy. They made us heavy enough to remain at our level in the water, neither floating to the surface nor sinking deeper. Weight is as much a factor underwater as it is in space. In one respect, I found that I could work better underwater because I could propel

One of the project's experiments involved underwater salvage operations. Here crew members fasten a patch on a simulated submarine with an explosive stud.

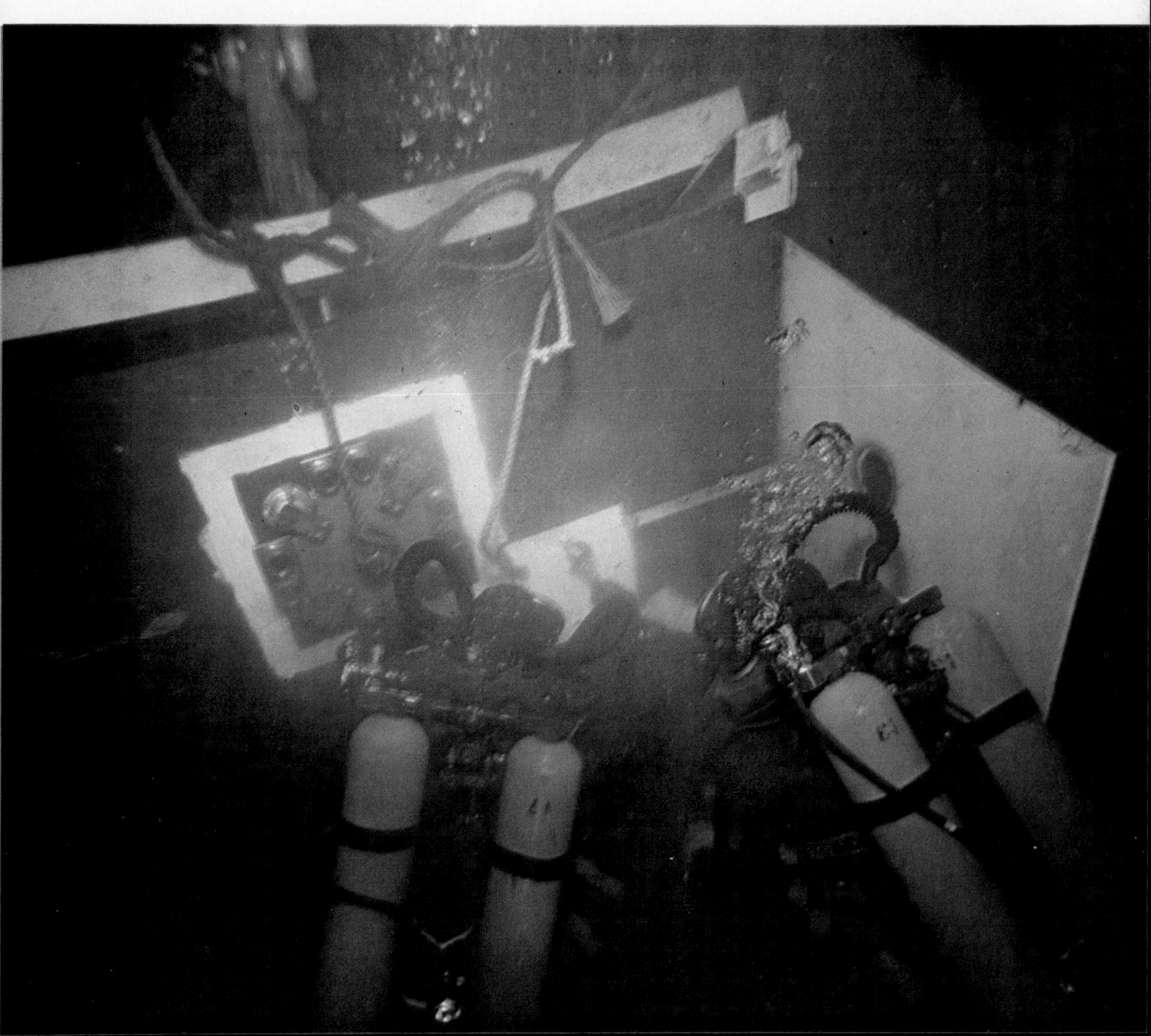

myself with fins. But, since water impairs movement, I became tired much more quickly than I did in normal weightless flight. However, I think that working in a pressurized spacesuit, as did the astronauts who "walked" in space, is the most difficult task of all.

Temperature control is, of course, vital in both environments. I had the problem at one point in my *Aurora 7* flight of being too hot. At the bottom of the Pacific it was just the opposite; I could not keep warm enough. We did experiment with a new wet suit made of latex foam sandwiched between two layers of rubber and containing electrically heated wires. One diver wore it and was able to stay out nearly four hours without getting uncomfortably cold. We were bitterly cold working without this suit—so cold, in fact, that our efficiency was limited. The frigid temperature and severe shivering, arising in part from our reaction to the helium, forced us to return for a hot shower and food after only about an hour in the water.

After their tour of duty was over, this capsule transported the divers to the decompression chamber where they decompressed without fear of the painful and dangerous bends.

There are always some dangers involved in the exploration of any new environment—up or down. While experimenting with the new suit, one diver temporarily lost his neutral buoyancy and started drifting upward to a point where bends could occur. Fortunately, his partner realized the situation and pulled him back down for adjustments to his equipment. Other risks were less serious, but important medically. Many of us got ear infections and skin rashes; a number suffered from headaches caused by the inability of our equipment to eliminate all the carbon monoxide from the breathing mixture. But we proved that man can overcome such obstacles as headaches, dangerous marine life, low water temperatures, and high pressures, just as he has learned to adapt to space flights.

Sealab II was a marked improvement over *Sealab I*, just as *Sealab III*, which is planned for a depth of 430 feet, will be an improvement over *Sealab II*. Then will come *Sealab IV* with a goal of 650 feet,

As the members of the Sealab team whiled away the hours, the pressure in the chamber was decreased from that of 205 feet below the surface back to sea level.

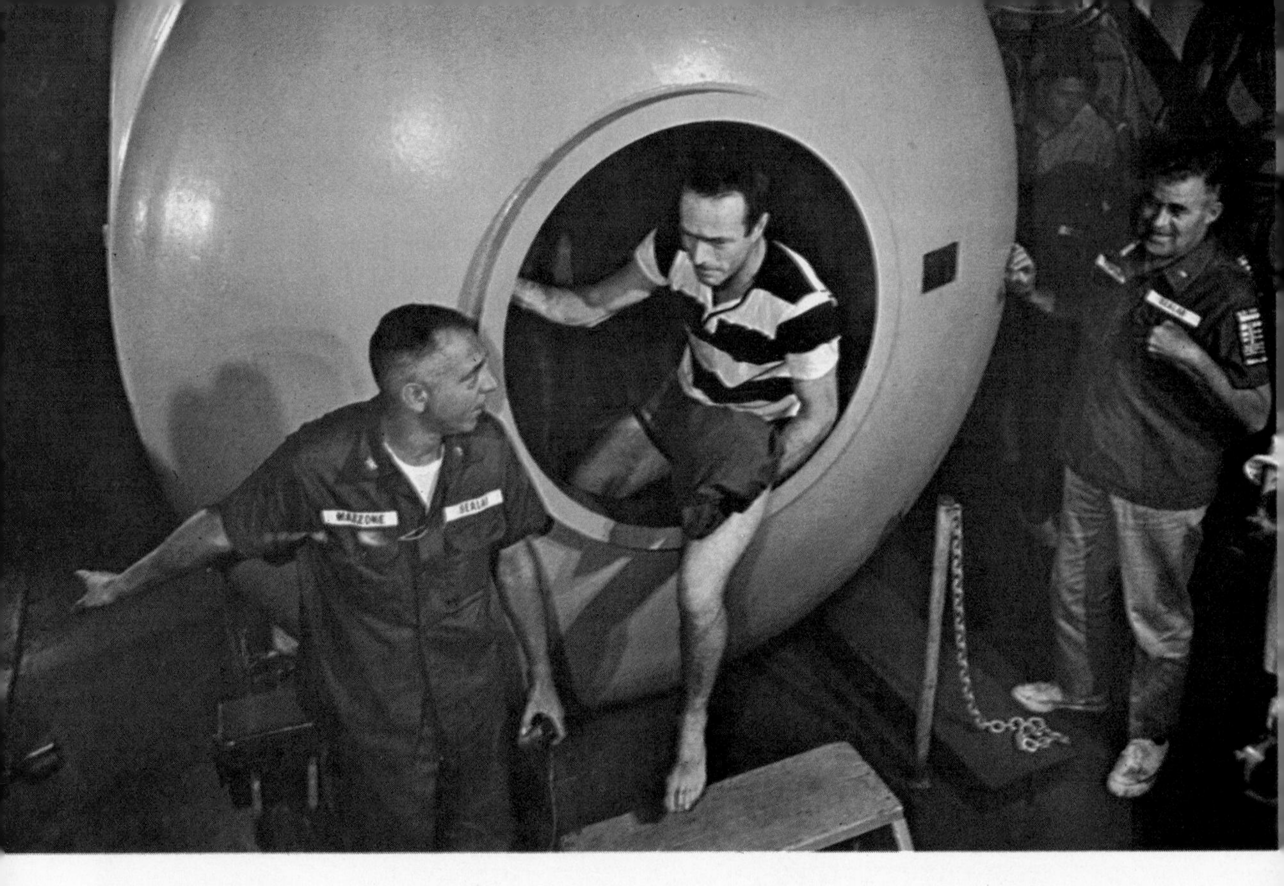

Finally, after spending 30 days in *Sealab II* and 33 hours in the decompression chamber, Commander Carpenter returns to earth.

followed by the highly sophisticated *Sealab V*, planned for 850 feet, with diving excursions to a depth of about 1,000 feet. This is well below the lower limits of the continental shelf.

These graduated and projected depths indicate a major difference in studying the contrasting environments of inner and outer space. Our training in the space program has already subjected us to virtually every condition we expect to find on the surface of the moon. In contrast, each Sealab project will subject us to a brand new, more hazardous and less known environment. While we can, for training purposes, simulate some of the first Sealab environments on land, we do not yet have equipment that can simulate the experience our crews will encounter in *Sealab V*. This means that we must not only improve our equipment and procedures after each experiment, but that we must also simultaneously redesign and replan for the unknown conditions of the next and more challenging phase.

Crew selection vital

Sealab II taught us many things, including the need for emphasis on crew selection and training. Underwater exploration requires men with a rare combination of stability, curiosity, courage, physical strength, stamina, and an innate fascination for the sea. If trouble arises underwater, your only salvation is the hatch in Sealab. You cannot obey a diver's natural instinct to go to the surface, or you will get the bends, possibly even explode. Crew members, therefore, need cool heads. Endless practice is also needed, as is experience with equipment, including the opportunity—which astronauts already have—of contributing to its design and safety features. Life underwater depends on an exotic, complicated piece of breathing apparatus that each participant must know how to operate. He must know its limits so precisely that he can sense a malfunction as quickly as he can sense fatigue and stress within his own body.

Sealab II taught us that we need better and more practical marine architecture, not only for the sake of efficiency, but also to make possible longer missions. We need more room, especially in work areas where we must spend endless hours assembling, checking, and repairing equipment. We need more effective humidity and temperature control. Also, the vessel should be designed so that it can remain submerged much longer and be stationed in a level position on a sloping terrain.

Navigation for the ocean explorer is still rudimentary; he relies heavily on simple visual guidelines. These are almost as elementary as the pearl diver's anchor line from a skiff. The ocean explorer obviously needs some kind of vehicle to extend his range since his anchored Sealab is immobile.

Whether the trip is into outer or inner space, Scott Carpenter is always glad to return to his Houston home. Here he is surrounded by his family, left to right: Candace Noxon, Marc Scott, Kristen Elaine, his wife Rene, and Robyn Jay.

Wet suit design lags far behind the well-conceived garments worn in space. Progress, however, is being made in this area, and by the time *Sealab V* submerges we may have a diver's suit that controls body temperature by circulating electrically heated water within the garment. Ultimately, we may have a suit heated by a compact unit that could substitute for one of the lead weights on a diver's belt. The heat would be produced by radioactive isotopes.

Divers cannot communicate underwater except with a few primitive gestures or sound-making devices, such as knife taps against the metal of a diver's air tank, or scuba bottle. Thus, two men working together on the ocean floor are essentially deaf-mutes. I am sure this is only a temporary technical problem, but it deserves serious study immediately in view of growing United States commitments to effective research beneath the seas.

Divers, like astronauts, are remarkable and highly adaptable men. Divers, however, have been forced to adopt a do-it-yourself philosophy, as opposed to aviators and space pilots who are able to turn design and maintenance problems over to others. If a pilot finds an unworkable piece of equipment in his cockpit, he simply writes it up on his Form 1. As an astronaut, I turned in reports on problems that I was confident others could solve better than I. A diver, on the other hand, is not accustomed to this kind of help and has learned to "make do" or fix it himself. While this is an admirable personal trait, it does not provide the engineering reliability he needs and deserves.

A rich harvest ahead

Once these technical problems are given adequate research and development funds and scientific attention, the rewards of future oceanographic research, like those of space research, are certain to be significant. One important difference between the two frontiers lies in the distances involved. Our nearest exploitable neighbor in space is vastly farther away than the richest part of the sea floor. The continental shelves that the future Sealabs will explore are comparatively shallow areas, generally defined as land in less than 600 feet of water. Yet the continental shelf around the United States is enormous. I am confident it will eventually produce vast resources.

Located on or under this virtually untouched fringe of our nation are vast petroleum deposits, untold mineral wealth, abundant sources of fresh water, a teaming jungle of edible fish and aquatic plants, and countless wreckages and artifacts of great interest to archaeologists.

Much has been written about the future harvest of the sea. Some of it is realistic, some undoubtedly highly visionary; yet the continental shelf represents a new frontier which we would be extremely shortsighted to ignore. If the Sealab studies and related scientific programs can solve the problems of living and working at an ocean depth of 850 feet, then we will have gained access to an area which must certainly prove to be an incalculable asset to our nation.

See also Section Three, OCEAN.

A Year Book Special Report

The Poetry Of the Body

An imaginative series of paintings by Dr. Paul Peck that captures the delicate complexities and inherent beauty of the organs and systems of the human body

For centuries artists have gained inspiration from the beauty of a landscape, the interest in a face weathered by experience and wisdom, the contours of the nude, and more recently, in attempts to render subjective states of feeling in abstract form. The paintings on the following pages derive their inspiration from another source: the beauty of the internal world of the human body.

The paintings are the work of Dr. Paul Peck of New York City, generally acknowledged to be among the finest medical artists of our time. They are the culmination of a lifetime of experience as an artist and teacher in the fields of anatomy, medical illustration, and fine art. To create these paintings, Dr. Peck employed not only his extensive medical knowledge and consummate skill as a painter, but most important of all, the vision of a poet. "I am enchanted," says Dr. Peck, "with the myriad colors and textures that exist in the human body, and the extraordinary world revealed by the microscope. The body rivals in intricacy, complexity, and symmetry anything that has been the traditional subject matter for artists."

In these paintings, Dr. Peck has exceeded the boundaries of medical illustration, which is concerned with the accurate depiction of what can be seen or is known to exist. Although this new art reflects profound anatomical knowledge, it uses reality merely as a starting point, infusing it with a vivid imagery which fires the imagination and creates a three-dimensional world of beauty and grace that lies beyond the present limits of observation.

To achieve this dramatic impact, Dr. Peck sometimes focuses on a single element, as with the enlarged glomerulus in the lower right-hand section of *The Kidney*. In *Urinary Stones*, a striking effect is achieved by combining several bladder and kidney stones in a single composition. Moreover, a few of the stones are shown cut open to reveal the complex patterns of their internal structure. In all the paintings, Dr. Peck has imparted a mood appropriate to the particular subject. *Blood Formation*, for instance, possesses a gay, exuberant quality which reflects the life-sustaining role of red blood cells. It contrasts strongly with the mysterious aura of *The Liver*, appropriate for an organ that still retains many unsolved riddles.

These paintings can be enjoyed on many levels. To the anatomist, they present a three-dimensional view of the complex microscopic world that he has known primarily as a series of two-dimensional fragments. To the physician, they offer insight into the visualization of biological processes. To the general viewer, for whom they are primarily intended, they open a doorway to the beauty inherent in the internal structure of the human body.

Urinary Stones

The cavernlike interior of the bladder is the setting for a collection of kidney and bladder stones, grouped together because they are formed by the accumulation of mineral salts within the same body system. The stones are accurately portrayed as to shape, color, and relative size. The contour of each stone is determined by the shape of the hollow space in which it is formed; the color by its chemical composition. The irritation caused by the presence of stones is symbolically portrayed by the frayed lining of the bladder and the enlarged veins beneath its surface.

CALCULI, Dr. Paul Peck, 1963, 15¼" x 21¾"

The Kidney

The internal structure of the kidney is depicted as though one were standing in the midst of the hundreds of thousands of nephron units which make up this organ. Each consists of a long graceful tube with an enclosed coil of capillaries, or glomerulus, at one end. The painting has as its focal point an enlarged view of a glomerulus, lower right, receiving blood for the filtering process which restores essential substances to the blood stream and conveys waste material to the urinary tract.

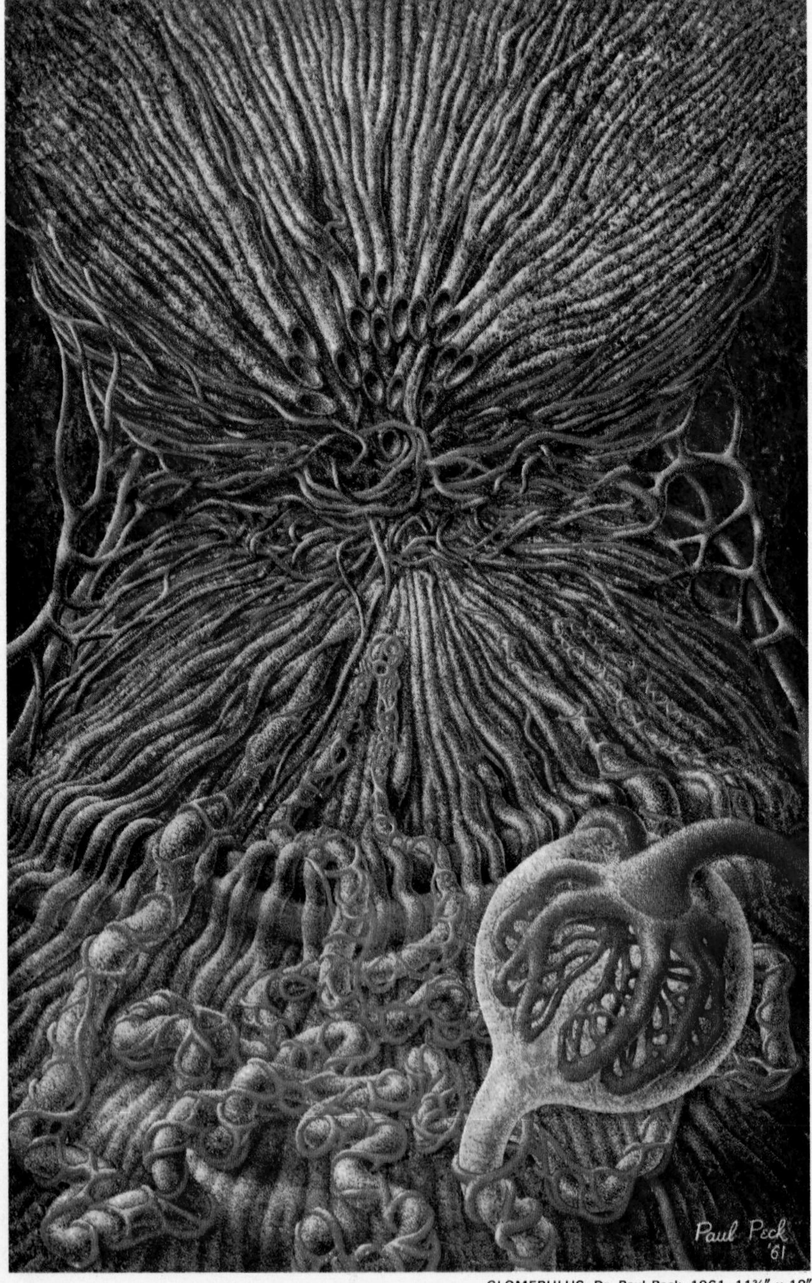

GLOMERULUS, Dr. Paul Peck, 1961, 11¾" x 18"

BONE, Dr. Paul Peck, 1962, 19⅞" x 25⅝"

Bone

The structure of bone is shown here in three aspects. Its external appearance is represented by a vertebra, upper left, shown actual size. The meshwork radiating in all directions is the spongy inner core of all bone, seen under low magnification. At lower right, under high magnification, is a cross section of compact bone which shows the concentric arrangement of cells which is the basis of all bone structure.

Blood Formation

Here, in lively and gay colors, we see the formation of red blood cells within the bone marrow, depicted as a white latticework. The various cells, accurate in color and relative size, show the transition from immature cells, through successively smaller stages, to the biconcave disks, the red blood cells. These are the functional units of the blood stream which carry oxygen to all parts of the body.

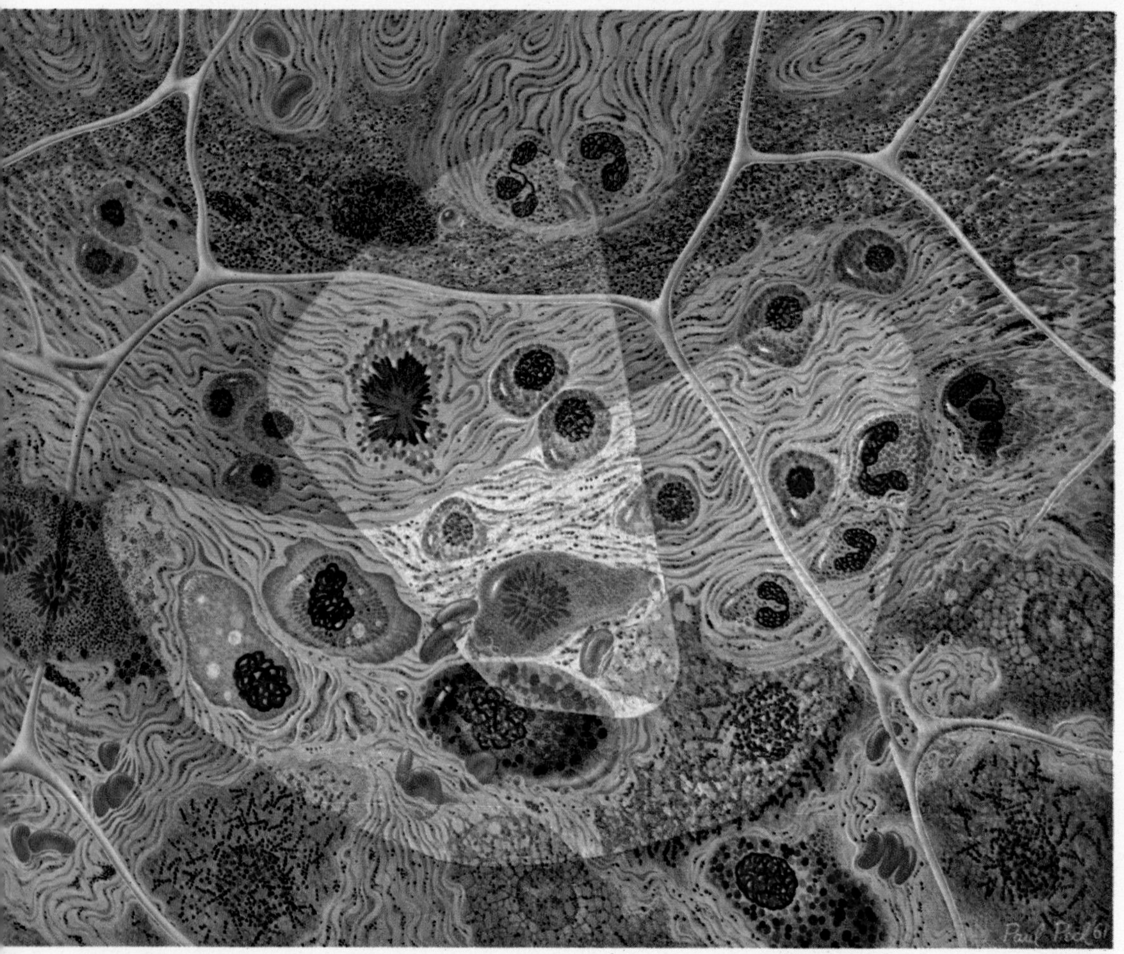

HEMATOPOIESIS, Dr. Paul Peck, 1961, 17¾" x 14"

SKIN, Dr. Paul Peck, 1965, 15⅛" x 18⅜"

The Skin

This painting symbolizes some characteristics of skin: its multilayer structure; its ability to shed dead surface cells; its reaction to injury, such as sunburn, by peeling; and its tendency to wrinkle in the aging process. Thus the composition consists of a series of layers. The uppermost shows a hair complete from its root to the scalp. A deeper layer, upper left, shows violet-stained hair follicles in cross section. At lower left, we see reddish-brown sebaceous glands, microscopically accurate, yet beautiful in their abstract design.

Nerve Cells

Like eerie undersea creatures, a group of *neurons*, or nerve cells, drift in a ganglion of the autonomic nervous system. Glistening with stored-up energy, the neurons are ready to transmit the vital impulses that control the body's involuntary processes. The other-worldly atmosphere of the painting suggests a stillness that may be broken at any moment by the crackling of an electric discharge.

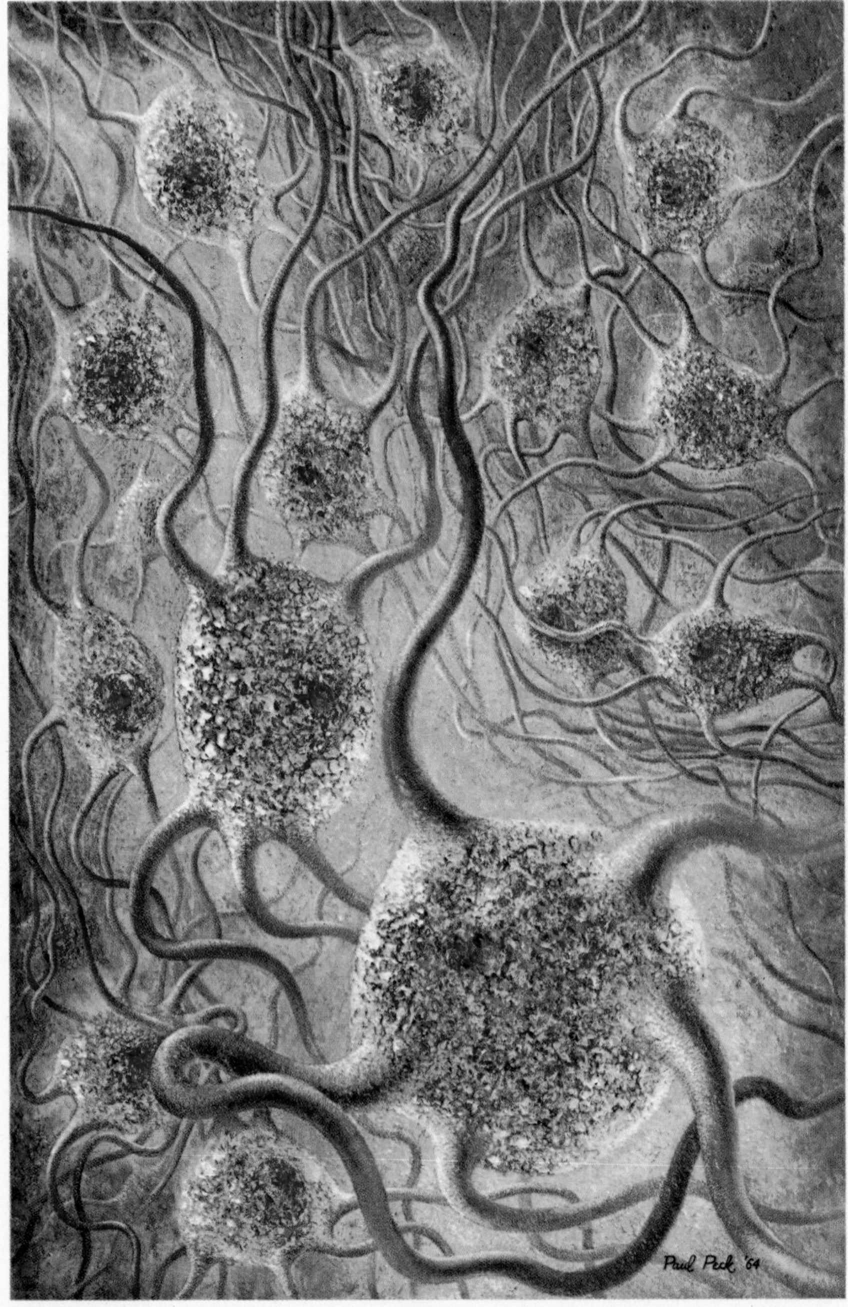

NEURONS, Dr. Paul Peck, 1964, 16" x 24"

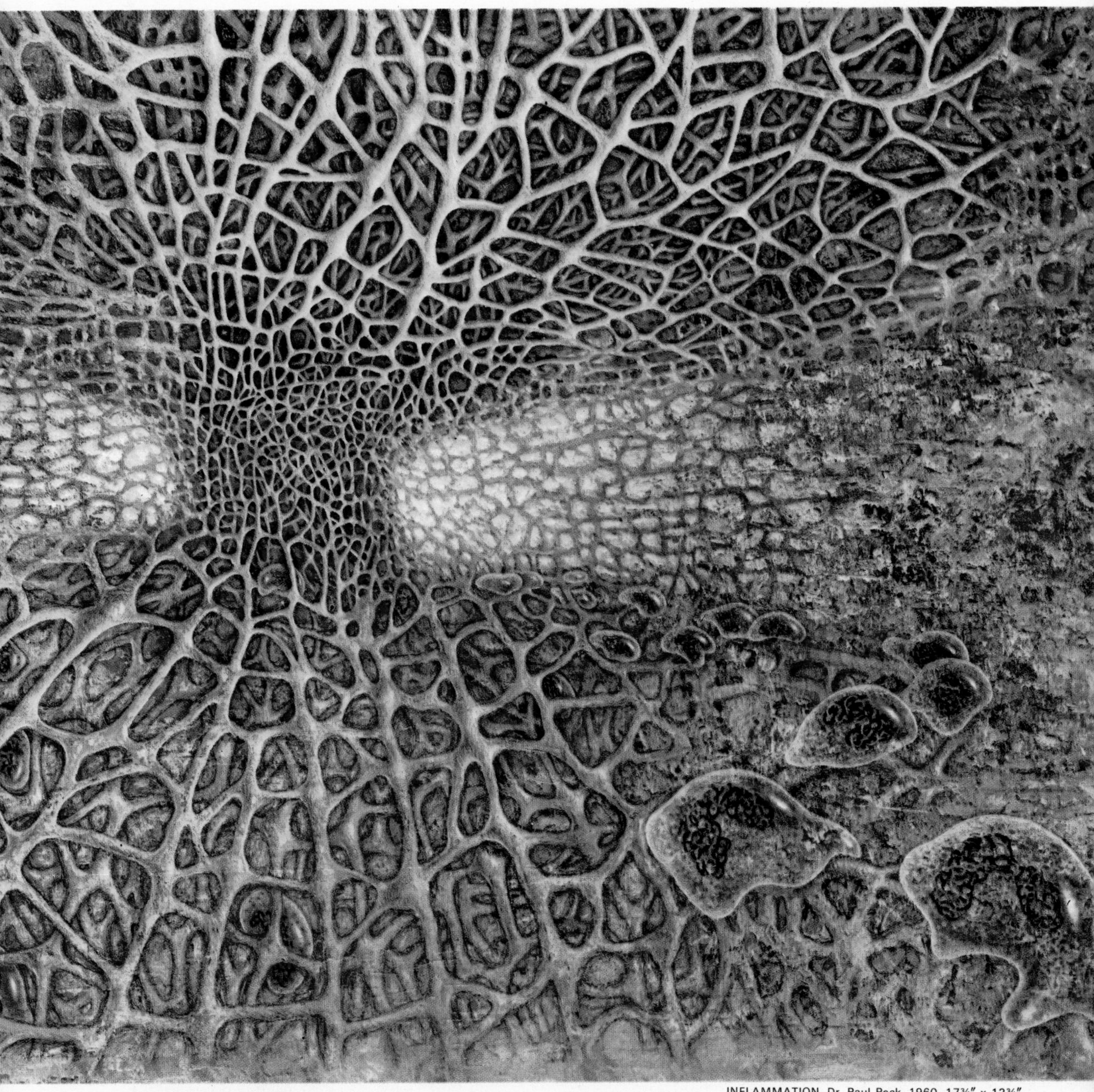

INFLAMMATION, Dr. Paul Peck, 1960, 17¾" x 12¾"

Inflammation

Inflammation is the reaction of tissue to injury or infection. We are witnessing a critical moment in the life of an individual. Invaded by hostile bacteria, the body counterattacks. Blood constituents erect a temporary latticework to control the spread of infection. Vast quantities of the body's defenders—the germ-destroying white blood cells—advance along the scaffolding toward the site of the infection, at center. On either side, the battleground is now strewn with fragments of dead bacteria and tissue cells, and the scaffolding has begun to dissolve.

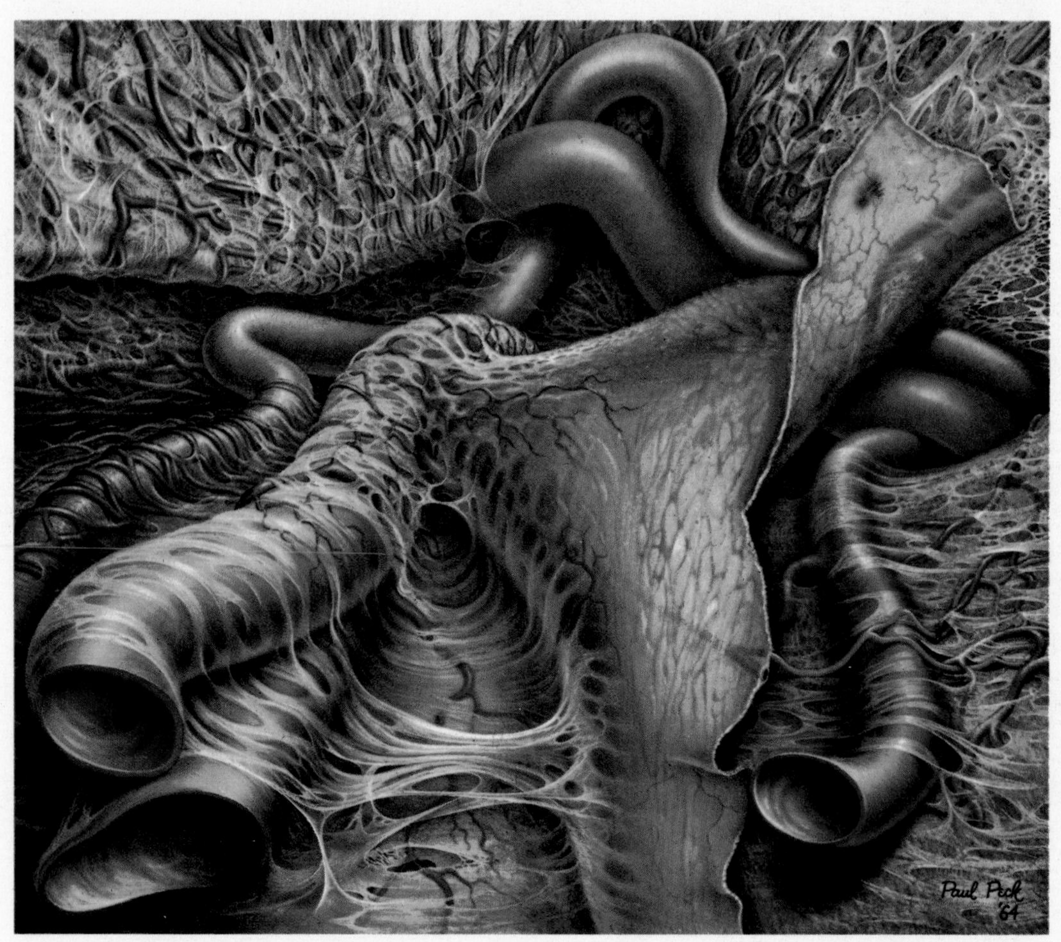

VASCULATURE, Dr. Paul Peck, 1964, 15¼" x 18"

Blood Vessels

This composition is based on patterns formed by the coursing of arteries (red) and veins (blue). An intricate pattern of some smaller vessels, enmeshed in connective sheaths, is seen at the upper left. Larger vessels which lie nearer to the surface of the internal organs and are more loosely covered, are seen in the foreground. Blood vessels are so numerous in the body that even the smallest ones–the capillaries, which are about one hundredth of an inch long–if placed end to end, would encircle the earth four times.

THE HEART, Dr. Paul Peck, 1958, 15⅝" x 15⅝"

The Heart

The heart is visualized solely by the form of the coronary vessels which nourish it. As a model for this composition, the artist carefully injected the coronary vessels of an actual heart with colored plastic; the arteries with the red, the veins with blue. The heart substance was then dissolved by a corrosion technique which left only the plastic network of veins and arteries. The realistic rendering of these vessels contrasts vividly with a background pattern that is symbolic of the body's circulatory system.

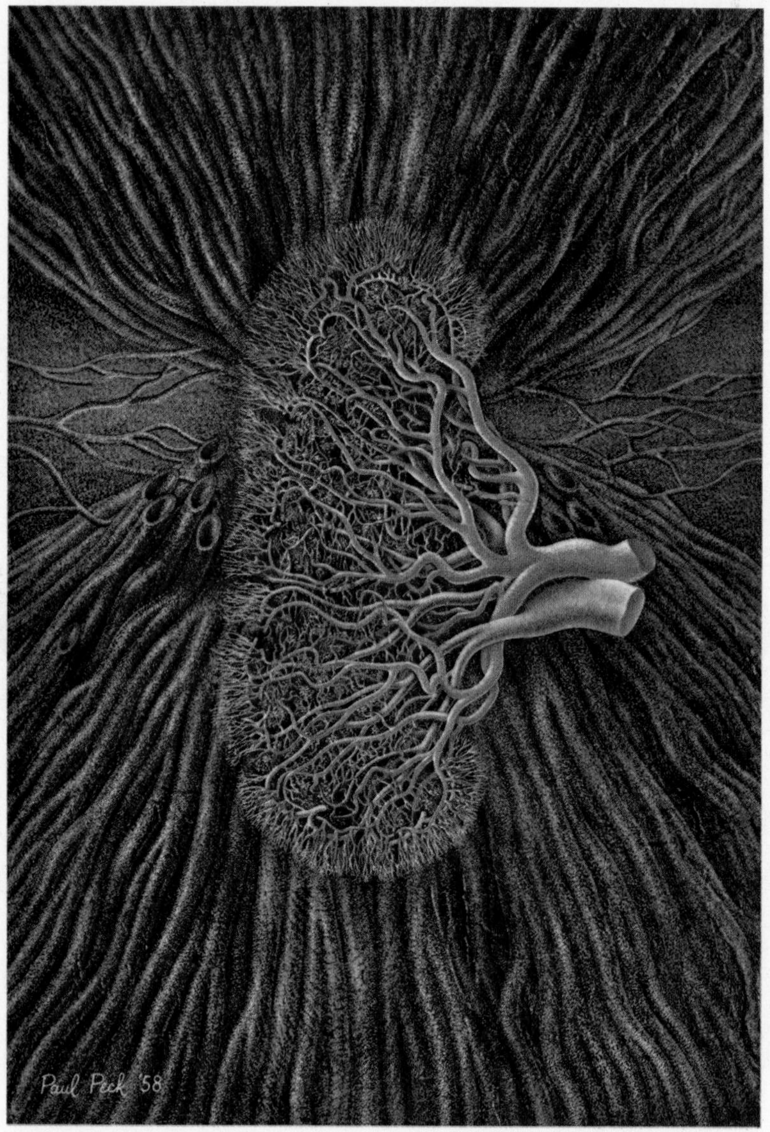

HYPERTENSION, Dr. Paul Peck, 1958, 11½" x 16½"

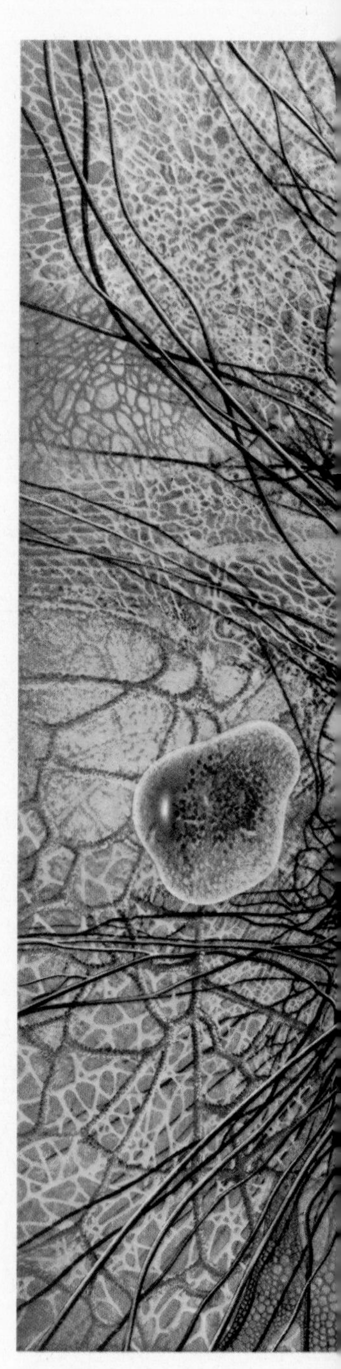

Hypertension

Some of the ravages of hypertension, a disease caused by excessive blood pressure, are revealed in this corrosion specimen of a kidney. Its frayed contour is due to the destruction of small arteries. The background, representative of the hundreds of thousands of tubules in a single kidney, reveals numerous gaps where the tubular elements have died as a result of impaired blood supply.

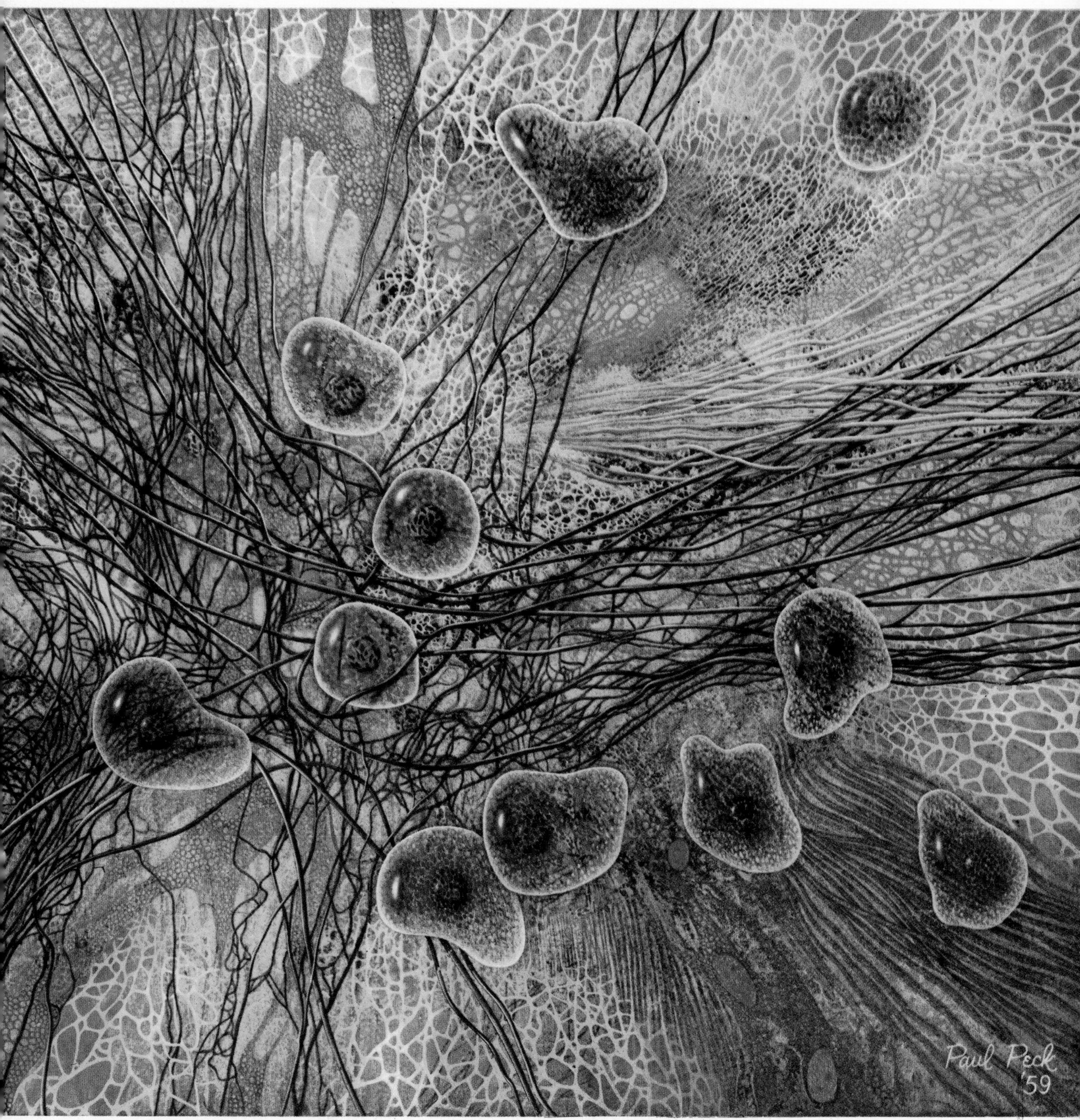

THE RETICULO-ENDOTHELIAL SYSTEM, Dr. Paul Peck, 1959, 13¼" x 17"

Connective Tissue

Connective tissue is the most widespread structure in the body, covering every organ, joint, bone, muscle, nerve, and blood vessel with a protective wrapping. The painting depicts various fibrous and netlike components of this tissue. The darkly stained fibers form a physical barrier to the spread of infection while the white blood cells scattered among its strands rid the body of invading organisms.

The Liver

The objects dramatically suspended in space are gallstones. The gall bladder and liver substance have been dissolved, leaving only a network of veins and the stones formed by the accumulation of bile salts. The pale green pervading the left portion of the painting emphasizes the bile-producing function of the liver, while the warm, reddish glow at the right is reminiscent of the liver substance itself. The painting has an air of mystery appropriate to an organ whose true nature is still not completely understood.

GALLSTONES, Dr. Paul Peck, 1966, 17" x 24"

PAUL PECK, B.Sc., M.A., Ph.D., is one of the outstanding medical artists of our time. He combines a thorough background in anatomy and the medical sciences with broad experience in the fine arts and education. After completing the premedical curriculum at New York University in 1929, he received graduate training in art education at Columbia University and in gross and microscopic anatomy at the Johns Hopkins Medical School. Thereafter, he continued his doctoral studies while teaching at New York University, Hunter College, Pratt Institute, and the Institute of Adult Education where he was both professor of art and chairman of the art department.

During World War II, Paul Peck served as chief medical artist in the Surgeon General's Office and in the Army Institute of Pathology, Washington, D.C., where he trained units of medical illustrators for service overseas. From 1945 to 1946 he was a member of a pathological investigation unit of the Army Institute of Pathology studying tropical diseases in Central America. For this work, he was awarded a special citation for outstanding achievement by the Office of Inter-American Affairs. Dr. Peck was later commissioned to do a series of paintings on tropical diseases for the Library of Congress. In 1945 he received an invitation from the World Health Organization to conduct medical art courses in various countries. For the last 15 years he has been engaged in the preparation of numerous atlases of anatomy, pathology, and surgery which have been translated into many languages and are used by doctors and medical students throughout the world.

Among numerous honors and awards that Dr. Peck has received are: First Prize in Mural Design, New York World's Fair, 1939; Anatomical paintings chosen to represent contemporary medical illustration in the permanent exhibit "Five Hundred Years in the History of Anatomical Art," Smithsonian Institution, 1954; Medical Art in the permanent collection, National Museum, Washington, D. C.; Eight annual awards for excellence in art in institutional advertising, 1953-1964; and a Gold Medal for Outstanding Achievement in Art awarded by the Art Directors' Club, 1965.

The Continuing Search for Knowledge

Man's quest for knowledge is a ceaseless and fascinating adventure which is unlimited by geographic boundaries or language barriers. As educational publishers, we feel that we have an important responsibility in this great human search.

In 1960 and 1961, THE WORLD BOOK ENCYCLOPEDIA sponsored an expedition led by Sir Edmund Hillary, the first conqueror of Mount Everest, into the Himalaya to test man's reactions in the thin air at the top of the world. Similarly, in 1965 and 1966, THE WORLD BOOK YEAR BOOK and WORLD BOOK ENCYCLOPEDIA SCIENCE SERVICE, INC., sponsored an African expedition led by Prince Boris de Rachewiltz, *left*, author of 20 books on archaeology, ethnology, and Egyptology, to study the history and customs of the mysterious Beja. The following is a report of the expedition by Pulitzer Prize winner George Weller of the *Chicago Daily News*, and photographed by Tor Eigeland. —The Editors

A Year Book Special Report

By George Weller

They Speak to No Strangers

The origins of the Beja are obscured by the mists of time, but these proud, Indo-European people have maintained their identity in a parched land for more than four thousand years

There are two Africas, the known and the unknown. Africa the continent has been explored. Yet the heritage of African man still awaits discovery. The semi-nations of the new Africa, hastily renamed for political distinction after independence, stir to a soft beating of old tribal drums. Their new names are only labels to sort out an Africa still unformed, burdened with a dark past, feeling for a dim future.

A hundred years from now, these artificial names may be worn away, revealing the old language-bound tribal states beneath. This underlying Africa is as changeless as a camel's cry or a sand-choked water hole. It is as crafty as men bargaining for a potent bull, a powerful amulet, or a weapon that has drawn blood.

Holding his staff of authority, a *kualay,* across his shoulders, a Beja tribesman walks in solitude toward the full African moon.

This is the Africa of the mysterious Beja, a people both wise and ignorant, fierce, independent, and having a tradition at least 20 times as old as that of the United States.

The Beja number about 700,000 people, with no capital or central power, a resilient network of tribes loosely bound by family relationships and a prehistoric language, but no writing. They are protected from assimilation by being spread out and isolated in a scorched land no man wants. Out of this 600-mile-wide, 1,000-mile-long belt of sand and thorns between the Red Sea and the Blue Nile (see map on opposite page), owned separately by Egypt and the Sudan, and often disputed at its frontiers, the hardy Beja somehow extract a sparse living as camel raisers and fishermen.

Anglo-Saxon history first recognized the Beja as the "Fuzzy-Wuzzies," the fierce guerillas of the Nile who fought the British in the days of Mohammed Ahmed (the Mahdi), Charles George Gordon, and Lord Kitchener. But the pharaohs of Egypt, the Romans, Greeks, Arabs, and Chinese had already known them.

These fuzzy-haired but far from fuzzy-minded Beja were sitting cross-legged in the shadows of their camels on the dun bluffs overlooking the Red Sea when the earliest Greek and Phoenician navigators threaded their way south among the blue-green coral reefs toward the Indian Ocean. Long before Christ was born, the first Chinese junks zigzagged up the Red Sea to the coves of Aidhab, the Beja port, offering the heavy black silk of Peking to the Beja for their little goatskin bags of emeralds and gold dust. In those days, the Beja sat at the yoke of the Orient and the West.

Today, giant tankers, long and low, creep along the same blue corridor. The Beja still sit on the same cliffs, watching the Soviet submarines and the American aircraft carriers that have replaced the triremes of Greece and Rome, and the galleys of the pharaohs.

By the Nile, western limit of their thirsty domain, the Beja were peering from the bluffs above the temples of Abu Simbel as the XIV Roman legion marched cautiously southward. Abu Simbel has been cut up into blocks and reassembled on the cliffs above the rising waters. The brown stone faces of Abu Simbel have lost their place, but the brown flesh faces of the Beja still keep their vigil above the sliding green river.

The Beja manner with strangers is not immediate hostility, but a guarded cordiality. Their wariness has met the test of survival for 4,000 years or more. When strangers are numerous, they vanish.

Ever watchful of raiders nosing along the edges of their parched sanctuary, the Beja gradually developed their eccentric hairdo, wild in appearance, but very practical for the desert. "We must always see strangers out in the sun before they see us," the Beja explain. "Wearing our hair this way is manly and beautiful. But mainly it protects our eyes. Arabs and westerners wear dark glasses. But real people of the desert like us scorn them."

The author:
George Weller has roamed the world as a foreign correspondent. He is a former Neiman Fellow at Harvard, a prize-winning journalist, and author of a number of distinguished books.

Why were the Beja, among the thousands of African tribes, singled out to be studied by a World Book Year Book mission?

They were chosen because they are racial strangers in Africa, mysterious in origin. They are not Semites or Negroes like their neighbors, but forgotten Indo-Europeans, lost cousins of the peoples of Western Europe and the United States. Their hair may make them appear savage, but their noses are narrow, their lips thin, their features delicate, though dark as walnut. When the Indo-European tribes were migrating to Europe's forests, the Beja, like the Kurds of northern Iraq, somehow got diverted southward from the main line of westward march, caught in a back eddy of their own. To discover them is like finding a lost column of Spartans or a Phoenician colony.

At least 4,000 years ago, and probably much earlier, the Beja seem to have paused on their way out of India in the mountains of southern Russia. They picked up place names in the Caucasus and brought them south into Africa. These names turn up in the Egyptian "Book of the Dead," the long papyrus of about 2,000 B.C.

Century after century, the Beja survive. Wherever their tall camels, with wrinkled, uplifted noses and faraway troubled eyes, discover today's grass and tomorrow's water, the Beja can endure.

J. Spencer Trimingham in *Islam in Ethiopia*, explaining the background of the Beja, says, "At some undetermined epoch, Africa was

Though dark-skinned, the Beja have narrow noses and thin lips; evidence of their Caucasian ancestry.

The Mystery of the Beja

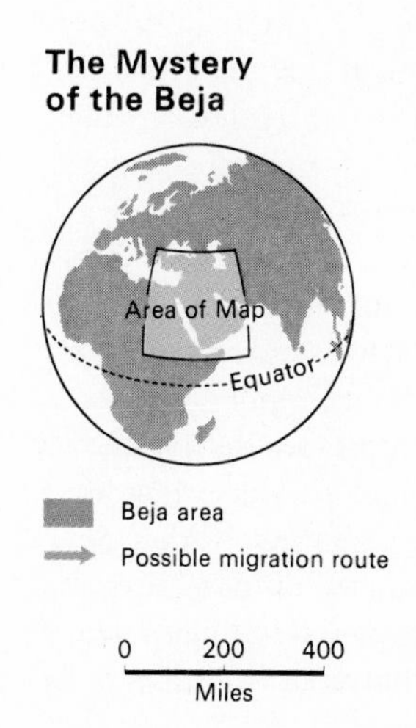

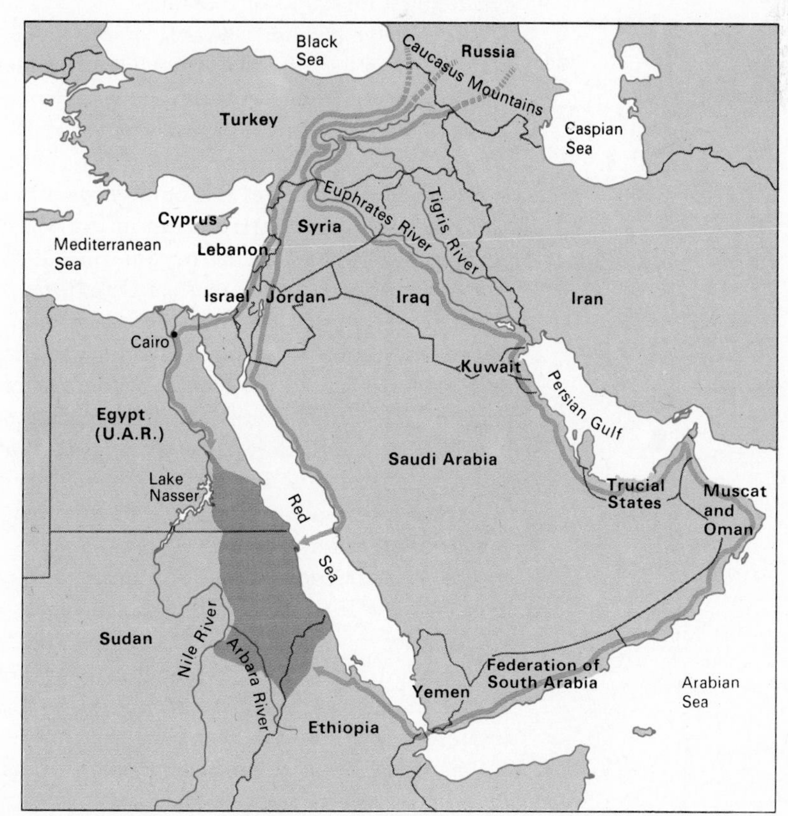

Map indicates the area in which the Beja live, as well as possible migration routes into their present region. How they arrived where they are today remains an intriguing mystery.

The Beja earn a spare living as camel raisers and fishermen. Pictured here is one of their villages in the Sudan.

invaded, possibly from South Arabia, by waves of Hamitic-Caucasians belonging to the same race of man as most Europeans. The pre-dynastic Egyptians in the past and the Beja today are the most unmodified members of this race."

To Ludwig Keimer, the first great scholar of the Beja, "they are men of Caucasian characteristics whose skin has been rendered brown by the sun, but have nevertheless retained their Caucasian appearance . . . Almost all ethnologists today regard these Hamites as being part of the Caucasian race."

De Rachewiltz shares this opinion with Keimer, whom he assisted from 1955 until the latter's death in 1957, and whose ethnological researches de Rachewiltz has been pursuing and enlarging.

Exactly how the Beja arrived where they are now, we do not know. Some were losers in the dynastic struggles in Egypt 4,000 years ago. This faction must have come directly from the Caucasus. Other Beja seem to have skirted the terrible wilderness of the Sinai desert reaching the Nile by the route that the Bronze Age people traveled from the Caucasus to Tahun in Palestine. Still another column appears to have gone down the Persian Gulf to southern Arabia, then followed the monsoon winds eastward to East Africa, like the early Chinese and Indian traders.

The World Book Year Book mission wanted to visit the Beja not only because they seem to be strayed blood relatives of the Atlantic community, but because their society is an open door to early Egypt. There are many words in their language, forgotten in the modern Egyptian language, which correspond to hieroglyphs in the tombs lining the west bank of the Nile.

The Beja language, To-Bedawi, classified as "hamito-cushitic," is a living reservoir of ancient Caucasian roots and Egyptian words of pharaonic times. Though older in Africa than the Semitic tongues, Hebrew and Arabic, To-Bedawi is easier for a European or American to learn and pronounce well. A Beja, conversely, learns English easily. But the Beja progress poorly in Sudanese and Egyptian schools because they come from homes where no Arabic is spoken. Nearly all the Beja we met spoke of the immense difficulty of going on into Arab high schools and colleges.

Our mission, led by Prince de Rachewiltz, stayed with the Beja from November, 1965 through March, 1966. We ate, traveled, bickered, dickered, and even danced with them. We did not merely accept the men's view of their history; we also listened and recorded the joys and griefs of their slim, articulate women. And our alert photographer, Tor Eigeland, found scores of ways to get around their aversion to being photographed.

The first Beja we found were selling camels in Embaba, the crumbling old meat market of Cairo. The camels provide meat protein for an Egypt fed by American wheat. These camels are raised by other Beja, their cousins, near the mountains of Ethiopia, far to the south.

A few Beja have settled in Aswan, near Egypt's great dam. Other Beja leave their families in Sudan's deserts and join stevedoring gangs in Port Sudan. Some are fishermen and smugglers of pilgrims.

A nomadic, desert people, the Beja carry their half-spherical, woven tents from camp to camp. Here one of them prepares coffee.

Most of the Beja are nomads, carrying their half spherical, woven tents from camp to camp along a triangular system of water holes in the desert. Their route has changed little in 4,000 years. By law, they are not allowed firearms. But they do not resent this; they protect themselves with ancient Crusader swords, daggers, and throwing clubs.

Our party was the first to be able to move around, making comparisons between the various subtribes of Beja. When the Bishari would not tell us something we wanted to know, de Rachewiltz gently pried the information out of them by indicating that we already knew half the secret from their rivals, the Ababda.

Our object was not simply to unwind the language and customs of the various Beja tribes, but to trace their meanderings in history. We knew that writers of pharaonic Egypt, and Greek and Roman historians and Arab chroniclers had mentioned the Beja. De Rachewiltz kept shuttling back to archives in Cairo and to libraries in Khartoum, checking clues. We soon won the heart and help of Mohammed Dirar, a retired railroad official living outside Port Sudan, a Beja himself, and their only tribal historian. At the same time we had Hassan Foda, our own historian, working in Egyptian archives. And in Khartoum we had Father Giovanni Vantini, a missionary who knows the urbanized Beja well, to provide us with the history of assimilation.

The governments of Egypt and the Sudan are wary about any publicity given the Beja. It took weeks to convince Arab officials of our scholarly purposes. These "developing" countries tend to impose an arid authority of what they call socialism on their simpler citizens. They are not eager to draw foreign attention to these dark-skinned

Camels, appropriately called "the ships of the desert," play an important role in the life of the Beja tribes.

early settlers who wear coiffures like dandelions, carry long swords like Christian knights, and are notably cool about serving pan-Arabism or the master state.

In Egypt, where economic and political pressures are strongest, some Beja have cut off their hair and donned sunglasses and long white galabiars, determined to lose themselves among the Arab Egyptians. In Sudan, however, they are themselves. There, a flourishing Beja Congress Party defends the right of this minority, though the party itself is split into pro- and anti-assimilationists. To refuse to assimilate, when it means losing a soft job in Arab bureaucracy, is a difficult test for the stubbornly independent Beja character.

As we traveled from one Beja tribe to another, we found it was of little use to carry letters of introduction. Few desert Beja can read. What was important was to carry a message between relatives, a baby's name, an elder's illness, or an important betrothal. Another way to gain their confidence was to wear some gift or token of esteem. For example, Sheik Ali Karrar, a leading Beja spokesman and our faithful friend, gave our researcher of women, Gioia Nalin, called Leila, two bracelets of hammered silver to use as her passport. He said to her benevolently, "Now you are a Beja, now you are Leila Ali Karrar." Hundreds of miles away, deep in Sudan, when she showed these bracelets to the Beja women, she was instantly able to gain entrance to their tents, to help them medically, and even to break their taboo against being photographed.

Village of Hatmia-Beni Amer in Sudan, *opposite page,* is a resting place for Beja camel caravans.

We chose Aswan for our first researches because, though the Beja in Egypt number hardly more than one-sixth of the population, this resort and industrial city just north of the First Cataract on the Nile is still a Beja crossroads. Here we met the caravans of camels, some loaded with needed firewood, as they came plodding in at the "gate of

the desert." The Beja drivers were slumped on the camels' brown humps wearing hand-carved wooden combs in their hair, jogging up and down, limp as rag dolls.

We followed the camels south from Aswan to Esnah, into the palm-rimmed market place where they were fattened, changed hands, and loaded aboard trains for Cairo. And then we went back to Aswan and trekked north along the Nile to where the thirsty caravans emerge from the desert. We traced this route to Kassala, the city near the base of Ethiopia's mountain rampart, where the camels are bred. There we found ourselves in the benevolent hands of Ali Karrar's son, married to the daughter of the largest Beja camel raiser. We brought the good news that his father had, at 70, just become the father of a daughter. Finally, we turned eastward to the Red Sea coast where there are five main tribes of Beja. The best known to historians are the 75,000 Bisharin. Farther north are the Ababda, a tribe of some 50,000 who are gradually being Arabized. Petty employment at the Aswan dam and in the Soviet-Egyptian installations on the Red Sea is swallowing their desert memories, softening their muscles, making them forget their tongue. The unspoiled Sudanese Beja derisively call them *Masr Effendi*, meaning "Mister Egyptian."

In the southern Sudan are four tribes of pure Beja, least known to history. They are the most remote. They are the 100,000 Amarar, the 105,000 Beni Amer, and the 270,000 Hadendowa. Finally, there are the Halanga who claim to be the oldest of all.

A musician plays at a pre-wedding dance near Atbara, Sudan. Beja men are entitled by religion to have four wives, but usually take only one.

Ali Karrar was an invaluable source of help to us in studying the Beja. Slim and courtly, he is an ardent Beja patriot and literally sleeps on Beja history. Under his head is a wooden pillow called a *miti-ras*, used by the early Bejas in Egypt to preserve alertness in sleep and to protect their flaring coiffure.

Ali Karrar is proud of the history of the Beja, but where their customs originated is beyond him. He told us that a Beja married couple sleeps their first night with a sword between them, symbolic of renunciation and sacrifice. De Rachewiltz informed the chief that this custom was also common in the Caucasus, and that it was probably related to the earlier Indian custom of separating newly married couples with the staff of Visvavau. Ali Karrar threw open his arms in a gesture of frank bafflement. "We don't know where these customs first came from," he said. "If you can find out, please tell us."

De Rachewiltz tried to extract tribal history from another Beja leader, less open and sophisticated than Ali Karrar. The chief waited until all the questions were recited. Apparently he wanted to know where they led. As he listened, waving his long *kualay*, his wooden staff of authority curved by tallow and heat, he gravely made notes in the sand at his feet in some code of his own. When the questions ended, he erased everything he had written. He refused to answer. By his standards, he had won this bout of intelligence. He had extracted the stranger's questions. He had also destroyed them so that they would

Pictures of Beja women are very rare. The one above shows smiling tribal beauties.

not intrude on him. He was doing what the Pennsylvania Amish call "shunning." The Beja are sustained in this carefully undocumented system of remembering and forgetting by the fact that most of their relationships are close. Any Beja can remember all members of his clan-group for generations. His interest in outsiders is merely polite.

Arabs use transistor radios like newspapers, listening attentively to the boiling intrigue that whirls through their unstable world. The Beja are more wary. Bodiless air voices, like letters, can mislead and betray. The familiar mind of a nearby relative is more trustworthy.

Beja girls like radios for music, but the only Beja we found who wanted a transistor for news was small, graceful Fakiyya who, at 80, walks with the swinging purposeful gait of a ballerina. She is the eccentric, emancipated innkeeper of the Beja suburb in Aswan. She is childless, husbandless, frolicsome, and free. In her mud hut, the camel drivers drink her sweet coffee from little brown pots. "Now if you would give me a tran*sees*tor," Fakiyya told de Rachewiltz, "I would hang it there"–she pointed through the murky shadows to a center tent pole rubbed shiny by the backs of squatting camel drivers–"and I would have more business." She is probably deceiving herself. She really wants the noisy gadget in order to listen to the world. Her mind is hungry for variety.

Fakiyya has a beauty advantage over her sisters of the Beja tribes. She can use city water for bathing. Her sisters depend on animal fats. To any Beja woman reared in the sand, bathing all over in water is as wasteful as a Western woman tubbing in milk. The right way for a woman to take a bath in the desert is to dig a small hearth about a foot deep inside the family tent. At the bottom of the hearth is a bed of grass which, when burning, keeps the "bath" dense and smoky.

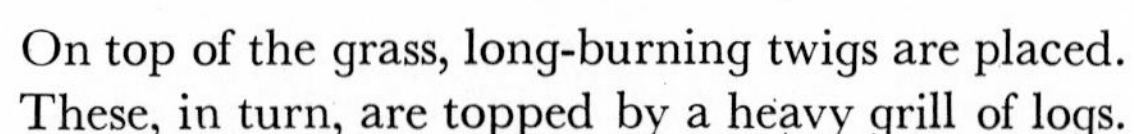

On top of the grass, long-burning twigs are placed. These, in turn, are topped by a heavy grill of logs.

As the fumes rise, the bather, her eyes smarting, has a good drenching sweat, then carefully wipes herself with clean rags. This is followed by another upward-directed shower of aromatic smoke. After this dry sauna, the woman rubs a smooth tallow in all her pores, either homemade or the fragrant expensive kind (25 cents a lump) that her husband has bought from Fakiyya on a trip to Aswan.

This mutton fat, called in Beja *gob*, just as it looks, is a sure wrinkle-remover. The glob of gob Fakiyya gave me looked and smelled like Camembert cheese that had been used as a football by two puppies. Gob removes not only wrinkles, but all human companions, except Beja. On me, it smelled blasphemously, but not on the Beja. Smoke, sweat, and gob, without water, keep the Beja as free of odors as any lotion-pampered westerner.

It is not easy, we discovered on leaving Aswan, to find a small Beja family in the desert. The Beja live quietly. They move unobtrusively in small groups of three or four families. All of them are at least cousins of some degree.

Dress, for both men and women, is loose and free; light, baggy trousers, a trim vest to show off the lean upper torso, and for men, the 30-foot-long white scarf that crosses over the chest and hips and falls in two elegant folds from the shoulders.

A Beja man usually takes one wife (renouncing his religious right to four), marrying as young as 18 and divorcing rarely. A man has first right to ask his girl cousin's hand in marriage. His uncle cannot refuse him if he has the money to buy her. This is a compact society preferring nearby familiar things, deliberately renouncing excursions beyond its limits.

A Beja herds camels at the animal market in Ed Damer, Sudan. Camels are a chief source of meat. They are also used for desert transport and can subsist for days without water. They are able to transport extremely heavy loads.

A newborn child remains nameless for 40 days. Then a relative, usually an uncle, comes to the tent of the parents and inquires politely, "How have you named your child?" The father answers, and the name of the newborn is indelibly written on the minds of his people.

Age, counted in years, is not important to a Beja. It is obvious to him. Just as he opens a camel's lips, he need only look at you to tell about how many years you have lived. The exact total is unimportant.

For the Beja, fire is a universal medicine. When a man has a mysterious pain, red-hot heat is the cure. The Beja take steel—any blade will do—and heat it in a fire. Then they touch the tip to one of their mysterious points of conduction that channel the flow of good and evil through the body. This hot point is a sort of Beja version of Chinese acupuncture, wherein needles are applied to the so-called poles of control, often far from the seat of pain. Did the early Beja learn this method from the Chinese silk merchants? The Beja do not remember. All they know is that the touch of hot metal is good for any ailment.

Though stubborn in their customs, the Beja are not stupid or slug-

The hair of the Beja, as on opposite page, appears wild, but it protects their eyes from the fierce desert sun. In picture at right, Bejas bargain with each other while seated among their camels.

gish, but alert, gifted, and teachable when they choose to learn. They simply object to sitting still, nosing into books in a place where government tax collectors can catch up with them. To collect anything, the government of Egypt and Sudan have had to hire Beja chiefs as tax collectors. They alone can trace delinquents across the desert's blank.

Their eyesight remains wonderful today. We met Beja trackers in Aswan who earn $40 a month pursuing criminals into the desert for the Egyptian police. In thousands of years, no eyes have surpassed theirs in reading the faint hint of a camel's hoof on stony ground or the imperceptible pressure of the sandal of an eloping woman. But these Beja sleuths carefully avoid getting into difficulties with their own people in the desert. They refuse to track beyond 15 miles outside a town, where tribal territorial rights begin. "To court a girl who has wakeful parents in her tent," says a Beja proverb, "a young man must learn to leap from stone to stone." The Beja prefer tracking Arab criminals. To become members of the Egyptian police, their hair must be partly subdued. But their eyes keep the alertness of desert falcons.

The mind of the Beja is a perfect record of what is important to him and of what he has heard. He does not distort, boast, or exaggerate. Listen to how two Beja from the same subtribe greet each other,

In moving to cities like Aswan, *below,* or Port Sudan to seek job opportunities, the Beja risk losing their long cultural traditions.

City Beja live in squalid quarters, but their families are tightly knit.

meeting in the desert four days out of Port Sudan. One man is city-bound for a job on the docks, having left his family and herds to earn money. The other has finished with his stint as a stevedore.

First the nomads exchange their low, almost expressionless litany of polite recognition. It is as formalized as two bureaucrats meeting in a corridor. Because there is no hurry in the desert, the greeting lasts much longer than it would elsewhere. There is a soft slurring undertone; both nomads speaking, neither really listening. It begins "Dabaiwa" (Are you well?) . . . "Gurha Kifaina" (I hope everything is going well) . . . "Hamdulillah" (Thanks be to God). Then the ritual goes around again, with each softly murmuring queries, until imagination flags. Gradually, the ritual runs down.

Then comes the real business; the exchange of information. The man from the city goes down the price list of each store in the bazaar, naming the commodity: salt, tea, sugar, and thick and thin cotton, where each comes from, and exactly what each costs. The man from the desert tells the outbound Beja where the grass is best, which wells still have water and which have dried up, what marriages have taken place, who has been born and what his name is, who has died and where he was buried in the simple Beja circle of cemetery stones. This interchange is the living newspaper of the Beja.

In Port Sudan, we found that the Beja of the sea resist and survive because they are adaptable. Once they sweated in the gold mines of the Red Sea coast for the Egyptians, Romans, Arabs, and Turks. Now they fish or dive for mother-of-pearl along the entire coast. Their slim

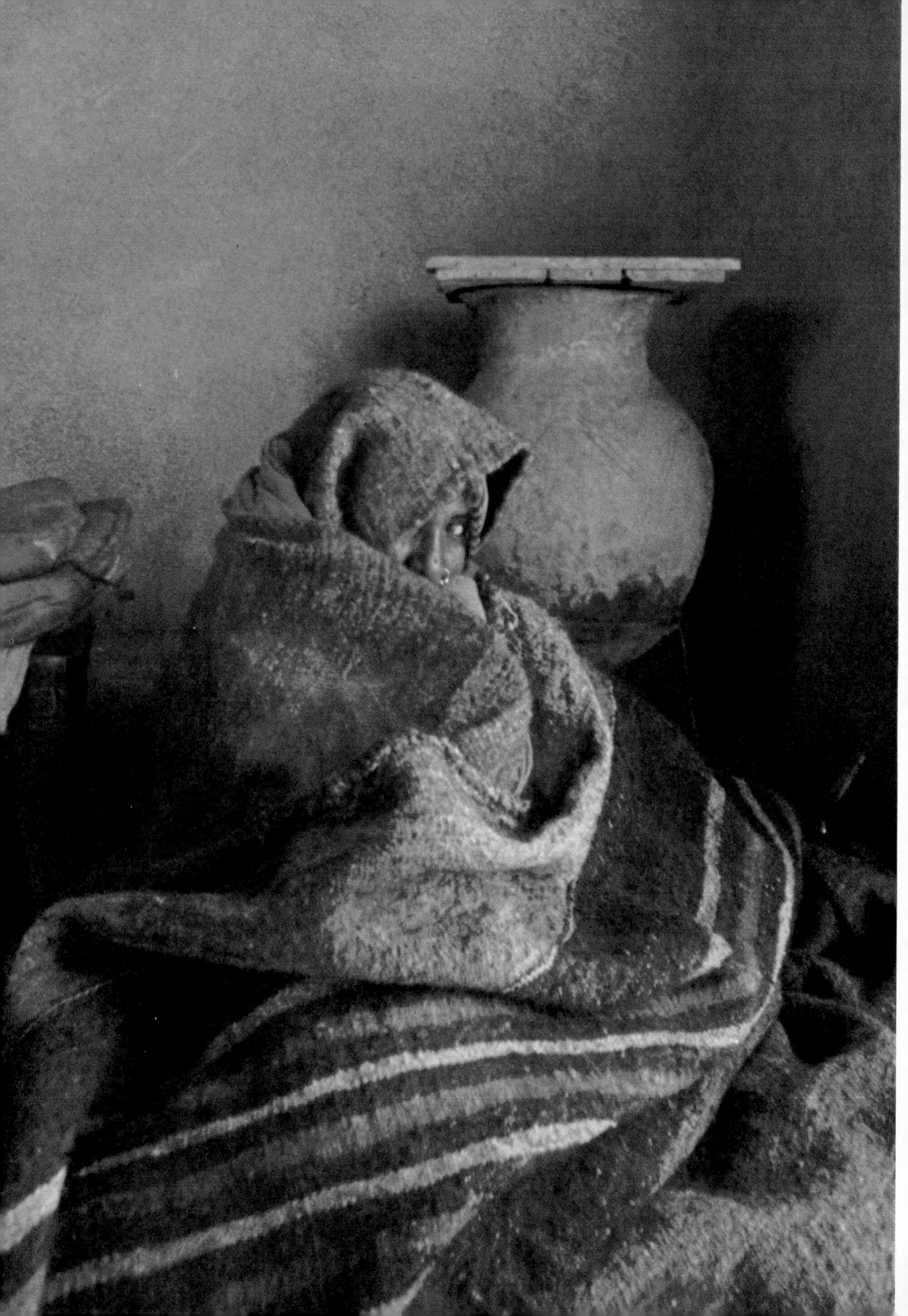

Even the Beja children, shown here in Aswan, display unusual but highly practical hairdos.

sailing wherries, the *mbeit*, steal out at dawn, and move eastward around ramparts of decaying old Suakin, remaining until sunset.

A Beja's job as a stevedore in Port Sudan is miserably paid. But in dingy Deim-el-Arab, the port's unpainted shantytown, a young Beja, needing $100 for bride money and a wedding banquet, can save that much in six months. Three-quarters of these city "warriors" are under 25 years old. They work in tight family clubs of 12 men, mostly cousins, near or far. When one has enough money, a brother or a cousin comes in from the desert to take his place.

If a Beja elects to remain in Port Sudan, however, forsaking the desert, national horizons begin to open for him. He votes. Hence the other 3,000,000 Sudanese are his suitors. The dominant Arabs and Nubians in the north, and the restless Negroes, partially Christianized, rebelling against them in the south, have one weakness in common—they must rely on the good will of the Beja minority to sell and buy abroad. Sudan's egress to the sea depends on the free passage of trucks and freight trains through Beja country to Port Sudan. The old railroad to Suakin has been torn up. Sudan's only sea exit is Port Sudan. As doorkeepers, the Beja are not a minority people who can be lightly brushed aside.

Not very eagerly, they now find themselves stumbling into politics. In the Sudanese parliament of 203 seats, the "Beja bloc" has 11 seats. Do they always vote alike? Usually. But being Beja, not always.

In religion, the Beja are unimpressed by the gentle teachings of Christianity, preferring the Moslem faith. The Koran acts as a restraint against their sinking into animism. But they are superstitious. They believe profoundly, for example, in the mandrake, the man-shaped root called in Beja *arta hindi* meaning "the root that gets the

Woman on opposite page is being treated for a cold. This process involves smearing her body with camel grease, lighting a fire, and then wrapping her in blankets to encourage perspiration.

girls." Before you get your girl, you must find your root. To do this, you must train a *shuckli* (black dog) to dig it up. The mandrake grows only in the yellow valley of the Atbai, the tributary of the Blue Nile.

The owner of a trained black dog asks a down payment of up to five camels to search for an unused mandrake. Any girl worth being chased by a mandrake costs three camels. Being a *homunculus* (little man), the mandrake cries in protest when it is pulled up to be sent on a quest for a girl for somebody else. Woe to the man who sees the root and greedily pulls it up with his bare hands. He risks his life, according to the beliefs of the Beja.

Recently Sheik Amin, a wealthy camel merchant, hired a used, but still lively mandrake at the high rate of a-camel-for-24-hours (about $100, Aswan price). The costly amulet was rented to him only long enough for a single, hard-selling approach to the family of the girl in question. A leather bag enclosed the lower half of the mandrake, the little root-man being cut off at the waist. Through the eloquent intervention of the *afrit* (ghost) living in the mandrake, and temporarily at his command, the sheik got the girl he was pursuing.

Today, when a Beja wants to explore the supernatural, he ignores Allah, Christianity, and science. He does not even bother to consult the stars. He disdains the researches in astronomy of the ambitious, desert-traveling Arabs. He regards *O-Trik* (the moon) as more meaningful. The moon determines the all-important time of a man's birth, whether rising (promising), full (lucky), or waning (unfortunate). The Beja, traveling for generations along the same routes, do not really need the stars as guides.

When they require an intimate job of divination, the Beja go to the tents of their camp followers, the Takruni. The Takruni, a small tribe

Working as a stevedore on the docks at Port Sudan, a Beja, though poorly paid, can save enough in six months to marry.

of sorcerers from the juju sects of West Africa, have managed to attach themselves to the Beja as wizards.

The Takruni are clever Negroes who migrated eastward several centuries ago, possibly from today's Ghana. They found an easy vocation practicing black arts among the Beja.

Freebooters in witchcraft, subtle in the psychology of the sands, the Takruni hold the Beja as clients by their occult management of family troubles. One day, as we watched, a Takruni woman threw out a handful of shells on a palm mat. Murmuring spells in her own tongue, she made the conches answer her, reading their arrangement. Then, speaking in Beja, she disclosed to a Beja woman, veiled like herself, what the future would bring. This prosperous, plump witch had little leather lockets for sale, love charms that would lure one man and repel another. Her neck was ringed with heavy silver coins, and her prices were high. "Why do you spend so much on this witch?" we asked her client. "Because," whispered the Beja woman, "if any Takruni doesn't like you, he can change your sex."

Can the Beja survive our enclosing civilization? Perhaps they have some protective assets. The worthlessness of their land and the humility and hardship of their work as raisers of cheap meat help to discourage conquest. When invasion has threatened in the past, they have always proved their willingness to fight–and fight fiercely–for what they hold dear: their camels, waterholes, and women.

But what about the voluntary desertion of their parched land for the white anthills of the city? This desertion can still entrap the Beja. If the tribes, in learning city Arabic, forget how to speak To-Bedawi, they can be swallowed up.

The highest rampart around the Beja is their sense of continuity, fostered by early, responsible marriage. They make demands of each new society that swirls past their corner of Africa. If the intruder does not meet Beja standards, they reject him and wait another 100 years. They survive because they have viable standards.

More than 40 years ago, Sheik Ali Karrar, then a vigorous young man, guessed that Cairo would pay well for fresh meat. He decided to lead a herd of 500 sheep across the desert from the Red Sea to the Nile, then 1,200 miles up to Cairo.

"After many days of walking," he recalls, "I finally saw the peaks of the pyramids in the sky to the north. I turned in at Gizeh and sold my sheep to a merchant. Then I rode quietly into Cairo. I sat down at a Greek coffee shop, looking for other Beja I could trust.

"The Greek gave me coffee and a glass of water. I noticed a hair floating in the water. I said, 'Give me water without a hair.' The Greek said, 'Why? By your looks, you have been living with sheep for months yourself. What is one hair to you?' I answered the Greek, 'Yes, I have been drinking dirty water for many months. But I swallowed it only to drink clean water from you.' "

The world must provide clean water, or the Beja will not drink.

A Year Book Special Report

By June Bingham

The Most Impossible Job In the World

As United Nations Secretary-General, U Thant, a mild-mannered Burmese, must try to deal with the often conflicting aspirations of 122 nations

East and West have met in the Glass House on 42nd Street. They have met in U Thant, an Asian steeped in British culture, and they have met in his 38th floor executive suite. So narrow is the United Nations building that the Secretary-General's office receives the morning sun while his adjoining dining room catches its afternoon rays.

Ever since he first occupied the post in 1961, U Thant has worked a six-day week, 52 weeks a year. The only exceptions were a week's vacation in the Caribbean, a short spell in a New York City hospital with an ulcer, and necessary trips outside the United States. On one of those trips, U Thant admitted that his was "a killing job." The UN's first Secretary-General, Trygve Lie, had called it, even more emphatically, "the most impossible job in the world."

U Thant, *seated at left,* confers with an aide as Australian Minister of External Affairs Paul Hasluck, *at podium,* addresses the General Assembly.

Trygve Lie, *left,* the first Secretary-General, laid the groundwork for the office. His successor, Dag Hammarskjöld, *right,* defined its limits.

Late in 1966, a reluctant U Thant heeded the pleas of a peace-hungry world to stay on in this "most impossible job." The scope of the job seems simple enough as it is defined in Chapter 15, Article 99, of the UN Charter. That article states: "The Secretary-General may bring to the attention of the Security Council any matter which in his opinion may threaten the maintenance of international peace and security." Yet, as Trygve Lie pointed out in his memoirs, *In the Cause of Peace,* Article 99 gave "the office of Secretary-General political responsibilities in the promotion and preservation of peace that the Secretaries-General of the League of Nations did not possess. . . . " Thus the Charter brought to the conduct of international affairs something unknown in the world before—an office held by one man who must be at once the symbol of the collective struggle for peace and spokesman for a world interest overriding any national interests in the councils of nations.

The Big Five Allies of World War II—the United States, the Soviet Union, France, Great Britain, and Nationalist China—at the time of the UN's birth in 1945, looked upon the role of the Secretary-General (S-G) a little more narrowly. They envisioned the Security Council as the UN's cabinet and the S-G merely as the cabinet's chief executive officer. In January, 1946, they agreed on a dark horse candidate—the stocky, blunt, union leader-turned-foreign minister, Trygve Lie of Norway. Lie tried—as much as the Russians would permit—to fill the role as it had been conceived.

Lie felt that "there were limits to the extent of the [S-G's] initiative," that his "was a moral power, not a physical one; moral power in this world is not conclusive. . . . But I was determined that the [S-G] should be a force for peace. How that force would be applied, I would find out—in the light of developments."

The developments were the Cold War, Mainland China going Communist, and the hot war in Korea. Soviet vetoes soon paralyzed the Security Council. Lie, as the Council's chief minister, acted for the

The author:
June Bingham, whose latest book, *U Thant, The Search for Peace,* was published in 1966, is a Barnard College graduate and wife of a New York congressman.

majority—the West. The Communist minority accordingly considered Lie an out-and-out Western partisan. Lie submitted his resignation in November, 1952.

It was in greeting the new S-G, Dag Hammarskjöld, at New York City's Idlewild Airport in March, 1953, that Lie warned the Swedish diplomat that he was stepping into the world's most impossible job. Slim, handsome, discreet Hammarskjöld was the epitome of European diplomacy; an intellectual, a poet, a lifelong bachelor who possessed enormous personal charm.

Hammarskjöld's main contribution to the UN was to stake out the far limits of the S-G's powers (some say he stretched them too far). This was an act of importance far beyond the context of the Congo crisis in which the stretching reached its farthest point. The Secretaries-General of the old League of Nations had never utilized their political power, and it had withered together with the organization.

In September, 1957, almost a year after the twin crises of Hungary and Suez, Hammarskjöld said it was the duty of the S-G "to use his office, and indeed the machinery of the [UN] to its utmost capacity and to the full extent permitted at each stage by practical circumstances . . . to act without [specific] guidance should this appear to him necessary . . ."

Later, during the Congo turmoil, which had begun in mid-1960, he described for an interviewer his conception of the S-G's position. "This is a political job and I am a political servant" . . . he said, thinking out loud. "The Secretary-General has to be available. [As a] go-between? That is a busybody. Catalytic agent? That is a little better. Clearing house? That is better still. It is an immensely important thing—the job, not the man—because in this . . . world split, there is nothing to take its place."

A weakness stemming from a virtue

Thus, more and more, Hammarskjöld acted on his own initiative. As a result, he won the support of many of the small and unaligned nations. But also at various times, he antagonized some of the major powers. Much more than Lie, he became a world figure in his own right. His principal weakness stemmed from a virtue: his insistence on doing things personally—on the double, on the spot. It led to many of his most startling successes—and to his death in a jungle airplane crash in 1961 on a UN mission of peace for the Congo. Only after the posthumous publication of his book, *Markings,* were many people made certain of the growing messianic strain they had suspected when he began assuming a superhuman series of burdens. In a curious way, Hammarskjöld, the Occidental, turned out to have been a more mysterious and inscrutable person than U Thant, the Oriental.

U Thant, in his own quiet manner, has shared Hammarskjöld's general conception of the office: The S-G should take initiatives in keeping the peace. But U Thant, with his self-effacing yet blunt approach—so unlike Hammarskjöld's—was able to win the confidence

U Thant breaks his day's routine and enjoys a cigar as he relaxes with a visitor in his 38th-floor office at UN headquarters.

of UN member nations large and small and of varying political persuasions. In the fall of 1966, a delegate from a small neutral nation remarked that U Thant "is respected as a man whose sincerity has never been challenged, and who has another quality needed now—great patience."

What sort of man is this who can command such respect and confidence? What hidden facets of character or background account for the intense faith that so many people of varied political persuasions have shown in this slight, mild-mannered Asian?

His face is round. His glasses are round. His mouth is round. One could caricature him by using only a draftsman's compass. His smile is warm, his handshake firm. He greets his guests in the anteroom of his office and insists that they precede him into the long, light, buff-colored room. He is, obviously, a gracious host.

His stark, handsome, Scandinavian modern desk and the matching round wooden table were chosen by Hammarskjöld. It is typical of U Thant that he has replaced neither of these objects. His office, which overlooks the East River and the roofs of the boroughs of Queens and Brooklyn, affords a more attractive view by night than by day. If the night is clear, he can see the beacons of Kennedy International Airport on Long Island. "The view," he says, "is conducive to meditation."

His day begins at 6 A.M. After washing, he practices meditation in a small room with a Buddhist shrine in the large ivy-covered house he rents in the Riverdale section of the Bronx. He then climbs onto his exercycle and, at the same time, watches the news on television. Later, while eating a Western breakfast, he reads the newspapers. He is not a fast reader. The phone from the office may ring with a report of overnight cables. He often dictates an answer right away lest the time difference in the receiver's part of the world mean the loss of valuable working hours there.

U Thant is driven to his UN office by car, a trip of about 25 minutes. On arrival, he confers with his top assistants. He likes to delegate authority. His *chef de cabinet*, Under-Secretary Chakravarthi V. Narasimhan of India, takes charge of most administrative decisions. But the political ones U Thant deals with himself.

When the General Assembly is in session, he is likely to attend. Between the speeches, he may retire to a semicircular room behind the

U Thant greets U.S. Ambassador Arthur J. Goldberg, *above*, as they prepare to enter the S-G's private dining room, *below*, to attend a luncheon for Canada's UN Ambassador, Paul Tremblay, seated at U Thant's right.

U Thant and his wife, Daw Thein Tin, entertain their grandson in the yard of their Riverdale (New York) home.

podium to sign his mail, to confer, or to receive dispatches. After the morning session, there is usually a luncheon in the S-G's dining room. Chiefs of mission are invited at least once a year, as are the top Secretariat officials. The difference between these two groups is that the delegates work at the UN on behalf of their governments, while the Secretariat officials, on the other hand, work for the UN on behalf of the organization itself.

After lunch there may be another session of the Assembly—or perhaps of the Security Council—at which the S-G is expected. Otherwise, he will tend to one of the many other aspects of his job. They include:

- Administering the Secretariat, which consists of 3,600 persons in New York and about 2,400 in the field, military as well as civilian.
- Following the instructions of the four main UN bodies: the General Assembly and its seven committees, the Security Council, the Economic and Social Council, and the Trusteeship Council.
- Preparing reports for those bodies.
- Initiating new proposals in problem areas.
- Negotiating behind the scenes in diplomatic and political crises.
- Preparing for press conferences or speaking engagements. (He likes to write his own speeches in longhand.)

In the evening, U Thant may attend a diplomatic reception. He attends these only when they are held at UN headquarters, and he stays but a short time. Then he returns to his papers. Finally, after 8 P.M., he is driven to Riverdale where he changes into Burmese dress, reads the evening newspapers, and dines on Burmese food, prepared under the supervision of his wife, Daw Thein Tin.

U Thant was born and grew up in Pantanaw, a small town in the rice-rich Irrawaddy delta, about 50 miles from Rangoon, Burma's chief port and capital. At the age of 19, after two years at University College, Rangoon, he returned to teach in Pantanaw. Three years later, he became headmaster of its National High School. In the meantime, he wrote prolifically, mostly for educational magazines.

For a short time in 1942, during the Japanese occupation of Burma, an old university friend, U Nu, persuaded U Thant to work in Rangoon on a reorganization plan for education. U Thant recalls:

"I was not happy at all. Conditions were much worse than under the British system. There were too many Japanese 'advisers.' . . . Life in Rangoon grew pretty hot. It was not only the bombing; I was a target of Japanese suspicion."

He returned again to Pantanaw and, despite Japanese surveillance, worked secretly for the Burmese underground. After the war, on Jan. 4, 1948, U Nu became the first prime minister of independent Burma and appointed U Thant its press officer. U Thant rose fast in his new calling. In 1953, he became secretary to the prime minister. In 1957, he was sent to the UN as Burma's permanent representative. He was glad to accept the post, although his wife, who still does not speak English, would have preferred to stay in Burma.

On Sept. 18, 1961, Secretary-General Dag Hammarskjöld was killed in an airplane crash in Northern Rhodesia (now Zambia). The Soviets tried to install their troika; namely, three Secretaries-General, one from each side of the Iron Curtain and one from the neutral nations. All three of them would have had to agree before the UN could have acted. But the nations outside the Soviet bloc stood firm. The principle of one Secretary-Generalship finally prevailed, and U Thant was elected acting S-G on Nov. 3, 1961. With typical modesty, he says he was chosen simply because he comes "from a nonaligned country in a strategic part of the world." A year later, Thant was unanimously elected the actual rather than acting S-G. He was formally sworn into office on Nov. 30, 1962.

Shedding the cares of office, U Thant heads for a swim in the pool at his home, a cigar in one hand and a transistor radio in the other.

The resourceful broker

U Thant, in running the office of S-G, has not been content to imitate his Scandinavian predecessors. He has played down the roles of both obedient servant or daring innovator. Instead, he has tried to act as the resourceful broker. His Burmese, Buddhist background of positive neutrality has helped him carry out that role. His main accomplishment is to have consolidated the gains made by Hammarskjöld, while reweaving the torn international fabric.

The Russians had refused even to speak to Hammarskjöld because of the UN's Congo actions, just as they had similarly refused to speak

The rays of the morning sun silhouette U Thant at his desk in his UN office. The desk had previously belonged to Dag Hammarskjöld.

to Lie because of UN action in Korea. But with U Thant, the Soviets have remained on polite terms despite his continuing refusal to give them all the Secretariat posts they have demanded. On Sept. 19, 1966, U Thant sharply criticized the Russians for imposing restraints on his initiative. (Moscow insists that the Security Council is the sole source of authority within the UN and that all peacekeeping actions must have the Council's sanction.) U Thant has also sharply criticized the United States for its Vietnam policies. Yet despite these controversies, he has thus far managed to keep the confidence of both East and West.

U Thant's main weakness, as in the case of Hammarskjöld, also stems from a virtue: A tendency to think first about how to patch up a difference, rather than how to support the more correct side. One diplomat observed that if U Thant were confronted by a nation saying that two plus two equals four and another saying that two plus two equals eight, his first impulse would be to sound out their interest in six. Actually, as U Thant himself has said:

"No difficult problem can be solved to the satisfaction of all sides. We live in an imperfect world and have to accept imperfect solutions, which become more acceptable as we learn to live with them . . . "

One difficult problem has been Vietnam. Partly because three of the four countries involved, Communist China and the two Vietnams, are not UN members, U Thant has thus far acted only in an unofficial capacity. In other crises, he is able to act officially. For example, he intervened in the Cuban crisis of 1962. At the height of the tension, his suggestion of a two- to three-week moratorium was accepted by both Soviet Premier Nikita S. Khrushchev and U.S. President John F. Kennedy. It gained the time for a solution that avoided nuclear confrontation. A similar success resulted from U Thant's visit to India and Pakistan in September, 1965, at the height of their fighting over Kashmir. He conferred with both governments and reported to the Security Council which called for a cease-fire.

An increasingly heavy burden

Despite these successes, the "impossible" aspects of U Thant's duties have weighed increasingly heavily on him. By Nov. 3, 1966–the expiration date of his first term–he could have honorably put his burden down. Matters other than the sheer workload were on his mind; matters involving the very existence of the UN itself. On Sept. 1, 1966, he notified all 117 UN delegations (grown to 122 by year's end) that "I have decided not to offer myself for a second term." He voiced his concern over the war in Vietnam, the continued exclusion of Communist China from the UN, the growing economic gulf between the poor and rich nations of the earth, and the lack of effective UN peacekeeping machinery. He concluded by insisting that there was no indispensable man for the S-G's job.

But the UN thought otherwise. Three months later, U Thant yielded to a unanimous recommendation by the Security Council. He had made the point that the S-G should not be a "glorified clerk." U Thant, it was agreed, would be allowed to take initiatives in emergencies to preserve world peace. U Thant then accepted a second five-year term as S-G on Dec. 2, 1966.

In the long run, Thant believes that the worst world tensions stem from the ever-widening economic and social gap between the "have-not" nations and the "haves." Compared to these tensions, the struggle in Vietnam, U Thant says, "is a passing phase."

To be able thus to view history through a telescopic lens while spending full time trying to improve its course is the result, in part, of U Thant's Buddhism and its emphasis on inner peace. In part, it results from his Burmese-type neutralism, and from the UN's emphasis on constructing "in the minds of men . . . the defenses of peace."

See also Section One, Paul-Henri Spaak: Focus on The World; Section Three, United Nations.

A Year Book Special Report

By Earl Ubell

Our Pill-Filled Lives

Drugs have played an important role in man's attempts to ease pain and suffering, but through increasing dependency and misuse, they can also pose serious health problems

Headache? Take a pill. Depressed, tense? Take a pill. Runny nose, arthritis, heart pain, stomach-ache–pills, pills, pills. And so it goes. Millions of Americans take pills on their own or on their doctors' say-so every day for every ill from an upset stomach to an upset psyche. We consume tons of drugs at a cost of almost $4,000,000,000 each year. An obvious result of all this pill-taking has been the alleviation of much suffering and the saving of many lives.

Now, however, many thoughtful leaders of the United States medical profession are having second thoughts about America's–and the world's–pill mania. They see a coming epidemic of pill-caused diseases. They worry about the silent and possibly deadly effects of long-term pill-taking. They fear that lifesaving pills can lose their

power through indiscriminate use. They even suspect that many medicines now prescribed have no beneficial effects at all. And they look with horror at the tendency of some physicians to overprescribe and the tendency of many patients to demand and often obtain unneeded and even dangerous drugs.

The concern of these medical leaders, as well as the enactment of new drug laws and the appointment of a new commissioner of the Food and Drug Administration (FDA), has spurred a surge of activity to control the use and remedy the abuse of drugs. Starting in January, 1966, just a few weeks after his appointment to the FDA, Dr. James Lee Goddard, the agency's young and articulate commissioner, banned one pill after another as either unsafe or ineffective. He also instructed his agency to review the scientific evidence on some 6,000 preparations – many in use for generations – to determine if they are really helpful.

It took a tragedy, caused by the drug thalidomide, to stimulate the Congress of the United States to apply the brakes on the nation's enthusiasm for drugs. The catastrophe struck Europe in 1961 and 1962. Thalidomide appeared on the market as a "safe" sedative and antinausea medicine. It did not hurt those who took it. But when the pills were swallowed by pregnant women, the drug seeped into the womb and prevented the development of the arms and legs of embryos. Only the stubborn suspicion of Dr. Frances O. Kelsey of the FDA, now head of the drug investigation division, kept the drug from being consumed by millions of American women. Prior to this episode, Congress had shown little interest in drug reform in spite of questions raised in an investigation of drug costs by the Senate Subcommittee on Antitrust and Monopoly headed by Senator Estes Kefauver. The thalidomide issue triggered congressmen into support for Kefauver's drug-reform amendments to the Federal Food, Drug, and Cosmetic Act. These were passed in August, 1962.

Since World War II, more than 600 new drugs have been injected into the stream of medicine throughout the world. These chemicals, plus new synthetics used as food additives, as well as insect sprays, and increased air and water pollution, have literally immersed the population in a totally novel chemical environment.

Until the 1920s, doctors had comparatively few chemical weapons to fight disease. Many of the existing drugs were ineffective. Dr. Oliver Wendell Holmes, the great physician and author of the 19th century, thought so little of the drugs of his time that he said if they "could be sunk to the bottom of the sea it would be all the better for mankind – all the worse for the fishes." In contrast, modern chemistry and biology have given doctors the equivalent of an arsenal of atomic weapons for their war against disease. Modern pills have conquered infections and slowed the progress of chronic illnesses. They have also afforded greater relief from pain. Their awesome power has changed not only American medicine but American life as well. For example:

The author:
Earl Ubell, former science editor of *The New York Herald Tribune,* and now science editor for CBS-TV in New York City, has received many awards for excellence in science writing.

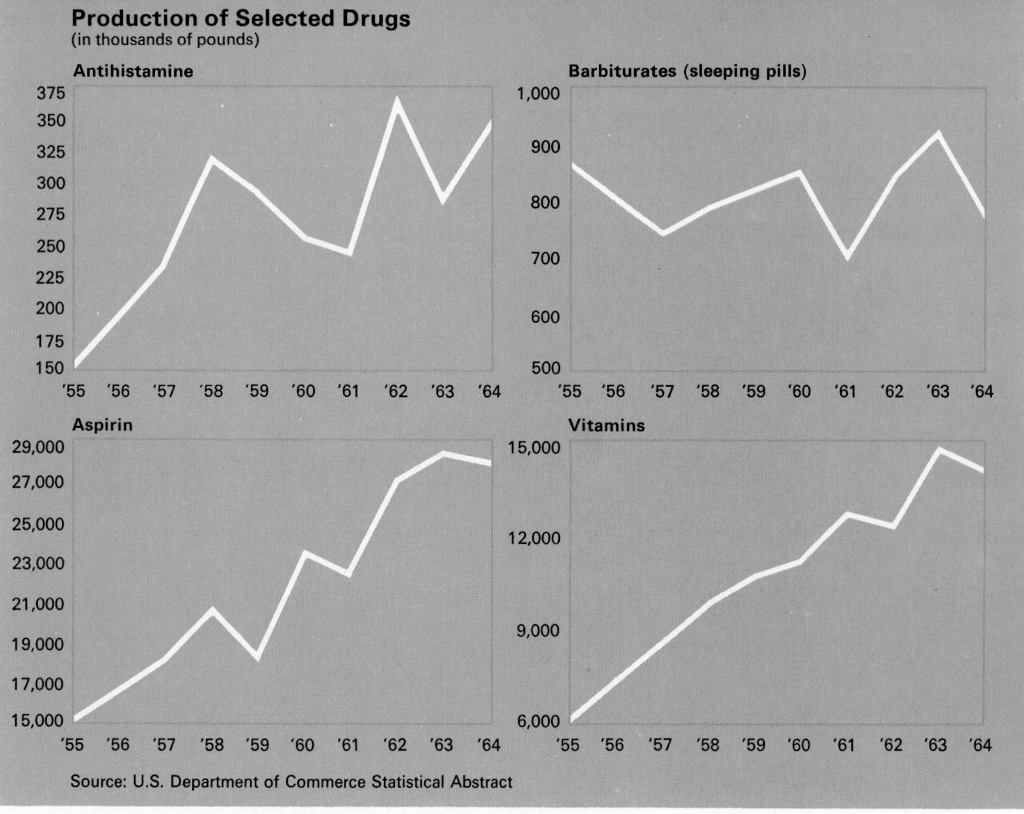

Drug production—represented here by antihistamines, aspirin, barbiturates, and vitamins—has generally increased in recent years. The figures depicted in this chart are based solely on the active chemical content of the drugs. They do not include the materials used for coating tablets or liquids used to dilute solutions.

■ Drugs have helped to extend the life span of an individual many years beyond his normal period of productive capacity. As a result, it has been necessary to institute social and economic reforms for the care of growing numbers of the aged.

■ In the short time since their introduction in 1954, tranquilizers and other psychoactive drugs, because of their effectiveness in the treatment of mental illness, have helped to change American attitudes toward emotional problems.

■ Contraceptive pills, taken regularly by an estimated 7,000,000 women, have raised moral questions, though there is little doubt about their effectiveness in preventing pregnancy. Their overall biological effects admittedly have not been fully determined.

■ Many pills now prolong the lives of victims of hereditary diseases. That, in turn, could increase the number of individuals with such maladies by allowing them to live long enough to pass on their illness to future generations. Some geneticists, projecting this effect into the future, foresee awesome consequences.

■ The effective use of antibiotics, vaccines, and other medicines to reduce the number of infections may eventually produce a society that lacks an inborn protection against infection. That, too, could have catastrophic consequences if a freak germ should develop against which no antibiotic is effective.

■ Because of the general availability of drugs, more and more persons

While the cost of prescription drugs has generally declined, increased consumption has resulted in a steady rise in consumer expenditures for drugs and surgical supplies.

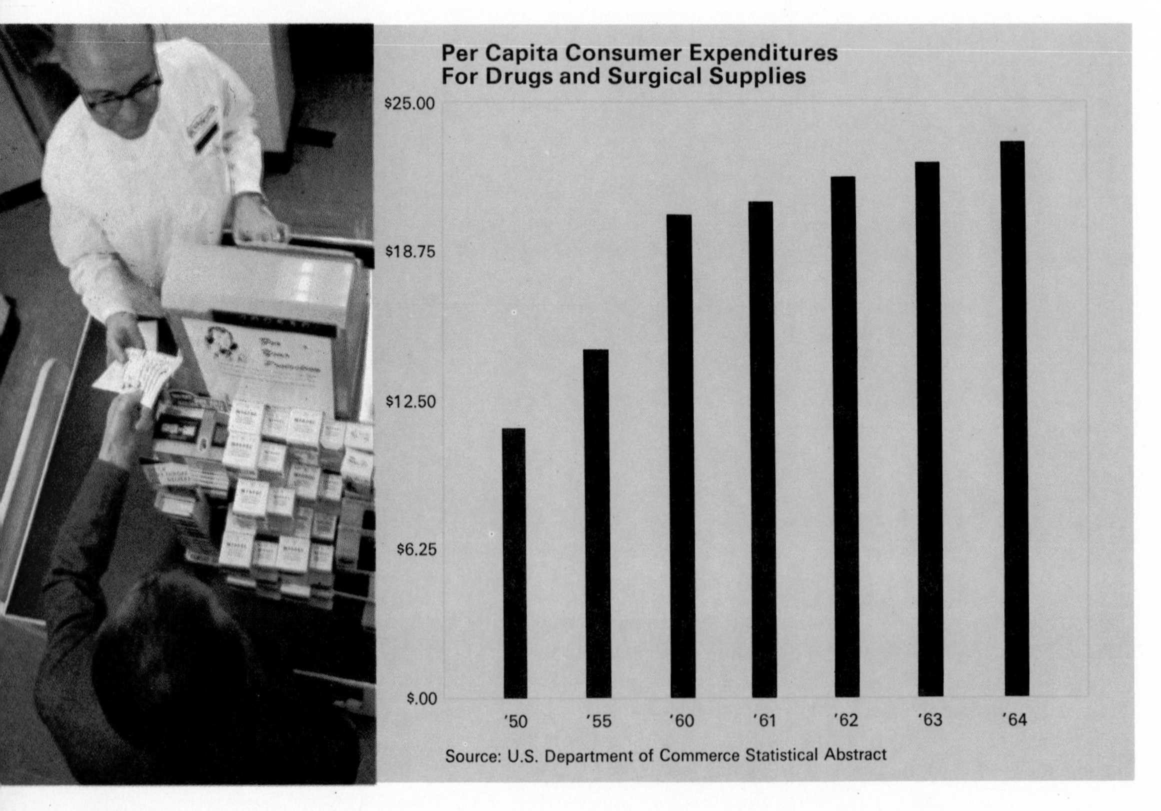

seek pill thrills, not only with the older narcotics such as opium or morphine, but with the newer amphetamines (pep pills), barbiturates, and the newest darling of the pill set, *lysergic acid diethylamide* (LSD). This latter chemical produces hallucinations and often, even more unfortunately, deep mental disturbances.

The 1962 amendments to the Food, Drug, and Cosmetic Act altered the government's role in medicine by greatly expanding the FDA's authority over drug labeling and advertising. Until then, the FDA checked only on the safety of drugs. The decision of a drug's effectiveness was left largely to the doctor. Now, each drug company has to prove that its product actually does what the manufacturer claims that it will do.

Dr. Goddard's appointment as commissioner of the FDA came at a time when the FDA needed a stronger hand. As the federal government's regulatory agency for drugs, the FDA is constantly under a barrage of criticism on all sides – congressional investigators, the drug industry, the medical profession, the general public, and even factions among its own personnel. Some accuse the FDA of being too easygoing in policing drug manufacturers. Others say it is too strict, charging that it blocks scientific progress and interferes with the relationship between a physician and his patient. Critics have objected to almost everything the FDA does, or fails to do.

When Dr. Goddard assumed his post, the staff was staggering under a backlog of applications for testing and marketing drugs. Pressing decisions were delayed and some matters that needed immediate attention were making the rounds of the agency from desk to desk. Conditions had become so inefficient that an advisory committee, appointed by John W. Gardner, Secretary of Health, Education, and Welfare, turned in a report urging a top-to-bottom reorganization of FDA procedures and personnel.

Dr. Goddard immediately asserted his own authority and that of the agency. Within two weeks, he held his first press conference and promptly suspended human tests of a new oral contraceptive because in massive doses it caused cancer in dogs. He reaffirmed the agency's stand against Krebiozen, the alleged anticancer substance, keeping the drug out of interstate commerce.

He then ordered dozens of brands of throat lozenges containing antibiotics off the market as ineffective for sore throats. He clamped down on certain drug companies that sell pills for heart pain. He warned them against making claims – without sufficient evidence – that the pills in question prolong life.

Not everyone in the agency approved of Dr. Goddard's leadership. A few key men resigned, and others were eased out of their jobs. Dr. Goddard asked Congress for $63,000,000 for the FDA in fiscal 1967, 12 times as much as the agency had been allotted a decade before. And so it has gone: new orders, new people, and new money have signaled a new attitude toward our pill-filled lives.

Dr. Goddard has charged that some members of the Pharmaceutical Manufacturers Association (PMA) suffer from a "disease of irresponsibility" in introducing new drugs. He also has charged that a third of the drug companies have violated FDA advertising codes in one way or another.

The FDA collects information on adverse drug reactions from 195 school-affiliated hospitals. As a new safeguard, it established five field offices in 1966 to handle and study illegal use of drugs. It has also tightened its standards of safety and strengthened its checks on prescription drugs and patent medicines. As in the past, it also inspects and regulates processed foods and food additives, cosmetics, and certain household items such as cleaning fluids. But almost all the controversies and criticism leveled against FDA, both past and present, concern its regulation of drugs.

The leaders of medicine and the pharmaceutical industry have reacted strongly to Goddard's first and subsequent actions. Dr. James Z. Appel, president of the American Medical Association (AMA) from 1965 to 1966, charged that Dr. Goddard's early campaign created hysteria and could eventually destroy the freedom of physicians to practice the most effective medicine.

In essence, the AMA's position holds that the doctor in his private office is in the best position to diagnose his patient's condition and prescribe any required medication. When the FDA issued a strong warning against the use of certain long acting sulfonamides (sulfa drugs), medical leaders said the warning was so strong doctors would be afraid to use the drugs even if they believed them best for a particular condition in a particular patient. They called the warning an interference with medical practice. To that Dr. Goddard replied: "It is the job of the FDA to interfere with the practice of medicine."

From their side, the drug manufacturers see great danger in the strict new regulations, danger to the vigor of the American drug industry. Through their spokesman, C. Joseph Stetler, president of the PMA, they charge that the commissioner overemphasizes "isolated instances without acknowledging the integrity and responsibility which our industry has consistently demonstrated." They point out that American manufacturers have developed more than half the world's new medicines since 1940. In contrast, Soviet industry has created only a few new compounds during the same period.

To that, Dr. Goddard answers, "I am not against profit in the drug or any other industry. Profit stimulates beneficial activity." His aim, he says, is simply to safeguard the public interest.

How does this profusion of new pills affect our everyday lives? Let us examine some of the more commonly used substances. Take for example the use of the antibiotics.

Ask any doctor what is the most wonderful medicine ever discovered, and the chances are he will answer "penicillin." By now every schoolboy knows how in 1928 an English bacteriologist, Sir

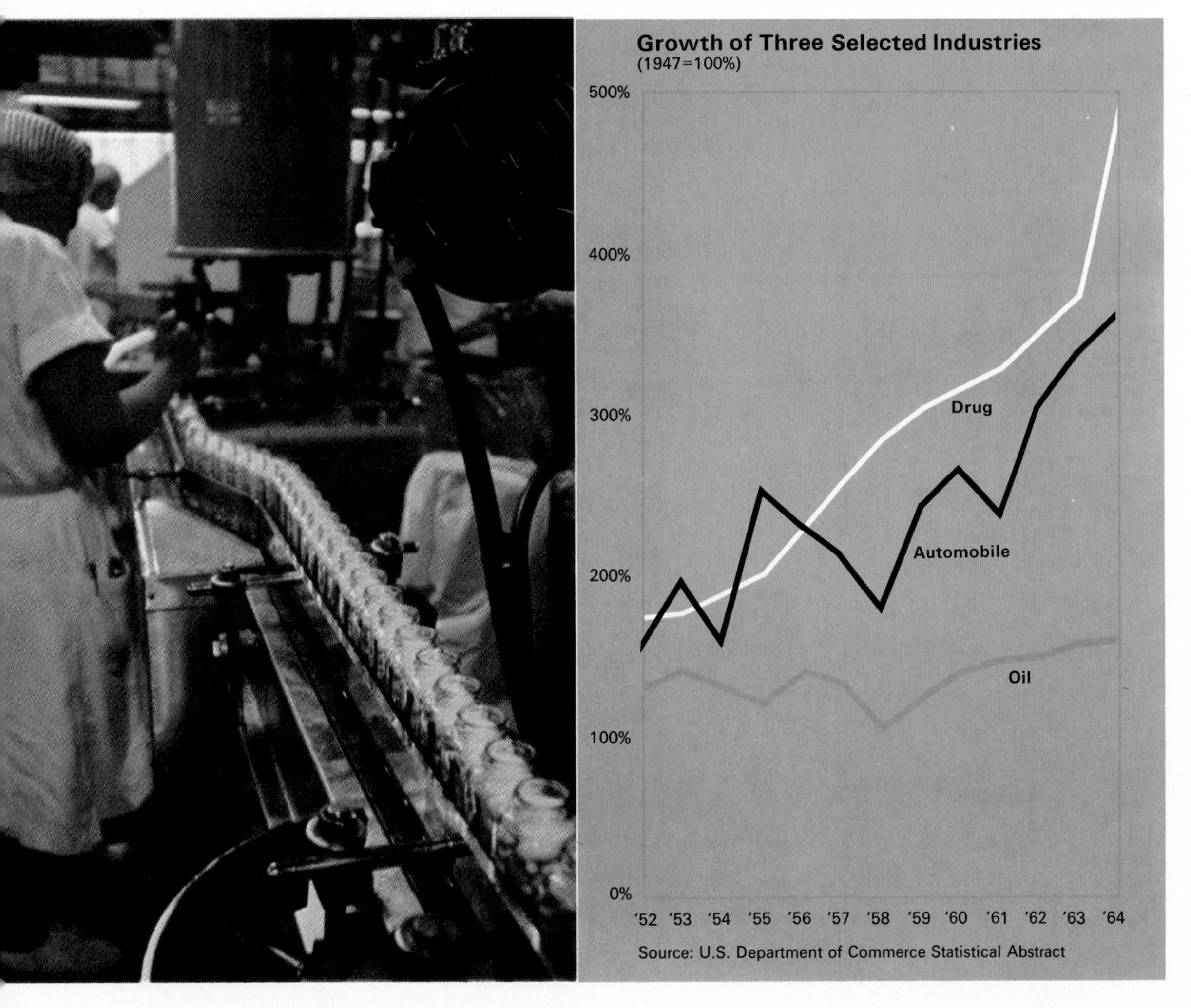

The drug industry, compared here with the oil, rubber, and automobile industries, has experienced a sharp rate of growth.

Alexander Fleming, discovered the first clue to that chemical in a culture plate of common bacteria. He found a mold growing on the bacteria, but no bacteria in a halo around the mold. The mold was giving off a substance that stopped the growth of germs.

Dr. Fleming tried to isolate the substance and failed. Beginning in 1938, Sir Howard W. Florey and Ernest Chain, working at Oxford University in Great Britain, took up the hunt and finally succeeded in extracting enough penicillin to save the life of a policeman suffering from a severe infection. Penicillin was the first antibiotic; a substance given off by one living organism to do battle against another.

Since then, penicillin has saved millions of lives throughout the world, thanks to an industrial effort that now produces tons of the drug at only a few cents a dose. Doctors have discovered that penicillin stops the growth of many varieties of bacteria, bacilli and germs that cause such diseases as diphtheria, gonorrhea, staphylococcus, streptococcus, and syphilis, to name but a few.

Developing A Drug

The concept for a new drug may stem from the hope of meeting a specific medical need, or it may simply be spurred by a research idea related to new chemical or medical theories. Concepts for new drugs come from physicians, industrial research laboratories, and other sources.

When a promising chemical compound is selected, it is evaluated and tested in a research laboratory on several species of animals. Tests determine the effects of the drug on various organs in the animal's body. These tests determine its effectiveness, as well as its safety. As an investigative new drug (IND), it is then submitted for approval to the Food and Drug Administration (FDA) for use in human tests.

Once approval is granted, tests on human subjects are conducted in hospitals throughout the country. The drugs are first used on healthy human volunteers to ascertain that the drugs are safe for further tests. Then they are used with a select group of sick patients. Finally, a large cross section of people is tested.

If human tests are satisfactory, the drug is resubmitted to the FDA as a new drug application (NDA). The FDA then evaluates research data pertaining to the drug, conducts tests on the substance, and examines proposed manufacturing and merchandising plans. If these and other considerations meet FDA standards, the NDA is approved and the drug is ready for production.

The analysis of drug compounds, *above left,* results in volumes of statistical data, *above*. A Swiss white mouse, *below left,* weighs in during testing phase. Manufacturing process begins with scooping proper ingredients into a tablet press, *below*.

New Drug Development

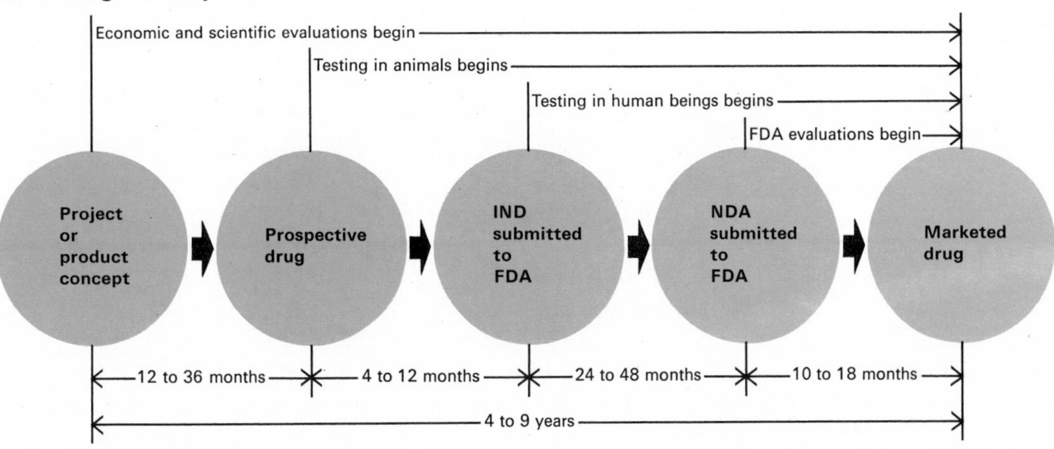

Developing a new drug is a costly and time-consuming process that may take nine years or more to go from concept to a marketable product.

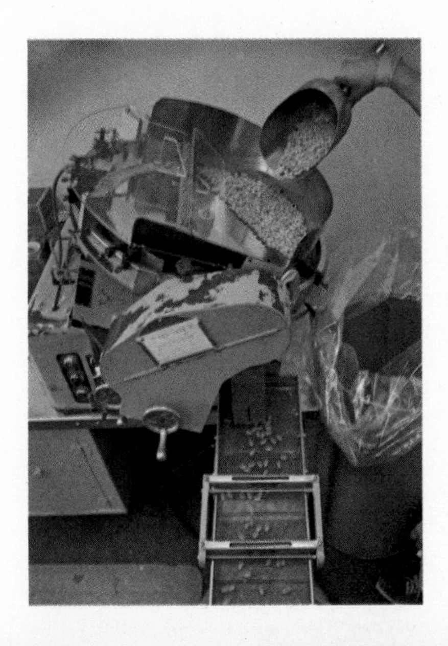

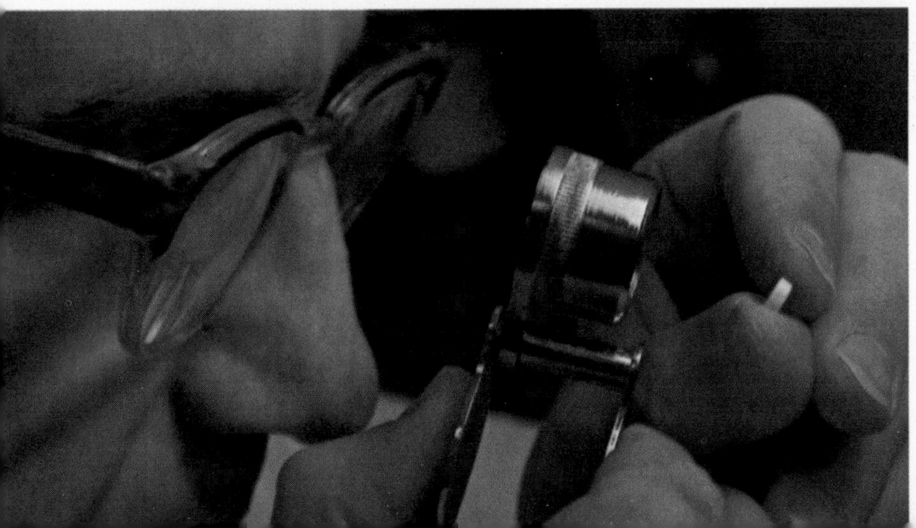

Imprinting machine, *above left,* stamps each pill with corporate symbol. Pills are counted on perforated trays, *above,* and then funneled into waiting bottles. One of many quality checks involves examining pills for physical defects under high magnification, *left.*

With the success of penicillin, the hunt for more antibiotics intensified. Scientists surveyed every type of microscopic mold, hoping to find more antibiotics of the penicillin type. They studied the stems of rotten cantaloupes; soils from Venezuela, the Philippines, and Colombia; the throats of chickens, and even sewage.

This vigorous search since 1940 has resulted in the discovery of more than 25 antibiotics now in use by doctors and hospitals throughout the world. These include the familiar chloramphenicol, streptomycin, tetracycline, and others not so familiar, such as kanamycin and polymyxin. There is scarcely an infection that can any longer escape the antibiotic armory.

For example, Dr. Louis Weinstein, professor of medicine at Tufts University (Boston branch), has produced a gigantic chart of some 50 infections and 24 antibiotics, plus six other antigerm chemicals. When a doctor uses this table, he can find at least two and sometimes as many as four drugs to fight a particular germ.

The glory of this achievement has been marred by three major complications of antibiotic therapy—resistance, superinfection, and allergy. Members of the medical profession fear that the power of the antibiotics may even be lost because of these problems.

Bacteria attempt to fight off penicillin, and in the process resistant strains develop that can destroy the penicillin. Many strains of staphylococcus, among which is the strain that causes boils, resist penicillin. The elimination of these germs has become a major problem in hospitals and in operating rooms. Recently, the FDA began to study the use of antibiotics in agriculture because new findings indicate that resistance can develop in animals, and the resistant germs can be carried to human beings through the consumption of various food products.

Doctors fight the problem of resistance by testing the susceptibility of the infecting germ to a variety of antibiotics and then using the most effective one. In the last five years, chemists have altered the molecular structure of penicillin to produce new types that can destroy previously resistant germs.

Superinfection is another complication in the use of antibiotics. It often upsets the delicate balance of bacteria inside human bodies. Usually, several varieties of germs live in harmony inside the digestive tract, each apparently secreting substances that keep the others in check. An antibiotic will destroy one group of bacteria and leave others untouched. The latter, unchecked, multiply rapidly and produce a superinfection.

The allergic response is still another problem the doctor must consider. Sensitive individuals who have taken penicillin for a minor illness often become allergic to it. Subsequent injections may produce not only hives but a type of shock, known to doctors as *anaphylactic shock*. Within minutes, the throat may choke up, and the victim may very possibly be dead.

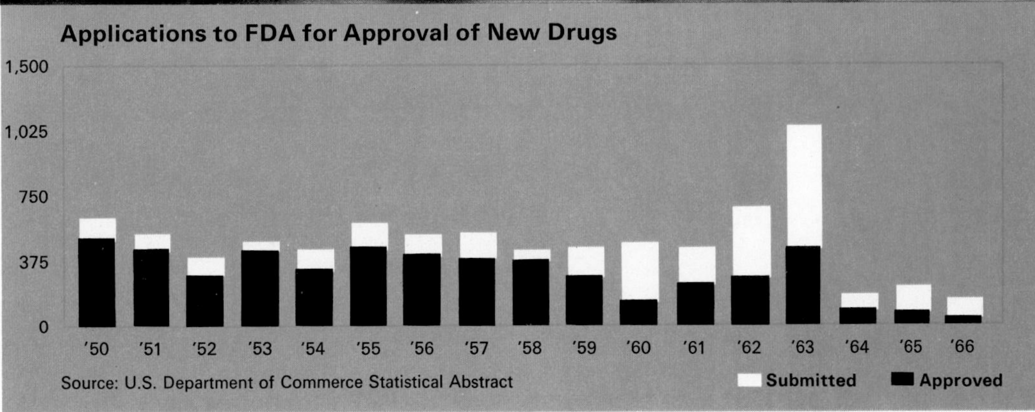

Prior to being marketed, a new drug must be approved by the Food and Drug Administration, headed by Dr. James L. Goddard, *pictured above*. Chart shows the ratio between the number of applications submitted and those approved.

Sometimes patients create health hazards for themselves with antibiotics. They save the medicine prescribed for a former illness and take it when they believe they have the same disease. What they do not know is that many antibiotics lose their effectiveness and sometimes change their chemical nature over extended periods of time.

For the scientists, the question remains: Will chemistry and medical science be able to solve the problems and increase the usefulness of the armory of antibiotics?

Next to antibiotics, the drugs acting on the mind have produced the greatest change in medical practice. In just one decade, chemistry has created a wide array of drugs that are of value in the treatment of various psychiatric disorders. They relieve confusion, hallucination, and agitated behavior. They tranquilize; that is, reduce anxiety. Scientists have also produced drugs that lift the depressed patient out of his psychological gloom.

The arrival of these chemicals in the mid-1950s completely reversed psychiatric practice. Earlier, psychiatrists relied on verbal therapy; a few sedatives, electric shock treatment, and the strait jacket. The psychoactive drugs have all but eliminated the jacket. They have reduced the need for electric shock and cut back the total number of inmates in state mental hospitals from a peak of 750,000 in 1957 to 534,000 in 1966. At the moment, perhaps 4,000,000 Americans take the antidepressant pills. An equal number consume other types of pills that act on the nervous system.

The chief drugs acting upon the mind belong to a class called phenothiazines. In the severely ill patient, these pills clear up thought disturbances, delusions, agitation, and anxiety.

The Role of The FDA

The Food and Drug Administration (FDA) enforces laws designed to protect purity and truthful labeling of foods, drugs, and cosmetics. No drug can be marketed until it has been approved by the FDA. Drug companies submit detailed reports of the tests they have conducted on any new drug. These reports include an analysis of the drug's chemical composition and methods of manufacture and packaging. Manufacturers also submit samples of each drug, the intended wording of its label, and the advertising material that will be used in promoting its sale.

The FDA examines the research reports supplied by the manufacturer to determine whether any dangers of the drug outweigh its usefulness. Samples of a drug are regularly analyzed for purity and correct chemical ingredients.

The FDA is authorized by law to determine whether a drug may be sold without a physician's prescription. The agency's decision is based on its opinion as to whether the drug could cause harm if taken without medical supervision.

Injecting fertile eggs with an antibiotic and then studying the development of the embryo is one method of checking whether the drug is safe for human consumption.

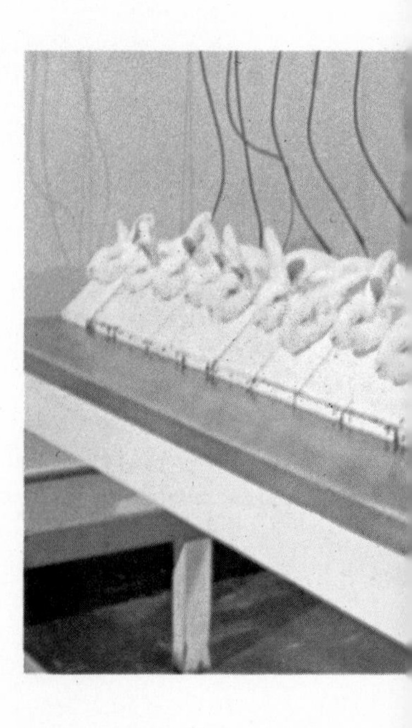

Rabbits are also used to test a drug's safety. These rabbits have been injected with a substance, and the effect on their temperature is being monitored.

In the antidepressant class, there are amitriptyline, imipramine, isocarboxid, and tranylcypromine. Each is somewhat different, but the surprising thing is that less than 10 years ago doctors had no drugs to fight depression. Now they have a dozen.

The pills known to relieve mild anxiety are the tranquilizers—chlordiazepoxide (Librium), diazepam (Valium), and meprobamate (Miltown), to name but three. These are swallowed by the millions each year. Although the evidence to support their antianxiety effects is not as good as the data for the other psychoactive drugs, doctors agree that they do help in the management of minor emotional problems.

However, the dangers of taking pills for every emotional upset are great. All the psychoactive drugs have side effects. Some, such as the minor tranquilizers, may be addicting.

In other instances, the side effects for a few people can be unexpected. The discovery of these side effects is scientifically important

Drug action is tested in these test tubes which simulate the chemical content of the human stomach.

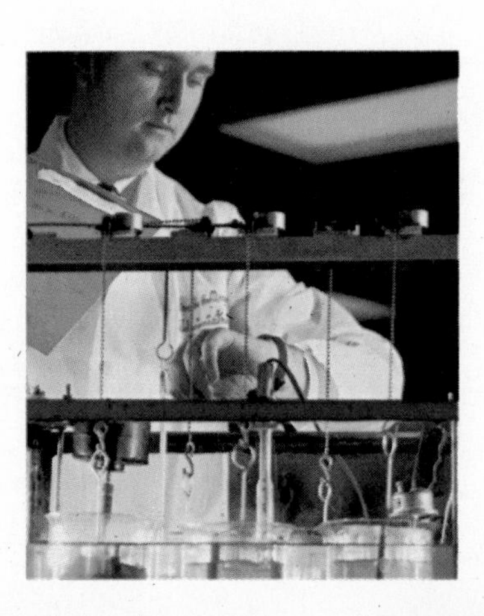

A researcher, *right,* checks the dissolving rate of a time capsule to see if it performs as advertised by the manufacturer.

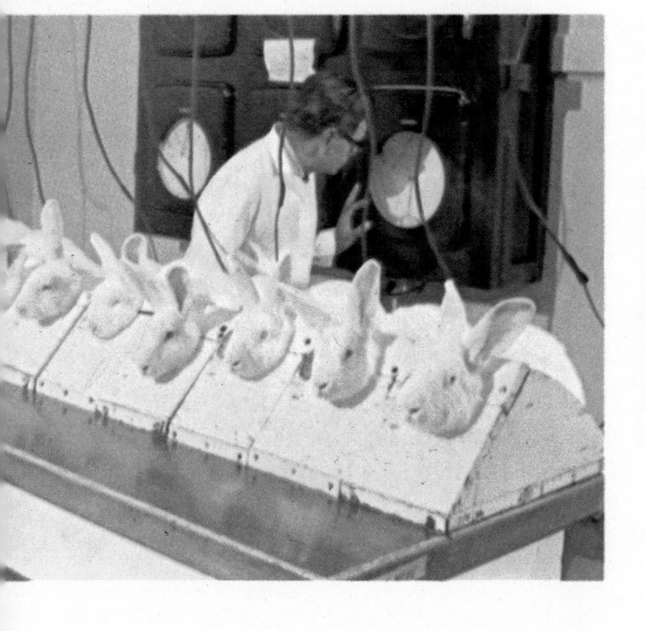

The many volumes of reports submitted by a drug manufacturer are carefully examined by the FDA. Reviewing the evidence, *above,* are members of the agency's division of neuropharmacological drugs.

even though the number of people affected may be small. For example, a few persons out of every 100,000, owing to a peculiar genetic defect in their biochemistry, find that the antidepressant Parnate is incompatible with blue cheese. If such a patient takes both, he may pass out from a surge of high blood pressure. For a few people, some of the major tranquilizers produce temporary shaking palsy. And recently, one of the major tranquilizers was found to produce minor changes in the lens and retina of the eye.

By studying the specific dimensions and characteristic markings of each manufacturer's pills, FDA officials can help identify counterfeits.

Nevertheless, Dr. Nathan S. Kline, the originator of one of the antidepressant pills, says the relief afforded by the mind pills far outweighs their dangers. When side effects occur, the doctor always has the option of switching to another pill.

Female sex hormones have been used to treat various feminine disorders for 20 years. In that period, chemists created synthetic counterparts to the natural hormones, estrogen and progesterone. Synthetic estrogens alleviate the difficulties of menopause. Other synthetic hormones have helped younger women with problems relating to their menstrual cycle.

In the last five years, however, sex hormones have opened a completely new way of life for many people. Biologists discovered that a synthetic hormone, progestin, combined with small amounts of estrogen, prevents ovulation. The combination, when it is taken orally, becomes a contraceptive.

Some authorities have always had doubts about the safety of the pill. Concern was aroused over the apparent increased numbers of blood clots in the lungs of women taking the pill. However, the evidence indicates that, on a statistical basis, the incidence is no greater than among those who do not use progestins.

In August, 1966, a Committee on Obstetrics and Gynecology, set up by the FDA, stated that there was no scientific evidence that the pills presented any danger of blood clotting or of cancer. The committee, however, urged prolonged caution and surveillance. Most authorities continue to advise against the use of the pills by patients suffering from *thrombophlebitis* (swelling and inflammation of the blood vessels), cancer of the breast, or cancer of the genital tract.

When questioned about the committee's report, Dr. Goddard said, "All other things being equal with a person in good health . . . I would recommend the pill."

Until 1922, a diagnosis of diabetes in any young person implied a short, gruesome life. Insulin, a hormone that helps the body use sugar, was unknown. In that year, two Canadian scientists, Sir Frederick G. Banting and Charles H. Best, extracted insulin from animal pancreases. They injected it into the body of a diabetic 14-year-old boy and saved his life. Since then, millions of diabetics have injected themselves with this hormone.

In 1955, German and French chemists discovered drugs, which in contrast to insulin, are effective when taken by mouth. They appear to act by stimulating the pancreas to produce insulin. For some diabetics, the oral drugs eliminate the need for regular injections.

Although the pills seem relatively safe, there may be a danger in relying on them exclusively for the treatment of diabetes in elderly patients, especially when effective control of the disease may be achieved by weight reduction. Also, pills are not usually effective in treating diabetes among the young.

Another triumph of 20th-century biology and medicine was the discovery of vitamins. In general, vitamins are chemicals the body needs in small amounts. In the United States, the vast majority of individuals get more than enough vitamins because of varied diets. Yet some Americans chew vitamin pills like candy; a practice that has been condemned by many health organizations, including the AMA.

Unlimited vitamin consumption by children may lead to poisoning by vitamins, mainly vitamins A and D which, unlike the others, tend to accumulate in the body over a period of time. Excessive vitamin consumption during certain stages of pregnancy can produce harmful effects on the fetus. To be sure, growing children, pregnant women, and persons suffering from malnutrition often need vitamin supplementation, but the amounts should be prescribed by a doctor.

In recent years, the Federal Trade Commission has severely limited the claims made by the producers of nonprescription brand drugs. Extensive claims were once made for the cold-relieving properties of antihistamines. However, careful tests showed that just as many individuals taking antihistamines came down with the common cold. The antihistamines relieved the symptoms but did not destroy the germs. At most, advertisers can now claim only to relieve the symptoms of a cold–and then not always.

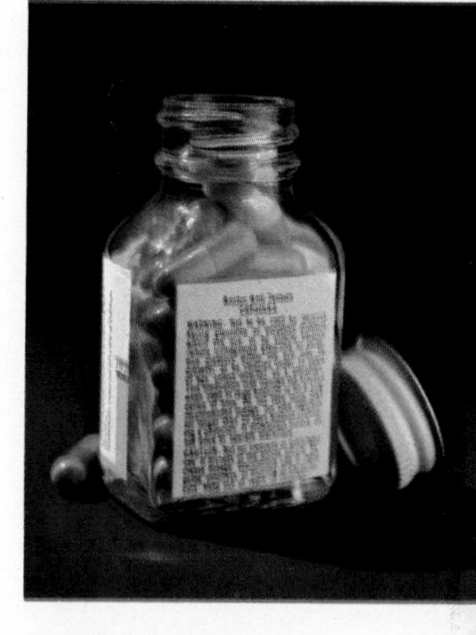

Drug laws require that appropriate warnings be included on all containers. The FDA approves labeling.

The most common nonprescription pill, of course, is aspirin. It has a wide variety of uses from the simple relief of headache and muscle pain, to reduction of fever, relief of gout, or the treatment of acute rheumatic fever. Yet even this common pill has its dangers. Fatal doses rarely occur in adults, but in children they are not uncommon. More than half the fatal poisonings reported by poison control centers involve aspirin.

Most of the laxatives, tonics, sleeping pills, and other over-the-counter items carry warnings to "see your doctor" if symptoms persist. Few persons do, with the result that more than one illness may continue for a long time unattended by a competent medical practitioner.

Drug abuse is an old problem that takes on new aspects whenever newly developed chemical compounds become available. Such is the case with the hallucinatory agent LSD. Taking LSD produces fantastic visions. Some psychologists say that these hallucinations extend the limits of perception and that properly administered, the drug can be useful in treating alcoholism and minor mental illnesses.

Most of the drug circulates illegally, however, and is being used by students and others for its hallucinatory effects. The persons refer

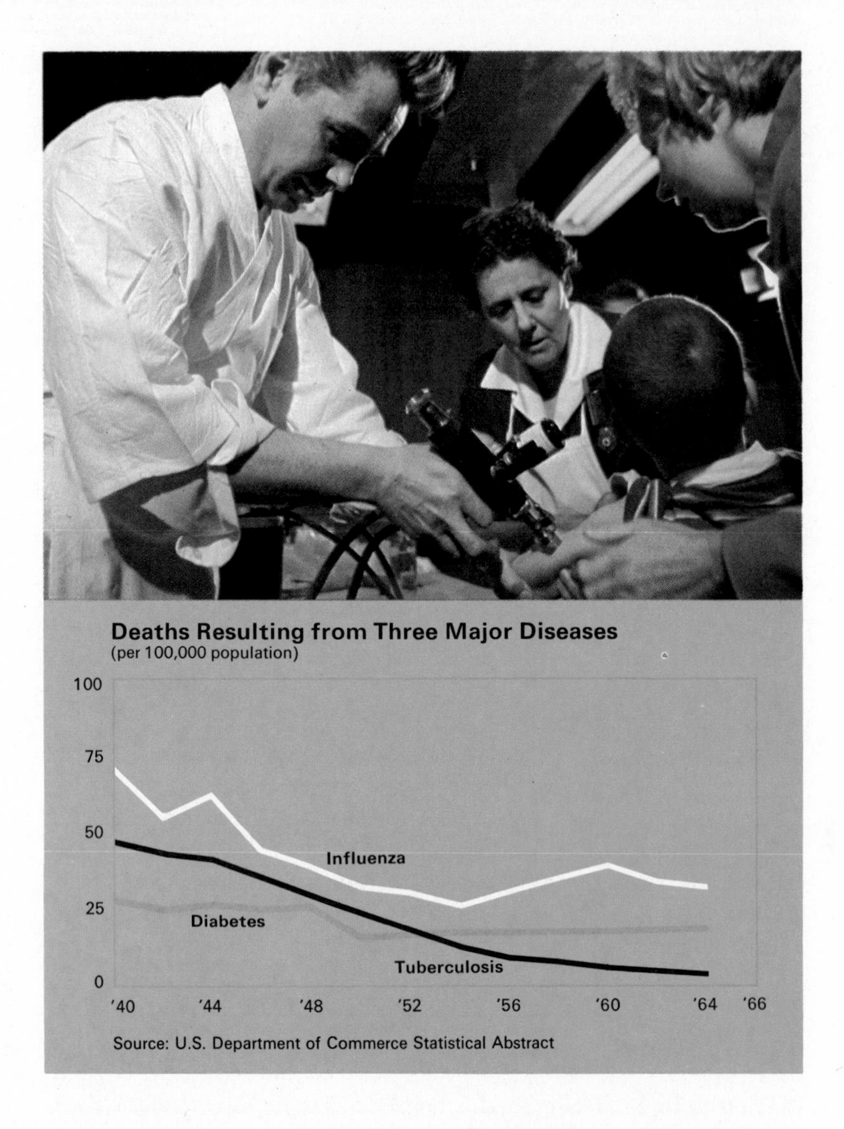

The effectiveness of drugs in controlling disease is forcefully demonstrated by the declining deaths from diabetes, influenza, and tuberculosis.

to the act as "taking a trip." At first believed to be safe, LSD trips turn out to have dangers. Reports from psychiatric hospitals indicate that significant numbers of young people do not return from their "trips." They suffer severe and prolonged mental breakdown, sometimes to the point of suicide. Many of the nation's leading psychiatrists have warned that indiscriminate and medically unsupervised use is clearly dangerous.

The FDA and other groups have sent out special warnings about LSD. Local police are moving against those who sell the drug illegally. The legal manufacturer withdrew from its role as supplier to the medical profession, and LSD can now be obtained only for experimental purposes from the U.S. Public Health Service.

The barbiturates, one of the most common families of sleep-producing drugs, are among the most widely abused. Many persons find that the drugs are habit-forming. Thousands die of overdosage each year.

Probably half are suicides. Some deaths are caused by automatic pill-taking. A patient swallows a couple of barbiturate pills to get to sleep. He finds they do not work. He takes one or two more. The effect of the drug is such that he forgets how many he has already taken. Soon he has an overdose. Some deaths are also caused by the combined consumption of barbiturates and alcohol.

Amphetamines, such as Dexedrine, are popular with college students and truck drivers who want to stay awake and with women who want to lose weight. Frequently, patients become addicted to the drugs as they take increasing amounts to get the same effects they first obtained with small doses. Panic, confusion, and delirium, followed by depression and fatigue, are just a few of the results of overdosage. Sometimes, severe mental disturbance occurs.

Not every drug, of course, nor even every class of drugs, can be covered in a review of our pill-filled lives. Too many have been discovered in a short time. That is what worries many physicians.

In particular, they fear the rise of drug-induced diseases. Their word for it is *iatrogenic* (*iatrose*, treatment; *genic*, generated). Dr. Louis Lasagna of the Department of Medicine, Pharmacology, and Experimental Therapeutics of the Johns Hopkins University medical faculty, in discussing the problem before the Kefauver Senate Subcommittee on Antitrust and Monopoly in 1961, cited studies that show that one hospital patient in five suffers from some sort of iatrogenic complication. In his own institution, an investigation of 100 randomly selected patients showed 7 per cent suffering from drug reactions, despite the fact that hospital personnel had indicated that each was free of untoward effects.

The problem is further complicated by patients' desires to medicate themselves. Doctors report that some patients have secretly taken anticoagulant drugs, leading to puzzling bleeding. Again, Dr. Lasagna reported to the Kefauver subcommittee that half of the patients cannot follow drug-taking instructions, thus usually overdosing or underdosing themselves. Individual responsibility in the use of drugs cannot be overemphasized. For while the proper use of drugs can do a great deal of good, their indiscriminate use can produce irreparable harm.

Dr. Lasagna also cited a study in his own hospital which showed that patients receiving one antibiotic were also taking at least five other drugs, and in one instance as many as 31 other medicines during the period they were hospitalized. "It is difficult to believe that all these drugs were truly indicated," he said. "One suspects rather that some drugs are given to relieve the symptoms of others."

While modern chemistry and biology have produced a magnificent array of lifesaving and pain-alleviating chemicals, today many are overused, and abused. If we wish to retain their power to do good, we must drastically cut their power to do harm. A start on that problem has now been made.

See also Section Three, Drugs, Medicine, Mental Health.

A Year Book Special Report

By Jerry Izenberg

The Other Face of Pro Sports

Under the guise of being "just sports," professional athletics have become lucrative business ventures

A successful young man of 31 returned from a Hawaiian vacation on Aug. 2, 1966, to sign a contract that would guarantee him almost $1,000,000. He was neither a movie star nor a business tycoon. John Riley Brodie was a football player, a quarterback for the San Francisco 49ers. By calling a touchdown play against the lucrative business of professional sports, he had become a Horatio Alger hero of the golden gridiron, a pigskin patriot of the American Dream.

Brodie had taken advantage of the free enterprise system. As star passer for the 49ers of the National Football League (NFL), he had been paid some $35,000 a year. The rival American Football League (AFL) had, however, offered him double that, plus a long term contract to play with the Houston Oilers. Brodie was set to jump from one league to the other. So were numerous other NFL stars, who saw in the competition between the two leagues an opportunity to share

The ever-present television camera buys its way into all the big sporting events, paying much more than the fans who attend.

CBS

in the prosperity of professional football. But now the jump was no longer possible, because the monopolistic sports business would tolerate competition only on the playing field.

Faced with the threat of player insurrection, the two leagues had announced on June 8, 1966, that they would merge. Just as in baseball, one group of owners, acting through an appointed commissioner, would have total control over the professional game. The merger would mean the end of competition, of free-enterprise football—and the end of the AFL offer to Brodie. Brodie blew the whistle and called his lawyer. By merging, football would rob him of his chance to earn more money. Pay up, he told the NFL, or he would take football to court. The league, fearful of a suit that might threaten its newly achieved monopoly, paid quickly—a five-year contract for $921,000.

Early in January, 1966, baseball pitchers Sandy Koufax and Don Drysdale, the left- and right-handers who had led the Los Angeles Dodgers' hitless wonders to victory in the 1965 World Series, had held a press conference. Advised by a Hollywood theatrical lawyer

The author:
Jerry Izenberg is a nationally syndicated sports columnist for the *Newark* (N.J.) *Star-Ledger*. His book, *Championship: The Complete NFL Title Story*, was published during 1966.

$800,000, $900,000, $1,000,000, HUT! San Francisco's star quarterback John Brodie profited by the merger of the two professional football leagues.

and bound together with a whither-thou-goest-I-will-go philosophy, Koufax and Drysdale launched their assault on the Dodgers' front office. They became the first two-man holdout in baseball history, demanding together more than $565,000 in an unheard-of three-year joint contract.

The two veteran ballplayers were winding up to hurl their money pitch not only at the Dodgers, but also against the entire structure of professional baseball. They would go to court if necessary, they said, and test baseball's right to indenture them to one team under its controversial reserve clause: Once a ballplayer signs a contract, he can never again freely seek employment with another team. Baseball settled by paying the holdouts $220,000 for the 1966 season.

With these challenges by top performers, the men who control professional sports in the United States found themselves in a dilemma that they had been approaching for more than a decade. How could they rake in enormous profits and yet cling to the traditional legal immunities offered a pure sport? How could they run their clubs for

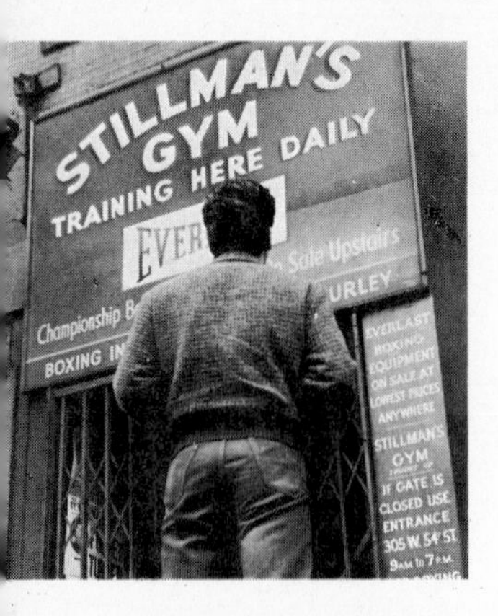

Boxing clubs, *above*, were virtually ruined by television. As a result, challengers for Cassius Clay, *below*, were difficult to find.

maximum profit and still build and hold the loyalty of the fans? Because of the greed of owners, absentee management, and, most important, the profitable concessions to television, professional sports are running the risk of alienating the fans who buy tickets at the stadium.

Professional boxing was the first to change under the impact of television. Just a decade ago, boxing had become so active on television that it had not one, but two, nationally televised fight cards each week. Matches were made for no other reason than to fill television commitments. Some of them were very bad. Hard-core fight fans who had supported the neighborhood clubs stayed at home to watch main events on television. With the failure of the clubs–the spawning grounds of champions–boxing soon found itself without talent.

Television used boxing, drained it, competed with its grass-roots' source of fighters, and then dropped it. Today, the big event in boxing, the heavyweight championship match, is geared to closed circuit theater television when fought in the United States. Consequently, the one-shot promoter, the hustler, can move in, promote the biggest

event in the industry, collect his profits, and not put a cent back for the development of future fighters.

Professional baseball's metamorphosis from a rich man's hobby into a big business was triggered in 1953 when Lou Perini moved his Boston Braves to Milwaukee and lumped them with his bulldozers and other assets of his construction business for tax reasons. It was the first baseball franchise shift since 1903. At his heels, like sod busters jockeying for position at the start of the 1889 Oklahoma land rush, other corporate interests converged on baseball. No less than 11 franchise changes have occurred since 1953.

For decades, baseball was run by families who were a loyal part of their communities. These were the Macks in Philadelphia, the Comiskeys in Chicago, the Griffiths in Washington, D.C., and, in New York City, the Stonehams in Manhattan and the Ebbetses in Brooklyn.

Baseball was fun for the fans then. It meant lively hours of excitement on a sunny afternoon. The owners cared about the towns in which they lived, and were not too concerned when a new thing called radio came along. Listening to a ball game was just not the same as going out to the ballpark.

Then television appeared, opening wide financial horizons. New interests moved in, and family ties began to disappear from the game. P. K. Wrigley still hung on in Chicago, but the others were gone. The Stonehams and the Griffiths, though still in baseball, now owned teams in other cities as business ventures.

Television buys the Yankees

With the purchase of the controlling interest in the New York Yankees by the Columbia Broadcasting System (CBS) in August, 1964, the transformation was virtually complete. The network had speculated in many types of businesses before, among them the Broadway show *My Fair Lady*. But when it purchased 80 per cent of the Yankees' stock from co-owners Del Webb and Dan Topping, it threw baseball's conflict of interest laws into the limelight. Many people–including Congressmen–felt that CBS, which was competing for sports events with other television and radio networks, would have an unfair, and possibly illegal, advantage.

It was not impossible that CBS wanted only its share in the profits of the Yankees. But these were not the Yankees of old: The team's standing in the league was falling and so was attendance at the park. Though operating control apparently remained in the hands of Webb and Topping, CBS could not stand by as the Yankees fell from profit and power. This truth emerged with the firing of Yankee manager Johnny Keane in early May, 1966.

The timing of Keane's demise was masterfully planned, and observers felt they detected the fine public relations hand of CBS. The Yankees, who once fired shortstop Phil Rizzuto on Old Timers Day, had never won awards for good public relations. But now, under CBS, Keane's firing was different. He was axed when the club was 3,000

Felipe Alou of the Milwaukee—no the Atlanta—Braves takes a big league cut for fans in the South.

miles from home, in Anaheim, Calif., on a Saturday afternoon. The three hour time difference between California and New York made coverage in the Saturday New York papers virtually impossible. And it was on the weekend when the Kentucky Derby dominated the sports sections. Thus, a minimal reaction from the fans was guaranteed. Not surprisingly, a CBS representative had been on the road with the club. If, skeptics reasoned, CBS had a part in the timing, it also had a part in the decision. And if this were so, they further argued, here at last was evidence that baseball is, indeed, a big business.

By September, 1966, of course, all pretense had faded. Webb and Topping had sold their remaining stock, and CBS had complete ownership of the club. A CBS vice-president became president of the once-proud, now last-place Yankees.

Elsewhere, the chase for profit had left abandoned ballparks in Boston, Philadelphia, St. Louis, New York, and, in 1966, Milwaukee, which had kidnaped the old Boston Braves.

Poor attendance at the park did not dictate the Braves' shift; poor "attendance" in the homes did. Geographically, Milwaukee was a bad television investment. With the Minnesota Twins (a transplant from Washington, D.C.) on one side, and the waters of Lake Michi-

gan and Chicago's two ball clubs on the other, the Braves simply could not find enough television viewers. The absentee owners, Chicago businessmen, succumbed quickly to a multimillion-dollar television deal in Atlanta, which would put the Braves in almost every living room in the southeastern states.

Baseball, though, was really in serious difficulty from television; a fact that, with typical short-sightedness, the owners long refused to acknowledge. In search of the easy dollar, they rushed to meet the demands of television. By doing so, they caused their teams to suffer from overexposure. Thus, baseball hurt itself at the gate, and became more and more dependent on the whims of television sponsors.

At the same time, baseball expanded its traditional two eight-team leagues to a pair of 10-team circuits. This move was the most amazing affront to the laws of nature since the Tower of Pisa began to lean. By wholesaling the major leagues on television, luring people out of Class B ballparks all over America, baseball virtually crippled its once vast minor league farm system. The minor leagues shrank from over 50 leagues in 1950 to roughly a dozen leagues by 1966. With myopic eyes fixed on the dollar, baseball bosses pinched off their source of skilled athletes, just as boxing bosses had done a decade before.

Because of an acute shortage of good players, the major league expansion had one immediate effect. It delayed by several years the departure of mediocre ballplayers to positions of trust at their neighborhood service stations. A great many minor leaguers were suddenly drawing major league paychecks. But despite the poor quality of play, the new teams made money. Perhaps this further lulled baseball into a false sense of security.

Baseball was smugly confident it would remain a sacred cow. Declared legally a sport rather than a business, it had long been exempt from normal antitrust business laws. But baseball must have had some doubts: witness the Danny Gardella affair.

Danny Gardella was a World War II outfielder with the New York Giants. Talent was at a minimum during the war years. Danny could hit a baseball great distances. It was when he tried to catch one that he got into trouble. With the end of the war and good players about to come marching home, Danny saw a limited future in New York. He jumped his contract and signed to play in the outlaw Mexican League.

Years later, he returned to the United States and again sought baseball employment. He was still bound to the Giants under the reserve clause, a peculiar section of every major league contract which grants the player to his last contract-holder—whether he signs or not—'til death or trade do they part. Should the contract be either sold or traded, the player becomes the sole property of the new owner. But more important, he agrees to "abide by the rules of baseball" when he signs. One of these rules makes him the property of the last club to hold his contract—whether or not he signs a new contract the next year. He cannot deal with anyone else. The Giants did not choose to employ Danny Gardella. Nor did they choose to release him. Later, when they said they would, nobody else wanted him. Danny went to court.

Baseball's protective cloak

Professional baseball functions under the protective cloak of a 1922 decision of the Supreme Court of the United States. This decision, apologists of the sport contended, settled for all time that baseball is not a business. Because of this, baseball was able to control competition, set prices and salaries, and deny players the right to shop around for a better deal. But the Court's decision, in truth, arrived at no such clear-cut conclusion.

The case had been brought against organized baseball by the Baltimore club of the now defunct Federal League—an independent, or "outlaw," group that functioned outside baseball's traditional two-league structure. Baltimore contended it had been deprived of the right to obtain players and playing sites. In the majority opinion, written by Justice Oliver Wendell Holmes, Jr., the Court said that baseball was so mild in its interstate aspects that it was clearly outside the aims of federal antitrust legislation. Armed with this decision, baseball continued to enforce its reserve clause and strengthen its grip on the location and ownership of franchises.

So Danny Gardella lost his challenge of this peculiar form of peonage, but he appealed, and baseball must have been worried, because one day Danny announced he was dropping the case.

"Did they pay you off?" a reporter asked him as he was packing one afternoon in 1948.

"You could say," and Danny did say it, "that they gave Danny Gardella a little something for his trouble." The best guess is $60,000.

Times have changed: Nationwide televising of the games has made baseball big business. The prospect of a court fight has it terrified. When the state of Wisconsin challenged the Braves' right to abandon Milwaukee for Atlanta–although the same state had encouraged the Braves to abandon Boston 12 years earlier–the full impact of baseball's privileged position was suddenly felt.

Baseball claimed it had the right to desert the fans and move where it could best profit. This claim came from the same people who had for years asserted they were not running a business at all, but a pure, all-American sport.

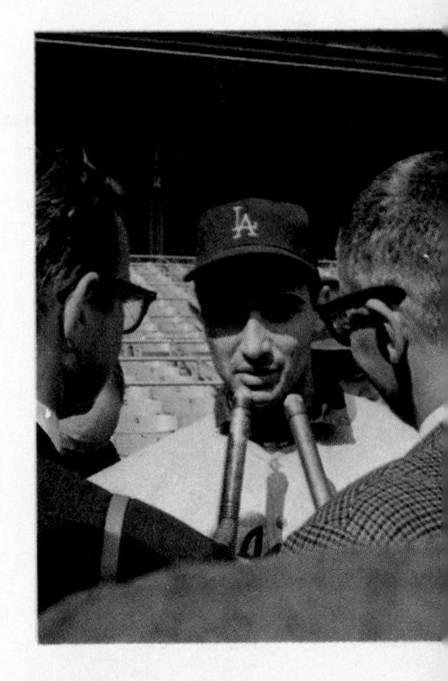

Dodger star Sandy Koufax held out for a larger share of his club's full coffers in his last season.

With the reserve clause in jeopardy and baseball's peculiar status challenged in the courts, here came Drysdale and Koufax, holding out and threatening legal action. Other players were confused and somewhat awed at the prospect of what their own moves might be the following year if the two holdouts outlasted the front office.

"It makes me a little uncomfortable," a player confessed to a reporter before an exhibition game in the spring of 1966. "I mean if two players can hold out, what could an entire infield accomplish?"

Ultimately, Sandy Koufax and Don Drysdale settled for less than they had asked, although nobody was sure what sub rosa terms were included in the settlement. Drysdale made a telling point when he said: "Every chapter in player disputes over salaries has ended with the player giving in. But someone wrote during this dispute that when they start putting maximums on what owners can earn, then they can put them on what players can earn."

With another pennant and a new attendance record in the stadium, Dodger owners had little doubt that Koufax and Drysdale had been worth their salaries despite a disastrous World Series.

Football's money war

The unrest that has swept through the baseball ranks was matched by the football dollar war between the NFL and the AFL. The older NFL, as with any monopoly, had been through wars before. During the 1920s, theatrical promoter C. C. "Cash and Carry" Pyle started a rival league. His chief weapon was Harold "Red" Grange, star of the Chicago Bears and then the biggest name in football. Both leagues suffered. Wellington Mara, president of the NFL New York Giants, remembers as a young man looking through binoculars from the Polo Grounds across the Harlem River at the competitor's Yankee Stadium game and saying to his father, Tim, who founded the Giants, "Don't worry, pop. They haven't got anybody in their park either."

After eight grinding seasons, Green Bay's Jim Taylor and Paul Hornung, *left,* have earned the hard way what their bonus-rich teammates, Donnie Anderson, *right,* and Jim Grabowski earned in their role as rookies.

The NFL won that war. Later, in the post-World War II boom years, it met and conquered another adversary, the All-America Conference, this time after costly spending.

At peace, the National Football League found itself in the best of all possible worlds. The late Bert Bell, Sr., then league commissioner, inaugurated a wise policy. He sold television rights only for road games. This served as a spur to fan interest, since the one way to see the home team score was to go to the park. Millions did. With no competition on the horizon, a steady flow of television money, and a monopoly on talent through its take-it-or-leave-it college draft, pro football soon became a gold mine.

When, in 1959, a new group of wealthy sportsmen were rejected in their bids to obtain expansion franchises from the smug NFL, they founded the American Football League. Under the old college draft, a player had to sign with the NFL club that had picked him or find other work. Now, with two leagues, clubs in rival circuits were vying

Today, roaring crowds quiet football's fear of overexposure on television.

to recruit him. Armed with tax lawyers and accountants, a lot of young fellows became rich through exploiting free-enterprise football.

In the first year of competition for talent, 1960, All-Americans Billy Cannon of Louisiana State University and Charlie Flowers of the University of Mississippi proved as quick with their pens as they were with their feet. They signed contracts with teams in both leagues. The American League had not yet bought its first $22 football, but already the war was on. Both leagues instituted a policy of baby-sitting, in which grown men followed beardless collegians around the country, bribing, deceiving, and, if necessary, blackmailing them into contracts. Free enterprise, football style, degenerated into a full-scale fiasco.

In New York, the AFL Jets had an image problem. They had risen like a phoenix out of the ashes of the defunct Titans, a financially disastrous franchise. David A. "Sonny" Werblin, president of the Jets and a former head of one of America's largest theatrical booking agencies, moved to fill Shea Stadium. He wanted headlines, and he got them.

In early January of 1965, Joe Willie Namath, a 21-year-old quarterback from the University of Alabama, sat down to luncheon with Werblin, Joe Willie's tax lawyer, and what seemed to be all the television cameras and sports reporters in New York City. By the time the trio finished their cherries jubilee, it was reported throughout football that Joe Willie Namath, who had never thrown a football in a professional game, had received $400,000 to sign with the Jets.

Whether Joe Willie actually got the full $400,000 is not important. What is important is that the announcement made a lot of veteran players re-examine their bruises. His contract became a rallying point for disgruntled veterans who were not getting big raises because the money was being put aside for untested rookies.

When the NFL Chicago Bears signed Dick Butkus, a rookie linebacker from the University of Illinois for a reported $250,000 in 1965, one professional player told a reporter,

"I'm All-League and what has it gotten me? I've proved myself. I want a piece of that money."

The bull market soars even higher

Following the 1965 season, bonuses got even bigger. College stars such as Tommy Nobis, University of Texas ($600,000) and Donnie Anderson, Texas Technical College ($711,000) rode the impetus provided by Namath to their huge bonuses.

The bitterness of the veterans sank deeper. Using it as a lever, several AFL teams signed veteran NFL players in the spring of 1966 to big 1967 contracts. Football players, unlike baseball players, can become free agents after one year, when they have fulfilled their contract. John Brodie, who was to make a lot of money, was just about to sign an AFL contract. But both leagues were by now financially exhausted, and as always in business, bankbooks prevailed over emotions. On June 8, the two leagues signed a peace treaty that retained all existing franchises and assured them of a common player draft.

The roughhouse of big league ice hockey is gaining hordes of rabid fans. This sport, too, wants its share from the seemingly bottomless television moneybag.

During the frantic days of spending that preceded the peace, a new kind of agent came upon the scene. Usually he was a lawyer. His primary job was to keep the bidding going between the leagues for his client's services. But with the merger of the two leagues, there is a return to the take-it-or-leave-it offer from a single club. The lawyers are ready. They consider this a restraint of trade. Somebody is going to bring it all into court soon. Football is keenly aware of the dangers. In a pre-election pressure play in October, 1966, the leagues forced legislation through Congress that they hope will protect the merger from antitrust action.

A fourth sport, professional hockey, is moving into the big time. Though it is a game imported from Canada, it combines the three elements that attract American sports fans–violence, speed, and wide-open play. In 1966, the National Hockey League voted to expand from its traditional six-team format. It will add clubs in Los Angeles, San Francisco, St. Louis, Pittsburgh, Philadelphia, and Minneapolis-St. Paul. Baltimore stands ready to pick up a franchise should any of the six fail to live up to its obligations. One should note here that six of these cities also have National Basketball Association teams. Pro basketball, plagued by a sameness of play and too much whistle-blowing has failed to get the full ride from the dollar boom. Nonetheless, it plans to add more franchises.

Hockey, with its climb to international prominence, has assumed the problems of a sport monopoly. In Canada itself there is great bitterness over the exclusion of Vancouver, B.C., from the list. This city had been the original home of the New York Rangers. It has supported a minor league team well and fully expected to be included in the new league. But it is not geographically in what research firms call the big television market areas. The league–dominated by Canadian players and Canadian business interests–turned its back on the Canadian city and went for the big Yankee dollar. Since then, the howls have been heard all the way up to the Canadian Parliament. In addition, National Hockey League television demands were considered so greedy that the National Broadcasting Company sent it back north to meditate during the summer of 1966.

Golfer-of-the-Year Billy Casper sinks a 25-foot putt. His $25,000 winner's share of the nationally televised U.S. Open tournament boosted his winnings to more than $120,000 for 1966.

Baseball, basketball, football, hockey, and other professional leagues insist they need the benefits of a monopoly. They want to hold the exclusive sale of television rights, the player draft and reserve clauses, the control of ownership and location of franchises, and of the rules of play. Some people who follow sports fear the professional game could not survive otherwise.

There are other privately owned monopolies. They control various utilities, such as electricity, gas, and telephones. These legal monopolies are permitted to exist, however, with one necessary condition: they must act responsibly, in the best interest of the public. Can American Telephone and Telegraph pull its telephones out of Milwaukee because of low profits there? If U.S. sports businesses are to keep their privileged position, they must act, first of all, for the fans who fill the seats.

Television has done much to trigger the swing from sport to business–and perhaps ruin. But television itself is not ruining professional sports. Professional sports, rather, are permitting themselves to be ruined by television. They have become completely dependent on it. Treading on familiar ground, pro football changed its shrewd TV policy in 1966 in order to pocket more than $30,000,000 a year for television rights. The two leagues scrapped the total blackout for 75 miles around home games, and now allow local stations to televise other league games. Soon, football may suffer the consequences. The lesson should have been learned.

If it is not learned soon, one day some advertising agency executive will say:

"Why do we pay them all that money for TV? Nobody goes to ball games any more."

By that time, the owners will not be worrying about the courts, and certainly not the fans. They will all be in other businesses.

See also Section One, Red Smith: Focus on Sports.

Russia:

Its Meaning For Our Time

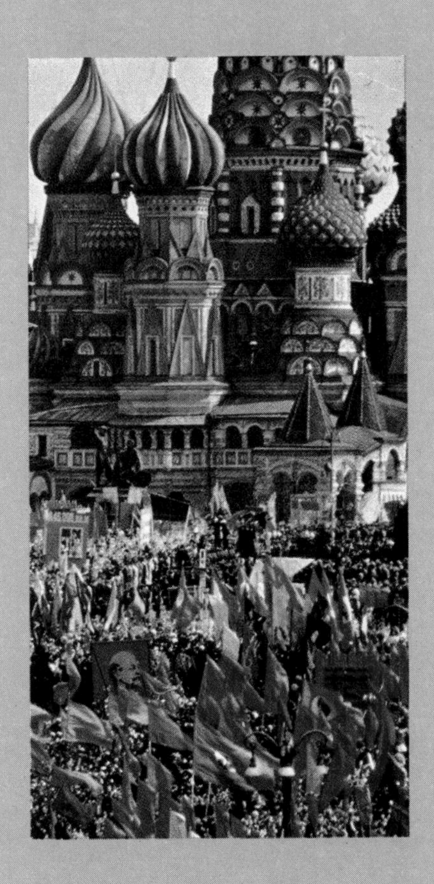

The rise and fall of nations is generally a slow process, but occasionally the pent-up resentments of a people erupt in sudden and violent revolution. Such an event took place in Russia just 50 years ago. American John Reed has described it as "*Ten Days That Shook The World*." Certainly the Russian revolution of 1917 was one of the most historic events of the 20th century. In the following pages, the editors of THE WORLD BOOK YEAR BOOK attempt to give added meaning to that event.

First, there is Edward Crankshaw's article "Russia: Fifty Years of Turmoil." In it, the author traces the highlights of a half-century of the Red Giant's relations with the United States. Crankshaw also speculates on the effect of the current Sino-Soviet struggle.

Next, there is the Trans-Vision® unit "Russia: The Growth of a Nation." Utilizing transparent overlays, this exclusive feature traces Russia's growth from its beginnings to the present day.

Finally, to keep your WORLD BOOK ENCYCLOPEDIA up to date, we have reprinted the new RUSSIA article from the 1967 edition of THE WORLD BOOK ENCYCLOPEDIA. This new article begins on page 556.

—The Editors

A Year Book Special Report

By Edward Crankshaw

Russia: Fifty Years Of Turmoil

A noted British commentator sees the recent rift between the Soviet Union and Red China as one of the turning points in history

Today we stand at one of the great turning points of history. The quarrel between China and the Soviet Union has decisively changed the world balance and shattered all conventional assumptions of past decades. It is an event of colossal magnitude. Its implications are almost too much to grasp.

For most of the past 20 years, the policies of the West have been based on the idea that two great powers, Russia and China, were ranged against the West in a single-minded, monolithic menace. Now they have split. The Communist world, which

Lenin returned to Russia from exile in 1917 on the now-famous "sealed train" to lead the Bolshevik revolution, an event that made Communism a world force.

was never actually as monolithic as it appeared, is now fragmented.

Communist China and Russia are at each other's throats, as they have been since 1959 when Nikita S. Khrushchev refused to share Soviet atomic weapons with Mao Tse-tung and took the first major step toward a tacit alliance with the United States. The Communist parties of the West, the Soviet fifth column, have thrown off their disciplinary bonds and have been written off by Moscow. The East European satellites find themselves in disarray. Moscow has lost its grip on the so-called underdeveloped countries. In addition, it has to dispute any remaining influence it may have with China.

On the Western side, The North Atlantic Treaty Organization (NATO) is falling apart because of lack of sufficient Russian pressure to hold it together. France is pursuing a highly personal line of its own. Cuba still stands, a Communist land on America's doorstep. The aspirations of the United States to be the bearer of concord and prosperity to the underprivileged nations have been clouded by events in Vietnam.

Despite this, many people continue to talk and think about the Soviet Union and the world Communist movement in terms of the Berlin blockade, which emphasized the depth of the chasm between the East and West.

Even now, it is common for people to ask whether the Russo-Chinese quarrel is really serious. The time lag between such a momentous event and public understanding is disturbing. The failure to appreciate not only the reality of the quarrel but also its inevitability, shows how far we are from knowing the nature of the Communist world. When the Chinese Communists took over China in 1949, Joseph Stalin made the greatest possible show of solidarity with China in order to terrify the West. The West was duly terrified. Even then, however, tension between Moscow and Peking existed. But, during the late 1940s and 1950s, the Chinese were so dependent on Russian aid that they had to defer to Moscow. Mao could do this without loss of face because Stalin was obviously the supreme leader of the Communist world. When Stalin died in 1953, however, circumstances were different. It was one matter for the proud Chinese to defer to Stalin, quite another to take orders from Georgi Malenkov, or Khrushchev. (Mao was a grander figure than either.) And so the tensions built up.

The author:
Edward Crankshaw is a frequent contributor to *The Observer,* London. His most recent book, *Khrushchev: A Career,* was published in 1966.

Illustrations by George Roth

At first they were concealed. But by 1956, Moscow and Peking were at loggerheads because of Khrushchev's announced policy of "peaceful co-existence" with the West. Chinese Communist leaders charged him with failing to carry out Communist ideals. Mao said war with the West could not be avoided and accused Khrushchev of fearing a "paper tiger." In 1959, the first explosion came. Khrushchev refused to share atomic weapons or know-how with the Chinese. The world did not learn of this until later. But it should have been obvious that something was amiss when the Russians withdrew their technicians from China that same year. Then, in 1960, came the Bucharest and Moscow conferences where Chinese delegates accused Khrushchev of treason to the revolutionary cause, and Khrushchev called Mao "another Stalin, spinning theories in a void." The proceedings of these conferences were not published in the West until February, 1961. By the winter of 1962-1963, the quarrel was out in the open. The seeming monolith was shattered.

Even now, roughly a decade after the quarrel started, it has not been accepted by the West as an event demanding a complete revision of earlier policies.

Can we learn from the past? Must we repeat old mistakes? There were earlier turning points in Russo-American relations that could have been useful. All were missed or discounted. For 50 years, mistakes on both sides have been almost continuous. Must this go on?

Once the second most powerful man in Russia and head of the Red Army, Leon Trotsky was later assassinated in Mexico, apparently by order of Joseph Stalin.

The most striking aspect of the whole period, in retrospect, is the quite remarkable absence of statesmanship on either side. Few people had anything to say that was remotely relevant or constructive. The turning points, as they arose, were simply overlooked in a general process of drift. There have been times when Soviet threats have been worse than Soviet deeds, and other times when Soviet deeds have appeared insufficiently prepared for by words. This produced confusion among those whose duty it was to interpret accurately Soviet words, attitudes, and actions by putting themselves into the minds of the Russians and trying to understand the principles behind the actions—the strains and contradictions between Soviet aspirations and reality.

There is one other important point. From 1917 to 1941, the supreme enemy in Moscow's eyes was not the United States, but Great Britain, regarded by Russia as the greatest imperial power. The United States was thought to be on the side lines; a potential source of technical aid and a counterweight to Japan. Britain, Germany, and France bulked much larger in Russian eyes.

American isolation during the period had certain unfortunate consequences. One was that it left Russia maneuvering between Nazi Germany, gaining impressively and dangerously in weight, and a Franco-British coalition divided between fear of a resurgent Germany and apprehension of Bolshevism. Full-scale American participation in the councils of Europe could have helped Europe to break out of its fears. It could have discouraged the rise of Fascism and broadened Europe's horizons. Such participation could have aided in establishing a more stable Western Europe and bringing Russia into the world family. It was not to be so.

The United States withdrew from world problems after the Treaty of Versailles in 1919. America's voice was not heard again until it spoke through President Franklin D. Roosevelt, at the time that Adolf Hitler swept through Europe.

Nikolai Lenin, returning from Switzerland in April, 1917, in the now-famous sealed train, had only to agitate and wait. In October, 1917, power fell into his hands. Dedicated as he was to the dream of world revolution, Lenin might have established a useful relationship

Prosecutor at the famous purge trials in the 1930s, Andrei Vishinsky later became chief Russian delegate to the United Nations where he was notorious for his tirades against the West.

with the United States if he had shown more wisdom. America, on the other hand, might have shown greater magnanimity had President Woodrow Wilson and his advisers possessed a truer picture of Russia and the Russians. On the Russian side, Lenin and Leon Trotsky made it almost inevitable that little or no fruitful cooperation would occur.

It is easy to say, and it has been said, that Russo-American relations since the revolution demonstrate that Washington, not Moscow has been to blame for everything that has gone wrong. It is equally easy to demonstrate the reverse. Both versions are false.

Prejudice, inertia, ignorance, and malice on both sides have been to blame. But, on the whole, it is fair to say that until comparatively recently, the errors of commission were mainly Russia's, while the errors of omission were American.

By an error of commission, I mean, for example, Stalin's encouragement of the subversive activities of the Comintern, whose role it was to organize Communist revolutions throughout the world. His invasion of Finland in 1939 was seen by the West as an action of overwhelming brutality; by Stalin it was viewed as a reluctant and strictly limited precautionary measure in the face of Adolf Hitler's invasion of Poland.

By an error of omission, I mean, for example, the failure of America to ask itself whether the stability of the world might not be best secured by extending material aid to a regime which was clearly destined to stay, regardless of its merits or demerits, and was, just as clearly, being driven to rash and brutal excesses by a sense of in-

security regarding Germany on the one hand, and Japan on the other. The United States had recognized the provisional government of Alexander F. Kerensky shortly after the fall of the czar, but it was not until 1933 that the U.S. officially recognized Stalin's Russia.

It is futile, and it would take volumes, to trace the errors on both sides, step by step, through the years. A few of the highlights will suffice. They began with Lenin's absurd, irrelevant, and wholly ruinous challenge to the Western Allies immediately after the revolution of 1917. Because of internal conditions, Lenin had to take Russia out of World War I. At the same time, he wanted Allied help. Instead of explaining the true circumstances and apologizing for his defection, he turned a necessary act into a demonstration of hostility against the very governments whose assistance he desperately needed—and which were going to suffer heavily from his action.

After the Bolshevik seizure of power, and without any formal warning to the Allies—Russia's allies—Lenin promulgated his "decree on peace," a demand for immediate peace without Allied annexations and indemnities. Furthermore, Lenin addressed himself not as one head of state to other heads of state. He chose instead to speak over the heads of established governments to the peoples, demanding that they should take matters into their own hands and set up their own ways of working out terms of peace. In other words, while seeking help from the United States government, he called on the American people to overthrow their government. Most dire of all, with regard to America, he soon repudiated all Russia's debts to the outside world.

It should have been plain that there was no chance that the workers of America, Great Britain, and France would rise against their governments and march under Lenin's banner to successful revolution. But in the terrible stress of those years, there were few clear-sighted on-lookers. Politicians everywhere were deeply engaged in a struggle to the death, and here was a man who, if he could not stimulate revolutions, clearly could and would do his best to weaken each country's war effort by trying to spread disaffection and industrial unrest. He was dangerous. He was a threat to social stability everywhere. It seemed inconceivable that a man of this type, flanked by a handful of fanatics, could keep his grip on the Russian people. But he did.

Here was a classic example of the way in which Soviet attitudes and actions were to deceive not only the West, but also the Russians themselves for decades to come. Even when, at the time of the Brest-Litovsk Treaty in 1918, Lenin was desperately begging for help against Germany, he could not refrain from biting the hand of help that he needed. When he cast his vote for acceptance of aid from France, he felt he had to say: "I request that my vote be added in favor of the acceptance of potatoes and arms from the bandits of Anglo-French imperialism." He was, of course, intensely suspicious of Allied motives in offering him assistance against the Germans. But he was unable to see clearly what he himself was doing. The Allies were equally unable to appreciate the stark realities which inevitably made Russia's bark worse than its bite, then and thereafter.

The impression created by Lenin's initial actions could not be erased. The Allies refused him help. In the summer of 1918, the Supreme Allied War

At Tehran, Iran, in 1943, Roosevelt, Churchill, and Stalin agreed to "work together in the war and in the peace." But even before the end of World War II, the Soviet leader had struck out on a separate course.

Council decided to intervene in the Russo-German conflict—first to build up a new front in Russia against Germany, and also to prevent vast quantities of Allied war materials from falling into German hands. The Allies joined the "Whites" in trying to destroy Bolshevik power.

American troops, with British, French, Czech, and Japanese, were allied with czarist generals in a vain campaign to destroy the new government of Russia headed by Lenin, himself very much a Russian in origin, character, and purpose. He was fighting with the aid of the Russian people, "in all their naive majesty and might"—a people who wanted only bread and land and peace. The people slowly united behind the Bolshevik leader, not because they believed in Bolshevism, but to throw out the landlords and the foreign interventionists. Lenin won. America never really had its heart in the job. It was over-persuaded by the British and the French or alarmed by the threat of Japanese expansion in Siberia. It was not until 1933, 16 years after the revolution, that an American administration at last brought itself to admit that Lenin's successor, Stalin, was the true ruler of Russia and accorded him official recognition.

These events, right or wrong, established the mood of the future. They were to poison all attempts to establish more reasonable and fruitful relations. Time and again, after the withdrawal of the Allied troops from Siberia in 1919, the Bolshevik government made overtures to Washington, but they were repulsed. It is true to say that prejudice, irrational fear, and sheer muddled thinking in America and the West in general have for 50 years stood in the way of reasonable relations with Russia. But these qualities are universal. Time and time again, when relations have appeared to be moving into smoother waters, the Russians have upset the apple cart by making usually meaningless but dangerous and seemingly hostile gestures.

The causes of this behavior lie deep in the realms of psychology. We cannot even try to unravel them here. It is as though Russian politicians find it impossible to make concessions to hard reality without loudly proclaiming what they would do if reality did not exist. The habit seems to be sort of a compulsive pride. It also seems to reflect in some esoteric way—almost a superstitious way—that they feel they are preserving their honor, their integrity, their ultimate freedom of action by abandoning their aspirations and conceding to hard reality only under violent protest. This makes it very difficult

One of the tensest moments of the Cold War took place in the Berlin blockade of 1948-1949. By blocking all rail, water, and highway routes, the Russians cut off the flow of supplies to West Berlin. But a massive allied airlift shattered Russia's hope of taking over the divided city.

to assess Russian words and actions. But it does not make it impossible. It is such a deep-seated and ancient characteristic that it can and should be studied and allowed for.

In 1921, for example, Lenin was compelled to retreat. In order to keep the Soviet Union afloat, he had to renounce his dreams for a Communist society and inaugurate a New Economic Policy. This policy, involving the practical restoration of free enterprise, was designed not only to harness anti-Communist traders and entrepreneurs in the Soviet Union to the economy, but also to reassure foreign governments, including the U.S., and persuade them to invest in the Soviet Union with credits and technical aid. The effect was spoiled by the continued harping on world revolution and the continued use of every opportunity, through the Comintern, to appeal to subversive elements to work against the very governments on whose stability Russia wanted to rest. Again, in 1928, while Stalin, by his words and the most important of his actions, indicated that he had abandoned all attempts to spread revolution and was concentrating on "building Socialism in one country." But he allowed the activities of the Comintern to continue. Thus he undermined the confidence he was trying to build up.

This perpetual contradiction, this constant discrepancy between actions and words, made it extremely difficult for an American statesman to know when to believe the Russians. American businessmen knew that once an agreement had been reached with the Russians, and a contract signed, the Bolsheviks were punctilious in observing it. The attitude of the United States government was that Russian economic stability could not be restored until the country abandoned its political system. Ironically, trade between the Bolsheviks and private firms in Europe and the U.S. was soon to expand.

The government's blindness seemed to stem from an unawareness that there was a very special danger in assuming that Russians think and speak as Americans do. I would not in the least defend the special Russian mixture of duplicity and self-deception; I am only suggesting that much more serious attempts should be made to understand it.

Throughout the 1930s and into the 1940s, Western distrust of Russia was great. The brutal elimination of the peasants in the 1930s and the purge trials, prosecuted by Andrei Vishinsky, resulting in millions of deaths, emphasized these fears. Russian feelings toward the West were equally intense.

Then came World War II and a seemingly dramatic reversal of relations. Russia and the United States became allies against Germany. For a time, there was cooperation between the two powers. But once the war was over, the situation deteriorated again. When President Franklin D. Roosevelt died in 1945, he was succeeded by Harry S. Truman. The latter did not share some of Roosevelt's illusions, but he did share Roosevelt's failure to understand the workings of Stalin's mind.

In fairness, it must be said that Stalin himself did nothing to clarify the difference between his real and his apparent purposes. Allied missions to Moscow had been frustrated at every turn in their efforts to seek useful cooperation against Germany. Second-front propaganda was continuous, and trouble-stirring. No spark of Russian gratitude was shown for Lend-Lease. The massacre of 15,000 Polish officers by the Russians, and Stalin's refusal to go to the help of the Poles at the time of the Warsaw uprising (or to let the Allied air forces help them effectively)—all these things and many more were enough to make any President of the United States conclude that the Soviet government was beyond the pale.

Indeed it was. The real failure of Western diplomacy then and in the following years (save for Winston S. Churchill's groping, alone and unsupported, in the right direction at the Tehran Conference and thereafter, until events bore him down), was the failure to sort out fact from fiction, reality from propaganda, and to analyze in the light of past Russian behavior the motivation behind Russian words.

While Stalin behaved like a brute (he knew no other way), he was a cautious and rational brute. He was clearly torn between the desire, the necessity indeed, for obtaining U.S. aid to rehabilitate his devastated country, and the determination to exploit in his interest the chaos of postwar Europe, using the power of the Soviet ground forces.

American policy was also full of contradictions. Even when Roosevelt knew that Russia had firm designs on Eastern Europe (Stalin never concealed these) and should have known that Stalin's behavior in territory controlled by him would differ in no way from his behavior at home, the U.S. was inviting him to move into Southeast Asia as an ally against Japan. In the next breath, as it were, President Truman was trying to bring economic pressure to bear by the abrupt cancellation of Lend-Lease. Stalin was later to tell W. Averell Harriman that he knew Lend-Lease had to end, but that the way it ended had been "unfortunate and even brutal"—an odd word for the supreme brute to use! When, on top of this, Washington contrived to "lose" for a whole year a formal request from Moscow for a $6,000,000,000 loan, the Russians not unnaturally concluded that Truman's actions were more closely calculated than in fact they were.

There were only two things that seriously mattered to Stalin at the end of the war: cash, whether from the Western Allies or from Germany as reparations, and insurance against the revival of Germany as a power. The last chance Washington had to get on good terms with Moscow was through an immediate and realistic discussion of how much aid could be given to Russia in return for certain assurances to be exactly defined. This chance was not taken. The Marshall Plan came just six months too late. Had General George C. Marshall been able to make his great gesture at the opening of the Conference of Foreign Ministers in Moscow in March, 1947, the course of history might have been changed. Instead, the ministers endlessly discussed a German peace treaty in an economic vacuum.

At the same time, President Truman proclaimed his doctrine, unilaterally guaranteeing the Free World (outside the framework of the United Nations) against Soviet aggression and adopting "containment" as official U.S. policy.

Thus the Cold War was born. History from 1947 until 1959 was a sad story of the inevitable escalation of the Cold War—exemplified by the Berlin blockade of 1948-1949—and its spasmodic, erratic, reluctant decline after Stalin's death. America and Russia, ranged against each other, sought to bring into their own orbits as much of the rest of the world as they could.

In 1959, three years after Khrushchev bowed to the facts of the Nuclear Age, and formally announced Russia's abandonment of the "fatal inevitability" of war and the necessity for "violent revolution," the stalemate under the nuclear umbrella was broken by the epoch-making quarrel between Moscow and Peking.

The Sino-Soviet split, when it came, resulted partly from Khrushchev's tentative efforts to achieve a détente with Washington, the supreme enemy; more particularly because of Khrushchev's refusal to share atomic secrets with Peking. Khrushchev pushed ahead.

Already, in the summer of 1959, he was infuriating the Chinese by speaking as leader of one of the two greatest powers collaborating with the leader of the other.

"Our country and the United States" he said that summer "are the two most mighty powers in the world. If other countries fight among themselves, they can be separated; but if war breaks out between America and our country, no one will be able to stop it. It will be catastrophe on a colossal scale."

China, the great ally, was just another country. Within three months, after meeting with President Eisenhower in the United States, Khrushchev was speaking of the latter as a wise and statesmanlike figure, a man of peace. Soon after that, Russian technicians were withdrawn from China, to the great detriment of Peking's economic planning.

There was a check on Khrushchev's approach following the U-2 airplane incident in May, 1960 and the planned fiasco of the Paris summit meeting. But immediately after Paris, Khrushchev went to Bucharest and, behind closed doors, in front of the Chinese delegation, accused Mao of being another Stalin, ignorant of the realities

After Stalin's death in 1953, China's Mao Tse-tung contested leadership of the Communist world with Stalin's successors. The result has been a serious fission in Sino-Soviet relations.

of war, "oblivious of any interests other than his own, spinning theories detached from the realities of the modern world."

Khrushchev still could not bring himself or his colleagues to take the next step–detach himself completely from past Soviet aspirations to be the headquarters of world revolution–and openly seek a reasoned agreement with America. He was largely a prisoner of his past, his own propaganda, and Stalin's past. Washington was likewise the prisoner of its past. The first meeting between President John F. Kennedy and Khrushchev in Vienna in the summer of 1961 was not a success. Khrushchev, not giving an inch, tried to sound out the new, young President and succeeded only in alarming him. "If Khrushchev means what he says about Berlin" said Kennedy afterward, "there will be war." Khrushchev, for his part, evidently thought he could push and rattle Kennedy. The muddle over the Bay of Pigs suggested to him not, as it should have, that Kennedy was a man who could learn by his mistakes, but rather that the President might be vulnerable in a war of nerves. Khrushchev still wanted a détente. But he was also greedy to get the best terms for Russia.

Cuba was his last fling. After Cuba, he showed that he, too, could learn his lessons. He began at last to go all out for a realignment with America–but too fast, and with too little response. He was in trouble already over his "harebrained" domestic policies. Men who were opposed to him for varying reasons drew together. He was pushing toward America, toward Germany, even, too rapidly–and with too little response. He was driving too fast toward the final break with China. He was leaving Vietnam to its fate, seemingly for no return.

When Khrushchev had gone, his successors made a sharp effort to damp down the quarrel with Peking. It was in vain. At the same time, they felt that to hold their own as pretenders to the leadership of the Communist world (which Khrushchev had been prepared to split irrevocably), they must assert themselves in Vietnam. By a twist of fate, the first American bombing raids in North Vietnam coincided with premier Aleksei Kosygin's visit to Hanoi. Kosygin did his best to persuade the North Vietnamese to negotiate. His efforts were in vain.

Today we have an ironic situation in which, unfortunately, both governments find themselves once more ranged implacably against each other over an issue which both would have liked to avoid. This occurs, again ironically, during a critical era of flux, when the Chinese breakaway has changed the face of international relations. If Moscow and Washington can bring themselves to an in-depth analysis of the real situation in Asia and have the courage to act on conclusions arrived at by clear thinking, they may yet come together and save the world. Have they the will to try again? This is what concerned observers wonder.

See also Section One, PAUL-HENRI SPAAK: FOCUS ON THE WORLD and Section Three, CHINA, COMMUNISM, and RUSSIA.

Russia:
The Growth of a Nation

Russia: The Growth of a Nation

The year 1967 marks the 50th anniversary of the Bolshevik Revolution, one of the most important events in modern history. Thus it seems appropriate to review the Russian past in order to understand its present condition.

The Union of Soviet Socialist Republics (U.S.S.R.) includes within its borders some 235,000,000 people. Straddling Europe and Asia, it embraces more than 100 different nationalities, but it was principally the Russian people who built this enormous empire. The Soviet Union is one of today's superpowers.

Russia did not always enjoy comparable status. From their first appearance until the 9th century, the Slavic ancestors of the Russians occupied only a small area of what is known today as the Soviet Union. Parts of Russia were repeatedly overrun by nomadic invaders. The creation of a stable state required the development of sufficient unity and strength to repel such attacks.

By the mid-17th century, Russia's security in the east had been won. But it was then confronted by more advanced neighbors to the west. To defend itself, and to attain its westward objectives, Russia was compelled to increase its strength by borrowing ideas from the West. It was thus able in the 18th century to expand far to the west and south.

The expansion of Russia was accompanied by the centralization of control in an increasingly despotic state and the reduction of the peasants to serfdom. This condemned the country to economic, military, and cultural backwardness. In the 19th century, serfdom was abolished, but Russia still lagged behind the major powers at the outbreak of World War I. Centuries of neglect of popular needs produced a potentially explosive domestic situation. Russia's defeats in World War I led to the overthrow of the imperial regime and then to a Communist revolution.

Under the Soviet regime, autocratic methods reappeared in modern forms. The population and resources of the country were mobilized as never before in a massive campaign of economic development. The new scale of Russia's power became apparent in World War II, when the Soviet Union helped to defeat the Nazi war machine and established its domination over most of Eastern Europe. Today the Communist empire appears to be receding, but Russian power is evidently here to stay.

Cover: Throughout much of its history, Russia has been involved in warfare. Young visitors to a Moscow art gallery study a painting of a 14th century battle between Russians and Mongols.
Cover photograph by Burt Glinn, Magnum.

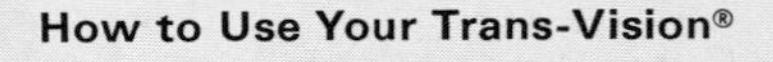

How to Use Your Trans-Vision®

Place your YEAR BOOK in a horizontal position. Read the introduction above. Then turn the lower page over and pull the gatefold page toward you (Fig. **1**). Study the physical features map and the text above it. Now turn the gatefold away from you. Also, pull out the gatefold page at the back of the unit (Fig. **2**). The text on these pages describes the periods shown on the maps. Place each of the transparent maps on top of the 1054 map (Fig. **3**). Any of the transparent maps may be placed over the physical features map by folding in the top gatefold page. To study Russia's economy, fold in the bottom gatefold page.

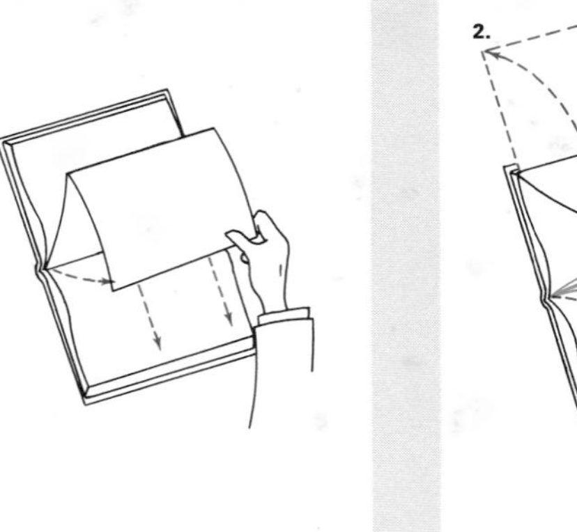

1.

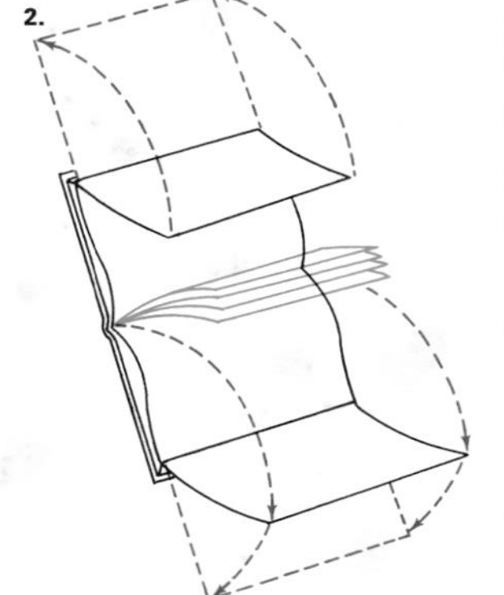

2.

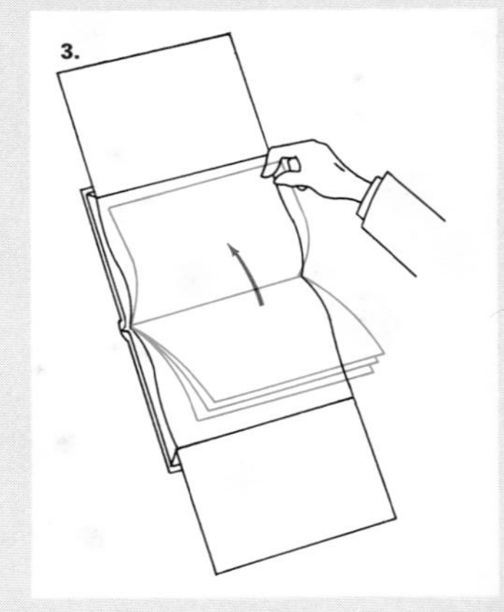

3.

Jerry Cooke, Pix/Publix

The vast sweep of the Russian heartland is shown in this photograph of a collective farm in Siberia.

Russia: The Land

Great size is the dominant physical feature of the Soviet Union. Included within its borders is more than one-seventh of the earth's land surface, more than the combined area of the United States and China. Its 8,649,500 square miles are wrapped almost halfway around the earth.

Its vast extent from north to south gives it successive zones of frozen tundra, forest, and steppe (grasslands). Its great east to west extent across the northern portion of Eurasia gives it continentality. It has extremes of temperature and a shortage of moisture in the interior. Millions of square miles are unsuitable for normal settlement and agriculture because of too little precipitation or too short growing seasons. Frozen arctic seas and rivers limit navigation to a few months each year. Nevertheless, the great zone of rich black grassland soils, when properly watered, and the warmer southern reaches provide a base for feeding its population. Insufficient moisture, however, remains a problem in many areas. Crop yields suffer from occasional drought. As a result, many areas must use irrigation or plant only crops that require little moisture.

Russia's topography consists essentially of a vast lowland lying north of a high mountain and plateau belt. This fact tends to isolate it from southern Asia. Only in the west do open lowlands continue. Internally the Ural Mountains, an old range worn down to rounded hills, and the mountains in the northeast, are the major exceptions to the general lowland character of the country. Waterways have been important transportation routes from early times, and they still exercise a vital role today.

Size brings diversity of minerals, as well as other resources. From ancient crystalline rocks, gold, iron, and other metallic minerals are obtained. From overlying sedimentary rocks coal, petroleum, and fertilizers are extracted. No nation is potentially more self-sufficient.

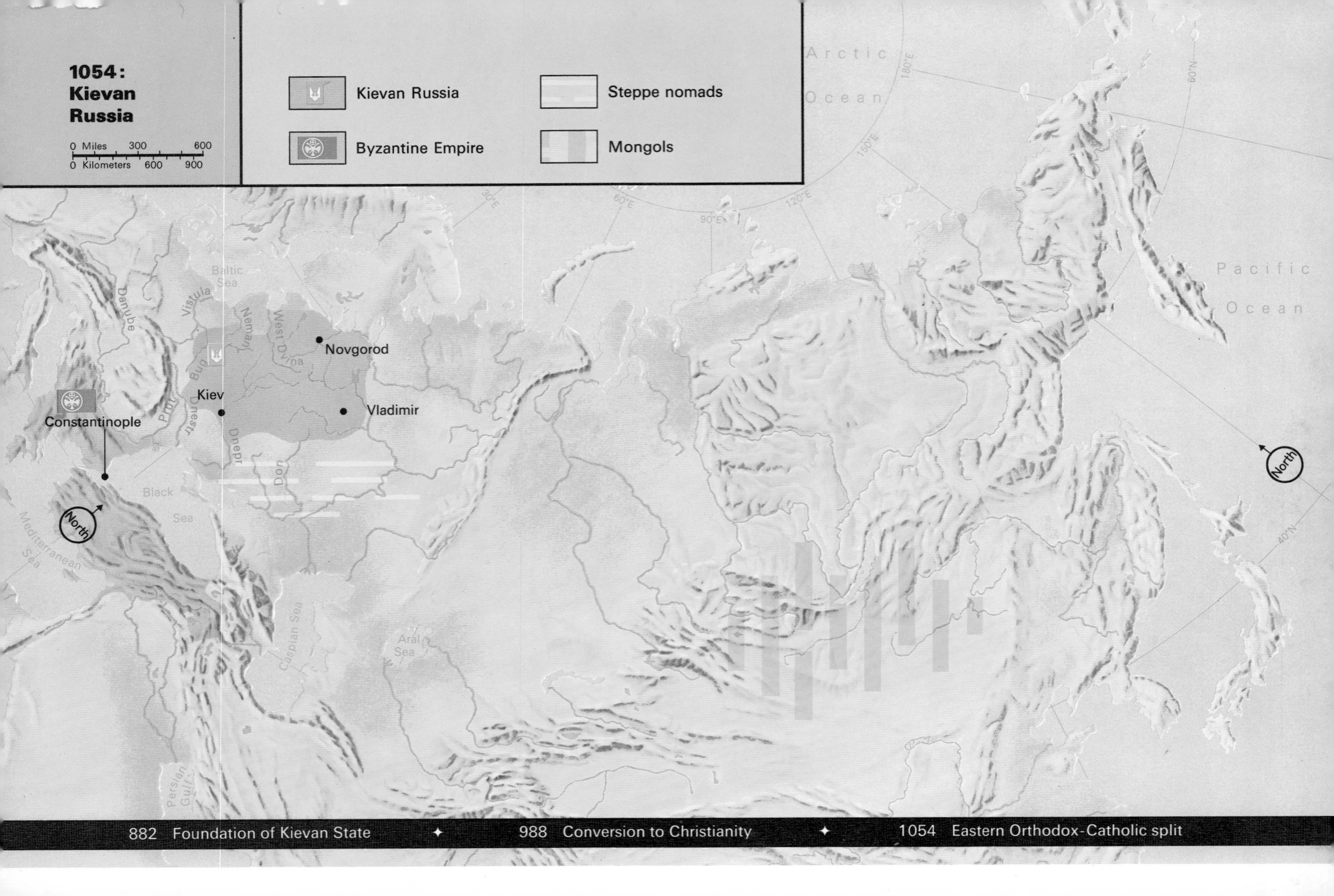

1054: Kievan Russia
0 Miles 300 600
0 Kilometers 600 900
Kievan Russia
Byzantine Empire
Steppe nomads
Mongols
Arctic Ocean
Pacific Ocean
Baltic Sea
Black Sea
Mediterranean Sea
Caspian Sea
Aral Sea
Persian Gulf
Danube
Vistula
Neman
West Dvina
Bug
Prut
Dnestr
Dnepr
Don
Novgorod
Kiev
Vladimir
Constantinople
North
30°E
60°E
90°E
120°E
150°E
180°E
60°N
40°N
882 Foundation of Kievan State
988 Conversion to Christianity
1054 Eastern Orthodox-Catholic split

Russia's Industrial Power

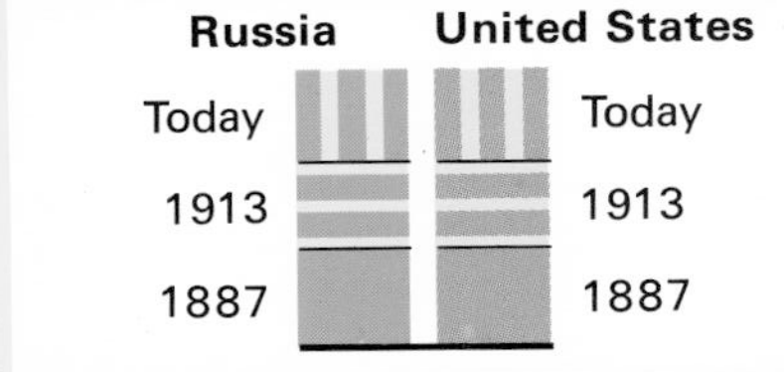

The economic power of the Soviet Union is second only to that of the United States. Since the late 19th century, and especially during the past generation, the Russian economy has enjoyed remarkable growth. Soviet coal production now exceeds that of the United States, which relies more on electric power. Conversely, the U.S.S.R. lags behind the United States in oil output. The Soviet Union's very limited transportation is a major problem. It has experienced repeated difficulty in feeding its people. Nonetheless, despite the economic problems it faces, it is the second major power in the world today.

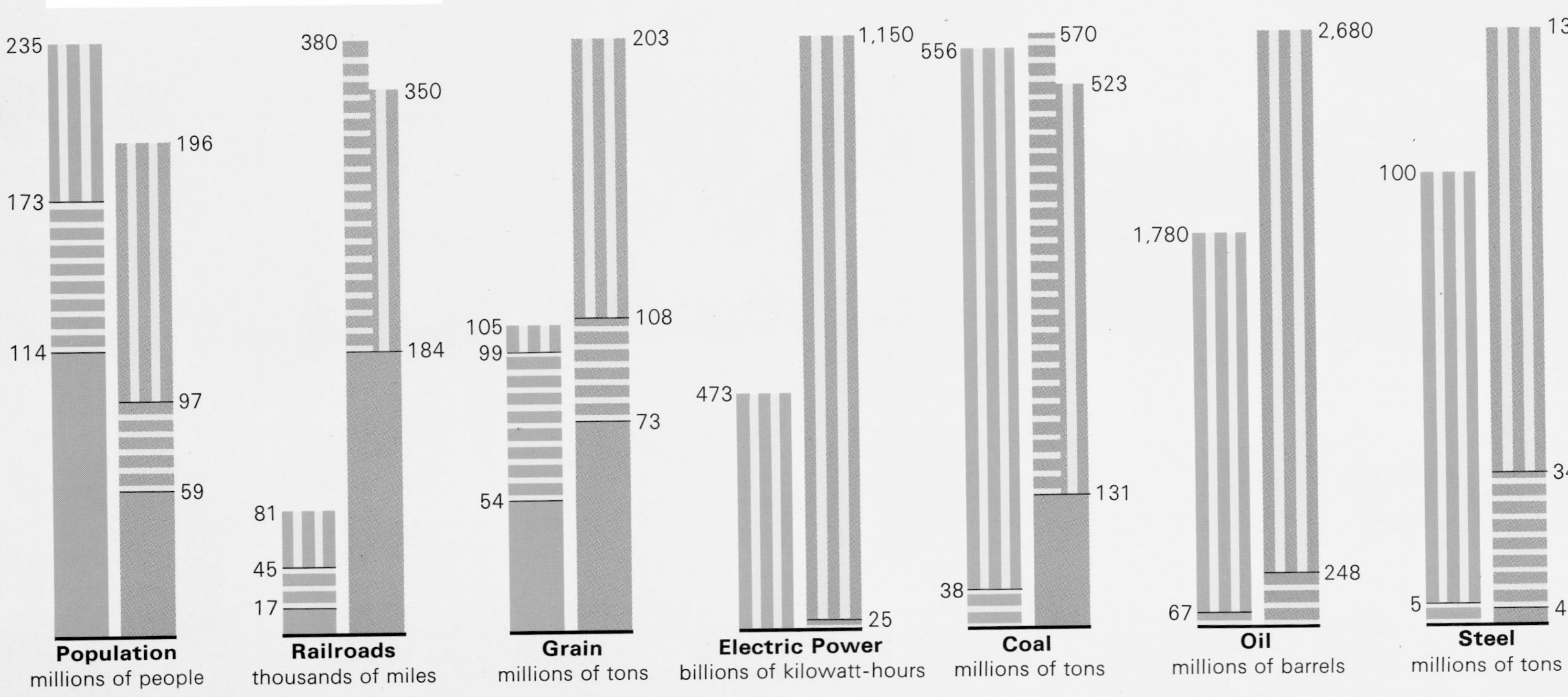

1815: Imperial Russia

Russian explorers had reached the shores of the Pacific Ocean in the 17th century. In the 18th century, they crossed the Bering Strait, staked a claim to Alaska, and even succeeded in planting a series of settlements in California.

More significant, however, was the Russians' westward expansion. Its advances were helped by waning Polish and Turkish power, but this was not the only reason. Russia's own power grew as it increasingly borrowed Western military and technological skills and made better use of the great natural resources within its boundaries.

Peter the Great, who reigned from 1682 until 1725, overcame much of the resistance to Western ideas. He modernized the army, created a navy, promoted industrial development, and reorganized the state. From Sweden he wrested an outlet to the Baltic and there established a new, westward-oriented capital, St. Petersburg. He made Russia a major European power.

Catherine the Great, who reigned from 1762 until 1796, helped bring about the partitions of Poland, a move that extended Russia's borders deep into Europe. Catherine also compelled the Turks to give Russia territory on the Black Sea and in the Crimea. Under Alexander I, czar from 1801 to 1825, Russia played an important role in defeating France in the Napoleonic wars, though Napoleon Bonaparte at one time occupied Moscow. As a result of these wars, Russia gained Finland, and at the Congress of Vienna in 1815, additional Polish territory.

For this expansion of state power, the Russian people paid dearly. Victories in the Napoleonic wars managed to conceal grave weaknesses in Russia's backward economic and social system. But once the wars were over, there began a century of revolutionary struggle to overthrow the czars.

1920: Lenin's Russia

During the 19th century, Russian expansion slowed down, then halted. In the early 20th century, the process went even further. In central and eastern Asia, Russia did seize vast new territories, but in the Balkans, and in its conflict with Japan over Korea and Manchuria, it was frustrated.

To Russia's defeat in the Crimean War (1853-1856), Czar Alexander II responded with a new dose of Westernization. But his reforms, including the abolition of serfdom, fell well short of restoring Russia's competitive position with the West.

Moreover, the economic condition of the peasants worsened after their emancipation. The new industrial working class was dissatisfied. Many of the empire's nationalities resented Russian domination. A radical intelligentsia strove to kindle a revolution. In 1905, a revolution occurred, but it failed to achieve its goals.

World War I broke the back of Russia's ramshackle society. In February, 1917 (old calendar), the embittered Russian people overthrew the imperial state. The moderate government that followed failed to satisfy the hopes of the masses. In October, 1917, it was toppled by the radical Bolshevik party under Lenin.

After the Bolshevik revolution, Russia was forced to sign a treaty with Germany that would have deprived it of all its European territorial gains of the previous two centuries. With Germany's defeat, the treaty was annulled, but Russia still lost Finland, the Baltic provinces, and its Polish territory.

In addition to making peace with Germany, the new Soviet regime decreed land reform and the nationalization of industry. But before it achieved real peace, it had to fight for its life (1918 through 1920) against counter-revolutionary forces partially supported by foreign powers.

1948: Stalin's Russia

Between 1921 and the outbreak of World War II, Russia's borders remained unchanged. Internal problems occupied the attention of the government and the people. The Union of Soviet Socialist Republics, as Russia was now called, launched a series of Five-Year Plans designed to step-up economic development. The output of industry increased tremendously. Agriculture was collectivized, but its productivity did not rise significantly.

Lenin's successor, Joseph Stalin, established a totalitarian dictatorship. Propaganda, welfare measures, and an attention to minority groups produced a measure of internal stability.

The Soviet government tried to stir up revolutions in several areas in the world, but its chief concern was with the security of Russia. Its diplomacy failed, and Russia became a principal participant in World War II. The country suffered huge losses, but had the vitality to rebound. The Russian army drove Nazi Germany back behind its own borders.

As a consequence of the war, Stalin's Russia regained the Baltic provinces and eastern Poland. Soviet military occupation transformed other east European countries into a Communist bloc. In Asia, the Chinese Communists were about to take over the vast reaches of China. Under Stalin's regime, the Soviet Union became, at enormous cost in human lives, a modern industrial power. In the process, there was a great migration of people from the countryside into the cities. The importance of education was emphasized. Many new opportunities were opened to promising young people.

Yet this modernized Russia was enclosed within a political system as harsh and autocratic as that of the ancient Principality of Moscow. As in that time, Russia's rulers remained suspicious of the West and isolated their people behind an "iron curtain."

Russia Today

By the time Joseph Stalin died in 1953, his policies had created deep hostilities, both at home and abroad. Alliances were set up to prevent the further extension of Soviet power, and the Cold War was on. In Russia's eastern European satellites, resistance to foreign domination was apparent. The first crack appeared in the Russian empire when Yugoslavia bolted the Communist bloc in the summer of 1948.

Stalin's domestic postwar policies reduced the prestige he had gained during World War II. He did achieve the economic recovery of Russia and stimulated further industrial expansion. While the Russian people were allowed a few more consumer goods, housing conditions continued bad. The development of agriculture lagged seriously. Intense political and cultural repression alienated many people. A host of problems was left to Stalin's successor, Nikita Khrushchev.

Khrushchev set out to de-Stalinize Russia. He possessed great power but used it with more restraint than his predecessor. Forced labor camps were closed; respect for legality increased; greater freedom was permitted in cultural life. But the Communist party made it plain that it did not intend to give up control.

Khrushchev encouraged continued economic development, but the rate of growth declined. Agriculture remained a bottleneck. On the other hand, the Russian people were provided with more goods, and the acute housing shortage was somewhat eased. The government's emphasis on heavy industry, the space race, and foreign aid prevented larger gains in other realms.

In Khrushchev's era, Soviet authority in the Communist world declined. In 1956, Poland asserted a measure of independence. A revolution was crushed in Hungary in the same year, but thereafter a somewhat more liberal regime emerged. This same tendency toward independence developed elsewhere in Eastern Europe.

To secure relaxation of relations with the West, the Soviet government participated in settlements of disputes in Austria, Indochina, and Korea. Now and again, as in Berlin and Cuba, Russia took the offensive. But, for the most part, Khrushchev advanced a policy of "peaceful coexistence." This change of attitude had the effect of easing tensions with the West. Khrushchev's successors continued his policies, even more cautiously.

Since Stalin's death, the trend of Soviet foreign policy has been more friendly toward the West. Russia appears to be somewhat more open to Western influences. But the distance between the Soviet Union and the West is still great.

The surge of Soviet economic growth is symbolized by this enormous hydroelectric plant at Bratsk, Siberia.

Burt Glinn, Magnum

Despite Soviet progress, many Russians lead primitive lives similar to these shepherds in their lonely camp.

Burt Glinn, Magnum

With flag held high, this monument in Vladivostok on the Pacific commemorates Russia's successful stand against foreign intervention after World War I.

Soviet Life Magazine, Sovfoto

Prepared by the editors of THE WORLD BOOK YEAR BOOK.

Consultants:
Samuel H. Baron, Chairman, Department of History, University of California, San Diego;
Edward B. Espenshade, Jr., Chairman, Department of Geography, Northwestern University;
Arthur P. Mendel, Department of History, University of Michigan.

Art Work:
Base art by Bernard Guiliano.
Historical overlays prepared by the art staff of THE WORLD BOOK YEAR BOOK
under the direction of Joe W. Gound.

Printed in U.S.A. by the Trans-Vision® Division, Milprint Incorporated.

Section Three

Contributors to THE WORLD BOOK YEAR BOOK report on the major developments of 1966 in their respective fields. The names of these contributors appear at the end of the articles they have written. A complete roster of contributors, giving their professional affiliation and listing the articles they have prepared, appears on pages 6 and 7.

The Year On File, 1966

Articles in this section are arranged alphabetically by subject matter. In most cases, titles refer directly to articles in THE WORLD BOOK ENCYCLOPEDIA. Numerous cross references (in bold type) are a part of this alphabetical listing. Their function is to guide the reader to a subject or to information that may be a part of some other article, or that may appear under an alternative title. *See* and *See also* cross references appear within and at the end of articles and similarly direct the reader to related information contained elsewhere in THE YEAR BOOK.

ACKLEY, (HUGH) GARDNER (1915-), battled against inflation throughout 1966 as the President's chief defender of the New Economics. It was up to Ackley, chairman of the Council of Economic Advisers (CEA) since November, 1964, to devise policies that would take the heat out of the boom without touching off a runaway inflation and without capping nearly six years of prosperity with a recession. He resisted the urgings of other new economists–such as his CEA predecessor, Walter W. Heller–to advise an income tax increase.

Ackley, born in Indianapolis, Ind., on June 30, 1915, was graduated from Western Michigan University in 1936. Four years later, he took his Ph.D. at the University of Michigan, where he taught for a year before going to Washington, D.C., and the Office of Price Administration.

In 1946, he resumed teaching at Michigan, with time out during the Korean War to serve as chief economist in the Office of Price Stabilization. He became economics department chairman at Michigan in 1955. In 1962, he joined the three-man CEA under chairman Heller.

As chairman, Ackley works 12 to 16 hours a day, six days a week. For relaxation, he plays the piano or putters in the garden of his Washington home. He married Bonnie A. Lowry on Sept. 18, 1937. They have two sons, David and Donald, both in college.

ADEN. See SOUTH ARABIA, FEDERATION OF.

ADVERTISING, as an industry, scored significant dollar gains in 1966. But industry leaders were not overjoyed at the results. They felt that advertising was merely keeping pace with an expanding economy–and with inflation. They feared that the failure of advertisers to accelerate their spending further reflected their uncertainty about the future.

In any event, total spending on advertising did go up significantly. According to estimates of *Printers' Ink*, the trade magazine, and the research department of McCann-Erickson, Inc., the grand total reached $16,335,000,000, an increase of 7 per cent over the $15,255,000,000 total for 1965.

On a percentage basis, television and radio made the biggest gains. Each gained 9 per cent in spot and network volume, with TV reaching $2,300,000,000 and radio $350,000,000. Nevertheless, print media did well. Magazines recorded a 7 per cent gain to $1,285,000,000. Newspapers showed an 8 per cent increase to $940,000,000, not counting an increase of 11 per cent in classified advertising–largely due to the stepped-up efforts of employers to find employees in a tight labor market.

Despite a strong campaign to upgrade the product in the face of criticism, outdoor advertising, alone among the media, suffered a slight decline. Its total volume was $118,000,000.

The Color Countdown was over, as Eastman Kodak Company said in advertising its color film for use in TV commercials. With nearly all prime-time TV presented in color in 1966, color was also making appearances elsewhere. For instance, partly in response to color advertising in various media, two out of five refrigerators sold in 1966 came in colors instead of the once traditional white. And SpectaColor–preprinted ads on coated paper with magazine quality color–became a frequent part of newspapers.

In the magazine world, another device for serving the needs of the advertiser seemed to have reached a stage of maturity. Regional and "spot" editions, with the help of the computer's ability to pinpoint regional subscribers and newsstand sales, allowed advertisers to reach specific markets or combinations of them. *Time* magazine, a pioneer in the field, increased the number of its metropolitan editions from three (New York, Chicago, Los Angeles) to eight, a move that was fairly typical. All told, close to 200 magazines were offering regional as well as spot editions to their advertisers by the close of the year.

The International Trend of the business continued as U.S. agencies followed their clients overseas. During the year, it was estimated that more than 50 U.S.-based agencies had one or more offices outside the country and that such overseas offices totaled 270. In some cases, an agency would

Watch Out For The Other Guy

Maybe you're a good driver. Many drivers aren't. So why put yourself at the mercy of some other guy's mistakes? Better to drive defensively. And expect the unexpected. After all, nearly half the drivers in fatal collisions are good drivers, and in the right. But being in the right isn't enough. You could be dead right.

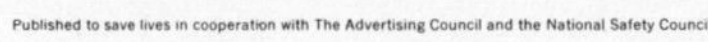

Schematic profile of an alert driver won Special Mention in the *Saturday Review's* 14th Annual Advertising Awards in April.

A Times Square landmark took its last puff in 1966. After 24 years of blowing smoke rings, New York City's famous billboard was dismantled.

simply open a branch in London, or Paris, or Montreal. Others might buy a part or a full interest in an existing foreign agency. The latter route was more popular because it gave the U.S. agency built-in knowledge of, and experience with, local customs and culture.

J. Walter Thompson retained its title as the largest U.S. advertising agency, in terms of either domestic billings or combined domestic and foreign. On the basis of domestic billings alone, Young and Rubicam was No. 2, but on a combined basis it was challenged for the second spot by McCann-Erickson.

The Leading Nations, after the United States, in the use of advertising in 1966 were Great Britain, West Germany, Japan, Canada, and France, in that order. Economic problems in both Great Britain and Japan held down expenditures. Nevertheless, Japan's great Dentsu Advertising remained the sixth largest agency in the world, while Britain's Lintas, Ltd., ranked in the top 20.

U.S. advertisers paid increasing attention to the Negro market numbering 21,500,000 persons and commanding an estimated gross income of $27,000,000,000. The evidence could be seen in the fat issues of *Ebony*, the *Life*-like monthly, and in the success of *Tuesday*, the weekly newspaper supplement devoted to Negroes. EDWIN W. DARBY

See also DRUGS; PUBLISHING; RADIO; RETAILING; TELEVISION.

AFGHANISTAN. In line with Prime Minister Mohammed Hashim Maiwandwal's publicized plan for "progressive democracy," the Afghan parliament authorized the establishment of political parties in July. The widening of political freedom, however, was not complete; a leftist newspaper was banned in May. In September, 23 judges were tried for corruption and three were convicted. Afghanistan appointed its first woman cabinet member.

Afghanistan signed a border agreement with Communist Chinese Foreign Minister Chen Yi during his state visit in April. Chen Yi's visit also produced a $28,000,000 loan to build a textile mill. Another neighbor, Russia, began construction of a fertilizer plant and the Shibarghān natural gas pipeline. In July, the U.S.-built highway from Kabul to Kandahar was opened to traffic. Pakistan agreed to allow shipment of Afghan fruit across Pakistani territory to Indian markets. A new rail link between Pakistan and Afghanistan will be built with U.S. assistance. On the lighter side, Metro-Goldwyn-Mayer will film James Michener's novel *Caravans* in Afghanistan.

Facts in Brief. Population: 16,400,000. Government: King Mohammed Zahir Shah; Prime Minister Mohammed Hashim Maiwandwal. Monetary Unit: afghani (74.75 = U.S. $1) Foreign Trade: exports, $73,100,000; imports, $63,900,000. Principal Exports: caracul, cotton, fruits, nuts. WILLIAM SPENCER

AFRICA

The march toward self-determination for all Africans moved forward in 1966. The year marked the independence of two new nations: Botswana, formerly Bechuanaland, and Lesotho, formerly Basutoland. They increased to 38 the number of struggling independent nations on the continent.

Increasing freedom, however, caused international concern over government policies that divided black and white Africans. Attempts in both the United Nations (UN) and the World Court failed to weaken the white-dominated rebel government of Rhodesia or to free South West Africa from the racist grip of the Republic of South Africa.

Two controversial personalities, a black and a white, fell from African leadership. Ghana's Kwame Nkrumah, advocate of pan-African unity, and for nine years president of the first independent nation in sub-Saharan Africa, was deposed on February 24. Prime Minister Hendrik F. Verwoerd of the Republic of South Africa, architect of his country's program of strict racial segregation, was assassinated on September 6.

Army leaders seized the Central African Republic, Ghana, Nigeria, and Upper Volta, but an attempt in Congo (Brazzaville) failed. Nigeria and Congo (Kinshasa, formerly Léopoldville) were torn by violent political clashes. The deposing of the mwami (king) in Burundi by his son, who in turn was deposed, also attracted world attention, as did a series of political and tribal tensions in Kenya and Uganda.

NORTHERN AFRICA

The North African countries, for the most part, maintained a smooth course in their domestic and foreign affairs. This was especially true of Algeria, Libya, Morocco, and Tunisia. Only the United Arab Republic, under President Abdel Gamal Nasser, continued to roil sensibilities in the Middle East. See ALGERIA; LIBYA; MOROCCO; TUNISIA; UNITED ARAB REPUBLIC (UAR).

WESTERN AFRICA

Political crises and bloody tribal clashes kept Nigeria in turmoil. But new army regimes in Ghana and Upper Volta appeared to have their countries under control. Guinea criticized moderate African states, and welcomed leftist Nkrumah when he was deposed by Ghana. See GHANA; GUINEA; NIGERIA; UPPER VOLTA.

Dahomey's General Christophe Soglo, empowered by a swift and peaceful takeover on the last day of 1965, appointed a 10-man civilian cabinet. The National Renovation Committee, which consults with Soglo on administration and economic development, was enlarged to 35 members on January 12. To curb Communist influence, diplomatic ties with Communist China were broken.

Liberia. Some 10,000 workers at the Firestone Rubber plantation struck for higher wages on February 1. After violence led to the death of one worker, Liberia's President William V. S. Tubman sent troops to the strike area. On February 8, the strike ended, but it had called to mind recent coups d'état elsewhere in Africa, and the parliament was quick to grant Tubman emergency powers for one year on February 9. Labor difficulties continued, nevertheless, with strikes at other plantations.

Mauritania. Fights between Negro African and Moorish high school students broke out February 8 in the capital city of Nouakchott. Cultural and

British pipeline in the sky carried needed oil to Zambia when Britain blockaded rebellious Rhodesia, Zambia's usual supplier.

racial differences, growing Moorish political power, and the use of Arabic in the schools were among the causes. Soon, fighting involved adults. Six persons were reported killed and dozens wounded. Despite a curfew and closed schools, intermittent fighting lasted until April. A cabinet reshuffle in February found new ministers of interior, justice, and foreign affairs.

Senegal. On January 16, Senegalese joined the previously all-French commission that runs the University of Dakar. On January 27, the French promised logistical support of Senegalese army and police units in return for landing rights for French military aircraft. The first World Festival of Negro Arts was held in Dakar from April 1 to 24.

Sierra Leone announced on February 3 that it would invest almost $3,000,000 in the development of orange plantations. On February 5, the United Nations Special Fund granted more than $2,000,000 to improve transportation and the fishing industry.

Ivory Coast. Tense relations with Ghana eased with the overthrow of Kwame Nkrumah on February 24. Ivory Coast sent a good-will mission to the new government. On March 23, the two nations planned defenses when Guinea threatened to send troops across the Ivory Coast to reinstate Nkrumah in Ghana. The board of governors of the African Development Bank, representing 23 African nations, held its first annual meeting in Abidjan, Ivory Coast, on April 18.

Mali's austerity measures included the closing of its embassies in the United States and seven other countries on February 9. One of the few remaining links with France was cut in February when the last French military forces left.

Togo. A U.S. treaty with Togo was signed on February 8 providing for friendship, commerce, and navigation between the two countries.

Gambia, Africa's smallest nation, held its first election since gaining independence on Feb. 18, 1965. The May voting returned Prime Minister David Jawara's People's Progressive party to power.

Niger was accused by Guinea of involvement in an alleged French plot against Guinea in May. Niger denied the charges.

CENTRAL AFRICA

Political and army leaders in Congo (Kinshasa) continued their struggle for power. The Central African Republic was taken over by military leaders in a swift coup on January 4. And Burundi held its place as one of the world's most unstable governments. See BURUNDI; CENTRAL AFRICAN REPUBLIC; CONGO (KINSHASA).

Two New African Nations

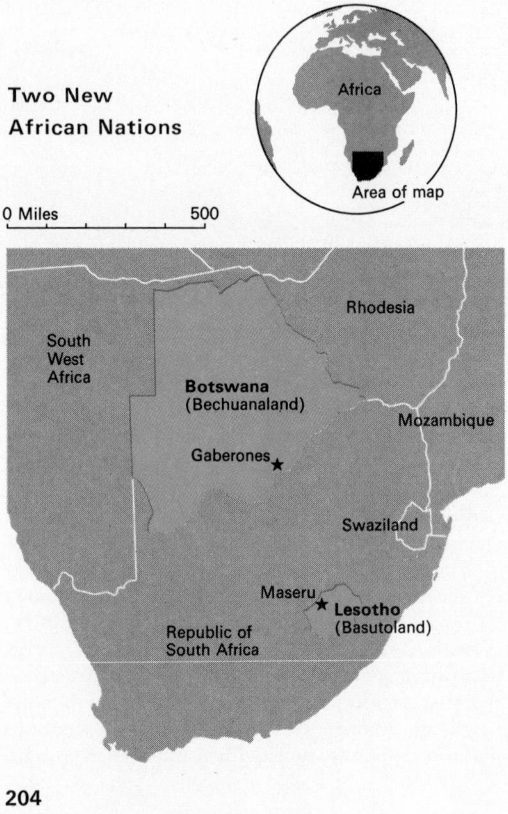

Rwanda and Burundi, after months of border raids between the two countries and verbal conflict over refugees, agreed in April to re-establish normal relations and ease tensions.

Congo (Brazzaville) army units attempted to seize the country on June 28 while President Alphonse Massemba-Débat and a number of senior cabinet members were in Tananarive, Malagasy Republic, for the Afro-Malagasy Common Organization meeting. The rebels, led by Captain Marien Ngoubi, objected to domination by the leftist Political Bureau and the Communists, the presence of Cubans in the president's private army, the arming of the government's youth movement, and the formation of a "political department" in the army to provide Marxist indoctrination. Massemba-Débat returned on July 3 and crushed the revolt.

Cameroon accepted $2,500,000 in French aid on January 29 to improve highways, railways, airports, and cotton production, and to construct a radio station and teacher training college. The Agency for International Development (AID) loaned $3,800,000 to Cameroon on February 22 for road building and economic development.

Chad. President François Tombalbaye reached an agreement with France on March 16 for $3,500,000 in grants and loans to improve veterinary medicine and to build a power plant, a textile mill, bridges, and buildings.

Gabon. A new port was under construction near Libreville to handle iron ore exports. Railway and mining improvements will be financed by a consortium of the World Bank (International Bank for Reconstruction and Development), AID, and other international agencies.

EASTERN AFRICA

President Jomo Kenyatta of Kenya took strong measures against his rivals, strengthening his party's control over the country. In Uganda, the leader of the internal kingdom of Buganda was deposed. Emperor Haile Selassie I of Ethiopia declared in September that a neighbor, French Somaliland, was an "integral part" of Ethiopia. Somaliland and France reacted quickly. See ETHIOPIA; KENYA; UGANDA.

Somalia-Kenya relations deteriorated after border raids accompanied Somalia's claim for parts of Kenya inhabited by Somalis. As a result, Kenya cut off all trade with Somalia on June 21.

Somalia continued to maintain its relations with both the East and the West. It had U.S.-trained policemen, U.S. Peace Corps teachers teaching English in the primary schools, and Russian doctors working in Somali hospitals. West Germany loaned Somalia more than $2,000,000 on March 15 for vehicles, agricultural equipment, a banana fiber processing plant, and a textile factory.

Tanzania, like Somalia, accepted assistance from the East, the West, and international agencies. A World Bank affiliate, the International Develop-

Facts in Brief on the African Countries

Country	Population	Government	Monetary Unit	Foreign Trade (million U.S. $)	
				Exports	Imports
Algeria*	13,100,000	President Houari Boumedienne	dinar (4.90 = $1)	689.7	731.3
Angola	4,995,000	Governor-General Silvino Silverio Marques	escudo (28.58 = $1)	183.6	185.4
Botswana*	514,378	President Seretse Khama	rand (1 = $1.41)	no information	
Burundi*	2,970,000	President Michel Micombero	franc (86.86 = $1)	30.2	21.6
Cameroon	5,103,000	President Ahmadou Ahidjo	CFA franc (245 = $1)	118.6	133.6
Central African Republic*	1,300,000	President and Premier Jean-Bedel Bokassa;	CFA franc (245 = $1)	26.1	27.2
Chad	2,945,000	President François Tombalbaye	CFA franc (245 = $1)	27.1	30.9
Congo (Brazzaville)	875,000	President Alphonse Massemba-Débat; Premier Ambroise Noumazalay	CFA franc (245 = $1)	42.7	59.7
Congo (Kinshasa)*	15,700,000	President Joseph Mobutu; Premier Leonard Mulamba	franc (150 = $1)	381.6	258.8
Dahomey	2,165,000	President and Premier Christophe Soglo	CFA franc (245 = $1)	13.7	34.1
Ethiopia*	22,350,000	Emperor Haile Selassie I	dollar (2.48 = $1)	101.7	145.7
Gabon	460,000	President Léon Mba	CFA franc (245 = $1)	105.	62.3
Gambia	357,000	Prime Minister David Jawara	pound (1 = $2.80)	9.1	12.2
Ghana*	8,164,000	National Liberation Council Chairman Joseph A. Ankrah	cedi (1 = $1.17)	317.8	448.
Guinea*	3,545,000	President Sékou Touré	CFA franc (245 = $1)	51.5	49.2
Ivory Coast	3,660,000	President Félix Houphouet-Boigny	CFA franc (245 = $1)	277.	235.9
Kenya*	9,500,000	President Jomo Kenyatta	shilling (7.09 = $1)	146.	249.4
Lesotho*	760,000	King Moshoeshoe II; Prime Minister Leabua Jonathan	rand (1 = $1.41)	no information	
Liberia	1,060,000	President William V. S. Tubman	dollar (1 = $1)	199.8	619.6
Libya*	1,708,000	King Idris I; Premier Hussein Mazik	pound (1 = $2.80)	796.5	320.
Malagasy Republic	6,655,000	President Philibert Tsiranana	CFA franc (245 = $1)	91.4	138.4
Malawi*	4,200,000	President Hastings Kamuzu Banda	pound (1 = $2.82)	30.9	50.2
Mali	4,655,000	President Modibo Keita	CFA franc (245 = $1)	15.5	42.8
Mauritania	895,000	President Mokhtar Ould Daddah	CFA franc (245 = $1)	65.7	23.3
Morocco*	14,300,000	King and Prime Minister Hassan II	dirham (4.98 = $1)	429.6	453.4
Mozambique	7,175,000	Governor-General General José da Costa Almeida	escudo (28.50 = $1)	103.3	174.5
Niger	3,220,000	President Hamani Diori	CFA franc (245 = $1)	25.2	37.2
Nigeria*	60,500,000	National Government Head Yakubu Gowon	pound (1 = $2.83)	750.	766.4
Rhodesia*	4,500,000	Prime Minister Ian D. Smith	pound (1 = $2.83)	441.7	368.6
Rwanda	2,900,000	President Grégoire Kayibanda	franc (115 = $1)	.4	5.8
Senegal	3,410,000	President Léopold Sédar Senghor	CFA franc (245 = $1)	128.6	163.8
Sierra Leone	2,790,000	Governor-General Justice H. J. Lightfoot-Boston; Prime Minister Albert M. Margai	leone (1 = $1.40)	82.1	107.9
Somalia	2,250,000	President Aden Abdullah Osman; Premier Abdirizak Haji Hussein	Somali shilling (7.14 = $1)	25.	30.6
South Africa*	18,700,000	President Charles R. Swart; Prime Minister Balthazar Johannes Vorster	rand (1 = $1.40)	1,426.9	2,487.3
Sudan	13,700,000	Supreme Council of State President Ismail al-Azhari; Premier Sadiq el Mahdi	pound (1 = $2.89)	195.1	207.9
Swaziland	310,000	Resident Commissioner Sir Francis Lloyd; Paramount Chief Sobhuza II	rand (1 = $1.41)	no information	
Tanzania	10,814,000	President Julius Nyerere	shilling (7.12 = $1)	179.6	140.3
Togo	1,630,000	President Nicolas Grunitzky	CFA franc (245 = $1)	26.9	44.9
Tunisia*	4,750,000	President Habib Bourguiba	dinar (1 = $1.92)	119.9	245.9
Uganda	7,550,000	President A. Milton Obote	shilling (7.12 = $1)	178.8	114.3
United Arab Republic*	31,150,000	President Gamal Abdel Nasser; Premier Zakariya Muhyi Al-Din	Egyptian pound (1 = $2.30)	605.2	933.2
Upper Volta*	4,805,000	President and Prime Minister Sangoulé Lamizana	CFA franc (245 = $1)	6.7	25.1
Zambia	3,825,000	President Kenneth Kaunda	pound (1 = $2.82)	425.6	228.3

*Indicates countries that have special articles.

ment Association, on January 13, extended $5,000,000 in credit to Tanzania for use in an agricultural program. In June, $7,800,000 in loans and grants were obtained from Communist China for agricultural education, economic planning, and roads. In October, university students rioted against compulsory national service following graduation.

Sudan. The constituent assembly on July 25 voted overwhelmingly to censure Premier Mohammed Ahmed Mahgoub. Mahgoub thereupon resigned, and Sadiq el Mahdi, 30 years old, was elected premier.

Sudan, weakened by a continuing civil war, and Chad signed agreements on air communications, trade, and frontier traffic on February 23.

SOUTHERN AFRICA

The two new nations, Botswana and Lesotho, political strife in Malawi, the assassination of South African Prime Minister Verwoerd, the Rhodesian crisis, and international struggles over the future of South West Africa commanded world-wide interest in 1966. See BOTSWANA; LESOTHO; MALAWI; RHODESIA; SOUTH AFRICA; SOUTH WEST AFRICA.

Zambia. Attempts by Great Britain and other nations to blockade Rhodesia without cutting the oil flow to neighboring Zambia led to a massive airlift. The British Royal Air Force was forced to end its oil-lift from Tanzania to Zambia on January 3 because Tanzania objected to the presence of British military personnel. A private British concern continued the airlift until May. After that, trucks from Tanzania, plus a train and truck route from Mozambique, supplied Zambia with oil.

Malagasy Republic allowed Great Britain to station Royal Air Force planes in Malagasy to patrol the sea routes used by tankers taking oil to Mozambique for blockaded Rhodesia.

Angola. Portugal and the rival exile governments of Angola and Mozambique issued conflicting reports of guerrilla warfare in these Portuguese African provinces. The two competing governments in exile claimed during the year that rebels had killed dozens of Portuguese soldiers in Angola. The formation of a third group, the Council of Angolan People, was reported in Kinshasa, Congo, in July.

Mozambique. A rebel government claimed in London on February 17 that its "freedom fighters" had killed some 2,000 Portuguese soldiers in 1964 and 1965 and had set up their own administrations in two northern provinces. Portugal had reported earlier, on February 15, that its casualties had been light and that over 100 "terrorists" had been captured during the previous two weeks.

Swaziland and Great Britain reviewed the Swaziland constitution and proposed in March that the mineral-rich country should have internal self-government in 1966 as a monarchy (Paramount Chief Sobhuza II) under British protection, leading to full independence by 1970. BENJAMIN E. THOMAS

AGNON, SHMUEL YOSEF (1888-), shared the 1966 Nobel prize for literature with Nelly Sachs of Stockholm. They were named on October 20 by the Swedish Academy of Literature as "two outstanding Jewish authors, each of whom represents Israel's message to our time."

Primarily a novelist and short-story writer, Agnon writes in Hebrew. His work, translated into 16 languages, has been called unique in the way it bridges the gap between European and Hebrew literature. It reflects a deep knowledge of the many strands of Jewish culture and tradition. Two of Agnon's best-known books are *Bridal Canopy* and *A Guest for the Night.*

A short, spry man with blue eyes, Agnon has lived some 40 years in Talpiot, a quiet section of Jerusalem, but his writings largely reflect his people's ancient ways, rather than the hum of contemporary activity in the relatively new nation of Israel.

S. Y. Agnon (which is the way he signs his books) was born on July 17, 1888, in Buczacz, a town in eastern Galicia. The region is now part of the Soviet Union, but in the author's early years it was part of the Austro-Hungarian Empire. He moved to Jerusalem in 1908, but in 1913 went to Berlin to study. There, in 1919, he married Esther Marx. The couple have lived in Jerusalem since 1924. Agnon is the first Israeli to win a Nobel prize. WALTER F. MORSE

See also SACHS, NELLY.

AGRICULTURE strained to meet the needs of the world's ever-rising numbers of hungry people in 1966. The U.S. Food for Freedom program was utilizing food production as a bold instrument of world politics, and one with a strong humanitarian appeal. A study of 26 developing countries–seven in Latin America, four in Africa, four in Europe, seven in the Middle East and South Asia, and four in the Far East–found their agricultural production to be increasing faster than that of the advanced countries, and even of the United States in its years of most rapid growth.

Secretary of Agriculture Orville L. Freeman noted during the year that U.S. agriculture was becoming increasingly world oriented. American farmers were the world's largest exporters, supplying more than 20 per cent of the world agricultural trade. By 1970, commercial export sales by U.S. farmers should reach $6,000,000,000 and total farm exports (including foreign aid) $8,000,000,000. Both figures are about 20 per cent above the levels of fiscal 1966.

Communist countries were still struggling to increase agricultural production. Even though the Soviet Union harvested bumper crops of grain in 1966, it felt the need to negotiate with Canada for a three-year contract for delivery of 9,000,000 tons of wheat and flour, 3,000,000 tons in the 1966-1967 crop year. The Soviet grain crop totaled more than 160,000,000 tons in 1966. Since 1963, the Soviet Union has purchased 478,000,000 bushels from Canada at a total cost of $1,000,000,000 (Canadian). See CANADA.

U.S. Farmers enjoyed a banner year in 1966. Production generally held up well, and prices rose to the highest level since 1947. Realized net incomes topped $16,000,000,000, up almost $2,000,-000,000 from 1965, and the highest since record 1947. And income per farm reached a record $4,900. Strong demand, along with about a 3 per cent decline in farm production, led to generally higher prices. Those two factors helped to eliminate most of the long-standing surpluses, with the exception of cotton.

Farm land values rose, and capital investment for the average farm reached $65,960. Man-hours of farm labor dropped about 4 per cent, to one-half the 1950 level. At the same time, output per man-hour increased to two and one-half times the 1950 level. One farmworker supplied farm products–food, fiber, and tobacco–for nearly 40 persons.

Crop Output suffered from unfavorable weather in 1966. Overall crop production fell about 4 per cent below the 1965 record high. Yields per acre also were lower, but still near the record 1965 levels.

Pasture conditions and hay yields were generally not as good as those of 1965. Record domestic and foreign consumption cut into grain supplies. Carry-over of wheat dropped to 536,000,000 bushels, down one-third from 1965 and two-thirds from 1961. Corn carry-over at the end of the crop year totaled only 866,000,000 bushels, down one-fourth from 1965. Carry-over was more than 2,000,000,000 bushels in 1961.

In face of the dwindling supplies of wheat, Secretary Freeman authorized the planting of 68,200,000 acres for the 1967 crop, a 32 per cent increase over 1965 and the most such acreage since 1953. But in surveys taken in the fall of 1966, the average wheat farmer said he intended to increase his planting by only 20 per cent.

Output of Major U.S. Crops
(millions of bushels)

Crop	1966*	1965	1960-1964‡
Corn	4,130	4,171	3,769
Sorghums	731	666	538
Oats	836	959	1,009
Wheat	1,296	1,327	1,224
Soybeans	931	844	661
Rice (a)	845	769	636
Potatoes (c)	300	290	266
Sugar (b)	5,425	5,371	4,781#
Cotton (d)	103	150	150
Tobacco (e)	1,844	1,855	2,178

*Preliminary; ‡average; #1961-1964 average
(a) 100,000 cwt; (b) 1,000 tons; (c) 1,000,000 cwt; (d) 100,000 bales; (e) 1,000,000 pounds

The U.S. Department of Agriculture, in its 1967 feed grain program, also took steps to encourage increased output. It eliminated its program of voluntary acreage retirements and increased price support for corn by 5 cents to $1.05 a bushel.

Cotton stocks during the 1966-1967 marketing year are expected to decline about 3,500,000 bales from the record August, 1966, carry-over of nearly 17,000,000 bales. The soybean harvest was up 10 per cent. Vegetable production dropped sharply.

The farmers' all-crop prices in October averaged 5½ per cent higher than in the 1965 month. Cotton price skids of about 20 per cent were more than offset by price increases in food and feed grains and fruits. Soybean prices at times skyrocketed to a peak of nearly $1 per bushel above 1965 levels.

Because livestock prices went up even more (10 per cent) than those of crops, the total of all farm prices averaged 7 per cent more than the previous year. Prices paid by farmers were up only about 3 per cent. As a result, their incomes were materially better. Farmers voiced concern, however, over higher interest rates and higher-priced farm labor.

Livestock. Output of poultry and meat animals rose 6 per cent and 1 per cent, respectively. Production of dairy products declined 4 per cent. Livestock prices reached their highest level in 14 years in the first quarter. Increased production of poultry and meat animals resulted in lower prices late in 1966, but dairy product prices remained

A ragged file of California grape pickers marched 300 miles to Sacramento–and to the first major U.S. farmworkers' contract.

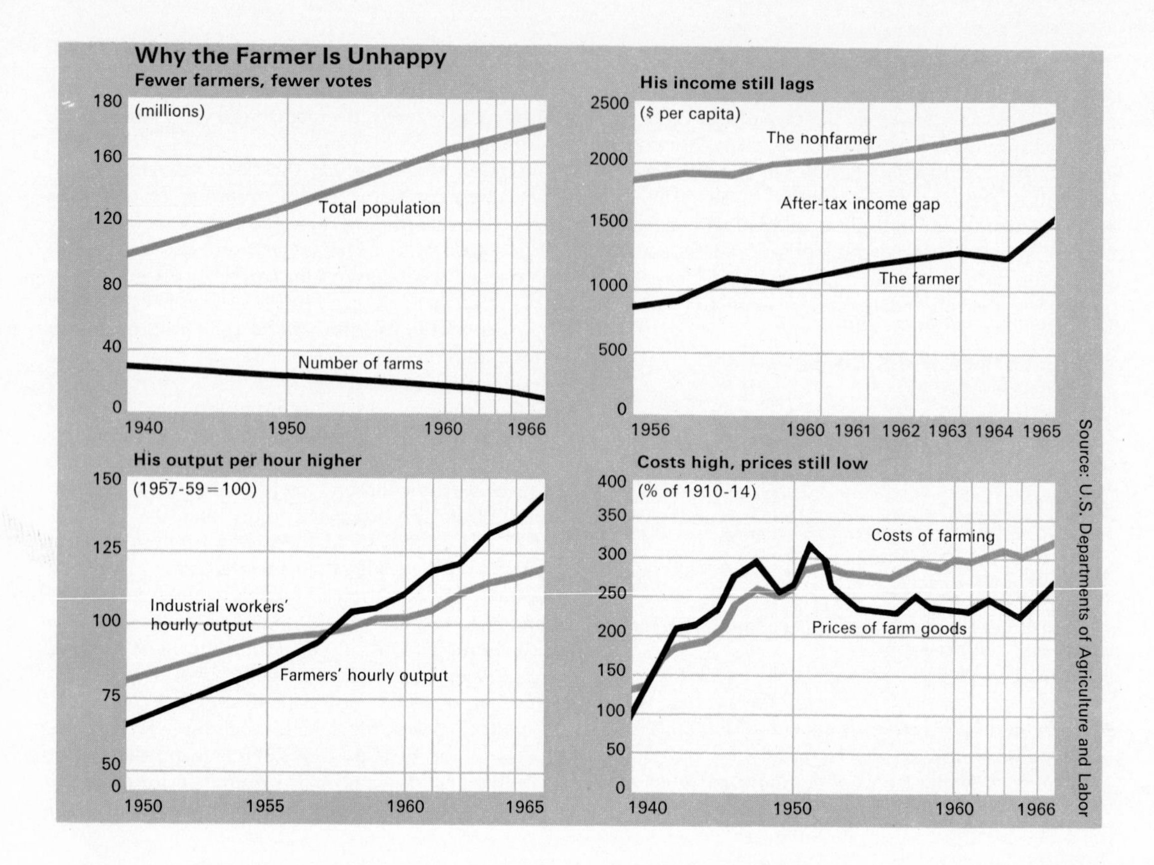

strong due to tight supplies and a June 30 increase in dairy price supports.

Per capita red meat consumption held at about 1965 levels, with beef up 3 pounds to 100 pounds per capita and pork down 1½ pounds to 57.3 pounds. Poultry (chicken and turkey) consumption continued to increase, gaining almost three pounds to 43½ pounds per person.

U.S. Production of Animal Products
(millions of pounds)

Product	1966*	1965	1957-1959‡
Beef	19,400	18,718	13,704
Veal	930	1,018	1,240
Lamb and mutton	640	651	711
Pork	11,150	11,173	10,957
Eggs (a)	5,375	5,382	5,475
Chicken	7,225	6,654	4,880
Turkey	1,680	1,508	1,065
Total milk (b)	1,215	1,251	1,233
Cheese	1,885	1,756	1,396
Ice cream	3,680	3,634	3,212
Butter	1,155	1,343	1,477

*Preliminary; ‡average
(a) 1,000,000 dozens; (b) 100,000,000 pounds

The number of cattle on farms declined during 1966 by more than 1,000,000 head for the second year in a row. On Jan. 1, 1966, there were 106,309,000 head of cattle on farms.

Hog slaughter in late 1966 moved well ahead of previous year levels as the 10 per cent larger pig crop began moving to market. For the year, however, hog slaughter was 75,000,000 head, down from 76,610,000 in 1965. The number of sheep and lambs on farms increased for the first time since 1959. Sheep and lamb slaughter through June, 1966, was down 3 per cent from the 13,306,000 total of a year earlier.

Marketing. The U.S. consumers' 1966 food bill totaled an estimated $91,000,000,000, up from $85,400,000,000 in 1965. Food took about 18.2 per cent of disposable income in both years. See Food.

Food prices became a national issue in 1966. Housewives in several cities across the nation organized protest demonstrations against rising food prices at supermarkets and other food stores. See Economy, The (Close-Up).

Retail food prices in the third quarter of 1966 reached a new high, 13.7 per cent above the 1957-1959 average and 4.5 per cent above a year earlier, as the farmer's prices were passed on to the consumer. How much they were being passed along was the subject of a study of bread and milk prices undertaken by the Federal Trade Commission (FTC) on August 4. In its report, issued October 25, the FTC found that retailers and processors were responsible for much of the rise in prices since Jan. 1, 1966. Of the average 1.7-cent increase in the price of a loaf of bread, farm ingredients accounted for 0.6 cent. The farmer got 2 cents of the 3.9-cent rise in the price of a half gallon of milk.

In June, the National Commission on Food Marketing issued a report on the structure and performance of the food industry. The 15-man commission had been authorized by Congress to make the two-year study. It described the food industry as generally efficient and progressive, but needing closer surveillance to keep prices down. High food prices were attributed partly to excessive spending for advertising, trading stamps, and other promotions by processors and retailers.

Technology continued to improve the farmer's products and increase his efficiency. Among the year's developments were:

- Successful large-scale trials of a synthetic compound called MATCH that brought groups of sows into heat simultaneously. This could lead to more efficient artificial insemination of sows.
- Discovery by a Finnish scientist that protein is not essential in a milk cow's diet.
- Breeding of a protein-rich strain of high-lysine corn into a nonhigh-lysine hybrid corn by scientists at Purdue University. The new corn, when fed to children in Guatemala, was found to provide almost the same protein value as skim milk.
- Yield tests on newly developed hybrid wheat showed increased yields between 15 per cent and 50 per cent over nonhybrids. Costs are still uneconomic and the seeds are not on the market.

Farm Legislation. The original Food for Peace Act of 1954, and expanded in 1960, underwent some major revisions in amendments signed into law on November 12. The new legislation shifted emphasis from a program of surplus disposal to one of planned production for export. Thus, food was being used as a major instrument of foreign policy. This made the American farmer a key figure in U.S. international relations.

The new policy was a positive one of encouraging output of specific foods for foreign aid. That policy – along with current good farm income, continued rising domestic incomes, increasing demand for food, and dwindling surplus stocks – seemed to hold a somewhat brighter future for agriculture over the next few years.

In other agricultural legislation the Congress:

- Appropriated $6,994,590,150 for the Department of Agriculture and the National Advisory Commission on Food and Fiber for fiscal 1967.
- Provided for a cotton research and promotion program to be financed by cotton growers. The program can be implemented only after a national referendum, which must win the approval of either two-thirds of all cotton farmers or of those farmers who grow two-thirds of the total cotton crop.
- Enacted a broader minimum wage bill that covers about 390,000 farmworkers. They will get a

Agrisculpture, titled *One Is Greater Than 100,* in Massey-Ferguson's Des Moines (Iowa) offices depicts the farm power revolution.

minimum wage of $1 an hour effective Feb. 1, 1967, increasing in steps to $1.30 by 1969.

Farm Labor made other gains in 1966. For the first time, the average farm wage exceeded $1 an hour. The 1966 level was $1.03, up 8 cents from 1965 and 13 cents above the 1964 average.

A grape pickers' union made the first breakthrough in organizing California's massive fieldworker force. The National Farm Workers Association (NFWA) signed a contract in June with Schenley Industries, Inc. It provided a 35-cent hourly wage increase, which raised the minimum rate to $1.75 an hour.

World Agriculture. Wheat production established a new record of 9,500,000,000 bushels, up from 9,000,000,000 in 1965 and the previous record of 9,300,000,000 in 1964. Russia made a striking recovery with a record grain crop of 171,000,000 metric (2,204-pound) tons. Free World cotton growers outside the United States produced 23,600,000 bales for the seventh new record in as many years.

World livestock numbers reached record levels in 1966. Hogs were estimated at 467,700,000 head, 9 per cent above the 1956-1960 average. Cattle increased 13 per cent from the 1956-1960 average to 1,103,500,000 head.

World Crop Production
(000,000 omitted)

Crop	1955-59	1965	1966 (est.)	% U.S.
Barley (bu.)	3,255	4,217	4,546	8.7
Corn (bu.)	6,480	8,182	8,507	48.2
Oats (bu.)	4,085	3,028	3,000	27.9
Soybeans (bu.)	894	1,185	1,273	72.8
Wheat (bu.)	7,969	9,000	9,500	13.1
Rice*	132.8	159.0	171.0	2.2
Sugar (tons)	49.6	68.8	72.8	7.4
Coffee (bags†)	58.3	80.9	65.2	—
Cotton (bales)	43.8	53.0	48.3	22.3

*Metric tons: Excluding Communist Asia. †132.276 lb.
Source: U.S. Department of Agriculture, Foreign Agricultural Service.

U.S. Exports and Imports of agricultural products remained high. Agricultural exports climbed to a record $6,700,000,000 in the year ended June 30, 1966, up 10 per cent from the previous year. Corn and grain sorghum exports shot up 40 per cent, as rising incomes throughout the world brought an increased demand for livestock products and, consequently, feed grains. Cotton exports fell more than 30 per cent.

Agricultural imports rose 12 per cent from a year earlier, the largest increase since 1950-1951, to a total of $4,454,000,000. Much of the increase was in animals and animal products, which climbed 36 per cent in the fiscal year. CHARLES E. FRENCH

See also INTERNATIONAL TRADE AND FINANCE.

AIR FORCE, U.S. See ARMED FORCES OF THE WORLD; NATIONAL DEFENSE.

AIR RACE. See AVIATION.

AIRPLANE. See ARMED FORCES OF THE WORLD; AVIATION.

ALBANIA continued on its strongly pro-Communist Chinese course in 1966, with Premier Mehmet Shehu and China's Premier Chou En-lai exchanging visits early in the year.

Trade relations between Albania and the East European Communist countries remained steady during the year. Political relations, however, did not improve. A Polish invitation to attend a Warsaw Treaty Organization meeting in February was rudely rejected by Albania as was an invitation to attend the 23rd Congress of the Soviet Communist party in Moscow from March 29 to April 8.

Albania was increasingly isolated in international affairs. At the fifth congress of the Albanian Communist party, held in November, only four Communist countries sent delegates: the People's Republic of China, North Korea, Romania, and North Vietnam.

During the year, the party celebrated its 25th anniversary. Although it was still under the firm grip of First Secretary Enver Hoxha, there was talk during the year of "enemies" in the party.

Facts in Brief. Population: 1,980,000. Government: Communist Party First Secretary Enver Hoxha; Premier Mehmet Shehu. Monetary Unit: lek (50=U.S. $1). Foreign Trade: exports, $4,500,-000; imports, $22,000,000. Principal Exports: tobacco, copper, wine, cigarettes. F. GORDON SKILLING

ALBERTA. See CANADA.

ALGERIA. The ruling military junta wrestled with the political and economic problems it inherited when it overthrew President Ahmed Ben Bella's "cult of personal power" in 1965. While Ben Bella remained under house arrest, his followers and other Algerian leaders broke with the new regime. Guerrilla leader Hocine Aït Ahmed escaped from jail in April and founded the Secret Organization of the Algerian Revolution (OCRA) in Luxembourg, to oppose both Ben Bella and President Houari Boumedienne. In October, a dispute over municipal elections split the National Revolutionary Council. Two council ministers, Bachir Boumaza and Ali Mahsas, fled to Luxembourg and joined OCRA. Boumedienne then scheduled elections for February, 1967.

Algeria's economic instability was shown in May when Boumedienne nationalized all mines in addition to property the French had abandoned. He declared "foreign ownership is incompatible with our sovereignty and choice of socialism." France retaliated by suspending its $96,000,000 aid program.

Increased Controls. In June, a new penal code defined offenses and crimes against the socialist system and the state. Three courts were set up to try offenders. The state took over all publications in September and restricted travel by foreign reporters to Algiers. Medical trainees were made civil servants and were required to serve the state.

Algeria's worst drought cut the wheat harvest from 2,000,000 to 800,000 tons. France relented and provided 80,000 tons. The United States pledged $12,594,000 for wheat under its Food for Peace Program and Canada granted $1,000,000.

Despite political uncertainty, Algeria continued to attract foreign investments. In February, a new pipeline began carrying oil from the Saharan oil fields to Arzew. It had been built with $70,000,000 of British-Kuwaiti capital. SONATRACH, the Algerian national oil company, contracted with two New York banks for $15,000,000 to build pumping stations on the line. It also allied with the Southeastern Drilling Company of Texas for joint Saharan drilling. Russia promised to finance 28 small dams to irrigate reclaimed land. It also supplied 11 MIG-21 fighter aircraft to the Algerian army.

Land Reform. In a significant step, Boumedienne proposed that all large farms be operated by workers' cooperatives, the expropriated land to be paid for with 15-year treasury bonds. Members of the National Revolutionary Council visited rural areas to explain the plan to Algeria's peasants.

Facts in Brief. Population: 13,100,000. Government: President Houari Boumedienne. Monetary Unit: dinar (4.90=U.S. $1). Foreign Trade: exports, $689,700,000; imports, $731,300,000. Principal Exports: citrus fruits, oil, wine. WILLIAM SPENCER

AMERICAN LEGION. See VETERANS.

AMERICAN LIBRARY ASSOCIATION (ALA) established its 14th division, Information Science and Automation, in 1966. It also organized the Office for Library Education, with Lester Asheim as director. The administrative changes accompanied the ALA's growth to more than 32,000 members in 1966, an increase of 26 per cent since 1961.

Officers of several national library associations met at ALA headquarters in Chicago on March 4 and 5 and formed the Joint Committee on National Library and Information Systems (CONLIS). The committee was assigned the task of drafting a program to improve the access to, and availability of, information through national communications systems linking libraries and information centers.

ALA Conference. At the 85th annual conference in New York City, July 10 to 15, members adopted revised standards for public libraries and library services to the blind, to be published in 1967.

The ALA council adopted a resolution requiring the suspension of members found guilty of violating civil rights laws. In addition, signed complaints against members would be forwarded to appropriate agencies for investigation and action.

The conference also adopted a new policy on international affairs. In it, ALA promised to continue to work with international library groups for the development of libraries and a library profession in countries where none exist.

At the conference, Congressman John E. Fogarty (D., R.I.) was awarded an honorary life membership "in recognition of his long and distinguished commitment to the cause of better libraries."

Other Developments. During 1966, the ALA continued to support legislation for library development. This legislation included the Library Services and Construction Act and the Higher Education Act. In addition, the National Books for the Blind Act was amended to include assistance for handicapped persons who cannot use conventional materials. See LIBRARY.

Mary V. Gaver, a professor of the Graduate School of Library Service, Rutgers University, was installed as president of the ALA. Foster E. Mohrhardt, director of the U.S. Department of Agriculture Library, was installed as vice-president.

The ALA's Library Technology Program continued its long-term studies of copying equipment and circulation control systems, surveys of library automation activities, and testing of library furniture and equipment.

Awards in 1966 included:

The Clarence Day Award of $1,000, to Mrs. Frances Clarke Sayers, former lecturer in the School Library Service, University of California at Los Angeles.

Melvil Dewey Medal for distinguished achievements in behalf of libraries and librarianship, to Lucile M. Morsch, retired chief of the Descriptive Cataloging Division of the Library of Congress.

E. P. Dutton-John Macrae Award of $1,000 for advanced study, to Mrs. Irene Gullette, coordinator of elementary library service for the Board of Public Instruction, Broward County, Florida.

Grolier Award of $1,000, to Mildred L. Batchelder, retired executive secretary of the Children's Services and Young Adult Services Divisions, for her 40 years of devoted attention to children's reading and books for young readers.

The J. Morris Jones-World Book Encyclopedia-ALA Goals Award for 1966, a sum of $25,000, was awarded to the American Association of School Librarians, a division of ALA, for the revision of the 1960 school library standards.

Lippincott Award of $1,000 for outstanding participation in professional library associations, notable published professional writing, and other significant activity in the profession, to Keyes De Witt Metcalf, librarian emeritus of the Harvard University library. He also received the $500 Scarecrow Press Award for a distinguished contribution to library literature.

Melcher Scholarships of $1,500 for graduate study in children's library services, to Mrs. Maureen Harris Davis of Bellingham, Wash., and $1,000 to Carol Senda of Shaker Heights, Ohio.

Halsey W. Wilson Library Recruitment Award $1,000, first given in 1966, to the Pennsylvania State Library for its especially imaginative training and recruiting program. RUTH M. WHITE

See also CANADIAN LIBRARY ASSOCIATION; CANADIAN LITERATURE; EDUCATION; LITERATURE FOR CHILDREN (Awards).

ANGOLA. See AFRICA.

ANIMAL. See AGRICULTURE; CONSERVATION; LIVESTOCK SHOW; PET; ZOOLOGY; ZOOS AND AQUARIUMS.

ANTARCTICA. See EXPLORATION.

ANTHROPOLOGY

The World's Vanishing Hunters

10,000 B.C.: World population 10,000,000 100% hunters

A.D. 1500: World population 350,000,000 1% hunters

Today: World population 3,300,000,000 .001% hunters

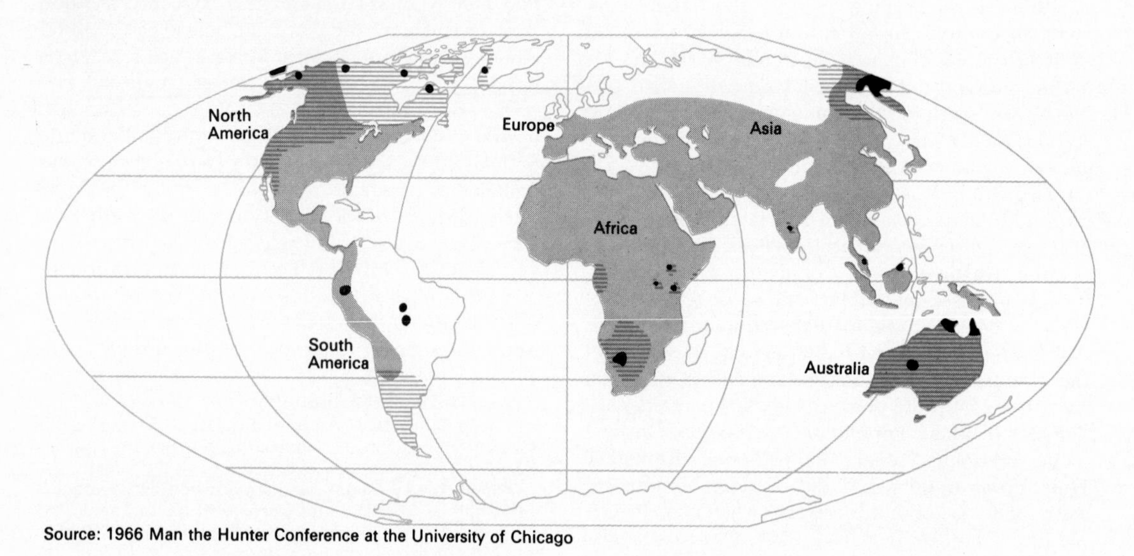

Source: 1966 Man the Hunter Conference at the University of Chicago

ANTHROPOLOGY. Scientists from the University of Minnesota uncovered the fossil remains of two ancient primates (the order of creatures that includes apes and man) in the Purgatory Hills of eastern Montana. Of a genus previously unknown, the primates lived when dinosaurs still roamed the earth–at a time much earlier than any other known primates. The two were given the genus name *Purgatorius* for the site where they were found.

Leigh Van Valen of the Department of Vertebrate Paleontology at the American Museum of Natural History in New York City studied the two specimens and described them as members of the paromomyid family of prosimian primates, possibly related to the tarsiers of today. The most recent of the two was named *Purgatorius unio.* It lived during the Paleocene Epoch of geologic history, between 50,000,000 and 63,000,000 years ago. The other was *Purgatorius ceratops*, and dates to the Cretaceous Period, more than 63,000,000 years ago.

Fossil Human Beings. Several important fossil remains of human beings were discovered in Europe and Africa. At the site of Vértesszöllös, Hungary, part of the occipital bone (the back of the skull) of a fossil man was uncovered late in 1965. Though the find has not been fully evaluated, it probably is the oldest human fossil yet found in Europe. At Salzgitter-Lebenstedt, in Germany, Adolf Kleinschmidt found two pieces of a Neanderthal skull in 1966. This discovery is significant because the site was apparently an open-air camp, and because it has yielded the well-preserved remains of animals and plants.

At the Olduvai Gorge in Tanzania, East Africa, Louis S. B. Leakey and his co-workers uncovered a right toe bone of an early manlike creature. Although it is not possible to say whether it belonged to an individual of the *Homo habilis* species or to an Australopithecine like *Zinjanthropus*, it does add to the evidence that hominids of this period (possibly 1,750,000 years ago) were able to walk erect.

Space in Culture. A new theory that will likely influence current ideas on overpopulation, as well as the work of architects and city planners, was presented by anthropologist Edward T. Hall of the Illinois Institute of Technology in his book *The Hidden Dimension* (1966). He pointed out that it has long been known that different animal species will tolerate different degrees of congestion and permit other animals to approach only within certain limits before fleeing or fighting.

Man, says Hall, exhibits the same behavior, though different cultures have different spacing tolerances. He refers to this distance regulation as "proxemic patterns." He shows that the proxemic patterns of Japanese culture permit what most North Americans would consider crowded conditions. Arabs in public places behave in ways that people in the United States consider rude and aggressive. This is because Arabs feel that an individual who is standing still does not have as much right to the space he occupies as does a mobile individual. People from the United States tend to treat standing objects and individuals with respect, moving around them at a distance.

Symposium on Hunters. Anthropologists from many parts of the world met for a three-day conference on "Man the Hunter" at the University of Chicago's Center for Continuing Education, in April, 1966. The participants discussed many aspects of the life of hunting and gathering peoples of the world from the present to prehistoric times. Many of the papers were directed at the problem of understanding how modern man came to be what he is, considering that the hunting way of life has dominated 99 per cent of man's history.

One important result of the conference was the realization that hunting groups are much more diverse and complex than had previously been suspected. No single group can be taken as typical of all the rest, and no analogy with the behavior of a modern hunting-gathering group can be used as the basis for interpreting the evidence of prehistory. This realization will certainly lead to new developments in anthropological theory. LESLIE G. FREEMAN, JR.

ANTI-POVERTY. See POVERTY.

ARABIA. See SAUDI ARABIA.

ARCHAEOLOGY. Mary Leakey, a distinguished prehistorian and wife of anthropologist Louis S. B. Leakey, published in 1966 a detailed analysis of the earliest Stone Age tools and artifacts ever found. The tools making up the Oldowan industrial complex were discovered at Olduvai Gorge in Tanzania, Africa. The complex contained a number of standardized types of stone tools found at other sites in the gorge. Some dated back nearly 2,000,000 years and some to only about 500,000 years.

Mrs. Leakey listed six major categories of tools:

1. Choppers and chopping tools made from cobblestones. The crude cutting edges were formed by chipping flakes from one or both sides of the stone.

2. Spheroids fashioned by battering and flaking stones into a nearly spherical shape.

3. Subspheroids made in the same way, but sufficiently different to form a separate category.

4. Proto-bifaces produced by flaking cobblestones until a rough, pointed cutting edge was formed.

5. Scrapers made by dulling the sharp cutting edge of a stone flake. This was done by removing a continuous series of chips along the cutting edge.

6. Proto-burins produced by shaping stones into crude chisel-edged pieces.

Each of these six categories contained a number of discrete types of tools. Mrs. Leakey also listed a series of stones that had been battered during use as toolmaking anvils, as well as stone flaking debris found at toolmaking sites. Although it is not yet possible to say which early man made these Oldowan tools, Mrs. Leakey believed that they were the handiwork of *Homo habilis*, an early type of man.

New World Discoveries. James W. Warnica, a highly competent amateur archaeologist, produced new evidence concerning the ways of life among the big-game hunters of the southwestern United States. Over a period of years, Warnica has conducted excavations at the well-known Clovis site in New Mexico, and has carefully mapped the location of every bone and artifact that has been found. The most recent discoveries were the remains of four mammoths and a bison that may have been killed by early man at what was once an ancient water hole.

Warnica's maps provided data on the association and distribution of the objects at the site–data essential to an understanding of the activities that produced such a distribution. The data suggested that the mammoths and the bison were butchered and eaten, because, with the bones, were found several Clovis-type spear points and other tools, including multiple perforators and a grindstone. Other bits of bone found with the tools included those of a horse, a peccary, a camel, an antelope, a deer, and reptiles. The find has been dated by the radiocarbon method at about 9220 B.C.

Another mammoth butchering site was uncovered in Oklahoma by archaeologists from the Museum of the Great Plains in Lawton, Okla. The Domebo site find was reported by Frank C. Leonhardy of the museum, who said that four projectile points were among the bones of a single mammoth. Radiocarbon dates show that the mammoth was killed between 9000 and 8000 B.C.

Stonehenge. The electronic computer has been used in archaeology for many purposes, particularly in the decoding of forgotten languages. In 1963, Gerald S. Hawkins of the Smithsonian Astrophysical Observatory published the results of his computer analysis of Stonehenge, the prehistoric monument on England's Salisbury Plain. He showed that there was a deliberate alignment of the stones in the monument, which might well have served as sighting points for determining sunrise, sunset, moonrise, and moonset on midsummer day and midwinter day (the solstices). In 1966, Hawkins published a book, *Stonehenge Decoded*, which summarized his work on the stones and holes at the monument. He revised his theory, speculating that the monument was used as a kind of prehistoric computer to predict the occurrence of solar and lunar eclipses. The book raised a great deal of controversy in scientific circles. Hawkins certainly demonstrates that certain features at Stonehenge do line up with certain astronomical phenomena, but it will never be possible to prove that the men who built Stonehenge actually used the monument to predict eclipses. LESLIE G. FREEMAN, JR.

"Habitat," built of prefabricated concrete cubes for Canada's Expo 67, represents an imaginative approach to urban housing.

ARCHITECTURE. The year signaled the growing recognition by a large segment of the profession of the critical problems of human settlement. Faced with an unsatisfactory man-made urban environment and the increasing number of people that must work and live in the city, a significant number of the world's architects directed their talents and resources toward seeking better ways of accommodating the rapidly expanding urban population. They did so through research, by leading and attending educational seminars, and by the imaginative efforts of their projects.

Nearly all the professional conferences, seminars, and meetings in the United States dealt with urban and regional topics, rather than with the planning of single buildings. Also, most of the meetings were attended by men in the many disciplines, including behavioral scientists, economists, and engineers. This multidisciplinary approach seemed to mark the end of attitudes and traditions in which creative architects worked in isolation.

Aspen Conference. Further evidence of this powerful shift of concern was noted by the announcement in May that the third annual Aspen Award had been won by Greek architect Constantinos A. Doxiadis, 53, for "Humanistic Achievement." His concern for design, from single family homes to new towns, and indeed to regional multicity growth, singled him out from his profession–not as one unique to such a comprehensive involvement–but as the man who directed the attention of the design professions to the problem of the population explosion and the resulting environment crises.

Expo 67. The Canadian World's Fair, Expo 67, which will open on April 28, 1967, provided the setting for a glimpse into the future of form and technology in architecture. Perhaps the most intriguing structure rising on the fairgrounds was "Habitat 67," a visionary attempt to achieve a new form of urban housing. The architect, Moshe Safdie of Israel, conceived a multilevel village incorporating outdoor as well as interior living spaces by allowing the roofs of one dwelling unit to serve as the terrace of the unit above. Complete needs for shops and services are contained within the village, which is composed of large prefabricated and prestressed concrete cubes. The cubes are equipped on an assembly line with kitchens, bathrooms, plumbing, wiring, windows, and finished surfaces. Then they are hoisted into place by cranes, very much like a child's building blocks. Habitat was significant as a demonstration of the imaginative application of modern technology to satisfy today's mass housing needs in a livable manner.

Instant City. Another example of the growing awareness of the urban problem was the commissioning of architects by several industries to execute visionary city projects. One such project was designed by Chicago architect Stanley Tigerman. He was commissioned by the Vermiculite Institute and W. R. Grace Company to design a project utilizing air rights above superhighways for a vertical city development. His plan allowed for most of the functions and services necessary for carrying on life in a self-contained city.

AIA Award. In the more traditional involvements of architects, notable accomplishments were made and honors were bestowed.

The American Institute of Architects (AIA) awarded its Gold Medal of Honor to Kenzo Tange, who became the first Japanese and one of the youngest architects to receive this award. Said AIA President Morris Ketchum, Jr., at the presentation: "To Kenzo Tange, architect, philosopher, teacher, writer–who has, through the poetry of his architecture, brought a dignity, grace and integrity to his own land and to men everywhere." Tange is the designer of many imaginative projects. He is best known for his sports arena built in Tokyo in 1964 for the Olympics Games.

Mies van der Rohe. Chicago, home of architectural titan Ludwig Mies van der Rohe, chose Mies' 80th birthday in 1966 to honor him as "The conscience of Chicago architecture." Mies' projects, personified by his philosophy, "less is more," have left their mark on most of the major cities of the West in sleek glass and steel towers of curtain wall construction. It was generally considered that no other modern architect accomplished such significant buildings with such economy of means, exquisite use of proportion, clarity of structure, and direct use of materials. Among his projects singled out for praise were the Illinois Institute of Technology Campus in Chicago, the Seagram Building in New York City, built in collaboration with Philip Johnson, and the Bacardi Building in Cuba.

Civic Center. As a further compliment to Mies' central role, Chicago dedicated a brawny new Civic Center. The building was designed by Jacques Brownson, a former student of Mies, for the C. F. Murphy firm. It is quite possibly the greatest of the towers constructed in the tradition of Mies' philosophy. See CHICAGO; CITY.

Exhibitions. Exhibitions of architecture are staged across the nation, but seldom do they attempt to present the creator as well as his creations to the public. But the Museum of Modern Art in Manhattan succeeded in conveying both the works of Louis J. Kahn, designer of many of the most notable buildings of this generation, as well as his philosophy. Kahn's profound ability as a teacher, philosopher, and architect was presented to the public in an exhibition that made clear his thought process, the evolution of his concepts, and his theories as reflected in his words and works. DONALD HANSEN

See also CITY; CITY AND REGIONAL PLANNING; Section One, ALISTAIR COOKE: FOCUS ON THE ARTS.

ARGENTINA. On June 28, a military junta ousted the civilian government of President Arturo Umberto Illia. Congress and the supreme court were dissolved and all political parties, of which there were about 200 in the nation, were abolished. Lieutenant General Juan Carlos Ongania, a retired army officer, took over the presidency.

The coup d'état, which was carried out swiftly and without bloodshed, had been encouraged by businessmen and landowners who were increasingly concerned over Illia's inability to control the nation's weakening economic situation. They were also impatient with the government's failure to check inflation and to control labor demands for higher wages in the face of declining productivity. Resentment was widespread, too, over the government's tolerance of left-wing activities as reflected in the provincial election victories of the Perónists.

Student Unrest. On taking office, President Ongania promised to institute a general program of austerity and reform. Within a month, however, mounting political and social unrest, and continuing inflation, had divided Ongania's supporters. The academic community was up in arms, too, over the military regime's seizure of the nation's eight nationally chartered universities in July because of alleged antigovernment leftist activities. Scores of professors and students who protested the seizure were beaten by the police. As a result, more than 900 of the 2,000 teachers at the University of Buenos Aires resigned. Unrest and violence continued despite such government moves as the disbanding of a number of student organizations and a government offer to restore most university privileges that had been abolished.

Economic Problems. Though the central bank's monetary reserves climbed amid a growing trade surplus ($467,000,000 for the first nine months), the foreign debt reached a staggering $2,400,000,000 to $3,200,000,000. Obligations maturing within the year were estimated at $700,000,000 to $998,000,000. Between January and September, living costs were up 20.2 per cent.

The gross national product, which had declined 1 per cent during that period, was expected to show a 2.2 per cent decrease for the year. Agricultural and livestock output fell 4.3 per cent, production of manufacturing industries decreased 0.9 per cent, and deficit financing assumed alarming proportions. By year's end, and despite the efforts of the Ongania regime, inflation continued to soar, labor relations remained tense, and business was generally in a growing recession.

Facts in Brief. Population: 23,408,000. Government: President Juan Carlos Ongania. Monetary Unit: peso (205=U.S. $1). Foreign Trade: exports, $1,492,500,000; imports, $1,198,600,000. Principal Exports: maize, meat, wool, wheat. MARY C. WEBSTER

ARMED FORCES OF THE WORLD. Asia became the focus of the world power conflict in 1966. The shift away from Europe was dramatically underscored late in the year, both by the appearance of President Lyndon B. Johnson at the Manila conference on U.S.-Asian defense policy, and by the explosion of Communist China's fourth nuclear bomb. The power shift could be seen further in the U.S. troop build-up in Southeast Asia to 500,000 men, as compared to the 375,000 men stationed in Europe. In addition, the United States was planning to reduce its strength in Europe to token force by 1970. See ASIA; NORTH ATLANTIC TREATY ORGANIZATION (NATO).

It was the Vietnamese war and the apparently lessening menace of Soviet power in Europe that spurred the U.S. commitment in Asia. By year-end, the United States had more than 380,000 men in South Vietnam, 31,000 in Thailand, and 70,000 with the Seventh Fleet supporting the bombing of North Vietnam.

U.S. Missile Lead. The United States retained its 3-to-1 lead in the number of intercontinental ballistic missiles (ICBM). The U.S. total was 1,004 ICBMs. This included 950 Minuteman and 54 Titan missiles. The Department of Defense planned to add 50 more Minuteman IIs to the 150 advanced-type already located deep in underground silos, and would modernize the earlier models. Russia also was improving the quality of its ICBM force, partly by installing underground missiles similar to the solid-fuel Minuteman. The Soviet total was approximately 350.

Missile Subs. In submarine-launched missiles, the United States held an impressive superiority with 40 operational Polaris submarines, each with 16 missiles aboard. The 41st and final Polaris was scheduled for completion in 1967. In 1966, 35 of the missile subs were deployed at sea. Russia, meanwhile, had 40 missile submarines, of which 15 were nuclear-powered. But its underwater vessels carried only three or four missiles each. These had ranges of 500 miles compared to the maximum 2,700-mile range of the Polaris.

Strategic Bombers in the United States were overshadowed by the awesome ICBM. The nation had 600 B-52 jet bombers and 80 B-58 medium-range jet bombers, compared to Russia's 150 long-range and 1,000 medium-range bombers.

Defense Systems. The future of collective defense systems became more clouded than ever in 1966. On both sides, nationalism and economic pressures eroded military unity and strength. France wrenched its forces out of NATO, and the United States and Great Britain prepared to cut their troops in West Germany because of the heavy drain in foreign monetary exchange. The United States continued to bolster NATO with 223,000 troops, 25,000 sailors, and 70,000 airmen, but the organization was a collective defense system largely on paper. It was made up of 24 divisions, including 12 German, five U.S., three British, two Netherland, two Belgian, plus one Canadian brigade. These ground forces, totaling about 850,000 men, faced some 800,000 Warsaw Pact troops.

Comparative Military Manpower
as of Oct. 31, 1966

	United States	Russia	Communist China
Army	1,362,812	2,000,000	2,300,000
Navy	1,026,274*	450,000	140,000
Air Force	904,432	700,000**	90,000
Total	3,293,518	3,150,000	2,530,000

*Includes 278,712 marines
**Includes 200,000 strategic rocket force

The Warsaw Pact nations made few gains in 1966. Russia continued to keep 20 divisions in East Germany, two in Poland, and four in Hungary. It also deployed some 15 divisions on its Chinese borders to check Peking's bellicosity. LLOYD NORMAN

See also NATIONAL DEFENSE.

ART. See ARCHITECTURE; DANCING; LITERATURE; MUSIC; PAINTING AND SCULPTURE.

ASIA

The massive struggle for ideological control over Asia's teeming millions entered a new phase during 1966. It saw a heightening of the conflict between the pro-Communist forces as led by the People's Republic of China and the anti-Communist elements that were headed primarily by the United States.

Most of the struggle revolved around the bitter conflict that was being waged within and, in part, along the borders of Vietnam. There, some 380,000

A Vietnamese mother and her children wade to safety during an attack. This picture won the 1966 Pulitzer prize for News Photography.

U.S. fighting men and about 500,000 South Vietnamese troops were pitted against an undetermined number of North Vietnamese and Viet Cong forces in a war that was alternately a direct slugging match between well-equipped troops and a clandestine guerrilla contest.

The extent of the American commitment, however, went far beyond the number of men engaged in the actual contest, for it embraced a far-reaching complex of advanced military weapons that excluded only atomic weapons. American airplanes, ranging thousands of miles from bases in Guam, swooped low over the jungles and the Mekong Delta of Vietnam, to bomb and destroy the areas held by the Communist Viet Cong. U.S. air power struck deep, too, in North Vietnam, carrying the war close to Communist China's borders.

Although the costs of the war mounted astronomically for the U.S. and its allies in 1966, they appeared to be paying dividends. No longer could the Viet Cong claim even the potential of a major military victory over American troops. Battalion, and even regimental-size attacks during 1966 had cost the Viet Cong so heavily that by year's end they were no longer engaging the Americans in sizable force. The success of the Americans in the military field did not mean success in the political one, however. Political dissatisfaction with the South Vietnamese regime of Premier Nguyen Cao Ky was still rife as Buddhists and leftists vied for power. In

World leaders, attending a summit conference held at Malacanang Palace in Manila in October, sign a joint communiqué on Vietnam.

this area, the war seemed further than ever from a solution. See KY, NGUYEN CAO; VIETNAM.

Political Uncertainty. The escalation of the war in Vietnam was only one aspect of the struggle. Elsewhere in Asia, the ideological confrontation took various forms. The most significant turnabout in Asia occurred in Indonesia, where the Sukarno brand of leftism was defeated by the Indonesian army. Under General Suharto, the army literally wiped out the Indonesian Communist Party (PKI) —the largest in Asia other than China—and set Indonesia on a new course. The reversal in Indonesia meant a new chance for Malaysia and Thailand, both of whom rapidly coalesced with the Indonesians and then brought in the Philippines to present a more solid front of regional cooperation.

Politically, the attraction of Communist China as the wave of the future was obviously on the wane as nation after nation in Asia, seeing through the glittering Chinese generalities, became anxious for its own safety. India and Pakistan, which had been at each other's throats in 1965, buried their differences and tried to work out their own problems during 1966 (see INDIA). Pakistan began to look elsewhere for support of its policies rather than to Peking (see PAKISTAN). Burma made increasingly friendly overtures to the West. Ceylon worked hard, too, to realign its Western ties. The Republic of Korea, long under Communist Chinese pressure,

"Who's winning—the Forces of Freedom or the People's Democracies?"

defiantly sent two divisions to South Vietnam to fight with the Americans and the Vietnamese. It urged even stronger measures to combat the influence of Communist China (see KOREA). Of all the Asian nations, only Japan continued to pursue a middle-of-the-road policy. See JAPAN.

Communist Chinese Threat. The key to the resistance confronting Communist China, however, was not found solely in the hardening position of the United States and its allies. It was also to be found in the open and growing hostility of the Soviet Union toward its former Chinese partners. See COMMUNISM; RUSSIA.

China's fifth atomic test, its advances in missilery, its military potential, and its bellicose statements all stimulated a greater awareness of the threat it poses to world peace. The political convulsions within China, as evidenced by Red Guard activity, and the struggle for power and leadership among the Chinese hierarchy stimulated world-wide anxiety. When the United Nations (UN) once again took up the perennial question of the admission of China to the UN, the Chinese lost by an even greater vote than in 1965. See UNITED NATIONS (UN).

Economic Agreements. The fear of Communist China stimulated more coordinated efforts on the part of the peripheral nations of Asia to band together in common purposes and goals during 1966. In June, the groundwork was laid for a greater degree of economic cooperation with the establishment of the Asian and Pacific Council (ASPAC). Members included Australia, Formosa (Taiwan), Japan, South Korea, Malaysia, New Zealand, the Philippines, and South Vietnam. Laos attended as an observer. The creation of the Asia Development Bank, with a subscribed capital of $1,000,000,000, was but another step indicating the willingness of Asian nations to work together.

Finally, a visit by President Lyndon B. Johnson to New Zealand, Australia, Malaysia, Thailand, the Philippines, Vietnam, and the Republic of Korea, in October, made it clear that the United States was determined to back its Asian allies in their efforts to raise their standards of living while resisting Communist aggression. See PRESIDENT OF THE UNITED STATES.

Population Growth. The most pressing and immediate need for regional development in Asia was in agriculture. Total food output in the area increased in 1966 but per capita production declined as the continent continued to lose ground in its desperate race with population expansion. Even Communist China was compelled once again to import grain from Canada (see CANADA). Food scarcities in India touched off riots in a number of cities during the year (see INDIA). Of all the Asian countries, only Formosa (Taiwan) remained a showcase of agricultural production. See FOOD; FORMOSA; POPULATION, WORLD.

JOHN N. STALKER

ASTRONAUTS. Three astronauts died in their Apollo capsule on Jan. 27, 1967, when fire swept through the spacecraft during a routine test for the mission. The three–Lieutenant Colonel Virgil I. "Gus" Grissom and Lieutenant Colonel Edward H. White II of the air force, and Lieut. Commander Roger B. Chaffee–were rehearsing for the first manned flight of Project Apollo. Grissom, 40, was one of the original Mercury space pilots and was command pilot of the first manned Gemini mission. White, 35, was the first American to "walk" in space. The flight was to have been the first for Chaffee, 31. Walter M. Schirra, Jr., Donn Eisele, and Walter Cunningham will take their place.

Two other astronauts had died in 1966. They were Elliot M. See, Jr., and Major Charles A. Bassett II, who were killed in the crash of their jet trainer. The two were buried with military honors at Arlington National Cemetery on March 4.

The National Aeronautics and Space Administration (NASA) selected 19 new astronauts in May, 1966. NASA also told of plans for the first three manned Apollo missions. The first was scheduled to be an earth orbital flight of up to 14 days duration.

Prime crew for the second manned flight will be composed of Lieutenant Colonel James A. McDivitt, Lieutenant Colonel David R. Scott and Russell Schweickart, a civilian. During the flight, planned to test rendezvous and docking procedures, the crew flying the command and service modules will dock with an unmanned lunar module. It will be the first manned operation of the lunar module.

The crew for the third flight: Colonel Frank Borman, Lieutenant Colonel Michael Collins, and Major William A. Anders. On this flight, events that will occur during an actual lunar landing will be conducted, but in earth orbit.

In January, NASA announced that the first astronauts that land on the moon will unload a 150-pound instrument package that, if all goes well, will perform "every basic observation in geophysics."

Space Rescue? The flight in March of Gemini VIII dramatically posed the question: Should a rescue system be built to return to earth an astronaut stranded in space? The issue received much notice because astronauts David R. Scott and Neil A. Armstrong encountered great difficulty when their craft veered into a violent tumble.

In the discussion that followed the flight, it was learned that a variety of space rescue systems had been under study by NASA for several years. One method would make an extra rocket and spacecraft available at every launch for earth-to-orbit rescues, another involved the "lifeboat" concept, in which a space vehicle would carry a smaller craft that would be ejected in an emergency.

Nevertheless, the question of the feasibility of such systems was answered in the negative by NASA's chief of manned space flight, Dr. George

ASTRONAUTS

The Gemini Mission—What It Has Accomplished

Spacecraft	Date	Orbits and Flight Time	Astronauts	Chief Accomplishments
Gemini I	April 8 to 12, 1964		Unmanned	Test of spacecraft and its modified Titan II launch vehicle.
Gemini II	Jan. 19, 1965		Unmanned	Suborbital test of spacecraft and heat shield.
Gemini III	March 23, 1965	3 4h.53m.	Virgil I. Grissom; John W. Young	Verifies design of craft, operation procedures. First to change orbit.
Gemini IV	June 3 to 7, 1965	62 97h.56m.	James A. McDivitt; Edward H. White II	White becomes first American to walk in space; 20 minutes.
Gemini V	Aug. 21 to 29, 1965	120 190h.56m.	L. Gordon Cooper, Jr.; Charles Conrad, Jr.	Proves man can withstand eight days needed for round trip to moon.
Gemini VI	Dec. 15 to 16, 1965	17 25h.51m.	Walter M. Schirra, Jr.; Thomas P. Stafford	Rendezvous with orbiting Gemini VII. Fly in formation six hours.
Gemini VII	Dec. 4 to 18, 1965	206 330h.35m.	Frank Borman; James A. Lovell, Jr.	Used as rendezvous vehicle during flight by Gemini VI.
Gemini VIII	March 16, 1966	7 10h.42m.	Neil A. Armstrong; David R. Scott	First docking with a target vehicle; creates concern over safety in space.
Gemini IX	June 3 to 6, 1966	46 72h.21m.	Thomas O. Stafford; Eugene A. Cernan	Cernan walks in space for record two hours nine minutes.
Gemini X	July 18 to 21, 1966	44 70h.46m.	John W. Young; Michael Collins	Agena vehicle used to blast docked Gemini/Agena 476 miles high.
Gemini XI	Sept. 12 to 15, 1966	45 71h.17m.	Charles Conrad, Jr.; Richard F. Gordon, Jr.	Power of Agena vehicle used to boost Gemini/Agena to record 851 miles.
Gemini XII	Nov. 11 to 15, 1966	59 94h.36m.	James A. Lovell, Jr.; Edwin E. Aldrin, Jr.	Aldrin first astronaut to work comfortably outside spacecraft.

Mueller. Speaking in Washington, D.C., in August, Mueller declared that the cost and complexity of such a system made it seem that the effort would be better spent in making space flight, itself, safer. Said Mueller: "We don't exactly have instant rescue for people flying around in airliners and this is a large segment of the population."

New Astronauts. The 19 new astronauts that joined NASA in May are: Vance Brand, 34, a Lockheed test pilot; Lieutenant John S. Bull, 31, a navy test pilot; Major Gerald P. Carr, 33, of the marine corps; Air Force Captain Charles M. Duke, Jr., 30, flight instructor; Air Force Captain Joe H. Engle, 33, X-15 test pilot; Lieutenant Commander Ronald E. Evans, Jr., 32; Major Edward G. Givens, Jr., 36, of NASA's Manned Spacecraft Center, Houston, Tex.; Fred W. Haise, Jr., 32, NASA test pilot; Air Force Major James B. Irwin, 35; Dr. Don L. Lind, 35, physicist at Goddard Space Flight Center, Beltsville, Md.; Marine Captain Jack R. Lousma, 30; Navy Lieutenant Thomas K. Mattingly, 30; Navy Lieutenant Bruce McCandless II, 28, youngest astronaut; Lieutenant Commander Edgar D. Mitchell, 35; Major William R. Pogue, 36, of the air force; Captain Stuart A. Roosa, 32, air force test pilot; John L. Swigert, Jr., 34, civilian test pilot; Lieutenant Commander Paul J. Weitz, 33; and Air Force Captain Alfred Worden, 34. MARK M. PERLBERG

See also SPACE EXPLORATION.

ASTRONOMY. Interest centered on both the closest celestial object, the moon, and what seem to be the most distant objects, the quasars.

The first series of pictures taken from the surface of the moon were transmitted by a Russian spacecraft, Luna IX. Launched from the earth on Jan. 31, 1966, Luna IX landed on the moon on February 3. On June 3, the U.S. spacecraft Surveyor I also landed successfully on the lunar surface, a few miles from the crater Flamsteed and about 500 miles from the Luna IX landing point. Surveyor I relayed a series of excellent photographs that gave the surface area the appearance of a "freshly turned field" with rocks and pebbles everywhere.

Two Lunar Orbiters were also launched, the first on August 10 and the second on November 6. Both took pictures of the unseen side of the moon. See SPACE EXPLORATION.

Quasars. The combination of enormous energy output, relatively small size, and apparent remoteness made *quasars* (quasi-stellar radio sources) one of the most widely discussed subjects in astronomy in 1966. Quasars emit energy in the form of light and radio waves equivalent to the total energy given off by millions of stars, or even by entire galaxies. Yet they appear to be so small as to be almost indistinguishable from stars.

The central region of a quasar is probably 100,-000,000 to several tens of billions of times as dense as the sun, and emits a great amount of radiation in the blue, or short wave length, end of the spectrum. This central region may fluctuate in brightness over a few months or years. It is apparently surrounded by an envelope of tenuous material that spreads over a distance of millions of light-years.

All the quasars seem to be moving away from our Milky Way galaxy at a tremendous speed. The evidence for this is inferred from their spectra, which show that the light they emit is shifted in wave length toward the red, or long wave length, end of the spectrum. The effect is analogous to the lowering pitch of an automobile horn when the automobile is rapidly receding from the listener. Because of their red shift, quasars seem to be receding faster than any other object in the universe.

Not all astronomers agree that this red shift is caused by the speed at which quasars are moving away from us, in some cases at a velocity of up to 80 per cent of the speed of light. The red shift could also be caused by extremely strong gravitational fields around the quasars, or by material rapidly collapsing toward the center of the quasar. It is possible, too, that the shift may also have some unknown origin.

In March, it was reported that Halton C. Arp of the Mount Wilson and Palomar Observatories had found evidence which indicated that radio sources, including several quasars, tend to be in the vicinity of certain unusual-looking galaxies, called "peculiar galaxies." This would mean that quasars are not at the farthest reaches of the universe, as had been assumed. He suggested that the quasars were ejected from these galaxies. If this were true, then the distances of the quasars and the peculiar galaxies from the earth probably would be comparable, only 30,000,000 to 300,000,000 light-years distant.

Quasi-stellar blue objects, related to quasars but which do not emit radio waves, were studied by Sidney Van Den Bergh of the David Dunlap Observatory at Richmond Hill, Ontario, Canada. These objects were first discovered by Allan Sandage of the Mount Wilson and Palomar Observatories in 1965. Van Den Bergh reported that he carefully searched a small part of the sky and counted all the quasi-stellar blue objects he could detect inside that selected area. He counted 33. From this, he calculated that the total number that could be detected over the entire sky would be about 400,000. Though the number may seem large, it is but a small fraction of the billions upon billions of stars and other luminous objects in the universe.

Hydrogen Clouds. S. Y. Meng of the radio telescope observatory at Ohio State University reported that a team of astronomers at the observatory's 26-foot radio telescope, located near Delaware, Ohio, had found huge clouds of gaseous hydrogen traveling toward the center of our Milky Way from all directions, at speeds of up to 500,000 mph. The

In August, the Lunar Orbiter spacecraft took the first photograph of the earth from vicinity of the moon (239,000 miles away).

clouds are composed of neutral hydrogen. The discovery showed for the first time that such clouds cover a large portion of the sky and are not restricted to certain areas as had been previously believed.

Neutral hydrogen consists of complete hydrogen atoms, whereas ionized hydrogen consists of charged atomic fragments of hydrogen. Both types are found separately in the universe in large clouds of gas.

Meng suggested that the neutral hydrogen clouds may be returning to the Milky Way after being ejected from it approximately 1,000,000 years ago.

Neutral Helium. Radio waves emitted by helium in the Milky Way have been detected by radio astronomers at Harvard University. The discovery confirms the prediction made in 1959 by Russian astronomer N. S. Kardashev that neutral helium atoms in interstellar space would emit certain radio waves as they changed from one highly excited electron state to another.

The discovery was considered important because the relative abundance of helium in the universe can now be measured and compared with the known abundance of hydrogen. This will help scientists to determine how the universe originated, how it is evolving, and how stars are born. Preliminary estimates of the ratio of hydrogen to helium were found to be about 10 to 1, as theory predicted.

X-Ray Source. Scientists at the Naval Research Laboratory's E. O. Hulbert Center for Space Research in Washington, D.C., determined that the strongest known source of X rays in the heavens is most probably a neutron star. This source, called Scorpius XR-1, is relatively close to the earth. It is theoretically about 10 miles in diameter and has a density so great that a cubic inch of its matter weighs 1,000,000,000 tons. The star is surrounded by clouds of material at a temperature of almost 100,000,000° F.

Unseen Companion. Peter van de Kamp, director of the Sproul Observatory at Swarthmore College, Swarthmore, Pa., has identified a fourth star having either a large planet or an extremely small star as an invisible companion. The three stars previously found to have unseen companions were also discovered at the Swarthmore observatory.

The new unseen companion revolves around a star named DB plus five degrees 1668. It is about 13 light-years from the earth. Unseen objects circling a star can be detected only by measuring the amount of wavering they produce in the motion of the star. The new unseen companion appears to have a mass about twice that of Jupiter.

Solar Eclipse. One of the most comprehensive studies of an eclipse took place on November 12, and involved 800 scientists and technicians and some $90,000,000 worth of equipment. The path of the total solar eclipse began in the Pacific Ocean, west of the Galápagos Islands, and passed southward to Peru. It also swept across western Bolivia, northern Argentina, southern Brazil, and into the Atlantic Ocean, where it ended south of Africa.

Rockets, high altitude laboratory airplanes, ships, balloons, a satellite, and ground stations were all used to gather data that was likely to be useful in radio communication, space travel, and weather prediction, as well as in knowledge of the solar forces and their effects on the earth's atmosphere.

Meteor Shower. The most spectacular celestial fireworks of the 20th century were observed in the early morning hours of November 18 over the southwestern United States. Clouds covering most of the rest of the United States and Europe prevented people elsewhere from seeing the spectacular display. The meteor shower was apparently caused by icy comet fragments that are in an elongated orbit around the sun. Each November, the earth passes through this orbit and some of the meteors plunge into the earth's upper atmosphere. Only occasionally, however, do the showers occur as spectacularly as they did in 1966. The phenomenon is known as the Leonid shower since the meteors appear to come from a point near the constellation Leo.

Astronomical Observatory. The United States launched an astronomical satellite, OAO-1, on April 9, but it failed to operate as planned. The observatory was reportedly the heaviest and most complicated unmanned spacecraft ever sent aloft by the United States. ROBERT I. JOHNSON

ATLANTA experienced not only growth in 1966, but also the turmoil of unrest for the first time in 60 years. On September 6, Negroes from the Summerhill district rioted after a detective wounded a fleeing Negro suspected of having stolen a car. Mayor Ivan Allen, Jr., rushed to the scene and climbed atop a police car to speak to the crowd but was toppled from his perch. The mayor was shaken but unhurt. Stokely Carmichael, youthful Negro leader of the Student Nonviolent Co-ordinating Committee (SNCC), was accused of helping foment the disturbance. Riots broke out again on the night of September 11, after a white motorist shot and killed a Negro youth who was standing with friends on a sidewalk. Mayor Allen offered a $10,000 reward for information on the killer.

Despite tight money and a carpenters' union strike, construction activity in 1966 set another record. At least six buildings of 21 stories were rising, and the 41-story First National Bank Building was nearly completed. Also, ground was broken on June 3 for a cultural center to be built as a memorial to the 106 art patrons who lost their lives in a Paris plane crash on June 3, 1962. In the planning stage was an 18-story devlopment called Park Place/Atlanta, which will be a $200,000,000 complex of offices, stores, apartments, and restaurants. It will rise in the shadow of the capitol and transform railroad property into a platform-city. DONALD W. LIEF

ATOMIC ENERGY. The year 1966 saw the arrival of commercial nuclear power on a broad scale. Orders for atomic reactors almost tripled those placed by utility companies during 1965, considered a banner year for nuclear power.

The 23 reactors ordered during the first 11 months of 1966 were accompanied by commitments and options for five more. Adding this to the 1965 total of eight, the new reactor orders brought the two-year total to 36 reactors capable of generating 28,059 megawatts by 1971. Though this megawattage accounted for only a small percentage of the nation's estimated total generating capability in 1971, it represented more than 50 per cent of all new large-plant generating stations ordered or committed during 1965-1966. Large-plant stations are units of 400 megawatts or more.

In December, the Atomic Energy Commission (AEC) announced the selection of Weston, Ill., west of Chicago, as the site for the world's largest atom smasher. See SCIENCE AND RESEARCH.

Uranium. An assessment of both U.S. uranium enrichment facilities and uranium ore deposits accompanied the upsurge in commitments to nuclear power generation. On the basis of the AEC's most recent forecasts of domestic requirements and estimates of present reserves, the mining industry has an 11-year supply of uranium ore on hand, according to Dean A. McGee, president of Kerr-McGee Corporation, one of the two largest producers of domestic uranium.

Breeder Reactors, dominating the horizon of advanced reactor concepts, received increased research and development in 1966. The breeder reactor is considered essential to the future of nuclear energy because it converts nonfissionable U-238 into fissionable plutonium, thus producing more fuel than it uses. As yet, the use of plutonium as fuel has been demonstrated only in experimental reactors, though it is a by-product of all uranium-fueled reactors and will provide a $1,000,000,000 stockpile of atomic fuel by 1980, according to officials of Westinghouse Electric Corporation.

Fusion Research. The United States is lagging in efforts to harness thermonuclear fusion, according to a report drafted in July by eight top scientists for the AEC. Thermonuclear fusion occurs in hydrogen bombs–the fusion of atoms of heavy hydrogen with a tremendous release of energy. The control of such thermonuclear reactions would provide man a virtually inexhaustible supply of energy, since heavy hydrogen is present in the oceans in quantities that would last billions of years. U.S. outlays for fusion research have declined since 1960, and are now insufficient to provide the necessary equipment and scientific talent to stay abreast of

Nuclear Electrical Power Comes of Age

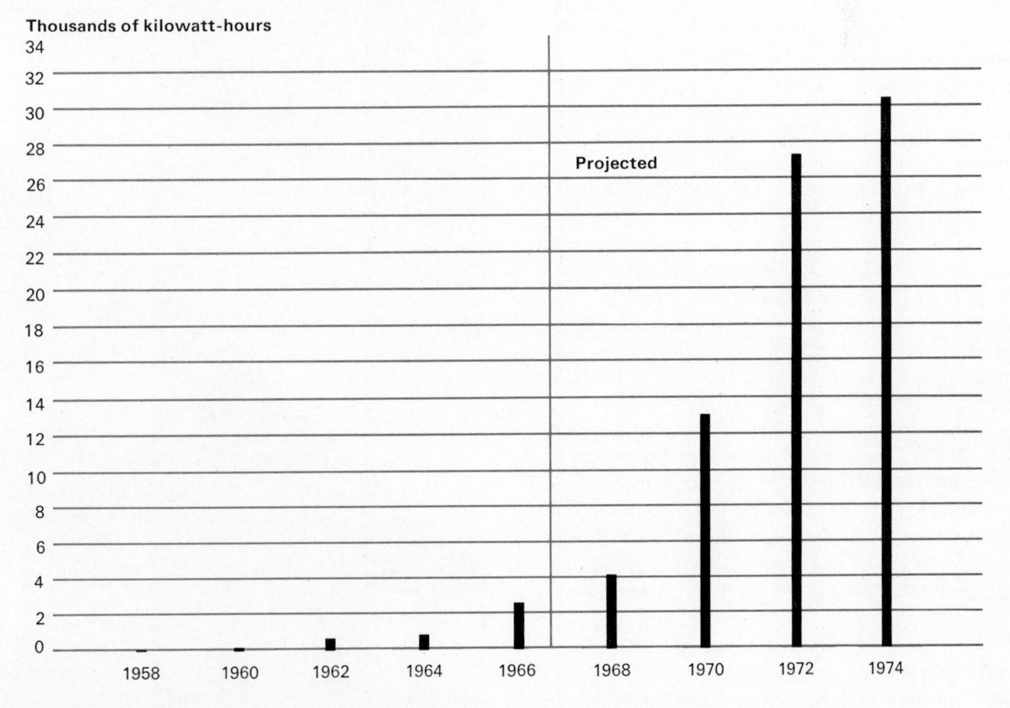

Source: Atomic Energy Commission

the field, the report said. By contrast, Russia, Great Britain, West Germany, and France have forged ahead with new facilities and research personnel. The panel recommended a 15 per cent annual increase in operating funds over the present $22,000,000 yearly budget, plus $3,000,000 to $4,000,000 more per year for building new experimental devices.

Desalination. In 1966, the Metropolitan Water District of Southern California and three utility companies embarked on a major project for desalting seawater as an auxiliary function of large nuclear power reactors. They plan to construct two giant reactors on a man-made island off Bolsa Chica Beach State Park near Los Angeles, Calif. These will each produce 900 megawatts of electric power and desalt 150,000,000 gallons of water per day. The first of the two units is to be completed in 1970 and the second is to be ready in 1977. The project will be subsidized by the U.S. Department of the Interior and the AEC. See CONSERVATION.

Appointments. The appointments of Samuel N. Nabrit and Wilfrid E. Johnson to the AEC ended speculation that the commission might be permitted to dwindle to a one-man body, and brought the AEC back to its five-seat complement. The appointees joined incumbent members James T. Ramey, Gerald F. Tape, and Chairman Glenn T. Seaborg just as the AEC reached its 20th anniversary on August 1. The commission was created by the Atomic Energy Act of 1946. Nabrit, an educator and administrator for more than 20 years, came to the AEC from Texas Southern University. Johnson had spent 17 years with General Electric's atomic energy facility at Hanford, Wash.

Awards. The Enrico Fermi Award of $50,000 was given to three internationally distinguished European nuclear scientists. The recipients were Professor Otto Hahn of Göttingen, West Germany; Professor Lise Meitner of Cambridge, England; and Professor Fritz Strassmann of Mainz, West Germany. The three were chosen for their combined and individual efforts in discovering nuclear fission and for their extensive experimental work.

Missing Bombs. Two U.S. Air Force planes collided on Jan. 17, 1966, while refueling in the air near Palomares Beach on the coast of Spain. The collision caused two hydrogen bombs to burst open and spread plutonium over the beach and nearby tomato fields. Two other bombs were recovered intact, one of these from the Mediterranean Sea.

To relieve the fears of Spanish fishermen and farmers, AEC officials ordered the mildly contaminated soil to be packed in steel drums and shipped to the United States. JAMES A. PEARRE

AUSTRALIA

The two-party coalition government of Australia's Prime Minister Harold E. Holt won another term of office in the general elections held on November 26. The election results were seen as a national endorsement of the government's policy of sending combat troops to Vietnam and a repudiation of the Labor party's opposition to such a policy. The election victory was also considered a mandate to the Holt government for closer cooperation with the United States.

Shilling-and-pence cash registers are being converted to accommodate Australia's switch to a dollars-and-cents currency.

Decimal Currency. Holt, a former federal treasurer, had been named prime minister by Governor-General Lord Richard Gardiner Casey following the resignation of Sir Robert Gordon Menzies in January (see HOLT, HAROLD E.). Shortly after taking his post, he presided over one of the most complex transactions in Australia's history – a changeover from the pounds-and-pence system to a dollars-and-cents currency. The switch, which had been planned for three years, had been prepared for extensively throughout 1965.

To help businesses convert their office machines to the decimal system, the government had provided a drawing fund of $60,000,000. In addition, $10,000,000 was spent on printing and stamping out the new money, one dollar of which was worth $1.13 in United States currency.

Economic Boom. Australia's switch to a new currency was symbolic of the change that was sweeping through the economy in general. Where the nation's prosperity had once been dependent largely on agriculture, it was now veering sharply to dependence on mineral wealth. In fact, mining and industry were threatening to outstrip the old standby, wool, as the country's main source of revenue.

The oil and gas industries, in particular, were enjoying an upsurge. In January, the nation's second commercial oil field – at Alton, Queensland – came into production and for the first time Australia's commercial crude oil output exceeded 10,000 bar-

Sail-like structural shells will form the roof of a new opera house that is being built near harbor bridge at Sydney, Australia.

rels a day. In March, a third oil field with commercial potential was discovered in the Bass Strait between Victoria and Tasmania. Yet another oil strike was made on Barrow Island, 40 miles off northwest Australia in June. The Bass Strait field was especially important because of its proximity to Melbourne and the heavily industrialized southeast corner of Australia.

Iron ore–once considered the country's scarcest resource–was being exported in large quantities, some 15,000,000 tons of it having been found in western Australia alone. In October, a trade agreement was signed with Japan. It provided for shipment over a 15-year period of 100,000,000 tons of iron ore worth approximately $896,000,000 from deposits at Mount Newman.

Bauxite and coal, too, were being mined at an increased rate. Foreign investments were pouring in to help produce the two commodities. Among the investors were such companies as Alcoa, Kaiser Aluminum, Mitsui, and Utah Mining and Construction. Altogether, about 1,000 U.S. corporations had interests in either the production or processing of Australia's largely untapped mineral wealth.

Livestock Production–once the nation's chief source of income–was in serious trouble in 1966 because of one of the worst droughts in Australia's history. In June, however, rains brought welcome relief to most of the affected areas.

Hardest hit by the drought were the owners of sheep and cattle stations in the vast back country. In New South Wales, the worst hit state, 11,800,000 sheep and lambs, 117,000 dairy cattle, and 860,000 beef cattle were lost. Drought losses in southwest Queensland and in central Australia were also severe. As a result, farm income was expected to fall from the $426,720,000 it had earned in 1965 to an estimated $230,680,000 in 1966.

With the help of government loans and relief payments, however, sheep and cattle owners in the stricken area were buying new stock for the long hard pull back to normal production.

Immigration Law Changes. Australia continued to encourage European immigrants in order to meet the labor shortages resulting from the industrial boom. Canberra, the federal capital, alone was employing 1,000 people and spending $40,000,000 a year on its immigration program.

In March, the nation relaxed its laws governing the entry of nonwhites. It announced that regulations for non-Europeans seeking limited residence permits had been eased and that the period of residence for citizenship had been shortened from 15 to five years. It also announced that under certain conditions no quotas would be imposed on Asians with special technical skills.

In August, concern was aroused over a government plan to conscript those immigrants who had

Shorts-clad Harold Holt, Australia's new prime minister, relaxes from the cares of office.

become permanent residents but not citizens. Many opponents of the plan felt that the decision would reduce immigration.

Defense Spending. The 1966-1967 budget provided for defense spending of $1,100,000,000–an increase of $282,200,000 over the previous year's record outlay. A good part of the money was to be spent abroad, especially for U.S.-made military aircraft and guided missiles.

Heavy defense expenditures, along with other allocations and large appropriations for drought relief, produced a budget that showed a record deficit of $496,400,000. The total budget of $6,600,000,000 was $672,000,000 higher than in 1965-1966.

A second space tracking station, established near Canberra by the U.S. National Aeronautics and Space Administration, officially opened on February 24. Construction was delayed, however, on a $74,000,000 U.S. Navy communications base being built on the west coast for Polaris submarines. Disputes over costs had held up work, and completion was not expected until 1967.

Facts in Brief. Population: 11,632,000. Government: Governor-General Lord Richard Gardiner Casey; Prime Minister Harold E. Holt. Monetary Unit: Australian dollar (1 = U.S. $1.13). Foreign Trade: exports, $3,013,900,000; imports, $3,711,-500,000. Principal Exports: wool, iron ore, minerals, meat. PAUL TULLIER

AUSTRIA. For the first time since 1945, the conservative People's party won a parliamentary majority in the national elections held in March. A new, one-party government was formed by Chancellor Josef Klaus, who was also head of the People's party. The new chancellor's action brought to a close an era of coalition with the Socialists which had lasted 21 years.

Economic Prosperity. Despite a balance of payments deficit and a labor shortage, Austria continued to prosper, with agriculture and the tourist trade showing profitable increases. Industry, too, was improving the nation's finances. Much of its success was attributable to technological leadership in the machine tools field and in new steel processes.

In order to maintain this flourishing economy, the government indicated that Austria would make every effort to become linked with the European Economic Community (EEC, or Common Market). Although Austria belonged to the rival European Free Trade Association (EFTA), its trade with the group only accounted for about 20 per cent of its total trade. The major part–more than 50 per cent–was with the Common Market.

The decision to seek closer collaboration with the Common Market was based on Austria's belief that the dynamic growth of the market would be helpful to the country's own development. By implication, Austria's trade with EFTA could not be expanded rapidly enough to meet the country's needs.

Border Problems. A new wave of violence erupted along Austria's border with Italy in September. The attacks were attributed to Austrian-based terrorists whose ultimate aim was the detachment from Italy of the Trentino-Adige region, a predominantly German-speaking area.

The terrorists' object in unleashing the attacks was twofold: (1) to block completion of an accord between Austria and Italy; and (2) to keep the leaders of the province's ethnically German two-thirds majority from working out a large measure of autonomy within the Italian republic.

State Visit. Federal President Franz Jonas paid a five-day official visit to Great Britain in May. Discussions were held regarding the problems Austria faced in seeking EEC membership.

In October, Archduke Otto of Hapsburg, the former claimant to the Austrian throne, visited Innsbruck. It was the archduke's first visit to Austria since the monarchy collapsed in 1919. His visit touched off protest strikes by about 250,000 workers who were opposed to the possibility of his resuming permanent residence in Austria.

Facts in Brief. Population: 7,247,000. Government: President Franz Jonas; Chancellor Josef Klaus. Monetary Unit: schilling (25.78 = U.S. $1). Foreign Trade: exports, $1,599,500,000; imports, $2,100,200,000. Principal Exports: iron and steel, timber, machinery. KENNETH BROWN

AUTOMOBILE. Safety was the main chapter of the automobile story in 1966 as the industry chalked up its second best sales and production year, topped only by record-setting 1965.

Virtually everyone talked about highway safety and the need for cutting down on the nation's traffic toll of about 1,000 deaths a week. Congress, at the request of President Lyndon B. Johnson, moved the federal government into the forefront of the battle.

Congress gave virtually unanimous endorsement to the Johnson-proposed Highway Safety Act of 1966 and the National Traffic and Motor Vehicle Safety Act, both of which the President signed on September 9. At the same time, he named William J. Haddon, Jr., as the National Highway Safety Agency's first administrator.

Auto Sales, which started out strong in the opening quarter of 1966, eased off in April just about the time maximum attention was focused on congressional auto safety hearings and on attorney-author Ralph Nader, whose book, *Unsafe at Any Speed*, sharply criticized the automobile industry as indifferent to the safeness of its cars.

Indications were that new car sales in the United States in 1966 would total about 9,000,000 units, including a record-breaking 640,000 imports. This would be about 300,000 cars short of the 9,332,945 cars (including 569,415 imports) sold in 1965.

Some auto industry leaders contended that overemphasis on the auto safety issue had scared some potential buyers out of the market. Other reasons listed for the sales drop were the war in Vietnam–which took thousands of young potential car buyers into military service–and tighter credit restrictions that made installment loans harder to get. Also in April, the 7 per cent federal excise tax was reimposed; it had dropped to 6 per cent on Jan. 1, 1966.

Even though car buyers bought fewer cars, they spent almost as much on them as they did in 1965. They were "trading up" and buying more extras. Cars with a list price above $2,500 accounted for 60 per cent of U.S. output in the first half of 1966, up from 52 per cent in the year-earlier period. In 1961, when the trend to higher priced cars started, the percentage figure was only 32. More than 29 per cent of the new cars produced in the first nine months of the 1966 model year were air-conditioned. Only 23 per cent of the 1965 line was so equipped.

Production. The slight slowdown in sales–in comparison with 1965's red-hot pace–showed up in downward adjustments in production schedules at the four major U.S. auto companies. They were expected to wind up 1966 with assemblies of about 8,600,000 cars, compared with 9,300,000 in 1965.

U.S. bus and truck production was expected to reach about 1,700,000 units, under the record

The 14 Most Frequent Causes of Auto Injury

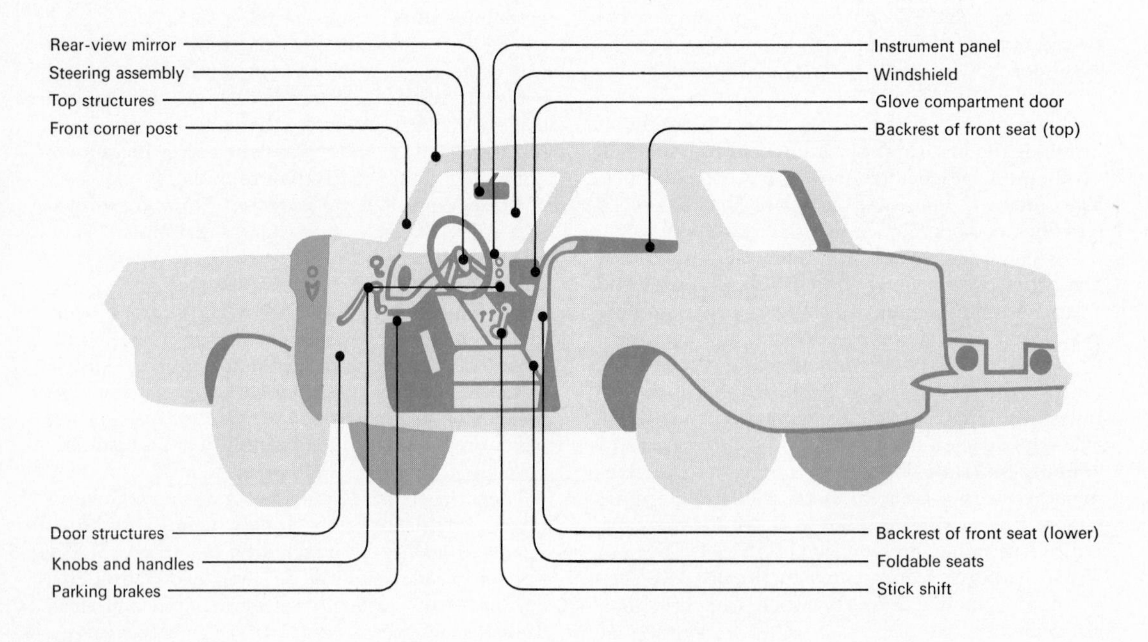

The Road To Safety

Three days after the nation had tallied its grimmest traffic death toll for any Labor Day weekend on record, the first comprehensive federal legislation for automobile and highway safety became law. President Lyndon B. Johnson, in signing the two bills on Sept. 9, 1966, noted that while 29 U.S. servicemen had died in Vietnam on the holiday weekend, "614 Americans died on our highways." He went on to cite the familiar grisly statistics of the "raging epidemic of highway death" and concluded that the two bills "promise . . . to cure the highway disease, to end the years of horror, and give us years of hope."

The next day, a National Safety Council spokesman forecast that the new legislation, when it became fully effective, would save at least 10,000 lives a year. The mandatory safety standards prescribed for U.S. and imported motor vehicles would be the chief lifesaving factor. They would go far to reduce the deaths and injuries caused by the *second collision* – the crash of the passenger against the car's interior that occurs less than a second after the car's initial impact with another object.

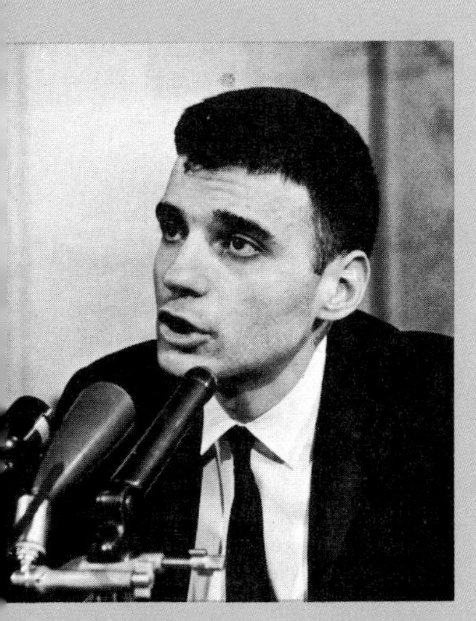

Ralph Nader, crusading auto industry critic, gave impetus to safety bills.

It was the National Traffic and Motor Vehicle Safety Act of 1966 that called for more safety in automotive design and equipment. Its companion bill, the Highway Safety Act of 1966, provided for $267,000,000 in federal grants to states for a coordinated program of highway safety. The Secretary of Commerce would establish uniform standards by Jan. 1, 1969, covering such items as highway design, vehicle inspection, education and licensing of drivers, and accident investigations and reports. States that failed to conform to these uniform standards would be subject to a 10 per cent reduction in federal aid for highway construction.

The first bill aimed at the car itself. It directed the Secretary of Commerce to devise safety standards for all new motor vehicles, including trucks and buses, by Jan. 31, 1967. They would take effect Jan. 31, 1968, by which date the Secretary would issue a revised list. The new standards would become effective six months to a year later. They would be based on research and testing authorized under the act.

The Motor Vehicle Safety Act also provided for:

- A National Traffic Safety Agency, under the Department of Commerce, to administer the act. The President immediately appointed Dr. William J. Haddon, Jr., a widely recognized safety expert, as administrator.
- Minimum safety standards for used cars by Sept. 9, 1967.
- Tire safety standards, to take effect before Jan. 31, 1968, and a uniform tire-quality grading system by Sept. 9, 1969.
- Notification to car buyers by manufacturers of any safety defects discovered after sale of the vehicle.
- Civil penalties of $1,000 for each violation of the act. However, it put on a $400,000 ceiling for any related series of violations.

The act leaves the spelling out of standards to the Secretary of Commerce. It was expected he would follow most or all of the 26 standards that the General Services Administration (GSA) adopted for the federal government's purchases of 1968 model cars. The first 17 of those standards took effect on GSA purchases of 1967 models. Among the less routine of the safety requirements were: anchorages for shoulder belts and seats, recessed control knobs, collapsible steering column, safety door latches and hinges, four-way flashers, dual brakes, standard bumper heights, uniform gearshift pattern, smog-control devices, and safety standards for tires and rims.

The remaining nine GSA standards applied to U.S. purchases of 1968 model vehicles. They included more extensive padding and recessing inside the car, turn signals visible from the side, rear window defoggers, and nonrupturing fuel tanks and pipes.

The carmakers feared the new safety standards would upset production schedules. On the 1967 models, however, the industry proved itself surprisingly adaptable. The collapsible steering column became standard. A year earlier, General Motors Corporation had said it was at least two years away. Detroit – which for years had insisted that "Safety doesn't sell" – was selling safety. Robert A. Irwin

"It's part of our new safety campaign."

1,802,603 assembled in 1965. The combined truck and passenger car output for 1966 came to about 10,370,000 units. World-wide, car and truck production in 1966 was estimated at 22,000,000 units, compared with about 23,000,000 in 1965.

In some other segments of the world auto market, Canada and notably Britain, motor vehicle production was trimmed in 1966. Britain, in retrenching its home economy to bolster its exports, tightened credit on purchases of cars. Higher down payments with shorter repayment periods, as well as a higher sales tax, effectively reduced sales. Britain's position as the world's No. 3 auto producer was challenged by Japan, whose output of cars and trucks was expected to total 2,200,000 units in 1966.

The 1967 Line. The U.S. auto companies offered 367 basic 1967 models, with scores of options. The two major sales themes were safety and sportiness.

Ford, which jumped into an early lead in the personalized, sporty car field with the Mustang two years ago, found itself with a bevy of challengers. One came from within its own family–Lincoln-Mercury's Cougar. Chevrolet came up with its Camaro, and Chrysler-Plymouth jazzed up and enlarged its Barracuda line, as it made a determined bid for a piece of the sporty car market, estimated at 1,000,000 units a year.

Prices ranged from $2,073 for a Rambler American 220 to $10,571 for a Cadillac Seventy-Five limousine. The design trend was toward a long hood, a short deck, and low and sleek profiles.

The 1967 models bore higher price tags. General Motors (GM) put its average increase at $54 a car. Chrysler estimated its at $64; Ford, $66; and American Motors, $67. Ford and Chrysler originally had announced larger price hikes, but trimmed them after GM's announcement of smaller figures.

The U.S. Bureau of Labor Statistics (BLS) backed up the industry's contention that most of the price increase stemmed from the inclusion of former optional safety features as standard equipment. The BLS said that after allowances for quality changes, the 1967 prices averaged only two-tenths of one per cent over those of the 1966 models. Prices that consumers actually paid for cars in 1966 were the lowest since 1957, according to the BLS. The Consumer Price Index for new cars in August, 1966, stood at 95.8 (1957-1959=100). For foods, it was 115.8.

Safety improvements of several types were made on the 1967 models. For the 1968 models–both U.S. and foreign–the safety act required the federal government to issue safety standards by Jan. 31, 1967. On December 1, U.S. Safety Administrator Haddon published a list of 23 requirements for the 1968 models. The automakers were given 30 days to present their countersuggestions.

The proposed standards differed somewhat from those set by the federal government on the cars it purchased. Not included in the new list were rear-window defoggers, standard bumper heights, and roll bars on Jeep-type vehicles. Added to the list were windshield defoggers and generally more stringent requirements for the car's interior: padding, recessing of knobs, and seat anchorage.

New Car Warranties were expanded and improved in 1966. For the first time, all four major car firms were guaranteeing the power train–engine, transmission, and rear axle–for five years or 50,000 miles, whichever came first. Chrysler–the first with such a warranty–and its three competitors extended it to the suspension and steering systems. All four companies guaranteed all the rest of the car except tires, upholstery, and some trim items for two years or 24,000 miles.

The Electric Car emerged on the automotive horizon in 1966. It was still years away from making an appearance in the showrooms, however. In September, Ford disclosed a laboratory model of a sodium-sulfur battery, 15 times lighter than the conventional lead variety. Company engineers said they would need at least two more years to develop a prototype car (see ENGINE AND ENERGY). In October, GM demonstrated two experimental electric vehicles. One, a Corvair, was powered by heavy, expensive ($15,000) silver-zinc batteries. The other, a small truck, was driven by hydrogen-oxygen fuel cells. Both had short ranges of from 40 to 150 miles.

CHARLES C. CAIN III

Wheels fly in all directions as cars pile up at beginning of the Indianapolis 500. Fortunately, no drivers were seriously injured.

AUTOMOBILE RACING. Jack Brabham, the Australian who won the World Grand Prix Drivers' championship in 1959 and 1960 with a Cooper-Climax car, captured the 1966 championship driving a Brabham-Repco designed and manufactured largely by himself. John Surtees of England, the 1964 champion, was second, driving a Ferrari. Third was Jochen Rindt of Austria in a Maserati-Cooper.

At the Indianapolis 500 on May 30, Jim Clark of Scotland just failed to repeat his 1965 victory, finishing a close second to Graham Hill of England. Hill, in a Lola-Ford, took the lead from Scot Jacky Stewart with only 10 laps to go. The event was marred by a first-lap crash involving 16 of the 33 cars in the race, but no one was seriously injured.

Surtees won the new Canadian-American Challenge Cup after winning three of the series of six approximately 200-mile races held on courses as far apart as St. Jovite, Quebec, and Riverside, Calif.

In the manufacturers' endurance contests, Ford became the first U.S. company ever to win the championship. Ford also had success in other racing categories. Mario Andretti of Nazareth, Pa., won his second U.S. Auto Club driving championship in a rear-engine Ford racer, and Charles Parsons of Carmel, Calif., won the U.S. road-racing title in a McLaren-Ford. In stock car racing, Richard Petty of Randleman, N.C., was the leading driver in a 1966 Plymouth.

JAMES O. DUNAWAY

AVIATION. The year 1966 may well be the year in which the Vertical Take-Off and Landing (VTOL) and the Short Take-Off and Landing (STOL) aircraft came of age. Helicopters with speeds of 200 mph to 400 mph, carrying 100 passengers, were in sight. Advanced design, 400 mph VTOLs were planned. Range was increasing, maintenance was becoming less costly, and more central-location heliports were being established. Jet engines were providing STOLs extra power for take-off and for higher cruising speeds. Some used rotor blades that fold in level flight.

The 17 manufacturers of VTOLs were seeking broader markets. Some concentrated on more efficient small utility-type helicopters; others were developing transport types. All based their optimism on the versatility of both the VTOL and STOL types of aircraft.

In a disaster test air exercise in New York City in November, a number of STOLs showed their capabilities. One landed on a 40-foot stretch of a Hudson River pier. Another, a 47-passenger De Havilland Buffalo, landed and took off using only 300 feet of a parking lot near the foot of Wall Street.

Airlines. A 43-day strike, from July 8 to August 19, halted what had started to be a record-breaking year for the five affected airlines–Trans World Airlines (TWA), Eastern, National, Northwest, and United. The walkout cost the industry more than

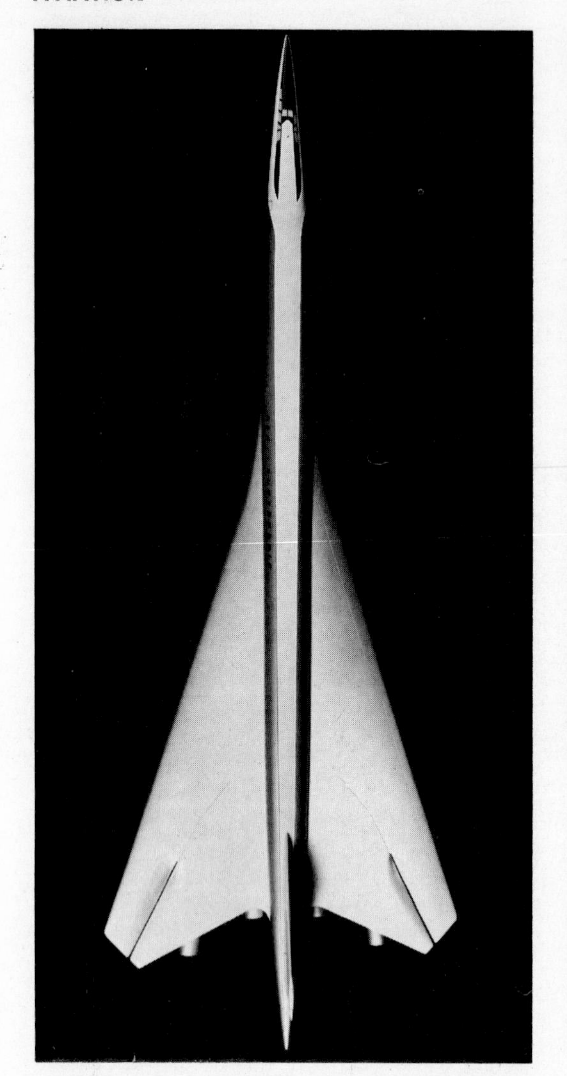

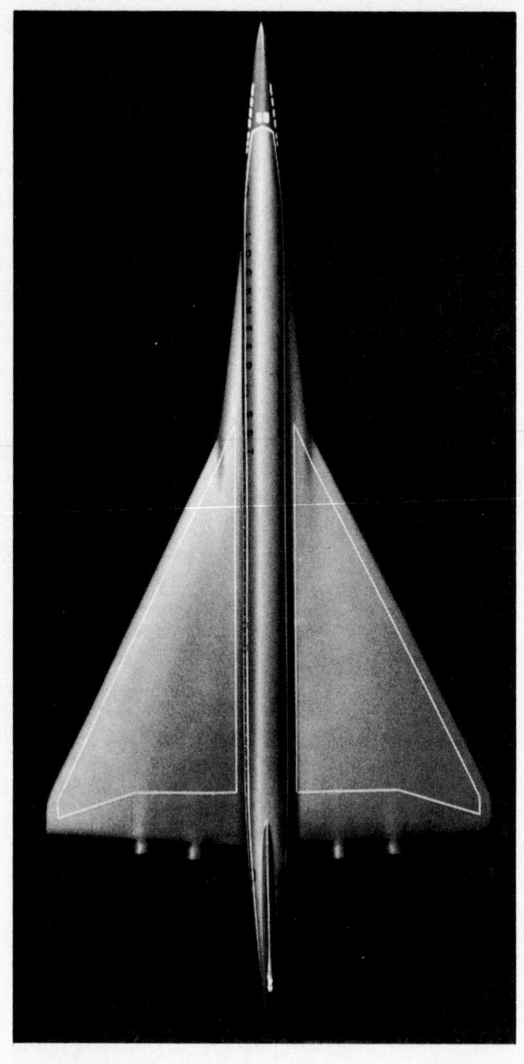

Boeing's variable sweep-wing model, *left,* won out against Lockheed's fixed, double-delta wing entry, *right,* as the U.S. choice for a supersonic transport—which may be flying the route, *below,* by 1974.

To Paris in Two Hours–by 1974

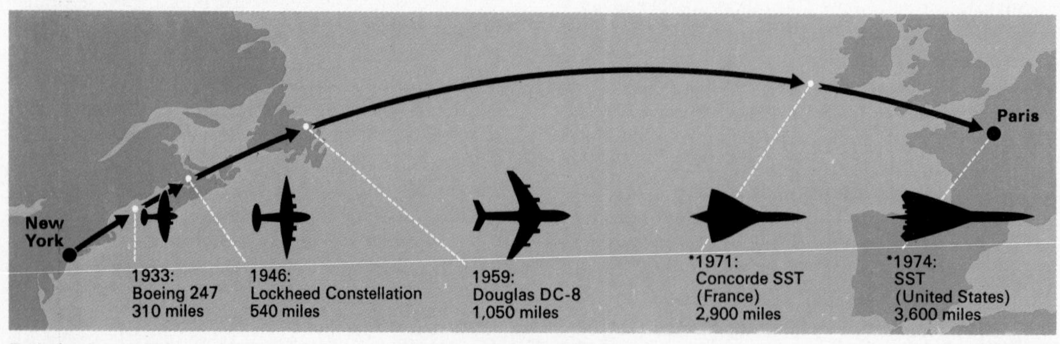

Typical two-hour flights, past, present, and future, compared on Great Circle Route

*estimate

$5,000,000 a day in lost passenger revenues. By year's end, all five lines were doing well again.

For the industry as a whole, the expansive pace of the previous year was maintained. Passenger-miles flown by U.S. scheduled airlines rose 17.4 per cent during 1965 to a total of 68,676,547,000. Net operating profits went up 42.9 per cent to $672,-467,000. World-wide, airline operating profits increased 37 per cent to $850,000,000 in 1965.

Supersonic Transport (SST) progress continued. The Russians announced late in May that they were entering the SST race. Their TU-144 will have a speed of 1,550 mph and a range of 4,000 miles–about the same as the British-French *Concorde*. Both are expected to be in service about 1971. Orders for the $16,000,000 *Concorde* were still about 10 below the break-even point of 70 aircraft.

The U.S. SST was not expected to be in service until 1974. About 100 have been ordered at an estimated price of $35,000,000 each, with 250 the break-even point from the standpoint of profits. President Lyndon B. Johnson was to decide between two competing designs by the end of 1966. Each would have a range of 4,000 miles at a cruising speed of 1,800 mph. The Boeing Company's design incorporating a movable wing–swept back for supersonic flight and extended for slower speeds–and with a capacity of about 350 passengers, won out. The President made his decision December 31. The losing Lockheed Corporation design utilized a fixed double-delta wing and seated about 275 passengers.

The Jumbo Jets. In April, as Boeing was rounding out its first 50 years in the aircraft business, it announced its first order for the B-747, a jumbo jet capable of carrying 490 persons. Pan American World Airways, Inc., placed the $525,000,000 order, with deliveries for the 25 jets to start in 1969. TWA ordered 12 in September. Other orders followed.

Orders were also being placed for a "stretched" version of Douglas Aircraft Company's DC-8. The new DC-8-60 will seat 250, or about 60 more passengers than the DC-8. Convertible passenger-freight airplanes, such as the Boeing 727-QC and the Lockheed Hercules, also were on 1966 order-books. The Air Transport Association predicted that 5,200,000,000 ton-miles of freight will move by air in 1970, against 1,700,000,000 ton-miles in 1965.

Government Activities. Thirty-one government agencies were consolidated into the new Department of Transportation late in the year (see TRANSPORTATION). The Federal Aviation Agency (FAA) was renamed the Federal Aviation Administration and became the dominant operating agency in the new department.

In the year ended June 30, 1966, the FAA issued 211,153 airman certificates. This was an increase of 25 per cent over 1965. Of these, 116,354 were student pilot certificates and 6,369 were air transport pilot certificates.

Under a new rule, the FAA declared any structure more than 2,000 feet above ground level a hazard to air navigation and an inefficient utilization of air space. Henceforth, any such installation must be proved efficient.

General Aviation flying, which includes all but military and airline operations, continued to expand. Landings and take-offs at the 303 airports with FAA control towers rose 27 per cent in the year. General aviation aircraft sales were up about 20 per cent for the second consecutive year, totaling nearly 16,000 aircraft with an average selling price of about $40,000 each. The top sellers were three Cessnas–the 150, 172, and 182–and the Piper Cherokee.

A new FAA study forecast a surge in the growth of general aviation by 1975. Its projections showed a fleet of 160,000 general aviation aircraft flying 30,000,000 hours, compared with 88,742 aircraft flying 15,700,000 hours in 1964. General aviation aircraft were expected to remain powered mostly by piston engines, although supercharging, range, and speed will increase. The number of turbine-engine aircraft will rise from 306 in 1964 to about 4,000 by 1975 and rotocraft from 1,306 to about 3,000.

In fiscal 1966, the FAA reported that general aviation pilots flew a record 2,600,000,000 miles in 16,700,000 hours with 95,442 aircraft. They also achieved their lowest fatal accident rate in history–one death for every 5,000,000 miles flown.

Airports. Flying activities at FAA control-tower airports broke all records. Landings and take-offs exceeded 45,000,000, a 19 per cent increase from fiscal 1965. In April, the FAA reported that as of Jan. 1, 1966, the total number of U.S. airports had risen to 9,566, a gain of 76 in a year.

The state of Ohio started a county airport investment program of $5,000,000. These airports are expected to draw as much as $2,000,000,000 in new industrial developments into the state. The program's goal is to assure each county of an airport of adequate size to handle all present-day aircraft, except executive jets or larger aircraft. Each county would receive a grant of not more than $100,000.

Chicago-O'Hare International Airport, the world's busiest airport, set a new single-day record on Sept. 9, 1966, when 2,006 landings and take-offs were recorded. Also, a new 24-hour record was set by handling 78,155 passengers. Fiscal 1966 take-offs and landings at O'Hare totaled 553,093.

Based on an FAA study of 1965 operations, delays at major U.S. airports cost the nation's aircraft operators an estimated $63,600,000. Airlines incurred 64.7 per cent of the total cost. The delays were attributed to air traffic control procedures, airport limitations, and weather conditions.

Work began on the development of two major Australian airports under a five-year program calling for the expenditure of $40,000,000 at Melbourne and $46,000,000 at Sydney.

AVIATION

International Air Transportation continued to make gains in 1966. Load factors increased slightly, and the financial results for the industry as a whole were better. Newly ordered equipment increased capacity. At the end of the year, International Air Transport Association (IATA) members were operating about 1,625 jets, with another 625 on order. During the first six months of 1966 the number of passengers on the heavily traveled North Atlantic Route totaled 1,761,122, an increase of 19.2 per cent from the year-earlier period.

In November, the United States and the Soviet Union signed an agreement to establish the first direct air service between New York and Moscow. Pan American and Russia's Aeroflot, the world's largest airline, were expected to begin flights in the spring of 1967, each with one round trip a week. Earlier, in July, Canada and the Soviets agreed to weekly air service between the two countries. An Air Canada DC-8 made the first flight from Montreal to Moscow on November 1. Three days later, an Aeroflot TU-114 made the reverse flight.

Pan American-Grace Airways, Inc. (Panagra), sold to Braniff International Airways in October, strengthened U.S. air routes to South America.

Noteworthy Flights. A Lear Jet Model 24 made an around-the-world flight, leaving Wichita, Kans., May 23 and returning May 26 with an elapsed time of 65 hours 39 minutes, and a total flight time of 50 hours 19 minutes. The distance flown was 22,992.9 statute miles. Pilots were John Lear, Rick King, and Henry Beaird. Average speed was 350.24 mph, and 18 records were set.

Sheilah Scott of Great Britain flew 29,055 solo miles around the world in a Piper Comanche, leaving London on May 18 and returning on June 20. She averaged 177 mph in flight, establishing 12 intercity records.

In July, Bernice Steadman, with Mary Clark as copilot, won the 20th Annual All-Woman's Transcontinental Air Race (Powder Puff Derby), from Seattle, Wash., to Clearwater, Fla.

Aviation Trophy and Award winners in 1966:

American Institute of Aeronautics and Astronautics Goddard Award to Hans J. P. von Ohain, A. W. Blackman, and George D. Lewis for their contributions to aircraft jet propulsion.

Frank G. Brewer Trophy to Mrs. Jane N. Marshall for her contributions as an editor and writer.

Robert J. Collier Trophy to James E. Webb, administrator of the National Aeronautics and Space Administration (NASA), and the late Hugh L. Dryden, former deputy administrator of NASA, for their contributions to human experiences in space flight.

Wright Brothers Memorial Trophy to Juan T. Trippe, chairman of Pan American Airways, for promoting international air commerce and good will.

Eugene M. Zuckert Award to General Bernard A. Schriever for outstanding contributions to air force professionalism.

LESLIE A. BRYAN

See also ARMED FORCES OF THE WORLD; DISASTERS; NATIONAL DEFENSE; SPACE EXPLORATION.

AWARDS AND PRIZES presented in 1966 included the following:

GENERAL AWARDS

Academy of American Poets Awards. *Fellowship*, for distinguished poetic achievement, to Archibald MacLeish. *Lamont Award* to Kenneth O. Hanson of the Reed College faculty for his first book of poems *The Distance Anywhere.*

American Academy of Arts and Letters and National Institute of Arts and Letters Awards. *Gold Medals* to Jacques Lipchitz, sculptor, and Virgil Thomson, composer. *Arnold W. Brunner Award in Architecture* to Romaldo Giurgola. *Majorie Peabody Waite Award*, for continuing integrity in his work, to Harry Partch, composer. *Rosenthal Foundation Awards* to painter Howard Hack, and Tom Cole for his first novel, *An End to Chivalry. Russell Loines Award in Poetry* to William Meredith. *Awards in Art* to Romare H. Bearden, Lee Bontecou, Carroll Cloar, Ray Johnson, Ezio Martinelli, Karl Schrag, and Richard C. Ziemann. *Awards in Literature* to poet-playwright William Alfred; novelists John Barth, Shirley Hazzard, and Josephine Herbst; poets James Dickey, Edwin Honig, and Gary Snyder; and poet-playwright M. B. Tolson. *Awards in Music* to Walter Aschaffenburg, Richard Hoffman, John MacIvor Perkins, and Ralph Shapey.

American Academy of Arts and Sciences Emerson-Thoreau Medal to Edmund Wilson, writer and literary and social critic.

American Institute of Architects Gold Medal to Kenzo Tange, designer of the Peace Memorial Hall and Museum in Hiroshima, the Olympics buildings in Tokyo, and other buildings in Japan.

Anisfield-Wolf Awards by the *Saturday Review*, for books that deal most creditably with race-relations problems, to Claude Brown for *Manchild in the Promised Land; The Autobiography of Malcolm X*, published by Grove Press; Amram Scheinfeld for *Your Heredity and Environment;* and H. C. Baldry of England for *The Unity of Mankind in Greek Thought.*

Aspen Institute for Humanistic Studies Award to Constantinos Doxiadis, architect who has designed communities in Greece, Iraq, Jordan, Lebanon, Pakistan, Syria, and the United States.

Brandeis University Awards. *Creative Arts Awards* to actress Eva LeGallienne, author Eudora Welty, sculptor Isamu Noguchi, and composer Stefan Wolpe. *Special Medal* to Meyer Schapiro, Columbia University art historian and fine arts professor. *Citations* to actor-director-teacher Alvin Epstein; composer Mario Davidovsky, sculptor Richard Stankiewicz, and novelist John Barth. *Medal for Distinguished Service to Higher Education*, awarded for the first time in 1966, to Mr. and Mrs. Jack I. Poses, who have supported the fine arts curriculum at Brandeis University for years.

British Royal Society of Literature Award to Derek Walcott of Trinidad, the first Negro honored with this award, for his poetry collection *The Castaway.*

College of Arts Association Charles Rufus Morey Book Award to Erwin Panofsky, German-born Institute for Advanced Study (Princeton, N.J.) Professor Emeritus, for *Tomb Sculpture*, cited as the "most distinguished work of scholarship in the history of art published in 1964."

Columbia University Frederic Bancroft Prizes, for studies in American diplomacy and international relations, to Richard B. Morris for *The Peacemakers: The Great Powers and American Independence;* and Theodore W. Friend III for *Between Two Empires: The Ordeal of the Philippines, 1926-1946.*

Denmark's Sonning Prize, for outstanding contributions to European culture, to Sir Laurence Olivier, internationally famous British actor and director.

Freedom House Freedom Award to President Lyndon B. Johnson for his support of civil rights, aid to education, and his "decisive stand on Vietnam."

Jawaharlal Nehru Award for International Understanding, established by the Government of India in memory of the country's first prime minister, Jawaharlal Nehru (1889-1964) and awarded for the first time in 1966, to United Nations Secretary-General U Thant of Burma. See Section Two, THE MOST IMPOSSIBLE JOB IN THE WORLD.

National Association for the Advancement of Colored People Spingarn Medal, honoring an American Negro for distinguished achievement, to John H. Johnson, publisher of *Ebony*, *Tan*, *Jet*, and *Negro Digest* magazines, for "his productive imagination, ingenuity and enterprise in the perilous field of publishing."

National Book Committee Awards. *National Book Awards: Fiction Award* to Katherine Anne Porter for *The Collected Stories of Katherine Anne Porter; Arts and Letters Award* to Janet Flanner (Genêt) for *Paris Journal, 1944-1965. History and Biography Award* to Arthur M. Schlesinger, Jr., for *A Thousand Days: John F. Kennedy in the White House* (see SCHLESINGER, ARTHUR M., JR.); and *Poetry Award* to James Dickey for *Buckdancer's Choice. National Medal for Literature*, for a lifetime of work, to Edmund Wilson, writer and critic.

National Gallery of Arts Awards, presented by Mrs. Lyndon B. Johnson and awarded for the first time to art scholars and teachers across the country, to: James S. Ackerman, Harvard University Fine Arts Department chairman; Helen Aupperle, Idaho Falls high school art teacher; Emma L. Bippus, Toledo (Ohio) Museum of Art Education Department Senior Lecturer; Sibyl Browne of San Antonio, Tex., retired University of Georgia Professor of Art Education; Martha Christensen, Louisville (Ky.) Schools Art Supervisor; Howard Conant, New York University Department of Art Education chairman; Victor D'Amico, New York Museum of Modern Art Department of Education director; Charles M. Dorn, National Art Education Association Executive Secretary; J. Eugene Grigsby, Jr., Union High School Art Department head, Phoenix, Ariz.; Robert Inglehart, University of Michigan Department of Art chairman; Marie L. Larkin, University of Missouri Professor of Art and St. Louis Public Schools Supervisor of Art; Frederick M. Logan, University of Wisconsin Professor of Art and Art Education, Madison; Doris W. Lough, Pacific Pre-Vocational School specialist art teacher, Seattle, Wash.; Edward Matill, Pennsylvania State University Art Education Department head; Mary Adeline McKibbin, University of Pittsburgh art teacher and retired Pittsburgh Public Schools art director; Erwin Panofsky, Institute for Advanced Study (Princeton, N.J.) Professor Emeritus; James A. Porter, Howard University Art Department head; Olga M. Schubkegel, Hammond (Ind.) School System Art Education director; Julia B. Schwartz, Florida State University art professor; Grace S. Smith, Houston (Texas) Independent School District Art Education director; John and Aurelia Socha (joint award), Minneapolis (Minn.) Public School art teachers; Wilber Moore Stilwell, University of South Dakota Art Department chairman; Ruth J. Stolle, Tripoli (Wis.) artist and retired rural art teacher; Frederick S. Wight, University of California (Los Angeles) Department of Art chairman; and Edwin Ziegfeld, Columbia University Teachers College Fine and Industrial Arts head.

Poetry Society of America Awards. *Alice Fay di Castagnola Award* to Edsel Ford for *A Landscape for Dante*, a group of sonnets (24 of his envisioned 70 have been completed). *Melville Cane Award* to James Dickey for *Buckdancer's Choice.*

Society of American Historians Awards. *Francis Parkman Prize* to Daniel J. Boorstin for *The Americans: The National Experience. Allan Nevins Prize* to Robert L. Beisner for *The Anti-Imperial Impulse: The Mugwumps and the Republicans, 1898-1900.*

Society of Architectural Historians Alice Davis Hitchcock Award to John McAndrew for *The Open Air Churches of Sixteenth Century Mexico* (1965).

West German Publishers and Booksellers Association International Peace Prize to Willem Adolf Visser't Hooft, Dutch Reformed theologian and General Secretary of the World Council of Churches; and Augustin Cardinal Bea, President of the Vatican Secretariat for Promoting Christian Unity, for their efforts to achieve understanding between the Catholic and Protestant churches.

Yale University Awards. *Henry Elias Howland Memorial Prize*, conferred every two years for distinguished achievement in literature, fine arts, or the science of government, to English actor-director Tyrone Guthrie. *School of Art and Architecture Gold Medal*, awarded for the first time in six years, to John D. Entenza, founder of the *Arts and Architecture* magazine, and executive director of the Graham Foundation for Advanced Studies in the Fine Arts. *Yale Series of Younger Poets Award* to James Tate for his book *The Lost Pilot*, which is to be published in early 1967.

SCIENCE AND INDUSTRY

Albert and Mary Lasker Foundation Awards. *Medical Journalism Awards: Newspaper Award* to Joann Rodgers and Louis Linley for their front-page series "Your Health and Medicine" in *The Baltimore* (Md.) *News American* (between Oct. 10-Nov. 9, 1965). *Magazine Award* to Gerald Astor, *Look* senior editor, for his article "Stroke: Second Greatest Crippler," June 15, 1965. *Television Award* to Station WABC-TV for "Who Will Tie My Shoe?" The mental retardation story first appeared on Channel 7 on Dec. 4, 1965. *Medical Research Awards:* For basic research to George E. Palade of Rockefeller University, among the first to use the electron microscope for cell studies. For clinical research to Sidney Farber of Harvard Medical School, who found (1955) the antibiotic actinomycin D effective against Wilms' tumor (a form of cancer) and aminopterin and methotrexate (1947) effective in checking acute leukemia. *Public Service Health Award* to Eunice Kennedy Shriver for her encouragement of national legislation and other work on behalf of the mentally retarded in many institutions and centers throughout the United States.

American Chemical Society Awards. *Priestley Medal* to William O. Baker, Bell Telephone Laboratories Vice-President for Research, for his research on long-chain molecules and electronic uses of plastics. *Irving Langmuir Award* to University of Illinois Physical Chemistry Professor Herbert S. Gutowsky, for identifying and analyzing complex chemical compounds. *James T. Grady Award* to The Associated Press science writer Frank E. Carey for his writing on chemical progress. *Willard Gibbs Medal* to U.S. Atomic Energy Commission chairman Glenn T. Seaborg, Nobel physics laureate (1951) and atomic scientist. *Gold Medal* to University of Chicago Biochemistry Professor Samuel B. Weiss for his work in enzyme chemistry. *Pure Chemistry Award* to Columbia University Professor Ronald Breslow, whose research includes biochemical model systems, small-ring compounds, and conjugation effects. *Fisher Award in Analytical Chemistry* to Lyman C. Craig of Rockefeller University. The countercurrent distribution apparatus was named for him. *Jacob F. Schoellkopf Medal* to Leon O. Winstrom for his original contributions in the development of low-pressure catalytic hydrogenation processes.

AWARDS AND PRIZES

American Institute of Physics and American Physical Society Dannie Heineman Prize to Nikolay N. Bogolyubov, Russian scientist, for his work in mathematical physics, including "the first rigorous proof of dispersion relations for the nonforward scattering of elementary particles."

American Medical Association Awards. *Scientific Achievement Award* to Wendell M. Stanley, University of California (Berkeley) biochemist and Nobel chemistry laureate (1946), for his virus research, including the preparation of enzymes and virus proteins in pure form and the isolation of the *tobacco mosaic virus* (1935). *Joseph Goldberger Award in Clinical Nutrition* to Harvard University Professor of Medicine William B. Castle for his studies of pernicious anemia and other blood diseases. *Distinguished Service Award* to the University of Illinois Department of Surgery head Warren H. Cole, for his writings on cancer, general surgery, and goiter treatment.

American Sociological Association MacIver Award to Canadian sociologist John Porter for his book, *The Vertical Mosaic.*

British Royal Geographical Society Awards. *Patron's Medal* to E. J. H. Corner, leader of expeditions to North Borneo and the Solomon Islands, for botanical exploration. *Founder's Medal* to G. Hattersley-Smith for glaciological investigations in the Canadian Arctic. *Victoria Medal* to G. R. Crone, librarian and map curator, for his contributions to historical cartography and the history of geographical thought. *Mrs. Patrick Ness Award* to E. C. Evans and J. P. M. Long of Australia for investigations of aboriginal territory in West Central Australia.

Case Institute of Technology Albert A. Michelson Award to Edwin H. Land, Polaroid Corporation president and director of research, as "a pioneer in optical research for the invention of polaroid and its wide application in science and technology, the design of the Land camera, his contributions to color vision, color photography, three-dimensional motion pictures, and for many innovations in basic and applied optics."

Columbia University Awards. *Vetlesen Prize*, awarded every two years, to University of Leiden (Netherlands) Observatory Director Jan Hendrik Oort, noted galaxy authority and pioneer in the science of radio astronomy. *Charles Frederick Chandler Medal* to University of California (San Diego) Chemistry Professor Joseph Edward Mayer, for "two decades of research in the behavior of gas molecules."

Franklin Institute Award. *Franklin Medal* to National Academy of Sciences President Frederick Seitz as a leader in science and in the field of physics, and for his work on the structure and properties of solid materials and his clear exposition of the new theory of the solid state and its applications.

International Congress of Mathematics J. C. Fields Medal, awarded every four years, to Stanford University Professor Paul J. Cohen for proving that the "continuum hypothesis" is independent of the axioms of set theory, and, therefore, cannot be proven until new axioms are formulated; and Stephen Smale of the University of California (Berkeley) for the Smale Theorem, which proves that a sphere can be turned inside out without forming a "crease."

National Academy of Sciences Awards. *Public Welfare Medal* to U.S. Secretary of Health, Education, and Welfare John W. Gardner "for eminence in the application of science to the public welfare." *Alexander Agassiz Medal* to University of California (San Diego) Geophysics Professor Carl Eckart, for his analysis of the motions of the sea and the forces behind them.

National Medal of Science, presented by President Johnson, to the following distinguished scientists: John Bardeen, University of Illinois Physics and Electrical Engineering Professor and Nobel physics laureate (1956), as coinventor of the transistor. Peter J. W. Debye, Cornell University Professor Emeritus of Chemistry and a Nobel chemistry laureate (see DEATHS OF NOTABLE PERSONS). Hugh L. Dryden (1898-1965), the late deputy administrator of the National Aeronautics and Space Administration and a physicist and engineer, who served in government posts for 47 years, was the first person awarded this medal posthumously. Clarence Leonard Johnson, Lockheed Aircraft Corporation vice-president, whose craft, such as the U-2 and A-11, advanced and revolutionized aircraft design. Leon Max Lederman, Columbia University Professor of Physics and Experimental Physicist, made recent discoveries in meson physics. Warren Kendall Lewis, Massachusetts Institute of Technology Professor Emeritus of Chemical Engineering, was cited as the father of modern chemical engineering. (Francis) Peyton Rous, noted Rockefeller University cancer research scientist (see ROUS, [FRANCIS] PEYTON). William W. Rubey, University of California geology and geophysics professor, noted for basic geological discoveries and work on "the transport of sediment and geologic history of sea water." George Gaylord Simpson, Harvard University Professor of Paleontology, noted for studies of vertebrate evolution through geologic time and for organic evolution based upon genetics and paleontology. Donald Dexter Van Slyke, Brookhaven National Laboratory research chemist, whose 55 years of biochemistry research includes "classic studies" on the physical chemistry of blood. Oscar Zeriski, Harvard University Professor of Mathematics, who has achieved international renown for his work in algebraic geometry.

Pacific Science Center Foundation Arches of Science Award to René Jules Dubos, Rockefeller University bacteriologist and pioneer in antibiotic drugs. See DUBOS, RENÉ JULES.

Passano Foundation Award to John T. Edsall, Harvard University Professor of Biological Chemistry, for research on the physical-chemical basis of the structure and biological activity of amino acids, peptides, and proteins.

Royal Canadian Geographical Society Massey Medal to Alf Erling Porsild, Danish-born chief botanist of the National Museum of Canada, for "his contributions to the knowledge of the Canadian Arctic, particularly its botany and the use of Arctic plants as food."

United Nations Educational, Scientific and Cultural Organization Kalinga Prize, for popularization of science, to Eugene Rabinowitch, scientist and editor of the *Bulletin of the Atomic Scientists.*

Vernon Stouffer Foundation Medical Prize, presented for the first time in 1966, to Harry Goldblatt, Mount Sinai Hospital in Cleveland, Ohio, whose hypertension research included producing high blood pressure in dogs (1934) and other animals; and Ernst Klenk, University of Cologne in West Germany, who stimulated research into cholesterol and other fatty materials and contributed to knowledge of arteriosclerosis.

West German Medical-Pharmaceutical Research Society Paul Ehrlich and Ludwig Darmstaedter Prize to (Francis) Peyton Rous. See ROUS, (FRANCIS) PEYTON.

World Meterology Organization Prize, for outstanding work and international collaboration, to Tor Bergeron of Sweden for pioneering new techniques in air mass analysis and the physics of precipitation.

See also NOBEL PRIZES; PULITZER PRIZES; and Awards sections of articles such as ATOMIC ENERGY, AVIATION, and LITERATURE FOR CHILDREN.

BAHAMAS. See WEST INDIES.

BALAGUER Y RICARDO, JÓAQUIN (1907-), was inaugurated July 1, 1966, as the 71st president of the 122-year-old Dominican Republic. Balaguer had been president from 1960 to 1962, but that was a figurehead post under Rafael Leonidas Trujillo y Molina. He succeeded President Héctor Garcia-Godoy. See DOMINICAN REPUBLIC.

Born in Santiago on Sept. 1, 1907, Balaguer received a B.A. degree in philosophy and letters in 1924 from Santiago's La Escuela Normal, and a law degree from the University of Santo Domingo in 1929. A precocious student, he wrote his first book when he was 14 years old. He is the author of numerous books in the fields of literature, history, politics, and biography.

Balaguer served as rector (president) of the University of Santo Domingo, then entered his government's foreign service. His posts included: alternate representative to the United Nations, minister to Colombia and later to Ecuador, and ambassador to Honduras and then Mexico. Returning home in 1949, he was appointed secretary of education and fine arts, and, in 1953, he became foreign minister.

Balaguer is a bachelor. He has worked long to reduce illiteracy in his nation. In May, while he was campaigning for office, his auto caravan was ambushed and one person was killed. WALTER F. MORSE

BALLET. See DANCING.

BALLOONS. See ASTRONOMY; WEATHER.

BANKS AND BANKING. Credit, the chief stock in trade of banks and other lenders, became a scarce commodity in 1966. And, as with any other item in short supply and strong demand, its price rose sharply. The *prime rate* (what banks charge on loans with the least risk of default) advanced from 5 per cent to 5½ per cent in March, to 5¾ per cent in June, and to 6 per cent in August.

Increased federal spending, especially for the war in Vietnam, and a burst of capital accumulation contributed to the tightest domestic credit pinch since the 1920s. In the ensuing competition for funds to lend, many banks began issuing certificates of deposit (CDs) in denominations as low as $25. Three-month Treasury bill yields went to an all-time peak of over 5½ per cent in September, while *federal funds* (one-day loans of bank reserves) traded above 6 per cent. Long-term Treasury bond rates rose to 4.8 per cent, well above the 4¼ per cent ceiling on new issues with more than five-year maturities.

The Federal Reserve Board (FRB), seeking to minimize inflationary pressures on the economy, followed a course of restraint. It would make reserves available to member banks—but not enough for banks to make all the loans businessmen sought. By May, the FRB was putting pressure on banks to ration credit to "select" borrowers.

This stimulated banks to compete vigorously for time deposits to increase their lending power. And compete they did. Banks added about $15,000,000,000 to time deposits in 1966, particularly CDs, accounting for half the liquid asset accumulation. Savings and loan association (SLA) shares increased only $5,000,000,000, and almost not at all after midyear. See chart.

The Pattern of tightness in the money market was set before the year began, on Dec. 5, 1965, when the FRB raised the *discount rate* from 4 per cent to 4½ per cent. (The discount rate is the rate of interest a member bank must pay for funds it borrows from the Federal Reserve banks.) The upper limit on interest that could be paid on time deposits was raised one full percentage point to a total of 5½ per cent.

Between late August and mid-September, the capital and money markets neared crisis conditions. Long-term bond yields reached 45-year highs late in August. In September, short-term money market interest rates reached the highs of the late 1920s.

Squeeze on SLAs. The Federal Home Loan Banks tried to hold down rising SLA dividend rates during the first half of the year. They threatened to deny the SLAs borrowing privileges if rates exceeded 4¾ per cent, or 5 per cent in some areas. But this policy was abandoned at midyear as SLAs faced unprecedented withdrawals. Top interest rates on government-guaranteed new home mort-

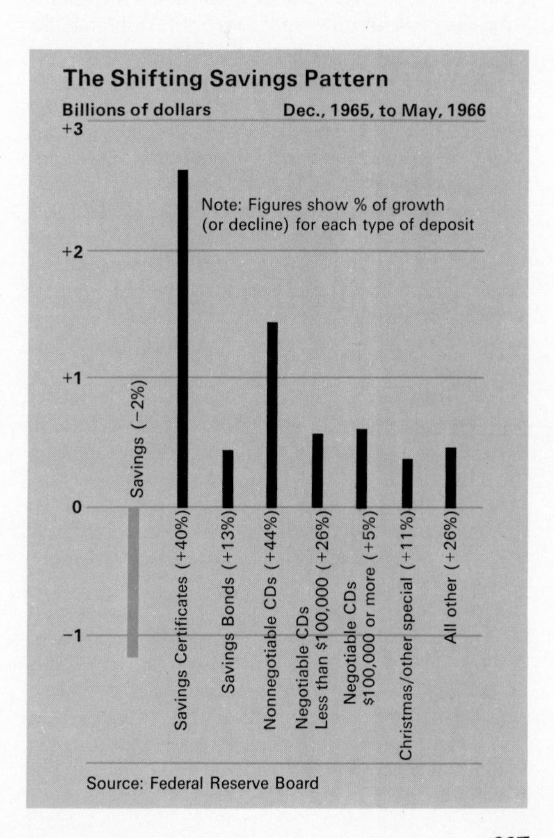

gages were increased from 5¼ per cent to 6 per cent. Because of discounts, mortgage yields rose to 6.6 per cent in September, up from 5.5 per cent the year before. Conventional mortgage rates went even higher. And housing starts dropped to an annual rate of less than 1,000,000 units in the fourth quarter. See HOUSING.

Counteractions. To limit the feverish competition for savings, the FRB reduced the ceilings on interest rates for some classes of CDs, and it ruled that banks' capital notes would be subject to reserve requirements.

On September 1, the presidents of each of the 12 district Federal Reserve banks sent letters to each member bank urging a slowdown in business loans. The letter also announced a new lending policy that would favor member banks that acted to reduce their business loans. Later in September, as SLA shareholders continued to transfer their funds to banks, Congress authorized federal regulatory agencies to limit rates paid to consumers to 5 per cent or less. A 5 per cent limit also was imposed on CDs with less than $100,000 face value. SLAs generally could pay no more than 4¾ per cent, except that those already with higher rates could pay up to 5 per cent or 5¼ per cent depending on their area.

Some Easing of tight money came in the year's last quarter, as President Lyndon B. Johnson let it be known that fiscal–rather than merely monetary –measures would be used to fight inflation. In October, Congress authorized temporary removal of the 7 per cent investment tax credit and a tightening of depreciation rules. As the year ended, the FRB revoked its September 1 directive, noting that bank expansion of business loans had moderated. See CONGRESS OF THE UNITED STATES; TAXATION.

Overseas Banks were caught in the same tight-money vise as banks in the United States. In some Western European countries interest rates touched their highest levels of the century before turning down by year's end. In Germany, for instance, long-term public authority bonds paid more than 8 per cent interest.

U.S. efforts to solve its balance of payments problems complicated the difficulties of foreign banks. U.S. banks, as in 1965, were encouraged by the administration guidelines to keep overseas loans below 107 per cent of the December, 1964, level. In the first half of 1966, U.S. businesses increased their borrowing of funds from foreign sources to more than the entire 1965 total.

European branches of U.S. banks began issuing CDs to attract *Euro-dollars* (European deposits of dollars in U.S. banks). All these activities put pressure on the European capital market. The giant Lebanese Intra Bank failed in mid-October, in part because of high-yielding, long-term assets it got with funds borrowed in the Euro-dollar market. See INTERNATIONAL TRADE AND FINANCE; LEBANON.

The Bank Merger Act of 1966, signed into law on February 21, excused from further prosecution the mergers of Manufacturer's Trust Company and Hanover Bank in New York City and First National Bank and Trust Company and Security Trust Company of Lexington, Ky. Both mergers had been found in violation of antitrust laws, and the banks had been ordered to be separated. The act instructed courts in the future to weigh financial and not just competitive factors.

Government Actions. Empire Trust and the Bank of New York merged on December 7. The FRB had approved the merger in November, but delayed 30 days under the new merger law to allow time for a challenge by the Department of Justice.

In a landmark decision, the U.S. Supreme Court on December 12 ruled that national banks were bound by the same branching rules as state banks.

Federal deposit insurance for banks and SLAs was increased from $10,000 to $15,000 in 1966. The Federal Deposit Insurance Corporation also dropped its challenge of claims where defunct banks had paid more than legal interest rates to depositors.

First National City Bank of New York City got Securities and Exchange Commission approval to provide the first bank-managed, "mutual fund" type of participation investments; and it pioneered trading in CDs of other banks for its own customers.

New Banks. The comptroller of the currency chartered only 15 national banks in the first half of 1966, well below the six-month average of 50 for the preceding two years. There were 13,802 commercial banks and 505 mutual savings banks as of June 30. Commercial banks added 528 new branches in the first six months; 319 of them national bank branches. On June 30, national banks accounted for 57 per cent of the 16,282 banking offices, but only 35 per cent of the commercial banks.

William B. Camp was named to succeed James J. Saxon as comptroller of the currency when his term expired on November 15. Camp was expected to follow most of Saxon's banking reform and liberalization policies. Andrew F. Brimmer was appointed on February 26 to the seven-man Board of Governors of the FRB. Brimmer a "moderate," replaced "conservative" C. Canby Balderston.

Credit Cards. First National City Bank agreed to operate its newly acquired Carte Blanche credit card business as an independent business pending outcome of an antitrust action. American Express, No. 1 in credit cards, began franchising banks to offer its cards, while the Bank of America considered going national with its California-based Bank Americard. To ward off that challenge, Chicago area banks began issuing credit cards late in the fall. Several types appeared, all under the Midwest Bank Card emblem. WILLIAM G. DEWALD

See also ECONOMY, THE; MONEY; Section One, SYLVIA PORTER: FOCUS ON THE ECONOMY.

BASEBALL. An interleague trade, four months before the season started, turned the Baltimore Orioles into baseball's team of the year. The traded player, outfielder Frank Robinson, came to the Orioles from the Cincinnati Reds. He promptly assumed leadership of the predominantly youthful Baltimore team and sparked the Orioles to their first American League pennant and a World Series rout of the world champions, the Los Angeles Dodgers.

The Dodgers' excellent pitching staff continued strongly in the series, but their weak attack collapsed completely and the Orioles whipped them in four straight games. Frank Robinson socked home runs in the first and fourth games, driving in three runs. He thus accounted for more runs than the entire Dodger team. After taking the opener in Los Angeles, 5-2, the Orioles blanked the Dodgers 6-0 in the second game there, and 1-0 in both the third and final games in their own stadium.

The American League. Led by Frank Robinson, third baseman Brooks Robinson, and first baseman John "Boog" Powell, the Orioles soared so high in the first few months of the season that they were able to coast for the final 10 weeks. Frank Robinson became the ninth major league player to win a batting Triple Crown as he topped his new league in batting average (.316), home runs (49), and runs batted in (122). He was an overwhelming choice for the Most Valuable Player award, which he had won in the National League five years earlier, thus becoming the first player to achieve this honor in both major leagues.

The once mighty New York Yankees lost 10 of their first 11 games. Less than a month after the season started, manager Johnny Keane was replaced by Ralph Houk. The Yanks spurted briefly but again sagged and finished last, something no Yankee team had done since 1912. See Section One, RED SMITH: FOCUS ON SPORTS.

The National League. Once again several contenders remained in the running until the last few days of the drive. The Pittsburgh Pirates faded late in the season and were finally eliminated on the next-to-last day, while the San Francisco Giants disappointed their fans with their third near-miss in three years. The Giants, written off prematurely by rivals, managed to keep their hopes up until the Dodgers snuffed out Philadelphia to end the season. The Dodgers reeled off eight victories in a row, in September, went to first place, and stayed there.

An arthritic condition in his left elbow continued to bother Sandy Koufax of the Dodgers throughout the year. By the end of the season, the 30-year-old ace was forced to resort to frequent injections of cortisone in order to keep pitching. Nonetheless, he won 27 games, struck out 317, and paced the Na-

Brooks Robinson of Orioles, leaping for joy, and Andy Etchebarren come in to congratulate pitcher Dave McNally at the close of World Series.

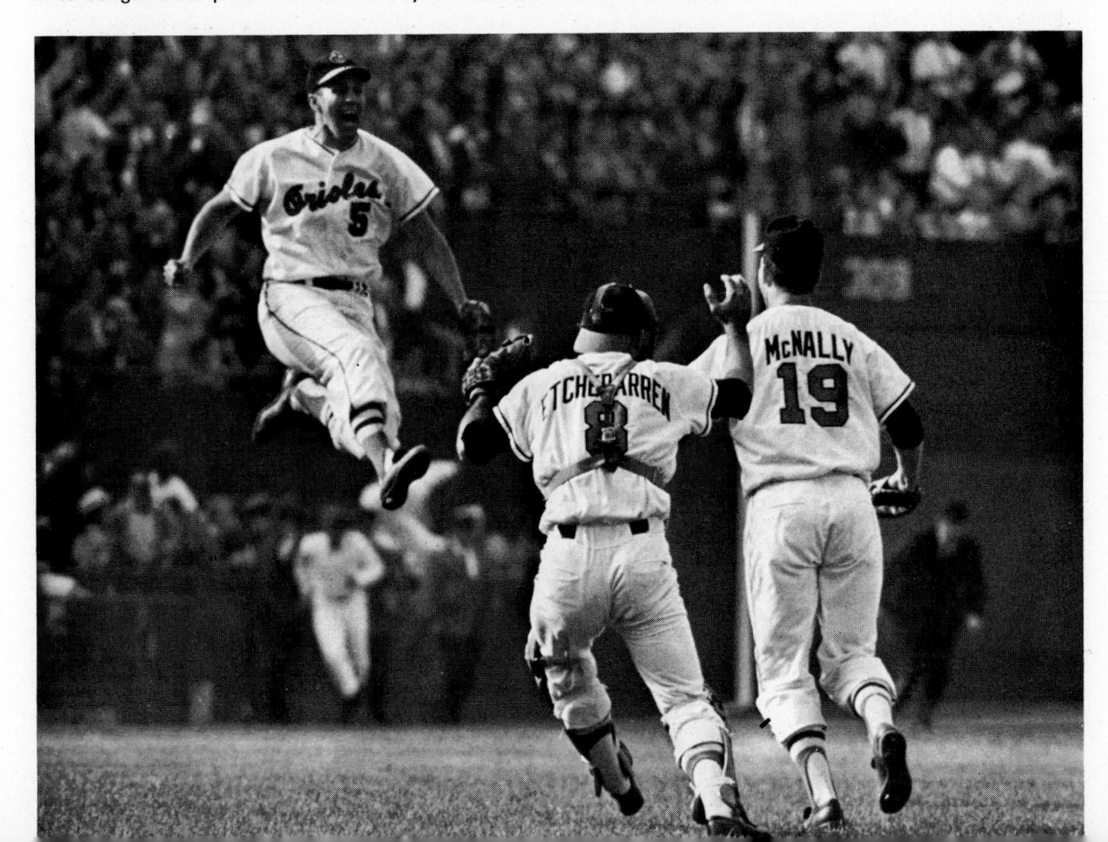

Final Standings In Major League Baseball

American League

	W.	L.	PCT.	GB.
Baltimore	97	63	.606	—
Minnesota	89	73	.549	9
Detroit	88	74	.543	10
Chicago	83	79	.512	15
Cleveland	81	81	.500	17
California	80	82	.494	18
Kansas City	74	86	.463	23
Washington	71	88	.447	25½
Boston	72	90	.444	26
New York	70	89	.440	26½

Leading Batters

Batting Average—Frank Robinson, Baltimore	.316
Home Runs—Frank Robinson, Baltimore	49
Runs Batted In—Frank Robinson, Baltimore	122
Hits—Tony Oliva, Minnesota	191
Runs—Frank Robinson, Baltimore	122

Leading Pitchers

Games Won—Jim Kaat, Minnesota	25
Win Average—Jim Nash, Kansas City (12-1)	.923
Earned Run Average—Gary Peters, Chicago	1.98
Strikeouts—Sam McDowell, Cleveland	225

National League

	W.	L.	PCT.	GB.
Los Angeles	95	67	.586	—
San Francisco	93	68	.578	1½
Pittsburgh	92	70	.568	3
Philadelphia	87	75	.537	8
Atlanta	85	77	.525	10
St. Louis	83	79	.512	12
Cincinnati	76	84	.475	18
Houston	72	90	.444	23
New York	66	95	.410	28½
Chicago	59	103	.364	36

Leading Batters

Batting Average—Mateo Alou, Pittsburgh	.342
Home Runs—Henry Aaron, Atlanta	44
Runs Batted In—Henry Aaron, Atlanta	127
Hits—Felipe Alou, Atlanta	218
Runs—Felipe Alou, Atlanta	122

Leading Pitchers

Games Won—Sandy Koufax, Los Angeles	27
Win Average—Phil Regan, Los Angeles (14-1)	.933
Earned Run Average—Sandy Koufax, Los Angeles	1.73
Strikeouts—Sandy Koufax, Los Angeles	317

tional League in earned-run average for the fifth consecutive year. After the season ended, Koufax announced his retirement from baseball.

Center fielder Willie Mays of the Giants clubbed 37 home runs, lifting his lifetime total to 542. During the season, Mays climbed from fifth to second on the all-time list, passing Mel Ott, Ted Williams, and Jimmy Foxx. At 35, the well-conditioned Mays had a slim chance of catching up with baseball's top home-run hitter, Babe Ruth, who slammed 714 during his career.

Attendance at major league games rose to a record total of 25,200,000. For the fifth consecutive year, the National League broke its own attendance record. The leaders, once again, were the Dodgers. They packed in 2,600,000 of the National League's 15,000,000 total. Another factor in establishing the record was the move of the former Milwaukee Braves to Atlanta. After a long court battle with the city of Milwaukee and the state of Wisconsin, the owners of the Braves finally secured their right to operate in the South. Despite numerous early season difficulties on the field, the Braves drew more than 1,500,000 at home.

The biggest reason for the jump in attendance in the American League from 8,900,000 to 10,200,000 was the shift of the Los Angeles franchise to Anaheim, where the newly-established California Angels played sixth-place ball and drew 1,400,000 onlookers. As tenants of the Dodgers' ballpark the previous year, they had pulled little more than 500,000 paid admissions.

All-Star Game. Another new ballpark, the Busch Memorial Stadium in St. Louis, was the scene of the midsummer All-Star game. The National League won in 10 innings, 2-1, for its fourth straight win and an edge of 19-17 (with one tie) over the American League. The outstanding player in the game was the Orioles' Brooks Robinson, who cracked a triple and two singles and made two spectacular fielding plays.

Hall of Fame. Also in midseason, 75-year-old Casey Stengel and 47-year-old Ted Williams were admitted to baseball's Hall of Fame in ceremonies at Cooperstown, N.Y. A rule requiring the lapse of five years after the end of an active career was waived for Stengel, permitting the garrulous former manager of four major league teams to join the ranks of the notables.

Front Office. The biggest front office news of the year was made after the World Series. President Dan Topping sold his 10 per cent interest in the New York Yankees, leaving the Columbia Broadcasting System (CBS) in complete control of the team. CBS executive Michael Burke became president and chairman of the board. Then the Yankees, indicating sweeping changes ahead in playing personnel, brought back their one-time director of farm opera-

Orioles' Frank Robinson hit three home runs in the 1966 World Series to help his team beat the Dodgers in four straight games.

tions, Lee MacPhail. During 1966, MacPhail had been an assistant to the new commissioner of baseball, William Eckert. But before that MacPhail had established a reputation as a highly capable executive in his six-year tenure as president and general manager of the Baltimore Orioles. One of MacPhail's final moves at Baltimore was to bring Frank Robinson to the Orioles.

Amateurs. Ohio State captured the National Collegiate Athletic Association (NCAA) title, and Linfield College of Oregon took the National Association of Intercollegiate Athletics (NAIA) championship. Houston won the annual Little League World Series.

Award Winners in the major leagues were:

National League Most Valuable Player–Roberto Clemente of the Pittsburgh Pirates.

American League Most Valuable Player–Frank Robinson of the Baltimore Orioles.

Cy Young Award, to the "pitcher of the year"–Sandy Koufax of the Los Angeles Dodgers.

National League Rookie of the Year–Tommy Helms of the Cincinnati Reds.

American League Rookie of the Year–Tommy Agee of the Chicago White Sox.

National League Manager of the Year–Walt Alston of the Los Angeles Dodgers.

American League Manager of the Year–Hank Bauer of the Baltimore Orioles.

JOHN LAKE

See also Section Two, THE OTHER FACE OF PRO SPORTS.

BASKETBALL. The 1965-1966 collegiate season turned out to be a Cinderella year for Texas Western University of El Paso, Tex., a team that had never before won any title of note. Coached by defense-minded Don Haskins, the Texas Western Miners squeezed through the National Collegiate Athletic Association (NCAA) Midwest Regional play-off with victories over Oklahoma City, Cincinnati, and Kansas, and reached the finals with an 85-78 victory over Utah at College Park, Md.

Then, led by Bobby Joe Hill and Willie Worsley, the Miners outshot and outhustled four-time winner Kentucky for the championship, 72-65. Duke, which had lost to Kentucky in the other semifinal, edged Utah for third place.

1966 College All-American Team

Players	School
Cazzie Russell	Michigan
Dave Schellhase	Purdue
Clyde Lee	Vanderbilt
Dave Bing	Syracuse
Jim Walker	Providence

(Source: NCAA consensus All-American)

Both Texas Western and Kentucky had come into the tournament with identical regular-season won-lost records of 23-1. But Kentucky was rated first and Texas Western third in both the Associated Press and United Press International final rating polls, and Kentucky's coach, Adolph Rupp, had been voted "Coach of the Year."

The leading collegiate scorer was Dave Schellhase of Purdue. But another Big Ten player, Cazzie Russell of Michigan, won all the polls for the season's outstanding player and set a Big Ten career scoring record of 2,164 points.

After the college season, Russell helped the Ford Mustangs of Dearborn, Mich., win the Amateur Athletic Union (AAU) championship. In September, Russell signed a 3-year, $200,000 professional contract with the New York Knickerbockers. To get him, the Knickerbockers had to outbid the Harlem Globetrotters with the highest price ever paid for a professional rookie.

In the world amateur tournament, held in Santiago, Chile, in April, Yugoslavia upset the American team, 69-59, and went on to win the championship. Both teams had 5-1 overall records, but the Yugoslavs' earlier victory over the U.S. gained them the title.

Professional. The Boston Celtics won their eighth consecutive National Basketball Association (NBA) championship, but not without a struggle. They were beaten for the Eastern Division title, for the first time in 10 years, by the Philadelphia 76ers. The Cincinnati Royals were third, and the New York Knickerbockers fourth and last.

In the play-offs, the Celtics beat the Royals, three games to two, earning another chance at the 76ers in the Eastern final. This time the Celtics won, four games to one, to gain the championship round.

In the Western Division, the Los Angeles Lakers breezed to a seven-game margin over the Baltimore Bullets. It was the Lakers' fourth divisional title in five years. Behind the Bullets came the St. Louis Hawks. The San Francisco Warriors were fourth, and the Detroit Pistons last.

The NBA championship was a seesaw seven-game struggle. The Celtics looked like easy winners as they built up a three to one lead, but the Lakers fought back to tie the series. The final game went down to the last seconds before the Celtics won 95-93.

Red Auerbach, the Celtics' coach for 16 years, retired after the season. He became Boston's general manager, and was replaced by Bill Russell, the first Negro coach of a major professional team.

Auerbach's retirement from coaching was expected, but Dolph Schayes' was not. Schayes, whose coaching of the 76ers to the Eastern title resulted in his being named "Coach of the Year," was fired when the team lost in the play-offs. Chamberlain won his seventh straight scoring title and was named "Player of the Year." Rick Barry of San Francisco, the "Rookie of the Year," became one of only four first-year men in league history to score more than 2,000 points in a season. The league continued its gradual expansion with the granting of a franchise to the Chicago Bulls. JAMES O. DUNAWAY

BASSETT, LESLIE (1923-), professor of music at the University of Michigan, received the Pulitzer prize in music in 1966 for his composition *Variations for Orchestra*. The composition was awarded the prize after its U.S. première in 1965 by the Philadelphia Orchestra, with Eugene Ormandy conducting. *Variations* had received its world première two years earlier in Rome where Bassett lived from 1961 to 1963 as a recipient of the Rome prize of the American Academy in Rome.

Leslie Bassett was born in Hanford, Calif., the son of a rancher. He began to study the piano when he was about five years of age. While in high school in Fresno, he played the trombone in local bands, jazz groups, and orchestras. From 1942 to 1946 he was trombonist in a U.S. Army band.

Bassett studied at Fresno State College, where he received his B.A. degree in 1947. He won his M.A. degree from the University of Michigan two years later. In 1950, he studied in Europe on a Fulbright grant under famed composer Arthur Honegger and also with Nadia Boulanger. The following year, he taught in the public schools of Fresno, and, in the fall of 1952, joined the faculty of the University of Michigan. Leslie Bassett is married to the former Anita Denniston.

See also PULITZER PRIZES.

BASUTOLAND. See LESOTHO.

BECHUANALAND. See BOTSWANA.

BELGIUM. A series of crises early in the year resulted in the resignation of Prime Minister Pierre Harmel and his cabinet. The government's resignation, after little more than six months in office, touched off a 33-day cabinet crisis.

The trouble began over an issue involving health insurance. The country's 9,000 physicians and the Christian Social party favored proposed "entry fees" of 60 cents a visit at clinics run by mutual insurance associations affiliated with the Socialist party. The Socialists, who felt the issue was an ideological one, opposed it. Angered by the government's attitude, the doctors threatened to strike. Simultaneously, hundreds of coal miners in northeast Belgium began rioting to protest the closing of a number of mines. There was a flare-up, too, in the Flemish-Walloon language war. Police used tear gas to quell Flemish nationalist demonstrators.

King Baudouin I, anxious to avert the collapse of the Socialist-Christian-Democrat government, refused to accept the cabinet's resignation. Instead, he asked Harmel to placate the miners and also seek a truce with the physicians. The 12 Socialist members of the coalition government refused, however, to accept such a move. Led by Foreign Minister Paul-Henri Spaak, they handed in a collective resignation to Harmel, who once again resigned. This time the king accepted the resignation.

Paul-Henri Spaak, Europe's "grand old man," resigned as foreign minister of Belgium in 1966, but remained a minister of state.

King Baudouin then called upon former Prime Minister Achille Van Acker to act as constitutional adviser and, with his help, a new coalition government was formed under the leadership of Paul Vanden Boeynants of the Christian Social party.

Balanced Budget. On September 29, the government presented–for the first time since 1964–a balanced budget to parliament. It called for about $4,400,000,000 in expenditures. Revenues were estimated at $2,000,000 above that amount. As promised earlier, the budget contained no increase in general and excise taxes. But some selective tax increases were in prospect.

NATO. Proposed transfer of the North Atlantic Treaty Organization's headquarters from Paris to Brussels was approved by the Belgian government in June. Subsequently, the government offered land near Casteau, outside Brussels, as a site for the new headquarters.

Royal Visit. Queen Elizabeth II of Great Britain paid a five-day state visit in May, the first such visit made to Belgium by a reigning British sovereign in 44 years. She visited World War I battle scenes.

Facts in Brief. Population: 9,430,000. Government: King Baudouin I; Prime Minister Paul Vanden Boeynants. Monetary Unit: Belgian franc (50.08 = U.S. $1). Foreign Trade: exports, $6,386,-900,000; imports, $6,373,400,000. Principal Exports: iron and steel, machinery. KENNETH BROWN

BIOCHEMISTRY. A team of biochemists working in China announced in 1966 that they had successfully achieved the total synthesis of an insulin molecule. Insulin is used in the treatment of diabetes, and is isolated from the pancreas of slaughtered cattle. The development of synthetic insulin as a means of increasing the supply and of modifying the molecule to produce a more effective hormone has been a long-sought goal.

Nobel prize winner Frederick Sanger, in 1954, unraveled the sequence of amino acids in insulin. The molecule consists of two distinct amino acid chains held together by a disulfide bridge. Teams of organic chemists, such as those headed by Panayotis G. Katsoyannis of Brookhaven National Laboratory, Gordon H. Dixon of the University of British Columbia, and Helmut Zahn of Aachen, Germany, have been successful in the synthesis of each chain, but the uniting of these two chains eluded their efforts.

The Chinese achievement of a totally synthesized insulin molecule with full biological activity opens the way to a study of the relationship between the structure and function of this protein hormone.

Unraveling Antibodies. The study of the structure of antibody proteins has been impeded by the inability to distinguish antibodies from other proteins in the blood. Antibodies are produced in the tissues of animals and human beings to ward off bacteria and other foreign substances. A protein resembling antibody proteins, called Bence-Jones protein, has been found in the urine of patients suffering from a cancer known as *myeloma*.

The amino acid sequence in Bence-Jones proteins was unraveled in 1966 by Frank W. Putnam and his colleagues at Indiana University, and by C. Milstein at Cambridge in England. They discovered that the Bence-Jones protein has a total of 214 amino acids and is similar to the smaller of two chains of amino acids that occur in normal antibodies. Variations in the amino acid sequence occur in a restricted portion of the molecule, a fact that provides new insight into the amount of genetic information needed to produce specific proteins involved in the immune response.

Radiation Effects. Scientists at Cornell University found that some of the harmful effects of radiation are due to newly created substances that react with the genetic material of the cell. Prior to this it had been assumed that such effects were always the result of radiation damage to the cell itself. The scientists, Richard Holstein, Michiyasu Sugii, and Frederick Steward, irradiated the coconut milk broth in which they grew normal plant cells.

Surprisingly, they found damaged chromosomes in the cells grown in this broth. Six unidentified substances, apparently formed by the action of radiation on sugars in coconut milk, were isolated. Further experiments showed that pure sugars, when irradiated, induce growth abnormalities and chromosome damage in plants and fruit flies. The pressing question raised by this finding is whether foods preserved by irradiation are necessarily safe for human consumption.

Hormone Regulation. Seymour Levine and Richard F. Mullins, Jr., of Stanford University, studied the far-reaching effects of hormones on the central nervous system of animals. They found that the presence of gonadal, adrenal, and thyroid hormones during critical periods of development produced permanent and profound alteration in the animal's psychophysiological processes. In newborn rats the hormonal system was apparently responsible, in part, for the early stages of development of the central nervous system.

Newborn rats of either sex have a common sexual control system. In females, this system becomes fixed shortly after birth, but in males it is changed by the advent of male sex hormones, secreted by the testes. When the testes were surgically removed at birth, depriving the male animal of testosterone, and female hormones were injected, the male rat exhibited complete female sexual behavior. Male rats, however, showed no response to female hormones if castration took place after the first five days of life. The difference in response demonstrated that a crucial period occurs shortly after birth during which the rat's sexual development may be influenced. It was also shown that the sexual pattern of newborn female rats could be altered by the administration of male sex hormones. Further research may lead to an understanding of how the central nervous system regulates behavioral patterns.

Advances in Photosynthesis. James A. Bassham and R. G. Jensen at Lawrence Radiation Laboratory of the University of California reported in November that they were able to carry out the photosynthesis outside a living cell at a rate not significantly different from that taking place inside the cell. In 1954, Daniel I. Arnon was the first to produce photosynthesis outside the cell, but this was at a very slow rate. One reason for the improved rate was the use of freshly cut spinach leaves grown under carefully controlled laboratory conditions. Chloroplasts isolated from the fresh leaves were shaken, in the presence of light, in a solution containing water and radioactive carbon dioxide.

The scientists also discovered two key points in the reactions regulating the synthesis of proteins and starches. They speculated that the proper chemicals, applied at the control points, could block the formation of starches, and possibly enhance the synthesis of proteins in green leaves. While this is speculative, such a change would result in greater production of protein, and thus increase the nutritive value of plants. HAROLD FEINBERG

See also BIOLOGY; BOTANY; CHEMISTRY.

BIOLOGY. A series of experiments with hydrogen cyanide, one of the most potent of poison gases, has led to a modification in the theory of the orgin of life on earth. The experiments were conducted by Clifford N. Matthews and his colleagues of the Monsanto Chemical Company. They subjected hydrogen cyanide to an energy source of ultraviolet light and then let the resultant material react with water. The experiment produced substances that were much like large segments of protein.

In 1952, an experiment by Stanley L. Miller and Nobel prize winner Harold C. Urey had demonstrated that heat and electrical fields can influence the inorganic elements in gases to form complex organic molecules. Matthews pointed out, however, that the effect of radiation on the earth's early methane and ammonia atmosphere would result in the production of large quantities of hydrogen cyanide. Thus any theory of the origin of life must include this gas. His work suggested that hydrogen cyanide was important in the creation of life.

Animal Communication. Various means of communication exist among animals of all species, even those of the lower life-forms. For example, slime molds, organisms classified as both plant and animal, communicate by chemical means. The slime mold's life cycle starts with individual ameboid cells. Some of these cells secrete a chemical, *acrasin*, which can attract neighboring cells, and thus form a colony of cells. Some cells of the colony are able to produce spores. When the spores are released, free-swimming ameboid cells hatch and repeat the life cycle.

Margaret Vince, Cambridge University research psychologist, discovered, in 1966, that communication can take place even between the embryos of birds. Biologists have long known that all of the eggs of game birds, such as the quail, hatch at approximately the same time, even though they may have been laid hours apart. This phenomenon allows the mother bird to leave her nest for food without worrying about any unhatched eggs.

Using sensitive instruments, the psychologist was able to detect a faint clicking sound that came from inside the quail eggs. These started about 24 hours before hatching, and stopped only minutes before the eggs hatched. The clicking sounds seem to trigger a more rapid development of less mature embryos in adjacent eggs. She proved this by showing that the incubation period of an egg could be shortened by placing it among eggs that had begun incubation at least a day earlier. The newer egg hatched at the same time as the older eggs. Close proximity of eggs is necessary for the signal to be transmitted. Eggs placed several inches apart hatched independently of each other, sometimes several days apart.

In Munich, Germany, Martin Lindauer has continued the studies with bees and their communication system that were initiated by his teacher Karl von Frisch. Von Frisch, in 1951, found that by certain dance routines a bee can tell others where it has found a rich store of nectar. Lindauer has discovered that dances are also used in searching for a new hive site. When they find a likely place, the worker bees return and dance before the swarm.

Mosquito Control. Mosquitoes that breed in the rice paddies of California's Sacramento Valley have largely become resistant to man-made insecticides. Entomologist Ernest Bay of the University of California has enlisted the help of the Argentine pearlfish, *Cynolebias bellottii*, in the fight against mosquitoes. These fish, which feed on larvae, keep large areas of Argentina and Brazil mosquito free.

At maturity, a single pearlfish can consume about 50 larvae per day. When a female pearlfish is three weeks old, it produces as many as 300 eggs a week. After the spring floodwaters recede, the eggs are preserved in the dried mud. The following year the eggs hatch about an hour after the area is once again inundated. Thus a new generation of larvae-eating fish is produced. So far, Bay has been able to breed pearlfish in water-covered rice fields; he now hopes to mass-breed the fish in his laboratory and stock the rice fields of California. This may prove to be a happy solution to pest control, since it does not involve noxious chemicals. HAROLD FEINBERG

See also BIOCHEMISTRY; BOTANY; INSECT.

BLAKE, EUGENE CARSON (1906-), stated clerk of the General Assembly of the United Presbyterian Church in the United States, was elected general secretary of the World Council of Churches. He succeeded the retiring Dutch theologian Willem A. Visser't Hooft. Blake has long been active in World Council of Churches affairs, and in 1961 headed the consultations that brought the Russian Orthodox Church into that body.

Blake was born in St. Louis on Nov. 7, 1906. He was graduated with honors in philosophy from Princeton University in 1928, where he returned to receive his Bachelor of Theology degree in 1932. He also studied in Edinburgh, Scotland, and later received a Doctor of Divinity degree from Occidental College in Los Angeles. He married the former Valina Gillespie in 1929.

As executive officer for some 3,000,000 Presbyterians, he has led his denomination through many years of ecumenical and social change. In 1960, he proposed a consultation to unite Protestant denominations in the United States. He has been a strong advocate of racial integration, and, in 1963, was arrested for leading Negro and white marchers in an attempt to desegregate Baltimore's Gwynn Oak Amusement Park.

The World Council of Churches encompasses 214 Protestant, Anglican, and Orthodox bodies. Its headquarters are in Geneva, Switzerland.

BLINDNESS. A large amount of legislation on health, education, and welfare, enacted into law by the 89th Congress, became operative during 1966. While much of the legislation did not deal primarily with services to blind persons, most of it will benefit them. As a result of the amendments, the number of blind persons rehabilitated into employment in the United States rose 11 per cent during 1966.

Education. The trend toward educating blind children with nonblind schoolmates in public schools continued to increase throughout the world. According to the American Printing House for the Blind, 7,119 blind children in the United States were being educated in boarding schools in 1966, as compared to 10,934 in the public school systems. In addition, 1,248 blind children attended public and private institutions caring for multihandicapped individuals. The increase was attributed largely to implementation of educational legislation.

International Programs. Illustrative of the many world conferences held in 1966 were two sponsored by the American Foundation for Overseas Blind. Representatives of 13 nations took part in the First African Conference on Work for the Blind in Lagos, Nigeria, in January, 1966. They developed a five-year plan to bring prevention, education, and rehabilitation services to African nations. In May, 1966, representatives of 17 Spanish-speaking countries met with U.S. delegates in Buenos Aires, Argentina, to consider cooperative undertakings in the printing of braille books and services for the blind.

Braille. The American Printing House for the Blind published the *Nemeth Code of Braille Mathematics and Scientific Notation* on May 15, 1966. The code was designed to clarify communications between blind mathematicians and scientists. On Aug. 18, 1966, Massachusetts Institute of Technology successfully demonstrated a new technique of converting computer output to Grade II braille, which is the most widely used form of braille. The development has many applications in addition to its vast potential for increasing the production of braille literature throughout the world.

World Blindness Estimates. The National Institute of Neurological Diseases and Blindness has been developing a model reporting registry of blind people for each state in the United States. This system has been adopted in other nations. One such project is a complete census of an urban-rural area in Egypt. Although the census is not finished, validated statistics thus far indicate a blindness prevalence rate of 14 per 1,000 (seven times that of the United States) in urban areas and 45 per 1,000 (almost 23 times the U.S. rate) in rural areas. Although a much wider world sampling should be made, the facts indicate that current estimates of 10,000,000 to 15,000,000 blind persons in the world should be increased. DOUGLAS C. MACFARLAND

BOATS AND BOATING activity expanded at a lively rate in 1966, as sales reached an estimated $2,817,000,000, a gain of more than 5 per cent over 1965. At the New York City National Boat Show alone, a record $46,600,000 in sales were made in just 12 days.

Among the most noticeable trends were a continuing increase in the use of fiberglass for hulls in both motorboats and sailboats, a 60 per cent jump in production of inboard-outboard propulsion units, and a significant growth in the number of houseboats made and sold.

The U.S. Coast Guard began a program of stricter enforcement of federal motorboat safety regulations. Special emphasis was placed on proper ventilation of bilges and space around engines and fuel tanks, and on proper lights for night cruising.

Motor Racing. Tragedy struck unlimited hydroplane racing at the height of its biggest season in history. Drivers Ron Musson, Rex Manchester, and Don Wilson died in accidents in the President's Cup race on the Potomac, on June 19. Musson, the champion driver in 1963, 1964, and 1965, was driving a new *Miss Bardahl* at 170 miles per hour when the boat nosed into the water and exploded. Three hours later, Manchester and Wilson collided in the final heat. Earlier in the year, Hank Bowman was killed while racing his hydroplane in the Orange Bowl Regatta on Biscayne Bay, near Miami.

Hydroplane driver Bill Legg was thrown into the air when his boat hit a wave on a turn in the National Hydro Limited race, July 31.

In the Gold Cup on July 3 at Detroit, Chuck Thompson was killed when *Smirnoff* blew up. The remaining nine drivers voted unanimously to resume the race the next day, and Mira Slovak, a 37-year-old airline pilot, drove *Tahoe Miss* to victory. Slovak finished the season as the year's leading driver.

In ocean racing, Jim Wynne of Miami won the world drivers' championship, scoring 36 points to 23 for runner-up Merrick Lewis of Alliance, Ohio. Wynne entered only four races during the year, but won them all. First he won the Sam Griffith Memorial between Miami and Bimini in a controversial gas-turbine powered craft called *Thunderbird*. Officials, however, awarded the prize money to Jerry Larger of Florida because they considered Wynne's boat experimental and ruled him ineligible. The race was marred by rough weather, as 20-foot waves swamped 28 of the 30 boats entered, including Dick Bertram's *Brave Moppie*, the top boat of 1965.

In subsequent races, Wynne switched to *Ghost Rider*, a boat with conventional gasoline engines, and won the Miami-to-Nassau, Cowes-to-Torquay (England), and Miami-to-Key West races.

Sailing. Sumner A. Long's 57-foot yawl *Ondine*, of Larchmont, N.Y., was the overall winner of the 3,400-mile Bermuda-to-Denmark transatlantic race. Robert Johnson of Portland, Ore., was first to finish in his 72-foot ketch *Ticonderoga*, but *Ondine* was placed first on corrected time. *Ondine* also won the 1,430-mile San Diego-to-Acapulco ocean race.

Winner of the men's North American sailing championship and the Mallory Cup was William S. Cox of Darien, Conn. Cox edged out John J. McNamara of Boston with slightly more consistent sailing in the eight-race series, although McNamara won three races to Cox's one.

Another successful sailor was Paul Elvstrom of Denmark, who won world championships in two classes. In August, Elvstrom skippered *Web III* to the 5.5-meter title at Skovshoved, Denmark. A month later he won the World Star class title, beating defending champion Lowell North of San Diego, Calif., by only three points, at Kiel, Germany.

Great Britain won the International Catamaran Challenge Trophy, known as the "Little America's Cup," for the sixth straight time. The British defender, *Lady Helmsman*, skippered by Reg White, defeated the American challenger, *Gamecock*, four races to two. The latter was sailed by Bob Shiels of Darien, Conn.

Preparations for Australia's second challenge for the America's Cup intensified. A syndicate of Melbourne yachtsmen built *Dame Pattie* to vie with a revamped *Gretel*, the 1964 challenger, for the right to represent the Aussies. The challenge series will begin Sept. 12, 1967, off Newport, R.I. JAMES O. DUNAWAY

BOLIVIA. See LATIN AMERICA.

BOOKS. See CANADIAN LITERATURE; LITERATURE; LITERATURE FOR CHILDREN.

BOSTON reduced its property tax 12 per cent to $101 per $1,000 valuation, as a result of a state-enacted $185,000,000 tax program. The purpose of the reduction was to improve chances of continuing investment in the city. The lawmakers, however, failed to extend the state's credit for a proposed $98,000,000 sports complex.

Also likely to spur the city and the metropolitan area's growth, was a $369,000,000 program of mass transit improvements announced in August by the Massachusetts Bay Transportation Authority.

Once a staid city, Boston was becoming a major convention site. In 1966, 289 conventions met there, attracting 225,000 persons who spent approximately $100,000,000 while visiting the city.

The beginning of rehabilitation in the central business district was marked by the temporary relocation of Raymond's, a leading department store, and completion of the downtown area's first high rise apartment tower. Adding to the activity in Government Center, was the 26-story John Fitzgerald Kennedy Federal Office Building tower, which was dedicated in May. A new city hall was scheduled for completion in 1967.

In September, an experimental program of busing more than 200 Negro children to suburban schools began. Approved by the state legislature, the entire tuition and transportation costs of $259,000 were financed by a U.S. grant. DONALD W. LIEF

BOTANY. Phytochrome, a complex molecule in plant cells, was further analyzed by scientists of the U.S. Department of Agriculture at Beltsville, Md., where it was first discovered in 1964. Phytochrome molecules regulate such processes as germination, growth, and flowering, turning these functions on and off in response to the length of days and nights. It is highly sensitive to light in the red and far-red wave lengths.

In September, Sterling B. Hendricks of the Beltsville laboratory reported at the 152nd meeting of the American Chemical Society that the *chromophore* (color-producing segment) of phytochrome had been identified. The chromophore is a blue pigment, related in structure to chlorophyll of plants and to the iron-containing constituent of blood.

Dormant Seeds. For the first time, a botanist succeeded in observing the internal cell structure of dormant plant seeds – a task that had previously defied electron microscope examination. Dormant seeds, in a state of suspended animation called *anabiosis*, are able to survive long periods under adverse conditions, and to revive years later. During anabiosis, the seed skin thickens and hardens and water content falls to about 10 per cent of normal. Scientists had failed when they tried to study seed cells in this state, primarily because the liquid solutions used in preparing slides for microscope inspection immediately revived the cells.

German botanist Ernst Perner successfully prepared anabiotic pea cells for electron microscope inspection by using dry osmic acid vapors for slide preparation. Perner's cell photographs reveal that cellular protein converts to an inactive, crystalline form during anabiosis. The pictures also show that the tiny sacs of fluid in the cells, called *vacuoles*, move to the inner cell walls during anabiosis, presumably to strengthen the wall and help provide insulation.

Pollution. Plants were mentioned in connection with air pollution as both friend and foe. University of Delaware plant pathologists experimented with test plots of pollution-sensitive plants in an attempt to develop a method for using plants to identify air pollutants. Plants under study included spinach, tobacco, annual bluegrass, and pine for detection of ozone; snapdragons and carnations for detection of ethylene; and tomatoes and alfalfa for detection of sulfur dioxide.

Certain trees, including the pine and sage, were accused of being the source of 10 times as much air pollution as man and machine combined. Botanist Frits W. Went of the University of Nevada told the Fourth International Bio-Meteorologist Congress, held at New Brunswick, N.J., in September, that the trees emit harmful molecular substances known as terpenes and esters. These substances then react with other airborne chemicals to form large amounts of pollutants. JAMES A. PEARRE

See also GARDEN AND LAWN.

BOTSWANA, formerly the British Protectorate of Bechuanaland, became Africa's 38th independent nation on September 30. The independence ceremony, ending 81 years of British rule, was held in Gaberones, Botswana's capital. Botswana is mostly a desert country, and independence came during a severe drought. Aided by $12,600,000 in funds from the United Nations (UN) World Food Program, its people worked hard throughout the year on water conservation programs to prevent severe famine. Great Britain promised economic aid of $36,400,000 over a three-year period.

Independence day marked a high point in the career of Sir Seretse Khama, the president of the new nation. Educated in South Africa and Britain, Khama was once banished from Bechuanaland for marrying a British white woman.

Botswana is landlocked and must use the seaports of the Republic of South Africa. Three days before Botswana's independence, Rhodesia moved to protect its own vital supply route to South African seaports by taking over operation of the railroad that crosses Botswana. In September, the UN General Assembly warned South Africa that any interference with Botswana would violate the UN Charter.

Facts in Brief. Population: 514,478. Government: President Seretse Khama. Monetary Unit: rand (1 = U.S. $1.41). Foreign Trade: no statistics available. Principal Export: beef. BENJAMIN E. THOMAS

BOWLING. Defending champion Dick Weber of St. Louis scored one of his most satisfying victories in the All-Star tournament at Lansing, Mich. By a narrow margin of 684 pins to 681 over Nelson Burton, Jr., also of St. Louis, Weber took the match-play final and gained his fourth All-Star title. He thus equaled the record of Don Carter, also from St. Louis. Joy Abel of Chicago won the women's title, defeating Bette Rockwell of Lynn, Mass.

Wayne Zahn of Atlanta earned $25,000 by beating Weber, 203 to 170, in the one-game final of the Firestone Tournament of Champions held annually at Akron, Ohio.

In the two-month American Bowling Congress (ABC) tournament at Rochester, N.Y., the Plaza Lanes Club of Sault Sainte Marie, Ont., won with a pin fall of 3,066 for its three games. A total of 26,040 men took part. Bob Strampe of Detroit won seven straight matches to earn the ABC Masters title.

In the Woman's International Bowling Congress (WIBC) tourney at New Orleans, the Gossards of Chicago scored 2,755 to pace a field of 4,083 teams. Judy Lee of Los Angeles won the match-game equivalent of the men's Masters.

In October, Carl Wilsing, a 226-average bowler, rolled games of 298, 300, and 278 at Sheboygan, Wis., for the second highest series recorded in ABC league bowling. The top mark was set in 1939 by Allie Brandt of Lockport, N.Y. JOHN LAKE

BOXING. Heavyweight champion Cassius Clay, who prefers to be called Muhammad Ali, took on virtually all comers in a feverish 12 months of activity inside and outside the ring. At Toronto, Clay outpointed George Chuvalo, and in London he stopped Henry Cooper and knocked out Brian London. At Frankfurt, Germany, he scored a technical knockout over Karl Mildenberger. Finally, he pounded out a technical knockout over Cleveland Williams at the Houston Astrodome.

In March, Illinois boxing officials revoked their approval for the Clay-Ernie Terrell fight scheduled for Chicago. Toronto finally accepted it, but by that time, Terrell, recognized as heavyweight champion by the World Boxing Association (WBA), had decided that the fight would not pay well, and he withdrew. Chuvalo, who lives in Toronto, took his place. The Clay-Terrell fight was rescheduled for Feb. 6, 1967, at Houston.

World Champion Boxers

Division	Champion	Where Fought	Year Won
Heavyweight	Muhammad Ali	Miami	1964
Light-heavyweight	Dick Tiger	New York	1966
Middleweight	Emile Griffith	New York	1966
Welterweight	Curtis Cokes	New Orleans	1966
Lightweight	Carlos Ortiz	San Juan	1965
Featherweight	Vincente Saldivar	Mexico City	1964
Bantamweight	Masahiko Harada	Nagoya, Japan	1965
Flyweight	Horacio Accavallo	Tokyo	1966

Other Champions. The year's most controversial fight occurred at Mexico City in October between lightweight champion Carlos Ortiz of New York and former featherweight ruler Sugar Ramos of Mexico City. Referee Billy Conn stopped the fight in the fifth round, awarding a technical knockout to Ortiz because of a cut over Ramos' left eye. Ramon Velazquez of the World Boxing Council then overruled Conn, and ordered Ortiz to return to the ring. When Ortiz refused, Velazquez declared Ramos the winner and new champion. In the rest of the boxing world however, Carlos Ortiz continued to be recognized as the champion.

Welterweight champion Emile Griffith of New York won the middleweight crown from Dick Tiger of Nigeria, and defended it against Joey Archer of the Bronx, winning both fights by decisions. Griffith was forced to give up his welterweight title, after he failed in a court appeal against the rule that a boxer can be champion of only one division at a time. Curtis Cokes of Dallas won the elimination for the vacant welterweight crown.

In December, Tiger moved up to the light-heavyweight class and outpointed Jose Torres of New York for the title. JAMES O. DUNAWAY

BOY SCOUTS OF AMERICA. See YOUTH ORGANIZATIONS.

BOYS' CLUBS OF AMERICA. See YOUTH ORGANIZATIONS.

BRAZIL. General Arthur Costa e Silva, a former minister of war, was elected president by a joint session of the Brazilian congress on Oct. 3, 1966. Costa, who was not to take office until March, 1967, was expected to continue the austerity program instituted by outgoing President Humberto de Alencar Castelo Branco.

In 1966, President Castelo Branco had taken strong action against military elements who, in the name of "anti-Communism," had repeatedly challenged his administration. In September, he relieved the commanding general of the Fourth Army of his post. The action followed an attempt by army officers to suppress a declaration made by Roman Catholic bishops denouncing "social injustices" and nonobservance of labor laws in the northeast area. President Castelo Branco had taken equally strong action against corruption in government. In one case, São Paulo's Governor Adhemar de Barros was removed from office and stripped of his political rights for 10 years for allegedly trying to buy votes in the gubernatorial election. However, the removal of six congressmen and four lesser elected officials from office in October, on the grounds of corruption and subversion, touched off an open revolt in congress. Castelo Branco immediately ordered that body to recess for a month. He appealed for understanding and support, saying he had acted in defense of the ideals of the 1964 revolution.

The Castelo Branco regime's unpopularity was due largely to its stiff but necessary austerity and stabilization measures. To make sure these policies would continue, the government decreed that in the future, the president, the governors of 11 states, and the mayors of state capitals would be chosen by both houses of congress. It did permit, however, the election of a new chamber of deputies by direct, popular vote on November 15. A committee of jurists was appointed to revise the 1946 constitution, incorporating into it the government's constitutional amendments and the permanent clauses of the institutional acts.

Brazil fought valiantly to stem its vicious inflationary spiral but the odds were formidable. It hoped to keep the rise in living costs down to 35 per cent in 1966 versus 45 per cent in 1965 and 85 per cent in 1964. But in the first nine months of 1966, these costs climbed by 35.2 per cent. On March 1, the country's great mass of poor, unskilled workers got some relief from rising prices through a 30 per cent hike in minimum wages and suspension of federal and state sales taxes on food essentials. But Brazilians continued to suffer from steadily dipping purchasing power. Discontent grew, while demonstrations and riots became more numerous.

Early in August, the government made another major move against spiraling costs. It imposed a one-year wage freeze and offered a 20 per cent cut in income tax assessments to companies that would refrain from raising their prices. In the fall, good climatic conditions raised hopes for bumper food crops that would help reduce living costs.

After a good performance in the first half of the year, business began to stall. Sales of durables were off 25 per cent, automobile inventories were building up, and the bankruptcy rate was rising as the credit squeeze was increasingly felt. On a more encouraging note, the treasury department's deficit for the first six months of 1966 was 50 per cent less than expected.

By August, Brazil's foreign exchange holdings were well past the $500,000,000 level and they were expected to be close to $800,000,000 by year's end. This was due largely to the fact that the republic's trade balance promised to be highly favorable. Also expected to improve the situation was a heavy inflow of foreign capital. In July, the finance minister presented plans to a foreign consortium calling for an economic development program that would cost an estimated $1,100,000,000.

Facts in Brief. Population: 85,011,000. Government: President Humberto de Alencar Castelo Branco. Monetary Unit: cruzeiro (2,200 = U.S. $1). Foreign Trade: exports, $1,595,700,000; imports, $1,097,500,000. Principal Exports: coffee, cotton, iron ore. MARY C. WEBSTER

BRIDGE AND TUNNEL. See BUILDING AND CONSTRUCTION.

BRIDGE, CONTRACT. Italy's famed Blue Team won its eighth consecutive world contract bridge championship at St. Vincent, Italy, in April and May. The North American team was second. The next event was set for Miami, Fla., in April, 1967.

The British Bridge League announced in August that an independent inquiry had resulted in the exoneration of Terrence Reese and Boris Schapiro, whom the World Bridge Federation had found guilty of cheating during the 1965 world contract bridge championship at Buenos Aires, Argentina. The federation said it seemed unlikely, however, that it would accept the results of the British inquiry.

At the spring tournament of the American Contract Bridge League (ACBL), held at Louisville, Ky., in March, the Harold S. Vanderbilt Cup was awarded to a team composed of Philip Feldesman of New York City; Ira Rubin of Paramus, N.J.; Lew Mathe and Robert Hamman of Los Angeles, Calif.; and Sammy Kehela of Toronto, Canada.

Winners of the Spingold trophy at the ACBL summer tournament in Denver, Colo., were Ira Rubin, Alvin Roth, and William Root of New York City, and Curtis Smith of Houston. THEODORE M. O'LEARY

BRITISH COLUMBIA. See CANADA.

BRITISH COMMONWEALTH OF NATIONS. See GREAT BRITAIN; and articles on various countries of the Commonwealth.

BRITISH GUIANA. See GUYANA.

BUILDING AND CONSTRUCTION expenditures reached an estimated high of $75,300,000,000 in 1966. This represented an increase of 4.9 per cent above the $71,900,000,000 spent in the preceding year, according to revised 1965 figures issued by the U.S. Bureau of the Census. On the basis of total construction contracts, the F. W. Dodge Company predicted a 3 per cent gain for 1967 expenditures.

Construction costs rose to record highs in 1966, as labor, materials, equipment, and money costs continued to climb. The 20-city construction cost index published by *Engineering News-Record* indicated an increase of 5.2 per cent in the first nine months of the year, almost double the rise in the comparable 1965 period. Labor shortages were acute in some areas, and wages climbed. Average hourly wage rates for common labor in the 20 cities were up 20 cents from the December, 1965, level, and skilled labor rates were up 23 cents. In addition to higher wages, a sharp uptrend in prices of materials (except lumber) and equipment pushed costs higher.

Tight money, with costs of borrowing the highest in decades, reduced housing starts to the lowest level in years (see HOUSING). Higher interest rates also curtailed borrowing of funds for public projects.

New Building Techniques. At the annual meeting of the American Institute of Steel Construction in Boston, the Tishman Research Corporation of New York City described a structural system utilizing metal-edged gypsum planks over steel bar joists. Its engineers said the system would make steel-frame construction competitive with *flat-plate* (reinforced concrete slab) construction.

An ancient type of construction, the masonry bearing wall, enjoyed a revival in 1966. This new-old method of building integrates floors and walls, allowing walls and partitions as thin as six inches to bear heavy loads. A 17-story apartment building with reinforced brick bearing walls was under construction in Denver. It was the first all-masonry "high-rise" to be built in the United States since Chicago's Monadnock Building was erected in 1891.

Building Codes were being overhauled in many U.S. cities, including Denver, Colo.; Houston, Tex.; and Philadelphia, Pa. Some of the new codes permit such sweeping changes as the use of plastic pipe for cold water, drainage, and vent systems. Most permit more use of prestressed and reinforced concrete. More than 150 communities have adopted a model code prepared by the Building Officials Conference of America.

Outstanding Projects. With the opening of the new Metropolitan Opera House on September 16, New York City's Lincoln Center for the Performing Arts neared completion. Only the Juilliard School of Music remained to be built. The seven-level, 3,800-

Drilling rig *Gem III* takes test bores of English Channel seabed to plot the route of a tunnel Britain and France hope to complete in 1975.

seat structure is the largest opera house yet built and the first to be air-conditioned. Its stage is the most highly mechanized of any in the world. See MUSIC (Close-Up).

Busch Memorial Stadium, a key structure in the master plan for St. Louis, was dedicated on May 8. Supporting facilities include shops, restaurants, and parking garages. The project will eventually take in 31 blocks and cost about $89,000,000.

The American Society of Civil Engineers' Outstanding Civil Engineering Achievement Award for 1966 went to a huge project, the National Aeronautics and Space Administration (NASA) Complex 39, the Apollo-Saturn assembly and launch facility at Cape Kennedy, Florida. The huge Space Age complex is dominated by the Vehicle Assembly Building, the world's largest in terms of volume of space. See SPACE EXPLORATION.

Bridges. Opening of two great European bridges – the Tejo (Tagus) River Bridge at Lisbon, Portugal, and the Severn River Bridge between southwest England and southern Wales – highlighted 1966's bridge building. Both were completed six months ahead of schedule.

The Tejo River Bridge, opened to traffic on August 6, has a center suspension span of 3,323 feet, the longest in Europe and the fifth longest in the world. The bridge also set records for the highest towers (625 feet) for any bridge in Europe; for the world's longest continuous truss (7,472 feet from anchorage to anchorage); and for the world's longest bridge designed for both highway and rail traffic.

The Severn River Bridge, dedicated by Queen Elizabeth II on September 8, is a link in the London-to-South Wales M4 Motorway. Its total length of 6,033 feet includes two side spans of 1,000 feet each and a main suspension span of 3,240 feet, the third longest in Europe. The bridge utilizes a continuous closed-box girder construction for a significant saving in weight and steel. It weighs about 36 per cent less than Scotland's new (1964) Forth Bridge, with a main span of 3,300 feet. A closed box structure is stronger than one with open ends or than the H-shape of the traditional girder. The bridge's deck was prefabricated on shore in 88 sections (or boxes). Each section was floated out into the river, hoisted up and welded into place.

A New U.S. Bridge, under construction across Narragansett Bay between Newport and Jamestown, R.I., employed a new, timesaving technique of installing suspension cables. The cables were fabricated in the Steelton (Pa.) plant of Bethlehem Steel Corporation and shipped to the site on reels. The 76 parallel-wire strands of 61 wires each were pulled off the reels and across the bridge spans instead of being spun in place wire by wire, as under the conventional (and more expensive) method. The contracts for the two-mile crossing's steel superstructure were awarded in June.

Also in June, plans for building a $40,000,000 toll crossing connecting San Diego and Coronado, Calif., over San Diego Bay were announced. The 2.1-mile, four-lane crossing will be the nation's third major orthotropic bridge, a type of bridge in which the flanged top of the girders form the road deck. Its three orthotropic spans will total 1,880 feet.

Farther north, the world's longest orthotropic span was on its way to completion sometime in mid-1967. The 7.4-mile San Mateo-to-Hayward (Calif.) crossing of lower San Francisco Bay will include a 5,500-foot orthotropic section.

And in the Pacific Northwest, the 4.2-mile bridge across the mouth of the Columbia River was dedicated August 27. The bridge, connecting Astoria, Ore., and Point Ellice, Washington, consists of two near-shore girder spans and a long causeway in between. The bridge closed the last gap in U.S. 101, the coastal highway from the Mexican border north to the northern shore of Olympic Peninsula in the state of Washington.

Dams. Ghana, on Jan. 22, 1966, dedicated its 370-foot-high Akosombo Dam, key structure in the West African nation's $200,000,000 Volta River power project. In August, U.S. Vice-President Hubert H. Humphrey dedicated the 10,180-foot-long Barkley Dam on Kentucky's Cumberland River. The multipurpose dam cost $142,000,000, $3,000,000 less than the original estimate.

Also in August, work got underway on the last of the four Columbia River Treaty dams – the $352,000,000 Libby (Mont.) Dam on the Kootenai River, a tributary of the Columbia. Work on the other three dams – Arrow, Duncan, and Mica, all in Canada – was underway, on or ahead of schedule.

The world's first tidal power dam was completed in March. By summer, the Rance River Dam at St. Malo, France, was harnessing tides, which have a daily rise and fall of 33 feet. Its *maremotrice* (sea motor) was generating enough electric power to supply a city the size of Boston.

New Tunnels. Selection of the designer for the $60,000,000 Cripple Creek Tunnel through the Rockies was announced in March by the Colorado Department of Highways. The two-lane, 1.7-mile-long tunnel, at an elevation of about 11,000 feet, will provide an all-weather crossing of the Continental Divide. When it is opened to traffic, perhaps in 1969, it will save 11 miles of travel, compared with the present route over Loveland Pass.

In late September, a 313-foot-long binocular-shaped section of steel tunnel was floated into position near Oakland, Calif., and lowered onto the floor of San Francisco Bay. It was the first of 57 segments of the four underwater miles of a six-mile tunnel link in the Bay Area Rapid Transit District's system.

M. E. JESSUP

See also ARCHITECTURE; CONSERVATION; TRANSPORTATION.

BULGARIA. The Central Committee, after much delay, approved far-reaching economic reforms in April. Under them, detailed planning functions were to be transferred from central agencies in Sofia to industrial branches. This decentralization goes far beyond that of the Soviet Union or the other Communist-bloc nations. See RUSSIA.

In foreign affairs, Bulgaria's official visiting list reflected the regime's new interest in widening its horizons. In February, it played host to a party-government delegation from Romania and in April, it sent a delegation to Yugoslavia. In July, diplomatic relations were initiated with Canada. In August, Bulgarian Foreign Minister Ivan Bashev visited Turkey. Party Leader Todor Zhivkov made an official visit to France in October.

None of these exchange visits, however, indicated any serious loosening of Bulgaria's ties with the Soviet Union. In the Soviet Union's conflict with Communist China, Bulgaria continued to give full support to the Soviet's position. Bulgaria also increased its aid to North Vietnam during the year by concluding two agreements for interest-free credit.

Facts in Brief. Population: 8,330,000. Government: Communist Party First Secretary Todor Zhivkov; President Georgi Traikov. Monetary Unit: lev (2=U.S. $1). Foreign Trade: exports, $196,400,000; imports, $302,800,000. Principal Exports: tobacco, clothing.

H. GORDON SKILLING

BUNDY, McGEORGE (1919-), last of the New Frontiersmen to leave the White House, took over the presidency of the Ford Foundation on March 1, 1966. As special assistant for national security affairs since 1961, he had exercised a great deal of influence on foreign policy. His success has been credited to a high intelligence and a talent for analyzing problems quickly and trenchantly.

Bundy was born in Boston, Mass., on March 30, 1919, a direct descendant of the Lowells and other "proper Bostonians." He is said to have earned the best grades on record at Groton School and Yale University, where he earned an A.B. degree in 1940.

He became a junior fellow at Harvard University in 1941. He served during World War II in army intelligence. From 1946 to 1948, he worked with Henry L. Stimson as co-author of the former Secretary of War's autobiography. He became a lecturer in government at Harvard in 1949, and four years later – at the age of 34 – was made dean of the faculty of arts and sciences.

The talent of this Yale man and Republican came to the notice of a famous Harvard man and Democrat. When John F. Kennedy became President, he called Bundy to the White House.

Bundy plays a fast game of tennis and likes to escape the tensions of work at parties. He married a Boston girl, Mary B. Lothrop, in 1950. They have four children – all boys.

BURMA continued to pursue a policy of isolationism toward its Asian neighbors as well as the nations of the West. Under its chief of state, General Ne Win, it also continued its efforts to nationalize the economy. The results were negligible.

Prices on basic foodstuffs reached new highs during 1966. Rice and timber production decreased. The Burmese, however, were not starving due, for the most part, to the basic natural wealth of the country. What was most urgently needed was managerial skills.

General Ne Win continued his tight and restrictive military rule. Former political leaders remained under house arrest or in prison. The press was carefully censored, and dissident organizations were either suppressed, harassed, or driven underground. Ne Win, however, unhesitatingly made trips to both the Communist and non-Communist world, seemingly confident of his ability to retain power, even while out of the country. As a result of his visits to the United States and Great Britain in 1966, his policy of neutrality was gaining acceptance and respect among the Western nations.

Facts in Brief. Population: 25,556,000. Government: Union Revolutionary Council Chairman Ne Win. Monetary Unit: kyat (4.72=U.S. $1). Foreign Trade: exports, $224,700,000; imports, $247,300,000. Principal Exports: lumber, oilseed cake and meal, rice.

H. GORDON SKILLING

BURUNDI. Crown Prince Charles Ndizeye, 19-year-old heir to the throne, seized the government on July 8. He formed a new cabinet and appointed Captain Michel Micombero to replace Leopold Biha as premier. Prince Charles' father, Mwami (King) Mwambutsa IV, was in Switzerland. On November 28, the young prince, now Mwami Mioame Ntare V, was himself overthrown by army forces led by Micombero. Military men were appointed to all key government positions. Upon naming himself president, Micombero established a 13-member National Revolutionary Council.

Burundi accused neighboring Rwanda in January of permitting armed bands to raid Burundi. Rwanda countercharged that armed Watusi refugees in northern Burundi were planning to invade Rwanda. The two countries agreed in April to re-establish peaceful relations. Then, in August, after signing a security pact with Congo (Kinshasa) and Rwanda, the prince's government announced it would resume relations with Communist China.

Facts in Brief. Population: 2,970,000. Government: President Michel Micombero. Monetary Unit: franc (86.86=U.S. $1). Foreign Trade: exports, $30,200,000; imports, $21,600,000. Principal Export: coffee.

BENJAMIN E. THOMAS

BUS. See TRANSPORTATION.

BUSINESS. See ECONOMY, THE; Section One, SYLVIA PORTER: FOCUS ON THE ECONOMY.

Alan S. Boyd, 44, was named by President Lyndon B. Johnson to head the new Cabinet-level Department of Transportation.

CABINET. On Nov. 6, 1966, President Lyndon B. Johnson selected Alan S. Boyd, undersecretary for transportation in the Department of Commerce, to head the new Department of Transportation.

The department, the 12th in the Cabinet, is also the fourth largest. When in full operation, it will employ nearly 100,000 people and spend about $6,000,000,000 a year. Much of the controversy over congressional approval of the new department centered about the various government agencies and bureaus it was to include.

U.S. Cabinet as of Dec. 31, 1966
(In order of succession to the presidency)

Secretary of State	Dean Rusk
Secretary of the Treasury	Henry H. Fowler
Secretary of Defense	Robert S. McNamara
Attorney General (acting)	Ramsey Clark
Postmaster General	Lawrence F. O'Brien
Secretary of the Interior	Stewart L. Udall
Secretary of Agriculture	Orville L. Freeman
Secretary of Commerce	John T. Connor
Secretary of Labor	W. Willard Wirtz
Secretary of Health, Education, and Welfare	John W. Gardner
Secretary of Housing and Urban Development	Robert C. Weaver
Secretary of Transportation	Alan S. Boyd

Among the agencies placed in the Department of Transportation were: the Federal Aviation Agency, Bureau of Public Roads, Coast Guard, Civil Aeronautics Board (safety functions only), Interstate Commerce Commission, and the National Transportation Safety Board. See TRANSPORTATION.

HUD. Robert C. Weaver became the first head of the Department of Housing and Urban Development (HUD) on Jan. 18, 1966. The post had been vacant since the department was created in November, 1965. The core of HUD was the Federal Housing and Home Finance Agency, which had been directed by Weaver since 1961. See CITY AND REGIONAL PLANNING.

Weaver, 59, was speedily confirmed by the Senate with hardly a murmur from Southern segregationists. He was the first Negro to be named to the Cabinet. The Senate also approved Robert C. Wood as undersecretary of the new department.

State. On Oct. 3, 1966, Nicholas deB. Katzenbach left his post as Attorney General of the United States to become undersecretary of state. As Katzenbach changed responsibilities, he was under presidential mandate to continue as chairman of the Justice Department's National Crime Commission until its work was completed early in 1967.

Justice. Ramsey Clark, son of Supreme Court Justice and former Attorney General Tom C. Clark, became acting Attorney General when Katzenbach's post became vacant.

CALDECOTT MEDAL. See LITERATURE FOR CHILDREN (Awards).

CAMBODIA found itself once again involved in a border dispute with the United States during 1966. On at least four occasions–July 31, August 2, September 7, and September 22–American aircraft had violated Cambodia's frontiers while in pursuit of North Vietnamese guerrillas who were using Cambodia as a base for forays into South Vietnam.

Although the United States subsequently apologized for the violations, its attempts to resume full diplomatic relations–ruptured in 1965–were rebuffed by Prince Norodom Sihanouk. A proposed visit by U.S. ambassador at large W. Averell Harriman was abruptly canceled. On September 30, Cambodia filed a protest with the United Nations in which it characterized U.S. actions as aggression. See UNITED NATIONS; VIETNAM.

The country continued to prosper as the economy made steady gains, especially in light industry. A rise in exports of rice, rubber, and pepper helped to increase its foreign exchange. Progress was also made in such social fields as health and education.

Facts in Brief. Population: 6,660,000. Government: Chief of State Norodom Sihanouk; Prime Minister Norodom Kantol. Monetary Unit: riel (34.93 = U.S. $1). Foreign Trade: exports, $105,300,000; imports, $103,100,000. Principal Exports: rice, rubber, maize, pepper. JOHN N. STALKER

CAMEROON. See AFRICA.

CAMP FIRE GIRLS. See YOUTH ORGANIZATIONS.

CANADA

Canada prepared to celebrate the 100th anniversary of the confederation of the provinces. The centennial was to be climaxed with a World's Fair, Expo 67, in Montreal from April 28 to Oct. 27, 1967. With the colorful observance, the country's unity seemed stronger; the drive to separate Quebec from the rest of Canada seemed to be dying, and a new balance of fiscal power between the provinces and the central government was emerging. Canadians were trying to hold back inflation in their booming economy. The population boomed as well, topping 20,000,000 in 1966.

The 27th Parliament opened on January 18, after the bitterly contested election of Canada's fourth minority government since 1957. The Liberals held 130 out of 265 seats, Conservatives 97, New Democratic party 21, Créditistes eight, Social Credit five, independents three, and one vacancy that was expected to go to the Liberals. Later, in September, Prime Minister Lester B. Pearson's Liberals captured a Quebec seat from the Conservatives. The victory edged them one seat closer to a voting majority in the House of Commons.

The Prime Minister had shuffled his cabinet on Dec. 17, 1965, naming Mitchell Sharp as minister of finance. Sharp left the Department of Trade and Commerce, which was taken over by Robert H. Winters, a Toronto businessman. Allan MacEachen, a Nova Scotian, moved from the Department of Labor to become minister of national health and welfare. A powerful new figure in the cabinet was Jean Marchand, a former Quebec labor leader, who became the first minister of manpower and immigration.

An Affair to Forget. Controversy erupted in Parliament over the Munsinger affair, Canada's first sex-and-security scandal. Early in March, Lucien Cardin, the minister of justice, challenged Conservative leader John G. Diefenbaker to reveal his participation in the case, which had occurred in the late 1950s, during Diefenbaker's tenure as Prime Minister. It was soon disclosed that Gerda Munsinger, an East German woman, had been allowed to enter Canada in 1955, although she had previously been denied entry to the country on security grounds.

Mrs. Munsinger, the former wife of a U.S. serviceman, had a police record in Europe of espionage for Russia, imprisonment for possessing faulty docu-

A potash plant rising from a Saskatchewan wheat field typifies industrial expansion into Canada's rapidly developing west.

ments, petty theft, and prostitution. In Canada, she associated with criminals in Montreal. It was alleged that she was intimate with Pierre Sévigny, the associate minister of national defense in the Diefenbaker government, and was known socially by other ministers and executive assistants in the Conservative government.

These revelations triggered a parliamentary uproar. Cardin claimed that Diefenbaker had failed to act decisively when there may have been a risk to Canadian security. The Pearson government directed an inquiry by Justice Wishart F. Spence of the Supreme Court of Canada. Justice Spence's 20,000-word report was issued on September 23. It confirmed the charge that Mrs. Munsinger's sensational relationship with Sévigny constituted a serious security risk.

"A more dangerous cabinet position than that of national defense, from the point of view of espionage by enemy agents or information-seeking by greedy racketeers could hardly be imagined," the report stated. It censured Diefenbaker for not dismissing Sévigny when he first learned about the relationship, and for not informing Douglas Harkness, the minister of national defense.

Though sensational, the Munsinger scandal led to no prosecutions. Mrs. Munsinger had returned to Germany in 1961, and Sévigny had resigned from the cabinet early in 1963. The case did however, impair the reputation of Diefenbaker, who, at the end of 1966, was facing several challenges to his leadership of the Conservative party. Many Canadians wondered why Cardin waited three years before making his charges. The Munsinger scandal was a sorry episode that most Canadians were anxious to forget. See ESPIONAGE.

A second, less sensational, security investigation concerned George Victor Spencer, a Vancouver postal clerk who was discovered to have passed harmless information to Russian agents for several years. The government dismissed him from the civil service but did not bring charges. Justice Dalton Wells of the Ontario Supreme Court investigated the case and stated that in his opinion the government had acted with fairness and forbearance in not prosecuting Spencer.

High Drama rocked the House of Commons on May 18. Paul Joseph Chartier, 45, died in an adjoining washroom when a bomb he was about to toss into the chamber exploded prematurely. Prime Minister Pearson, Opposition Leader Diefenbaker, and many members of Parliament were in the chamber at the time. Chartier, a former mental patient, stated in a note that he intended "to drop a bomb and kill as many as possible for the rotten way you are running this country."

New Legislation. Despite the time lost dealing with scandals, the 1966 session of the 27th Parliament passed much constructive legislation. Heading the list of social welfare measures was the Canada Assistance Plan. It draws together and extends programs covering a variety of payments, including allowances to mothers and blind and disabled persons. Almost 1,000,000 Canadians were expected to benefit from the plan, which will cost an estimated $250,000,000 for the first year.

A national medicare plan (insurance covering physicians' services for all persons) was given first reading by the House of Commons. Medicare was approved by the Commons and Senate before the year ended, but the danger of mounting inflation prompted the government to postpone the starting date for the program from July 1, 1967, to no later than July 1, 1968.

During the autumn session, the House dealt with supplementing the $75-a-month pension for needy persons too old to benefit from the Canada Pension Plan. It was hoped that they could be guaranteed an income of $105 a month. The cost of the supplement would be $225,000,000.

Aid to Education. Legislation to establish a health resources fund was approved as a companion piece to medicare. The fund is a huge new source of money for the provinces to train physicians, nurses, and medical research workers over the next 15 years.

The new Training Allowance Act enabled the federal government to help retrain workers displaced by automation. Operating grants to universities were increased from $3 to $5 per Canadian. An amendment to the Canada Student Loan Act boosted federal loans to university students.

Banking Legislation. After two years of study by House and Senate committees, Parliament chartered Canada's first new banks since 1938, the Bank of Western Canada, with headquarters at Winnipeg, and the Bank of British Columbia, with head offices in Victoria. Legislation to allow chartered banks to increase interest rates from 6 to 7 per cent and eventually remove the interest ceiling was introduced by Finance Minister Sharp and given first reading. This was one of several changes planned as part of the government's decennial review of the Bank Act, then two years overdue.

Federal-Provincial Relations. Two major conferences between the federal government and the 10 provinces were held in Ottawa. The first was the tax structure committee meeting on September 14 and 15. Finance Minister Sharp offered the provinces a sweeping new tax-sharing formula, to pay for certain shared responsibilities that the federal government would relinquish. These included hospital insurance, the national health grants, and the Canada Assistance Plan. Sharp stated that responsibilities were within the provinces' jurisdiction and that the federal role had constituted "a continuing influence on provincial decision-making." To pay for the full cost of these programs, Ottawa would reduce the personal income tax 17 per cent. The provinces would then levy this share of the tax. Sharp suggested that the transfer take place on Jan. 1, 1967.

A second conference, on education, was held from October 24 to 28. The provinces were offered $194,000,000 in federal grants to improve public services in low-income areas and $204,000,000 to aid higher education. Part of the money would come from the transfer of 4 per cent of the personal income tax and 1 per cent of taxable corporation profits from the government to the provinces. At present, the federal government gives 24 per cent of the personal income tax to the provinces. Three provinces, however, take more. Quebec receives an additional 23 per cent because it had withdrawn from certain shared cost programs. The federal proposals meant a loss to the provinces of $49,000,000 in federal grants for technical and vocational training. Though disappointed with the federal offer, the provinces were expected to accept the proposed changes.

The new division of taxes will end the separate status enjoyed by Quebec. In the future, all the provinces will have the same fiscal freedom and responsibility. The offer was the federal response to Quebec Premier Daniel Johnson's demand that Quebec be allowed to levy 100 per cent of personal and corporate income taxes and succession duties. If it had surrendered all taxing authority to Quebec, the federal government would have granted the province virtual independence as an associate state. Thus, the federal government, in its proposals, asserted its supremacy in the federation. "We must somehow fashion machinery," Sharp said, "which will permit a strong federal government to accomplish the economic and social responsibilities which properly belong to it, but without impairing the fiscal freedom and responsibility of the provinces." The federal action was an important shift in "co-operative federalism," developed by the Pearson government since 1963.

Foreign Affairs. Canada continued to express its concern over the growing seriousness of the war in Vietnam. Chester Ronning, a veteran Canadian diplomat with extensive experience in Asia, made two confidential visits to Hanoi, North Vietnam, to explore the possibility of a settlement.

Canadian-Russian relations were enhanced by the visit in July of Dmitri Polyansky, first deputy chairman of the U.S.S.R. Council of Ministers and the most important Russian official ever to come to Canada. External Affairs Minister Paul Martin paid a return visit to Russia in November.

Debate over whether Canada should strive to free its industry from U.S. control continued, but advocates, led by former Finance Minister Walter Gordon, seemed to be losing ground. Prime Minister Pearson stated on several occasions that this policy would be fatal, and that Canada must maintain a hospitable climate for foreign investment. In April, Minister of Trade and Commerce Robert Winters sent a letter to Canadian subsidiaries of foreign corporations describing 12 ways in which the companies could become better corporate citizens of Canada.

National Defense. Minister of National Defense Paul Hellyer's controversial plan to unify Canada's three armed services moved forward. A bill to establish the Canadian Armed Forces was introduced in Parliament in November and was referred to the House's Defense Committee for study. Under the bill, navy and air force ranks would disappear, a common service uniform would be chosen, and all 105,000 Canadian servicemen would assume army ranks from private to general. The Canadian Armed Forces would have three components: the regular force, the reserve force, and the special force. The latter would be activated in time of emergency for collective defense under international agreements. Hellyer contended that the merger will provide Canada with greater flexibility to meet the military requirements of the future. He also said that the integrated force will make Canada "the unquestionable leader in the field of military organization." The plan was proposed in 1964, after which the commands of the three forces were integrated. In 1966, Lieutenant

Daniel Johnson, sworn in on June 16 as 20th premier of Quebec was frustrated in his drive for more self-rule in the province.

France's Expo 67 pavilion, with the theme "Tradition and Invention," will highlight the 1967 World's Fair in French-speaking Montreal.

General J. V. Allard succeeded Air Chief Marshal Frank R. Miller as Chief of Defense Staff.

In a "revolt of the admirals" during the summer, several senior navy officers resigned in protest against Hellyer's scheme. Rear Admiral William Landymore, commander of sea operations at Halifax, was dismissed in July when he objected to the navy's loss of identity, charging that the unification scheme would endanger morale without reducing defense spending.

The Budget. Mitchell Sharp's first budget, announced on March 29, applied the brakes to Canada's rapid economic growth. Without slowing the economy, the finance minister warned, the gross national product would rise by 9 per cent, half due to rising prices. Sharp's "brakes" included a tax increase on medium and upper personal income brackets, expected to cost taxpayers $140,000,000 in the fiscal year. Other measures encouraged businesses to delay capital outlays. The government also postponed 10 per cent of its construction projects. Sharp forecast a budgetary deficit of $150,000,000 for fiscal 1966-1967, based on expenditures of $8,450,000,000 and revenues of $8,300,000,000.

Later, on September 8, Sharp's "baby budget" speech to the House announced further anti-inflation measures, since "all Canadians will suffer if a continued boom should lead to bust." Pay raises for the armed forces and the supplement for old age pensioners would increase expenditures by $375,000,000. To prevent inflationary consequences, Sharp proposed a general tax increase to cover them. He promised to announce the exact nature of the tax changes when the state of the economy was clearer. On December 19, Sharp announced an increase of 1 per cent on the old age security tax and 1 per cent on the federal sales tax.

The Domestic Economy started strong in the first quarter of 1966, slackened in the second, then picked up speed again in the third. For the full year, the gross national product was expected to reach about $54,600,000,000, a whopping 10½ per cent increase over 1965. Almost 4 per cent of this increase was from a rise in prices. Exports increased more than had been expected. They totaled $6,588,800,000, up 24 per cent, in the first eight months.

A heavy increase in U.S. defense spending in Canada helped boost third quarter exports. The prairie wheat crop was expected to total 825,000,000 bushels, 14 per cent more than in the previous record year of 1963. This was good news for Canadian farmers, who must deliver $800,000,000 worth of wheat and flour to Russia over the next three years. The sale, concluded in June, was the largest commercial wheat transaction in history.

The year saw a leveling in business capital investment. After three years of annual gains of 20 per cent, capital spending in 1966 was expected to be up by only about 10 per cent. Unemployment in September totaled 2.7 per cent of the labor force, slightly above the figure in 1965. But economists were concerned over the fact that wages were rising twice as fast as national output. In the first half of 1966, for instance, wages and salaries rose 12 per cent over 1965; output was up only 6 per cent. The difference was attributed to a strong inflationary pressure, primarily due to rising prices.

Wage increases came, in many cases, after strike action. A 39-day strike brought Quebec longshoremen wage increases of 80 cents an hour in a two-year contract. Shortly afterward, the government settled a threatened strike by 1,200 employees of the St. Lawrence Seaway Authority. A 30 per cent wage increase was provided, 20 per cent retroactive to Jan. 1, 1966, and 10 per cent on Jan. 1, 1967.

On August 26, nearly 118,000 railway workers walked off their jobs in a strike that might have crippled the Canadian economy. Pearson summoned Parliament to meet on August 29. After four days of debate, Parliament passed a bill ordering railway men back to work and guaranteeing a minimum wage boost of 18 per cent in four stages during 1966 and 1967. Compulsory arbitration would be imposed if bargaining did not settle other aspects of the dispute by mid-November. Trains began moving again on September 2. Negotiations concluded in mid-December gave two groups of railway unions a further 6 per cent pay increase by 1968.

THE PROVINCES

Alberta saw a rich oil field, Rainbow Lake, come into production in the spring. The field may hold more than 6,000,000,000 barrels of oil. Forest fires farther north in the province consumed over 100,000 acres in June, destroying $30,000,000 worth of prime timber.

British Columbia. Premier William A. C. Bennett led his Social Credit government to its sixth consecutive election victory on September 12. It won 33 of 55 seats, the New Democratic party 16, and the Liberals 6. Although the government's share of the popular vote increased to 45 per cent, its majority in the legislature dropped because of an increase in the total number of seats. The main government casualty was Attorney General Robert Bonner, who was defeated in Vancouver but later found a constituency to represent in the northern part of the province.

Manitoba was another of the five Canadian provinces that held elections in 1966. Premier Dufferin Roblin's Conservative government won a fourth term on June 23, capturing 31 seats out of the 57 in the legislature. But the party's share of the popular vote dropped from 45 to 39 per cent. The New Democratic party increased its support substantially, especially in the Greater Winnipeg area, winning 11 seats, while the Liberals elected 14. A member of the Social Credit party held one seat. Roblin named Thelma Forbes, former speaker of the legislature, head of the Department of Municipal Affairs. She thus became Manitoba's first woman cabinet minister.

New Brunswick. Premier Louis J. Robichaud's Liberal government won legislative approval for a sweeping program of municipal reform. Under the mandate, the provincial government will be responsible for assessment, taxation, education, welfare, justice, and health on the municipal level. The Assessment Act, a key item in the program, was only one of 146 bills passed by the legislature during its first session in 1966. The program is to provide a minimum standard of social services throughout the province. The government won a by-election in Saint John in September in the first test of its strength at the polls after the reforms were adopted. The need for additional revenue forced the province's sales tax up from 3 to 6 per cent.

Premiers of Canadian Provinces

Province	Premier	Political Party
Alberta	Ernest C. Manning	Social Credit
British Columbia	William A. C. Bennett	Social Credit
Manitoba	Dufferin Roblin	Conservative
New Brunswick	Louis J. Robichaud	Liberal
Newfoundland	Joseph R. Smallwood	Liberal
Nova Scotia	Robert L. Stanfield	Conservative
Ontario	John P. Robarts	Conservative
Prince Edward Is.	Alexander B. Campbell	Liberal
Quebec	Daniel Johnson	Union Nationale
Saskatchewan	Ross Thatcher	Liberal

Newfoundland. Premier Joseph R. Smallwood won his "greatest victory since Confederation" in a provincial election held September 8. Smallwood, in power since the island became a province in 1949, saw his Conservative opposition in the legislature drop to only three members, all from St. John's. The Liberals won 39 seats.

Newfoundland suffered two economic blows: the U.S. Air Force announced it would abandon its base at Stephenville, which employs 1,000 civilians, and Dosco Industries stopped mining iron ore on Bell Island on June 30. Iron mines in the Conception Bay area were closed because of limited markets for low-quality ore. Efforts to find another operator were unsuccessful.

Nova Scotia. The Nova Scotia legislature held a special session in September to ensure local control of the Maritime Telegraph and Telephone Company, Ltd. The Bell Telephone Company had previously acquired 51 per cent of the shares of Maritime, but is prevented by the new legislation from voting more than 1,000 shares. Bell announced that it would challenge the legislation.

A second auto assembly plant was established on the site of a dormant naval base. Its output in the first year would be 1,000 units of a Japanese automobile, the Isuzu Bellet. Volvo Canada, Ltd., is already assembling cars at Dartmouth.

Ontario. Canada's most populous province, with a gross provincial product of over $20,000,000,000 in 1965, had record provincial government expenditures of $1,846,000,000 in 1966. Taxes were increased on a number of items and the provincial sales tax was raised from 3 to 5 per cent. Social welfare was extended through the Medical Services Insurance Act, which began on July 1. The plan supplements existing private plans.

Prince Edward Island. Canada's smallest province replaced the oldest premier in the country with the youngest. Conservative Premier Walter Shaw, 78, was succeeded by Alexander B. Campbell, 32, when the Liberals won 17 seats to the Conservatives 15 in the island legislature. The election of May 30 resulted in a tie, but a deferred election of July 11 gave the Liberals two more members. The victory ended seven years of Conservative rule.

Quebec. In a dramatic election upset, the Union Nationale party, led by Daniel Johnson, defeated Jean Lesage's six-year-old Liberal government on June 5. Quebec's first Sunday election gave the Union Nationale 56 legislative seats, the Liberals 50, and the independents two. The winning Union Nationale, though, took only 41 per cent of the vote to the Liberals' 47 per cent. Two rabid separatist parties had less than 9 per cent and failed to win a seat. Johnson's campaign platform called for Quebec's take-over of all direct taxation from the central government.

In October, a 40-year agreement was signed whereby Quebec will purchase electric power from the gigantic Churchill Falls hydroelectric project in Labrador. The power would be generated by a Newfoundland company, but its transmission would be handled by Quebec. The project should at first produce about 6,000,000 horsepower, and will relieve the serious power shortage predicted for the Montreal area.

Saskatchewan. The rural province passed controversial labor legislation after employees of the Saskatchewan Power Corporation struck in early September, demanding a wage increase of 8 per cent. Premier Ross Thatcher immediately called a special session of the legislature. It voted to make arbitration compulsory and without appeal in labor disputes involving essential services, such as heat, water, and electricity, as well as hospitals and nursing homes. The 1,200 strikers rejected a government offer of a 6 per cent wage increase, but returned to their jobs after the legislation was passed. An arbitration board was to settle the dispute.

Facts in Brief. Population: 20,357,000. Government: Governor General George P. Vanier; Prime Minister Lester B. Pearson. Monetary Unit: Canadian dollar (1.08=U.S. $1). Foreign Trade: exports, $8,745,000,000; imports, $8,627,000,000. Principal Exports: nonferrous metals, paper and pulp, wheat. DAVID M. L. FARR

CANADIAN LIBRARY ASSOCIATION (CLA) held its 21st annual conference in Calgary, Alberta, in June, 1966, with "Manpower and Education for Library Service" as its theme. At the conference, the CLA reaffirmed its position on intellectual freedom and library standards. "Libraries," it said, "have a primary role to play in the maintenance and nurture of intellectual freedom."

The Book of the Year for Children medals were presented to Mme. Monique Corriveau for *Le Wapiti*, James McNeill for *The Double Knights*, Mme. Andrée Maillet for *Le Chêne des Tempêtes*, and James Houston for *Tiktáliktak*.

Young Canada's Book Week was celebrated Nov. 15 to 22, 1966, under the patronage of John Hayes, a popular writer of Canadian historical tales for young readers. CLA was one of several sponsors of Canadian Library Week. The week's theme was "Reading–the Key to a Changing World."

Library buildings were dedicated at Brock University, St. Catharines, Ont.; Simon Fraser University, Burnaby, B.C.; University of Victoria, Victoria, B.C.; and Loyola College, Montreal, Que. New buildings were also opened for the Saskatoon Public Library, and branch public libraries in Ottawa, Ont.; North York, Ont.; Calgary, Alta.; Halifax, N.S.; and Saint John, N.B. The National Library building in Ottawa, Ont., was completed in December. ELIZABETH H. MORTON

CANADIAN LITERATURE. The approaching centennial of Canadian Confederation in 1967 influenced the output of publishers in 1965 and 1966. The arts, biography, contemporary affairs, history, literature, and outdoor life were among the categories covered.

The Arts. *Painting in Canada; A History* by J. Russell Harper, authoritatively covers 300 years of painting. *On the Enjoyment of Modern Art* by Jerrold Morriss is an enthusiastic discussion of modern art by a Canadian.

Biography. *The Dictionary of Canadian Biography*, Volume 1, A.D. 1000-1700, edited by George W. Brown, deals mainly with the first French and English discoverers and settlers and early Indian leaders. Some 19 volumes will follow.

Mrs. Simcoe's Diary, edited by Mary E. (Quayle) Innis, describes Canadian life of two centuries ago. *I, Nuligak* is an autobiography of a Canadian Eskimo who was born in primitive surroundings. The story was edited and translated by Morris Metayer, and is illustrated by the Eskimo, Ekootak.

Here Are the News was written by Edith Josie, an Indian reporter, whose own story was a feature in *Life* magazine. It tells the daily life of Old Crow, a settlement situated north of the Arctic Circle.

Contemporary Affairs received wide attention in 1966. Among those books published were: *A Choice for Canada* by Walter Gordon; *The Shape of*

Scandal by Richard J. Gwyn; *This Game of Politics* by Pierre Sévigny; *Neighbours Taken for Granted–Canada and the United States*, edited by Livingston P. Merchant; and *Canada's Role as a Middle Power*, edited by John King Gordon.

Fiction. *The Road Past Altamont* by Gabrielle Roy, *A Jest of God* by Margaret Laurence, *Hangman's Beach* by Thomas H. Raddell, and *Mallabec* by David Walker captured the regionalism of Manitoba, Halifax, and New Brunswick. Leonard N. Cohen, who is best known as a poet, published his first novel, *Beautiful Losers*, in 1966.

History. *Montreal, Island City of the St. Lawrence*, by Kathleen Jenkins, won praise for capturing in one volume the essential history of the second largest French-speaking city in the world, from the moment of its discovery to its role as host of Expo 67.

The Governor-General's Literary Awards for 1966 went to James Eayrs for *In Defence of Canada* (English nonfiction); Alfred Purdy for *The Cariboo Horses* (English poetry); André Vachon for *Le Temps et L'Espace dans l'Oeuvre de Paul Claudel* (French nonfiction); Gilles Vegneault for *Quand les Bateaux s'en Vont* (French poetry); and Gerard Bessette for *L'Incubation* (French fiction). No awards were made in 1966 for fiction in the English language. ELIZABETH H. MORTON

CARNEGIE MEDAL. See LITERATURE FOR CHILDREN (Awards).

CELEBRATIONS and anniversaries observed in 1966 included the following:

YEAR-LONG CELEBRATIONS

American Bible Society Sesquicentennial. Founded in New York City in May, 1816, the society has as its main purpose the translation, publication, and distribution of the Bible. In the past 150 years, it has distributed some 750,000,000 Bibles, Testaments, Scripture portions, and selections throughout the world. A new 12-story Bible House, located near Lincoln Center for the Performing Arts, was dedicated on April 3, 1966.

American Methodism Bicentennial. One April Sunday in 1766, Philip Embury preached in New York City to a group, which constituted the first Methodist society in the New World. He was a disciple of John Wesley, the Church of England priest who founded the Methodist movement in England. Two years later, Embury opened New York's first Methodist Chapel at 44 John Street, site of the present John Street Methodist Church (built in 1841). Embury, Francis Asbury, Thomas Coke, and many others rode "circuits" on horseback, preaching and organizing churches and congregations wherever they went. As part of the bicentennial celebration in 1966, 12 Methodist clergymen in various parts of the United States acted as circuit riders. They traveled on horseback and preached in villages, towns, and cities along their way to Baltimore, Md. All arrived on April 21, for the Methodist conference. The oldest rider, the Rev. Sumner L. Martin, age 78, began his journey at Greencastle, Ind., on January 9, and traveled 740 miles.

Argentina Sesquicentennial commemorated the country's declaration of independence in 1816 after nearly 300 years as a Spanish colony. The United Provinces of La Plata became Argentina in 1862.

Christian Science Centennial. The Christian Science movement was founded in 1866 by Mrs. Mary Baker Eddy, who suffered a severe injury and was healed while reading about Jesus' healing power in Matthew 9:1-8. Her *Science and Health with Key to the Scriptures* contains Christian Science beliefs. The Mother Church, the First Church of Christ, Scientist, was built in Boston, Mass., in 1894. In 1966 there are some 3,300 churches and societies in 48 countries. Publications include *The Christian Science Monitor*, the international daily newspaper founded in 1908. A centennial book, *Mary Baker Eddy: The Golden Days* was published in April, 1966. A marble bust of Mrs. Eddy was presented to the National Portrait Gallery, Smithsonian Institution, in Washington, D.C.

Columbia University College of Physicians and Surgeons Bicentennial. The first medical school in the United States was founded in 1767 as King's College Medical School. Its first home was a building in lower Manhattan, New York City, where the Woolworth Building now stands. The year-long bicentennial celebration, "Two Hundred Years of Medical Progress," began in September, 1966.

Indiana Sesquicentennial. On April 19, 1816, President James Madison signed the proclamation authorizing Indiana Territory to prepare for statehood. The state constitution was drafted at the territorial capital in Corydon, and signed on June 23. Indiana was admitted as the 19th state of the Union on Dec. 11, 1816. The state legislature selected Indianapolis as the capital in 1821.

Poland's Millennium commemorated its 1,000th year as a Christian nation, dating back to the conversion of Prince Mieszko in 966. Associated with his conversion is the Black Madonna portrait of the Virgin Mary, accredited to St. Luke and enshrined in Jasna Gora Monastery at Częstochowa. Ceremonies there on May 3, 1966, climaxed the year-long observances. Stefan Cardinal Wyszyński, Roman Catholic Primate of Poland and Archbishop of Warsaw, was not permitted to attend millennium ceremonies in other countries. Foreign high church officials were barred from Poland. The Communist government observed the millennium as Poland's 1,000th year as a nation. See POLAND.

Rutgers Bicentennial Year was proclaimed on Jan. 4, 1966. The 12th oldest college in the United States was founded as Queen's College in New Brunswick, N.J., and renamed Rutgers for a benefactor in 1825. It is now Rutgers, The State University.

Westminster Abbey 900th Anniversary began on Dec. 28, 1965, and continued through 1966. Queen Elizabeth II was the first to make a pilgrimage to Britain's national church during the celebration. Accompanied by representatives of most of the churches in Christendom, she placed roses on the shrine of Edward the Confessor, who built a church on the Westminster site (1042-1065). The first English monarch crowned there was William (I) the Conqueror on Dec. 25, 1066. A bishopric was established there in 1539, which made the abbey a cathedral. Its official title is the Collegiate Church of St. Peter.

Winston-Salem Bicentennial commemorated the founding of Salem in 1766 by Moravians from Pennsylvania. The settlers purchased the 100,000-acre tract of land in North Carolina in 1752, established a few small communities, and then the town of Salem. The Home Moravian Church, still the headquarters of the Moravian Church South, was built in 1800. In 1813, Salem and Winston (founded 1849) consolidated to form the present city of Winston-Salem. A new Greek-design amphitheater in the May Dell was the scene of the bicentennial drama *Till the Day Break*. The Early American Moravian Music Festival and Seminar held at Salem College's new Fine Arts Center in June was also part of the bicentennial observance.

SHORTER CELEBRATIONS

April 20-21—Harvard University Divinity School Sesquicentennial was observed at a two-day convocation. The school was founded in 1816, and became known as a "fortress of liberal outlook and faith."

May 17—Pearl Harbor Naval Base 50th Anniversary. The United States base in Hawaii, where most of the major Pacific commands have headquarters, was established on the southern coast of Oahu Island in 1916. There were only six ships there at the time. The first dry dock was not built until 1919.

May 18—Newark Tercentennial. The New Jersey city was founded by a group of Connecticut Puritans, led by Robert Treat, in May, 1666. The community, first called Milford, was renamed for its first minister, Abraham Pierson, who was ordained at Newark-on-Trent in England. The present mayor of Newark-on-Trent, William Kerr, was a guest at Newark's 300th anniversary celebration in 1966.

May 25-Oct. 14—Battle of Hastings 900th Anniversary was celebrated in England and France. The English observance began with the unveiling of the Hastings Embroidery, commissioned for the occasion. It depicted 81 scenes in English history from William (I) the Conqueror to Queen Elizabeth II. Bayeux, William's home in Normandy, France, exhibited its famous tapestry of 72 scenes from the life of King Harold II and the invasion and conquest of England by William, Duke of Normandy. King Harold II ascended the English throne in January, 1066. He defeated a Norwegian invasion in Yorkshire, and then hurried to Sussex to fight the Normans. The two armies met on Oct. 14, 1066, near Hastings at a point now known as Battle. Harold was killed and his forces defeated. William was crowned King of England on Dec. 25, 1066.

May 31—Battle of Jutland 50th Anniversary was commemorated by Great Britain and West Germany. The greatest naval battle of World War I was fought on May 31-June 1, 1916, at Skagerrak Strait in the North Sea. Both claimed victory, but Great Britain retained control of the high seas.

September 9—Great London Fire Tercentennial which also honored the centennial of the London Fire Brigade, was commemorated with a great pageant on the River Thames. The fire began in a wooden house on Pudding Lane on Sept. 9, 1666, and burned for nearly a week. Most of the city was destroyed, including Old Saint Paul's Cathedral and the Guildhall. Sir Christopher Wren designed the rebuilt (1675-1710) Saint Paul's Cathedral and other famous churches.

Oct. 26-28—Peabody Museum of Natural History Centennial was observed with scientific meetings at Yale University. The Kline Biology Tower was dedicated, completing the $18,000,000 Kline Science Center. The museum was established in 1866 with a gift from merchant-financier George Peabody (1795-1869).

Dec. 7—Japanese Attack on Pearl Harbor 25th Anniversary was commemorated in Honolulu. Taking part in the service at the National Memorial Cemetery of the Pacific was Mitsuo Fuchida of Japan. He was the young naval commander who led the first air formation over Pearl Harbor on Dec. 7, 1941. Fuchida is now a Christian evangelist.

Dec. 15—U.S. Bill of Rights 175th Anniversary. The first 10 amendments to the U.S. Constitution, known as the Bill of Rights, came into effect on Dec. 15, 1791. Actually, the first eight, which set forth the people's basic rights, are the Bill of Rights. Amendments 9 and 10 prohibit Congress from passing laws that would violate these rights.

The U.S. Department of Commerce unveiled its new "census clock" on Sept. 16, 1966. The counter records changes in population.

CENSUS. As of Dec. 31, 1966, the population of the 50 states, the District of Columbia, and Americans in the armed forces abroad was estimated at 198,000,000. A year earlier the estimate stood at 195,800,000. The 1.1 per cent increase compared with 1.2 per cent in 1965 and represented a continuation of the slowdown in U.S. population growth. The 10-year annual average increase (1956-1966) was 1.53 per cent.

The gradual decrease in population growth was principally attributed to the drop in number of births—from 3,948,000 in the year ended June 30, 1965, to 3,697,000 in fiscal 1966.

Plans for the 1970 Census. In 1966, the Bureau of the Census reported to Congress on plans for the 1970 Census of Population and Housing. For the first time, the census of every U.S. household will be conducted by mail, although enumerators will visit homes which file incomplete returns or fail to respond. Enumerators will also canvass some rural and special areas which do not lend themselves to a mail-type census.

In a series of regional meetings, institutions and individuals suggested ways in which the 1970 census data could be made more useful to them.

Local officials were asked to cooperate in revising maps of their areas and in establishing address guides that will make it possible for electronic computers to provide special tabulations at the request and expense of the sponsors for such areas as school zones, police precincts, and traffic zones.

A special census of New Haven, Conn., and its surrounding metropolitan areas will be conducted in April, 1967. This census will provide a test of questions tentatively selected for the 1970 census, a test of computerized coding of addresses, and an opportunity to evaluate the feasibility of conducting a census principally by mail.

Census officials repeated their deep concern over the protection of the privacy of all persons and families. These officials were supported in their views on privacy by the Federal Census Act, which prohibits the use of any census information for taxation, investigation, or regulation.

Other Censuses. During 1966, the bureau published preliminary reports of the 1964 Census of Agriculture covering 50 states and over 3,000 counties. It continued publication of final results from the 1963 censuses of manufacturing, business, and mineral industries. Looking ahead to 1967, plans were made to complete new censuses of the same categories, plus transportation and governments.

New Economic Document. In October, 1966, the Bureau of the Census published a new book, *Long-Term Economic Growth,* which provides a 105-year view of many factors affecting U.S. economic growth. The book brings together a series of 400 aggregate annual statistical data. JOHN C. BAKER

CENTRAL AFRICAN REPUBLIC started a new year with a new government: the army seized power on Jan. 1, 1966. With only 450 soldiers, it wrested control of key government offices and abducted President David Dacko. Cabinet ministers were also arrested, but were soon released. The nation's constitution was abolished and the Legislative Assembly was dissolved. Colonel Jean-Bedel Bokassa, army chief of staff, became president, premier, minister of defense, and minister of justice. Bokassa appointed a 10-man revolutionary council to assist him.

On January 6, the new government broke diplomatic relations with Communist China and ordered all Chinese nationals out of the country, alleging a Chinese plan to intervene in the government. Army officers who had cooperated with the Chinese were dismissed or tried by courts-martial.

The presidents of Chad and the Central African Republic announced on April 6 that their two countries would build a road between their capital cities and cooperate on economic and cultural matters.

Facts in Brief. Population: 1,300,000. Government: President and Premier Jean-Bedel Bokassa. Monetary Unit: CFA franc (245=U.S. $1). Foreign Trade: exports, $26,100,000; imports, $27,200,000. Principal Exports: coffee, cotton, diamonds. BENJAMIN E. THOMAS

CENTRAL AMERICA. See LATIN AMERICA.

CEYLON saw its once-shaky economy becoming increasingly stable in 1966. The coalition government of Prime Minister Dudley Senanayake, showing both resiliency and strength, brought a measure of political security to the nation.

In January, the government settled a bitter language feud by giving the Tamil minority the right to transact official business in its own language instead of in Sinhalese. Even more serious than the language problem, however, was an attempted coup d'état which leftists and a portion of the army launched while Senanayake was abroad during the summer. The conspiracy was discovered, however, and the plot forestalled.

The government undertook even more determined measures in 1966 to encourage foreign investment. Special legislation pertaining to American companies was passed, and a white paper issued, setting forth guarantees for foreign investors. Loans were promptly forthcoming from the United States as were special food credits. India as well as Communist China also extended credit.

Facts in Brief. Population: 12,030,000. Government: Governor-General William Gopallawa; Prime Minister Dudley Senanayake. Monetary Unit: rupee (4.75=U.S. $1). Foreign Trade: exports, $409,600,000; imports, $309,800,000. Principal Exports: tea, rubber. JOHN N. STALKER

CHAD. See AFRICA.

CHEMICAL INDUSTRY growth was solid rather than spectacular in 1966. Demand for chemical products grew. Production rose about 10 per cent, and plants generally operated at 90 per cent of capacity or better. Shipments of chemical products climbed to a value of about $39,000,000,000 in 1966 from a bit over $36,000,000,000 the year before.

The industry's outlays for building new plants and modernizing old ones, at home and abroad, reached an all-time high of approximately $3,000,000,000. Virtually two-fifths of its plants at the end of 1966 had been installed since 1961. Trends toward large-capacity plants and computer-controlled processes continued strong. All reflected the industry's drive to specialize in product line and achieve the economies of large-scale output–integrated all the way from raw material to final product.

Prices for chemicals rose slightly during the year, a welcome change after several years of decline. There was a steady parade of price rises throughout the year on basic chemicals. On April 1, for instance, prices went up on four sodium phosphates, styrene, caustic soda, and two plasticizers. The combination of firming prices and high production assured the chemical makers of profits of more than $3,500,000,000 for the year, or about 10 per cent above the level of 1965.

Sulfur Turnabout. One of the most widely used of chemical raw materials, sulfur, came into short supply in 1966. Because of expanding mine and refinery capacities, sulfur had been in oversupply. However, growing demands from the fertilizer,

Production of Leading Chemicals

Inorganic (1,000 tons)	1964	1965	1966*
Ammonia	7,634	8,607	9,890
Chlorine	5,945	6,439	6,700
Hydrochloric acid	1,264	1,310	1,419
Nitric acid	4,733	4,860	5,156
Phosphoric acid	3,283	3,845	4,306
Sodium carbonate	4,948	4,931	5,054
Sodium hydroxide	6,389	6,724	7,015
Sulfuric acid	22,924	24,822	26,361
Organic (million lb.)			
Acetic anhydride	1,399	1,534	1,583
Formaldehyde	2,840	3,086	3,367
Methanol	398	433	462
Phthalic anhydride	556	579	627

*12 months ended July 31. Source: U.S. Dept. of Commerce

chemical, steel, pulp and paper, and munitions industries overtook the supply, which grew 6 per cent in the United States in 1966.

Sulfur prices rose sharply on foreign markets, but only moderately in the United States, where producers were under federal pressure to dampen inflationary increases. Sulfuric acid, produced from sulfur and itself a basic component of thousands of industrial products, moved up in price over the year.

THOMAS E. FEARE

See also MANUFACTURING; PETROLEUM AND GAS.

CHEMISTRY. Workers at the California Institute of Technology (Caltech) made the first direct measurement of the minimum energy needed to initiate a chemical reaction. John M. White, a graduate student working under the direction of chemical physicist Aron Kuppermann, found that an absolute minimum of one-third of an electron volt of energy is needed to split a hydrogen molecule into two hydrogen atoms and to combine one of them with an atom of deuterium (heavy hydrogen) to form deuterium hydride. The reaction will not occur with any less energy.

White focused light from a 200-watt mercury lamp on a diffraction grating, which, like a prism, broke the beam into its separate wave lengths of light–each with its specific energy level. He then aimed the beam of light, one wave length at a time, at a cylinder containing hydrogen and deuterium iodide gas. When molecules of deuterium iodide were struck by sufficiently energetic photons in the light beam, they split into fast-moving atoms of deuterium and sluggish, heavier atoms of iodine. The speeding deuterium atoms in turn collided with hydrogen molecules and split them. Some deuterium atoms then combined with some of the unattached hydrogen atoms to form deuterium hydride. In this way, it was possible to determine the minimum energy needed for the creation of deuterium hydride.

Photosynthesis. The complex chemical process of photosynthesis, the means by which plant cells make carbohydrates from carbon dioxide and water, was unraveled in 1955 by Nobel prize winner Melvin Calvin. In 1966, another method for such reactions was found by Daniel I. Arnon and his coworkers at the University of California (Berkeley). They found this in photosynthetic bacteria rather than in green plants. The bacteria they used was *Chlorobium thiosulfatophilum*, which, like a green plant, uses light energy to convert carbon dioxide to carboxylic acids and eventually into amino acids and other cellular components.

In the method discovered by Calvin, known as the Calvin cycle, light energy provides the basis for the production of triphosphopyridine nucleotide ($TPNH_2$), which in turn converts carbon dioxide to a triose sugar with the help of the high energy substance adinosine triphosphate (ATP). In photosynthesis involving bacteria, Arnon found that powerful reducing agents known as ferredoxins are produced during the photosynthetic reaction. Ferredoxins in turn are capable of producing ATP and $TPNH_2$, which are then used directly to convert carbon dioxide to carboxylic acids.

Ferredoxins are probably the most powerful reducing agents found in a cell. Though first discovered several years ago, no ferredoxin structure has yet been fully analyzed, although it is known that they are proteins of low molecular weight and contain iron.

The new method is of interest also because it appears to be, in part, a reversal of the well-known Krebs citric acid cycle. This was outlined in 1937 by the German-born British chemist, Sir Hans Krebs, who later shared a Nobel prize for his work. The Krebs cycle is found throughout all living tissue and involves energy release during oxidation. The new cycle discovered by Arnon appears to feed energy into a step of the Krebs cycle and get back in return a more highly reduced carbon compound.

Instruments. Chemical research in 1966 was characterized by the appearance of an ever-increasing number of sophisticated and complex tools.

At Pennsylvania State University, an instrument that combines a mass spectrometer with a high energy laser was developed for the analysis of matter. A laser beam can vaporize solid samples in a time period of about one-half a millisecond. As the sample is vaporized, the light it emits is separated into its wave lengths by the mass spectrometer. Each type of matter has its specific light spectrum, so that the analysis by the spectrometer will determine its constituents. The advantage of the laser beam over other means of vaporizing matter for study by spectrometer is that a laser beam only vaporizes small areas at a time, 10 microns or less in diameter.

ROBERT A. UPHAUS

See also BIOCHEMISTRY.

CHESS. Tigran Petrosian of the Soviet Union retained the world chess championship by defeating his countryman, Boris Spassky, in a 24-game match concluded in June at Moscow's Variety Theater. Spassky had won the right to challenge Petrosian by surviving a series of elimination matches with most of the world's leading players.

Petrosian fared badly, however, in the Piatigorsky Cup international tournament played at Santa Monica, Calif., in July and August, for prizes totaling $20,000. Many experts regarded the tournament as the most illustrious ever played in the United States, involving as it did 10 grand masters from many parts of the world. Petrosian was able to do no better than a tie for sixth.

Spassky, the winner of the 18-round, 27-day event, was the only player to go through the tournament without a defeat (he drew 13). He finished with 11½ points, one-half point more than the total tallied by Bobby Fischer, the U.S. champion. Fischer rallied after being tied for last place at the end of eight rounds. Going into the final round, he and Spassky were tied, but the Russian defeated Jan Donner of Holland while Fischer obtained a draw with Petrosian. Denmark's Bent Larsen was third.

At Seattle in August, Robert Byrne of Indianapolis, Ind., and Pal Benko of New York City tied for first place in the U.S. Open. Mrs. Mary Bain of New York won the women's title. THEODORE M. O'LEARY

CHICAGO. The city's downtown building boom got a major boost on September 23. An Illinois Supreme Court decision gave the green light for an estimated $1,000,000,000 worth of construction on air rights over 186 acres of railroad property fronting Lake Michigan.

In other activity, the 100-story John Hancock Center resumed construction after delays due to faulty caissons. Steel work was topped out on another 20-story unit of the Gateway Center, built on air rights above other railroad property, and work started on a second (45 stories) federal office building, expected to cost $43,000,000. Work also began on the so-called "free-form" 70-story Lake Point Tower. The structure reportedly will be the world's tallest reinforced-concrete building.

In art, the city accepted with delight a monumental gift from the Spanish artist Pablo Picasso: a design for a 50-foot high steel sculpture created especially for the city, to stand in the plaza fronting the new Civic Center. The center, the tallest building in the city (698 feet), was dedicated with appropriate fanfare on May 2. See ARCHITECTURE; PAINTING AND SCULPTURE.

In August, the city's highly controversial school superintendent, Benjamin Willis, resigned under pressure. He was replaced by James F. Redmond, who had been previously in charge of schools in Syosset, N.Y.

Daley's Troubles. In his 12th year as mayor, Richard J. Daley gained solid endorsement of his program when, on June 14, voters strongly approved a multipurpose $195,000,000 bond issue. But in the weeks that followed, a long, tense summer began. First, sporadic disturbances in Puerto Rican and Negro neighborhoods occupied the mayor's and the nation's attention.

Then came efforts to make housing for Negroes available in white working-class neighborhoods. A series of marches led by Dr. Martin Luther King, Jr., were met with great hostility. The most serious event occurred when Negroes, marching into neighboring Cicero, Ill., were attacked with rocks and bottles. Although this demonstration was not sanctioned by Dr. King, it seemed to hasten an agreement between Mayor Daley and civil rights groups to work for open occupancy in Chicago.

Nevertheless, the aftermath was felt on election day, November 8. The power of the Democratic organization, led by the mayor, was notably weakened. Both Negroes and white working-class voters defected, keeping down the typical Democratic landslide in the city.

At year-end the Chicago area was selected as the site of the world's largest atomic reactor. To be built in suburban Weston, Ill., the project will cost some $375,000,000. DONALD W. LIEF

See also SCIENCE AND RESEARCH.

CHILD GUIDANCE. A Joint Committee on Mental Health of Children, authorized and funded by the Congress of the United States, began its work in 1966. Reginald Lurie, a psychiatrist, was chosen as committee chairman. Psychologist Joseph Bobbitt, associate director of the National Institute of Child Health and Human Development, was named executive director.

Nationally, children with mental health problems will find more services available to them. Recent federal legislation authorized contributions to the states toward the development of "comprehensive community mental health centers." The financial aid approved amounted to $50,000,000 for 1966 and $65,000,000 for 1967. This legislation requires all 50 states and three territories to draft broad new programs with the major emphasis on services for children.

Handicapped Children. Progress in guidance and education for handicapped children was expected to continue as a result of the 1966 amendments to the Elementary and Secondary School Improvement Act. A new Title VI authorized $50,000,000 the first year and increasing sums thereafter.

Two books of special value to parents were Lawrence K. Frank's *On the Importance of Infancy*, a basic reference on infant care and development; and H. G. Ginott's *Between Parent and Child*, which provides information in such matters as sex education, sibling rivalry, and discipline. Professionals and parents with special interests in handicapped children found value in such 1966 publications as *Mental Deficiency, the Changing Outlook* by Ann M. Clarke and Alan D. B. Clarke; *The Disabled Reader: Education of the Dyslexic Child* by John Money; *Thinking Without Language, Psychological Implications of Deafness* by Hans G. Furth; and *Psychopathology of Childhood* by Jane W. Kessler.

Behavior. The perennial controversy over the relative importance of nature and nurture in the development of a child's personality received fresh fuel in a 1966 research report by Dr. D. H. Stott. In his *Studies of Troublesome Children*, Dr. Stott argued that environmental explanations of behavioral difficulties have been overstressed. He concluded that disturbing behavior results not only from exposure to stress, but also from a congenital impairment of temperament.

Child guidance clinics were increasingly adopting group treatment methods in preference to individual treatment in 1966. The Flint (Mich.) Child Guidance Clinic reported that group treatment was not only more economical in use of professional time, but actually more effective in improving the adjustment of "hard-to-reach" preadolescent boys and girls. The interaction of boys and girls on each other in the course of group treatment appeared to be an essential ingredient. FRANCES A. MULLEN

CHILD WELFARE. A National Adoption Resource Exchange was formed and put into operation in the fall of 1966 by the Child Welfare League of America. A nationwide information system, the exchange was designed to help balance the uneven distribution of homeless children in the United States and families desiring to adopt them. The Field Foundation provided some of the funds.

In 1965, the last year for which figures were available, federal, state, and local public welfare agencies spent $352,000,000 for child welfare services. The figure represented an increase of 12.5 per cent above 1964. The contribution of $34,200,000 by the U.S. government rose $5,400,000 over the previous year. The U.S. Department of Health, Education, and Welfare provided $3 of every $4 expended by the individual states for financial assistance programs for children.

Cooperatoin between social agencies and schools was increased by the Elementary and Secondary School Improvement Act of 1965. The act provided aid to school systems having special programs for disadvantaged children. FRANCES A. MULLEN

CHILDREN'S BOOKS. See LITERATURE FOR CHILDREN.

CHILE. See LATIN AMERICA.

CHRONOLOGY. See pages 8 to 12.

CHURCHES. See EASTERN ORTHODOX; JEWS AND JUDAISM; PROTESTANT; RELIGION; ROMAN CATHOLIC.

CHINA

The façade of China's once monolithic Communist party was cracked wide open in 1966 by a violent power struggle between Mao Tse-tung and opponents of his policies. In the political convulsions that attended the struggle, new leaders rose to the front ranks; a "Great Proletarian Cultural Revolution" was launched, and the nation seemingly was set on a course the outcome of which few persons in the Western world were able or even willing to predict.

Young Red Guards, carrying a huge picture of Karl Marx, march in Peking. Each waves a copy of Mao Tse-tung's selected sayings.

Intellectuals Attacked. In perspective, the events of 1966 were presaged by a significant incident that took place in November of the preceding year. In Shanghai, a journalistic attack was launched against a respected historian named Wu Han, who had written some tongue-in-cheek plays that seemed to deal with ancient characters but which really appeared to mock Chairman Mao Tse-tung, as well as the Communist party and some of its most cherished slogans. The attacks on Wu Han, which were followed by increasingly shrill tirades against other literary notables, were clearly a warning of an impending purge of those intellectuals and party leaders who had been questioning Mao's policies abroad and at home.

Source of Doubts. The immediate origins of the doubts arising from Mao's policies could be traced to the United States' military build-up in Vietnam early in 1965. The sound of American bombs exploding just south of China's border produced acute alarm in Peking. Mao and his companions had always preached that "Wall Street Imperialism" would someday try to destroy their revolution. Now they wondered if the fateful day had come. Would China have to fight in Vietnam, as 15 years earlier it had been impelled to fight in Korea? And if the answer was "yes," how could the nation best prepare for this mortal conflict?

The debate in Peking dragged on inconclusively through the summer of 1965. In September, the party's central committee met, but it, too, could not make up its mind either on U.S. intentions or on what to do.

Army Affected. Inevitably, however, the debate on war or peace began to leave its imprint on many areas. One was on the intellectual life, as epitomized by such notable writers as Wu Han. A parallel debate flared up in the army. There, the professionals — undeterred by two purges since the Korean war – again began to demand a compact, highly trained, modern army. The army commissars countered with the argument that it was men and not weapons that won wars. Fueled by the seeming U.S. threat from the south, this debate raged through the early fall of 1965. In the end, the army politicians, led by Defense Minister Lin Piao – a staunch supporter of Mao – ousted the spokesman of the professionals, Chief of Staff Lo Jui-ching.

All these signs of strain revived Mao's own fears and hopes. For years he had been increasingly alarmed by what he regarded as the decay of his revolution. The new urban society had somehow lost its revolutionary fervor. The intellectual elite seemed to be looking down its collective nose on the nation's half a billion peasants. The youth of the nation had grown soft, selfish, and disinterested in the revolution.

Young Blood. Mao had long felt that the peasant revolts in China's past had failed because they had gone flabby. He was determined to save his revolution from this fate – or the fate that, he insisted, had befallen the Soviet Union's revolution. In 1966, his solution was to inject the serum of youth into his own revolution, to revive the fervor, purity, and discipline that it displayed in its decades in the wilderness between 1927 and 1949. What Mao demanded was a sharp swing to the left. The slogan would be, "Put Politics in Command," and dogma would prevail over all else in the army barracks, the theaters, the schools, and in the factories.

For once, however, Mao ran into strong opposition. Some Chinese leaders did not share Mao's nostalgia for the glorious years in the mountains. Others believed that after the hungry years between 1959 and 1962, it was time to let the "expert" rather than the "Red" take a hand at managing things. Still others apparently felt that the methods, ideas, and slogans that Mao had used in the countryside during his fugitive years were not suitable in the nuclear 1960s.

A personal factor also may have been involved among the dissatisfied; Mao was 72 years old and ailing. He was still a political giant, but he was no longer the supreme arbiter who for 30 years had

Mao Tse-tung, applauding in response to cheers, leaves a Communist rally. Behind him is Lin Piao, a newly emerged party leader.

The Rise Of Lin Piao

Marshal Lin Piao's sudden emergence as Mao Tse-tung's political heir provided China with its most dramatic success story of 1966.

Only a year earlier, Lin Piao had been sixth in the set of seven official portraits of the men who govern China. The second place for 20 years had belonged to the president, Liu Shao-chi. In August, 1966, Liu was demoted to eighth place, just beyond the circle of power, and Lin Piao moved to the second spot.

The nation was made aware of this change at a series of immense rallies in Peking. At these meetings, Lin appeared at Mao's elbow, and spoke in his name. Official reports referred to him as "Mao's close comrade in arms," and Lin become the principal interpreter of Maoism.

Hindsight suggests that Lin's rise began in 1965, and involved fierce conflicts within the party and the army. On Sept. 3, 1965, Lin's now-famous speech, "Long Live the Victory of the People's War," was published. This 30,000-word statement was described by some Western observers as "China's *Mein Kampf*." But in 1966, it became obvious that it was Lin's argument in his struggle with army professionals. The latter wanted to reshape China's obsolete army into a smaller, highly trained force equipped with modern weapons. Lin, like Mao, regarded this as heresy. He insisted that it is man, and not arms, that decides the outcome of wars; that the modern "imperalist" armies can be overcome by guerrillas in a "people's war;" and that in all fields, including that of battle, it is more important to understand Communist theory than to be a military expert.

This was not a new argument for Lin. He had become defense minister in September, 1959, as a result of his advocacy of these principles. His statement of 1965 was notice that nothing had changed. Shortly thereafter, Marshal Lin's (and Mao's) doctrine of "the people's war" was reaffirmed as the keystone of Peking's strategy.

In 1966, Lin's army became Mao's principal political tool. The army newspaper, *Liberation Army Daily*, emerged as the main oracle of Chinese Communist theory. Lin himself issued directives to moviemakers and railroad workers, and he urged China's millions to "study the thought of Mao Tse-tung." Lin also became the hero of the young Red Guards, whom he used to rally support for Mao's policies and to intimidate the opposition.

Lin was born in 1908, one of four sons of a felt factory owner in a village in Hupeh province. He left home at the age of 10, completed middle school, and was then caught up in the revolutionary turmoil of the mid-1920s. He actively supported Sun Yat-sen in the civil war, and in 1924 enrolled in the first class of the newly established Whampoa Military Academy set up by the Nationalists. There, he was a brilliant student.

In 1926, he joined the Communist party, and a year later took part in the abortive Communist uprising in Nanchang. For two decades after that, he was a member of the Communist guerrilla armies that fought Chiang Kai-shek and the Japanese in various parts of China. Lin became an army commander at 20; at 29 he defeated the Japanese in an important battle; and at 40, at the head of a 1,000,000-man army, he swept across China in pursuit of Chiang Kai-shek's defeated forces.

Lin is a soft-spoken, slight, frail man. In 1939, he was wounded by the Japanese, and had to spend three years recuperating. In the early 1950s, he was again gravely ill, reportedly with tuberculosis. While serving as head of a military and political university in 1937, he married his pupil, Liu Hsi-ming. They have a son and a daughter.

Beyond doubt, Lin is one of Asia's great generals, accustomed to both power and struggle. Like Mao, he has made the Chinese village the center of his universe, and he distrusts the city and the intellectual. At the head of China, he can thus provide that unchanged continuity for which Mao has long yearned. But the question is whether he can long prevail over his new allies, who are likely more skillful at machine politics and who may not back him in the future as they did in 1966.

MARK GAYN

Young Chinese Communist, a member of the Red Guard, yells enthusiastically during a demonstration in Peking.

made the final decisions. The party leaders now looked ahead to the day when other men and other policies would prevail.

Sometime early in 1966, the men in Peking decided that the United States, after all, did not mean to go to war with China now. But they were already immersed in the internal struggle. In this, the most important and possibly the last conflict of his life, Mao had only one major ally, Lin Piao; opposing him were most of his old companions who had traveled with him on the long, cruel road to power. These men controlled much of the immense party machine, in Peking and in the provinces.

Power Shift. The party had been Mao's power base ever since he had taken it over from his rivals in 1935. Now no longer able to depend on it, he set about building a new base. First, Lin Piao's army replaced the party as Mao's principal political tool. By mid-spring, 1966, it was no longer the party's *People's Daily* but the army's newspaper that handed down pronouncements of true faith. By mid-fall, it was army officers who sat in banks and newspaper offices, in factories and ministries. Army men took over formal direction of culture. The people were told to emulate the soldiers, and to listen to Lin Piao.

A key role in the drama in Peking was assigned to Madame Mao, also known as Chiang Ching. Once an obscure stage and movie actress in Shanghai, she had drifted into the Communist-held areas of China in the late 1930s. In 1939, she became the fourth Mme. Mao Tse-tung. Never active in politics until 1966, she suddenly emerged in May as the top leader of a purge being conducted at the University of Peking. Her rise thereafter was spectacular. She presided at some of the great rallies in Peking, became the second in command of the "cultural revolution," and when the army took control of the arts, Mme. Mao was the authority the army's consultants turned to for advice.

Red Guards Emerge. Army backing alone was not enough for Mao's purposes. In May, 1966, almost surreptitiously, the first unit of the teen-age Red Guards was organized in a middle (high) school in Peking. By August 18, when the movement was formally unveiled at a huge rally, its strength was already thought to exceed 1,000,000. Only three months later, the number of the Red Guards was put at 22,000,000, and one estimate said one-fifth of the nation's transport was engaged in moving them on their missions of persuasion and violence. Lin Piao became their patron, and in effect they became the army's reserve.

With the schools and universities closed by government order, these millions of youngsters had ample time to write their posters attacking this or that party boss; take part in almost continuous demonstrations against the "old" culture and China's "ancestral" traditions; recite Mao's works to anyone within the sound of their voices; and now and then "bombard" some party bastion still opposed to Mao. The Red Guards, acting as Mao's shock troops, altered the "bourgeois" names of streets and shops; they smashed ancestral tablets and defaced China's ancient temples. By late summer, they were further emboldened to storm provincial party offices believed to be unfriendly to Mao Tse-tung.

The army and the Red Guards became Mao's prime tools, but they were not the only ones. Unable to seize control of the entire party machine, he captured some of its key components. One was the seven-man standing committee of the Politburo, which he packed with his allies. Another was the party's propaganda committee, through which he was now able to deny public forum to his opponents. He had also created "cultural revolution committees," with vast if purposely vague powers.

Mao's first major opponent to be ousted was Mayor Peng Chen of Peking, who, until then, had been regarded as one of the men likeliest to succeed Mao. All through the spring of 1966, a bitter campaign was waged against the top political thinkers in Peng's municipal party machine. Once this "black gang" was destroyed, Peng's own turn came in late May, 1966. This was only the beginning of his ordeal. According to Red Guard posters, he was dragged out of his bed one December night, and the following day put on "public trial" at a stadium filled with aroused Red Guards.

Mao's other top opponents were for months described only as "party authorities who have taken the capitalist path." In November, 1966, to no one's surprise, posters finally identified these mysterious figures as Chief of State Liu Shao-chi and the party's General Secretary Teng Hsiao-ping. By December, huge rallies of Red Guards were being held to demand that these two veterans of the revolution – both of whom were once Mao's closest companions – be arrested, tried, and put before the firing squad.

As 1966 came to an end, Mao's opposition was in disarray, even if it was still holding out in the provinces. But even Mao's complete victory would not restore order to the political scene. There were many signs that the rot of dissension had sprouted in the ranks of his own political allies. Still ahead, too, was the shock the nation would experience when Mao made his promised sharp swing to the left. The shock would be felt through the whole spectrum of life, from education (which was to be radically reorganized) to agriculture (where the peasant's tiny private plot was being denounced as a vestige of capitalism).

But there was a reverse side. Mao's proudest achievement since 1949 had been the bringing of order and stability to a nation that had not known them for nearly 30 years. Now, overnight, this gain seemed to have been thrown to the winds. Encouraged by Mao and Lin Piao, bands of Red Guards challenged authority, besieged party offices, and fought pitched battles with rival youth groups or with workers. The public, accustomed to party control, now saw party officials hesitant, frightened, or publicly humbled. This loss of public confidence would be difficult to restore. Production was bound to suffer because of the turmoil in the streets and with countless young workers away from their jobs (but still drawing their pay). Finally, because of the prolonged school holiday, an entire generation faced the loss of perhaps a year's education, a loss that would contribute little to the nation's progress.

Communist China's Party Chairman Mao Tse-tung, *foreground,* takes a swim in the Yangtze River to dispel rumors of his failing health.

Domestic Economy. Most of the damage done by the conflict in Peking was political and psychological. Despite drought, Peking claimed a harvest as good as that of 1957 (though China's population has grown by at least 120,000,000 since then). Industry appeared to be making modest progress. China also continued to make spectacular advances in the development of its nuclear arsenal. On Oct. 27, 1966, Chinese scientists fired a guided missile with a nuclear warhead in Sinkiang province. On December 28, China carried out its fifth successful nuclear test. See ATOMIC ENERGY.

In Foreign Affairs, China's isolation deepened as the number of nations and Communist parties friendly to it continued to shrink. During 1966, the North Korean and Japanese Communist parties parted company with Peking (see KOREA). The chasm dividing China and the Soviet Union also continued to widen, and Moscow continued its efforts to organize a new world Communist congress at which Peking could be read out of the party.

Facts in Brief. Population: 709,000,000. Government: Communist Party Chairman Mao Tse-tung; Chairman of the Republic Liu Shao-chi; Premier Chou En-lai. Monetary Unit: yuan (2.50 = U.S. $1). Foreign Trade: exports, $1,110,500,000; imports, $1,328,900,000. Principal Exports: coal, metal ores and concentrates, rice, textiles. MARK GAYN

See also COMMUNISM; RUSSIA.

CITY. The White House and the Congress of the United States worked together to pass a legislative landmark, the Demonstration Cities and Metropolitan Development Act of 1966. The measure introduced a new approach toward revitalizing entire slum neighborhoods. The act authorized $900,000,000 a year for two years to aid selected cities to make a comprehensive attack on physical and social blight. Congress also voted continuation of many programs of importance to cities. Extended were aid for anti-poverty efforts, mass transit, air pollution control, libraries, law enforcement, highways, and airports. To help clean up the nation's waterways, Congress went beyond administration budget requests.

Of major importance to local police forces were two decisions of the Supreme Court of the United States. *Miranda vs. Arizona* spelled out the rights of a suspect in police custody. And in *Sheppard vs. Ohio*, the Court held that pretrial publicity could make a fair trial impossible. See SUPREME COURT OF THE UNITED STATES.

The Economic Picture of tight money and rising costs had its impact in cities. The scarcity of mortgage money caused housing construction to drop off sharply in many metropolitan areas. Dozens of public works projects–stadiums, bridges, schools, waterworks–were postponed as contractors' bids soared over estimated costs. Local governments had difficulty selling bonds to finance construction. Despite a 32-year high in average interest rates, many issues failed to get any bids from banks.

Faced with a steadily rising cost of living, some of the 1,844,000 municipal employees firmly sought pay increases. The year opened with a paralyzing transit workers strike in New York City. Firemen walked out in Atlanta, Ga.; St. Louis, Mo.; and Kansas City, Mo. The nation's first full-scale police strike in 47 years very nearly occurred in Pontiac, Mich. Other cities with labor unrest included Detroit, Mich.; San Francisco, Calif.; Dayton, Ohio; Lansing, Mich; and Los Angeles, Calif.

The Ghetto. The troubled slums of 38 cities erupted into violence during the summer months. While none compared in intensity with the 1965 Watts outbreak in Los Angeles, National Guardsmen were needed to restore order in Cleveland, Chicago, and San Francisco. In almost all instances, the riots began in Negro neighborhoods. Growth of the nonwhite ghetto was examined in a study, published in August, which forecast that at least 14 big cities will have Negro populations of 40 per cent or higher by 1970. Another 23 cities with over 100,000 population will be more than 30 per cent Negro.

The explosiveness of the situation led to hearings by a Senate subcommittee headed by Senator Abraham A. Ribicoff (D., Conn.). For three weeks, Cabinet officials, mayors, and slum residents gave testimony on "the crisis of the cities."

Metropolitan Affairs. While the ghetto remained largely a central city problem, other regional issues were met in some locations by a relatively new agency of local government, the voluntary council of government. These groups were composed of officials representing both cities and suburbs. The Advisory Commission on Intergovernmental Relations viewed these councils as one means of resolving pressing area-wide problems without resorting to fully realized metropolitan governments. At year's end, some 23 councils were active. Some of the newest were in central Oklahoma; Topeka, Kans.; and Hartford, Conn. Older councils in Washington, D.C., and New York City moved to take on primary planning responsibilities for their entire area. North America's first metropolitan government, Toronto, Ont., further consolidated its suburbs and central city. The region was reorganized into six boroughs instead of 13 municipal corporations.

CED Story. The influential Committee for Economic Development (CED) stimulated widespread interest with its recommendations to modernize local government. A CED report urged cutting the number of local governments (91,000 in 1962) by 80 per cent. DONALD W. LIEF

See also CONGRESS OF THE UNITED STATES; Section One, ALISTAIR COOKE: FOCUS ON THE ARTS.

CITY AND REGIONAL PLANNING. "The Great Society and Its Implications for Planning" was the main theme of the annual conference of the American Society of Planning Officials, held in Chicago in December, 1966. The 2,300 delegates were told by Robert C. Weaver, Secretary of the Department of Housing and Urban Development, " . . . the sort of planning and programming needed to make demonstration cities work represents a drastic departure from most of the city planning that has ever been done before."

Calling for a closer working relationship between city planning officials, other municipal agency officials, and representatives of private organizations, Weaver said, "I firmly believe that planners, at this crucial point in time, will either have to get deeply involved in the full range of problems afflicting our cities or they must risk the abrogation of their traditional role." See ARCHITECTURE; CITY.

More New Towns. General Electric Company (GE) announced its plans to develop several "new towns" within reasonable commuting distance of major metropolitan centers. Construction of the first of GE's planned cities will be underway in 1967, but the location has not yet been announced. The initial project will take 15 to 20 years to complete and will cost close to $1,000,000,000, with GE furnishing an unspecified share of the funds. The first GE-sponsored new town will have a population of approximately 100,000 people, contain its own industrial community, business establishments, recreational and educational facilities, and consist of a variety of housing styles ranging from single-family units to a diverse selection of apartments.

The action by GE is not unique in American industry. Goodyear Tire and Rubber Company, Humble Oil and Refining Company, and American-Hawaiian Steamship Company have similar projects underway or in the planning stage. The new town of Reston, Va., a section of which opened in 1966, is financed in part by a $15,000,000 investment of the Gulf Oil Corporation.

Montreal. "Even now, few people in Montreal seem to realize that they are building the most advanced urban core of our time." Thus did the September issue of the *Architectural Forum* magazine hail the city planning and redevelopment accomplishments of the Canadian city. Describing Montreal's efforts, which are centered around the Place Ville Marie project in the central business district, Peter Blake, editor of the highly respected publication, wrote, "What is happening in this approximately 200-acre core of Montreal is that the vision of a multilevel metropolis is finally being realized." Editor Blake credited Vincent Ponte, who planned the "new" Montreal, with making "downtown pedestrianism more comfortable than it has ever been made in any North American city in this century."

J. ROBERT DUMOUCHEL

CIVIL RIGHTS. Racial riots in major cities across the nation and cries of "black power" made civil rights a leading concern in the United States in 1966. An agenda for new national policy was offered in President Lyndon B. Johnson's State of the Union Message, calling for strict federal laws against those who "murder, attack, or intimidate" civil rights workers and for laws establishing "unavoidable requirements for nondiscriminatory jury selection" in the South. The most controversial feature of the message was the President's request that discrimination in housing sales and rentals be prohibited.

Legislation introduced in the Congress of the United States, based upon the President's proposals, prohibited discrimination on racial or religious grounds in the "purchase, rental, lease, financing, use, and occupancy of all housing." The bill promised to affect the North more than any previous civil rights measure. Public opinion, tolerant of other civil rights legislation in recent years, failed to rally behind the bill. Although it passed the House, it never came to a vote in the Senate. This proved to be the first failure of a civil rights measure in Congress in nine years.

Kentucky's Plan. The year's most impressive civil rights legislation was adopted by the state of Kentucky. The first state south of the Ohio River to enact such a law, Kentucky went farther toward barring discrimination in public accommodations and hiring practices than the Civil Rights Act of 1964. The Kentucky statute opened to Negroes all businesses serving the public except barbershops, beauty shops, and small boarding houses. It guaranteed fair employment standards to the 90 per cent of the labor force that works for businesses employing eight or more persons. (The federal civil rights act, even when fully extended in 1967, will cover only businesses employing 25 or more persons.)

Court Battles. The courts continued to be a principal arena of the civil rights struggle. In *South Carolina vs. Nicholas deB. Katzenbach*, the Supreme Court of the United States upheld the Voting Rights Act of 1965, which outlawed literacy tests and other registration practices used in Southern states to keep Negroes from voting, and authorized the entry of federal registrars to enroll new voters. The Court ruled in March that these "stringent remedies" were a valid means for carrying out the commands of Section 2 of Amendment 15, which empowers Congress to take "appropriate" measures to bar voting discrimination.

The Court continued to throw out Southern convictions of persons seized in nearly every kind of civil rights demonstration. In *Brown vs. Louisiana*, Congress of Racial Equality (CORE) demonstrators, who staged a "stand-up" in a Clinton (La.) public library, had been convicted for disturbing the peace. Yet the closeness of the vote, 5 to 4, suggested some disenchantment by the Court with ever-bolder

Where Race Riots Struck in 1966

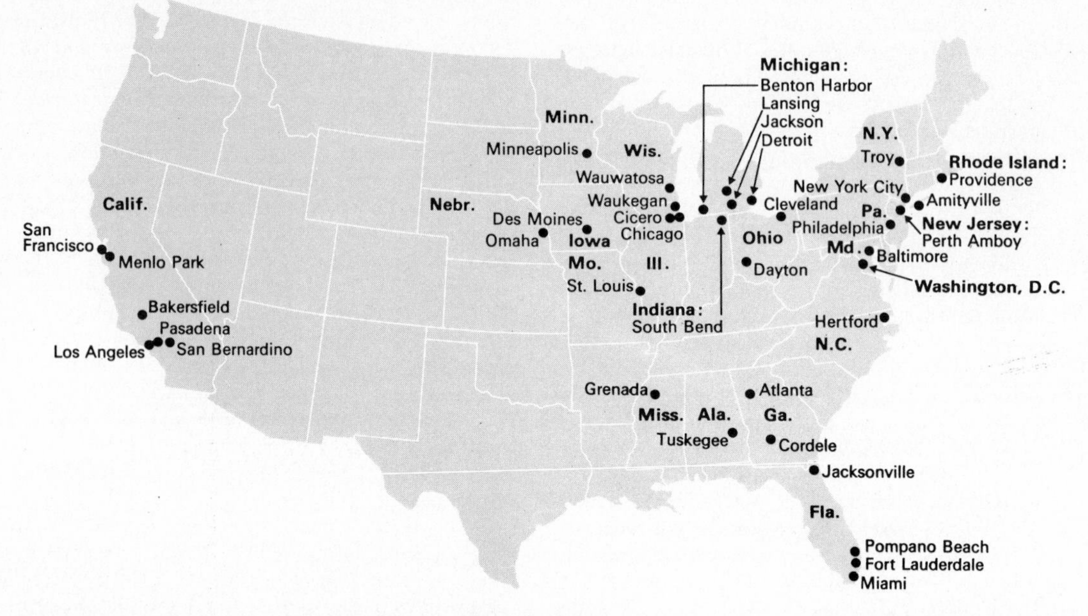

Racial disturbances flared in 38 U.S. cities in 1966, but most significantly in the North. The National Guard was called to quell riots in Chicago, Cleveland, San Francisco, and elsewhere.

civil rights demonstrations. Justice Hugo Black, an ardent supporter of civil rights, wrote in dissent: "It has become automatic for people to be turned loose as long as whatever they do has something to do with race. This is not the way I read the Constitution."

Early in 1966, the United States Civil Rights Commission noted that after more than a decade following the Court's school desegregation decisions only one of every 13 Negro children in the 11 states of the Old Confederacy was attending schools with white students. This was the case despite the 1964 Civil Rights Act, which empowered the U.S. Office of Education to withhold federal funds from segregated school districts. The commission attributed the poor record to the Office of Education's faulty guidelines, which permitted Negroes to attend any schools that had vacant space. This placed the burden of integration upon the Negro, who usually did not seek to integrate for fear of retaliation.

Controversial Guidelines. Thus, the Office of Education quickly issued new and tighter guidelines in March, suggesting: (1) that Southern school officials step-up the pace of integration of selected school faculties within a district, or risk losing federal aid; (2) that the one- and two-room shacks typifying many all-Negro schools in the South be closed and their students transferred to other schools; and (3) that Negroes must not be intimidated in the development of local desegregation plans. The efficacy of the new guidelines was evidenced by the outcry from Southern legislators in Congress.

Hospital's Role. In a parallel development, the U.S. Public Health Service sent "a medical facilities compliance report" to some 7,600 hospitals throughout the nation, and announced that those practicing segregation will be denied federal funds. Billions of dollars of newly available Medicare benefits gave extra effect to the threat. See MEDICARE.

White House Conference on Civil Rights, headed by a 35-man council of civil rights leaders, businessmen, educators, labor union representatives, and public officials, declared in May that the federal government's civil rights progress had not been matched "by state and local government, by business and labor, the housing industry, educational institutions, and the wide spectrum of voluntary organizations that, through united effort, have the power to improve our society."

The civil rights scene provided ready illustration for the conference's contention. During the year, many Southern restaurants were turned into "clubs" to avoid compliance with the 1964 Civil Rights Act barring discrimination in public accommodations. The U.S. Department of Justice filed suits against restaurant owners following this practice.

Grenada Violence. In the civil rights field, 1966 was above all a year of violence. Atlanta, Chicago,

Cleveland, Dayton, San Francisco, and St. Louis erupted with racial violence. And the nation and the world was shocked to see grown men kick and strike Negro children with pipes and clubs when they entered a former all-white school in Grenada, Miss., under a court order. One youngster suffered a broken leg.

The Meredith March. James H. Meredith, 32, first Negro to study at the University of Mississippi, was shot from ambush near Hernando, Miss., during a march he undertook in June to encourage Negroes to register to vote. Meredith's march was taken up by other Negro leaders, and he was able to complete the march himself. His assailant, Aubrey James Norvell, 40, of Memphis, Tenn., was sentenced in November to five years in prison for the highway shooting.

Black Power. A schism in the Negro civil rights movement over the issue of "black power" developed in 1966. Leaders of the more radical organizations, such as Floyd McKissick, 44, of CORE, and Stokely Carmichael, 25, of the Student Nonviolent Coordinating Committee (SNCC), pleaded for black power, or for Negroes to build their own bases of power. West-Indian-born Carmichael declared that black power was intended to end the Negro's sense of inferiority in predominantly white America. In political terms, it meant seeking to take over government whereever Negroes were a majority, organizing economic boycotts, and the creation of all-Negro financial institutions.

Moderate organizations rejected the black power theme. Roy Wilkins, executive director of the National Association for the Advancement of Colored People (NAACP), said that black power "can mean in the end only black death." Martin Luther King, Jr., warned that the black power issue might split the civil rights movement permanently. A. Philip Randolph, president of the Brotherhood of Sleeping Car Porters, urged Negro leaders to "take great care against overheating the ghettos," lest they precipitate "a race war in this nation which could become a catastrophe."

Public opinion seemed to weaken in its tolerance of Negro civil rights. Reports from university campuses indicated a decline of student interest in the subject. A backlash vote developed in several urban areas in the November elections. Primaries for the congressional elections provided scant comfort. In Louisiana, 12-term Congressman James Morrison paid for his moderate racial record by losing the Democratic primary to segregationist John Rarick. In Georgia, a strident racist, Lester Maddox, was locked in a gubernatorial race that would have to be decided by the courts or the state legislature.

Elsewhere in the World, civil rights seemed healthiest in traditionally democratic countries. Generally, the new governments of Africa compiled

Negroes march in tense Cicero, Ill., which has a history of racial violence. *Below,* white onlooker is restrained by police during another demonstration.

"Man, this stuff's been aging for 100 years."

a grim record. In South Africa and Rhodesia, white dominance tightened its grip. In Russia, the persecution of Jews continued. Communist China underwent a vast purge of dissident opinion.

But there were favorable developments, too. A severe test of civil rights is a general election, with its enormous stakes of power. One of the better elections of the year was brought off in the Dominican Republic. Tensions ran high, and to keep the proceedings honest, numerous foreign and diplomatic "observers" were on hand. The election was deemed an honest one and was widely hailed as the country's second free election since 1924.

In Spain, the Franco dictatorship took an encouraging turn when the *Cortes* (legislature) enacted a new press law under which publications no longer need to secure clearance prior to their appearance in print. Although the Ministry of Information can still seize an entire press run, it now must take its case promptly to the courts. LOUIS W. KOENIG

See also COURTS AND LAWS; DEMOCRACY; SUPREME COURT OF THE UNITED STATES; and related country articles.

CLOTHING. See FASHION; MANUFACTURING (Textile).

CLUBS, BOYS' AND GIRLS'. See YOUTH ORGANIZATIONS.

COAL. See MINES AND MINING.

COIN COLLECTING. See HOBBIES.

COLOMBIA. National Front presidential candidate Carlos Lleras Restrepo won office in the May 1 elections. However, approximately three-fourths of the electorate showed their disillusionment with the government either by not voting at all or by voting for a return to authoritarian ways. In earlier elections held on March 20, the National Front had failed to win a two-thirds majority in both houses of the legislature and it was thus feared that paralysis in government would block needed legislation.

Austerity Program. Lleras was sworn in on August 7 for a four-year term. A trained economist and a supporter of private enterprise, he stressed the importance of creating more jobs in the industrial sector, and made it clear that efficiency and production costs were a matter of public interest. He emphasized the need for agrarian reform, the introduction of new forms of capitalization, and easy access to education by the masses.

Lleras sought congressional authorization to rule by decree until July, 1967, on matters of economic development and administrative reorganization. He also sought a constitutional reform under which the required two-thirds congressional majority for major decisions would be reduced to a simple majority. These efforts, however, were blocked by opposition forces who feared Lleras wanted dictatorial powers.

The republic suffered from a tight credit and profit squeeze, the latter caused by rising costs of raw materials and wage pressures, as well as by governmental price controls on finished products. Import restrictions were liberalized but became subject to a higher exchange rate. To stimulate coffee exports, the rate paid for dollars earned by the commodity was raised 4.6 per cent in August to 9.35 pesos to the U.S. $1. Despite only a 2.3 per cent rise in the money supply in the first seven months of 1966, prices rose 13 per cent in the same period, revealing a serious inflationary trend.

Development Program. The Lleras administration prepared an economic program which was to be presented to various international lending agencies. The program called for $6,000,000,000 in foreign aid over four years. To attract foreign oil capital, Colombia began revising its oil legislation: it expected to sign some 250 new oil exploration contracts with foreign firms by the end of the year.

On August 30, the government closed the University of Antioquia for the rest of the semester following a month-long student strike. The students were (1) protesting a government decree requiring student attendance at 80 per cent of their classes, and (2) a ruling on the repayment of tuition fees.

Facts in Brief. Population: 18,566,000. Government: President Carlos Lleras Restrepo. Monetary Unit: peso (18.20 = U.S. $1). Foreign Trade: exports, $538,900,000; imports, $453,400,000. Principal Exports: bananas, coffee, crude oil. MARY C. WEBSTER

See LLERAS RESTREPO, CARLOS; LATIN AMERICA.

COMMUNICATIONS on a global scale was advanced late in 1966 when the 55-nation International Telecommunications Satellite Consortium began using its satellite Intelsat II, or Lani Bird, to relay signals over the Pacific Ocean. The October 26 launch, however, was not a complete success. Intelsat II failed to go into a perfect, circular orbit in step with the rotation of the earth. Such an orbit would have allowed it to hover 22,300 miles directly above a point in the mid-Pacific. Its forerunner, Early Bird, achieved such an orbit and was giving around-the-clock transatlantic service. Because of Intelsat II's imperfect, elliptical orbit, it was able to relay telephone calls, data, television, and other communications traffic only on a part-time basis.

A similar space achievement was recorded June 14, 1966, when the U.S. Department of Defense shot a group of seven communications satellites into space on a Titan IIIC rocket. The satellites were released at equal intervals to link ground stations as far as 10,000 miles apart. The system was set up to handle the military's top-priority command and control traffic. It was first successfully used on October 17 as a link between Vietnam and the United States. Voice messages traveled 50,000 miles via satellite between an earth station near the battlefront and another at Camp Roberts, Calif.

Earthly Advances in the communications art were also recorded. They included these firsts:

- Customer-dialed U.S.-European telephone calls during a demonstration in Philadelphia, Pa., in June. A "limited trial" was to begin in 1967.
- An undersea telephone cable connecting North America and South America, a 550-nautical-mile span that was formally put into service in August.
- Direct-dialing between the United States and the Virgin Islands, in September.
- A submarine cable system between Israel and France. A contract for this link was let in July.

The British Commonwealth, meanwhile, was moving forward with its cable-laying program to link Australia, Britain, Canada, and South Pacific and Southeast Asian nations.

Growth. When U.S. overseas telephone service was introduced in 1927–only to points in Great Britain and Cuba–11,750 calls were made that year. During the 12 months ended in March, 1966–when Americans could reach 97 per cent of all telephones in the world–some 8,390,000 calls were completed. Some of this growth, of course, stemmed from the fact that in 1927 New York-to-London calls cost $75. In 1966, the weekday rate for three minutes was $12.

Domestically, the American Telephone & Telegraph Company (AT&T) reported that interstate long-distance messages increased about 16 per cent from 1965. The number of telephones in service in the United States at the end of 1966 approached 96,000,000, almost 80,000,000 by the Bell System and the remainder by the some 2,400 independent companies. Bell System companies spent approximately $4,200,000,000 on construction in the year, while the independents' outlay was $900,000,000.

New Information Service. The Western Union Telegraph Company took its first step to establish a nationwide "information utility" in March when it opened a computer center at its New York City offices. Its aim was to provide the information service needs of business and government through a multiple-access computer communications network on a *real-time* (instant-response) basis. Initially, it served customers in eight Eastern cities. By year's end, the system covered about 200 cities.

Government Action. The Federal Communications Commission (FCC) opened its long-heralded investigation into AT&T's telephone rates on June 7. By the end of the year, the extensive hearings had produced a transcript in excess of 6,000 pages.

Congress restored the 10 per cent federal excise tax on local and long-distance telephone and teletypewriter exchange service. In 1965, the tax had been cut from 10 per cent to 3 per cent, effective Jan. 1, 1966. The new legislation returned the tax to 10 per cent on April 1. On April 1, 1968, it will drop to 1 per cent for the rest of that year, after which it will be eliminated entirely. THOMAS M. MALIA

See also ELECTRONICS; FOUNDATIONS; RADIO; TELEVISION; WEATHER.

COMMUNISM. The two monoliths of international Communism seemed to be moving steadily toward a final and irrevocable split during 1966. The links still remaining between the two giants–the People's Republic of China and the Soviet Union–had worn so thin by the end of the year that almost nothing was lacking but a formal act of rupture. See CHINA, PEOPLE'S REPUBLIC OF; RUSSIA.

Throughout the year, successive events widened the gulf between Chinese Communism and most of the rest of the world movement. In March, when the 23rd congress of the Communist Party of the Soviet Union (CPSU) opened in Moscow, the Chinese were not represented. The fact that the parties of Albania, Burma, Japan, Malaysia, New Zealand, the Philippines, and Thailand were also absent and that North Vietnam and North Korea did send only fraternal delegates, testified to the disunity of the international Communist movement. See Section Two, RUSSIA: FIFTY YEARS OF TURMOIL.

Chinese Accusations. In replying to the CPSU invitation, the Chinese bitterly accused the Soviet leaders of proceeding farther down the road of revisionism, collaborating with the United States for world domination, and undermining the struggle in Vietnam. In a letter sent to other parties, the Soviet party had attacked the Chinese Communist party for refusing to hold bilateral discussions and for its open defiance of the CPSU.

Vietnamese delegate to a Communist youth congress in Moscow gets a traditional "toss-up" after he predicts victory in Vietnam.

Pro-Moscow Leanings. The position of the Soviet Union, meanwhile, was substantially strengthened. From actions taken during the party congress, and subsequent events, there were indications that the Soviet party had marshaled the support of the majority of the world's Communist parties. The North Korean Communist party, in August, proclaimed its independence of the Chinese as well as the Soviet leaderships, and, while it criticized both, its denunciation of Peking was more vigorous.

North Vietnam, with its borders adjoining China's, but with its economy dependent on Soviet aid, had also adopted, by August, a more pro-Soviet attitude. Twice during the year, delegations from Hanoi visited China, North Korea, and the Mongolian People's Republic. But they also paid calls on the Soviet Union and other East European countries (including Hungary, Bulgaria, Romania, East Germany, Albania, and Poland) where they concluded agreements for increased assistance.

Position Weakens. Conversely, the Chinese position was weakened when Indonesia's Communist party was physically destroyed during the year and the powerful Japanese party, one of China's closest supporters in the Sino-Soviet rift, moved to the middle of the road. With India's Communist party continuing to follow a pro-Soviet course, China lacked strong support from any significant Asian movement. An open break also occurred in February with Cuba (see CUBA).

In Europe, Albania remained the only ally of Peking. Even in Romania, which had continued to play a neutral role in the ideological dispute between Moscow and Peking, Chinese influence waned. When Communist Chinese Premier Chou En-lai paid a long visit to Bucharest in June, he failed to wean the Romanians away from Moscow. In Albania, however, which he visited immediately after, Chou En-lai enjoyed a more fruitful reception. See ROMANIA.

Accusations Exchanged. The "cultural revolution" in China in the late summer further aggravated the situation within the international Communist movement. In August, the central committee of the CPSU issued a condemnation of Chinese policy, the first public statement of its kind since the ouster of Soviet Premier Nikita S. Khrushchev.

Denying Soviet collusion with American "imperialism," the Soviet leadership blamed the Chinese for having rejected all proposals for united action in support of Vietnam and for causing a serious split in the world Communist movement. One after another, the Moscow-oriented Communist parties joined in denouncing China. In Europe, only Romania refrained from such action.

Reciprocal Walkouts. Although diplomatic relations continued between Moscow and Peking, they were greatly strained by these events and by the activities of the Red Guards who demonstrated frequently outside the Soviet embassy in Peking. In October, at a celebration marking the 17th anniversary of the Chinese regime in Peking, Soviet and other delegates walked out in anger over remarks made by Chinese Premier Chou En-lai. In November, Chinese delegates retaliated by walking out on a celebration of the 49th anniversary of the Soviet revolution in Moscow.

Despite widespread support in the world Communist movement, Moscow was unable to achieve a united strategy for dealing with the Chinese challenge. An assemblage of East Europe's Communist leaders in Moscow in October disbanded with a noncommittal communiqué. Although it was reported that more aid to Hanoi had been pledged, there were rumors from Poland that the delegates had urged North Vietnam to soften its line on peace terms. Publicly, however, the Soviet Union persisted in its hard line on the question, and rebuffed American overtures for improved U.S.-Soviet relations as long as the war in Vietnam continued.

Schism Remains. Appeals were made at party congresses held in Bulgaria and Hungary in November for a world Communist conference to deal with the Chinese question. Strong support was forthcoming from some parties, notably the Hungarian and Bulgarian. But others, including the Romanian, Polish, and Yugoslavian, in Europe, and the Mongolian and North Korean, in Asia, responded with indifference or open hostility. H. GORDON SKILLING

COMPUTERS may soon be able to display all the "thinking" processes of man according to Marvin L. Minsky, professor of electrical engineering and director of the artificial intelligence group at Massachusetts Institute of Technology (M.I.T.). In the September issue of *Scientific American*, he stated that a profound change in computers occurred with the discovery that human thought processes can be turned into prescriptions for the design of computer programs, and that these machines are already being used to set goals, make plans, consider hypotheses, and recognize relationships.

"It is unreasonable to think machines could become nearly as intelligent as man is and then stop, or to suppose we will always be able to compete with them in wit or wisdom," he said. He further pointed out that computers have been programmed to win consistently at checkers, to solve complex algebraic word problems, and to score at the 10th grade level on college entrance exams. Computers eventually will be built that can apply the experience gained in solving one type of problem to the solution of different problems, he predicted.

However, philosophy professor Hubert L. Dreyfus, a fellow faculty member of Professor Minsky at M.I.T., expressed the opposite view, comparing a computer enthusiast to a man who inches up a tree believing he will reach the moon. Dreyfus said that human intelligence cannot even be approximated on a computer because of the vast chasm between the most complex computers and thinking.

Memory Units. Computer data memory units, the heart of computing machines, have traditionally consisted of tiny doughnut-shaped cores made of ferrite and threaded in a matrix of wires. In 1966, scientists at the Univac Division of Sperry Rand in New York City developed special plated wires to replace ferrite cores in the memory system of an engineering model computer they built for the U.S. Navy. Each plated wire is half as big, half as heavy, and requires one-tenth the power of a ferrite core memory with the same capacity.

Other methods for making smaller memory units with larger capacity were also being developed. These included the use of magnetic films and integrated circuits. However, several promising techniques embrace the traditional doughnut-shaped core principle, but with a new twist. In one, the cores are chemically grown around tiny gold wires.

Giant Brain. A giant computer expected to perform calculations 50 times faster than any existing computer will be built by the University of Illinois under an $8,000,000 contract to the U.S. Air Force. Heading the team to build "Illiac IV" is Professor Daniel L. Slotnik, who explained that speeds of over 1,000,000,000 computations per second will be achieved through a central control unit linked with many storage units. JAMES A. PEARRE

CONGO (BRAZZAVILLE). See AFRICA.

CONGO (KINSHASA, formerly Léopoldville). Joseph Mobuto took drastic steps to control his turbulent country in 1966. Four Congolese leaders, including former Premier Evariste Kimba, were arrested for plotting to overthrow the government on May 30, sentenced on June 1, and publicly hanged on June 2. On October 26, Mobutu dismissed Premier Leonard Mulamba, abolished his position, and took over as president of the cabinet.

Federal troops clashed with guerrilla forces in Katanga and in eastern Congo in January. The Katanga revolt was soon put down. But north and east of Stanleyville, the government could hold only the major towns. On March 12, Premier Mulamba accused Fidel Castro of Cuba of sending Cubans to teach guerrilla warfare to the rebels.

The assembly, after a recess of nearly three months, was reconvened by Mobutu on March 7. But the president stripped the assembly of its legislative powers on March 22, because of political intrigue and lack of cooperation. He then governed by decree.

On April 6, Mobutu reduced the 21 provinces established in 1963 to 12 in order to save money and ease tribal and political conflicts. The Congo renamed its major cities on Independence Day, June 30, to eradicate reminders of its colonial past. Léopoldville was changed to Kinshasa, Elisabethville to Lubumbashi, and Stanleyville to Kisangani.

About 700 police, supported by some 30 white mercenaries, mutinied in Kisangani (Stanleyville) July 23, saying they had not been paid for three months. Mulamba compromised with the mutineers to re-establish government control. Former Premier Moise Tshombe was accused of plotting the Kisangani mutiny.

In September, the Mobutu government announced that Tshombe would be tried in absentia for high treason, and that it was severing diplomatic relations with Portugal, claiming Portuguese Angola was harboring Tshombe's mercenaries. Then, in a September strike against Tshombe's power, Congolese army units attacked and crushed the rebels in Kisangani.

Aid from the United Nations technical assistance mission had dropped from 2,500 workers in mid-1964 to about 700 in early 1966. By the end of the year, Congolese had replaced foreigners in most of the programs.

Facts in Brief: Population: 15,700,000. Government: President Joseph Mobutu. Monetary Unit: franc (150=U.S.$1). Foreign Trade: exports, $381,-600,000; imports, $258,800,000. Principal Exports: copper, diamonds, palm oil. BENJAMIN E. THOMAS

CONGRESS OF THE UNITED STATES

By the time the second session of the "fabulous 89th Congress" adjourned on Oct. 22, 1966, it had shown a certain amount of independence and a general lack of enthusiasm for some of President Lyndon B. Johnson's Great Society proposals. Seventeen days later, that disenchantment was registered by the voters themselves as they rejected scores of the President's Democratic supporters.

The Nation was gripped by the "Senate's teach-in" on Vietnam, as were, *from left,* Senators Aiken, Hickenlooper, and Fulbright.

The Democratic majority in the House was cut from a total of 295 seats to 248. The Republicans had picked up 47 seats, increasing their representation to 187.

In the Senate, the Republicans gained three seats, raising the Republican-to-Democratic ratio from 33-67 to 36-64. The President a few days later had to concede that the 90th Congress "will be more difficult for any new legislation we might propose." See DEMOCRATIC PARTY; ELECTIONS; REPUBLICAN PARTY.

The 89th, indeed, was remarkable. Its first session had enacted some 90 major bills. Its second session added significantly to the Great Society legislative score–a demonstration cities plan, creation of a Department of Transportation, tax revisions, and funds for aid to education, for rental supplements for the poor, for a Teachers Corps, and for combating air and water pollution. Yet the Congress, as though attempting to free itself of the presidential grip, struck out on its own. The toughness of its auto safety bill far exceeded the administration's version. On other bills, it refused to go along with the White House–notably in its rejection of the civil rights bill with its provision for open housing.

The Second Session of the 89th Congress convened on Jan. 10, 1966, after a 78-day recess. It opened with the Democrats outnumbering the Republicans 68 to 32 in the Senate, and 293 to 140 in the House–with two vacancies, caused by the

PICTURES OF THE YEAR/Stanley Tretick,

death of Herbert C. Bonner (D., N.C.) and the resignation of John V. Lindsay (R., N.Y.). The Republicans got their 33rd seat in the Senate when Robert P. Griffin was appointed after the death of Patrick V. McNamara (D., Mich.).

In his State of the Union message to Congress in January, President Johnson called for expansion of the Great Society at home. At the same time, he pledged that U.S. forces would stay in Vietnam "until aggression is stopped." All told, the President asked for passage of 25 major bills.

Budget and Finance. The U.S. budget for the fiscal year ending June 30, 1967, was estimated in January, 1966, at $112,800,000,000, up some $4,200,000,000 over fiscal 1966. An increase of $3,000,000,000 was sought for domestic Great Society programs. From an anticipated gross national product of about $740,000,000,000, or $59,000,000,000 above the 1965 record, the administration foresaw enough revenue to hold the deficit for fiscal 1967 at $1,800,000,000.

The second session appropriated a record $130,281,568,480, including $58,067,472,000 for defense and some $16,000,000,000 in supplemental funds for 1966. Congress authorized $17,480,759,000 for arms and military research, and voted a 3.2 per cent across-the-board pay increase for all uniformed personnel. A similar increase was voted for all federal employees, effective July 1, 1966.

Foreign Policy. In January, 53 senators supported a resolution favoring negotiation of a treaty with the Soviet Union to limit the spread of nuclear weapons. In March, Congress authorized U.S. participation in the Asian Development Bank (see ASIA). In April, a program of supplying emergency food for famine-stricken India was approved by joint resolution.

In September, Congress voted its lowest foreign aid appropriation since 1957. It cut the administration's lowest request in 18 years – for $3,387,000,000 – to $2,936,490,500 for fiscal 1967. The following month it extended the Food for Peace Program for two years, authorizing expenditures of almost $7,500,000,000, including $5,000,000,000 in new commitments. Both bills authorized the federal government to offer birth control data and other assistance in population control to foreign governments that ask for such help.

Taxes. On March 15, the President signed tax legislation that would increase revenues by an estimated $1,100,000,000 in fiscal 1966 and $4,800,000,000 in fiscal 1967. Excise taxes, which had been reduced or eliminated in 1965, were raised or restored on new cars and telephone service. Increased withholdings of taxes on personal income were authorized, and corporations with large annual tax liabilities were required to pay taxes quarterly. Both steps were taken to collect taxes sooner, not to raise the tax rates. A *rider*, or amendment, to this legislation also increased Social Security coverage (see SOCIAL SECURITY).

In October, Congress suspended for 15 months both the special 7 per cent tax credit for business investment in new plant and equipment and the fast write-offs that had been allowed for depreciation of new commercial and industrial buildings. Both actions were attempts to restrain inflationary tendencies in the national economy. See ECONOMY, THE.

And in its final bill, Congress revised revenue laws to stimulate foreign investment in the United States. So many riders allowing special tax benefits were attached to this legislation, however, that it became known as the "Christmas Tree Bill." One rider that broke new ground authorized setting up a fund to finance presidential campaigns. Starting with 1967 income tax returns filed in 1968, taxpayers may indicate whether they wish $1 (or $2 if a joint return) of their tax to go into a fund to be divided between the major candidates and their running mates. See TAXATION.

Aid to Education was increased by the second session. In October, Congress passed a $6,100,000,000 program of aid to elementary and secondary schools. It also provided $3,970,000,000 in federal funds to aid the nation's colleges. See EDUCATION.

A new GI Bill of Rights, signed by the President in March, provided educational, health, housing, and job benefits – at a cost estimated at $358,000,000 in the first year – for veterans with more than 180 days of active service since Jan. 31, 1955, the expiration date of the old GI Bill. See VETERANS.

Welfare Legislation. Congress authorized $1,750,000,000 for the War on Poverty in fiscal 1967. But it kept tight rein on the money by earmarking separate amounts for particular parts of the program. As in the foreign aid program, Congress approved the use of some funds for local family-planning programs.

The second session also voted funds for the National Teachers Corps – to supply low-income school districts with specially trained teachers – and for the rent subsidy program in which a tenant in a nonslum flat pays 25 per cent of his income toward the rent with the federal government paying the balance. Both programs were authorized but not funded by the first session of the 89th Congress (see POVERTY).

The highly controversial Demonstration Cities and Metropolitan Development Act passed in October. Congress voted funds for a two-year, $1,260,000,000 attack on urban slum problems. From 60 to 70 cities were expected to be aided in developing ways of improving and rebuilding specific "demonstration neighborhoods." See CITY; HOUSING.

Transportation. The Urban Mass Transportation Act, signed by the President on September 8, provided federal grants to state and local public agencies to help finance capital expenditures on

Members of the United States House

The House of Representatives of the 90th Congress consists of 248 Democrats and 187 Republicans, compared with 295 Democrats and 140 Republicans for the 89th Congress. Table shows congressional districts, winner, and party affiliation. Asterisk denotes those who served in the 89th Congress. AL denotes "At Large."

ALABAMA

1. Jack Edwards, R.*
2. William L. Dickinson, R.*
3. George W. Andrews, D.*
4. William Nichols, D.
5. Armistead I. Selden, Jr., D.*
6. John H. Buchanan, Jr., R.*
7. Tom Bevill, D.
8. Robert E. Jones, D.*

ALASKA

(AL) Howard W. Pollock, R.

ARIZONA

1. John J. Rhodes, R.*
2. Morris K. Udall, D.*
3. Sam Steiger, R.

ARKANSAS

1. E. C. Gathings, D.*
2. Wilbur D. Mills, D.*
3. J. P. Hammerschmidt, R.
4. David Pryor, D.

CALIFORNIA

1. Don H. Clausen, R.*
2. Harold T. Johnson, D.*
3. John E. Moss, D.*
4. Robert L. Leggett, D.*
5. Phillip Burton, D.*
6. William S. Mailliard, R.*
7. Jeffery Cohelan, D.*
8. George P. Miller, D.*
9. Don Edwards, D.*
10. Charles S. Gubser, R.*
11. J. Arthur Younger, R.*
12. Burt L. Talcott, R.*
13. Charles M. Teague, R.*
14. Jerome R. Waldie, D.*
15. John J. McFall, D.*
16. B. F. Sisk, D.*
17. Cecil R. King, D.*
18. Robert B. Mathias, R.
19. Chet Holifield, D.*
20. H. Allen Smith, R.*
21. Augustus F. Hawkins, D.*
22. James C. Corman, D.*
23. Del M. Clawson, R.*
24. Glenard P. Lipscomb, R.*
25. Charles E. Wiggins, R.
26. Thomas M. Rees, D.*
27. Ed Reinecke, R.*
28. Alphonzo Bell, R.*
29. George E. Brown, Jr., D.*
30. Edward R. Roybal, D.*
31. Charles H. Wilson, D.*
32. Craig Hosmer, R.*
33. Jerry L. Pettis, R.
34. Richard T. Hanna, D.*
35. James B. Utt, R.*
36. Bob Wilson, R.*
37. Lionel Van Deerlin, D.*
38. John V. Tunney, D.*

COLORADO

1. Byron G. Rogers, D.*
2. Donald G. Brotzman, R.
3. Frank E. Evans, D.*
4. Wayne N. Aspinall, D.*

CONNECTICUT

1. Emilio Q. Daddario, D.*
2. William L. St. Onge, D.*
3. Robert N. Giaimo, D.*
4. Donald J. Irwin, D.*
5. John S. Monagan, D.*
6. Thomas J. Meskill, R.

DELAWARE

(AL) William V. Roth, Jr., R.

FLORIDA

1. Robert L. F. Sikes, D.*
2. Don Fuqua, D.*
3. Charles E. Bennett, D.*
4. A. Sydney Herlong, Jr., D.*
5. Edward J. Gurney, R.*
6. Sam M. Gibbons, D.*
7. James A. Haley, D.*
8. William C. Cramer, R.*
9. Paul G. Rogers, D.*
10. J. Herbert Burke, R.
11. Claude D. Pepper, D.*
12. Dante B. Fascell, D.*

GEORGIA

1. G. Elliott Hagan, D.*
2. Maston E. O'Neal, Jr., D.*
3. Jack Brinkley, D.
4. Benjamin Blackburn, R.
5. S. F. Thompson, R.
6. John J. Flynt, Jr., D.*
7. John W. Davis, D.*
8. Williamson S. Stuckey, Jr., D.
9. Phillip M. Landrum, D.*
10. Robert G. Stephens, Jr., D.*

HAWAII

(AL) Spark M. Matsunaga, D.*
(AL) Patsy T. Mink, D.*

IDAHO

1. James A. McClure, R.
2. George V. Hansen, R.*

ILLINOIS

1. William L. Dawson, D.*
2. Barratt O'Hara, D.*
3. William T. Murphy, D.*
4. Edward J. Derwinski, R.*
5. John C. Kluczynski, D.*
6. Daniel J. Ronan, D.*
7. Frank Annunzio, D.*
8. Daniel D. Rostenkowski, D.*
9. Sidney R. Yates, D.*
10. Harold R. Collier, R.*
11. Roman C. Pucinski, D.*
12. Robert McClory, R.*
13. Donald Rumsfeld, R.*
14. John N. Erlenborn, R.*
15. Charlotte T. Reid, R.*
16. John B. Anderson, R.*
17. Leslie C. Arends, R.*
18. Robert H. Michel, R.*
19. Thomas F. Railsback, R.
20. Paul Findley, R.*
21. Kenneth J. Gray, D.*
22. William L. Springer, R.*
23. George E. Shipley, D.*
24. Charles Melvin Price, D.*

INDIANA

1. Ray J. Madden, D.*
2. Charles A. Halleck, R.*
3. John Brademas, D.*
4. E. Ross Adair, R.*
5. J. Edward Roush, D.*
6. William G. Bray, R.*
7. John T. Meyers, R.
8. Roger H. Zion, R.
9. Lee H. Hamilton, D.*
10. Richard L. Roudebush, R.*
11. Andrew Jacobs, Jr., D.*

IOWA

1. Fred D. Schwengel, R.
2. John C. Culver, D.*
3. H. R. Gross, R.*
4. John H. Kyl, R.
5. Neal Smith, D.*
6. Wiley E. Mayne, R.
7. William J. Scherle, R.

KANSAS

1. Robert J. Dole, R.*
2. Chester L. Mize, R.*
3. Larry Winn, Jr., R.
4. Garner E. Shriver, R.*
5. Joe Skubitz, R.*

KENTUCKY

1. Frank A. Stubblefield, D.*
2. William H. Natcher, D.*
3. William O. Cowger, R.
4. Gene Snyder, R.
5. Tim Lee Carter, R.*
6. John C. Watts, D.*
7. Carl D. Perkins, D.*

LOUISIANA

1. F. Edward Hébert, D.*
2. Hale Boggs, D.*
3. Edwin E. Willis, D.*
4. Joe D. Waggonner, Jr., D.*
5. Otto E. Passman, D.*
6. John R. Rarick, D.
7. Edwin W. Edwards, D.*
8. Speedy O. Long, D.*

MAINE

1. Peter N. Kyros, D.
2. William D. Hathaway, D.*

MARYLAND

1. Rogers C. B. Morton, R.*
2. Clarence D. Long, D.*
3. Edward A. Garmatz, D.*
4. George H. Fallon, D.*
5. Hervey G. Machen, D.*
6. Charles McC. Mathias, Jr., R.*
7. Samuel N. Friedel, D.*
8. Gilbert Gude, R.

MASSACHUSETTS

1. Silvio O. Conte, R.*
2. Edward P. Boland, D.*
3. Philip J. Philbin, D.*
4. Harold D. Donohue, D.*
5. F. Bradford Morse, R.*
6. William H. Bates, R.*
7. Torbert H. Macdonald, D.*
8. Thomas P. O'Neill, Jr., D.*
9. John W. McCormack, D.*
10. Margaret M. Heckler, R.
11. James A. Burke, D.*
12. Hastings Keith, R.*

MICHIGAN

1. John Conyers, Jr., D.*
2. Marvin L. Esch, R.
3. Gary E. Brown, R.
4. Edward Hutchinson, R.*
5. Gerald R. Ford, R.*
6. Charles E. Chamberlain, R.*
7. Donald W. Riegle, Jr., R.
8. James Harvey, R.*
9. Guy Vander Jagt, R.
10. Elford A. Cederberg, R.*
11. Philip E. Ruppe, R.
12. James G. O'Hara, D.*
13. Charles C. Diggs, Jr., D.*
14. Lucien N. Nedzi, D.*
15. William D. Ford, D.*
16. John D. Dingell, D.*
17. Martha W. Griffiths, D.*
18. William S. Broomfield, R.*
19. Jack H. McDonald, R.

MINNESOTA

1. Albert H. Quie, R.*
2. Ancher Nelsen, R.*
3. Clark MacGregor, R.*
4. Joseph E. Karth, D.*
5. Donald M. Fraser, D.*
6. John M. Zwach, R.
7. Odin Langen, R.*
8. John A. Blatnik, D.*

MISSISSIPPI

1. Thomas G. Abernethy, D.*
2. Jamie L. Whitten, D.*
3. John Bell Williams, D.*
4. G. V. Montgomery, D.
5. William M. Colmer, D.*

MISSOURI

1. Frank M. Karsten, D.*
2. Thomas B. Curtis, R.*
3. Leonor K. (Mrs. John B.) Sullivan, D.*
4. Wm. J. Randall, D.*
5. Richard Bolling, D.*
6. W. R. Hull, Jr., D.*
7. Durward G. Hall, R.*
8. Richard H. Ichord, D.*
9. William L. Hungate, D.*
10. Paul C. Jones, D.*

MONTANA

1. Arnold Olsen, D.*
2. James F. Battin, R.*

NEBRASKA

1. Robert V. Denney, R.
2. Glenn C. Cunningham, R.*
3. David T. Martin, R.*

NEVADA

(AL) Walter S. Baring, D.*

NEW HAMPSHIRE

1. Louis C. Wyman, R.
2. James C. Cleveland, R.*

NEW JERSEY

1. John E. Hunt, R.
2. Charles W. Sandman, Jr., R.
3. James J. Howard, D.*
4. Frank Thompson, Jr., D.*
5. Peter H. B. Frelinghuysen, R.*
6. William T. Cahill, R.*
7. William B. Widnall, R.*
8. Charles S. Joelson, D.*
9. Henry Helstoski, D.*
10. Peter W. Rodino, Jr., D.*
11. Joseph G. Minish, D.*
12. Florence P. Dwyer, R.*
13. Cornelius E. Gallagher, D.*
14. Dominick V. Daniels, D.*
15. Edward J. Patten, D.*

NEW MEXICO

(AL) Thomas G. Morris, D.*
(AL) E. S. Johnny Walker, D.*

NEW YORK

1. Otis G. Pike, D.*
2. James R. Grover, Jr., R.*
3. Lester L. Wolff, D.*
4. John W. Wydler, R.*
5. Herbert Tenzer, D.*
6. Seymour Halpern, R.*
7. Joseph P. Addabbo, D.*
8. Benjamin S. Rosenthal, D.*
9. James J. Delaney, D.*
10. Emanuel Celler, D.*
11. Frank J. Brasco, D.
12. Edna F. Kelly, D.*
13. Abraham J. Multer D.*
14. John J. Rooney, D.*
15. Hugh L. Carey, D.*
16. John M. Murphy, D.*
17. Theodore Kupferman, R.*
18. Adam C. Powell, D.*
19. Leonard Farbstein, D.*
20. William F. Ryan, D.*
21. James H. Scheuer, D.*
22. Jacob H. Gilbert, D.*
23. Jonathan B. Bingham, D.*
24. Paul A. Fino, R.*
25. Richard L. Ottinger, D.*
26. Ogden R. Reid, R.*
27. John G. Dow, D.*
28. Joseph Y. Resnick, D.*
29. Daniel E. Button, Jr., R.
30. Carleton J. King, R.*
31. Robert C. McEwen, R.*
32. Alexander Pirnie, R.*
33. Howard W. Robison, R.*
34. James M. Hanley, D.*
35. Samuel S. Stratton, D.*
36. Frank Horton, R.*
37. Barber B. Conable, Jr., R.*
38. Charles E. Goodell, R.*
39. Richard D. McCarthy, D.*
40. Henry P. Smith III, R.*
41. Thaddeus J. Dulski, D.*

NORTH CAROLINA

1. Walter B. Jones, D.*
2. L. H. Fountain, D.*
3. David N. Henderson, D.*
4. James C. Gardner, R.
5. Nick Galifianakis, D.
6. Horace R. Kornegay, D.*
7. Alton Asa Lennon, D.*
8. Charles Raper Jonas, R.*
9. James T. Broyhill, R.*
10. Basil L. Whitener, D.*
11. Roy A. Taylor, D.*

NORTH DAKOTA

1. Mark Andrews, R.*
2. Thomas S. Kleppe, R.

OHIO

1. Robert A. Taft, Jr., R.
2. Donald D. Clancy, R.*
3. Charles W. Whalen, Jr., R.
4. William M. McCulloch, R.*
5. Delbert L. Latta, R.*
6. William H. Harsha, R.*
7. Clarence J. Brown, Jr., R.*
8. Jackson E. Betts, R.*
9. Thomas L. Ashley, D.*
10. Clarence E. Miller, R.
11. J. William Stanton, R.*
12. Samuel L. Devine, R.*
13. Charles A. Mosher, R.*
14. William H. Ayres, R.*
15. Chalmers P. Wylie, R.
16. Frank T. Bow, R.*
17. John M. Ashbrook, R.*
18. Wayne L. Hays, D.*
19. Michael J. Kirwan, D.*
20. Michael A. Feighan, D.*
21. Charles A. Vanik, D.*
22. Frances P. Bolton, R.*
23. William E. Minshall, R.*
24. Donald E. Lukens, R.

OKLAHOMA

1. Page Belcher, R.*
2. Ed Edmondson, D.*
3. Carl B. Albert, D.*
4. Tom Steed, D.*
5. John Jarman, D.*
6. James V. Smith, R.

OREGON

1. Wendell Wyatt, R.*
2. Al Ullman, D.*
3. Edith Green, D.*
4. John R. Dellenback, R.

PENNSYLVANIA

1. William A. Barrett, D.*
2. Robert N. C. Nix, D.*
3. James A. Byrne, D.*
4. Joshua Eilberg, D.
5. William J. Green III, D.*
6. George M. Rhodes, D.*
7. Lawrence G. Williams, R.
8. Edward G. Biester, Jr., R.
9. G. Robert Watkins, R.*
10. Joseph M. McDade, R.*
11. Daniel J. Flood, D.*
12. J. Irving Whalley, R.*
13. Richard S. Schweiker, R.*
14. William S. Moorhead, D.*
15. Fred B. Rooney, D.*
16. Edwin D. Eshleman, R.
17. Herman T. Schneebeli, R.*
18. Robert J. Corbett, R.*
19. George A. Goodling, R.
20. Elmer J. Holland, D.*
21. John H. Dent, D.*
22. John P. Saylor, R.*
23. Albert W. Johnson, R.*
24. Joseph P. Vigorito, D.*
25. Frank M. Clark, D.*
26. Thomas E. Morgan, D.*
27. James G. Fulton, R.*

RHODE ISLAND

1. Fernand J. St. Germain, D.*
2. John E. Fogarty, D.*

SOUTH CAROLINA

1. L. Mendel Rivers, D.*
2. Albert W. Watson, R.*
3. W. J. Bryan Dorn, D.*
4. Robert T. Ashmore, D.*
5. Thomas S. Gettys, D.*
6. John L. McMillan, D.*

SOUTH DAKOTA

1. Benjamin Reifel, R.*
2. E. Y. Berry, R.*

TENNESSEE

1. James H. (Jimmy) Quillen, R.*
2. John J. Duncan, R.*
3. W. E. (Bill) Brock III, R.*
4. Joe L. Evins, D.*
5. Richard H. Fulton, D.*
6. William R. Anderson, D.*
7. Ray Blanton, D.
8. Robert A. Everett, D.*
9. Dan Kuykendall, R.

TEXAS

1. Wright Patman, D.*
2. John Dowdy, D.*
3. Joe R. Pool, D.*
4. Ray Roberts, D.*
5. Earle Cabell, D.*
6. Olin E. Teague, D.*
7. George Bush, R.
8. Robert C. Eckhardt, D.
9. Jack Brooks, D.*
10. J. J. Pickle, D.*
11. W. R. Poage, D.*
12. James C. Wright, Jr., D.*
13. Graham Purcell, D.*
14. John Young, D.*
15. Eligio de la Garza, D.*
16. Richard C. White, D.*
17. Omar Burleson, D.*
18. Robert D. Price, R.
19. George H. Mahon, D.*
20. Henry B. Gonzalez, D.*
21. O. C. Fisher, D.*
22. Robert R. Casey, D.*
23. Abraham Kazen, D.*

UTAH

1. Laurence J. Burton, R.*
2. Sherman P. Lloyd, R.

VERMONT

(AL) Robert T. Stafford, R.*

VIRGINIA

1. Thomas N. Downing, D.*
2. Porter Hardy, Jr., D.*
3. David E. Satterfield III, D.*
4. Watkins M. Abbitt, D.*
5. William M. Tuck, D.*
6. Richard H. Poff, R.*
7. John O. Marsh, Jr., D.*
8. William L. Scott, R.
9. William C. Wampler, R.
10. Joel T. Broyhill, R.*

WASHINGTON

1. Thomas M. Pelly, R.*
2. Lloyd Meeds, D.*
3. Julia Butler Hansen, D.*
4. Catherine May, R.*
5. Thomas S. Foley, D.*
6. Floyd V. Hicks, D.*
7. Brock Adams, D.*

WEST VIRGINIA

1. Arch A. Moore, Jr., R.*
2. Harley O. Staggers, D.*
3. John M. Slack, Jr., D.*
4. Ken Hechler, D.*
5. James Kee, D.*

WISCONSIN

1. Henry C. Schadeberg, R.
2. Robert W. Kastenmeier, D.*
3. Vernon W. Thomson, R.*
4. Clement J. Zablocki, D.*
5. Henry S. Reuss, D.*
6. William A. Steiger, R.
7. Melvin R. Laird, R.*
8. John W. Byrnes, R.*
9. Glenn R. Davis, R.*
10. Alvin E. O'Konski, R.*

WYOMING

(AL) William Henry Harrison, R.

PUERTO RICO

Resident Commissioner

Santiago Polanco-Abreu, D.*

transit systems (see TRANSPORTATION [Transit]). The next day, two far-reaching automobile and highway safety laws were enacted. One required manufacturers to conform to federal minimum safety standards for cars and tires, effective Jan. 31, 1968. The other encouraged the states to develop more effective highway safety programs (see AUTOMOBILE [Close-Up]). And in October, Congress established a Cabinet-level Department of Transportation (see CABINET; TRANSPORTATION).

Labor and Consumers. Congress voted to increase the minimum wage and extend the wages and hours law to another 8,000,000 workers—some 390,000 of them on farms. The minimum wage for workers already covered was raised from $1.25 an hour to $1.40, effective Feb. 1, 1967, and to $1.60 a year later. See AGRICULTURE; LABOR.

The Fair Packaging and Labeling Act, passed in October, required manufacturers of some 8,000 household items to label the contents of their packages more truthfully, clearly, and prominently. Size and weight standards were to be developed by the food and drug industries. The Secretary of Commerce could request legislation if the voluntary system failed. A ban on the sale of hazardous toys and warning labels on dangerous products were made mandatory in related legislation, voted also in October. See FOOD; RETAILING.

Conservation. Five additions to the National Park System were authorized: the Indiana Dunes National Lakeshore, North Carolina's Cape Lookout National Seashore, Guadalupe Mountain National Park in Texas, the Bighorn Canyon National Recreation Area in Montana and Wyoming, and Michigan's Pictured Rocks National Lakeshore.

In October, a $3,600,000,000, five-year program against water pollution was established in the Clean Rivers Restoration Act. Congress also authorized a $186,000,000, three-year program to clear up air pollution. See CONSERVATION.

Daylight Saving Time. The Uniform Time Act of 1966, signed by the President on April 13, aimed to end the confusion over schedules, phone service, and timetables caused by the hodgepodge pattern of different times prevailing within various states. Effective in 1967, daylight saving time will run from the last Sunday in April to the last Sunday in October in every state, unless a state's legislature votes to keep the entire state on standard time.

Citizens' Rights. In June, the Bail Reform Act of 1966 provided that under some circumstances indigent defendants awaiting trial in the federal courts could be released without having to put up a cash bond.

On July 4, the President signed a bill providing that any government decision to withhold federal records from public scrutiny can be challenged by a private citizen and is subject to judicial review. The act goes into effect July 4, 1967.

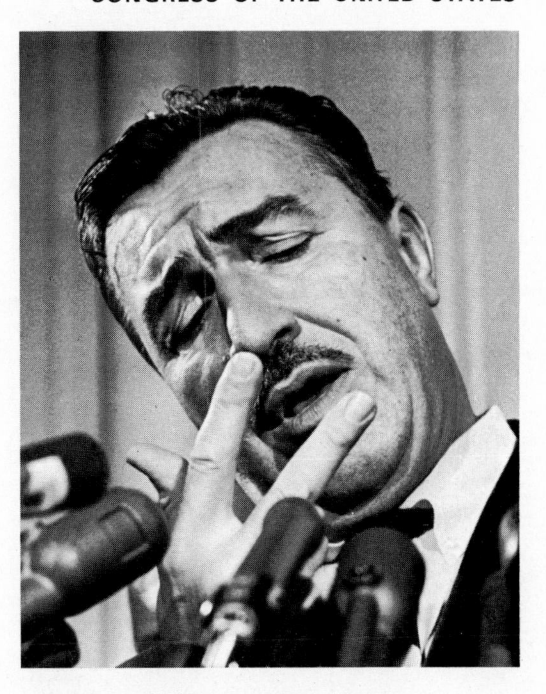

Representative Adam C. Powell (D., N.Y.) reacts to House curbs on his powers as Education and Labor Committee chairman.

Four bills enacted July 19 gave private citizens increased legal rights in civil litigation against the federal government. In October, Congress provided funds for civil commitment and rehabilitation instead of prison terms for drug addicts. See CRIME; COURTS AND LAWS.

Other Legislation:

- Increased protection for animals used in research.
- Strengthened regulations dealing with the activities of foreign lobbyists.
- Tightened federal supervision of bank mergers.
- Ended the little-used postal savings system.
- Authorized a third hydroelectric plant for the Grand Coulee Dam on the Columbia River.
- Boosted federal insurance on savings accounts from $10,000 to $15,000.
- Extended the exclusive U.S. fishing zone to 12 miles from its former three-mile limit.
- Established relief procedures for victims of major natural disasters.
- Provided for the protection of about 75 species of wildlife threatened with extinction, authorizing $15,000,000 to acquire land for refuges.
- Authorized federal regulatory agencies to set ceilings of from 4¾ per cent to 5¼ per cent on interest rates paid to depositors by banks or savings and loan associations.
- Increased most parcel post package rates effective Jan. 15, 1967.

Members of the United States Senate

The Senate of the 90th Congress consists of 64 Democrats and 36 Republicans, compared with 67 Democrats and 33 Republicans for the 89th Congress. Senators shown starting their terms in 1967 were elected for the first time in the Nov. 8, 1966, elections. Those shown ending their current terms in 1973 were re-elected to the Senate in the same balloting. The second date in each listing shows when the term of a previously elected Senator expires.

State	Term
ALABAMA	
Lister Hill, D.	1938–1969
John J. Sparkman, D.	1946–1973
ALASKA	
E. L. "Bob" Bartlett, D.	1959–1973
Ernest Gruening, D.	1959–1969
ARIZONA	
Carl T. Hayden, D.	1927–1969
Paul J. Fannin, R.	1965–1971
ARKANSAS	
John L. McClellan, D.	1943–1973
J. William Fulbright, D.	1945–1969
CALIFORNIA	
Thomas H. Kuchel, R.	1953–1969
George L. Murphy, R.	1965–1971
COLORADO	
Gordon L. Allott, R.	1955–1973
Peter H. Dominick, R.	1963–1969
CONNECTICUT	
Thomas J. Dodd, D.	1959–1971
Abraham A. Ribicoff, D.	1963–1969
DELAWARE	
John J. Williams, R.	1947–1971
J. Caleb Boggs, R.	1961–1973
FLORIDA	
Spessard L. Holland, D.	1946–1971
George A. Smathers, D.	1951–1969
GEORGIA	
Richard B. Russell, D.	1933–1973
Herman E. Talmadge, D.	1957–1969
HAWAII	
Hiram L. Fong, R.	1959–1971
Daniel Ken Inouye, D.	1963–1969
IDAHO	
Frank Church, D.	1957–1969
Len B. Jordan, R.	1962–1973
ILLINOIS	
Everett M. Dirksen, R.	1951–1969
Charles H. Percy, R.	1967–1973
INDIANA	
R. Vance Hartke, D.	1959–1971
Birch E. Bayh, D.	1963–1969
IOWA	
Bourke B. Hickenlooper, R.	1945–1969
Jack R. Miller, R.	1961–1973
KANSAS	
Frank Carlson, R.	1950–1969
James B. Pearson, R.	1962–1973
KENTUCKY	
John Sherman Cooper, R.	1956–1973
Thruston B. Morton, R.	1957–1969
LOUISIANA	
Allen J. Ellender, Sr., D.	1937–1973
Russell B. Long, D.	1948–1969
MAINE	
Margaret Chase Smith, R.	1949–1973
Edmund S. Muskie, D.	1959–1971
MARYLAND	
Daniel B. Brewster, D.	1963–1969
Joseph D. Tydings, D.	1965–1971
MASSACHUSETTS	
Edward M. Kennedy, D.	1962–1971
Edward W. Brooke, R.	1967–1973
MICHIGAN	
Philip A. Hart, D.	1959–1971
Robert P. Griffin, R.	1966–1973
MINNESOTA	
Eugene J. McCarthy, D.	1959–1971
Walter F. Mondale, D.	1964–1973
MISSISSIPPI	
James O. Eastland, D.	1943–1973
John Cornelius Stennis, D.	1947–1971
MISSOURI	
Stuart Symington, D.	1953–1971
Edward V. Long, D.	1960–1969
MONTANA	
Mike J. Mansfield, D.	1953–1971
Lee Metcalf, D.	1961–1973
NEBRASKA	
Roman Lee Hruska, R.	1954–1971
Carl T. Curtis, R.	1955–1973
NEVADA	
Alan Bible, D.	1954–1969
Howard W. Cannon, D.	1959–1971
NEW HAMPSHIRE	
Norris Cotton, R.	1954–1969
Thomas J. McIntyre, D.	1962–1973
NEW JERSEY	
Clifford P. Case, R.	1955–1973
Harrison A. Williams, Jr., D.	1959–1971
NEW MEXICO	
Clinton P. Anderson, D.	1949–1973
Joseph M. Montoya, D.	1965–1971
NEW YORK	
Jacob K. Javits, R.	1957–1969
Robert F. Kennedy, D.	1965–1971
NORTH CAROLINA	
Sam J. Ervin, Jr., D.	1954–1969
B. Everett Jordan, D.	1958–1973
NORTH DAKOTA	
Milton R. Young, R.	1945–1969
Quentin N. Burdick, D.	1960–1971
OHIO	
Frank J. Lausche, D.	1957–1969
Stephen M. Young, D.	1959–1971
OKLAHOMA	
A. S. Mike Monroney, D.	1951–1969
Fred R. Harris, D.	1965–1973
OREGON	
Wayne L. Morse, D.	1945–1969
Mark O. Hatfield, R.	1967–1973
PENNSYLVANIA	
Joseph S. Clark, Jr., D.	1957–1969
Hugh D. Scott, Jr., R.	1959–1971
RHODE ISLAND	
John O. Pastore, D.	1950–1971
Claiborne de Borda Pell, D.	1961–1973
SOUTH CAROLINA	
Strom Thurmond, R.	1956–1973
Ernest F. Hollings, D.	1967–1969
SOUTH DAKOTA	
Karl E. Mundt, R.	1948–1973
George S. McGovern, D.	1963–1969
TENNESSEE	
Albert A. Gore, D.	1953–1971
Howard Baker, Jr., R.	1967–1973
TEXAS	
Ralph W. Yarborough, D.	1957–1971
John G. Tower, R.	1961–1973
UTAH	
Wallace F. Bennett, R.	1951–1969
Frank E. Moss, D.	1959–1971
VERMONT	
George D. Aiken, R.	1941–1969
Winston L. Prouty, R.	1959–1971
VIRGINIA	
Harry F. Byrd, Jr., D.	1966–1971
William B. Spong, Jr., D.	1967–1973
WASHINGTON	
Warren G. Magnuson, D.	1944–1969
Henry M. Jackson, D.	1953–1971
WEST VIRGINIA	
Jennings Randolph, D.	1958–1973
Robert C. Byrd, D.	1959–1971
WISCONSIN	
William Proxmire, D.	1957–1971
Gaylord A. Nelson, D.	1963–1969
WYOMING	
Gale W. McGee, D.	1959–1971
Clifford P. Hansen, R.	1967–1973

Bills That Failed. The civil rights bill died in the Senate on September 19 because of opposition to controversial Title IV, which forbade racial discrimination in the sale or rental of housing. A Senate filibuster against the bill prevailed. Two attempts to shut off debate by invoking cloture failed. See CIVIL RIGHTS.

The administration failed again in its effort to repeal Section 14(b) of the Taft-Hartley Act, which allows states to pass right-to-work laws that bar union shops. Two proposals for constitutional amendments made by Senate Minority Leader Everett M. Dirksen (R., Ill.) were defeated. One would have allowed citizens in each state to decide by vote whether factors other than population should provide the basis for apportioning one house of their state legislature. The other would have permitted voluntary prayer in schools. Both moves were attempts to nullify Supreme Court decisions.

Other failures included: federal control of the sale of firearms; home rule for Washington, D.C.; "truth-in-lending" legislation; four-year terms for U.S. representatives; the extension of "most favored nation" tariff treatment to some Soviet-bloc countries; authorization of two dams in the Grand Canyon of the Colorado; increases in veterans' pensions; strengthening provisions against discrimination in employment; and authorizations of several park and recreation proposals, notably the Oregon Dunes National Seashore, the Redwood National Park, and a nationwide hiking trail system.

Vetoed Legislation was rare in the 89th Congress. President Johnson vetoed only 17 of the second session's host of bills. Two were notable. On September 12, he took Congress to task for "fueling the fires of inflation" in its passage of a bill to increase life insurance coverage of federal employees and members of Congress by more than 30 per cent. He put its annual cost at $90,000,000.

The second major veto came on November 13. It was on the District of Columbia crime bill, which would have allowed the district's police to interrogate a suspect for a total of 10 hours before his arraignment. This, plus a provision allowing police to hold material witnesses for six hours, went "far beyond the necessities of interrogation," the President said. The Supreme Court, in its so-called Mallory Rule of 1957, had required that a suspect be arraigned "without unnecessary delay." The legislation would have nullified that ruling.

Hearings. Committees of the 89th Congress conducted a wide range of hearings during the second session. The widely publicized and sometimes televised hearings chaired by Senator J. William Fulbright (D., Ark.) challenged the administration's policies in Vietnam and toward Communist China. It developed into a full-scale national debate and touched on such issues as foreign aid policies and programs and the ethics and politics involved in the supplying of medical and other aid to the Viet Cong by private groups in the United States.

Hearings on auto safety stimulated public demands for federal minimum safety standards that went far beyond the limited proposals of President Johnson. Extensive Senate hearings on urban problems highlighted the difficulties faced by slum-ridden cities and shortcomings of the War on Poverty program. The senators, under Abraham A. Ribicoff (D., Conn.), offered a thoroughgoing, no-holds-barred critique of administration policy.

Other investigations were concerned with the activities of the Ku Klux Klan; a way to control the Central Intelligence Agency; the possibility of improving the Selective Service Act; the alleged misconduct of Senator Thomas J. Dodd (D., Conn.) in his relations with a lobbyist and in his use of campaign contributions and proceeds from testimonial dinners.

In September, the House Education and Labor Committee stripped its chairman, Adam Clayton Powell (D., N.Y.), of most of his authority to delay legislation. Powell's former absolute power to hire, fire, and set salaries for his staff also was curbed and subjected to committee review and approval.

The New Congress. The Republicans won 52 House seats from the Democrats in the November 8 election. Of those 52, many had been elected in the Johnson landslide of 1964. Five Democrats also took seats from Republicans.

In the Senate, only one incumbent was defeated – Paul H. Douglas (D., Ill.) by 47-year-old Charles H. Percy, millionaire industrialist. Other new Republican senators were Governor Mark Hatfield of Oregon; Howard H. Baker, Jr., of Tennessee; Edward W. Brooke, attorney general of Massachusetts and the first Negro senator since Reconstruction; and Clifford P. Hansen, governor of Wyoming. New Democratic senators were William B. Spong, Jr., of Virginia and Ernest F. Hollings of South Carolina. See BROOKE, EDWARD W.

Leaders of the second session of the 89th Congress included:

In the Senate, Carl Hayden, Arizona, president *pro tempore;* Mike Mansfield, Montana, majority leader; Russell B. Long, Louisiana, majority whip; four new assistant majority whips: Daniel B. Brewster, Maryland; Philip A. Hart, Michigan; Daniel K. Inonye, Hawaii; and Edmund S. Muskie, Maine. Everett M. Dirksen, Illinois, was minority leader; Thomas H. Kuchel, California, minority whip.

In the House, John W. McCormack, Massachusetts, Speaker; Carl Albert, Oklahoma, majority leader; T. Hale Boggs, Louisiana, majority whip; Gerald R. Ford, Michigan, minority leader; Leslie C. Arends, Illinois, minority whip. CAROL L. THOMPSON

See also JOHNSON, LYNDON B.; PRESIDENT OF THE UNITED STATES; U.S. GOVERNMENT; Section One, JAMES B. RESTON: FOCUS ON THE NATION.

CONSERVATION

Conservation adjusted itself to new goals in 1966. President Lyndon B. Johnson had keynoted the new approach a year earlier when he addressed delegates to the White House Conference on Natural Beauty in May, 1965. "I have called for a new conservation to restore as well as to protect," the President told the delegates, "to bring beauty to the cities as well as to keep it in the countryside, to handle the waste products of technology as well as the waste of natural resources."

In 1966, this "new conservation" inspired action in Congress and at all levels of government. But perhaps most significant was renewed public support of conservation causes. On the local level, aroused citizens battled bulldozer and chain saw to save parkland and trees from highway builders and commercial developers. Nationally, conservationists fought to save California's redwoods and to keep two dams out of the Grand Canyon. The 89th Congress failed to act on either issue. But in a surge of action in the final weeks of its second session, it enacted a number of other conservation measures.

WATER

Water – and keeping it clean – was one of the last major items of business for the Congress. In October,

Despite hazings by U.S. game wardens, these geese refuse to fly south and give up the good life at the Horicon (Wis.) refuge.

it passed the Clean Rivers Restoration Act of 1966. It provided $3,900,000,000 over a period of five years for a massive attack on water pollution.

The act, by eliminating the former dollar ceilings on federal grants, enormously stepped-up aid to communities in building water-purifying and sewage-treatment plants. It was estimated that New York City, for example, would receive between 30 per cent and 55 per cent in U.S. aid on such projects, instead of the 1.1 per cent it had been averaging.

On May 10, the Federal Water Pollution Control Administration, established under the Water Quality Act of 1965, was transferred to the Department of the Interior from the Public Health Service. By October 2, all 50 states had decided to set their own water quality standards by June, 1967, rather than rely on the federal government.

The drought in the Northeast continued into its sixth year, spreading into Virginia and Maryland. The Potomac River reached an all-time low flow at Washington, D.C., on September 7. And in York, Pa., water was being trucked in at a cost of $25,000 a day, before heavy rains ended the emergency.

Flood Losses in the year, estimated at under $100,000,000, were well below the more than $750,000,000 1965 total. Most destructive of the 1966 floods occurred in April and May in eastern Texas, with 27 deaths and damage of $18,000,000 reported (see DISASTERS). The U.S. Army Corps of Engineers reported its 1966 flood control program cost about $1,300,000,000.

Battle of the Dams. The failure of Congress to act on the Colorado River Basin Project was a major victory for the Sierra Club and other conservation organizations. They had attacked the legislation's aim to authorize two dams, which, they said would forever harm the natural beauty of the Grand Canyon and the free-flowing Colorado River.

The complex legislation package, with an initial total cost of $1,700,000,000, sought to authorize a $500,000,000 aqueduct for the Central Arizona Project (CAP), other dams in Arizona and in the upper Colorado River basin states, and a feasibility study of importing Columbia River water to the Colorado. The two controversial dams–Bridge Canyon (or Hualapai), downstream from Grand Canyon National Park, and Marble Canyon, upstream from the park–would not be used for irrigation water storage, but for hydroelectric power to help finance the CAP. For that reason the Department of the Interior's Bureau of Reclamation, which would do the building, called them "cash register" dams.

New legislation is expected to be introduced in the 90th Congress. But in the meantime, the Department of the Interior was reviewing the whole basin project, including such alternatives as nuclear or coal-fired generating plants–which some engineers have called more economical than dams.

Desalination. Agreement was reached in August to build the world's largest nuclear fueled desalting and electric power plant. The $435,000,000 facility will be constructed on a man-made island south of Los Angeles by the Metropolitan Water District of Southern California, with federal and public utility industry participation. It will provide 150,000,000 gallons of fresh water a day–enough to meet the needs of a city of 750,000 and more than double the capacities of all existing desalting plants. Its target

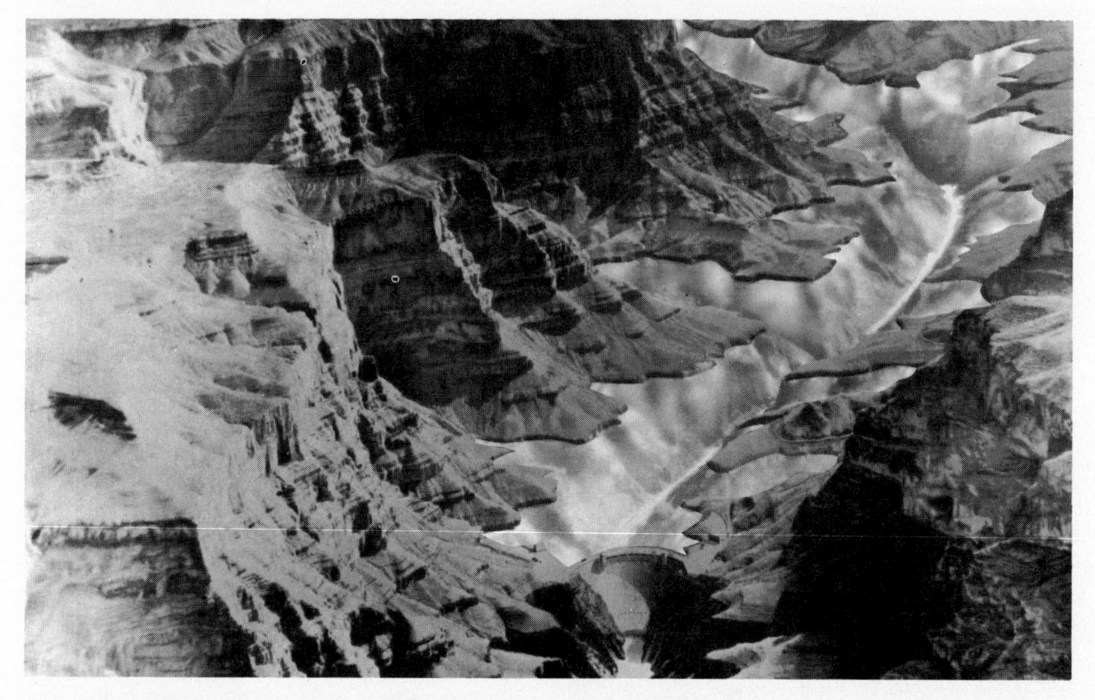

How Grand Canyon would look if the proposed Bridge Canyon dam were built. It and a second dam would flood half the 280-mile canyon gorge.

date is 1971. Engineers expect the cost per 1,000 gallons of fresh water to range from 22 cents to 30 cents, compared with $1 using today's desalters. See ATOMIC ENERGY.

PARKS AND OUTDOOR RECREATION

For the second year in a row, more undeveloped land (1,246,957 acres in the year ended June 30, 1966) was set aside for parks and other recreational uses than was used for urban development and highways (about 1,000,000 acres a year since 1950).

The Land and Water Conservation Fund, which began operating in 1965, funneled $59,132,700 to the states in 1966 for acquisition and development of outdoor recreation areas. Receipts from admission fees to federal recreation areas to support the fund reached $9,000,000 during the 1966 vacation season. This was $2,000,000 more than in 1965, but still well below the annual $13,000,000 goal.

National Park attendance zoomed to an estimated record 137,000,000 visits, up from 121,312,000 in 1965 and 80,000,000 visits in 1960.

Congress helped the National Park Service (NPS) celebrate its golden jubilee–the NPS was established on Aug. 25, 1916–by approving a number of additions to the park system. The first to be authorized was Cape Lookout National Seashore, extending 58 miles south of Cape Hatteras along North Carolina's Outer Banks. The President signed the bill on March 10.

Other additions approved in Congress' October rush to adjourn included:

- The Pictured Rocks National Lakeshore in Upper Michigan, a 67,000-acre wooded park along 39 miles of Lake Superior's southern shore.
- The Guadalupe Mountains National Park, 77,000 acres of mountain wilderness in west Texas.
- The Big Horn Canyon National Recreation Area, 63,000 acres in Montana and Wyoming bordering the reservoir of the Yellowtail Dam, now under construction. Part of its development will be handled by the National Park Service.
- The Indiana Dunes National Lakeshore, setting aside about 10 miles of Lake Michigan shoreline east of Gary, Ind. The area to be acquired totals 6,539 acres. The existing Indiana Dunes State Park with its 2,181 acres of duneland may be added if the state of Indiana donates it to the NPS.

WILDLIFE

Congress also took steps to protect wildlife. In October, it authorized a $15,000,000 program for the conservation and propagation of endangered species of fish and wildlife. The action recognized that despite stepped-up conservation action, the nation was, in the words of Secretary of the Interior Stewart L. Udall, "still losing the overall battle to save America's endangered wildlife from extinction."

The polar bear received protection on two fronts. Early in 1966, the Boone and Crockett Club, official keeper of North America's big game records, decided to eliminate the polar bear from its eligibility list. Alaska tightened its hunting regulations on the big bear. It instituted a permit system, with a limit of 350 permits, effective Jan. 1, 1967. An estimated 400 polar bears were killed in Alaska in 1966.

Whooping cranes seemed to be winning the battle of survival, with more than 40 birds wintering at the Aransas National Wildlife Refuge in Texas. But the future of such species as Florida's key deer, the bald and golden eagles, and the California condor still appeared bleak.

Also on the more optimistic side, a good nesting season for migratory waterfowl permitted an increase in the permissible bag of most duck species in the Department of the Interior's 1966 duck hunting regulations. The rate of wetlands acquisition accelerated during 1966. About 207,000 acres costing $13,250,000 were acquired for waterfowl habitat and wildlife refuges. See HUNTING AND FISHING.

FORESTS

A major battle between preservationists and some California lumbermen ended in September with at least a temporary victory for conservation. The Miller Redwood Company of Crescent City, Calif., and four other redwood-harvesting firms farther south agreed to halt cutting of "park quality" trees in areas proposed for a Redwood National Park.

An administration-sponsored bill called for a 43,000-acre park in the Mill Creek area around the present Jedediah Smith and the Del Norte Coast Redwoods State parks. A rival–and more expensive–park proposal was the 90,000-acre Redwoods Creek area farther south, incorporating the existing Prairie Creek Redwoods State Park.

The truce allowed time for the new 90th Congress to give calm consideration to both proposals and to determine how much of the remaining 300,000 acres of the original stand of 2,000,000 acres of coastal redwoods should be preserved.

The legislation needed to create some kind of a Redwood National Park was expected to be approved by Congress in 1967.

Forest Fires. Public forest lands suffered the most destructive fire season in years. More than 1,000,000 acres in five states were burned over. The heaviest damage was in Alaska (709,000 acres) and Idaho (248,000 acres). In 1965, fires burned only 147,000 acres of federal forest lands.

An unusual number of forest fires in 1966 were set by arsonists. In Happy Camp, Calif., a timed incendiary device was used to touch off a six-day, 12,000-acre blaze that destroyed $3,200,000 worth of Douglas fir. Two other arson-caused fires were reported in the same period in the Sequoia National Forest in central California. And in southern Cali-

Strip mining devastates the once-green countryside near Paradise in western Kentucky and pollutes the formerly clear fishing stream.

fornia, in November, 14 fire fighters lost their lives battling extensive brush fires.

MINERALS AND FUELS

Federal resource agencies in September revealed an ambitious plan to study the earth's natural resources from space. Water, oil, mineral, agricultural, and even human resources would come under the scrutiny of sophisticated remote-sensing instruments aboard earth-orbiting satellites. Space photographs, for instance, would disclose earth faults associated with metallic ore deposits and the large folds in the earth's crust that commonly serve as reservoirs for petroleum. The project, named Eros (earth resources observation satellites), was expected to get underway in 1969.

Kentucky's tough new restrictions on strip mining went into effect in June. Under the law, mine operators generally must restore the land to its original contours. In mountainous areas, backfilling, gentle terracing, and revegetation must be carried out.

In July, Secretary Udall recommended a $250,000,000 program to regulate strip mining and to reclaim mine-devastated lands in 12 Appalachian states. He urged enactment of state laws (similar to Kentucky's) and the establishment of a central federal agency to correlate the program. A. L. NEWMAN

See also AGRICULTURE; FISHERY; FOREST PRODUCTS; MINES AND MINING; PETROLEUM AND GAS.

COSTA RICA. See LATIN AMERICA.

COURTS AND LAWS. The Texas Court of Criminal Appeals, on Oct. 5, 1966, reversed the conviction of Jack Ruby, who had been sentenced in 1964 to die for the murder of Lee Harvey Oswald, accused assassin of President John F. Kennedy. The court also ruled that a retrial must take place outside of Dallas County, where the shootings occurred.

The conviction was upset because the judges held that a Texas law was violated during the trial. The law requires that confessions in a murder case be voluntary and spontaneous. This was violated, the judges ruled, when the court that tried Ruby allowed as testimony a confession Ruby made to Dallas Detective Sergeant Patrick T. Dean. Dean had told the trial court that Ruby confessed to him that he had plotted for two days to kill Oswald.

According to Presiding Judge W. A. Morrison, the statement should not have been introduced, because no evidence was presented at the trial to show that the confession had been made freely and spontaneously. Hence, Ruby's statement, a confession of premeditated murder, which carries the death penalty in Texas, was ruled out of order. The court's decision removed the question of premeditation from the case. He could thus be charged only with "murder without malice," which is punishable in Texas by five years in prison. However, Ruby would never come to trial. He died in a Dallas hospital on Jan. 3, 1967, ravaged by cancer.

New Bond Law. President Lyndon B. Johnson signed a bail bond reform measure on June 22. It will affect defendants in federal cases. The law includes a provision for giving credit toward the sentence for time spent awaiting trial. It also provides for the release of federal prisoners charged with noncapital crimes, unless the judge determines that the defendant might flee.

Court Reform. Voters in Colorado and in Kansas City, Mo., approved a new judicial selection plan in the November (1966) election. Under the plan, a nonpartisan commission will submit nominees for judgeships to an appointing official who will fill vacancies from the list. After a period of service, the new judges will run for election on their records. Such nonpartisan commissions already exist for some courts in Alaska, Florida, Iowa, Kansas, Missouri, and Nebraska.

New Mexico abolished justice of the peace courts in which laymen, who were paid by fees, presided. A new lower court manned by lawyer-judges will be created. Justice of the peace courts were also removed from the constitution in Wyoming.

Juries Upheld. Law professors Harry Kalven, Jr., and Hans Zeisel of the University of Chicago, weighted the scales in favor of the jury system in their book *The American Jury*, published in 1966. Their 10-year study revealed that judge and jury agree at least 75 per cent of the time. Further, they found that jurors are not swayed by skillful lawyers, pregnant mothers, attractive blondes, or the Christmas season. The jury emerged in the study as a defender of the American principle that a man is presumed innocent until proved guilty. Yet, jurors have freed only 5 per cent of the accused tried before them.

The American Bar Association (ABA) Criminal Justice Project, which aims to propose rules and policies for all who share in the responsibility for the proper administration of criminal justice, published a report, "Fair Trial–Free Press" in October. Although the report placed the burden for ensuring a fair trial on lawyers and policemen, it recommended that the judge punish newsmen who try to affect the outcome of a trial and suggested that such offenders reimburse the defendant for expenses incurred in obtaining a new trial.

World Law. At a meeting held in Geneva, Switzerland, in March, high court judges from all over the world voted for the formation of a World Association of Judges. Chief Justice Earl Warren of the United States was elected chairman. The judges will seek to improve the administration of justice by promoting communication between judges of all nations. The conference was sponsored by the World Peace Through Law Center, which is computerizing the national laws of more than 100 nations. Though the center's headquarters are at Geneva, it established reference service for judges from all countries at Harvard University Law School. FANNIE J. KLEIN

Confessions and the Law

A far-reaching decision made by the Supreme Court of the United States on June 13, 1966, stirred controversy in judicial circles and alarm in many police departments throughout the nation. The decision, in effect, broke new constitutional ground by declaring that the Fifth Amendment's privileges against self-incrimination came into play as soon as a person was taken into custody.

Actually, the decision was the latest of a series that dealt with police interrogation procedures. The parent case of the decision had been *Escobedo vs. Illinois*, in which the Court had ruled out a confession primarily because the defendant's right to see his lawyer—under Amendment 6–had been violated. In its 1966 opinion, the Court disposed of four more appeals by prisoners who had confessed after having been interrogated by police under circumstances which indicated that their civil rights had been violated.

Within the Supreme Court itself there was a sharp split–5 to 4–over the decision in which the Court also spelled out specific rules the police were to follow in questioning suspects. Chief Justice Earl Warren, speaking for the majority, said the new rules were necessary to protect an individual's right–under the Fifth Amendment to the U.S. Constitution –"not to be compelled to incriminate himself." The Chief Justice insisted that the rules would "not constitute an undue interference with a proper system of law enforcement." Justice Abe Fortas called the rules "the Magna Carta of our times."

Each of the four dissenting Justices, however, criticized the ruling bitterly in separate opinions. They contended that the Constitution did not require such sharp restrictions on police. They warned that the ruling would weaken law enforcement and bring "harmful consequences for the country at large." Justice John M. Harlan said, "This doctrine . . . has no sanction . . . as a legitimate tool of law enforcement." And Justice Byron R. White predicted that "in some unknown number of cases, the Court's rule will return a killer, a rapist or other criminal, to the streets."

The new rules certainly made it harder–if not impossible, as many law enforcement officers contended–to get a confession at all. From now on, the Court had held, police could not question a suspect until they had first told him that he had a right to remain silent. They must also tell him that anything he said might be used against him, and that he had a right to have an attorney present at the questioning–and that, if he could not afford to hire an attorney, one would be provided for him at public expense. If the suspect then "knowingly and intelligently" waived his rights, the police could question him all they wanted. But they carried the "heavy burden" of proving that the suspect was not tricked or bullied into submitting to the questioning. Even if a suspect started to talk, he could stop the questioning at any time by invoking the Fifth Amendment privilege of silence or by asking for a lawyer.

Though there was much criticism of the Supreme Court's action, support for it came from several quarters. U.S. Attorney General Nicholas deB. Katzenbach said, "It makes the job for law-enforcement officers more difficult. There's no question about that. But that in itself does not mean that it is a bad decision or poorly conceived." He pointed out that it would help to "assure equality to rich and poor in the criminal process," and predicted that it would not make "a tremendous amount of difference" in law enforcement. "The hardened criminal never talks anyway," the Attorney General said.

California's Attorney General Thomas Lynch said that "the decision is helpful because it lays down definite guidelines."

How well it had done so proved true when, on Nov. 12, 1966, a man was picked up in Chicago near the scene of a crime. Allegedly armed, and in hiding, he promptly reminded the arresting officers of the *Escobedo vs. Illinois* decision and demanded a lawyer. No one was more familiar with it–his name was Danny Escobedo, and he was the man whose case had set the Supreme Court on its course.

FOSTER STOCKWELL

CRIME. Three of the worst mass murders in America's history occurred within a period of four months in 1966.

In Chicago, eight student nurses were murdered in their apartment July 14. Identified by fingerprints and a tattoo after he was hospitalized in an apparent suicide attempt, Richard Franklin Speck, 24, a drifter, was arrested and charged with the multiple slayings.

In Austin, Tex., Charles Joseph Whitman, also 24, hauled an arsenal of guns to the top of the University of Texas Tower on August 1. From his secluded perch, he terrorized the campus with gunfire for 90 minutes. Before he was shot by stalking police, Whitman killed 14 people and wounded 31.

In Mesa, Ariz., 18-year-old Robert Benjamin Smith entered a beauty school on November 12. Forcing his hapless victims to lie head to head in a macabre circle of death, he shot and killed four women and a child and seriously wounded two others. Smith asserted he had been planning the killing for three months after getting the idea from the mass murders in Chicago and Austin.

Gun Law? The mass slaughter revived interest in a proposed statute that was before the Congress of the United States during the year. Sponsored by Senator Thomas S. Dodd (R., Conn.) it would: (1) limit interstate mail-order traffic in hand guns; (2) limit the inflow of military-surplus firearms from abroad; (3) ban over-the-counter hand gun sales to out-of-state buyers and persons under 21; and (4) prohibit sales of rifles to persons under 18.

British Police Killing. For the first time in over more than 50 years, Great Britain witnessed the killing of three unarmed policemen in a single incident. They were killed on August 12 in a working class section of London when they attempted to check a parked car. After a massive manhunt the three men–34-year-old Harry M. Roberts, a former convict listed as Britain's most wanted man, and his two associates, John Edward Witney and John Duddy–were arrested. They were tried and sentenced to life imprisonment on December 12. Before capital punishment was abolished in 1965 in England, the murder of a policeman was punishable by hanging.

Police Guidelines. The Supreme Court of the United States, in its June 13 opinion in *Miranda vs. Arizona*, set forth police guidelines which are designed to protect the rights of a suspect after he has been arrested. The ruling was certain to have a profound effect on law enforcement (see SUPREME COURT OF THE UNITED STATES). The decision paralleled an action of the British courts half a century ago, the Magistrates Rules of 1912, which set down guidelines for the police.

Banking and Organized Crime. On February 28, Chairman Wright Patman of the U.S. House of Representatives Banking Committee, issued a report of the committees' investigation into the collapse of federally insured banking institutions. Patman asserted that there was evidence that banks were being subjected to Jet Age criminal activity, and that federal banking agencies are using horse-and-buggy methods to combat the menace. The committee reported on the collapse of a Newport News (Va.) bank, which helped finance and otherwise aid large-scale criminal activities. He observed that there are as many as 194 "problem banks" in the United States.

U.S. Prison Reorganization. A major reorganization of the U.S. Bureau of Prisons was announced by President Lyndon B. Johnson on November 30. The reorganization is designed to bring about more effective use of new techniques of rehabilitation. It was prompted by concern over a high percentage of habitual offenders. Among other things, the reorganization provided for the creation of a division of community services to administer work-release programs and prerelease guidance centers.

Crime and Alcoholism. On April 1, the U.S. Fourth Circuit Court of Appeals in the District of Columbia moved the U.S. system of criminal justice onto new legal ground. It ruled, in the case of 59-year-old Dewitt Easter, a North Carolinian who had been arrested 200 times for public drunkenness, that chronic alcoholism is a disease not subject to criminal prosecution. JOSEPH D. LOHMAN

CUBA. Mounting economic and political troubles plagued the island during 1966, with the Castro regime possibly going through its greatest internal crisis in several years. Reports spoke of the arrest of army officers and the erratic behavior of Premier Fidel Castro.

Communist China announced in the early part of 1966 that it planned to cut trade with Cuba from a $250,000,000 exchange of goods to $170,000,000. Seemingly, it was loosening its ties with the island as an ally in its ideological feud with the Soviet Union. The cutback meant, among other things, that Cuba would have to reduce its rice rations. Castro accused Peking of using trade to blackmail the island.

Cuba's all-important sugar crop reached scarcely 4,500,000 tons in 1966. This was nearly one-third below its 6,500,000-ton goal and less than half the 10,000,000 tons promised for 1970. With over half of the crop pledged to the Soviet Union, and with prices at rock bottom on the world market, Cuba was hard-pressed financially.

Facts in Brief. Population: 7,750,000. Government: President Osvaldo Dorticos Torrado; Premier Fidel Castro. Monetary Unit: peso (1 = U.S. $1). Foreign Trade: exports, $155,800,000; imports, $219,400,000. Principal Exports: beet and cane sugar, tobacco. MARY C. WEBSTER

See also LATIN AMERICA.

CYPRUS. See GREAT BRITAIN.

CZECHOSLOVAKIA continued to follow basic Soviet policies in 1966. In March, it rejected a formal note from West Germany containing peace and disarmament proposals that might have led to a rapprochement between the two countries. In its rejection, the Czech government indicated no such proposals could be considered as long as West Germany refused to recognize East Germany.

In June, the Czech Communist party held its 13th congress in Prague. Party Secretary Antonín Novotny was reconfirmed as the head of the government. Plans for a wider implementation of the nation's "new economic model," including a reformed wholesale-retail price system, were set for 1967. The congress also approved directives calling for new methods of agricultural management.

On party orders, the literary journal *Tvar* ceased publication. Changes were made in the editorial boards of other magazines, and warnings were issued to the newspapers to follow the party line.

Facts in Brief. Population: 14,290,000. Government: President Antonín Novotny; Premier Josef Lenart. Monetary Unit: crown (16.16=U.S. $1). Foreign Trade: exports, $628,200,000; imports, $774,900,000. Principal Exports: machinery, textiles, leather footwear. H. GORDON SKILLING

DAHOMEY. See AFRICA.

DAIRYING. See AGRICULTURE.

DAM. See BUILDING AND CONSTRUCTION.

DANCING. Federal agencies and private foundations contributed heavily to the support of the dance in the United States in 1966. Early in the year, the American Ballet Theatre received an emergency grant of $100,000 and a subsidy of $250,000, both from the National Council on the Arts. At the same time, the Ford Foundation gave $3,200,000 to the New York City Center of Music and Drama. This gift enabled its two resident companies, New York City Ballet and New York City Opera, to expand their operations at the New York State Theater in Lincoln Center for the Performing Arts.

More Grants. In mid-February, the National Council on the Arts announced further grants: $142,500 to enable the Martha Graham Company to tour the United States for the first time in 15 years, and an additional grant-in-aid of $40,000 to the same company for the creation of two works.

Recipients of smaller grants (for the creation of new works or the revival of old ones) were José Limón, $23,000; Anna Sokolow and Antony Tudor, $10,000; Alvin Ailey, Paul Taylor, Merce Cunningham, and Alwin Nikolais, $5,000 each. These grants were contingent on the raising of supplementary funds.

National Foundation on the Arts and Humanities made an outright $300,000 grant for the development of the American Theater Laboratory, headed by Jerome Robbins. The laboratory is an experimental workshop, to which Robbins has promised to devote his full time for the next several years. Rockefeller Foundation awarded the University of Utah $370,000 for a resident modern dance repertory company. The money will be administered over a four-year period.

The Ford Foundation announced new grants to three companies on Aug. 1, 1966. The Robert Joffrey Ballet received $500,000, the Pennsylvania Ballet $450,000, and the Boston Ballet $300,000. Earlier, the Ford Foundation awarded a $1,500,000 matching grant (over a five-year period) to the North Carolina School of the Arts, Winston-Salem.

New Association. National Endowment for the Arts (a part of the National Foundation) underwrote the costs of the first National Dance Conference, which was held June 2 and 3, 1966, in New York City. The conference brought together for the first time dancers, choreographers, and directors of ballet, modern dance, and ethnic companies from all sections of the country. The meeting resulted in the formation of the first service organization for the dance, the Association of American Dance Companies. William Habich, who has long been associated with the regional dance movement, was elected president.

Artistic Accomplishments. In the spring, the American Ballet Theatre ended its second suc-

Robert Joffrey's ballet, *Gamelan*, which was inspired by the Joffrey company's Far East tour, reflects Oriental dancing and drama.

cessful season at New York State Theater. Particularly brilliant was the revival of Antony Tudor's *Pillar of Fire*. The company successfully toured the Soviet Union for a second time under the cultural exchange program of the U.S. Department of State. On its return, the company set off in September on its longest U.S. tour, covering about 100 cities.

Paul Taylor's modern dance company traveled to the Near East, North Africa, and Europe during the summer on a cultural exchange program.

New York City Ballet had the distinction of opening the new Saratoga Performing Arts Center during the month of July. Also during the summer, George Balanchine's ballet, *A Midsummer Night's Dream*, was filmed by Oberon Productions, a specially formed company. This first American ballet film will be distributed by Columbia Pictures.

The Robert Joffrey Ballet proved so successful during its March 30 to April 3 performances at New York City Center that it was invited to become the resident company, with two three-week seasons annually. The company gave its first season under its new name, City Center Joffrey Ballet, in September, and then began a U.S. tour.

Harkness Ballet toured Europe a second time before beginning its first long U.S. tour in September. Martha Graham's U.S. tour in 1966 commemorated her 50th anniversary as a dancer. In contrast to the reception often accorded her earlier in her career, Miss Graham was received warmly by understanding audiences.

Cultural Exchange. The most eminent visiting company was the Bolshoi Ballet from Moscow, with the dazzling Maya Plisetskaya, Ekaterina Maximova, and Vladimir Vasiliev. The young ballerina Natalia Bessmertnova made an unforgettable impression in her first U.S. performance of *Giselle*. Yuri Grigorivich's stunning new production of the *Nutcracker* ballet provided the most hopeful sign that a major new choreographer is emerging.

National Dance Foundation. The formation of the National Dance Foundation was announced October 13, with Charles Reinhart, manager of the Paul Taylor company, as president. Dancer-choreographers involved were: Alvin Ailey, Merce Cunningham, Murray Louis, Alwin Nikolais, and Paul Taylor. Its purpose is to produce as well as to present American modern dance around the country to regular theatergoers rather than only to specialized audiences.

Other Developments. The first Pacific Western Regional Ballet Festival was held in Sacramento, Calif., May 27 to 29, 1966.

Martha Graham received an honorary degree of Doctor of Arts at Harvard University in June. Agnes de Mille was the 1966 recipient of the Capezio Award. Helen Tamiris, the great modern dancer and choreographer, died August 4, at the age of 61.

P. W. MANCHESTER

DEATHS OF NOTABLE PERSONS in 1966 included those listed below. An asterisk (*) means the person has a biography in THE WORLD BOOK ENCYCLOPEDIA. Persons listed were Americans unless otherwise indicated.

Aaltonen, Wäinö (1894-May 29), Finnish sculptor noted for portraits, free-standing figures, and large monuments, carved in stone. He won international fame with the *Paavo Nurmi* (Finnish Olympic long-distance runner, 1920s) bronze figure. Bridgehead figures in Tampere, *Aleksis Kivi* monuments, *Friendship* monuments (Göteborg, Sweden, and Turku), and the *Delaware Monument* (Chester, Pa.) are some of his other works.

Akhmatova, Anna (1888-Mar. 5), Russia's greatest woman poet (real name Anna Andreevna Gorenko), won fame with her first volumes of verse, *Evening* (1912) and *The Rosary* (1914). Then came *The White Flock*, *The Plantain*, *Anno Domini* (1916-1922), and *The Willow* (1940), *Selected Verse* (1943), and *Tashkent Poems* (1944). *Poem Without a Hero* and *Requiem* are more recent works. The poetess suffered long periods of silence during Stalin's time, but in 1965 she visited Italy to receive the Taormina prize and England for an honorary doctorate at Oxford University.

Albareda, Anselmo Maria Cardinal (1892-July 20), Prefect of the Apostolic Vatican Library for nearly 30 years, was a native of Barcelona, Spain.

Allen, Florence E. (1884-Sept. 12), the first woman appointed to a United States Court of Appeals (sixth Circuit, Cincinnati, 1934-1959), also was the first woman elected to the Court of Common Pleas in Cleveland (1920-1922), and the first elected to the Ohio Supreme Court (1922-1934).

Allingham, Margery Louise (1904-June 30), English creator of detective Albert Campion (in *The Crime at Black Dudley*, 1929), wrote many mystery novels. *The Tiger in the Smoke* (1952) was filmed (1956).

Arden, Elizabeth (1884-Oct. 18), founder, president, and board chairman of the international beauty and cosmetics enterprise, was born Florence Nightingale Graham near Toronto, Canada. She opened her first business in New York City about 1910.

Arp, Jean (Hans) (1887-June 7), French abstract painter and sculptor known as a great innovator, was a founder of the Dada movement in art and a leader in surrealism. His exceptionally original collages were widely imitated. *Mythical Sculpture* (1949), *Configuration of Serpent Movements* (1950), and *Cobra-Centaur* (1952) were among his later sculptures.

Astor, William Waldorf (1907-Mar. 7), third Viscount of Hever Castle, was a House of Lords member. He and Lady Nancy Astor (1879-1964) were the first mother and son to serve together in the British House of Commons (1935-1945).

Auriol, Vincent (1884-Jan. 1), French Socialist party leader, served as the first President of the Fourth French Republic (1947-1954).

Bashir, Antony (1898-Feb. 15), Lebanese-born Metropolitan Archbishop of the Syrian Antiochian Orthodox Church of North America since 1936, came to the United States in 1922. He was founder and publisher of the Arabic monthly *Al-Khalidat* and also the founder and the publisher of the Eastern Orthodox English monthly *The Word*.

***Beebe, Lucius Morris** (1902-Feb. 4), newspaper columnist known for his elegant dress, wrote books about the American West and railroads. He owned and published (with Charles Clegg, editor) *The Territorial Enterprise* newspaper (1952-1960), and wrote *Comstock Commotion: The Story of the Territorial Enterprise and Virginia City News* (1954).

British novelist Evelyn Waugh, world-famous for satirical writings, died at the age of 62.

Martha Holmes, *Life* © Time Inc.

Sophie Tucker, vaudeville singing star, was known as the last of the "Red Hot Mamas."

Paul Reynaud, premier of France when it was overrun by the Nazis in 1940, died at age 87.

Belaúnde, Victor Andrés (1883-Dec. 14), Peruvian diplomat, had served as his country's permanent representative to the United Nations since 1945. He was president of the General Assembly (1959-1960).

Berg, Gertrude (1899-Sept. 14), made her debut as Molly on "The Goldbergs" (also author-producer) radio program in 1929 (television, 1949). She was author-producer of *The House of Glass* (radio, 1935), author of *Me and Molly* (Broadway, 1948), co-author of *Molly* (Goldbergs film, 1951), and appeared in the Broadway plays *A Majority of One* (1959-1962), and *Dear Me, the Sky Is Falling* (1963).

Bhabha, Homi Jehangir (1909-Jan. 24), physicist and chairman of India's Atomic Energy Commission (since 1948) and the Department of Atomic Energy (since 1954), was president of the United Nations International Conference on Peaceful Uses of Atomic Energy in 1955.

Birnbaum, Abe (1899-June 19), did hundreds of covers and other art work for *The New Yorker* in the past 39 years; contributed to other magazines and *The New York Times* (Sunday drama section); and illustrated Ann Rand's *Did a Bear Just Walk There?* and other children's books.

Blanton, Smiley (1882-Oct. 30), psychiatrist, with the Rev. Norman Vincent Peale founded (1937) the Religio-Psychiatric Clinic at the Marble Collegiate Church and the American Foundation of Religion and Psychiatry (1951) in New York City. They wrote *Faith Is the Answer* (1940) and *The Art of Real Happiness* (1950). He also wrote *Love or Perish* (1956).

Bosworth, William W. (1869?-June 3), architect, directed such restorations in France as the Reims Cathedral and Châteaux of Versailles and Fontainebleau. He designed buildings in the United States and the *Major L'Enfant Monument* in Arlington (Va.) National Cemetery.

Braley, Berton (1882-Jan. 23), prolific author of verses, short stories, and books, wrote the popular long narrative poem about pirate Henry Morgan, *Morgan Sails the Caribbean.*

Brauner, Victor (1904?-Mar. 11), Romanian-born surrealist painter widely known in Europe, recently was given an exhibition in New York City.

Breton, André (1896-Sept. 28), French poet and critic, was considered the father of surrealism. His major writings include *Manifesto of Surrealism* (1924); critical and autobiographical essays *Les Pas Perdus* (1924); *Second Manifesto of Surrealism* (1930); *Immaculate Conception* (1930); and *Communicating Vessels* (1932), a study of dreams. The novel *Nadja* (1928) is considered his most important work.

Brouwer, Dirk (1902-Jan. 31), Netherlands-born Yale University Professor of Astronomy and observatory director since 1941, also had edited the *Astronomical Journal* since 1941.

Brown, Arthur William (1881-Oct. 24), Canadian-born magazine illustrator known for such characters as "Ephraim Tutt" (*Saturday Evening Post*) and "Claudia" (*Red Book*), illustrated books for such authors as Booth Tarkington, Ring Lardner, and Irvin S. Cobb.

Brunner, Emil H. (1889-Apr. 6), Swiss Protestant theologian, wrote such works as *The Mediator* (1928); the great *Divine Imperative* (1932, 1934) on Christian ethics; *Justice and the Social Order* (1943, 1945); *Natural Theology* (with noted Karl Barth, 1946); *The Christian Doctrine of God* (1946, 1949); and *Christianity and Civilization* (1948, 1949).

Bushman, Francis Xavier (1883-Aug. 23), silent screen idol known as the handsomest man in the world, starred in some 400 films. He later appeared in radio plays and on television.

***Byrd, Harry Flood** (1887-Oct. 20), Democratic U.S. Senator from Virginia (1933-1965) known as "Mr. Economy," opposed excessive government spending. He was chairman of the Senate Finance Committee for 10 years. Byrd was a state senator (1915-1925) and governor of Virginia (1926-1930).

Camm, Sir Sidney (1893-Mar. 12), designed Britain's World War II *Hurricane* fighter plane, the revolutionary Hawker Siddeley P-1127 (vertical take-off strike plane), and other airplanes.

Carrà, Carlo (1881-Apr. 13), Italian painter, was the last surviving founder (Umberto Boccioni, Luigi Russolo, Giacomo Balla, and Gino Severini) of the futurist movement. He and Giorgio de Chirico originated the Italian school of metaphysical painting.

Castaldo, Alfonso Cardinal (1890-Mar. 3), Archbishop of Naples since 1958, was elevated to the Sacred College of Cardinals in 1958.

Chaikoff, Israel Lyon (1902-Jan. 25), English-born University of California (Berkeley) physiology professor noted for gland research, discovered how thyroid hormones are formed in the body.

Montgomery Clift, a leading man in films and on the stage, died at the age of 45.

Hedda Hopper, movie columnist, died at the age of 75. She was known for her outrageous hats.

Steve Shapiro, *Life* © Time Inc.

Buster Keaton, comedy star of the silent screen, died in Hollywood at age 70.

Chalmers, Thomas (1884-June 11), operatic baritone (1911-1922) and character actor, during a long stage career appeared in *Mourning Becomes Electra* (1931), *Death of a Salesman* (1949), *All the Way Home* (1960), and many other plays. He played the father in *Pepper Young's Family* (radio, 1934-1952), and had written, directed, and produced films.

Cherkasov, Nikolai K. (1903-Sept. 14), Russian actor and member of the Pushkin Drama Theatre (in Leningrad) since 1933, also played in *The Conquests of Peter the Great* and other films.

Clift, Montgomery (1920-July 23), played Erik Valkonen in *There Shall Be No Night* (1940). Other plays include *Skin of Our Teeth* (1942), *The Searching Wind* (1944), and *The Seagull* (1954). His films include *Red River* (his first, 1948), *A Place in the Sun* (1951), *From Here to Eternity* (1953), *Judgment at Nuremberg* (1961), and *Freud* (1962).

Cory, David (1873-July 4), author of 50 books for children, wrote the Jack Rabbit stories (syndicated in newspapers 40 years) and a series on Sioux Indians.

***Craig, Edward Gordon** (1872-July 29), son of the famous English actress Ellen Terry, was noted for his scene design and stagecraft theories. He created three-dimensional stage effects (in *Hamlet* at Moscow Arts Theatre, 1911), and founded *The Mask* (journal, 1908-1929) and School for the Art of the Theatre (1913) in Florence, Italy.

***Crouse, Russel** (1893-Apr. 3), wrote and produced Broadway plays with Howard Lindsay, including *Anything Goes* (their first, libretto, 1934), *Life with Father* (1939-1947), *Arsenic and Old Lace* (produced, 1941), *State of the Union* (1945, awarded Pulitzer drama prize in 1946), *Call Me Madam* (1950), and *The Sound of Music* (libretto, 1959).

***Debye, Peter Joseph William** (1884-Nov. 2), Netherlands physicist and chemist, was awarded the Nobel chemistry prize (1936) for his studies of molecular structure.

Demerec, Milislav (1895-Apr. 12), Yugoslavian-born geneticist, was a discoverer of mutable genes.

Dennis, Wesley (1903-Sept. 3), known for his pictures of horses in motion, illustrated 15 of Marguerite Henry's books (such as *Misty of Chincoteague*) and John Steinbeck's *The Red Pony*. Dennis wrote the *Flip* series and other children's books. His last one is *Tumble: The Story of a Mustang* (1966).

Devine, George (1910-Jan. 20), first an actor, was manager-producer of the London Theatre Studio (1936-1939). He was artistic director of the Old Vic (1946-1951), founder of the Young Vic, and artistic director of the English Stage Company (Royal Court Theatre, 1955-1965).

***Disney, "Walt," Walter E.** (1901-Dec. 15), see Close-Up on page 302.

Duhamel, Georges (1884-Apr. 13), French poet, novelist, essayist, and surgeon, is best remembered for his autobiographical novel series *The Pasquier Chronicles*. *The New Books of Martyrs* (as Denis Thévenin) and *Civilization* (winner of Goncourt prize) were World War I reflections.

Edson, Gus (1901-Sept. 26), former sports cartoonist, did *The Gumps* after Sidney Smith died in 1935 until the strip ended in 1959. He created (1955) the *Dondi* strip (filmed), done with Irwin Hasen.

Faulkner, Barry (1881-Oct. 27), the first artist awarded the American Academy of Arts and Letters Prix de Rome fellowship in painting (1907), did murals for the National Archives Building in Washington, D.C.; and *The Signing of the Declaration of Independence* in the John Hancock Building in Boston.

Fields, Joseph (1895-Mar. 3), playwright, producer, and director, wrote such Broadway hits (with Jerome Chodorov) as *My Sister Eileen* (1940), *Junior Miss* (1941), *Wonderful Town* (1953), and *Anniversary Waltz* (1954), all filmed, and *Louisiana Purchase* (film 1941). He wrote *Flower Drum Song* (libretto, 1958) and directed *The Desk Set* (1955).

Fitzsimmons, James Edward (1874-Mar. 11), "Grand Old Man of Thoroughbred Racing" and known as "Sunny Jim," retired in 1963. He began as an errand boy in 1885, and was a jockey (1889-1894). His 2,275 race winners included Gallant Fox, Omaha, and Nashua.

Fleming, Eric (1925?-Sept. 28), star of the television series *Rawhide*, played in such Broadway productions as *My Three Angels* and *Stalag 17*.

Ford, Wallace (1898-June 11), born Samuel Jones in England, played on Broadway in *Seventeen* (1918), as Abie in *Abie's Irish Rose* (1922-1923), George in *Of Mice and Men* (1937), and as Doc in *Come Back, Little Sheba* (1950). His many films include *The Lost Patrol* (1943), *Harvey* (1950), *The Last Hurrah* (1958), and *Tess of the Storm Country* (1961). He also appeared on some 150 television programs.

***Forester, Cecil Scott** (1899-Apr. 2), English author, wrote the famed Horatio Hornblower novels (1937-1964) about English naval life. His first success was *Payment Deferred* (1925, stage and screen versions starred Charles Laughton). *The African Queen* (1935), *The General* (1936), *Captain Horatio Hornblower* (1939), and *The Good Shepherd* (1955) were filmed.

Frank, Philipp (1884-July 21), Austrian-born mathematician, physicist, and renowned philosopher of science, wrote *Philosophy of Science* (textbook) and many other scientific works.

Frawley, William (1894?-Mar. 3), played in such Broadway musicals as *Sons o' Guns* and *She's My Baby*. *The General Died at Dawn*, *My Wild Irish Rose*, and *The Babe Ruth Story* were among his many films. He played in *I Love Lucy* (1951-1960) and *My Three Sons* television series.

Friedlander, Leo (1890-Oct. 24), sculptor, designed *Valor and Sacrifice*, two equestrian groups for the Arlington Memorial Bridge (Washington, D.C.); the Oregon State Capitol (Salem) panel *The Covered Wagon*; and other heroic figures and monuments.

Fuller, John Frederick Charles (1878-Feb. 10), English soldier and military historian, wrote *The Decisive Battles of the United States* (1942), *The Decisive Battles of the Western World and Their Influence upon History* (three volumes 1954, 1955, 1958), and numerous other works.

Gates, Ruth (1888-May 23), made her Broadway debut in Belasco's *The Music Master* (1906), created the Aunt Jenny role in *I Remember Mama* (1944), and last played in *Opening Night* (off-Broadway, 1963).

***Giacometti, Alberto** (1901-Jan. 11), Swiss-born Italian painter and sculptor, was noted for the extreme elongation and thinness of his figures. Examples are *The Pointing Man*, *Persons Traversing a Square*, and *Seven Figures and a Head*. He first experimented in impressionism and cubism, and was a leading surrealist.

Giannini, Vittorio (1903-Nov. 28), music educator known for *The Taming of the Shrew* and other operas, just completed *The Servant with Two Masters*. He composed symphonies, concertos, and choral and chamber works. *Canticle of the Martyrs* is among his best works.

Gimbel, Bernard F. (1885-Sept. 29), was president (1927-1953) and then board chairman of Gimbel Brothers, Inc. His grandfather opened the first Gimbel store at Vincennes, Ind., in the mid-1800s.

Gowers, Sir Ernest Arthur (1880-Apr. 16), proponent of simple and direct English, revised the 1965 edition of Henry Watson Fowler's *Modern English Usage*. He wrote *The Complete Plain Words* (1954).

***Green, Theodore Francis** (1867-May 19), Democratic U.S. Senator from Rhode Island (1937-1961), was the oldest person ever to serve in Congress.

***Grosvenor, Gilbert Hovey** (1875-Feb. 4), National Geographic Society president (1920-1954) and then board chairman, joined its magazine staff in 1899 and was editor in chief (1903-1954).

Guggenheimer, Minnie (1882-May 23), music patron and philanthropist, had served as chairman and chief fund-raiser for the Lewisohn Stadium summer symphony concerts in New York City since 1918.

Gunn, Ross (1897-Oct. 15), United States Naval Research Laboratory physicist (1926-1957), credited as being one of the "true fathers of the nuclear submarine" did work on the separation of isotopes of uranium for the atomic bomb and started work on atomic power for submarines in 1939.

Hadas, Moses (1900-Aug. 17), Columbia University Professor of Greek, translated and edited many classical works, and Jakob Christopher Burckhardt's *Age of Constantine the Great* (from the German) and Joseph ben Meir Zabara's *The Book of Delight* (from the Hebrew). He also wrote *Aristeas to Philocrates*.

Hageman, Richard (1882-Mar. 6), Netherlands-born musician, conducted the Amsterdam Royal Orchestra (1899-1903), the New York Metropolitan Opera Company (1914-1926), and other orchestras. He wrote *The Crucible* and other orchestral works; *Caponsacchi* (opera); and scores for many films.

Harrigan, William (1894-Feb. 1), remembered as the captain in *Mister Roberts* (1948-1951, 1956), made his stage debut in 1898. He starred in *The Great God Brown* (1928), played Charlie Chan in *Keeper of the Keys* (1933), and appeared in films.

Harris, Elmer Blaney (1878-Sept. 6), author of many plays, wrote *So Long, Letty* (starring Charlotte Greenwood, 1916), *The Modern Virgin* and *Young Sinners* (1931), *The Man Who Killed Lincoln* (1940), *Johnny Belinda* (1941, filmed 1948), and screen scripts.

***Herter, Christian Archibald** (1895-Dec. 30), the President's Special Representative for Trade Negotiations for the past five years, served as Secretary of State (1959-1961) and Undersecretary of State (1957-1959). The former governor of Massachusetts (1953-1957) also was Republican U.S. Representative from Massachusetts (1943-1953).

***Hevesy, Georg von** (1885-July 5), Hungarian-born scientist, was awarded the Nobel chemistry prize (1943) for using radioactive isotopes as indicators in the study of chemical processes. He and Dirk Coster discovered the element hafnium (1923).

Higgins, Marguerite (1920-Jan. 3), newspaperwoman, received a Pulitzer prize in international reporting (1951) on the Korean War.

Hocking, William Ernest (1873-June 12), eminent philosopher, wrote such major works as *The Meaning of God in Human Experience* (1912), *The Coming World Civilization* (1956), and *The Meaning of Immorality in Human Experience* (1957).

***Hoffman, Malvina** (1887-July 10), internationally noted sculptress, did *The Races of Mankind* collection of 101 bronze figures and heads in the Field Museum of Natural History in Chicago.

Hoffmann, Arnold (1886-Aug. 21), Russian-born artist first known for landscapes and portraits, did such World War II paintings as *Civilization, 1940*, of Jews at a concentration camp, and *The Destruction of Lidice* (now in the National Museum in Prague).

***Hofmann, Hans** (1880-Feb. 17), German-born painter and teacher, founded art schools in Europe and in New York City and Provincetown, Mass. He greatly influenced the development of abstract art in the United States.

Hopper, Hedda (1890-Feb. 1), former stage and screen actress, won fame as a Hollywood gossip columnist. She is remembered for her fabulous hats and a 10-year feud with another Hollywood columnist, Louella O. Parsons.

Jarvis, DeForest Clinton (1881-Aug. 18), a country doctor in Barre, Vt., came to fame with *Folk Medicine: A Vermont Doctor's Guide to Good Health* (1958). It was followed by *Arthritis and Folk Medicine* (1960).

Johnson, Hewlett (1874-Oct. 22), English Anglican minister and Dean of Canterbury (1931-1963), was known as the "Red Dean" because of his Communist associations, speeches, and writings.

Kane, Helen (1910-Sept. 26), petite brunette who punctuated songs ("I Wanna Be Loved By You," "That's My Weakness Now," and others) with a babyish "boop-boop-a-doop," won fame on stage, screen, radio, and television.

Keaton, Joseph Francis "Buster" (1895-Feb. 1), was one of the three (Charlie Chaplin and Harold Lloyd) great comics of silent films. *The General*, *Steamboat Bill, Jr.*, *The Passionate Plumber*, and *The Navigator* were among his best pictures.

Ed Wynn, noted comedian and veteran of 64 years of show business, died in California.

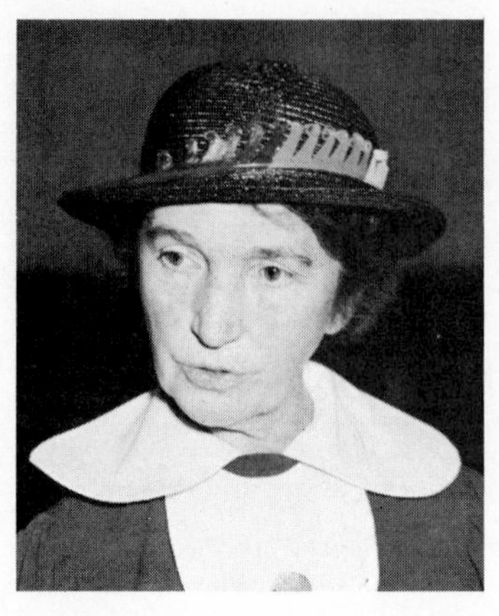

Margaret Sanger, pioneer in field of planned parenthood, died at 82 in Tucson, Ariz.

Cecil S. Forester, author of the well-known Captain Horatio Hornblower sea stories, died.

***Kiepura, Jan** (1902-Aug. 15), tenor known as "the Polish Caruso," sang in the world's major opera houses. His most popular role was Prince Danilo (1,000 or more times in seven languages) in *The Merry Widow* operetta with his wife, Hungarian soprano Marta Eggerth. He also appeared in films.

King-Hall, Sir Stephen (1893-June 2), retired British naval officer internationally known as an author and commentator on warfare and world affairs, wrote *The War at Sea, 1914-1918, Power Politics in the Nuclear Age,* and many other notable works.

Kolehmainen, Hannes (1890?-Jan. 11), the first of the "Flying Finns," won the 1912 Olympic 5,000-meter (14:36.6) and 10,000-meter (31:20.8) runs, and the 8,000-meter cross-country race (45:11.6, not recognized for world marks); and the 1920 Olympic marathon (26 miles 385 yards in 2 h. 32 m. 35.8 s.).

Korolev, Sergey P. (1906-Jan. 14), designed the rocket and space system for Russia's first earth satellites, and directed the designing of such manned spaceships as the Vostok and Voskhod.

Kraeling, Carl Herman (1897-Nov. 14), Yale University Divinity School theologian (1929-1950) and Buckingham Professor of New Testament Criticism and Interpretation (1941-1950), was founder-director of its Near Eastern Languages and Literature Department. He was a University of Chicago archaeology professor (1950-1962) and director of its Oriental Institute (1950-1960).

Kresge, Sebastian S. (1867-Oct. 18), founder of the S. S. Kresge chain stores, opened his first one in Detroit, Mich., in 1899. He established the Kresge Foundation (1924) for philanthropic purposes.

Lloyd George, Lady Megan (1902-May 14), daughter of British Prime Minister David Lloyd George (1916-1922), served in the House of Commons as a Liberal for Anglesey (Wales, 1929-1951) and as a Labour party member for Carmarthen since 1957.

Long, Marguerite (1874-Feb. 13), French pianist renowned as an interpreter of the romantic composers, was the first woman professor at the Paris Conservatory of Music (1920) and the first woman awarded the Legion of Honor for music.

Loomis, Roger Sherman (1887-Oct. 11), world authority on Arthurian legends, wrote 10 scholarly volumes such as *Arthurian Tradition and Chrétien de Troyes* and *A Mirror of Chaucer's World.*

***Luckner, Count Felix von** (1881-Apr. 13), German naval hero, fought in the Battle of Jutland (1916). He then disguised a small ship as a Norwegian fishing vessel, got through the British North Sea blockade, and sank 25 Allied ships without loss of life. He was captured in August, 1917.

Lurcat, Jean-Marie (1892-Jan. 6), French painter famed for his tapestries, designed *L'Orage* (*Thunderstorm,* Paris Museum of Modern Art), the large four-seasons (Château de la Muette, Paris), *Apocalypse* (Church of Assy, Haute Savoie), and others.

Macmillan, Lady Dorothy Evelyn Cavendish (1901?-May 21), was the wife of former British Prime Minister Harold Macmillan.

Maddy, Joseph Edgar (1891-Apr. 18), music educator and president of the famed National Music Camp (founded with Thaddeus P. Giddings, 1928) at Interlochen, Mich., organized and conducted the first national high school orchestra (230 youngsters from 30 states) at Detroit in 1926.

***Manship, Paul** (1885-Feb. 1), sculptor, did the *Celestial Sphere* (Woodrow Wilson memorial) in Geneva, Switzerland, and memorials in the United States. His *Prometheus* is in New York's Rockefeller Center.

Marshall, Herbert (1890-Jan. 22), English actor known for his romantic roles, made his stage debut in 1911. *The High Road* (1928) and *A Bill of Divorcement* (1929 revival, film 1940) are some of his many successes. His films include *The Razor's Edge* and *Duel in the Sun* (1946). He played Ken Thurston in "The Man Called X" radio series, and appeared in television plays.

Masaryk, Alice G. (1879?-Nov. 29), educator, sociologist, and author, was president of the Czechoslovak Red Cross (1918-1938). She was a daughter of Tomás G. Masaryk, a founder and first president of Czechoslovakia (1918-1935) and a sister of Jan G. Masaryk, foreign minister (1945-1948).

McLean, Kathryn Forbes (1909-May 15), wrote *Mama's Bank Account* (1943), seen on Broadway as *I Remember Mama* (1944-1951) and on the screen.

McNamara, Patrick V. (1894-Apr. 30), had been Democratic U.S. Senator from Michigan since 1955.

***McNaughton, Andrew George Latta** (1887-July 11), commanded Canadian overseas forces (1939-1944), and represented Canada at the United Nations (Atomic Energy Commission 1946-1950, permanent delegate 1948-1949) and on Canadian-U.S. commissions.

Billy Rose, Broadway producer and composer of many popular song hits, died at age 67.

Francis X. Bushman died after a distinguished career in both silent and talking films.

Admiral Chester W. Nimitz was fleet commander when he signed Japanese surrender documents.

Menken, Helen (1901-Mar. 27), began as a child actress in New York City (1904). She was the original Diane in *Seventh Heaven* (New York 1922, London 1927), Elizabeth Tudor in *Mary of Scotland* (1933), and produced *Stage Door Canteen* (1942-1946).

***Menninger, William Claire** (1899-Sept. 6), psychiatrist and president of the Menninger Clinic (founded with father and brother Karl A.) at Topeka, Kans., was president of the Menninger Foundation.

Meriwether, Lee (1862-Mar. 12), a St. Louis (Mo.) lawyer for 70 years and traveler, wrote *A Tramp Trip—How to See Europe on Fifty Cents a Day* (1887, popular for years), and about 30 other books. *My First 100 Years, 1862-1962* was followed by *A Postscript to My Long Life.*

Miller, Warren (1921-Apr. 20), journalist, wrote such books as *Cool World* (1959) and *The Siege of Harlem* (1964), and several children's books.

Montet, Pierre (1885-June 19), French Egyptologist, made such archaeological finds as royal tombs at Byblos, now in Lebanon (1922), a silver sarcophagus of King Sheshonq (1939), and the tomb of King Psousennes I (1940) near Tanis, Egypt.

Morrison, Charles Clayton (1875?-Mar. 2), Disciples of Christ minister, was editor of *The Christian Century* (1908-1947). He made it a nondenominational (1915), influential Protestant journal.

Nichols, Anne (1896-Sept. 15), actress and author of plays and scenarios, came to fame as author of *Abie's Irish Rose*, the Broadway comedy (1922-1927) that "never stopped playing somewhere." There were revivals (1937, 1954), films (1928, 1946), radio series, and many touring productions.

***Nimitz, Chester William** (1885-Feb. 20), U.S. Pacific Fleet Commander in Chief (1941-1945) and a signer of the Japanese surrender documents (Sept. 2, 1945), was chief of naval operations (1945-1947).

***Norris, Kathleen** (1880-Jan. 18), author of some 80 romantic novels (*Mother* 1911, *The Venables* 1941, and *Family Gathering* 1959), was the wife of novelist Charles Gilman Norris (1881-1945).

O'Connor, Frank (1903-Mar. 10), Irish writer (born Michael John O'Donovan), was a librarian (1925-1938) and director of the Abbey Theatre (1936-1939) in Dublin. His many novels and short-story collections include *The Guests of the Nation* (1931), *The Saint and Mary Kate* (1932), and *The Mirror in the Roadway* (1956). He also wrote plays.

O'Kelly, Seán Thomas (1882-Nov. 23), second President of Ireland (1945-1959), served in the Dáil Éireann (House of Deputies, 1918-1945) and held many government posts.

Orr, Douglas William (1892-July 29), architect, designed the Robert A. Taft Memorial Tower in Washington, D.C., Yale University buildings, and was vice-chairman of the commission on the renovation of the White House (1949-1950).

Orr, Louis (1879-Feb. 18), noted for his etchings of the Reims Cathedral done under German artillery fire in 1917, is represented in the Louvre in Paris and other art museums in France.

Palombo, David (1920?-Aug. 13), Israeli sculptor, made the parliament building's courtyard gates in Jerusalem and the *Burning Bush* sculpture there.

***Parrish, Maxfield** (1870-Mar. 30), was known for his rich glowing colors, especially the "Maxfield Parrish blue." His paintings include *The Garden of Allah* and *The Land of Make-Believe*, and the famous *Old King Cole* mural. He also illustrated books, and did posters, magazine covers, and calendars.

Patterson, Arthur Lindo (1902-Nov. 6), New Zealand-born crystallographer, devised the Patterson synthesis for applying X-ray diffraction to analysis of crystalline structure.

Patterson, Elizabeth (1874-Jan. 31), actress noted for mother and other gentlewomen roles, played in *Yankee Point* (1942), and many other New York productions. Her many films include *My Sister Eileen* (1942), *Little Women* (1949), and *Intruder in the Dust* (1949).

Pearce, Alice (1917-Mar. 3), comic actress, played in *On the Town* (1944, film 1949), *Sail Away* (1961), and other Broadway productions, and on television in "Bewitched." She last appeared in motion pictures in *The Glass Bottom Boat* (1966).

Peugeot, Jean-Pierre (1896-Oct. 18), retired as Peugeot Automobile Company president in 1964. His grandfather and granduncle, Eugéne and Armand, built the first French automobile in 1898.

Phillips, Duncan (1886-May 9), founded the Phillips Gallery in Washington, D.C. (1918), one of the world's noted galleries.

Pininfarina, Battista (1895-Apr. 3), Italian automobile designer, pioneered the streamlined body style and designed car bodies for manufacturers in Britain, France, and the United States.

Porter, Quincy (1897-Nov. 12), composer of chamber music, received the Pulitzer music prize (1954) for *Concerto for Two Pianos and Orchestra*. His other works include *Music for Antony and Cleopatra* and *The Moving Tide* for orchestra.

Reynaud, Paul (1878-Sept. 21), prominent French statesman, resigned as premier in 1940 rather than surrender to the Germans. He broke with President De Gaulle (1962) over foreign and other policies.

Robinson, Fred Norris (1871-July 21), Chaucer and Celtic philology authority, introduced Celtic studies at Harvard University in 1896.

Rogoff, Julius M. (1884-June 25), Latvian-born pioneer in adrenal gland research, discovered endocrine (interrenalin of the adrenal cortex) and originated the modern treatment for Addison's disease.

Rorimer, James J. (1905-May 11), director of New York's Metropolitan Museum of Art since 1955, wrote *Survival: The Salvage and Protection of Art in War* on his search for art work stolen by the Nazis.

Rose, Billy (1899-Feb. 10), producer and composer born William Samuel Rosenberg, came to fame as a lyricist. His 400 or more songs include "That Old Gang of Mine," "Barney Google," "Without a Song," and "It's Only a Paper Moon." He produced many musicals, and was an art patron.

Rossen, Robert (1908-Feb. 18), screen writer, director, and producer, is remembered for *Body and Soul* (1947), *All the King's Men* (1949 Academy award winner), and *The Hustler* (1961).

***Sandoz, Mari Susette** (1901-Mar. 10), biographer and novelist, wrote *Old Jules*, *Crazy Horse*, *Buffalo Hunters*, *The Horsecatcher*, *Love Song to the Plains*, *The Battle of The Little Big Horn*, and other books about the Nebraska plains and the Old West.

***Sanger, Margaret** (1883-Sept. 6), a nurse, pioneered the birth control movement. She and her sister opened the nation's first birth control clinic in New York City (1916). Her Birth Control League (1921) became the Planned Parenthood Federation of America (1946).

Scherchen, Hermann (1891-June 12), German interpreter of ultramodern music, conducted in the major European music centers. He was chief of the Musikkollegium, Winterthur, Switzerland, and wrote *Handbook of Conducting* and *On the Nature of Music*.

Severini, Gino (1883-Feb. 26), Italian painter and a founder of futurism (1910), did *Dynamic Hieroglyph of the Bal Tabarin* (1912) in the New York Museum of Modern Art. His reconstructed *Le Panpan à Monico* (original in Berlin gallery destroyed by Hitler) is in the Paris Museum of Modern Art.

Shaporin, Yuri A. (1889-Dec. 11), conductor at the Maly Drama Theatre (Petrograd 1919-1928) and the Pushkin Theatre (Leningrad 1928-1934), composed such works as *The Decembrists* (opera), *Saga of the Battle for the Russian Land* (oratorio), *On the Field of Kulikov* (symphony-cantata), and *The Flea* (orchestra suite).

***Shastri, Lal Bahadur** (1904-Jan. 11), was Prime Minister of India. See INDIA.

Sirén, Osvald (1879-June 12), Finnish-born Stockholm University Fine Arts Professor (1908-1925) and Oriental art expert, wrote such monumental works as *Imperial Palaces of Peking* and *Chinese Painting, Leading Masters and Principles*.

***Sloan, Alfred Pritchard, Jr.** (1875-Feb. 17), who pioneered roller bearings, four-wheel brakes, and other developments for automobiles, was president (1923-1937) and chairman (1937-1956) of the General Motors Corporation.

A Maker Of Dreams

Walt Disney (1901–1966)

Walt Disney produced fairy tales on film that entertained countless millions throughout the world. He was a motion picture pioneer who delighted the children of one generation with the antics of a squeaky-voiced mouse named Mickey and the world's first full-length animated motion picture. The children of another generation crowed with delight over his version of *Mary Poppins*, in which he blended cartoon characters with real people and introduced a catchy, new word into the vocabulary of the young: *supercalifragilisticexpialidocious*(!).

Disney filled his cartoon films with cuddly birds and animals. A cross between Hans Christian Andersen and Henry Ford, he and his staff created products that brought in an estimated $100,000,000 yearly. Among them was Disneyland, an amusement park near Los Angeles.

Walter Elias Disney was born in Chicago on Dec. 5, 1901. He spent most of his boyhood on a farm in Missouri. Later, he studied cartooning at night at the Chicago Academy of Fine Arts. During World War I, he drove an ambulance in France for the Red Cross. In 1920, he organized his own company to make cartoon versions of fairy tales.

It was in 1928, with a sound film called *Steamboat Bill*, in which Disney introduced Mickey Mouse, that his career began to boom. That cheerful saucer-eared fellow was soon a popular figure all over the world. After Mickey, and Minnie Mouse, came fractious Donald Duck, and two early Disney dogs, Pluto and Goofy.

In the late 1940s and 1950s, Disney produced several widely praised nature films (among them *Water Birds*, *Beaver Valley*). Later he made conventional films as well (*Huck Finn*, *Davy Crockett*). Always at the head of his profession, he was among the first big producers to make films for TV.

The only Disney story with an unhappy ending occurred on Dec. 15, 1966, when the master of fantasy died of lung cancer. MARK M. PERLBERG

Smith, Lillian (1897-Sept. 28), early civil rights spokesman, won world acclaim as the author of the controversial novel *Strange Fruit* (1944, dramatized 1945). Later books include *Killers of the Dream*, *Now Is the Time*, and *Memory of a Large Christmas.*

Sterry, Charlotte Reinagle-Cooper (1870?-Oct. 10), English tennis star, won her first open singles title at Ilkley in 1893 and the Wimbledon singles in 1895, 1896, and 1898 as Miss Cooper, and in 1901 and 1908 as Mrs. Sterry.

***Taylor, (Joseph) Deems** (1885-July 3), music critic and commentator, composed the orchestral suite *Through the Looking Glass* (1922) and the operas *The King's Henchman* (libretto by Edna St. Vincent Millay, 1927) and *Peter Ibbetson* (1931). His books include *Some Enchanted Evening* and *Of Men and Music.*

Thomas, Albert (1898-Feb. 15), Democratic U.S. Representative from Texas, was first elected in 1936.

Treece, Henry (1912-June 10), British poet and historical novelist, wrote stories of early Britain and the Vikings. His best children's books are *The Burning of Njal* and *Horned Helmet. The Green Man* is a 1966 book. Treece also wrote two studies of Dylan Thomas' works.

Tucker, Sophie (1884-Feb. 9), known for her big voice and flamboyant dress and jewels, was a star entertainer for 60 years. Among her most popular songs were "Some of These Days" and "I'm the Last of the Red Hot Mamas."

Veksler, Vladimir I. (1907-Sept. 22), Russian nuclear physicist, and Edwin M. McMillan of the University of California shared the United States Atoms for Peace Award in 1963.

Vening Meinesz, Felix Andries (1887-Aug. 12), Netherlands geophysicist and geodesist, pioneered in a method of studying the earth's interior beneath ocean beds, developed a theory of the origin of mountains, and made possible the accurate calculation of the earth's shape.

Vittorini, Elio (1908-Feb. 13), Italian novelist known internationally for *In Sicily* (1941) and *The Red Carnation* (1948), did translations of U. S. and British writers.

Wagner, Wieland (Adolf Gottfried) (1917-Oct. 16), co-director of the Wagner Festival at Bayreuth, was the grandson of the famous composer Richard Wagner and great-grandson of Franz Liszt. Wieland and his brother Wolfgang introduced a new style of opera staging at Bayreuth in 1951, retaining little of the traditional scenery and props.

Waley, Arthur David (1889-June 27), English translator of Chinese and Japanese literature, wrote on Far Eastern art and literature. His translations include *The Tale of Genji* (six volumes), *The Book of Songs*, and the allegorical fairy story *Monkey*. He wrote *The Opium War Through Chinese Eyes.*

Walker, Kenneth Macfarlane (1882-Jan. 22), English genitourinary surgeon, wrote *The Physiology of Sex*, *The Making of Man*, and other books.

***Waugh, Evelyn Arthur St. John** (1903-Apr. 10), British satirical novelist and great literary figure, came to fame with *Decline and Fall* (1928) and other books. *Brideshead Revisited* (1945) is considered his best book. *The Loved One* (1948) is a satire. *Men at Arms* (1952), *Officers and Gentlemen* (1955), and *The End of the Battle* (1962) is a trilogy on army life in World War II.

Webb, Clifton (1893-Oct. 13), born Webb Parmelee Hollenbeck, began his career as a child actor. He sang in grand opera, and starred in *As Thousands Cheer* and other musical comedies. His first film was *Laura* (1944). Lynn Belvedere in *Sitting Pretty* was his most popular screen role.

Wellman, Paul I. (1898-Sept. 16), author of 27 books, wrote *Death on the Prairie* (1934), *The Walls of Jericho* (1947, filmed), *The Iron Mistress* (1951, filmed), and *The Greatest Cattle Drive* (1964). He also wrote the films *Cheyenne*, *Red Gold*, and *Jubal.*

Westover, Russ (1887?-Mar. 5), originated the syndicated comic strip "Tillie the Toiler" (1921-1959).

Wilkinson, Louis U. (1881-Sept. 12), also wrote as Louis Marlow. His novels include *The Puppets' Dallying* (1905), *The Buffoon* (1916), and *Swan's Milk* (1934). *Welsh Ambassadors* (1936) is a study of the noted Powys brothers. He edited *The Letters of Llewelyn Powys* and *The Letters of John Cowper Powys to Louis Wilkinson.*

***Wynn, Ed** (1886-June 19), comedian of vaudeville, stage, screen, radio, and television, was born Isaiah Edwin Leopold. *Ed Wynn's Carnival* (1920) and *The Perfect Fool* (1921) were among his most memorable Broadway productions. The "Perfect Fool" turned serious in *The Great Man* (1956), *Marjorie Morningstar* (1958), and *The Diary of Anne Frank* (1959).

Young, Desmond (1892-June 27), English adventurer and soldier, wrote the famed *Rommel, The Desert Fox* (1950, also filmed) about his German captor in North Africa, General Erwin Rommel of World War II.

***Zernike, Frits** (1888-Mar. 10), Netherlands scientist and Nobel physics laureate (1953), developed the phase contrast microscope and made possible the study of living cells.

***Zorach, William** (1887-Nov. 15), Lithuanian-born artist known for realistic human and animal sculptures, carved in stone (also worked in wood and metal). He just completed *Wisdom of Solomon* (two women and child) for a New York showing in 1967. His famed *Mother and Child* (1927-1930) is in New York's Metropolitan Museum of Art. Other works include the *Kiener Memorial Fountain* (1965, St. Louis, Mo.), and the aluminum *Spirit of the Dance* (1932, New York Radio City Music Hall).

DEMOCRACY. In a world of rising expectations, sensitive economies, and prickly political issues, democracy was under challenge on many fronts in 1966. In nations where it is a familiar way of life, democracy acquitted itself well. In Great Britain, for example, where the Labour government had been ruling with a razor-thin majority in the House of Commons – a tribute to British political discipline – the government improved its position enormously by a sweeping victory in the national elections of March 31. Then, in the face of mounting national economic problems, the government advanced a broad austerity program. Despite the severity of the austerity measures to the worker and his union, which are the bastions of the Labour party's strength, the government pushed ahead with party and legislative support.

West Germany. In nations where democracy was unfamiliar, the political seas were also rough. In West Germany, Chancellor Ludwig Erhard found himself at the helm of a minority government when, on October 27, four of his cabinet ministers, members of the Free Democratic party, resigned. This left Erhard, head of the Christian Democratic Union, which had run West Germany since its birth, in control of a minority government. On December 1, a new coalition government of Christian Democrats and Social Democrats, with Kurt Georg Kiesinger as chancellor, took over the reins of state (see KIESINGER, KURT GEORG). But it remained to be seen how the Germans would weather the change.

There was cause for alarm in Germany when the "neo-Nazi" National Democratic party elected eight members to the parliament in the state of Hesse in November. It was the first time any National Democrats had been elected above the local level. Two weeks later, the party elected candidates to the state parliament of Bavaria. Outgoing Chancellor Ludwig Erhard warned of the increased rightist strength.

Africa. Among the new nations, particularly those of Africa, 1966 was a poor year for democracy. In Nigeria, the most populous African nation, a budding democracy was crushed in a military takeover. Dahomey, the Central African Republic, Upper Volta, and other countries suffered military coups. Rhodesia and the Republic of South Africa persisted in their course of white autocracy.

Elsewhere, improvements that contributed to democratic health were afoot. President Ferdinand Marcos moved to weed out corrupt officials in the Philippines. Austria revitalized its parliament, which had played a minor part in policymaking.

In the United States, President Lyndon B. Johnson's Great Society program contributed to the ideal of a citizenry of quality–in mind, health, and economic well-being–as a way to more complete democracy. The President's program incorporated recommendations for new legislation aimed to give U.S. citizens more wholesome cities in which to live, better medical care, and less poverty.

But the administrative actions of agencies of the U.S. government sometimes were considered dubious in their fidelity to the democratic ideal. Revelations in the Senate showed that the Internal Revenue Service and the Federal Bureau of Investigation (FBI) utilized the facilities of the American Telephone and Telegraph Company in its extensive monitoring of telephone calls, reportedly to improve its service. In December, it was disclosed that the FBI had "bugged" the embassy of the Dominican Republic since the 1950s. In the Department of State, Abba Schwartz, administrator of the Bureau of Security and Consular Affairs, appeared to have been forced out of his post by a reorganization. He had worked toward a relaxation of curbs on immigration, travel, and admission of refugees.

Political discussion in the United States centered upon civil rights questions and the war in Vietnam. Senator J. William Fulbright (D., Ark.), chairman of the Senate Foreign Relations Committee, affirmed the right to dissent in a democracy by publicly examining and criticizing the administration's policy on Vietnam. LOUIS W. KOENIG

See also CIVIL RIGHTS; COURTS AND LAWS; SUPREME COURT OF THE UNITED STATES; and articles on the various countries.

DEMOCRATIC PARTY candidates on November 8 suffered their worst defeat at the polls in two decades with a net loss of 47 seats in the House of Representatives, three seats in the Senate, and eight governorships.

Democrats retained control of Congress, however, and still enjoyed a top-heavy majority of 64 to 36 in the Senate compared to the old division of 67 to 33. In the House, however, the reduction of the lopsided 295-to-140 Democratic majority to one of 248 to 187 spelled potential trouble. This dramatic shift in congressional power was expected to revive the conservative coalition of Republicans and Southern Democrats that proved so troublesome to the administration of President John F. Kennedy. See CONGRESS OF THE UNITED STATES.

In another major shift of party control, the Democrats lost 10 gubernatorial races to the Republicans and won only two. They held the top job in only 24 of the 50 states–until Georgia decided its race in January, 1967. Previously, 33 states had Democratic governors and 17 Republican. Five of the seven most populous states, which would cast more than half of the electoral votes needed to elect a President, chose Republican governors in 1966. See GOVERNORS OF THE STATES.

Party Organization was shattered in many states by the Republicans' comeback. And the Republicans moved into a position to make a much stronger challenge for the White House in 1968 than was thought likely before the 1966 elections. In fact, some of President Johnson's fellow Democrats, who blamed him in part for the 1966 setback, appeared to feel that his re-election could be threatened in 1968 unless he took a personal hand in reorganizing the party. See REPUBLICAN PARTY.

The Democratic campaign was neither as well-organized nor as well-financed as the Republican. Many Democratic candidates for Congress received only small sums of $1,400 to $2,000, or no help at all, from the national organization, while some of their Republican challengers had as much as $16,000 to spend. The President's Democratic critics quarreled with his policy of stinting on the 1966 campaign and diverting part of the funds toward reducing the $4,000,000 1964 campaign deficit. Democratic spokesmen reported that the deficit, which had been reduced to about $2,400,000 by April, was down to just under $1,000,000 as 1966 drew to a close.

The President was also held responsible for the Democratic National Committee's minor role in the campaign and its meager efforts for an extensive voter registration drive in 1966. Critics charged that the national committee had fallen into neglect under the Johnson administration and that its Kennedy-appointed chairman, John M. Bailey of Connecticut, had become a mere figurehead. The President was being urged to revive the committee,

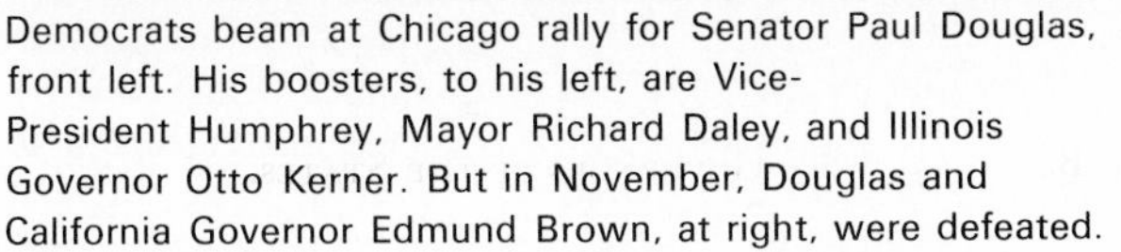

Democrats beam at Chicago rally for Senator Paul Douglas, front left. His boosters, to his left, are Vice-President Humphrey, Mayor Richard Daley, and Illinois Governor Otto Kerner. But in November, Douglas and California Governor Edmund Brown, at right, were defeated.

place a strong man at its head, and take steps himself to reconcile feuding Democratic politicians.

President Johnson stumped energetically at the start of the 1966 campaign but dropped out during its crucial last three weeks. He left for the Manila conference on Vietnam on October 17, and returned on November 2. His announcement that he was to have surgery and that he was going to his Texas ranch to rest disappointed a number of hard-pressed Democratic candidates. They had been counting on his winding up the campaign with a 12- to 15-state whirlwind tour. Altogether in the campaign, he had appeared in person in 19 states and spoken on behalf of 54 candidates. Only 29 of them won, however. See PRESIDENT OF THE UNITED STATES.

Campaigner Kennedy. The phenomenon of the campaign was Democratic Senator Robert F. Kennedy of New York. He drew enormous, wildly enthusiastic crowds, full of young people waving signs that urged him to run for President as early as 1968. Kennedy, however, was unable to prevent a Republican victory in New York state, and he had a lower batting average than the President. Only 18 of the candidates he supported were successful, while 28 failed to win election.

Nor was Kennedy the only big-name campaigner who had difficulty in transferring his personal popularity to Democratic candidates. His brother, Senator Edward M. Kennedy of Massachusetts, was unable to prevent a Republican sweep in the home state of the Kennedy clan. Vice-President Hubert H. Humphrey failed to save his native Minnesota from a Republican triumph. President Johnson was unable to dissuade his fellow Texans from re-electing Republican Senator John G. Tower.

Strength in the South, once solid Democratic territory, was further eroded as the Republicans elected two governors and a senator for the first time since Reconstruction and picked up nine House seats for a new total of 28. There was a portent of trouble ahead for President Johnson in the victory of Mrs. Lurleen Wallace to succeed her husband as governor of Alabama. Governor George C. Wallace, barred by state law from succeeding himself, threatened to run for President in 1968.

In surveying the damage after November 8, the President suggested that the Democrats were hurt by a good many factors, including the coattail power of the popular Republican candidates for governor in Michigan, Ohio, and California, and the tendency of the voters to support the party out of power. "Over a period of years the American people have a way of balancing things," he said. "When a pendulum swings one way, as it did in 1964 pretty strongly, it has a tendency to swing back." WILLIAM MCGAFFIN

See also ELECTIONS; U.S. GOVERNMENT.

DENMARK. In a sudden, unexpected move, Prime Minister Jens Otto Krag and his cabinet resigned on November 2, after encountering strong opposition from the right-wing Conservative and Social Liberal parties over a proposed pay-as-you-go-tax plan. In a general election on November 22, Krag won another four years in office. His party's representation was sharply reduced, however, and Krag found himself the head of a minority government.

Inflation problems, meanwhile, plagued the nation's economy, with the cost of living up about 7 per cent over the preceding year. Because living costs were tied to wages by law, some 2,000,000 Danes received an increase in earnings totaling about $102,500,000 in midyear. This nullified an earlier government move to combat inflation by levying a $64,500,000 increase in direct taxation.

In September, Princess Margrethe, heir to the Danish throne, announced her engagement to Count Henri de Laborde de Monpezet. The count, who is a French citizen and a Roman Catholic, planned to apply for Danish citizenship and join the Lutheran State Church before the wedding.

Facts in Brief. Population: 4,780,000. Government: King Frederik IX; Prime Minister Jens Otto Krag. Monetary Unit: krone (6.88 = U.S. $1). Foreign Trade: exports, $2,319,500,000; imports, $2,822,100,000. Principal Exports: dairy products, machinery, meat. KENNETH BROWN

DENTISTRY. A proposal for a national dental health program for children, "particularly the needy and underprivileged," was adopted by the American Dental Association (ADA) House of Delegates. ADA officials noted that the "United States, of all the well developed countries of the world, is the only one which does not have such a program." They hoped that pilot projects on a major scale could be initiated in 1967. Financing is expected to be largely on the traditional grant-in-aid basis, and responsibility for planning will rest heavily at the state and local levels.

The ADA estimated that 50 per cent of all two-year-olds have decayed teeth, the average child entering school has three decayed teeth, and by age 15 has 11 decayed, missing, or filled teeth.

Dental Manpower. In planning the national dental health program for children, the ADA faced the problem of expanding existing dental manpower resources. In 1966, 88,500 dentists were actively engaged in private practice in the United States, and 95 per cent of these accepted children for treatment. But, according to the ADA, there is need for many more dentists because the population per dentist has increased by 25 per cent since 1930. They hope that through a broad construction program for new teaching facilities the number of dental school graduates can be increased from 3,800 in the 1965-1966 academic year to 4,500 by 1972.

Oral Cancer. Smokers who give up cigarettes and switch to pipes or cigars do not lessen their chances of developing oral cancer. The warning came from 1966 ADA president Dr. Maynard K. Hine at the annual meeting of the Maryland State Dental Association in Baltimore on Sept. 21, 1966. He pointed out that "recent studies of smoking and oral cancer show no significant difference in the development of oral cancer between cigarette smokers and those who smoke pipes or cigars."

Dental Research. A superstrength steel created for space rockets and deep-diving undersea crafts has been tested in dental bridgework and caps for teeth, Dr. Edward G. Kaufman of the New York University College of Dentistry told the International Association for Dental Research in March. The appliances are stronger, thinner, lighter, and less expensive than those that are made with other dental materials.

International Dentistry. The Féderation Dentaire Internationale held its 54th annual session in Tel Aviv, Israel, in June. Delegates discussed ways to adopt uniform standards of dental education and licensure. Five of the six European Economic Community nations–Belgium, France, Luxembourg, The Netherlands, and West Germany–agreed to recognize the dental certification of any dentist from their respective countries on a reciprocal basis by 1967. LOU JOSEPH

DETROIT added to its cultural stature in June with the opening of the handsome, new south wing of the city's Institute of Arts. Faced with highly polished granite, the new wing's 389 galleries doubled the museum's space. Work also started on a $7,000,000 north wing. Nearby, Wayne State University, its enrollment swollen to 30,000, announced a $150,000,000 building program.

In an April election, voters approved the establishment of a Community College Authority to meet growing educational demands. Detroit's largest community college, Henry Ford, doubled its enrollment in the past five years to 10,000 students.

Police. In a highly successful program dubbed "Impact," the city's police department launched efforts to modernize its law enforcement. An emergency telephone system allowed patrol cars to respond more quickly to serious trouble, resulting in lower crime rates and more efficient use of policemen. "Impact" also equipped patrolmen with electronic communications and overhauled the department's administration.

Renewal. Detroit's second downtown residential redevelopment project, Elmwood Park, won an award for architectural quality. The first of its 1,070 apartments opened, with some apartments designed for the elderly. DONALD W. LIEF

DICTIONARY. See SECTION FIVE: DICTIONARY SUPPLEMENT.

DIPLOMAT. Several countries were created in 1966, thus increasing the number of states with which the United States exchanges ambassadors. Among these was British Guiana, which proclaimed its independence at Guyana in May. Bechuanaland became Botswana in September. Ambassadors representing President Lyndon B. Johnson and the United States in other countries and their counterparts from those countries to the United States, in January, 1967, included the following:

Country	From U.S.A.	To U.S.A.
Afghanistan	Robert G. Neumann	Abdul Majid
Algeria	John D. Jernegan	Cherif Guellal
Argentina	Edwin M. Martin	Alvaro C. Alsogaray
Australia	Edward W. Clark	John Keith Waller
Austria	J. W. Riddleberger	Ernst Lemberger
Belgium	Ridgway B. Knight	Baron Louis Scheyven
Bolivia	Douglas Henderson	Julio Sanjines-Goytia
Botswana	Vacant	Zachariah K. Matthews
Brazil	John W. Tuthill	Vasco Leitão da Cunha
Bulgaria	John M. McSweeney	Luben Guerassimov
Burma	Henry A. Byroade	U Tun Win
Burundi	Vacant	Vacant
Cameroon	Vacant	Joseph N. Owono
Canada	W. Walton Butterworth	A. Edgar Ritchie
Cen. African Rep.	Claude G. Ross	Michel Gallin-Douathe
Ceylon	Cecil B. Lyon	Oliver Weerasinghe
Chad	Brewster H. Morris	Boukar Abdoul
Chile	Ralph A. Dungan	Radomiro Tomic
Colombia	Reynold E. Carlson	Eduardo Uribe
Congo (Kinshasa)	G. McMurtrie Godley	Cyrille Adoula
Costa Rica	Raymond L. Telles, Jr.	Fernando Ortuño
Cyprus	Taylor G. Belcher	Zenon Rossides
Czechoslovakia	Jacob D. Beam	Karel Duda
Dahomey	Clinton E. Knox	Louis Ignacio-Pinto
Denmark	Katharine Elkus White	Torben Rønne
Dominican Rep.	John Hugh Crimmins	Héctor Frederico Garcia-Godoy
Ecuador	Wymberley Coerr	Gustavo Larrea
El Salvador	Raul H. Castro	Ramon de Clairmont-Duenas
Ethiopia	Edward M. Korry	Tashoma Haile-Mariam
Finland	Tyler Thompson	Olavi Munkki
Formosa	W. P. McConaughy	Chow Shu-kai
France	Charles E. Bohlen	Charles E. Lucet
Gabon	David M. Bane	Louis Owanga
Gambia	William R. Rivkin	Vacant
Germany, West	George C. McGhee	Heinrich Knappstein
Ghana	Franklin H. Williams	Abraham Benjamin Bah Kofi
Great Britain	David K. E. Bruce	Sir Patrick Dean
Greece	Phillips Talbot	Alexander A. Matsas
Guatemala	John Gordon Mein	Francisco Javier Linares Aranda
Guinea	Robinson McIlvaine	Karim Bangoura
Guyana	Delmar R. Carlson	Sir John Carter
Haiti	B. E. L. Timmons III	Vacant
Honduras	Joseph J. Jova	Ricardo Midence Soto
Iceland	James K. Penfield	Petur Thorsteinsson
India	Chester Bowles	Braj Kumar Nehru
Indonesia	Marshall Green	Vacant
Iran	Armin H. Meyer	Khosro Khosrovani
Iraq	Robert C. Strong	Nasir Hani
Ireland	Raymond R. Guest	William P. Fay
Israel	Walworth Barbour	Avraham Harman
Italy	G. Frederick Reinhardt	Sergio Fenoaltea
Ivory Coast	George A. Morgan	Vacant
Jamaica	Wilson T. M. Beale, Jr.	Sir Neville Noel Ashenheim
Japan	U. Alexis Johnson	Ryuji Takeuchi
Jordan	Findley Burns, Jr.	Farhan Shubeilat
Kenya	Glenn W. Ferguson	Burudi Nabwera
Korea, South	Winthrop G. Brown	Hyun Chul Kim
Kuwait	Howard Rex Cottam	Talat Al-Ghoussein
Laos	William H. Sullivan	Khamking Souvanlasy
Lebanon	Dwight J. Porter	Ibrahim Hussein El-Ahdab
Liberia	Ben H. Brown, Jr.	S. Edward Peal
Libya	David D. Newsom	Fathi Abidia
Luxembourg	Patricia Roberts Harris	Maurice Steinmetz
Malagasy	Vacant	Louis Rakotomalala
Malawi	Marshall P. Jones	Vincent H. B. Gondwe
Malaysia	James D. Bell	Tan Sri Ong Yoke Lin
Mali	C. Robert Moore	Moussa Leó Keita
Mauritania	Geoffrey W. Lewis	Abdallahi Ould Daddah
Mexico	Fulton Freeman	Hugo B. Margáin
Morocco	Henry J. Tasca	Ahmed Laraki
Nepal	Carol C. Laise	Padma Bahadur Khatri
Netherlands	William R. Tyler	Carl W. A. Schurmann
New Zealand	Herbert B. Powell	George R. Laking
Nicaragua	Aaron S. Brown	G. Sevilla-Sacasa
Niger	Robert J. Ryan	Adamou Mayaki
Nigeria	Elbert G. Mathews	N. Ade Martins
Norway	Margaret Joy Tibbetts	Arne Gunneng
Pakistan	Eugene M. Locke	Agha Hilaly
Panama	Charles W. Adair, Jr.	Ricardo M. Arias E.
Paraguay	William P. Snow	Juan Plate
Peru	J. Wesley Jones	Celso Pastor
Philippines	Wm. McC. Blair, Jr.	Vacant
Poland	John A. Gronouski, Jr.	Vacant
Portugal	W. Tapley Bennett, Jr.	Vasco Vieira Garin
Romania	Richard H. Davis	Petre Bălăceanu
Russia	L. E. Thompson, Jr.	Anatoliy F. Dobrynin
Rwanda	Leo G. Cyr	Celestin Kabanda
Saudi Arabia	Hermann F. Eilts	Ibrahim Al-Sowayel
Senegal	William R. Rivkin	Ousmane Socé Diop
Sierra Leone	Andrew V. Corry	Gershon B. O. Collier
Singapore	Francis J. Galbraith	Vacant
Somalia	Raymond L. Thurston	Ahmed Mohamed Adan
So. Africa, Rep. of	William M. Rountree	H. L. T. Taswell
Spain	Angier Biddle Duke	The Marquis de Merry Del Val
Sudan	William H. Weathersby	Amin Ahmad Hussein
Sweden	J. Graham Parsons	Hubert de Besche
Switzerland	John S. Hayes	Felix Schnyder
Syria	Hugh H. Smythe	Vacant
Thailand	Graham A. Martin	Sukich Nimmanheminda
Togo	William Witman II	Robert Ajavon
Tunisia	Francis H. Russell	Rachid Driss
Turkey	Parker T. Hart	Turgut Menemencioğlu
Uganda	Henry E. Stebbins	Otema Allimadi
United Arab Rep.	Lucius D. Battle	Mostafa Kamel
Upper Volta, Rep. of	Elliott P. Skinner	Paul Rouamba
Uruguay	Henry A. Hoyt	Juan Felipe Yriart
Venezuela	Maurice M. Bernbaum	E. Tejera-Paris
Vietnam, So.	Henry Cabot Lodge, Jr.	Bui Diem
Yugoslavia	C. Burke Elbrick	Veljko Micunovic

DISARMAMENT. A historic treaty banning nuclear weapons from space and from using either the moon or other celestial bodies as military bases was negotiated by the United States and the Soviet Union in 1966. The 2,000-word treaty, which contained a preamble and 17 articles, was hailed by President of the United States Lyndon B. Johnson as "the most important arms-control development since the limited test-ban treaty of 1963."

The Text of the Treaty was put together over a five-month period within the framework of the United Nations (UN) Committee on the Peaceful Uses of Outer Space and its 28-member subcommittee of legal experts. The chief negotiator for the United States was Ambassador to the UN Arthur J. Goldberg. He worked closely with Platon D. Morozov, second in command of the Soviet Union's UN delegation. Before the treaty could become effective, however, it would have to be ratified by five nations, including Great Britain, the Soviet Union, and the United States.

Other Actions. On January 27, after a five-month recess, the regular UN Disarmament Committee reconvened in Geneva, Switzerland. Only 17 of the 18 member nations were present. The French seat remained vacant, as it had for a number of years.

Two main issues confronted the conference during the seven months it was in session. One issue was a proposed treaty to halt the spread of nuclear weapons. The other was a treaty to ban underground nuclear tests. On the first issue, the United States and the Soviet Union presented rival draft treaties but progress was blocked because the Soviets felt the United States intended to permit the Federal Republic of (West) Germany access to U.S. nuclear weapons through the North Atlantic Treaty Organization. See GERMANY; NORTH ATLANTIC TREATY ORGANIZATION (NATO). On the question of underground tests, the Soviet Union still rejected U.S. insistence on international inspection. On August 29, when the conference recessed, discussions had reached a stalemate.

The Arms Race continued during 1966 largely because of an escalation of the war in Vietnam (see VIETNAM). The menacing role of Communist China, too, was a deterrent to any significant reduction in arms during the year. Its successful firing of a nuclear-tipped missile and its explosion of another atomic device were equal causes for caution in the area of disarmament. See ATOMIC ENERGY; CHINA, PEOPLE'S REPUBLIC OF.

There were indications that the arms race would continue to spiral upward as reports began to spread in international circles that the Soviet Union was beginning to deploy an antiballistic missile (ABM) defense system along the approaches to its heartland.

MILT FREUDENHEIM

See also ARMED FORCES OF THE WORLD; UNITED NATIONS (UN); NATIONAL DEFENSE.

DISASTERS

A devastating mine-slag avalanche, which took the lives of 116 schoolchildren in Aberfan, South Wales, proved to be one of the most shocking disasters of 1966. Another disaster that shocked the world was the flood in Italy. The damage to irreplaceable art treasures in Florence was impossible to estimate. Large crop and other property damage seriously affected the country's economy. See ITALY; PAINTING AND SCULPTURE.

Hurricane *Inez* in the Caribbean area caused extensive damage. The year's worst earthquake took a heavy toll of life in Turkey. Japan was the scene of two of the worst airplane disasters of the year, and India was plagued with a series of train wrecks that took more than 300 lives.

Major disasters included the following:

AIRCRAFT CRASHES

Jan. 14—Cartagena, Colombia. An Avianca DC-4 broke in two and fell in the Caribbean Sea, killing 51 of the 61 persons aboard.

Jan. 22—Haiti. A Haitian airliner crashed in the Duchiti area and killed 30 persons.

Jan. 24—French-Swiss Border. An Air India Boeing 707 crashed into a ridge near the summit of Mont Blanc, killing 117 persons.

Jan. 28—Bremen, West Germany. A Lufthansa German Airlines plane crashed while attempting to land at the airport; 46 persons were killed.

Feb. 2—Near Faridpur, East Pakistan. A vulture flew into the blades of a helicopter, causing it to crash; 23 persons were killed.

Feb. 4—Tokyo Bay, Japan. An All-Nippon Airways Boeing 727 crashed and killed 133 persons.

Feb. 7—India. An Indian Airline Corporation F27 disappeared in the Banihal Pass of the Himalaya mountains with 37 persons aboard.

Feb. 17—Moscow, Russia. A Soviet TU-114, the world's largest airliner, crashed on take-off from Sheremetyevo Airport, killing 38 persons.

Mar. 4—Tokyo, Japan. A Canadian Pacific DC-8 jetliner hit approach lights at the International Airport and crashed; 64 persons were killed.

Mar. 5—Japan. A British Overseas Airways Corporation Boeing 707 jetliner caught fire and crashed on the eastern side of Mount Fujiyama, killing 124 persons.

Mar. 18—Near Cairo, United Arab Republic. An Egyptian airliner (Russian-built Antonov 24-B) crashed and burned, killing 30 persons.

Apr. 22—Arbuckle Mountains, Southern Oklahoma. An American Flyers Airline Lockheed Electro crashed and burned in the foothills. Many servicemen were among the 81 persons killed.

Apr. 27—Between Huampara and Omas, Peru. A Lansa Airlines Constellation crashed in the Andes Mountains, killing 49 persons. Among them were three American Peace Corps volunteers.

More than 150 townspeople, most of them children, perished when a century-old slag heap slid into the heart of Aberfan, Wales.

Terence Spencer, *Life* © Time Inc.

Aug. 6—Near Falls City, Nebr. A Braniff International Airways jet airliner came down in flames, killing all 42 persons aboard.

Aug. 11—Romania. A Romanian airliner crashed on a flight from Cluj to Bucharest, killing 24 persons.

Sept. 1—Ljubljana, Yugoslavia. A Britannia Airways turboprop crashed, killing 97 persons.

Sept. 22—Queensland, Australia. An Ansett-A.N.A. Viscount airliner crashed and killed 24 persons.

Nov. 13—Matsuyama, Japan. An All-Nippon Airways YS-11 turboprop plane crashed and killed all 50 persons aboard.

Nov. 22—Aden, South Arabia. An Aden Airways plane crashed after take-off, killing 28 persons.

Nov. 24—Near Bratislava, Czechoslovakia. A Tabso Airways IL-18 turboprop plane crashed after take-off, killing 82 persons.

Nov. 26—North of Tansonnhut, South Vietnam. A U.S. Air Force C-47 transport plane crashed and burned; all 27 persons killed were Americans.

Dec. 24—Da Nang, South Vietnam. A Flying Tiger Airlines cargo plane crashed in a residential area, killing four crewmen and 125 civilians.

BLIZZARDS AND STORMS

Jan. 28-Feb. 2—United States. Snow and cold in the Midwest and the Atlantic states killed about 200 persons, including 106 in the South.

Mar. 3-7—United States. Snowstorms and bitter cold in the Upper Midwest area killed 20 persons.

Mar. 23-24—United States. A blizzard moved across the northern Midwest, killing at least 28 persons.

BUS AND TRUCK WRECKS

Feb. 1—South of Miami, Fla. A bus collided with a train engine; 18 Puerto Rican farmworkers were killed.

Feb. 3—Brooksville, Fla. A school bus collided with a truck, killing three pupils and the woman bus driver.

Apr. 28—Ribeirão Préto, Brazil. A truck with 19 sugar plantation workers hit a fallen high-tension cable. All 19 were electrocuted.

July 25—Niederbrechen, West Germany. A bus plunged from the highway through a bridge guard onto a road below; 28 of the 33 dead were children.

Oct. 7—Dorion, Quebec. A bus was struck by a Canadian National Railways train; 19 high school students were killed.

Nov. 18—Near Ngomweni, South Africa. A bus rolled down an embankment into the Jmhloti River, killing 40 persons.

Dec. 21—East of Windsor, Ont. A truck loaded with sand hit a school bus, tearing a hole in it. Sand poured in on the children, killing eight.

CYCLONES, HURRICANES, TYPHOONS

Jan. 31—Samoan Islands. A weekend hurricane killed about 90 persons.

June 8-9—Caribbean Area. The season's first hurricane, *Alma*, killed 12 persons in Cuba and three in Florida.

June 28—Honshu, Japan. Typhoon *Kit* swept the east central Pacific coast, killing at least 32 persons.

Sept. 25—Japan. Typhoons *Helen* and *Ida* battered parts of the country, taking 174 lives.

Sept. 25-Oct. 11—Caribbean Area. Hurricane *Inez* spawned in the Atlantic and hit the Guadalupe Islands, the Virgin Islands, Puerto Rico, the eastern tip of the Dominican Republic, and southeast Oriente province in Cuba, moved toward the Bahamas and the Florida Keys, crossed the Gulf of Mexico, and struck Mexico. The estimated death toll for the Caribbean area was 293.

Her village was one of 24 leveled in the province of Varta, Turkey, by a series of earthquakes that killed 2,480 people in August.

EARTHQUAKES

Mar. 20-22—Western Uganda. Earthquakes destroyed the towns of Bwamba and Bundibugyo, and killed at least 19 persons.

May 18—Beni, North Kivu Province, Congo. An earthquake killed 90 persons.

June 27—Western Nepal. An earthquake killed 80 persons.

Aug. 19-20—Eastern Turkey. An earthquake killed about 2,480 persons in a four-province area.

Oct. 17—Lima and Coastal Area, Peru. An earthquake killed about 100 persons.

EXPLOSIONS AND FIRES

Jan. 6—St. Paul, Minn. Fire in the Carleton Hotel killed nine persons.

Jan. 18—Taipei, Formosa. Fire in the Shin Sheng Building killed 28 persons.

Jan. 28—Boston, Mass. An explosion and fire in the Plymouth Hotel's cocktail lounge killed 10 persons.

Feb. 4—Buenos Aires, Argentina. A factory explosion killed 13 persons.

Green Bay, Wis. Fire destroyed the city's historic Astor Hotel and killed eight persons.

Mar. 11—Minakami, Japan. Fire destroyed two ski resort hotels, and killed 31 persons.

Apr. 23—Lapinlahti, Finland. Fire in a mental hospital almost destroyed the building and took the lives of 29 persons.

Apr. 26—Amraoti, India. An explosion and fire at a cottonseed oil mill killed 32 persons.

Sept. 12—Anchorage, Alaska. Fire in the Lane Hotel killed 14 persons.

Oct. 9—Bulacan Province, Philippines. The explosion of half a ton of firecrackers killed 14 persons.

Oct. 13—Montreal, Quebec. A chemical plant explosion and fire in suburban LaSalle killed 11 persons.

Oct. 17—New York City. Fire destroyed three buildings in the Madison Square area and took the lives of 12 firemen. It was the highest toll in the city's fire department history of 101 years.

FLOODS

Jan. 11—Rio de Janeiro, Brazil. Heavy rain flooded the city and set off landslides, which killed 239 persons.

Mar. 11—South Jordan. A flood in the desert area took the lives of 57 persons.

May 27-31—Recife, Brazil. Heavy rain and floods took the lives of at least 90 persons.

June 5-6—San Rafael, Honduras. A 30-inch rainfall nearly destroyed the town, and killed 73 persons.

Sept. 10—Vientiane, Laos. The Mekong River flood took 34 lives in two weeks.

Nov. 3-5—Italy. Heavy rains caused the Po, Arno, and other rivers to flood vast areas. Seawater, swept in by high winds, added to the disaster which took at least 100 lives. Art treasures in Florence were heavily damaged.

Nov. 4-5—Eastern Panama. Floods in the Pacora-Chepo area took about 50 lives.

SHIPWRECKS

Jan. 10-11—Atlantic Ocean. The Spanish freighter *Monte Palomares* sank about 40 miles east-northeast of Bermuda. Only six of its crew of 38 were rescued.

Jan. 25—North Sumatra, Indonesia. The *Permina* sank near the port of Belawan. Only 89 of its 200 or more passengers were rescued.

Jan. 29—Near Chandpur, East Pakistan. A river launch collided with a steamer and sank. About 100 persons drowned.

Mar. 24—Nicaragua. The motor launch *Elizabeth* sank in the Escondido River, drowning 19 persons.

June 16—Kill van Kull Channel between New Jersey and Staten Island, New York City. Tankers *Alva Cape*, carrying flammable naphtha, and *Texaco Massa-*

BOAC jetliner, trailing fire from its wing tanks, crashed into Mt. Fuji, Japan, on March 5, and killed all 124 passengers.

chusetts collided near the Bayonne (N.J.) Bridge. Explosion and fire followed, killing 33 men.

July 31—English Channel. The *Darwin*, a pleasure boat, vanished in a storm off the Cornwall coast with 31 passengers aboard.

Sept. 14—North Sea. The West German Navy Submarine *Hai* (*Shark*) sank near the Dogger Bank about 200 miles off the British coast; 20 crewmen drowned.

Oct. 22—Near Cavite, Philippines. The American-owned freighter *Golden State* collided with the Philippines coastal steamer *Pioneer Leyte*; 26 persons on the steamer were killed.

Nov. 2—Gulf of Mexico. The oil barge *Mercury* sank off Lobos Island, with 28 men aboard.

Nov. 29—Lake Huron, 200 miles off Harbor Beach, Mich. The ore freighter *Daniel J. Morrell* broke in two and sank, taking 28 lives.

Dec. 8—Aegean Sea. The car and passenger ferry *Heraklion* sank near Milos Island during a storm. About 230 persons were reported dead or missing.

Dec. 31—Bering Sea. A Russian refrigerator ship sank, taking the lives of 50 seamen.

TORNADOES

Mar. 3—Central Mississippi. Tornadoes, which swept the area at dusk, killed 52 persons.

Apr. 4—Central Florida. Tornadoes cut across the state from west to east, killing 11 persons.

June 8—Topeka, Kans. A tornado cut through the center of the city, killing 17 persons.

TRAIN WRECKS

Feb. 16—Split, Yugoslavia. A 19-car coal train sped down a steep grade and struck an oncoming passenger train; 29 persons were killed.

Apr. 20—Lumding, Assam, India. An explosion on a train killed 55 persons.

Apr. 23—Diphu, Assam, India. An explosion on a train killed 40 persons.

May 26—Near Belgaum, Mysore, India. An express train left the rails, killing at least 22 persons.

May 31—Near Bucharest, Romania. The collision of an express and a local train took the lives of 38 persons.

June 13—Near Bombay, India. Two suburban trains collided, killing 60 persons.

Oct. 12—North of Hyderabad, India. A passenger train ran into a freight train; 70 persons were killed.

Oct. 23—Lakhisarai, Bihar, India. An Eastern Railway express train ran into a group of persons standing on a railroad track, killing at least 35 of them.

Nov. 16—Near Rio de Janeiro, Brazil. Two commuter trains collided, killing at least 34 persons.

VOLCANOES

Apr. 24—Central Java, Indonesia. Mount Kelut began erupting, pouring lava on the villages below; 90 persons had been killed there by May.

Aug. 12—North Sangi Island, Indonesia. Mount Awu erupted, killing 28 persons; 60 children were reported missing.

OTHER DISASTERS

Feb. 15—Switzerland. Gas swept through a tunnel under construction near the Saint Gotthard Pass in the Alps, killing 17 men.

May 14—Near Quito, Ecuador. A landslide crushed the huts of sleeping road workers, killing 52 of them.

July 8—Monomura, Japan. Walls in a section of an irrigation tunnel caved in, killing 25 workers.

Oct. 21—Aberfan, South Wales. An avalanche of coal slag buried the Pantglas Junior School, a farmhouse, and 16 miners' cottages; 116 children and 28 adults were killed. Heavy rains were thought to have caused the slide which struck at 9:30 A.M. Coal mine waste towered to 400 feet.

DOMINICAN REPUBLIC. A measure of political stability returned to the nation on July 1 when Joaquin Balaguer was sworn into office as president. Balaguer, who had been overwhelmingly elected on June 1, succeeded provisional president Hector Garcia-Godoy (see BALAGUER, JOAQUIN).

Garcia-Godoy paved the way for the elections when, early in the year, he issued an order calling for self-exile by a number of military leaders. The move touched off uprisings, particularly in Santo Domingo, the capital. In their wake, a general strike spread from Santo Domingo to the interior. The strike, and continuing acts of terrorism, placed the government in jeopardy. Backed, however, by the Inter-American Peace Force, which had been sent to maintain order following the outbreak of civil war in 1965, the government survived.

On April 24, Dominicans staged a potentially riotous "Yankee Go Home" rally in the capital, but with the Peace Force again in the background, there were no large-scale disorders. On April 28, however, a more serious demonstration involving several thousand young leftists took place in the capital. The wounding of six Dominicans by two U.S. servicemen prompted Garcia-Godoy to place security in the hands of the Dominican police. Later, the armed forces were restricted to their barracks until after the presidential election in order to avoid involvement in any new incidents.

Austerity Measures. On June 24, the Organization of American States voted to end its military and political intervention, and, on September 19, the last of the Peace Force troops were withdrawn. In the interim, Balaguer had restored the country's confidence in its ability to recover from the aftereffects of almost two years of turmoil.

In his inaugural speech, Balaguer promised a regime of reform and austerity designed to get the country back on its feet. Subsequently, he halved his own salary, cut the salaries of all other higher paid government workers, and clamped a ceiling on pensions. A central auditing system was set up to combat corruption and inefficiency in government operations. Later, Balaguer introduced far-reaching reforms in the armed forces. Price cuts and a price freeze were decreed for edible oil, meats, and rice, while new austerity taxes were announced. The president also had 26 women sworn in as governors of the republic's provinces—the first time in Dominican history that all the provincial governors were women.

On August 19, the debt-ridden state-owned Dominican Sugar Corporation was dissolved on Balaguer's orders and replaced by a State Sugar Council which would supervise the 12 mills previously operated by the corporation. Each mill was to manage itself. To provide jobs for any sugar workers that were laid off, the government planned a $40,000,000 public works program.

In August, renewed violence prompted Balaguer to announce that he planned to ask congress to "procure a real political truce" until 1968 by prohibiting "all public political activities that may alter the spirit of democratic living and the atmosphere of order and security within which the country now lives."

Economic Moves. The economy, which had been drained by the civil war, gradually began to display signs of recovery. Balaguer helped by beginning to pay off some government debts, thus attacking at its roots the shortage of liquid cash that had put a brake on business activity. Export earnings, which began to climb in the last quarter of the year, were bolstered further by a U.S. decision to raise the Dominican Republic's 1966 sugar quota in the U.S. market by 30 per cent, for a total of 578,411 tons over the preceding year.

Many problems remained at year's end, however, one of the foremost being unemployment which stood at 30 per cent of the 1,500,000-man labor force. At midyear, per capita income was believed to have dropped 15 per cent (to $205) during the preceding 12-month period.

Facts in Brief. Population: 3,783,000. Government: President Joaquin Balaguer. Monetary Unit: peso (1 = U.S. $1). Foreign Trade: exports, $135,300,000; imports, $135,000,000. Principal Exports: cane sugar, cocoa, coffee. MARY C. WEBSTER

DRUGS. From January 17, when Dr. James L. Goddard was sworn in as commissioner of the Food and Drug Administration (FDA), through the end of 1966, the U.S. drug industry became increasingly aware of the tough-minded new administrator.

On April 6, in a blunt speech to the Pharmaceutical Manufacturers Association (PMA) at Boca Raton, Fla., he said he was "frankly alarmed" at the state of the industry. The industry expressed alarm at his actions as well.

Early in the year, Dr. Goddard charged the industry with violations of drug advertising rules. He said that in 1965 "one-third" of the members of the PMA were found to have ads in violation of the regulations. When pressed by industry, however, the FDA was unable to substantiate the charge.

The commissioner's tough, regulatory ways persisted for the rest of the year. For instance, he later ordered a review of about 4,000 pre-1962 drugs, and the FDA proposed restrictions on food supplements and vitamins. See GODDARD, JAMES L.

Generic Drugs. As Medicare got underway in July, the old generic-versus-brand name drug controversy arose again. With the federal government footing the bill for an increasing portion of prescription drugs, pressure mounted to hold down their costs. In July, Senator Russell B. Long (D., La.), introduced a bill that would require doctors to prescribe by generic, or common chemical, name if the drugs were to be paid for with federal funds. The Senate Finance Committee was to hold hearings on his bill early in 1967. See MEDICARE.

The drug industry took a dim view of this move, equating generic drugs with poor quality. However, with many important drugs available from only one maker, the amount of savings to the government would be conjectural.

New Drugs. In the first half of 1966, only six new drugs (single chemical entities) got FDA clearance. In the 1965 period, there were 14. The yearly average of 1948-1964 had been 38. The amount spent on ethical drug research, however, rose 8½ per cent in 1966, to about $353,000,000.

Total Sales of all products–drugs, cosmetics, toiletries, chemicals–were estimated at a record $7,000,000,000, up $800,000,000 from 1965. Manufacturers' U.S. sales of ethical drugs for human use were put at $3,200,000,000, against $2,900,000,000 in 1965. Veterinary drug sales totaled about another $200,000,000.

Despite the industry's travails with the FDA and Dr. Goddard, it rolled up a 10 per cent gain in profits in 1966. Total earnings for all products were expected to reach $770,000,000. JOHN J. ELSBREE

See also CHEMICAL INDUSTRY; HEALTH; HOSPITAL; MEDICINE; MENTAL HEALTH; Section Two, OUR PILL-FILLED LIVES.

EARTHQUAKES. See DISASTERS; GEOLOGY.

EASTERN ORTHODOX. Metropolitan Antony Bashir, archbishop of the Syrian Antiochian Church in America, died in Boston on Feb. 15, 1966. For more than 30 years, he was one of the most articulate exponents and defenders of Orthodox unity in America and the main architect of the Standing Conference of Orthodox Canonical Bishops in the United States. In March, a special convention of the archdiocese nominated three candidates to fill his post. From among them, the Holy Synod of the Church of Antioch in Damascus chose the Right Reverend Archimandrite Philip Saliba. He was consecrated by the Patriarch Theodosius in Damascus and enthroned in New York City on October 13. Metropolitan Philip is a native of Syria.

On September 29, the first joint meeting of the Ecumenical Commission, appointed by the Standing Conference of Orthodox Bishops and the Roman Catholic hierarchy of the United States, was held under the chairmanship of Archbishop Iakovos and Bishop Flanagan of Worcester, Mass. The commission established an agenda which included both the discussion of theological problems and practical concerns.

Another significant development was the publication by the Standing Conference of Orthodox Bishops of *Ecumenical Guidelines for Clergy and Laity.* The purpose of the document was to channel and control the ecumenical work in America.

Open Letter. At the end of December, 1965, two young priests of the diocese of Moscow–Fathers Gleb Yakunin and Nickolai Eshliman–sent "open letters" to the chairman of the Presidium of the Supreme Soviet, Nikolai Podgorny, and to the head of the Moscow patriarchate, Alexis, denouncing the "unconstitutional and illegal interference of the state into church affairs" as well as the virtual surrender of the Russian hierarchy to state pressures.

In May, the priests were summoned to the patriarchate and ordered to withdraw their accusations. Upon their refusal, they were suspended from priestly duties but they addressed a solemn appeal to an improbable general synod of the Russian Church. These events, widely publicized both in the Soviet Union and abroad, seem to have provoked a deep crisis in the Russian Church. The incident indicated an increasingly vocal opposition by the younger clergy to the hierarchical leadership of those accused of compromising with the atheistic Soviet regime.

Antioch. In addition to Metropolitan Philip (Saliba), two other young metropolitans were elected by the Synod of Damascus: Ignatius Hazim, for the diocese of Lattakie in Syria; and Spiridon Khouri, for the diocese of Zahle in Lebanon. These elections seemed to strengthen the group of bishops which opposes the growing influence of the Moscow patriarchate in the East. ALEXANDER SCHMEMANN

EBERHART, RICHARD (1904-), was awarded the Pulitzer prize in poetry in 1966 for his *Selected Poems, (1930-1965)*. Long a leading figure on the U.S. literary scene, Eberhart received the Bollingen prize in poetry in 1962 and was chosen to succeed Robert Frost as poetry consultant for the Library of Congress (1959 to 1961). His several books include *A Bravery of Earth* (1930); *Great Praises* (1957); and *The Quarry* (1964). Eberhart's poetry combines both lyric and metaphysical concerns. Among his best-known poems are "The Groundhog" and "The Horse Chestnut Tree."

Richard Ghormley Eberhart was born in Austin, Minn. He took his B.A. degree from Dartmouth College, in 1926. The following year he sailed around the world as a deck hand on a tramp steamer. In 1929, Eberhart received another B.A. degree, this time from Cambridge University in England. Back in the United States in 1930, he served in Washington, D.C., as a tutor to the son of King Prajadhipok of Siam, now Thailand. From 1933 to 1941, he taught at St. Mark's School, in Southboro, Mass.

In 1941, the poet married Helen Elizabeth Butcher. The couple have two sons. In 1946, he became an officer in the Butcher Polish Company. Since 1956, Eberhart has spent most of his time as poet in residence at Dartmouth.

See also PULITZER PRIZES.

THE ECONOMY

When 1966 came to an end, the United States had marked up another record year for its economy. Its gross national product (GNP) had risen nearly 8.7 per cent to approximately $740,000,000,000. But price increases reduced the rate of real growth in GNP (the total output of goods and services) to less than 5 per cent, slightly below the 5½ per cent growth of the previous year.

For the rest of the industrialized world, the picture was mixed. Great Britain, fighting to preserve the international status of the pound sterling, was forced to impose severe deflationary measures. Its GNP increased less than 2 per cent. Even in West Germany, the prize example of post-1950 growth, the increase over 1965 was only 2½ per cent. On the other hand, both Italy and Japan achieved rates that approached 8 per cent. Canada matched the U.S. rate of approximately 5 per cent.

In the less developed nations, inflation continued to be the primary problem, especially in South America. Economists were generally coming to agreement that inflationary pressures, especially when they were intense, limited rather than improved the possibilities for real growth in output.

President Johnson, *right*, and his four top advisers on the economy grapple with the problem of how to hold down inflation.

Based on the sketchy information available on Communist countries, Western experts estimated a Russian growth rate of 5 per cent. A record grain crop in the Soviet Union plus the increasing emphasis the Soviets were placing on earning a profit were cited as major contributing factors.

The U.S. Economy, as in 1965, proved far more robust than was forecast at the beginning of the year. In January, 1966, the President's Council of Economic Advisers (CEA) had estimated a 1966 GNP of $722,000,000,000, plus or minus $5,000,-000,000. Most private forecasts were higher.

Perhaps the major cause for failing to come closer to the actual $740,000,000,000 mark lay in the stepped-up outlays for the war in Vietnam. By year's end, these war expenses were running at the rate of $20,000,000,000 per year, contrasted with a previous estimate of $10,000,000,000. This additional pressure on the economy contributed to the 3½ to 4 per cent increase in consumer prices; only a 2 per cent rise had been forecast at the beginning of the year. Other pressures included record high levels of personal income and corporate profits, the lowest rate of unemployment since 1953, and the heavy expenditures on new plant and equipment.

Fiscal Actions were taken in October to remove some of the inflationary pressures. Congress suspended for 15 months the 7 per cent investment tax credit that had been applicable on purchases of new machinery and equipment. It also disallowed some of the accelerated depreciation on new buildings. Economists thereupon began to question whether these curbs on business investment would actually serve to reduce or increase inflationary pressures. Most believed they would tend to "cool off" the economy, but that postponing capital investment also would build up inflationary pressures later on.

After the election, speculation heightened on whether the President would ask for a general tax increase in 1967. Economists were split on the issue. Gardner Ackley, chairman of the CEA, told President Lyndon B. Johnson in December that he expected a moderate, balanced growth in the economy in 1967–seeming to indicate continued opposition to a tax increase (see ACKLEY, GARDNER).

A few days earlier, Ackley's predecessor as CEA chief, Walter W. Heller, also agreed that inflationary pressure had eased. Nevertheless, he said, a tax increase was still necessary. He urged a tighter fiscal policy but a more relaxed monetary policy.

Rising Prices. During the fall, housewives began picketing supermarkets because of the rising cost of food. In 12 months, food prices had increased an average of 4 per cent. But prices received by farmers had risen more, nearly 10 per cent. The picketing, which achieved some price cuts, at least was symptomatic of the discontent over the squeeze on the pocketbook. See AGRICULTURE; FOOD.

The fact was that the paycheck was not going as far as it had. For the first time since 1957, *real wages* (the amount of goods and services a week's work would purchase) showed a decline. In December, 1965, the average weekly factory earnings in terms of 1957-1959 prices were $99.93. By August, 1966, they had dropped to $98.22. They recovered only slightly by the end of the year. One effect was the virtual rejection of the administration's wage guidelines, which called for a 3.2 per cent a year limit on wage increases. That amount, roughly equal to the estimated annual increase in productivity, could be granted without inflationary consequences. These guidelines were breached first in the airline mechanics' strike, and then in the electrical equipment industry. The ultimate settlements approximated 5 per cent. See LABOR.

The price protests and shrinking buying power of the dollar, however, seemed not to curtail the consumers' desire to spend. Although automobile sales lagged behind the record 1965 pace, total consumer expenditures on durables rose more than 5 per cent during the year, and expenditures on nondurables and services rose by approximately 8 per cent. Despite personal incomes totaling more than $600,000,000,000 a year–an all-time high–consumers were saving less than 5 per cent of their *disposable* (after-tax) income. This rate of saving was lower than at any time in the previous 10 years.

Corporate Profits, in the meantime, continued to rise. They climbed about 10 per cent during the year, reaching $48,000,000,000 after taxes. As a result, a vigorous debate ensued. Was inflation created by a rise in wages or in profits? Both sides, however, tended to ignore the facts. The major area of rising prices had little relation to union gains or corporate profits.

The consumer price index (CPI) for all items rose by 4 percentage points from October, 1965, to October, 1966. The CPI for commodities, however, went up only about 3 points. If food is excluded, commodity prices rose less than 2 percentage points. The goods in this category are those produced mostly by union labor in industry. In contrast, all services exclusive of rent rose about 6 per cent during the same period. Yet corporate profits and union-negotiated wages had the smallest impact in the service category. The facts indicated that the largest price increases tended to occur in those areas that lacked an adequate supply of resources and skills to meet consumers' rising demands (see chart).

Consumer Spending Climbs — and So Do Prices

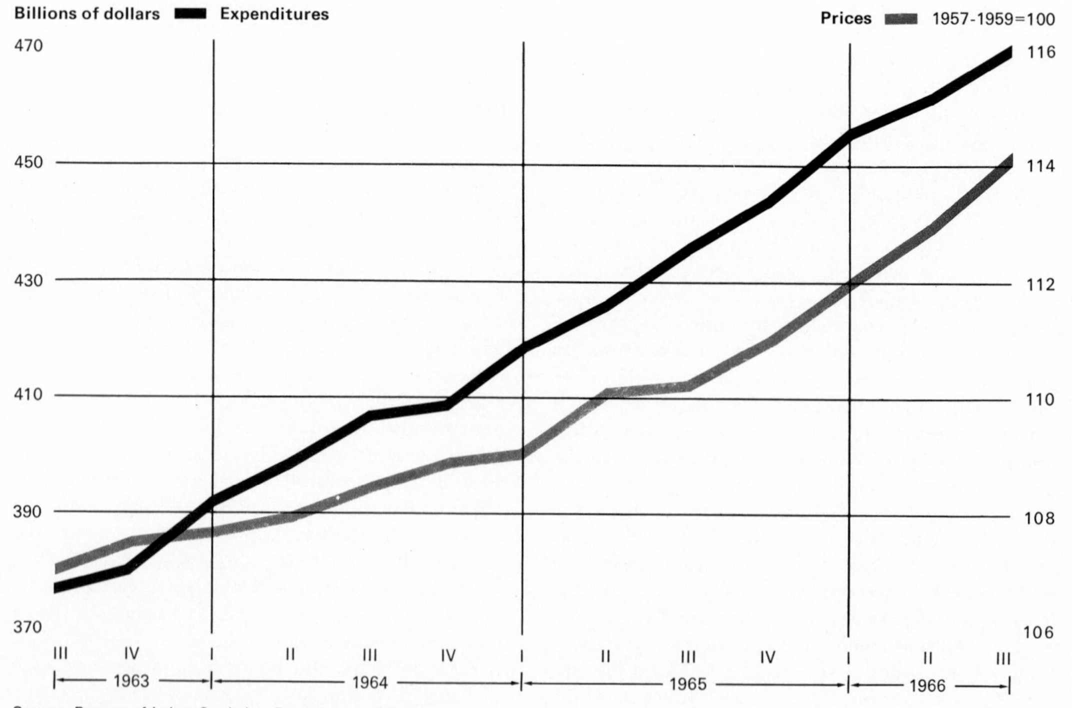

Source: Bureau of Labor Statistics; Department of Commerce

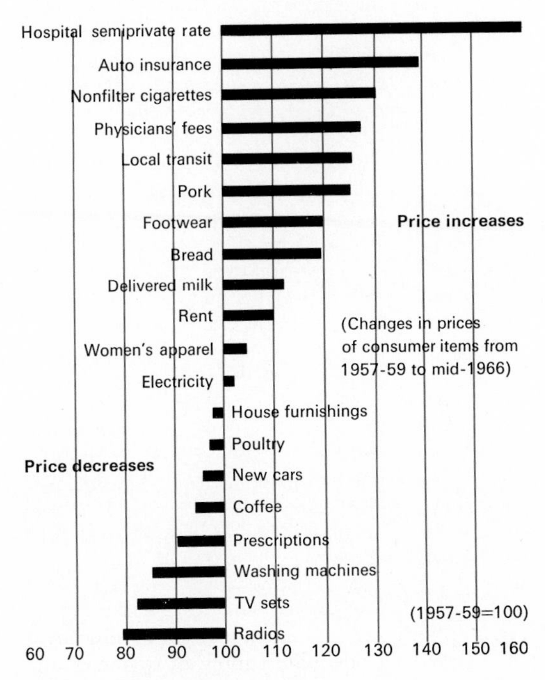

been racing ahead at rates of well over 10 per cent during 1964 and 1965, slowed their increase to about 6 per cent.

Money and credit came under heavy demand–for national defense, for expanding production facilities, for building business inventories, and for satisfying the cravings of the prosperous consumers. U.S. Department of Defense spending soared $10,600,000,000 in 12 months, to $61,300,000,000 at the end of the third quarter. Industry's investment in new plant and equipment rose to an estimated annual rate of $62,600,000,000 at the end of 1966, from $55,350,000,000 a year earlier. Manufacturing and business inventories increased more than $12,800,000,000, third quarter to third quarter. Personal spending rose a modest 5 per cent, compared with the increases for the other three categories–from almost 11 per cent to nearly 21 per cent.

All this put tremendous pressure on the banks' ability to supply funds. The Federal Reserve Board (FRB), in attempting to keep inflation in check, took various actions to discourage the rapid expansion of credit by banks. This counter-pressure from the FRB had the effect of driving all interest rates up. Even the banks' *prime* (best-risk) customers had to pay 6 per cent. See BANKS AND BANKING.

Slumping Indicators. The principal casualty of this tight squeeze on money was residential housing.

How Much Inflation? That question was a principal topic of conversation in the United States and became a campaign issue in the November elections. But the U.S. variety of inflation was notable for its remarkable stability in comparison with price rises in the rest of the world. With 1958 prices as a base, the January (1966) U.S. price level was 10 per cent lower than that of any other major industrial country. And of those nations, only Italy experienced a lower increase in prices–2 per cent–than the United States.

At the other extreme, despite efforts to contain them, prices in Brazil appeared to be rising at the rate of 50 per cent per year. In India, after a year of moderate inflation, the upward movement of prices continued, running about 11 per cent above corresponding months of 1965. See chart.

High Cost of Money. The concern over inflation in the United States may have been excessive, but the monetary authorities seemed determined to check price increases before they could escalate and seriously endanger the economy. They used the control of credit as their chief weapon. As a result of their action, as well as of the heavy demand for funds, the money supply (consisting of currency and demand deposits) rose less than 1½ per cent from January to September–from $168,000,000,000 to $170,500,000,000. September's figure was actually lower than June's. Even time deposits, which had

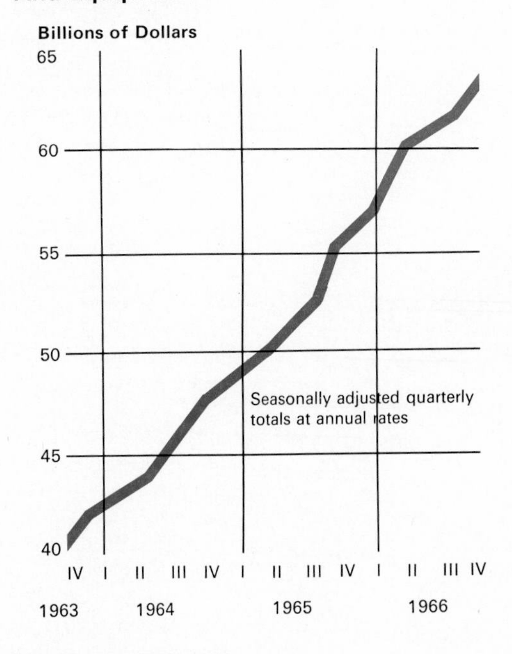

Housewives In Revolt

In October, 1966, U.S. housewives resorted to picket lines and boycotts in an effort to stem the rising cost of living. The boycotts started in Denver, Colo., and spread east and west. Organizations such as HELP (Housewives to Enact Lower Prices) and YELP (You're Enlisted to Help Lower Prices) picketed supermarkets and called upon grocers to abandon promotional "gimmicks" and reduce food prices instead.

In some cases, food prices came down, but government economists warned that the price reductions were probably temporary.

The rapid rise in food prices over the previous 18 months brought complaints in the Congress of the United States where there were warnings that "inflationary pressures have reached crisis proportions." Accordingly, the U.S. Department of Agriculture (USDA) and the Federal Trade Commission began separate investigations into food retailing and manufacturing practices.

"Don't make the farmer the scapegoat for increases in the cost of living," said Secretary of Agriculture Orville L. Freeman. "The recent modest farm price increases have been too long delayed."

USDA calculations showed that the farmer received 41 per cent of the amount the consumer paid in 1966 for a "market basket" containing 62 representative foods. According to this figure, the farmer's share had increased somewhat since 1963, but it was still considerably lower than the farmer's portion from 1947 to 1949, when it was 51 per cent.

Some of the rising cost of food could be traced to the shift in consumer preferences. The average family, enjoying the benefits of increased income, steadily improved the quality of the food it consumed. Meat and other high protein foods gradually displaced the less expensive wheat-based products, and highly processed "convenience" foods grew in popularity.

Originally limited to frozen vegetables and other simple items, convenience foods are becoming increasingly sophisticated–and more expensive. Among the specialized items recently marketed are: breakfast cereals with freeze-dried fruits, vegetables frozen in butter sauce and sealed in plastic cooking pouches, and frozen corn on the cob. In addition, new recipes often call for the combined use of convenience foods. A popular torte recipe, for example, combines French cherry vanilla pudding mix, frozen raspberries, and frozen pound cake.

These convenience foods appeal to the busy housewife because they are easy to prepare, add variety to menus, and save time. Despite the added cost, the housewife is likely to buy such foods in increasing amounts.

In 1966, more than 30,000 companies were involved in handling, processing, manufacturing, and transporting the items Americans ate. The labor force required by the huge food industry was more than twice the size of the force employed in the automotive industry.

Close inspection by government agencies showed that the increasing costs sustained by the food manufacturing industry for additives, transportation, processing, and handling accounted for much of the price spread between what the farmer received and what the consumer paid. Other factors, labor in particular, were becoming increasingly important factors in rising costs. It was estimated that labor accounted for 50 per cent of the cost of moving food from the farmer to the ultimate consumer. And as the consumer buys more processed foods, the percentage represented by labor is expected to increase even more.

In 1965, the last year for which figures are available, consumers spent $85,000,000,000 on food–far more than they spent on the products of any other single industry. Or, to put it another way, food items accounted for one-third of all consumer purchases. In this light, it was difficult for the consumers—such as the housewives on the picket lines—to realize that they actually paid out more for goods and services than for food.

Yet Americans actually were spending only about 18 per cent of their net income on food–the lowest percentage in U.S. history. In 1947, the figure was 26 per cent. Ruth L. Henoch

Mortgage rates approached 7 per cent. Even at those rates, potential home buyers had difficulty finding lenders. Housing starts dropped to their lowest level in 20 years, with an annual rate of a little over 800,000 in October. (They recovered to about 1,000,000 by November.) Building permits also fell to 750,000 annually in October. Heavy construction and commercial and industrial building, however, more than made up for the housing decline and pushed total new construction for the year to a record of nearly $75,000,000,000. See BUILDING AND CONSTRUCTION; HOUSING.

Another segment of the economy that failed to reflect prosperity and rising prices was the stock market. Stock prices reached an all-time high in February with the Dow-Jones industrial average hitting 995. But a sharp, almost continuous sell-off soon set in. By December, the average had dropped more than 20 per cent. See STOCKS AND BONDS.

Thus the cliché that inflation always brings higher stock prices was smashed. The future would have to tell whether the stock market was accurately predicting general economic conditions for 1967. The declining rate of increase in profits during the last half of the year was disquieting. It gave no encouragement that stock prices would quickly rebound to the high levels of early 1966. Industrials closed 1966 still 215 points shy of the magic 1000 level.

The consumer sector of the economy fared well on balance. Despite the stock market decline, at the end of the third quarter shareholders were receiving $1,600,000,000 more per year in dividends than they had the year before. Although prices were about 4 per cent higher, employees were earning about $36,000,000,000, or 10 per cent, more per year than in 1965. Farmers' incomes also rose to the highest level since 1947 (see AGRICULTURE).

U.S. Consumer Income and Outgo

	Calendar Year			3d Quarter Rate		
	1961	1965	Change	1965	1966	Change
	($ billions)		%	($ billions)		%
Personal Income	416.8	535.1	28.4	552.8	585.2	5.9
Less Taxes...	52.4	66.0	26.0	66.7	77.4	16.0
Disposable Income......	364.4	469.1	28.7	486.1	507.8	4.5
in 1958 dollars	*350.7*	*426.9*	*21.7*	*440.9*	*444.8*	*0.9*
Personal Outlays	343.2	443.4	29.2	457.6	483.3	5.6
Savings.......	21.2	25.7	21.2	28.5	24.5	−14.0
Nonmortgage Debt........	57.7	87.9	52.3	83.8	91.6	9.3
Prices and Jobs						
Consumer Price Index (1957-59=100)....	104.2	109.9	5.5	110.2	114.1	3.5
Employed (millions)....	66.8	72.2	8.1	72.3	74.2	2.6
Unemployed (millions)....	4.8	3.5	−27.1	3.3	2.9	−12.1

Empty shopping carts outside a Denver (Colo.) supermarket testify to the effectiveness of a housewives' boycott for lower food prices.

U.S. and World Inflation 1965-1966

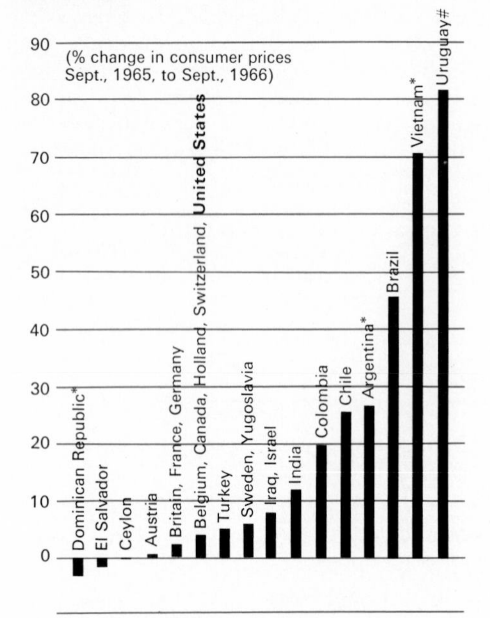

* to August; # to July
Source: The International Monetary Fund

The sharp decline in new home buying, the lagging purchase of new cars, and the slowing growth of installment debt–all pointed to some consumer uneasiness or doubts. Such pessimism was confirmed in a University of Michigan Research Center consumer survey around September 1. It found that an "increasing minority" believed a recession was coming in the months ahead.

Another survey, reported by the National Industrial Conference Board late in the year, noted that U.S. consumers had substantially less *discretionary income* than they had in the fourth quarter of 1965. Discretionary income consists of what is left for spending and saving after paying for basic necessities and fixed obligations. It dropped from $220,-800,000,000 on an annual basis in the final quarter of 1965 to $218,000,000,000 in 1966's second quarter. This occurred despite a rise in gross income.

Boom for Labor. The virtually steady drop in unemployment aided the labor force as a whole by putting more money in more workers' pockets. The overall jobless rate held at 4 per cent or less all through the year, compared with a 4.6 per cent average for 1965. Unemployment among married men dropped to 1.9 per cent in October. The continued shortage of skilled and experienced workers was evidenced by the record volume of unfilled jobs.

Further reductions in unemployment seemed possible only at the expense of increasing inflationary pressures. With U.S. factories working at 91.2 per cent of capacity and the rate of long-term unemployment down to 0.6 per cent of the working force, there seemed little possibility of further expansion of production without pushing costs higher and thus generating tremendous upward pressures on prices. See MANUFACTURING.

In a major change of policy, CEA chief Ackley on October 26 declared that retraining and education –not government action to expand the economy– were the only sound ways to reduce unemployment significantly below the 4 per cent level. This same fullness of employment would put a ceiling of 4 per cent on the economy's growth rate until 1970, according to a mid-December study by the Department of Labor. It said any growth would have to depend on the new entries into the labor force. This projected 4 per cent growth rate was sharply under the 5.5 per cent of 1964, 1965, and 1966 and well below other estimates for the immediate years ahead. If the 4 per cent rate should prove correct, federal revenues–and Great Society programs–might suffer severely.

The Government Sector of the economy grew to about 21 per cent of total GNP in 1966, from about 20 per cent in 1965. Total government purchases of goods and services reached a record high of more than $153,000,000,000. In a reversal of 1965, the federal government spent slightly more than the state and local governments combined. National defense accounted for three quarters of federal expenditures.

Gross National Product By Sectors of the Economy

Sector	Calendar Years			3d Quarter Annual Rate		
	1961	1965	Change	1965	1966	Change
	($ billions)		%	($ billlions)		%
Consumer	335.2	431.5	28.7	435.0	469.9	8.0
Durables	44.2	66.1	49.5	66.7	70.2	5.2
Nondurables	155.9	190.6	22.3	191.4	208.1	8.7
Services	135.1	174.8	29.4	176.9	191.5	8.3
Business	71.7	106.6	48.7	106.7	115.0	7.8
Fixed						
Investments	69.7	97.5	39.9	98.0	105.1	7.2
Housing	22.6	27.8	23.0	27.8	24.8	–10.8
Other bldg.	18.4	24.9	35.3	24.4	27.7	13.5
Equipment	28.6	44.8	56.6	45.8	52.6	14.8
Inventory						
change	2.0	9.1	*	8.7	9.9	*
Net Exports	5.6	7.0	2.5	7.1	4.2	–40.8
Government	107.6	136.2	26.6	137.7	155.5	12.9
Federal	57.4	66.8	16.4	67.5	78.3	16.0
State, local	50.2	69.4	38.2	70.2	77.2	10.0
TOTAL	520.1	681.2	31.0	686.5	744.6	8.5
Total in 1958						
prices	497.3	614.4	23.5	618.2	649.3	5.0

*Not applicable
Source: U.S. Department of Commerce.

These greatly increased outlays were largely offset by tax revenues, which also climbed in step with the economy. On a cash budget basis, the federal deficit was expected to be somewhat smaller than the $4,544,000,000 deficit of 1965. On a *national income and product accounts* basis, federal receipts topped expenditures by $300,000,000 annually by the end of September. This accounting basis includes only the federal revenues and outlays that affect current output or income earned in production.

The Business Sector, straining to meet the expanding needs of government and consumer, showed signs of slowing down toward the end of the year. In November, the Federal Reserve index of industrial production declined three-tenths of a point to 158.3 of its 1957-1959 base of 100. Except for a hestitation in September, the index had climbed steadily from 149 at the end of 1965.

The corporate profit rate faltered for the first time since 1964. In the third quarter, the adjusted annual level of profits dipped to $48,300,000,000 from the record $48,700,000,000 rate for the first and second quarters of 1966. Other business indicators that were slipping or flattening out late in the year included retail sales, wholesale prices, and bank loans to business.

Business spending for capital improvements rose impressively throughout the year. The estimated total for 1966 was $60,560,000,000, up 17 per cent from $51,960,000,000 in 1965. But for 1967, the gain was expected to be only 5 per cent, according to a survey late in 1966 by McGraw-Hill, Inc., economists. It would be the slimmest gain since 1963. The major reason cited for the more modest 1967 expansion plans was the suspension of the 7 per cent investment credit and of accelerated depreciation allowances.

Total spending by the business sector reached an annual rate of $115,000,000,000, or 15.7 per cent of GNP, in the third quarter of 1966, up $8,300,000,000 from the rate 12 months earlier. But the annual rate at midyear had reached a record high of $118,500,000,000–another example of slippage in the latter part of the year.

The Net Export Sector lost ground in 1966. The U.S. favorable balance of trade in goods and services shrank from a final 1965 figure of $6,957,000,000 to an estimated $4,000,000,000 for 1966. An accelerating increase in imports contributed the most to the narrowing margin.

The U.S. position in its overall balance of payments, on the other hand, showed some further improvement. The 1965 debit of $1,337,000,000 had been less than half of 1964's unfavorable balance. At the end of the 1966 third quarter, the indicated annual figure was $868,000,000. The voluntary restraints on the outflow of U.S. capital, plus high U.S. interest rates, apparently were taking effect. See Banks and Banking; International Trade and Finance.

As 1966 drew to a close, uncertainty remained high. Many economic indicators had turned down, most having hit their highs during 1966. No one expected a significant recession, and some estimates of GNP for 1967 ran as high as $790,000,000,000. The consensus seemed to be that some of the "heat" had been taken out of the economy. Interest rates were easing and mortgage money becoming at least possible as 1966 ended.

It was fair to say that 1966 represented another extremely good year for the economy, and that the problems encountered in maintaining a low level of unemployment, together with stable prices, were not unexpected. Warren W. Shearer

See also Section One, Sylvia Porter: Focus on The Economy; and articles on the various countries.

ECUADOR. See Latin America.

The Pulse of Business

	Bottom of the 1961 Recession (Feb., 1961, or 1st quarter)	1965 (October or 3rd quarter)	1966 (October or 3rd quarter)
Total output (GNP, billion, annual rate)	$503.6	$686.5	$744.6
Outputs of industry (1957=100)	102.1	145.5	158.6
Autos, other hard goods	94.3	150.8	168.9
Clothing, other soft goods	110.8	142.3	151.4
Unemployment (per cent of civilian labor force)	6.8	4.3	3.9
Farm net income (billions, annual rate)	$ 12.8	$ 14.2	$ 16.0*
Retail trade (billions, monthly)	$ 17.8	$ 24.2	$ 25.6
New construction (billions, annual rate)	$ 54.6	$ 72.7	$ 71.8
Housing starts, private (millions, annual rate)	1.2	1.4	0.8
Business inventories (billions)	$ 93.4	$118.4	$132.2
Factories' new orders (billions, monthly)	$ 29.1	$ 41.8	$ 45.1
Unfilled orders, hard goods (billions, end of month)	$ 42.8	$ 60.7	$ 76.2
Factory workweek (avg. hrs.)	39.3	41.3	41.4
Corporation profits (billions, annual rate)			
Before taxes	$ 45.0	$ 75.0	$ 81.9
After taxes	$ 24.0	$ 44.1	$ 48.2
Spending for plant and equipment (billions, annual rate, December)	$ 33.8	$ 55.35	$ 62.60
Exports of goods (billions, monthly)	$ 1.7	$ 2.4	$ 2.7
Imports of goods (billions, monthly)	$ 1.1	$ 1.8	$ 2.3

*Preliminary

EDUCATION in the United States was marked in 1966 by another round of increases in federal support of local schools and of higher education, and, at the same time, by heated controversy over the government's role in bringing about school desegregation in the South.

Official estimates indicated that about $45,100,000,000, or 6.7 per cent of the gross national product, was spent in 1965-1966 for the operation of all schools, including public and private institutions of higher learning. This total was expected to rise to $48,800,000,000 in 1966-1967. The federal part of this enormous expenditure amounted to $6,100,000,000 in fiscal 1966, thus helping greatly to stimulate what is perhaps the most significant trend in American education: the extension of years of schooling downward to the preschool level and upward to graduate and postdoctoral study.

Legislation. The Congress of the United States went considerably beyond President Lyndon B. Johnson's recommendations for educational spending in 1966. In the face of White House efforts to keep domestic budgets down, both in response to inflationary trends and to the needs of the war in Vietnam, Congress authorized $700,000,000 more for education than the President had asked.

In its renewal of the Elementary and Secondary School Improvement Act, Congress allotted $6,100,000,000 to the nation's schools over a two-year period. In addition, the Higher Education Facilities Act was carried forward with an authorization of $3,600,000,000 for three years. And the student loan provision of the National Defense Education Act was allowed $190,000,000 for 1967 and $225,000,000 for the following year. But the Congress served notice that it intends to have a careful look at the loan picture after 1968 to determine whether a substantial part of the total might be taken over by private moneylending institutions.

Teacher Corps Loss. The only legislation that fared badly during the year was the National Teacher Corps. The measure was proposed by President Johnson in 1965 as a means of coming to the aid of urban slum schools and needy rural school districts. But it was opposed by many congressional observers as a potential source of excessive federal control, even though the bill specifically gave local school authorities full command over the Corps teachers and met the demands that they be paid at the local rate. The original proposal to put some 4,000 teachers in the field in 1966 was reduced through budget cuts to only 1,200. An initial appropriation of $9,500,000 for selection, training, and administration was supplemented by only $7,500,000–barely enough to see the first contingent through the 1966-1967 school year.

International Education Act. On the other hand, Congress passed the International Education Act of 1966 which provided funds and authorized plans to improve the teaching of international affairs in schools and colleges. Although not provided by the bill itself, President Johnson announced that he would create by executive order a special center for international education within the Department of Health, Education, and Welfare. This center would take on many of the functions of educational and cultural exchanges that are now largely in the hands of the U.S. Department of State and therefore subject to frequent charges abroad that American scholars on foreign soil are merely an extension of American foreign policies.

Civil Rights Controversy. Heated debate arose from the fact that the U.S. Education Commissioner must, under Title VI of the Civil Rights Act of 1964, enforce the act's guidelines regarding the desegregation of schools. The law specifies that no federal funds may be given to schools which remain segregated by law. Although the Supreme Court of the United States had ruled against school segregation in 1954, only 2.5 per cent of the 2,943,102 Negro children in the former Confederate states were attending school with white youngsters. It was only after the guidelines went into effect that this total rose to 6 per cent, and it was expected to rise above 10 per cent by the end of 1966.

Some Southern Congressmen, however, complained that the commissioner's field representatives were acting too harshly, and Commissioner Harold Howe II had to bear the brunt of Southern displeasure during two days of stormy hearings before the House Rules Committee. Nevertheless, efforts to deprive him of the right to defer funds without prior hearings failed. Instead, an amendment to the education legislation was passed that limited to 90 days the period during which the commissioner may defer funds before a hearing is held. By November, only 13 districts were barred from receiving federal funds.

Controversy in the North. The integration controversy was not confined to the South, however. Northern communities heard new demands for greater efforts to increase integration in the schools curtailed by *de facto* segregated housing. New patterns emerged in two areas, in Boston, Mass., and in Hartford, Conn. Under a so-called metropolitan plan, Negro children from the slum schools in the cities were assigned, and transported daily by bus, to a number of high-income suburban communities.

In New York City, controversy arose over Intermediate School 201 in East Harlem, a supermodern, windowless air-conditioned structure that was intended by the board of education as a showcase of quality education. But Negro parents organized effective opposition on the grounds that they had been promised an integrated school. They insisted that unless that promise was met they be granted, in place of integration, a substantial measure of control over the school.

Out of the battle emerged the appointment of a high-prestige task force of eminent citizens who would seek to determine how education in urban slum areas might be improved and ways that local parents might be given a greater share in the process. At the same time, new calls went out to the local universities to take a lead in such educational upgrading. New York University (NYU), with the approval of the board of education and aided by federal and foundation funds, "adopted" a school in the tough and predominantly Negro Bedford-Stuyvesant section of Brooklyn.

Along similar lines, the Ford Foundation, in giving Columbia University an unprecedented $35,000,000 grant toward a $200,000,000 fund drive, earmarked $10,000,000 of the grant for special efforts in urban and minority affairs. Columbia, like other urban universities, has long suffered because of the declining neighborhoods bordering it. Ford Foundation president McGeorge Bundy underlined the importance of the grant by calling it a test of what might be done by universities elsewhere (see BUNDY, MCGEORGE).

Enrollments. When the 1966-1967 academic year opened, enrollments in all institutions on all levels reached 56,000,000, an increase of about 2.6 per cent over the previous year. The steepest enrollment increase was in higher education—up 500,000 over the previous year's total of 5,526,000. This was a record rise of 9.1 per cent. In substantial measure, this gain was the result of the mushrooming of two-year junior or community colleges.

A total of 36,600,000 children were enrolled in the elementary grades, from kindergarten through grade eight. This was a gain of 600,000 over the previous year. Enrollment in private schools was 5,400,000, about 100,000 more than the year before. About 4,500,000 of this total was enrolled in Roman Catholic parochial schools.

High schools enrolled 13,300,000 pupils, an increase of 2.3 per cent. Of this total, about 1,300,000 was accounted for by nonpublic schools, of which slightly more than 1,000,000 were Roman Catholic parochial school students.

Teacher Shortage. Despite record increases in college graduating classes in recent years, the nation's schools suffered the worst teacher shortage in a decade. Many states began the year with thousands of teachers below the number needed. Hence appeals went out to retired teachers and to college-educated women to staff the classrooms.

Economic Reward. Job opportunities remained highly favorable for college graduates, with beginning salaries at the bachelor's level ranging from $5,400 for teachers and some government positions to an occasional $8,000. Computer jobs generally brought about $7,800 in annual salaries.

Great gains in faculty salaries were reported by the American Association of University Professors.

Parents picket Harlem's ultramodern Intermediate School 201, which was a focus of racial problems in New York in 1966.

The group noted a 7.3 per cent overall gain above the previous year. In the top-rated colleges and universities, full professors averaged $23,290, but at the lowest institutional level the same faculty rank still averaged only $7,160. Some of the weaker institutions were part of the lower economic standards prevalent in parts of the South. Thus, a Ford Foundation grant of $33,500,000 to colleges and universities in the South assumed special importance.

Extended Schooling. The Educational Policies Commission, an agency of the National Education Association, which earlier had thrown its weight behind the extension of public education through the community college movement, in 1966 emphasized the first rungs of the ladder. It called for universally available preschool and prekindergarten education for children at the age of 4. The commission reported that of the nation's 8,400,000 children between the ages of 4 and 5, about 3,400,000 were enrolled in private or public preschool classes.

Preschool education, largely through the popular Head Start Project, continued to enroll well over 500,000 youngsters in its eight-week summer program. Another 150,000 or more were going to all-year Head Start centers. The program did not escape some criticism, however. A survey, financed with federal funds and carried out by sociologist Max Wolff, indicated that too many of the preschool programs lacked expert and properly prepared teachers. It also reported that even if preschool programs were well planned and staffed, the benefits would be quickly wiped out unless similar understanding instruction followed the deprived youngsters through the early grades in school.

At the other end of the educational spectrum, graduate school attendance was reported to have increased by 10 per cent over the previous year. Some observers attributed the increase to a student desire to avoid the military draft. This theory lost support, however, because the trend was almost as strong in the women's colleges.

College Reform. The undergraduate rebellion against college administration appeared to have lost some of its steam. Some of the earlier undergraduate militancy seemed to have been translated, however, into reform action in some colleges. In an increasing number of institutions, students were given the option of taking some courses in which they would not be marked in letter or percentage grades, but rather on a pass-fail basis. This thus reduced the extreme competitive pressures found in higher education today. FRED M. HECHINGER

See also Section One, LAWRENCE A. CREMIN: FOCUS ON EDUCATION.

EDUCATIONAL FOUNDATIONS. See FOUNDATIONS.

EGYPT. See UNITED ARAB REPUBLIC (UAR).

EIRE. See IRELAND.

EISENHOWER, DWIGHT D. (1890-), celebrated his 50th wedding anniversary (July 1) and his 76th birthday (October 14) in 1966. In his position as an elder statesman, General Eisenhower approved the administration's foreign policy and gave vocal support to President Lyndon B. Johnson's conduct of the war in Vietnam.

In January, Eisenhower praised the President's decision to resume air attacks on North Vietnam; to have acted otherwise, he declared, would be to offer "sanctuary to those responsible for sending guerrilla forces and supplies to South Vietnam."

In a magazine article published in March, the former President criticized pacifists who burned their draft cards to protest the Vietnamese war. Again, in October, he declared that the United States should "use as much force as we need to win" in Vietnam.

In May, in a letter to the House Foreign Affairs Subcommittee on Europe, Eisenhower recommended "drastic amendment" of the 1951 Atomic Energy Act to give the United States more flexibility in nuclear matters.

In November, 1966, Eisenhower visited President Johnson. The two announced that the former President may make an official good-will tour later.

Surgeons at Walter Reed Hospital removed General Eisenhower's gall bladder on Dec. 12, 1966, without complications. CAROL L. THOMPSON

ELECTIONS

Elections held Nov. 8, 1966, restored the Republican party as a major force in U.S. politics. The Republicans made net gains of 47 seats in the House of Representatives, three seats in the Senate, and eight governorships.

Nearly 56,000,000 votes were cast, a record high for a midterm election. It was a turnout of 48 per cent of the 116,400,000 Americans eligible to vote. When the ballots were counted, the Republicans were jubilant and the Democrats dismayed. In the past half century, the party in power has lost an average of 38 seats in the House in off-year elections. Since 1932, the average has been 33. The Republican gain represented an impressive comeback from the 1964 disaster under former Senator Barry M. Goldwater. They lost 38 seats in the House then.

Two Parties Again. While the Republicans failed to capture control of Congress, their party was re-established as an effective opposition. President Lyndon B. Johnson at a postelection news conference said the Democratic losses "somewhat exceeded" his expectations and would make the passage of any new legislation "more difficult."

The elections invigorated the two-party system on a national scale, gave the Republicans some promising presidential hopefuls, and improved their chances in the 1968 election. Republicans now occupy the governor's chair in 25 states, five of which – California, New York, Pennsylvania, Ohio, and Michigan – control 159 electoral votes, or more than half of the 270 needed to elect a President.

The Republicans cut into the Democratic vote in the cities, in the rural Midwest, in the West, and in the South. They elected governors in Florida and Arkansas and a U.S. senator in Tennessee for the first time since Reconstruction. They also increased their Southern congressional representation from 19 in the old Congress to 28 in the new.

Major Results. At stake in the midterm elections were all 435 seats in the House of Representatives and 35 of the 100 seats in the Senate. In the House, the Democrats won 248 seats and the Republicans 187. The previous ratio had been 295 to 140, respectively. The Democrats' share of the total House vote fell to 52 per cent from 54 per cent in 1964.

In the Senate, the Democrats won 17 seats and the Republicans 18, reducing the Democratic 67-to-33 majority to 64 to 36. Only one incumbent senator was defeated, Paul H. Douglas (D., Ill.). He lost his fourth-term bid to Charles H. Percy, 47-year-old millionaire industrialist. Other new Republican Senators are Governor Mark Hatfield of Oregon; Howard H. Baker, Jr., of Tennessee; Edward W. Brooke, attorney general of Massachusetts,

Republicans won top jobs in three states in November. Ronald Reagan, *upper left,* became California's governor; Charles H. Percy, *upper right,* won Illinois Senate seat; George W. Romney and Robert P. Griffin *(glasses)* became Michigan's governor and senator respectively.

the first Negro senator since Reconstruction; and Clifford P. Hansen, governor of Wyoming. William B. Spong, Jr., of Virginia and Ernest F. Hollings of South Carolina were the only new Democratic Senators elected. See CONGRESS OF THE UNITED STATES.

In the 35 gubernatorial races, 12 states switched party control. The Republicans won 10 and the Democrats two. Republicans elected 23 governors, the Democrats 11, and one contest, in Georgia, was undecided. Neither of the two leading contestants there, Democrat Lester G. Maddox and Republican Howard H. Callaway – both segregationists – scored the required 50 per cent of the vote. The dispute went to the Supreme Court of the United States. It upheld Georgia's provision to throw the election into the legislature, which on Jan. 10, 1967, put Maddox into office by a 182-to-66 vote.

The gubernatorial race that drew probably the most national attention was in California. There, Ronald Reagan, a former film and television star, swamped two-term Democratic Governor Edmund G. "Pat" Brown with a plurality of nearly 850,000 votes. See GOVERNORS OF THE STATES.

Referendums resulted in a number of unexpected outcomes. New York City voters, by a 2-to-1 margin, scuttled that city's police civilian review board. In Dearborn (Mich.) vote on the war in Vietnam, the hawks prevailed, 3 to 2, over the doves. Colorado voters refused to abolish the death penalty. And, generally, the voters said "no" to plans for reforming state and local governments.

Negro Voters strayed slightly from the Democratic column. Governors George W. Romney and Nelson A. Rockefeller each captured 34 per cent of the Negro vote. Nationwide, Negro support of Democratic candidates fell 8 per cent from 1964.

In the South, newly won voting rights put some Negroes into office. Alabama elected its first Negro sheriff since Reconstruction, when Lucius D. Amerson defeated his two white opponents in Macon County. Three Negroes were elected to school boards in Louisiana.

Campaign Issues were not clear-cut in the 1966 midterm elections. The Republicans capitalized on voter discontent with the Johnson administration, particularly with the war in Vietnam and high prices. One Democratic congressional leader commented acidly: "This has been an anti-Lyndon Johnson election. Even the survivors are laying the disaster right in his lap."

Voter resentment over race riots and assorted civil rights problems – the "white backlash" – was not as large a factor as many expected it to be. In California, Illinois, and parts of the South, however, it may have helped the Republicans in some contests. In Maryland and Arkansas, on the other

The Grand Old Party Rocks the Great Society in 1966

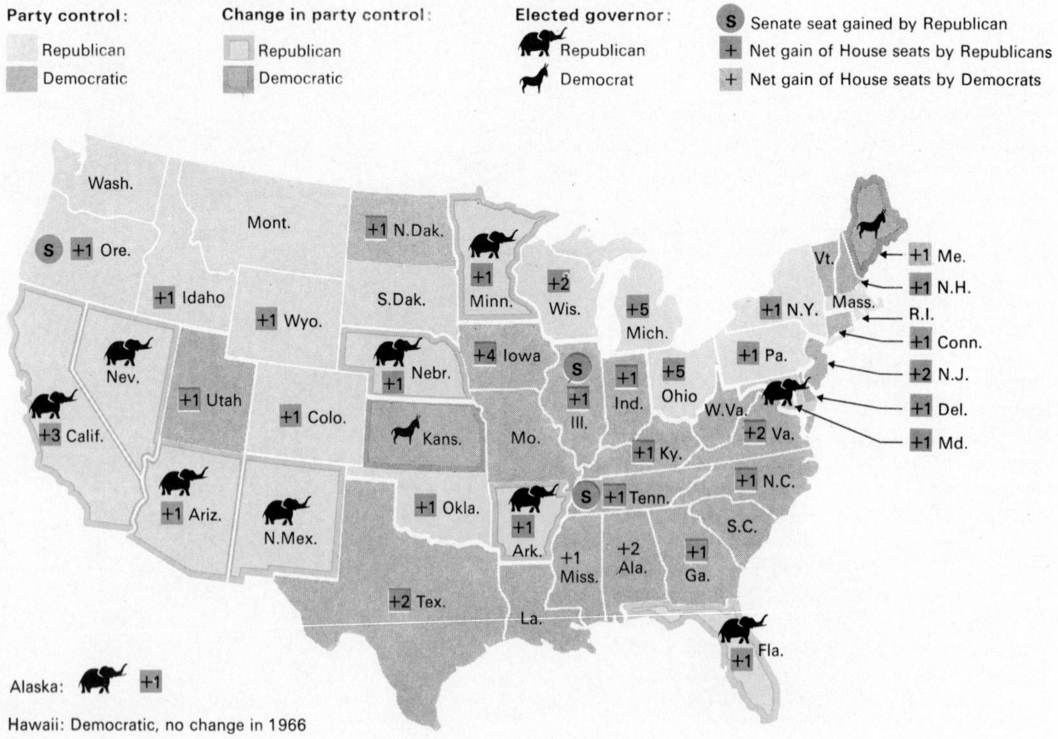

Party control: Republican; Democratic
Change in party control: Republican; Democratic
Elected governor: Republican; Democrat
S Senate seat gained by Republican
+ Net gain of House seats by Republicans
+ Net gain of House seats by Democrats

Alaska: Republican governor elected, +1

Hawaii: Democratic, no change in 1966

A New Voice In the Senate

Edward W. Brooke, 47, the new Republican Senator from Massachusetts, became the first Negro to sit in the U.S. Senate since Reconstruction. Winding up his second term as attorney general of Massachusetts, he defeated former Governor Endicott Peabody, 46, on Nov. 8, 1966, by a margin of more than 400,000 votes. The seat had been vacated by 74-year-old Republican Senator Leverett Saltonstall.

Brooke also was the first Negro to be popularly elected and the first ever to be sent to the Senate from the North. Two other Negroes, Hiram R. Revels (1870-1871) and Blanche K. Bruce (1874-1881), were Republicans from Mississippi. In those days, senators were elected by state legislatures, not by popular vote.

Brooke can best be described as a Negro in politics, not a Negro politician. He is a realist. His Massachusetts constituency is only about 2 per cent Negro. He points out that since Negroes make up only 10 per cent to 12 per cent of the U.S. population, it will be the white majority that will decide on civil rights progress.

Edward W. Brooke thanks Massachusetts voters on his election to Senate.

In his personal life, he has escaped being scarred by racial bigotry. Although he knows the "dreadful discrimination" that many of his race have suffered, he says that "honestly I cannot claim that this has had any shattering effect on me."

He recalls that his early years were spent in a "segregated cocoon," while he was growing up in Washington, D.C., where he was born on Oct. 26, 1919. His was a middle class background. His late father, Edward, was a Veterans Administration lawyer. His mother used to take him to New York City to attend the opera and concerts; the color bar prevented their attending musical events in the nation's capital.

He earned his B.Sc. degree at Howard University in 1941 and went off to war. He entered the army as a private and emerged as a captain. He distinguished himself by working behind enemy lines with the partisans in Italy. It was there that he met a Genoese girl, Remigia Ferrari Scacco, whom he married after the war, on June 7, 1947.

During his army service, a group of young Negroes from Boston influenced Brooke to settle in their city after the war and study law. He entered Boston University Law School in 1946, became editor of its *Law Review*, and received a Master of Laws degree in 1950. Then Brooke settled down to private law practice in Boston.

Brooke was catapulted into public prominence in 1961, when Governor John A. Volpe named him to head the watchdog Boston Finance Agency. After its exposure of several civic scandals, Brooke was a sure winner for the attorney general post. He won it in 1962 with a plurality of 259,355 votes—the only Republican to win a state-wide office that year.

Two years later, Brooke won reelection with a plurality of nearly 800,000 votes. It was the largest plurality registered by any Republican in the history of Massachusetts. It was the same election in which the state's voters gave Lyndon B. Johnson a landslide victory. And by 1964—if not before—the voters were fully aware of the light-skinned Brooke's Negro ancestry.

In his 1966 Senate campaign, Brooke for the first time became concerned over the threat of "white backlash." He has never been a militant on civil rights. He, his wife, and two teen-age daughters, Remi and Edwina, live quietly in Newton Centre, an upper middle-class, predominantly white, Boston suburb.

In an election eve telecast, in a subtle allusion to his race, he quipped, "Well, Mother, I guess you never thought you'd see your son running for the U.S. Senate." His mother and the rest of his family were on the program with him.

In the Senate, his will be a voice of moderation. One of his ambitions is to reverse the extreme "Black Power" militancy that has crept into the civil rights movement. Another is to make sure the Republicans name a presidential candidate in 1968 who will appeal to the nation's minority groups. And, as for himself, he does not hide his ambition to become his party's vice-presidential candidate one day.

WILLIAM McGAFFIN

hand, Democrats who attempted to exploit it were defeated by moderate Republicans.

The Republicans attracted voters by fielding a large number of new and attractive candidates. While somewhat more conservative than the President and his administration, many if not most of those who won seemed to have rejected the ultra-conservative Goldwater ideology.

Winning Women. All 11 incumbent woman representatives won their races for the House. There was one new member, Mrs. Margaret M. Heckler, a Republican from Massachusetts. She defeated Republican Joseph W. Martin, Jr., in the Republican primary and ended his 42-year congressional career. Altogether, 26 women ran for the House and two for the Senate. The lone victor in the Senate, Republican Margaret Chase Smith of Maine, won re-election to a fourth term. She is the only woman in the new Senate.

In Alabama, Mrs. Lurleen Wallace, a Democrat, won a campaign to succeed her husband George C. Wallace, as governor. He was barred by state law from the race. Mrs. Wallace will be the third woman governor in U.S. history. Her husband was expected to keep on running the state by serving as her dollar-a-year "assistant." WILLIAM MCGAFFIN

See also DEMOCRATIC PARTY; PRESIDENT OF THE UNITED STATES; REPUBLICAN PARTY; STATE GOVERNMENT.

ELECTRIC POWER AND EQUIPMENT. In 1966, the major deciding factors in ordering electric power generating equipment centered around two economic facts: (1) the importance of bigness, through the efficiency to be obtained by adopting larger unit size, and (2) the first real economic competitiveness of nuclear power for units of 400,000,000 watts, or 400 megawatts (mw), and larger. For nuclear units below this size, reactor fuel costs may fail to match those of fossil fuels (coal, oil, and gas). See ATOMIC ENERGY.

The economies of bigness came from two factors. One, common to all industry, was the marked reduction in operating costs with increased unit size. The other was the development of widespread utility system interconnections, which allow swaps of power between systems during emergencies or periods of peak demand. Utilities in Western states stood ready to link their transmission lines to power systems across the United States. The intertie, planned for early 1967, would synchronize 94 per cent of the nation's generating capacity.

The Unit Size of turbine-generators has been increasing dramatically. More than half the electric generating capacity on order in 1966 was for units of 500 mw or more. Large thermal generating units earn their keep while delivering close to a full load for almost 24 hours a day. Thus, they are called base load units. But their low overall operating costs rise startlingly when forced to match fluctuating load requirements. Peaking loads, during daytime and early evening, may be taken by gas turbine, diesel, or small fossil-fueled units or pumped storage hydro. With the increased size of generating units and with the U.S. electrical load about doubling every 10 years, the problem of meeting "peak load" demands will become more urgent.

Blackout: One Year Later. Since that memorable Tuesday evening of Nov. 9, 1965, when the lights went out over an 80,000 square-mile area of the Northeast, the electric utilities have worked to reduce the chances of a repeat occurrence. To date, nearly all changes have been voluntary. The Federal Power Commission was expected to issue a final report with its recommendations by early 1967.

The utilities, more deeply concerned with the integrity of their systems than anyone else, took action in 1966 to meet future emergencies. They looked at their arrangements with utility neighbors as well as at their own systems.

Consolidated Edison Company in New York City placed 24 diesel engine generator sets at various stations for safe shutdown, plus auxiliary power and light for rapid restoration of service. It had two 15,000-kw gas turbine sets on order. Many companies that escaped the blackout also added or improved equipment. Public Service Electric and Gas Company of New Jersey, for instance, installed additional units totaling 360 mw at six more stations –all were to be in service by the end of 1967.

The Power Industry as a whole put in another profitable year. Its record for the fiscal year ended June 30 follows:

	1965	1966	% Gain
	(in millions)		
Total production (kwh)	1,116,826	1,200,479	7.5
Utilities' output (kwh)	1,016,031	1,096,999	8.0
Utilities' revenues	$13,026	$13,808	6.0
Utilities' net income	$ 2,499	$ 2,648	6.0

Electric apparatus manufacturers did well–shipments up 17 per cent, prices 2 per cent, and output 20 per cent from 1965. The industry's two leaders, General Electric Company (GE) and Westinghouse Electric Corporation, however, were beset by strikes late in the year. Wage-increase settlements costing about 5 per cent a year were well above the 3.2 per cent U.S. guidelines (see LABOR).

In June, GE was awarded a contract to furnish the electric generators and nuclear reactors for the world's largest nuclear-powered plant. GE will receive about half of the total $247,000,000 contract for the Tennessee Valley Authority (TVA) plant at Browns Ferry, Ala. The two units, with a total capacity of about 2,200 mw, were to begin operating in 1970 and 1971. The TVA expects savings of $100,000,000 over a 12-year period from using nuclear-reactor instead of coal-fired steam generators. The costs of the nuclear fuel are guaranteed through 1982. JAMES J. O'CONNOR

Integrated circuit chip, so small it can pass through eye of needle, contains two logic circuits with 15 transistors, 13 resistors.

ELECTRONICS. Tiny devices called integrated circuits (ICs) were successfully used in microwave equipment–a new area for IC technology. The components of ICs are built as inseparable parts of one solid chip. Though they have been widely used for lower frequency applications, such as satellite communications, computers, home radio receivers, television, and desk-top calculators, the technical advances needed to adapt ICs to microwave equipment such as radar and radio relay stations were achieved only after 1964. (Microwaves are that portion of the electromagnetic spectrum ranging from as low as 230,000,000 cycles a second up to 300,000,000,000 cycles a second.) Radio Corporation of America (RCA) announced a two-pound, hand-held radar system for military applications, made possible by ICs and Texas Instruments, Inc., of Dallas, was developing an IC radar system for jet aircraft. In addition to compactness, ICs offer greater reliability and require no maintenance.

New uses for microwaves in fields other than communications were also reported. Heat-generating microwaves were used in drying paper, removing solvents from magnetic tapes during production, and controlling milk pasteurization.

Miniaturization. Physicists at Raytheon Company of South Norwalk, Conn., teamed up with doctors on the staff of Tufts University School of Dental Medicine in Boston, Mass., to design a radio transmitter that can be inserted in the gap left by a lost tooth. The transmitter, which will be used to aid dental research, beams information on chewing, swallowing, and biting to external receivers.

A new transistor the size of a pinhead was developed by engineers at Westinghouse Electric Corporation, of Pittsburgh, Pa. The device, called a "resonant gate transistor," greatly extends the range of working frequencies for transistors, and has immediate application in devices ranging from spacecraft telemetry systems to touch-tone telephones. A key part of the device is a vibrating gold whisker one-tenth the diameter of a human hair.

Lasers. New uses demonstrated for lasers included "bloodless surgery" with a laser "knife" developed at Bell Telephone Laboratories. The beam from the experimental laser cut through flesh during a tumor removal operation. It left a clean incision and cauterized the wound, thus stemming blood flow.

Perkin-Elmer Corporation of Norwalk, Conn., demonstrated a laser television system capable of scanning a subject in complete darkness and then producing an image on a screen as sharp as any taken in daylight brightness.

Two methods for rapidly changing the direction of laser beams in a laser television system were reported during the year. Zenith Radio Corporation employed ultrasonic waves to move a laser beam back and forth. The system, which eliminates the need for a picture tube and many other electronic components now built into TV sets, was demonstrated in Chicago in October. It produces TV pictures on a screen with a beam which scans across the screen 15,750 times a second. The beam is moved up and down by mechanical means. International Business Machines Corporation (IBM) announced a "scanlaser" capable of aiming a laser beam in any one of roughly 14,500 directions represented by a grid of about 120 x 120 units.

D.C. Transformer. A transformer which operates on direct current, long thought to be technically impossible, was built and demonstrated by Ivar Giaever of the General Electric Company. The device uses glass slides on which extremely thin films of tin have been deposited. These form both the primary and secondary cells of the transformer. When the device is cooled to about 38° F., the metal films become superconducting and a direct current passed through the tin primary gives rise to a voltage in the secondary. By placing a number of secondary films in series, Giaever was able to develop a secondary voltage many times higher than the primary voltage.

JAMES A. PEARRE

ELIZABETH II, QUEEN. See GREAT BRITAIN.

EL SALVADOR. See LATIN AMERICA.

EMPLOYMENT. See ECONOMY, THE; EDUCATION; LABOR; SOCIAL SECURITY; SOCIAL WELFARE; Section One, SYLVIA PORTER: FOCUS ON THE ECONOMY.

ENGINE AND ENERGY. Scientists at the Intersociety Energy Conversion Conference, held in Los Angeles in September, reported that solar cells would continue to be the main energy sources for long-lived satellites. They based their prediction on continued progress in the field. In one development, engineers at Westinghouse Electric Corporation designed solar cells with a built-in electrical field to increase resistance to radiation which reduces power output.

Batteries. The search for high energy density battery systems has led to the use of highly active metals and unconventional compounds for anodes, cathodes, and electrolytes. Among anode materials being used were lithium, liquid sulfur, and zinc. Cathodes of liquid sodium, nickel halides, cupric chloride, and porous nickel were also reported. Electrolytes included conducting ceramics, aqueous potassium hydroxide, and organic compounds.

Ford Motor Company engineers predicted that a fully engineered prototype of the battery they are developing will have an actual energy density of up to 150 watt-hours per pound. A typical lead-acid battery now used in automobile electrical systems produces only from 7 to 12 watt-hours per pound.

The demand for high energy density batteries was stimulated by military requirements and by the predicted return of electric automobiles. George A. Hoffman of the Institute of Government and Public Affairs at the University of California at Los Angeles cited rapid advances in electric motor design, reduction in weight of batteries and regenerative fuel cells, and increases in air pollution as reasons for the renewed interest in electric automobiles. See AUTOMOBILE.

A 2½-ton electric truck successfully completed three years of road tests. It was developed for the U.S. Army by Lear-Siegler, Inc., of El Segundo, Calif. Each of the six-wheel assemblies was driven by a separate squirrel-cage alternating current motor. Power was supplied by a generator.

Electrogasdynamics. The U.S. Department of the Interior granted $680,500 to Gourdine Systems, Inc., a newly organized New Jersey company, to demonstrate the feasibility of transforming coal directly into cheaply transmittable electricity at the mine by using electrogasdynamic (EGD) generators. Under the guidance of Meredith Gourdine, physicist-president of Gourdine Systems, prototype EGD generators have been built for production of high voltage alternating current and direct current electricity, and for transforming low voltage electricity into high voltage electricity. EGD basically involves injecting ions from a corona discharge electrode into a high speed flow of gas. The moving gas drives the ions along a narrow tube, forming a high voltage electric current. JAMES A. PEARRE

Sodium Sulfur Battery

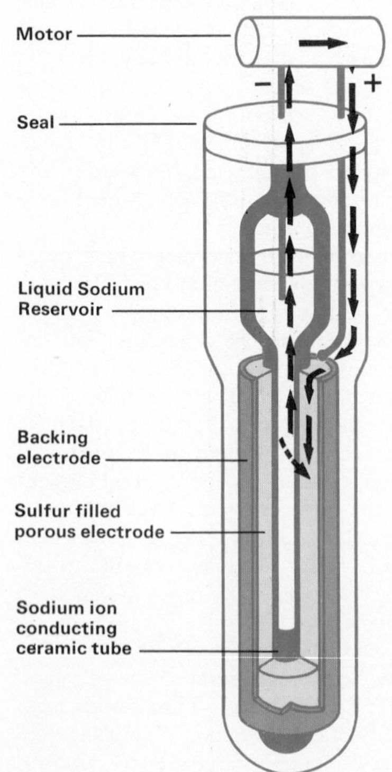

ENGINEERING. The need to develop programs of continuing education for practicing engineers, as a means of keeping them up-to-date on technological developments, dominated the discussion at meetings of professional engineering societies in 1966. One study made by a joint advisory committee of the Engineers' Council for Professional Development showed that industry, government, academic institutions, and engineering societies were all engaged in setting up continuing education programs. The advisory committee reported that most big industries were offering courses for employees, tuition-refund plans, time off for professional meetings, and leaves for full-time study. A number of government agencies also offered their engineers similar incentives to continue their education.

World Engineering. On the international scene there also was interest in continuing education. At the Fifth Education Conference of Engineering Societies of Western Europe and the United States held in Copenhagen, Denmark, in September, 22 professional engineering societies agreed to assume responsibility for encouraging and developing programs of continuing study in their home countries.

The formation of a world-wide federation of engineers was authorized at meetings of engineering societies held in Paris, France, and Mexico City, Mexico, under sponsorship of the United Nations Educational, Scientific, and Cultural Organization

(UNESCO). To be known as the International Conference of Engineering Societies (ICES), the new organization will consist initially of the four existing regional engineering federations, embracing North and South America and Western Europe. The primary purpose of ICES will be to promote international understanding by strengthening professional understanding.

Engineer Shortage. A survey made by the Engineering Manpower Commission of the Engineers' Joint Council showed that the demand for engineers, especially new graduates with bachelor degrees, was substantially greater than in 1965, and that there were fewer young engineers to meet the increased demand. The commission said there were only about 9,000 engineering graduates available in the United States to fill the demands of industry for 14,000 graduates. Electrical engineers received the most job offers.

Starting Salaries were also at an all-time high. The survey compiled by the College Placement Council showed an increase of 4.5 per cent over 1965 in offers to engineer graduates with a bachelor's degree. The survey encompassed 110 colleges and universities. Beginning salaries offered to chemical engineers averaged $677 a month. Aeronautical engineers were next at $670 a month, followed by metallurgical engineers at $662, and electrical engineers at $661. Mary E. Jessup

ESPIONAGE. Fictional spy tales and filmed spoofs became more and more outlandish in 1966, but the practice of real-life espionage ran the authors and the moviewriters a close second.

In November, Federal Bureau of Investigation (FBI) agents arrested U.S. Air Force Staff Sergeant Herbert William Boeckenhaupt, 23, at March Air Force Base, Riverside, Calif. The gaunt, dark-browed airman, who was born in Mannheim, Germany, had come to the United States in 1947. He was a communications radio specialist who tended teletype and cryptographic machines in the air force's command post in the Pentagon's subbasement. Boeckenhaupt was accused by the FBI of conspiring to furnish defense secrets to Aleksei R. Malinin, assistant commercial counselor of the Soviet embassy in Washington, D.C. A few days after the sergeant's arrest, British police picked up Cecil W. Mulvena, a 47-year-old real estate dealer, in London. Mulvena was reported to be Boeckenhaupt's link in Great Britain.

A second Pentagon spy case involved retired U.S. Army Lieutenant Colonel William Henry Whalen, 51, who was accused by the FBI in July of conspiring with two Soviet agents, Major General Sergei A. Edemski and Mikhail A. Shumaev. The Russians also worked in the Soviet embassy, but had since departed. Whalen, who had served with the Joint Chiefs of Staff at the Pentagon, was accused of having received $5,500 from the Russians for data on atomic weapons and the Strategic Air Command. He allegedly passed material to the Russians in meetings at shopping centers.

In a bizarre case unmasking one of its own agents, the U.S. Central Intelligence Agency (CIA) fired Hans V. Tofte, Danish-born espionage expert. The CIA claimed it found secret papers in Tofte's home in the Georgetown section of Washington. Tofte said the CIA had staged an "amateurish raid" on his home and had taken papers he was using to prepare a report suggesting improvements in the CIA.

Elusive Agent. The daring escape of George Blake, Soviet master spy, from England's Wormwood Scrubs prison in October, seemed like an incident out of a James Bond thriller. The 44-year-old Englishman had served only 5½ years of his 42-year term for feeding crucial information to Russia on the British spy apparatus.

Canada saw the belated unfolding in 1966 of the activities of Mrs. Gerda Munsinger, a 36-year-old German woman who was described as having been a "frequent companion" of Associate Defense Minister Pierre Sevigny during 1959. Sevigny admitted a "social relationship" with Mrs. Munsinger, who was a waitress, secretary, model, and according to Royal Canadian Mounted Police, a Communist agent. But he denied that he gave Mrs. Munsinger any state secrets during their affair. Lloyd Norman

ETHIOPIA. Important changes were made by Emperor Haile Selassie I in 1966 to help Ethiopia in its gradual approach to democracy. One was a three-year study, begun in February, to prepare several unnamed provinces within the empire for self-government. Selassie also permitted Premier Akilou Abde Wold to name his own cabinet. Formed in April, it included five new ministries: planning, land reform, public works, information, and tourism.

Clashes continued during the year between Ethiopia and Somalia over the latter's claims to border territory in Ethiopia. Somalia claimed the disputed area was largely inhabited by people of Somali origin. At year's end the problem remained unresolved.

Ethiopia and the U.S. Export-Import Bank issued $1,700,000 in public shares in a new paper mill. The bank also granted $4,300,000 for machinery. Ethiopia received $798,000 for wheat purchases from the Food for Peace program, and $7,200,000 for educational assistance from the Association for International Development.

Ethiopia acted as host to the 15th annual Pugwash Conference for scientists—a "first" for Africa.

Facts in Brief. Population: 22,350,000. Government: Emperor Haile Selassie I; Premier Akilou Abde Wold. Monetary Unit: dollar (2.48 = U.S. $1). Foreign Trade: exports, $101,700,000; imports, $145,700,000. Principal Exports: coffee, hides and skins, oilseeds. William Spencer

EUROPE

There were signs and portents that a new Europe was in the making in 1966. Politically, the continent remained divided into two ideological camps: In Western Europe, the democratic processes continued to flourish; Eastern Europe remained oriented to the Communist policies of the Soviet Union. But in 1966, for the first time since the end of World War II, there was an upswing in trade relations between the two blocs indicating that some light was beginning to pierce the Iron Curtain. See BULGARIA; HUNGARY; ROMANIA; RUSSIA.

In Western Europe, two factors blocked any real progress toward economic integration during the year. One was the uncompromising attitude of President Charles de Gaulle of France, whose fear of supranationalism led him to threaten the future of the North Atlantic Treaty Organization (NATO) and to bog down further development of the European Economic Community (EEC, or Common Market). The other factor was the financial difficulties of Great Britain, which had to seek protection for its pound sterling, a reserve currency among the other nations of Europe. See FRANCE; GREAT BRITAIN.

Trade Blocs. Efforts were made during the year to heal the trade split between Western Europe's two trade blocs: the European Free Trade Association (EFTA) and the EEC. At a conference held in Bergen, Norway, ministers of EFTA pledged their governments "to pursue by all available means" the integration of EFTA into the Common Market.

Before such an integration could take place, however, the Common Market first had to solve some of the problems which threatened its own security. In the opening months of the year, plans had been made to reconstitute the six-member Common Market as a five-power body if talks with France concerning President Charles de Gaulle's uncongenial attitude toward the community ended in failure. A later conference in Luxembourg, however, resulted in a compromise agreement which temporarily eased the crisis. De Gaulle was persuaded to end his seven-month boycott of the market's institutions. In return, however, he laid down terms which, it was felt, might seriously weaken the EEC's decision-making and policy-initiating institutions.

De Gaulle's terms, all directed toward key sectors of the Common Market's supranational system, gave France a continuing right to veto decisions affecting its "important interests." After lengthy debate, a compromise was reached: the Five could by-pass the French veto by putting an important issue to a majority vote if no decision was reached in "a reasonable time."

Agreement Reached. The real stumbling blocks toward progress in the Common Market have been the questions of farm financing and farm prices. On May 11, however, the Council of Ministers adopted financial regulations covering the community's common agricultural program. This agreement, which involved a complicated system of agricultural subsidies, marked a major breakthrough for the EEC, which had been deadlocked on the issue since June

Hubert Le Campion, *Life* © Time Inc.

United States jeeps await removal from France after President Charles de Gaulle ordered NATO forces to leave the country.

30, 1965, when the previous farm finance regulations had expired. The new agreement provided for gradually increasing coverage of the program's costs through levies on individual members.

The other stumbling block – farm prices – was removed on July 24 when the Council of Ministers reached final agreement on common prices for most farm products of the bloc. Under the interlocking agreements, the Six would integrate their 13,000,000 farmers and the whole of their produce in a single agricultural system. Thus, all farm produce of the member countries would flow freely across their borders.

New Members. Meanwhile, Britain indicated that since the agricultural crisis had been resolved, it would make a definite move toward reopening negotiations for entry into the Common Market. At the same time, efforts were made to integrate the EEC and EFTA. At the Council of Europe Assembly in Strasbourg, France, in September, Jens Krag, the Danish prime minister, proposed that Norway, Sweden, and Denmark should break their ties with Britain and the other EFTA countries and join the Common Market. He made a similar statement on his return to Copenhagen. Ministers of other nations, particularly of the Low Countries, were fearful that the opportunity to join the Common Market might be lost if protracted negotiations for Britain's entry continued. They made it quite clear that the entry of other countries into the Common

European nobility poses for official portrait at wedding of Princess Beatrix of The Netherlands to Claus von Amsberg of Germany.

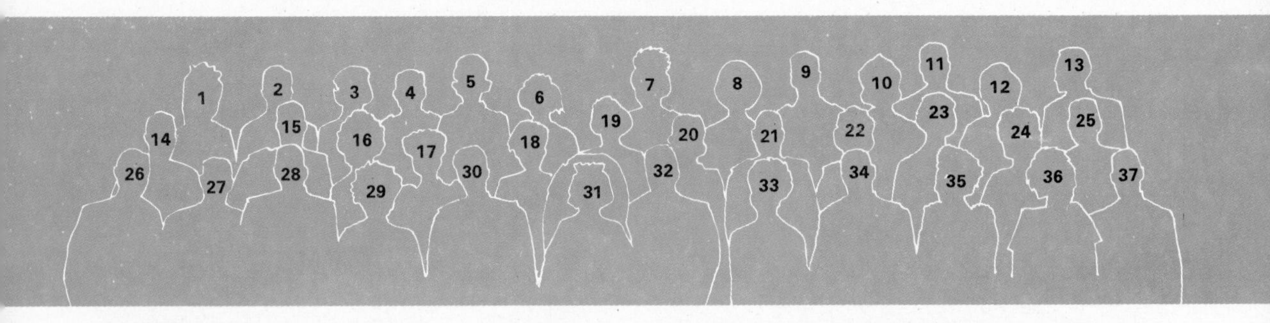

Key to the picture: **(1)** Princess Irene of The Netherlands; **(2)** the Aga Khan; **(3)** Princess Irene of Greece; **(4)** Prince Charles of Luxembourg; **(5)** Princess Benedikte of Denmark; **(6)** Princess Christina of Sweden; **(7)** Fraulein Christine von Amsberg; **(8)** Princess Paola of Liège; **(9)** Prince Albert of Liège; **(10)** Princess Sophie of Greece; **(11)** her husband, Don Juan Carlos of Spain; **(12)** Princess Aschwin of Lippe-Biesterfeld; **(13)** Prince Aschwin of Lippe-Biesterfeld; **(14)** Don Hugo Carlos of Bourbon-Parma; **(15)** Prince Harald of Norway; **(16)** Princess Marina, Duchess of Kent; **(17)** Princess Armgard of Lippe-Biesterfeld, mother of Prince Bernhard; **(18)** Frau von Amsberg, mother of the groom; **(19)** Princess Christina of The Netherlands; **(20)** Grand Duchess Josephine Charlotte of Luxembourg; **(21)** Grand Duke Jean of Luxembourg; **(22)** the Infanta Pilar; **(23)** Princess Margaretha of Sweden (Mrs. John Ambler); **(24)** Princess Margriet of The Netherlands; **(25)** her fiance, Mijnheer Pieter van Vollenhoven; **(26)** Mr. John Ambler; **(27)** the Hon. Angus Ogilvy; **(28)** King Constantine of Greece; **(29)** Queen Juliana; **(30)** King Baudouin of Belgium; **(31)** Princess Beatrix; **(32)** Prince Claus; **(33)** Queen Fabiola of Belgium; **(34)** Prince Bernhard of The Netherlands; **(35)** Queen Anne Marie of Greece; **(36)** Princess Alexandra; **(37)** Prince Michael of Kent.

Market should not be made contingent on the prior entry of Great Britain.

GATT. A big step forward came with the decision of the six Common Market countries to end their year-long deadlock over their joint negotiating position in the Kennedy Round of tariff-cutting talks, within the framework of the General Agreement on Tariffs and Trade (GATT). Once the deadlock had ended, a 50 per cent reduction in tariffs on an important range of products of special importance to Britain and the rest of Europe was made possible. In addition, the way was opened for intensive negotiations on agricultural products. By December, however, no substantial progress had been made in the tariff-cutting talks between GATT and the EEC.

International Economy. The EFTA made another 10 per cent cut in tariffs on manufactured goods traded within the Association at the end of 1965, thus paving the way for the EFTA's 1966-1967 objective of a single, free trade market for manufactured goods produced by almost 100,000,000 people. The British government's decision to lift the temporary extra tariff on imports of manufactured goods, which was made at the end of November, was a move welcomed by EFTA.

Since 1959, trade among EFTA countries had approximately doubled; it had increased by 150 per cent among the four Nordic countries. This broad upward trend in EFTA trade continued throughout 1966. Exports rose by about 10 per cent and imports by 9 per cent. During the 12 months ended in March, intra-EFTA imports reached a monthly average of $612,000,000. Total EFTA exports amounted to $6,831,000,000. EFTA trade with the EEC continued its growth rate of 10 per cent, but EFTA's deficit with the Common Market increased by 5 per cent in the first six months of the year to $190,000,000.

European Defense. Cracks in the Western alliance appeared wider in 1966. De Gaulle's insistence that the days of an "Americanized Europe" were over, led him to withdraw French forces from NATO and to order NATO forces to vacate French soil by April 1, 1967. The NATO defense ministers decided on a new NATO strategic concept based on political and psychological assessments of the international situation, and not on the full war potential of Russia and her allies. At the same time, plans were made for the transfer of Supreme Headquarters, Allied Powers in Europe (SHAPE), from Rocquencourt, near Paris, to Casteau, near Mons, Belgium. See BELGIUM; NORTH ATLANTIC TREATY ORGANIZATION (NATO).

Talks on Troops. In September, U.S. President Lyndon B. Johnson and Chancellor Ludwig Erhard of West Germany met in Washington, D.C. After two days of talks, they agreed to invite Britain to a series of tripartite talks to a review of the Communist threat in Europe, the forces required to meet it, and the problem of financing them. Erhard advised President Johnson that West Germany would be unable to maintain its present contributions toward keeping American forces in Europe once the present agreement expired in 1967. But he assured the President that every effort would be made to meet the current foreign exchange offset arrangement that called for the purchase of $1,350,000,000 worth of military equipment in the two-year period ending June 30, 1967. At year's end, negotiations between Washington and Bonn were being conducted to achieve that end.

West Germany also faced a cut in British forces. Bonn, however, moved only a small way toward bridging the annual foreign exchange costs which were worrying Britain. Its offer of $72,000,000 was increased to $92,000,000, but it still left Britain with $212,000,000 short even after projected economies had been made. Consequently, Britain planned cuts in its military commitments to Germany which would save $30,000,000 a year in foreign currency.

Space Projects. Britain shocked the rest of Europe in June by deciding to abandon the communications satellite program of the European Launcher Development Organization (ELDO). Reaction in Bonn, Paris, and Rome was so strong that the decision was rescinded and a compromise reached. KENNETH BROWN

EXPLORATION. See OCEAN; SPACE EXPLORATION.

EXPLOSION. See DISASTERS.

FAIRS AND EXHIBITIONS. Two Montreal islands, one man-made and the other enlarged by some 200 acres, are to be the site of the Canadian Universal and International Exhibition of 1967. Popularly known as Expo 67, it is the first "first category" world's fair ever to be held in the Western Hemisphere. Other world's fairs in this part of the world had not been approved by the Bureau of International Expositions in Paris, France. Therefore, they were not officially classified and could not obtain representative participation by foreign governments.

Expo 67, integrated around the general theme of "Man and His World," was planned as part of the Canadian Confederation Centennial. Ile Sainte Helene, which was enlarged, and Ile Notre-Dame, wholly man-made, make up most of the 998-acre site of the Montreal fair. The two St. Lawrence River islands are connected to the mainland by motor causeways and an overhead monorail.

Running six months, from April 28 through October 27, Expo 67 will be the central attraction of a vast Canadian effort to earn $1,000,000,000 from foreign visitors during the 1967 Centennial Year. Major exhibits from about 75 countries will include the Soviet Union, the United States, and most European, Latin-American, and Asian countries as well as exhibits of about 50 religious and social and other private institutions. Paid admissions totaling 30,000,000 are anticipated from some 10,000,000 visitors divided as follows: 4,100,000 Canadians; 5,600,000 U.S. citizens; and 350,000 other foreign visitors. Massive promotional efforts were mounted in the United States, Mexico, Europe, and the Far East in 1966.

1966 Fairs and Exhibitions. Though there was no official world's fair in 1966, the enormous variety of trade, industrial, agricultural, and regional fairs in some 50 countries seemed more active and successful than ever.

The U.S. government participated in 19 international fairs and exhibitions that attracted about 2,000,000 visitors in 15 countries. In addition, 48 exhibitions enabled U.S. businesses to test and sell foreign markets in six permanent U.S. trade centers the Department of Commerce maintains in Bangkok, Frankfurt, London, Milan, Stockholm, and Tokyo. The United States was officially represented in major fairs held in El Salvador, France, West Germany, Israel, Japan, Libya, Mexico, Thailand, and Turkey.

Fair Growth. The basic tasks of fairs and exhibitions are to promote understanding of the cultural and scientific achievements of the country, and to stimulate sales of the products and services of both governmental and commercial exhibitors.

In recent years, this activity has expanded greatly throughout the world, partly as a by-product of accelerated foreign travel and investment and trade

since the end of World War II. This has been especially true of the United States, which participates in such activities overseas as part of its broad drive to build up export trade. Accordingly, 1967 promises to be a record year for U.S. participation in international exhibitions.

Thus far, 49 nations have scheduled 650 fairs and exhibitions of all types during 1967. The first official World's Fair in Asia is scheduled for Osaka, Japan, in 1970. Originally, the 1967 World's Fair was to be held in Moscow as part of the Soviet Union's 50th anniversary celebrations, but the Russians dropped their project in favor of Canada's centennial observance. According to international agreement, there can be only one official World's Fair in any given year.

Meanwhile, plans moved ahead in the organizing and promoting of HemisFair, a major international exhibition scheduled to run for 184 days (April 6 to Oct. 6, 1968) in San Antonio, Tex. The fair will feature the changing relationships, progress, and diversity of the nations of the Western Hemisphere. It is expected to attract several million visitors from Latin America as well as Canada and the United States.

Other Benefits. Business was not usually the chief concern of many fairs and exhibitions. Many clearly had an educational, political, or cultural

West Germany's pavilion, *above,* nears completion at Canada's Expo 67. The site of the fair is two islands, *below,* in the St. Lawrence River opposite Montreal. The fair will begin in April, 1967, and will include exhibits from more than 70 nations.

purpose. To these ends, the U.S. Information Agency participated in scores of fairs in which the basic purpose was to promote the understanding of policies, aims, and cultural achievements of the American people.

The postwar expansion of U.S. involvement with the world went hand in hand with the steady growth of world travel to a record-breaking volume of $13,200,000,000 in 1965, and the buoyant surge of Free World trade to an unprecedented total of $174,000,000,000.

Business and pleasure travelers, reaching a global total of 80,000,000, helped generate attendance for the fairs, and the expansion of trade. This, coupled with the diversification of U.S. industry overseas, made the economic stakes in successful trade promotions through fairs and exhibitions higher than ever. See TRAVEL.

For similar reasons other countries increased their participation in fairs, especially Great Britain, Japan, the Soviet Union, and West Germany. While there was no exact inventory of the number of fairs and exhibitions held throughout the world in 1966, official observers generally agreed that more than 500 exhibitions attracted the greatest attendance ever. WILLIAM D. PATTERSON

See also ARCHITECTURE; CANADA; MUSEUMS; PAINTING AND SCULPTURE.

FARM EQUIPMENT. See MANUFACTURING.

FASHION designers revolted against tradition in 1966. The thunder was first heard in England, where a youth rebellion resulted in world-wide recognition and profits for designers and manufacturers of the Mod look in clothes. Although the fashion rebellion began in London in 1965, it became more intense and widespread elsewhere during 1966.

Throughout the world, girls enjoyed the Mod look. The look required abbreviated skirts, or miniskirts, and pale colored fishnet or lacy textured hosiery, cut-out, low-heeled "little girl" shoes, mannish jackets, and ties or French "undershirt" tops. Accessories included over-the-shoulder handbags and gaudy jewelry, which ranged from antique pins and necklaces to modern styled geometric earrings.

Young men also went Mod via low slung, wide belted, skinny, fitted pants, to which they added extra-wide, flashy printed ties that contrasted with the wallpaper floral prints of their shirts. Boots, vests, London caps, and narrow Carnaby jackets were also worn by the young men who took part in the rebellion against traditional men's clothes and conservative ways.

Youth's Uniform. In the United States, the Mod look became one of the clothing industry's biggest promotions. Both young men and women picked up the look. American youth became infatuated with the exotic, offbeat image, using it as a means of differentiating themselves from the adult

Chicago breezes ruffled the hair but not the hemline of a miniskirt wearer as she walked along Michigan Avenue in the summer.

Henry Grossman, *Life* © Time Inc.

The Mod look for men–polka-dotted shirts with contrasting collars and cuffs–spread from London's Carnaby Street to the U.S.

generation. Miniskirts, associated with Mod fashions, were adapted to more conservative styles with the length modified to two inches above the knee.

The new short-short skirt fashion resulted in mixed emotions everywhere. In the United States, some schools found it necessary to regulate permissible skirt lengths. In Iran, the education minister labeled the miniskirt "improper and indecent" and said any girl who insisted on wearing it would be denied admission to educational institutions.

The Cone Shape. The uplifted hemlines were also a part of Paris' haute couture fashions, but these were less radical, yet still very youthful. Paris designers Yves St. Laurent and Cardin not only raised hems to above the knees but also uplifted entire silhouettes of dresses for styles with high cuts, narrow shoulders, and gliding but controlled cone shapes. Revolting against the short skirt trend was designer Marc Bohan of the House of Dior, who lengthened his coats to midcalf, but had his models wear them over shorter skirted dresses.

A look that was a combination of Mod and haute couture was the most popular fashion for women past their teens. Cone shape dresses, often with halter necklines, came with above-the-knee hemlines. Women living active lives chose them not only for their fashion interest but also for their relaxed, mobile silhouettes. The look of glittering silver was a popular, young, and swinging look for evening. The metallic mood was completed with silver shoes and shiny, wet-looking lipstick.

Mannish and Military Styles. Women borrowed suit styles from men. They wore straight-legged pant suits, often of men's fabrics, for day-wear. For evening and at-home, they wore them in more elaborate fabrics and in wide, fluid shapes. Pant suits provided a fashionable means of comfort. They were worn and accepted everywhere.

The military look was also popular. Army pockets, brass buttons, epaulets, and trench coat treatments were featured on coats, suits, and sportswear.

Paper dresses came to the fore in 1966. They were initiated by such offbeat designers as Californian Judy Brewer. Women purchased the paper garments for ease, amusement, and as conversation pieces.

White House Bride. Of importance to the fashion world was the wedding of Luci Baines Johnson, the younger daughter of President and Mrs. Lyndon B. Johnson, to Patrick Nugent, on Aug. 6, 1966. The design of Luci's traditional, high-necked, long-sleeved, lace gown was kept secret until the wedding day. Her attendants wore floor-length dresses of deep pink moire, with long "cage" type veils. The First Lady wore a "Yellow Rose of Texas" coat, dress, and matching turban.

The 1966 Coty Award was shared by California designer Rudi Gernreich and New York designer Geoffrey Beane. ROCHELLE HASSON

FINLAND. In the general elections held in March, the Socialist parties won 103 of the 200 seats in parliament, thus ending years of political domination by the leftist Centre party. A four-party coalition government was formed on May 27 under Rafael Paasio, a Social Democrat (see PAASIO, RAFAEL). For the first time since 1948, the cabinet included four Communists.

The new government faced an imbalance of foreign trade and continuing agitation for price increases for the already heavily subsidized farming industry. The economic boom that had begun in in 1964 showed signs of slackening. A lessening demand for import goods helped the trade balance. In order to keep valuable foreign currency from flowing out of the country, the government also cut automobile imports by one-third.

A feature of the import-export picture during 1966 was a marked increase in demand for agricultural products by countries belonging to the European Economic Community. See EUROPE.

Facts in Brief. Population: 4,690,000. Government: President Urho K. Kekkonen; Premier Rafael Paasio. Monetary Unit: markka (3.20 = U.S. $1). Foreign Trade: exports, $1,427,000,000; imports, $1,646,100,000. Principal Exports: lumber, paper and pulp, boats and ships, agricultural products. KENNETH BROWN

FIRE. See CONSERVATION; DISASTERS; SAFETY.

Airborne scientists off New Jersey coast use infrared device to study effect of sea temperatures on the migration of fish.

FISHERY. The United States extended its exclusive fishing zone to 12 miles off its coasts in legislation enacted in October. The law, however, did not extend U.S. sovereignty beyond the historical three-mile limit. Pacific Northwest salmon fishermen had sought the 12-mile zone to prevent intensive coastal fishing by Russian and Japanese fleets.

Also in October, Congress authorized an $8,800,000, five-year program for developing a fish protein concentrate, including a $1,000,000 plant to produce fish flour. In the meantime, the Food and Drug Administration was holding up its approval on marketing the product for human consumption.

The Inter-American Tropical Tuna Commission acted in April to limit the 1966 catch of yellow-fin tuna in the eastern tropical Pacific Ocean to 79,300 short tons. The restrictions, designed to restore diminishing stocks, went into effect in September.

The 1966 U.S. fish catch declined to a postwar low of about 4,200,000,000 pounds. The 1965 catch of 4,700,000,000 pounds had brought U.S. fishermen a record $451,000,000. The United States remained fifth among the world's fishing nations–behind Peru, Japan, China, and the Soviet Union, in that order. In 1965, for the first time, imports exceeded U.S.-produced fish products. A. L. NEWMAN

FISHING. See HUNTING AND FISHING.

FLOOD. See CONSERVATION; DISASTERS.

FLOWER. See GARDEN AND LAWN.

FOOD. Consumer food prices in the first part of 1966 increased on an average of 5 per cent over those of 1965. Bread prices jumped by three cents a loaf, milk by two or three cents a quart, and a head of lettuce often cost as much as 40 cents. These general price increases were met by widespread buyer resistance. Some chain stores tried to overcome the resistance by lowering prices or by increasing cash contests, premiums, and stamps.

Toward the end of 1966, housewives took the matter of food prices into their own hands and picketed food stores across the country. Grocers responded with temporary price reductions, but officials in Washington, D.C., predicted that food prices would continue to rise into 1967. See ECONOMY, THE (Close-Up).

The World Food Crisis worsened in 1966. India suffered its worst famine in years, and there were shortages in many other places. As surplus foods in America were siphoned off to foreign consumers, U.S. officials directed their efforts to meeting specific dietary deficiencies in other lands.

American companies were encouraged to build plants abroad for the production of protein-rich foods. The Agency for International Development (AID) will reimburse such companies up to 75 per cent of any losses incurred.

New Protein Sources. Nutritionists continued to search for new and cheaper sources of high quality protein. The United States Department of Agriculture distributed 40,000,000 pounds of a new, corn-based food intended for use by infants and children overseas. Called *CSM*, the powdered product is composed of precooked corn meal to which soybean flour, dry milk, calcium carbonate, vitamins, and minerals have been added. CSM contains 20 per cent protein and can be served as a thin cereal or beverage.

A companion product, *Ceplapro*, was developed for use in rice-consuming countries. Just 113 grams of Ceplapro kernels per day will provide one quarter of the energy needs of a preschool child and about one half of his other nutritional requirements. Both of these formula foods have high protein efficiency ratios, making them well-suited for feeding undernourished populations.

To assure a continuing supply of shrimp, a good source of protein, Russian scientists developed a new technique for raising shrimps in reservoirs under controlled conditions.

In the United States, the argument between industry and government officials over the use of fish concentrates as food material was expected to be resolved and the material released for public use. The Food and Drug Administration (FDA) was to decide which of two methods of preparation it will accept. The powdered concentrate, about 80 per cent protein, is a valuable agent for enriching breads, noodles, cookies, and other foods.

Technical Advances. A new, solvent-extraction milling process for rice was introduced by Truman Wayne of Houston, Tex. The process produces a whiter rice, a protein-rich rice bran, and an inexpensive rice oil in the same operation. It also permits a longer shelf life for the rice.

The broiler industry announced a new microwave cooking process for precooked, frozen chicken parts which significantly reduces cooking losses and eliminates darkening caused by bone porosity.

Packaging and Advertising Regulations. Dr. James L. Goddard, new chief of the FDA, struck out aggressively against misleading and false packaging and advertising (see GODDARD, JAMES L.). In July, 1966, the FDA filed suit against a spaghetti maker, charging that the company was guilty of misbranding the product. The description on the package, disputed by the FDA, claimed that the spaghetti was low in calories, high in protein, and of significant value in reducing weight. The move was one of a number of similar actions taken by the FDA to protect the consumer. Goddard also suggested that candy cigarettes, pills, and other children's items simulating products for adults might well be removed from the food market.

The FDA also enforced stringent new regulations on dietary foods and supplements. It allowed the label "low calorie" to be used on food and drink only if the average serving contained no more than 15 calories. The term "reduced in calories" could be used only if the calories were fewer than one-half the number of calories in standard counterparts. The elements allowed in foods labeled "fortified" were to be strictly controlled.

After 25 years, the term "minimum daily requirements," established by the government during the depression years and used in connection with vitamins and minerals, was dropped as misleading.

New Products met wide acceptance in 1966. Among these were:

- Instant freeze-dried coffee, introduced by General Foods.
- A new liquid margarine, packaged in square, plastic bottles to better fit into a refrigerator. It was marketed as a substitute for cooking oil.
- Fluid shortenings, used by commercial bakers and housewives to improve icings.
- Vegetables canned in real butter sauce to compete with frozen foods similarly treated, packed under pressure or in a vacuum for quick cooking.

The "red-hot" (hot dog) was changed in color by the adoption of a new coloring called Orange B. This new coloring effectively dyes all casings, whether artificial cellulose, artificial protein, or animal. Its penetration into the meat is within the penetration restriction of one micron, yet the loss of color is virtually nil when the meats are cooked in water.

ALMA LACH

See also AGRICULTURE.

FOOTBALL. Notre Dame and Michigan State battled to a 10-to-10 tie in the most discussed college football game of the decade. The rivals came to their mid-November meeting at East Lansing, Mich., with unbeaten and untied records. In the first quarter, Michigan State built a 10-to-0 lead on a touchdown by Regis Cavender and a 47-yard field goal by Dick Kenney. At half time, the score was 10 to 7. The Irish tied the score on a 28-yard field goal by Joe Azzaro in the final quarter.

Late in the game, Spartan quarterback Jimmy Raye tried a running play on fourth down at his own 29-yard line and made the first down. But Notre Dame's defense held at midfield and the Irish regained the ball. Notre Dame coach Ara Parseghian then decided to settle for a tie and ran out the clock.

1966 Conference Champions

Conference	School
Big Ten	Michigan State
Southeastern	Alabama, Georgia (tie)
Southwest	Southern Methodist
Big Eight	Nebraska
Atlantic Coast	Clemson
Ivy League	Dartmouth, Harvard, Princeton (tie)
Middle Atlantic	Delaware
Southern	William & Mary
Missouri Valley	North Texas State, Tulsa (tie)
Western Athletic	Wyoming
Yankee	Massachusetts
Pacific Eight	Southern California
Mid-American	Miami, Western Michigan (tie)

In wire-service ratings after the game, Notre Dame was named No. 1 by one poll–the Associated Press rankings selected by sportswriters and broadcasters–while Michigan State was No. 1 in the other –the United Press International balloting done by a board of coaches. The following week, the Fighting Irish traveled to Los Angeles and blistered Southern California, 51 to 0, in their last game of the season. In the balloting after that, Notre Dame was voted No. 1 by both the services.

The competition recalled a somewhat similar situation that developed in 1965. At the end of the regular season, Michigan State headed the polls, only to be replaced by Alabama when Michigan State lost to UCLA in the Rose Bowl game and Alabama defeated Nebraska in the Orange Bowl.

The Bowl Games

Bowl	Winner	Loser
Liberty	Miami, 14	Virginia Tech, 7
Bluebonnet	Texas, 19	Mississippi, 0
Sun	Wyoming, 28	Florida State, 20
Gator	Tennessee, 18	Syracuse, 12
Cotton	Georgia, 24	Southern Methodist, 9
Sugar	Alabama, 34	Nebraska, 7
Rose	Purdue, 14	Southern Calif., 13
Orange	Florida, 27	Georgia Tech, 12

Other Results. Two other undefeated, untied teams were beaten in their final games. On Thanks-

Bob Gomel, *Life* © Time Inc.

Michigan State's Phil Hoag (36) and Jeff Richardson (57) corner Notre Dame passer Coley O'Brien (3) in the college "Game of the Year."

giving Day, Mike Vachon of Oklahoma kicked a 21-yard field goal with only 48 seconds left, to hand Nebraska its first setback, 10 to 9. Two days later, Georgia upset Georgia Tech, 23 to 14, and spoiled the Engineers' hopes for a perfect season. At the end of the campaign, only third-ranked Alabama, with a 10-and-0 record, could claim a perfect mark.

Steve Spurrier, University of Florida quarterback from Johnson City, Tenn., received the Heisman Trophy, awarded annually to the outstanding college football player.

Professional. In June, the bitter and expensive battle between the two professional leagues ended abruptly in a merger that amounted to an eventual absorption of the seven-year-old American Football League (AFL) by the 46-year-old National Football League (NFL). The agreement called for a common draft in 1967, halting the competitive bidding that had enabled players such as Donnie Anderson of Texas Tech, Tom Nobis of Texas, Jim Grabowski of Illinois, and Joe Namath of Alabama to secure six-figure contracts in the two previous years. See Section Two, The Other Face of Pro Sports.

Another facet of the agreement called for the addition of two teams no later than 1968 and the expectation of more to follow. The NFL promptly added New Orleans as its 16th team for 1967.

From the standpoint of the fans, the most interesting aspects of the merger was the provision for a common schedule by 1970 and the provision for a game between the 1966 champions of each league, a long-awaited confrontation that was immediately dubbed "The Superbowl Game."

Antitrust Immunity. Commissioner Pete Rozelle of the NFL, designated as the top executive of the merged leagues, sought to gain antitrust immunity from Congress similar to the protection granted organized baseball by a 1922 decision of the U.S. Supreme Court. Congressman Emanuel Celler (D., N.Y.) fought the move, but had to concede defeat after the U.S. Senate approved it as a rider to President Lyndon B. Johnson's anti-inflation bill.

In the NFL, the Dallas Cowboys took the Eastern title, while the Green Bay Packers captured the Western crown. Green Bay won the title game by a score of 34 to 27. Gayle Sayers of the Chicago Bears was the league's leading rusher with a total of 1,231 yards, while Bart Starr of Green Bay was the best passer with a record of 156 completions out of 251 attempts. Starr was also voted the most valuable player in the league. Bruce Gossett of Los Angeles led all scorers with 113 points, and Charlie Taylor of Washington won pass receiving honors with 72 catches for 1,119 yards.

All-America Team

Offense

Ends—Jack Clancy, Michigan; and Gene Washington, Michigan State.

Tackles—Ron Yary, U.S.C.; and Wayne Mass, Clemson.

Guards—Tom Regner, Notre Dame; and Cecil Dowdy, Alabama.

Center—Jim Breland, Georgia Tech.

Quarterbacks—Steve Spurrier, Florida; and Bob Griese, Purdue.

Halfbacks—Mell Farr, UCLA; and Floyd Little, Syracuse.

Flanker—Ray Perkins, Alabama.

Fullback—Nick Eddy, Notre Dame.

Defense

Ends—Bubba Smith, Michigan State; and Tom Greenlee, Washington.

Tackles—Pete Duranko, Notre Dame; Loyd Phillips, Arkansas; and Wayne Meylan, Nebraska.

Middle Guard—John Lagrone, SMU.

Linebackers—John Lynch, Notre Dame; and Paul Naumoff, Tennessee.

Halfbacks—George Webster, Michigan State; Tom Beier, Miami (Fla.); Nate Shaw, Southern California; and Martine Bercher, Arkansas.

Standings in National Football League

Eastern Conference	W.	L.	T.	Pc.
Dallas	10	3	1	.769
Cleveland	9	5	0	.643
Philadelphia	9	5	0	.643
St. Louis	8	5	1	.615
Washington	7	7	0	.500
Pittsburgh	5	8	1	.385
Atlanta	3	11	0	.214
New York	1	12	1	.077
Western Conference	**W.**	**L.**	**T.**	**Pc.**
Green Bay	12	2	0	.857
Baltimore	9	5	0	.643
Los Angeles	8	6	0	.571
San Francisco	6	6	2	.500
Chicago	5	7	2	.417
Minnesota	4	9	1	.308
Detroit	4	9	1	.308

The Kansas City Chiefs took the Western title in the AFL, and the Buffalo Bills won the Eastern crown. The play-off was won by Kansas City by a score of 31 to 7. Jim Nance of the Boston Patriots was the AFL's foremost ground-gainer with a total of 1,458 yards, and Len Dawson of Kansas City, voted the league's most valuable player, was top passer with 159 completions in 284 attempts. Gino Capelletti captured the scoring title with 119 points, while Lance Alworth of San Diego was top pass receiver with 73 catches for 1,383 yards. John Lake

Standings in American Football League

Eastern Division	W.	L.	T.	Pc.
Buffalo	9	4	1	.692
Boston	8	4	2	.667
New York	6	6	2	.500
Houston	3	11	0	.214
Miami	3	11	0	.214
Western Division	**W.**	**L.**	**T.**	**Pc.**
Kansas City	11	2	1	.846
Oakland	8	5	1	.615
San Diego	7	6	1	.538
Denver	4	10	0	.286

FOREST PRODUCTS. Despite a decline in home building, total expenditures for new construction increased and overall production and consumption of timber and lumber rose slightly in 1966. Prices for most forest products also increased during the year.

The Paper Explosion. The United Nations Food and Agriculture Organization (FAO) reported in June that world output of pulp, paper, and paperboard was expected to approach 128,000,000 tons by 1968, or 4,000,000 above the estimate FAO had made a year earlier. The total for 1966 was 114,000,000 tons, up from 83,000,000 tons in 1960.

With Americans using an average of nearly 500 pounds of paper per person a year—compared with 50 pounds at the turn of the century—the industry was pushing research to increase sources of paper pulp. In order to accomplish this, a number of firms operating in the Southeast put their foresters to work at developing supertrees. The aim is for faster growing, taller, sturdier, more disease-resistant specimens. The increase in yield, in terms of cords of pulpwood per acre of forestland, was expected to do for forestry what hybrid corn had done for agriculture.

1966 Timber Output of U.S. forests totaled about 11,700,000,000 cubic feet, about 3 per cent over 1965 and 11 per cent more than the average for the previous decade. Timber consumption exceeded U.S. production, rising 4 per cent in the year to a new high of 12,300,000,000 cubic feet. Total use of all industrial roundwood, including fuel wood, reached 13,400,000,000 cubic feet.

Production of lumber also increased slightly during the year. At 37,100,000,000 board feet, it was 2,400,000,000 board feet higher than the average for the previous decade. Output of pulpwood, including roundwood and chips, increased to 55,000,000 cords, a 10 per cent gain for the year. Consumption of lumber, at 33,500,000,000 board feet, held at about the 1965 level, but pulpwood consumption, at 55,800,000 cords, increased about 5 per cent.

Prices for most forest products have been rising in the past five years. That trend continued in 1966. Stumpage prices exceeded the previous highs set in the mid-1950s. Early in 1966, wholesale prices of softwood lumber advanced rapidly as the result of a shortage of railway cars, military buying, and inventory building in anticipation of labor disputes. But by fall, prices had eased to 1965 levels. Prices of southern pine rose from about $16 a cord to $17.

Net imports of timber products reached a new high of 1,900,000,000 cubic feet, about 11 per cent above 1965. Imports of softwood lumber rose about 6 per cent over 1965, to 5,200,000,000 board feet.

National forest timber cut in the year, ended June 30, 1966, totaled 12,100,000,000 board feet, a new record. A. L. NEWMAN

FORMOSA, or **TAIWAN,** enjoyed a modest boom in its economy and a spectacular one in its political hopes during 1966. The tempest caused by Communist China's "cultural revolution" had led President Chiang Kai-shek to predict that "the days of Mao Tse-tung are numbered."

While the government's leaders dreamed of a return to the mainland, most of the nation's 12,632,000 people were preoccupied with problems closer to home. With more than half of the population under 20 years of age, the Nationalist government was under heavy pressure to create jobs. So far, it had been able to do so, with economic growth keeping ahead of increases in the working population. But with an annual birth rate of 3 per cent and the number of employable youths increasing steadily, there was concern for the future.

The economy was hurt by the declining price of sugar and the price Japan's wholesalers were willing to pay for the island's banana crop. These losses were offset, however, by growing exports of industrial products.

Facts in Brief. Population: 12,632,000. Government: President Chiang Kai-shek; Vice-President and President of the Executive Yuan: Yen Chia-kan (C. K. Yen). Monetary Unit: NT dollar (40 = U.S. $1). Foreign Trade: exports, $449,600,000; imports, $556,700,000. Principal Exports: bananas, electrical goods, chemical products, sugar. MARK GAYN

FOUNDATIONS. A revolutionary nationwide satellite television system that would use profits from the relay of commercial television shows to finance noncommercial video was proposed on August 1 by the Ford Foundation. The suggestion was presented by the foundation's new president, McGeorge Bundy (see BUNDY, MCGEORGE).

Over a 15-year period, the Ford Foundation had invested about $100,000,000 in educational television. It was still contributing about $7,000,000 annually to the National Educational Television network. It was partly to reduce its philanthropic role and partly to stimulate a wider interest in educational and cultural telecasting that the foundation presented its revolutionary program.

In an 80-page brief submitted to the Federal Communications Commission (FCC), the foundation proposed the establishment of a new television system that would use four synchronous-broadcast orbiting satellites – one for each U.S. time zone. By establishing such a system and placing its operation under a nonprofit organization, the foundation believed the commercial networks – which pay the American Telephone and Telegraph Company about $65,000,000 a year for ground transmission – could reduce their own operating costs to $45,000,000. The resulting savings could be used to finance coast-to-coast educational television. A U.S. Senate committee took the proposal under advisement and announced that plans to hold public hearings on the Ford Foundation's suggestion would be forthcoming.

Major educational foundations reporting on their activities in 1966 included the following:

Alfred P. Sloan Foundation, New York City, announced a grant of $315,000 for a three-year program for executive development fellowships, to be established at the London Graduate School of Business Studies. The Deafness Research Foundation received a grant of $316,250. Unrestricted grants totaling $1,400,000 were made to 90 researchers from universities in the United States and Canada.

Carnegie Corporation of New York announced a grant of $300,000 to the Southern Regional Education Board for the improvement of Negro higher education in the South. Another grant of $350,000 was made to eight Philadelphia schools for "exceptionable excellence" programs. Carnegie also contributed $100,000 to the White House Fellows in Government program for 1966-1967.

The Commonwealth Fund, New York City, reported assets of $90,455,747 as of June 30, 1966. Income totaled $5,927,589, and appropriations, $7,001,915. Grants included $5,326,770 for medical education and community health; $350,000 for fellowships and awards in the health field; and $935,000 for the Division of International Fellowships.

Field Foundation, Inc., New York City, reported assets of $42,286,787 as of Sept. 30, 1965, and a net income of $2,714,122. Grants included $1,579,515 for intercultural and interracial relations, $243,837 for child welfare, and $334,160 for other social services. Field Foundation observed its 25th anniversary in 1965. Since it was founded in 1940 by Marshall Field III, publisher, grants totaling $19,584,429 have been made for child welfare, and intercultural and interracial relations.

Ford Foundation, New York City, reported assets of $3,015,055,893 as of Sept. 30, 1965, and an income of $145,406,691. New appropriations came to $155,058,-938. Grants included $23,954,215 for education; $87,-975,000 for special programs; $23,732,542 for public affairs; $6,452,038 for economic development and ad-

Important American Foundations

Foundations with more than $100,000,000 in assets as of January, 1965 (the latest year available):

	Year founded	Estimated assets (in millions)
*1. Ford Foundation	1936	$3,871
*2. Rockefeller Foundation	1913	862
*3. Duke Endowment	1924	596
*4. Kellogg Foundation, W. K.	1930	492
5. Mott Foundation, Charles Stewart	1926	418
*6. Hartford Foundation, John A.	1942	397
7. Carnegie Corporation of New York	1911	344
*8. Sloan Foundation, Alfred P.	1934	298
9. Bishop Foundation, Bernice P.	1953	287
10. Pew Memorial Trust	1957	263
11. Longwood Foundation	1937	251
12. Moody Foundation	1942	242
*13. Lilly Endowment, Inc.	1937	234
14. Rockefeller Brothers Fund	1940	210
*15. Commonwealth Fund	1918	156
16. Danforth Foundation, The	1927	146
17. Avalon Foundation	1940	138
18. Waterman (Phoebe) Foundation	1945	134
19. Kettering Foundation, Charles F.	1927	121
*20. Carnegie Institution of Washington	1902	113
21. Old Dominion Foundation	1941	103
22. Fleischmann Foundation of Nevada, Max C.	1951	103
23. Cleveland Foundation	1914	102

*Asterisk indicates the corporation has a separate article in THE WORLD BOOK ENCYCLOPEDIA.

ministration; $8,922,876 for science and engineering; $7,842,877 for humanities and the arts; $52,085,235 for international training and research; $8,216,200 for population; $12,385,790 for international affairs, and $48,692,306 for overseas development.

John A. Hartford Foundation, New York City, reported assets of $183,216,645 as of Dec. 31, 1965. Total income was $14,357,416. Appropriations of $14,033,-520 were made for medical research and clinical and other programs.

John and Mary R. Markle Foundation, New York City, reported assets of $32,530,124 as of June 30, 1966. Income came to $1,660,370. Twenty-five new scholars in academic medicine received grants totaling $750,-000. Grants of $707,500 were made for medical libraries and other purposes.

Rockefeller Foundation, New York City, reported an income of $29,100,000 for the year ending Dec. 31, 1965. Appropriations approved came to $35,900,000. Grants for world-wide programs included $8,500,000 toward the conquest of hunger; $2,600,000 for university development; $3,100,000 for population problems; $2,800,000 for equal opportunity programs; and $3,400,000 for aid to cultural development.

FOUR-H CLUBS. See YOUTH ORGANIZATIONS.

FRANCE

France pursued its independent, often unpredictable, ways in international relations in 1966. The key figure in France–76-year-old President Charles de Gaulle–continued to champion his concept of a Third World, in which France would play a leading role. He remained firmly opposed to any moves toward supranationalism in Europe, yet he softened his attitude toward the European Economic Community (EEC, or Common Market) and he even talked of Great Britain reapplying for EEC membership (see EUROPE). His firm stand against the North Atlantic Treaty Organization (NATO) saw its removal from French soil begin in the fall, yet he enabled the Kennedy Round of tariff cutting negotiations to resume in earnest in Geneva, Switzerland, and, surprisingly, agreed to the use of French gold reserves to support the British pound sterling along with other Western bankers (see GREAT BRITAIN; INTERNATIONAL TRADE AND FINANCE).

NATO. President De Gaulle declared in February that France's association with NATO would end on April 4, 1969, and that meanwhile France would gradually cut down its commitments by withdrawing completely from military activities and ending its financial contributions. De Gaulle described the Atlantic Treaty of 1949 as "unrealistic" in the light of current conditions. "An alliance cannot be kept immutable when the conditions prevailing at the time it was formed have changed," he told a press conference. "The West is not threatened today as it was when an American protectorate was established in Europe under cover of NATO."

Supreme Headquarters, Allied Powers in Europe (SHAPE) began preparing for its move from Rocquencourt to Casteau, near Brussels, Belgium, and the Central European Military headquarters at Fontainebleu also began negotiating for Belgian headquarters (see BELGIUM). The SHAPE move was slowed, however, after protests from General Lyman L. Lemnitzer, Supreme Allied Commander, Europe (SACEUR), that the abrupt withdrawal of the entire French staff would cause confusion. U.S. forces began to cross the English Channel to Britain in the summer, with France calling for their complete withdrawal by April, 1967. French troops in Germany were withdrawn from NATO command in July. In that same month, De Gaulle visited Bonn, West Germany, for talks about the future of French forces stationed there. Germany was in-

Monumental statues frame French President Charles de Gaulle as he emerges from a museum during his visit to Leningrad.

World Tour of Charles de Gaulle

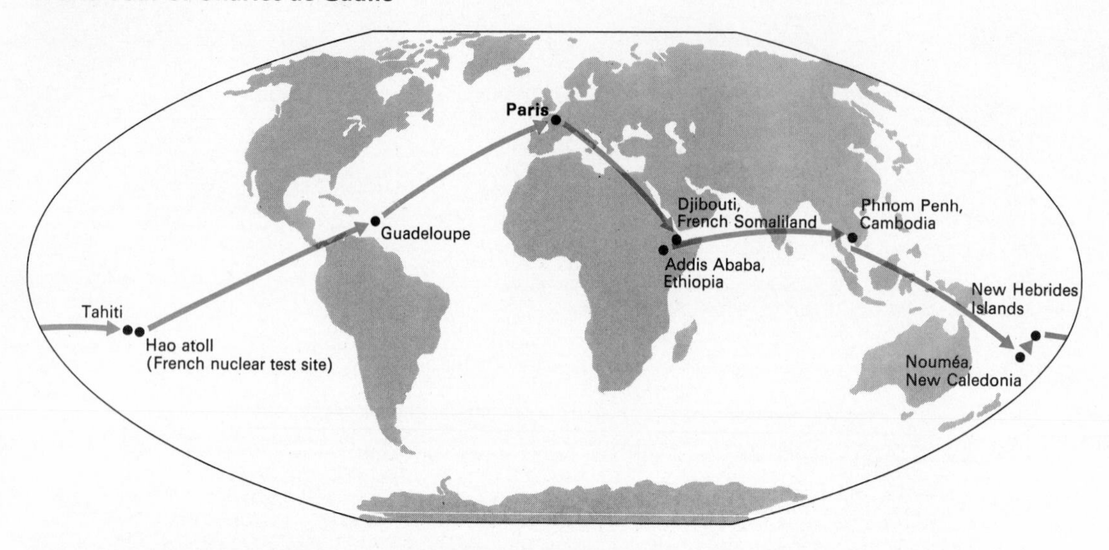

French President Charles de Gaulle made a 19-day world tour in the fall of 1966. During his voyage, he traveled about 27,000 miles through Africa, Asia, Oceania, and the Caribbean. A highlight of De Gaulle's tour occurred in the Pacific where he watched an atomic bomb test; a low point occurred in French Somaliland where his arrival was greeted by riots.

formed that some units would be withdrawn. Nevertheless, in September, France's permanent representative on the Atlantic Council announced that France would be represented by "liaison missions" at the Chiefs of Staff Committee in Washington, D.C., as well as Supreme Allied Headquarters, Europe, and Supreme Allied Command, Atlantic.

Domestic Economy. With the 1967 elections in mind, the government announced a domestic social program in January based on higher minimum salaries, improved pensions, and industrial and agricultural expansion. There also was a substantial freeing of government credits. As a result of these moves—part of the nation's Fifth Plan—industrial production rose by 8.2 per cent; the cost of living was up by only 2.5 per cent. The import-export gap was narrowed: imports were covered by exports by 97 per cent, compared with 89 per cent in 1965.

Foreign Visits. President De Gaulle made two international journeys during the year. In June, he visited the Soviet Union for 12 days. At its conclusion, a joint Franco-Soviet declaration was published pledging greater understanding between the two nations, and two agreements were signed. The first related to scientific, technical, and economic cooperation; the second agreement called for the launching of a French satellite by the Soviet Union as well as for the exchange of information and technical advisers.

In a tour made in September, De Gaulle assailed American policy in Vietnam, and made innumerable speeches about France's "world" role and influence. French nuclear intentions were underscored by De Gaulle's visit to a testing site in the Pacific where he watched an atomic bomb explosion. The tour, however, was not without mishaps. In Djibouti, French Somaliland, De Gaulle was greeted by rioting Somalis who were demanding independence. An immediate aftermath of the disorders was the dismissal of the governor, René Tirant, who was blamed for the outburst. Subsequently, a tentative offer of independence was made to French Somaliland. See AFRICA.

The Ben Barka Affair. Widespread police reforms were instituted in France in 1966 as a result of "the Ben Barka affair," which began in October, 1965, when Mehdi Ben Barka, an exiled Moroccan left-wing leader, was kidnaped in Paris. His disappearance touched off a manhunt during which it was disclosed that the French police had participated in the kidnaping. When questioned, they confessed that Ben Barka had been handed over to the Moroccans. Subsequently, De Gaulle dismissed General Paul Jacquier, 55-year-old head of the French counter-espionage service, and he suspended the deputy head, Commandant Marcel Finville, who said that he had been informed in advance of the kidnap plot. The Moroccan envoy in Paris was

Europe's Last Patriarch

Since the days of World War II, except for one period of eclipse, the outsized, improbable figure of France's 76-year-old President Charles de Gaulle has loomed increasingly large on the European scene. In 1966, it loomed larger than ever.

Having led the Free French movement in World War II, De Gaulle emerged from that conflict as a man of considerable importance. For 12 years, he sat in the shadows of retirement while such leaders as Great Britain's Winston S. Churchill and Konrad Adenauer of West Germany dominated postwar Europe. Then, in May, 1958, General De Gaulle was asked to take command of his nation. In June, he accepted.

The Fifth Republic was soon established, and the bitter war in Algeria was subsequently terminated – the latter situation being one which, observers agreed, only De Gaulle could have resolved.

De Gaulle's subsequent actions have angered many, mystified others, and pleased his large following of admirers. Whatever the response to his decisions, one thing was clear: his primary objective was to promote the greater glory of France; to achieve for his nation, despite its limited power, a major role in today's world. As 1966 closed, he stood alone as the last living patriarch of Europe.

A deeply religious man, De Gaulle had spent most of his adult life in the military until he assumed his position as a statesman. An honor graduate of St. Cyr, France's equivalent of West Point, he had won high respect as a soldier and military strategist. At times, however, his manner was abrasive; almost always he appeared arrogant. President Franklin D. Roosevelt reportedly once said of him that the General thought of himself as a direct descendent of Joan of Arc. At Casablanca in 1943, when France was stripped of military power, Churchill turned to his personal physician, Lord Moran, and said of De Gaulle: "Well, just look at him! Look at him! He might be Stalin with 200 divisions behind his words."

But the hauteur, the stubbornness, the plans for "the grand design," paid dividends – at least for France. Once more, the nation gained a voice in the top councils of the world. Its government was stabilized; its economy revived. De Gaulle's rule, however autocratic, brought order out of chaos.

All his moves were allegedly aimed at transforming Europe – a Europe which, of course, would be led by France – into a "third force" between the United States and the Soviet Union.

France, an early member of the North Atlantic Treaty Organization (NATO), later became disenchanted with the alliance which was by then regarded by De Gaulle as obsolescent. In 1966, the General took the radical step of ordering U.S. troops to withdraw from French soil. Economically, France helped to organize the European Economic Community (EEC, or Common Market), but later proved a disruptive force when Gaullist policies met with resistance from other nations. On another front, France pushed ahead to develop its own nuclear capability.

It recognized Communist China, to the dismay of some. De Gaulle built closer ties with West Germany, though the two peoples had formerly been bitter enemies. He sought more harmonious relations with Russia. Increasingly, particularly in 1966, he attacked U.S. policy in Vietnam as being both impractical and brutal.

Whatever De Gaulle's critics might say, it seemed certain that the General would not be deterred from his chosen path. Historian Arthur M. Schlesinger, Jr., in his book, *A Thousand Days: John F. Kennedy in the White House*, recounts a conversation between President Kennedy and the General that illustrates the point. De Gaulle, Schlesinger reports, suggested to the President that the latter should not rely too much on his advisers. The important thing for every man, De Gaulle said, was his own judgment. "He was expounding, of course," Schlesinger adds, "the Gaullist philosophy of leadership."

As long as he remains at the head of the French government, Charles André Joseph Marie de Gaulle is not likely to budge one inch from that philosophy.

C. C. Renshaw, Jr.

Banner-carrying union workers at a Renault automobile plant in France demonstrate against rising living costs and low paychecks.

recalled after King Hassan I of Morocco rejected a French demand for the arrest of General Oufkir, his minister of the interior. The French government had called for Oufkir's arrest because of his involvement in the kidnaping. See MOROCCO.

Anglo-French Projects. Anglo-French cooperation in aircraft and in aerospace industries encountered difficulties, notably over the development of a medium-range, large capacity airliner. Rolls-Royce had designed a $90,000,000 engine for it, but, to save costs, it was suggested that U.S.-made Pratt and Whitney engines be used instead.

Further meetings were held to determine the future of the variable-geometry "swing-wing" plane, another joint project. Proposals were made, too, for the joint building of a Jaguar tactical fighter, a support trainer, and a radar warning plane.

Facts in Brief. Population: 48,300,000. Government: President Charles de Gaulle; Premier Georges Pompidou. Monetary Unit: franc (4.89 = U.S. $1). Foreign Trade: exports, $10,055,400,000; imports, $10,344,600,000. Principal Exports: chemicals, iron and steel, machinery, wines. KENNETH BROWN

FUTURE FARMERS OF AMERICA (FFA). See YOUTH ORGANIZATIONS.

FUTURE HOMEMAKERS OF AMERICA (FHA). See YOUTH ORGANIZATIONS.

GABON. See AFRICA.

GAMBIA. See AFRICA.

GAMES, MODELS, AND TOYS. The wild skate board craze appeared to be dying out in 1966, as had hula hoops and other fads in earlier years. Interest in slot car racing remained high but had leveled off with approximately 3,000 raceways operating across the United States.

Batman and secret agents invaded the toy field. There were Batman art toys, games, costumes, wheel toys, model kits, and a Batman walkie-talkie. There were also Batman figures, airplanes, radios, hats, a dart launcher, and a Batman city, all on display at the 1966 Toy Fair in New York City in March. See TELEVISION (Close-Up).

And there were not only more spy toys this year, but more toy spies. At least 11 different undercover agents, including a stuffed cat with a secret agent outfit, were available. They were equipped with every known espionage device, and some that even the fiction writers had not thought of, such as secret printing putty.

Battery operated automobiles that run on a track of tubing were a popular addition to the toy field. Compressed air in the tubing, activated by pushing a switch button, enabled the operator to control the car's course.

The trend toward realism in dolls continued, with toy manufacturers introducing dolls whose facial expressions could be changed by moving an arm or leg.

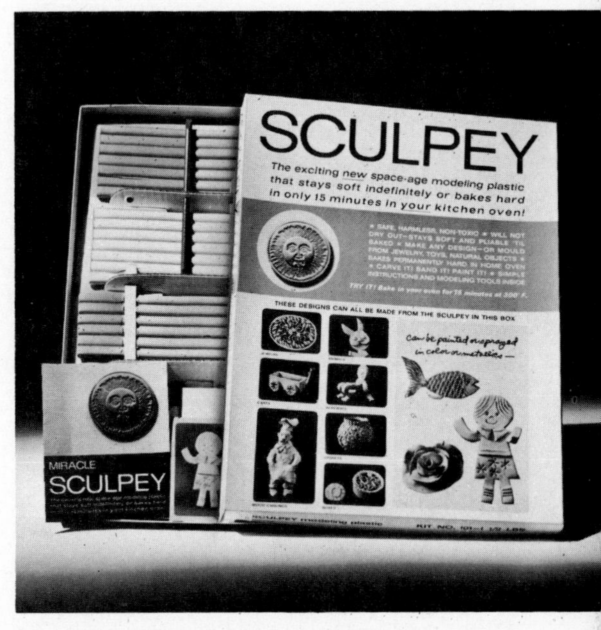

Games based on TV and comic book heroes, a James Bond 007 model auto, and a special modeling plastic were exciting 1966 toys.

One of the most popular action games was Twister, played on a color-marked plastic surface spread across the floor. Its players took awkward and contorted positions according to directions based on the spinning of a dial.

Model Making. Robert Sifleet of Baltimore, Md., won both the Grand National and the Open National championships at the National Model Airplane contest at Glenview, Ill., in July. Dubby Jett of Seagoville, Tex., retained his senior championship, and the junior title went to Randy Richmond of Bensenville, Ill. The Dallas Aeromodelers Association won the club championship and the U.S. Air Force Team Four took the team title.

Marbles Title. Melvin Garland, 14, of Pittsburgh, Pa., won the boys' division of the 43rd National Marbles tournament at Wildwood, N.J., in June. Marcella Elliott, 13, of New Castle, Del., took the girls' title.

Other Awards in 1966 included:

Craftsman's Guild Winners. In the annual Fisher Body Craftsman's model car building competition, university scholarships went to: *Senior Division*—Ovid O. Ward, Roanoke, Va., $5,000; John M. Mellberg, Park Ridge, Ill., $4,000; Kenneth A. Kelly, St. Petersburg, Fla., $3,000; and Joseph W. D'Mura, East Gary, Ind., $2,000. *Junior Division*—Dale Gnage, Rochester, N.Y., $5,000; Bruno Bottarelli, Chicago, Ill., $4,000; Larry Hagen, New Brighton, Minn., $3,000; Leonard Constance, Flint, Mich., and Carl LaRoche, Franklin, N.H., each $2,000.

THEODORE M. O'LEARY

GANDHI, INDIRA NEHRU (1917-), was sworn in as prime minister of India on Jan. 24, 1966. She succeeded the late Lal Bahadur Shastri, who died on January 11 while settling the Pakistan-India border dispute at Tashkent (see INDIA).

The first woman ever to become the head of a major country, Mrs. Gandhi was born Nov. 19, 1917, at Allahabad, the only child of Jawaharlal Nehru. She was educated in Switzerland and later at Oxford University in England, but returned to her native country at the onset of World War II.

Mrs. Gandhi's family had long been active in India's struggle for independence. She joined the movement in 1941 and continued to be active in politics after India achieved its freedom in 1947. In February, 1959, Mrs. Gandhi became president of the Congress party, the third generation of her family to serve in that position. She eventually left this post to assist her father, who was then prime minister. When Nehru died in 1964, his successor, Shastri, appointed Mrs. Gandhi minister of information and broadcasting.

Mrs. Gandhi's election as prime minister came at a time when her country faced its most severe problems since becoming independent. Chief among these was a major food shortage.

In February, 1942, she was married to Feroze Gandhi, a lawyer, who died in 1960. Mrs. Gandhi has two sons, Rajiv, 21, and Sanjay, 19.

GARDEN AND LAWN. The ancient Japanese art of bonsai attracted an ever-widening circle of devotees during 1966. Bonsai is the patient and skillful art of dwarfing trees through a combination of root confinement and starvation. Almost any variety of seedling can be used, and the miniature plant in time resembles a full-grown tree.

More than 20 bonsai clubs exist in the United States, most of them formed within the last three years. The largest, the Bonsai Society of Greater New York, claims a membership of 555 compared to 18 in 1963.

International Congress. The first meeting of the International Horticultural Congress ever held in the Western Hemisphere took place in August at the University of Maryland, College Park, Md. Among the papers presented at the meeting was a study of fire resistance in plants. Another stressed the importance of developing a wider variety of tropical trees suitable for home environment that is too dry for tropical foliage plants.

Another important event, the annual Northeastern Florists' Association United Trade Fair and School, held in October at Boston, was climaxed with a wedding spectacular titled "First Ladies and Flowers." Models wore reproductions of the bridal gowns worn by the wives of U.S. Presidents, and carried floral arrangements of their favorite blooms.

Correspondence Courses for gardeners increased in popularity in 1966. Subjects included rose gardening, trees for the home grounds, plant propagation, the home greenhouse, and landscape planning for small properties. Pennsylvania State University, as well as a number of other schools and individuals, provided the courses which were used by many people throughout the United States and in other countries.

New Flowers announced in 1966 included the first F1 hybrid carnation, the fragrant "Petite Pink"; the first dwarf species of marigold, "Yellow Nugget"; and the first in a series of low asters covered with large blooms, "Snow White." The All-America Gold Medal, awarded only twice since 1939, was presented to the new cosmos, "Sunset."

House plant enthusiasts were introduced to an evergreen amaryllis, "Apricot Lily," which apparently needed no resting period. It blooms repeatedly if given the proper temperature and light conditions. "Queen Fabiola," a tuberous begonia, blossoms three weeks earlier than other begonia varieties and continually produces coral-pink flushed with gold flowers throughout the summer months.

All-America Rose Selections for 1966 were: "Bewitched," a clear, bright phlox-pink hybrid tea with gracefully pointed, medium-long buds, 35 to 40 petals, and long stems; "Gay Princess," a soft, shell pink floribunda with large hybrid tea-shaped flowers; "Roman Holiday," a brilliant orange-red floribunda with urn-shaped buds, 25 to 30 petals, and an elusive tea fragrance; and "Lucky Lady," a free-blooming bicolor grandiflora, light, clear pink on the face of the petal and deeply suffused with red on the reverse.

Fruits and Vegetables introduced to gardeners in 1966 included a new "Sunrise" strawberry, which has early, bright red, sweet berries on robust, disease-resistant plants, and "Clyde Purple," a new raspberry, which bears large, dark berries. Among the new vegetables were "Butter King" lettuce, and a larger headed "White Boston" type that is slower to bolt and more resistant to sun or tip burn. The unusual "Kabob" tomato, with fruits that average one and a half inches in diameter, was developed particularly for barbecue skewers. The "Superman Hybrid" tomato is resistant to both the fusarium and verticillium wilts. "Gold Nugget, "a small winter squash weighing about two pounds, stores well, and makes two or three servings.

Medicinal Plants. Much activity went into the search for medicinal properties in plants found throughout the world. One research laboratory in a school of pharmacy reported that it was testing a wide variety of plant materials to determine their medicinal value against 45 different disease-producing organisms, six types of cancer, and six viruses. It was also seeking to determine behavioral effects on laboratory animals. ELIZABETH HIGGINS

See also AGRICULTURE; BOTANY.

GAUD, WILLIAM S. (1907-), moved up to the post of administrator of the U.S. Agency for International Development (AID) on August 1. Gaud had been deputy administrator since 1964 under David E. Bell, who resigned to become vice-president of the Ford Foundation. Bell had promoted Gaud from the post of assistant administrator.

Gaud had been recruited to AID in 1961 by Secretary of State Dean Rusk and the then Attorney General, Robert F. Kennedy. From the end of World War II until his call to Washington, D.C., Gaud had been with a New York City law firm.

He was born in New York City on Aug. 9, 1907. He earned his bachelor of laws degree at Yale University law school in 1931. He served as an instructor at the law school and as assistant corporation counsel under Mayor Fiorello H. LaGuardia.

During World War II, Gaud served under Major General Joseph W. "Vinegar Joe" Stilwell in the China-Burma-India theater. It was there that he acquired his experience in foreign aid. Under Stilwell, he was responsible for military assistance to the three countries.

A lean, craggy six-footer, with a full shock of sandy hair, Gaud carries his 59 years well. He puts in a 10- to 11-hour day. Occasionally, he and his wife, the former Eleanor Smith, slip away for a long weekend of sailing down the Potomac. They were married in 1935 and have one daughter.

Reversal of Direction of Earth's Magnetism

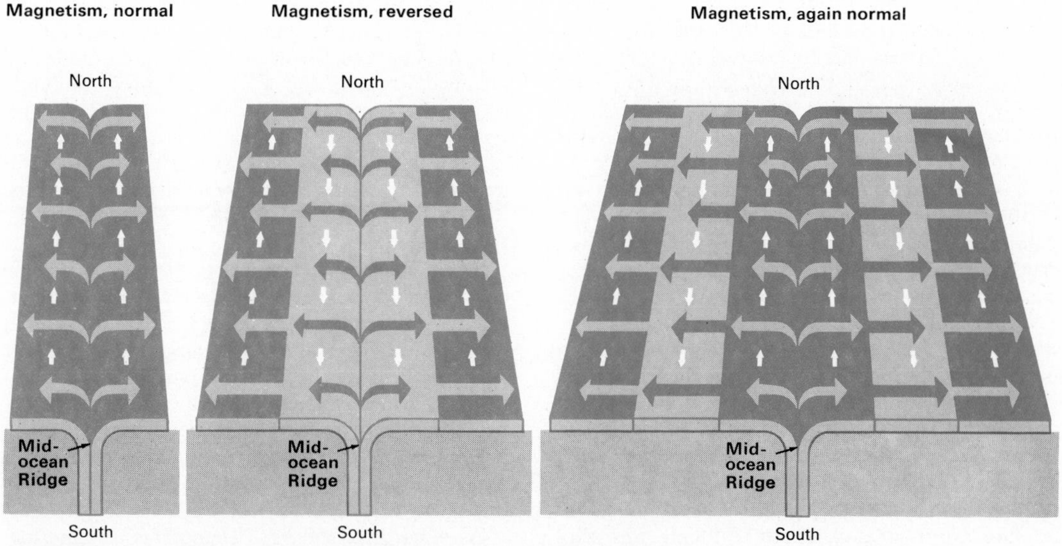

Magnetism, normal **Magnetism, reversed** **Magnetism, again normal**

North North North

Mid-ocean Ridge Mid-ocean Ridge Mid-ocean Ridge

South South South

Plans were developed in 1966 for studies of the ocean floor to see if the theory that the earth's magnetic field reverses every 700,000 to 1,000,000 years is correct. The dating of igneous rocks, formed from lava exuded under the sea, will show the direction of the field at times when the rocks solidified, and show any reversal.

GEOLOGY. The centuries-old theory that a rock breaks apart because of freezing and thawing of water in its cracks was overturned by two scientists at Rensselaer Polytechnic Institute at Troy, N.Y. James R. Dunn and Peter P. Hudec found that the breakdown is not due to freezing, but to the fact that the water molecules in the cracks come under the influence of negatively charged clay particles that lie along crystal boundaries in rock. The water molecules, bipolar in nature, orient themselves in a quasi-crystalline manner along the crystal boundaries and exert an expansive force, eventually causing cracks. These findings may prove valuable to the limestone and dolomite industries.

Cooler Core. A new method for calculating the temperature of the earth's core, developed by Professor George Kennedy of the University of California at Los Angeles (UCLA), lowered previous estimates by half. Professor Kennedy questioned the long-assumed direct relationship between the melting point of a substance and the amount of pressure upon it. After careful laboratory tests, he found that the relationship was between the melting point and the density, not pressure. Using his new formula and the experimentally derived value for the density of the earth's core, he calculated the core temperature to be 6700° F. The old value was 13,500° F. The new estimates will likely influence most theories about the geological history of the earth, and aid in studies of the way the earth loses its internal heat by radiation.

Trench Discovered. Scientists of the U.S. Coast and Geodetic Survey discovered an 800-mile-long fracture zone in the Pacific Ocean floor between the Hawaiian and Aleutian Islands. The trench, up to 15 miles wide at points, is the northernmost of four fracture zones that have been found in the seabed north of Hawaii. Geologists believe the trench resulted from a geologic upheaval occurring more than 50,000,000 years ago.

Volcanoes. After a study of the action of water in a silicate system resembling volcanic lava, Hatten S. Yoder at the Geophysical Laboratory of the Carnegie Institution of Washington proposed a new theory for volcanic eruption. He suggested that molten volcanic material, as it pushes up through the earth's crust, may suddenly enter a cavity or chamber, or suddenly deform the surrounding strata, so that a sharp drop in pressure occurs. Under these conditions the molten material changes to *magma* (a fluid mass) and releases a large amount of water vapor. The freeing of water from the magma and its conversion to steam takes place so rapidly that the magma is driven to the volcano mouth in an explosive eruption.

Earthquakes. A puzzling series of earthquakes, which began in the Denver, Colo., area in 1962, were found to be caused by the pumping of waste fluids into a deep disposal well at the Rocky Mountain Arsenal. More than 700 small earthquakes occurred, about 75 of them severe enough to be felt by local residents. Studies by scientists of the U.S. Geological Survey, in cooperation with the Colorado School of Mines, Regis College, and the University of Colorado, led to the solution of the problem. The well has since been closed and the quakes have ceased.

A National Earthquake Information Center was established by the Environmental Science Services Administration. The center will issue information regarding earthquakes of magnitude 6.5 or larger occurring anywhere in the world.

Other Developments. Secretary of the Interior Stewart L. Udall announced, in September, that earth-orbiting satellites will be launched to gather data about the natural resources of our planet including facts on the distribution of minerals and water. The first of these earth resources observation satellites (EROS) will be launched in 1969.

After years of planning, political squabbling, and administrative turmoil, Project Mohole was crippled in August when Congress refused to appropriate any more funds for the deep drilling project. The plan to sink a drill into the earth's mantle from an oceanborne platform in the Pacific fell prey to spending pressures of the space program and U.S. military operations in Southeast Asia. JAMES A. PEARRE

GERMANY remained a divided nation during 1966. Politically, there seemed little hope of a reconciliation between the two Germanys. But there were indications that in at least one area–trade–the division was no longer as deep as it had been.

Trade between the Federal Republic of (West) Germany and the (East) German Democratic Republic quietly increased during the first nine months of the year. Volume for 1966 was expected to reach about $700,000,000–close to $100,000,000 more than the total in 1965. For the East Germans, trade with West Germany was profitable; altogether, West Germany absorbed about 11 per cent of East Germany's total trade. For West Germany, however, the transactions had only a limited business value. Primarily, Bonn and West Berlin regarded the trading arrangement as an aspect of politics since it was linked indirectly with free access to the isolated city of Berlin. "No traffic, no trade," was the way West German officials explained the situation to the East Germans.

The Berlin Wall, despite breaches of trade, remained the symbol of a divided Germany. In August, steel-helmeted East German soldiers marched with guns in their hands and flowers in their belts in a celebration marking the fifth anniversary of the building of the Berlin Wall. Since its erection in 1961, 135 East Germans have lost their lives trying to escape to the West.

Early in 1966, West Germany "purchased" the release of 2,600 political prisoners from East German jails in return for goods worth $27,000,000. This "ransom-trading" was followed by plans for a meeting between Berlin's Mayor Willy Brandt and Walter Ulbricht, the East German Communist leader. To reassure the East Germans of its good intentions, the West German government passed a bill that would give the East German visitors immunity from arrest. After several postponements, the East Germans eventually backed out of the talks altogether.

West Germany, while preoccupied with the continuing existence of the Berlin Wall, found its attention diverted in the fall when the government was plunged into a major political crisis by the resignation of the Free Democrats from the coalition government. Their withdrawal was ostensibly prompted by plans of Chancellor Ludwig Erhard and his ruling Christian Democrats to meet a deficit of $1,000,000,000 in the proposed 1967 budget by raising taxes.

As a result of the Free Democrats' resignation, Erhard became head of a minority government. As such, he faced a legislative impasse, one that was compounded further when he stubbornly insisted on clinging to office despite pressures for his resignation. On November 8, the executive committee of his own party acted to end the crisis by nominating four candidates to succeed him. Two days later, Kurt Georg Kiesinger was named as Erhard's replacement, despite his record as a former member of the Nazi party. See KIESINGER, KURT GEORG.

After considerable behind-the-scenes maneuvering, Kiesinger was able to persuade the Social Democrats–the former opposition party–to participate in a coalition government with his own Christian Democrats party. Willy Brandt was named vice-chancellor.

The New Government faced serious economic problems as the threat of inflation continued to grow. The cost of living was higher and had risen faster in 1966 than in any year since the Korean War. Imports had increased at twice the rate of exports. Hourly wages were higher than in any other Common Market country and they tended to go higher as a labor shortage grew. Out of a total labor force of 26,000,000, only 216,000 were unemployed.

To head off inflation, the Kiesinger government drew up a program calling for higher taxes, the setting of credit ceilings, a cutback in expenditures for social services, and reduced defense spending.

Defense Cuts. In the fall, Germany, Great Britain, and the United States held discussions on the costs of keeping Allied troops in Germany. The German government indicated that it could not continue to offset foreign exchange costs at the level it had maintained during the preceding years. The United States and Britain insisted, however, that unless Germany continued to offset such costs they would be forced to reduce their forces in the republic. The United States maintained an estimated 300,000 troops in Germany; the foreign exchange costs of maintaining them were about $675,000,000. The British had about 59,000 troops in the country; their costs were about $263,000,000 a year. Late in the year, both the United States and Britain announced that unless some compromise could be reached they would have to cut back their troops when the current agreement expired in June, 1967.

The Starfighter Affair. The long-smoldering antagonism between the military command and the civilian defense ministry broke out in the open in August over the crash of a supersonic F-104G Starfighter. The crash was one in a series that had begun in 1961 and which, altogether, had cost the nation 62 planes and 40 deaths.

Immediately following the latest crash, Lieutenant General Werner Panitzki gave an interview in which he accused the defense ministry of inefficiency and delay in installing safety devices on the Starfighters. He also demanded a reorganization of the ministry. As a result, he was temporarily relieved as commander of the West German Air Force. Shortly thereafter, three top army generals quit over a decision by the civilian minister of defense, Kai-Uwe von Hassel, to allow trade union activities at army, navy, and air force installations. Despite an outcry in public and in parliament, Chancellor Erhard backed Von Hassel and approved his choice of successors to the generals. On December 6, however, the Luftwaffe's entire fleet of F-104G Starfighters was grounded for an indefinite period following another crash and another death on November 28.

East Germany's economy continued to grow during 1966, as did its standard of living. Food was plentiful and cheap with the exception of such tropical imports as coffee, which retailed for $10 a pound. Other durable consumer goods were also expensive. A television set, for example, cost $500.

Facts in Brief. Germany (East). Population: 17,300,000. Government: Communist Party First Secretary Walter Ulbricht; Prime Minister Willi Stoph. Monetary Unit: deutsche mark (4.19=U.S. $1). Foreign Trade: exports, $408,800,000; imports, $534,600,000. Principal Exports: machinery, fuel, clothing.

Germany (West). Population: 58,100,000. Government: President Heinrich Luebke; Chancellor Kurt Georg Kiesinger. Monetary Unit: deutsche mark (4=U.S. $1). Foreign Trade: exports, $17,911,300,000; imports, $17,611,000,000. Principal Exports: iron and steel, motor vehicles, chemicals, machinery.

KENNETH BROWN

Germany's past, present, and future leaders meet in Bonn. Former Chancellor Konrad Adenauer, *left*, and Chancellor Ludwig Erhard flank Kurt G. Kiesinger, who succeeded Erhard on December 1.

Ghanaian children cavort on ex-leader Kwame Nkrumah's statue after an army uprising had toppled him, and his monument, in February.

GHANA. Colonel Emmanuel R. Kotoka led an attack by army and police units on the main government buildings in Accra on February 24. The only resistance came from President Kwame Nkrumah's special guard and other security forces. Kotoka announced on the government radio that the victorious rebels had suspended the constitution, dismissed Nkrumah and all his ministers, dissolved parliament, and abolished Nkrumah's dominant Convention People's party. Kotoka contended that Nkrumah's dictatorial reign had brought Ghana close to economic disaster. Lieutenant General Joseph A. Ankrah, who became commander of the army and chairman of the National Liberation Council, pledged a future return to civil rule.

The rebellion took place while Nkrumah was in Peking, China, en route to Hanoi, North Vietnam, where he had hoped to arrange a truce in the Vietnamese war. Barred from returning to Ghana, he went to Guinea, where President Sékou Touré welcomed him and threatened to invade Ghana to restore Nkrumah to power. See GUINEA.

The government freed more than 700 prisoners of the Nkrumah regime, and placed in custody several hundred associates of Nkrumah. Alex Quaison-Sackey, Nkrumah's foreign minister and a former president of the United Nations General Assembly, was among those arrested. Later, he, former cabinet member Kojo Botsio, and others were freed.

Ankrah announced on March 2 that Ghana would resume negotiations with the World Bank and the International Monetary Fund to obtain urgently needed aid. The fund granted $36,400,000 in stand-by credits.

In February and March, the new government re-established diplomatic relations with Great Britain, and expelled more than 130 Russian technicians and their families. Communist China withdrew 125 technicians. The University of Ghana recruited British and U.S. professors to replace the Russians.

The giant $168,000,000 Volta River hydroelectric project was inaugurated by Nkrumah on January 22. U.S. agencies were expected to invest $164,000,000 in an aluminum smelter at Tema that will use Volta River power.

Ghana seized Guinean officials at Accra airport on October 29 to force the release of Ghanaians held in Guinea. The Guineans were released in November after world-wide protests.

Facts in Brief. Population: 8,164,000. Government: National Liberation Council Chairman Joseph A. Ankrah. Monetary Unit: cedi (1 = U.S. $1.17). Foreign Trade: exports, $317,800,000; imports, $448,000,000. Principal Exports: cocoa, diamonds, lumber, manganese. BENJAMIN E. THOMAS

GIRL SCOUTS. See YOUTH ORGANIZATIONS.

GIRLS' CLUBS OF AMERICA. See YOUTH ORGANIZATIONS.

GODDARD, JAMES LEE (1923-), took over as commissioner of the U.S. Food and Drug Administration (FDA) on Jan. 17, 1966. And immediately, the drug industry, doctors, the public, and the FDA itself had to take notice of him.

The wiry, prematurely gray-haired administrator was the first physician to head the FDA since 1921, and he aimed to impose high professional standards on the regulatory organization. In so doing, he showed a low tolerance for incompetence, bureaucratic delays, or ignorance. He had drugs taken off the market as unsafe or ineffective, lashed out at misleading advertising, and ordered relabeling of dangerous drugs.

Dr. Goddard was born in Alliance, Ohio, on Aug. 24, 1923. He got his M.D. from George Washington University in 1949, and his Master of Public Health degree, *magna cum laude*, from Harvard University in 1955. He joined the U.S. Public Health Service in 1951, became a civilian air surgeon in the Federal Aviation Agency in 1959, and was appointed head of the Communicable Disease Center, Atlanta, Ga., in 1962.

He married Mildred Mae Miller, a nurse, in 1945 while they were both serving in the army. He takes an occasional weekend off for hiking and camping with his wife and three teen-age children.

See also DRUGS; Section Two, OUR PILL-FILLED LIVES.

GOLF. Jack Nicklaus and Billy Casper were the big winners in 1966, the richest year ever recorded in professional golf. Nicklaus passed up a number of tournaments but competed in all the major ones, winning two of the top four – the Masters at Augusta, Ga., and the British Open at Muirfield, Scotland. Casper, winner of the 1966 U.S. Open title at San Francisco's Olympic Club, played more often, however, and managed to keep his name at the top of the earnings list for most of the year. His total earnings of $121,944 topped those of Nicklaus by $10,525.

The victory by Nicklaus at Augusta firmly established the 26-year-old golfer from Columbus, Ohio, as the master of the Masters. It was his third triumph in this event over the past four years. To win, he just had to survive an 18-hole play-off with Tommy Jacobs and Gay Brewer, Jr. After observing flaws in his own putting technique while watching a television rerun of a previous round, Nicklaus changed his putting stance in the play-off and putted superbly the following day.

The failure of Arnold Palmer to win the U.S. Open disappointed millions of his fans who watched the event on television. Most remembered how he had made golf history by making up seven strokes on the last round to win the 1960 Open at Cherry Hills Golf Club at Denver, Colo. During the 1966 Open, however, Palmer lost the lead three times. At one point in the fourth round he led Casper by seven strokes, but Casper rallied to tie him. In the decisive play-off, Casper won by four strokes.

PGA Victory. Al Geiberger of California captured the Professional Golfers Association (PGA) championship at Akron's lengthy Firestone course. He won his first major title by four strokes.

On the night of Geiberger's victory, professional golf lost one of its most personable players, Tony Lema. The 32-year-old Lema was killed in a plane crash along with his wife, Betty, a woman pilot, and a co-pilot. Lema's private plane crashed on a golf course that straddled the Indiana-Illinois state line. He had been scheduled to play in a one-day tournament on that very course the next day.

Jack Nicklaus' winning feat in the British Open was just as satisfying as Geiberger's at Akron, even though the British tournament offered only a small purse by escalated U.S. standards. It had been the only one of the four major professional golf tournaments that Nicklaus had not yet won.

South African Gary Player appeared infrequently on courses in the United States during 1966. He proved, however, that he could still win when competing with the top U.S. golfers. In a relatively new tournament in England, an eight-man affair called the Piccadilly World Tournament, Player eliminated Palmer in one semifinal match while Nicklaus was beating Casper. Then Player scored a surprisingly easy victory over Nicklaus to win the title.

Women's Play. Kathy Whitworth of San Antonio, Tex., led in earnings for professional women golfers, with $33,517, but the major titles were taken by lesser-known players.

Sandra Spuzich of Indianapolis, Ind., won the Women's Open at Chaska, Minn., edging Carol Mann of Towson, Md., by a single stroke. Gloria Ehret of Danbury, Conn., scored an upset in the Ladies PGA championship at the Stardust Golf Club in Las Vegas.

Amateur Golf. In the longest U.S. Woman's Amateur final ever played, Mrs. JoAnne Gunderson Carner of Seekonk, Mass., won her fourth title, defeating Mrs. Marlene Stewart Streit of Canada on the 41st hole of a scheduled 36-hole match. The same two had met in the final 10 years earlier, and Mrs. Streit had won it. Mrs. Streit won the 1966 medal honors in the World Women's Amateur tournament at Mexico City in October. She lives in Willowdale, Ont., and was playing for Canada. The United States won team honors.

The U.S. Men's Amateur championship played at Ardmore, Pa., was also won by a Canadian. Gary Cowan of Kitchener, Ont., became the first foreigner in 34 years to take the title. He tied Deane Beman of Bethesda, Md., in regulation play and then edged him by one stroke in the 18-hole play-off.

The University of Houston won the National Collegiate Athletic Association (NCAA) championship for the ninth time in 11 years. JOHN LAKE

GOVERNORS OF THE STATES holding office in 1967 are listed below, with their political affiliations and their years in office. Governors were elected in 35 states on Nov. 8, 1966. The Republicans won 23 governorships, and, with two incumbents, now have a total of 25. The Democrats won 12. With 13 incumbents, they hold a total of 25 governorships. Beginning in 1967, governors in Massachusetts, Michigan, and Nebraska will serve four-year terms. See ELECTIONS.

Governors of the 50 States

State	Governor	Terms
Ala.	Lurleen Wallace, D.	1967-1971
Alaska	Walter J. Hickel, R.	1966-1970
Ariz.	John R. Williams, R.	1967-1969
Ark.	Winthrop Rockefeller, R.	1967-1969
Calif.	Ronald Reagan, R.	1967-1971
Colo.	John A. Love, R.	1963-1971
Conn.	John N. Dempsey, D.	1961-1971
Del.	Charles L. Terry, Jr., D.	1965-1969
Fla.	Claude R. Kirk, Jr., R.	1967-1971
Ga.	Lester G. Maddox, D.	1967-1971
Hawaii	John A. Burns, D.	1963-1971
Idaho	Don W. Samuelson, R.	1967-1971
Ill.	Otto J. Kerner, Jr., D.	1961-1969
Ind.	Roger D. Branigin, D.	1965-1969
Iowa	Harold E. Hughes, D.	1963-1969
Kans.	Robert Docking, D.	1967-1969
Ky.	Edward T. Breathitt, Jr., D.	1963-1967
La.	John J. McKeithen, D.	1964-1968
Me.	Kenneth M. Curtis, D.	1967-1971
Md.	Spiro T. Agnew, R.	1967-1971
Mass.	John A. Volpe, R.	*1965-1971
Mich.	George W. Romney, R.	1963-1971
Minn.	Harold E. Le Vander, R.	1967-1971
Miss.	Paul B. Johnson, Jr., D.	1964-1968
Mo.	Warren E. Hearnes, D.	1965-1969
Mont.	Tim M. Babcock, R.	1962-1969
Nebr.	Norbert T. Tiemann, R.	1967-1971
Nev.	Paul Laxalt, R.	1967-1971
N.H.	John W. King, D.	1963-1969
N.J.	Richard J. Hughes, D.	1962-1970
N.Mex.	David F. Cargo, R.	1967-1969
N.Y.	Nelson A. Rockefeller, R.	1959-1971
N.C.	Daniel K. Moore, D.	1965-1969
N.Dak.	William L. Guy, D.	1961-1969
Ohio	James A. Rhodes, R.	1963-1971
Okla.	Dewey Bartlett, R.	1967-1971
Ore.	Tom McCall, R.	1967-1971
Pa.	Raymond P. Shafer, R.	1967-1971
R.I.	John H. Chafee, R.	1963-1969
S.C.	Robert E. McNair, D.	1965-1971
S.Dak.	Nils A. Boe, R.	1965-1969
Tenn.	Buford Ellington, D.	†1967-1971
Tex.	John B. Connally, Jr., D.	1963-1969
Utah	Calvin L. Rampton, D.	1965-1969
Vt.	Philip H. Hoff, D.	1963-1969
Va.	Mills E. Godwin, Jr., D.	1966-1970
Wash.	Daniel J. Evans, R.	1965-1969
W.Va.	Hulett C. Smith, D.	1965-1969
Wis.	Warren P. Knowles, R.	1965-1969
Wyo.	Stanley K. Hathaway, R.	1967-1971

*Served previous term (1961-1963).
†Served previous term (1959-1963).

GREAT BRITAIN

British voters supported the Labour party government in general elections on March 31. Prime Minister Harold Wilson saw his majority in the House of Commons leap from three to 97 as Labour won 363 seats. The Conservatives, under a new leader, Edward Heath, lost 51 seats, leaving them with 253. The Liberals increased their representation by two seats to 12. The Irish Republican Labour party won one seat. Thus, Labour was virtually guaranteed five more years of rule.

It was a singular success for Wilson. He had not only mastered the timing of the election, but had also judged that a quiet, even a dull campaign would best serve his party. Try as Heath did to raise major election issues – the dire problems of the economy and whether Britain should enter the European Common Market – the voters insisted that Labour, and Wilson, deserved an extended run in office. Nationally, Labour received 13,057,000 votes, the Conservatives 11,418,000, and the Liberals, 2,327,000. The turnout of 75.9 per cent was slightly down from the last general election in 1964.

Labour's majority was cut to 95 when a Welsh Nationalist won a by-election at Carmarthen, South Wales, on July 14. It was the first time the Welsh party was represented in Parliament.

Economic Crisis. Almost as soon as he returned to his desk, Wilson ran into the most severe financial crisis since 1949, when the value of the pound sterling was forced down. The pound had been faltering on the international exchange since February, reflecting the economy's generally poor performance and Britain's imbalance of trade.

Though industrial production had leveled off in the 15 months from January, 1965, to March, 1966, hourly wages, assisted by full employment and a shorter workweek, were rising 9 per cent a year. By July, inflation had put the pound under heavy strain, the precise loss of value being concealed by support from the Bank of England. Britain's creditors, principally U.S. and European central banks, voiced their growing dissatisfaction. Further credits to help stabilize the pound, they said, would depend on the Labour government's internal action.

July Measures. Wilson had committed himself, both in London and in Washington, D.C., to keep the pound's existing $2.80 exchange rate. He first sought to minimize the international loss of confidence in the economy, but on July 14 was forced to

Stalled ships crammed London's docks in June when a seamen's strike hit hard at Britain's already beleaguered economy.

raise the bank rate from 6 to 7 per cent to reduce borrowing. He then left for a weekend of diplomatic talks in Moscow. On his return, he found that the fiscal situation had gravely deteriorated.

The government's economic advisers were now insisting on immediate deflation. Wilson agreed, and faced the House of Commons on July 20 with a package of measures taking 600,000,000 pounds out of circulation. He wanted, and got, stringent restrictions on purchases, higher taxes on liquor and gasoline, a 10 per cent surcharge on the surtax paid by top-bracket taxpayers, cuts in public expenditures, and a reduction in the overseas holiday travel allowance from 250 pounds to 50.

In addition, the government locked the economy in a six-month freeze of incomes and prices (excluding, of course, prices raised by its own measures). This was to be followed by six more months of severe restraint. The voluntary curb of wage increases had plainly failed. The government tacked the powers it needed to enforce the freeze to its Prices and Incomes Bill, then in the Commons, and forced its passage against strong opposition.

Into Recession. The consequences of Wilson's deflationary policy were soon visible. There was a sharp slump in industrial investment plans and layoffs of workers by large firms. Labour's ambitious national economic plan of 1965 was dead. Unemployment, which had been running at 1.5 per cent, rose to 2.4 per cent by mid-December.

Loud outcries were heard from trade unions, which feared that unemployment would rise to even higher levels. Wilson spoke before the Trades Union Congress on September 5, and again at the Labour party conference October 4, securing the unions' endorsement of his anti-inflationary policies. His government did not dare to reduce the squeeze on credit or to modify the wage freeze until the end of November, the date it had promised to lift the remaining 10 per cent surcharge on imports. If the pound survived the expected rise in imports, the government might relax other restrictions. But the most the government would say was that it hoped the country's balance of payments would be in the black in 1967.

Payroll Tax. In the budget announced by Chancellor of the Exchequer James Callaghan on May 3, employers were to pay a selective tax for each employee. The tax began September 5, but was to be refunded, with a bonus, only to manufacturers after February, 1967.

The aim of the tax, attributed to Callaghan's aide, Nicholas Kaldor, was to make service industries pay a greater share of the tax burden and thus encourage manufacturing–and export–with a shift of service workers into manufacturing work. But the

Prime Minister Harold Wilson, victorious in March elections, was soon frustrated by severe crises, both at home and in the Commonwealth.

Blood, Sweat, and Tears

notion that all types of services should be equally burdened, and all types of manufacturers equally privileged, served to deteriorate further British industry's relations with the Labour government.

Cabinet Shake-Out. Despite the election success, Wilson's cabinet remained under constant strain. Frank Cousins, left-wing leader of the giant Transport and General Workers' Union, resigned from his cabinet post as technology minister on July 3, contending that Wilson's policy of restraining wage increases was "fundamentally wrong." At the height of the economic tension, on July 20, First Secretary of State George Brown submitted his resignation, but withdrew it within hours. Callaghan also indicated dissatisfaction.

On August 10, Wilson hastily reshuffled his team. Brown took over the foreign office, a post he had long wanted, exchanging cabinet seats with Michael Stewart, who succeeded him as first secretary and minister of economic affairs. Left-inclined political theorist Richard Crossman advanced to become leader of the House of Commons.

The government announced in March that the pound–whatever its value–would be divided in 1971 into 100 pence under the decimal system.

Rhodesia Holds Out. British economic sanctions failed to bring down the illegal white government of Prime Minister Ian Smith in Rhodesia. Smith's rebels had broken with Britain in November, 1965, rather than agree to future rule by the black majority. Wilson forecast in January that his economic measures "might well bring the rebellion to an end within a matter of weeks rather than months." But by April 9, he was forced to go to the United Nations (UN) Security Council for permission to use force, if necessary, to keep tankers from carrying oil for Rhodesia. See UNITED NATIONS (UN).

He was further embarrassed when the Commonwealth prime ministers assembled in London from September 6 to 14. Afro-Asian Commonwealth nations demanded military action against Smith. Wilson agreed that if Smith did not take "the initial and indispensable steps" to end the rebellion by the end of the year, Britain would withdraw its existing proposals and seek mandatory economic sanctions at the UN.

A further British plan for a settlement, including guaranteed advancement of black Africans to political equality, was offered to Smith in Salisbury, Rhodesia, in September by Commonwealth Secretary Herbert Bowden. Smith answered that the two sides might not be far from agreement. But it seemed clear that he refused to give up his government's independence.

In December, Smith met with Wilson aboard a British warship where they drafted last-ditch proposals to end the revolt. The British Commons accepted them unanimously, but on December 5, Rhodesia rejected the terms. True to Wilson's promise to the Commonwealth Nations, Britain went before the UN Security Council. For the first time in its history, the Council voted mandatory economic sanctions against a country, banning UN members from selling oil to Rhodesia or purchasing 12 basic Rhodesian exports.

Gibraltar Blockaded. Britain and Spain remained at loggerheads over the future of Gibraltar, the historic British fortress at the western entrance to the Mediterranean.

Spanish Caudillo Francisco Franco claimed The Rock for "natural unity and territorial integrity." He accused the Gibraltarians of smuggling, and the British of flying over Spanish territory near the Gibraltar air base. Britain offered Spain a permanent representative in Gibraltar and the use of both port and airfield on the same terms given to North Atlantic Treaty Organization (NATO) members. The Spaniards refused, and set up a land blockade.

Defense Controversy. Britain's continued military role east of Suez created mounting controversy within the Labour party. Minister of Defense for the Navy Christopher Mayhew resigned February 19 in protest of the decision by Defense Secretary Denis Healey to phase out the aircraft carrier force by the mid-1970s. Healey stated on February 22 that the Indian Ocean area would be defended by a force of 50 F-111A fighter-bombers to be bought from the United States.

At the Labour party conference on October 6, Mayhew joined union leader Frank Cousins to defeat Healey's east-of-Suez policy. Cousins' argument, shared throughout the Labour left, was that the defense budget should be reduced.

Crime in the Headlines. The nation was shocked when three plainclothes policemen were shot dead on August 12, outside Wormwood Scrubs prison, London. Two men were swiftly arrested but a third, Harry Roberts, was seized only after a nationwide search. See CRIME.

The killings aroused strong demands for a return to capital punishment for the murder of Britain's unarmed policemen. The move was resisted by Home Secretary Roy Jenkins. An inquiry revealed that none of Britain's prisons was secure.

World Cup Win. To the delight of soccer fans, England won the Jules Rimet Trophy for the first time in the World Cup competition in London in July. Before the games, the trophy itself was stolen from an exhibit, and remained missing until sniffed out by a dog taking his master for an evening stroll.

Facts in Brief. Population: 54,300,000. Government: Queen Elizabeth II; Prime Minister Harold Wilson. Monetary Unit: pound (1 = U.S. $2.80). Foreign Trade: exports, $13,710,900,000; imports, $16,137,700,000. Principal Exports: chemicals, machinery, motor vehicles, textiles. ALASTAIR BURNET

See also FASHION; SOCCER.

GREECE enjoyed a relatively quiet year, free from the parliamentary crises and public riots that had marred 1965. It remained preoccupied, however, with the problem of Cyprus.

Acrimony over military control of the island and plans for its future continued in 1966 between Archbishop Makarios, the Cypriot president, and General George Grivas, the Athens-appointed Cypriot commander of an army which included 10,000 Greek "volunteers." The archbishop charged that the general was planning to depose him.

In a parliamentary debate over the issue, Prime Minister Stephanos Christos Stephenopoulos, who sided with Grivas, lost his one-man majority when two ministers "defected" during a vote on the issue. He regained the balance when an adherent from the Centre Union party swung over to his side. In December, however, Stephenopoulos lost a substantial part of his parliamentary support and he was forced to resign. An interim government was set up under Ioannis Paraskevopoulos to prepare for general elections in May, 1967.

Facts in Brief. Population: 8,710,000. Government: King Constantine XIII; Prime Minister Ioannis Paraskevopoulos. Monetary Unit: drachma (29.85 = U.S. $1). Foreign Trade: exports, $327,600,000; imports, $1,133,900,000. Principal Exports: cotton, dried fruit, tobacco. KENNETH BROWN

GUATEMALA. See LATIN AMERICA.

GUINEA welcomed Kwame Nkrumah on March 2 after he had been deposed by Ghana. President Sékou Touré created confusion by declaring Nkrumah president of Guinea, but it was soon clear that this was an honorary position and that Touré still ruled Guinea. Touré accused Britain of planning Nkrumah's ouster and threatened to send troops across Ivory Coast to Ghana to return Nkrumah to power. He then said France had sent troops in disguise to support an Ivory Coast attack on Guinea. Guinea did not mobilize its troops, however, though the state radio continued to denounce Britain, France, and conservative African countries. Nkrumah's broadcasts urging Ghanaians to rebel caused Ghana to protest to the United Nations.

On October 29, Foreign Minister Louis Beavogui and 18 other Guinean officials were seized at Accra, Ghana, while en route to an Organization of African Unity parley in Ethiopia (see GHANA). Guinea charged that the United States was behind the Accra incident. It detained the U.S. ambassador for 24 hours, and later expelled the U.S. Peace Corps mission. The Guinean hostages were released on November 5, following international protests.

Facts in Brief. Population: 3,545,000. Government: President Sékou Touré. Monetary Unit: CFA franc (245 = U.S. $1). Foreign Trade: exports, $51,500,000; imports, $49,200,000. Principal Exports: aluminum, bananas, coffee. BENJAMIN E. THOMAS

GUYANA, a former British colonial possession on the northeast coast of South America, became an independent nation on May 26, 1966. Guyana, which means "land of waters," was formerly known as British Guiana.

Guyana's admission as the 23rd member of the British Commonwealth of Nations was announced on May 26. A referendum was scheduled for 1967 to decide whether Guyana would remain a constitutional monarchy or become a republic.

The 620-man British military garrison was to have remained in the country only until October. But, in November, the stay was extended for an indefinite period. A state of emergency declared by Great Britain in 1964 was to remain in effect until the 63-man parliament could enact similar emergency measures. It was not until December, however, that a security bill was introduced in parliament to give broad powers to the government.

On May 26, the United States turned over Atkinson Field in Georgetown to Guyana. It had obtained a lease on the airport during World War II.

Facts in Brief. Population: 683,000. Government: Governor-General Sir Richard Luyt; Prime Minister Forbes Burnham. Monetary Unit: Guyana dollar (1.71 = U.S. $1). Foreign Trade: exports, $97,300,000; imports, $104,400,000. Principal Exports: bauxite, cane sugar, rice. PAUL TULLIER

HAITI. See LATIN AMERICA.

HANDICAPPED, THE. The U.S. program of services for the handicapped was expanded in 1966 under the Vocational Rehabilitation Act, which became law in November, 1965. The new legislation authorized federal grants for the construction and staffing of rehabilitation workshops. It also made it possible for the states to provide up to six months of vocational rehabilitation services for severely disabled persons. U.S. officials hoped that, with the enlarged federal-state programs, their goal of rehabilitating 300,000 disabled Americans can be reached by 1975.

During the fiscal year ended June 30, 1966, a record total of 154,000 mentally or physically handicapped persons returned to gainful employment. Pennsylvania, with 12,338 persons rehabilitated, led the list of states for the fourth year in succession. New York was second with 9,512; North Carolina, third with 9,184; and Illinois, fourth with 8,302.

Outstanding advances in rehabilitation techniques were reported at the 10th triennial world congress of the International Society for Rehabilitation of the Disabled. More than 2,500 delegates from 61 countries attended the convention in Wiesbaden, Germany, Sept. 11 to 17, 1966. Results of research projects being financed by U.S. funds in Egypt, India, Israel, Pakistan, Poland, and Yugoslavia were reported. JOSEPH P. ANDERSON

HARNESS RACING. See HORSE RACING.

An Air Force plane sprays Dallas, Tex., with an anti-mosquito insecticide in attempt to eradicate an epidemic of encephalitis.

HEALTH AND DISEASE. Members of the 89th Congress of the United States, which adjourned Oct. 22, 1966, took an interest in the health of the nation as no previous Congress ever had. More than 1,500 "health" bills were introduced, and during the first session, Congress enacted into law more national health measures than had all previous Congresses in the last decade. Congress also appropriated more dollars for health than it had in all of the 168 years since the U.S. Public Health Service (PHS) was formed.

Among the more important of the new laws were Medicare; the Comprehensive Public Health Amendments; the Heart Disease, Cancer, and Stroke program; the Drug Abuse Control Amendments; and the Child Safety Act of 1966 (see MEDICARE; SOCIAL WELFARE).

In many quarters, concern was expressed over the cost of Medicaid, as well as Medicare, and the fact that national expenditures for all forms of medical care, public and private, had tripled since 1950. On August 23, John W. Gardner, Secretary of Health, Education, and Welfare, was directed by President Lyndon B. Johnson to begin a major study of rising health costs.

Respiratory Diseases. The PHS announced a new program in February to deal with chronic respiratory diseases. The remedial and control program, with an appropriation of $1,000,000 for the first year, will complement the extensive research that the PHS regularly conducts on such diseases. The most common are chronic bronchitis and emphysema, which probably to some degree affect at least 10 per cent of the middle and older age groups.

Obesity. A panel of experts appointed by the PHS concluded that obesity is a major public health problem among Americans. It is a problem, they said, that will probably get worse as the nation eats more and exercises less. The best way to lose weight and to keep it off, the experts said, is to step-up physical activity and to make a permanent change in eating habits under medical supervision.

Epidemics. Flooding in Texas in the spring of 1966 led to a proliferation of Culex mosquitoes, the carrier of encephalitis. This resulted in an encephalitis epidemic during the summer in which 104 suspected cases were reported and 11 deaths recorded. The spraying of wide areas with malathion to eradicate the mosquitoes succeeded in halting the spread of the disease.

An influenza epidemic occurred in March with 715 deaths reported from 122 cities during one week. It is hoped that a new medication (Amantadine hydrochloride), administered in pill form, will serve to minimize future outbreaks of type A influenza, known as Asian flu. THEODORE F. TREUTING

See also DENTISTRY; HOSPITAL; MEDICINE; MENTAL HEALTH.

HELMS, RICHARD M. (1913-   ), a career intelligence officer, took command of the Central Intelligence Agency (CIA) on June 30, 1966. He had been deputy for a year to Vice-Admiral William F. Raborn, who resigned as director after serving 13 months. Raborn had had no previous experience in either intelligence or foreign affairs, and CIA morale had been widely reported as low. Helms, on the other hand, was the first professional to have come up from the ranks to head the CIA.

His experience in the field started in World War II when the former foreign correspondent served as a naval intelligence officer. He joined the CIA when it was established in 1947.

Helms was born in Saint Davids, Pa., on March 30, 1913. He received his high school education in Germany and Switzerland and speaks French and German fluently. He was graduated with honors from Williams College in Williamstown, Mass., in 1935. After working with United Press and the *Indianapolis Times*, he joined the navy in 1942. In August, 1943, he was assigned to the Office of Strategic Services (OSS).

Helms married Julia Bretzman Shields of Indianapolis in 1939. They live in Washington, D.C., with their son Dennis and a son and daughter from a previous marriage of Mrs. Helms.

HIGHWAY. See TRANSPORTATION.

HOBBIES. Comparative stability returned to the coin collecting market in 1966, as the coin shortage ended and frenzied hoarding diminished. Plaguing dealers and collectors was an increase in thefts of coin collections and the appearance of forged coins. Another concern was an increase in the minting of "fantasy coins," which were being issued by some countries for sale to collectors rather than for use as legal tender.

In January, the U.S. Department of the Treasury announced that it would date all coins 1965 until August, when they would be dated 1966. Prior to this announcement, coin dating had been frozen at 1964 to lessen the demand by collectors during the shortage. Other evidence that the shortage had ended came from Canada, where it was announced in January that the government would accept orders for proof sets of its 1966 coins. In contrast to 1965, only a few orders arrived.

Despite the end of the coin shortage, few Kennedy half dollars showed up in general circulation although more than 390,000,000 had been minted in 1964 and 1965. Obviously many were being hoarded.

Although the U.S. Department of the Treasury adhered to its policy of not offering proof sets for sale, it did accept orders for mint sets of 1965 coins in March and later for 1966 issues. Produced at the San Francisco mint, these sets of five coins were of

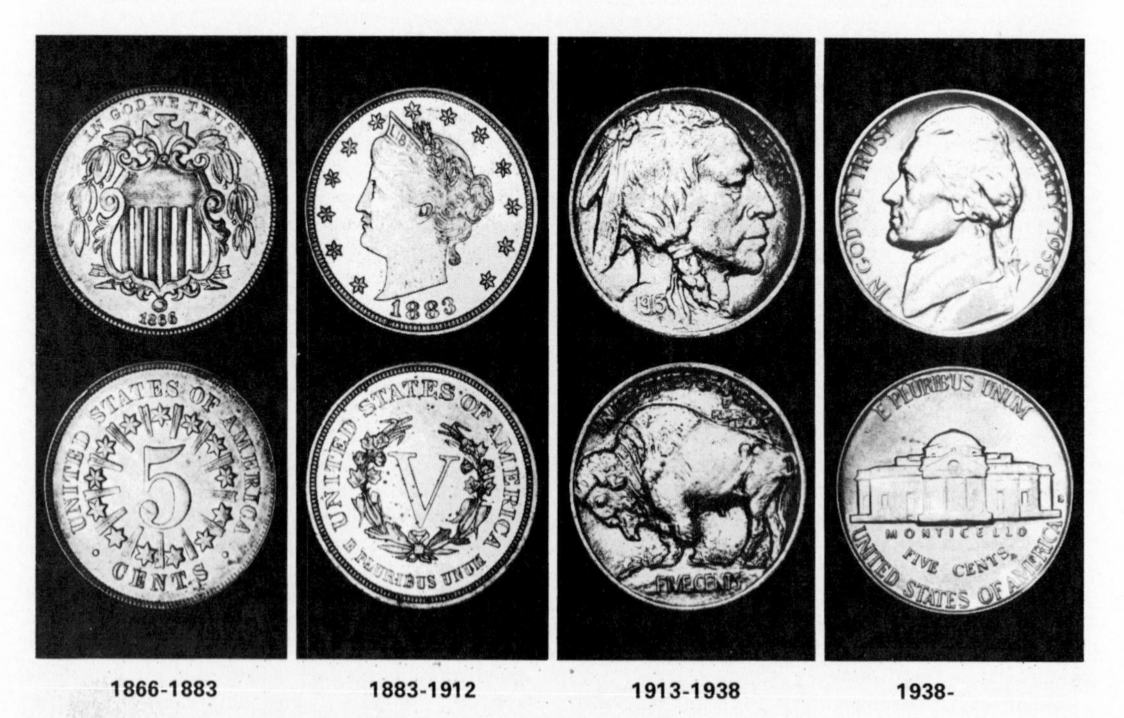

1866-1883 **1883-1912** **1913-1938** **1938-**

The nickel celebrated its 100th birthday in 1966. The four major nickels issued during the 100-year period are shown above. The dates indicate the years in which each coin was minted and circulated.

unusually high quality because they were produced on former ammunition presses. The powerful striking pressure of these machines produced coins with a higher relief and a shinier surface than previous mint sets. By April, 2,000,000 of the 1965 sets had been ordered at $4 a set.

The American Numismatic Association set up a coin theft reward fund as an incentive to the apprehension of coin thieves and their accomplices. The International Association of Professional Numismatists created a committee to deal with the problem of "fantasy coins." Members voted that, after May 18, they would refuse to handle issues so designated by the committee.

Stamps. Stamp collectors were concerned with the philatelic equivalent of "fantasy coins," stamps issued primarily for sale to collectors rather than for use as postage. With more than 4,000 different stamps being issued annually, it has become increasingly difficult for the collector of average means to maintain a complete general collection. For example, a collector who wished to obtain a complete set of stamps honoring the late President John F. Kennedy had to spend about $500. The American Philatelic Association decided to continue its use of the "black blot" symbol to indicate "unneeded" stamps.

The first stamp auction ever held at sea was conducted aboard the *Queen Mary*, which was bringing collectors to the Sixth International Philatelic Exhibition at Washington, D.C., in May. Collectors on land were able to bid by radiotelephone. Roger Weill of New Orleans, aboard the ship, paid $56,000 for a block of 21 of the 90-cent blues of 1860. Joel Olsson of Boras, Sweden, won the top award at the exhibition for a specialized collection of 1855-1858 Skilling-Banco issues and 1856-1862 local issue rarities. American winners were Mr. and Mrs. Charles E. Kilbourne of Schenectady, N.Y., and General Robert J. Gill of Baltimore, Md.

In May, the United States issued its first international air mail postal card. The 11-cent card was also the first ever printed by a duotone process and the first U.S. card with a *cachet*, a four-paneled pictorial of outstanding sights for visitors.

Great Britain, in June, issued its first sports stamps, commemorating the world soccer championships. When England subsequently won the event, one of the stamps was reissued with the overprint, "England-Winner!"

One of the year's most unusual stamps was issued by Czechoslovakia to commemorate the 30th anniversary of the International Brigade which fought in the Spanish Civil War. It bore Pablo Picasso's famous painting *Guernica*, which hangs in New York City's Museum of Modern Art. It was issued in sheets of 15. In the right margin of five, appeared Picasso's signature plus a detail from the painting, a hand holding a broken sword. THEODORE M. O'LEARY

HOLT, HAROLD EDWARD (1908-), a lawyer and political leader, became prime minister of Australia Jan. 26, 1966. He had served in the cabinet of his predecessor, Sir Robert Menzies.

Harold Edward Holt was born in Sydney, Australia, Aug. 5, 1908. He attended Wesley College in Melbourne, and Queen's College of the University of Melbourne, where he received his law degree. He was elected to the federal parliament in 1935 and four years later was invited to join the first Menzies cabinet. In March, 1940, Holt, a Liberal, was dropped from Menzies' coalition government to accommodate a leader of the Country party. He then volunteered for overseas duty. In October, 1940, Holt was recalled to head a new ministry. He remained in parliament as a member of the opposition after the Menzies government fell in 1941.

When Menzies regained power in 1949, Holt was appointed to the cabinet as minister for immigration. He became treasurer in 1958. In 1960, he risked his popularity with the voters by introducing a deflationary budget. He represented Australia at the Manila conference on Vietnam in October, 1966. Holt's wife, Zara, is a dress designer.

HOME ECONOMICS. See FASHION; FOOD; INTERIOR DESIGN; YOUTH ORGANIZATIONS (Future Homemakers of America).

HOME FURNISHINGS. See INTERIOR DESIGN.

HONDURAS. See LATIN AMERICA.

HORSE RACING. The horse of the year was Buckpasser, three-year-old son of Tom Fool and Busanda, owned by Ogden Phipps. Although he missed three months of the season (including the triple crown races) because of an injury, Buckpasser won 11 stakes races, was the year's leading money-winner, and set a new world record for the mile.

Buckpasser and Graustark, owned by John Galbreath, were the early favorites for the Kentucky Derby. But in March, Buckpasser developed a quarter crack in his right front hoof that sidelined him until June. Then, on April 30, a week before the Derby, Graustark suffered a broken bone in his left front foot, and was retired to stud.

Major Foreign Races of 1966

Race	Winner	Value to Winner
Epsom Derby	Charlottown	$208,570
Grand National Steeplechase	Anglo	62,535
Grand Prix de Paris	Danseur	144,000
Irish Derby	Sodium	145,600
Prix de l'Arc de Triomphe	Bon Mot	219,000

Kauai King, owned by Michael Ford, won the Kentucky Derby and the Preakness. He failed in a bid to become the first triple crown winner in 18 years, however, running fourth in the Belmont Stakes, which went to Amberoid.

Buckpasser returned to the races in June and began an impressive winning streak. At year's end, he

Buckpasser, the horse of the year, won the Mile-long Arlington Classic in a world record time of 1 minute $32\frac{3}{5}$ seconds.

had earned $649,921 in winning 13 out of 14 races. This gave him a career total of $1,237,174.

In their only meeting of the year, Buckpasser beat Kauai King and won the Arlington Classic in world record time for the mile, 1 minute $32\frac{3}{5}$ seconds.

Eddie Neloy, Buckpasser's trainer, also saddled the year's best two-year-old, the aptly named Successor. Successor earned $441,404, winning four of nine starts and finishing in the money in all the others. Neloy set records himself by becoming the first trainer to saddle 40 stakes winners in a year.

Harness Racing. Bret Hanover became the top money-winner in harness racing history. Before the four-year-old pacer was retired in November, he had amassed $922,616 in earnings and had lowered the world pacing record for the mile to 1 minute $53\frac{3}{5}$ seconds. In 68 races over a three-year period, Bret Hanover won 62 times, was second five times, and third only once. Ironically, the third place was in his final race, at Hollywood Park, Inglewood, Calif. In this race he set such a fast pace, however, that the winner, True Duane, broke the world record for the $1\frac{1}{8}$ mile distance by two full seconds.

Romeo Hanover became the third horse (after Adios Butler and Bret Hanover) to win pacing's triple crown for three-year-olds, scoring easy victories in the Cane Futurity at Yonkers Raceway, the Little Brown Jug at Delaware, Ohio, and the Messenger Stakes at Roosevelt Raceway.

Major U.S. Races of 1966

Race	Winner	Value to Winner
Arlington Classic	Buckpasser	$ 63,000
Arlington-Washington Futurity	Diplomat Way	195,200
Belmont Stakes	Amberoid	117,700
Brooklyn Handicap	Buckpasser	69,615
Champagne Stakes	Successor	148,325
Delaware Handicap	Open Fire	79,930
Flamingo Stakes	Buckpasser	88,660
Garden State Stakes	Successor	188,475
Gardenia Stakes	Pepperwood	117,612
Gulfstream Handicap	First Family	74,200
Hollywood Derby	Fleet Host	75,500
Hollywood Gold Cup	Native Diver	102,100
Jockey Club Gold Cup	Buckpasser	71,825
Kentucky Derby	Kauai King	120,500
Metropolitan Handicap	Bold Lad	75,140
New Hampshire Sweepstakes	Buffle	180,212
Preakness	Kauai King	129,000
Santa Anita Derby	Boldnesian	96,900
Santa Anita Handicap	Lucky Debonair	100,000
Suburban Handicap	Buffle	72,085
Widener Handicap	Pia Star	87,620
Woodward Stakes	Buckpasser	73,190

In trotting, the triple crown races were won by three different three-year-olds. Polaris took the Yonkers Futurity, Kerry Way the Hambletonian at DuQuoin, Ill., and Governor Armbro the Kentucky Futurity at Lexington, Ky. Kerry Way was the first filly to win the Hambletonian in eight years.

Noble Victory set a world trotting record for the mile in 1 minute $55\frac{3}{5}$ seconds. James O. Dunaway

HOSPITAL. The implementation of Medicare in 1966 focused attention on the obsolete and inadequate facilities in many U.S. hospitals, and on the acute shortage of manpower–particularly of nursing personnel. By July 1, facilities containing more than 92 per cent of the nation's hospital beds had been approved for participation in the Medicare program, as a result of their compliance with the Civil Rights Act of 1964. See CIVIL RIGHTS.

Nurses from New York City to San Francisco went on strike for higher pay. Their actions pointed up the severe shortage of nurses, as well as the financial dilemma faced by those who provide health services. The new militancy on the part of nurses coincided with the start of Medicare, which will eventually require a sharp increase in the number of registered nurses.

In New York City, the Department of Hospitals announced a $1,300,000 program in March to train and license nurse's aides, many of whom already perform jobs for which they should be trained and licensed. The federal government will assist the city in financing the program.

What is apparently the nation's first "trauma center" for the intensive treatment of seriously injured and shock patients was established at Cook County Hospital in Chicago. THEODORE F. TREUTING

See also HEALTH; MEDICARE; MEDICINE.

HOTEL. See TRAVEL.

HOUSING activity in 1966 dropped to its lowest level since World War II. In October, for the first time since November, 1946, private housing starts dropped below 1,000,000 units a year, sinking to an annual rate of 841,000. They then rose to 1,000,000 in November, but were still down 35.4 per cent from the 1,547,000-unit pace of November, 1965.

Nor did the reports on new building permits give encouragement for any near-future upswing. The annual rate for permits sagged to 714,000 in October and inched back up to 717,600 in November. It had been 1,280,000 in November, 1965. Total outlays for new private, nonfarm residences also fell–from a seasonally adjusted annual rate of $21,500,000 in the first quarter of 1966 to $18,200,000 in the third quarter.

High interest rates, a tight money situation that limited borrowing even at high rates, increasing costs of building materials, and tax considerations all were factors in the slump (see BANKS AND BANKING; BUILDING AND CONSTRUCTION). The total number of private nonfarm housing starts in 1965 had been 1,482,300. Those for all of 1966 were estimated at 1,225,000, a 19 per cent drop for the year. Market analyses indicated there was demand, however, for nearly 1,600,000 units.

A National Housing Shortage and a substantial increase in housing costs were clearly indicated for 1967. The rental housing vacancy rate, which had not dipped below 7.2 per cent in any quarter since 1961, fell below 6.8 per cent in the second quarter of 1966. It was expected to remain low as long as new construction lagged.

President Lyndon B. Johnson, late in July, authorized the Department of Housing and Urban Development (HUD) to release–through the Federal National Mortgage Association (FNMA)–$250,000,000 in special assistance funds for financing the construction of some 15,000 low to moderately priced housing units. The funds, released on November 28, allowed FNMA to purchase mortgages from lending institutions.

Early in December, the President announced that the Federal Home Loan Bank Board would release an additional $500,000,000 to savings and loan associations and mutual savings banks. The amount should finance an additional 30,000 new homes and further stimulate the industry.

The Demonstration Cities and Metropolitan Development Act, or Public Law 89-754, enacted Nov. 3, 1966, gave promise of a long-run spur to housing. It was approved in October by a Congress that for months had scrutinized every facet of the complex program. Under the new law, some 60 to 70 cities of all sizes and in all parts of the country will be selected by HUD's Secretary to plan, develop, and execute comprehensive demonstration projects that, in turn, will lead to the development of "model" neighborhoods.

HUD was to coordinate the program in order to help cities "improve their physical environment, increase their supply of adequate housing for low- and moderate-income people, and provide educational and social services vital to health and welfare." Federal grants-in-aid will provide up to 80 per cent of the local share of the costs of the demonstration projects. Chosen cities will rebuild or restore–physically and socially–entire slum and blighted sections. They will have the help of 170 federal aid programs. See CITY.

Urban Renewal Funds. A survey conducted in mid-1966 by the National Association of Housing and Redevelopment Officials, the U.S. Conference of Mayors, and the National League of Cities indicated that the federally assisted urban renewal program was suffering a setback because of lack of federal funding. The survey revealed that 445 of the 800 cities with urban renewal projects will need $5,100,000,000 to plan and execute their new projects before June, 1969. Congress in 1966 failed to supplement the total of $2,200,000,000 that had already been authorized for 1965-1969.

Robert C. Weaver was sworn in on Jan. 18, 1966, as HUD's first Secretary a little more than four months after HUD had been authorized. Weaver, the first Negro to hold Cabinet rank, had served as administrator of the Housing and Home Finance Agency since 1961. J. ROBERT DUMOUCHEL

The $7,400,000 Jesse H. Jones Hall for the Performing Arts, the major cultural facility in the Southwest, opened in October, 1966.

HOUSTON gained a major cultural facility on October 3 with the opening of the Jesse H. Jones Hall for the Performing Arts. Its acoustics, elegance, and flexible design won national acclaim from critics who gathered for the gala event. The 3,001-seat hall, faced with Italian marble, cost $6,600,000 and was the first new structure in a proposed $40,-000,000 Civic Center. The next element, a convention center, was scheduled for completion in 1967.

Economic and population growth continued in Houston. Year-end estimates put the city's population at 1,192,000 and its metropolitan environs at 560,000. To support a range of expanded public facilities and services for the area, voters approved city and county bond issues totaling $138,600,000.

Construction activity downtown included work on two 28-floor office towers, one of which, the Houston Natural Gas Building, was topped out on October 7, just 10 months after excavation began. Shell Oil Company announced that it will build a 47-story building, said to be the tallest west of the Mississippi River. Industrial construction featured completion of a $32,000,000 brewery. Also, plans were made to build two steel mills.

Despite the presence of fuming petrochemical industries, a community air pollution survey released late in the year indicated that Houstonites, unlike dwellers in other U.S. cities of similar size, breathe relatively clean air. DONALD W. LIEF

HUGGINS, CHARLES BRENTON (1901-), who has devoted his life to combating cancer through surgery and medicine, was awarded a Nobel prize in physiology and medicine on Oct. 13, 1966. He shares the award with Peyton Rous of Rockefeller University in New York City.

Huggins is William B. Ogden Distinguished Service Professor of Surgery at the University of Chicago and director of the university's Ben May Laboratory for Cancer Research. When September brought his 65th birthday, he refused a retirement offer, saying that, "the cancer problem isn't licked yet." The university extended his contract.

Huggins was honored specifically for his work in hormone treatment of cancer of the prostate. He discovered, in 1941, that female sex hormones could be used to retard prostate cancers. This was the first nonradioactive substance to be found effective in the control of cancer.

Huggins was born in Halifax, Nova Scotia. He attended Acadia University there, and then obtained an M.D. degree from Harvard in 1924. He was an instructor in surgery at the University of Michigan's medical school before moving to Chicago in 1927.

Huggins and his wife, the former Margaret Wellman, have a son, Dr. Charles Edward Huggins of Harvard Medical School, and a daughter, Mrs. Emily Wellman Huggins Fine. WALTER F. MORSE

HUMPHREY, HUBERT HORATIO (1911-), returned on Jan. 3, 1966, from a tour of Japan, Formosa, the Philippines, and South Korea. En route, the Vice-President received an honorary degree from the University of Hawaii. Later in January, Humphrey and Secretary of State Dean Rusk represented the United States at the funeral of Indian Prime Minister Lal Bahadur Shastri in New Delhi. After the funeral, Humphrey conferred with Soviet Premier Aleksei Kosygin.

Then in February, Humphrey made another trip to the Far East. In 15 days, he visited South Vietnam, Thailand, Laos, Pakistan, India, Australia, New Zealand, the Philippines and, finally, South Korea. Highlight was an inspection of rural pacification programs and troop installations in South Vietnam. On his return, he briefed President Lyndon B. Johnson and congressional leaders of both parties.

Humphrey also spearheaded the administration's War on Poverty program; addressed the National Association for the Advancement of Colored People (NAACP) and the White House conference on civil rights; and headed a Cabinet-level commission to study social unrest in city slum areas.

The Vice-President made the headlines in July, 1966, when he called for a drive to eliminate slum housing, saying that if he lived in a slum he might "lead a mighty good revolt." CAROL L. THOMPSON

HUNGARY. In May, 1966, after long discussion and delay, economic reform measures were approved by the government. Scheduled to take effect on Jan. 1, 1968, the reforms called for the transfer of considerable autonomy to various enterprises. They also called for the introduction of a freer system of price setting. At the same time, a new five-year plan for 1966-1970 was adopted.

The close association between Hungary and the Soviet Union remained unchanged during 1966. First Secretary János Kádár, in a speech made at the 23rd congress of the Communist Party of the Soviet Union in Moscow, gave full support to the Soviet Union in its dispute with Communist China. Hungarian aid to North Vietnam was increased in 1966 following two visits by delegations from Hanoi.

Visits exchanged with other Communist states during the year testified to Hungary's solidarity with its neighbors. Kádár visited Romania, Yugoslavia, and the (East) German Democratic Republic; Premier Guyla Kállai the United Arab Republic (UAR) and India.

Facts in Brief. Population: 10,225,000. Government: Communist Party First Secretary János Kádár; President Istvan Dobi; Premier Guyla Kállai. Monetary Unit: forint (23.48=U.S. $1). Foreign Trade: exports, $350,000,000; imports, $442,800,000. Principal Exports: meat, metals, motor vehicles. H. GORDON SKILLING

HUNTING AND FISHING. A total of 34,827,066 hunters and fishermen in the United States spent a record $138,000,000 on hunting and fishing licenses and permits during 1965, according to the U.S. Department of the Interior. Complete 1965 figures were not available until May, 1966.

The expenditures were almost $6,000,000 over the previous high set in 1964. As might be expected, the number of persons fishing, 20,496,517, and the number of persons hunting, 14,330,549, also were new highs. Neither total included several million more unlicensed hunters and fishermen.

In hunting, however, the total big-game bag was less in 1965 than in 1964–down 3.1 per cent. The take was up 5.6 per cent for whitetail deer, 16.7 per cent for caribou, 21.3 per cent for grizzly bear, 33.2 per cent for polar bear, and 18.2 per cent for wild boar. The big-game harvest was down 10.5 per cent for elk, 14.9 per cent for mule deer, 13.4 per cent for blacktail deer, 18.7 per cent for antelope, and 65.3 per cent for bighorn sheep. The take of wild turkey increased by 3.3 per cent.

The most bagged big-game animal in the United States traditionally is the whitetail deer, and in 1965 the Big-Game Inventory issued by the U.S. Fish and Wildlife Service showed that 1,160,691 of these deer were taken.

Trophies. In the Twelfth North American Big-Game Competition of trophy animals, sponsored by the Boone and Crockett Club, two whitetail deer heads were recognized as larger than the previous world record holders. Since the club is interested in trophies and not when they were taken, the new world record was awarded to a deer taken several years ago in Minnesota. However, the second place head was bagged in 1965 by a bow-and-arrow hunter, Melvin Johnson, near Peoria, Ill.

Other new world records were awarded for a Columbian blacktail deer bagged in 1963 by Woodrow W. Gibbs in Oregon; for a bighorn sheep taken in 1911 by Clarence Baird in Alberta, Canada; for a cougar bagged in 1964 in Utah by Garth Roberts; for a jaguar bagged in Sinaloa, Mexico, in 1965, by C. J. McElroy; and for a black bear taken in 1964 in Colorado by W. L. Cave.

Fishing Records. Only one major change occurred in 1966 in the official fresh-water world records kept by *Field & Stream* magazine. This was a new record spotted black bass of eight pounds caught by Bob Hamilton in Smith Lake, Ala. The catch replaced a record seven-pound spotted bass also caught in 1966 in the same lake.

In July, 1966, the International Game Fish Association, official records keeper for salt-water species, listed only two new world records. These were a 1,100-pound Pacific blue marlin taken by Andre D'Hotman at Le Morne, Mauritius; and a 22-pound 1 ounce flounder taken by F. I. Aguirrezabal at Caleta Horcon, Chile. CLARE CONLEY

HYDE, ROSEL HERSCHEL (1900-), was appointed chairman of the Federal Communications Commission (FCC) by President Lyndon B. Johnson, on June 27, 1966. The appointment marked Hyde's fourth consecutive term as a member of the regulatory agency and his second term as chairman.

Rosel H. Hyde was born in Bannock County, Idaho, April 12, 1900, and entered government service in 1924, while still a student. He attended Utah Agricultural College and George Washington University, from which he was graduated in 1929. He was admitted to the bar of the District of Columbia in 1928 and to practice before the Supreme Court of the United States in 1945.

Hyde has been associated with the FCC since its inception in 1934, advancing from general counsel to commissioner in 1946. On April 18, 1953, he was named to a one-year term as chairman by President Dwight D. Eisenhower. He then became acting chairman until Oct. 4, 1954. His present term expires June 30, 1969.

During 1966, Hyde presided over the FCC's widely publicized investigation of the American Telephone and Telegraph Company.

Hyde is a member of the Federal Bar Association and has served with the U.S. Civil Service Commission and the Office of Public Buildings and Parks. He and the former Mary Henderson were married on Sept. 3, 1924. They have four children.

ICE HOCKEY. In a memorable National Hockey League (NHL) season, veterans Gordie Howe of the Detroit Red Wings and Bobby Hull of the Chicago Black Hawks set new scoring records.

Howe, a 37-year-old rightwinger playing his 20th NHL season, scored 29 goals to raise his own mark for total career goals to 624, a league record.

Hull, 10 years younger, scored 54 goals from his left wing position, despite missing five games because of a torn knee ligament. This broke the season record of 50 set by Maurice "Rocket" Richard in 1945 and equaled by Bernard "Boom Boom" Geoffrion in 1961 and by Hull himself in 1962. In addition, Hull set a new record of 97 total points (goals plus assists). His career goals stood at 318.

But not even Hull's superlative scoring could prevent the Montreal Canadiens from winning both the league championship and the Stanley Cup. A three-game winning streak enabled the Canadiens to pull away from the Black Hawks after a close, season-long struggle. It was their seventh title in nine years.

The Canadiens then gained the Stanley Cup finals with four straight victories over the Toronto Maple Leafs. After losing the first two games in the finals, the Canadiens rallied and took four straight to win the Cup for the second time in a row.

The Canadiens scored 90 points in winning the league title. Behind them came the Black Hawks with 82, the Maple Leafs with 79, and the Red Wings with 74. The Boston Bruins, perennial cellar dwellers, squeaked into fifth place over the New York Rangers, 48-47.

Chicago put four players on the league's six-man all-star team: goalie Glenn Hall, center Stan Mikita, defenseman Pierre Pilote, and left wing Hull. Others on the squad were Howe of Detroit at right wing and Jacques Laperriere of Montreal as the other defenseman.

Expansion. The NHL completed its plans for expansion in 1967 from six teams to 12. To the present cities of Boston, Chicago, Detroit, Montreal, New York, and Toronto will be added six American cities: two from the East (Philadelphia and Pittsburgh); two from the Midwest (Minneapolis-St. Paul and St. Louis); and two from the West Coast (Los Angeles and San Francisco).

The newly completed Oakland Coliseum will be the home of the San Francisco team, the California Seals. An arena was under construction for the Philadelphia Fliers in South Philadelphia near the John F. Kennedy Stadium, the scene of the annual Army-Navy football game. In Inglewood, Calif., a part of the Greater Los Angeles area, a multipurpose sports arena called The Forum was planned for the Los Angeles Kings, and the Minneapolis-St. Paul (Minn.) North Stars were also to move into a new arena. The St. Louis Blues and the Pittsburgh team will use existing buildings.

The league signed a three-year, $3,500,000 television agreement with the Columbia Broadcasting System (CBS) in September. Previously, the NHL had been the only major professional sports conference without a television commitment.

Other Winners. In the American Hockey League, the Rochester Americans won their second straight Calder Cup, defeating the Cleveland Barons 4-2 in the play-off series. Michigan State defeated Clarkson College of Technology (Potsdam, N.Y.) in the finals at Minneapolis to win the National Collegiate Athletic Association (NCAA) championship.

Russia continued its domination of world amateur hockey, winning its fourth consecutive International Tournament title at Ljubljana, Yugoslavia. Czechoslovakia was second, and Canada third. The U.S. team tied for sixth with Finland.

Awards in the National Hockey League:

Calder Trophy (best rookie), Brit Selby, Toronto.
Hart Trophy (most valuable player), Bobby Hull, Chicago.
Lady Byng Trophy (sportsmanship), Alex Delvecchio, Detroit.
Norris Trophy (best defenseman), Jacques Laperriere, Montreal.
Ross Trophy (leading scorer), Hull, Chicago.
Smythe Trophy (most valuable in Stanley Cup play), Roger Crozier, Detroit.
Vezina Trophy (leading goalie), Lorne Worsley and Charlie Hodge, Montreal.

JAMES O. DUNAWAY

Peggy Fleming, *above, center,* won the woman's world figure skating competition at Davos, Switzerland in 1966. At right she demonstrates her championship form.

Pierre Boulat, *Time* Magazine © Time Inc.

ICE SKATING. Peggy Fleming, a willowy 17-year-old high school senior from Colorado Springs, Colo., became the first American to win a World Figure Skating gold medal since the 1960 Olympics. Her victory by a wide margin at Davos, Switzerland, in 1966, capped a five-year comeback for American skaters following the 1961 plane crash which killed the entire U.S. team.

European champion Emmerich Danzer of Austria took the men's title, defeating Wolfgang Schwartz, another Austrian. Gary Visconti of Detroit was third, and Scott Allen of Smoke Rise, N.J., was fourth. The Russian husband-and-wife team of Oleg Protopopov and Lyudmilla Belousova Protopopov won their third straight world pairs championship. Bernard Ford and Diana Towler of Great Britain won the ice dance competition.

A few weeks earlier, at Berkeley, Calif., Miss Fleming won her third North American championship in a row. Allen regained the men's title he had lost to Visconti in 1965, and the pairs crown was won by Cynthia and Ronald Kauffmann.

Speed Skating. Cees Verkerk of Holland captured the men's world championship at Göteborg, Sweden, by finishing first in three of the four races. The 500-meter sprint went to Tom Gray of Minneapolis, Minn., and the women's world championship was won for the third time by Valentina Stenina of the Soviet Union.

James O. Dunaway

ICELAND. Late in December, the government took steps to end an upward spiral in the cost of living. It introduced in the *Althing* (parliament) a bill that would freeze prices at the August 1 level for one year. Government officials said the step was necessary because an economic boom appeared to be faltering. The cause was a decline in export prices on fish and fish products. These products account for 95 per cent of Iceland's exports.

To peg prices at the August 1 level, Iceland's government would have to step-up its subsidies on consumer items such as milk, butter, cheese, and meat. The cost for one year was estimated at about $8,400,000 – an outstanding sum for the island country.

Construction was begun on an aluminum plant which, when completed, was expected to produce 60,000 tons of the metal annually. It was hoped that the new plant, which was to be hydroelectrically operated, would help diversify the economy and end Iceland's dependency on one major export as its source of earnings. Meanwhile, the introduction of better equipment and more up-to-date methods had helped to reduce fluctuations in the fish catch.

Facts in Brief. Population: 195,000. Government: President Asgeir Asgeirsson; Prime Minister Bjarni Benediktsson. Monetary Unit: krona (42.95 = U.S. $1). Foreign Trade: exports, $129,100,000; imports, $137,300,000. Principal Exports: fish and fish products, animal oils and fats. KENNETH BROWN

IMMIGRATION AND EMIGRATION. The immigration reform bill signed into law by President Lyndon B. Johnson on Oct. 3, 1965, brought 7,096 alien parents of U.S. citizens to this country in 1966. The figure was 87 per cent more than in 1965 and more than double the average number admitted in the past 10 years. Four times as many other relatives of U.S. citizens were admitted in 1966 as in the previous year. The number of aliens admitted to the United States because of their skills more than doubled, from 2,376 in 1965 to 5,716 in 1966.

The first few months of operations under the new law "clearly indicate that it is performing the function hoped for by President Johnson," commented Mrs. Helen F. Eckerson, head of the Statistics Branch of the Immigration and Naturalization Service. "It is bringing to this country close relatives of citizens and permanent resident aliens, and bringing to the economy the persons having needed skills."

Besides putting alien relatives in a favored category, the new law abolished the national origins quota system which for 40 years had favored immigrants from the British Isles and Northern Europe over immigrants from Italy, Greece, and other Western European countries. Under the old law, only 5,666 Italians and 308 Greeks could enter the U.S. each year. In fiscal 1966, 25,154 Italians and 8,265 Greeks were admitted. WILLIAM MCGAFFIN

INCOME TAX. See TAXATION.

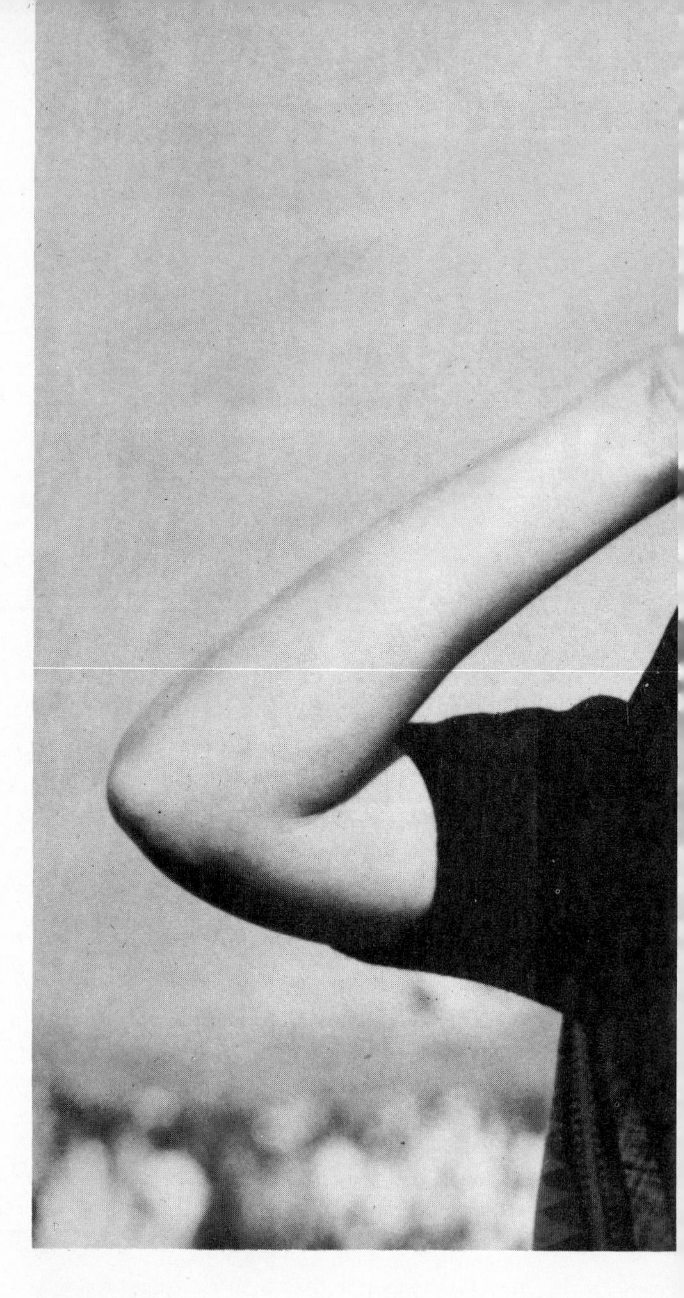

INDIA

On January 24, Indira Gandhi became the third prime minister of India and the second woman in modern history to head a major government. The first had been Mrs. Sirimavo Bandaranaike of Ceylon. Mrs. Gandhi, whose father, Jawaharlal Nehru, had held the prime ministership for 17 years, succeeded Lal Bahadur Shastri who died on January 11 in Tashkent, Russia, after signing a troop-withdrawal agreement with Pakistan. See DEATHS OF NOTABLE PERSONS; GANDHI, INDIRA; PAKISTAN.

India's Prime Minister Indira Gandhi salutes her troops during a review held near the Assam-Pakistan border.

Mrs. Gandhi was elected by the ruling Congress party in the first direct contest ever held for the prime ministership. She received a vote of 355 as compared to 169 for her chief rival–former finance minister Borarji Desai. With a spirit of independence, Mrs. Ghandi began economic reforms.

Economic Reforms. Foremost among the reforms was the devaluation of the rupee from 4.76 to 7.5 to the U.S. dollar. The government had tried less drastic measures such as direct subsidization of exports and tax credits. But a harsh devaluation of the rupee was the only way to boost India's sagging exports and curb a thriving black market.

Simultaneously, the government liberalized imports for 59 priority industries in a partial freeing of what many considered an over-regulated "license economy." Again, in the matter of fertilizer production–a key to India's agricultural future–Mrs. Gandhi allowed American investments to come in and compete with the inefficient public sector in an effort to boost fertilizer output from its present 450,000 tons per year to at least 1,000,000 tons.

Political Back-Pedaling. These moves raised a hornet's nest of protest. The opposition benches, Communists, and even the left-wing elements of her own party accused Indira Gandhi of "selling out" to U.S. and world bank pressures. Her two principal advisers, Asoka Mehta, minister for planning and C. Subramaniam, minister for agriculture, bore the brunt of the attacks.

The government held firm on its economic reforms, but with the February (1967) elections looming large, it back-pedaled on the more political issues. It shelved an offer made by U.S. President Lyndon B. Johnson in April, to establish an India-America Education Foundation using the vast rupee funds that the United States had accumulated in India. The offer had been criticized in some quarters as imposing American control over India's internal affairs.

Food-Population Problem. Advances were made in solving India's twin-headed problem of food and population. Food production, which in 1965-1966 had dipped below 76,000,000 tons because of the worst drought of the century, was back up to the 1964-1965 level of 89,000,000 tons. But in the opinion of many observers, India's bureaucracy needed to be overhauled and streamlined if it was to achieve a significant breakthrough on the food front. Because of an intrauterine device known as the Lippes loop, however, India seemed on the verge of effecting population control. Since the loop's introduction in Bombay, the city had reduced its birth rate to 28 per 1,000 population as compared to the national average of 40 per 1,000.

Rioting Mobs continued to plague the nation during 1966. Bengal and Kerala experienced widespread food riots, during which post offices and railway stations were favorite targets for mob demonstrations. Punjab state, ostensibly divided lingually into Punjabi Subha, Haryana, and Himachal Pradesh, was in fact divided between Sikhs and Hindus, setting off a series of protests and violence. Students also churned up trouble. Late in the year, there was considerable agitation over the slaughter of cows, which are raised as symbols of abundance by the Hindus. On November 7, demonstrations against cow slaughter deteriorated into violent rioting in which eight people were killed and 47 were injured. A reshuffling of the cabinet resulted.

Border Troubles. To the long-standing Naga revolts were added the guerrilla activities of the Mizo tribes near the Pakistan-Burma border. The Indian government openly accused Pakistan and Communist China of fomenting guerrilla terrorism.

Facts in Brief. Population: 500,200,000. Government: President Sarvepalli Radhakrishnan; Prime Minister Mrs. Indira Gandhi. Monetary Unit: rupee (7.5 = U.S. $1). Foreign Trade: exports, $1,686,100,000; imports, $2,818,600,000. Principal Exports: jute, tea, textiles.

KEKI R. BHOTE

Indian dockworkers, ankle-deep in wheat, unload a shipment sent by the United States to relieve a famine threat to India's millions.

Louis Kraar, *Time* Magazine © Time Inc.
Indonesian President Sukarno, *left,* addresses a political rally in Djakarta. General Suharto, his rival for power, listens intently.

INDIAN, AMERICAN. An energetic new effort to get the Indian people into the mainstream of national progress was spurred in the spring of 1966 by some sharp criticism of the Bureau of Indian Affairs from the Senate Committee on Interior and Insular Affairs. It charged: "Indians remain at the bottom of the economic ladder, have the highest rate of unemployment, live in the poorest housing, and suffer chronic poverty." Shortly thereafter, on April 13, the Senate confirmed Robert Lafollette Bennett of Alaska, an Oneida Indian and a career civil servant, as commissioner of Indian Affairs–the first Indian to fill the post in almost 100 years.

At a major conference on Indian affairs at Santa Fe, N.Mex., in April, Secretary of the Interior Stewart L. Udall called for a revitalization of the 142-year-old bureau. The new approach–expected to be spelled out in legislative proposals early in 1967–will be to give Indians more of a voice in developing their own programs. They would also fashion new economic tools to help Indians become self-supporting. Termination of federal authority–unwanted by the Indians themselves–is not envisioned.

A preview of the new program came in August when the Hopi Indians of Arizona signed a contract to invest $1,500,000 of tribal funds to build a new garment factory. The plant, to be operated by a subsidiary of the B.V.D. Company, will provide more than 400 new jobs. A. L. NEWMAN

INDONESIA abruptly changed its political course in 1966. In the changeover, President Sukarno retained his title but relinquished much of his power to Lieutenant General Suharto, an ardent anti-Communist who had charted the government's new course. The switchover began early in the year when the Indonesian army, lead by Suharto, began consolidating police power in its hands. To accomplish this, however, the generals, who were embittered by Sukarno's permissive attitude toward the Communists, had to move quickly against the 3,000,000-strong Indonesian Communist Party (PKI) stronghold in Java. In retaliation for the murder of six of their leaders, army units moved into the Communist-dominated areas, seized PKI leaders, and summarily executed them via the firing squad. Included among them was P. N. Aidit, head of the PKI and Indonesia's top Communist leader. Although estimates of the number executed varied, most sources agreed that about 300,000 PKI's were killed during the operation.

President Sukarno at first showed no inclination to fight back and in March he signed a decree transferring his presidential powers to General Suharto and his military junta. Suharto promptly created a three-man presidium, which included Adam Malik as foreign minister, the Sultan of Djakarta as minister of internal affairs and economic problems, and himself. This three-man team, backed by the tough Indonesian army and Moslem student groups as well as other Moslem organizations, seized control of the country and maintained its power throughout the year.

Suharto, meanwhile, had promptly set about reversing the course that Sukarno had charted for Indonesia. He entered into negotiations with Malaysia to end the "crush Malaysia" policy that Sukarno had formulated. By June, a formal cease-fire had been arranged, and in August a long-range agreement was concluded. Suharto also made it clear that he wanted to establish closer ties with the Philippines and also with Thailand. See ASIA; PHILIPPINES; THAILAND.

These moves, however, proved too much for Sukarno who lashed back at Suharto and his junta in an annual Independence Day speech he delivered in September. In it, Sukarno repeated his old policies: crush Malaysia; side with Communist China; throw out the Western colonialists. He also asked that he be returned to power. But this time the Sukarno magic failed. Some five major organizations representing some 6,000,000 people denounced the speech and demanded his ouster.

General Suharto, convinced of public support in his fight against left-leaning elements in the country, began moving against various former left-leaning cabinet ministers and Sukarno favorites. A number of them were brought to trial, including former Foreign Minister Subandrio, who was eventually sentenced to be executed.

Foreign Affairs. Important moves were made by Suharto in international relations. Indonesia quickly rejoined the United Nations. Simultaneously, it began re-establishing relations with the West while curtailing relations with the Communist world. Suharto let it be known that Indonesia wanted a renewal of economic aid and foreign investment. Owners of companies that had been confiscated by the government under President Sukarno were informed of the government's desire to return them to their owners. Vast public building plans were quickly halted and the private economic sector was encouraged to become more active. One situation that might hinder the economy's recovery was the anger felt by many Indonesians toward the Chinese residents who, they felt, were implicated in an attempted Communist take-over early in the year. This resulted in confiscations of Chinese-held property and business, the interning of thousands of Chinese, and their gradual repatriation to Communist China.

Facts in Brief. Population: 109,220,000. Government: President Sukarno; Chairman of the Presidium, First Minister of Defense and Security Sector Suharto. Monetary Unit: rupiah (44.64= U.S. $1). Foreign Trade: exports, $678,000,000; imports, $597,400,000. Principal Exports: rubber, petroleum and petroleum products. JOHN N. STALKER

INSECT. Insects are able to synchronize their activities with the seasons through a mechanism that precisely measures the relative length of daylight and darkness, according to Perry L. Adkisson, a Texas A&M University entomologist. He said that insects possess a biological clock that programs the flow of brain hormone which in turn controls the insect's growth, reproduction, and dormant periods.

The screwworm fly population in the United States was completely eradicated in 1966 as a result of a U.S. Department of Agriculture program begun in 1957. The livestock pest once cost farmers $100,000,000 a year. It was eliminated by releasing millions of male screwworm flies that had been sterilized by radiation. The sterile males mated ineffectually, and the population was depleted.

Two insect hormones were synthesized for the first time in 1966. Ecdysone, a steroid that regulates the development of the insect from larva to adult (metamorphosis) was prepared at the Syntex Research laboratory, in Palo Alto, Calif. The chemical is useful in the study of chromosomes. The second insect chemical, called the juvenile hormone, was prepared at Harvard University. It is necessary for premetamorphic insect development, but will prevent metamorphosis if its secretion does not cease at the correct time. Researchers believe this hormone may be used in the development of new insecticides. JAMES A. PEARRE

INSURANCE. Life insurance became a trillion dollar industry in 1966. By the end of the year, life insurance protection in force for U.S. families had increased at least $125,000,000,000, outstripping the optimistic industry estimates at the beginning of 1966, when the total had reached $900,554,000,000.

Policies issued by legal reserve life insurance companies totaled more than $985,000,000,000. The balance of $55,000,000,000 or so included all other types of life insurance, mainly GI and fraternal organization policies. As recently as 1958, total life insurance in force was less than half the 1966 record. In 1950, it was less than $250,000,000,000.

Benefits paid to policyholders and beneficiaries came to $12,400,000,000 for the year, up from $11,-416,000,000 in 1965. At the end of 1966, six out of seven U.S. families had some form of life insurance protection, and the average insured family held approximately $20,000 worth of life insurance, up from $18,300 a year earlier.

Canada Still Led the United States and the world, according to one measure accepted by the industry: the ratio of life insurance in force to total national income. By that standard, the United States was second, followed by Sweden, New Zealand, and The Netherlands. In total volume, however, Canada was a long way from the U.S. mark, with about $82,000,000,000 (Canadian) of life insurance in force.

Total Assets–investments in stocks, bonds, mortgages, policy loans, property–of U.S. life insurance companies have shown almost as spectacular total growth as total insurance in force. At $165,000,000,000 or more at year's end, they had about doubled since 1954. With the fire and casualty companies' more than $41,000,000,000 counted in, the industry's total assets came to $206,000,000,000–somewhere near 10 per cent of the nation's estimated total wealth.

Profits of life insurance companies in general rose more than usual in 1966, despite rising costs and increased benefits. One of the major reasons, paradoxically, was "tight" money–a hardship for many other businesses (see BANKS AND BANKING). Insurance companies, however, take in large amounts of money. And it comes in regularly, no matter whether money is tight or easy. When it is tight, the returns they receive on new mortgages and loans to corporations rise in step with interest rates. As a result, in 1966 they were able to earn the highest yields on their investments in 35 years.

This was one big reason that life insurance stocks–and stocks of fire and casualty companies, too–broke out of a long bear market in late 1966 and started to climb once again. The advance actually was led by the fire and casualty companies. The breakout came when the hurricane season closed without major damage. In 1965, the companies had had catastrophic losses on their policies from Hurricane Betsy's still incomplete toll of $715,000,000, the largest single insured loss in history.

But the losses from highway deaths and accidents remained tragically high. Deaths, injuries, and insurance payments broke all previous records.

Federal Regulation? Congress made moves late in the year to look into the insurance industry, the regulation of which it had left up to the states by the McCarran-Ferguson Act of 1945. The Senate Commerce Committee was to open hearings early in 1967 on whether "state laws regulating insurance are adequate." Or if they were adequate, the committee would see if they were really being enforced.

In the House, Chairman Wright Patman (D., Tex.) of the Banking and Currency Committee planned to examine what he called "the interlocking control between banks and insurance companies." His staff also would look into "credit life insurance" bought by consumers as a condition of getting loans from banks or finance companies.

A book that appeared in the fall of 1966 could be the augury of some major changes for insurance. *Pay Now, Die Later*, by insurance man James Gollin, took a sharply critical view of the industry's selling practice. Whether it would have the same catalytic effect on insurance as Ralph Nader's *Unsafe at Any Speed* had on the automobile industry remained to be seen. EDWIN W. DARBY

See also MEDICARE; SOCIAL SECURITY.

INTERIOR DESIGN. Interior designers, furniture manufacturers, and others in the home furnishings industry joined forces in 1966 to supply an eclectic look for the homes of affluent, individualistic, young consumers. The combined effort culled the best designs from many sources to provide a feeling of luxury and sophistication.

The trend in home design leaned toward 18th century English and French furniture, with French lines becoming most popular. Several French styles were reproduced, all with subtle curves, delicate moldings, hand carving, and romantic motifs and patterns. Antique painted furniture also reflected the French trend, and there was an abundance of French-inspired wall and floor decoration.

However, the Mod look in the clothing and fashion industry proved popular in upholstery and drapery fabrics, as well as in floor and wall coverings. Op and Pop Art designs–black and white, bright and shiny–appeared along with furry upholstery fabrics and simulated animal skins.

The Mod appearance was accented with plush fabrics. However, the same velvets and simulated furs were also designed in traditional patterns.

Spanish and Mediterranean styles also won favor with many consumers. The dark, massive wood pieces with heavy carvings were warm and comfortable, and also handsome. Many elements of

Attractive 19-inch transistorized portable television set won an international design award for research and development in 1966.

World's bankers gather in Washington, D.C., for the annual meetings of the International Monetary Fund and World Bank in September.

these styles also fit in well with eclectic settings. The previously popular Scandinavian styles were featured mainly as accessories and lighting fixtures.

Italian and Oriental or bamboo pieces appeared to be moving into furniture markets at the year's end, with Italian designs following the French trend in appearance and appeal. Considered a versatile wood, bamboo fit in everywhere, usable with modern, English, or Oriental furniture.

Technology brought several new words into the consumer's vocabulary. Fabrics acquired "durable" or "permanent press" finishes after being chemically treated. The finishes eliminated much maintenance and care when they were applied to curtains, draperies, and bedspreads. Another was "solid state," an engineering term applied to electronic devices that eliminated vacuum tubes and other bulky parts from radios, televisions, and other appliances. Solid state components provided greater efficiency with a minimum of breakdown.

Awards in interior design, given annually by the American Institute of Interior Designers were: residential furniture, Howard Yarme and Ira Saltz; business furniture, George Nelson and Robert Propst; drapery fabric and wall covering, Jack L. Larson; upholstery fabrics, Design Studio of Clarence House; soft surface floor covering (rugs), Paul E. Letz; and glassware, Professor Claus J. Fiedel.

HELEN SCHUBERT

INTERNATIONAL TRADE AND FINANCE. While governments argued and negotiated through 1966 on ways to reduce trade barriers and to improve the international monetary mechanism, the economy of the industrial world continued to prosper and world trade to flourish. The only major threat to a continuation of the steady advance in exchanges among nations came from yet another crisis of the British pound sterling, but once again an international rescue operation saved the pound (see GREAT BRITAIN).

Total world trade, as measured by the exports of all nations combined, rose about 10 per cent in 1966 to between $180,000,000,000 and $184,000,000,000. This followed a rise of 9 per cent in 1965. Year after year, this growth of trade has been a major element in continuing prosperity.

For the United States, 1966 was an unusual year in international trade and finance. Its imports rose sharply, about 18 per cent. Exports did amazingly well considering the robust state of domestic demand, rising by slightly over 10 per cent. The growth of imports seriously narrowed the all-important trade surplus to a little more than $3,000,000,000, compared with the recent peak in 1964 of nearly $7,000,000,000. See ECONOMY, THE.

Fortunately for the U.S. balance of payments, there was a reversal in the flow of capital. Largely because of tight money and high interest rates at home, the outflow of dollars for lending and investing abroad lessened, and the inflow of foreign money increased. The government's voluntary program for limiting direct investment by business firms abroad also played a role in the markedly improved balance of payments situation. See BANKS AND BANKING.

The result was that, despite the reduced trade surplus and the $900,000,000 cost in foreign exchange of the war in Vietnam, the U.S. balance of payments deficit was about the same as the $1,300,000,000 of 1965, which in turn was by far the smallest since the balance of payments became a serious problem in 1958. The loss of gold by the United States was only about half as large in 1966 as in 1965. France once again was the major converter of dollars into gold, and hence it was the source of the bulk of the U.S. loss of slightly more than $500,000,000 in bullion. See FRANCE.

While the official U.S. goal continued to be the elimination of the payments deficit altogether, and while European nations continued to urge the priority of doing so, there were signs that the United States was finding a deficit in the range of 1965 and 1966 tolerable. Secretary of the Treasury Henry H. Fowler said officially that the goal of absolute balance probably could not be attained so long as the war in Vietnam continued.

Meanwhile, the dollar was generally strong throughout the year compared with other currencies in the foreign exchange markets. However, a reversion to the higher deficits of the years 1958 through 1964 could bring a return to a crisis atmosphere, at home and abroad.

In International Negotiations, there were three main strands. None were decisive in 1966. But all represented a continuing evolution, with the final outcome still in doubt.

First, the European Economic Community (EEC, or Common Market) got back in business as France ended its boycott, which had begun in mid-1965. The other EEC members are Belgium, Italy, Luxembourg, The Netherlands, and West Germany. Arguing and struggling as always, the six nations managed to complete their common agricultural price support system, with its apparatus of barriers against imports. And they also finally agreed upon their "offers" in the Kennedy Round of world-wide tariff negotiations, over a year late.

Although the Common Market experienced more quarreling than unity, it promised to achieve at least its main economic purpose of a European customs union, with free trade internally and a common tariff against imports, by mid-1968. Thus Britain, in November once again indicated its interest in joining the EEC. In December, its six partners in the European Free Trade Association–Austria, Denmark, Norway, Portugal, Sweden, and Switzerland–met in London and declared that they "welcomed" the British move. Actual negotiations for the entry of Britain or its partners, however, remained well in the future.

The Kennedy Round of talks in Geneva, Switzerland, moved to a climax but did not reach it. The tariff-reducing offers of the Common Market were viewed by the United States and other negotiating partners as seriously deficient. In agriculture, where the issue is not mainly tariffs but other protective devices such as import levies that vary with world prices, the offers for most products were regarded as almost worthless. Farm products amount to about 30 per cent of U.S. exports to the Common Market nations.

Thus it became increasingly clear as 1966 ended that nothing like the original Kennedy Round aim of a sweeping reduction of tariff barriers–by 50 per cent with a minimum of exceptions–would be realized. However, outright failure of the negotiation also seemed unlikely. Much will depend on the kind of U.S. decisions made. The United States and the rest of the 60-odd non-EEC nations in the General Agreement on Tariffs and Trade (GATT) will probably be faced with two choices: (1) accept a fairly useful tariff reduction by the Common Market on industrial products with very little in agriculture, or (2) condemn the whole four-year negotiation to failure. The year 1967 will tell the story. At midyear, the U.S. authority under the 1962 Trade Expansion Act to negotiate across-the-board tariff reductions will expire. See EUROPE.

"Paper Gold"? Negotiations on international monetary reform continued to make slow progress. At issue was the creation of a new international reserve asset, often dubbed "paper gold," to supplement gold, dollars, and pounds sterling for settling international accounts. Shortage of such reserves could hamper world trade. The negotiators were largely agreed that there was no urgency as long as U.S. balance of payments deficits continued. But if the United States started to take in more dollars than it paid out to other countries, the world's supply of reserves (dollars) would shrink. The aim was to set up a "contingency plan" for creating new international money, backed by the leading currencies, to be used when the U.S. deficit ended.

In 1966, the "Group of Ten" leading financial nations, with France a notable exception, came closer to agreeing on many of the major principles of a contingency plan. The nine other nations are Belgium, Canada, Great Britain, Italy, Japan, Sweden, The Netherlands, United States, and West Germany. For the last three days in November the "Ten" met for the first time with representatives of the poorer countries in Washington, D.C. In joint negotiations with the executive directors of the International Monetary Fund (IMF) both groups found a broad basis of agreement on creating additional reserves, universally available to all 105 IMF member nations. Yet there was doubt that a treaty would be ready for approval at the next IMF annual meeting in Rio de Janeiro in September, 1967.

The chief stumbling block continued to be the issue of control: who shall decide, and by what system of weighted majority voting, when to create "paper gold" and how much? It is an issue that goes to the roots of national sovereignty.

East-West Trade. While U.S. trade with Russia and Eastern Europe picked up in 1966, it still represented only 0.76 per cent of total U.S. exports and imports for the first half. It had been 0.56 per cent in the 1965 period. In a major foreign policy address on October 7, President Lyndon B. Johnson proposed strengthening trade and cultural ties with the Eastern bloc nations. Five days later, he lifted restrictions on 400 nonstrategic items for export to those nations. But a bill that would have permitted freer trade and authorized "most favored nation" status for Communist countries failed to pass.

In the meantime, Eastern Europe's trade with Western Europe and Japan continued its slow but steady growth. It was still less than 5 per cent of total world trade, however. The chief problem remained one of the West's finding enough East-bloc goods to import. If the Communist nations' goods do not sell, they cannot earn the hard currencies needed to pay for imports. EDWIN L. DALE, JR.

See also articles on the individual countries.

INVENTION. The Supreme Court of the United States handed down its first decisions on patent legality in 15 years in February, 1966. The rulings, which voided two patents–a clamp for vibrating shank plows and a plastic finger sprayer–prompted U.S. Patent Commissioner Edward J. Brenner to urge his staff to adhere strictly to standards governing the granting of patents. The key issue in the patent decisions was the "obviousness" standard, a requirement set by patent law that an invention be "not obvious" in order to be granted a patent.

The Patent Office continued efforts to reduce a backlog of over 200,000 pending applications in anticipation of a transition to an international patent system. Commissioner Brenner estimated that a truly international patent system will begin to operate in about five years.

At a meeting in Geneva, Switzerland, in October, the 18-nation executive committee of the Paris Convention for the Protection of Industrial Property unanimously called for efforts on the part of all members to work toward standardization of patent filing procedures and coordination of patent examination systems. It was announced that the 74 member nations of the Paris Convention will send representatives to a meeting in Vienna, Austria, in 1970, to begin implementation of the system.

Among the measures taken by the Patent Office to streamline its operations was the decision to microfilm all 19,000,000 pages of the existing U.S. patents on file at the office. The microfilm system will make it possible to supply a copy of any patent issued since 1790 immediately on request. The system will become fully operational in 1968.

Top Inventor. Samuel Ruben of New Rochelle, N.Y., who holds over 300 patents, was presented the 1966 award as inventor of the year by the Patent, Trademark, and Copyright Research Institute of George Washington University in Washington, D.C. Ruben is known for inventions in the electrochemical and electronics fields. His dry electrolytic condenser is used in nearly every radio set.

Unusual Patents. Peter J. Booras of Keene, N.H., patented a process for producing bread in a continuous loaf. The loaf is cut and packaged as it emerges from the oven.

An electronic computer system that has successfully predicted common stock prices for five years was patented by John M. Lambert of Rockville Center, Long Island, N.Y. The system has been used under contract by many of the nation's largest mutual funds, banks, and professional investors.

An automatic barber, which can be programmed to give haircuts according to a customer's special hair pattern, was patented by a French engineer. According to the patent, the customer is expected to keep his head in contact with the machine's "feelers." JAMES A. PEARRE

IRAN patched up its troubles with Iraq, which had accused Iran of giving equipment and a "haven" to rebellious Kurdish tribesmen. Iran had countered with charges that Iraqi planes had bombed Iranian villages in May. The two countries formed a joint commission to police the border.

Propagandists from the United Arab Republic (UAR) demanded the overthrow of Iran's Shah Mohammed Riza Pahlevi. Charging conspiracy, the police seized and imprisoned 55 members of the underground Islamic Nations party in January.

Though the UAR appeals fell on deaf ears, the shah requested U.S. military aid. When the United States hedged, he turned to Russia. In September, however, the United States made a counteroffer. As a result, Iran will buy U.S. F-5 interceptors, plus a destroyer and four corvettes from Britain, to defend the Kharg Island oil installations.

Economic gains were impressive. The refinery expansion at Kharg was completed. Four foreign auto firms–American Motors, Citroën, Rootes, and Volkswagen–arranged to assemble cars in Iran for the Iranian market.

Facts in Brief. Population: 23,400,000. Government: Shah Mohammed Riza Pahlevi; Premier Amir Abbas Hoveida. Monetary Unit: rial (75 = U.S. $1). Foreign Trade: exports, $1,302,200,000; imports, $859,500,000. Principal Exports: carpets, petroleum and petroleum products. WILLIAM SPENCER

IRAQ concluded a cease-fire with its rebellious Kurds in June, 1966, after months of sporadic but fierce fighting. Kurdish Mullah Mustafa al-Barzani accepted the truce as a prelude to restoration of Kurdish rights, which Premier Abdul Rahman al-Bazzaz outlined in a 12-point program. Local autonomy was pledged for Kurdistan, but the instability of the Iraqi government slowed the program.

President Abdul Salam Muhammad Arif died in a helicopter crash in April. He was succeeded by his brother, Abdul Rahman Arif. In June, Bazzaz's predecessor, Brigadier General Arif Abdel Razzak, launched a coup against the government, but the plot was thwarted by quick government action.

Iraq's problems were far from settled. Bazzaz unexpectedly resigned in August. Naji Talib replaced him and organized a new 18-member cabinet that included three Kurdish ministers.

The government increased its capital in the World Bank from $55,000,000 to $64,000,000, and contributed $50,000 to the World Food Program. It also gave a $56,000,000 contract to Lebanese and West German firms for a paper mill at Basra.

Facts in Brief. Population: 8,600,000. Government: President Abdul Rahman Arif; Premier Naji Talib. Monetary Unit: dinar (1 = U.S. $2.80). Foreign Trade: exports, $866,100,000; imports, $297,-300,000. Principal Exports: cement, crude petroleum, dates, raw wool. WILLIAM SPENCER

IRELAND. An explosion on March 8, 1966 shattered the towering Nelson Pillar in the heart of Dublin. The police blamed the outlawed Irish Republican Army (IRA) for the blast which brought down the 20-foot statue of Lord Nelson atop it.

The bombing touched off fears of further IRA violence as Ireland neared the 50th anniversary of the 1916 uprising that had led to southern Ireland's independence from Great Britain. However, on Independence Day–April 10–there were no incidents.

On June 25, 83-year-old Éamon de Valéra was inaugurated as president of the republic for a second seven-year term. In the elections, which were held on June 2, he narrowly defeated Thomas F. O'Higgins, candidate of the *Fine Gael* (United Ireland) party. In November, Seán F. Lemass resigned as prime minister, and the *Dáil Éireann* (house of deputies), by a 71 to 64 vote, elected John Lynch to succeed him.

Earlier in the year, Lynch, who was then finance minister, announced that Ireland would switch to a decimal coinage system to coincide with Britain's planned changeover in 1971.

Facts in Brief. Population: 2,830,000. Government: President Éamon de Valéra; Prime Minister John Lynch. Monetary Unit: pound (1 = U.S. $2.80). Foreign Trade: exports, $626,700,000; imports, $1,040,600,000. Principal Exports: meat and dairy products, alcoholic beverages. PAUL TULLIER

ISRAEL. Clashes with Arab infiltrators along its borders with Syria and Jordan provoked a retaliatory attack by Israel on a Jordanian village in November. The United Nations Security Council and most of the world's nations censured Israel for the action. See JORDAN, MIDDLE EAST, UNITED NATIONS (UN).

Oddly, in December, 1965, before trouble grew at the border, Israel had ended the military control of its Arab minority, in effect since 1948. Israel's Arabs, including Bedouins of the Negev Desert, could travel freely throughout the nation.

Domestic problems, however, were potentially more dangerous to Israel than the continuing strife with its Arab neighbors. The high cost of military preparedness and a severe balance of payments deficit continued to plague the economy. To slow the recession, the Labor Federation agreed to waive cost of living wage allowances, but higher taxes and the 8 per cent salary increase parliament voted for itself kept Israelis from supporting a voluntary pay cut. Israel applied for associate membership in the European Common Market as a last-ditch effort to even its balance of payments, since there seemed no way to reduce military spending.

There were some bright spots. The West Germans granted $40,000,000 in credits, and the United States loaned Israel $52,000,000 for grain imports under the Food for Peace Program.

Economic difficulties revived Israel's self-help tradition. A group of young American volunteers assisted by building a children's playground for Upper Nazareth village during their summer stay as paying guests of local families. Another group of Americans began building Israel's largest public recreation area, Bible Land, which will meet the increasing demands of Israelis for family entertainment. In the Negev, a new irrigation device, developed by an Israeli inventor, Simha Blass, was introduced. In tests, it doubled yields per acre while using 20 per cent less water. The Jewish Agency announced a pilot project that will help new immigrants adjust to Israel. The project will provide language and vocational training.

Former Prime Minister David Ben-Gurion's 80th birthday drew only grudging tribute from the Israeli cabinet primarily because Ben-Gurion's Rafi party had aligned with the Herut party to challenge Prime Minister Levi Eshkol's Mapai government.

The John F. Kennedy Information Center in Jerusalem opened in November. Hadassah, the women's Zionist group, built the memorial; artist Marc Chagall designed the stained-glass windows.

Facts in Brief. Population: 2,435,000. Government: President Shneor Zalman Shazar; Prime Minister Levi Eshkol. Monetary Unit: pound (3 = U.S. $1). Foreign Trade: exports, $430,100,000; imports, $834,900,000. Principal Exports: diamonds, fruit and nuts, textiles. WILLIAM SPENCER

ITALY

Italy was struck by disaster in November when storm winds up to 90 miles an hour battered its west coast from the Alps to Sicily. As a result of the torrential rains that accompanied the storm, scores of people died and thousands were made homeless. Florence was ravaged by a flood that caused irreparable damage to some of the world's great art treasures, including Renaissance paintings and books that dated back to the 12th century (see LITERATURE; PAINTING AND SCULPTURE).

Landslides in Sicily as well as in northern Italy devoured or threatened to engulf entire villages. Rampaging rivers destroyed bridges, roads, buildings, and railroads, and thousands of livestock perished in the waters that, in places, rose 20 feet. The canal city of Venice was badly damaged by the record-breaking tides that swept in from the Adriatic. Thousands of square miles of farmland, ruined by seawater, would be uncultivatable for almost a decade. At year's end, with 18 provinces flooded, the magnitude of the disaster was only just beginning to be realized. All that was known with any certainty was that a third of Italy's economy had been wrecked by the worst storm in centuries.

The Italian government, acting quickly, appropriated $330,000,000 for immediate relief work and, later, it approved a $700,000,000 appropriation for a three-year program of flood relief reconstruction and flood control works. But some government sources placed the damage at a minimum of $1,600,000,000 and predicted that the job of rehabilitation would require at least two decades to complete. See DISASTERS.

Prior to the disaster, Italy had enjoyed a wave of prosperity. Celebrating 20 years as a republic, it had consolidated the economic expansion of the previous year, with a general rise of 8 per cent in industrial production. Its foreign exchange position was excellent, due largely to a large amount of revenue received from tourism – 904,700 more visitors, and an increased revenue over the previous year of $235,000,000. There was also a dramatic upswing in the balance of payments credit from $774,000,000 to $1,595,000,000.

Government Crisis. The year opened with a series of governmental crises, and Premier Aldo Moro resigned following a rebellion in his own Christian Democratic party. Three times within a month, President Giuseppe Saragat asked Moro to form a new government. Twice Moro failed. On his third attempt, however, he succeeded in forming a center-left coalition of the biggest party, the Christian Democrats, with the Socialists, Social Democrats, and Republicans. When parliament approved the new government, Premier Moro described it as "corresponding to a precise long-term program which opens new horizons as regards economic recovery and civic advancement." He also called attention to its anti-Communist composition. Later, plans were made to merge the Socialist and Social Democrat parties.

Party Revitalized. In October, delegates representing the former Italian Socialist party and the Italian Democratic Socialist party met at suburban Eur, just outside Rome, to heal a 19-year-old breach that had weakened the Socialist movement and made its separate factions ineffectual minor partners of the Christian Democrats or the Communists. At the conclusion of the meeting, it was announced

that both parties had agreed to form one united Socialist party. Leaders promised that the unified party would continue to work with the Christian Democrats as long as the coalition made reasonable progress toward reforms of the government structure and social organization as outlined in an agreed program. The delegates elected 75-year-old Pietro Nenni as president of the party.

Foreign Accord. In April, Foreign Minister Amintore Fanfani and the Soviet Union's Foreign Minister Andrei Gromyko held a three-day series of talks in Rome, during which they stressed their mutual desire for peace. Later that month, in a statement to parliament, however, Moro reaffirmed Italy's ties with the West by announcing that Italian foreign policy would continue to be founded on loyalty toward the Atlantic Alliance.

Disastrous high tides from the Adriatic Sea flooded Venice's famed Piazza of St. Mark and inundated the Doges Palace, in November.

Frontier Incidents. A series of incidents in the Trentino-Alto Adige region, formerly the Austrian South Tyrol, disturbed Austro-Italian relations just as the two countries were reaching tentative agreement on the disputed area. Terrorists want the province returned to Austria, from which it was torn in 1919 by the Treaty of St. Germain. Moro, however, promised that the area would remain Italian.

Scientific Research. A survey made during the year revealed that Italy would spend $291,000,000 on scientific research in 1966. Under a joint program sponsored by the European Organization for the Launching of Space Vehicles (ELDO), Italy had assumed partial responsibility for a 160-kgm satellite to be launched for telecommunications, radio transmissions, and atmospheric research.

Overseas Projects. Work contracted abroad by Italian firms rose sharply during the year, with Africa as the chief site of operations. Included were the Khashm-el-Girba and Roseires dams in the Sudan, roads in the United Arab Republic (UAR) and Uganda, and hydroelectric works in the various parts of the Middle East. The Fiat Motor Company signed a $97,000,000 contract with the Soviet Union, calling for the construction of an automobile factory that, when in operation, would produce 600,000 cars a year. An industrial group, GIE-Impregilo, won a $200,000,000 power station contract in the Andes, in South America.

Facts in Brief. Population: 53,800,000. Government: President Giuseppe Saragat; Premier Aldo Moro. Monetary Unit: lira (623 = U.S. $1.). Foreign Trade: exports, $7,187,200,000; imports, $7,347,-700,000. Principal Exports: chemicals, machinery, motor vehicles, textiles. KENNETH BROWN

IVORY COAST. See AFRICA.

JAMAICA. See WEST INDIES.

Japan's vast shipbuilding industry gets a boost with the launching of the *Tokyo Maru*, a giant, 1,005-foot-long tanker.

JAPAN continued to play a role of increasing importance in Asian and world affairs. Possessing only limited military strength, Japan relied on diplomacy and its position as the world's sixth ranking economic power to spread its influence in international politics. During the year, high-level economic, educational, and cultural conferences were held between the United States and Japan, with Secretary of State Dean Rusk attending the economic conference held in July. The United States agreed late in 1965 to allow Japanese commercial planes to fly across the continental United States.

A visit by Andrei Gromyko in July was the first ever made by a foreign minister of the Soviet Union to Japan. He was returning an earlier visit made to Moscow by Japanese Foreign Minister Etsusaburo Shiina. An agreement was signed early in 1966 establishing a Tokyo-Moscow air connection. At the same time, a five-year trade agreement calling for $2,100,000,000 in two-way trade was concluded.

Sino-Japanese Relations. Informal relations between Japan and Communist China increased during 1966. More Japanese journalists, businessmen, scholars, and political figures visited China than ever before. Trade was up, too. Significantly, leading factions within the ruling and conservative Liberal-Democratic party increasingly demanded the establishment of normal relations with Communist China.

Japan was elected late in 1965 to a two-year term in the United Nations Security Council and UN Ambassador Akira Matsui served as Council president for February, 1966. Ambassador Hiro Aoki, chief of Japan's Permanent Delegation to the International Labor Organization (ILO) in Geneva, Switzerland, was elected chairman of the ILO.

In Asia, Japan took the initiative in an attempt to assist Indonesia with its economic problems. It participated in establishing the nine-nation Asia and Pacific Council in Seoul, Korea, in July. It also sponsored the Ministerial Conference on the Economic Development of Southeast Asia. In addition, Japan sent the first of its Overseas Cooperation Volunteers to Asia and Africa during the year.

Political Moves. The growing unpopularity and poor health of Prime Minister Eisaku Sato, together with a series of scandals involving some of his cabinet ministers, a factional strike inside his Liberal-Democratic party, and popular discontent over the rising cost of living were all part of the political scene in Japan in 1966. These factors, plus a constitutional requirement that a general election be held at least once every four years, guaranteed that an election for the house of representatives would be held in 1967. An informal coalition of the Socialist party, the moderate Democratic Socialist party, and the Kōmeitō party made up the principal opposition to the Liberal-Democrats.

By midyear, the government was confident that the country had emerged from the economic recession of the past few years. The gross national product, the rate of economic growth, consumer spending, per capita income, and foreign trade were up. The great popular concern was with the continuing rise in consumer prices; yet much of it seemed to be balanced by increased personal income.

Other Developments. The 1972 Winter Olympic Games will be held in Sapporo on the northern island of Hokkaido. "Progress and Harmony of Mankind" will be the theme of the 1970 Osaka World's Fair. The government officially designated 1968 as "Meiji Centennial Year" to commemorate the accession to the throne of the Emperior Meiji (Mutsuhito) under whose reign Japan became a modern nation. The first state-owned National Theatre, designed to preserve the traditional dramatic forms, was opened in November.

Edwin O. Reischauer resigned as U.S. ambassador to Japan after six years of service. His successor was U. Alexis Johnson, a career diplomat with long experience in Asia and Japan.

Facts in Brief. Population: 98,682,000. Government: Emperor Hirohito; Prime Minister Eisaku Sato. Monetary Unit: yen (360=U.S. $1). Foreign Trade: exports, $8,456,200,000; imports, $8,167,-800,000. Principal Exports: iron and steel, ships, metals products, textiles. JOHN M. MAKI

JEWS AND JUDAISM. Jewish intellectual leaders in 1966 were engaged in an examination of the fundamental theological grounds of Judaism, and were concerned over the nature and possible effects of interreligious dialogue.

The majority of Orthodox rabbis were opposed to theological dialogue between Judaism and Christianity. In the words of Rabbi Joseph Soloveitchik, acknowledged leader of Orthodoxy in the United States, "There cannot be mutual understanding" between Jews and Christians on questions of dogma and doctrine, because "Jews and Christians will employ different categories and will move within incommensurate frames of reference . . ." According to Rabbi Soloveitchik, Orthodox Jews would be prepared to discuss such topics as war, peace, freedom, civil rights, and secularism with their Christian neighbors. But any searching encounter on such theological issues as the idea of covenant, the nature of Jesus, the doctrine of the Trinity or Jewish ethical monotheism, and the meaning of messianism, could result only in misunderstanding or subtle attempts at conversion.

Difference of Opinions. Conservative and Reform rabbis, however, vigorously opposed any diminution in the intensity or scope of the ongoing dialogue. Indeed, Rabbi Abraham Joshua Heschel of the Jewish Theological Seminary of America, in New York City, viewed premature closure of such discussions as unwise practically, and untrue religiously. Said Rabbi Heschel, "To refuse contact with Christian theologians is to my mind barbarous."

To illustrate the wisdom and impact of interreligious dialogue, as he saw it, Rabbi Heschel accepted the invitation extended by Union Theological Seminary (Protestant) to become its first Jewish visiting professor (for the academic year ended in June, 1966). The vigor of Rabbi Heschels' exposition of the basic insights of Judaism and his soaring linguistic style seemed to have a decisive impact upon the Christian seminarians.

As if to illustrate the possibilities of internal dialogue among the various interpretations by Jews of Judaism, the Rabbinical Assembly (Conservative), at its annual convention, held in Toronto in May, was host to speakers from the leadership of both the Orthodox and Reform wings of Judaism.

Seminary Fire. The vigorous debates regarding the virtues of reaching outward were dimmed somewhat by the tragedy that struck the Jewish Theological Seminary on April 18. A fire of unknown origin broke out in the library, destroying some 70,000 volumes and several irreplaceable periodical collections. Also, the blaze inflicted water damage on no fewer than 120,000 additional books. But the magnitude of the loss and the possibility of still further losses by mildew of the water-soaked books brought a quick and heartening response. Hundreds of Jewish and Christian seminarians, college students, adult members of churches and synagogues, and even children, worked 24 hours a day for one week drying every page of the damaged books by hand. Thus the world's greatest collection of Judaica was rescued from total disaster.

Chairs of Judaica. Although the major rabbinical schools (Hebrew Union College in Cincinnati, Jewish Theological Seminary and Yeshiva University in New York City) remained the prime sources for study and research into the traditions and insights of Judaism, their sway did not remain unchallenged in 1966. During the past decade, numerous chairs of Judaica have been endowed in leading universities. In 1966, Dr. Zvi Ankori of the Hebrew University of Jerusalem, was named the first Melton Visiting Professor of Jewish History at Ohio State University. Similar professorial posts had already been created at Yale, Vanderbilt, Dartmouth, and Stanford. Hence, the seminaries would have to train young scholars to fill these posts and provide replacements for their senior faculty members. It was believed that this broadening of the base for scholarly research would affect recruitment for the rabbinate and would raise the level of religious literacy among Jewish collegians, some of whom would eventually become leaders of secular Jewish organizations. It was thought that this development would play a decisive role on the congregational scene. DAVID WOLF SILVERMAN

Honeymoon-bound Luci embraces her father, while her mother, Mrs. Lyndon B. Johnson, shakes hand of groom, Patrick J. Nugent.

JOHNSON, LYNDON BAINES, worried about the war in Vietnam, rising prices, and his declining popularity in 1966. His energy continued to astound the public. He drove himself, and his associates, hard; he conferred tirelessly with congressional leaders; and he traveled widely in the United States and abroad.

Anxious to be well-liked, he was concerned when polls showed his popularity ratings on a downswing. In September, the Louis Harris poll reported that only 50 per cent of the U.S. public approved of the way he was doing his job. In February, 1964, he had rated 83 per cent. *Time* magazine called this shrinkage "the affection gap." After his personal campaigning for Democratic candidates, Republican victories were not reassuring. Nevertheless, despite some congressional opposition, the President's program was largely successful in the second session of the 89th Congress. And by and large, the nation supported his decision to escalate the war in Vietnam. See CONGRESS OF THE UNITED STATES.

A Highlight of the President's year was his historic trip to attend a seven-nation conference in Manila. On October 17, he and Mrs. Johnson began a 31,500-mile journey that took them to Manila in the Philippines and to six other Asian and Pacific nations. The President made the 17-day trip to talk with U.S. allies on the progress of the war in Vietnam and to get their views on a unified effort to develop the economies of Southeast Asia.

On his return, Mr. Johnson disclosed that he would have to undergo surgery for repair of an abdominal hernia–the result of his 1965 gall bladder operation–and for removal of a small polyp in his throat. His general health was excellent. His only chronic health problem seemed to be overweight–a problem shared by many other well-fed middle-aged Americans.

After a few days of rest at his Texas ranch, he entered the Naval Hospital at Bethesda, Md., on November 15. The successful 53-minute operation was performed the next day. Again, as in 1965, the President spent the last weeks of the year recuperating; and again, the President's health proved equal to the surgery and to the tasks and strains of his office.

The Social High Point for the Johnson family was the marriage on August 6 of Luci, younger daughter of the President, to Patrick J. Nugent, 23, of Waukegan, Ill. Nineteen-year-old Luci was the first daughter of a President to marry while her father was in office since Eleanor Wilson's wedding in 1914. More than 700 invitations bearing the presidential seal summoned family friends to Luci's wedding at the Shrine of the Immaculate Conception in Washington, the largest Roman Catholic church in the United States. The White House reception that followed was a highly publicized gala.

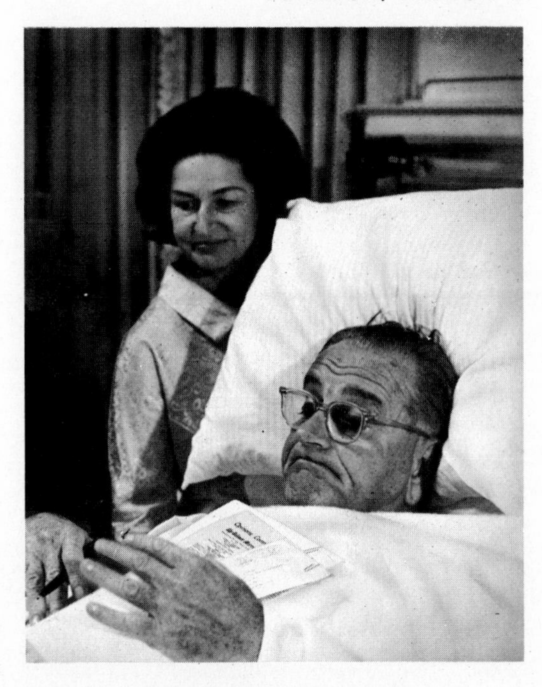

President Lyndon B. Johnson catches up on his paperwork, hours after undergoing surgery. Mrs. Johnson is at his side.

Bulldogger

The LBJ Ranch. The President spent Easter at his ranch in Texas and returned in July for a vacation. He fished, went speedboating, and held his first live television press conference in almost a year. On August 27, he was back at the ranch, with Mrs. Johnson and older daughter Lynda, to celebrate his 58th birthday with barbecued beef and ice cream.

The Johnson Family. Mrs. Johnson was her husband's almost constant companion in 1966. At the same time, she continued her keen interest in beautification and conservation of natural resources. In April, she turned on a new scenic lighting system for the San Antonio River at San Antonio, Tex. Then, with a 70-member party, she went to Big Bend National Park, where she hiked along mountain trails, floated down the Rio Grande on a raft, and dined by the light of a campfire. Later that month, Mrs. Johnson and daughters Lynda and Luci accompanied the President to Mexico City.

Daughter Lynda received a B.A. degree *cum laude* in history from the University of Texas at Austin in June. In July, she took a two-week holiday in Madrid, a graduation gift from her father. In the fall, Lynda accepted a part-time position on the staff of *McCall's* magazine, after reportedly considering offers from the *National Geographic* and the Ford Foundation. CAROL L. THOMPSON

See also DEMOCRATIC PARTY; ELECTIONS; PRESIDENT OF THE UNITED STATES; VIETNAM.

JORDAN. The borders of Jordan were violated in November when Israeli units attacked the town of Es Samu in Jordanian Palestine in retaliation of Arab guerrilla raids on Israel. Jordan's protest brought United Nations condemnation of Israel and placed King Hussein I under strong internal pressures to strike back. See MIDDLE EAST.

Jordan celebrated 20 years of statehood with economic progress but in an atmosphere of political uncertainty. In April, about 100 people were arrested for belonging to political groups banned since 1957.

King Hussein celebrated Jordan's 20th anniversary by digging the first spadeful of earth for the Mukhaiba Dam on the Yarmuk River. The dam's $31,000,000 cost will be shared by all the Arab states. In another action, the king also ordered parliament to amend the laws to allow women to vote.

Jordan received $30,000,000 in aid from the United States in 1966. In addition, the United States and United Nations Food and Agriculture Organization jointly provided $2,150,000 in credits for wheat purchases made necessary by a drought and poor harvests.

Facts in Brief. Population: 2,100,000. Government: King Hussein I; Premier Wasfi al-Tell. Monetary Unit: dinar (1 = U.S. $2.82). Foreign Trade: exports, $21,400,000; imports, $157,900,000. Principal Exports: fruits, phosphates, and tomatoes. WILLIAM SPENCER

JUNIOR ACHIEVEMENT (JA) held its 23rd National Junior Achievers Conference on the campus of Indiana University in Bloomington from Aug. 16 to 21, 1966. A record number, 1,822 persons, attended the only teen-age business conference in the world. The delegates represented 410 JA communities in 48 states and five provinces in Canada. Visitors from Germany, Mexico, and Venezuela also attended.

The theme of the 1966 JA conference was "Business and Youth–Partners in Progress" and it featured workshops and seminars in public relations, management, and marketing. The delegates not only discussed common business problems but aired their opinions of the free enterprise system and the JA program.

Many of those attending competed for scholarships and other awards by demonstrating their individual abilities and business achievements. The highest award given at the 1966 National Junior Achievers Conference went to Terry Opdendyk, 18, of Grand Rapids, Mich. He was named "JA President of the Year" and received a $1,500 college scholarship from the Young Presidents Organization. Judy Edstrom, 17, of Lafayette, Ind., was awarded the title of "Miss Junior Achievement" and received $250. JOSEPH P. ANDERSON

JUVENILE DELINQUENCY. See CRIME.
KASHMIR. See INDIA; PAKISTAN.

KASTLER, ALFRED (1902-), credited with the discovery of the principle that led to development of the laser beam, was awarded the 1966 Nobel physics prize on December 10. The principle dealt with "optical pumping," a method for raising atoms to particular energy levels.

Kastler is on the faculty of L'École Normale Superieure of Paris, where he heads a 20-man laboratory staff that continues his work on "optical pumping." This research has not only proved useful in the development of the laser, but it has also been fruitful in studying the fine structure of atomic states.

Kastler is widely known in France for taking stands, in print and vocally, on nonlaboratory issues. He wants the war in Vietnam ended and the atomic bomb done away with.

Kastler was born in Guebwiller, a village in Alsace, which then was a part of Germany. In 1920, the L'École Normale admitted a few Alsatians who could not pass the French language examinations, and Kastler was among them. After graduation he taught at Louvain, Belgium, and at Bordeaux and Clermont-Ferrand in France. He joined L'École Normale's faculty in 1941.

Kastler is a member of the French Academy of Sciences and an officer of the French Legion of Honor. He and his wife, the former Elise Cosset, who is a high school teacher, have three children and six grandchildren. WALTER F. MORSE

KENYA. President Jomo Kenyatta survived leftist Oginga Odinga's attempt to unseat him in June elections and emerged even more firmly established as the leader of his country in 1966. Before the challenge, Kenyatta's Kenya African National Union (KANU) had maintained one-party control for 18 months. Three months before the election, Odinga resigned from KANU when he was dropped as vice-president of the party. In April, he was elected president of the new socialist and anti-Western Kenya People's Union party (KPU) and persuaded 28 other dissident KANU members of parliament to join KPU.

By the move, Odinga hoped to control enough members to gain a vote of no confidence against Kenyatta's government. But KANU members hastily passed a constitutional amendment requiring members of parliament who leave their party to seek re-election at the end of the session. The elections, held in June, returned only Odinga and eight other KPU members.

Intermittent Fighting broke out early in the year between army and police units and Somali nomads in Kenya's northeastern province. Radio Mogadiscio in Somalia announced in February that the Somali "nationalists" had killed 41 Kenyan troops. The defense minister of Kenya countered by claiming that his forces had killed 105 Somali "bandits." Somali ambushes and Kenyan counterattacks continued throughout the summer. Kenya charged that the increasing strength of Somali attacks was due to secret support from the Somali Republic. Though Somalia denied the charges, Kenya prohibited Somali Airlines flights over Kenya and, on June 21, cut off all trade with Somalia.

Kenya decreased Communist contacts in February and March by expelling Czech, Communist Chinese, and Russian diplomats, as well as correspondents for Czech and Soviet news agencies.

Other Developments. Food shortages caused by two years of severe drought were partly relieved by the Food for Peace program of the U.S. Agency for International Development (AID). The program provided more than $2,000,000 worth of corn, nonfat dry milk, and vegetable oil.

Kenya deprived American-born Mrs. Ernestine Hammond Kiano, wife of the minister of labor, Gikonyo Kiano, of her Kenya citizenship on June 8 on charges of disloyalty. Six Asians, two of whom were Kenya citizens, were deported on August 14 "for reasons of national security." The moves brought criticism from the foreign press and created concern among Asian citizens of Kenya.

Facts in Brief. Population: 9,500,000. Government: President Jomo Kenyatta. Monetary Unit: shilling (7.09=U.S. $1). Foreign Trade: exports, $146,000,000; imports, $249,400,000. Principal Exports: coffee, sisal, tea. BENJAMIN E. THOMAS

KIESINGER, KURT GEORG (1904-), succeeded Ludwig Erhard as chancellor of the Federal Republic of (West) Germany on Dec. 1, 1966. A former Nazi, Kiesinger had joined the party in 1933 as a 29-year-old lawyer. He insisted, however, that after the bloody Nazi putsch of 1934, he stood opposed to the Hitler regime. See GERMANY.

Kiesinger was born on April 6, 1904, of a Roman Catholic family in Ebingen, Swabia, in southwest Germany. He studied law at the universities of Tübingen and Berlin. After graduation, he set up practice in Tübingen, where he later entered politics as a local Christian Democratic Union leader. He was first elected to the Bundestag (parliament) in 1949 and later re-elected with 75 per cent of the total vote cast in his district.

As a favorite of former chancellor Konrad Adenauer, Kiesinger enjoyed a succession of high government posts including the chairmanship of the Bundestag's foreign relations committee. In the mid-1950s, when an expected call to serve as minister of justice failed to materialize, Kiesinger returned to his home where he ran for and was elected minister-president of the state of Baden-Württemberg–a position he occupied at the time of his appointment as chancellor.

Married, with two children, Kiesinger lives in a Swabian-type house in Tübingen. PAUL TULLIER

KIWANIS INTERNATIONAL. See SERVICE CLUBS.

KOREA. On September 22, North Korea's Prime Minister Chung Il-kwon and his cabinet submitted their resignations because of insults they had received in the national assembly during heated hearings on a smuggling scandal.

The scandal, which involved the smuggling into Korea of about $120,000 worth of raw saccharin from Japan, allegedly involved South Korea's largest business combine. Some legislators charged that cabinet members were guilty of collusion in bringing the saccharin into the country surreptitiously. President Chung Hee Park rejected the resignations and the cabinet agreed to stay on after assurances that they would not again be subjected to insults by the legislature.

Presidential Visit. A million Koreans welcomed U.S. President Lyndon B. Johnson to Seoul in November. They did so in a mood of jubilation. With the help of U.S. aid, the gross national product had been growing at about 9 per cent annually for the previous four years. Average per capita income was rising at the annual rate of 6.4 per cent. During the President's visit, which was part of an Asian tour, he indicated that the United States would continue to aid Korea's economic efforts.

Such efforts had been most apparent in August when, after almost a year of exacting work, the South Korean government completed the compilation of a five-year economic development plan covering 1967 to 1971. It was worked out with American advisers, World Bank representatives, and other foreign experts. Among the new plan's goals was the achievement of a 7 per cent annual growth rate.

Late in the year, and shortly after President Johnson's visit, two skirmishes occurred along the demilitarized zone separating North Korea from South Korea. In one incident, four U.S. soldiers were killed. U.S. and South Korean officials saw no indications, however, that North Korea was preparing to launch any major hostilities.

North Korea remained firmly oriented to Communism. At a party congress held on October 17, North Korean Prime Minister Kim Il-sung, who was head of the party, confirmed North Korea's ideological independence from both Communist China and the Soviet Union.

Facts in Brief. Korea (North): Population: 11,534,000. Government: Chairman of the Presidium Choe Yong Kun; Prime Minister Kim Il-sung. Monetary Unit: won (1.20=U.S. $1). Foreign Trade: exports, $18,300,000; imports, $34,200,000. Principal Exports: metals, agricultural products.

Korea (South): Population: 30,357,000. Government: President Chung Hee Park; Prime Minister Chung Il-kwon. Monetary Unit: won (270.27=U.S. $1). Foreign Trade: exports, $176,600,000; imports, $449,700,000. Principal Exports: cotton fabrics, iron ore, raw silk. PAUL TULLIER

KUWAIT

KUWAIT played the role of inter-Arab broker in both economic and political affairs in 1966. The national assembly increased the capital of the Kuwait Fund for Arab Economic Development (KFAED) to $560,000,000. KFAED loaned $6,700,000 to Lebanon, $42,000,000 to the United Arab Republic (UAR), and $28,000,000 to Morocco.

The neutral zone between Kuwait and Saudi Arabia was eliminated, thereby allowing the two countries to share the area's petroleum resources. Kuwait also proposed a solution designed to end the Yemen civil war by partition and to improve relations between Saudi Arabia and the UAR (see Middle East).

The assembly passed a new nationality law limiting citizenship to 50 aliens annually. General elections were scheduled for January, 1967. Prime Minister Jabr al-Ahmad al-Sabah was named crown prince by Sheik Sabah al-Salim al-Sabah.

In November, Kuwait inaugurated its National University; the faculty included one American professor. The first Sheraton Hotel in the Arab world also opened in Kuwait.

Facts in Brief. Population: 564,000. Government: Sheik Sabah al-Salim al-Sabah; Prime Minister Jabr al-Ahmad al-Sabah. Monetary Unit: dinar (1 = U.S. $2.81). Foreign Trade: exports, $1,311,500,000; imports, $340,200,000. Principal Export: petroleum. William Spencer

Passengers stranded in Philadelphia by an airline machinists' strike linger disconsolately at closed ticket counter.

KY, NGUYEN CAO (1930-), premier of South Vietnam, celebrated the anniversary of his first year in office on June 19, 1966. Under Ky's leadership, the nation had taken an important step toward democracy in September when some 80 per cent of its eligible voters had turned out to elect a National Assembly to draft a constitution. See Vietnam.

Premier Ky was born on Sept. 8, 1930, in Son Tay, French Indochina, just outside of Hanoi, the present capital of North Vietnam. His father was a schoolteacher. Ky attended local primary and high schools until 1948 when he enrolled in the Nam Dinh Reserve Officer's School. He completed his studies there in June, 1952, and subsequently received military training in France, North Africa, and the United States. In December, 1954, Ky returned to Vietnam which, in the meantime, had become independent. He subsequently joined the air force where he held relatively unimportant commands until November, 1963, when President Ngo Dinh Diem was overthrown. Thereafter, Ky's rise was rapid. In June, 1965, as a member of the junta that had overthrown the civilian government of Pham Huy Quat, he was named premier.

Ky married Dang Tuyet Mai, a Vietnamese airline hostess, in 1964. He lives with his wife and six children (five of them by a previous marriage) in a three-bedroom bungalow on Tan Son Nhut Air Base on the outskirts of Saigon. Walter F. Morse

LABOR force changes followed the pattern of the previous year in 1966. Civilian employment increased by 1,800,000 between the third quarters of 1965 and 1966 to 74,200,000 jobs. Unemployment continued to drop. The average rate for all of 1966 was slightly under 4 per cent, for the first time since 1953. The average number of unemployed persons was slightly under 3,000,000. Late in the year, government economists stressed that further reductions in unemployment should be accomplished by improved training, counseling, and job placement efforts rather than by stimulating economic growth. They cited the danger of inflation, with industry already operating at near-capacity levels. See Economy, The.

Average hourly earnings of production workers in manufacturing increased by about 10 cents in 1966; the 1964-1965 gain was eight cents. Hours worked per week also increased slightly, so that gross weekly wages rose $5 to about $114 a week in the 12 months to October. But price boosts of 3.7 per cent and higher Social Security taxes offset these gains. Thus, the real spendable weekly pay of the typical factory worker with three dependents at $88 (based on 1957-1959 prices) was slightly less than a year earlier. Likewise, the real spendable earnings of workers in mining, construction, trade, and finance showed little change from October, 1965, to October, 1966.

Fallen Guideposts. Wage settlements in major collective bargaining agreements in 1966 ran higher than in the previous few years, in part because of sharp price increases. Transit workers in New York City opened the new year with a settlement providing for three annual increases: 4 per cent the first and second years and 7 per cent the last year (see NEW YORK CITY). Airline mechanics settled in midsummer for three annual increases of about 5 per cent each year (see AVIATION). Settlements in the construction industry generally exceeded this figure. In manufacturing, many new labor contracts were negotiated. The one in the electrical industry provided for an immediate 4 per cent increase, extra money for skilled workers, an additional paid holiday, and other improvements.

These increases exceeded the raises suggested by the government guideposts, which had called for average increases in wages of 3.2 per cent and stable prices. Despite government pressures on management to keep prices from rising and on labor to keep wage demands in line with gains in national productivity, the guideposts were toppled. A median wage increase of 3.8 per cent was provided in major settlements in the first nine months of 1966.

Reflecting higher wages and near-capacity operating rates, unit labor costs in manufacturing began to climb in the second half of 1966. The index, which had been relatively stable since 1960, reached 102 per cent of its 1957-1959 base in November (see MANUFACTURING [chart]). Wages were starting to rise faster than productivity, or gains in output per man-hour of labor. The long period of stable U.S. labor costs was in marked contrast to the rise in other industrial nations. The average U.S. annual change in unit labor costs between 1957 and 1964 ranged from −0.2 per cent to +0.6 per cent, versus increases of 4.5 per cent for The Netherlands, 4.4 per cent for West Germany, 2.3 per cent for Great Britain, and 1.6 per cent for Japan.

Industrialized countries in Western Europe also struggled to prevent inflation and were using voluntary wage and price guides to help achieve price stability. Britain announced a compulsory six-month wage freeze in the middle of 1966 and late in the year extended it on a slightly modified basis for another six months. See EUROPE; GREAT BRITAIN.

Strikes in 1966, in terms of man-days of idleness, amounted to less than .20 of 1 per cent of total time worked. This was at about the same level as in each year since 1959, when it stood at .61 of 1 per cent. There was widespread sentiment for restricting strikes, however, because several had noticeably inconvenienced the public in 1966.

The New York City newspaper and transit strikes early in the year, the strike against five of the na-

The Shifting Pattern of Jobs
Major occupation groups–1955 to 1975

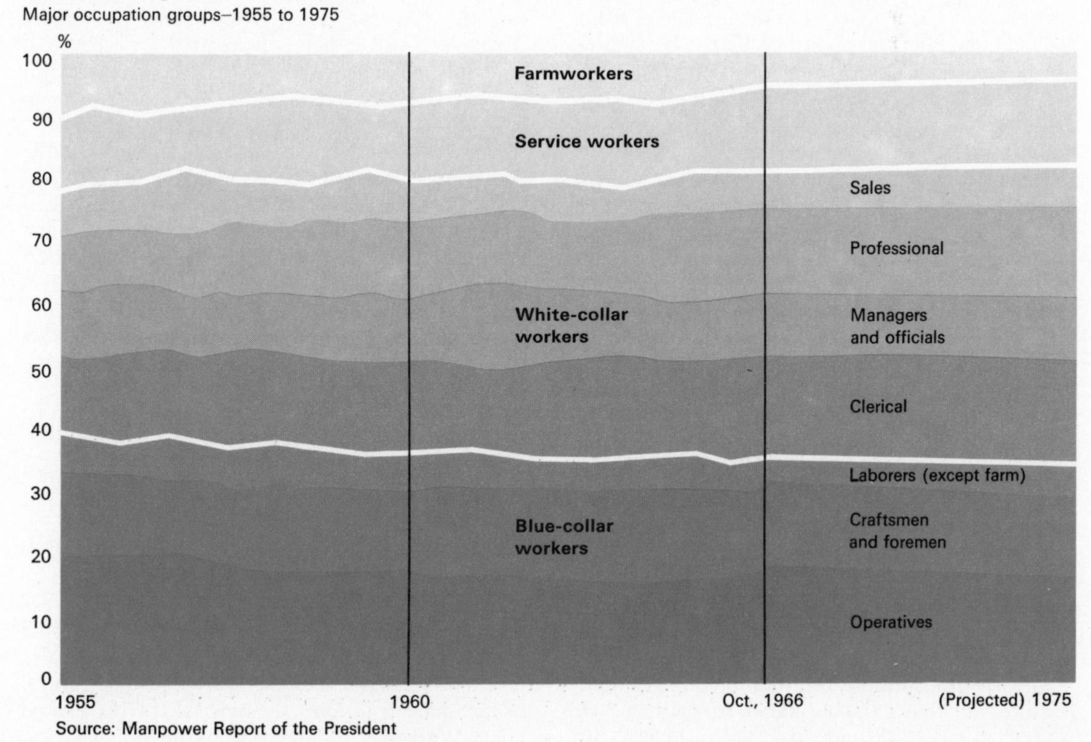

Source: Manpower Report of the President

During New York City's 12-day transit strike, people used bicycles, their feet, or–as this woman did–they hitchhiked to get around.

tion's major airlines, and a number of work stoppages by hospital employees were illustrative of this problem. Despite the suggestions that strike legislation be enacted, Congress took no action in 1966.

For 1967, labor-management relations experts expected tougher bargaining. Strikes may increase because major contracts covering about 3,000,000 workers–twice as many as in 1966–were due to expire in 1967. They were in such key industries as automobiles, rubber, trucking, and meat packing. Union negotiators were under pressure to obtain substantial increases to offset the rise in living costs and large corporate profits. Pressure also was on management to resist any demands that would cause further increases in unit costs, because of uncertainty about future business prospects.

The 11½-year labor dispute between the Kohler Company, Wisconsin plumbingware maker, and the United Auto Workers (UAW) came to an end in 1966, when the company agreed to settle all outstanding unfair labor practice claims. In November, it began distributing $3,000,000 in back pay and wage adjustments to 1,349 former and present employees. It added another $1,500,000 to the pension fund to make up for pension credits lost during the six years of the strike.

A New Bargaining Technique was tried successfully in 1966. "Coordinated bargaining" by representatives of 11 unions won a contract in October from the electrical industry's toughest negotiator, the General Electric Company. A federal appellate court earlier had vacated an injunction requiring management to bargain on this basis. But because both sides reached agreement, the legal basis of this new technique was not fully tested.

The historic five-year agreement between the Pacific Maritime Industry Association and the West Coast Longshoremen's Union was renegotiated without a strike. The former agreement contained a mechanization and modernization (M&M) fund that provided for employment security guarantees and pension supplements. The new agreement continued the M&M fund but dropped the employment security guarantees, presumably because the union believed that employment prospects in the industry were good enough to warrant putting the money to other uses.

A Major Breakthrough in bargaining occurred in agriculture. California grape pickers struck for union recognition in the fall of 1965. After six months, they won an agreement, first by one large grower and then by others. Their union would be recognized if a majority voted for the union in representation elections. The independent National Farm Association Workers won elections at various locations and later merged with other agricultural worker groups to form the new AFL-CIO United Farm Workers Organizing Committee.

Collective bargaining spread further in the public sector in 1966 as teachers, nurses, and other public employees turned more frequently to bargaining as the procedure to use in solving their problems.

State of the Unions. Late in November, the American Federation of Labor-Congress of Industrial Organizations (AFL-CIO) reported that its total U.S. membership had risen by about 250,000 in a year to 13,500,000 as of June 30, 1966. It was an increase of about 1,100,000 dues-paying members since 1963, which was the lowest year since the AFL-CIO was founded in 1955. The federation added that its rolls had "continued to move upward" in the last half of 1966.

Government statistics on membership trends between 1961 and 1964 (the latest year available) supported the AFL-CIO claim to substantial gains. It should be emphasized, however, that as a per cent of total U.S. nonagricultural employment, union membership had declined from the 1954 peak of 33.4 per cent to 28.9 per cent in 1964. This is relatively on the low side, compared with such countries as Britain and Sweden.

Union leadership saw few changes in 1966. David Dubinsky, 74, resigned as president of the International Ladies Garment Workers Union, a post he had held since 1932. Louis Stulberg, 64, a former garment cutter, succeeded him on July 15. And the United Rubber Workers union chose Peter Bommarito to succeed George Burdon as president.

James R. Hoffa, president of the independent International Brotherhood of Teamsters, won reelection to a five-year term by acclamation in July. But in December, the Supreme Court of the United States upheld his 1964 conviction for jury tampering. He was granted a rehearing in February, but was expected to have to start serving his eight-year prison sentence sometime in 1967.

Minimum Wage. Congress raised the minimum wage from $1.25 to $1.40 effective February, 1967, and to $1.60 in February, 1968, for the 29,500,000 workers already covered under the Fair Labor Standards Act. Also, an additional 8,100,000 workers were brought under the act, including 390,000 farmworkers, with minimums rising at a slower rate, to $1 in February, 1967, and not reaching $1.60 until 1971. The farmworkers' minimums would stop at $1.30 in 1969.

Automation and Technological Change generally posed few problems for the economy in 1966 because of the continued high rate of newly created jobs. Disputes arose, however, where technological change and other factors led to a reduction in jobs. For example, the merger of four New York City newspapers led to the longest major newspaper strike in U.S. history (see PUBLISHING).

Technology and the American Economy, the 1966 report of the National Commission on Technology, Automation, and Economic Progress, was much more cheerful in its outlook than studies of automation made five years earlier. Point No. 1 of its 20 major conclusions and recommendations was that: "There has been some increase in the pace of technological change. The most useful measure of this increase for policy purposes is the annual growth of output per man-hour in the private economy. If 1947 is chosen as a dividing point, the trend rate of increase from 1909 to that date was 2 per cent per year; from 1947 to 1965 it was 3.2 per cent per year. This is a substantial increase, but there has not been and there is no evidence that there will be in the decade ahead an acceleration in technological change more rapid than the growth of demand can offset, given adequate public policies."

The last sentence reflected the increasing acceptance of the idea that public policies stimulating the growth of demand for goods and services can create sufficient jobs to offset those wiped out by the introduction of machinery and automated systems–both at the present pace and at the pace anticipated in the next 10 years.

In point No. 9, the panel noted that many people have not shared in the wealth made possible by technological change and recommended that "economic opportunity be guaranteed by a floor under family income." JAMES L. STERN

See also COMPUTERS; SOCIAL SECURITY; Section One, SYLVIA PORTER: FOCUS ON THE ECONOMY.

LAOS. Under the coalition government of Prince Souvanna Phouma, the nation continued its efforts to achieve political stability. The pro-Communist Pathet Lao still held approximately two-fifths of the country but they were less active than in previous years. This was due in part to the lack of continuing support from the North Vietnamese, who were forced to concentrate their efforts on their own war in South Vietnam. The lull in Pathet Lao activities was also related to the decreasing importance of the Ho Chi Minh supply route which ran through part of Laos. See VIETNAM.

Souvanna Phouma pressed ahead with development plans for the country, particularly in education and agriculture. These plans, which called for large expenditures, received a setback, however, in September when the national assembly refused to approve Phouma's annual budget. Despite the repeated urgings of King Savang Vathana, the assembly would not yield and it subsequently was dissolved in order to prevent the fall of the government. In December, plans to elect a new 59-seat assembly were announced by the king.

Facts in Brief. Population: 2,070,000. Government: King Savang Vathana; Premier Souvanna Phouma. Monetary Unit: kip (240=U.S. $1). Foreign Trade: exports, $1,400,000; imports, $29,900,000. Principal Exports: gums, resins, tin, ore, wood. JOHN N. STALKER

LATIN AMERICA continued to seek hemispheric unity in various ways in 1966. In some of its efforts, the area achieved notable successes; in others, success proved elusive.

In the spring, the United States and its Latin American neighbors found themselves stalemated at two conferences. One was held in Panama for the purpose of drafting proposed amendments to the Charter of the Organization of American States (OAS). The other was held in Buenos Aires to discuss certain policies of the Alliance for Progress program. The Latin-American countries wanted to set down in treaty form specific economic policies by which the United States would be committed to help its neighbors. The United States wanted more general phrasing; it also urged the Latin Americans to make greater efforts toward self-help so as to mobilize their resources. In addition, the United States also wanted to strengthen the OAS' powers to maintain peace in the hemisphere and deal with problems involving Communist subversion. But it was too soon after U.S. intervention in the Dominican Republic for the Latin Americans to reach agreement.

Later, a compromise resolution was reached: Washington agreed to put into treaty form a commitment to continue its long-term aid program, plus a pledge to help Latin America achieve economic integration and better access to world markets for its commodity exports. The Latin Americans dropped their insistence that the U.S. be more specific in its commitments and that it give the region drastic trade concessions. They also endorsed a series of self-help measures involving controls on inflation, effective tax systems, agrarian reform, and education. The hemisphere's foreign ministers had been expected to endorse the draft treaty in August, as well as adopt modifications to the OAS Charter and plan a summit meeting of the hemisphere's presidents, but the ministers' meeting was indefinitely postponed.

Common Market Plan. In June, Felipe Herrera, president of the Inter-American Development Bank proposed the formation of a Latin American Common Market which would gradually eliminate tariffs in internal trade and erect a common external tariff. On August 17, the fifth anniversary of the Alliance for Progress, U.S. President Lyndon B. Johnson called for the economic integration of the 19 republics and the raising of the 2.5 per cent annual per capita growth target for the region to 4 to 6 per cent. This came just after the presidents of Chile, Colombia, and Venezuela, and the presidential delegates of Peru and Ecuador, in a joint "Declaration of Bogotá," advocated the need for integration and cooperation at various levels, modifications of the Latin American Free Trade Association (LAFTA), closer cooperation between that body and the Central American Common Market (CACM), and the eventual union of the two. It pinpointed eight main areas for joint industrial development: cellulose, chemicals and petrochemicals, electronics, fertilizers, food, manufactured metal products, metallurgy, and timber. Later, the five nations agreed to set up a common market in petrochemical products, anticipating an exchange of items valued at about $45,000,000 by 1970.

The Bogotá Declaration was of major importance in view of the barren results of negotiations in LAFTA, where agreement was getting more difficult to achieve, notably on questions involving lower tariffs. Among other things, the Bogotá accord indicated that of the 10 republics associated with LAFTA, half had decided to avoid further delays in achieving economic, social, and cultural coordination in such areas as trade liberalization, industrial development, transportation, communications, and interchange of technological data.

The CACM, five years old in July, had trade restrictions remaining on only 27 items. In these five years, the CACM index of economic growth rose 5.5 per cent annually, as against 4.5 per cent in the 1950s, and the figure was expected to be 6.4 per cent per annum in the future. Panama signed an agreement to eventually become a member. And to woo this market, Mexico's President Díaz Ordaz made a two week tour of Central America in January, promising technical aid, preferential tariffs, and private Mexican venture capital for developing industries. Mexico lent $5,000,000 to the Central American Economic Integration Bank, while the Bank of Mexico subscribed to the first bond issue made by the Central American Bank. See MEXICO.

CENTRAL AMERICA

Costa Rica. José Joaquin Trejos Fernández, a political novice, was inaugurated as president on May 8, his main objective being national unity. Foremost on his agenda was a banking reform to allow private and foreign banks to operate in the nation and accept deposits, thus indirectly improving the tight credit situation. The International Monetary Fund (IMF) approved a one-year $10,000,000 stand-by credit. The Ford Motor Company and Kaiser Jeep planned assembly plants in San José, while the Firestone Company was building a $7,000,000 tire plant nearby. On June 1, an 8,000 barrel-per-day oil refinery and associated asphalt plant was completed.

El Salvador. The governing party retained a legislative majority and won most of the municipal contests in the elections held March 13. The government maintained stringent exchange controls due to balance of payments problems resulting from poor coffee and cotton crops–the republic's principal exchange earners–and to the low market prices for coffee.

Guatemala returned to constitutional government after three years of military rule, during which

Facts in Brief on the Latin-American Countries

Country	Population	Government	Monetary Unit	Foreign Trade (million U.S. $) Exports	Imports
Argentina*	23,408,000	President Juan C. Ongania	peso (205=$1)	1,492.5	1,198.6
Bolivia	4,286,000	President René Barrientos Ortuño General Alfred Obando Candia	peso (11.86=$1)	131.9	134.1
Brazil*	85,011,000	President Humberto de Alencar Castelo Branco	cruzeiro (2,200=$1)	1,595.7	1,097.5
Chile	8,950,000	President Eduardo Frei Montalva	escudo (4.29=$1)	687.8	603.6
Colombia*	18,566,000	President Carlos Lleras Restrepo	peso (18.20=$1)	538.9	453.4
Costa Rica	1,507,000	President José Joaquin Fernandez Trejos	colon (6.62=$1)	109.2	160.2
Cuba*	7,750,000	President Osvaldo Dorticós Torrado Premier Fidel Castro	peso (1=$1)	155.8	219.4
Dominican Republic*	3,783,000	President Joaquin Balaguer	peso (1=$1)	135.3	135
Ecuador	5,243,000	President Otto Arosemana Gomez	sucre (17.82=$1)	222.7	172.3
El Salvador	2,997,000	President Julio Adalberto Rivera	colon (2.50=$1)	188.4	200.2
Guatemala	4,540,000	Chief of State Julio Cesar Mendez Montenegro	quetzal (1=$1)	185.9	229.7
Haiti	4,820,000	President François Duvalier	gourde (5=$1)	45	39
Honduras	2,298,000	President Osvaldo López Arellano	lempira (2=$1)	139.8	113.8
Mexico*	43,675,000	President Gustavo Díaz Ordaz	peso (12.49=$1)	1,142	1,559.1
Nicaragua	1,754,000	President Lorenzo Guerrero Gutierrez	cordoba (7=$1)	149	152.5
Panama*	1,308,000	President Marco Aurelio Robles	balboa (1=$1)	132.2	378.6
Paraguay	2,033,000	President Alfredo Stroessner	guaraní (125=$1)	57.3	48.7
Peru	12,087,000	President Fernando Belaúnde Terry	sol (26.80=$1)	667.6	729.8
Uruguay	2,788,000	National Council of Government President Alberto Heber Usher	peso (70=$1)	191.3	150.9
Venezuela*	9,228,000	President Raúl Leoni	bolívar (4.48=$1)	2,558.5	1,296.6

*Indicates countries that have special articles.

it was plagued by killings, bombings, and kidnappings carried out by a few hundred Communist-led terrorists. On July 1, non-Communist leftist Julio César Méndez Montenegro became the republic's first civilian president since 1951 and the first government opposition candidate to win in modern history. He immediately cracked down on the pro-Communist guerrillas, instructing the army and the police to maintain order and quell any uprisings, from either the right or the left. He launched an agrarian reform program, made plans to reduce the nation's sizable debts, a budget deficit, and a widening balance of payments gap. The country's gross monetary reserves had reached a record $95,200,000 by June 30, aided by peak export income from coffee and cotton, heavy borrowings from abroad, and an overflow of private capital investment.

Honduras. The country's gross monetary reserves, heavily bolstered by foreign loans, were at a record $45,300,000 at the end of July, reflecting a fairly satisfactory trade balance, a slowdown in the utilization of central bank credit by the public sector, and the accumulation of public sector deposits. Texaco was authorized to build an $8,000,000 refinery at Puerto Cortes, while the World Bank lent $4,800,000 to help finance the expansion and improvement of the port.

Nicaragua. President René Schick Gutierrez died on August 3 of a heart attack; his term, ending April 30, 1967, was filled by Vice-President Lorenzo Guerrero. Overall, the nation was enjoying its fifth successive year of economic expansion, prosperity, and general price stability.

CARIBBEAN ISLANDS

Haiti reportedly executed eight plotters against the regime in March. Other reports spoke of unusual clandestine activity by opponents of President François Duvalier, who had proclaimed himself dictator for life. Haiti suffered from reduction of its tourist trade, the withholding of foreign aid, a decline in business activity, a poor coffee crop, and disorganized government finances. The IMF approved a one-year $4,000,000 stand-by arrangement, but the island remained close to bankruptcy.

Puerto Rico. The annual growth rate of about 9.3 per cent placed the island second only to Japan in a global comparison of economic growth. Its industrialization program completed its fifth record-breaking year, with 412 plant promotions for the fiscal year ended June 30, including huge chemical facilities and Puerto Rico's first full-fledged aircraft (helicopter) manufacturing plant. Construction also surged ahead, but the agricultural picture was different, especially regarding the important sugar crop which has been unable to fill its mainland sugar quota over a period of 10 years. In August, after a two year study, a joint U.S.-Puerto Rican commission recommended that the islanders should decide by popular vote whether to continue as a commonwealth territory, become an independent nation, or apply for U.S. statehood.

SOUTH AMERICA

Bolivia. General René Barrientos Ortuño was elected president on July 3 and took office August 6 for a four-year term. His principal goal was economic development, and he offered ample guarantees to private capital to help achieve it. The economy was growing at a satisfactory rate of 5½ per cent annually. The peso boliviano remained free and steady, monetary reserves were up, and the foreign debt at the end of March, 1966, was only $280,000,000 compared to $278,000,000 in 1965.

Chile. An 88-day strike by the copper miners ended late in March; it had cost the country $38,500,000 in production and nearly $19,000,000 in tax revenues. Despite this setback, the republic expected to record a $90,000,000-plus balance of payments surplus in 1966, up from $80,000,000 in 1965. Industrial production for the first six months of 1966 was up 9.6 per cent. But inflation proved a problem; living costs for the first nine months jumped 21 per cent, thus exceeding the 15 per cent figure at which the government had hoped to hold it. President Eduardo Frei Montalva ordered the implementation of a wage policy and curbs on government spending. Money remained very tight and interest rates edged upward. To spur business, Chile banned the traditional Latin-American siesta during the working day. During the year, fresh water was found in the nitrate-rich Atacama desert, a discovery which could dramatically transform northern Chile's economy.

Ecuador. On March 29, the armed forces high command deposed the military junta and announced full restoration of civil rights. Clemente Yerovi Indaburu, a Guayaquil businessman, was named provisional president. Yerovi canceled plans for a scheduled presidential election. He did, however, permit the election of a new constituent assembly. In October, at a special session, the assembly elected Otto Arosemana Gomez as provisional president to succeed Yerovi.

Paraguay on August 19 received a $7,500,000 one year IMF stand-by credit to help it meet any difficulties in its international payments. Spain granted the nation $15,000,000 for various industrial and transport projects, while the International Development Association lent $7,500,000 for a program to increase livestock production. Paraguay became an oil-refining country during the year when a plant near Asúncion, operating on Algerian crude oil, began producing 10,000 barrels per day.

Peru enjoyed an economic growth rate of around 6.2 per cent for 1966. Although it struggled with a balance of payments problem and budget deficits, its currency–the sol–remained stable. The IMF granted a $37,500,000 stand-by credit to support the government's anti-inflation campaign; the World Bank lent $10,000,000 for an electric power expansion program and $9,100,000 to build a $14,700,000 port at Pejerry. The Inter-American Development Bank lent $20,000,000 to help finance a $39,500,000 program to improve living standards in seven Indian communities.

Uruguay. On November 27, after 12 years of political instability, the country voted on whether it would retain its unworkable nine-man national council system of government or revert to a one-man presidential set-up. The coalition of two main political parties had declined into unstable and separate groupings. By a large majority, the voters replaced the Swiss-style rotating system with a one-man chief executive. They elected Oscar Daniel Gestido, a retired air force general. He was to serve a five-year term beginning March 1, 1967.

Industrial and agricultural output were virtually stagnant, although the country did enjoy excellent returns for its vital wool clip. The only growth was in the national debt (more than $550,000,000), in bureaucracy (over 19 per cent of the labor force), in the circulation of money (which skyrocketed by 69.3 per cent in a 12-month period ended June 30), and in living costs (up an average 6 per cent a month in the first six months). MARY C. WEBSTER

LAW. See CIVIL RIGHTS; COURTS AND LAWS; CRIME; SUPREME COURT OF THE UNITED STATES.

LEBANON. The country's traditional role as regional banker was shaken by a financial crisis in October, 1966. The country's largest private bank, Intra, shut down. Withdrawals of nearly $30,000,000 during the previous month had left Intra without enough cash to meet its liabilities. The government ordered a three-day bank holiday to prevent a run on other banks, but the expected panic did not develop. In fact, a new private bank, Transorient, a joint venture of Arab and U.S. investors, was dedicated 10 days after the crisis. See MIDDLE EAST.

Premier Rachid Karamí resigned in April to allow parliament to elect a cabinet from among its own members; Karamí's cabinet consisted of nonpolitical technicians. Abdullah Yafi, a six-time premier between 1938 and 1956, succeeded Karamí. Yafi resigned in November and Karamí returned. The new cabinet dismissed more than 150 officials.

Strikes plagued the economy. Transport workers struck for higher pay in July, paralyzing transportation. A one-week strike at the state-run electric company in September forced the government to draft clerks to provide electricity.

Facts in Brief. Population: 2,150,000. Government: President Charles Helou; Premier Rachid Karamí. Monetary Unit: pound (3.08 = U.S. $1). Foreign Trade: exports, $105,500,000; imports, $475,200,000. Principal Exports: fruits, raw cotton, vegetables. WILLIAM SPENCER

LESOTHO, formerly the British protectorate Basutoland, became independent on Oct. 4, 1966. But the last steps to independence were marred by political strife. Chief Leabua Jonathan, prime minister of the former protectorate, was supported by the Basutoland National party, which had only a slight majority in the national assembly.

Jonathan was locked in a bitter power struggle with the Basutoland Congress party and its leader, Oxford-educated Paramount Chief Moshoeshoe II. In the new government, Moshoeshoe became a constitutional monarch with limited authority and Jonathan became prime minister with major governmental responsibility.

In the weeks preceding independence, Moshoeshoe had demanded executive powers. When Jonathan refused to yield, supporters of Moshoeshoe tried to disrupt the independence ceremonies. In December, violence broke out, but was quickly crushed by Jonathan's forces. Moshoeshoe was placed in "protective custody" for a short time.

Jonathan maintained good relations with the Republic of South Africa, which surrounds Lesotho.

Facts in Brief. Population: 760,000. Government: King Moshoeshoe II; Prime Minister Leabua Jonathan. Monetary Unit: rand (1 = U.S. $1.41). Foreign Trade: no statistics available. Principal Exports: cattle, mohair, wool. BENJAMIN E. THOMAS

LIBERIA. See AFRICA.

LIBRARY. Public libraries will benefit for the next five years from the expanded Library Services and Construction Act passed by Congress in 1966. The two existing programs for library services and construction were expanded in the new act, and two new programs were added. The new programs provide for inter-library cooperation in establishing and operating networks of libraries and for extension of library services to the institutionalized and the handicapped.

The National Books for the Blind Act was amended to allow the Library of Congress to serve other physically handicapped persons who cannot use conventionally printed materials. It also provided funds for grants to the states for library services to the physically handicapped.

College Libraries. Higher Education Act grants were distributed again in 1966 to help strengthen college and university library resources. Grants under the act also provided funds for institutional and graduate level fellowship awards in library and information science training. Graduate and undergraduate institutions were also allocated funds from the Higher Education Facilities Act of 1965 for new construction and for remodeling of libraries.

Advisory Committees. President Lyndon B. Johnson appointed several new national advisory groups in 1966. Two of them, the President's Committee on Libraries and the National Advisory Commission on Libraries, were to assess the role and adequacy of the nation's libraries. The President also appointed the two advisory councils authorized by the Higher Education Act. They are the Advisory Council on College Library Resources and the Advisory Committee on Library Research and Training Projects.

Library cooperation on a nationwide scale will be fostered by the establishment of the Joint Committee on Library and Information Systems (CONLIS). This committee is composed of representatives from six national library associations. See AMERICAN LIBRARY ASSOCIATION (ALA).

Anti-Poverty Programs. Numerous local libraries participated actively in providing reading materials for the disadvantaged. Nationally, there were two significant anti-poverty programs related to libraries, and the National Book Committee participated in each of them.

The Office of Economic Opportunity and the Community Action Program worked with the National Book Committee to establish guidelines for library services in neighborhood centers. The National Book Committee then compiled lists of books for kits which were distributed to disadvantaged groups by the Volunteers in Service to America (VISTA). Funds for this project were made available by a $200,000 grant from the Fund for the Advancement of Education. MIRIAM DONAHOE

LIBYA issued new oil concessions to 23 foreign companies under the terms of the law passed in November, 1965. The new law increases Libya's oil tax and will make funds available to further buoy Libyan economic development. The government formed a state-owned oil company to sell oil directly to Western European markets.

Oil companies in Libya made several new strikes. British Petroleum, Ltd., struck oil in April, as did Socony Mobil Oil Company and E.N.I., the Italian concessionaire. Standard Oil Company of New Jersey and its subsidiary, Esso Standard Libya, announced new natural gas strikes in their areas. As a consequence, the Libyan government negotiated a contract with the Illinois Institute of Technology in Chicago to study new methods of utilizing the natural gas.

Parliament approved a record budget of $523,600,000 for 1966-1967, $386,400,000 of it to come from oil royalties. In a move against growing inflation, the Bank of Libya acted in June to increase the reserves required by commercial banks by 50 per cent. It also required a 25 per cent minimum cash deposit by importers of consumer goods.

Facts in Brief. Population: 1,708,000. Government: King Idris I; Premier Hussein Mazik. Monetary Unit: pound (1 = U.S. $2.80). Foreign Trade: exports, $796,500,000; imports, $320,000,000. Principal Export: crude petroleum. WILLIAM SPENCER

LINDLEY, JONATHAN (1931-), a staff member of the U.S. Senate Committee on Banking and Currency, was appointed director of the U.S. Department of Commerce's Office of Regional Economic Development.

In this post he will coordinate the work of various regional planning commissions that are now being established. The commissions, provided for under the Public Works and Economic Development Act of 1965, are to deal with states that have common ties but have lagged behind the nation in economic growth. They will plan long-range programs that may be financed by private capital, or through existing local, state, and federal programs.

In his previous post on the U.S. Senate Committee on Banking and Currency, Lindley assisted in formulating general committee policy on area redevelopment and economic growth, and was closely involved with the Economic Development Act during the process of its enactment.

He attended George Washington University in Washington, D.C., where he received a bachelor's degree in economics and did graduate work in the field of economic policy. As a member of the Senate committee staff, he was awarded a Congressional Staff Fellowship by the American Political Science Association. Lindley is married, has two children, and lives in Alexandria, Va.

LIONS INTERNATIONAL. See SERVICE CLUBS.

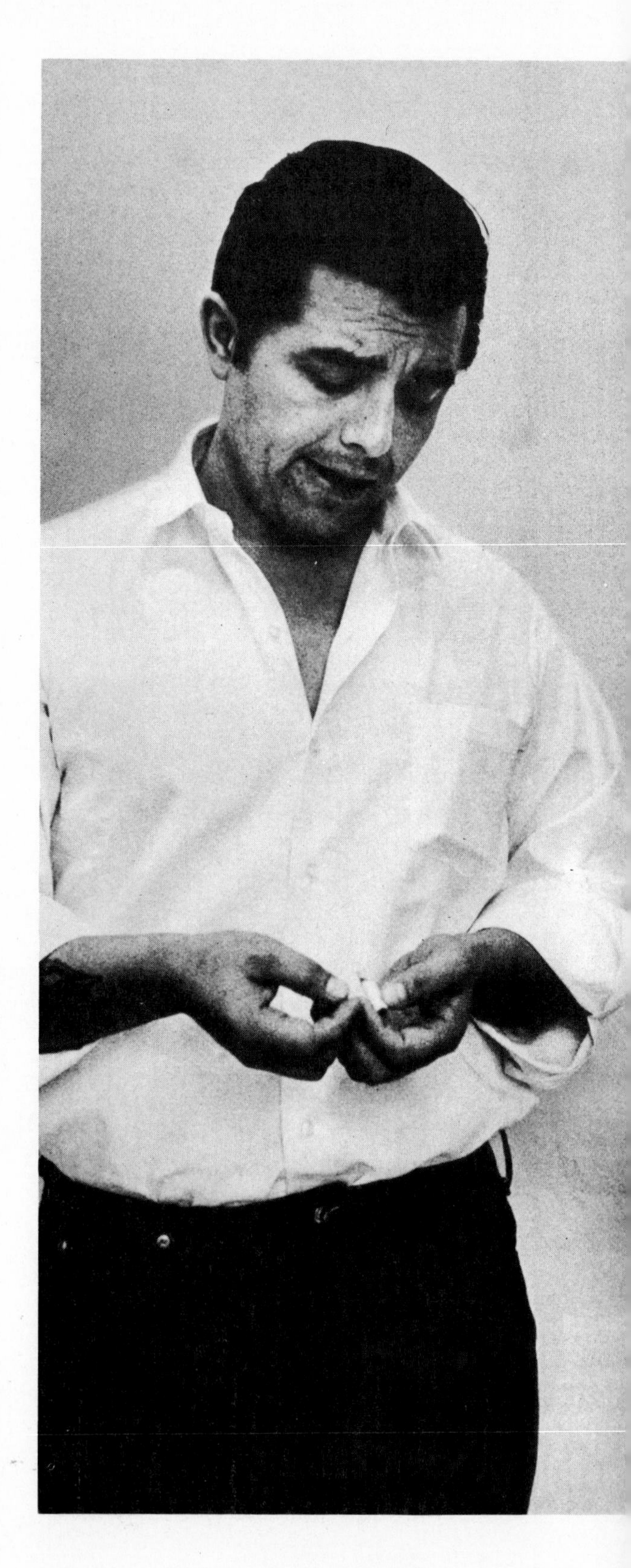

LITERATURE. The British critic Walter Allen, writing in *The New York Times Book Review* at the close of 1966, made three observations on British book publishing that might well apply to the situation in the United States. The first was that "too many books are published in Britain anyway"; the second, "as the number of books published creeps up year by year, the number of novels among them falls slightly but steadily"; and the third, "fiction is becoming an increasingly less important element in publishing." Certainly the experience of 1966 would indicate a parallel trend in the United States where, despite a tremendous outpouring of new titles, there was a notably scanty list of offerings in the field of fiction.

On the whole it was a good year for publishers. Preliminary estimates at the year's end indicated that U.S. book buyers in 1966 paid close to $2,500,000,000 for 2,200,000,000 books.

FICTION

In the area of the novel, it was one of those years in which the reader had very little from which to choose, either in the field of quality fiction, or in mere entertainment. The top-rated best seller in December was Robert Crichton's first novel, *The Secret of Santa Vittoria*, an amusing, highly readable and unpretentious story of an Italian village's fight to save its wine supplies during World War II. It shared first novel honors for the year with two

others which were written with more grace and literary distinction. They were William H. Gass' *Omensetter's Luck* and Sylvia Wilkinson's *Moss on the North Side*. *Omensetter's Luck*, a beautifully written philosophical story of a fortunate man and the envy his luck inspired among his neighbors in a small Ohio community, was clearly one of the better novels of the year. Miss Wilkinson's tale of a young girl's search for identity exhibited a fresh and original talent.

Among the established U.S. novelists, the best work came from Bernard Malamud and John Barth. Malamud's *The Fixer*, the story of a Russian Jew falsely accused of a ritual murder in the Czarist days, was a graceful and moving work. Barth's *Giles Goat-Boy, or The Revised New Syllabus* was a remarkable and controversial allegory in which the world is satirically pictured as a university. But its wit stumbled too often on pedantry to make it wholly successful.

Two other well-known veterans who published new novels were Louis Auchincloss, whose *The Embezzler* was another of his competently written "novel of manners," and Walker Percy, whose *The Last Gentleman* told the story of a young Southerner in search of a life worth living.

Four younger writers who had been steadily advancing their careers published creditable works in 1966. Harry Mark Petrakis, in *A Dream of Kings*, created a new and appealing hero in Chicago's Greek-American community, which has become his special world. Thomas Pynchon, author of the widely hailed *V*, continued to explore the complexities of existence in *The Crying of Lot 49*. Wilfrid Sheed again exhibited his gift for satire in *Office Politics*, the story of interrelationships among the staff of a liberal New York magazine. Reynolds Price, with *A Generous Man*, offered new evidence of his narrative powers in a tale of a boy's coming of age in the North Carolina backwoods.

Importations. The offerings from abroad were generous if not spectacular. The best of them included Graham Greene's *The Comedians*, a smoothly written story of modern Haiti by one of England's ablest storytellers; and Doris Lessing's *Children of Violence*: Vol. 3, *A Ripple from the Storm*, and Vol. 4, *Landlocked*, the third and fourth in her series of novels about the life of an Englishwoman involved in left-wing politics.

Much publicity preceded Rebecca West's novel, *The Birds Fall Down*, a rather old-fashioned spy tale, but, in the main, it disappointed American readers who had expected more from the elderly Dame Rebecca. Another English spy story which seemed

Truman Capote, *right*, author of *In Cold Blood*, interviews convicted murderer Perry Smith whose story is revealed in the book.

largely unworthy of its talented author was Kingsley Amis' *The Anti-Death League.*

Of the other novels from abroad, perhaps the most notable were Jakov Lind's *Landscape in Concrete*, a devastatingly bitter story of a Nazi soldier in World War II; the New Zealand novelist Sylvia Ashton-Warner's *Greenstone*, a delightful adult fable of family relationships; and the French novelist Alain Robbe-Grillet's *La Maison de Rendez-Vous*, a Hong Kong tale in the style of the so-called "objective" French novel.

Short Stories. The year was exceptionally rich in short story collections. Two posthumous gatherings were among the best. They were *Alpha and Omega*, by Isaac Rosenfeld, and *The Big Knockover*, a selection of short stories and novels from the work of Dashiell Hammett, the dean of American detective story writers. The Hammett volume was edited by Lillian Hellman. Another posthumous story collection was *The Magic of Shirley Jackson*, edited by her husband, literary critic Stanley Edgar Hyman. It included her famous tale, "The Lottery."

Nine of Stanley Elkin's better short stories were offered in *Criers and Kibitzers, Kibitzers and Criers*, while John Updike and R. V. Cassill, two other well-regarded writers in this genre, offered new selections in *The Music School* and *The Happy Marriage and Other Stories*, respectively.

From Europe came Heinrich Boll's *18 Stories*, a collection covering 15 years; Sean O'Faolain's *The Heat of the Sun*, a miscellany showing the Irish storyteller's varied gifts; and Sylvia Townsend Warner's *Swans on an Autumn River*, a seventh collection by a masterly English stylist.

Two veteran U.S. short-story writers who brought out new collections were John O'Hara with *Waiting for Winter*, and Kay Boyle with *Nothing Ever Breaks Except the Heart.*

NONFICTION

Autobiography, Biography, Diaries, and Letters. As usual, nothing was more interesting than people in the nonfiction of 1966. Statesmen and literary figures, again as usual, dominated the field, with honors for coverage going to the late Sir Winston Churchill, about whom two of the more readable books of the year were written. The first to appear–and one that caused an international furor–was *Churchill: Taken from the Diaries of Lord Moran: The Struggle for Survival, 1940-65.* An intimate and revealing portrait by the personal physician to the late British prime minister, it was criticized by some as an unseemly violation of privacy. The other Churchill book was the first volume of the official biography being written by his son. It was Randolph S. Churchill's *Winston S. Churchill: Youth, 1874-1900.* Detailed and ably written, it leaned heavily on Sir Winston's own written records.

Two other British statesmen were represented in important offerings. Former Prime Minister Harold Macmillan's *Winds of Change* was a notable chronicle of British political events from 1914 to 1939. Another fateful period of modern history was covered in *Harold Nicolson: Diaries and Letters, 1930-1939*, edited by Nigel Nicolson.

Among the books by and about literary figures the one that received the most attention was A. E. Hotchner's *Papa Hemingway: A Personal Memoir*, an account of some events in the last 14 years of the late Ernest Hemingway's life by one of the novelist's latter-day companions. It was a blazingly frank book and, like Lord Moran's book on Sir Winston Churchill, was criticized as an invasion of privacy. But legal action against it by the novelist's widow came to no avail.

One of the year's outstanding literary biographies was Lawrance Thompson's *Robert Frost: The Early Years, 1874-1915*, the first volume of what promises to be a definitive work on the New England poet. Malcolm Cowley, whose *Viking Portable Faulkner* is credited with broadening William Faulkner's literary reputation, published an important record of his friendship with the Mississippi novelist in *The Faulkner-Cowley File: Letters and Memories, 1944-1962.* Justin Kaplan's *Mr. Clemens and Mark Twain*, the first important new biography of Samuel L. Clemens in years, offered fresh insights into the personality of the author of *Huckleberry Finn.*

Theodore Roethke's posthumous book of *Collected Poems* was a publishing highlight of 1966. Roethke, *above*, died in 1963.

The National Book Award Winners, *left to right,* were James Dickey, poet; Katherine Anne Porter, novelist and short-story writer; Janet Flanner, journalist; and Arthur M. Schlesinger, Jr., historian. Dickey won the prize for *Buckdancer's Choice;* Porter for *The Collected Stories of Katherine Anne Porter;* Flanner, writing under the name of Genêt, for *Paris Journal of 1944–1965;* and Schlesinger for *A Thousand Days: John F. Kennedy in the White House.*

André Maurois continued his career as a biographer with *Prometheus: The Life of Balzac*, a portrait of characteristic brilliance. The life of a little-known poet and novelist who knew a number of the important literary figures in the Paris of the 1930s was laid bare in the first volume of *The Diary of Anais Nin*, edited by Gunther Stuhlmann. Richard Ellmann published the second and third volumes of the *Letters of James Joyce*, an important record of the Dublin novelist's life and work.

The lives of two musicians, one a contemporary and one an old master, were published. They were *Virgil Thomson*, a lively autobiography by the well-known music critic and composer, and Paul Henry Lang's *George Friderick Handel*, the best biography of that great musician yet to appear.

Raymond Moley's *The First New Deal* was an important and revealing record of the early New Deal days, when he was an adviser to Franklin D. Roosevelt. Another onetime New Dealer, David E. Lilienthal, published the third volume of his *The Diary of David E. Lilienthal*. Subtitled "The Venturesome Years, 1950-55," it covered his removal from public service (as Atomic Energy Commission chairman) and return to private business.

John F. Kennedy's press secretary, Pierre Salinger, added his bit to the story of Kennedy's presidency with a modest but, nevertheless, useful memoir, *With Kennedy*.

A memorable autobiography by Isaac Bashevis Singer, author of *Gimpel the Fool*, *The Magician of Lublin*, and other masterly tales on Jewry, appeared. It is called *In My Father's Court*.

Essays and Criticism. The rather thin field of critical works for the year included a handful of important books, notably two volumes by Wallace Fowlie entitled *Rimbaud* and *Rimbaud: Complete Works, Selected Letters*. The latter was a companion piece to the former, a critical study. Joseph N. Riddel published his able *The Clairvoyant Style*, a criticism of the poetics of Wallace Stevens, and Norman Mailer brought out *Cannibals and Christians*, a free-swinging commentary on the times which included both literary and political targets within its focus. Susan Sontag, a novelist, caused a stir with her collection of essays, *Against Interpretation*.

History. Barbara W. Tuchman, whose writing on World War I had won her international acclaim, went back beyond the turn of the century to write *The Proud Tower: A Portrait of the World Before the War, 1890-1914*. The book was an excellent analysis of the forces that shaped the modern world. One of the year's more readable histories was Cornelius Ryan's *The Last Battle*, which described the events leading up to the Battle of Berlin in April, 1945. Cabell Phillips contributed a noteworthy portrait of Harry S. Truman in *The Truman Presidency: The History of a Triumphant Succession*.

LITERATURE

The American Scene. Two literary men who chose to write about subjects usually covered by journalists scored success in 1966. One was the novelist Truman Capote, whose *In Cold Blood* was a detailed and skillfully written account of a multiple murder and its aftermath in a small Kansas community. The other was George Plimpton, editor of the *Paris Review*, who posed as a rookie quarterback with the Detroit Lions professional football team and came up with a fascinating account of his experiences in *Paper Lion*.

The Kennedy assassination continued to bring forth controversial challenges to the Warren Commission Report. Edward Jay Epstein's *Inquest* challenged the adequacy of the investigation by the commission, while Mark Lane's *Rush to Judgment* was an outright attack on the findings themselves.

If the importance of books is measured by their ability to cause social change, Ralph Nader's *Unsafe at Any Speed* was the year's most important book. It attacked the automobile industry frontally for its apathetic attitude in building safety into its cars and it brought immediate government action to ensure greater automobile safety in the future. See AUTOMOBILE (Close-Up).

The Arts. In the deluge of publishers' "merchandise" published for the gift-giving season at the end of the year, there were at least two art books worthy of survival. One was a facsimile reproduction of *The Hours of Catherine of Cleves*, one of the most beautiful of all illuminated manuscripts. John Plummer supplied a useful introduction. The other was a two-volume set, *The Original Water-Color Paintings by John James Audubon for "The Birds of America."* It was reproduced in color from Audubon's original paintings in the collection of the New York Historical Society. It included all except three of the ornithologist's famous water colors. The color reproduction was superb. VAN ALLEN BRADLEY

POETRY

American enthusiasm for public readings by poets reached a height in 1966 that surpassed anything the country had known since the great days of "platform culture" during the Chautauqua movement. As in the past, big-name poets continued their junkets from campus to campus, but what characterized the new interest in poetry readings was the large number of less well-known poets who sought, and found, an audience. Highly organized poetry-reading circuits brought whole companies of poets into even remote areas. For example, a nationwide system of regional circuits was administered by the Academy of American poets in New York City. Students gave public readings on many campuses to enthusiastic audiences of their fellows. Most universities undertook poetry festivals as regular extracurricular features. These generally included readings, lectures, workshops, and informal get-togethers of poets and students.

Inevitably, performances improved and interest in dramatic reading revived. Ronald Bayes, a theatrical director, presented two successful performances by student-actors reading the works of older poets, "An Evening with Ezra Pound" and "An Evening with William Carlos Williams." The poet and anthologist Donald Hall won success with "An Evening's Frost," a dramatic selection from the poems of Robert Frost.

The theater itself paid more attention to poets. Experimental theaters for verse drama sprang up widely, some operating in the relative luxury of foundation grants, others maintained only by their members' zeal. Two of the best known were the Judson Poets' Theatre and the American Place Theatre, both in New York City.

U.S. audiences in 1966 were introduced to the work of the young Russian poet, Andrei Voznesensky, who read his poems before enthusiastic audiences in New York City, Chicago, and Washington, D.C. His book, *Antiworlds*, appeared with translations by leading U.S. poets.

In addition, readings by poets were turned to other than cultural ends. Poets Robert Bly and David Ray organized a series of "read-ins" in opposition to U.S. policy in Vietnam. More than 50 poets, including many of the country's best known, participated.

Other Events. Three well-liked poets died during 1966: Delmore Schwartz, winner of the Bollingen award; Hubert Creekmore, known equally for his poetry and his fiction; and Arthur Waley, whose translations from the Chinese had set the tone for dozens of younger Orientalists.

Perhaps the most important book of the year was the *Collected Poems* of Theodore Roethke, winner of the 1953 Pulitzer prize in poetry, who died in 1963. The volume contained all his previously published work plus a section of posthumous poems. It was destined, critics said almost unanimously, for a secure place among American classics. Also notable was the appearance of another volume of verse and prose by Marianne Moore, *Tell Me, Tell Me: Granite, Steel, and Other Topics*. A collection that caused considerable comment was a posthumous volume of intense, highly personal poems, *Ariel*, by the late Sylvia Plath.

Robert Lowell became the first American poet to be seriously considered for the honorary Professorship of Poetry at Oxford, an elective chair filled by secret ballot of the dons. The vote went to Edmund Blunden, an older British poet, but Americans were aware of the honor paid to them. And James Dickey became the first of a younger generation of U.S. poets to be named poetry consultant to the Library of Congress. HAYDEN CARRUTH

See also EBERHART, RICHARD.

LITERATURE, CANADIAN. See CANADIAN LIBRARY ASSOCIATION; CANADIAN LITERATURE.

LITERATURE FOR CHILDREN. Of interest to parents, grandparents, and other adults in 1966 were two anniversaries in children's literature as well as several books for family sharing, and two concerning children's literature and art. For teachers and others who work with children, and the children themselves, there were the rich collections of picture books and tales, and collections for the story hour.

The 900th anniversary of the Battle of Hastings is celebrated by several new titles. *The Bayeux Tapestry: The Story of the Norman Conquest: 1066*, by Norman Denny and Josephine Filmer-Sankey, is reproduced in color with explanatory text, and concerns Harold's visit to William of Normandy. Then follows the pictorial tale of Harold's return to England, and his succession to the throne upon the death of Edward the Confessor.

Place, contestants, and the battle are portrayed in narrative and dramatic pictures in *The Norman Conquest* by C. Walter Hodges. *The Silver King: Edward the Confessor, the Last Great Anglo-Saxon Ruler*, by Margaret Stanley-Wrench, pictures England under a king, who was exiled in Normandy in his youth. His relationships to Harold as well as to William of Normandy are related.

The Last Viking, by the late Henry Treece, begins as Harald Hardrada and his allies await the approach of Edward's successor, King Harold II, followed by the battle that weakened the Saxon army for the Battle of Hastings. Elizabeth Luckock's *William the Conqueror*, illustrated from the "tapestry," as the famous embroidered history is called, details the early life of William. Although unwelcome in England at the time, William helped make it the strong nation it became.

O. G. Tomkeieff's *Life in Norman England*, the era of Edward the Confessor beginning in 1042, relates the heritage from the Anglo-Saxons and the introduction of the feudal system following the conquest. The text concerns village, town, church and educational life, medical and legal practice, architecture, fine arts, and amusements. Alfred Duggan's *Growing Up with the Norman Conquest* gives a chatty account of everyday life in the England of 1087, the last year of William the Conqueror's reign. Clothing, food, and transportation of knights and lesser landholders, London burgesses, the cloister, and the peasantry are discussed.

The 100th anniversary of the birth of Beatrix Potter (1866-1943), whose *The Tale of Peter Rabbit* has been beloved by small children, is remembered with *Beatrix Potter, 1866-1943*, a centenary catalog lovingly prepared by Leslie Linder and published in London.

Also for adults interested in children's books, the Library of Congress issued a pamphlet *Fables from Incunabula to Modern Picture Books*, a fascinating annotated bibliography by Barbara Quinnam. Would-be authors and illustrators for children will welcome *Writing, Illustrating and Editing Children's Books* by Jean P. Colby as well as *The Art of Art for Children's Books: A Contemporary Survey* by Diana Klemin.

Books for family sharing include *The Mother Goose Treasury*, illustrated by Raymond Briggs with lively pictures and containing more than 400 rhymes. Also, there is an edition of Robert Louis Stevenson's *A Child's Garden of Verses*, colorfully illustrated by Brian Wildsmith.

The Odyssey World Atlas is a beautiful, well-printed oversize book, which many families may enjoy as an educational and artistic treat to be shared at many age levels.

A new award was established in 1966 in honor of the recently retired executive secretary of the Children's and Young Adult services divisions of the American Library Association. The Mildred L. Batchelder Award will be made to "an American publisher for a children's book considered to be the most outstanding of those books 'originally published

From *The Monster Den*, drawings by Edward Gorey; poems about naughty children by John Ciardi. Publisher: J. B. Lippincott.

From *Ananse the Spider.* Pictures by Peggy Wilson. African folk tales retold by Peggy Appiah. Publisher: Pantheon.

in a foreign language, in a foreign country, and subsequently published in the United States . . . ' "

TRANSLATIONS

Golden Island by Katherine Allfrey. This winner of the German Children's Book prize is a fantasy about a Greek girl and a dolphin.

You Have a Friend, Pietro, by Josef Carl Grund, is the tale of a Corsican vendetta, as told by an Italian stonecutter.

Pappa Pellerin's Daughter by Maria Gripe. A young Swedish girl, Loella, longs for her father and adopts a scarecrow, whom she calls Pappa Pellerin.

The Sun Train by Renée Reggiani. Detailed plot and characterization pictures a Sicilian family trying to improve their financial and social status.

The Happy Islands Behind the Winds by James Krüss. Original tales from the German, in which privileged visitors may converse with intelligent animals about such things as art and poetry.

The Little Man by Erich Kästner. This circus fantasy by a popular German author has an adventurous "Tom Thumb" size hero.

The Gold Coin by Reidar Brodtkorb. This translation from the Norwegian is about two children's long search for their parents after a raid in the Estonia of the 1600s.

My Name Is Pablo by Aimée Sommerfelt. Translated from the Norwegian. A shoeshine boy in Mexico City is befriended by a Norwegian family.

SOME NEW EDITIONS AND REPRINTS

A Christmas Carol. A ghost story of Christmas by Charles Dickens. Illustrated by Philip Reed.

No Room, retold by Rose Dobbs, is an old tale about the peasant's crowded house and the baby and animals underfoot.

Calico Bush by Rachel Field. A powerful novel of early Maine for adults as well as teens. The author considered it her best writing.

Household Stories from the collection of the Bros. Grimm. Translated from the German by Lucy Crane, and done into pictures by Walter Crane. A republication of an important 1866 edition.

The Trumpeter of Krakow by Eric P. Kelly. A beautiful edition of this Polish history story, with a foreword by Louise Seaman Bechtel, editor of the book when it won the Newbery medal (1929).

The Amiable Giant, by Louis Slobodkin, tells of the giant's birthday party for Gwendolyn, who was not afraid.

ART AND MUSIC

Drawings to Live With by Bryan Holme. An exquisite collection from prehistoric rock drawings, Da Vinci and Dürer, to Paul Klee and Ludwig Bemelmans. Briefly annotated.

Paint, Brush and Palette by Harvey Weiss. A basic book on fundamental techniques of painting and use of color. Includes plastic paints and marker pens.

The Ingenious John Banvard by Nan H. Agle and Frances A. Bacon. Frontier history as pictured in Banvard's panoramas of the Mississippi.

The Troll Music. Story and pictures by Anita Lobel. The musicians in this fantasy produce a symphony after the troll restores tone to their instruments.

The Sound of Bells, by Eric Sloane, relates how musical bells are replacing discordant sounds again.

PICTURE BOOKS

Billy the Littlest One by Miriam Schlein. Illustrated by Lucy Hawkinson. How the tiniest child always longs to grow.

ABC, An Alphabet Book by Thomas Matthiesen. Colored photographs of everyday objects, such as dolls and eggs, make this just right for the very young. Artists, as well as adults and children, will pore over the brilliantly colored pictures in Celestino Piatti's *Animal ABC.* English text by John Reid.

Pinkety, Pinkety: A Practical Guide to Wishing by Sesyle Joslin. Illus. by Luciana Roselli. A small princess knows exactly what to do with stars and rainbows.

Mr. Tall and Mr. Small by Barbara Brenner. Illus. by Tomi Ungerer. How the giraffe and the mouse escape from the forest fire is fun to tell or read.

Farewell to Shady Glade by Bill Peet. Monster machines destroy their homes and 16 animals journey far.

One Wide River to Cross by Barbara and Ed Emberley. All can sing this folk song as Noah's animals march across the pages in bold black woodcuts on bright colors.

Jennie's Hat by Ezra Jack Keats. Her plain straw hat was disappointing until the birds brought colorful things to trim it.

Sumi's Special Happening by Yoshiko Uchida. Illustrated by Kazue Mizumura. Oji Chan celebrates his 99th birthday with noise, food, and fun.

Sam, Bangs & Moonshine by Evaline Ness. A lonesome little girl and her cat live near the sea. Imagination and an incoming tide almost cause disaster. Perfect "wet" and sunny illustrations.

POETRY

The Golden Hive by Harry Behn. There is real empathy with childhood in these nature poems.

Songs of Innocence by William Blake. Music and illustrations by Ellen Raskin. Guitar arrangements by Dick Weissman. This volume belongs on the piano, and its companion volume, with text and large woodcuts, is ideal for a child's hands.

Oh, What Nonsense! by William Cole. Drawings by Tomi Ungerer. Nonsense from Laura Richards to John Ciardi for family sharing.

I See the Winds by Kazue Mizumura. These follow the form of Haiku, and encourage children to try to create their own poems.

Poems to Solve by May Swenson. Chosen to present visual imagery and stimulate thinking.

The Silver Swan. Compiled by Horace Gregory and Marya Zaturenska. Poems of appeal to young teens.

The Paths of Poetry: Twenty-Five Poets and Their Poems, by Louis Untermeyer, is an introduction to their lives in relationship to their poetry.

TALES FOR MANY AGES

Billy Boy, verses selected by Richard Chase. A picture book illustrated by Glen Rounds, with the Southern mountain version of the folk song.

Baba Yaga by Ernest Small. Humorous woodcuts by Blair Lent decorate this Russian witch tale.

Snow-White and Rose-Red by the Bros. Grimm. A picture book by Barbara Cooney.

Pangur Ban by Joan Balfour Payne. "Once long ago in old and holy Ireland there lived a little white cat" introduces a beautifully illustrated story.

The Black Heart of Indri, adapted by Dorothy Hoge, is a delicately illustrated Oriental love story.

The Carpet of Solomon: A Hebrew Legend by Sulamith Ish-Kishor. Tells of the time when King Solomon became humble and his kingdom was restored.

Backbone of the King: The Story of Paka'a and His Son Ku by Marcia Brown. An outstanding new classic created from an Hawaiian epic.

COLLECTIONS FOR THE STORY HOUR

Joy to the World, Christmas Legends by Ruth Sawyer. A carol accompanies each miracle tale.

Favorite Fairy Tales Told in Czechoslovakia and *Told in Sweden.* Two new volumes by Virginia Haviland for telling to, or reading by, children.

The Giant Who Drank from His Shoe and Other Stories by Léonce Bourliaguet. Translated from the French. Another attractive collection about giants is *The Giant Book* by Beatrice Schenk de Regniers.

The Hungry Moon, Mexican Nursery Tales by Patricia F. Ross. It is a long-awaited reprint of the tales, each accompanied by a verse in English and Spanish.

Palace in Bagdad: Seven Tales from Arabia by Jean R. Larson. Tales with lessons, flavored with humor.

Philip and the Pooka and Other Irish Fairy Tales by Kathleen Green. In *The Stone of Victory and Other Tales,* Padraic Colum has chosen 13 magic stories from his collections.

The Three Sorrowful Tales of Erin by F. M. Pilkington. Exquisite telling from the Irish sagas of the Children of Tuireann, the Children of Lir, and the Sons of Uisne.

From *The Jazz Man.* Woodcuts by Ann Grifalconi. Mary Hays Weik writes of the troubled life of a Negro child. Publisher: Atheneum.

From *The Magic Flute*, the Mozart opera, illustrated by Beni Montresor and told in a new version by poet Stephen Spender. Publisher: Putnam.

Once There Was and Was Not: Armenian Tales Retold by Virginia A. Tashjian. A fascinating and varied collection that is just right for telling.

Australian Legendary Tales. Collected by K. L. Parker. Edited by H. Drake-Brockman. Authoritative, comprehensive collection for storytellers.

FANTASIES, FABLES, AND TALL TALES

McBroom Tells the Truth by Sid Fleischmann. An Iowa family of 12 is helped by the weather in this tall tale.

Emily's Voyage by Emma Smith. Emily was a delightful "Guinea Pig" who loved to travel.

The Kelpie's Pearls by Mollie Hunter. A delightful tale of magic from the Scottish highlands.

The Magic Finger by Roald Dahl. An eight-year-old girl changes Mr. Gregg, his wife, and son into ducks in this animal fable about hunters.

Gaetano the Pheasant: A Hunting Fable, by Guido Rocca, teaches the dangers of conformity. It is beautifully illustrated.

Andy Buckram's Tin Men by Carol R. Brink. Andy, boy-baby sitter, is mechanically minded.

Nightbirds on Nantucket by Joan Aiken. In a sea adventure, Dido, Nate, and Dutiful are involved with Hanoverian plotters and a pink whale.

Viollet by Julia Cunningham. A fable of the grape harvest as the thrush, the dog, the fox, and the old count thwart the villain.

The Cloud Forest by Joan North. In this tale of foreboding, a magic ring helps a boy overcome evil.

The Castle of Llyr by Lloyd Alexander. Princess Eilonwy is growing up in this third tale of Prydain, a mythical kingdom.

PEOPLE ARE IMPORTANT

Did You Carry the Flag Today, Charley? by Rebecca Caudill. Responsibility wins over curiosity, and makes everyone proud of small Charley.

The Street of the Flower Boxes by Peggy Mann. Paint, flowers, and interested children help transform a slum.

Sailor's Choice, by Natalie S. Carlson, is about a stowaway boy, a Newfoundland sea captain, and a dog named Sailor.

Lapland Outlaw by Arthur Catherall. A boy's fast-paced chase after a dishonest trader who swindled his father of his reindeer.

Chauncy and the Grand Rascal by Sid Fleischman. An orphan travels down the Ohio to the West, encountering unusual people and tall-tale adventure.

David in Silence by Veronica Robinson. Realistic story of problems and emotions of a deaf boy, his friends, and family.

The Witch's Daughter by Nina Bawden. An intriguing mystery involving some thieves, a boy, a blind girl, and an orphan.

A Candle in Her Room by Ruth M. Arthur. Hate caused by the doll, Dido, spans three generations until the granddaughter, Nina, destroys Dido.

Queenie Peavy by Robert Burch. An eighth-grade girl in rural Georgia defies teachers, and is blamed for some things she has not done.

Second-hand Family by Richard Parker. An English orphan boy from the "Home" is sent to a family to board, and finds a place for himself.

Trust a City Kid by Anne Huston and Jane Yolen. An old horse is important to a Harlem boy who visits a Quaker farm.

SCIENCE AND CONSERVATION

Hurry Spring! by Sterling North. An idyllic diary of a season and a lifetime is for families to read aloud together.

The Hunt for the Whooping Cranes: A Natural History Detective Story, by J. J. McCoy, is a detailed account of a continent-wide conservation project.

Ladybug by Robert M. McClung. Notes at the end explain the history and folklore of ladybugs.

The Travels of Monarch X by Ross E. Hutchins. A reconstructed four-month, 2,000-mile migration flight of a Monarch butterfly from Toronto to Mexico.

The Ocean World by Vladimir and Nada Kovalik. Oceanography, involving all the sciences, is a challenge to exploration.

Sea Monsters, by Walter Buehr, tells how further development of oceanography may explain the fabulous creatures of the sea.

Race Against Time: The Story of Salvage Archaeology by Gordon C. Baldwin. The young person feels the urgency to save before excavations destroy.

How Fast, How Far, How Much: The How of Scientific Measurements by William Moore. About human, geologic, astronomic, and other measurements.

How Animals Communicate by Bil Gilbert. A fascinating account of research with bees, birds, dogs, apes, and dolphins.

From *Zlateh the Goat*, illustrated by Maurice Sendak. Tales of Middle Europe's Jews by Isaac B. Singer. Publisher: Harper & Row.

TEEN STORIES

Skald of the Vikings by Louise E. Schaff. Young Thrain's adventures in Vinland in 1007.

Crimson Moccasins by Wayne D. Doughty. An adopted white son of Blue Heron, a Miami, fails his manhood test. In Conrad Richter's *The Light in the Forest*, a beautiful new edition illustrated by Warren Chappell, a white boy is raised as a Leni-Lenape.

The Blood of the Brave by Betty Baker. The story of Juan, who acted as interpreter for Cortes.

The King's Fifth by Scott O'Dell. Estéban, maker of Coronado's maps, tells his story of the gold when he is accused of withholding the king's share.

The Secret Sea by Richard Armstrong. Stark tale of a whaling voyage in a dangerous sea.

Canalboat to Freedom by Thomas Fall. A Scottish emigrant boy helps the underground railroad.

The Plan for Birdsmarsh by K. M. Peyton. Two boys on an English coastal farm encounter criminals.

Head into the Wind by Robinson Barnwell. How Toby grew up in the South during the depression. Jimmy in *The Rough Road*, by Margaret McPherson, faces the depression on the Island of Skye.

Pastures of the Blue Crane by J. F. Brinsmead. Outstanding story of Ryl and her grandfather on the beautiful north coast of Australia.

Bride at Eighteen by Hila Colman. Teens may view thoughtfully the problems of Kate's marriage to Mike, a law student.

A Girl Like Me by Jeannette Eyerly. In a timely novel, teen-age Robin drops the fast crowd, but finds her friend has become an unwed mother.

THE ANCIENT WORLD AND OTHER TOPICS

The Roman Republic by Isaac Asimov. Mediterranean civilization from 1000 B.C. to Augustus.

The King of Men by Olivia Coolidge. Novel by a student of the ancient world is based on the Agamemnon story.

Roman Roads by Victor W. Von Hagen. Why highways and bridges of 2,000 years ago still survive.

Ancient Crete, by Frances Wilkens, tells of Sir Arthur Evans' explorations at Knossos.

God Is in the Mountain compiled by Ezra Jack Keats. Religions of the world accent brotherhood in this important pictorial presentation.

God and His People, edited by Harold Bassage. Taken from the King James Version of the Old Testament, and attractively illustrated.

A Matter of Life and Death: How Wars Get Started—or Are Prevented by Albert Z. Carr. Teens and their elders will enjoy discussing this together.

Spinning Tops by Larry Kettelkamp. Fascinating games which children from everywhere can share.

Japan: Crossroads of East and West, by Ruth Kirk, gives the human side of the country, with its old ways and the new.

Perez y Martina: Un Cuento Folklorico Puertorriqueno by Pura Belpré. A classic tale told in Spanish.

Awards in 1966 included:

American Library Association Children's Services Division Awards: *Caldecott Medal*, for the most distinguished American picture book in 1965, to Nonny Hogrogian, illustrator of *Always Room for One More* by Sorche Nic Leodhas. *Newbery Medal*, for the most distinguished contribution to American literature for children in 1965, to Elizabeth Borton de Treviño for *I, Juan de Pareja.*

British Library Association Awards: *Carnegie Medal*, for an outstanding book for children, to Philip Turner for *The Grange at High Force. Kate Greenaway Medal*, for the most distinguished illustrated book for children, to Victor G. Ambrus, illustrator-author of *The Three Poor Tailors.*

Canadian Library Association Book of the Year for Children Awards. See Canadian Library Association.

Catholic Library Association Regina Medal, for a lifetime dedication to the highest standards of literature for children, to Leo Politi, noted American author and illustrator of children's books.

Child Study Association of America Children's Book Award to Natalie S. Carlson for *The Empty Schoolhouse*.

Hans Christian Andersen Medals are awarded every two years by the International Board on Books for Young People to a living author and a living illustrator who, by outstanding value of their complete works, have made the most distinguished contribution to international children's literature. *Author's Medal* to Tove Jansson of Finland, known for *Finn Family Moomintroll* and other Moomin books. *Illustrator's Medal*, to Alois Carigiet of Switzerland, who illustrated *A Bell for Ursli* and other Selina Chönz books.

The New York Herald Tribune Awards, presented at the newspaper's Spring Festival of Children's Books: *Picture Books* to Ellen Raskin, author-illustrator of *Nothing Ever Happens on My Block. For Children 8 to 12* to Reginald Ottley for *Boy Alone. For Older Boys and Girls* to Geoffrey Trease for *This Is Your Century*.

Thomas Alva Edison Foundation National Mass Media Awards: *For the Best Children's Book on Natural Science* to J. Bronowski and Millicent E. Selsam for *Biography of an Atom. For the Best Science Book for Youth* to Charles A. Gray for *Explorations in Chemistry. For Excellence in Portraying America's Past* to Milton Meltzer, editor of *In Their Own Words: A History of the American Negro, 1865-1916. For Special Excellence in Contributing to the Character Development of Children* to Phillip Viereck for *The Summer I Was Lost.*

Eloise Rue

LIVESTOCK. See Agriculture.

LIVESTOCK SHOW. Once again an Aberdeen-Angus steer was named grand champion of the International Live Stock Exposition. The 67th annual show was held in Chicago from Nov. 25 to Dec. 3, 1966. Blackie, the winner, weighed in at 1,275 pounds – the show's heaviest champion steer in 15 years. The Chicago Mercantile Exchange paid Blackie's owner, Harvey Hartter, Carlock, Ill., $15 a pound, and planned to exhibit the steer to publicize its trading in cattle futures.

A black Hampshire pig exhibited by the University of Wisconsin was judged the best of show among more than 500 barrows in the open market swine competition. Sensation, Jr., the Chester White pig shown by 14-year-old Debra Pichner of Owatonna, Minn., became grand champion in the junior swine competition and the reserve grand champion.

A Polled Hereford steer became grand champion of the 68th American Royal Live Stock Show and Horse Show in Kansas City, Mo. The steer, weighing 1,155 pounds, brought its owners, Emery Tuttle & Sons of Arcola, Ill., $5,655.

The Royal Agricultural Winter Fair was held in Toronto, Ont., Canada, from Nov. 11 to 19, 1966. Quebec took the prize for the first time in the show's history with an Aberdeen-Angus senior calf, Desourdymere 3150. It brought $13.25 per pound, the highest price ever paid for a show animal at this fair.

Sandy Klime and her livestock show entry, *above*, take a break during the judging. Blackie, *right*, was named Grand Champion.

LLERAS RESTREPO, CARLOS (1908-), took office as the 11th president of Colombia on Aug. 7, 1966. He was overwhelmingly elected to a four-year term on May 1, succeeding Guillermo Léon Valencia. See COLOMBIA.

An economist, Lleras was born in Bogotá, Colombia, on April 11, 1908. His family was well-to-do, and today Lleras has substantial business interests. He taught public finance at the National University and had been editor of the Liberal party's newspaper, *Tiempo*.

During his 30 years of government service, Lleras served three times as minister of finance and was for many years a senator, a position from which he campaigned hard for the presidency. He has also been president of Colombia's National Committee for Coffee Growers and of a business enterprise.

Lleras, a supporter of low-cost housing, was a leader in the National Land Reform Institute, which distributed arable land to 100,000 peasants. In his campaign, he emphasized the need for radical changes in Colombia, and pledged a "national transformation" if he were elected.

Although Colombia has a long history of political violence, Lleras is the antithesis of the political strongman. On the other hand, he must maintain order while accomplishing his economic goals in the face of heavy pressures from right-wing and Communist factions. WALTER F. MORSE

LOS ANGELES, the city of the automobile, gave the pedestrian his day on May 18, 1966, when the first phase of the Civic Center Mall was dedicated. Built at a cost of $6,900,000 and including a two-level underground garage, this section will be joined by others until a broad expanse of landscaped walkways connects the $35,000,000 Los Angeles County Music Center with city hall.

Watts. Much of the nation looked at the Watts section of Los Angeles as the Negro ghetto's most explosive situation, and, indeed, Watts erupted again on March 15. Two men, one white and one Negro, were killed. But, the area remained generally quiet, although tense, for the rest of the year.

A Watts Summer Festival brought in speakers, music, and a makeshift movie theater, the only one serving the district. The nearest hospital was still far away. But public transportation, cited in the post-riots investigations as a contributing cause of poverty, got a boost. A $2,700,000 federal mass transit grant started improved bus service July 5, so that Watts residents could have greater access to jobs elsewhere in the metropolitan area.

Also in July, a controversial symbol of law and order, Chief of Police William H. Parker, died of a heart attack. During his long tenure, he built the city's police force into a model of efficiency. However, his gruff, no-nonsense attitude caused great resentment among Negroes.

Other Developments. Mayor Samuel W. Yorty appeared in August before a highly critical Senate subcommittee investigating the problems of cities. He pointed out his limited authority under a 41-year-old city charter.

Within the mayor's bailiwick of recreation was the new Los Angeles Zoo that opened in November at a cost of some $9,000,000. Among its 2,200 specimens were a variety of rare apes, a fine collection of equines, and hundreds of species of birds.

At Century City in west Los Angeles, the nation's largest privately financed urban development project was showing how planning can make the central city exciting. The 180-acre tract, under development by the Aluminum Company of America, had 12 of its 88 planned structures underway or completed. Opened in 1966 was the 20-floor Century Plaza Hotel, designed by architect Minoru Yamasaki, and the Century Tower Apartments. The basic plan of Century City is composed of "superblocks," to reduce traffic congestion and encourage pedestrian movement, and make possible more flexible use of land. Nearly all parking will be below ground.

In urban renewal, the city's largest project, Bunker Hill, was beginning to rise on 130 acres of land. And the tallest building in Southern California, the 536-foot Union Bank Square Building, was topped out in October. DONALD W. LIEF

LUMBER. See FOREST PRODUCTS.

LUXEMBOURG. An order to draft 400 men into the army touched off a political crisis which toppled the government in November, 1966. The order had been made as a move to fulfill Luxembourg's troop commitments to the North Atlantic Treaty Organization (NATO).

Members of the Socialist party believed the draft should be ended. The Christian Socialists agreed but wanted to discuss the matter with NATO members before taking action. Unable to resolve the dispute, Premier Pierre Werner resigned.

Luxembourg enjoyed continuing prosperity during 1966. Iron and steel output continued to increase. The nation also continued to benefit from its membership in Benelux.

Doubts about the future of the European Coal and Steel Community (ECSC) caused some concern in the nation. Headquartered in Luxembourg City, ECSC faced the prospect of a merger that would require its relocation in Brussels, Belgium.

Facts in Brief. Population: 337,000. Government: Grand Duke Jean; Premier Pierre Werner. Monetary Unit: franc (50.10=U.S. $1). Foreign Trade (including Belgium): exports, $6,386,900,000; imports, $6,373,400,000. Principal Exports: steel products, agricultural products, textiles, ceramics. KENNETH BROWN

MAGAZINE. See PUBLISHING.

MALAGASY REPUBLIC. See AFRICA.

MALAWI became a republic on July 6, 1966. Under its constitution, parliament elected Hastings Kamuzu Banda, the prime minister, to serve as the nation's first president. Formerly a constitutional monarchy, the country remained within the British Commonwealth of Nations. Earlier in the year, Banda had accused Tanzania of harboring Malawi rebels who, he said, planned to attack Malawi with guerrilla fighters trained in Cuba and Communist China. In February, Banda broke off relations with the United Arab Republic (UAR). While no reason was given, the break apparently was made because he suspected the UAR of supporting exiled Malawi rebels.

On February 1, Malawi executed Medson Silombela for treason and murder. He was an associate of former education minister Henry Masauko Chipembere, now in the United States, who led an unsuccessful revolt against Banda in 1964.

Malawi supported British attempts to overthrow the rebel white government in nearby Rhodesia through economic sanctions, but maintained that African nations did not have the military strength to invade Rhodesia.

Facts in Brief. Population: 4,200,000. Government: President Hastings Kamuzu Banda. Monetary Unit: pound (1 = U.S. $2.82). Foreign Trade: exports, $30,900,000; imports, $50,200,000. Principal Exports: cotton, peanuts, tea. BENJAMIN E. THOMAS

MALAYSIA, FEDERATION OF, enjoyed a relatively quiet year due largely to a relaxation of pressures from Indonesia. In August, Indonesia formally terminated its "confrontation" with Malaysia by signing a peace accord in Djakarta. It marked the end of an undeclared war which had taken about 700 lives. British troops who had held the jungle defense line in Borneo against Indonesian infiltrators began a phased withdrawal from Malaysia. See INDONESIA.

Although Malaysia's most pressing problem was thus solved, it faced others almost as grave. Communist guerrilla activity continued along its borders with Thailand, thus necessitating large expenditures for defense. Singapore also posed a security problem because of its Chinese population which continued to infiltrate Malaysia's borders in the state of Sarawak. Altogether, Prime Minister Tunku Abdul Rahman estimated that there were about 20,000 Communists in Malaysia. About 10,000 of them were hard-core, card-carrying members of the banned Malaysian Communist party.

The basic wealth of Malaysia continued to buoy the nation's economy, however. Exports of agricultural products, rubber, tin, and timber continued high. To encourage a flow of development capital into the country, the government also provided for special rebates on foreign investments. Meanwhile, under a five-year, $3,400,000,000 economic development program, nearly $2,000,000,000 was earmarked for investment in private enterprises.

British troops, dispatched to Malaysia when Malaysian-Indonesian tensions flared, return to their station in Singapore.

Facts in Brief. Population: 9,834,000. Government: Paramount Ruler Shah Ismail Nasiruddin; Prime Minister Tunku Abdul Rahman. Monetary Unit: dollar (3.03 = U.S. $1). Foreign Trade: exports, $1,107,300,000; imports, $1,332,900,000. Principal Exports: lumber, rubber, tin. JOHN N. STALKER

MALI. See AFRICA.

MALTA held its first general election since independence in March, 1966. Prime Minister Borg Oliver's Nationalist party increased its seats in parliament from 25 to 28. The Labour party gained six seats, but three other parties failed to win any.

The significance of the results lay in the Labour party's success. Malta's population was mostly Roman Catholic and many parish priests had warned their congregations that it would be a mortal sin to vote the Labour ticket.

Strong objections were made to Great Britain in midsummer when it revealed plans to cut defense spending in Malta from $43,500,000 to about $20,000,000. The Maltese government pointed out that nearly 10,000 of the island's 80,000 workers were employed by the armed services and that the cutback would present the Mediterranean island a serious unemployment problem.

In August, Lord Berwick, parliamentary secretary of the Commonwealth office, visited Malta to discuss the matter with Prime Minister Oliver and representatives of the General Workers' Union. Their talks were inconclusive and at year's end Malta still faced a serious economic problem.

Facts in Brief. Population: 338,000. Government: Prime Minister Borg Oliver. Monetary Unit: pound (2.80 = U.S. $1). Foreign Trade: exports, $18,597,000; imports, $105,432,000. Principal Exports: textiles, scrap metal. KENNETH BROWN

MANITOBA. See CANADA.

MANUFACTURING output and sales continued to surge during 1966. But there were signs that this longest of postwar economic booms was topping out. Inflation and the increasing U.S. commitment in Vietnam were putting strains on the economy.

Figures released in October by the Department of Commerce on new factory orders underscored the suspicion of a leveling-off in business. While the record $46,293,000,000 in new orders booked by all factories in September rose $1,451,000,000 from August, there would have been a decline without the unusually high gain of $1,501,000,000 in defense orders.

Defense buying accounted for much of the build-up in manufacturers' unfilled-order backlogs. By the end of September, the backlog had risen about $16,500,000,000 in 12 months to a total of $79,200,000,000. Administration experts feared this rise was putting heavy inflationary strains on plant capacity and the labor markets. Nearly half of the build-up was due to a $7,500,000,000 increase in unfilled defense orders, which exceeded $31,000,000,000 by the end of September.

Productivity of U.S. factory workers seemed to be leveling off for the first time since 1961. Nonfarm output per man-hour rose between 2.1 per cent and 4.6 per cent annually from 1961 through 1965. In the three months of the 1965 fourth quarter alone, productivity climbed a steep 1.4 per cent. But, in the 10 months through October, 1966, productivity had posted only a 0.6 per cent gain. Moreover, third quarter productivity was down slightly from the first quarter.

The lag in productivity gains was attributed to the shortage of skilled labor and the near-capacity operations that reduced efficiency in many plants. For the first time since 1960, this combination of factors began to outweigh the productivity gains realized from new manufacturing processes and modern production equipment. Machine tool maker, Warner and Swasey Company, reported that output per man-hour during the year had dropped 8 per cent below the 1965 level at its main plant in Cleveland, Ohio.

U.S. factories ran closer to capacity in each of the first three quarters of 1966 than at any time since 1955. The 1966 seasonally adjusted rates were 91 per cent of capacity, the same as the last quarter

U.S. Factory Production
(1957-59=100)

Products	% of Output 1957-59	1961-64 Average	Sept. '65*	Sept. '66*
Durables	**48.07**	**121**	**148**	**167**
Iron and Steel	5.45	108	125	139
Other metals	1.50	123	152	164
Fabricated metal	5.37	120	147	163
Electrical machinery	6.37	130	162	189
Other machinery	8.43	124	162	189
Motor vehicles	4.68	138	175	165
Aircraft, etc.	5.26	106	126	171
Instruments	1.71	124	156	180
Clay, glass, stone	2.99	115	134	141
Lumber	1.73	107	116	110
Furniture	1.54	129	157	173
Miscellaneous	1.51	121	147	157
Nondurables	**38.38**	**123**	**141**	**151**
Textiles	2.90	116	136	142
Apparel	3.59	123	144	148
Leather goods	1.11	101	108	109
Paper	3.43	123	144	151
Printing, publishing	4.74	117	129	144
Chemicals	7.58	142	177	194
Petroleum	1.97	115	125	131
Rubber, plastics	1.99	135	171	194
Foods	8.64	116	122	127
Beverages	1.61	116	131	139
Tobacco	.82	115	121	119
All Manufactures	**86.45**	**121**	**145**	**160**
Other U.S. Production				
Mining	**8.23**	**106.7**	**112.5**	**121.0**
Coal	1.16	98.7	108.1	114.7
Oil and natural gas	5.64	106.8	110.1	119.7
Metals	.61	113.5	122.4	128.6
Stone and minerals	.82	112.5	127.4	133.5
Utilities	**5.32**	**136.4**	**164.4**	**177.4**
Electric power	4.04	138.2	169.8	182.4
Gas	1.28	130.7	147.7	154.1†

Source: Federal Reserve Board *Seasonally adjusted. †June.

After Years of Stability–Labor Costs per Unit of Output Start to Climb

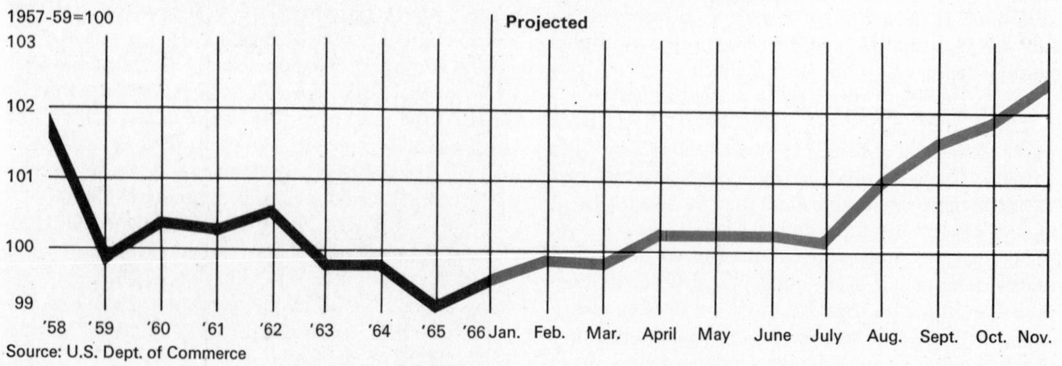

Source: U.S. Dept. of Commerce

of 1955. Yet industry had not lagged in plant expansion. According to a McGraw-Hill, Inc., survey in November, 36 per cent of all U.S. manufacturing capacity had been installed since December, 1961. Since December, 1950, the figure was 76 per cent. The auto industry's plant was the newest, with 58 per cent of its capacity five years old or less. Next was the chemical industry, about 39 per cent; followed by textiles, 38 per cent. The same survey also disclosed that about 22 per cent of industry's 1966 capital expenditures went for automated equipment.

Zero Defects. Not only new capacity, but new methods and systems were helping manufacturers increase efficiency. One such system was Zero Defects (ZD), a program for motivating workers toward higher quality output to help reduce waste. It was estimated that each mistake by an employee costs an average of $25. ZD program costs run no higher than $5 per employee. By year's end, about 12,000 plants had ZD programs. The major impetus for ZD came from its endorsement by the Department of Defense and from industry's never-ending battle to reduce the astronomical $9,000,-000,000-a-year bill for quality assurance alone.

Tube by the Mile. Chase Brass & Copper Company developed a method to extrude copper tubing in 10,000-foot and 20,000-foot lengths, compared with the former maximum of 2,200 feet. The greater lengths permit plumbing contractors to order the copper tube in the lengths they require, avoiding the expense of joining several short pieces.

The new process also has permitted Chase to convert its Cleveland tube mill from a job shop to an automated production plant, putting copper processing almost in the same league as steelmaking. Within 24 hours, Chase can fill an order that once took three to 14 days.

Machine Tools. New orders for machine tools showed signs of flattening out late in the year. They had rebounded sharply in September after two months of decline. But in October, they slipped again, and fell 17 per cent in November – the first 1966 month to be below the level of a year earlier. November's new orders totaled $126,355,000. For the first 11 months, net new orders totaled $1,721,-949,000, 29 per cent above bookings for the similar period of 1965. One tool builder welcomed the slowdown as a "wonderful" chance to whittle down his backlog a little.

The 1966 machine tools had increased power, were capable of faster loading and unloading, possessed greater precision, flexibility and versatility – all of which made them more productive than their predecessors. Numerical control machining was gaining wider acceptance.

Electrical Machinery. In November, the National Electrical Manufacturers Association (NEMA) estimated 1966 sales of electrical products at a record $36,300,000,000, up 12 per cent from 1965's previous high mark. For the two big categories, consumer products and industrial electronics and communications, increases of 9 per cent and 10 per cent, respectively, to $8,390,000,000 and $10,950,-000,000 were expected.

Television set sales soared over the 13,000,000 mark for the first time. Color TV sales accounted for 4,800,000 units. Manufacturers said a shortage of picture tubes and other components prevented sales from exceeding 5,000,000 sets. In Western Europe, where viewers were preparing to watch their first color telecasts in the spring of 1967, approximately $1,800,000,000 was spent by consumers on TV sets in 1966. See TELEVISION.

Communications equipment and electronics manufacturers reached for new markets with such products as data phones, facsimile transmission apparatus, telemetering equipment, and the substitution of electronic telephone switching for electromechanical systems. They were stepping up their use of microcircuits and other miniaturization devices. See COMMUNICATIONS; ELECTRONICS.

Apparel Manufacturers pointed to a number of factors that gave an extra push to their sales in 1966. They included high consumer income, full employ-

Men per Unit of Output – U.S. vs. Europe

	Steel	Chemicals	Metal products	Electrical machinery	Transport equipment	Nonelectrical machinery
United States	1.0	1.0	1.0	1.0	1.0	1.0
Great Britain	2.3	3.4	2.2	4.2	3.2	3.5
West Germany	1.7	2.6	3.2	3.8	2.4	3.2
France	1.6	3.0	3.1	2.6	2.0	2.3
Italy	1.2	2.5	4.2	2.3	2.1	2.4

Source: *The Economist*

ment, a growing population (particularly in the young adult category), large military expenditures, and a trend away from durables into soft goods and services. Apparel sales increased 5 per cent in the year to a total of $32,800,000,000.

Clothing makers were modernizing their production techniques. Die-cutting machines were replacing hand methods of cutting garment components. New pattern-marking systems used photographs of miniaturized patterns to preplan the marking of actual size patterns. Larger firms also were increasing their use of electric cloth-spreading machines, which, they reported, doubled worker productivity.

In Textile Design, International Business Machines Corporation (IBM) developed a computerized "drawing board" that saves hundreds of hours in laying out patterns of fabrics. It usually requires a designer 200 hours to lay out the design of a necktie. He must fill in and color the 600,000 tiny rectangles needed to make a tie design. The new IBM process pares the job to 20 minutes.

Instead of painting the design on fine graph paper, the designer uses a light-sensitive pen that writes on a cathode-ray tube "drawing board" linked to a computer. He can select a weave pattern from the computer's memory and insert it wherever he wants it in the design.

Rubber and Rubber Products. U.S. consumption of new rubber–synthetic and natural–in 1966 was estimated to total 2,215,000 long (2,240-pound) tons. This marked the fifth consecutive year new annual highs were reached. World production of synthetic rubber accounted for 57.1 per cent of total rubber output; it was 56.4 per cent in 1965. Total rubber consumption in the Free World, plus imports by Soviet-bloc nations, totaled 5,625,000 tons, of which 3,190,000 long tons were synthetic.

Synthetic rubber consumption accounted for 74.9 per cent of the total U.S. volume. Consumption of styrene-butadiene rubber (SBR), used primarily in tires, amounted to 1,130,000 long tons. But this dominance of SBR in the U.S. rubber market was in jeopardy.

The trend to radial-ply tires could slash the use of SBR. In 1966, radial-ply tires were offered for the first time by U.S. automobile makers as standard equipment on some 1967 models. SBR has neither the strength nor heat resistance necessary for use in radial-ply, or "belted," tires, which automotive engineers rate high in safety, durability, traction, and fuel economy. The strongest candidates to supplant SBR are polyisoprene and/or ethylene-propylene terpolymer (EPT).

In the huge 186,700,000-unit-a-year (1966) tire market, the battle of materials was not limited to rubber. In tire cords, polyester, nylon, or a combination of the two, all vied to replace rayon in the original equipment (OE) market. In mid-May, a drop in its hitherto prohibitive price enhanced polyester's chances. In November, Goodyear Tire and Rubber Company said it was switching two of its tire lines to polyester. That would give a quarter of the OE market to the new fiber. Polyester cord also was finding new use as reinforcement in hose and other industrial rubber products.

Farm Machinery makers completed one of their best years since World War II. Their total sales, including farm tractors, rose 15 per cent to another record high of $3,850,000,000 in 1966. Profits for all but one of the industry's Big Four reached new heights. Deere & Company's sales for the fiscal year ended Oct. 31, 1966, passed the $1,000,000,000 mark for the first time, and its profits rose to $78,708,570 from the $51,034,619 of fiscal 1965.

The world-wide push for food, expanding economies, the trend toward larger and more prosperous U.S. farms–all have made supplying the farmer a major growth industry. One illustration of this growth is the ever-rising sales of mechanical pickers –ranging from $500 cranberry pickers to $40,000 celery harvesters. In the California tomato fields, sophisticated machines that could choose as well as pick, moved in to save the crop imperiled by a lack of labor. The Department of Labor calls this shift to mechanization "agrimation." GEORGE J. BERKWITT

MARINE CORPS, U.S. See ARMED FORCES OF THE WORLD; NATIONAL DEFENSE.

MAURITANIA. See AFRICA.

MEDICARE, the program of health benefits for persons aged 65 and older that was passed by the Congress of the United States in 1965, went into operation on July 1, 1966. By the end of the year more than 2,000,000 people had received hospital services and more than $500,000,000 had been paid by the U.S. government in hospital and medical bills. Approximately 98 per cent of the nation's hospitals had joined the program, and virtually all doctors were participating, according to Dr. Philip R. Lee of the U.S. Department of Health, Education, and Welfare.

The overwhelming success of the program was not fully expected by federal officials or medical personnel, who had expressed two serious concerns as the opening date for Medicare approached. The first was that the demand for hospital care would increase so drastically that existing facilities would not stand the strain and a breakdown in health services would result. However, after three months of operation, during which time more than 1,000,000 Medicare patients were treated, admissions had risen only 3 per cent, and except for certain rural areas where shortages of facilities existed before the law was passed, there was little overcrowding.

The second concern was that an actual shortage of hospital beds would be created in certain sections of the country because of the requirement of nondiscrimination in the Medicare program. This problem did not materialize. The provision of the law which calls for compliance with all civil rights laws, and prohibits discrimination because of race, color, or national origin, was accepted by an overwhelming majority of the nation's hospitals.

Emergency Center. Despite careful planning and excellent cooperation from hospital administrations and physicians, problems did arise in certain communities where hospitals did not wish to participate in Medicare. To make sure that maximum service would be available to Medicare patients during the first months of operation, a referral center was established in the National Institutes of Health at Bethesda, Md., to handle emergency cases. With telephones manned on a 24-hour basis, the center served as a clearing house for doctors and patients who could not find hospital space and were faced with medical emergencies. If no other hospital was available, the doctor was referred to the nearest federal hospital.

Rising Costs. Of concern to patients and government officials was a report released by the Bureau of Labor Statistics which showed that for the 12-month period ended Aug. 31, 1966, costs of hospital care increased by 7.7 per cent and physician's fees had increased 5.7 per cent. With the start of the Medicare program, a minority of the nation's doctors reportedly raised their fees for patients 65 and over, and New York City health officials, in August, confirmed reports that some

Former First Lady Bess Truman received Medicare Card No. 2 from President Lyndon B. Johnson at ceremony in Independence, Mo.

physicians in that city had raised their fees for older patients as much as 300 per cent.

The city physicians contended that they had raised the fees of only those patients whom they had carried at lower fees than prevailed in the rest of their practice. Many were long-standing patients who were retired or financially dependent, they said. Under the Medicare plan, the government pays 80 per cent of a physician's bills after the first $50. These physicians said that they had raised their fees so that they could accept the government fee as full payment and not attempt to collect the 20 per cent from the patients.

On August 23, President Lyndon B. Johnson requested John W. Gardner, Secretary of Health, Education, and Welfare, to undertake a study of the rising hospital and medical costs. The study will be conducted in cooperation with the President's Council of Economic Advisers, the Department of Labor, and other federal agencies.

Administrative Problems. After three months of Medicare, the principal complaint voiced by patients, doctors, and hospital administrators was that there were too many forms to fill out and too many records to keep. By the year's end government officials had promised to try to reduce the number of forms and to simplify the procedure. They pointed out, however, that where tax money is involved, adequate records must be kept to make careful accounting possible.

The implementation of Medicare brought to light the shortage of physicians, nurses, social workers, medical technicians, and other medical personnel. As a result, federal officials began a "crash" campaign to train more medical workers. The goal was to nearly double the 100,000 nurses and "subprofessional" personnel – aides, orderlies, and technicians – now graduated annually from a variety of government-supported training programs.

Court Test. A three-judge federal court in Los Angeles ruled, in November, that a loyalty oath required by applicants for Medicare benefits was unconstitutional. The suit, one of the first test cases regarding any part of the Medicare act, was filed for a 65-year-old Los Angeles housewife, Mrs. Alda T. Reed, by the American Civil Liberties Union. Mrs. Reed had declined to answer the disputed loyalty oath question "as a matter of conscience and constitutional rights."

Medicaid, the little-understood but related program to Medicare, was not doing well. Medicaid provides benefits for needy persons under 65 who cannot get Medicare. It is administered by state governments and was approved by Congress in 1965 as Title 19 when Medicare was added to the Social Security Act of 1935. Only 19 states have established plans to meet the 1970 deadline for the adoption of Medicaid programs.

JOSEPH P. ANDERSON

See also CIVIL RIGHTS; OLD AGE.

MEDICINE

Artificial transplants of organs, the latest findings in cancer research, and the development of new vaccines encouraged optimistic predictions on the part of many medical researchers. Dr. Edward L. Tatum, noted geneticist and 1958 Nobel prize winner, suggested that within the "next few decades" the causes of many, if not all, forms of cancer will be understood. He also predicted that most virus diseases, as well as many of mankind's genetically determined ills, will have been conquered. Dr. Tatum made the prediction at a symposium on the Future of Medicine held in New York City in May.

A less optimistic note, however, was sounded by Sir George Pickering, Regius Professor of Medicine at Oxford University and a participant in the same forum. He said that recent trends in medicine suggest that man eventually will have a much extended life span, "perhaps in the end with somebody else's heart or liver, somebody else's arteries, but not with somebody else's brain." He found terrifying the prospect of a future in which those with senile brains and behavior would form an ever-increasing portion of the earth's inhabitants.

Artificial Heart. Early in 1966, Dr. Michael E. DeBakey, Houston heart surgeon, announced that within a month it would be possible to install an artificial heart in a human patient. Doctors at Maimonides Hospital in New York, meanwhile, reported the development of a mechanical heart that could be placed inside the chest to help a weak heart pump blood. Their device had proved effective in dogs, though it had not yet been used on human patients.

In April, Dr. DeBakey successfully implanted an artificial heart in a 65-year-old man. This was the third known attempt to save a life through the use of an auxiliary heart. Though the surgical procedure was successful, the man died several days later of a ruptured lung. Shortly thereafter, two other patients were implanted with artificial hearts, but each died within days because of other complications. Then, in August, a 37-year-old Mexican woman, Mrs. Esperanza del Valle Vasquez, successfully recovered from a heart operation in which an artificial heart was used as a temporary measure. Dr. DeBakey was the surgeon. She left the hospital fully recovered after a stay of about one month.

Cancer Research increasingly turned to what scientists believe are defects in the cancer victims' self-defense mechanisms, more familiarly known as

Famed Texas surgeon, Dr. Michael E. DeBakey, inserted a partial "artificial heart" in the chest of an Illinois miner in April, 1966.

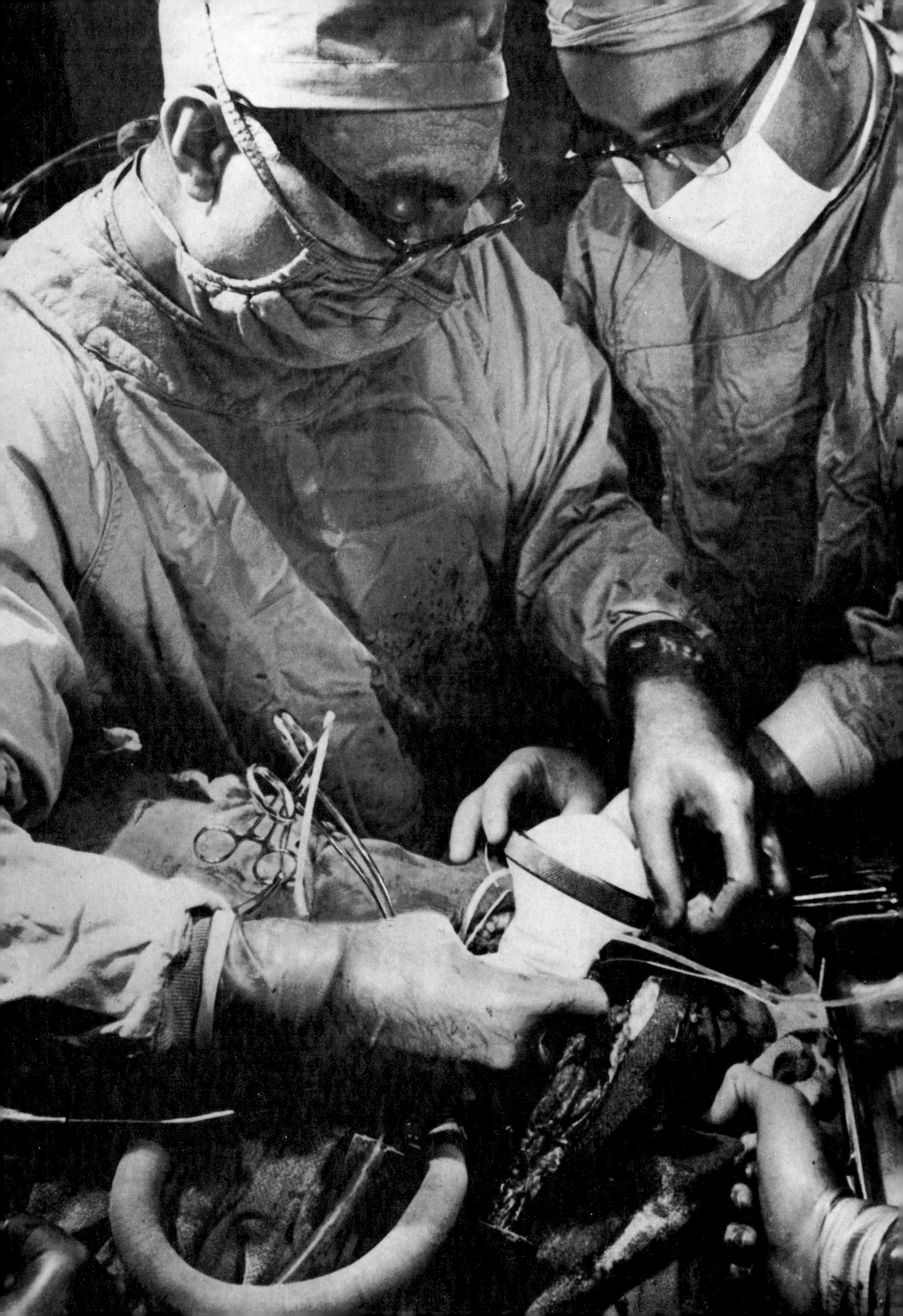

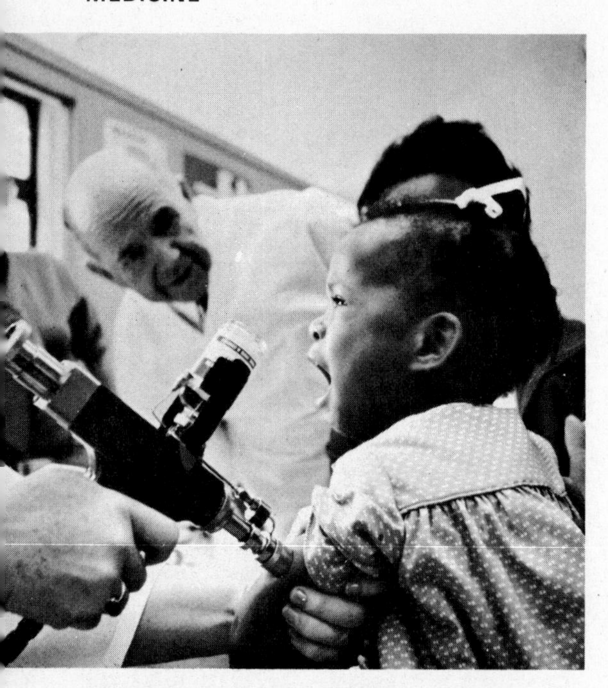

There were fewer cases of measles in 1966 because more than 12,000,000 U.S. children had been inoculated with a measles vaccine.

the immune response. Various experiments were carried out that were designed to stimulate the defective immune system. One project, conducted by researchers at Wayne State University in Detroit, involved the injection into a patient of a small portion of his own tumor cells combined with gamma globulin from the blood serum of rabbits. Such injections were given to each patient over several weeks, and the patient's immune system responded by producing three types of antibodies–one against the gamma globulin-tumor cell combination, and one against each of the separate substances.

In another study, made by Dr. Elaine Levi of the Cedars-Sinai Medical Center in Los Angeles, Calif., newborn rabbits were inoculated with human white cells. At that age, the immune system of the rabbit is not yet working, and fails to build up defenses against the human characteristics of the cells. Then at a later date, when the rabbits were capable of producing antibodies, they were injected with cells from specific human cancers. It is expected that the animals so treated will respond by producing antibodies against these cancer cells. Serum from the rabbits with the cancer-fighting antibodies, can then be injected into patients suffering from cancer.

Organ Transplants. The greatest difficulty encountered in transplanting organs from one person to another is the rejection of the donor's tissue by the tissue of the recipient. At the Seventh International Transplantation Conference, held in New York in February, a new way of producing tolerance to foreign tissues was reported. Dr. Felix T. Rappaport and Dr. Randolph M. Chase, Jr., of New York University School of Medicine, found substances in bacteria that can sensitize an animal against living tissue from another animal, when introduced in small amounts. Previously, researchers had found that foreign substances, which were rejected in small doses, would sometimes be tolerated by the body when introduced in large doses. The reasons for this paradoxical effect are not clear, but some specialists believe that the recipient's internal defenses are overcome by the invasion of such large amounts of the foreign substance. It is probable that tolerance to foreign tissue can be induced, at least in animal research, by introducing large amounts of the new bacterial substances.

Mumps Vaccine. A safe and effective live virus vaccine against mumps was developed by Maurice R. Hilleman and Eugene Buynak of the Merck Institute for Therapeutic Research in West Point, Pa. In field trials, the vaccine has proved at least 97 per cent effective in protecting children against the disease, and the tests have also shown the substance to be noncontagious. The new vaccine is likely to be available in 1967. THEODORE F. TREUTING

See also BIOCHEMISTRY; DENTISTRY; HOSPITAL.

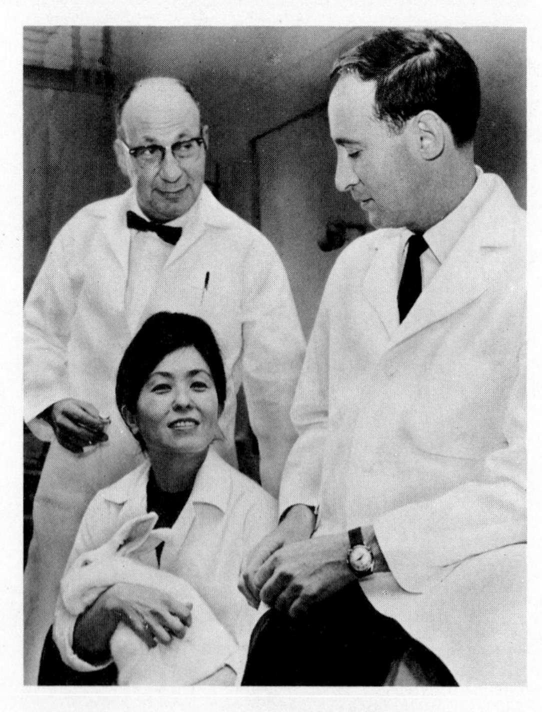

A rheumatic fever vaccine was developed by Chicago scientists, *left to right,* Albert Dorffman, M. K. Wittner, and Eugene Fox.

David Rubinger, *Life* © Time Inc.

Israel dedicated a monument to John F. Kennedy on July 4. Designed by David Reznik, it will be surrounded by a forest of saplings.

MEMORIALS dedicated or announced in 1966 included the following:

American War Memorial in the National Memorial Cemetery of the Pacific, Honolulu, Hawaii, was dedicated on May 2, in honor of the Americans of World War II and the Korean war who are buried there. The dominant feature of the memorial is a 30-foot statue of Columbia.

Anna Eleanor Roosevelt Memorial Monument in the United Nations garden was dedicated on April 23. "1884—Anna Eleanor Roosevelt—1962" is inscribed on the semicircular granite bench. Opposite the bench is a large granite slab engraved with a flame and a quotation from the late Adlai E. Stevenson's eulogy to the distinguished world figure and First Lady of the United States (1933-1945): "She would rather light candles than curse the darkness, and her glow warmed the world."

Estes Kefauver Memorial Library was dedicated at the University of Tennessee on June 25. The entire office of the late Democratic U.S. Senator (1903-1963) was reconstructed in the library wing, which is to house his papers and mementos.

Harry S. Truman Center for the Advancement of Peace was announced by President Lyndon B. Johnson on January 20. The center for international studies is to be established at the Hebrew University in Jerusalem, Israel.

James Joyce Statue was unveiled on June 16, in the Fluntern Cemetery, Zurich, Switzerland, where the Irish novelist (1882-1941) was buried. The bronze life-size figure was designed by American sculptor Milton Hebold.

John F. Kennedy Memorial, near Jerusalem, Israel, was dedicated on July 4. It stands on a Judean hill at the entrance of what is to be the John F. Kennedy Peace Forest. The 60-foot-high memorial resembles a tree trunk. It is surrounded by 51 concrete pillars separated by tinted panels that represent the District of Columbia and the 50 states of the United States of America. Inside is a portrait bust of the late President, illuminated by a single shaft of light from the ceiling. Excerpts from Kennedy's major public addresses are inscribed on the walls. Israeli architect David Reznik designed the memorial.

Sir Winston Churchill Monument was unveiled in Washington, D.C., on April 9. The nine-foot high memorial, in front of the British embassy garden fence overlooking Massachusetts Avenue, stands on British and American soil to symbolize the great statesman's Anglo-American parentage and his honorary U.S. citizenship. The right hand is raised in a V-for-Victory salute. William M. McVey of Cleveland, Ohio, designed the monument.

Ulysses S. Grant Murals were dedicated at Grant's Tomb in New York City on May 26. The three marble and glass mosaics, each 9 by 18 feet and made from the paintings by New York artist Allyn Cox, depict the Union general at Vicksburg, Chattanooga, and his meeting with Confederate General Robert E. Lee at Appomattox.

Woodrow Wilson Ancestral Home in County Tyrone, near Strabane, Northern Ireland, was dedicated as a national monument, on June 17, by his grandson, the Rev. Francis B. Sayre, Jr., Dean of Washington (D.C.) Cathedral. James Wilson, grandfather of President Woodrow Wilson, left his farm home and migrated to the United States in 1807. He became a noted Ohio newspaperman and legislator. A small printing shop in Strabane, where James Wilson learned the printing trade, also was dedicated as a memorial.

MÉNDEZ MONTENEGRO, JULIO CÉSAR (1916-), dean of the law school of the University of Guatemala, was sworn in as president of Guatemala on July 1, 1966. A candidate of the liberal Revolutionary party, he had won a plurality but not the majority necessary for election in a vote held on March 6. He was elected to office, however, in a run-off election held on May 10. Méndez succeeded Colonel Enrique Peralta Azurdia, head of the military regime that had seized power in 1963. See LATIN AMERICA.

The new president, a small, wiry man, was born in Guatemala City, the son of a well-to-do family. He attended elementary and high schools there, as well as the University of Guatemala from which he earned his degree in law in 1940. A man who had been interested in politics most of his adult life, Méndez–with his brother Mario–was one of the founders of Guatemala's Revolutionary party in 1958. Méndez' candidature for the presidency was based in part on indignation over Mario's death under mysterious circumstances in 1965.

Guatemala's new president is described as a man who lives simply. Married, and the father of three children, he takes a fatherly interest in his law students. His favorite activities, aside from the art of politics, include trips to archaeological sites in Guatemala. He is also an omnivorous reader and a lover of concert music. WALTER F. MORSE

MENTAL HEALTH. In May, 1966, President Lyndon B. Johnson created a committee on mental retardation to evaluate programs in the field and to advise him on new national efforts needed to cope with the problem. He named as chairman John W. Gardner, Secretary of the Department of Health, Education, and Welfare (HEW). Also in May, the Joint Commission on Mental Health of Children was started with a $1,000,000 grant from the National Institute of Mental Health.

A report of the National Institute of Mental Health issued in February, confirmed the experience of many state welfare departments. The institute pointed out that federal and state assistance designed to overcome the economic poverty magnified a natural epidemic of disabling psychiatric and emotional problems in the Appalachia area. Dependency upon welfare checks is encouraged by the lack of available jobs and the fact that the men learn that in order to be eligible for public assistance they must be "sick."

Mental Retardation. Scientists at Harvard Medical School and Massachusetts General Hospital in Boston discovered a hereditary disease that causes one form of mental retardation. Children afflicted with this condition have a natural aversion to meat, milk, and milk products. After eating such foods they can go into coma. The scientists hope a special diet will be devised for the disease.

Drug Addiction. Daytop Village, a rehabilitation center for narcotic addicts on Staten Island, announced plans in June to establish seven satellites in upstate New York, New Jersey, Washington, D.C., and Chicago. The first of these was opened at Swan Lake in Sullivan County, a New York resort. Funds for the centers are provided by grants from national, local, and private institutions.

In New York City, a treatment program of group psychotherapy, with the participation of former addicts as therapists, was initiated in July. Dr. Efren Ramirez, the city's narcotics coordinator, said that he expected 5,000 addicts to be involved in the program by the end of the year. The initial appropriation was $5,500,000 for the fiscal year that began July 1. In subsequent years, up to $100,000,000 will be required annually, according to Dr. Ramirez.

Alcoholism. In an experimental program at St. Vincent's Hospital in New York, whose alcoholic rehabilitation unit is one of the oldest in the nation, alcoholics received an electric shock every time they reached for a highball. The electric shock therapy was used in place of drugs which cause extensive vomiting.

On October 20, HEW director Gardner announced the start of a major federal program to combat alcoholism. It will involve research, education, and professional training. THEODORE F. TREUTING

See also HANDICAPPED, THE; PSYCHOLOGY.

METALLURGY. Die casting of ferrous metals, such as iron and steel, was made feasible for the first time in 1966 through the use of alloy steel dies consisting of refractory metals such as molybdenum, tantalum, and tungsten. Die casting formerly was restricted to metals having low melting points. The new dies can be used at 2000° F., according to General Electric Company researchers.

A method for accurately determining the energies that hold atoms of a given metal or alloy together was announced by two members of the faculty of Pennsylvania State University. Lawrence E. Murr and Maurice C. Inman reported that they employed an electron microscope and computer programming in a new three-dimensional analysis technique enabling them to predict the strength and performance of metals under impact.

Certain "metal-eating" bacteria, which accidentally consume specific metals along with nutrients, may provide an inexpensive method for prying apart metals that are abundant but expensive to separate, according to scientists at the U.S. Bureau of Mines. Such microorganisms have been used to separate columbium and tantalum, and similar experiments with zirconium and hafnium were being conducted by Walter N. Ezekiel at University of Maryland laboratories. JAMES A. PEARRE

See also MINES AND MINING; STEEL INDUSTRY.

METEOROLOGY. See WEATHER.

Smiling President Gustavo Díaz Ordaz acknowledges the cheers of Mexico's congressmen after delivering his state of the union message.

MEXICO continued to enjoy a growth rate that outpaced most of the other Latin-American countries. Industrial investments climbed notably in 1966. The gross national product was expected to rise by more than 6 per cent–up from 5.1 per cent in 1965. Prices remained stable and the peso was stronger than at any time since it was devalued in 1954. The key factors were industrialization and tourism. An anticipated 1,500,000 visitors were expected to spend a record $747,000,000.

Government spending was under restraint, thus keeping a monetary reserve strength for stimulating business when needed. The foreign debt–$1,768,000 as of Dec. 31, 1965–was being shifted from a short-term to a long-term repayment basis and was very much within manageable limits. There were bumper farm crops, although the drop in the world market price for cotton, Mexico's principal export crop, aggravated farm unemployment. As of September 1, the republic's gold and currency reserves were at a near-record high of $566,500,000, with additional stand-by credits of $435,000,000 available from the U.S. Treasury, the Export-Import Bank, and the International Monetary Fund.

Development Plan. On September 5, President Gustavo Díaz Ordaz announced a five-year (1966-1970) $22,000,000,000 national development plan aimed at maintaining an annual growth rate of 6 per cent. About $14,400,000,000 of the total was to come from private capital. The funds would be invested in industry (40 per cent), in communications and transport (23 per cent), in agriculture, cattle raising, and fishing (14 per cent), in social welfare (22 per cent), and in administration and defense (1 per cent). The planned expansion of Pemex, the national oil industry, and various electrical projects would absorb 84 per cent of the state industrial investments.

In May, the campus of Mexico's National University was the scene of a violent student riot. Originally, the students had gathered to protest the use of campus police at the university and to denounce the introduction of entrance examinations intended to raise the school's quality. Communist agitators in the crowd, however, ignited the tension into rioting, during which the famous outdoor murals of Diego Rivera and others were smeared with slogans such as "Death to Yankee Imperialism." After days of turmoil, the university president resigned.

Mine Take-Over. In June, between 500 and 800 students seized the Cerro de Mercado iron ore plant and mine belonging to the Compañia Fundidora de Fierro y Acero in Durango state. They remained there until the government agreed that it would put up two-thirds of the capital for a steel mill in Durango provided studies proved such a project practical. The state had been in economic trouble for several years, and the students believed a steel plant would bring prosperity. The state governor was later impeached by direct request of President Díaz because of his "lack of interest, irresponsibility, and ineptitude."

Land Redistribution. In 1966, the government acknowledged the fact that land reform, the nation's most sacred of revolutionary tenets, had not created a farm system capable of feeding the burgeoning population. Accordingly, it began making fundamental changes in its land-distribution program. The first changes involved the granting of individual, rather than communal, titles, in the hope that such a move would spur farm output.

The Lerma Plan received a great deal of attention in 1966. Under it, the living conditions of 8,000,000 people in the 50,000 square-mile Lerma-Chapala-Santiago area would be vastly improved. The plan covered such needs as housing and educational facilities. Private sources would be depended upon to develop industry and agriculture. Mexico planned to invest $145,000,000 and the Inter-American Development Bank $150,000,000 in the extensive project.

Facts in Brief. Population: 43,675,000. Government: President Gustavo Díaz Ordaz. Monetary Unit: peso (12.49=U.S. $1). Foreign Trade: exports, $1,142,000,000; imports, $1,559,100,000. Principal Exports: cotton, coffee, fish, sugar, petroleum.

MARY C. WEBSTER

MIDDLE EAST. The most dangerous escalation of the Arab-Israeli conflict since the invasions of Suez in 1956 threatened to bring war to Palestine in 1966. Exactly 10 years to the month after the Suez incident, Israel struck again. Israeli commandos mounted a massive raid on the Jordanian village of Es Samu, three miles over the border, on November 13. The village of 4,000 was heavily damaged, with over 100 buildings destroyed. Jordanian troops moving to its relief were ambushed by the Israelis; 15 soldiers were killed. Israel asserted that its action was justified by the continuing attacks by Arabs infiltrating from guerrilla bases inside Arab territory.

World Reaction deplored Israel's move. Acting upon a complaint from Jordan, the United Nations (UN) Security Council unanimously condemned Israel for the raid on November 16. It warned Israel that future reprisals would not be tolerated, and that the raid was a clear violation of both the UN Charter and the Israel-Jordan armistice agreement. The censure resolution, sponsored by the African states of Mali and Nigeria, was unique in that it was supported by all five permanent members of the council. Earlier in November, a resolution of censure against Syria, requested by Israel, was vetoed by Russia.

Arab Riots. Ironically, the Es Samu raid shook the throne of the one Arab leader, King Hussein I of Jordan, whose policies toward Israel emphasized moderation and willingness to control the borders against infiltration. Following the Israeli attack, antigovernment riots broke out in Jerusalem, Nablus, and other cities in the Jordanian part of Palestine. The rioters shouted for arms to fight Israel and denounced Hussein. Martial law was declared, and troops patrolled the streets.

The underground Palestine Liberation Organization assailed Hussein and urged Palestinian Arabs to overthrow him. The diminutive king stood firm for moderation, although he approved military conscription for Jordanians between 18 and 40 years of age, issued guns to border villagers, and accepted Saudi Arabia's offer of 20,000 troops to help defend Jordan's borders.

Division over Yemen. Trouble with Jewish Israel obscured the fundamental lack of unity among the Arabs themselves. The split between monarchies and "republics," with Saudi Arabia and Jordan on one side, Syria and the United Arab Republic (UAR) on the other, grew deeper. The civil war in Yemen sharpened their differences.

The Jiddah agreement of August, 1965, for a truce in the fighting between Saudi-backed royalists and republicans supported by Egyptian forces was observed for a time. But in September, the UAR clamped a firm hold on Yemen. It arrested republican Yemeni ministers, headed by Premier Hassan al-Amri, in Cairo. Yemeni President Abdullah al-Salal, after a year of medical treatment in the UAR, returned to Yemen to establish a strongly pro-Egyptian government.

Arab States. Arab unity remained a vocal exercise, with little positive agreement. Relations between Syria and the UAR improved slightly. The Syrian government that overthrew President Amin el-Hafez in February, after months of anti-Nasser propaganda, switched its position enough to approve a joint military command with the UAR.

An unexpected financial crisis struck Lebanon in October. Lebanon's largest private bank, Intra, closed when sudden withdrawals of $30,000,000 in one month exceeded its cash reserves.

The Arab Economic Boycott of firms dealing with Israel struck at many companies. An Arab League conference held in Kuwait in November, voted to ban the Ford Motor Company, Coca-Cola, and the Radio Corporation of America from doing business in Arab countries. They joined U.S. firms Kaiser-Fraser, Sears Roebuck, Zenith, Alka Seltzer, and Helena Rubenstein on the prohibited list. The ban on 90 other international companies was lifted after they had complied with boycott regulations.

The UAR and Pan-American Oil Company signed an agreement on long-term export rights and financing for a new UAR oil field in the Gulf of Suez. Estimates of 300,000 barrels a day would triple national production, making the UAR a net oil exporter by late 1968.

The Suez Canal handled more than 20,000 ships in the year ended June 30, with an almost 50 per cent increase in transit fees. Yet, potential oil revenues and $197,300,000 in canal income were hardly enough to meet the UAR's mounting deficit.

Non-Arab States in the Middle East went their separate ways with relative stability, and chalked up significant gains in their development. Despite a barrage of personal attacks by Arab radio, Shah Mohammed Riza Pahlevi of Iran proceeded with his reform program. The shah stressed Iranian neutrality by accepting aid from both the East and the West. His only recognition of Arab hostility was a request for U.S. arms.

Turkey struck oil and natural gas in quantity. The consortium of countries aiding the Turks under the Organization for Economic Cooperation and Development (OECD) granted $330,000,000 to continue Turkey's economic development program.

President Abdul Salam Muhammad Arif of Iraq died in a helicopter crash in April. Arif's brother and successor, Abdul Rahman Arif, made a truce with Iraq's rebellious Kurds, reversing the previous government's hard-line policy toward the rebellion. So, until the lid blew off on Israel's Jordan border late in the year, organized military conflict was strangely absent from the region. WILLIAM SPENCER

See also articles on the related countries.

MILLER, PERRY (1905-1963), a top-ranking scholar in American literature and the history of ideas, was posthumously awarded the 1966 Pulitzer prize in history for *The Life of the Mind in America.* His wife helped complete the book, which was unfinished at his death. It was the first volume of a projected series on the intellectual history of the nation.

Perry Miller was a foremost figure in American studies. He was best known for his two-volume work, *The New England Mind,* in which he set forth the intellectual achievements of the New England Puritans, showing their European roots, and making clear that they were interested in more than keeping to rigid codes of morality and burning witches. Dr. Miller also wrote biographies of the early New England theologian, Jonathan Edwards, and Roger Williams, founder of the colony of Rhode Island. He edited the anthologies, *The American Puritans* and *The Transcendentalists.*

Perry Miller was born in Chicago, Ill., Feb. 25, 1905. He entered the University of Chicago, but left after his freshman year to go to sea on an oil tanker. He returned and took his B.A. degree there in 1928 and his Ph.D. in 1931. Soon after, he joined the Harvard University faculty, where he was Powell M. Cabot Professor of American Literature.

MINERALOGY. See GEOLOGY; METALLURGY; MINES AND MINING.

Tensions between Israel and its Arab neighbors mounted late in 1966.
Here, armed Israeli troops scan their country's Syrian border.

MINES AND MINING. Copper and aluminum took center stage in the mineral world in 1966, but for entirely different reasons. The copper industry collided with the soaring needs of the Vietnamese war and a torrent of labor strife to produce one of the most erratic years in recent history.

A rash of strikes in the United States, Chile, and Zambia disrupted production at a time when demand for the red metal was at an all-time high. To add to the turbulence, a major African mine was shut down by a flood. The resulting scarcity of supplies–world production was down about 30,000 tons from 1965–spawned sporadic price increases, pushing prices as high as $1 and more a pound on the world market.

In the United States, both production and prices remained fairly stable despite the closing of one major mine after a strike. Two small companies did raise prices from 36 cents a pound to 38 cents, but none of the major producers followed suit. U.S. government actions in releasing 520,000 tons from its stockpiles and in suspending import tariffs suppressed any wider rises.

Aluminum recorded the best year in its history. Free World production climbed from 3,921,000 tons in 1960 to 5,506,100 tons in 1965. Enormous demand from aluminum's major markets helped raise production in the United States to over 2,960,000 tons. Shipments of finished products were 4,500,000 tons. This growth was augmented by a switch from copper to aluminum by many users and by a boom in its use for transportation equipment, which, for the first time, caught up with the building and construction industry as a major outlet for aluminum products.

Metal Output. In the United States, primary production and prices of various metals were:

	Average Monthly Output (thousands of tons)		Price Per Pound (October)	
	1965	1966	1965	1966
Aluminum	226.2	246.7	$.245	$.245
Copper	113.4	111.4	.3568	.36
Lead	37.8	39.2	.16	.14
Zinc	88.2	88.2	.15	.15

Expansion Programs to boost mine and refinery capacity were unveiled frequently during 1966. Anaconda Company planned to expand copper output in Montana, Arizona, and Nevada. New copper mines were in development by Phelps Dodge Corporation at Tyrone, N. Mex.; American Metal Climax, Inc., in Puerto Rico; and Calumet & Hecla Company in Michigan. International Nickel Company planned a big copper- and nickel-mining development near Ely, Minn.

Most aluminum producers were expanding capacity, and several new companies reported they would enter the aluminum producing business. Intalco, a joint U.S.-French enterprise, dedicated a $150,000,000 primary aluminum reduction plant in Washington state in September.

Titanium and Uranium, the mining industry's faded glamor products of the early postwar years, made comebacks in 1966. Supersonic aircraft and aerospace hardware uses, along with technological advances in the metal's production, gave titanium new status. The economic breakthrough in nuclear power restored uranium to a growth industry (see Atomic Energy).

Coal Production of all types continued to rise. Some 533,000,000 tons of bituminous was produced, up sharply from 1965's 512,000,000 tons. And despite the fears for its future from nuclear power plants, several companies were entering the coal business for the first time. Kerr-McGee Corporation–a principal uranium producer–planned to open mines in Oklahoma.

Congress enacted two mine safety measures in 1966. One extended the federal safety provisions to coal mines employing fewer than 15 persons. The other made the Federal Bureau of Mines responsible for setting health and safety standards for the nation's 250,000 noncoal-digging miners.

Texas Gulf Sulphur Company and all but two of 12 accused officials were exonerated in August by a federal court of profiting in its stock by using inside information about its major 1964 copper and lead discovery at Timmins, Ontario. In September, the mine began its first production. Thomas J. Murray

See also Petroleum and Gas; Steel Industry.

MONACO celebrated its 100th anniversary as one of the world's leading playgrounds in 1966. It did so against the background of a bitter dispute between Prince Rainier III, ruler of the principality, and Aristotle S. Onassis, Greek shipping magnate.

Prince Rainier was anxious to put into effect an ambitious program that would expand the principality's tourist facilities. By so doing, he hoped to make them competitive with the flourishing French and Italian resorts along the Mediterranean.

Onassis was opposed to the program, largely because it would depend on financial support from the Société des Bains de Mer, a corporation which operates the lucrative Monte Carlo casino and other major properties in Monte Carlo. Inasmuch as Onassis owned 52 per cent of the shares in the company–the principality's chief source of income–the prince's program had little hope of succeeding.

To break the deadlock, both of the disputants engaged in a series of legal maneuvers during which neither quite succeeded in outwitting the other. Toward the end of the year, however, Onassis announced that he no longer intended to participate in any action concerning the management of the controversial company.

Facts in Brief. Population: 24,000. Government: Prince Rainier III. Monetary Unit: franc (4.90=U.S. $1). Principal Sources of Income: tourism and shipping. Kenneth Brown

U.S. $2 bills became a "dead issue" in 1966, when the Treasury Department ceased printing them. The bills had fallen into disuse.

MONEY. Australia and the Bahamas joined the list of countries with decimal currency in 1966. On February 14, Australia made its new dollar equal to half of its old pound, or about $1.11 (U.S.). The Bahamas switched to a dollar pegged to the British pound sterling and worth seven shillings, or about 98 U.S. cents, effective May 25. New Zealand will change to dollars in 1967, Zambia in 1968, Fiji in 1969, and Great Britain and Ireland in 1971.

The newly designed Australian notes varied from tan, green, blue, and orange over the $1, $2, $10, and $20 denominations. By June, only 15 per cent of the note circulation was of the old pound form. Over 400,000,000 new decimal coins–1, 2, 5, 10, 20, and 50 cents–took 10 weeks to distribute.

Major Changes in Foreign Exchange Rates
(in U.S. cents)

Nation (and unit)	1965	1966
Argentina (peso*)	.535	.410
Chile (escudo*)	24.25	20.25
Colombia (peso*)	5.55	6.17
Ecuador (sucre)	5.50	4.85
India (rupee†)	21.02	13.30
Uruguay (peso*)	1.55	1.40
Yugoslavia (dinar†)	.08	8.00

* Free, or spot, quote at end of year. † Revalued.

The Bahamas made the $3 bill a reality in its decimal switch. Its other notes, printed in four colors, were 50 cents and $1, $5, $10, $20, $50, and $100. It issued nine denominations of coins: 1, 5, 10, 15, 25, and 50 cents, and $1, $2, and $5.

The U.S. Money Supply totaled a seasonally adjusted $170,000,000,000 in September, $38,000,000,000 in notes and coin and the rest in checking accounts. Curbed by the Federal Reserve Board's tight money policy, the increase for the 12 months through October was about $4,400,000,000, well below the $7,500,000,000 advance for calendar 1965.

The Treasury made a massive effort to step-up its minting of coins. The value of coins in circulation increased over 15 per cent in 1966, to account for more than 10 per cent of total currency.

New silverless dimes and quarters and silver-saving half dollars cut the U.S. Mint's use of silver to about 60,000,000 ounces in 1966, down from the unsustainable 320,000,000 ounces in 1965. Treasury silver stocks dropped 370,000,000 ounces in 1964, 400,000,000 in 1965, but only about 150,000,000 in 1966. This left the Treasury with less than 650,000,000 ounces. By offering to sell silver from this dwindling supply at the present monetary price of $1.293 an ounce, it hoped to be able to hold the lid on silver prices.

WILLIAM G. DEWALD

See also BANKS AND BANKING; Section One, SYLVIA PORTER: FOCUS ON THE ECONOMY; and country articles and tables for other foreign exchange rates.

MONGOLIAN PEOPLE'S REPUBLIC. See OUTER MONGOLIA.

MOROCCO. The strange twists of the Ben Barka affair involved Moroccan officials in French justice. In September, 1966, six persons went on trial in Paris, France, for the 1965 abduction and presumed murder of the exiled Moroccan leftist. But after seven weeks of testimony, another suspect, Ahmed Dlimi, Morocco's deputy minister of interior, unexpectedly flew to Paris and surrendered. The trial was recessed pending an investigation.

Although the affair had soured French-Moroccan relations, it aroused little interest in Morocco. King Hassan II retained Minister of the Interior Mohammed Oufkir, who also had been linked with the murder, in his post in a minor cabinet shuffle in February. In March, Omar Benjelloun, Mehdi Ben Barka's successor as head of the National Union of Popular Forces, was arrested after demanding an investigation of Oufkir.

In May, Algeria's nationalization of mines set off a new border dispute; two mines were in territory claimed by Morocco. One of Morocco's favorite Americans was honored with the opening of John F. Kennedy Boulevard in Casablanca.

Facts in Brief. Population: 14,300,000. Government: King and Premier Hassan II. Monetary Unit: dirham (4.98=U.S. $1). Foreign Trade: exports, $429,600,000; imports, $453,400,000. Principal Exports: fruits and nuts, natural phosphates, vegetables.

WILLIAM SPENCER

MOTION PICTURES

On the surface, 1966 turned out to be an excellent year for the American motion picture industry. The recovery spiral, begun in 1965, continued on all fronts in 1966—more films, more theaters, and record grosses. Leading the list was *The Sound of Music*, which, although still in limited release throughout the year, was expected to earn some $90,000,000 before its world-wide run was completed. If so, it would topple the memorable *Gone with the Wind* from its long-held position as all-time champion at the box office.

Dr. Zhivago, with an assist from its six Academy Awards, seemed destined to gross at least $25,000,000 in the domestic market alone, while the producers of *Hawaii* and *Who's Afraid of Virginia Woolf?* were each anticipating returns of some $20,000,000, merely from performances in the United States. Most impressive of all was the success of the James Bond thriller, *Thunderball*. It racked up U.S. grosses of $26,000,000 on its relatively modest $3,000,000 investment, and brought the grand total on all four Bond movies to about $100,000,000.

As usual, the studios withheld some of their biggest releases, *A Man for All Seasons*, *Grand Prix* (in Cinerama), and *The Sand Pebbles*, until the rich, year-end holiday season. Outstanding returns were anticipated on these as well.

Feature Film Riches. Television, once looked upon as the movies' nemesis, in 1966 contributed strongly to the new prosperity. In some motion picture studios, production of films for TV and outright sales from their libraries of old films accounted for as much as a third of the year's income. This percentage might well rise if the trend set by the American Broadcasting Company (ABC), which paid $2,000,000 for two showings of *The Bridge on the River Kwai* and $5,000,000 for *Cleopatra*, continues. So spectacular were the ratings on *Kwai*, that within days the TV networks had bought 118 more pictures for a record $92,500,000.

In a variation of this trend, the National Broadcasting Company (NBC) contracted with MCA-Universal for a series of 30 two-hour feature films. When the motion picture *Fame Is the Name of the Game* introduced the series in November, it topped all expectations in the ratings department. Hence, ABC-TV promptly negotiated with Metro-Goldwyn-Mayer (MGM) for a similar program on its network. In all, the movie studios had network

Miniaturized participants of *Fantastic Voyage* have been injected into a vein of a scientist's body to remove blood clot.

commitments of over $205,000,000 for filmed TV shows for the 1966-1967 season–up some $25,000,000 from the year before.

Hollywood Troubles. Despite this apparent prosperity, all was far from well within the studios themselves. With the sole exception of Music Corporation of America (MCA), owned by Universal, every major company in Hollywood was plagued by proxy battles, stockholder suits, and attempts by dissident directors to seize control.

By the end of the year, the old order had almost passed completely. Jack L. Warner, the last of the movie moguls, had sold his studio to former tire tycoon Eliot Hyman, of Seven Arts. Paramount had gone to Charles Bluhdorn of Gulf & Western Industries. United Artists was on the verge of becoming a wholly owned subsidiary of Transamerica Corporation, a holding company; Columbia had achieved an uneasy peace with the Swiss Banque de Paris, which had spearheaded an outright take-over earlier in the year; and there were persistent rumors that the venerable lion of studios, MGM, would merge with U.S. Smelting, Refining & Mining early in 1967.

What worried the movie veterans more than the newness of the corporate ownership was the realization that, because of assets such as studios, real estate, and libraries of old films, most of the film companies were actually worth more dead than alive. Thus if their new pictures failed to return a profit, the astute businessmen-owners would probably not hesitate to stop producing new films.

Liberalized Movie Code. Another new face, as far as Hollywood was concerned in 1966, was that of Jack A. Valenti, an aide to President Lyndon B. Johnson before his June appointment as president of the Motion Picture Association of America (MPAA). No sooner had Valenti assumed office than he unveiled a vastly liberalized Production Code, one that substituted the criterion of "good taste" for the numerous specific restrictions of the former code, and which set up a system of voluntary film classification to replace the "voluntary self-censorship" introduced by Will H. Hays almost 40 years ago. The new code applied only to MPAA members (and, at that, not to their foreign importation branches). See VALENTI, JACK A.

Georgy Girl, a British-made Columbia release, was the first film to receive the "Suggested for Mature Audiences" classification; United Artists' bawdy *A Funny Thing Happened on the Way to the Forum* was the second.

Meanwhile, the producers, long restive under the original code, and aware that a more permissive one was underway, were already beginning to explore the limits of their new freedom. One character in *The Group* and the leading man in *Inside Daisy Clover* were depicted as sex deviates. Abortion figured prominently in *Alfie*, and adultery was only one of the ways in which the ill-sorted quartet of *Who's Afraid of Virginia Woolf?* gave vent to their neuroses. Promiscuity, a basic element of all the James Bond movies, was even more in evidence in such frankly imitative efforts as *Our Man Flint*, *Modesty Blaise*, *The Silencers*, and *The Liquidator*. Outright nudity turned up in a number of diverse, big-budgeted offerings, among them *The Bible*, *The Professionals*, and *Hawaii*.

Nudity was even more prominently featured in the year's foreign imports, in *Dear John* and the controversial *Night Games* from Sweden; in *Galia*, *Mademoiselle*, and *The Game Is Over* from France; and even in the popular *Loves of a Blonde* from Czechoslovakia. Needless to say, all went promptly on the National Catholic Office's "condemned" list. But since none of these were–or could be–affected by the MPAA's "voluntary" code, one could understand why states like New York and Pennsylvania were busily preparing legislation calling for compulsory classification in 1967.

Awards in 1966 included:

Academy of Motion Picture Arts and Sciences Awards for 1965 to: *The Sound of Music*, best film; Julie Christie in *Darling*, best actress; Lee Marvin in *Cat Ballou*, best actor; Robert Wise, *The Sound of Music*, best director; Shelley Winters in *A Patch of Blue*, best supporting actress; Martin Balsam in *A Thousand Clowns*, best supporting actor; *The Shop on Main Street*, best foreign film.

ARTHUR KNIGHT

MOTLEY, CONSTANCE BAKER (1921-   ), New York attorney, became the first Negro woman federal judge in September. She was appointed U.S. district judge for southern New York. Until the assignment, she was president of the Borough of Manhattan and had been a New York state senator.

Mrs. Motley was born in New Haven, Conn., her parents having migrated from the British West Indies. Her father, a chef, lacked funds to send her or her five sisters and two brothers through college. At 18, however, she made a speech on civil rights that so impressed a white businessman that he offered to finance her education.

She studied at Fisk University and at New York University, where she earned a degree in economics. She then studied at Columbia University and received her law degree in 1946. Her first job was as clerk in the office of the National Association for the Advancement of Colored People (NAACP) Legal Defense and Educational Fund.

In civil rights cases, she became known as a persistent interrogator, one who was often quite witty and always direct in summations. In 1962, she represented James H. Meredith, the Negro who won admission to the University of Mississippi.

Mrs. Motley was married to Joel Motley, an insurance and real estate broker, in 1946.

MOTORBOAT RACING. See BOATS AND BOATING.

MOZAMBIQUE. See AFRICA.

MULLIKEN, ROBERT SANDERSON (1896-), distinguished service professor of physics and chemistry at the University of Chicago, was awarded the 1966 Nobel chemistry prize on November 3. He was honored for his "fundamental work concerning chemical bonds and the electronic structure of molecules by the molecular orbital method." His principal work involves the concept that the valence electrons in molecules are not bound to a particular atom, but travel in orbits around two or more atomic nuclei.

Mulliken was in Tallahassee, Fla., when the award was announced. Since 1965, he has been dividing his time between Chicago and Florida State University's Institute of Molecular Biophysics. From 1942 to 1945, Mulliken was on leave from the University of Chicago to work on the project that developed the atomic bomb.

Mulliken was born in Newburyport, Mass., the son of a professor of organic chemistry at Massachusetts Institute of Technology. He received his Ph.D. from the University of Chicago in 1921. He was a research fellow there and at Harvard until 1926, then assistant professor of physics at Washington Square College of New York University until 1928, when he joined the University of Chicago faculty. Mulliken and his wife, the former Mary Helen von Noé, have two daughters. WALTER F. MORSE

MUNICIPAL GOVERNMENT. See CITY.

The new Whitney Museum of American Art, designed by Marcel Breuer, was opened in New York City in September, 1966.

MUSEUMS. The National Gallery of Art in Washington, D.C., celebrated its 25th anniversary in 1966. The museum marked the occasion by recognizing 25 teachers and scholars who had been outstanding in art education. Each received a specially designed medal and a $500 award from Mrs. Lyndon B. Johnson in a ceremony at the White House. See AWARDS AND PRIZES.

Building Projects. New Yorkers crowded into the Whitney Museum of American Art at the opening of its new home on September 27. They found architect Marcel Breuer's granite and concrete structure bold on the outside, but the simple interior galleries quietly efficient. The opening exhibition brought together an unequaled representation of American art from 1670 to 1966. Meanwhile, the Museum of Modern Art in New York City began remodeling the old Whitney building as part of its expansion program.

New art museums were dedicated by Princeton University and the University of Pittsburgh. In Detroit, Mich., the Institute of Arts completed the construction of a wing costing $3,785,000. The M. H. De Young Memorial Museum in San Francisco, Calif., built a large addition to house Oriental art.

The largest project of the year began in Toronto, where the Ontario provincial government let a $21,700,000 contract to erect the Centennial Centre of Science and Technology.

Attendance. The American Association of Museums estimated that 300,000,000 persons attended approximately 4,500 bona fide museums in the United States and Canada in 1966. The National Museum in Washington, D.C., reported 13,000,000 visits, an increase of 812,000 over the previous year. More than 7,800,000 visitors were counted at the National Park Service's historic house museums.

Support. In spite of this evidence of public interest, museums needed more money to carry on their programs. After 50 years, the Boston Museum of Fine Arts began charging an entrance fee to reduce its annual operating deficit. One U.S. museum in four now charges admission.

Museums also received support from government. The state of New York appropriated $600,000 to its Council on the Arts for grants to local museums. The National Science Foundation granted more than $1,000,000 to the Florida State Museum. Many museums cooperated with schools to develop experimental programs under the Elementary and Secondary Education Act of 1965. The new National Council on the Humanities proposed a training program for museum personnel.

New Administration. Late in December, 1966, Thomas P. F. Hoving, New York City's administrator of recreational and cultural affairs, was named director of the Metropolitan Museum of Art. RALPH H. LEWIS

MUSIC

Artistic achievement and financial strain made up the most conspicuous elements of musical life in the United States during 1966. There was no question that further great things lay ahead, but the issue of paying the bills became paramount as production costs continued to soar and musicians demanded a larger share in the expanding national economy.

Moreover, a report from The Twentieth Century Fund, prepared by Princeton University economists William J. Baumol and William G. Bowen, indicated that the gap between possible box office income and the cost of producing serious musical events showed no signs of closing in the immediate future. In fact, the report stated that by 1975, the gap for all the major performing arts would probably amount to $60,000,000 annually.

The Met's Opening. The big event of the year was itself a symbol of affluence, the opening of a new, $45,700,000 Metropolitan Opera House at the Lincoln Center for the Performing Arts, in New York City. An American soprano, Leontyne Price, starred in the première of an American opera, Samuel Barber's *Antony and Cleopatra.* Celebrities of the arts and international society were on hand for the performance. See Close-Up.

The glittering new Met was "a building with a smile on its face" to assistant manager Herman E. Krawitz, who observed there had not been a strike in all the years of construction. Instead, there was a strike opening night, which arose from the orchestra's demands for a new contract. The strike was settled verbally in time for an announcement between the acts of *Antony and Cleopatra,* but the settlement between the Met and the musicians did not become final until December.

By that time the Metropolitan was facing serious budget problems that required a 20 per cent hike in ticket prices at midseason. Although the new theater permitted lavish productions, such as the company's success with its staging of Richard Strauss' symbolic opera, *Die Frau ohne Schatten,* it was not an inexpensive place in which to work.

The Met's Old Home. The historic old Metropolitan Opera House, scheduled to be demolished for an office building, was the scene of prolonged and tearful farewells on its last night, in April. And, early in the New Year, despite a campaign to save it, the process of demolition began.

On its last evening in the historic old Metropolitan Opera House, the company joined hands and voices in "Auld Lang Syne."

First-nighters enter the glittering new home of the Metropolitan Opera at Lincoln Center for the Performing Arts, in New York City.

With the demise of the old Met, two of the company's great prima donnas, Licia Albanese and Zinka Milanov, ended their Metropolitan careers.

National Company's Demise. The Met encountered two severe setbacks in 1966. The first was the acid reception it received in Paris in the spring during its first visit in more than 50 years. A still bleaker note was the cancellation of the 1967-1968 season of its national company because of an operating deficit of $800,000 incurred in the first season. The company, which was drawing well, was only in its second year on the road.

U.S. Opera Boom. Despite these difficulties, the United States was in the midst of an opera boom in which there was unusual audience support for unfamiliar repertory. The New York City Opera, now the Met's nearest neighbor (and closest rival) on the other side of Lincoln Center Plaza, offered in its spring season the American première of Von Einem's *Danton's Death* and the North American première of Ginastera's *Don Rodrigo*.

The San Francisco Spring Opera was picketed when demonstrators protested that it only presented modern works that were conservative in style. But the fall schedule brought some unorthodox fare, Berlioz's *The Trojans* and the U.S. première of Janáček's *The Makropoulos Case*. The Lyric Opera of Chicago offered Prokofiev's *The Angel of Fire* and Monteverdi's *The Coronation of Poppea*, in addition to standard repertory works. Perhaps the biggest prize of all went to the Opera Company of Boston, which invested $500,000 and months of work on the U.S. première of Schönberg's monumental *Moses and Aaron*, which finally reached the public in November, some seven months after the originally scheduled date.

Wagner Dies. The real operatic tragedy of the year was the death at 49 of Wieland Wagner who had revolutionized the staging of his grandfather's music dramas and, indeed, provided fresh approaches to the very meaning of opera.

On Strike. Few seasons have brought the concentration of labor troubles that accompanied 1966. The Philadelphia Orchestra was on strike for eight weeks–the longest walkout of any major U.S. orchestra on record. Other strikes included the New York City Opera Orchestra, the Indianapolis Symphony, and the Los Angeles Philharmonic. The Kansas City (Mo.) Philharmonic also had negotiation troubles.

Earlier in the year, when the going was less strenuous, the Philadelphia Orchestra had made a successful tour in May and June that took them to 13 cities in 10 Latin-American countries. In August, the orchestra offered its first season in its new summer home at the Saratoga (N.Y.) performing arts center. In August, the Cincinnati Symphony began a 10-week, round-the-world tour with Max Rudolf conducting. Sponsored by the U.S. Department of State, it was the first globe-circling junket by an ensemble from the United States. Meanwhile, the Boston Symphony was launching an unusual cultural exchange, a short-term swap of players with the Japan Philharmonic.

Two major European orchestras made extensive visits in the United States during the summer, a new development that made the London Symphony available for a festival in Daytona Beach, Fla., and the Orchestre de la Suisse Romande, under the distinguished Ernest Ansermet, an attraction in Palo Alto, Calif.

The New York Philharmonic offered an impressive month of music in early summer to illustrate the heritage and legacy of Igor Stravinsky. Later, its free park concerts in the New York area drew audiences as large as 80,000. The big news came in November when Leonard Bernstein announced that in 1969, at the close of his 10th season as music director, he would become laureate conductor, passing the primary responsibility to a successor. William Steinberg, with the title of principal guest conductor, will share the podium with Bernstein for the 1966-1967 and 1967-1968 programs.

Concert Halls were topics of brisk discussion. Two of the oldest and best known, Carnegie Hall, the 75-year-old monument to music on 57th Street in New York City, got a complete renovation, as did Orchestra Hall, the 62-year-old home of the Chi-

The New Home of The Met

The opening on September 16 of the Metropolitan Opera Company's new home at the Lincoln Center for the Performing Arts in New York City was the most glittering event in the U.S. musical world in years. Guests on that cool autumnal evening included Mrs. Lyndon B. Johnson, the president and the first lady of the Philippines, the Secretary-General of the United Nations, a large contingent of Washington, New York City and state dignitaries, and members of many of the nation's most prominent families.

The bejeweled audience heard the première of a new opera, *Antony and Cleopatra*, written for the occasion by U.S. composer Samuel Barber, and it saw on stage some of the effects made possible by the technical marvels of the $45,700,000 opera house. Cleopatra's barge floated toward the audience on a silver Nile, its oars dipping in unison. A large sphinx turned now its profile, now its full face to the audience. In the distance, the Egyptian fleet sailed off to encounter the Romans.

If most critics found Barber's music wanting and the production overblown, nearly everyone agreed that it accomplished a prime purpose of the evening: to display the facilities of the new house. Hence, the company on that opening night was a little like a Cinderella grown a bit boisterous, because at long last she could wear bright clothes and have the run of a king's palace.

The new opera house was built to replace the famed Grand Old Lady of 39th Street, the creaking old home that was built in 1883 and found wanting even on its opening night. At the old Met, scenery had to be stored in a separate building. Some of its 3,500 seats were located behind posts, and more seriously, the house lacked adequate facilities of almost every kind for its performing artists.

The new building (seating capacity 3,800) has changed all that–and more. Designed as the focal point of the nation's largest culture center, its facilities make it the most modern opera house in the world. Only one-third of the volume of the building is used for its public spaces and auditorium. Two-thirds are used for space the audience never sees. In the old building, these proportions were reversed.

The stage area of the new house is six times that of the old. The 81-foot main stage is divided into seven sections that can be raised to different elevations. It is backed by another stage 66 feet deep and flanked by two large additional stages in each wing. The latter are known as stagewagons. These can be set up for the later acts of an opera. When the main stage is cleared of its scenery for one act, the stagewagons can be noiselessly rolled out onto the main stage, at the touch of a button, with the scenery for the following act.

The house contains 20 soundproof rehearsal rooms, space for storing 25 complete sets, a carpenter shop 10 times the size of the old one, and motel-like apartments, each equipped with a shower, a piano, and an electronic device that emits an always accurate "A," the note by which musicians establish pitch.

The house, which all but completes the overall plan for Lincoln Center (the Juilliard School of Music is still to be built), was designed by Wallace K. Harrison, a chief designer of Manhattan's United Nations complex and Rockefeller Center. Although some criticized the opera house because it did not break fresh architectural ground, the public seemed satisfied. It thoroughly enjoyed its graceful arched façade, its gold and scarlet paneled auditorium, its starburst chandeliers presented by the Austrian government, its spiral staircase, and its colorfully swirling murals by the painter, Marc Chagall. And both public and artists agreed that the building's acoustics were superb.

Said Architect Harrison: "The design of the building was based entirely on acoustics, sightlines, and lighting. The shape was determined by the lowest frequency of sound a man can hear . . . we framed the hall in wood, like a violin."

It was clear on opening night, and as the season progressed, that nowhere did grand opera have a grander home than at the Lincoln Center for the Performing Arts. MARK M. PERLBERG cago Symphony. The Jesse H. Jones Hall for the Performing Arts opened in October to provide Houston, Tex., with the major cultural facility of the Southwest. See HOUSTON (Picture).

The Tchaikovsky Competition in Moscow brought a U.S. winner, 24-year-old soprano Jane Marsh. The contest's piano division, which brought fame to Van Cliburn in 1958, was won by a Russian teen-ager, Gregory Sokolov. In Fort Worth, Tex., the contest established by Cliburn was won by a Romanian, Radu Lupu.

The current increase in interest in chamber music was acknowledged by a $400,000 grant from the National Arts Endowment to further the cause. Mozart was flourishing, too. During the season, Manhattan was to hear all 27 piano concertos by the master played by Lili Kraus.

Swatch of Gold. Best selling classical album of the season, surprisingly, was neither a stereo nor a hi-fi production, but *Opening Nights at the Metropolitan*, a nostalgic collection of famous voices from 1893 to 1959. Part of its appeal was the inclusion in the albums of a swatch from the famed gold curtain of the old theater. Elsewhere in recordings, one could note the baroque boom was still going strong and in 1966 it entered the operatic field. But significant contemporary music, as usual, was still poorly represented on record. ROBERT C. MARSH

MUSIC, POPULAR. Performances aimed at teenage audiences dominated the pop scene in 1966, but there were signs of growing sophistication in some of the music, and of amalgamation with other idioms. The *sitar* (an Indian stringed instrument) was heard in performances by the Beatles, who also had a hit ("Michelle") in which a string quartet participated.

The pop world was invaded by jazz groups. Ramsey Lewis, Count Basie, Chet Baker, and Bud Shank recorded songs introduced by the Byrds, the Rolling Stones, and other rock groups. This gave the performers greater exposure on AM radio, which normally leans to pop artists.

Blues. Rhythm and blues songs exerted a major influence on music during the year. They were performed often by single singers, while vocal groups continued to dominate in the rock and folk rock fields. Leading artists were organist Jimmy Smith, making his vocal debut in "Got My Mojo Working"; Billy Larkin and the Delegates, Wilson Pickett, James Brown, Otis Redding, and an important new performer from Alabama, Percy Sledge. A jazz-influenced pop blues singer, Lou Rawls, became a hit on both singles and on LPs.

The success of Herb Alpert's Tijuana Brass instrumental group, with its multimillion record sales, bridged the gap between adult and teen audiences.

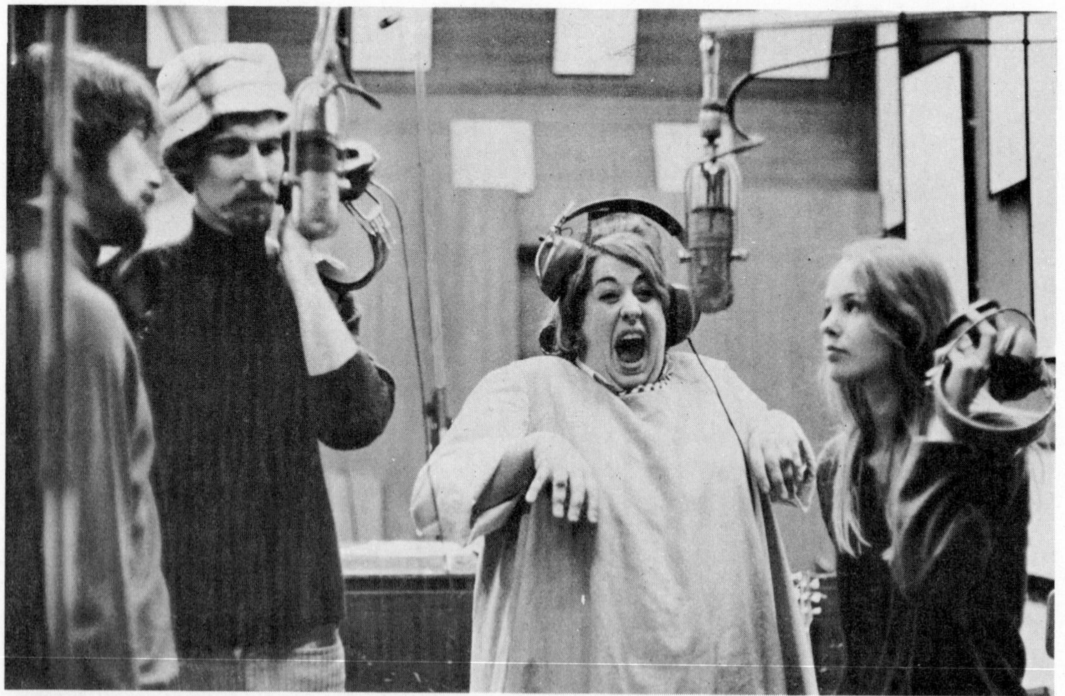

Lee B. Johnson, *Life* © Time Inc.

The Mamas and Papas recording their second album, "Words of Love." Issued in 1966, it had advance sales of over a million records.

Beatle fans in Fort Oglethorpe, Ga., burned pictures of their favorites after John Lennon's remark that they were "more popular than Jesus."

Their Mexican-influenced sound featured two trumpets and bright rhythms. Sergio Méndes, a young pianist from Brazil, toured the United States as a supporting act in Alpert's concerts and made a strong impression in person and on records, usually leading a small instrumental and vocal combo known as "Brasil 66." Other prominent instrumental groups were the orchestras of Mantovani and Bert Kaempfert.

Rock. Though the Beatles and a few other British groups retained their popularity with the American public, there was a noticeable trend toward domestic rock units. One, the Monkees, was created specially as the subject of a television series and was simultaneously launched on records. The Monkees came from Hollywood, Calif., the point of origin of several other top groups such as Paul Revere and the Raiders, and Gary Lewis and the Playboys.

Some newly popular units used a loud, heavily amplified sound; among them was a semijazz, semirock outfit known as the Butterfield Blues Band. But, in general, there was a slight decline in the raucousness of pop music. This was detectable in the softer sound of The Sandpipers, The Mamas and The Papas, and Simon and Garfunkel, whose provocative version of "Silent Night" (sung to the background of a news bulletin detailing tragic events in the 1966 world) was a much-discussed Christmas item.

Jazz. A greatly increased acceptance of jazz was noted in U.S. universities and schools in 1966. Lectures, concerts, and credit courses in the theory and art of jazz were presented. At Stanford University, Palo Alto, Calif., students successfully completed their "Jazz Year" project in the spring of 1966.

In July, veteran pianist Earl "Fatha" Hines took a small band and jazz singer Clea Bradford on a six-week tour of the Soviet Union. In October, the Stan Getz Quartet flew to Bangkok to play at a state dinner given by President Lyndon B. Johnson for the king and queen of Thailand. The king is a noted jazz expert and saxophonist.

Friedrich Gulda, the celebrated classical and jazz pianist, organized an ambitious International Competition for Modern Jazz, held in Vienna, Austria, in May. Cash prizes and scholarships were offered to young musicians.

The ties between jazz and religion grew closer than ever. Duke Ellington and his band performed their program of sacred music at Coventry Cathedral in England and at a synagogue in Beverly Hills, Calif. Father Tom Vaughn, an Episcopalian curate in Midland, Mich., played jazz piano at Newport, R.I. Another Episcopalian priest, Father Malcolm Boyd, read a series of prayers on contemporary subjects to the accompaniment of jazz guitarist Charlie Byrd. Many jazz works were performed in houses of worship. LEONARD G. FEATHER

NATIONAL DEFENSE. The ugly "little" war in South Vietnam, Communist China's test of an atomic missile, and a menacing new stage in the nuclear arms race pushed U.S. defense policymakers to the brink of critical new decisions in 1966. These military pressures were forcing the defense budget well above the $70,000,000,000 level at a time when President Lyndon B. Johnson was trying to hold a firm line against a continuing military build-up and the resulting inflationary expenditures.

In Vietnam, the United States, the world's leading military power with more than 3,300,000 men spread around the globe, found itself entangled in a murky conflict with a minor power that did not yield to a strategy of gradual escalation. The war, costing $15,000,000,000 to $24,000,000,000 a year, according to various estimates, had outgrown the dimensions of guerrilla battle and had become, in the words of Secretary of Defense Robert S. McNamara, a "quasi-conventional war." The massive fire and air power of the United States could crush the Viet Cong and North Vietnamese regulars when they could be found in the dense jungles, the soggy rice fields, and the forbidding highlands of South Vietnam. But the hard core guerrilla force of some 110,000 men plus 170,000 irregulars kept on fighting.

U.S. strategists believed that until the back of the main force could be broken by "hunter-killer" and "spoiling" operations, and until the infiltration rate of 8,000 a month could be curtailed sharply, the effort to restore peace to Vietnam would be frustrated. Hence, the United States increased the number of its troops in South Vietnam during 1966 by more than 200,000, to a total of more than 380,000. This force, larger than the number of men the United States had in Korea, was backed by more than 1,000 combat planes, 2,000 helicopters, and several thousand artillery pieces. In addition, there were 35,000 troops in Thailand, and 40,000 men with the Seventh Fleet off Vietnam.

The build-up was scheduled to lessen in 1967. Fewer than 100,000 troops were expected to be sent to Vietnam, bringing the total of U.S. forces there to 480,000 by year-end. Secretary of Defense McNamara predicted that draft calls would drop by nearly half, to about 25,000 a month, early in 1967. Although he declined to forecast future U.S. strength in Vietnam, it was apparent from other Pentagon data that the war was entering a new stage at the end of 1966. The Viet Cong and North Vietnam regulars had been defeated soundly in some 150 operations during the year. Communist dead averaged 4,500 a month. According to U.S. intelligence estimates, the Viet Cong were losing about as many men, killed and captured, as the number that was infiltrating from the north.

1967 Turning Point? Because of the heavy enemy losses, U.S. strategists looked for a turning point in the war to come in the spring of 1967. During 1966, spoiling raids pounced on Viet Cong and North Vietnamese units before they could stage the expected spring and summer monsoon offensive. And, when the North Vietnamese 324B division tried to cross the demilitarized zone at the 17th parallel in July, U.S. Marines and South Vietnamese troops drove it back across the border, taking a heavy toll of lives. The Communists had prepared for the drive for months, building bunkers and fortified villages in the zone. Two other North Vietnamese divisions were believed to be near the zone, waiting to take part in a breakthrough that never came. But stout defense by seven marine battalions and eight South Vietnamese army battalions repulsed the invasion attempt.

Operations Irving and Attleboro. In two other strategic operations, U.S. and allied forces scored important victories. In Operation Irving, during October, the U.S. 1st Air Cavalry Division and other units killed 1,973 enemy troops and captured a record haul of 1,765 prisoners and 5,712 suspects in 23 days of heavy fighting. The fighting took place in Binh Dinh province, a rich rice area. In Operation Attleboro, in Tay Ninh forest, the Viet Cong headquarters area and hideout of the elite 9th Viet Cong Division, the U.S. 196th Light Infantry Brigade, and parts of the 25th Infantry and 1st Infantry divisions, killed about 1,000 guerrillas.

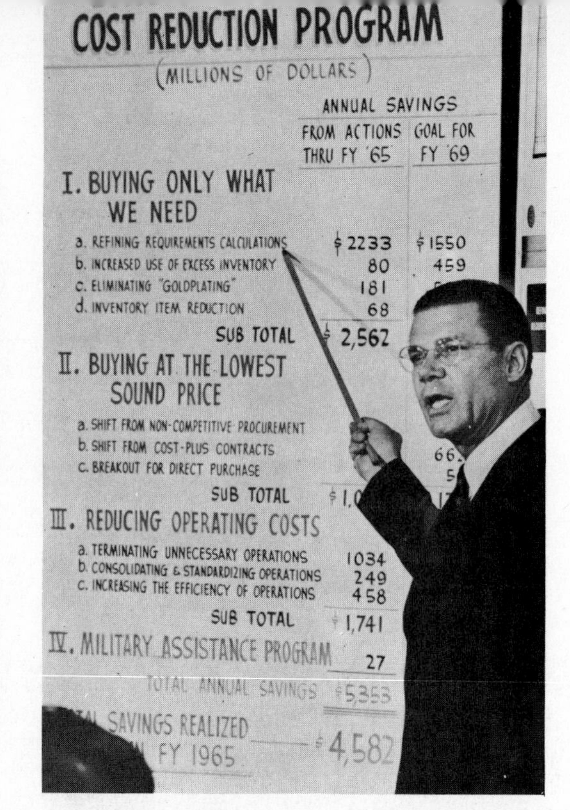

A cost reduction program suggested by U.S. Secretary of Defense Robert S. McNamara raised controversy in Congress in 1966.

U.S. Strategy in Vietnam was to knock out the hard core guerrillas and regulars by search and destroy attacks, to head off enemy raids, and to deny food sources to the enemy by controlling highways and cutting off supplies. Although these kinds of operations would continue in 1967, the U.S. command in Saigon near year-end was shifting to a new phase. This would involve using most of the 300,000 men in the South Vietnamese army in so-called pacification operations, which is current military jargon for seizing rural areas and replacing the Viet Cong political administrations of the villages with South Vietnamese officials. The goal of this new strategy was to extend the Saigon government's control beyond the 57 per cent of the population it controlled at year-end. The idea was to push the Viet Cong guerrillas out of the villages where they often rule politically if not militarily, and drive them into the rugged hills where they face constant pursuit and bombardment.

Planning Options. With the Vietnamese war expected to evolve into the pacification stage, U.S. defense planners were confronted with major decisions in other areas.

Secretary McNamara, at a November press conference at the LBJ Ranch, disclosed that the Russians were installing an antimissile defense system, although there was some doubt about its nature and capability. Nevertheless, McNamara indicated that he probably would recommend deployment of the Poseidon submarine missile as an answer to a Soviet antimissile system. Poseidon, an improvement on Polaris, has multiple warheads and decoy devices.

Still, an improved offense against a Soviet defense network would not provide protection against Russian ICBMs, or a possible Communist Chinese missile. Hence, Pentagon planners weighed the relative advantages, effectiveness, and cost (some $25,000,000,000) of a Nike-X antimissile system that could provide some defense against a large-scale attack. Strategists were also weighing the merits of a smaller $3,000,000,000 to $4,000,000,000 Nike-X system to parry a limited Chinese missile threat, expected to be in evidence by 1975 to 1980.

The planners also evaluated an air force proposal for a manned bomber for the late 1970s that would have a range of 6,000 miles and carry about two dozen of the new short-range attack missiles (SRAM). The aircraft would fly at more than 1,500 mph and have swivel wings like the F-111 to enable it to fly slower at lower altitudes. It would also carry a heavy load of nonnuclear bombs for tactical support missions. The air force argued that manned bombers would be needed to complement the big missiles and to force an enemy to maintain a costly air defense system.

Polaris vs Poseidon

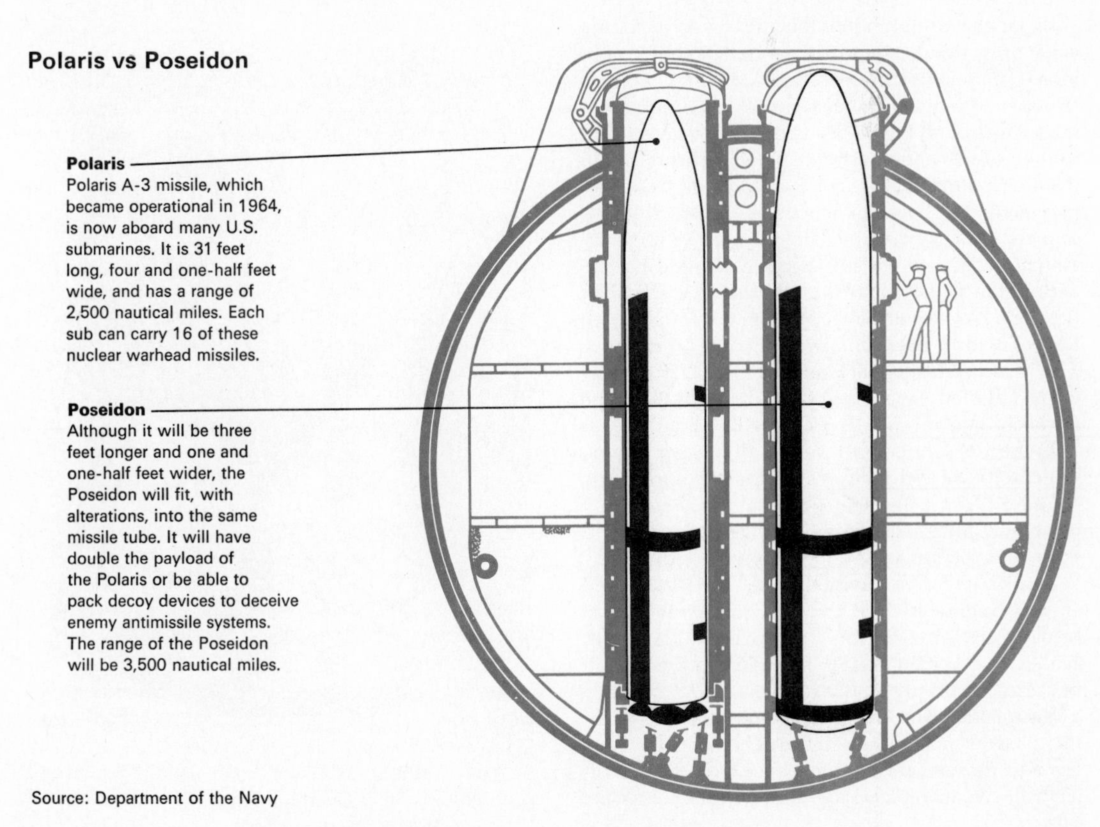

Source: Department of the Navy

NATIONAL DEFENSE

Defense Spending. U.S. concern with the rising spiral of the nuclear arms competition was evident in its effort to stop the spread of such weapons, to promote a lessening of tensions, and to end the Vietnamese war. The prospects for a reduction of arms costs did not seem bright, however. In some quarters, optimism as to Soviet intentions was a reflection of a desire to cut U.S. troops below the 225,000 level in West Germany. Both the United States and Britain were urgently trying to slash the expenses of their troops in Germany.

But there was little hope that the U.S. defense budget could be reduced. Defense spending for fiscal 1967 was expected to reach $68,000,000,000, compared to $55,300,000,000 of fiscal 1966.

Congress voted $58,067,472,000 in defense appropriations for fiscal 1967, $403,119,000 more than the Johnson administration requested. This fund included $17,165,065,000 for the army, $16,826,700,000 for the navy, $20,805,900,000 for the air force, and $3,269,807,000 for defense agencies. Congress also provided $792,000,000 for military aid, $101,100,000 for civil defense, and $979,600,000 for military construction.

U.S. military forces, authorized to reach 3,093,000 men by mid-1967, were permitted to climb past 3,325,000 in 1966, to support the Vietnam war build-up. See Armed Forces of the World.

U.S. ARMY

By far the largest unit of the military services, the army grew rapidly to provide about 250,000 troops in Vietnam by the end of 1966, besides 223,000 troops in Germany, 50,000 in Korea, and lesser numbers around the globe. The army was stretched thin in officers and noncommissioned officers and in training resources as it tried to meet its troop deployment and rotation schedules. About 700,000 soldiers had to be trained in the year. The army augmented its forces in Vietnam by adding the 25th Infantry Division, the 4th Infantry Division, the 11th Armored Cavalry Regiment, the 196th Light Infantry Brigade, and numerous other units. The units already there included the 173rd Airborne Division, the 1st Brigade of the 101st Airborne Division, and the 1st Air Cavalry Division.

In Europe, the army drained off at least 15,000 skilled officers and noncoms to staff the expanding training bases in the United States. This cut army personnel in West Germany to 210,000 early in 1966, but the loss was restored by year-end.

Besides the five divisions and three armored cavalry regiments in Germany, the army had a brigade in West Berlin, two divisions in South Korea, a Sergeant missile battalion in Italy, and brigades in Hawaii, Alaska, and the Canal Zone.

New Weapons being developed for the army included the Chaparral infrared missile for low-level air defense; the 20-foot Lance battlefield artillery missile to replace the Honest John; and the Maw and Tow antitank missiles. Others include the Cobra helicopter aerial gun ship for close air support and a more advanced helicopter capable of flying 220 mph. It is designed as a heavy gun ship, and can carry machine guns, grenade launchers, rockets, and antitank missiles.

U.S. NAVY

The navy's major combat role in the Vietnam war was in air support, sealift, and bombing operations. Three or four navy attack carriers of Task Force 77 accounted for nearly half the raids on North Vietnam. But the navy's A-4 Skyhawk and F-4 Phantom II bombers sustained substantial losses over the heavily defended targets. Increased exposure of the navy planes required orders for 280 planes to replace losses expected in 1967.

With combat operations tying up five of the eight flattops in the Pacific (the United States has 15 attack carriers altogether), the navy pressed one of its smaller antisubmarine carriers into duty. Also, the war prevented the retirement of two big carriers in an economy move planned in 1965.

The budget for fiscal 1967 provided the navy with $428,000,000 for a second nuclear powered aircraft carrier. The first nuclear carrier, the *Enterprise*, which entered combat duty for the first time on Dec. 3, 1965, established new records in sorties and endurance.

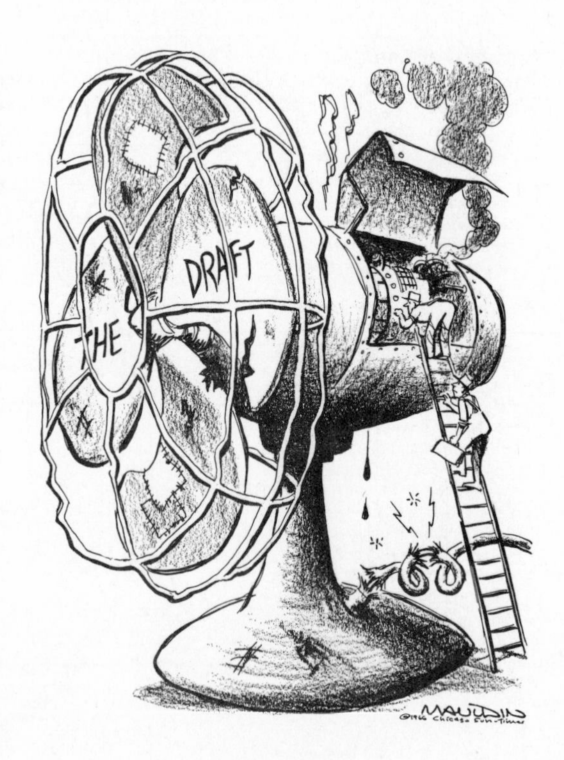

Overhaul Time

The Draft Controversy

The nation's draft system came under increasing criticism in 1966, a year of big draft calls as the war in Vietnam continued to escalate.

Numerous critics contended that the system was unfair because it selected some young men for military duty, while permitting others to continue their education and careers without interruption. On May 18, Secretary of Defense Robert S. McNamara himself complained in a speech in Montreal, Que., that there was an "inequity" in the present system.

Much of the criticism was caused by the fact that 1,900,000 college students had been deferred from the draft. It was contended that they were given an unfair advantage over young people who could not afford to go to college.

The controversy over the war in Vietnam added to the controversy over the draft. Some students objected to being drafted because it might involve them in a war they bitterly oppose. Negro Congressman Adam Clayton Powell (D., N.Y.) declared that a higher percentage of Negroes was packed off to Vietnam "to be killed," because the inferior education provided them did not give them a chance in the deferment tests.

Draft boards were empowered to defer a student if he ranked high enough in his class, or if he received a high enough grade in the College Qualification Draft test.

Nearly 1,000,000 students took the qualification test in 1966. But on numerous college campuses both the test system and the class rank system were strongly criticized. At the University of Chicago, a group of students formed a militant organization called "Students Against the Rank." Also, the 150-question qualification test was under attack partly on grounds that it was unfair since it discriminated against the nonscience students.

There also was bitterness over the large number of young people who escaped military service because of lack of mental or physical requirements. In fiscal 1965, about 1,500,000 men came of military age. But it was estimated that about 32 per cent of these would be rejected as unsuitable either physically or mentally, about 25 per cent would be acceptable but would not be called, and only about 43 per cent would do military service before they were out of the military age bracket.

Still another reason for the mounting draft controversy was the exemptions granted wealthy young personalities such as George Hamilton and Cassius Clay (Muhammad Ali). Hamilton, a film star who has been a frequent escort of Lynda Bird Johnson, the President's daughter, was given deferred status on the grounds that he was the sole support of his mother. His draft board finally ordered him to report for a physical examination. Heavyweight boxing champion Clay was originally exempted because he could not pass the mental tests.

Despite these criticisms, Lieutenant General Lewis B. Hershey, the director of the Selective Service System, vigorously defended student deferments in testimony before the House Armed Services Committee. This policy was in the "national interest," he declared, since it permits the educating of "physicians, dentists, and allied specialists, scientists, engineers, teachers, and others whose skills may be critical in the future."

He pointed out that a student who is deferred is not exempt from the possibility of being drafted after he completes his education. About 56 per cent of those who are deferred do their military service later. Of those who never get to college, only about 46 per cent enter the military.

There were a number of proposals made for reforming the draft system. For example, Senator Edward M. Kennedy (D., Mass.) favored a national lottery which would give all an equal chance of being drafted. Anthropologist Margaret Mead suggested that young men be drafted and then be given the opportunity to serve either in the military or in organizations such as the Peace Corps.

At year's end, President Lyndon B. Johnson awaited the results of a National Advisory Commission that, it was hoped, would shed light on the problem of the draft. William McGaffin

A tunnel in Colorado's Cheyenne Mountain leads to the operations center of the North American Air Defense Command. Computers, *right*, will help warn of an enemy attack.

Destroyers and cruisers supported ground forces in Vietnam with their heavy guns. Other warships joined the South Vietnamese vessels in coastal surveillance, in river assault groups, and in interdicting, or intercepting Viet Cong gunrunners from North Vietnam.

The navy's fleet of 900 warships included 40 Polaris submarines, 26 nuclear powered attack submarines, and 8,300 aircraft. The navy was spending $2,000,000,000 for ships, including five nuclear submarines, two missile destroyers, and two fast deployment ships that would be loaded with arms for rapid sealift to troops in remote hot spots.

The Marines, with 2⅓ divisions and an air wing in South Vietnam, joined with South Vietnamese forces to extend control of their areas from the coastal enclaves. They worked with the South Vietnamese units in pacification programs. The new 5th Marine Division neared completion of its organization and training at Camp Pendleton, Calif. It had one brigade in South Vietnam and one in Hawaii.

U.S. AIR FORCE

The air force had more than 800 fighter-bomber, photo reconnaissance, and escort planes in South Vietnam and Thailand and was heavily burdened by the war. It flew an average of 400 sorties a day against road networks, bridges, railroads, military bases, petroleum storage areas, and other targets in North Vietnam, Laos, and South Vietnam.

Airpower advocates, dismayed by public doubt and skepticism about the effect of air attacks, urged more intensive and wider choice of targets in North Vietnam. Hence, bombings of the petroleum dumps near Hanoi and Haiphong, long exempt under the restrictions ordered by President Johnson, were finally authorized.

Overshadowed by the guerrilla war, the Strategic Air Command (SAC) won praise from Saigon for bombing by its big B-52 jet bombers, normally reserved for a possible nuclear strike. SAC began operations in Vietnam with the new SR-71, a 2,000-mph photo reconnaissance plane.

The air force had 14,000 planes in inventory and was planning to buy 600 more, including the new A-7 Corsair II jet bomber, which was scheduled to become operational in 1969. The new SRAM was ordered from the Boeing Company. The still-unbuilt FB-111 bomber and the B-52 bomber could carry dozens of these missiles, designed to be launched beyond the reach of enemy air defenses.

Coast Guard. Admiral Willard J. Smith replaced Admiral E. J. Roland as commandant of the coast guard in June, 1966. The sea patroling service, with 35,300 men and 325 ships, had 26 patrol boats and about 400 sailors assigned to South Vietnam. In 1966, jurisdiction over the coast guard passed from the Department of the Treasury to the new Department of Transportation. LLOYD NORMAN

NEPAL. The landlocked nation enjoyed a favorable year due to a variety of moves made by the increasingly responsible government. The economy was approaching what could be termed a transitional stage as compared to former almost primitive conditions. Nepalese currency, rather than India's rupees or other species, became the only legal tender. Irrigation and hydroelectric projects begun by India were completed despite a cutback in aid from India.

Most important to Nepal was the gradual resumption of trade relations with Tibet. It signed a new trade agreement in May with the Tibet Autonomous Region–the Communist Chinese regional government. Economic development suffered something of a setback in June, however, when a severe earthquake destroyed thousands of homes.

Nepal was active on the international scene in 1966. State visits from Yugoslavian and Israeli delegations resulted in the signing of new trade agreements. Nepal's envoys made repeated visits to India, as a result of which Indo-Nepalese relations grew more cordial in 1966.

Facts in Brief. Population: 10,400,000. Government: King Mahendra; Council of Ministers Chairman Surya Bahadur Thapa. Monetary Unit: rupee (7.60 = U.S. $1). Foreign Trade: exports, $22,800,000; imports, $38,900,000. Principal Exports: jute, oilseeds, rice. JOHN N. STALKER

NETHERLANDS, THE, suffered from the disruptive activities of the Provos, an anarchist youth civil disobedience movement. Their first hostile demonstration was at the March wedding in Amsterdam of Crown Princess Beatrix to Claus von Amsberg, a former German soldier and diplomat. The Provos threw smoke bombs at the bridal coach and clashed with police on the wedding route.

In June, the Provos were involved in a demonstration by building workers against a 2 per cent bonus cut. A worker had lost his life from natural causes, but the Provos blamed the police and rioted in the capital. During two nights of terror and looting, more than 100 persons were injured. In September, smoke bombs were thrown at the carriage taking Queen Juliana to the opening of parliament in The Hague. The police arrested 80 Provos.

The government was defeated in October, by a vote of 75 to 62, in a debate on its financial policies. As a result, Premier Joseph Cals resigned. On November 21, Jelle Zijlstra was named premier of an interim cabinet pending elections in 1967.

Facts in Brief. Population: 12,350,000. Government: Queen Juliana; Premier Jelle Zijlstra. Monetary Unit: guilder (3.62 = U.S. $1). Foreign Trade: exports, $6,392,500,000; imports, $7,462,500,000. Principal Exports: iron and steel, petroleum products, agricultural produce. KENNETH BROWN

NEW BRUNSWICK. See CANADA.

NEW GUINEA, a vast tropical island in the Pacific, remained under the joint control of Australia and Indonesia. West Irian, which was under Indonesian administration, was almost completely cut off from the rest of the world. This was particularly true following a political crisis involving a change in Indonesia's government (see INDONESIA). But the eastern portion of New Guinea, which included the Territory of Papua, continued to move ahead under a United Nations (UN) trusteeship administered by Australia.

The recently elected house of assembly laid the groundwork for eventual independence for the area, though no specific timetable was set. Nor was the eventual relationship with Australia precisely defined. Indications were that the Papuans would vote for self-governing status, while continuing economic and political ties with Australia. Studies on constitutional development continued meanwhile by a 14-man committee which had been appointed during the preceding year by the New Guinea house of assembly.

Australian financial support was the major source of public funds for the territory's government. But there was some optimism that, with intelligent development, the area could not only sustain itself, but also become relatively prosperous. Timber resources, in particular, showed promise of providing an economic base for the area. JOHN N. STALKER

NEW ORLEANS continued to shake off the devastation of 1965's Hurricane *Betsy* by bustling ahead with port development and increasing efforts to bolster its stature as a trade and tourist center. The first tenants moved into the International Trade Mart Tower, a 33-floor landmark overlooking the Mississippi. Near the Trade Mart, the Rivergate, a convention and exhibition facility, was rising. It includes a 17,666-seat auditorium.

New buildings and rehabilitation marked the historic French Quarter. Scores of old structures were remodeled as homes, apartments, and hotels. A major hotel is under construction on Bourbon Street on a site formerly occupied by a brewery.

To support the city's rejuvenation, Mayor Victor Schiro proposed a record five-year capital spending program of $190,640,000. And to help finance needed public improvements, Louisiana voters, on November 8, approved a state constitutional amendment to permit, in effect, a 50 per cent increase in the city's authority to issue bonds. Thanks to a favorable vote on another amendment, the city would also be able to build an all-weather domed stadium. Just a week earlier, New Orleans was selected as a site for a major league football team which will eventually use the $35,000,000 stadium.

Three uprated Saturn boosters, built at NASA's huge Michoud plant in New Orleans East, were launched at Cape Kennedy. DONALD W. LIEF

NEW YORK CITY. Mayor John V. Lindsay, who took office on Jan. 1, 1966, found that campaign enthusiasm did not automatically achieve results in office. Lindsay's term began amidst a paralyzing 12-day strike by transit workers that cost the city untold millions in economic loss. Despite emergency regulations which accommodated a 43 per cent increase in Manhattan's traffic volume, monumental tie-ups resulted. The strike saw transit union president Michael Quill jailed for contempt of court. After settlement, which involved a pay raise for transit workers, the fiery Quill died of a heart attack. The pay raise led to a 20-cent subway fare that began on July 5, ending Lindsay's campaign pledge to preserve the 15-cent ride.

Two other Lindsay pledges floundered during the year: a civilian board to review complaints against police and an end to the city's fiscal chaos. Although Lindsay created a panel to investigate citizens' complaints of police brutality and discourtesy, police and other groups campaigned to kill it. In a November referendum, a large majority of voters defeated the plan. Despite this action, Lindsay's new Police Chief Howard Leary quickly named a similar panel composed of five veteran police employees–three of them now civilians.

In finance, Lindsay found it difficult to slice the city's swollen budget. After a tough fight with the state legislature, he gained an income tax levied on both residents and commuters. But he conceded that a massive $300,000,000 deficit loomed without more state and federal aid. See TAXATION.

The Lindsay administration made vigorous efforts to recruit strong executive talent from business, other cities, and the federal government. It also moved firmly to streamline and consolidate a sprawling structure of 99 city agencies and departments into 10 administrations. Said *The New York Times:* "Reform is on the move in New York."

The saddest day of the mayor's year came in late October when he led a funeral procession behind the coffins of 12 firemen killed in a blaze near Madison Square Park. It was the worst tragedy in the fire department's 101-year history.

Air Pollution. On Thanksgiving Day, smog indexes hit the danger point, bringing about an alert for the entire New York-New Jersey-Connecticut metropolitan area. The murky smog dispersed, however, before it could have significant impact upon persons with heart or respiratory diseases. The near-disaster spurred clean-up measures, including a budget request for $5,000,000 for air pollution control and a limited merger of the air pollution agency with Cooper Union School of Engineering.

The *New York Herald Tribune* died, a victim of publishing economics. A happier event was the opening, in September, of the new Metropolitan Opera House at Lincoln Center. DONALD W. LIEF

See also MUSIC; PUBLISHING.

NEW ZEALAND re-examined its traditional economic ties with Great Britain with increasing anxiety during the year. Britain, faced by its own problems involving a balance of trade deficit, was tightening its restrictions on imports; as a result, New Zealand–which considered Britain its best customer–faced the possibility of a serious trade deficit of its own.

While a 10-year free trade agreement with Australia would help make up some of the deficit, New Zealanders were acutely aware of the fact that they would have to seek other markets for their principal exports of dairy products and wool. Japan was one such possibility, and accordingly, trade missions were sent to explore the Japanese potential. Similarly, missions were sent to the United States to investigate the possibility of opening up certain American markets for their products. New Zealand was also one of the founding members of the Asian and Pacific Council which was established in June. Member nations were to establish closer economic ties. See ASIA.

The government of Prime Minister Keith J. Holyoake continued to support the U.S. position on Vietnam, though it was subjected to some sharp domestic criticism for it, notably from the Labour party. In the November elections, however, Holyoake and his National party were easily returned to office even though the Vietnamese war had been made a political issue.

The visit of U.S. President Lyndon B. Johnson in October was a reminder of the possibility of more fruitful cooperation between New Zealand and the United States. There was a growing recognition of the necessity for such cooperation, particularly because of the economic and social commitments both the United States and New Zealand had in the Pacific Ocean area.

New Queen. On June 6, 1966, Kuini Te Ata-i-rangi-kaahu succeeded her father, after his death, as head of the King Movement, a confederation of Maori tribes. The new ruler, whose names mean the Soaring Bird of Dawn, is the fifth monarch in a dynasty that for more than a century has exerted a strong influence on relations between the Maoris, New Zealand's native Polynesians, and the white population.

Facts in Brief. Population: 2,741,000. Government: Governor-General Sir Bernard Fergusson; Prime Minister Keith J. Holyoake. Monetary Unit: pound (1 = U.S. $2.80). Foreign Trade: exports, $1,002,100; imports, $1,065,000. Principal Exports: meat, wool, dairy products. JOHN N. STALKER

NEWBERY MEDAL. See LITERATURE FOR CHILDREN (AWARDS).

NEWFOUNDLAND. See CANADA.

NEWSPAPER. See PUBLISHING.

NICARAGUA. See LATIN AMERICA.

NIGER. See AFRICA.

NIGERIA. A political crisis that had been simmering in Nigeria's Western Region for weeks sparked a military uprising on Jan. 15, 1966. The crisis had been precipitated by the re-election in October, 1965, of Western Regional Premier Chief Samuel L. Akintola. The opposition charged that the voting had been rigged.

In the outbreak of terrorism that immediately followed the military coup d'état, federal Prime Minister Sir Abubakar Tafawa Balewa was assassinated as were Akintola and another regional premier. Major General Johnson T. U. Aguiyi-Ironsi, one of the military dissidents, assumed control of the government, placed the country under martial law, and announced plans for a constitutional reform.

On May 24, Aguiyi-Ironsi issued a decree (1) reducing the Northern, Eastern, Western, and Midwestern Regions to provinces; (2) placing them under stricter central government control; (3) dissolving the federation of Nigeria and declaring the country a republic; and (4) abolishing all political parties. The decree touched off a new wave of disturbances, notably in Nigeria's Northern Region where the Moslem Hausa tribesmen feared that the more educated Ibos would replace them in government jobs and eventually control the region. By June 1, however, Northern Region police and army troops had restored order but it was estimated that about 300 persons had been killed in the rioting.

At a meeting held on June 16, the Aguiyi-Ironsi government was able to allay, temporarily, the fears of tribal leaders in the Northern Region. Aguiyi-Ironsi, during a nationwide tour he made in July, appealed to the various chiefs to end tribalism. He promised to consult with the leadership in all regions before adopting either a new constitution or a number of contemplated civil rights laws.

The Second Mutiny. On July 29, Northern soldiers stationed at Abeokuta (in the Western Region) mutinied, and the government of Aguiyi-Ironsi was overthrown. On August 1, Lieutenant Colonel Yakubu Gowon, a Northerner, assumed control. He announced plans for a return to civilian rule and repealed many measures of the former regime.

Despite efforts of Northern leaders, hundreds of Easterners in the Northern Region were killed in September and thousands fled to Eastern Nigeria. On October 1, Northern troops in Kano mutinied and joined civilian mobs attacking the Ibos. Although the mutinous soldiers were soon brought under control by the Gowon government, sporadic clashes continued.

Facts in Brief. Population: 60,500,000. Government: National Military Government Head and Supreme Commander of Armed Forces Yakubu Gowon. Monetary Unit: pound (1 = U.S. $2.83). Foreign Trade: exports, $750,000,000; imports, $766,400,000. Principal Exports: cocoa beans, palm kernels, peanuts, petroleum. BENJAMIN E. THOMAS

NOBEL PRIZES in literature and science were presented at ceremonies in Stockholm, Sweden, on Dec. 10, 1966. It was the 65th anniversary of the first presentation of the prizes in 1901. The Norwegian *storting* (parliament) Nobel Committee in Oslo, Norway, withheld the peace prize in 1966, and, as is its custom, the committee gave no reason for its decision.

Awards in 1966 included:

Literature Prize was presented to two "outstanding Jewish authors." Shmuel Yosef Agnon, a Hebrew writer now living in Jerusalem, is the first person in Israel ever to receive a Nobel prize. Sharing the literature prize with him was Nelly Sachs, a Jewish author of poetry, who fled her native Germany in 1940, and is now a resident of Stockholm, Sweden.

Science Prizes were presented to a French and three American scientists. *Chemistry Prize* was awarded to Robert Sanderson Mulliken, University of Chicago Distinguished Service Professor of Physics and Chemistry. *Medicine Prize* was shared by Charles Brenton Huggins, University of Chicago William B. Ogden Distinguished Service Professor of Surgery and director of the Ben May Laboratory of Cancer Research; and (Francis) Peyton Rous, pathologist, who for many years did cancer research at the Rockefeller Institute (now University) in New York City. *Physics Prize* was awarded to Alfred Kastler of L'Ecole Normale Supérieure in Paris, France.

See also AGNON, SHMUEL YOSEF; HUGGINS, CHARLES BRENTON; KASTLER, ALFRED; MULLIKEN, ROBERT SANDERSON; ROUS, (FRANCIS) PEYTON; and SACHS, NELLY.

NORTH ATLANTIC TREATY ORGANIZATION (NATO). On March 9, 17 years after the North Atlantic Treaty was signed, the French government formally announced its intention to withdraw all its armed forces from the 15-nation integrated military command. It simultaneously announced that all NATO commands and installations located on French territory would either be required to come under French command or leave French soil.

The French government, however, said France would not quit the alliance. NATO was given 12 months in which to evacuate its military establishments, which included Supreme Headquarters, Allied Powers in Europe (SHAPE) outside Paris, and the Central European Command at Fontainebleau. France set July 31 as the date for the withdrawal of its forces from NATO command; the United States was given 12 months to remove its 26,000 troops from France. Although the United States protested that the deadline was too short, an extension of time was refused.

In June, at a NATO meeting held in Brussels, it was decided that on leaving France, the three Central European Headquarters would be amalgamated under a single commander. The NATO Military College, it was agreed, would be moved to Rome, Italy.

On July 1, the U.S. nuclear support for French forces in Germany, consisting of atomic bombs for

"We've done our job too well."

use by aircraft committed to NATO and nuclear warheads for missiles, was withdrawn. The withdrawal of U.S. Air Force reconnaissance squadrons from France began in August. Three squadrons went to Britain, two to the United States, and one was disbanded. Two transport sections went to British bases.

In September, it was agreed that SHAPE would be moved to Casteau, in Belgium. The North Atlantic Council headquarters were to be relocated in Brussels, 40 miles from Casteau. Both moves were scheduled to take place in 1967.

Exercises. From February 27 to March 26, NATO forces held exercises in the Bardufosa area of northern Norway. Planned as a test of NATO's mobile forces, the exercise involved about 10,000 officers and men from six NATO countries.

A five-nation, 31-ship multinational exercise known as "Straight Laced" was held off Norway in August. British and U.S. destroyers armed with guided missiles took part. It was later reported that a Russian destroyer and three Russian submarines were in the area during part of the exercise.

Total Strength: land forces, 2,850,000 (estimated); naval forces, 33 carriers, 30 cruisers, 181 submarines, 56 nuclear submarines; air forces, 925 ICBMs, 480 fleet ballistic missiles, and 1,100 long-range and medium-range bombers. KENNETH BROWN

Dilemma of NATO Alliance

Map of Europe shows how France's withdrawal of its territory and armed strength from NATO leaves a gaping hole in the European defense system of the Western Allies.

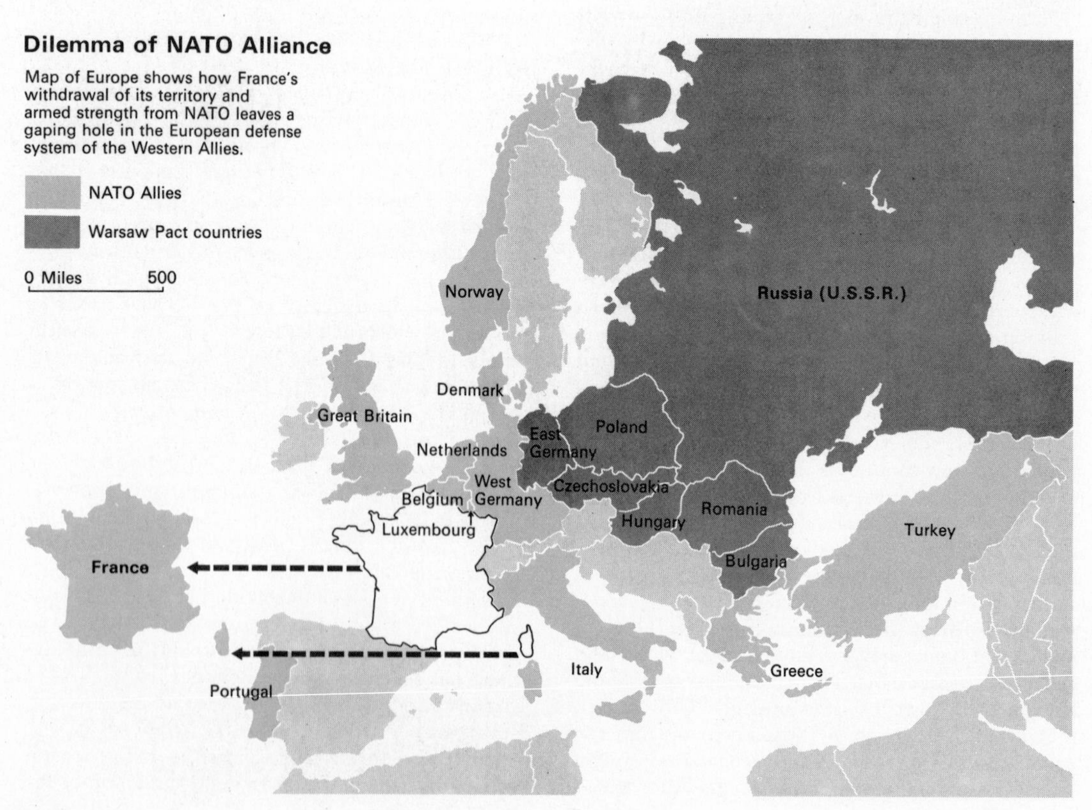

NORWAY. An economic boom continued without any signs of diminishing, despite fears of some exporters that credit restrictions by importing countries would reduce demand later. Unemployment fell to 0.2 per cent of the labor force. There were renewed fears of inflation, and the coalition government's main task was to curtail domestic demand.

Protracted negotiations took place in the spring involving new labor contracts that would affect about 5,000 companies and 260,000 workers. The national mediation commission imposed a ban on strikes when the negotiations broke down. Later, it proposed a two-year wage agreement. When this was rejected, the unions called for a number of strikes. The government, however, averted them by rushing a bill through the *storting* (parliament) making arbitration compulsory. Following a compulsory settlement, increased taxes were levied on gasoline, alcoholic beverages, and tobacco.

In June, a national pensions plan described as the greatest single social reform in the history of Norway, was adopted. It will begin on Jan. 1, 1967.

Facts in Brief. Population: 3,785,000. Government: King Olav V; Prime Minister Per Borten. Monetary Unit: krone (7.12=U.S. $1). Foreign Trade: exports, $1,442,900,000; imports, $2,205,600,000. Principal Exports: metals, wood and paper products, fish, ships, machinery. KENNETH BROWN

NOVA SCOTIA. See CANADA.

OCEAN. More than 1,700 scientists from 57 nations attended the Second International Oceanographic Congress, held at the University of Moscow from May 31 to June 9. The congress was convened under the auspices of the United Nations Educational, Scientific, and Cultural Organization (UNESCO) by the Soviet Academy of Sciences. Although the meeting was devoted to "ocean research to the benefit of mankind," most of the 500 papers presented were concerned with the purely scientific aspects of oceanography.

Advances in marine geology and geophysics, reported at the congress, included new data on the composition of the rock and sediment layers underlying the ocean. This was secured through echo-sounding techniques using explosives and high-powered electrical arcs. Other investigations revealed the pattern of climatic variations during the last 700,000 years. Scientists can now date marine sediments by the warm and cold species of fossil plankton that are found in them. The reversal of the direction of earth magnetism, occurring every 700,000 to 1,000,000 years, was also established as an indicator of age. Evidence of such reversals are found in the sediments of the ocean just as they are found in rocks on all the continents.

Deep Drilling. This method for dating marine sediments will be used in the planned 1968 and 1969 drilling operation of the Joint Oceanographic

Flip Schulke, *Life* © Time Inc.

Jacques Mayol descended 198 feet into the ocean off the Bahamas without breathing apparatus to establish a free dive record.

Institutions Deep Earth Sampling (JOIDES). This will be conducted by the Scripps Institution at La Jolla, Calif.; the Woods Hole Oceanographic Institution at Woods Hole, Mass.; the Institute of Marine Sciences of the University of Miami, Coral Gables, Fla., and the Lamont Geological Observatory of Columbia University in New York City. The National Science Foundation is funding this large drilling endeavor, which will recover about 50 sediment cores of varying lengths. They will be taken from a maximum of several thousand feet, thus allowing the study of sediments and underlying rock which are now accessible only by indirect means.

It is hoped that the results of JOIDES will shed light on another question under lively discussion in Moscow, the theory of continental drift. The reversal of the magnetic field, since it is an earth-wide phenomenon, was used by proponents to substantiate the theory of continental drift, or at least the motion of the sea floor from the midoceanic ridges toward the continents. However, there was great disagreement, and more direct evidence will be needed before the theory of continental drift can be accepted or rejected. The evidence may be obtained from sediment cores of the ocean floor.

The results in physical and chemical oceanography, presented at the congress, were just as varied as the geological reports. They were not, however, characterized by as much controversy. Many delegates emphasized the need for large-scale studies of ocean currents for which buoy systems would be designed and improved so that they could be anchored for long periods of time in the deepest part of the oceans. Until recently, the currents on the ocean floor were believed to be rather slow. New measurements indicate currents up to half a knot on the ocean floor. Acoustical methods for studying this movement and the structure of large water masses were reported at the congress. Such studies have been initiated across the Straits of Florida.

Legislation. The Congress of the United States showed interest in oceanography by passing a bill that established a National Oceanographic Council with membership at Cabinet level and Vice-President Hubert H. Humphrey as chairman. The council will study the steps necessary for the organization of oceanography at the overall governmental level. A committee report supporting this action was made by the President's Scientific Advisory Council, Panel on Oceanography, under the chairmanship of Gordon J. F. MacDonald.

A bill for the establishment of Sea Grant Colleges was also passed. It was signed by President Lyndon B. Johnson on October 15. Colleges established and supported under this bill will have programs that cover somewhat the same range of activities as those developed under the Land Grant College system, including oceanographic engineering, economy, law, medicine, and fishery science. F. F. KOCZY

OLD AGE. Federal government programs involving the elderly figured prominently in legislation passed by the Congress of the United States during 1966. Medicare was firmly established and other Social Security benefits were increased. The War on Poverty provided activity and assistance for many older people, and most of the states started community services under the Older Americans Act of 1965.

The federal government spends $25,000,000,000 each year to serve people over 65 years of age. Half of this amount consists of Social Security benefit payments; the remainder is used for services and salary payments to older people.

Medicare. Despite the concern expressed by opponents of Medicare, the program got off to a smooth start on July 1. Hospitals and doctors reported only slight increases in numbers of patients aged 65 and over, although Social Security offices were kept busy with the work of enrolling millions of people in the program. Approximately 90 per cent of the population over 65 enrolled in the voluntary portion of Medicare. See MEDICARE.

Social Security. The Congress of the United States raised Social Security benefits 7 per cent for most retirees. It also liberalized other provisions, including an increase in the nonpenalty earnings of retirees under 72 from $1,200 to $1,500 a year.

War on Poverty. The War on Poverty enlisted a number of people over 65 as "warriors" and gave direct benefits to persons over 65 who are "poor" as defined by the Economic Opportunity Act.

In 1966, the Office of Economic Opportunity (OED) employed about 19,000 people over 65 in Community Action Programs (CAP). The number included 12,500 who were paid to work in one of the 467 local community "Medicare Alert" programs. Together with 21,000 nonpaid volunteers, they called on 4,300,000 persons to inform them about Medicare and to urge them to join the voluntary part of the plan.

Several other similar projects also employed older people, providing them with opportunity for activity and a chance to supplement income. In terms of numbers, the most important of these was the Health-Aid program. Under this program, about $20,000,000 will be spent in 1966-1967 for the special training of nonprofessional health workers over 45 years of age for jobs in hospitals, nursing homes, and private homes. Another was the Foster Grandparents program, which employed about 2,000 persons over 60 to work with handicapped children. About 350 persons over 65 worked for the Volunteers in Service to America (VISTA) program in 1966. An experimental program for retired farmers, called Operation Green Thumb, paid men to plant trees and shrubs along highways and in parks.

The Older Americans Act of 1965 stimulated most of the states in 1966 to set up Councils on Aging to plan community service centers for senior

Senior citizens can aid underprivileged children in many parts of the United States through VISTA (Volunteers in Service to America). Workers serve for a one-year period.

citizens. The service centers will be supported jointly by the local communities and by a federal fund of $5,000,000.

Wasted Talent. The government's search for active civic roles for retired people was dramatized by a bill, introduced in the Congress on March 8, 1966, by Senator George A. Smathers (D., Fla.). The bill proposed to establish the Talented American Senior Corps. The corps would use $15,000,000 a year to employ older persons for a variety of social services. The aim of the proposal is to illustrate the conviction of those who study the processes of aging that older people will benefit themselves as well as society by keeping active.

A report published during the year by Professor Wayne Dennis, professor of psychology at Brooklyn College, Brooklyn, N.Y., shed light on a much-debated question: At what age are creative scholars, scientists, and artists most productive? He reported on the ages at which 738 prominent persons had their works published. Most of them lived in the 19th century and all had lived to age 79 or over. He found that writers of literature and music reached their peak mainly in their 40s. Scientists, he said, reached their peak in their 40s, and historians and philosophers in their 60s. ROBERT J. HAVIGHURST

ONTARIO. See CANADA.
OPERA. See MUSIC.
OUTDOOR RECREATION. See CONSERVATION.

OUTER MONGOLIA, PEOPLE'S REPUBLIC OF, was the focus of ever-increasing attention by the Soviet Union because of its position along Communist China's northern borders. As Sino-Soviet relations continued to deteriorate, the Soviet Union sent top officials to Ulan Bator, Mongolia's capital, to conclude agreements–such as the one signed in January which called for a 20-year treaty of friendship and mutual assistance. To shore up security in the area, Russia was reportedly deploying troops along the Mongolian-Chinese borders.

In June, at the 15th Congress of the Mongolian Communist party held at Ulan Bator, determined efforts were made by the Mongolians to iron out Chinese and Russian differences. The results were negligible, however, as the Chinese refused to attend and the North Vietnamese walked out.

Massive floods hit the eastern areas during the late summer and Russian assistance was extensive. The United States offered help, but this was refused by the Mongolians.

Facts in Brief. Population: 1,100,000. Government: Chairman of the Presidium of the Great People's Khural Zhamsarangin Sambu; First Secretary of the People's Revolutionary Party and Premier Yumzhagin Tsedenbal. Monetary Unit: tughrik (4=U.S. $1). Foreign Trade: exports, $7,300,000; imports, $1,000,000. Principal Exports: cattle, hides, wool. JOHN N. STALKER

PAASIO, RAFAEL (1903-), a former printer who rose through the ranks in journalism and politics, was sworn in on May 27, 1966, as prime minister of Finland. His Social Democratic party, of which he had been chairman since 1963, had won an overwhelming victory in the elections held in March. As party chairman, Paasio succeeded Vaino Tanner, an outspoken anti-Communist. The change improved Finland's relations with its neighbor, the Soviet Union. See FINLAND.

Paasio was born in Uskela, Finland, in 1903. A printer during the 1920s and 1930s, he became editor in chief of the Labor party's newspaper, *Youth*, in 1938. In 1942, Paasio was made the editor in chief of a daily newspaper in Turku, the *Turun Paivalehti*.

Paasio was first elected to parliament in 1948. He was second minister for social affairs in two cabinets, one in 1951 and the other in 1958. From 1949 to 1966, he was chairman of parliament's foreign affairs committee.

Paasio was chairman of the Young Social Democratic Workers from 1941 to 1945. He has been a member of the Social Democratic Party Council since 1957. He was a member of the supervising board of the Finnish Broadcasting Corporation from 1949 to 1964, and board chairman from 1961 to 1964. His political outlook is regarded as slightly left of center. WALTER F. MORSE

PACIFIC ISLANDS received international attention in July, September, and October, when the French set off a series of nuclear explosions in the Society Islands. President Charles de Gaulle, on a world tour, witnessed a test there on September 11.

Other areas in the Pacific showed increasing development and self-dependence during 1966, with Samoa and the Fiji Islands leading the way. Australia, New Zealand, and the United States worked closely to bring these Southwest Pacific areas into closer relationship with each other.

The United States, as trustee of the vast reaches of Micronesia, faced perhaps one of the most difficult tasks of any nation with trusteeships in the Pacific. During the year, a new high commissioner was appointed for the area to streamline the trusteeship government. A substantial budget increase to facilitate health and educational development was also expected to follow. To stimulate Micronesian participation in various projects, the introduction of a large number of U.S. Peace Corps volunteers was also planned. The Congress of Micronesia also played an important role in administering some 30,000 islands in the area. JOHN N. STALKER

PAINTING AND SCULPTURE

The most dramatic, indeed tragic, story in the visual arts in 1966 was the flooding of Florence, Italy, by the waters of the Arno. Swollen by rains, the river overflowed its banks from November 3 to 5 and poured vast amounts of water, mud, and oil into the city, considered the Athens of the Renaissance. Buildings, sculpture, and paintings on fragile wood panels were damaged, some beyond repair. Still worse havoc seems to have been wreaked on the great libraries, which drew scholars from all over the world.

Among the paintings, the most serious loss was Cimabue's 13th century *Crucifixion*, in the Church of Santa Croce. Fra Angelico's 15th century *Crucifixion* was badly damaged, as was Uccello's fresco *Sacrifice and Drunkenness of Noah*, in the Santa Maria Novella, and Ghirlandaio's *Pietà*. Five of the 10 panels from the Ghiberti bronze doors of the Baptistery were torn off and buried in mud, but were later recovered. Many precious lesser works and articles of the decorative arts were damaged or lost.

The Beanery, an eerie example of "environmental art" by Edward Kienholz, drew crowds at Chicago's Art Institute.

Exhibitions. The first and largest of the loan exhibitions in the United States was the colossal retrospective of Matisse organized by the Art Gallery of the University of California, Los Angeles, to open its new galleries. It was also shown afterward at The Art Institute of Chicago and the Museum of Fine Arts, Boston. It included material from Matisse's family and a fine, middle period work from Picasso's collection. The show was very successful, but informed opinion insisted that the much smaller exhibition held later at the Museum of Modern Art in New York City gave a better impression of the artist's work.

The displays of Mondrian, organized in Toronto, Ont., and of Münch at the Guggenheim Museum in New York City revealed these northern masters at their most appealing. The long-awaited and longer-planned Turner show at the Museum of Modern Art in New York City was also immensely successful. Some viewers saw in Turner's swirling canvasses an example of certain phases of contemporary art that were more than a century ahead of their time.

The Art Institute of Chicago organized "Treasures from Poland," an exhibition covering eight centuries of Polish art, from the earlier Middle Ages through the end of the Romantic period. The great drawing card of the show was the superb group of 12 views of Warsaw and its vicinity by Bernardo Bellotto. The group reaffirmed Bellotto's claim to being the greatest of the Venetian view painters.

Show of Shows. The Philadelphia Museum of Art presented its long-planned examination of Manet; and the Mauritshuis in The Hague, The Netherlands, organized a justly praised exhibition devoted to Vermeer and his tradition. But the major show of the year was that held in Stockholm, Sweden. It was dedicated to Queen Christina, perhaps the greatest art patron and collector of the 17th century. The show was another of the brilliant series sponsored by the Council of Europe.

Anniversaries. The Cleveland Museum held an exhibition of its accessions of the last five years to commemorate its 50th anniversary, and the National Gallery of Art in Washington, D.C., celebrated its 25th anniversary. That so many fine things could still be acquired was itself a revealing fact. The Whitney Museum of American Art opened its new home with a controversial exterior but a superb interior admirably adapted to the showing of works of art (see MUSEUMS). The new wing of the Detroit Institute of Arts proved less successful.

The Market and Monet. The market continued on its ever-rising way and broke more records. The auctions of the G. David Thompson collection and that of Helena Rubenstein added unnecessary demonstrations that early 20th century art might as

Ready-Made Bouquet, a painting by the Belgian surrealist, René Magritte, was included in a U.S. exhibition of his works.

well be made of platinum or uranium, as far as commercial values go. And the prices of fine old masters kept rising, too. Actually, the fine master works really are scarcer than ever, and unless major discoveries are made, the end of the road is not far off in certain categories. But discoveries are still being made, as, for example, the collection of Monet's son which emerged in February from the almost total obscurity of his country house. It contained many paintings by Monet and others by Renoir, Delacroix, Gauguin, Manet, and Pissaro.

Public Sculpture. In the rather neglected and difficult field of public art, the main plaza of Lincoln Center in New York City showed as its principal ornament an especially dull Henry Moore bronze. The one exciting moment in the field of public ornament came in Chicago in the early autumn, when it was announced that Picasso had presented the city his design for a monumental steel decoration, some 50 feet high, for the new Civic Center. He gave the original design to The Art Institute of Chicago. The design and the model suggest that the old magician has created something that will both enchant and delight when it is seen in front of an enormous steel building done in the now standard and rather monotonous modern vernacular (see CHICAGO). See also DEATHS OF NOTABLE PERSONS.

JOHN MAXON

The *Crucifixion* by Cimabue, *left,* was among works ravaged by floods that struck Florence in November. Detail, *right,* shows extent of the damage wrought upon this Masterwork of 13th century art.

PAKISTAN remained a country divided, geographically as well as politically, in 1966. Only a sense of patriotism, and a common faith–the Islamic religion–held East and West Pakistan together as a nation. East Pakistan, with 55 per cent of the population, earns most of Pakistan's foreign exchange. Yet 70 per cent of the civil service, 90 per cent of the army, and most business and industry was in West Pakistani hands. In the war with India over Kashmir, that erupted in 1965, East Pakistan–guarded by only one of Pakistan's nine divisions–felt isolated and unprotected. Its economy, which depended heavily on trade with India, was badly dislocated by the war.

East Pakistan's leading political party, the Awami League, under the leadership of Sheik Mujibur Rahman, continued to press for full autonomy, except in the areas of defense and foreign affairs. Rahman's arrest, along with 20 other leaders of the party, led to widespread riots in Dacca, Narayanganj, and Tejgaon. President Mohammed Ayub Khan, however, quickly quelled the disturbances.

Bhutto Resigns. President Ayub Khan also effected the resignation of Foreign Minister Zulfikar Ali Bhutto, whose strong anti-Indian sentiments and resentment over the signing of the Tashkent Agreements with India were not in keeping with the peaceful "Spirit of Tashkent" (see INDIA).

Economic Momentum. Pakistan experienced none of the economic slowdown that struck India after the Kashmir war. On the contrary, its gross national product increased by 4.8 per cent as compared with 4.1 per cent for the previous year. It did so despite a slowdown in foreign aid and a sharp decline in food output brought on by the worst drought of the century. Most of the economic upsurge was attributed to the government's encouragement of the free enterprise system and its drive for exports through imaginative laws.

Tashkent. In January, President Ayub Khan and the late Prime Minister Lal Bahadur Shastri of India signed the Tashkent Agreements, with the Soviet Union acting as mediator. The agreements called for mutual troop withdrawals; restoration of trade, travel, and communications; and a number of other steps designed to improve economic and social relations. But with the exception of troop withdrawals, which helped reduce tensions, peace remained elusive. Kashmir still continued to be a center of controversy and dozens of border incidents kept relations strained. India accused Pakistan of receiving arms from Communist China. Pakistan in turn protested Soviet arms aid to India.

Facts in Brief. Population: 109,800,000. Government: President Mohammed Ayub Khan. Monetary Unit: rupee (4.72 = U.S. $1). Foreign Trade: exports, $529,900,000; imports, $1,042,000,000. Principal Exports: cotton and cotton yarn, raw jute, tea, textiles. KEKI R. BHOTE

PANAMA. President Marco Aurelio Robles ordered the national guard into action early in June when student disorders flared up. The demonstrations, which were touched off by antigovernment agitators, were quickly suppressed.

Along with increasing internal and political stability, a new wave of prosperity was apparent. Economic growth was steady, and most Panamanians were enjoying better living standards than ever before. There was an apparent awareness that upheavals might compel the United States to look elsewhere for a new Atlantic-Pacific sea-level canal –a step the Panamanian government wished to avoid. During 1966, the United States and Panama held discussions regarding a change of status for the canal, as well as U.S. military bases and forces in the Canal Zone. There was also talk of a new sea-level canal. An executive agreement was reached for an on-the-ground site survey for a new passage.

Panama's gross national product rose an estimated 7 to 7.5 per cent in 1966 over the $615,000,000 figure for 1965, and it was expected to continue rising at this rate over the next few years.

Facts in Brief. Population: 1,308,000. Government: President Marco Aurelio Robles. Monetary Unit: balboa (1 = U.S. $1). Foreign Trade: exports, $132,200,000; imports, $378,600,000. Principal Exports: bananas, cotton, fish. MARY C. WEBSTER

PARAGUAY. See LATIN AMERICA.

PARENTS AND TEACHERS, NATIONAL CONGRESS OF (PTA) began a three-year program in 1966 to keep 7th and 8th grade children from smoking. Keys to the success of the project will be "room mothers" who are PTA representatives assigned to individual classrooms. These mothers will help to develop special school and home activities designed to involve other parents, teachers, and the children themselves.

The campaign will include three steps: (1) discussion of ways to help parents keep their children from smoking; (2) how to educate children to the hazards of smoking; and (3) how to develop specific community-wide programs related to the effort.

Initially, the program will be launched in the junior high schools in 20 states. The number will be increased annually, until 1969, when it is planned to have PTA no-smoking programs in all 50 states. During its first year, the project will be supported by a grant from the U.S. Public Health Service.

A major PTA project, one planned "to strengthen and expand community resources to safeguard the emotional health of children" was co-sponsored with the American Child Guidance Foundation. A booklet entitled "A PTA Guide for Community Services" was distributed to all local and state PTA units. In addition, a pilot project was planned which would enlist the cooperation of state PTA presidents, mental health associations, and parent and family life education groups. The three states initially selected for the pilot project were Connecticut, Kansas, and North Carolina.

About 2,000 members, representing 6,000 PTA groups from all sections of the United States and American schools overseas, attended the association's 70th annual convention. Meeting in Baltimore, Md., May 15 to 18, the group elected four regional vice-presidents: Mrs. W. J. Danforth, Ft. Worth, Tex.; Dr. Milton R. Litterst, Peoria, Ill.; Mrs. John M. Mallory, Endicott, N.Y.; and Joseph W. Showalter, Port Republic, Md.

Mrs. Jennelle Morehead, national PTA president, blamed "extremists" that "have infiltrated some PTAs and persuaded some to withdraw from the state and national congresses" for the loss of 81,000 members during the year. Such groups, she said, attempted to dictate material to be taught.

Delegates to the convention approved a change in the by-laws to increase the annual dues for the 11,710,000 members from five cents to 10 cents.

Awards. Ardath Ann Goldstein, 17, Community High School South, Downers Grove, Ill., won first prize in a PTA student essay contest with "Americans Not Everybody Knows." Other award winners were: Rose Sharp, 16, and Nancy Stack, 17, both of Mesquite High School, Mesquite, Tex.; and Joseph A. Spalding, 17, of St. Charles High School, Lebanon, Ky. JOSEPH P. ANDERSON

PAZHWAK, ABDUL RAHMAN (1918-), chairman of the Afghanistan delegation to the United Nations (UN) since 1958, became president of the UN General Assembly Sept. 20, 1966. He succeeded Muhammad Zafruli Khan of Pakistan. See UNITED NATIONS (UN).

Pazhwak is known as an expert parliamentarian and a hard worker. He was born in Kabul on March 7, 1918, and was educated in Afghanistan and Great Britain. Before he entered diplomatic service in 1946, he was editor of the daily newspaper *Islah.* He has written books in English and Persian.

Pazhwak was press attaché at the Afghan embassy in Washington, D.C., from 1949 to 1951, when he returned to Afghanistan to become a member of the foreign ministry. He also has been press attaché at Afghanistan's embassy in London and served briefly with the International Labor Organization. As chairman of the UN Human Rights Commission, he headed a mission of inquiry to South Vietnam in 1963 to study difficulties involving the Buddhists. He was also Afghanistan's representative to the Bandung Conference of Asian and African Nations in 1955.

A devout Moslem, Pazhwak often has shown little enthusiasm in dealing with women in public affairs. He has a family in Afghanistan, but his wife is not known to have accompanied him to New York City at any time. WALTER F. MORSE

PEACE CORPS. The largest agricultural effort ever undertaken by the Peace Corps was organized to help India cope with the critical problem of feeding its fast-growing population. The project was set in motion after a request was made to President Lyndon B. Johnson by Mrs. Indira Gandhi, the prime minister of India, during her visit to Washington, D.C., in March, 1966.

At the time of Mrs. Gandhi's visit, about 700 Peace Corps volunteers were in India. By the end of the year, the total reached 1,600 – more than in any other country – and 1,100 of these were occupied in an assault on the twin problems of agriculture and nutrition. Peace Corps volunteers worked at the village level, within the Indian government's Agricultural Extension Service, trying to motivate individual farmers to adopt modern methods and tools. New seeds were introduced, and instruction was given in irrigation and fertilization.

The volunteers also worked with the women of the villages, teaching them to prepare balanced meals for their children out of available food supplies. Some volunteers were engaged in a small pilot program in family planning.

Work Abroad. During 1966, the 25,000th volunteer left for overseas assignment and the 10,000th volunteer to complete a two-year tour returned to the United States. A record 10,000 volunteers were accepted and trained from the 42,223 persons who applied for service.

By the end of 1966, 12,006 volunteers were serving in 53 countries, compared to 9,912 in 46 countries at the end of 1965. Another 1,769 were in training in the United States.

Other Developments. Jack Hood Vaughn, 46-year-old career officer in the U.S. Department of State, was sworn in as the new director of the Peace Corps on its fifth anniversary, March 1, 1966. He succeeded R. Sargent Shriver, who had headed the agency since its creation. Shriver resigned so that he could devote full time to his other position as director of the Office of Economic Opportunity (OEO).

Thomas R. Dawson, 24, of Annapolis, Md., a Peace Corps volunteer stationed in Iran, was arrested by Russian border guards at Baku, U.S.S.R., on September 11, after he crossed the border without realizing it. The Russians kept him in jail for more than three weeks, and then released him.

During the year, volunteers were sent for the first time to Micronesia, the U.S.-administered Trust Territory of the Pacific, after a request from the United Nations in May. Some 3,000 applications were received. By the year's end, about 400 volunteers were on duty in the islands.

Volunteers were also sent for the first time to Chad, Botswana (formerly Bechuanaland), Mauritania and Libya, in Africa; Guyana (formerly British Guiana) and Paraguay in Latin America; and South Korea. WILLIAM MCGAFFIN

PERSONALITIES OF 1966. Americans chose President Lyndon B. Johnson as the man they admired most in 1966 for the fourth consecutive year. Second on the list for the fifth time in six years was former President Dwight D. Eisenhower, according to the Gallup Poll. Senator Robert F. Kennedy of New York was third for the second consecutive year. Newcomers to the list and their ranks were: United Nations Secretary-General U Thant (sixth), Senator Everett M. Dirksen of Illinois (seventh), Michigan Governor George W. Romney (eighth), and California Governor Ronald Reagan (tenth).

Former First Lady Mrs. Jacqueline Kennedy was the most admired woman for the fifth consecutive year, and First Lady Mrs. Lyndon B. Johnson was the second choice among Americans for the fourth consecutive year. Newcomer Mrs. Indira Gandhi, prime minister of India, was third. Mrs. George C. (Lurleen) Wallace, now governor of Alabama and also new on the list, was sixth.

Other personalities in the news during 1966 included the following:

Arntz, Heinz, of West Germany, played the piano for 1,054 hours between August 18 and October 1. He began his marathon in Düsseldorf, playing 22 hours a day. He maintained this routine while going by truck to Bremerhaven, and on board the liner *United States* across the Atlantic to New York City. From there he went by truck to the Long Island Fair at the Roosevelt Raceway grounds. He ended his marathon at 1:00 P.M. on October 1, saying, "I think I'll play concerts now." Arntz, age 67, played for 1,003 hours in Nancy, France, in December, 1965.

Bennett, Charles E., Democratic U.S. Representative from Florida, on June 6, completed 15 years in the House of Representatives without missing a roll call vote, setting a congressional record. He cast 1,554 votes. His last miss was on June 5, 1951, when he went to Michigan after learning no roll calls were scheduled. But during his absence the House voted on a District of Columbia traffic law. Bennett was first elected to the House on Nov. 2, 1948.

Boone, Daniel VI, operates a self-built model Union Pacific train for tourists at Burnsville, N.C. He is a direct descendant of Kentucky frontiersman Daniel Boone (1734-1820). Daniel VI also has a log cabin museum in Burnsville, and displays such novelties as his first model engine and antique forging tools.

Bradley, Reginald, received a U.S. Army medal for service in an Indian campaign on May 11, 72 years after he was discharged as a cavalry sergeant. Oliver E. Meadows, staff director of the House Committee on Veterans Affairs, went to San Francisco to present the medal to Bradley. He is now 98 years old.

Calver, George W., the first official "family doctor" for the Congress of the United States, retired on October 11. He began what was to be a routine three-year tour of navy duty as attending physician to Congress in 1928. He became such a favorite that Congress enacted a law to prevent his assignment elsewhere. He also was advanced in rank to rear admiral, and voted $1,500 annual pay in addition to his admiral salary. Dr. Calver had been on active duty as a naval medical officer since 1913.

Clark, June, made medical history by sneezing some 150,000 times during a 154-day period, between early January and June. The efforts of 130 doctors failed to stop her sneezing. Six days of chemically induced sleep gave the 17-year-old Miami (Fla.) girl relief, but failed as a cure. Finally, June was treated with an operant conditioning device at the Coral Gables Veterans Administration Hospital. The abnormal sneezes, which were occurring every 40 seconds, stopped after five hours of the mild electric-shock treatment.

Cole, George, and his family migrated from Kenya in Africa to New Zealand. They sailed from their home near Mombasa in a homemade, 40-foot boat *Galinule* on January 8, and arrived in northern New Zealand on November 8. Aboard was Mrs. Cole, a daughter and son in their 20s, and Mrs. Emily Cole, age 92. Grandmother Cole knitted sweaters during the 10,400-mile ocean voyage.

Another Custer Gets Scalped

James Holly Custer II was born in March. His birth announcement read:

Old Sitting Bull got Uncle George,
Finished him off at his last stand.
But here am I all safe and sound,
A wee bit small, but in command.

Young Custer is a great-great-great-great-great nephew of Indian-fighter George A. Custer who was killed in the Battle of the Little Big Horn (Montana, 1876). James was subjected to his first haircut in September. An Apache-Navaho-Mohave barber, Sally Fraijo, did the scalping in Phoenix, Ariz.

Dayton, Mona, was presented with the Teacher-of-the-Year award at a White House ceremony on April 5. The first grade teacher of Tucson, Ariz., gave President Johnson an album of drawings and letters from her pupils at the Walter Douglas School. Mrs. Dayton,

New York Mayor John Lindsay, *left,* led his city hall team against members of the press in a touch football game in Central Park.

the mother of four grown children, first attempts to stimulate "the often-neglected imaginations" of her pupils. "Some have never been talked to. They've never heard the *Three Little Bears*. All they have is television, or a baby-sitter, or an empty house," she said. She teaches children to speak full sentences and express their ideas before teaching them to read and write. "It's *their* experience, *their* world, that's the important thing," Mrs. Dayton explained.

Dinges, Madeline, won first place in the national collegiate sculpture competition with her portrait bust of U.S. Senator Everett M. Dirksen (R., Ill.). It features the Senate Minority Leader speaking, with mouth open. Asked if he objected, Dirksen said, "Oh no, it wouldn't be natural without it." Miss Dinges is a graduate of Monticello College, Godfrey, Ill. Her prize sculpture was to be placed in the Cape Coral (Fla.) "Garden of Patriots."

Durham, Elliot, Sheriff of Nottingham, England, issued a pardon to Robin Hood and his merry men in October. "I, the sheriff of Nottingham, do hereby exonerate Robin Hood and your archers from all accusations of acts contrary to law and order of the past." He read it in Sherwood Forest, the legendary gentleman outlaw's base of operation back in the 1100s and the 1200s.

Edwards, Hartley Benson, bugler for General of the Armies John J. Pershing in World War I, played *Taps* on his old instrument for the last time on May 29. He then presented it to the Smithsonian Institution in Washington, D.C. Edwards, now 71, blew *Taps* on the same bugle at 11:00 A.M., Nov. 11, 1918, beside an old boxcar near Toul, France, marking the end of fighting in that first great world war.

Fuqua, Janice, of Valley, Wyo., was the only graduate at the town's elementary school in May. U.S. Senator Milward Lee Simpson (R., Wyo.) delivered the commencement address. He is an old friend of the Fuqua family.

Banana Serenade

Ted Hamey, a New South Wales (Australia) farmer serenades his banana crop to get bigger and better production. The "music" is a loud brass blast broadcast through a loudspeaker system. The area that was exposed to this music for a 15-month period produced the best crop on his plantation, which is located at Coff's Harbor.

Hockenjos, William, of Florham Park (N.J.) turned in his driver's license in November to the New Jersey Automobile Club, and also his annual membership bill. Enclosed was the following explanation: "I'm returning the bill because I am 96, and I think it's about time I stopped driving."

Holt, Bertha M., of Creswell, Ore., was chosen American Mother of the Year by the American Mothers Committee, Inc. She is the mother of six children, and eight adopted Korean war orphans.

Houchens, Mary, of Cincinnati, Ohio, a housewife and mother of seven children, had a telephone booth installed in her farmhouse kitchen. "Now I can look through the glass and keep an eye on the children (ages 10 and under), and still have privacy."

A Cool, Cool Wedding

Sharon Ice and **Wesley Blizzard,** teachers in Columbus, Ohio, were married in June. They started dating because their fellow teachers thought there was humor in their names.

Johnson, Susan, of Baltimore, Md., and Curt Nagel were married on August 6, the same day that President

With Broadway star Carol Channing as his partner, Secretary of the Treasury Henry Fowler proved he could dance the frug.

Johnson's daughter Luci Baines and Patrick John Nugent were married. Susan, unaware of Luci's plans, chose August 6 because Curt was expecting to be sent to South Vietnam. It turned out that Susan and Luci were both born on July 2, 1947, both are Roman Catholics, both planned a nursing career, and both their husbands entered military service on Nov. 28, 1965. Luci chose the Immaculate Heart of Mary's (Susan's church in Baltimore) choir and organist to sing and play at her wedding. Susan's father, Albert W. Johnson, is also a Democrat.

Katzen, Sally, was elected editor in chief of the *Michigan Law Review* in April, the first girl to head the scholarly 65-year-old publication. The University of Michigan second-year law student directs an eight-member staff and 24 associate and assistant editors. They are all men.

Koufax, Sandy, the Los Angeles Dodgers' star pitcher, signed a 10-year contract with the National Broadcasting Company just before the end of the year. He expects to do NBC's baseball color commentary at first, and hopes it works into other things. Koufax, who quit the game after the 1966 season because of arthritis, said, "I don't want to maim myself. I might throw a pitch and shatter the arm." See BASEBALL.

Laise, Carol (Caroline) C., the first woman to serve as U.S. Ambassador to the Himalayan kingdom of Nepal, assumed her new duties in October. She and U.S. Ambassador-at-Large Ellsworth Bunker were married in Miss Laise's official residence in Katmandu (Nepal capital) on Jan. 3, 1967. This is believed to be the first time that two U.S. ambassadors were married to each other while both were on active duty. Madame Ambassador will continue to use her maiden name professionally.

Lopez, John, of Brooklyn, N.Y., is the first Puerto Rican to serve as a page in the U.S. Congress. He was sworn into office on March 28, by U.S. Senator Jacob J. Javits (R., N.Y.). He appointed John a Senate page.

McVeigh, Linda, is the first girl to serve as managing editor of Harvard University's 93-year-old student daily newspaper, the *Crimson*. She is a National Merit scholar from Los Angeles, majoring in American history and literature at Radcliffe College.

Nun Joins Actors Equity

Sister Marita Michenfelder of the Sisters of Loretto Roman Catholic religious order and a teacher at the Webster College for women in Webster Groves, Mo., qualified for Actors Equity membership as director of *Twelfth Night*. The play was produced at Webster's new Loretto-Hilton Center on July 1.

Poff, Richard H., Republican U.S. Representative from Virginia, was initiated into the Phi Kappa Phi social fraternity in November. He had been a pledge since his undergraduate days at Roanoke College in the early 1940s. World War II service and other things delayed the initiation. Poff was first elected to Congress in 1952.

Post, Mrs. Elizabeth L., a granddaughter-in-law of the late Emily Price Post (1873?-1960), supervised the 1965 (11th) edition of *Etiquette* (first published in 1922). She added new chapters on such subjects as servantless entertaining and teen-agers, and gave less space to information no longer needed today. "The single greatest change in etiquette," Elizabeth Post said, "is that effected by the informality of our life today. . . . In every way we are less rigid and formal than when Emily Post was in her prime."

Senator Everett M. Dirksen of Illinois poses with a prize-winning likeness created by Madeline Dinges, a student at Monticello College.

During the celebration of American Week in Monaco, Princess Grace demonstrated how baseball is played in the United States.

Ryan, Sister Michael Thérèse, of Worcester, Mass., is perhaps Africa's only flying nun. She has been flying in supplies and taking out the sick from the tiny Roman Catholic mission at Lorugumu, Kenya, since learning to pilot an airplane in 1963. She and three other nuns have living quarters at the mission, and operate a school and a four-bed dispensary.

A Dream Come True

Pamela Sue Smith attended the wedding of Netherlands Crown Princess Beatrix in Amsterdam on March 10. It all started with a 7th grade project of writing to important people in foreign countries. Pamela, who lives in Patchogue, N.Y., chose Queen Juliana of The Netherlands. She received replies from a lady-in-waiting. Then there was a rumor that the 12-year-old girl had been invited to the royal wedding. She confided to the director of The Netherlands Tourist Office that it was not true. He complimented her on her honesty, and then said, "Let's make a dream come true." Pamela was provided with a passport, a plane ticket, an official wedding invitation, and arrived in time for the ceremonies. Pamela Sue's visit to The Netherlands did not end until March 12, when she took a plane back to New York City.

Steinbeck, John, a 19-year-old army private and son of author John Steinbeck, was sent to South Vietnam in the summer. His father, who says no war is good, was unhappy, but said the boy wanted to go. He further explained, "If your country's in it, you're in it."

Swansburg, Jr., Mr. and Mrs. Donald E., the parents of two boys in Winthrop, Mass., were expecting another boy in July. But to everyone's surprise, Mrs. Swansburg had twin daughters, the first girls born in the Swansburg family in 78 years.

Watts, Sergeant Custer, serving with the U.S. Army in South Vietnam, received a letter from his draft board in Tazewell, Tenn., asking why he had not registered for the draft. The sergeant decided to ask the board to defer his case until he returned home. Custer is a veteran of the World War II D-Day landing in Normandy, and the possessor of two Silver Stars and three Purple Hearts.

Wilson, Mary, wife of the British Prime Minister Harold Wilson, received her first check as a poet and it came from Moscow. The Wilsons visited Russia in February, and the Soviet government newspaper *Izvestia* published her 18-line "After the Bomb." The poem begins:

After the bomb had fallen,
After the last sad cry
When the earth was a burnt-out cinder
Drifting across the sky . . .

Wylie, Barbara, and Gyale Lama were married on May 16, in the village of Phaphlu, Nepal. It was reported to be the first marriage between an American woman and a Sherpa. Miss Wylie, formerly of Ypsilanti, Mich., was serving as a United States Peace Corps teacher in the mountain village. The Sherpa people are noted mountain climbers, and often serve as guides with expeditions in the Himalayas.

York, William, is serving in South Vietnam in the Marine Corps. His father, Woodrow Wilson York of Rockwood, Tenn., and four uncles all served in the army as did their famous father, World War I Congressional Medal of Honor infantryman Sergeant Alvin C. York (1887-1964). William broke family tradition and enlisted in the marines in 1965. "I heard the Marine Corps was the best outfit, and I wanted to be part of the best."

PERU. See Latin America.

PET. A law to prevent the use of stolen pets in medical research and to require humane care and treatment of all animals used in such research was passed by Congress in 1966. President Lyndon B. Johnson, in signing the measure in August, noted that medical and scientific progress requires a use of animals and the law will not interfere with legitimate research. "But," he added, "science and research do not compel us to tolerate the kind of inhumanity which has been involved in the business of supplying stolen animals to laboratories or which is sometimes involved in the careless and callous handling of animals in some of our laboratories."

At the 90th Westminster Kennel Club dog show in New York City in February, best-in-show honors went to Champion Zeloy Mooremaides, a wire-haired fox terrier owned by Mrs. Marion G. Bunker of Pebble Beach, Calif. It was the 16th time a fox terrier had taken best-in-show honors, and the 12th time a wire-haired variety had won. No other breed has taken as many best-in-show honors in the New York show. The Westminster show drew 2,557 entries.

At the country's biggest dog show (3,420 entries), the International Kennel Club event at Chicago in April, best-in-show went to an old English sheep dog, Champion Fezziwig Raggedy Andy, owned by Mr. and Mrs. Hendrik Van Rensselaer of Basking Ridge, N.J.

Three of President Lyndon B. Johnson's beagle puppies romp on the White House lawn with a group of admiring press photographers.

American Kennel Club registration figures showed the poodle continuing as the most popular breed of dog in the United States. Next in line, in the same order as they had been since 1963, were German shepherds, beagles, dachshunds, and chihuahuas. American Kennel Club reached a milestone in its 82-year history in April when it registered its 10,000,000th dog, Eddie's Ginger, a golden retriever owned by 11-year-old Edwin L. Miller, of Pawling, N.Y.

Him, the famous pet beagle of President Johnson and his family, was killed in June when it was hit by a White House limousine while chasing a squirrel on the White House grounds. Him left two daughters, Pecosa and Kim, both White House pets. Him's equally famous sister, Her, died in 1964 after swallowing a stone.

A collie, appropriately named Hero, was awarded the 13th annual Ken-L-Ration Dog Hero medal. The collie, owned by the George Jolley family of Priest River, Idaho, saved the life of the Jolley's three-year-old son by diverting a horse that was charging at the boy. The dog bit the horse's nose to turn it away.

Cats. In winning *Cat of the Year* honors, Quadruple Grand Champion and International Champion Pharaoh Ramses II, a ruddy Abyssinian male, became the highest scoring cat in U.S. cat show history by running up 4,449 points in certified cat shows. No other cat ever scored more than 3,475 points in any season. Pharaoh is owned by Mrs. Kim Everett of Portland, Ore. *Opposite Sex Cat of the Year* was Grand Champion MaKhan-Da Willa, a seal point Siamese female, owned by Mary Frances Platt of Houston, Tex. *Longhair of the Year* was Grand Champion Larks-Purr Precious of Castilia, a blue cream female Persian that won Kitten of the Year honors in 1965 and is owned by Marcena Myers of Aliquippa, Pa., and Mrs. Merald Hoag of Rockville, Md. Mrs. Hoag also owned the *Opposite Sex Longhair of the Year*, Skyway's Eric of Normont, a red Persian male. Designated *Kitten of the Year* was Gray-Ivy Wee Wonder, a chinchilla Persian female, owned by Grace Over of Pasadena, Calif.

Gerbils. A desert rodent that is clean, odorless, friendly, eats little, and never bites invaded the pet market during 1966. Called the Mongolian gerbil, the animal is only four inches long (plus three inches of tufted tail), looks like a cross between a hamster and a rat, and leaps like a tiny kangaroo. Gerbils were first brought to the United States for medical research 11 years ago, but only recently moved into the pet market.

All these animals seem to need to be happy is an 8 x 21-inch cage carpeted with wood shavings and some objects to run around and jump over. They are indefatigably curious. They are also monogamous.

THEODORE M. O'LEARY

PETROLEUM AND GAS. U.S. motorists spent nearly $18,000,000,000 (including taxes) to buy gasoline in 1966. There were 2,000,000 persons working directly or indirectly in the U.S. oil industry. More than 300,000 gas stations served the public. Nearly 3,000,000 persons owned oil company stock, valued at more than $80,000,000,000. And the industry spent an average of $18,000,000 a day on exploration, development, and new facilities.

Despite the expenditures to expand supplies and facilities, production could not keep pace with the increasing demand. With continued general prosperity and an ever-greater number of automobiles on the road, demand jumped 4.7 per cent during the year to 11,800,000 barrels a day–substantially above the recent yearly increases of about 3 per cent. Consequently, prices of most oil products firmed. Gasoline "price wars" were rare in 1966. Virtually every major oil company reported substantial increases in sales and profits. The 15 major domestic producers' first nine-month earnings were 17.5 per cent higher than those of the 1965 period. The five major U.S. firms in the international group posted profit gains of 11 per cent.

World Oil. Outside the United States, consumption of petroleum products continued to spurt. In 1966, "Free Foreign World" demand jumped about 10 per cent–more than double the U.S. rate. Daily demand rose to nearly 16,000,000 barrels; the U.S. demand was less than 12,000,000 barrels a day. As short a time ago as 1955, that relationship was reversed: 8,460,000 U.S. barrels to 6,027,000 other.

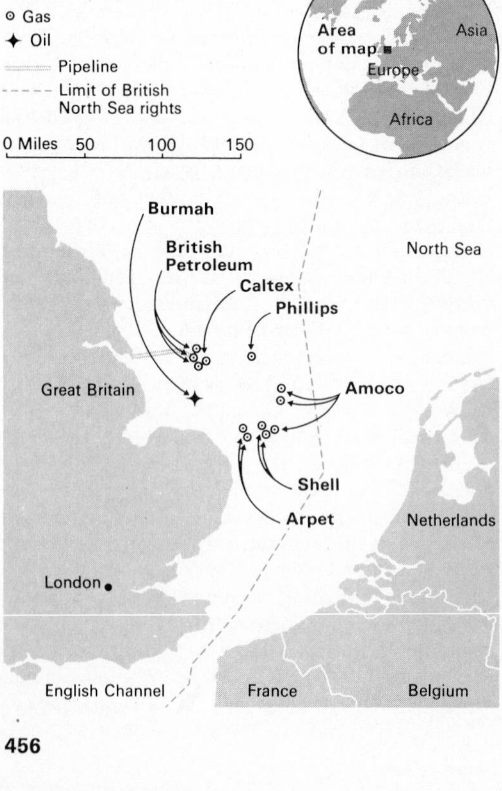

Exploration for new sources of petroleum continued apace, to meet rising world-wide demand. Within the United States, however, it was clear in 1966 that truly major increases in petroleum supplies were going to have to come largely from improved methods of recovering oil from old fields, from Alaskan reserves, and from offshore drilling. To date, only Louisiana has developed significant offshore production. Drilling off Texas has discovered more natural gas than oil, while the California effort mostly held promise for the future. During the year, the first significant production started flowing from Alaska's Cook Inlet, with its estimated reserves of 500,000,000 barrels of oil and a trillion cubic feet of gas.

The total U.S. proven oil reserves–in 30 states–at the end of 1966 stood at about 41,000,000,000 barrels. In the rest of the Free World total reserves probably amounted to something like 300,000,000,000 barrels, mostly in the Middle East, Canada, North Africa, and Venezuela.

Australia was one of the hottest areas for exploration in 1966. A first major strike in Egypt's western desert was reported by Phillips Petroleum Company in December. Russia was said to have brought major new oil fields into production during the year, mainly in Siberia. But Soviet exports of oil slowed in 1966. And in Canada, the $240,000,000 Athabascan oil sands project neared completion. More than $160,000,000 had been spent by the end of 1966 to build steam and other processing plants to extract oil from Alberta's bituminous oil sands.

Natural Gas. Great Britain's hopes for supplies of North Sea gas in commercial quantities were confirmed in 1966 by a succession of offshore strikes. Since the first strike, by the British Petroleum Company (BP) in December, 1965, seven fields in all have been brought in, and BP has begun construction of a pipeline to England's mainland (see map). In December, the British Gas Council established a price to utilities ranging from 17.5 cents to 35 cents per 1,000 cubic feet. Corresponding prices for manufactured gas were $1.44 and $1.68. By the end of 1967, it was expected that more than half of Great Britain would be receiving North Sea gas and that total gas use would increase fourfold.

Across the North Sea, The Netherlands reported the discovery of a new gas field in Friesland province with estimated reserves of nine trillion cubic feet. That, added to the 39 trillion-cubic-foot Groningen field, gave a huge boost to the European Economic Community (EEC, or Common Market) supply. The EEC estimated that natural gas would supply 8 per cent of all its energy needs by 1970, double the 4 per cent level of 1965.

EDWIN W. DARBY

Britain's North Sea Gas and Oil Discoveries

PHILADELPHIA, its sights fixed on hopes for a big bicentennial observance of American Independence in 1976, revealed sweeping plans for improvement in regional mass transit and downtown redevelopment. Each plan hinges on the other. Together, they promised an approach to metropolitan and central city development that was said to be unsurpassed in the United States.

For commuters, a 10-year $460,000,000 program was announced in September by the Southeastern Pennsylvania Transportation Authority. It will bring Reading and Pennsylvania Railroad passengers directly into the city's main shopping district for the first time, extend the Broad Street Subway to the northeast and south, and make rail and bus fleets almost fully air-conditioned.

As detailed by the city's redevelopment authority and planning commission in October, a 15-year plan for the downtown Market Street East area will require $500,000,000 in public and private money. Some 28 blocks will be razed and rebuilt. The core of the project will be an eight-block-long air-conditioned link between City Hall, Independence Hall, and present transportation systems.

On November 8, Philadelphians approved bond issues totaling $115,250,000. Largest item was $46,000,000 for improvements to quadruple passenger capacity at Philadelphia International Airport by 1973. DONALD W. LIEF

Philippine President Ferdinand Marcos closes the Manila summit conference on Vietnam with the firm rap of his gavel.

PHILIPPINES, THE. President Ferdinand E. Marcos re-emphasized his nation's alliance with the United States during the year. Under his guidance, the nation took an active role in foreign affairs.

On July 14, the Philippines became the fourth foreign nation to commit a sizable force to South Vietnam, joining the United States, Australia, and South Korea. On that date, President Marcos signed into law a bill authorizing the dispatch of 2,000 combat engineers and security troops to the war-torn nation.

Most of the troops were to be used as engineers on military construction projects and on irrigation ditches in Tayninh province near the Cambodian border. Others would serve as security guards. The first contingent arrived in Saigon on September 11.

Asian Role. The growing importance of the Philippines' role in Southeast Asia was emphasized in September when the United States announced a heavy increase in its economic assistance. The United States agreed to provide approximately $45,000,000 for a series of agricultural, highway, and rural electrification programs. It was also agreed that the United States would equip the Philippine army – over a two-year period – with supplies necessary to carry out a rural construction program and simultaneously reduce Communist guerrilla influence in central Luzon. The cost would be between $16,000,000 and $20,000,000.

U.S. Visit. Shortly after the U.S.-Philippines pact was announced, President Marcos and his wife paid an official 17-day state visit to the United States. After a four-day stay in Washington, D.C., where he conferred with U.S. President Lyndon B. Johnson and addressed a joint session of Congress, Marcos and his wife visited New York City, Chicago, Ill., and Ann Arbor, Mich. Marcos addressed the United Nations General Assembly.

In October, Manila was the scene of a summit conference on the war in Vietnam. The participants included representatives of Australia, New Zealand, Thailand, South Korea, and South Vietnam. President Johnson represented the United States. See JOHNSON, LYNDON B.

Smuggling Problem. On the domestic front, smuggling remained a major problem. It was estimated that the evasion of customs duties in 1965 had cost the public treasury nearly $125,000,000. To tighten the government's antismuggling measures, President Marcos reshuffled command of the Philippine constabulary, the branch of government charged with combating smuggling.

Facts in Brief. Population: 34,041,000. Government: President Ferdinand Marcos. Monetary Unit: peso (3.89 = U.S. $1). Foreign Trade: exports, $768,000,000; imports, $895,100,000. Principal Exports: copra, sugar, wood. PAUL TULLIER

PHONOGRAPH RECORD. See RECORDINGS.

PHOTOGRAPHY, in 1966, saw the introduction of many camera models and accessories, and a veritable boom in lenses and electronics. Some manufacturers saved their unveilings for Photokina 66, the world's largest photo show, held in October at Cologne, Germany. There, 597 exhibitors from 23 countries showed over 1,000 cameras and countless other photographic items. New merchandise revealed the general swing to electronics for increased automation and better exposure control.

New Cameras included:

- Zeiss Ikon Contarex Electronic "35," first single-lens reflex with electronic focal-plane shutter, fully electronic self-timer, automatic exposure control, and remote release system.
- Rolleiflex SL 66, first 2¼ x 2¼-inch single-lens reflex with integral bellows, tilting lens board, and features obviating the need for accessories.
- Rollei 35, smallest full-frame 35mm camera taking standard 20- and 36-exposure film loads.
- Konica Auto-Reflex, fully automatic single-lens reflex with electric eye which couples automatically to a full range of interchangeable lenses.
- Kodak Instamatic 324 flashcube camera with *f*/2.8 lens and automatic exposure control, which sets proper film speed when a cartridge is inserted.
- The Linhof 220, medium format camera (2¼ x 2¾-inch) with automatic cocking and film transport, using 120 or 220 film, and with a new departure in design including a movie-type handgrip.
- General Aniline & Film Corp.'s Anscomatic 726 for 126 instant-load cartridges, with photo-cell control of exposure and flashcube advance.

Many of the cameras were immediately available, while others were not expected to reach U.S. dealers until the spring of 1967.

Lenses introduced in 1966 included the Zeiss Planar 50mm *f*/0.7, fastest camera lens in the world; Leitz Noctilux 50mm *f*/1.2, first high-quality aspheric lens; and Zeiss Hologon 15mm *f*/8, a completely new type of lens, 35mm format, distortion-free, and with a field of 110 degrees.

New exposure meters included the Zeiss Ikon Ikophot T, the first fully transistorized electronic meter with no moving parts. Signal lights on the meter indicate proper exposure, and scales range from two hours to 1/1,000 second, while ASA is from 6 to 3200. The Weston Ranger 9, with large computer dial, eye-level finder, and candles-per-square-foot indicator (for determining brightness range of subject) is versatile and easy to handle.

Film News. Kodak announced an improved high speed Ektachrome film, Type B, that provides better color reproduction with improved sharpness, less granularity, and no loss in film speed (ASA 125). Both the improved high speed Ektachrome (daylight) and Kodacolor-X became available in Kodapak cartridges for Instamatic cameras. General Aniline announced that its Super Hypan (ASA 500) and Versipan (ASA 125) black-and-white films were available for the first time in all sizes–sheets, rolls, and the new 4 x 5, 16-exposure film packs. An Anscochrome film developing outfit for processing color slides also was available.

Awards in 1966 in various categories of photography included the following:

28th Annual Newspaper National Snapshot Awards. Grand Prize Winners ($1,000 plus 30-day around-the-world photo safari for two): *Color*–Carl M. Steubing, Jr., Scotia, N.Y.; *Black-and-white*–William T. Hubbard, Akron, Ohio. Second Prize ($500 plus 21-day trip to Europe for two): *Color*–Tally O. Bowman, Hickory, N.C.; *Black-and-white*–Martin H. Miller, Silver Spring, Md. Third Prize ($250 plus 14-day deluxe trip to Mexico for two): *Color*–Harold Atkins, Wasilla, Alaska; *Black-and-white*–Martin Doll, Patterson, N.C. Fourth Prize ($100 plus 7-day trip to Hawaii for two): *Color*–W. R. Warren, Hamilton, Ont.; *Black-and-white*–Kenneth Watson, Madison, Wis. Fifth Prize ($100 plus 7-day trip to West Indies for two): *Color*–Mrs. Jane Clayton, Memphis, Tenn.; *Black-and-white*–Norman R. Settle, Hutchinson, Kans.

1966 Scholastic Photography Awards, sponsored by *Scholastic Magazine* and Eastman Kodak Co. $1,000 senior scholarship to Shelby Wilson, Palo Verde High School, Tucson, Ariz.; $100 first awards in three categories, plus three honorable mentions, to John Shearer, Woodlands High School, Hartsdale, N.Y.; five junior awards out of 15 won by 8 entrants from his school to Harold Pfohl, Benjamin Franklin Junior High School, San Francisco. There were a total of 305 national award winners representing 164 schools in 36 states.

21st Annual Collegiate Competition, sponsored by Kappa Alpha Mu (KAM), National Press Photographers Association (NPPA), University of Missouri School of Journalism, and World Book Encyclopedia Science Service, Inc. NPPA's Colonel William Lookadoo $500 Scholarship to Robert Madden, University of Missouri. First place winners–from Georgia State College: *Feature*, Noel Davis; from the University of Maryland: *News*, Ken Firestone; from Southern Illinois University: *Category X*, John Richardson; from the University of Missouri: *Portfolio* and *Picture Story*, Robert Madden; *Portrait/Personality*, Barry Fitzgerald; *Sports*, Mike Anderson; *Pictorial*, H. Edward Kim; *College Life*, Brad Bliss.

Third Annual High School Photographers' Competition, sponsored by KAM and NPPA: Top award winner and recipient of the Honeywell Academic Grant ($500 scholarship) to Hugh S. Tessendorf, Topeka (Kans.) High School; first and second place plaques to Richard Greenawalt, West High School, Davenport, Iowa; third place plaque to Paul Rohadfox, Central Technical High School, Syracuse, N.Y.

Photographic Society of America 1966 Progress Medal Award to Adolf Fassbender, Hon. FPSA, New York, master pictorialist, teacher, and international lecturer.

White House News Photographers Association 1966 Grand Award to NBC News cameraman Richard V. Norling.

1966 Pulitzer Prize for News Photography to Kyoichi Sawada, United Press International, for distinguished pictures from Vietnam.

Joseph A. Sprague Memorial Award by NPPA, to James R. Bennett of KLZ-TV, Denver, Colo.; Gail William Churchill of the *Nashville Tennessean.*

Sixth Annual Anscochrome of the Year Competition, sponsored by Ansco: $1,000 Grand Prize to Mrs. Ann Zaiser, of the Kelowna Camera Club in British Columbia, Canada.

FRANK E. FENNER

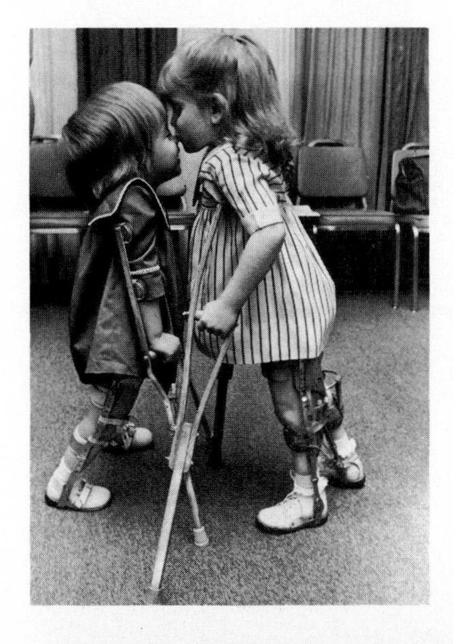

PICTURES OF THE YEAR/Larry Burrows, *Life* © Time Inc.

Among the award-winning pictures of 1966 were a picture of the March of Dimes poster girls greeting each other, by Tom Colburn of the *Houston Chronicle, upper left;* "Happy Birthday," by Mrs. Ann Zaiser of Kelowna, British Columbia, Canada, *upper right;* an unusual backlighted, downhill setting that was taken by William T. Hubbard of Akron, Ohio, *center;* and Shastri's widow in mourning as her husband lies in state, by Larry Burrows of *Life* magazine.

PHYSICS. Much attention was focused by physicists, in 1966, on the possibility that our universe existed in a contracted, intensely hot state at some time in the remote past. Robert H. Dicke of Princeton University, in 1965, suggested that if there ever was such a primordial "fireball," its thermal radiation might still be detectable in the form of microwaves. He published a discussion of this theory with three other Princeton colleagues, Phillip J. E. Peebles, Peter G. Roll, and David T. Wilkinson. They pointed out that if the universe were at one time filled by radiation from such a cosmic fireball with a temperature in excess of 10,000,000,000° K. (Kelvin scale, degrees centigrade above absolute zero), then the subsequent expansion of the universe would lower the energy of the radiation. It might now be detected by characteristic wave lengths of its electromagnetic spectrum.

Using a large antenna, Arno A. Penzias and Robert W. Wilson of the Bell Telephone Laboratories found a significant amount of cosmic background radiation at a wave length of 7.3 centimeters. During 1966, two more direct observations at different wave lengths were also reported. Roll and Wilkinson found radiation at 3.2 centimeters, and a team of British investigators reported radiation at a wave length of 20.7 centimeters.

Indirect evidence of possible background radiation resulted from studies of the absorption spectrum of interstellar cyanogen. Astronomers had long known that cyanogen molecules in interstellar space produce two lines on the absorption spectrum, indicating that some of the molecules are in a higher energy state than expected. The source of energy that produces this extra line had always been a mystery. Physicists at the University of California, Berkeley, and Columbia University studied the cyanogen line and found it showed a temperature of about 3° K., which could have been produced by cosmic radiation of .26 centimeter wave length.

All the reported data strongly support the theory that many billions of years ago the universe existed as a fireball. The question is still open as to whether this fireball was a single stage in the expansion of the universe or a recurring event in a periodically oscillating universe.

Matter-Antimatter Asymmetry. In scientific research it is not unusual for an experimental result, regarded as conclusive, to be called into question by the results of further experimentation. Such was the case, in 1966, with experiments involving the study of the neutral eta meson, a tiny short-lived particle which can decay into three pi mesons: one positively charged, one negatively charged, and one neutral. If the theory of matter-antimatter symmetry holds true in eta decay, the positive and negative pi mesons (which are antiparticles of one another) would on the average carry away equal amounts of energy in the decay.

By July, the most significant results had been reported by a collaboration of physicists from Columbia University and the State University of New York at Stony Brook. Eta mesons for this experiment were produced in a deuterium-filled bubble chamber at the Brookhaven National Laboratory. After a painstaking study of particle tracks in the bubble chamber, the experimenters were able to find 1,351 cases of eta decay. They found that the pi meson carried away a greater amount of energy 7.2 per cent more often than did the negative pi meson.

In September, however, physicists at the High Energy Physics Conference in Berkeley, Calif., reported contrary results obtained from other eta decay experiments. The most important of these took place at the Centre Europėen pour Recherches Nucléaires (CERN) in Geneva, Switzerland, where 10,665 eta decays were measured. In this experiment, positive pi mesons were found to have no significant excess energy whatever – a result consistent with the theory of matter-antimatter symmetry.

Thus the question of whether matter-antimatter symmetry or asymmetry exists in eta decay is unsettled, and physicists will continue to search for clarification. THOMAS O. WHITE

See also SCIENCE AND RESEARCH.

PLASTICS. See CHEMICAL INDUSTRY; MANUFACTURING.

POETRY. See EBERHART, RICHARD; LITERATURE.

POLAND celebrated the 1,000th anniversary of its founding as a Polish state as well as the nation's conversion to Christianity. The Roman Catholic Church stressed the religious aspects of the millennium and sought to demonstrate the continuing strength of Polish Catholicism. Official state ceremonies, however, put all the millennium emphases on Polish statehood, and linked them with the anniversary of victory in 1945.

Pope Paul VI was not permitted to come to Poland for celebrations, nor was Stefan Cardinal Wyszynski allowed to attend international ceremonies marking the anniversary in Italy and in the United States. Throughout the spring and summer, rival church and state celebrations often occurred in the same cities, symbolizing the conflict between the two entities.

Party Secretary Wladyslaw Gomulka lashed out on many occasions at the political role of the church and its alleged efforts to shift Poland's orientation to the West. Cardinal Wyszynski responded by sharply criticizing the state's harassment of the church and the officially promulgated atheism of the regime.

The 10th anniversary of the historic events of October, 1956, passed without any official notice, and with many of the achievements won that year partly lost. Agriculture had remained in private hands, and there was no sign of a desire to resume

Upturned sea of faces greets Stefan Cardinal Wyszyński during a rally celebrating the millennium of Roman Catholicism in Poland.

collectivization. But Poland continued to lag behind other Communist countries in the implementation of economic reforms.

Freedom of expression in the arts and in scholarship was subjected to increasing restrictions. Open police terror was not restored, but in January, three university lecturers were sentenced to three years in prison for disseminating opposition views.

Even the independent international position won for Poland in 1956 gave way to full support of the Soviet Union in all matters of foreign policy. Poland was slow in taking an openly critical stance in regard to Communist China, but in September it officially placed itself at the side of the Soviet Union. The restoration of diplomatic relations with Albania early in the year was followed almost immediately by a renewed breach (see ALBANIA). For undisclosed reasons, Poland did not take part in the military maneuvers of the Warsaw Pact powers. Relations between Poland and France remained satisfactory during the year.

Facts in Brief. Population: 32,100,000. Government: Communist Party First Secretary Wladyslaw Gomulka; Premier Josef Cyrankiewicz; President (Chairman of the State Council) Edward Ochab. Monetary Unit: zloty (23.94=U.S. $1). Foreign Trade: exports, $791,000,000; imports, $866,600,000. Principal Exports: coal and coke, freight cars, vegetables and fruits.

H. GORDON SKILLING

POPULATION, WORLD. The relentless growth in world population that had characterized previous years continued in 1966. At the end of World War II, the number of people in the world was increasing annually by 25,000,000. By 1966, the annual increase was 60,000,000, with the prospect of a population approaching 7,000,000,000 by the year 2000. Altogether, there were about 3,300,000,000 people on earth in mid-1966–or approximately 1,000,000,000 more than there were at the end of World War II.

Latin America continued to lead the world in the rate of population increase, with Africa and Asia not far behind. Birth rates in the three continents ranged from 30 to over 50 per 1,000 population; in the industrialized countries of the West, the rate ranged from 16 to 22. World-wide death rates continued to decline. According to a United Nations estimate, the world death rate was 20 per 1,000 before World War II, 19 per 1,000 in 1955, and 16 per 1,000 in 1966.

Because human numbers threatened to outrun the available food supply, there was growing concern over population growth among the world's leaders. During the past two years, food production had scarcely increased in Asia, Africa, and Latin America. World food reserves had been substantially depleted to feed more hungry mouths; U.S. grain stores that totaled about 115,000,000 metric tons in 1960 were perilously low. There were no substantial food reserves anywhere on earth; no sudden increase in world food production was in prospect. In India, there were serious food riots in 1966. See INDIA.

U.S. Concern. President Lyndon B. Johnson, who had repeatedly stressed the need for action on the population question, continued to do so in 1966. The Congress of the United States also was alert to the danger of the population crisis. It provided for making birth control information available to countries getting foreign aid and also set up procedures for birth control in anti-poverty programs. The Comstock Law of 1873, which barred distribution of birth control information and supplies, had been invalidated by court decisions. The Cone Law in Connecticut had been declared unconstitutional by the Supreme Court of the United States in 1965.

In recent years, 16 states had either repealed or amended laws barring dissemination of contraceptive information. By 1966, 21 states had made family planning a part of their health services.

The U.S. Department of Health, Education, and Welfare, the Department of the Interior, and the Department of Defense were all committed in various ways to support birth control programs. The Bureau of the Budget estimated that in fiscal 1967 the federal government would spend $25,300,000 on population control. ROBERT C. COOK

PORTER, KATHERINE ANNE (1890-), a distinguished writer of short stories, received the Pulitzer prize in fiction in 1966 for her volume, *The Collected Stories of Katherine Anne Porter*. Miss Porter had won wide popular acclaim for her first novel, *Ship of Fools* (1962). The book was some 20 years in the making. Based on a voyage to Germany just before World War II, it was made into a motion picture in 1966.

Miss Porter is best known for her short stories. Her first book, *Flowering Judas*, was published in 1930 and brought her wide critical praise, as did the publication of *Noon Wine* (1937). Her reputation was further enhanced by *Pale Horse, Pale Rider* (1939), and *The Leaning Tower* (1944). She is noted for the economy and polish of her style and her psychological insight in her portrayal of characters.

The writer was born Katherine Anne Maria Veronica Callista Russell Porter in Indian Creek, near San Antonio, Tex. Some of her best known stories are set in the Southwest. She is a descendant of a brother of Daniel Boone. The famous short-story writer O. Henry (William Sydney Porter) was her father's cousin.

Katherine Anne Porter was educated in private schools and in convents. Though she did not attend college, she holds honorary degrees from a number of colleges and universities.

See also PULITZER PRIZES.

PORTUGAL remained preoccupied with Angola and Mozambique during 1966. It stood firm on its policies toward the two overseas provinces in Africa but it did so in the face of uprisings, guerrilla warfare, and general condemnation by the African nations. The Portuguese government was particularly concerned over a British oil embargo on Rhodesia which involved the blocking of a pipeline from Beira, in Mozambique, to Feruka, Rhodesia. Aside from the fact that Mozambique's balance of payments was running at a monthly deficit of $3,750,000 because of the embargo, Portugal feared that the boycott would escalate into a blockade of Portuguese Africa. See AFRICA; RHODESIA.

Although Portugal was spending a third of its national income on defense, the economy was buoyant. Receipts from tourism were up 21 per cent over the preceding year, and industrial production had increased by 6.5 per cent. Inflation remained in check, while gold and foreign exchange reserves on hand were sufficient to finance imports for 15 months. In August, a consumer tax on luxury items took the place of the former general sales tax.

Facts in Brief. Population: 9,180,000. Government: President Américo Deus Rodrigues Tomaz; Premier António de Oliveira Salazar. Monetary Unit: escudo (28.64=U.S. $1). Foreign Trade: exports, $569,300,000; imports, $895,800,000. Principal Exports: cork, fish, wines. KENNETH BROWN

POST OFFICE. Nearly 10,000,000 pieces of mail lay undistributed in the post office at Chicago, Ill., during a mail slowdown in October, 1966. Three weeks passed before the emergency was over in spite of the hiring of extra help and the rerouting of incoming mail. At least four other big cities–Washington, D.C.; Milwaukee, Wis.; San Francisco, Calif.; and New York City–also reported record volumes of mail and corresponding processing problems during 1966.

Members of both houses of Congress promised to investigate the postal pile-up. "There is a backlog of mail in almost every major post office in the country," reported Senator Daniel Brewster (D., Md.). "What is going to happen as mail volume continues to skyrocket is collapse and chaos–unless we do something about it in a hurry."

Late in October, the Post Office Department moved to prevent a recurrence of the postal emergency during the Christmas season. With third-class mail up 10 per cent over 1965, Postmaster General Lawrence F. O'Brien borrowed $30,000,000 from the department's fourth quarter appropriation, "to move an unprecedented deluge" of early Christmas mail.

In a long-term effort to improve postal service, the Post Office Department signed a $22,700,000 contract for a source data system in May, 1966. In addition to supplying facts for decision-making, the

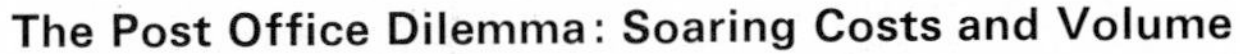

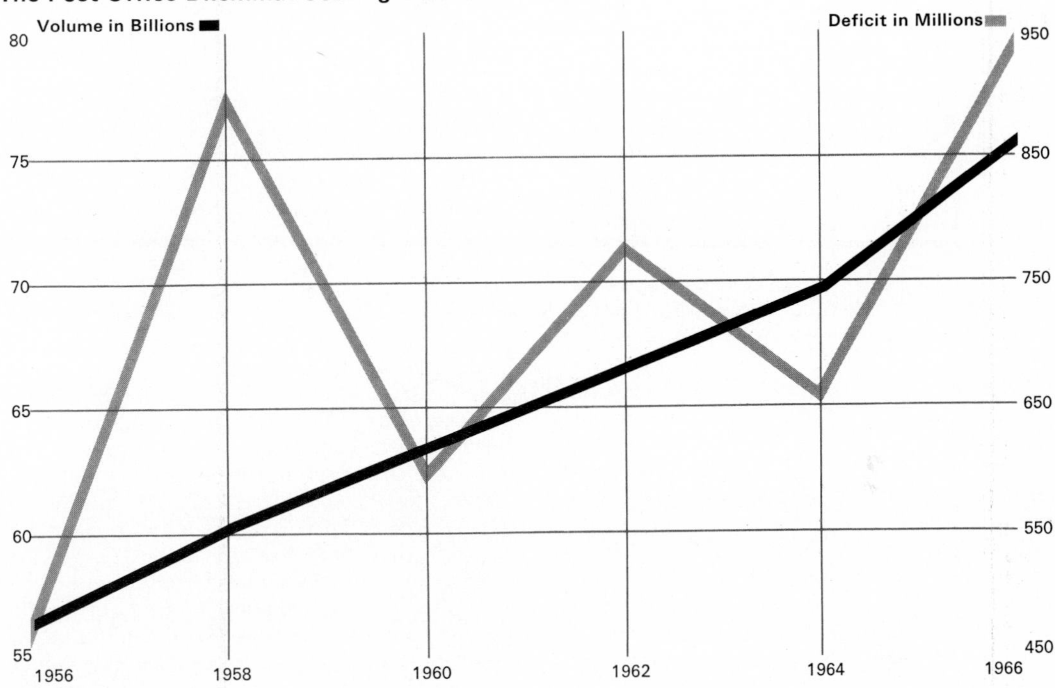

Source: Post Office Department

The great mail slowdown clogged the Chicago, Ill., post office in October, 1966, causing delays in delivery up to 10 days.

system will collect, classify, and analyze data such as mail volume, workloads, manpower fluctuations, and attendance records.

The department continued to promote use of the ZIP Code, in anticipation of the Jan. 1, 1967, deadline for mandatory coding of all bulk second- and third-class mail. It also announced in December that it would build and maintain its own new buildings as an economy measure.

End of Postal Savings. Congress terminated the postal savings system on March 28, 1966, because it has "outlived its usefulness." The system, instituted in 1911, had paid 2 per cent interest since its inception. At the time of closing, more than $147,000,000 in unredeemed certificates was still on deposit at post offices across the country.

New Postmasters. John R. Strachan became the first Negro to head the country's largest postal installation when he was sworn in as acting postmaster of New York City in November. Negro postmasters also head the offices at Chicago, Ill., and Los Angeles, Calif., the next largest cities in the United States, and 11 other first-class post offices.

Statistics. The 666,504 employees in the Post Office Department handled a total of 75,800,000,000 pieces of mail in fiscal 1966. The department received $5,840,000,000 in appropriations for fiscal 1967, an increase of $261,000,000 over 1966.

POULTRY. See AGRICULTURE.

POVERTY. President Lyndon B. Johnson continued to wage war on poverty in the United States, but at a pace only slightly greater than the previous year. Because of the budget problems posed by the costly war in Vietnam and inflationary pressures on the home front, the President decided to ask Congress for only $1,750,000,000 to finance the anti-poverty campaign in fiscal 1967. Congress responded by appropriating $1,600,000,000, which was only $100,000,000 more than the sum it allocated in the previous fiscal year.

The campaign to rescue millions of Americans who exist in conditions of poverty was as controversial in 1966 as it has been from its beginning, in 1964. The vast program was often criticized by Republicans, but generally defended by Democrats.

During the year the Office of Economic Opportunity (OEO), headed by 51-year-old R. Sargent Shriver, Jr., and allied government departments, carried out a wide variety of programs designed to root out poverty among Americans of all ages.

Head Start. In the summer of 1966, 573,000 prekindergarten children were sent to summer school for eight weeks and given medical and dental attention, at a cost of $97,000,000, to prepare them for entry into the public schools in September. In addition, 178,000 children were enrolled in a year-round, $83,000,000 Head Start program. Head Start was the most popular and most successful of the anti-poverty programs. A study of it, undertaken with OEO funds, concluded that it provided the preschool child with a thirst for further knowledge. It also concluded, however, that this thirst went largely unquenched, either because of subsequent poor teaching, or because of an uninspired curriculum in the public schools. See EDUCATION.

Community Action Programs (CAP) included a series of programs designed to mobilize public and private resources to fight poverty under local leadership. Head Start was one of these. In addition, free legal services for the poor were provided by 1,000 lawyers in 43 states, at a cost of $27,522, 944.

Upward Bound gave motivation and "catch-up" knowledge for a college career to 20,429 high school students on 225 college campuses in the summer of 1966. Its cost: $28,006,138.

Foster Grandparents Program furnished $5,089,003 for the employment of 3,000 low-income persons in their 60s to work with 6,000 neglected and deprived children in 27 states and in Puerto Rico.

Migrant and Seasonal Farmworkers were widely benefited by a $25,285,000 program of assistance in education, housing, and sanitation. About 800 centers were set up in more than 200 communities to provide a variety of services, including a preventive health program and counseling services.

The Nation's Economically Deprived

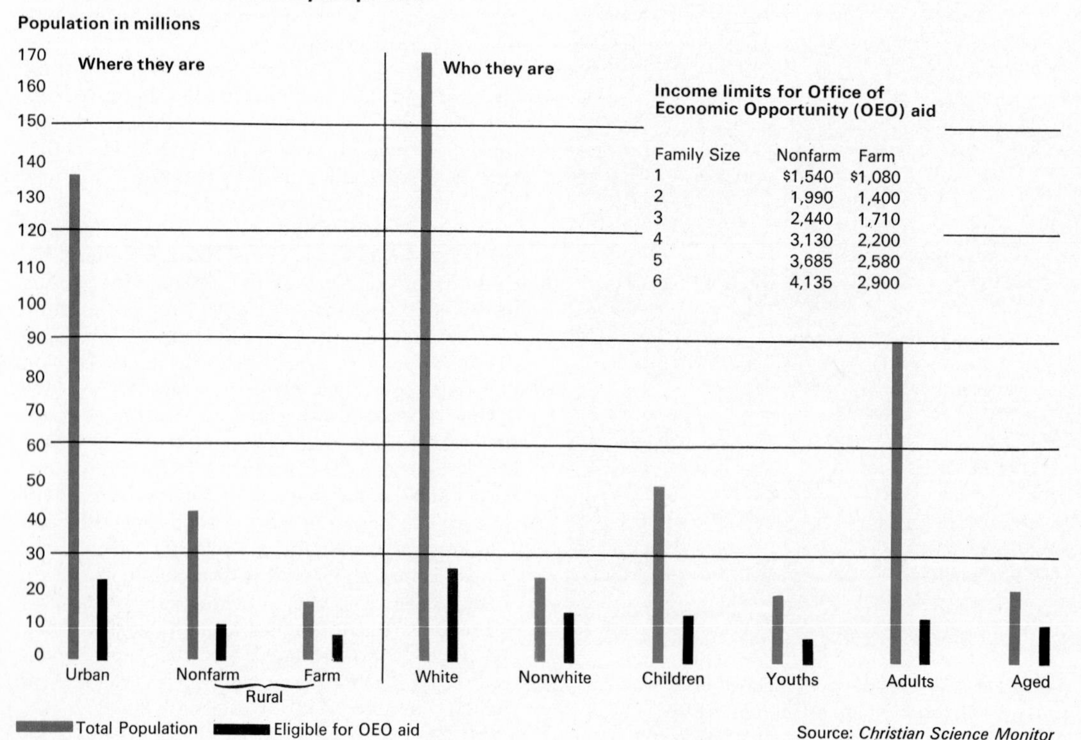

Income limits for Office of Economic Opportunity (OEO) aid

Family Size	Nonfarm	Farm
1	$1,540	$1,080
2	1,990	1,400
3	2,440	1,710
4	3,130	2,200
5	3,685	2,580
6	4,135	2,900

Source: *Christian Science Monitor*

Neighborhood Health Centers were set up on an experimental basis with $9,295,746 of OEO money in Denver, Colo.; Boston, Mass.; Chicago, Ill.; New York City; the Watts section of Los Angeles, Calif.; and in Bolivar County, Mississippi. These were intended to offer virtually all non-hospital medical services within one centrally located facility for all members of a family.

Job Corps. High school drop-outs from poor families were given a new chance with this program for young men and women, aged 16 to 22. Job Corps centers trained 25,341 young men and 3,676 young women for new vocational careers, at a cost of $303,277,417.

Some of the men at conservation centers concentrated on projects to preserve areas of natural beauty. Others, in urban centers, learned how to repair and maintain automobiles and boats; work as cooks and waiters; service appliances; work in machine shops; do welding, landscape gardening, and building maintenance. The young women were taught to be secretaries, store saleswomen, waitresses, cooks, hairdressers, and health workers.

VISTA. Trained specialists to work with the poor on 334 projects in 44 states were provided by the Volunteers in Service to America (VISTA) program, which cost $15,955,803. There were 3,592 volunteers from this domestic Peace Corps helping in both rural and urban areas.

Neighborhood Youth Corps, administered by the Department of Labor, created 528,672 part-time community service jobs for impoverished young persons, aged 16 through 21. The federal government contributed $266,139,096 of the total cost of the 1,478 hometown projects. Most of the youths were paid $1.25 an hour, which helped some stay in school, and others to return.

Adult Basic Education. About 11,000,000 American men and women over 18 have less than a sixth grade education. Hence, $34,122,227 was spent to provide instruction for about 335,700 adults to help them overcome illiteracy, which is both a cause and an effect of poverty.

Work Experience. Administered by the U.S. Department of Health, Education, and Welfare, this program provided work experience, training, and education for 84,820 unemployable heads of families on 274 projects. It cost $111,400,000.

Rural Loans. Farmers in the poverty belts were aided with 17,073 individual loans, totaling $27,264,266. In addition, rural cooperatives were benefited by 391 loans, totaling $4,708,461.

Small Business Loans. Small businessmen in poverty areas were helped with $17,251,184 in loans made, not on the applicants' credit rating, but on their character and know-how.

Outspoken Criticism of the anti-poverty program concentrated on about a half dozen Job Corps centers, where rough and rowdy behavior (rock throwing, car stoning, promiscuous behavior of some women in some of the camps) brought protests.

Hence, a new policy, raising the physical and mental requirements for acceptance in the Job Corps, was put into effect on June 13. Also, it was announced that corpsmen would be stationed at centers closer to their homes, with the hope that this would reduce the number of incidents between corpsmen and residents of surrounding neighborhoods.

In response to these difficulties, Congress gave the directors of Job Corps centers stronger authority to maintain discipline. It also enacted a new provision barring anti-poverty money to any persons who have promoted a riot or taken part in one, or who have engaged in activity which has damaged property or injured people.

Demonstrations, to air their grievances, were resorted to by some of the poor and some anti-poverty workers during the year. In April, 90 unemployed Negro plantation workers from Mississippi camped for five days in Lafayette Square, directly across from the White House. They were protesting a delay in the handling of their applications for $1,300,000 in anti-poverty funds. In May, about 300 anti-poverty workers picketed an OEO office in New York City to protest the OEO's $36,000,000 ceiling on funds for the city's war on poverty. The city had finally settled for this sum, although it originally requested $55,000,000.

Adam Clayton Powell (D., N.Y.), chairman of the House Education and Labor Committee, conducted an investigation into the administration of the War on Poverty. He failed to uncover any serious faults or wrongdoings. But the Republicans charged that the investigation was a whitewash. They contended that the OEO had fallen down on the administration of some of its programs. They urged the transfer of the Job Corps to the Department of Labor, and of Head Start to the Office of Education. They also declared that the anti-poverty program needed to be "liberated" from "waste, controversy, and the bad odor of political bossism."

OEO Director Shriver touched off a public quarrel when he cut off Head Start funds for the Child Development Group of Mississippi (CDGM). His action brought to a halt a program for 12,000 preschool children, most of them Negroes, in 28 Mississippi counties which had received some $7,000,000 in OEO funds during 1966.

CDGM representatives asserted that the funds were unfairly cut off. Labor leader Walter Reuther and a large number of religious leaders took a full-page advertisement in *The New York Times* on October 19 to suggest that Shriver may have knuckled under because of pressure from some political leaders. Shriver, in a letter to the *Times*, denied this. He said "payroll padding, nepotism, conflict of interest, and misuse of property" had forced him to take the action.

William McGaffin

101AB
HQ
HQ
1
ARMY

PRESIDENT OF THE UNITED STATES

President Lyndon Baines Johnson was first and foremost commander in chief of the armed forces during 1966. Criticism of U.S. policy in Vietnam mounted as the bombing of North Vietnam resumed early in the year and the number of U.S. soldiers at the fighting front increased. Most Americans, however, supported the President. Because of the grim reality of the Asian war and the threat of inflation, the President's plans for the Great Society were somewhat curtailed.

Early in the year, and again in the fall, President Johnson flew to the Pacific to confer with U.S. allies on the conduct of the war. On October 17, he left for a 17-day trip to Southeast Asia. He met for two days in Manila with six Asian allies–Australia, New Zealand, the Philippines, South Korea, South Vietnam, and Thailand.

At the close of the conference, on October 25, the allies issued a communiqué reaffirming their determination to secure freedom for South Vietnam and their concern for the future of all Asian and Pacific peoples. It declared that the people of South Vietnam would ask the allies to remove their troops within six months after "the military and subversive forces of North Vietnam are withdrawn, infiltration ceases, and the level of violence thus subsides."

On his way to the conference, President Johnson visited Samoa, New Zealand, and Australia. When the conference ended, he paid a surprise visit to U.S. troops in South Vietnam, and then traveled to Thailand, Malaysia, and South Korea before returning home via Alaska. Wherever he went, the President was welcomed by cheering crowds.

Declaration of Honolulu. Earlier in the year, on February 7 and 8, he conferred with South Vietnamese Premier Nguyen Cao Ky in Honolulu, Hawaii. At the close of the two-day conference, the two leaders issued the Declaration of Honolulu, stressing the importance of a combination of military action and civic reform to defeat the Communist forces of the National Liberation Front and North Vietnam.

The President moved immediately to implement the Declaration. Vice-President Hubert H. Humphrey and Secretary of Agriculture Orville L. Freeman, among others, left the next day (February 9)

Rain or shine, the press covers the goings and comings of the President. Here, he reviews troops at Fort Campbell, Kentucky.

The President, in a midsummer speechmaking swing into the Midwest's farms and cities, greets well-wishers during one of his motorcade's frequent stops in the streets of Des Moines, Iowa.

for Vietnam to make concrete suggestions for reform and reconstruction. See HUMPHREY, HUBERT H.; VIETNAM.

In March, President Johnson sent a civilian task force headed by Secretary of Health, Education, and Welfare John W. Gardner to Saigon. Later that same month, he announced that Robert W. Komer would be his special assistant for "peaceful reconstruction in Vietnam" and would go to Vietnam to study its needs along with Deputy Secretary of Defense Cyrus R. Vance.

In July, the President said, "We are ready to sit down at a conference table," under Red Cross auspices, to discuss treatment of war prisoners with North Vietnam. His suggestion was ignored by Hanoi. Responding to pressure at home and overseas to negotiate with North Vietnam, President Johnson stated firmly in September that the United States would offer a timetable for troop withdrawal when a similar Communist timetable was published. A month later, in Manila, the closely hedged six-month withdrawal timetable was offered.

In August, the President conferred at his Texas ranch with General William C. Westmoreland, commander of U.S. forces in Vietnam. After the conference, he asserted that a "Communist military take-over of South Vietnam is now impossible," but he admitted that there would be no quick victory.

Criticism of his Asian policy troubled the President throughout the year. It came from the aca-

demic world, from Republicans, and from prominent members of his own Democratic party, such as Senators J. William Fulbright of Arkansas and Robert F. Kennedy of New York. Late in February, the President dismissed any worry that the continuing public debate on Vietnam seriously challenged U.S. policy or would mislead the enemy into believing that America was divided. In March, he asked for–and got–a pledge of support for his Vietnam policy from a conference of 41 governors.

In May, at a speech at Princeton University, the President asked for support and understanding from the academic world. He took issue with Senator Fulbright's charge that the nation was "succumbing to the arrogance of power." Mr. Johnson said, "The exercise of power has meant for all of us . . . not arrogance but agony." Later that month, speaking to Democrats in Chicago, he attacked his critics as "nervous Nellies." After the bombing of fuel dumps and military installations near Hanoi and Haiphong in June and as the elections drew nearer, he defended his foreign policy more vigorously.

Foreign Policy. In other actions, the President:

- Ordered shipment of 3,000,000 additional tons of grain to India for famine relief, in February.
- Rejected French President Charles de Gaulle's bid for a bilateral approach to collective security and reaffirmed support for the North Atlantic Treaty Organization (NATO) with or without France, in an exchange of letters in March.

- Made his first major speech on African policy (to envoys from the member nations of the Organization of African Unity in May) and declared that the doctrine of white supremacy was repugnant to the United States.
- Proposed to the United Nations that a space treaty be negotiated declaring the moon and other celestial bodies off limits for military activity. In December, the United Nations General Assembly approved a treaty that would prohibit orbiting weapons of mass destruction or the placing of such weapons on the moon or other bodies in space. The President hailed the step as "the most important arms control development" since the 1963 limited atom-test ban treaty. He added that he would ask the Senate to ratify it by early in 1967. See DISARMAMENT; UNITED NATIONS.
- Made a major policy speech on China, declaring that "cooperation, not hostility, is the way of the future," in July.
- Wrote an article proposing a new era of Soviet-U.S. friendship in the September issue of *Amerika*, a U.S.-sponsored Russian-language publication distributed in the U.S.S.R.
- Called for a major shift in U.S. policy toward Eastern Europe and Germany. In a speech on October 7 in New York City, the President said that "the wound in Europe" must be healed through a growing reconciliation between West and East before Germany can be reunited. It was a bid for fostering more trade and closer ties between the United States and Western Europe, on one side, and Russia and its Eastern European satellites, on the other. See EUROPE; GERMANY; RUSSIA.

Travel Abroad. In April, the President and his entire family visited Mexico City, where some 25,000 cheering Mexicans met him at the airport. It was his first visit to a foreign capital since he assumed the presidency. In August, he met Canadian Prime Minister Lester B. Pearson at Campobello, New Brunswick, their sixth meeting.

In December, he walked half way across a bridge over the Rio Grande to greet Mexico's President, Gustavo Díaz Ordaz. The two chiefs of state then went to Ciudad Acuña to celebrate the joint construction of the Amistad (friendship) Dam. They called the project "an outstanding example of how two neighbor countries can resolve their common boundary problems with benefits to both."

Congress and the President did not harmonize as well as they did in 1965. He sent 25 major bills to Congress, but did not succeed in getting his way on all of them. His request for foreign aid was reduced. Congress said "no" to new civil rights legislation, repeal of Section 14 (b) of the Taft-Hartley Act, home rule for the District of Columbia, and federal control of gun sales.

Still, President Johnson professed himself well pleased with the second session of the 89th, the "Great Congress," he termed it. His budget for fiscal 1967, some $112,800,000,000, included a request for a $3,000,000,000 increase for welfare programs to further the Great Society. Congress gave the President most of what he asked for, including appropriations to meet the needs of the escalating war. See CONGRESS OF THE UNITED STATES.

Inflation was the President's most perplexing domestic problem in 1966. Butter, milk, automobiles, steel, and cigarettes–hundreds of items–carried higher price tags. The voluntary wage and price guidelines set up by the President's Council of Economic Advisers were defended by the President, criticized by some economists, and ignored by unions seeking higher wages and corporations seeking increased profits. See ECONOMY, THE.

In January, the administration reached a compromise with the steel companies to hold the line on steel prices, which they did until August. The President made a plea in March to all Americans, asking them to cut down on their buying because prices were "moving up too fast for comfort." He repeated the plea in May and July. Tobacco companies were urged by the White House to rescind a cigarette price rise scheduled for March 21. R. J. Reynolds Tobacco Company agreed, and five other companies trimmed the increase by 50 per cent. When price increases for the new 1967 cars were announced in September, the President was critical. Some of the increases later were revised downward (see AUTOMOBILE).

In September, the President asked Congress to suspend–until Jan. 1, 1968–tax incentives offered for business investment in new equipment and construction. Congress complied. On November 29, he announced at a press conference that federal programs totaling $5,300,000,000 would be cut back or canceled. Savings for the year ending June 30, 1967, would be about $3,000,000,000, he added.

Labor. The President intervened in two labor disputes during 1966. In July, he tried to help negotiate the airline strike that tied up the nation's air traffic for 43 days. But the settlement proposed by his advisers was rejected by the striking International Association of Machinists, who held out for a settlement that amounted to about 5 per cent in increased benefits–well above the President's wage-price guidelines of 3.2 per cent.

On October 17, President Johnson issued a Taft-Hartley Act injunction against electrical workers in scattered local strikes at General Electric plants. He declared that they were endangering production needed for the nation's war effort. See LABOR.

Civil Rights. The President asked Congress to ban racial discrimination in the selection of juries and in the sale, rental, and financing of all types of housing. He also requested better protection for civil rights workers and more power for federal enforcement of civil rights legislation. Congressional

A President is ever on duty, even in his White House bedroom, where he and former presidential aide Jack J. Valenti check official papers.

defeat of the Civil Rights Act of 1966 was attributed partly to white anxiety over race rioting and black racist propaganda. But some observers felt that the President did not push Congress hard enough to win passage of the bill.

Social unrest and racial rioting in urban slums in the summer provoked a presidential warning. He pointed out that Negroes are in a minority, only 10 per cent of the population, and that race rioting might endanger civil rights gains. See CIVIL RIGHTS.

The Campaigner. Between January 1 and the end of September, the President and Mrs. Johnson made 41 appearances in 23 states. In July, he took a 12-hour, nine-speech tour of Indiana, Kentucky, and Illinois. In August, his itinerary included an eight-speech trip to New York and all New England states but Connecticut and Massachusetts. Later, "nonpolitical" tours took him to Idaho, Colorado, and Oklahoma. In September, he stumped in Pennsylvania, West Virginia, Michigan, and Ohio.

Before he left for the Manila conference in October, the President said that his campaigning in the few days before the election would be limited. When he returned, impending surgery prevented him from further campaigning. See DEMOCRATIC PARTY; ELECTIONS; JOHNSON, LYNDON BAINES; REPUBLICAN PARTY.

The Draft. On July 2, the President appointed a National Advisory Commission on Selective Service to study the draft and make suggestions. In August, the President assured the nation that a "practical system of nonmilitary alternatives to the draft" was under study. See NATIONAL DEFENSE.

Visitors to the President in 1966 included:

In *March*, Indian Prime Minister Indira Gandhi; *April*, Southeast Asia Treaty Organization Secretary-General Jesús Vargas; *Late May and early June*, British Conservative party leader Edward Heath; *June*, First Deputy Chairman Rainer Barzel of the West German Christian Democratic Union, Nicaragua's president, the late René Schick Gutiérrez, Saudi Arabian King Faisal, and Australian Prime Minister Harold E. Holt.

July, British Prime Minister Harold Wilson, Bolivian President-elect René Barrientos Ortuño, and Guyana's Prime Minister Forbes Burnham; *August*, Israeli President Schneor Zalman Shazar; *September*, Philippine President Ferdinand E. Marcos, West German Chancellor Ludwig Erhard, Senegal's President Léopold S. Senghor, Indonesian Foreign Minister Adam Malik, Burmese Chief of State General Ne Win.

October, French Foreign Minister Maurice Couve de Murville, Soviet Foreign Minister Andrei A. Gromyko, British Foreign Secretary George Brown; and–in New York–UN Secretary-General U Thant and Laotian Premier Souvanna Phouma. CAROL L. THOMPSON

See also JOHNSON, LYNDON BAINES; U.S. GOVERNMENT; Section One, JAMES B. RESTON: FOCUS ON THE NATION.

PRINCE EDWARD ISLAND. See CANADA.

PRISON. See CRIME.

PRIZES. See AWARDS AND PRIZES; NOBEL PRIZES; PULITZER PRIZES.

PROTESTANT. Two conferences held in Europe in the summer and fall of 1966 dramatized differences among contemporary Protestants. They served to symbolize the two poles around which most Protestants organize their activity and orient their thought. In July, Protestant (and Orthodox) Christians met in Geneva, Switzerland, under the auspices of the World Council of Churches to discuss the role of Christians in today's revolutionary world. And in late October at Berlin, "conservative evangelicals" convened to discuss the role of individual Christians in evangelism today. The honorary chairman of the Berlin meeting was Billy Graham.

The Geneva Conference was ecumenical and socially oriented. It differed from previous convocations of its type in several respects. For the first time, such a conference was made up largely of laymen, young people, technical experts, and representatives of churches from "the Third World" of political neutralism and anticolonial social revolution. Only 173 of the 410 participants, including press-based observers, were clerics or were professional theologians.

Given the background of the delegates, Western churchmen were in the minority, and the social and political positions of their nations came under sharp attack. Many expressed surprise over the wide gap which exists in the interpretation of Christianity in the "developed" nations and in the nations of "the Third World."

Singled out for consistent scrutiny and attack was the Vietnamese policy of the U.S. government. Historic theological concerns seemed to be neglected as the churchmen hurried to understand the belligerence of the newer nations to Christianity and to propose policies which apply Christian norms to new social situations.

The Berlin Conference, on the other hand, was critical of ecumenism and concentrated exclusively (at least in intention) on nonpolitical matters. Its single concern was to equip Christian persons for evangelism on an individualistic basis. The conference was conservative, clerical, and American-dominated. Most of the papers read called for traditional theology and considered radical and new "secular" theologies threats to the Protestant faith. See RELIGION.

Graham in London. Evangelical Christians were in the limelight earlier in the year when Billy Graham held a crusade at Earl's Court in London, England. Graham expressed pleasure over the relative youth of the respondents and the measure of support he received from British churches. The total attendance was 1,055,368. Many more watched on television, and 42,487 made "decisions for Christ."

External Pressures. If some division within Protestantism was occasioned by internal matters, such as differences of opinion concerning the nature and mission of the church, other divisions occurred for external, and especially political, reasons. And these divisions burdened Protestants.

Relations of Protestants to the predominantly Roman Catholic government and environment of Spain remained problematic. Reformed Episcopal Bishop Santos Molina was among those who remarked on some easing of tensions between the 30,000 Protestants of Spain and the authorities. But others were more pessimistic over the degree to which the Vatican Council's decree on religious liberty would be made to work in Spain.

In most Communist-dominated countries, Protestants did not fare well. In East Germany, the government withdrew permission, which it had previously granted, to the Lutheran World Federation to hold its 1969 convention in Weimar. When Kurt Scharf, 63, was selected to succeed 85-year-old anti-Communist church leader Otto Dibelius in the Berlin-Brandenburg Evangelical Church (with its 5,000,000 members mostly in the Eastern zone), the act was seen as a provocation to East German authorities. Scharf had long been criticized by Communists because he headed the Evangelical Church in Germany, which provides chaplains for the West German army.

Farther east, in Poland, the 140,000 Protestants (a dwindling 0.4 per cent of the population) used the year of the Polish millennium to call attention to their church life as one lived in a "zone of silence." Congregations are far apart; pastors are in short supply and overworked. Because of their minority status in a nation which is both Communist and Catholic, Protestants there are often lonely and feel beleaguered. Similarly, in Cuba, Protestants announced that they had difficulty keeping their churches in repair. Their pastors are conscripted into the army or sentenced to labor camps; congregations are divided over their attitudes to the regime of Fidel Castro.

Unitive Efforts. Divided as they were both by internal choice and external necessity, Protestants continued to work for unity among themselves and then with Roman Catholics. Anglican primate Dr. Arthur Michael Ramsey, Archbishop of Canterbury, met with Pope Paul VI for a fruitful two-day visit at the Vatican in March. It was the first official meeting of the heads of these churches since the 16th century. The constructive spirit of such talks was seconded in countless conferences around the world. See ROMAN CATHOLIC.

Internal Ecumenism in Protestantism advanced apace on the basis of groundwork laid in previous years. Canadian Anglicans and the United Church of Canada made progress in their talks toward unity. In the United States, the Consultation on Church Union, which involves eight churches, met at Dallas in May to help nudge their denominations toward formulation of a detailed plan for the union of their churches.

Dr. Eugene Carson Blake, *left,* new World Council of Churches general secretary, is congratulated by his predecessor, Dr. Visser't Hooft.

A 15,000-word document, "Principles of Church Union," was adopted. But Dr. Albert C. Outler, Methodist leader, warned participants: "We must be careful not to outdistance our constituencies." The African Methodist Episcopal Church with its 1,250,000 members became the first largely Negro member of the Consultation. The Roman Catholic Church sent official observers, as did the Lutheran Church-Missouri Synod, which had also traditionally remained remote from such discussions.

New Leader of WCC. The World Council of Churches (WCC), to which the majority of the world's Protestant churches belong, turned for the first time to an American for leadership. Dr. Eugene Carson Blake, who had been stated clerk of the United Presbyterian Church in the U.S.A., was named to succeed pioneering Willem A. Visser't Hooft, the Dutch theologian who served as general secretary since the group was founded in 1948.

Blake was expected to bring distinctive American social and Christian activist concerns to the post. At the same time, he had long been regarded as a theologically motivated churchman and thus was acceptable to those who sought a leader in the mold of Visser't Hooft. See BLAKE, EUGENE CARSON.

The ecumenical organizations sometimes met opposition for their social expression, particularly in the fields of race relations and the quest for peace. The Central Committee of the WCC in February made a 10-point proposal urging immediate steps toward peace in Vietnam, stressing de-escalation. Two months earlier, the General Board of the National Council of Churches of Christ in America had set forth similar proposals. These were given wide publicity, but were attacked by those who wanted church leaders to support U.S. military policy or to remain silent on public moral issues.

Theological Controversy. The stresses of theological change revolved around the "death of God" controversy and were evident in disputes centering around James A. Pike. He resigned his post as Bishop of the Episcopal Diocese of California at San Francisco during the year to enable him to take a long look at Christian teachings in the secular context of the Center for the Study of Democratic Institutions in California. But before the year was out he was involved in a fracas with other Episcopal bishops who regarded him as a heretic because of his radical views on basic Christian teachings.

Statistical Data. The *1967 Yearbook of American Churches* noted that in 1965, 205 Protestant bodies reported a total clergy of 335,461, with 239,743 pastors with active charges. A total of 222 Protestant bodies reported 296,406 churches with 69,088,183 members. The 19 Eastern bodies reported 1,529 churches with 3,172,163 members and 1,948 clergy, 1,458 with active charges. MARTIN E. MARTY

PSYCHIATRY. See MENTAL HEALTH; PSYCHOLOGY.

PSYCHOLOGY. Investigators at the Oregon Primate Research Center near Portland, Ore., conducted an extensive study of the behavior patterns of infant rhesus monkeys in the hope of determining the physiological factors leading to sex differences. They found that the nervous system of a male at birth is qualitatively different from that of a female. Prior to this it had generally been thought that such behavior differences were the result of maturity.

The psychologists discovered that males even early in life behave differently from females. Males play more frequently and vigorously, and chase and threaten other monkeys more often than do females. Females, however, are more passive, groom other monkeys more, and flee from rough play more often than males. These behavioral differences cannot be ascribed to the type of hormones present during infancy, since the scientists found that male monkeys castrated soon after birth behave in a manner completely characteristic of normal males.

What was most surprising was that despite the unimportance of hormones after birth (when the behavior is actually being displayed), hormones before birth were crucial to the development of the type of behavior specific to each sex. If normal female monkeys were treated with a male hormone before they were born, their body structure was transformed almost completely into that of an ordinary-appearing male. The treated females also behaved much more like normal males.

Brain Control in Weight. Many experiments have shown that the destruction of a particular brain area (the ventro-medial nucleus of the hypothalamus) will cause animals to overeat until they become obese. This area of the brain apparently sends the signals to stop eating when an animal has eaten to excess. It does not do so, however, until some signal indicating satiation has been received, such as a high level of glucose in the blood, slight deviations of body temperature, or accumulation of body fat.

Bartley Hoebel of Princeton University and Philip Teitelbaum of the University of Pennsylvania demonstrated, in 1966, that body weight is perhaps the most important regulator of feeding behavior. They showed that normal rats, made obese by insulin injections, would stop eating after cessation of the injections until they returned to a normal body weight. Destruction of the brain area in insulin-obese rats, however, did not cause marked overeating, as it does in rats of normal weight. The scientists force-fed some of their experimental rats, made obese by the destruction of the brain area, until they became "superobese." Others they starved until they lost weight. In each instance, the rat corrected the deviation from its typical obese weight by appropriately decreasing or increasing its feeding behavior. ROBERT W. GOY

See also BIOCHEMISTRY; MENTAL HEALTH.

PUBLISHING. In 1900, there were 15 major daily newspapers in New York City. In 1966, at year's end, there were only four daily newspapers in the nation's largest city, down two from 1965. *The New York Times* and the *Daily News* were still publishing in the morning field, and the *New York Post* appeared in the evening. But the *World Telegram and Sun* merged with the *Journal-American* to form a single afternoon newspaper, and the morning *Herald Tribune* expired. See Close-Up.

The death of the *Herald Tribune* on August 15 brought to an end a newspaper rich in tradition. The paper traced its lineage back to the *Herald*, founded in 1835 by James Gordon Bennett, and to the *Tribune*, founded in 1841 by Horace Greeley.

The three newspapers (*Herald Tribune*, *Journal-American* and *World Telegram and Sun*) were each beset by dwindling circulation and advertising revenues. In March, 1966, they formed a new corporation that had planned to publish one morning and one afternoon newspaper. They estimated that the merger would save them $15,000,000 a year. But the new enterprise, called the *World Journal Tribune*, was unable to reach agreement for new contracts with newspaper unions, and a 140-day strike ensued. This strike, the longest in a major city in the United States, forced the *Herald Tribune* to close down, according to its publisher, John Hay Whitney.

But the strike was only part of the 1966 newspaper story. Papers in large cities have been consolidating for a decade as the population has moved from city to suburbs, and as competition for advertising income has stiffened. In the New York City area, for example, daily newspapers must compete with nine television stations, more than 70 radio stations, and almost 40 daily newspapers ranging from the suburban dailies to specialty newspapers.

However, the city got its fourth paper when the new *World Journal Tribune* finally did appear. Vol. 1, No. 1 was published in the evening of September 12. The public eagerly bought up some 930,000 copies of the first edition. Critics of the early numbers of the paper felt it was short on hard news, and long on the columnists from the defunct *Trib*, the *Journal-American*, and the *World Telegram and Sun*.

Suburban Papers. The move of businesses and families to the suburbs has been followed by newspapers, and 1966 saw four new suburban newspapers launched. Cowles Communications founded *The Suffolk Sun* on Long Island. It will compete with the financially successful *Newsday*. Day Publications, a subsidiary of Field Enterprises, founded two newspapers, *The Arlington Day* and *The Prospect Day*, in the suburbs of Chicago. The Gannett Company launched *Today* in Brevard County, Florida, home of the Cape Kennedy space projects.

Overall Newspaper Circulation in the United States was 60,357,563, down 54,703 from 1965, according to *Editor & Publisher*. There were 1,751

Death of a Newspaper

In August, 1966, the *New York Herald Tribune*, one of the nation's leading newspapers and often the editorial conscience of the Republican party, died. Like scores of other newspapers, the *Trib* had become the victim of rising costs, population changes, and the shift of advertising dollars to television. For eight years, publisher John Hay Whitney had tried unsuccessfully to compete with *The New York Times* (circulation: 725,480) and the *Daily News* (circulation: 2,031,380). Finally, he decided to merge his morning paper (circulation: 331,341) with two evening dailies: Scripps-Howard's *World Telegram and Sun* and the Hearst-owned *Journal-American*. But a crippling pressmen's strike prevented the merged paper from appearing on the newsstands. By the time the merged evening paper was published, in September, the *New York Herald Tribune* had closed forever.

The *Herald Tribune* traced its ancestry to two very special newspapers: the *New York Herald*, founded by James Gordon Bennett, Sr., in 1835, and the *New York Tribune*, started by Horace Greeley in 1841. The first was noted for its wit, style, Wall Street news, and the introduction of murder trial coverage. Greeley's paper was the symbol of popular causes, the proponent of the Western frontier ("Go West, Young Man"), and the voice of the infant Republican party. The *Herald* sent Stanley to Africa to find Livingstone, while the *Tribune* found room in its columns for a then unknown London correspondent named Karl Marx.

Horace Greeley founded the *New York Tribune* in 1841.

When Greeley died in 1872, Civil War reporter Whitelaw Reid became the *Tribune's* owner and editor. His son Ogden succeeded him in 1912, and bought the *Herald* 12 years later. The combined paper became widely known for its excellent writers, including Robert Benchley, John Lardner, John O'Hara, Grantland Rice, and Deems Taylor. In fact, the reporters were so good that it is said rival newsmen carried the *Trib* with them on reporting assignments so that they could consult it for research.

Reid died in 1947 and his widow, Helen, assumed direction of the company. Mrs. Reid, however, faced financial troubles because the Reid estate had steadily diminished over the years. She instituted a radical economy wave at a time when *The New York Times* was aggressively pursuing advertisers and expanding its staff. By 1954, the *Trib's* circulation had dropped to the lowest of any of the seven dailies in New York City. The paper was floundering and staff morale sank, even though it still had some of the best feature writers of any paper in the country: Judith Crist (movies), John Crosby (television), Walter Kerr (drama), Clementine Paddleford (food), Eugenia Sheppard (fashion), and Earl Ubell (science), columnists Joe Alsop, Art Buchwald, Jimmy Breslin, Walter Lippmann, and Red Smith, and the well known Korean War correspondents Homer Bigart and the late Marguerite Higgins.

In 1958, Whitney purchased controlling interest in the company and assumed control. He brought in a succession of new editors, and briefly the paper's circulation rose. Then, in 1962, all the New York papers were shut down by a 114-day printers' strike. At the end of this strike, *Herald Tribune* readers found that their paper had raised its price from a nickel to a dime. The paper's circulation continued to decline steadily. At the end, Whitney said, "I have never been involved in a more difficult or painful decision than the one . . . not to resume publication."

With the death of the *Herald Tribune*, the city of New York was left with but four regular dailies, compared with the 15 that flourished in 1900. Many on the staff did not think the death was really necessary. "I can't believe it was," said Red Smith, "I think it underlines the spectacular immaturity, the complete childishness of labor-management relations in the newspaper business here." Some remembered that Heywood Broun, one of the most widely read newspaper columnists of the 1930s and a member of the *Tribune's* staff in 1912, once said that the death of a newspaper, unlike the closing of a shoe factory, was just cause for weeping. FOSTER P. STOCKWELL daily newspapers publishing during the year, which was a decrease of 12 from the year before. Some large newspapers grew still larger in 1966, and staff members expect them to continue growing in 1967. *The New York Times* daily edition and the *Wall Street Journal*, according to predictions of some experts, will become newspaper giants in 1967 with weekday circulations of over 1,000,000. At present, only the *New York Daily News* is in that class.

One of the most prestigious columnists in the country, Arthur Krock of *The New York Times*, retired on October 1. Winner of three Pulitzer prizes for distinguished reporting, Krock had been a journalist for nearly 60 years. His column had appeared on the *Times* editorial page since 1934.

Abroad, the influential but somewhat impoverished *Times of London* was sold. The buyer: Roy Thomson, owner of newspapers over the world. He planned to merge the money-losing *Times of London* with his *London Sunday Times*. Also, for the first time in its 181-year history, the *Times of London* began to print news regularly on page one. Dropping its "magnificent isolation," Editor Sir William Haley moved its "personals" and most of its ads inside the paper.

Magazines did well in 1966. According to Publisher's Information Bureau, general magazines attracted more than $1,000,000,000 in advertising revenues for the first time. This was a rise of 8 per cent over 1965. Even the *Saturday Evening Post*, long a money loser, was buoyed by a 20 per cent advertising revenue increase for the year. Its parent company, Curtis, reflected the upturn with its first revenue gain in years.

The small magazines, those that appealed to special groups of readers, did well, too. *Ramparts*, edited by Roman Catholic political activists, raised its circulation to 65,000, with articles critical of policies of the church, and of the government's role in Vietnam.

Book Sales mirrored the public's interest in reading matter. For the 14th straight year, sales were at record levels, estimated for 1966 at $2,500,000,000, a 10 per cent increase over 1965. Some 26,000 new titles appeared in the year.

Again, textbooks and encyclopedias accounted for a bit more than half the sales of book publishers. The breakdown of other categories: professional, 2 per cent; religious, 4 per cent; adult trade (fiction) books, 11 per cent; juveniles, 23 per cent. Book club editions and the output of university presses constituted the remainder.

The trend toward consolidation in the industry continued. Radio Corporation of America acquired Random House. The electronics industry has been interested in publishing, for the two, according to

New York City's Vanishing Newspapers

Year merged or ceased publishing

Date founded in parentheses

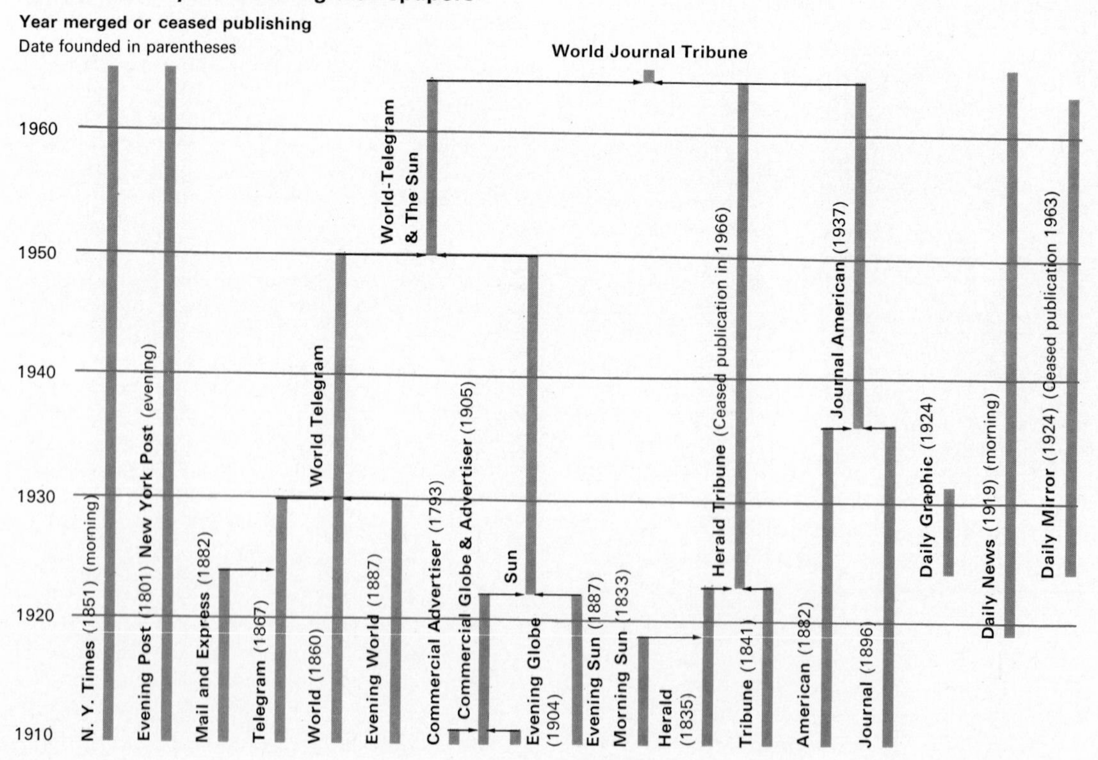

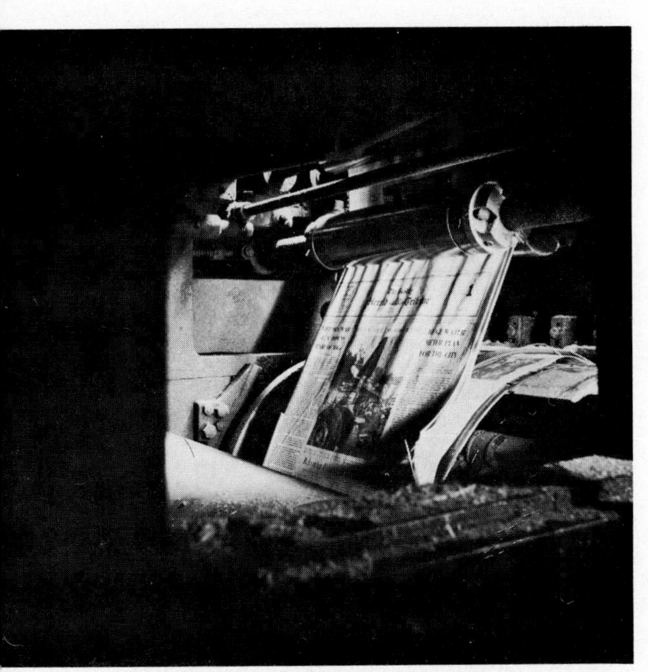

PICTURES OF THE YEAR/Bill Eppridge, *Life* © Time Inc.
The last edition of the *New York Herald Tribune* lies on an idle press. The historic newspaper ceased publication in 1966.

Bennett Cerf, Random House chairman, are "natural partners for the incredible expansion immediately ahead for every phase of education."

At Simon and Schuster, Inc., another consolidation took place. M. Lincoln Schuster sold his half interest in the firm to his partner, Leon Shimkin, who thereupon linked the firm to Pocket Books, Inc.

The Kennedy Book. But in the book field, all events paled before those surrounding one unpublished volume, William Manchester's *Death of a President*. Manchester was a journalist who had contracted with the Kennedys to write the authorized story of the assassination of President John F. Kennedy. He used material from 10 hours of recorded interviews with Jacqueline Kennedy in the book, which is to be published by Harper & Row. Serialization rights were bought by *Look* magazine for an unprecedented $650,000.

But in December, Mrs. Kennedy filed suit in Manhattan to hold up publication because it contained matter that she felt was too personal for print. Grounds for the suit included the contention that the author violated a contract which gave the Kennedy family control over the book. At year-end, *Look* bowed to Mrs. Kennedy's wishes, and deleted the disputed material from its manuscript, and Harper & Row indicated it would do the same in the book, scheduled for 1967. MELVIN MENCHER

PUERTO RICO. See LATIN AMERICA.

PULITZER PRIZES in journalism, literature, music, and art were announced on May 2, 1966, following recommendations by the Advisory Board of the Pulitzer School of Journalism at Columbia University. No prize was awarded for drama. The other prizes were conferred as follows:

For the Most Disinterested and Meritorious Public Service Rendered by a U.S. Newspaper: a gold medal to the *Boston Globe* for its campaign to prevent confirmation of Francis X. Morrissey as a federal judge in Massachusetts.

For a Distinguished Example of Reporting on International Affairs: $1,000 to New Zealander Peter Arnett of the Associated Press for reports on the war in Vietnam.

For a Distinguished Example of Reporting on National Affairs: $1,000 to Haynes Johnson of the *Washington* (D.C.) *Star* for his special report on "Selma (Ala.) Revisited."

For a Distinguished Example of Local Reporting: *General Reporting*, $1,000 to *The Los Angeles Times* staff for its coverage of the Watts riots of August, 1965. *For Special Reporting*, $1,000 to John A. Frasca of the *Tampa* (Fla.) *Tribune*. His articles on two robberies were followed by the confession of a guilty man and the freeing of a wrongly convicted man.

For a Distinguished Example of Editorial Writing: $1,000 to Robert Lasch of the *St. Louis Post-Dispatch* for an editorial on the war in Vietnam.

For an Outstanding Example of News Photography: $1,000 to Japanese Kyoichi Sawada of the United Press International for his Vietnam combat photography.

For an Outstanding Example of a Cartoonist's Work Published in a U.S. Newspaper: $1,000 to Don Wright of the *Miami* (Fla.) *News* for his editorial cartoons. One of his cartoons pictures a war scene with two injured men walking toward each other, captioned "You Mean You Were Bluffing?"

For the Best Fiction by an American Author: $500 to Katherine Anne Porter for *The Collected Stories of Katherine Anne Porter*. See PORTER, KATHERINE ANNE.

For the Best Nonfiction by an American Author: $500 to Edwin Way Teale for *Wandering Through Winter*. See TEALE, EDWIN WAY.

For a Distinguished Book of the Year on U.S. History: $500 to the late Perry Miller for *The Life of the Mind in America: From the Revolution to the Civil War*. See MILLER, PERRY.

For a Distinguished Biography or Autobiography Preferably on an American Subject: $500 to Arthur M. Schlesinger, Jr., for *A Thousand Days: John F. Kennedy in the White House*. See SCHLESINGER, ARTHUR M., JR.

For a Distinguished Volume of Verse by an American Author: $500 to Richard Eberhart for *Selected Poems (1930-1965)*. See EBERHART, RICHARD.

For a Distinguished Musical Composition: $500 to Leslie Bassett for *Variations for Orchestra*. See BASSETT, LESLIE.

Traveling Fellowships to the highest ranking graduates of the Columbia University Graduate School of Journalism for a year of travel and study abroad, $1,500 each to: Michael J. Leahy, James G. Lubetkin, and David B. Mangurian.

Fellowship in Critical Writing, $1,500 to Bill J. Perkins, who is studying for a career in the field of theater criticism.

QUEBEC. See CANADA

RACING. See AUTOMOBILE RACING; BOATS AND BOATING; HORSE RACING; TRACK AND FIELD.

RADIO. The Federal Communications Commission (FCC) ruled, in 1966, that as of December 31, FM-AM stations under common ownership in 222 large market areas must offer different programs during at least 50 per cent of the broadcast day. This meant that AM stations could not rebroadcast their programs simultaneously over their FM bands, but had to produce different material for FM listeners. All the areas designated by the FCC had populations of 100,000 or more. In anticipation of the deadline, most stations introduced separate FM programing earlier in the year.

Several group broadcasters entered the previously staid FM market with a dazzling array of different programing formats, ranging from rock and roll to girl disk jockeys.

FM radio set retail sales in 1966 increased 37 per cent over those of 1965. Combined AM-FM radio set sales were also up over 1965 (the previous record year), in which 31,000,000 radio sets were sold.

"Hot line" talk shows continued to be strong in local programing. One outlet was so entranced with the format that, in February, it adopted a 24-hour-a-day telephone talk only policy.

One of the most important industry sales took place July 1, 1966, when Minnesota Mining and Manufacturing Company (3M) sold the Mutual Broadcasting System for $3,100,000 to Mutual Industries, Inc., a newly formed corporation.

Station Income. According to the Radio Advertising Bureau, radio advertising (network, spot, and local) was running about 13 per cent ahead of 1965 during the first six months of 1966. Indications were that sales in the second half of the year would be equally good. Total sales for the first half of 1966 were set at $477,400,000, with local programs accounting for about $295,000,000 of that figure.

Official FCC figures on AM-FM advertising for 1965 put total radio revenue at $792,500,000, with "before federal income tax" profits of $77,800,000. However, profit was restricted to local and spot sales. The four radio networks (ABC, NBC, CBS, and Mutual), as a group, reported a loss in sales.

Other Events. The 1966 Peabody Awards were given to CBS and American Airlines for "Music 'Til Dawn," an all-night "good music" disk show carried by seven CBS outlets. A Radio Public Service award was also given to WCCO, Minneapolis, Minn., for its coverage of three major disasters.

The Mutual network's conservative, sometimes controversial, radio commentator, Fulton Lewis, Jr., died August 22. At the time of his death, Lewis was broadcasting twice daily over 500 stations.

In December, the U.S. Bureau of Standards radio station, WWV, moved to Fort Collins, Colo. The government station's time and frequency signals are used by ships, aircraft, radio and TV stations, utilities, and electronics laboratories. June Bundy Csida

RAILROAD. See Transportation.

RECORDINGS. Large-scale merchandising of records in supermarkets, drug stores, and record shops helped boost total record sales to $675,000,000 for 1966. On the basis of the increase in sales it was predicted that the $1,000,000,000 mark would be reached by 1970. By that time, according to some experts, tapes may have replaced disks as the dominant sound reproduction system.

Tapes. Such major record companies as Capitol, Decca, Columbia, and Liberty released their first tape cartridges during the year. As 1966 ended, 250,000 cartridge tape units were in use in automobiles alone. Eight-track tape players were optional in several new car models.

Though the eight-track stereo-cartridge system, introduced in 1965, gained rapidly on the four-track cartridges, it appeared that both would continue to flourish, along with the reel-to-reel two-track monaural tapes for home use.

Recording companies invested more money than ever in Broadway musical shows, backing them partly for the purpose of acquiring the rights to albums by the original casts. Two original cast albums popular during the year were those of *Man of La Mancha*, a musical about Don Quixote, and *Mame*, a musical version of *Auntie Mame*.

The most remarkable individual success of the year was scored by Bill Cosby, the comedian. Because of the great popularity he achieved as star of the television series, "I Spy," all four of his comedy albums received $1,000,000 sales certifications by the Record Industry Association of America, an unprecedented figure for a spoken-word recording artist. Comedy was also strong in the areas of political satire (LPs concerning President Lyndon B. Johnson and other public figures) and specialized albums performed by comedy production groups.

The most popular motion picture sound-track album was that of *Dr. Zhivago*. Other important LPs of film industry origin were provided by the music from *Hawaii*, *The Bible*, and *Alfie*. The music for *Alfie* was written and played by a jazz saxophonist, Sonny Rollins.

In the Classical Music Field, an outstanding success was an album of three LPs entitled *Opening Nights at the Met* (see Music). In an unprecedented move, Capitol Records leased from the Soviet government the rights to classical music recorded by the official U.S.S.R. record company.

Two late releases became the biggest hits of the year. Leader in the spoken category was "Gallant Men," which was recorded by U.S. Senator Everett M. Dirksen (R., Ill.), for Capitol records. "Winchester Cathedral," a number done in the style of old-time vaudeville band music, sold more than 2,500,000 copies. The New Vaudeville Band recorded it in London for Fontana. Leonard G. Feather

RECREATION. See Conservation; Fairs and Exhibitions; Hunting and Fishing.

RED CROSS. In 1966, the Red Cross observed 50 years of formal service to U.S. military personnel and their families. The organization marked the occasion by expanding service to the Vietnamese and to the growing number of U.S. soldiers in Vietnam.

The Red Cross field service staff in South Vietnam was increased to 200 members, stationed in 41 locations. Red Cross personnel also were on duty in six military hospitals and aboard the U.S. Navy hospital ship *Repose*. In addition, recreation workers provided activities for troops in base recreation centers and at remote outposts.

At the request of the U.S. Department of Defense, the American Red Cross provided 177,000 units of blood for treatment of sick and injured servicemen in the Vietnam conflict.

Under contract with the U.S. Agency for International Development (AID), the Red Cross took over management of several refugee centers in South Vietnam. Basic AID subsistence rations were distributed, refugees registered, sanitation improved, and medical aid provided.

Delegates to the 1966 National Red Cross Convention, held May 8 to 11 in San Diego, Calif., were told that Hurricane *Betsy* and other similar disasters had drained the financial resources of the agency. To offset this, the organization conducted a special campaign in 1966 to raise an additional $9,000,000.

JOSEPH P. ANDERSON

RELIGION. "God Is Dead." This headline on the front page of newspapers and on the front cover of mass circulation magazines startled America early in 1966. A *Catholic Digest* poll indicated that 97 per cent of the nation's people professed belief in God. Perhaps for this reason Americans were surprised to hear statements concerning "the death of God" from the lips of theologians, men who are supposed to be formally relating the ways of God to men.

The controversy over atheism was not confined to Protestantism, though William Hamilton and Thomas J. J. Altizer, the most publicized spokesmen of the "God Is Dead" movement, were Protestants. Rabbi Richard Rubenstein of Pittsburgh, Pa., in his book *After Auschwitz* gave evidence that atheism was also present in Jewish thought. While no Roman Catholic thinker was directly related to the radical movement, Catholic college students were among those most eager to give the "God Is Dead" spokesmen a hearing. Public attention peaked at the time of spring religious holidays, when a national news magazine devoted its Easter cover to a survey of the new theology.

The "death of God" slogan was merely the most dramatic and attention-getting evidence of a widespread attempt by theologians to relate their studies to the ways people think and act in a technological and affluent society. Influenced by profound thinkers such as Dietrich Bonhoeffer and Paul Tillich in

U.S. Church Membership Reported for Bodies with 150,000 or more members.*

Adventists, Seventh Day	364,666
Armenian Church, Diocese of America	163,960
Assemblies of God	572,123
Baptist Bodies	
American Baptist Association	726,112
American Baptist Convention	1,495,326
Conservative Baptist Association of America	325,000
Free Will Baptists	173,275
General Association of Regular Baptist Churches	154,767
National Baptist Convention of America	2,668,799
National Baptist Convention, U.S.A., Inc.	5,500,000
National Primitive Baptist Convention in the U.S.A.	768,800
North American Baptist Association	174,000
Progressive National Baptist Convention, Inc.	516,400
Southern Baptist Convention	10,770,573
Brethren (German Baptists)	
Church of the Brethren	198,815
Christian Churches (Disciples of Christ) International Convention	1,981,471
Churches of God	
Church of God (Cleveland, Tenn.)	205,465
Church of God in Christ	425,500
Church of the Nazarene	343,380
Churches of Christ	2,350,000
Eastern Churches	
Greek Orthodox Archdiocese of North and South America	1,770,000
Russian Orthodox Catholic Church in America Patriarchal Exarchate	152,973
Russian Orthodox Greek Catholic Church of America, The	('64) 600,000
Evangelical United Brethren Church	735,723
Jehovah's Witnesses	330,358
Jewish Congregations	('63) 5,600,000
Latter-Day Saints	
Church of Jesus Christ of the Latter-Day Saints	1,789,175
Reorganized Church of Jesus Christ of Latter-Day Saints	168,355
Lutherans	
Lutheran Council in the U.S.A.	
American Lutheran Church, The	2,541,546
Lutheran Church in America	3,142,752
Lutheran Church—Missouri Synod	2,692,889
Other Lutheran Bodies	
Wisconsin Evangelical Lutheran Synod	358,466
Methodist Bodies	
African Methodist Episcopal Church	1,166,301
African Methodist Episcopal Zion Church	1,100,000
Christian Methodist Episcopal Church	466,718
The Methodist Church	10,331,574
Polish National Catholic Church of America	282,411
Presbyterian Bodies	
The United Presbyterian Church in the U.S.A.	3,304,321
Protestant Episcopal Church	3,410,657
Reformed Bodies	
Christian Reformed Church	272,461
Reformed Church in America	232,414
Roman Catholic Church	46,246,175
Salvation Army	287,991
Spiritualists, International General Assembly of	164,072
Unitarian Universalist Association	166,622
United Church of Christ	2,070,413

*Statistics mainly for calendar year 1965
Source: 1967 Yearbook of American Churches

Protestantism, Pierre Teilhard de Chardin in Roman Catholicism, or Franz Rosenzweig in Judaism, they concentrated on the meaning of life in this world, rather than on a spatial "beyond," or a life after this one. Most serious theologians shunned the "death of God" terminology and pondered what it meant to be believers who might speak the name of God in a time when it seemed as if God did not make a practical difference in the affairs of men.

The National Context. Efforts by Illinois Republican Senator Everett McK. Dirksen to begin to take steps toward a constitutional amendment that would allow prayers in the public schools were frustrated when the senator's resolution failed by nine votes to receive a two-thirds majority. His amendment in effect would have nullified Supreme Court of the United States decisions of 1962 and 1963 against devotional exercises in tax-supported schools and similar public institutions.

Americans remained uncertain and divided over the role of the federal government in support of religious institutions. Debate ensued when the U.S. Office of Education revealed that about 7 per cent of the children in federally financed education programs attended private and especially Catholic parochial schools. When the U.S. House of Representatives appointed a new chaplain, the question of the propriety of continuing the practice which called for tax-supported chaplaincies in Congress again divided some citizens.

Americans also began to debate whether the federal census of 1970 could properly ask questions seeking information concerning religious affiliation from the people. As controversy mounted, A. Ross Eckler, census director, predicted that the question would not be included.

Social and Political Disputes. During 1966 many articles noting a growing gap between socially oriented clergymen and others appeared. When the civil rights movement moved into a new (Black Power) phase, or when riots in urban ghettoes were associated by many with civil rights, a "white backlash" was directed at socially oriented religious leaders of all faiths. Debated with equal fervor was the interfaith support by clergymen given to activities critical of the United States' part in escalating the war in Vietnam.

Among the Religions. While the ecumenical movement and the efforts at brotherhood between religions made progress, evidence of some resistance appeared during 1966. When the book *Christian Beliefs and Anti-Semitism* by Charles Y. Glock and Rodney Stark was published in 1966 by the B'nai B'rith, conservative Christians complained that it seemed to imply that anti-Semitism could be overcome only if Christians surrendered basic beliefs. This surrender they felt was not necessary, though few of them controverted the Glock-Stark findings of continued anti-Semitism. MARTIN E. MARTY

REPUBLICAN PARTY. Republicans made a striking comeback in the 1966 midterm elections from the debacle of 1964 under the presidential candidacy of former Senator Barry M. Goldwater of Arizona.

The party made an above-average net increase of 47 seats in the House of Representatives and picked up three seats in the Senate. Republicans wrested 10 governorships from the Democrats – who took two from them – for a net Republican gain of eight. The strong showing produced several presidential hopefuls and bolstered the party's prospects for 1968.

Republican National Chairman Ray C. Bliss recalled that when he took over his job in the spring of 1965 reporters asked him whether the Republican party was going to survive. After the 1966 vote was in, he said, "It looks to me as if we have a very live elephant."

In the 90th Congress, Republicans occupy 187 seats in the House and the Democrats 248, against a 140 to 295 division in the 89th. The party's 47-seat gain more than compensated for its 38-seat loss in 1964. In the new Senate, the Democrats hold 64 seats to the Republicans' 36, in contrast to the 67 to 33 advantage they had in the old Senate. See CONGRESS OF THE UNITED STATES.

In 25 of the 50 states, Republicans now sit as governors as a consequence of victories in 23 races together with two holdovers. Five of these 25 states – California, Michigan, New York, Ohio, and Pennsylvania – would cast more than half of the 270 electoral votes needed to elect a President. See GOVERNORS OF THE STATES.

1968 Hopefuls. Probably the leading contender for the 1968 Republican presidential nomination was Michigan's 59-year-old Governor George W. Romney. He won re-election to a third term with a landslide 61.4 per cent majority. He also dispelled his image as a political lone wolf by lending his coattails to six successful candidates on his ticket.

Other presidential possibilities included:

- Ronald Reagan of California, a 55-year-old former film actor who shed the ultraconservative image he had as a Goldwater lieutenant in 1964. He went on in 1966 to defeat Democratic Governor Edmund G. "Pat" Brown by nearly 1,000,000 votes.
- Charles H. Percy, 47, a self-made millionaire Illinois industrialist, who defeated veteran Democratic Senator Paul H. Douglas, with a majority of more than 400,000 votes.
- Former Vice-President Richard M. Nixon, 53, regarded by many as Romney's greatest rival. Nixon was not a candidate himself but campaigned arduously for other Republicans. Of the 86 candidates he supported, 58 were elected. Repayment of those political debts may put him in a strong position at the party's 1968 convention, despite the handicap of his record as a two-time loser.

At Republican governors' meeting in Puerto Rico, George W. Romney of Michigan, *left*, and New York's Nelson Rockefeller meet the press.

The Moderate Forces gained an important ally with Governor Nelson A. Rockefeller's upset re-election to a third term as governor of New York. Rockefeller, 58, has renounced presidential ambitions for himself. But he will control the powerful New York delegation at the 1968 convention. Opposed to Reagan and his old foe Nixon, Rockefeller was expected to throw his support to Romney.

Among the successful Republicans more or less in mid-position in the party's fractional strife were Ohio's Governor James A. Rhodes, who won re-election with the largest majority in his state's history, and Robert A. Taft, Jr., of Ohio, 49-year-old son of the late Senator Taft, who won back a House seat he had left two years before for an unsuccessful Senate bid. Another in this middle-ground group, Howard H. Baker, Jr., upset Tennessee Governor Frank G. Clement for a Senate seat.

The Liberal Wing of the party was strengthened by the triumph of Massachusetts Attorney General Edward W. Brooke, 47, the first Negro to win a Senate seat since Reconstruction (see BROOKE, EDWARD W.), and by the successful Senate campaign of Governor Mark O. Hatfield, 44, of Oregon.

The conservatives were helped by the election of Don Samuelson as governor of Idaho, John R. Williams as governor of Arizona, and the re-election of Senators John G. Tower (Tex.), Carl T. Curtis (Nebr.), and Karl E. Mundt (S.Dak.).

Southern Inroads by the Republicans continued as the party won 28 House seats, for a gain of 9. Once-solid Democratic Dixie also elected its first two Republican governors since Reconstruction– Winthrop Rockefeller of Arkansas, a moderate and a brother of Governor Rockefeller of New York, and Claude R. Kirk, Jr., of Florida, a conservative.

Other new Republican governors were Walter J. Hickel of Alaska, Spiro T. Agnew of Maryland, Harold E. LeVander of Minnesota, Norbert T. Tiemann of Nebraska, Paul Laxalt of Nevada, and David F. Cargo of New Mexico. Another new Republican in the Senate, Wyoming Governor Clifford P. Hansen, was elected to the seat vacated by Senator Milward L. Simpson because of ill health.

State Legislature net gains by Republicans were estimated to be 677 seats, compared with the loss of more than 500 in 1964. Republicans increased their control of both chambers of state legislatures from six to 15 states. See STATE GOVERNMENT.

The Republican campaign was better organized than the Democrats', and had considerably stronger financing, according to reports filed with the clerk of the U.S. House. Four Democratic groups reported a total of $276,040 in receipts and $504,876 in expenditures. Three Republican groups reported receipts totaling $1,777,103 and expenditures of $1,765,910. WILLIAM MCGAFFIN

See also DEMOCRATIC PARTY; ELECTIONS.

RETAILING. In a year of growing price inflation and increasingly tight money, the consumer was spending more of his income for day-to-day living – the nondurables, food and clothing – and less for durables, the big ticket items – furniture, refrigerators, cars, and major appliances.

For 1966 as a whole, retail sales increased 7 per cent to about $303,868,000,000. Wholesale trade, at $426,000,000,000, increased less, 6.8 per cent. Total retail sales by various outlets (in billions of dollars) and their percentage changes were:

Type of store	1965	1966	Gain
Department	$23.7	$29.9	13.9%
Variety	5.3	6.1	6.8
Women's apparel	6.2	6.6	5.1
Men's apparel	3.3	3.5	5.0
Grocery	61.1	66.3	8.6
Drug	8.9	9.8	9.6
Hardware	2.8	3.0	5.6
Appliance	3.0	3.3	8.9

Retail business gains slipped, however, toward the end of the year. For November, sales were only 3 per cent above the 1965 month. The trend was apparent in the sales of the nation's No. 1 retailer, Sears, Roebuck and Company. For the first half of the year, Sears' combined sales rose close to 10 per cent, but only about 6 per cent in the last half.

However, in the still very affluent 1966 economy consumers were willing to pay for what they wanted. Sales of air conditioners went up an amazing 30 per cent and color television up fully 80 per cent to nearly 5,000,000 sets. Retailers noted, however, that the high priced sets ($800 and up) were moving much slower later in the year.

Back to Downtown. During 1966, it became evident that city retailing was at last making a comeback. Some companies were even building new stores downtown. R. H. Macy & Company, for example, moved into central New Haven, Conn.

Fred Lazarus, Jr., chairman of Federated Department Stores, Inc., observed that "despite the growth of suburban shopping, and the increasing number of Federated branches, more people are apparently responding to the excitement of shopping in our main stores."

U.S.-style retailing continued to spread around the world with more supermarkets and shopping centers opening every place, from Austria to Japan. Sears was only months away at year's end from opening its first European store – in Barcelona, Spain. F. W. Woolworth planned to open its first Woolco department store in England late in 1967.

Profits for most big department store and variety chains lagged behind gains in sales. The outstanding performer, S. S. Kresge Company, increased its first nine months' sales 30 per cent and its earnings 29 per cent above the 1965 period.

Two retailing pioneers, Sebastian S. Kresge, 99, and Bernard F. Gimbel, 81, died in 1966 (see DEATHS OF NOTABLE PERSONS). EDWIN W. DARBY

RHODESIA. A unilateral declaration of independence by Rhodesia in November, 1965, caused Great Britain no end of frustration throughout 1966. Under the white-dominated regime of Rhodesia's Prime Minister Ian Smith, the nation's 95 per cent black population had little hope of improving its inferior economic and social position, or of gaining more than token representation in the government. Britain, however, was determined to withhold its official recognition of Rhodesia's independence, which it considered illegal, until some provisions had been made for majority rule by the black population.

Commonwealth Repercussions. In January, and again in September, member nations of the British Commonwealth met in Lagos, Nigeria, and in London, to discuss the Rhodesian situation. Some nations, notably the African, advocated the use of force as a means of bringing down the Smith government. This was a step, however, that British Prime Minister Harold Wilson was reluctant to take. He was equally lukewarm toward suggestions that mandatory sanctions be applied against Rhodesia, although Britain's previously applied oil embargo and economic sanctions were not as effective in bringing the Smith government to terms as had been hoped. Nor were trade bans instituted by the United States, Canada, and most of the African nations any more successful. They merely caused inconvenience, higher prices, and a dip in jobs.

Bilateral talks to reach a compromise were held between British and Rhodesian delegates in May, June, and July. They proved fruitless. Subsequently, in December – at Britain's request – the United Nations (UN) Security Council voted mandatory sanctions against selling oil to Rhodesia or buying 12 Rhodesian exports. See UNITED NATIONS (UN).

Domestic Problems. Within Rhodesia, military and police units were enlarged to maintain order among the restless black population. Emergency security laws were enacted, enabling the government to detain people without trial. Stringent censorship was imposed on newspapers. Newsmen and British residents who were critical of Smith's government were expelled.

Smith, meanwhile, continued to receive support from the white minority. On September 9, his government was declared illegal but nevertheless in power by Rhodesia's High Court. Two months later, he was given a unanimous vote of confidence by the ruling Rhodesian National Front party.

Facts in Brief. Population: 4,500,000. Government: Prime Minister Ian D. Smith. Monetary Unit: pound (1 = U.S. $2.83). Foreign Trade: exports, $441,700,000; imports, $368,600,000. Principal Exports: tobacco, asbestos, chrome, gold, iron and steel. BENJAMIN E. THOMAS

ROADS AND HIGHWAYS. See BUILDING AND CONSTRUCTION; TRANSPORTATION.

ROMAN CATHOLIC. Just as peace was Pope Paul VI's last concern at the end of the year 1965, so it was his first in 1966 when on January 1 he sent messages reflecting his deep anxiety to the leaders of the United States, the Soviet Union, Communist China, and North Vietnam, pleading for settlement of the war in Vietnam.

Peace was the theme later in the month when Pope Paul VI addressed the general Italian press, suggesting that a solution might be achieved through arbitration by neutral nations in the United Nations. The pope regretted that his "peace offensive" had not been positively accepted, but nevertheless expressed gratitude toward "those who responded to our appeal for peace." He then added: "Many statesmen echoed our humble voice." The pope's message at Easter was that "Christ's Resurrection should unite all men in peace." The same message was sent to the people of Vietnam later in the year, and also to the Council of Religions of Vietnam. He expressed approval of the council's efforts for "collaboration of all citizens."

Peace Efforts. Pope Paul's new encyclical *Christi Matri Rosarii* (Rosaries to the Mother of Christ), dated September 15, urged Catholics to say the rosary for peace during the month of October and to dedicate October 4, the anniversary of his 1965 peace mission to the United Nations, as a day of prayer for peace. Peace, he stated, "must rest on justice and the liberty of mankind and take into account the rights of individuals and communities otherwise it will be shifting and unstable." On the anniversary of his New York visit, he repeated his words, "No more war, war never again," at a Mass in St. Peter's. During his address, the pope expressed regret that during the past year the conditions which make peace a possibility had not improved. But he said that "peace is not impossible because what is impossible for man is not impossible for God. Thus is explained the solemn act we are now engaged in: praying for peace." Year-end peace pleas by Pope Paul VI included an appeal on December 2 for peace between Arabs and Jews in the Holy Land.

Implementation of Council Decrees. In order to put into practice the conclusions reached by Vatican Council II, which ended on Dec. 8, 1965, the pope established six post-conciliar commissions, including a central commission and five others. He did so through a *Motu Proprio* entitled *Finis Concilio*, dated Jan. 3, 1966. The central commission was established to coordinate the other five, which deal with bishops and the government of dioceses, the lay apostolate, religious missions, and Christian education, respectively.

Another *Motu Proprio* dated August 4 and entitled *Ecclesiae Sanctae* implements four decrees of the Council. Among the suggestions made in this 8,000-word document are the following: that local episcopal conferences propose to the Holy See the names of priests to be made bishops, and that priests and bishops retire voluntarily at the age of 75. The section dealing with coordination of missionary work recommends the establishment of a 24-man commission to assist the Congregation of the Propagation of the Faith. It will include 12 bishops from mission lands, four from nonmission lands, and four from missionary congregations and orders.

Historical Meeting. As the memorable two-day March visit to Rome by Archbishop Arthur Michael Ramsey of Canterbury drew to a close, the Anglican leader and Pope Paul VI signed a declaration thanking God for "a new spirit of Christian fellowship between the Roman Catholic Church and the churches of the Anglican Communion." They expressed their intention of "inaugurating a serious dialogue which, founded on the Gospels and on the ancient common tradition, may lead to that unity in truth, for which Christ prayed."

One Christian Bible. The commissioning by the Pope of the Vatican Secretariat Promoting Christian Unity to study all possibilities of a common Protestant-Catholic Bible was another post-conciliar event of the greatest importance. This Bible is to be published in all languages.

World-Wide Ministry. During 1966, Poland observed the millennium of her conversion to Christianity. Pope Paul VI was to have led a pilgrimage in honor of the occasion, but the visit did not take place because the Polish government had declared the visit "inopportune." See POLAND.

A 14-year rupture of diplomatic relations between the Holy See and Yugoslavia ended when an agreement was signed by respective representatives as part of an effort to solve mutual problems. Soviet Foreign Minister Andrei Gromyko was received by Pope Paul VI in another manifestation of the pope's concern for peace and for the Catholics of the Soviet Union. Peace with justice was clearly defined by the pope as he spoke to 15,000 representatives of Christian labor on May 22. During his discourse, Paul VI described the Church's opposition to "the false conception of man, history, and the world which is typical of radical Marxism."

The church continued to face hardships in the Congo, where another Congolese priest was slain. In southern Sudan, violations of churches continued and Catholics were forced to hide in jungles, or flee to neighboring countries. In Burma, Protestant and Catholic missionaries alike were affected by a ruling directing 230 priests and missionaries to leave the country by December. In Shanghai, both Protestant and Catholic churches were despoiled by members of the Communist Youth Movement, and another priest died in a Chinese labor camp where he had been imprisoned for 10 years.

Auxiliary Bishop Harold R. Perry of New Orleans, the first Negro in the United States hierarchy

during the 20th century, was consecrated in January. In August, Luci Baines Johnson, the President's daughter, was married to Patrick Nugent at the National Shrine of the Immaculate Conception, Washington, D.C. U.S. bishops elected Archbishop John F. Dearden as president of the National Conference of Catholic Bishops in November. In October, The Most Reverend Fulton J. Sheen, Auxiliary Bishop of the Roman Catholic Diocese of New York and the national director of the Society for the Propagation of the Faith, was named Bishop of the Diocese of Rochester, N.Y., by Pope Paul VI. He was also elected U.S. chairman of the Society for the Propagation of the Faith.

Year-End Events. In a discourse made two days before Christmas, Pope Paul VI announced that the first synod of bishops established during Vatican Council II will meet in Rome Sept. 29, 1967. In addition, the holy father announced the establishment of a layman's council to help with the lay apostolate movement and of a commission to work for social justice.

Decrees pertaining to the Curia reform are to be published in the near future. The pope expressed his intention of visiting many parishes of Rome in 1967 in order to meet with the bishops of the Roman vicariate to attain a "more direct contact with all sectors of the city, with their problems and their needs." The pontiff celebrated Christmas midnight Mass among the people of Florence during his Christmas visit to the flood-ravaged regions of Italy. See ITALY; PAINTING AND SCULPTURE.

U.S. Catholics. The total Catholic population of the United States reached 46,246,175, representing a 605,756 increase over 1965. The year brought 123,149 converts to the Catholic faith. U.S. personnel, including religious and laity working in Latin America, numbered 4,332, which represented a 45 per cent increase over 1950. The total number of teachers in Catholic educational institutions numbered 203,791, an increase of 5,035 over the previous year.

In the ecumenical spirit of the Council, a first full meeting between members of the National Council of Churches, including Orthodox, Anglicans, and Protestants, and the members of the Catholic Bishops Commission was held in New York.

The Catholics of the United States were no longer obliged to abstain from meat on Fridays, excepting the Fridays during Lent. Again in the spirit of the Council, they were urged to voluntarily practice self-denial in observing Christ's Crucifixion on Good Friday through self-sacrifice and through acts of charity to those less fortunate. FULTON J. SHEEN

With Vatican frescoes for a background, a Pope of Rome meets with an Archbishop of Canterbury for the first time since 1534.

ROMANIA. The independent position Romania occupied within the Communist world was underscored by visits from Yugoslavia's President Tito in April, Leonid I. Brezhnev of the Soviet Union in May, and Communist China's Chou En-lai in June. It was also enhanced by the holding of the Warsaw Treaty Organization conference in Bucharest in July. At that meeting, Soviet proposals for a strengthening of the Warsaw Pact were seemingly frustrated by Romania's resistance. But rumors of a Romanian withdrawal from the alliance proved baseless.

On the domestic scene, the position of Party Secretary-General Nicolae Ceausescu remained unshaken. At the celebration of the 45th anniversary of the Romanian Communist party on May 7, his major speech struck a strongly nationalistic note.

There was little evidence of any significant liberalization in the economic or cultural life of the nation, but significant innovations were made in state administration, agricultural agencies, and in mass organizations such as the trade unions.

Facts in Brief. Population: 19,600,000. Government: Communist Party Secretary-General Nicolae Ceausescu; Prime Minister Ion Gheorghe Maurer; Chairman of State Council (President) Chivu Stoica. Monetary Unit: lei (12=U.S. $1). Foreign Trade: exports, $317,300,000; imports, $425,900,000. Principal Exports: machinery, petroleum products, cement, cereals. H. GORDON SKILLING

ROSTOW, WALT WHITMAN (1916-   ), became a special assistant to President Lyndon B. Johnson on March 31. He was appointed to develop plans for long-range U.S. foreign policy, particularly in Latin America. Rostow moved to the White House from the Department of State. In 1961, he was named deputy special assistant to the President for national security affairs and later that year became counselor and chairman of the Policy Planning Council in the Department of State.

A Yale man and a Rhodes scholar, he returned to Yale and earned his Ph.D. degree in economics in 1940. During World War II, he was a major in the Office of Strategic Services. After the war, he held a number of government and teaching jobs both in England and in the United States. He became professor of economic history at the Massachusetts Institute of Technology (M.I.T.) and a member of M.I.T.'s Center for International Studies in 1950.

When John F. Kennedy assumed the presidency in 1961, he brought Rostow to Washington as deputy special assistant to the President for national security affairs. In May, 1965, Rostow became a member of the Inter-American Committee on the Alliance for Progress. Rostow is the author of several influential books on economics.

Rostow married Elspeth Vaughan Davies in 1947; they have two children.

ROTARY INTERNATIONAL. See SERVICE CLUBS.

ROUS, (FRANCIS) PEYTON (1879-), a specialist in cancer research since 1910, was awarded the Nobel prize in medicine in December, 1966. He shared the award with Charles B. Huggins of the University of Chicago.

Rous was honored for his discovery of tumor-inducing viruses. He is a pathologist at Rockefeller University in New York City, formerly the Rockefeller Institute. He joined the institute as a medical researcher in 1909. In 1911, he discovered that he could transmit a tumor from one chicken to another. The infective agent was evidently a virus, but such an organism was then little understood. It was thought that cancer was a disease within the cells. Rous' report on the transfer of tumors, published in 1912, was a medical milestone, though it was only with the 1951 discovery of a type of leukemia-causing virus that his early work was recognized.

Rous was born in Baltimore, Md. He received his Doctor of Medicine degree in 1905 from Johns Hopkins University in that city. He was an instructor in pathology at the University of Michigan before joining the Rockefeller Institute. Rous and his wife, the former Marion Eckford de Kay, have three daughters. WALTER F. MORSE

ROWING. See SPORTS.

RUBBER. See MANUFACTURING.

RULERS OF THE WORLD. See Facts in Brief tabs under various country articles.

RUSSIA. The post-Khrushchev collective leadership weathered its second year without major crises. The team of Leonid I. Brezhnev and Aleksei N. Kosygin represented a kind of balancing of party and state and a division of functions between the two top Soviet leaders. Their predecessor, Nikita S. Khrushchev, living in retirement since Oct. 15, 1964, emerged into the public view only to cast his vote in the national elections. The new leaders did not mount a major attack on him, although they did criticize and reverse some of his principal policies. The general style of the regime continued to be quiet, cautious, and pragmatic, as it followed a newly discovered slogan of Lenin's: "Fewer loud phrases, more genuine action."

Yet significant deeds were, in fact, few and far between during 1966, and changes were minimal in almost all spheres of Soviet life. Foreign observers noted a kind of paralysis of the system in the absence of initiative by the leaders. This was most noticeable at the 23rd Communist Party Congress, an occasion usually marking a major turning point, but one which, in 1966, passed off quietly and uneventfully. Successive meetings of the Central Committee were equally dull and concentrated on questions such as the Five-Year Plan directives (February), land reclamation (May), and Supreme Soviet business (August). Only the growing conflict with Communist China, which reached new dimensions toward the end of the year, broke the calm and the dull surface of public life. See CHINA, PEOPLE'S REPUBLIC OF.

Political System. No fundamental change in the political structure occurred. The enactment of a new constitution, as planned by Khrushchev, did not materialize. Work went on in the Constitutional Commission, now headed by Brezhnev, and in legal circles. But there were only a few public hints of the nature of impending changes.

Meanwhile, the elections to the Supreme Soviet on June 12 suggested that little or no basic reform was likely. In characteristic fashion, the single candidates in each electoral district were almost unanimously endorsed by the electorate, of which 99.94 per cent were reported to have voted. In the ensuing session of the Supreme Soviet in August, contrary to rumors in the West, Kosygin was again endorsed as Chairman of the Council of Ministers. The slate of nominees for the Council, numbering 84 members, was adopted without a dissenting voice, as was the slate for the Presidium, increased in size to 37, and headed by Nikolai V. Podgorny.

The business of the Supreme Soviet was on the whole routine during 1966.

The Communist Party remained the leading force in Soviet political life. As of Jan. 1, 1966, it included 12,471,000 members, of whom 797,400 were probationary. More than half of the members were under 40 years of age, and nearly half had been in the party for less than two years. At the 23rd congress, held in late March and early April, modifications were made in the party's rules, some of them codifying changes already made during 1965. Abolished were the Bureau for the RSFSR, the joint party-state control committee, and other innovations introduced by Khrushchev. There was some stiffening of the rules concerning admission to party membership, and a relaxation of Khrushchev's principle of periodic renewal of leadership. Most striking was the restoration of the title General Secretary (in place of First Secretary), and of the name, Politburo (in place of Presidium). This seemed to some to smack of a reversion to Stalinist practice, at least verbally. Others, however, felt the changes were probably designed to denigrate Khrushchev and to emphasize the return to Leninist principles.

More important than any of the semantic or organizational changes was the fact that no serious changes occurred in the ranks of the newly elected top organs. With the retirement of the elderly Shvernik and Anastas Mikoyan, and the appointment of A. Y. Pelshe (from Latvia), the Politburo numbered 11 full members, and eight candidates. The key figures appeared to be Brezhnev, Kosygin, Podgorny, and Suslov. The Secretariat numbered 10, in addition to Brezhnev, who, with Suslov and Shelepin, constituted the inner core. The new Central Committee included 195 full members, and 165 candidates, representing a shift of approximately one in five of the earlier roster of full members, and one in four of the candidates.

Economic Policy. There were no dramatic shifts in economic policy. Official statistics claimed that there had been a recovery in the rate of growth of the national income during 1964 and 1965 from the disastrously low figures of 1962 and 1963. A new Five-Year Plan, for the years 1966 to 1970, was adopted by the party congress, and was designed to correct the alleged imbalances of the Khrushchev period. The targets for both industry and agriculture were significantly reduced, and more consumer goods were to be provided.

Meanwhile, such moves were being introduced cautiously in certain selected enterprises in specific industries. Prominent economists, such as Lev Leontyev and Yevsei Liberman, voiced doubts about the pace of economic reforms and the lack of measures to free prices from government regulation. At the end of September, Vladimir Sitnin, chairman of the Committee on Prices, announced sweeping increases in wholesale prices for heavy industry effective July 1, but gave only vague hints of a future lessening of government control over prices.

In January, a committee of 149 members was set up, with Brezhnev as chairman, to study revision of the model statute of the collective farm. There was no indication, however, that this committee would ultimately recommend major changes in the collective system, or in the role of the private plots of individual farmers. Meanwhile, significant measures were taken to improve the income of collective farmworkers and to stimulate production. As of July 1, collective farmers were to receive guaranteed monthly payments in cash and in kind, corresponding to the rate of pay of the hitherto more highly paid state farmworkers.

Even more significant for the future was the far-reaching 10-year land reclamation program approved at the Central Committee meeting in May. About 15,000,000 rubles would be invested over the next five years in clearing and draining lands in the north, and irrigating those in the south. Finally, October 9 was set aside as a new national holiday to honor farmworkers. The regime was entitled to do a little boasting on this occasion. It produced a bumper grain crop of 171,000,000 tons in 1966.

Cultural Life. The outstanding event in the cultural sphere, and one of the most dramatic of the year, was the trial of two Soviet writers, Andrei D. Sinyavsky (alias Abram Tertz) and Yuli M. Daniel (alias N. Arzhak). They were accused of conducting agitation or propaganda with a view to subverting the Soviet regime, by publishing abroad, under pseudonyms, books regarded as anti-Soviet.

Polish and Russian leaders meet at the 23rd Congress of the Soviet Union's Communist party held in Moscow. Poland's Wladyslaw Gomulka, *second from left,* is flanked by Russia's Aleksei Kosygin, *left,* and Leonid Brezhnev. Polish Premier Josef Cyrankiewicz is at far right.

Delegates to the Soviet Communist Party's 23rd Congress converge on the new Hall of Congress. Flags are those of the Soviet republics.

During a four-day trial, both refused to admit their guilt, denied that their writings were anti-Soviet, and made spirited appeals for literary freedom. Their pleas, circulated privately, became widely known at home and abroad. They were found guilty, and sentenced to hard labor.

Foreign Relations. The year opened with the Soviet Union successfully mediating between India and Pakistan at the Tashkent Conference (see INDIA). Another evidence of Soviet influence was the signing, in January, of a new 20-year treaty with the Mongolian People's Republic (see OUTER MONGOLIA). In February, the soft landing of Luna IX on the moon was a space feat not without repercussions in foreign affairs (see SPACE EXPLORATION). The visit of Kosygin to the United Arab Republic in May, and of President Charles de Gaulle to the Soviet Union in June, demonstrated that the Soviet Union had other friends in the world (see FRANCE).

Another Soviet traveler abroad, D. S. Polyansky, deputy prime minister, after a long trip in Canada, signed an agreement for the opening of an air link between Montreal and Moscow. A similar aviation agreement was signed with the United States during the year.

None of these commercial successes could fully balance the fact that the Soviet Union had not been able to achieve similar results in its diplomatic relations with either the United States or Communist China. The continuance of war in North Vietnam stood in the way of improving relations with the United States (see VIETNAM). With China, conditions worsened steadily with the beginning of the cultural revolution and the actions of the Red Guard. The Soviet press, having until then avoided polemics, now began to report fully the events in Peking and, in August, the government protested strongly the action of the Red Guards outside the Soviet embassy. In September, Chinese students were ordered out of Russia. See CHINA, PEOPLE'S REPUBLIC OF; COMMUNISM.

Meanwhile, all was not well for the Soviet Union on its own doorstep in Europe. The conference of the Warsaw Pact countries, held in Bucharest in July, agreed on common declarations in support of North Vietnam and in favor of a European security conference. Soviet efforts to tighten the military organization of the Warsaw Pact, however, met with resistance, and no changes were made.

Facts in Brief. Population: 235,300,000. Government: General Secretary of the Communist Party Leonid I. Brezhnev; Premier Aleksei N. Kosygin; Chairman of the Presidium of the Supreme Soviet Nikolai Podgorny. Monetary Unit: ruble (1 = U.S. $1.11). Foreign Trade: exports, $2,176,-900,000; imports, $2,448,500,000. Principal Exports: machinery and equipment, crude oil and petroleum products, rolled steel. H. GORDON SKILLING

RYUN, JIM (1947-), a sophomore at the University of Kansas, became the first U.S. track star in 29 years to hold the world record for running the mile. In 1966 he not only broke the world record for the mile, but he also set a world record for the half mile and a U.S. record for the two-mile race.

Ryun ran the mile in only 3 minutes 51.3 seconds, more than two seconds faster than Michel Jazy of France, who set the old record in 1965. Just 12 years ago, England's Roger Bannister first ran the mile in less than 4 minutes (3:59.4) a feat long thought impossible. Since then more than 70 runners have done this, and two years ago Ryun became the first high school boy to do it. He has since run the mile nine times in less than four minutes. In May, 1966, Ryun ran the half mile in 1 minute 44.9 seconds, and in June he ran the two-mile in 8 minutes 25.2 seconds.

His home is in Wichita, Kans., where his father, Gerald Ryun, is a parts inspector at the Boeing aircraft plant. Jim attended Wichita East High School, where Coach Bob Timmons (now at the University of Kansas) first recognized his potential as a runner.

Ryun is far from husky—he weighs 155 pounds and is 6 feet 1½-inches tall—but careful training and exercise have given him strength and stamina. Throughout the year he rises early each morning to practice running. Besides running, his main hobby is photography, and several of his photographs have appeared in national magazines.

SACHS, NELLY (1891-), a refugee from Nazi Germany who became a Swedish citizen, was awarded the 1966 Nobel prize in literature on Oct. 20, 1966. She shared the honor with Shmuel Yosef Agnon of Israel (see AGNON, SHMUEL YOSEF). The joint award was only the third Nobel literature prize to be shared since the award was first offered in 1901. See NOBEL PRIZES.

Miss Sachs, a frail little woman with brown eyes, was born in Berlin on Dec. 10, 1891. Her father was a manufacturer with several inventions to his credit. Miss Sachs, who was then known as Leonie, was educated by private tutors who, like her parents, encouraged her interests in music, poetry, literature, and drama. At the age of 17, she began writing plays and verse, little of which appeared in print.

With the advent of Adolf Hitler, Miss Sachs' life was rudely changed. She lived in isolation for seven years, increasingly threatened by deportation. In 1940, she escaped to Sweden just before the Nazis were about to place her in a concentration camp.

Miss Sachs writes only in German. She has published several anthologies, among them *Eclipsed Stars* in 1945 and *The Habitation of Death* in 1947. A new collection of her poetry was published in December, 1966. In announcing the award, Dr. Anders Osterling of the Nobel committee praised her work "for expressing the tragedy of the Jewish people in lyrical laments of a painful beauty." WALTER F. MORSE

SAFETY. In 1966, the U.S. death toll from accidents increased in all four major categories. All types of accidents took the lives of an estimated 112,000 persons, an increase of 4.6 per cent over 1965. The death rate climbed a little slower—for a 3.6 per cent gain—to 57.2 per 100,000 population. That, however, was the highest rate since 1953, when it reached 60.1 per 100,000.

Deaths from public, nonroad accidents increased 2.6 per cent; motor vehicle deaths, 7.1 per cent; deaths from accidents at home, 3.6 per cent; and fatalities at work, 2.8 per cent. About 10,8000,000 persons were injured in accidents that disabled them beyond the day of the accident.

Fires, during 1966, killed about 7,800 Americans, some 600 more than in 1965. The monetary loss from fires was about 2 per cent higher than in 1965.

The total cost of all accidents was estimated at $19,500,000,000. The largest part—$5,800,000,000—was realized in loss of wages. Medical expenses accounted for $2,100,000,000; overhead costs of insurance, $3,900,000,000; property damage in motor vehicle accidents, $3,300,000,000; property loss in fires, $1,480,000,000. The "indirect" costs of work accidents were put at $2,900,000,000.

Accidental Deaths and Death Rates

	1965		1966	
Type of Accident	**Number**	**Rate†**	**Number**	**Rate†**
Motor Vehicle	49,000	25.3	52,500	26.8
Public Nonroad	19,000	9.8	19,500	10.0
Home	28,000	14.4	29,000	14.8
Work	14,100	7.3	14,500	7.4
TOTAL*	107,000	55.2	112,000	57.2

*Total does not add up because of duplications of motor vehicle and home and work deaths.
†Deaths per 100,000 population.
Source: National Safety Council.

Motor Vehicle accidents killed about 52,500 persons during the year, an all-time high. Several important steps were taken to help attack this mounting toll. In September, both houses of Congress passed the National Traffic and Motor Vehicle Safety Act and the National Highway Safety Act with hardly a dissenting vote. The highway measure provided the impetus and the means for the federal government to develop and encourage a comprehensive, yet individualized, safety program in each state.

President Lyndon B. Johnson named Dr. William J. Haddon, Jr., a nationally recognized safety authority, as head of the National Traffic Safety Agency, which was established by the safety legislation.

The Motor Vehicle Safety Act imposes mandatory changes on the 1968 models of both American and foreign-made cars. The Highway Safety Act of 1966 authorizes appropriations of $322,000,000 to the individual states over the next three fiscal years. Of this amount, $267,000,000 is earmarked for highway safety programs. The remaining $55,000,000 is for highway safety research and development.

Death is no stranger to California's "Slaughter Alley," the section of U.S. 101 where this multiple collision occurred in February, 1966.

The Defensive Driving Course of the National Safety Council was given to 195,227 persons in the year, almost five times as many as in 1965. Some 6,400 persons, including representatives from business, industry, government, the armed services, and religious and service groups, have been trained as course instructors.

The growing public concern over safety has spread to areas other than highway accidents. Congress, in 1966, extended federal safety provisions to small coal mines that employ fewer than 15 miners. Also, it brought the nation's 250,000 metal-ore and other noncoal miners under the protection of federal health and safety standards, New legislation tightened U.S. safety restrictions on all passenger ships sailing to or from U.S. ports. Vessels that failed to comply with international safety standards could be barred from leaving a U.S. port.

The Child Protection Act of 1966, amending the Federal Hazardous Labeling Act, banned the sale of hazardous children's toys and required warning labels on other dangerous articles and household materials. Drug manufacturers, late in the year, agreed upon more stringent bottling and labeling procedures for children's aspirin.

Awards. The National Safety Council's Trustees Awards for 1965 went to Delaware and Indianapolis, Ind., as the state and city, respectively, with the best all-round accident prevention programs. HOWARD PYLE

SAILING. See BOATS AND BOATING.

SAINT LOUIS. Major investments in a renewed waterfront, including a new 49,500-seat stadium, spurred metropolitan growth in 1966. In November, a survey showed more than $2,320,000,000 in major industrial, commercial, or public facilities were being constructed or planned. Suburban communities felt the impact of an office building boom and long-term growth was also forecast for the relatively undeveloped east side of the Mississippi.

To help support continued growth, the Chamber of Commerce and Mayor Alfonso J. Cervantes gave solid backing to 18 bond proposals, but voters in November approved only six, totaling $54,380,000. These will permit improvements in hospitals and health care, airports, street lighting, waterworks, and other municipal services. Although all proposals received more than 50 per cent of the total vote, legal requirements of a two-thirds majority killed the other 12 proposals.

Mayor Cervantes, himself of Spanish descent, scored a personal coup by negotiating to have the Spanish Pavilion–"the jewel of the New York World's Fair"–rebuilt on a downtown site. The much-applauded structure will house restaurants, a library, and a theater. The pavilion will have to share the spotlight, not only with the soaring 630-foot Gateway Arch, but also with three historic water towers built in the late 1800s. They were officially designated as landmarks. DONALD W. LIEF

SALVATION ARMY began its second century of international service by initiating a new program called the Salvationist Service Corps (SSC). The new activity, patterned after the Peace Corps, gives college students an opportunity to work with people in another country.

The first SSC group was composed of 12 students from California universities. After receiving special training, they were given summer assignments in Bolivia, Chile, and Peru. The SSC was officially approved by international headquarters during 1966 and will be included in Salvation Army programs in all parts of the world.

The Salvation Army received two awards in 1966. The first was a Certificate of Commendation from William J. Driver, administrator of the U.S. Veterans Administration, for its work with hospitalized veterans. The second was the Outstanding Service Award of the American Veterans of World War II and Korea. This award was given "in recognition of devoted and continuing service to humanity without regard to race, creed, or color for 100 years, and for the special services provided by the Salvation Army to American servicemen in three major wars and conflicts."

On Jan. 27, 1966, Commissioner Samuel Hepburn became national commander of the Salvation Army in the United States. He succeeded Commissioner Holland French. JOSEPH P. ANDERSON

SAN FRANCISCO experienced some tense nights of racial violence in the poverty-ridden Hunter's Point section from September 27 to 29. Injuries and damage were held to a minimum due to the presence of 1,200 National Guardsmen.

A major urban renewal project for Yerba Buena Center got the go-ahead from the board of supervisors. Its 80 acres south of Market Street will be converted at a cost of $31,000,000 to a planned mixture of commercial, cultural, educational, and public facilities. Less clear was the future of the proposed 423-acre Inner Mission redevelopment project. A wide assortment of citizen demands have held up the project.

The Bay Area Rapid Transit (BART) system was attacked for lack of aesthetic concern. Its consulting architect and landscape architect resigned, and the city rejected designs for two BART subway stations to be built under Market Street. Also, voters in Berkeley approved by 80 per cent a $20,000,000 bond issue raised to bury a part of the BART rail line, rather than having to look at what citizens considered an ugly overhead track.

However, San Franciscans rejected two large bond issues. A $96,500,000 proposal unrelated to BART to extend subway lines throughout the city went down to defeat, as did a $95,000,000 plan for improvements at International Airport. DONALD W. LIEF

SASKATCHEWAN. See CANADA.

SAUDI ARABIA. King Faisal, at a press conference held during his official 10-day visit to the United States in June, set off a storm of controversy. A statement by him, which was considered extremely anti-Semitic, aroused such a storm of protest that New York City's Mayor John V. Lindsay canceled a state dinner as well as all other official honors under pressure from Jewish groups. To smooth over relations with the Arab world's leading monarchy, however, President Lyndon B. Johnson later gave a stag dinner for Faisal, and New York Governor Nelson Rockefeller organized a seminar with leading U.S. specialists on Arab affairs.

The Saudi Arabian struggle with the United Arab Republic (UAR) over the civil war in neighboring Yemen sharpened. The two Arab countries supported opposing sides and committed troops and arms to the fighting. Saudi Arabia made aid agreements providing it with increased military power. Great Britain sold jet aircraft and Thunderbird ground-to-air missiles to the Saudi Arabians, and, in addition, agreed to build a military airfield near Yemen's border and set up an emergency defense system. The Raytheon Company of Lexington, Mass., sold the Saudi Arabian government Hawk antiaircraft missiles valued at about $126,000,000. In September, the United States promised to sell Saudi Arabia $100,000,000 worth of trucks and armored personnel carriers. The moves reflected international concern over a renewed UAR troop build-up there and the bombing of the Arabian oasis of Nejran in September, which threatened to cut off the flow of Arabian oil (see MIDDLE EAST).

A new leftist organization, the Federation of the People of the Arabian Peninsula, took credit in December for cutting pipelines and committing terrorist acts against Faisal's monarchy. The organization was the first of its type in Arabia.

The Saudi General Petroleum and Mineral Organization (Petromin) opened a new steel mill near Jiddah. To increase Arabia's revenues, Petromin also revised the Arabian American Oil Company (Aramco) concession agreement to tax Aramco sales at the posted price rather than at the actual discount price. Agreements were signed with Occidental Petroleum for a $19,000,000 sulfur recovery plant in Dammam, with West Germany for the al-Hasa irrigation project, and with an international consortium of companies for a $5,600,000 desalination project.

A potentially rich vein of silver and gold was found in the government's continuing search for mineral resources.

Facts in Brief. Population: 6,950,000. Government: King Faisal. Monetary Unit: riyal (4.47= U.S.$1). Foreign Trade: exports, $1,301,100,000; imports, $447,100,000. Principal Exports: petroleum and petroleum products. WILLIAM SPENCER

SAUL, RALPH SOUTHEY (1922-), a lawyer and a former federal Securities and Exchange Commission (SEC) official, became president of the American Stock Exchange (Amex) on November 7. The exchange's board of governors elected Saul to be the fifth president of the second largest U.S. securities market. He succeeded Edwin D. Etherington, who resigned to become president of Wesleyan University, Middletown, Conn.

Saul's election attracted special attention because he was a principal author of a 1963 SEC report that accused some Amex traders of "manifold and prolonged abuses." Some of the traders went to jail. Saul said as president he would manage "this market place" carefully, and tighten Amex standards for listing and rejecting stocks.

Saul was born May 21, 1922, in Brooklyn, N.Y., and served with the navy in World War II. He received his B.A. degree in 1947, and a LL.B in 1951.

After a year with the U.S. Foreign Service at Prague, Czechoslovakia, Saul began practicing law in New York City. He became an assistant counselor to Governor Thomas E. Dewey of New York. In 1958, Saul joined the SEC and rose to director of its trading and markets division in 1963. He left the SEC in 1965 to become an executive of Investors Diversified Service, Inc., of Minneapolis, Minn., which manages mutual funds. WALTER F. MORSE

Saudi Arabia's King Faisal, *left*, and Jordan's King Hussein I, *right*, were targets of the Middle East's anti-royalists in 1966.

SAUTER, ARNOLD (1908-), who has served as the Director General of Switzerland's Federal Public Health Service (FPHS) since 1955, was elected president of the 19th World Health Assembly on May 3, 1966. The assembly is a meeting held annually by the World Health Organization (WHO), an agency of the United Nations. Its 1966 meeting, which was held in Geneva, Switzerland, was attended by about 400 delegates representing WHO's 123 member nations and three associate members. The vote for Sauter, who succeeded V. V. Olguin of Argentina, was unanimous. See POPULATION, WORLD; UNITED NATIONS (UN).

Sauter was born in 1908 at Rickenbach, Thurgovie, Switzerland. The son of a physician, he became interested in medicine at an early age. Subsequently, he studied at the Faculties of Medicine at the University of Geneva and Zurich. He received his doctor of medicine degree at the world renowned University of Basel.

Shortly after graduating, Sauter set up a private practice. He had, however, always been intensely interested in problems involving public health and when he was offered the directorship of Switzerland's FPHS in 1955, he readily accepted. Sauter has written extensively on public health problems, chiefly tuberculosis, and many of his published works are used as textbooks in Switzerland's medical schools. WALTER F. MORSE

SCHLESINGER, ARTHUR M. JR. (1917-), won the 1966 Pulitzer prize in the field of biography of an American subject, with his book, *A Thousand Days: John F. Kennedy in the White House*. The book told the story of the Kennedy administration as seen by an insider who served the President as a special assistant and who was also an experienced author and historian. Schlesinger, in fact, had won the 1946 Pulitzer prize in history for *The Age of Jackson*, published when he was only 28, and had published three volumes of *The Age of Roosevelt* before he worked in the Kennedy government. His experience in government caused him to emphasize the "role of chance and contingency, the sheer intricacy of situations, the murk of battle," as heavily influencing the decisions made by the men who hold power.

Born in Columbus, Ohio, on Oct. 15, 1917, the son of a man who became a famous historian, Arthur Meier Schlesinger, Jr., graduated *summa cum laude* from Harvard University in 1938. He was a professor of history at Harvard from 1947 to 1961. In 1940, he married Marian Cannon. They have four children. During World War II, he served with the Office of Strategic Services (OSS). He served on the campaign staff of Adlai E. Stevenson in the elections of 1952 and 1956. Schlesinger holds a chair in the humanities at the City University of New York.

SCHOOL. See CIVIL RIGHTS; EDUCATION; Section One, LAWRENCE A. CREMIN: FOCUS ON EDUCATION.

SCIENCE AND RESEARCH. A two-year search for a site for the world's largest atom smasher ended on Dec. 16, 1966, with the announcement that Weston, Ill., a tiny village west of Chicago, had been selected by the Atomic Energy Commission (AEC).

The huge 200,000,000,000-electron-volt proton accelerator will consist, in part, of a ring of magnets a mile in diameter. Protons accelerated in this ring will be used to study the tiny subatomic particles. The construction of the accelerator complex is expected to cost about $360,000,000. It will have an annual budget of around $60,000,000.

The accelerator was a highly sought-after scientific prize. Some 150 sites were proposed by 43 states. In 1965, the AEC visited the sites and reported its findings to the National Academy of Sciences (NAS). By April, 1966, the Site Evaluation Committee of the NAS had pared the list to seven possibilities–Ann Arbor, Mich.; the Brookhaven National Laboratory at Upton, N.Y.; Denver, Colo.; Madison, Wis.; the Sierra foothills near Sacramento, Calif.; and South Barrington or Weston, near Chicago.

Following the publication of this list, South Barrington withdrew, stating that the accelerator and its staff would adversely affect the community's residential character. The other communities, however, avidly sought the project because of its cultural and economic benefits.

The criteria for the site selection included: 3,000 level acres of stable land; adequate power, water, and industrial facilities for the machine; and suitable educational, cultural, and transportation facilities for its staff and users.

Appropriations. Federal funds for research and development in 1966 did not increase, for the first time since the mid-1950s. Appropriations leveled at $15,900,000,000. According to *Science*, the journal of the American Association for the Advancement of Science, this was due mostly to U.S. commitments in Southeast Asia and the administration's desire not to cut funds for education and welfare.

The National Science Foundation pointed out that basic research was getting favorable attention and a higher percentage of the total research and development budget than ever before, because of Space Age demands and the government's drive to upgrade the nation's colleges and universities. It indicated that the outlook is for development's share of the research dollar to decline eventually to 60 per cent or slightly less. Its share was 79 per cent in 1959 and 66 per cent in 1966.

Currently, the fastest growth in government science funding is in the psychological and social sciences. Significant funding increases are also expected for research on environmental pollution, urban transportation, and water resources.

Pollution. Environmental pollution and waste management was an ever-growing concern of the

The tiny village of Weston, Ill., *above*, 30 miles west of Chicago, won out as the site of the Atomic Energy Commission's proposed 200 bev accelerator, *right*. It is expected to be completed by 1975.

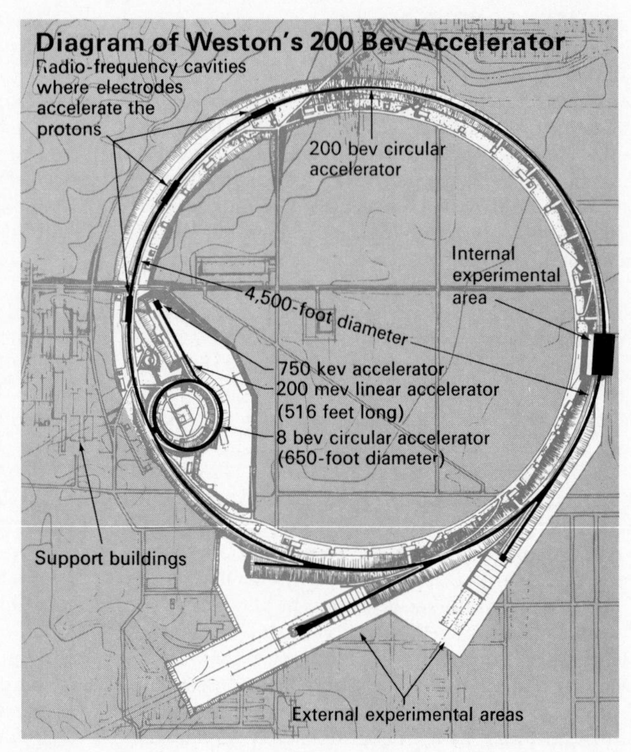

scientific community in 1966. A NAS committee on pollution headed by Athelstan F. Spilhaus of the University of Minnesota issued a report early in the year titled "Waste Management and Control." The committee contended that "our whole economy is based on taking natural resources, converting them into things that are consumer products, selling them to the consumer, and then forgetting about them." It pointed out, however, that there are in fact no "consumers" but only "users," and that the time has come to develop "the ultimate system that closes the loop from user back to resource and reuse."

The report recommended federal initiatives to bring about the application of modern technology to pollution control. Among the specific recommendations were the use of organic wastes to fertilize barren land and the segregation of metallic wastes so they can be reused. A National Commission for Environmental Protection, to be appointed by the President, was also suggested.

A symposium at the December meeting of The American Association for the Advancement of Science focused on the subject "Science in Pollution Control." The sessions dealt with pollution and health, atmospheric and radioactive pollution, and industry's role in environmental pollution.

International Cooperation. A group of scientists who helped organize the International Geophysical Year (IGY) and the International Years of the Quiet Sun (IYQS) appealed to governments, in a letter to *The Times* of London in July, to make such scientific cooperation permanent. The appeal was signed by two Russians, four Americans, one Briton, one Belgian, and one Italian. In reference to past collaboration, they wrote, "These world-wide cooperative scientific projects have shown conclusively that, however many and serious are the political problems that trouble the human race, it is possible for all the nations of the world to work closely together in great enterprises for the common good."

Such cooperation was also urged by Italy's Foreign Minister Amintore Fanfani, who proposed a Technological Marshall Plan for Western Europe. President Johnson took official notice of the Fanfani proposal in a speech to the National Conference of Editorial Writers on October 7, in New York City. He emphasized his desire to maintain close relations with the nations of Europe. He also said, "We are exploring how best to develop science and technology as a common resource. Recently the Italian government suggested an approach to narrowing the gap in technology between the United States and Western Europe. That proposal deserves careful study. The United States is ready to cooperate with the European nations on all aspects of this problem."

Science of Science. In recent years a new scientific discipline has been evolving in the hands of a small group of research investigators, administrators, and journalists. It is called "the science of science," and was institutionalized in 1964 by the formation of the Science of Science Foundation in London. During 1966, J. D. Bernal and A. L. Mackay of the University of London wrote an article for the British journal *The Technologist* that sharpened this somewhat hazy concept.

"Science must examine itself," they wrote, "in order to learn how science works and to make it work better." They asserted that the preconditions for a science of science now exist because there is enough scientific knowledge to be studied statistically and enough case histories of scientific discovery to identify and classify common elements. The foundation, with Bernal and Mackay among the members of its advisory council, promotes investigations that range from the analysis of the flow of scientific information to the relationship between science and technology.

Columbia University set up an institute to study the ethical and humanistic implications of the scientific revolution. Named the Institute for the Study of Science in Human Affairs, it was made possible by a $1,000,000 founding grant from the Alfred P. Sloan Foundation. The stated objectives of the new institute are the study of social and economic changes as they are related to scientific and technological advances.

JAMES A. PEARRE

See also Section One, Harrison Brown: FOCUS ON SCIENCE.

SCIENCE CLUBS OF AMERICA held the 17th National Science Fair–International in Dallas, Tex., in May, to honor the most promising student-scientists of the year.

Top Winners from among 419 finalists were:

Edward J. Emery, 17, of New Albany, Ind., for *L Forms and Gonidial Variants of Strain B6 of Agrobacterium Tumefaciens Produced by Glycine.*

Melinda L. Warner, 16, of Dallas, Tex., for *Hemerocallis Hybridizing.*

Carolyn C. Gerhardt, 18, of Jacksonville, Fla., for *Amminization of Transition Metal Sulfates.*

Robert Michael Swift, 15, of Chicago, Ill., for *Biochemical Study of Crown Gall Bacteria.*

Scott A. Jenkins, 15, of Albuquerque, N.Mex., for *Disturbance Theory for Rocket Drag Reduction.*

Frank R. Rudy, 17, of Harrisburg, Pa., for *Polymorphous DNA Molecules Adapted to Experiments on the Cause, Annihilation, and Prevention of Malignancies.*

Mary L. Wade, 18, of Gilmer, Tex., for *Oral Roentgenotherapy.*

James Kopel, 18, of Miami Beach, Fla., for *Experimental Confirmation of Wave-Particle Duality by the Use of Electron and Ion.*

Joseph F. Leykam, 18, of St. Louis, Mo., for *Design and Construction of an Electron Microscope.*

Dennis A. Hejhal, 17, of Chicago, Ill., for *Selected Topics in Complex Analysis.*

Mary D. R. Ruggere, 16, of Kingston, Pa., for *Expansion of the Moebius Strip in Dimension and Genus.*

Dena Lyn Ditzenberger, 16, of Terre Haute, Ind., for *Trichinosis in Non-Mammalian Vertebrates.*

N. Morris Summers, Jr., 16, of Jacksonville, Fla., for *Enzymic Basis for Melanization and Sclerotization in Fiddler Crab, Uca Pugnax.*

Health Awards were given by the following organizations: *American Dental Association*–Mary Lallier Schilling of Northfield, Minn., and Mary Lorie Wade of Gilmer, Tex. *American Medical Association*–Mary Lallier Schilling of Northfield, Minn., and Robert Carter Dillingham of Tallahassee, Fla. *American Pharmaceutical Association*–Dan Bradley Dydek of Fort Worth, Tex. *American Veterinary Medical Association*–Edwin Ronnie Collier of Mesquite, Tex.

Special Awards were made by the following organizations: *American Association of Petroleum Geologists*–Larry Chick of Lynnwood, Wash. *American Chemical Society*–Paul R. Herstein of Flint, Mich., and Sharon L. Payne of McLean, Va. *American Institute of Chemical Engineers*–to Scott A. Jenkins of Albuquerque, N.Mex. *American Institute of Mining, Metallurgical, and Petroleum Engineers*–Donald R. Chesnut of London, Ky.; Richard W. Edelman of Glendale, Wis.; and Gregory A. Snoke of Fort Wayne, Ind. *American Patent Law Association*–Carl H. Fromer of Staten Island, N.Y. *American Psychological Association*–Stuart Craig Jarvis of Louisville, Ky. *American Society for Metals*–Richard Wayne Edelman of Glendale, Wis. *American Society for Microbiology*– Robert M. Swift of Chicago, Ill. *Entomological Society of America*–Theodore I. King of Battle Creek, Mich. *National Committee for Careers in Medical Technology*–Edwin R. Collier of Mesquite, Tex. *National Pest Control Association*–Donald Howard Atha of San Diego, Calif. *Optical Society of America*–Henry B. Garrett of Roswell, N.Mex. *Society of Women Engineers*–Carolyn A. Ross of Berkeley Heights, N.J.

The National Aeronautics and Space Administration (NASA) awarded two-day visits to NASA facilities to: James Duggan of Alexandria, Va.; Jeffrey S. Harris of Albuquerque, N.Mex.; H. Grady Rylander of Austin, Tex.; Edward C. Svendsen of Arlington, Va.; Theodore M. Willer of Pine Village, Ind.; and Michael C. Yaksh of Atlanta, Ga.

The Atomic Energy Commission awarded trips to the Argonne National Laboratory to: Dwight N. Bass of Decatur, Ala.; John W. Benge of Lovington, N.Mex.; David C. Church of Louisville, Ky.; Mel Graham of Baton Rouge, La.; Barbara A. Hanson of Albuquerque, N.Mex.; James Kopel of Miami Beach, Fla.; Eddie G. Napps of Longview, Tex.; Frank W. Nobles of Hereford, Tex.; Edward C. Svendsen of Arlington, Va.; and Mary L. Wade of Gilmer, Tex.;

The U.S. Air Force (USAF) honored finalists in 10 special categories with plaques and expense-paid trips to USAF research facilities. The 10 and their categories were: *Aerospace Biological Sciences*–Jeffrey S. Harris of Albuquerque, N.Mex. *Aerospace Chemistry*—Steven G. O'Neal of Michigan City, Ind. *Aerospace Dynamics*–Scott A. Jenkins of Albuquerque, N.Mex. *Aerospace Electronics and Communications*–Howard S. Katz of Silver Spring, Md. *Aerospace Environmental Sciences*–Curtis Bryant of Le Mars, Iowa. *Aerospace Medicine*–Letantia B. Jankowski of Lodi, N.J. *Aerospace Physics*–H. Grady Rylander of Austin, Tex. *Aerospace Psychological and Social Sciences*–Rick P. Johnson of Evansville, Ind. *Aerospace Propulsion*–Jeffrey B. Bentley of Temple, Tex. *Mathematical and Computational Sciences*–John Pitts of Austin, Tex.

Westinghouse 25th Annual Science Talent Search scholarships went to: Henry Wagner, Jr., 16, of Gwynedd Valley, Pa., $7,500; Barry J. Klyde, 17, of Flushing, N.Y., $6,000; David R. Jefferson, 17, of Beltsville, Md., $5,000; Kevin R. Binns, 18, of Des Moines, Iowa, $4,000; and Linda Sue Powers, 18, of Beckley, W.Va., $3,000.

FOSTER P. STOCKWELL

SCULPTURE. See PAINTING AND SCULPTURE.

SENEGAL. See AFRICA.

SERVICE CLUBS and organizations in 1966 gave special attention to activities designed to promote international understanding and cooperation and to preserve freedom. Service clubs outside the United States grew rapidly, requiring increased liaison between newly formed clubs and international headquarters.

Kiwanis International inaugurated a Freedom Leadership Program. Its major objectives are: to identify the heritage of freedom in our nation; to provide leadership to increase understanding of the essential elements of our freedom; and to provide the leadership to increase respect and appreciation for our freedoms to the end that they will be defended, strengthened, and perpetuated. A Freedom Leadership manual explains the three objectives and suggests specific projects.

The rapid growth of Kiwanis Clubs overseas led to the authorization of a plan for a new European affiliate. It would divide Europe into six provisional Kiwanis districts. When four such districts have a combined total of at least 100 clubs, the parent organization's board of trustees will direct that Kiwanis International-Europe be established. The board authorized the establishment of the office of European administrator and named Kenneth P. Greenaway to the new position.

R. Glenn Reed, Jr., of Marietta, Ga., was elected head of Kiwanis International. James M. Moler of Charleston, W.Va., was named president-elect.

Lions International began the observance of its 50th anniversary by announcing a world-wide essay contest. In keeping with the Golden Anniversary year motto "Search for Peace," the international essay competition was on the topic "Peace Is Attainable." The contest was open to boys and girls 14 to 21 years of age in 132 countries. Its goal was to obtain a design for world peace; to create an understanding on the part of young people about the challenge of peace.

All entrants submitted essays no longer than 5,000 words to their local Lions Club. After the papers have been judged at the club and district levels, contest winners will be selected in eight world regions. All division winners will receive $1,000 and travel expenses to Chicago where the final judging will take place during the Lions' 50th annual convention in 1967. The winner will receive a $25,000 first prize and will present his essay to the convention.

As the organization entered its 50th year, it had nearly 800,000 members in 20,200 clubs in 132 countries and geographical locations. The largest Lions Club was in Monterrey, Mexico, with 1,011 members. The 49th annual convention of Lions International was held in New York City, July 6 to 9, 1966. Delegates elected Edward M. Lindsey of Lawrenceburg, Tenn., international president.

Rotary International, in cooperation with the Rotary Foundation, began a program called "Awards for Technical Training." The program is designed to help men 21 to 35 years of age working in technical fields to improve their vocational skills through a one-year study program in a country other than their own. The first 40 technical trainees were chosen from 23 countries.

Rotary Foundation Fellowships for International Understanding for 1966-1967 were awarded to 147 young men and women. The students spend a year abroad pursuing academic specialties, and getting acquainted with people and institutions in their host countries. They receive about $3,120 annually.

Interact, Rotary's organization for high school age boys, continued its steady growth. During the week of October 2 to 8, 1966, 34,000 boys in 1,400 clubs in 51 countries participated in Interact Week.

In July, 1966, there were 12,469 Rotary Clubs and an estimated 598,000 Rotarians in 133 countries and geographical regions. The 57th annual convention of Rotary International was held in Denver, Colo., June 12 to 16. Richard L. Evans, of Salt Lake City, Utah, was elected president. He outlined a 10-point program that emphasized Rotary's World Community Service projects. JOSEPH P. ANDERSON

SHIPS AND SHIPPING. See TRANSPORTATION.

SHIPWRECK. See DISASTERS.

SHOOTING. See SPORTS.

SIERRA LEONE. See AFRICA.

SKATING. See ICE HOCKEY; ICE SKATING.

SKIING. The French national ski team in 1966 took most of the Alpine skiing honors in the World Championships, held in Portillo, Chile, in August. The French won six of the eight gold medals, seven of the eight silver medals, and three bronzes.

Jean-Claude Killy and Marielle Goitschel led the team. Killy, best known as a slalom racer, scored a surprising win in the downhill, then eased his way to fifth- and eighth-place finishes in the two slalom races to take the men's combined title. His countryman, Leo LaCroix, was second, with Ludwig Leitner of Germany third and Jim Huega of the United States fourth. Miss Goitschel won the giant slalom and finished second in the downhill and special slalom to take the women's combined.

Other French victories were scored by Guy Perillat in the men's giant slalom and Annie Famose in the women's special slalom. Miss Famose also was second in the women's combined. The only non-French victories were scored by Carlo Senoner of Italy in the men's special slalom and 18-year-old Erika Schinegger of Austria in the women's downhill.

The best U.S. skier, Billy Kidd of Stowe, Vt., broke his leg in a training session at Portillo and could not compete. Also missing because of a broken leg was France's multiple Olympic medalist, Christine Goitschel, Marielle's sister.

Earlier, the French won most of the honors in the winter's big meets. Killy and Perillat shared laurels

The French team, which dominated the World Ski Championships held at Portillo, Chile, in August, 1966, marches in the opening ceremonies.

among the men with Kidd and Karl Schranz of Austria, while Miss Goitschel and her teammates stood out in the women's events. The French team edged Austria in the five-nation Werner Cup meet at Sun Valley, Idaho.

Nordic Skiing was dominated by the Norwegians who won five gold medals in the world championships at Holmenkollen, near Oslo, Norway.

Gjermund Eggen, a forester, led the way with victories in the 15- and 50-kilometer cross-country races. He also was a member of Norway's winning 40-kilometer relay team. Bjorn Wirkola won Norway's other gold medals in the 70- and 90-meter jumping events, while Georg Thoma of West Germany won his fourth straight world Nordic combined title. Russia swept the women's events, held in cross-country only. Alevtina Kolchina won the 5-kilometer race, and Claudia Boyarskikh the 10-kilometer; then they teamed up to form two-thirds of the winning 15-kilometer relay team.

A few weeks later, Wirkola made the longest ski jump in history at Vikersund Hill in Norway. His leap of 479 feet beat the previous record of 475.7 feet set by Peter Lesser of East Germany in 1965.

The University of Denver won its sixth straight National Collegiate Athletic Association (NCAA) championship. They took first place in jumping, cross-country, and downhill. James O. Dunaway

SOAP BOX DERBY. See Sports.

SOCCER. England played host to the World Cup tournament in July, 1966, and captured its first championship in a series of matches that attracted world-wide attention. The final game, played before 97,000 spectators at London's Wembley Stadium, was seen by a television audience estimated at 400,000,000. Queen Elizabeth II attended the matches and Prime Minister Harold Wilson returned from his meetings in the United States with President Lyndon B. Johnson to see the final game.

The championship game required a 30-minute overtime period. West Germany's Wolfgang Weber scored with only 30 seconds left in regulation time, tying the score at 2 to 2. Geoffrey Hurst, who made one goal during regulation play, then added two more in the extra period to win the coveted world title for England, 4 to 2.

Defending champion Brazil failed to reach the quarterfinal round. The famous King Pelé, whose speed and skill had led the Brazilian national team to World Cup triumphs in both 1958 and 1962, was injured in the first-round game. Without him in the lineup, Brazil was beaten by Hungary, 3 to 1. Then Portugal, whose star player Eusébio Ferreira da Silva replaced Pelé as the fans' favorite, eliminated the Brazilians by beating them, 3 to 1. Portugal then became the choice to take the cup. They defeated North Korea in the quarterfinal, 5 to 3, while the Soviet Union nipped Hungary, 2 to 1, West Germany routed Uruguay, 4 to 0, and England advanced with a 1 to 0 win over Argentina. In the semifinals, West Germany beat the Soviet Union and England eliminated Portugal, both by 2 to 1 scores.

World Soccer Standings
World Cup

Group 1 Standings	W	L	T	GF	GA	Pts
England	2	0	1	4	0	5
Uruguay	1	0	2	2	1	4
Mexico	0	1	2	1	3	2
France	0	2	1	2	5	1
Group 2						
West Germany	2	0	1	7	1	5
Argentina	2	0	1	4	1	5
Spain	1	2	0	4	5	2
Switzerland	0	3	0	1	9	0
Group 3						
Portugal	3	0	0	9	2	6
Hungary	2	1	0	7	5	4
Brazil	1	2	0	4	6	2
Bulgaria	0	3	0	1	8	0
Group 4						
U.S.S.R.	3	0	0	6	1	6
North Korea	1	1	1	2	4	3
Italy	1	2	0	2	2	2
Chile	0	2	1	2	5	1

Code: W (won), L (lost), T (tied), GF (goals for), GA (goals against), Pts (points)
Source: U.S. Soccer Football Association

New Leagues. The World Cup television ratings demonstrated the appeal of soccer as a specatator sport in the United States, as elsewhere. Two professional leagues were formed in the United States during 1966. Not long after the tournament ended in England, the National Professional Soccer League signed a contract with the Columbia Broadcasting System to televise one Sunday afternoon game each week from May to September, 1967. The league, however, did not receive recognition from the international federation that governs soccer. Its rival, the North American Soccer League, was recognized, but planned to wait until May, 1968, before starting to play. Since a number of cities were represented in both leagues, rumors of an eventual merger arose.

The National Professional Soccer League denied them and initiated an expensive, international talent hunt. It offered big salaries to coaches and players hoping to lure them to the United States.

The National Professional Soccer League planned to begin play with teams in New York City, Washington, D.C., Philadelphia, Pittsburgh, Atlanta, St. Louis, Chicago, Los Angeles, San Francisco, and Toronto. The North American Soccer League listed New York City, Washington, D.C., Philadelphia, Boston, Detroit, Cleveland, Chicago, Houston, Los Angeles, San Francisco, Vancouver, and Toronto. Two others were yet to be named.

JOHN LAKE

England's Geoffrey Hurst, *left,* scored two goals in overtime play to defeat the West German team 4 to 2 and win the world soccer cup.

SOCIAL SECURITY. In 1966, leaders of both major political parties promised Social Security beneficiaries a substantial increase in their monthly checks. President Lyndon B. Johnson announced that he would submit to the incoming 90th Congress legislation providing higher benefits. The same bill would allow persons of retirement age who continue working to increase their outside earnings without losing their Social Security benefits.

The President's plan, which would become effective Jan. 1, 1968, called for:

- An average increase of 10 to 15 per cent in monthly benefits, at a cost of $2,200,000,000 a year.
- A guaranteed minimum monthly benefit of $100 for each worker who has paid Social Security taxes for 25 years; the minimum is now $44 per month.
- An increase in the annual income ceiling from $1,500 to $2,400. This would make possible a higher income for those under Social Security who continue working after reaching retirement age.
- Extension of hospital and medical care coverage to approximately 1,000,000 disabled Social Security recipients under 65.

An increase in Social Security taxes went into effect on Jan. 1, 1966. The new tax schedule provided for a tax rate of 4.2 per cent each for employer and employee on earnings up to $6,600. The increase was one of the 1965 amendments to the Social Security Act which not only added Medicare but changed many of the provisions of the original act, passed in 1935, and gave an across-the-board increase of 7 per cent in all cash benefits. See MEDICARE.

The only amendment to the Social Security Act signed into law in 1966 extended coverage to men and women 72 years old or older who have never worked, or who have been in occupations not covered by Social Security and therefore have never paid Social Security taxes.

Commissioner Robert M. Ball estimated that about 370,000 persons were eligible for the new program at the outset. Monthly cash payments, which began in November, 1966, ranged from $35.00 for single persons to $52.50 for a married couple. The initial enrollment period will end Dec. 31, 1967.

These additional benefits will not be generally available to individuals receiving regular payments from other government retirement programs, regardless of whether they are federal, state, or local. However, in instances where the amount of the benefits received is less than the amount paid under Social Security, the Social Security Administration will make up the difference. The program will be financed out of general federal revenues.

During 1966, Social Security beneficiaries increased at the rate of 100,000 each month. By the end of the year there were more than 22,000,000 Americans who were receiving amounts from $44 to $309.20 per month, for a total cost estimated at $1,600,000,000.

JOSEPH P. ANDERSON

SOCIAL WELFARE leaders from 74 countries attended the 13th Biennial International Conference of Social Work in Washington, D.C., Sept. 4 to 10, 1966. The 3,000 delegates represented public and private social welfare agencies in all parts of the world. Two other international social welfare organizations, the International Association of Schools of Social Work and the International Federation of Social Workers, met at the same time.

Ruth Williams, former associate director of the National Conference of Social Workers, succeeded Joe R. Hoffer as secretary general of the International Conference of Social Work. Nelson C. Jackson, assistant executive director of the National Association of Social Workers, was elected secretary general of the International Federation of Social Workers.

Three Studies with far-reaching implications for social welfare policies and programs were completed in 1966. The first was made by the Advisory Council on Public Welfare, which was created by the U.S. Congress in 1964, "to review the administration of federally aided public welfare programs." The council's findings and recommendations were based on written and oral testimony presented over a two-year period by agency representatives, private citizens, and welfare recipients.

The council reported that 34,000,000 Americans were still living in poverty and that social services for the protection of children, families, the aged, and disabled were inadequate. Further, it said the lack of such services contributes to crime, delinquency, mental illness, and illegitimacy.

The second study was made by a Department of Health, Education, and Welfare task force on social work, education, and manpower. The findings revealed that the gap between the increasing demand and available supply of social welfare manpower was growing larger at all levels.

The third study, financed by the Ford Foundation, explored the feasibility of establishing neighborhood information centers as a part of a network of welfare services and facilities in urban communities. The study urged experimentation with neighborhood information centers under public and voluntary auspices. They would be staffed largely by nonprofessional personnel and adequately financed so that volunteer assistance would not be necessary to carry on the work.

Awards in 1966 included:

International Conference of Social Work René Sand Award to Jane M. Hoey, New York City, for outstanding leadership in developing national and international programs of social welfare.

National Conference on Social Welfare 1966 Distinguished Service Award to U.S. Representative Wilbur D. Mills (D., Ark.), "for his distinctive contribution toward the enactment of several of the most significant pieces of legislation in our time."

JOSEPH P. ANDERSON

SOMALIA. See AFRICA.

SOUTH AFRICA, REPUBLIC OF. Prime Minister Hendrik F. Verwoerd was stabbed to death in the Parliament building in Cape Town on Sept. 6, 1966. His assassin, Dimitri Tsafendas, was arrested on the spot, and on October 20, was judged insane. Balthazar Johannes Vorster, minister of justice, police, and prisons, and a strong believer in *apartheid* (racial segregation and separate development of the races) succeeded Verwoerd. See VORSTER, BALTHAZAR JOHANNES.

On January 21, South Africa again stated that it would not intervene in the affairs of other states or participate in boycotts. South Africa supplied the illegal government of Rhodesia with oil and other necessities throughout the year despite attempts by Britain and the United Nations (UN) to enforce a trade boycott (see RHODESIA). At the same time, it attempted to maintain good relations with other African nations, many of which were ruled by black Africans.

Conflicts. South Africa's control of South West Africa was a center of controversy throughout 1966. A former German colony, it was given to South Africa after World War I to be administered as a mandate of the League of Nations. Ethiopia and Liberia, strongly opposed to South Africa's policies of racial segregation, brought suit in the International Court of Justice at The Hague, The Netherlands, to end the mandate.

South Africa's new Prime Minister, Balthazar Johannes Vorster, promised no change in his country's strict apartheid policies.

Casket of Hendrik F. Verwoerd, slain South African Prime Minister, is carried by military leaders during rites in Pretoria.

The court dismissed the case on July 18, 1966, after deciding that Ethiopia and Liberia had no legal right to present the claims. Though the decision was celebrated in South Africa, other African nations condemned the action as a miscarriage of justice, and took the case to the United Nations (UN). On October 27, the UN General Assembly voted 114 to 2, with three abstentions–Great Britain, France, and Malawi–to end the 46-year-old mandate and bring South West Africa under UN administration.

South Africa declared that the UN had no legal right to order the change, and that any attempt to remove South West Africa from its control would be resisted with force. At year's end, approval for either economic sanctions or military intervention was being sought at the UN Security Council, though support from Britain and France, two council members, was doubtful since both had abstained from voting to end the mandate. See UNITED NATIONS (UN).

U.S. Senator and Mrs. Robert F. Kennedy visited South Africa in June and met with opposition leaders, editors, and students. He appealed for racial cooperation and equal rights. The government, opposed to such ideas, regarded the Kennedy visit as "purely private," and refused the senator's request to meet with government officials.

Emergency Measures. The government used its emergency powers to restrict outspoken advocates of equal rights for black Africans and other "disloyal" critics. Prohibitions against political meetings by black Africans who opposed government policies, and prompt arrest of those who tried to organize protests or create disorders resulted in outward calm and repressed opposition. Minister of Justice Vorster reported on August 2 that 125 people were being held for investigation under 180-day detention powers.

Backed by its enormous gold resources, the South African economy continued to expand at an inflationary rate. A World Bank loan of $20,000,000 was granted on July 29 to help finance a $176,000,000 power plant at Camden. Because of the ever-present threat of a boycott by nations opposed to South African racial policies, the search for oil was intensified. A minor discovery was reported.

Facts in Brief. Population: 18,700,000. Government: President Charles R. Swart; Prime Minister Balthazar Johannes Vorster. Monetary Unit: rand (1 = U.S. $1.40). Foreign Trade: exports, $1,426,900,000; imports, $2,487,300,000. Principal Exports: diamonds, gold, uranium. BENJAMIN E. THOMAS

SOUTH AMERICA. See LATIN AMERICA and articles on various countries.

SOUTH ARABIA, FEDERATION OF, was a major trouble spot in the Middle East during 1966. In January, two anti-British guerrilla organizations in neighboring Yemen merged to form the Front for the Liberation of Occupied South Yemen (FLOSY). Thereafter, assassinations and acts of terrorism increased steadily in the federation's British-protected state of Aden. The victims included the chief of the Aden Trades (union), the secretary of the bank employees union, and a member of Aden's federal council. FLOSY also took credit for the murder of the British commander of the Hadhramaut Bedouin Legion. Numerous grenade attacks were made against British troops stationed there. In August, the government sealed off the federation's border with Yemen and banned all trade.

Great Britain, meanwhile, proceeded with plans to withdraw its forces from Aden and grant the federation its independence by 1968. Britain promised $11,700,000 to help finance the federation's three-year development program.

Facts in Brief. Population: 1,150,000. Government: British High Commissioner Sir Richard Turnbull. Monetary Unit: dinar (1 = U.S. $2.82). Foreign Trade: exports, $49,600,000; imports, $51,200,000. Principal Exports: coffee, cotton, petroleum products. WILLIAM SPENCER

SOUTH WEST AFRICA. See SOUTH AFRICA, REPUBLIC OF; UNITED NATIONS.

SPACE EXPLORATION

The nation's exploits in space in 1966 were overshadowed early in 1967 by the tragic deaths of three U.S. astronauts in a routine test for what was to have been the first manned Apollo flight. Dead in a flash fire that swept the command module of their Apollo craft on Jan. 27, 1967, were: Virgil I. "Gus" Grissom, a veteran of both Gemini and Mercury; Edward H. White II, the first American to "walk" in space; and rookie astronaut Roger Chaffee. President Lyndon B. Johnson led the nation in mourning its fallen space pioneers. The tragedy seemed especially poignant because it came on the heels of a highly significant year in space, a year that saw the successful closing out of Project Gemini.

Besides knowledge gained in Project Gemini, these other accomplishments occurred in 1966:

- The moon was studied by unmanned spacecraft on its surface and by spacecraft in lunar orbit.
- Weather prediction was supported by operational spacecraft.
- New knowledge was gained of the environment of outer space.
- A major phase of unmanned flight was completed in the Apollo program of manned lunar exploration.

Gemini Highlights. The five missions in 1966 wound up the $1,300,000,000 Gemini program with resounding success. All six major program objectives were achieved. They were:

- Verification of man's ability to live and work on a flight that lasts longer than the time needed for a round trip to the moon.
- Use of the separately launched Agena vehicle as a propulsion unit for major changes in the orbit of a spacecraft.
- Rendezvous and docking.
- Manned operations in space outside the orbiting vehicle.
- Guided re-entry to a surface target.

Long-Duration Flight. The first objective of Gemini, a demonstration that man can live and work in space for up to 14 days, was accomplished by Astronauts Frank Borman and James A. Lovell, Jr., in the Gemini VII flight that took place in December, 1965.

Assembly in Space. Twice during 1966, flight, altitude, and speed records were exceeded with the

Panoramic view of India and Ceylon was taken by Gemini XI crewmen in orbit 460 nautical miles above the earth's surface.

use of the Agena as a space propulsion unit. On the Gemini X mission of July 18 to 21, Astronauts John W. Young and Michael Collins docked with their Agena target and then fired the Agena to add 400 mph to their 17,300-mile orbital speed. This caused them to reach an altitude of 476 miles. Later, on the Gemini XI mission of September 12 to 15, Astronauts Charles Conrad and Richard Gordon achieved an altitude of 851 miles and a speed of 17,943 mph. They also used the main engine of their Agena target vehicle to propel them to a higher altitude in space.

Rendezvous and Docking. Following the first achievement of rendezvous by Astronauts Walter M. Schirra, Jr., and Thomas P. Stafford in the Gemini VI flight in December, 1965, Gemini astronauts performed rendezvous in various ways on each of the five 1966 missions. The most impressive of the five maneuvers occurred during Gemini XI (September 12 to 15) when Charles Conrad, Jr., and Richard F. Gordon, Jr., linked up with their Agena on the first orbit—only an hour and 34 minutes after lift-off.

Docking was accomplished on four of the five missions. The only disappointment was on the June 3 to 6 Gemini IX flight of Astronauts Stafford and Eugene Cernan. They were prevented from nudging the nose of Gemini into the Agena's docking port because it was blocked by the gaping jaws of a protective cover that had failed to separate from

Historic close-up of the moon's Copernicus crater was taken by Lunar Orbiter II. It revealed 1,000-foot-high peaks, *center,* jutting from the floor. Peaks on the horizon are part of the Carpathian range.

the Agena vehicle, causing it to look like "an angry alligator," Stafford said.

Extra Vehicular Activity. Four U.S. astronauts ventured outside their Gemini spacecraft into the vastness of space during 1966, but it was not until the final Gemini XII mission of Lovell and Edwin E. Aldrin, Jr., from November 11 to 15, that satisfactory progress was achieved. On the earlier flights, Cernan on Gemini IX, Collins on Gemini X, and Gordon on Gemini XI, all found that simple activities in space outside the craft were quite exhausting.

But Aldrin had prepared carefully for his three ventures into the void. He spent more than five hours outside (including time standing up in his seat with the hatch open) and obtained valuable data on the performance of basic tasks in space. Aldrin was more successful than the others during his space walk because he took more frequent rests, had the use of extra handgrips on the outside of the craft, and wore a chest pack that absorbed perspiration and moisture from his breath.

Controlled Re-Entry. All of the last four Gemini missions returned to earth within a few miles of the waiting aircraft carrier. On the Gemini XI and XII flights, the astronauts allowed their computer to take over and fire the re-entry rockets. This had previously been done by the space pilots themselves.

Experiments. Also during the Gemini flights, astronauts conducted scores of scientific, technological, and operational experiments. Possibly the most impressive occurred on the second day of Gemini XII, when Lovell and Aldrin took photographs of a total eclipse of the sun.

In flying the 10 manned Gemini missions, the United States gained 1,940 man-hours of space flight experience that, combined with that of the Mercury program, brought the U.S. total to 2,000 hours.

Somewhat surprisingly, rendezvous had proved to be a little easier than expected, while extra vehicular activity was far more difficult.

The Gemini Emergency. Perhaps the most noteworthy event of Gemini was the nation's first space emergency. It occurred on the Gemini VIII mission of March 16. On this flight, Astronauts Neil A. Armstrong and David R. Scott accomplished docking for the first time, with the Agena target vehicle. But soon after, an electrical malfunction ignited a small rocket intended for maneuvering the spacecraft; it sent the craft into a rapid and accelerating roll. Armstrong and Scott identified the difficulty during a hair-raising half hour and overcame the spin by prematurely firing their re-entry control rockets. Hence, two orbits later, they had to return to earth in the western Pacific, after experiencing less than 11 hours of a scheduled three-day mission.

The successful handling of the Gemini VIII crisis confirmed the wisdom of the program's intensive contingency planning and training of astronauts and ground crews. But it focused increased attention on the potential need of rescue operations on more complex future space missions.

Another significant accomplishment was in the area of management. The original plan called for the spacing of flight missions three months apart. But technical and other difficulties delayed the beginning of manned flights more than a year after the time originally intended. But through concerted action by the National Aeronautics and Space Administration (NASA) and its contractors, the average time between launches was reduced to two months and the program was completed on schedule.

Lunar Studies advanced in 1966. Both Russia and the United States sent unmanned spacecraft to the moon to seek information for their manned lunar programs. Surveyor I soft-landed on the moon and sent to earth over 11,000 photos. Lunar Orbiter I photographed the earth from the moon. Lunar Orbiter II transmitted the first close-up photos of the greater crater Copernicus. See Close-Up.

Weather Operations. The Environmental Science Services Administration (ESSA) of the U.S. Department of Commerce orbited its first three operational weather satellites in 1966, as a part of the routine activities of the Weather Bureau. The ESSA satellites transmit pictures of cloud cover to the weather services of many countries. Also during the year, the United States and the Soviet Union began exchanging weather information from space on a "cold line" cable link established by agreement.

An improved weather satellite, Nimbus II, was orbited by NASA on May 15. Crossing the poles on each revolution and constantly pointed toward earth, Nimbus supplied continuous day and night weather pictures.

On December 6, the first Applications Technology Satellite was launched to a stationary orbit at an altitude of 22,300 miles. There it performend communications experiments and obtained pictures of the entire earth.

Science Satellites. Good results were obtained with several unmanned spacecraft. The Orbiting Geophysical Observatory (OGO) III operated for 50 days after its June 6 launch with an advanced stabilization system that kept it pointed toward the earth. After this period, it was stabilized in a simpler fashion. Its 21 experiments provided correlated measurements of the earth's magnetic field, radiation belt, and its relationship to the sun.

Explorer XXXII, a 495-pound satellite orbited May 25, carried eight experiments to collect data needed for understanding changes in the upper atmosphere and to study the effects of short-term atmospheric disturbances caused by radiation from solar storms. The flight was timed for the beginning of a new period of solar activity, expected to reach the maximum in 1968-1969.

The Passive Geodetic Earth Orbiting Satellite (PAGEOS) I, launched June 23, is a plastic balloon

The Mystery Of the Moon

The "Queen of the Night," as poets have called the moon, lost much of her glamor in 1966. No fewer than eight "suitors" called on her and agreed that she was scarred, bleak, airless, dry, and totally hostile. But then these suitors were no handsome knights either; they were an odd assortment of craft guided to the moon by American and Russian space engineers.

The visitors to the moon were:

Luna IX soft-landed Feb. 23
Luna X orbited the moon April 4
Surveyor I soft-landed June 2
Lunar Orbiter I orbited Aug. 10
Luna XI orbited Aug. 28
Luna XII orbited Oct. 25
Lunar Orbiter II orbited Nov. 9
Luna XIII soft-landed Dec. 24

Russia again jumped to an early lead. A Russian Luna was the first craft ever to soft-land outside the earth; another was the first to orbit the moon. Lagging, but not far, the U.S. Surveyor and Lunar Orbiters sent back tens of thousands of television pictures, including detailed views of the moon's rugged far side. Some were among the most dramatic and informative ever taken.

The mooncraft were searching for safe spots on which men could land. As a bonus to scientists, the search revealed the moon itself in great detail. The relatively smooth areas—the maria—were found to be undulating, dark gray-brown plains littered with rocks and pock-marked with shallow craters. Lunar uplands showed rugged mountains rounded by erosion, looking much like some on earth.

These vistas generally confirmed science's pre-Space Age notions: the moon has been cratered and worn through eons of siege by huge boulder- and rock-sized meteorites, sand-like micrometeorites, and even atoms in the solar wind.

Would they beat the surface into a fluffy dust that would envelop a descending spacecraft? Surveyor I was not even dusty after its jolting landing, and a surface-directed gas jet could not stir the grit.

No one knows how deep this lunar "soil" is. Radar and infrared measurements made from earth indicate that solid material starts, on the average, about three feet down. Luna XIII found that the soil beneath it is at least a foot deep. Whatever its depth, though, the soil compacts well enough to support a spacecraft or a walking man.

The surface minerals, which pictures cannot identify, are probably unlike those found on earth. A key to the origin and history of the solar system, they might be identified by comparing their radioactivity with that of earth minerals. But the moon's low radiation, measured by the Russian Lunas, gave inconclusive results.

The pictures did prove, though, what the plummeting Ranger spacecraft had indicated in 1965; the craters vary in size from miles-wide bowls to pits only inches across. Their various shapes indicate that some craters were not formed by meteoric impact, but by volcanic eruption.

Many of the craters were found to lie in rows, far too evenly to be formed by random bombardment. Small ridges, similar to those formed by the erosion of solidified lava, were also photographed.

Surveyor I focused on large rocks with rounded surfaces. They were similar to rocks thrust from volcanoes, but could possibly have been thrown from the white-hot impacts of meteorites. In startling photographs by Lunar Orbiters I and II, numerous volcanolike domes could be seen, as well as ridges and rills—the latter evidence of moonquakes.

Widespread volcanism, gave—or gives—the moon a continually changing, highly varied surface. Its core may still be molten. Certainly the vast maria are the results of past upwellings of liquid rock that flooded the large lowland areas and then became solidified.

The present surface, then, is clearly the result of several processes: volcanism, meteorite impacts, moonquakes, and erosion. The erosion is caused not by wind and water, as on earth, but by meteorite-chipped material sliding down slopes, softening surface features, rounding peaks, and filling in craters.

But, if the Queen has lost her court of poets, she found replacements in the selenologists. As 1966 ended, they were deep in controversy over these new findings and her role in the history of the universe. WADE TILLEUX similar to Echo I, the satellite visible to the naked eye, launched in August 1960. It is used as a target for sightings from various points on earth to obtain precise earth measurements through triangulation.

Pioneer VII was launched on August 17 to a solar orbit that swings outward one-eighth again as far from the sun as the earth's distance. Together with Pioneer VI, launched Dec. 16, 1965, it is observing the revival of solar activity.

The major disappointments of the year were the failure of instruments aboard the Orbiting Astronomical Observatory (OAO) I, two days after its April 8 launching, and the malfunction of a retrorocket supposed to have returned the first Biosatellite to earth three days after its December 14 launch. Biosatellite I carried plants and insects into space.

Apollo Progress. The first major phase of unmanned flight tests was completed in the Apollo program. This phase consisted of three flights of the uprated Saturn I launch vehicle. Two carried the Apollo spacecraft on suborbital flights to test the heat shield and the spacecraft, and one verified the operation of the upper stage of Saturn as a launch vehicle. On completion of the three tests, the Apollo/Saturn I was declared qualified to boost manned Apollo flights into earth orbit.

Also during 1966, the three-stage Saturn V, the launch vehicle intended for the lunar missions, neared the time of its first flight. The first and third stages were assembled on the launch platform at Merritt Island, Fla., separated by a dummy second-stage. The actual second stage underwent two successful ground firings at the Mississippi Test Facility and was being prepared at year's end for shipment to Cape Kennedy.

The Apollo/Saturn V launch complex, including the world's largest building, was placed in operation on May 25, five years to the day after the late President John F. Kennedy proposed the lunar mission. A giant crawler transporter emerged from the 525-foot high Vehicle Assembly Building, and carried the launch tower and a test version of the Apollo/Saturn V more than three miles to the launch pad.

A Moon Pack. With the completion of Gemini, all U.S. astronauts plunged into intensive training for Apollo. Detailed plans, including computer programs, were established for the first lunar mission, in which two astronauts are to spend 18 hours 22 minutes on the moon's surface, while a third orbits the moon overhead. Spacesuit development advanced. A package of instruments to be deposited on the surface and left behind to operate after their departure was under test. See ASTRONAUTS.

Soviet Activity. The hiatus in Soviet manned flight that began after the two-man flight of

Gemini IX astronauts Eugene Cernan, *left,* and Thomas Stafford await pickup after their splashdown 345 miles east of Cape Kennedy.

The hardware for the Apollo phase of the U.S. manned space program—the Uprated Saturn I booster, *left,* and the command module, *above*—were tested in 1966.

Voskhod II in March 1965, continued in 1966. But the Soviets were busy in unmanned flights.

In addition to their lunar explorations, Russian space scientists, in a fine exploit of space marksmanship, struck Venus with a satellite that was to have transmitted information on the planet, but failed to do so. Nevertheless, it was man's first contact with another planet. Russia also transmitted color television with the Molniya communications satellite and continued the general-purpose Cosmos series of unmanned scientific earth-orbital flights. Another noteworthy Soviet accomplishment was the 22-day flight of two dogs, Ugolyok and Veterok, and their safe return on the Cosmos mission of February 22 to March 16.

U.S. Defense Activity. Numerous space projects of the U.S. Department of Defense made progress in 1966, most notably the Manned Orbiting Laboratory (MOL). In the MOL program a modified Gemini spacecraft and a large attached section will be used as a manned space laboratory. In November, the re-entry capability of the modified Gemini craft was successfully tested.

Space Budget. The NASA appropriation for the fiscal year beginning July 1, 1966, was $4,968,000,000. Together with expenditures of the Department of Defense and other agencies the space budget was a little under $7,000,000,000. JAY HOLMES

See also Section One, JOHN GLENN: FOCUS ON SPACE.

General Francisco Franco, speaking before the Spanish parliament, outlines his proposals for sweeping changes in the constitution.

SPAIN. A new constitution was approved by 95.9 per cent of the voters in a national referendum held on Dec. 14, 1966. It was the first such referendum called in more than 19 years. The last one, which took place in July, 1947, had resulted in General Francisco Franco being named chief of state for life.

Prior to the election, the constitution had been approved by acclamation and without debate by the Cortes (legislature). Basically, it reformed the succession procedure and introduced a limited measure of liberalization to Spanish politics. But it also emphasized that Franco would remain chief of state–and retain his legislative powers–until his death.

World interest was focused on Spain in January when two United States Air Force B-52s crashed near Palomares Beach. Three of the four hydrogen bombs lost in the crash were quickly accounted for. One, however, was the object of a vast search which eventually cost the United States $70,500,000. See Atomic Energy.

Spain continued to press for the return of Gibraltar. However, talks with Britain proved fruitless.

Facts in Brief. Population: 32,100,000. Government: Chief of State and Premier Francisco Franco; Vice-Premier Agustin Muñoz Grandes. Monetary Unit: peseta (59.80 = U.S. $1). Foreign Trade: exports, $944,600,000; imports, $3,024,600,000. Principal Exports: cork, fruits and nuts, olives and olive oil, wine.

Kenneth Brown

SPORTS. The International Olympic Committee (IOC), in April, 1966, awarded the 1972 Summer Olympics to Munich, Germany. Munich was selected over Madrid and Montreal. Detroit, making its ninth bid for the games, finished last in the voting. Munich's winning plan included proposed expenditures of $145,000,000 to prepare for the thousands of athletes and spectators expected to attend.

Sapporo, Japan, won the 1972 winter games after a close competition with Banff, Canada.

The IOC also voted to investigate racial discrimination in South African sports before deciding whether South Africa would be eligible to enter the 1968 games to be held in Mexico City. The country was banned from the 1964 Olympics because it applied its policy on racial segregation to team selection. Avery Brundage, the Chicagoan who is president of the IOC, will head the investigating panel.

Meanwhile, at Mexico City, preparations quickened for the 1968 games. A second "Little Olympics" was held there in October, again revealing the need for improved organization, but showing progress over the "Little Olympics" that were held in October, 1965.

Athletes from throughout the world continued to protest against having to compete at Mexico City's 7,500-foot altitude without long preparation, but the IOC maintained its limit of four weeks' high-altitude training.

The International Equestrian Federation showed its concern about altitude problems by asking that the three-day event of the 1968 Olympics be held at an elevation lower than that of Mexico City. In December, the Mexicans partly complied by agreeing to move the equestrian events to Oaxtepec, only 4,500 feet above sea level.

The American Broadcasting Company (ABC) promised to give sports fans in every state the best view they have ever had of the Olympics. ABC-TV won the right to telecast the Mexico City games with a bid of $4,500,000. Earlier, the network had captured the right to broadcast the winter Olympics for 1968 (from Grenoble, France). The coverage from Mexico City will be live and in color, said a spokesman for ABC, and will amount to at least 40 hours of viewing.

Other Games. In addition to the European Games held at Budapest, in September, and the British Commonwealth Games at Kingston, Jamaica, in August, several other Olympic-style regional games were held. Japan dominated the Asian Games, held in Bangkok, Thailand, in December. The Japanese won 78 of the 140 gold medals, including all 28 in the swimming events. Two world records were broken, both in weight lifting. In the Central American and Caribbean Games, Mexico scored a close victory over Puerto Rico, the host country, in the unofficial point standings.

The International Brotherhood of Teamsters, which does not often turn up on the sports pages, did in 1966. James Hoffa, the Teamsters' controversial president, threw a scare into the managerial ranks of professional sports by announcing a campaign to organize players in "baseball, football, basketball, hockey, et cetera."

Awards. Jim Ryun, new world record holder in the mile and half-mile runs, was named Sportsman of the Year by *Sports Illustrated* (see RYUN, JIM). In the vote for Athlete of the Year, conducted by the Associated Press, Frank Robinson of the Baltimore Orioles baseball team was the winner.

Among the 1966 Sports Results were:

Curling. The world championship Scotch Cup was won by Canada for the seventh time in eight years. The U.S. men's championship was won by the Fargo Club of Fargo, N. Dak., and the women's title by St. Paul.

Handball. Paul Haber of San Jose, Calif., won the U.S. Handball Association's four-wall singles title, while Bob Lindsay and Pete Tyson of San Antonio, Tex., took the doubles crown. In the Amateur Athletic Union (AAU) competition, the champions were Steve Sandler of New York City in the one-wall singles, and Ken Holmes and Walt Ulbrich, also of New York City, in the one-wall doubles.

Rowing. The Intercollegiate Rowing Association regatta was won by the University of Wisconsin, but Harvard, unbeaten for the third straight year, was considered the best collegiate eight. In the world championships at Bled, Yugoslavia, West Germany won the eight-oared championship, and Don Spero of the New York Athletic Club won the single sculls.

Soap Box Derby. David Krussow, 12, of Tacoma, Wash., was the winner of the 1966 All-American Soap Box Derby at Akron, Ohio. Robert Logan of Santa Ana, Calif., had been the 1965 winner.

Joe Balsis of Minersville, Pa., won the $20,000 World's All-Round Pocket Billiard Championship at Johnston City, Ill.

Shooting. Stephen Hanzel of San Antonio, Tex., won the National Skeet Shooting Association all-around championship for men, and Mrs. Clarine Menzel of Oshkosh, Wis., won the women's title. In trapshooting, the men's Grand American was captured by Delbert Grim of Lincoln, Nebr., and the women's by Annie Gray of Seabrook, Md. The national service-rifle championship went to Capt. M. R. Menlove of the U.S. Army, and long-time pistol champion W. B. Blankenship again won the National Trophy match. In international competition, the United States won 17 gold medals at the world championships in Germany.

Weight Lifting. Russia won the team title by 10 points over Poland at the 1966 world championships held in East Berlin. Olympic champion Leonid Zhabotinsky again won the heavyweight title to give the Soviet team five gold medals in the seven events. Another Olympic titleholder, Yoshinobu Miyake of Japan, won the featherweight crown. In the AAU championships at York, Pa., Gary Gubner of New York City won the heavyweight title after completing three lifts for a total of 1,170 pounds.

Wrestling. Turkey took one gold medal (Atalay Mahmut, 171.5-pound) and placed in all seven other classes to score 34 points for the team title at the world free-style championships in Toledo, Ohio. Russia, with three gold medals, finished second with 28½ points, and the U.S. team placed third with 23 points. It was the first world wrestling title for Turkey since 1957, when the meet was held in Istanbul. Also at Toledo, Russia won the world Greco-Roman title for the 13th consecutive year. The team gained 39 points and three gold medals. Bulgaria, with two gold medals and 19 points, was runner-up. Larry Kristoff of Chicago was the heavyweight winner in both the AAU free-style and Greco-Roman championships at Lincoln, Nebr. Oklahoma State took its 25th National Collegiate Athletic Association (NCAA) title at Ames, Iowa, with 79 points. The team was paced by winners Yojiro Uetake (130-pound), Gene Davis (137-pound), Greg Ruth (160-pound), and Bill Harlow (191-pound).

Other Champions. *Archery*, U.S. championships: men, Hardy Ward, Mt. Pleasant, Tex.; women, Mrs. Helen Thornton, Tahlequah, Okla. *Bicycling*, Tour de France winner, Lucien Aimar, France. *Billiards*, world professional pocket title: Luther Lassiter, Elizabeth City, N.C. *Bobsledding*, world two-man: Italy. *Canoeing*, U.S. singles: James O'Rourke, New York. *Fencing*, world championships: foil, Russia; épée, France; saber, Hungary; women's foil, Russia; NCAA champion, New York University. *Gymnastics*, world championships: men's all-around, Mikhail Voronin, Russia; team, Japan; women's all-around, Vera Caslavska, Czechoslovakia; team, Czechoslovakia. AAU champions: men's all-around, Makoto Sakamoto, Los Angeles; team, Southern Connecticut G.C.; women's all-around, Linda Metheny, Tuscola, Illinois; team, Southern Illinois. NCAA champions: all-around, Steve Cohen, Penn State; team, Southern Illinois. *Judo*, AAU Grand Champion: Motohiko Eguchi, New York. *Lacrosse*, intercollegiate and open: Navy. *Modern Pentathlon*, world championships: individual, Andras Balczo, Hungary; team, Hungary. U.S. individual: Lt. James Coots, Ft. Lauderdale, Fla. *Polo*, open: Tulsa intercollegiate; Cornell Cup of the Americas: Argentina. *Volleyball*, world championship: Czechoslovakia. U.S. Open: Sand and Sea Club, Santa Monica, Calif. intercollegiate: Santa Monica City College. James O. Dunaway

See also the articles on various sports.

STAMP COLLECTING. See Hobbies.

STATE GOVERNMENT. In 28 states during 1966, official groups composed of legislators, citizens, legislative staffs, or all three, explored ways in which legislators may be helped in their work and more adequately rewarded for their services. Present biennial compensation for the typical legislator varies widely, from $200 in New Hampshire to $25,000 in Michigan. Twelve states looked at the need for staff and other services. Others examined requirements for office space and other physical facilities. Most legislators have neither offices nor staffs to serve them, although legislative research agencies operate in 42 states. Tennessee voters approved constitutional amendments providing for longer sessions, larger salaries, and reapportionment of districts.

The effort to provide more effective legislatures was due partly to the greater burdens of state government as a whole. It was also due to the influence of new members elected as a result of reapportionment of nearly all the state legislative bodies done in recent years.

Reapportionment Accepted. Population was finally accepted as the basis for apportioning legislative seats. All but one state established districts of equal population for each house of the legislature. Mississippi was ordered by a federal court to redistrict before electing legislators again.

An amendment to the U.S. Constitution to permit states to choose one legislative house on a basis other than population was defeated in the U.S. Senate. The amendment failed by seven votes to win the required two-thirds majority. See Congress of the United States.

More than half the states turned to management consultants and volunteers from business to suggest ways to improve procedures and cut expenditures without reducing services. Some were asked to suggest ways to improve the efficiency of computer systems. The states now spend over $90,000,000 each year to operate more than 300 computer systems.

Education First. In spite of efforts to improve efficiency, state spending continued to rise as a result of growing populations and expanding programs. Figures released in 1966 showed that general expenditures for all states in fiscal 1965 totaled $40,300,000,000, an increase of 8.3 per cent over 1964.

Education, including state support of local schools as well as junior colleges and state universities, continued to be the largest object of expenditure, accounting for 36 per cent of the total. Other major expenditures were for highways, accounting for 24 per cent of the total, and public welfare, 13 per cent. Expenditures for education and public welfare rose about 10.8 per cent above the previous year, more than double the 5 per cent increase for highways. Spending for most other categories also showed substantial increases.

State Revenues Rose to meet spending. General revenue for fiscal 1965 was $40,900,000,000, almost 9 per cent higher than the previous year. Taxes accounted for 64 per cent of this amount; 24 per cent came from federal funds, the rest from service charges. As in the past, the general sales tax produced more than any other tax, yielding 25 per cent of total tax revenue even though it is levied in only 37 states. Three states adopted the general sales tax in 1966. New Jersey and Massachusetts set a 3 per cent rate with exemptions for prescription drugs and food consumed at home. Virginia passed a 2 per cent tax without exempting food.

Referendums on tax questions were held in 18 states in November, 1966. Constitutional amendments permitting income tax legislation were defeated by voters in Illinois and Nebraska. New York voters approved a constitutional provision permitting a state lottery as long as the proceeds are spent for education. New Hampshire, which enacted a lottery in 1964, expected it to produce well over $2,000,000 for its education fund in 1966.

Barriers to Voting by Negro citizens were lower in 1966. The poll tax in state elections was abolished as a result of a Supreme Court of the U.S. decision which held that a Virginia poll tax law was unconstitutional. Seven other Southern states and Vermont repealed similar laws. Amendment 24 to the U.S. Constitution, ratified in 1964, prohibits a poll tax in national elections. James H. Andrews

See also Civil Rights; Taxation.

STEEL INDUSTRY expectations of a sharp drop in output in 1966 turned out to be pleasantly wrong when its mills went on to pour a record 134,069,605 tons of ingots and castings. Shipments of finished steel were 91,000,000 tons, just a shade below the all-time high of 92,700,000 tons in 1965.

The surprising performance stemmed from an uninterrupted and unanticipated strong demand from a number of sectors of the economy through the first nine months of 1966. As the year began, it was expected that major steel users such as automobile manufacturers would cut back on new orders while they used up the huge 25,500,000-ton inventory built up in anticipation of a steel strike.

Instead, a surging growth in durable goods manufacture, nonresidential building, and needs of the war in Vietnam accelerated the demand for steel. In the last quarter, production and shipments began to decline as car makers and the construction industry curtailed purchases. The steel mills were running at 84.5 per cent of capacity in December.

A Slight Profit Rise was expected by steelmakers despite total sales of about $17,900,000,000 and the broadest price increases since 1963. They attributed the small increase to higher labor costs. At midyear, pension payouts to steelworkers nearly doubled. Over the full year, moreover, average wages rose an estimated 3 per cent.

The price increases ranged over a selected number of products, including bars, cold-rolled sheet, and stainless. The overall rise was about 2 per cent. Many economists felt they would unduly inflate the prices of products made of steel and deal a severe blow to the administration's guidelines. But the only government action was a compromise maneuver in January after Bethlehem Steel Corporation had announced a $5-a-ton increase on structural steel. Bethlehem and the rest of the industry agreed to a more modest $2.75 boost a few days later.

Imports provided another surprise in 1966. Instead of dropping 2,000,000 to 4,000,000 tons below the 1965 level, they exceeded that year's 10,400,000 tons. Most significant has been the increase in imports of flat-rolled steel (tin mill products and sheet and strip)–to 33.4 per cent of steel imports in 1966, from 10.3 per cent in 1959. U.S. producers have traditionally held a competitive edge on this type.

For the first time, U.S. steelmakers outpaced Japan's in production under the new basic oxygen process, more efficient and less expensive than by open hearth. U.S. plants made 33,000,000 tons.

World capacity for making steel in 1966 exceeded demand for many items, particularly for cold-rolled sheet. World steel production, excluding China, slipped just below 500,000,000 tons in 1966. Western Europe's business slowdown was the main cause. The United States remained the top producer, with a quarter of the total. Russia was next, with an estimated 100,000,000 tons.

THOMAS J. MURRAY

STOCKS AND BONDS. The year 1966 found the United States with a booming economy and a slumping stock market. After-tax profits of U.S. corporations were running at a record annual rate of $48,700,000,000 in the first six months, but in the third quarter the pace had eased to $48,300,000,000. See ECONOMY, THE.

During most of 1966, tight money and uncertainty over taxes and business prospects pushed down both stock and bond values. In August and September, bond prices fell to lows unmatched since the 1920s. The Dow-Jones Index (DJI) average fell to a low of 744.32 on October 7. Early in the year, there had been several near-misses at penetrating the seemingly important 1000 barrier. The nearest came on February 9, when it hit the year's high of 995.15. By December 30, it stood at 785.69, a loss of 173.74 points for the year. Overseas, most stock markets finished 1966 with as lackluster performances as Wall Street's.

New Market Yardsticks were fashioned in 1966. Such indexes as the DJI, covering 30 stocks, have been criticized as being too narrow to reflect the activity of the more than 1,250 common stock issues traded on the New York Stock Exchange (NYSE). On June 15, the American Stock Exchange (Amex) became the first to use an all-stock index, covering its 950 issues.

On July 14, the NYSE put its Common Stock Index into use. It was given a value of 50.00 as of Dec. 31, 1965. It closed 1966 at 43.72. The index takes into account the changes in aggregate market value of all stocks–the price per share multiplied by the total number of shares outstanding in each listing. The Amex index ignores the total number of shares, counting only the gain or loss in each listing to find the day's total net change, which then is divided by the number of listed stocks.

Another Measure held more meaning for the ordinary stockholder: How did his own stocks do? The indexes do not necessarily tell what happened to the most popular stocks. This is the way the five most actively traded stocks on the NYSE fared by the end of 1966:

Stock	Volume	Close	Net Change
Sperry Rand	30,317,200	29¾	+7¾
AT&T	19,384,700	55	−5¾
SCM Corp.	17,095,400	56⅞	+3⅜
Chrysler	16,834,000	30¾	−22⅝
Pan Am. Air.	1,052,600	54¾	+3⅝

Total trade on the NYSE reached record highs in 1966–1,899,495,014 shares of stock and $3,092,789,700 in par value of bonds. As a result, brokers were swamped with paperwork. Major brokerage houses inaugurated a clearing system that eliminated the physical transfer of stock certificates.

New Issues of stocks totaled $1,870,000,000 in the first 10 months; the total for all 1965 was $1,547,000,000. New corporate bond issues gained less–to $13,121,000,000 in the 10 months, versus $13,720,-

An enterprising brokerage house made the most of the sliding stock market and publicized the "markdowns" available to its customers.

000,000 for all 1965. High long-term interest costs had made bonds less attractive than usual (see BANKS AND BANKING). New issues of state and local government securities totaled $9,200,000,000 in the first 10 months, about equal to the year-earlier period.

Liberalizing of Trading rules of the NYSE was allowed, effective Nov. 7, 1966, by the Securities and Exchange Commission (SEC). Well capitalized nonmember firms were permitted to make listed security transactions with member firms off the exchange. The new rules were adopted to facilitate moving large blocks of stock, which cannot always be handled on the exchange floor.

N.Y. Tax Skirmish. After bitterly fighting the proposed 50 per cent increase in the New York state stock transfer tax with threats to move out of the state–or at least set up a satellite trading floor in New Jersey to handle some transactions–Wall Street on July 1 quietly began paying the tax increase. The boost, which had been held to 25 per cent, amounted, at most, to an additional 1 cent a share.

Odd-lot trading fees were cut by the major exchanges under the pressure building up since the SEC's 1963 investigation. In addition to regular commissions, purchasers formerly had to pay fees on odd lots (less than 100 shares) of 12½ cents a share for stock priced below $40, and 25 cents a share otherwise. The reduction, on July 1, extended the 12½-cent fee to shares priced below $55.

Mutual Fund Report. The SEC released its long-awaited report on mutual funds in December. It asked that Congress enact sweeping changes to protect the public against "excessive" sales charges and to reduce management and advisers' fees to a "reasonable" level. It particularly criticized "front-end load" plans, in which half of the investor's first year payments go for sales commissions.

The 346-page report also urged a ceiling of 5 per cent on sales charges. Some of those charges, the SEC maintained, were as much as nine times higher than brokerage commissions on equivalent sales.

In other actions, the SEC extended its rules to cover all mutual fund dealers, not just those in the National Association of Security Dealers. Also, Congress extended the tax-free exchange of stocks for shares in mutual funds. The provision allows an owner of stocks with large capital gains to find a tax shelter and at the same time diversify his holdings.

People. Ralph S. Saul, a vice-president of Investors Diversified Services, Inc., and a former SEC official, was named in August to succeed Edwin D. Etherington as American Stock Exchange president. See SAUL, RALPH S.

Louis E. Wolfson, chairman of Merritt-Chapman & Scott Corporation, and four others were indicted in October on charges of conspiracy to defraud company stockholders.

WILLIAM G. DEWALD

SUDAN. See AFRICA.

SUNAY, CEVDET (1900-), was elected to a seven-year term as president of the Republic of Turkey on March 28, 1966. He had been chief of the Turkish armed forces general staff since 1960. The Turkish grand national assembly gave Sunay 461 of 532 votes to succeed the aging Cemal Gursel who was too ill, after a series of strokes, to continue in office.

Sunay was the fourth general among the five presidents elected since the Turkish republic was established in 1923. He was born in Trabzon, Turkey. After studying at the Kuleli Military High School at Istanbul, he entered army service during World War I. During the war, Sunay advanced to second lieutenant, then was wounded and taken prisoner by the British. On his release, he fought under Kemal Atatürk in the Greco-Turkish War in Asia Minor.

He was graduated from the Turkish Military Academy in 1930. After holding a series of commands and rising to the rank of lieutenant colonel, he was appointed, in 1942, assistant teacher of strategy at the military academy.

Sunay wrote two books on military skills while on the faculty. He returned to command posts in 1947 and was promoted to brigadier general in 1949 and to full general in 1959. In 1963, Sunay, a political moderate, put down two attempts by dissident army officers and cadets to seize the government. He is married and has two children. WALTER F. MORSE

SUPREME COURT OF THE UNITED STATES. From the standpoint of public impact, the most important opinion handed down by the Supreme Court of the United States in 1966 was the decision in the *Miranda vs. Arizona* case. It limited police questioning of accused persons. Chief Justice Earl Warren wrote the majority opinion in this 5 to 4 decision.

The Court held that the constitutional privilege against self-incrimination requires that the accused, when arrested and before being questioned by police, be told (1) of his right to remain silent; (2) of his right to the services of a lawyer during interrogation; (3) of his right to be provided with a lawyer if he cannot afford one; and (4) of the possible use against him of any incriminating statements made by him. Furthermore, it was held that if the accused "indicates in any manner, at any time prior to or during questioning, that he wishes to remain silent, the interrogation must cease." See COURTS AND LAWS.

Retroactivity. The Court refused, 7 to 2, to make the *Miranda* case retroactive. That is, it refused to make the decision apply to verdicts arrived at before the Miranda decision. Also, the Court decided, 5 to 2, not to make retroactive its recent ruling that adverse comment by a judge or prosecutor on a defendant's failure to testify violates the privilege against self-incrimination. The basis for these rulings is the Court's desire to avoid serious disruption of criminal law administration.

Free Press. In a landmark opinion in the field of free press and fair trial the Court reversed, 8 to 1, the 11-year-old murder conviction of Dr. Samuel Sheppard of Cleveland, Ohio. The Court ruled that inflammatory newspaper coverage denied Sheppard a fair trial consistent with the due process clause of Amendment 14. (Sheppard was subsequently released, retried, and acquitted of the 1954 slaying of his first wife.) At the same time the Court laid down guidelines to prevent press publicity that could affect the verdicts of criminal trials.

Obscenity. On March 21, 1966, the High Court announced that additional standards would be used to determine whether publications contain obscene material, within the meaning of Amendment 1. First, in the controversial *Ginzburg* case, decided 5 to 4, the Court stated that an obscenity test includes the advertising used to promote its sales. Second, in the *Fanny Hill* case, decided 6 to 3, the Court stated that it must be shown that a publication is "utterly" without redeeming social value before it can be banned as obscene.

In Other Significant Decisions the Supreme Court ruled that:

- Arizona's public employee loyalty oath law was unconstitutional, 5 to 4. The majority held that the act as drawn threatened the right of freedom of association guaranteed by Amendment 1.
- A blood test administered by law enforcement authorities to an accused drunk driver over his objection did not violate either the privilege against self-incrimination, the protection against unreasonable searches and seizures, or the due process clause of the Amendment 14. The vote was 5 to 4.
- Several key sections of the 1965 Voting Rights Act that protect the franchise of the Negro in the South were held constitutional, 8 to 1. In addition the Court held invalid, 7 to 2, New York's English literacy requirement for voting, so far as it is inconsistent with the provisions of the Voting Rights Act.
- The 17 defendants charged with conspiracy in the deaths of three Northern civil rights workers near Philadelphia, Miss., in 1964, were properly indicted. The Court based its decision on a federal civil rights statute enacted soon after the Civil War.

Justice Fortas. The Court continued to sustain tough government actions in the antitrust area. Despite a strong New Deal background, Justice Abe Fortas, the Court's newest member, voiced his dissatisfaction with an approach that automatically equates bigness with badness in two stinging dissents.

The 1966 Court consisted of Chief Justice Earl Warren and, in order of seniority, Associate Justices Hugo Black, William O. Douglas, Tom C. Clark, John Marshall Harlan, William J. Brennan, Jr., Potter Stewart, Byron Raymond White, and Abe Fortas. ALLEN HARRIS

SWAZILAND. See AFRICA.

High-spirited students give Sweden's 20-year-old Crown Prince Carl Gustav V a traditional Swedish toss-up to celebrate his graduation.

SWEDEN. Labor problems plagued the nation for most of 1966. They began early in January, when government-appointed arbiters tried to break a 52-day-old deadlock between unions and employers involving a national wage agreement. The workers, worried about a 6 per cent rise in the cost of living, wanted 10 to 30 per cent wage increases. The employers replied that any increases at all would price Sweden out of her export markets. Efforts to arbitrate the dispute proved unsuccessful, however, until April, when a worker-employer agreement was signed cutting hours and giving wage increases of 6½ cents an hour in 1966, and 5 cents an hour in 1967.

In October, about 1,300 university and secondary school teachers went on strike in protest against the adding of one week to the academic year and a request that teachers spend two summer holiday weeks on refresher courses. Among the striking teachers was Mrs. Aina Erlander, wife of the prime minister, who is a chemistry teacher in a Stockholm school. The strike led to a lockout of 20,800 teachers which, in turn, led to a protest strike by civil servants.

Facts in Brief. Population: 7,770,000. Government: King Gustav VI Adolf; Prime Minister Tage E. Erlander. Monetary Unit: krona (5.16 = U.S. $1). Foreign Trade: exports, $3,970,900,000; imports, $4,376,500,000. Principal Exports: iron and steel, engineering and manufactured products, paper and pulp. KENNETH BROWN

SWIMMING. It was the halfway year between the 1964 and 1968 Olympics, but the world's swimmers worked to set new records as if the Mexico City event were just around the corner. More than half the existing world records were broken, with the men's 400-meter free-style mark taking the worst beating.

The previous record of 4 minutes 12.2 seconds had been set by Don Schollander of Lake Oswego, Ore., in winning the 1964 Olympics. John Nelson, of Pompano Beach, Fla., brought it down to 4 minutes 11.8 seconds in a heat of the Amateur Athletic Union (AAU) outdoor championships at Lincoln, Nebr., on August 18. Schollander reclaimed it with a 4 minute 11.6 second performance in the final of the same evening. A week later, in the European championships at Utrecht, The Netherlands, Frank Wiegand of East Germany swam the distance in 4 minutes 11.1 seconds. Finally, Alain Mosconi of France cut the record to 4 minutes 10.5 seconds in a meet at Acapulco, Mex., on October 24.

Schollander, a 20-year-old sophomore at Yale, continued to rate as the world's best sprinter. In his specialties, the 200-meter and 220-yard free-style, he set new world marks of 1 minute 56.2 seconds and 1 minute 57 seconds, respectively. He also had the world's fastest 100-meter time, 53.2 seconds.

Another outstanding record was set by Mike Burton of Santa Clara, Calif., who swam 1,500 meters in 16 minutes 41.6 seconds.

Martha Randall showed both speed and form at the AAU meet as she tied her own world record in the women's 400-meter free-style.

International Meets. Both Australia and Russia showed strength in international competition. The Aussie men won 10 of the 13 gold medals and set eight world records at the British Commonwealth Games at Kingston, Jamaica, in August. Later the same month, Russian swimmers and divers won 12 out of 23 gold medals at the European championships in Holland.

However, in what was perhaps the most important international meet of the year, the Russians lost to the United States. The Five Nations meet, held July 16 and 17 in Moscow, saw the U.S. team win 11 events to the Soviet's six.

Women's Records. In women's swimming, U.S. teen-agers continued to stand out in the free-style and butterfly. World records were set by Pokey Watson in the 200-meter free-style (2 minutes 10.5 seconds) and Patty Caretto in the 1,500-meter free-style (18 minutes 12.9 seconds). Both were veterans at age 15. Russia's Galina Prozumenshchikova set world breast stroke marks for 100 meters (1 minute 15.7 seconds) and 200 meters (2 minutes 40.8 seconds), and South Africans Ann Fairlie and Karen Muir lowered the world backstroke standards to 1 minute 7.4 seconds for 100 meters and 2 minutes 26.4 seconds for 200 meters, respectively.

The Santa Clara Swim Club won both the men's and women's AAU outdoor team titles for the third year in a row. JAMES O. DUNAWAY

SWITZERLAND ended the last of the restrictions on foreign investments that it had imposed in 1964. As a result, interest on foreign deposits in 1966 would again be payable by Swiss banks. Foreigners would be able to buy Swiss shares, investment trust certificates, and mortgages. The anti-inflationary restrictions, which had been imposed to correct an imbalance in the economy and to curb over-financing from abroad, had proved successful in the goals set for them. At year's end, the National Bank held $3,245,000,000 in gold and foreign exchange reserves.

Two problems carried over from the preceding year troubled the economy. One was the cost of living, which continued to rise rapidly. The other carry-over concerned the labor force, a large percentage of which consisted of foreigners. Rigorous controls over their entry into Switzerland continued in effect, and only those arriving with contracts of employment were being admitted. To further discourage the influx, the government continued to rigidly enforce a law obliging alien nonresidents to obtain authorization before being permitted to purchase Swiss real estate.

Facts in Brief. Population: 6,188,000. Government: President Hans Schaffner. Monetary Unit: Swiss franc (4.30 = U.S. $1). Foreign Trade: exports, $2,993,100,000; imports, $3,705,000,000. Principal Exports: chemicals, machines, watches and clocks, textiles. KENNETH BROWN

SYRIA. A series of border incidents and repeated outbreaks of gun duels raised tension to a near-war level between Syria and Israel in 1966. Syria's domestic problems were equally serious because of a split between moderate and leftist elements in the ruling Ba'ath Party.

In February, the leftists in the party revolted and overthrew President Amin el-Hafez. Yusuf Zuayn, who had been ousted in December of the preceding year, was returned to office. Under the new regime's policies, Khalid Baqdash, the head of Syria's Communist party, was permitted to return from exile. Arrests reduced the moderates in the Ba'ath party.

The Zuayn government won few friends. In September, followers of the deposed Bitar and army officers loyal to him tried to unseat the government, whose pro-Communist leanings were apparent. Twice within a week, however, they failed to unseat it.

Surprisingly, Syria's relations with the United Arab Republic improved during 1966. The two countries agreed to coordinate their armed forces under a joint high command.

Facts in Brief. Population: 5,750,000. Government: Chief of State Nur al-Din al-Atasi; Premier Yusuf Zuayn. Monetary Unit: pound (4.10 = U.S. $1). Foreign Trade: exports, $168,700,000; imports, $212,600,000. Principal Exports: cotton, wheat, barley, wools. WILLIAM SPENCER

TANZANIA. See AFRICA.

TAXATION–whether to raise income taxes and if so, by how much–was avoided as a political issue in 1966. Total federal cash spending for the fiscal year ended June 30, 1966, was reported at $137,600,-000,000, up $15,200,000,000 from fiscal 1965. Cash receipts rose, too, but not enough to prevent a cash deficit of $3,200,000,000.

Expenses for the Great Society and, more particularly, for the war in Vietnam rose sharply. Final budget figures revealed that the fiscal 1966 Vietnam military effort cost some $5,800,000,000, or $1,100,-000,000 more than had been estimated. The Treasury estimated in October, 1966, that military expenditures for fiscal 1967 would reach a record "peacetime" total of at least $63,000,000,000. The U.S. cost of the Vietnam fighting was estimated at some $2,000,000,000 monthly.

Federal tax receipts in fiscal 1966 totaled a record $128,897,961,000, up $14,444,961,000 over fiscal 1965. But despite increasing revenues, inflation and the rising cost of the war forced minor tax increases.

Excise taxes on new cars were increased from 6 per cent to 7 per cent, effective March 15, 1966. They are scheduled to drop to 1 per cent on April 1, 1968. Taxes on telephone service were raised once again to 10 per cent from 3 per cent, effective on April, 1966, bills. The tax would expire altogether April 1, 1968. Both taxes had been reduced in 1965.

The rates of withholding of taxes on personal income were increased from the former flat 14 per cent to a graduated scale ranging up to 30 per cent, effective May 1, 1966. Corporations with annual tax liabilities over $100,000 were required to pay their taxes every three months. Both provisions sped up tax collection, but did not increase total tax bills.

Fiscal 1966 Federal Tax Collections
(millions of dollars)

Type of Tax	Amount	Change in Year
Corporation income	$30,834	+18.0%
Individual income	61,298	+14.2%
Employment	20,256	+18.4%
Estate and gift	3,094	+12.7%
Excise and other	13,398	− 9.4%
Total	$128,880	+12.6%

In October, Congress suspended for 15 months the 7 per cent tax credit for business outlays on capital equipment and the accelerated depreciation allowance on new business or industrial construction.

State Tax Collections rose 12.4 per cent–almost equal to the federal gain–in fiscal 1966, totaling $29,400,000,000. The five top states in percentage gains were: Idaho (31.5 per cent), Kansas (30.8), Iowa (26.2), Hawaii (22.1), and Arkansas (21.6). California collected the most, $3,438,000,000, and New York was close behind, with $3,430,000,000, followed, in order, by Pennsylvania, Michigan, Illinois, Texas, and Ohio.

In 27 states, both retail sales and personal incomes were taxed in 1966. Some taxpayers in four states–Kentucky, Maryland, Missouri, and New York–had to file three separate income tax returns: federal, state, and local.

Local Taxes. On Sept. 1, 1966, New York City began the withholding of its new tax on residents' incomes and out-of-city commuters' earnings. A New Yorker earning $150 a week and having three dependents, for instance, paid 95 cents a week. A commuter with the same salary paid 35 cents, regardless of the size of his family.

States' Major Tax Sources in Fiscal 1966
(millions of dollars)

Type of tax*	Amount	Rise in Year
General sales (40)	$7,873	17.3%
Selective sales:		
Motor fuels (50)	9,168	9.8%
Tobacco products (48)	1,541	20.1%
Alcoholic beverages (50)	985	7.4%
Insurance (50)	812	9.2%
Individual income (36)	4,303	17.7%
Corporation income (38)	2,037	5.6%
Property (44)	833	8.6%
Death and gift (49)	808	10.5%
Severance (29)	545	8.3%

*Number of states with tax shown in parentheses.

Municipal and County Governments in fiscal 1966 collected about $27,200,000,000 in taxes. Thus the total tax take of all government came to $185,-000,000,000, or one quarter of the gross national product. See CITY. CAROL L. THOMPSON

See also CONGRESS OF THE U.S.; SOCIAL SECURITY.

TEALE, EDWIN WAY (1899-), an author and naturalist, was awarded the 1966 Pulitzer prize for nonfiction for his book *Wandering Through Winter*.

Teale, who was born in Joliet, Ill., June 2, 1899, was educated at the University of Illinois, Earlham College (A.B. 1922), and Columbia University (A.M. 1926). A former instructor of public speaking and a feature writer for *Popular Science Monthly*, Teale has been a free-lance writer since 1941. He has written 20 books, all dealing with various aspects of science. His works have won him the John Burroughs Medal for distinguished nature writing (1943), the Christopher Award (1957), and the Sarah Chapman Francis Medal (1965).

Wandering Through Winter is the final volume in Teale's 15-year effort to describe the four seasons in America from a naturalist's point of view. His earlier works in the series were *North with the Spring* (1951), *Autumn Across America* (1956), and *Journey into Summer* (1960). Teale traveled nearly 20,000 miles throughout the United States in preparation for each book.

Although Teale first became noted as an insect photographer, he is now one of the world's best known nature writers.

Teale and his wife, the former Nellie Imogene Donovan, live in a rustic setting at Trail Wood, their Hampton, Conn., home.

TELEPHONE AND TELEGRAPH. See COMMUNICATIONS; TELEVISION.

TELEVISION

In 1966, there was growing evidence that a vast number of the nation's living rooms were becoming family motion picture theaters. More and more, the three television networks (NBC, CBS, and ABC) were devoting prime evening time to old movies, and the ratings achieved by these films, which had reposed quietly in Hollywood vaults for many years, were indeed startling.

A nine-year-old film, the Academy Award winning *The Bridge on the River Kwai*, gave the most impressive proof of the public's taste for movies, as opposed to the best of television's own specially created programs. *Kwai* was seen by an estimated 65,000,000 viewers on September 25, trouncing "Bonanza," television's perennial No. 1 program.

By fall, 1966, motion pictures filled prime evening time periods five nights a week and consistently scored high among the 15 most popular programs. After the success of *Kwai*, the three networks spent almost $92,500,000 in a single week for TV rights to more than 100 movies. See MOTION PICTURE.

NBC also negotiated a multimillion dollar deal with Universal Television to produce a series of two-hour films expressly for television. *Fame Is the Name of the Game*, the first movie made especially for television, received its world première on November 26. In the main, it received poor critical notices. Nevertheless, it chalked up a respectable rating.

Short, Unhappy Life. "Batman," a campy version of the comic strip, was the surprise hit of the 1965-1966 "second season." Batman's rating wings drooped as the year progressed, however, and the top-rated shows were mainly holdovers from 1965, among them "Lucy," "Bonanza," "Green Acres," "Red Skelton," "Gomer Pyle," and "Andy Griffith." The more successful of the new offerings included "A Family Affair" and "Rat Patrol."

Specials. Some of the most impressive specials were *Death of a Salesman*, Sir John Gielgud's *Ages of Man*, Barbra Streisand's "Color Me Barbra," *The Glass Menagerie*, "Beethoven: Ordeal and Triumph," and "Frank Sinatra–The Man and His Music, Part II," *Brigadoon*, "Lucy in London," and Jim Nabors' "Friends and Nabors."

News. Two news programs won special acclaim. These were the historic, live network-pool transmittal of the first moon surface close-ups in June and the first live telecast of a Gemini space capsule's safe return to earth. But the continuing coverage of the Vietnamese war by all three networks was also impressive and necessarily painful to watch.

Luci Baines Johnson's wedding in Washington, D.C., was a popular TV attraction in August. The growing stature of football on network TV was marked by the increased programming of both college and professional games in prime time periods. Reporting of the elections was outstanding, but some of the networks' computer-based predictions were in glaring error.

Emmy Awards. "The Dick Van Dyke Show" (CBS) ended its final season by winning four more Emmy Awards. Emmies also went to *Ages of Man* (CBS); "A Charlie Brown Christmas" (CBS); "Frank Sinatra–The Man and His Music" (NBC); Barbara Stanwyck, "Big Valley" (ABC); and Bill Cosby, "I Spy" (NBC).

Color TV continued to grow in 1966. By fall, programming on all three networks was virtually 100 per cent color in prime evening time periods. NBC also carried most of its daytime shows in color.

The public was buying color TV sets so fast that manufacturers had difficulty keeping up with the orders. By November, about 8,590,000 households, representing 15 per cent of all television homes, owned color sets. This represented a growth of 85 per cent, as compared to the ownership of color television sets in the same 1965 period. According to industry sources, the number could very well be double that total by the end of 1967.

Business for TV sales—network, spot, and local—was better than ever. Aggregate TV program sales, which totaled a record of $1,670,000,000 in 1965, were expected to reach $1,800,000,000 in 1966. The world market for U.S. TV programs also boomed in 1966. Early indications were that international sales of U.S. shows would total $80,000,000, as compared to $75,000,000 in 1965.

On the network executive front, CBS-TV had three different presidents. John A. Schneider, who succeeded James T. Aubrey in 1965, moved up to head the new CBS/Broadcast Group in February. He was succeeded by John Reynolds, who resigned in December. Reynolds' post was taken by Thomas H. Dawson. Fred W. Friendly resigned as president of CBS News in February and subsequently was named adviser on television to the Ford Foundation.

Educational Television (ETV), is the Ford Foundation's major single financial program. Ford has given U.S. ETV more than $100,000,000 since 1952. On August 1, the Ford Foundation startled the industry by proposing a plan to set up a nonprofit domestic-TV satellite which would operate in the interests of national educational television.

The Communications Satellite Corporation immediately proposed an extra assessment to its own satellite users to help finance ETV. At year's end, both plans were still pending Federal Communications Commission approval. JUNE BUNDY CSIDA

Mildred Dunnock and Lee Cobb provided some of the finest hours of 1966 television in the CBS production of *Death of a Salesman*.

"Holy Flypaper! We're Stuck!"

Holy phenomenon! Were American men in their 30s and 40s entering a second childhood? For, twice each week during 1966, one could enter millions of homes across the nation and find Daddy staring at the TV set with the same avidity as the children sitting beside him. And what was the family watching? A documentary on the war in Vietnam? A master class in violin? Not by a long shot. It was engrossed in "Batman," by all odds the 1965-1966 season's biggest hit.

There, running about the little screen in the living room, was the Caped Crusader himself, complete with Batcape, Batarang, tights, mask, and his faithful young ward, Robin, similarly costumed.

The youngsters on the living room floor were delighted. They could watch Batman battle the forces of evil in the persons of the sinister Joker, curvaceous Catwoman, chilly Mr. Freeze, or the sly Bookworm. And when Batman's gloved fist connected with the jaw of one evildoer or another, words such as "Zap," "Splat," or "Zonk" flashed across the TV screen—just like in the comic books! And perhaps that was what so delighted the children's elders. Batman was indeed right out of the popular Batman comic books that appeared before World War II, when there was no TV, and when the grownup generation was made up of boys and girls clustered around the radio, listening to "I Love a Mystery," "The Shadow," and "Lights Out." For what the producers of Batman had succeeded in doing was to translate one medium—comic books—almost directly into another—television.

A few concessions were made to modernity. Millionaire socialite and philanthropist Bruce Wayne, who fought crime in Gotham City as the Caped Crusader, roared to the scene of TV action in a jet-powered Batmobile. And the Batcave in the basement of the Batmansion was filled with all kinds of up-to-date gadgetry, including an atomic reactor. But the secret of the program's success seemed to be its old-fashioned comic book style: the Zonks and Splats splashed across the screen; the righteous stiffness of the hero ordering orange juice in a bar; the general bumbling of the police; and exclamations from Robin, such as, "Gleeps!", "Holy Barracuda!", or "Holy Flypaper! We're stuck!"

Other explanations were advanced to explain the sudden, immense popularity of the series. A favorite: "Batman" was supposed to have been part of the ultramodern "camp" movement, in which something usually considered to be in poor taste is somehow thought of as being either "in," "good," or just plain amusing. But whatever the reason, the Batman caper was successful indeed. Records of Batman theme music climbed the best-seller lists. Batman pins and sweatshirts flooded the land, and a new dance, the batusi, was born.

Most surprising of all, perhaps, was that big name stars vied to play the villains to the Dynamic Duo. Frank Sinatra was reported to have been upset because he was not selected to play the Joker. That suddenly coveted role went to Cesar Romero. Burgess Meredith played the Penguin, George Sanders was Mr. Freeze, and seemingly, whole studios of stars appeared in bit parts, including Sammy Davis, Jr., and Phyllis Diller.

Since TV more than any of the other media believes that nothing succeeds like success, it was inevitable that other characters from out of the childhood of the older generation be prepared for living room screens. Hence, in 1966, Tarzan, the apeman of old, appeared on TV, but without his mate, Jane. "The Green Hornet," one of the radio shows of the 1930s, got a new lease on life on television, and the children sat in their livingrooms and watched another two-fisted, crime-fighting hero out of their father's past. The Hornet in "private life," of course, was newspaper publisher Britt Reid. He rode to battle in a souped-up Chrysler called Black Beauty, with his trusty chauffeur Kato at his side.

Would the whole cast of comic book characters of the 1930s and 1940s be resurrected for television? It was rumored that Dick Tracy and Wonder Woman were waiting in the wings. Only time and the all-powerful ratings would tell.

MARK M. PERLBERG

Defending champion Roy Emerson was eliminated by Owen Davidson at Wimbledon, England, after crashing into the umpire's chair.

TENNIS. It was a topsy-turvy year for the world's best amateur tennis players. In the four major tournaments, the men's and women's championships were won by eight different players.

The year started off normally enough, with Australians Roy Emerson and Margaret Smith winning the Australian championships, Emerson for the fifth time and Miss Smith for the seventh. In the French championships, another Australian, Tony Roche, won the men's title, while Ann Haydon Jones of England took the women's title.

At Wimbledon, the tournament which is generally considered the "world championship," Emerson lost in the quarterfinals after he was injured from running into an umpire's chair. The men's crown went to Manuel Santana of Spain. Miss Smith ran into Billie Jean King of the United States and also lost. Mrs. King went on to beat Maria Bueno of Brazil in the final.

In the American championships at Forest Hills, Long Island, two more Australians fought it out for the men's title. Fred Stolle defeated John Newcombe, and Miss Bueno defeated Nancy Richey of the United States to take the women's championship for the fourth time.

Miss Smith did not compete at Forest Hills, and later announced her retirement. Emerson said he planned to cut down his schedule and would play only on a limited basis in 1967.

A new system of ranking the world's amateurs, based on points gained in tournaments, was announced by the Lawn Tennis Writers of America. Santana won with 130 points to 120 for Stolle, 104 for Roche, and 86 for Emerson.

Davis Cup. Australia won the Davis Cup for the seventh time in eight years. The team defeated India 4 to 1 at Melbourne, Australia, in December. India had reached the challenge round for the first time in history by upsetting Brazil earlier in the month.

The United States once again failed to reach the challenge round, losing 3 to 2 to Brazil in the interzone semifinal. It marked the fifth time in the last seven years that the U.S. team had not played in the Davis Cup final.

The U.S. women's team had better fortune. They beat Britain, 4 to 3, to win the Wightman Cup for the seventh straight year. They also won the new Federation Cup (women's version of the Davis Cup) with a 3 to 0 victory over West Germany. Mrs. King was the U.S. star in both competitions.

Professional. In professional tennis, Rodney Laver was the top player. Laver's wins included the U.S. championship and a special round-robin tournament at Forest Hills in which he won 10 straight matches from the best players in the world. Richard (Pancho) Gonzales, now 37 and making a comeback, played well all year, and upset Laver to win the London indoor title. JAMES O. DUNAWAY

THAILAND was increasingly, if unofficially, involved in the efforts of the United States to subdue the Communists in Vietnam during 1966. About 35,000 U.S. servicemen were stationed there and many U.S. construction workers were building a number of air bases, most of which were capable of accommodating B-52 bombers. See VIETNAM.

The economy remained stable during the year, due largely to rising exports of rice, rubber, and timber. Industrial development also made progress as a number of projects such as paper manufacturing plants and oil refineries neared completion.

The northeastern area was plagued by guerrilla activities conducted by members of the two-year-old, Communist-led Thai Patriotic Front. Communist guerrillas were also active along Thailand's border with Malaysia. Late in the year, the Thai government intensified its fight against the insurgents with the aid of a U.S. Air Force helicopter squadron which began flying Thai police and army units into action. However, persistent reports of increasing terrorism in the remote villages kept Thailand in an uneasy state of alert.

Facts in Brief. Population: 32,608,000. Government: King Phumiphon Aduldet; Premier Thanom Kittikachorn. Monetary Unit: baht (20.65=U.S. $1). Foreign Trade: exports, $617,800,000; imports, $731,300,000. Principal Exports: maize, rice, rubber, tin. JOHN N. STALKER

THEATER

The most eagerly awaited American play of the fall season was Edward Albee's *A Delicate Balance*. Audiences wanted to see how he would shore up his reputation, which had slipped badly with the earlier unmistakable failure of his adaptation, *Malcolm*. Albee retrieved his position as the most gifted of the younger American playwrights and accumulated some enthusiastic endorsements of *A Delicate Balance*, but in it he did not meet rigorous standards of play construction.

What he did achieve was a family drama of tense relationships that aroused interest with several strands of theme. One strand referred to the problem of friendship. It raised the question of how far we may presume upon friendship, and at what point it can become insufferable. This problem was posed by the invasion of the home of the chief characters, played by Jessica Tandy and Hume Cronyn, by two friends. The presence of the friends becomes so upsetting to the entire household that it becomes necessary to tell them to leave. This painful duty falls upon Tobias, the husband and father, who had idealized friendship as a means of compensating for his loneliness and the failure of his marriage.

The "delicate balance" of the title may well be life as a whole, or the sanity of human beings, which remains precarious even under the comfortable circumstances of an upper middle-class existence.

Other Plays. Among other ambitiously conceived U.S. plays, James Goldman's *The Lion in Winter* was distinguished by witty dialogue and keen thrusts of conflict. It dealt with the domestic life and political intrigues of Henry II and his spirited queen, Eleanor of Aquitaine.

But more often than not, ambitiousness on the part of native writers remained unrewarded. Even so adept a playwright as Tennessee Williams suffered one of his worst defeats with his *Slapstick Tragedy*, the common title for two one-act plays in which the author overextended himself in the pursuit of bizarre but largely wasted effects that seemed to imitate the European "theater of the absurd" and "theater of cruelty." But Williams recovered his professional standing late in the year with an excellent revival of his 15-year-old comedy, *The Rose Tattoo*. In the Broadway production, actress Maureen Stapleton achieved a personal triumph.

Other writers were less fortunate, and among these was the late Maxwell Anderson, whose celebrated verse tragedy *Winterset*, twice as old as Williams' comedy, proved painfully dated when revived in New York. His still older verse drama *Elizabeth the Queen*, given a more professional production starring Judith Anderson, also proved shopworn.

Mark Kauffman, *Life* © Time Inc.

Despite the success of some musical comedies, notably Gwen Verdon's dance vehicle *Sweet Charity*, and *Mame*, which was enlivened by the virtuosity of Angela Lansbury, the American stage in 1966 continued to rely as heavily as ever on imports.

Even the institutional theaters did not greatly enrich U.S. stage production, except at the Tyrone Guthrie Theatre in Minneapolis, where its productions continued to win acclaim. The Shakespeare Festival Theatre at Stratford, Conn., succeeded only modestly with a familiar repertory, to which the management added T. S. Eliot's *Murder in the Cathedral*. It was a ritualistic production staged by John Houseman, with Joseph Wiseman distinguishing himself as St. Thomas à Becket.

Actress Angela Lansbury, *center,* was a hit in *Mame,* the musical adaptation of the novel, *Auntie Mame,* by Patrick Dennis.

Lincoln Center. The most lavishly supported enterprise, the Lincoln Center Repertory Company, in New York City, under the directorship of Herbert Blau and Jules Irving, continued to be more distinguished in its choice of plays than in its actual productions. Jean-Paul Sartre's *The Condemned of Altona,* an intense study of guilt and remorse in postwar Germany, was replete with thematic interest but seemed discursively static at Lincoln Center. Bertolt Brecht's *The Caucasian Chalk Circle,* given for the first time in New York City, was cumbersomely staged and only moderately well acted. It was followed in the fall of the year by Ben Jonson's *The Alchemist.* But this effort succeeded far more as vaudeville than as a satire on human vanity and credulity.

Most Gratifying Plays originated abroad. The most appealing was the new Irish playwright Brian Friel's *Philadelphia, Here I Come!*, a rueful comedy of a boy's departure from Ireland. It was enriched by tenderly conceived character studies of the youth's inarticulate father and a disgraced former schoolmaster, as well as by a less successfully managed but theatrically lively Pirandellian splitting of the young hero into two personalities–his private and public selves–played by two different actors.

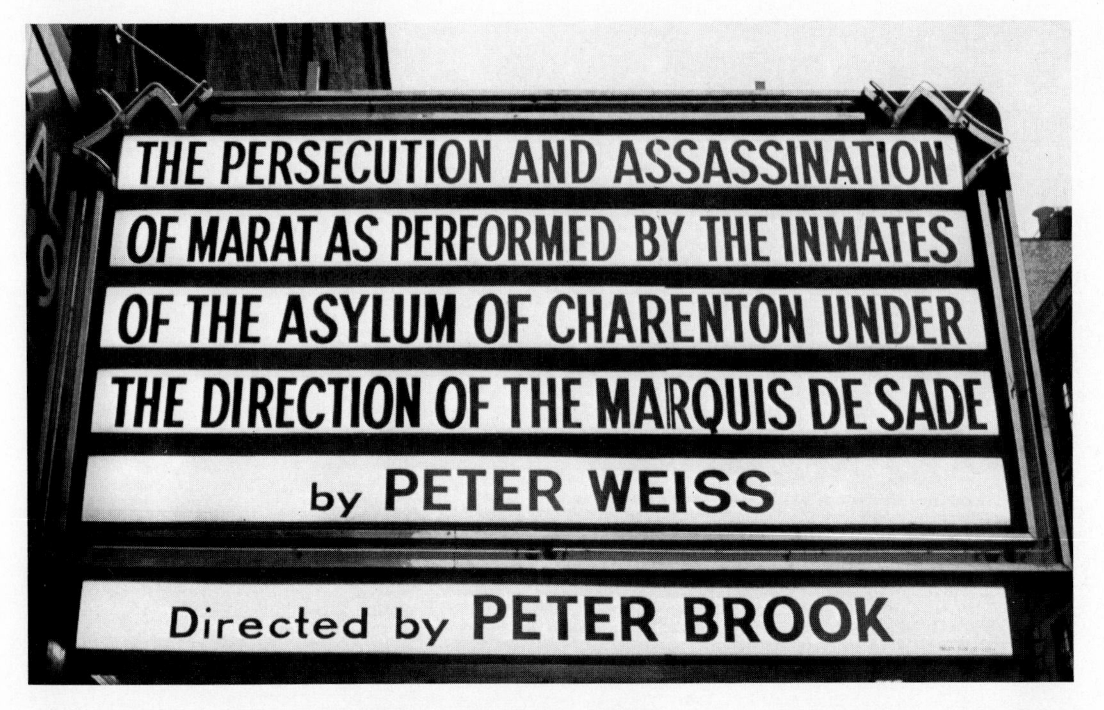

This hit play, with the longest title ever on a New York marquee, was a vivid mixture of philosophy, violence, and sensational effects.

The most incisive import was *The Killing of Sister George*, a British "black comedy" by Frank Marcus, in which a popular British Broadcasting Company (BBC) impersonator of a village nurse is deprived of her program and demoted to playing an absurd role in another serial. A mordant character study as well as a satire on popular entertainment, the play was particularly remarkable for being able to command sympathy for a thoroughly unsavory character. A belated British arrival was Arnold Wesker's early play, *The Kitchen*, which had been first seen in England in 1959. As staged in New York by Jack Gelber (author of *The Connection*), this seemingly slight play set in the kitchen of a restaurant was both a simple naturalistic picture of commonplace life and a Kafka-like representation of the stalemate of most peoples' lives.

The most notable British play to arrive in New York in 1966, was, however, John Arden's powerful pacifist drama *Serjeant Musgrave's Dance*. Somewhat muddled and difficult to follow, this play, first produced in England in 1960, deals essentially with the violence that defiles the world and the overpowering urge we sometimes feel to retaliate with even more outrageous violence. Arden's "serjeant" is moved to such retaliation when he returns from some unidentified war to Victorian England with the intention of executing a number of smug local citizens to avenge an equal number of lives sacrificed to the cause of British imperialism. Written under the influence of Brechtian drama, the play was both didactic and imaginative.

Didactic but not imaginative and actually a documentary exposition, *The Investigation*, by Peter Weiss, the German author of *Marat/Sade*, presented a chilling account of the horrors of Hitler's extermination camp at Auschwitz. The production evoked thought and emotion with its factuality. Without ever crystallizing into a play, its stark documentary presentation of the bestialization of the world was nonetheless evocative and frightening.

Foreign companies also enriched playgoing, at least in New York City, as was the case when the *Comédie Française* brought over a small part of its repertory. This included not only Corneille and Molière classics, but a modern farce by Feydeau and a 20th century tragedy by Henri de Montherlant that was called *La Reine Morte*.

Awards for the 1965-1966 Season included: **New York Drama Critics Circle Award** to: best play, *The Persecution and Assassination of Marat as Performed by the Inmates of the Asylum of Charenton Under the Direction of the Marquis de Sade*, by Peter Weiss; best musical, *Man of La Mancha*, by Dale Wasserman, Mitch Leigh, and Joe Darion.

The Antoinette Perry (Tony) Awards were given to the same plays in the same categories as the Drama Critics Circle Award.

John Gassner

THEATER, AMATEUR. Actors, directors, and technicians from the professional stage worked more closely with college and community theaters in 1966 than ever before. Eight young men and women received two-year McKnight Fellowships to study for one year in the graduate theater program of the University of Minnesota and to spend the second year as interns in acting, directing, or designing with the professional repertory company at the Tyrone Guthrie Theatre in Minneapolis, Minn. One of the directors of that company, Edward Call, staged a play for the university theater's 1966-1967 season and took part in classes at the university.

A professional repertory theater on the campus of Stanford University, in California, rang down the curtain on its first successful season and began its second, scheduling six plays, among them, *Antony and Cleopatra*, *The Cherry Orchard*, and John Osborne's *Inadmissible Evidence*. Gerald Hiken, Paul E. Richards, and other actors in the company worked with the students who then participated in the productions.

"Drama and the Church" became a living rather than a theoretical subject to students of Valparaiso (Ind.) University. They traveled to Coventry, England, in the fall for classes, conferences, and theater productions held at Coventry Cathedral.

Ties with the playwright were encouraged at the University of Utah, when that university commissioned Norman Corwin to write *The Hyphen* especially for production at the Pioneer Memorial Theater. It was seen in March and April. Corwin also was in residence at the university.

The federal government granted $60,000 through the Office of Education to encourage continuing cooperation between professional and educational theaters. The fund covered conferences on the subject held at the University of Minnesota in February and May.

Statistics released in 1966 showed that Shakespeare was again the favorite playwright of college theaters. A total of 567 college theaters (out of some 2,500) reported 201 productions of 29 of the Bard's works. These theaters, in the season preceding the report, staged a total of 2,988 full-length plays for audiences totaling 7,176,999.

Community Theaters continued to open across the nation. One of them, the Oakland (Calif.) Civic Theater Association, was formed to concentrate exclusively on the production of American plays. The opening season included Albee's *The Death of Bessie Smith* and Lillian Hellman's *Toys in the Attic*.

Columbus, Ga., was representative of the increasing number of towns acquiring their own community theater buildings. There, dedicated citizens completed their exacting restoration of the 94-year-old Springer Opera House. ALICE GRIFFIN

TOGO. See AFRICA.

TORNADOES. See DISASTERS; WEATHER.

TOYS. See GAMES, MODELS, AND TOYS.

TRACK AND FIELD. Jim Ryun, in 1966, brought the world record for the mile back to the United States for the first time since 1937. His time of 3 minutes 51.3 seconds, made on July 17, at Berkeley, Calif., smashed Michel Jazy's previous mark of 3 minutes 53.6 seconds by 2.3 seconds. He was timed at the quarter mile posts in 57.6 seconds, 1 minute 55.5 seconds, and 2 minutes 55.3 seconds. Ryun also set a world record in the half-mile of 1 minute 44.9 seconds, and a U.S. record in the two-mile of 8 minutes 25.2 seconds (see RYUN, JIM).

Only one other athlete, sprinter Tommy Smith of San Jose State College, seriously challenged Ryun's supremacy on the track. Smith set four world records at 200 meters and 220 yards. On May 7, he lowered the standard for the straightaway race from 20 to 19.5 seconds, and on June 11 he ran around a full turn in 20 seconds to take .2 of a second off the world record. Both marks were set at 220 yards, thus automatically applying to the shorter 200-meter distance (218 yards 2 feet 2 inches).

Smith also excelled as a member of the U.S. team that set a world record for the 1,600-meter relay with a clocking of 2 minutes 59.6 seconds. His 400-meter leg of the relay took only 43.8 seconds, the fastest ever.

Other World Records. Five other world records were set by three great distance runners. In the final race of his career, Michel Jazy of France reclaimed the 2,000-meter record by running the race in 4 minutes 56.2 seconds. Australia's Ron Clarke ran three miles in 12 minutes 50.4 seconds and 5,000 meters in 13 minutes 16.6 seconds. And Gaston Roelants of Belgium, world record holder and Olympic champion in the steeplechase, captured the records for 20,000 meters and the one-hour race, covering nearly 13 miles in the latter. Both records had been held by Clarke.

The only world record in a field event was set by pole vaulter John Pennel of Los Angeles, Calif., who cleared 17 feet 6¼ inches. This bettered the mark of 17 feet 5½ inches set by his roommate, Bob Seagren, earlier in the year.

Another pair of roommates made news in the decathlon. In the Amateur Athletic Union (AAU) championship at Salina, Kans., Bill Toomey of Santa Barbara, Calif., scored a record 8,234 points to Russ Hodge's 8,130. But the record was disallowed because the meet officials had provided substandard equipment. Three weeks later, with proper equipment, Hodge claimed the record with 8,230 points, defeating his roommate, Toomey, by only 11 points.

Political Feuds. The political aspects of track and field continued to make news. In July, Russia suddenly canceled its dual meet with the United States, which was to be held that month in Los Angeles. They said the cancellation was in protest of the U.S. role in Vietnam. Poland quickly followed suit. The canceled meets were replaced by an All-

American meet at Berkeley, Calif., on July 16 and 17, and an International meet between U.S. and British Commonwealth teams a week later at Los Angeles. Ryun set his mile record in the All-American meet. Hodge, Pennel, and the 1,600-meter relay team produced their marks at Los Angeles.

In the five-year-old dispute between the AAU and the National Collegiate Athletic Association (NCAA) there was little progress. An impartial five-man panel, appointed in 1965 by Vice-President Hubert H. Humphrey to settle the disagreement, held hearings throughout the year. A possible settlement in 1967 was forecast by Theodore Kheel, head of the panel. Originally, he had expected to achieve a settlement by March, 1966.

Pre-Olympic Meets. Some of the year's most important competitions took place in regional Olympic-style meets. East and West German athletes led the medal winners at the European championships in Budapest, Hungary, while favored Russia won only three of the 24 men's gold medals. In the British Commonwealth Games at Kingston, Jamaica, Kenya's distance runners showed exceptional strength. Naftali Temu defeated Australia's Ron Clarke, the world record holder, in the six-mile race; and Kipchoge Keino did the same in the three-mile race. Keino came back to win the mile, too, running it in 3 minutes 55.3 seconds in the final after a 3-minute, 57.4-second qualifying heat. Keino also ran the year's second fastest mile a few days later in London in 3 minutes 53.4 seconds.

The Kenyans' success in distance running focused attention on the altitude problem involved in holding the 1968 Olympic Games in Mexico City, which is some 7,500 feet above sea level. The Kenyans maintain that their training facilities, at 6,200 feet and higher, give them an advantage in oxygen utilization when running at any altitude. Most coaches and athletes agree, and the distance runs at Mexico City's "Little Olympics," held in October, seemed to confirm their opinions. These races were won in relatively slow times by Alvaro Mejia of Colombia, who trains at a near 9,000-foot altitude in Bogotá. Mejia, a little-known runner, defeated several of the world's best distance men at Mexico City.

In team competition, the Southern California Striders won the AAU indoor and outdoor titles. Kansas won the NCAA indoor team title, while the University of California at Los Angeles (UCLA) easily won the NCAA outdoor crown.

Cross Country. Gerry Lindgren of Washington State University won the NCAA individual cross country title, with Villanova winning the team title. In the AAU race, Ron Larrieu of the Striders won his second straight individual championship, and led the Striders to a team victory.

JAMES O. DUNAWAY

New World Track and Field Records Established in 1966

Subject to recognition by the International Amateur Athletic Federation (IAAF)

Men

Event	Holder	Country	Where Made	Date	Record
200 Meters and 220 Yards (straightaway)	Tommy Smith	U.S.A.	San Jose, Calif.	May 7	0:19.5
200 Meters and 220 Yards (turn)	Tommy Smith	U.S.A.	Sacramento, Calif.	June 11	0:20.0
880 Yards	Jim Ryun	U.S.A.	Terre Haute, Indiana	June 10	1:44.9
Mile	Jim Ryun	U.S.A.	Berkeley, Calif.	July 17	3:51.3
2,000 Meters	Michel Jazy	France	St. Maur, France	October 12	4:56.2
3 Miles	Ron Clarke	Australia	Stockholm, Sweden	July 5	12:50.4
5,000 Meters	Ron Clarke	Australia	Stockholm, Sweden	July 5	13:16.6
20,000 Meters	Gaston Roelants	Belgium	Louvain, Belgium	October 28	58:06.2
1 Hour	Gaston Roelants	Belgium	Louvain, Belgium	Oct. 28	12 mi., 1,168 yds.
30,000 Meters	Jim Hogan	England	Walton-on-Thames, England	Nov. 12	1:32:25.4
440 Yard Relay	Southern U. (Nairn, Harris, Johnson, Anderson)	U.S.A.	Modesto, Calif.	May 28	0:39.6
1,600 Meter Relay	U.S.A. (Frey, Evans, Smith, Lewis)	U.S.A.	Los, Angeles, Calif.	July 24	2:59.6
Mile Relay	Trinidad (Yearwood, Bernard, Roberts, Mottley)	Trinidad	Kingston, Jamaica	August 13	3:02.8
3,200 Meter Relay	W. Germany (Kinder, Adams, Bogatzki, Kemper)	W. Germany	Wiesbaden, Germany	August 13	7:08.6
Two Mile Relay	Southern California (Link, Bess, Buck, Carr)	U.S.A.	Los Angeles, Calif.	May 13	7:17.4
Pole Vault	John Pennel	U.S.A.	Los Angeles, Calif.	July 23	17 feet 6¼ Inches
Decathlon	Russ Hodge	U.S.A.	Los Angeles, Calif.	July 23-24	8,230 points

Women

None broken.

TRANSPORTATION, for the fourth straight year, continued to grow faster than the gross national product (GNP). For 1966, overall freight volume rose 6.8 per cent from the 1965 high–outpacing the 5.5 per cent gain in GNP (as it was measured in constant 1958 dollars). Overall passenger volume rose 5.7 per cent, as the airlines continued to widen their lead over all other modes of public transportation.

The Transportation Association of America (TAA) estimated the nation's total transportation bill for 1966 at $146,500,000,000, including outlays for all types of private and for-hire transport. Of that total, $67,300,000,000 was spent for freight and $79,200,000,000 for passenger transportation. Its estimates on total U.S. traffic volume follow:

Freight	**1965**	**1966**
(billions of intercity ton-miles)		
Rail	709	757
Truck	371	396
Pipeline	310	332
Barge	147	158
Lakes	109	115
Air	2	2
Total freight	1,648	1,760
Passenger		
(billions of intercity passenger-miles)		
Auto	817	880
Air	57	68.7
Bus	22.5	25.0
Rail	17.5	17.3
Water	3	3.3
Total passenger	917	994.3

The Department of Transportation (DOT) was created with the October 15 signing of H.R. Bill 15963. It was the culmination of at least 17 years of recommendations. In 1949, the Hoover Commission urged centralization, and in 1958, the Rockefeller Report proposed a separate transportation department. The need for coordination of agencies and functions had become obvious by 1966.

In signing the bill, President Lyndon B. Johnson said: "The problem of untangling, coordinating, and building a national transportation system worthy of America is a monumental task." He said transportation was the nation's biggest industry, accounting for $1 out of every $5 in the economy and employing more than 2,500,000 people. Although "... our system of transportation is the greatest in the world ... it is no longer adequate," President Johnson added.

The DOT became the fourth largest Cabinet-level department. In 1967, it will employ nearly 100,000 persons and spend almost $6,000,000,000. Its long-range task will be to coordinate the diverse functions of its 31 agencies and to develop a systematic approach to transportation. On November 6, the President named Undersecretary of Commerce Alan S. Boyd, an ex-chairman of the Civil Aeronautics Board (CAB), as Secretary of Transportation.

DOT took over civilian transport nonregulatory functions, such as promotion, safety, research, enforcement, and operations. The Bureau of Public Roads, the Federal Aviation Agency, the Coast Guard, and the St. Lawrence Seaway Corporation were transferred intact, and a department of Railroad Administration was established. The safety, but not rate-setting, responsibilities of the Interstate Commerce Commission (ICC) and the CAB were also transferred to the new department. The Maritime Administration was left in the Department of Commerce.

AIRLINES

The regularly scheduled U.S. domestic airlines–stimulated by the increasing popularity of air travel, promotional fares, and a healthy economy–flew a record 80,026,901,000 passenger-miles, 16.5 per cent above the 1965 level (see AVIATION).

The first "quick change" (QC) jets, passenger planes that can be converted for cargo in a matter of minutes, went into service in 1966. QC jets can expand air cargo service to small cities. Total air cargo volume for 1966 increased by more than 29 per cent, but was still only 7.3 per cent of air carrier dollar volume. In November, citing new technology such as the QC jets, CAB Chairman Charles S.

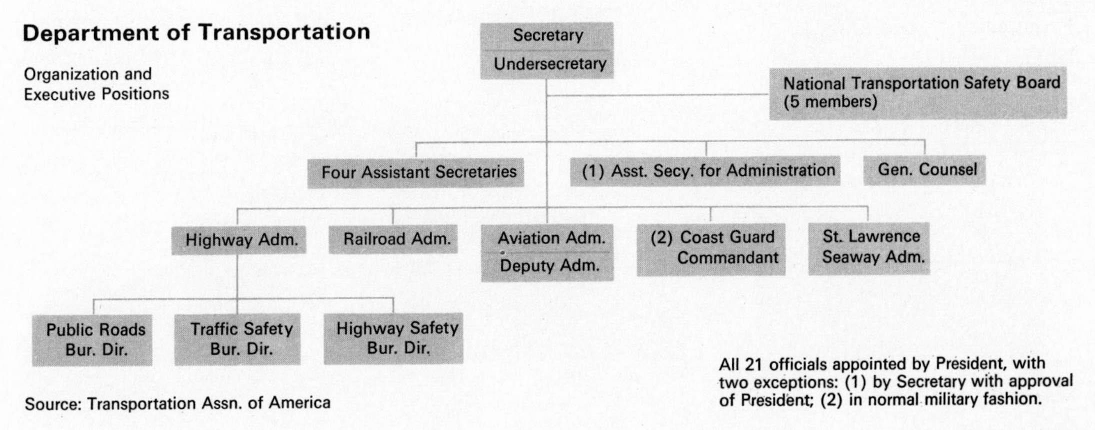

Source: Transportation Assn. of America

Murphy predicted that air cargo might surpass passenger volume by 1980.

RAILROADS

The nation's railroads wound up 1966 with their second most prosperous peacetime year on record. Freight volume, at 744,000,000,000 ton-miles and 6.6 per cent above 1965, for the first time exceeded the previous record of wartime 1944. Gross revenues of $10,675,000,000 exceeded 1953's record by $11,000,000. Net profits of about $925,000,000 neared the previous high of $927,000,000 set in 1955.

The year's heavy freight traffic was supported by increased grain and military shipments, lower rates, and the benefits from new equipment—estimated at a total investment of $1,947,000,000, up 19.3 per cent from 1965. Yet the industry was concerned about the slowdown in profits in the second half of the year. It cited rising labor and maintenance expenses, a decline of grain traffic to more normal levels, and a falling off of the movements of construction industry materials due to the slump in new housing starts.

Rising Labor Costs became one of the most pressing problems facing management at year's end. There was little leeway for cutting payrolls, with employment already down 40 per cent from 1956 to a total of about 632,000. Late in 1966, two of the largest unions, the trainmen and firemen, accepted a 5 per cent pay increase, retroactive to Aug. 12, 1966. Later, the Railway Clerks and the carriers reached a similar agreement, but with an effective date of Jan. 1, 1967. The pattern of these agreements indicated that total railroad labor costs in 1967 would increase by $240,000,000.

Legislation. Early in the year, the railroads' shortage of freight cars reached the crisis stage. It chiefly hampered the movement of grain and of forest products from the Northwest. In May, Congress authorized the ICC to increase per diem rentals on freight cars effective Sept. 1, 1966. It was reported that 90 per cent of all rolling stock carried a $3-a-day, or less, charge. It was cheaper, therefore, for some railroads not to return cars to the owning line but to keep using them at the bargain rentals. The law called for "incentive" charges to "encourage" railroads to return the cars and buy their own.

The Merger Trend, stalled since the marriage of the Wabash, Nickel Plate, and Norfolk & Western in late 1964, seemed likely to resume in 1967. The Pennsylvania-New York Central merger had been approved by the ICC and was ready to take place in 1966, but court appeals delayed it. The Supreme Court of the United States agreed to review the case early in 1967.

Late in the year, the ICC agreed to a new hearing of the proposed merger of the "Northern Lines"—made up of the Great Northern, Northern Pacific, and the Chicago, Burlington & Quincy—which it had rejected earlier.

Super-Speed Trains. In May, the Pennsylvania Railroad signed a two-year, $96,000,000 government contract to provide 100 mph hourly rail passenger service between New York City and Washington, D.C., to begin in October, 1967. The New York Central tested a 170 mph jet-propelled locomotive, to run on magnetized tracks. The Central also postponed its plan to discontinue long-haul passenger runs.

In October, Pullman, Inc., and United Aircraft Corporation unveiled a turbotrain for use in the Northeast Corridor. They said it would cost about 30 per cent less to operate than conventional trains and weigh only 60 per cent as much.

TRUCKING

Although motor carrier revenues moved ahead during the year, profit performance was uneven, particularly by short-haul carriers. Major productivity strides remained in over-the-road—rather than terminal—operations. Gross 1966 revenues reached an all-time high of $11,000,000,000, an increase of 8.9 per cent over 1965. Non-common-carrier, or private carriage, operations expanded even faster. Their ton-mileage increased an estimated 5.9 per cent in 1966. The merger trend among

Prosperity on the Rails

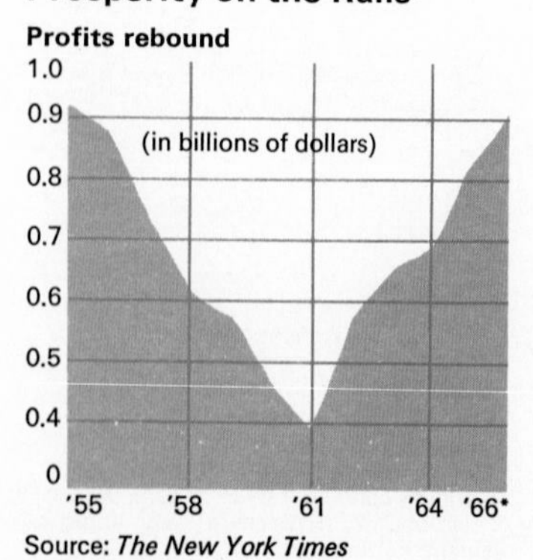

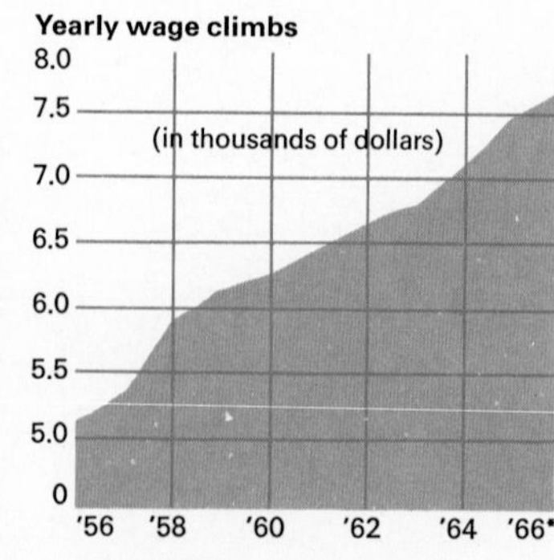

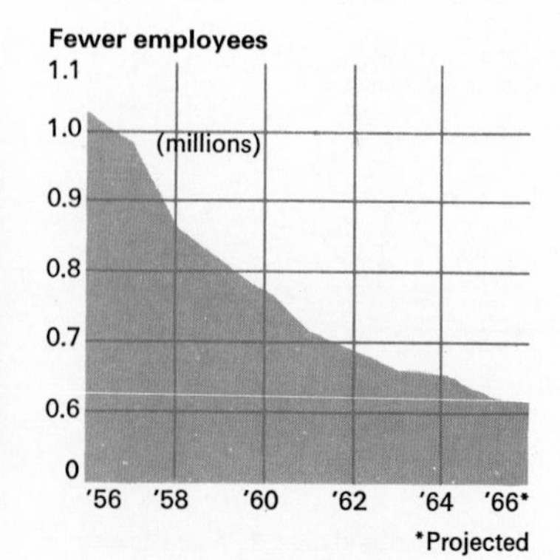

Source: *The New York Times*

*Projected

motor carriers also rolled along; the ICC approved 10 major mergers in the year ended June 30, 1966.

Fleet Acquisition and modernization continued apace. Manufacturers sold 1,700,000 trucks in 1966, not much change from banner 1965, but up from 1,500,000 in 1963. Truckers expanded their use of double-bottom equipment. These tandem-trailer trucks carry substantially greater payloads. They can drop one unit at a given destination and proceed to the next without pausing to unload. In July, Michigan became the 21st state to approve use of the 65-foot tandems on designated highways.

In September, the CAB opened hearings in San Francisco on the request of four long-haul truckers to enter the air freight forwarding business. A forwarder picks up air cargo shipments and consolidates them into larger loads for delivery to the airlines. Since air freight per-pound costs fall as the load gets bigger, this differential affords the forwarder his profit. Existing air freight forwarders and airlines opposed the move, which, if approved, would open new markets for trucking companies.

ROADS AND HIGHWAYS

Congress authorized $19,700,000,000 in federal aid for highway construction for fiscal years 1968-1972. It also extended the Interstate highway program for an additional year, to Oct. 1, 1973. That program, for building the 41,000-mile National System of Interstate and Defense Highways, was begun in 1956. By Sept. 30, 1966, traffic was running on 22,141 miles, or 54 per cent, of the system. In the preceding 12 months, 2,155 miles of right-of-way had been opened.

To ease inflationary pressures, the President, late in November ordered a 21.2 per cent cutback in federal highway spending for fiscal 1967. Project obligations totaling $4,000,000,000 were cut to $3,300,000,000. See AUTOMOBILE; SAFETY.

OCEAN SHIPPING

For the maritime industry, 1966 was a profitable year of recovery from the strikes of 1965. Management was concerned, however, over continued criticism of the subsidized third of the industry. The Department of Defense (DOD) questioned why only about one-fifth of the merchant ships in service in Vietnam were operated by subsidized lines. Shipowners said they stood to lose their regular customers in any massive switch to military service.

The DOD began exploring other forms of water transport such as "fast deployment logistics" (FDL) ships. These fast, efficient vessels, costing about $40,000,000 each, would be loaded with military equipment and stay at sea indefinitely–ready at a moment's notice to put supplies ashore in any crisis area. In July, the navy awarded three identical $5,000,000 contracts–all to aerospace firms–to develop plans for FDL ships. The final contract, to be awarded in mid-1967, will be worth about $1,000,000,000.

The unsubsidized two-thirds of the industry faced formidable problems. Most of its aging fleet will be 25 years old or older within the next few years. The lines face extinction in the 1970s unless drastic remedies are found and applied.

Containerization could be one of those remedies. Containers, cargo boxes generally 8 x 8 x 20 feet in size, allow efficient handling economies. They save time in ports, prevent pilferage and damage, and can be transferred directly to trucks or railroad cars. Problems still remaining include disagreements over the merits of roll-on wheeled units versus lift-on containers, resistance of labor unions, and difficulties in attracting private financing.

At the end of 1966, all but two of the 14 subsidized lines had plans to interchange containers and/or related equipment with foreign lines. In November, a Federal Maritime Commission official predicted that the containerization trend might lead to the development of only a few highly efficient "giant" U.S.- and foreign-flag shipping companies.

World Shipping under construction on Sept. 30, 1966, reached a new high of 1,807 ships totaling 12,118,668 gross tons, according to *Lloyd's Register of Shipping*. Japan continued in first place with 3,542,210 tons of merchant vessel construction, Britain held second. The United States slipped from 10th to 11th place with 383,227 tons. Russia's and Communist China's figures were not tallied.

In total existing fleets, however, Britain held onto first place with 21,542,000 tons. The U.S. merchant fleet was second, with 20,797,000, followed by Liberia, Norway, Japan, and Russia. *Lloyd's* reported total tonnage of the 22 principal shipping nations at 171,129,000 gross tons, up 10,738,000 tons in the year.

WATERWAYS

Barge traffic on the nation's inland waterways rose 7.4 per cent in 1966. Between 1950 and 1965 barge lines' share of all intercity freight shipments expanded from 5 per cent to almost 10 per cent. The railroads' share dropped from 56 per cent to 43 per cent in 1965. Barge traffic, over the 15 years, grew 196 per cent to 151,000,000,000 ton-miles, its rate of growth exceeded only by air freight. However, since barges carry largely low-cost, bulk commodities–such as sand and gravel, coal, grain, and ores–their revenue and profit gains have not kept pace with their increases in volume.

The economies of barge shipping have encouraged a growing number of industrial plants to locate near waterways. The American Waterways Operators cited an increase from 512 such locations in 1965 to 533 in 1966.

St. Lawrence Seaway traffic was estimated at a record high of 48,000,000 tons in 1966, more than 10 per cent above the 44,000,000 tons of 1965. Total Great Lakes shipping reached an all-time peak of 221,627,881 tons in the year, up from 206,498,825 in

1965. See BUILDING AND CONSTRUCTION; CONSERVATION.

KENNETH E. SCHAEFLE

TRANSIT

The Urban Mass Transportation Act of 1966, signed September 8, authorized $150,000,000 in federal grants for each of the fiscal years 1968 and 1969. Most will be used for capital improvements.

Mass transit's vital role was brought painfully home to millions of people when subway and bus employees went out on strike Jan. 1, 1966, paralyzing New York City for 12 days. The total cost in terms of lost business was put at $1,000,000,000. Another cost was the nickel hike in fares to 20 cents in July. See NEW YORK CITY.

Transit Advances in 1966 included:

- The February 26 opening of the 8-mile Bloor-Danforth crosstown line in Toronto's subway system.
- Initial construction in March of a rapid transit tunnel under San Francisco Bay (see BUILDING AND CONSTRUCTION).
- Chicago voter approval in June of a $26,000,000 bond issue for extension of two rapid transit routes.
- The opening of Montreal's first subway, the Metro, on October 17. It was the first system, except for Paris's, to use rubber-tired trains.
- Approval in November by the Southern California Rapid Transit District of $2,625,000 in contracts for developing plans for a $1,000,000,000 mass transportation system.

EUGENE B. MCCAUL

TRAVEL, having easily surpassed its 1965 record volume by a wide margin, was looking ahead optimistically as 1966 ended. In all, 80,000,000 residents of 128 countries spent $12,300,000,000 on foreign travel in 1966, compared with 75,000,000 who spent $11,460,000,000 in 1965. Of all those 1966 tourists, 15,600,000 were Americans. Although there were only 6 per cent more of them than in 1965, their total spending on international tourism rose 9.6 per cent—to an unprecedented $4,100,000,000.

The Travel Gap. Travel not only continued to be the single largest item in world trade, but the largest red-ink entry in the U.S. balance of trade. It was estimated at $1,830,000,000, even though the United States was again the world's No. 1 host country. Eight million foreign visitors spent $1,250,000,000 here plus $185,000,000 for fares on U.S. ships and aircraft.

Despite official concern over the steadily widening travel gap, the administration gave repeated assurances in 1966 that it planned no restrictions on outbound travel by Americans. This stand was a tribute to the leadership of Vice-President Hubert H. Humphrey, chairman of a presidential task force on travel. Humphrey has consistently urged that the United States expand travel from abroad rather than restrict U.S. outbound travel.

Yet Congress has failed to provide sufficient funds for the U.S. Travel Service (USTS) in the Department of Commerce to adequately promote foreign travel to the United States. Despite its budget of only $3,000,000 a year, this small professional agency has skillfully promoted and facilitated tourism from abroad. Canada spends nearly $5,000,000 in the United States alone to lure Americans across the border. Industry experts believe the USTS should have at least $10,000,000 a year to do its job.

The United Nations General Assembly, at the urging of the International Union of Official Travel Organizations, in November approved by acclamation a proposal to proclaim 1967 as International Tourist Year. That UN action was expected to increase world travel greatly. Yet its chief impact may well be to lure more Americans than ever abroad—and make the job of the USTS all the more difficult.

"Discover America," the originally promising program set up by private industry on the initiative of President Lyndon B. Johnson to persuade Americans to travel at home instead of abroad, has been handicapped by organizational difficulties and serious internal policy differences. Nevertheless, domestic U.S. travel expenditures in 1966 rose 10 per cent to $22,500,000,000. An estimated 127,000,000 travelers took business or pleasure trips in the year.

Hotel Expansion continued. Los Angeles got a new $32,000,000 hostelry in midsummer, the Century Plaza. Hilton Hotels International gave Paris

Suggested signs to help the traveler break the language barrier. Their meanings: 1) stairway, 2) elevator, 3) restaurant, 4) rail crossing, 5) no smoking, 6) exit.

its first major new hotel in over 30 years in April, and opened the Barbados Hilton in December. Inter-Continental opened new hotels in Bangkok, Thailand; Dacca, East Pakistan; and Bali, Indonesia. Sheraton acquired the luxurious St. Regis in New York City, and, late in the year, began operating its new circular "hotel in the clouds" on a mountaintop near Caracas, Venezuela.

Other Highlights of the 1966 travel year were:

- U.S.-Soviet agreement for direct air service between Moscow and New York, to start in the spring of 1967. Moscow-Montreal service began in November, 1966. See AVIATION.
- The successful switch to cruising by U.S. and foreign-flag steamship lines to replace the transoceanic express traffic lost to airlines. A record 320,000 Americans went on cruises in 1966.
- U.S. airlines' new, stand-by Youth Fare (one-half the regular fare) in 1966 increased by 71 per cent the number of 18-to-24-year-olds taking a commercial air trip for the first time.
- Britain slashed the amount of money its tourists could take out of the country from £250 to £50.
- To promote travel to the United States, the American Express Company invited 500 European travel agents and 30 foreign travel writers to visit the United States as its guests. WILLIAM D. PATTERSON

See also CONSERVATION; FAIRS AND EXHIBITIONS; TRANSPORTATION.

TREJOS FERNÁNDEZ, JOSÉ JOAQUIN (1917-), an economics and mathematics professor at the University of Costa Rica, and candidate of the National Unification coalition, was elected president of Costa Rica on Feb. 6, 1966. He defeated ex-Foreign Minister Daniel Odubar Quirós of the incumbent National Liberation Movement party. Although Trejos' vote margin over Odubar was only 0.6 per cent, Costa Rica's Supreme Electoral Tribunal certified his election on February 27. He was sworn into office on May 8, succeeding Francisco José Orlich Bolmarcich. See LATIN AMERICA.

Tejos was born in San José on April 18, 1917. After receiving his degree in economics from the University of Costa Rica, he matriculated at the University of Chicago where he studied in the mathematics department from 1946 to 1947. Returning to Costa Rica, he was instrumental in founding the School of Economics and Social Sciences at the University of Costa Rica in San José.

An expert mathematician, Trejos is also extremely interested in the intricacies of international finance. In 1961, as a member of the board of the central bank of Costa Rica, he took an active part in an International Monetary Fund conference held in Washington, D.C. He has also represented his nation's financial interests abroad. WALTER F. MORSE

TRINIDAD AND TOBAGO. See WEST INDIES.

TRUCKING. See TRANSPORTATION.

TRUMAN, HARRY S. (1884-), 33rd President of the United States, celebrated his 82nd birthday on May 8, 1966. In January, President Lyndon B. Johnson flew to Missouri to visit the former President on the announcement of a plan to establish the Harry S. Truman Center for the Advancement of Peace, at Hebrew University in Jerusalem, Israel. At the same time, President Johnson gave Truman Medicare card No. 1, in recognition of his efforts to establish a Medicare program during his presidency. Medicare card No. 2 went to Mrs. Truman.

During 1966, the former President voiced support for President Johnson's decision to resume bombing North Vietnam. As interest rates rose, he worried about inflation. In August, he warned that a rise in interest rates causes "hardship on the consuming public. It only benefits the privileged few." He maintained that if high interest practices persisted, "the result could be a serious depression." President Johnson subsequently disagreed publicly with Mr. Truman's analysis of the economy.

A study of the Truman administration, *The Truman Presidency: The History of a Triumphant Succession*, by Cabell Phillips, was published in May, 1966. It was followed in August, 1966, by a collection of readings, *The Truman Administration*, edited by Barton Bernstein and Allen Matusow. Early in 1966, a Gallup Poll listed Mr. Truman as the 10th most admired living American man. CAROL L. THOMPSON

TUNISIA, a former French colony, celebrated the 10th anniversary of its independence in April, 1966. In a celebration speech, President Habib Bourguiba listed some of the decade's accomplishments. Among them were a 62 per cent increase in the gross national product; a 112 per cent rise in industrial output–to $114,400,000 in 1966; a growth in primary school enrollment from 200,000 pupils to 734,000; and an increase in secondary school enrollment from 15,000 in 1956 to 80,000 in 1966.

In foreign affairs, Bourguiba made good-will visits to the Benelux countries and West Germany during the year. As a result, the Dutch agreed to accept Tunisian workers, and France promised to set duty-free quotas on its farm products. Tunisia shunned inter-Arab quarrels; it boycotted the Arab League and, in October, broke diplomatic relations with the United Arab Republic over Cairo's refusal to consider negotiating the Arab-Israeli conflict.

In May, Bourguiba inaugurated Tunisia's first nuclear research center located in Tunis. During the year, a plant in Sousse began assembling Ford and Fiat trucks. A U.S. firm agreed to convert the Bizerte military base into a naval repair yard.

Facts in Brief. Population: 4,750,000. Government: President Habib Bourguiba. Monetary Unit: dinar (1 = U.S. $1.92). Foreign Trade: exports, $119,900,000; imports, $245,900,000. Principal Exports: phosphates, olive oil, wine. WILLIAM SPENCER

TURKEY. Anti-American incidents were prevalent in 1966 as bitterness grew over the absence of Western support of the Turks in their dispute with Greece over Cyprus. A United States Information Agency library was bombed and the American Sixth Fleet, on a good-will mission to Istanbul, was met by students shouting, "Yankee Go Home!"

President Cemal Gursel died in July. Earlier, the assembly elected General Cevdet Sunay as his successor (see SUNAY, CEVDET). One of Sunay's first acts was to grant a full pardon to ex-President Celâl Bayar, who had been serving a life sentence.

In a disastrous earthquake that struck in eastern Turkey in August, thousands of villagers were left homeless and nearly 2,500 persons were killed (see DISASTERS). Concern, meanwhile, continued over Turkey's growing population. During the year, a family-planning agency began distributing birth control devices. See POPULATION, WORLD.

Facts in Brief. Population: 33,162,000. Government: President Cevdet Sunay; Prime Minister Suleyman Demirel. Monetary Unit: lira (9=U.S. $1). Foreign Trade: exports, $459,000,000; imports, $576,500,000. Principal Exports: tobacco, cotton, fruits, nuts. WILLIAM SPENCER

TYPHOONS. See DISASTERS; WEATHER.

UGANDA. See AFRICA.

UNION OF SOVIET SOCIALIST REPUBLICS (U.S.S.R.). See RUSSIA.

UNITED ARAB REPUBLIC (UAR). Conspiracies, political rivalries, and economic problems plagued President Gamal Abdel Nasser's regime in 1966. The prolonged trials of more than 100 members of the outlawed Muslim Brotherhood who had been arrested in December, 1965, ended in September. Three of them were hanged for attempting to alter the constitution by force and assassinate President Nasser; the others were given jail terms. In a trial involving another plot, Mustafa Amin, editor of the Cairo newspaper *Al-Akbar*, was convicted in August of having conspired with the U.S. Central Intelligence Agency. He was sentenced to life imprisonment. Life terms were also meted out to 10 others found guilty in another attempt on Nasser's life.

In July, the government drafted a new penal code to cover the growing number of economic and social crimes. By doing so, it hoped to reduce profiteering and corruption that had resulted from shortages, especially of rice, as well as from the country's strict anti-inflationary controls.

President Nasser grew concerned over Egypt's "brain drain" which continued in 1966. In August, he met privately with 200 foreign-trained student leaders. In order to discourage emigration, he agreed to raise student allowances and authorize draft exemptions and customs exemptions.

During the year, the 70,000-man UAR expeditionary force stationed in Yemen was recalled from

The discovery of a reservoir of underground fresh water in the UAR's western desert has triggered a large reclamation project.

various outlying positions, and regrouped to form a defensive triangle around the principal Yemeni cities. The move was made to reduce Egyptian casualties. See MIDDLE EAST; SAUDI ARABIA; YEMEN.

New Leaders. The UAR premier, Zakkaria Mohieddin, resigned in September. He was replaced by Mohammed Sidki Suleiman, an engineer who had been minister in charge of the Aswan High Dam.

Important oil strikes were made by Pan American Oil Co. in the Gulf of Suez, by the state-owned General Petroleum in Ras el-Bihar, and by Phillips Petroleum in the Egyptian desert. An accord between Pan American and the UAR in October permitted Pan American's Morgan field to start production in early 1967.

Nevertheless, the UAR's economic prospects were grim. The International Monetary Fund rejected a request for a $70,000,000 loan because of the government's slow progress in economic reforms and its over-commitment in Yemen. The central bank of Egypt had to sell $25,000,000 in gold for Egyptian currency in October to meet its trade deficit and current debts.

Facts in Brief. Population: 31,150,000. Government: President Gamal Abdel Nasser; Premier Mohammed Sidki Suleiman. Monetary Unit: pound (1 = U.S.$2.30). Foreign Trade: exports, $605,200,000; imports, $933,300,000. Principal Exports: cotton, rice, textiles. WILLIAM SPENCER

UNITED COMMUNITY FUNDS AND COUNCILS (UCFC) aided 12 graduate schools of social work in their scholarship program for young men and women seeking a career in fund-raising and community planning. In 1966, the program, called Fund and Council Training Scholarships (FACTS) made grants amounting to $15,400 to eight students, who were selected from a group of 37 applicants. Since the first grants, made in 1961, more than 50 graduate students have received scholarships totaling nearly $100,000.

A total of $625,548,625 was raised in the 1966 campaigns of the 2,200 United Funds, Community Councils, and Community Chests throughout the nation. The chairman for the 1966 campaign was Milton C. Mumford of Darien, Conn., chairman of the board of Lever Brothers Company.

The UCFC biennial conference was held in Toronto, Ont., in February, 1966. Joseph A. Beirne of Washington D.C., president of the Communications Workers of America, AFL-CIO, was elected president. He was the first representative from organized labor to be elected to this post.

The UCFC National Community Service Award for "distinguished leadership in furthering the United way" was given to Ralph Lazarus, Cincinnati, Ohio, and to Hess T. Sears, Des Moines, Iowa. The Newton D. Baker II Award went to Dean Phillips of Columbus, Ohio. JOSEPH P. ANDERSON

UNITED NATIONS (UN). A crisis involving the UN's secretary-generalship aroused world-wide concern in 1966, when on September 1, Secretary-General U Thant announced he would not be available for re-election as the UN's chief operating officer. Worried about the expanding war in Vietnam, U Thant had grown discouraged by the fact that the UN was not being asked to play a larger role in achieving peace there. Nearly every UN member nation appealed to Thant to remain in his post and work to strengthen the organization. The big powers endorsed his right to make independent peace moves. He then agreed to stay on in the post. On December 2, he was unanimously re-elected by the 21st General Assembly after the 15-nation Security Council had formally re-endorsed him. See *Special Report*, Section Two: THE MOST IMPOSSIBLE JOB IN THE WORLD.

Space Treaty. The UN, performing one of its major functions as "a center for harmonizing the actions of nations," provided a meeting place where the Soviet Union and the United States could negotiate many of their differences. As a result, an important new treaty directly involving U.S.-Soviet relations was drafted late in the year to bar nuclear and other mass-destruction weapons from deployment in space and on the moon. The UN General Assembly unanimously commended the treaty and urged the widest possible adherence to it. See Close-Up.

The Assembly unanimously called for early agreement on a measure to prevent the spread of nuclear weapons to additional countries. It also asked the 18-nation Disarmament Committee to consider a proposal binding nuclear-armed nations to refrain from using these weapons against nonnuclear countries. See DISARMAMENT.

Middle East Crisis. Arab terrorist raids against Israel, and Israeli reprisal actions against Syria and Jordan, were called to the attention of the Security Council repeatedly during the year. The hostilities had been launched in mid-July when terrorists from Syria laid mines inside Israel. In retaliation, Israeli planes destroyed Syrian construction equipment. Subsequently, Israel complained to the Council that armed groups from Syria had committed aggression against Israel, and that Syria, too, was threatening to do likewise. In the ensuing tensions, Israel launched new reprisals against the village of Es Samu, in Jordan, which was allegedly being used as an anti-Israeli base by Arab commandos who were believed to be infiltrating the area from Syria. The failure of Jordanian King Hussein's Western-oriented forces to defend Es Samu touched off discord within Jordan and among the other Arab countries. There were demands by the 13-nation Arab League that outside forces be sent into Jordan, including units of the Palestine Liberation Organization which were dedicated to war with Israel.

The opening of the 21st session of the United Nations General Assembly is presided over by Abdul Rahman Pazhwak, *center,* the new president.

Although the Security Council had been balked in its previous efforts to act on the dispute, this time it censured Israel for the attack on Es Samu. The vote was 14 to 0, with New Zealand abstaining. See ISRAEL; JORDAN; MIDDLE EAST; SYRIA.

Meanwhile, the Assembly sent a UN mission to soon-to-be independent Aden to study possible UN supervision of elections when British rule ended in that part of South Arabia. On Cyprus, an agreement covering the presence of a UN peacekeeping force there was renewed.

African Tensions. The successful survival of the white minority government in Rhodesia despite British and UN-established "voluntary" embargoes led to demands by the African nation members for stronger measures. On December 16, the Security Council voted unprecedented mandatory sanctions against Rhodesia, banning the supplying of oil to it and forbidding the purchase of 12 key Rhodesian exports by UN members. It was the first application of mandatory sanctions in the UN's history. See RHODESIA.

The independent African nations wanted the UN to go further, making Britain responsible for keeping oil from Rhodesia–even to the point of manning a naval blockade against South Africa. The sanctions were intended to oblige the minority government to submit to British rule until Rhodesia could be set on a course toward government by its black African majority. By year's end, however, talks between Rhodesian Prime Minister Ian Smith and British Prime Minister Harold Wilson had failed to produce a satisfactory agreement.

South West Africa. In another unprecedented action, the Assembly voted 114 to 2, with 3 abstentions, to revoke South Africa's mandate to govern the territory of South West Africa, a mandate which had been given it by the now-defunct League of Nations after World War I.

The General Assembly had reacted angrily after the UN-affiliated International Court of Justice at The Hague, The Netherlands, had thrown out a six-year-old suit which contended that South Africa had violated its mandate by imposing *apartheid* (racial segregation) on South West Africa. The Court had rejected the suit by a close 7-to-6 vote, with its president, Sir Percy Spender of Australia, voting twice (according to the Court's rules). Philip Jessup, the U.S. judge on the Court, was in the group backing the suit against South Africa. It had been initiated by Liberia and Ethiopia, the only black African members of the former League of Nations.

In the UN, where the African group numbered 38, a special 14-nation committee, which included the United States, was formed to report to a special session of the Assembly in April, 1967, on how to try to cope with South Africa's policy of ignoring UN demands.

Meanwhile, the African nations showed their anger toward the World Court by organizing a committee vote in which a supplementary budget request made by the World Court to cover its costs of conducting the South West Africa case was rejected. The Court's makeup was altered with the election of five new judges–one each from Poland, Nigeria, Sweden, the Philippines, and the United Arab Republic. See SOUTH AFRICA, REPUBLIC OF.

Turning to Portugal, the Africans won approval for an Assembly demand that the North Atlantic Treaty Organization (NATO) countries stop supplying arms to Portugal. The arms allegedly were being used to maintain Portuguese rule in Africa. Most NATO nations voted against the measure. See PORTUGAL.

Membership Issues. With nuclear-armed Communist China bulking large in major issues, such as Vietnam and disarmament, the annual debate on a UN seat for Peking disclosed a new American policy emphasis. A pro-Peking membership proposal calling for the ousting of Nationalist (Formosa) China was defeated by a vote of 56 to 47, with 17 countries abstaining. This was a larger margin of defeat for the proposal than that of 1965. Then the vote was 47 to 47, blocking the seating of Communist China. A two-thirds majority was required.

Asian Issues. Despite an American request, the Security Council failed to take up the Vietnam question after having put the issue on its agenda on February 2. It was argued that UN organs such as the Council could not deal usefully with Vietnam as long as Communist China and North Vietnam were not represented. (South Vietnam has observer status at the UN.) See VIETNAM.

In late 1966, India and Pakistan ratified and carried out a mutual withdrawal of forces ordered by the Security Council. Compliance followed a meeting between Pakistan's President Mohammad Ayub Khan and India's Prime Minister Lal Bahadur Shastri at Tashkent in January, 1966. See INDIA.

Korean Question. A Soviet effort to end the UN's role in Korea was rebuffed in the General Assembly political committee. Traditional UN support was reaffirmed, however, for UN-supervised elections and the eventual reunification of (Communist) North and South Korea.

Asian Development Bank. Under auspices of the UN Economic Commission for Asia and the Far East, the Asian Development Bank became a reality on August 22 when its charter was ratified by 15 nations who subscribed $650,000,000 of its $1,000,000,000 authorized capitalization. The United States and Japan each put in an initial $200,000,000 with promises of more to come.

In another important Asian membership development, Indonesia, the first country ever to withdraw from the UN, was welcomed back to active membership on September 28. After the change in govern-

Peace In Space

On December 8, the United Nations announced that agreement had been reached on the first international treaty governing space exploration. The text included these major points:

- Outer space, including the moon and other celestial bodies, shall be free for exploration and use by all states without discrimination of any kind, on a basis of equality . . . and there shall be free access to all areas of celestial bodies.
- There shall be freedom of scientific investigation in outer space . . . and states shall facilitate and encourage international cooperation in such investigation.
- Outer space, including the moon and other celestial bodies, is not subject to national appropriation by claim of sovereignty, by means of use or occupation, or by any other means.
- Parties to the treaty will not undertake to place any objects in orbit around the earth carrying nuclear weapons or any other kinds of weapons of mass destruction, install such weapons on celestial bodies, or station such weapons in outer space in any other manner.
- The moon and other celestial bodies shall be used exclusively for peaceful purposes by all parties to the treaty. The establishment of military bases, installations, and fortifications, the testing of any type of weapons and the conduct of military maneuvers on celestial bodies shall be forbidden.
- Parties to the treaty shall regard astronauts as envoys of mankind in outer space and shall render to them all possible assistance in the event of accident, distress, or emergency landing.
- All stations, installations, equipment, and space vehicles on the moon and other celestial bodies shall be open to representatives of other parties to the treaty on a basis of reciprocity. Such representatives shall give reasonable advance notice of a projected visit, in order . . . to avoid interference with normal operations in the facility to be visited.

MILT FREUDENHEIM

ment in Indonesia, it was announced that its withdrawal from the UN Jan. 21, 1965, now was considered as only a temporary "cessation of cooperation." See INDONESIA.

New Members. The newly independent countries of Guyana and Barbados from Latin America and Lesotho and Botswana from southern Africa were admitted during the year, bringing the General Assembly's membership to 122.

Financial and Peacekeeping Deadlock. The Soviet Union and France failed to make the voluntary donations to the UN they had promised in place of the assessments for UN peace forces in the Congo and Middle East which they considered illegal. Moscow and Paris argued that only the Security Council, with its big-power veto, could order and finance UN peacekeeping operations. A proposal made by Canada in the General Assembly would have established in advance a model scale of payments for peacekeeping forces. Avoiding the issue, the Assembly decided to postpone action until the special session scheduled for April, 1967.

Human Rights Covenants. Two covenants (draft treaties) to give the force of law to the 18-year-old Universal Declaration of Human Rights were approved by the Assembly. They covered the guaranteeing of rights to life, liberty, personal security, freedom from slavery and arbitrary arrest, and detention, to all people without regard to race,

Seating Arrangement

sex, language, or religion. They were subject to ratification by the U.S. and other governments.

Population Control. The General Assembly for the first time endorsed action by UN agencies to set up population control programs in countries requesting them. The Assembly measure, following approval by the Economic and Social Council, focused world attention on the urgent problem of rapid population growth and limited food supplies. See POPULATION, WORLD.

International Law. The drawing up of a "treaty on treaties," designed to set up rules on the validity, interpretation, and effect of treaties, was planned for a conference scheduled in 1968. The Assembly also set up a Commission on International Trade Law to bring harmony to existing laws in this field.

Elections. The 21st General Assembly unanimously elected as its president, UN Ambassador Abdul Rahman Pazhwak of Afghanistan. He succeeded Amintore Fanfani of Italy. See PAZHWAK, ABDUL RAHMAN.

To replace Jordan, The Netherlands, New Zealand, Uganda, and Uruguay on the Security Council in 1967, the Assembly elected Brazil, Canada, Denmark, Ethiopia, and India. (The other members are the United States, Britain, France, Soviet Union, and China [Formosa], all permanent; and Argentina, Bulgaria, Japan, Mali, and Nigeria.) MILT FREUDENHEIM

U.S. GOVERNMENT. The threat of inflation at home, and the escalating war in Vietnam, cast shadows on America's Great Society in 1966. At year's end, the United States and the Vietnams–North and South–seemed no nearer to the conference table than they were when the year began. News that Communist China had tested its fifth nuclear device–its third successful test of 1966–increased the anxiety of those who saw China, not North Vietnam, as America's real enemy.

At home, the elections of 1966 strengthened the Republicans in Congress, indicating rough going for Great Society legislation and for funds to nourish it. The vote outcome indicated some discontent with President Lyndon B. Johnson and his administration. See CONGRESS; ECONOMY, THE; ELECTIONS; PRESIDENT; VIETNAM.

The White House in the first three years of the Johnson presidency lost 15 members of its staff. In December, 1966, Bill D. Moyers, presidential press secretary and one of the President's closest associates, resigned effective Feb. 1, 1967, to become publisher of the Long Island (N.Y.) newspaper *Newsday*. The fourth press secretary to serve President Johnson would be George Christian, 39, a one-time International News Service (INS) reporter, formerly on the staff of Texas Governor John B. Connally, Jr.

Two others retired in April: Jack J. Valenti, special assistant, and George E. Reedy, Johnson's second press secretary, who had been working for the President on long-range projects. In March, the President named Walt W. Rostow and Robert E. Kintner as his special assistants.

The Cabinet. During the year, the top posts of two new departments were filled: Robert C. Weaver in Housing and Urban Development, and Alan S. Boyd in Transportation. See CABINET.

Department of State. Abba P. Schwartz resigned as head of the Bureau of Security and Consular Affairs in March, after he was informed that a reorganization plan would eliminate his bureau. His liberal supporters contended that Schwartz had been eased out because he favored relaxed regulation of travel and immigration.

In April, after some criticism of procedures of the Passport Office and its director, Miss Frances G. Knight, Senator Edward M. Kennedy (D., Mass.) announced that Miss Knight's office would no longer be able to request overseas diplomatic personnel to get reports on Americans traveling abroad for the Federal Bureau of Investigation (FBI) as a matter of routine. Thereafter, the department's Bureau of Research and Development would have to approve any such FBI request, which would have to conform to clear criteria, not simply the fact that the FBI had asked for it.

In a surprise announcement in September, the President named Attorney General Nicholas deB. Katzenbach to succeed George W. Ball as undersecretary of State, No. 2 man in the department. Eugene V. Rostow was named undersecretary for political affairs, succeeding Thomas C. Mann, and Foy D. Kohler replaced U. Alexis Johnson as deputy undersecretary for political affairs.

Other departmental appointments included:

In January, Lincoln Gordon as assistant secretary of State for inter-American affairs, replacing Jack Hood Vaughn, who became director of the Peace Corps.

In March, Joseph Palmer II succeeded G. Mennen Williams as assistant secretary of State for African affairs; James W. Symington was appointed chief of protocol.

Major diplomatic appointments in 1966 included:

Llewellyn E. Thompson, Jr., as Ambassador to Russia, succeeding Foy D. Kohler; Ellsworth Bunker as Ambassador-at-Large, succeeding Llewellyn E. Thompson; Sol M. Linowitz, as Ambassador to the Organization of American States; U. Alexis Johnson as Ambassador to Japan; John W. Tuthill as Ambassador to Brazil. See DIPLOMAT.

Housing and Urban Development (HUD), the 11th Cabinet-level department, established in 1965, was staffed early in 1966. President Johnson named Robert C. Weaver, its first Secretary and the first Negro to fill a Cabinet post. Weaver was sworn in on Jan. 18, 1966. He formerly headed the Housing and Home Finance Agency. See CITY; HOUSING.

The Department of Transportation (DOT) became the 12th department, by act of Congress on October 15. More than 30 federal agencies were transferred to DOT, with the conspicuous exception of the Federal Maritime Commission. The President named Alan S. Boyd as Secretary on November 6. See TRANSPORTATION.

Department of Health, Education, and Welfare (HEW) Secretary John W. Gardner in November announced plans for a major reorganization of his department. Its eight major bureaus and agencies would be consolidated into three sections or departments: health, education, and individual and family services. HEW's Food and Drug Administration, for the first time since 1921, was headed by a physician when the President named Dr. James L. Goddard as its commissioner in January. See CIVIL RIGHTS; DRUGS; GODDARD, JAMES L.; HEALTH AND DISEASE; MEDICARE; OLD AGE; SOCIAL SECURITY.

Other Federal Appointments in 1966 included:

In January, Mrs. Constance B. Motley to the U.S. District Court in New York City, the first Negro woman ever to sit on a federal bench; *in February*, presidential counsel Lee C. White as chairman of the Federal Power Commission; Elmer B. Staats, deputy director of the budget, as Comptroller General; Andrew F. Brimmer, assistant secretary of Commerce for economic affairs, to the Federal Reserve Board; *in March*, Bernard Zagorin as U.S. director of the Asian Development Bank; *in June*, Rosel H. Hyde as chairman of the Federal Communications Commission; Richard M. Helms as director of the Central Intelligence Agency (see HELMS, RICHARD M.); William S. Gaud as head of the Agency for International Development (see GAUD, WILLIAM S.); *in November*, William B. Camp as Comptroller of the Currency. CAROL L. THOMPSON

UPPER VOLTA. Lieutenant Colonel Sangoulé Lamizana, the army chief of staff, assumed control of the government on Jan. 4, 1966. He did so to end the threat of serious riots. Trouble had begun on December 30 of the preceding year when the government cut the salaries of government employees by 20 per cent and reduced their family allowances. Union leaders then called for a strike. A state of emergency was declared and the strike was banned.

On January 3, in defiance of the government's edict, the workers struck. The police force, using tear gas, dispersed the demonstrators, who had surrounded the presidential palace. In the afternoon, Lamizana and the army took control.

Labor leaders announced on January 4 that the order reducing family allowances and wages had been rescinded. They urged civil servants to return to their jobs and support the new government. On January 9, a provisional government was formed under Lamizana.

Facts in Brief. Population: 4,805,000. Government: President and Prime Minister Sangoulé Lamizana. Monetary Unit: CFA franc (245=U.S.$1). Foreign Trade: exports, $6,700,000; imports, $25,100,000. Principal Exports: fish, livestock, peanuts. BENJAMIN E. THOMAS

URUGUAY. See LATIN AMERICA.

UTILITIES. See COMMUNICATIONS; ELECTRIC POWER; PETROLEUM AND GAS.

VALENTI, JACK JOSEPH (1921-) left his job as special assistant to President Lyndon B. Johnson to become president of the Motion Picture Association of America on June 1, 1966. The association is the industry's voluntary self-regulatory body.

The ebullient 44-year-old former public relations and advertising executive was born in Houston, Tex., on Sept. 5, 1921. After supporting himself through high school, he joined the air force and became a bomber pilot during World War II. He flew 51 combat missions and received the Distinguished Flying Cross. After the war, he studied at Harvard University where he graduated from its business school. He then returned to Houston to head the Humble Oil Company's advertising department, and later founded his own advertising agency.

An unabashed admirer and friend of President Johnson, Valenti handled political advertising for the Kennedy-Johnson campaign in 1960. At Johnson's invitation, Valenti was in the Dallas motorcade on Nov. 22, 1963, when President Kennedy was assassinated, and was immediately drafted by the new President as his personal assistant. He served as a speech writer, editor, trouble shooter, and, perhaps most important, a social companion and confidant of the President.

He married Mary Margaret Wiley, secretary to the then Vice-President Johnson, in 1962. They have two children.

VANDEN BOEYNANTS, PAUL (1919-), was sworn in as prime minister of Belgium on March 19, 1966. Vanden Boeynants, who had been president of the Christian Social party since 1961, had accepted King Baudouin's request to form a new government after Prime Minister Pierre Harmel had resigned. See BELGIUM.

The new Belgian prime minister was born in Vorst, a small town near Brussels, on May 5, 1919. He attended the College St. Michel, a Jesuit secondary school, where he learned to speak French in addition to his native Flemish tongue. After finishing school, Vanden Boeynants went into business as a maker and exporter of sausages. At the age of 30, he became interested in politics and was elected to parliament. He was 34 when the Brussels Town Council made him one of its six aldermen. He became a cabinet officer at the age of 39. In 1961, he was elected president of the Christian Social party, a position that vaulted him into his new post.

Vanden Boeynants is a vigorous advocate of a businesslike operation of government. Of an energetic temperament, he visits a gymnasium almost daily for weight-lifting and volley ball workouts. Because of a childhood affliction which impaired his hearing, he wears a hearing aid. The new leader, who heads a company that makes and exports 90 kinds of sausages, is a butcher's son who married a meat dealer's daughter. WALTER F. MORSE

VAUGHN, JACK HOOD (1920-), assistant secretary of State for inter-American affairs, was sworn in as the new director of the Peace Corps on March 1, 1966. He succeeded R. Sargent Shriver, who resigned in order to devote full time to the Office of Economic Opportunity (see PEACE CORPS).

Vaughn was born in Columbus, Mont., Aug. 18, 1920. He served with the marines in the Pacific during World War II. After the war, he worked for his M.A. degree in Latin American studies at the University of Michigan, and spent his summers in Mexico, studying at the National University and boxing professionally.

Vaughn directed U.S. Information Agency programs in Bolivia and Costa Rica (1949 to 1952). He later served with the International Cooperation Administration in Panama, Bolivia, Mali, and Senegal. He returned to Washington in October, 1961, to become regional director for Peace Corps programs in Latin America. In 1964, he was named U.S. ambassador to Panama, where he earned the country's Vasco Núñez de Balboa medal for his handling of the U.S.-Panama dispute over the Canal Zone. In March, 1965, he became assistant secretary of State and the U.S. coordinator of the Alliance for Progress.

Vaughn's favorite relaxations are gardening and poker. He married Joanne Cordes Smith in 1946. They have two daughters.

VENEZUELA. On Oct. 30, 1966, the government crushed an attempted military uprising by members of the National Guard headquarters garrison stationed near Caracas. It was the first uprising of any size against the rule of President Raúl Leoni since he had taken office from Rómulo Betancourt in 1964.

Guerrilla activity, meanwhile, persisted in the mountainous countryside. In November, it erupted in Caracas when members of the antigovernment underground Armed Forces for National Liberation attacked a number of public buildings. The new outburst, however, failed to alarm the government which estimated the terrorists' strength at about 200 full-time members.

Policies Questioned. The government was more concerned in 1966 with opposition to its oil and tax policies, which had dismayed businessmen and politicians alike. In a critical showdown with the foreign oil companies, the republic in late 1965 had made claims for back taxes involving an unofficially estimated $100,000,000-plus for the years 1958 to 1960. It also limited discounts from posted prices on exports of residual fuel. Foreign oil interests, alarmed both by the size of the tax claims and the arbitrary methods for determining the amounts, believed that to accede would be tacit endorsement of price-fixing by government decree. Any such precedent in Venezuela could cause them endless troubles in other oil-producing nations of the world.

Venezuela also refused to grant new petroleum concessions, even though the competitive position of its oil abroad had deteriorated, proven reserves had decreased, and the level of exploration and drilling activities was receding. Meantime, the oil companies were squeezed by a new three-year labor contract which added some $80,000,000 to their labor costs.

On top of all this, the government sent a sweeping tax reform bill to congress under which the oil concerns, already covering 64 per cent of the government's $1,700,000,000 budget, would have to provide up to 70 per cent of the additional revenues (or $70,000,000 to $80,000,000) the regime intended to raise. Business in general was alarmed by the legislation. While there was little question that the government needed more revenue, the solution, government opponents felt, was not a mountain of new taxes but a closer look at government spending and the more efficient use of existing resources. The government and the oil firms then worked out a tentative agreement covering back taxes, proposed new taxes, and government price-setting for tax purposes; the suggested tax increases were modified.

Facts in Brief. Population: 9,228,000. Government: President Raúl Leoni. Monetary Unit: bolívar (4.48=U.S.$1). Foreign Trade: exports, $2,558,500,000; imports, $1,296,600,000. Principal Exports: petroleum and petroleum products, coffee, iron ore. MARY C. WEBSTER

VETERANS. When President Lyndon B. Johnson signed the Veterans Readjustment Act of 1966, veterans organizations achieved a goal they had been working toward for 10 years. The legislation has been called the "Cold War GI Bill." It provided benefits—similar to those given World War II and Korean War veterans—to ex-servicemen with at least 180 days of active duty since Jan. 31, 1955.

The new act's provisions include:

- One month of schooling for each month of active service up to a maximum of 36 months. This applies to those wishing to complete high school as well as college, in U.S. or foreign schools. Educational benefits for full-time students range from $100 per month, if there are no dependents, to $150 per month for two or more dependents. Scaled-down benefits are provided for part-time students. Veterans are allowed eight years to complete their education from the date of their discharge from their last active duty, or from June 1, 1966, whichever date is later.
- Medical care in Veterans Administration hospitals for nonservice-connected disabilities, if there is room and the veteran can demonstrate financial need.
- Job counseling and assistance in placement by the U.S. Department of Labor.
- An extra five points on scores for veterans taking competitive Civil Service tests. Those with service-connected disabilities will receive 10 points.

- Loans for home and farm purchases up to $7,500 if the loan is made by a private lender. The new law authorizes direct loans up to $17,500 for veterans living in small towns or rural areas where loans from private lending institutions are not available.

Other legislation passed by the Congress increased monthly dependency and indemnity payments to parents and children of veterans whose deaths were service-connected. The increases are designed to offset the rise in living costs.

The Veterans Administration (VA) budget for the fiscal year beginning July 1, 1966, was $5,900,000,000, an increase of $17,000,000 over the previous year. Of this amount, $1,250,000,000 was earmarked for an expanded medical care program.

The VA's Voluntary Service National Advisory Committee celebrated its 20th anniversary by sponsoring its first national convention, April 18 to 20, in Washington, D.C. The program was started in 1946 by General Omar N. Bradley.

American Legion posts and auxiliary units began a campaign to inform servicemen about the educational benefits under the new GI Bill.

The 48th American Legion national convention was held in Washington, D.C., August 29 to September 2. John E. Davis, former governor of North Dakota, was elected national commander.

While the convention was in session, President Johnson signed a bill allowing Vietnam veterans to become members of the Legion. Gordon Saffold of Saltville, Va., was the first Vietnam veteran to be admitted under the revised charter. The Legion's Distinguished Service Medal was awarded to Captain Roger H. C. Donlon, the first Medal of Honor winner in Vietnam.

American Veterans Committee (AVC) in 1966 amended its constitution to accept Vietnam veterans into membership. The organization's 1966 annual convention was held in Washington, D.C., February 11 to 13. John S. Stillman of New York City was re-elected national chairman.

American Veterans of World War II and Korea (AMVETS), through its national commander, Ralph E. Hall, urged negotiations between the United States and Canada to stop young Americans from dodging the draft by moving across the border. The convention was held August 15 to 21 in Columbus, Ohio, and A. Leo Anderson of Washington, D.C., was elected national commander.

Veterans of Foreign Wars (VFW) held its 67th annual convention in New York City, August 19 to 26. The delegates resolved that no college student be exempted from the draft unless he was enrolled in an officer training program. They also opposed admission of Red China to the United Nations, and condemned U.S. policy permitting the sale of foreign-made drugs in the United States. Leslie M. Fry, an attorney from Reno, Nev., was elected commander in chief.

JOSEPH P. ANDERSON

VIETNAM

The real, if undeclared, war involving the United States in Southeast Asia and specifically in Vietnam continued throughout 1966. As in all open hostilities, battles were fought and men died. Policies were questioned and sides taken. Despite its battle losses and criticism at home and abroad, the United States remained determined to prevent the take-over of South Vietnam by the North Vietnamese Communists.

Search for Peace. The year began with a peace offensive initiated by the United States. For 37 days, the United States called a halt to its air raids on North Vietnamese targets while American peace emissaries visited various world capitals to explore the possibilities of getting the North Vietnamese to negotiate a cease-fire and a peaceful settlement of the war. By the end of January, however, it had become obvious that the moves were doomed to failure. The North Vietnamese had continued to build up their military strength. They increased their terrorist activities against the South Vietnamese.

On January 31, the United States resumed its air attacks against North Vietnam, in what became known as "escalating" the war. The United States also began a steady troop build-up. Where there had been some 200,000 troops by the end of 1965, the number had nearly doubled in 1966. Some 380,000 were serving by the end of the year, with projections being made which would bring the number to 500,000 by sometime in 1967. By April of 1966, the cost of the war to the United States had mounted to an average daily expenditure of some $33,000,000.

U.S. War Efforts. The massive amount of military power which the United States was pouring into Vietnam meant not only a tremendous troop build-up, but the creation of huge port installations to handle the volume of supplies necessary to keep its troops in the field. The expansion of harbor facilities, such as those at Cam Ranh Bay, were an indication that the United States was determined to stay and to support its war effort. As U.S. troops carried the war to the Viet Cong, however, the American casualty rate began to mount. In one week in December, about 800 U.S. servicemen died in Vietnam; the estimated total since Jan. 1, 1961, was about 6,000.

During 1966, the United States began to use incredibly mobile infantry and artillery units, whose effectiveness derived largely from the use of heli-

A direct hit by U.S. bombers explodes North Vietnam's second biggest oil storage complex on the outskirts of Hanoi.

PICTURES OF THE YEAR/Larry Burrows, *Life* © Time Inc.

Determined to vote, a Vietnamese soldier whose hands were injured in battle uses his teeth to drop his ballot into the box.

copters and air support. It was this mobility that resulted in some of the major victories of the war against large-scale attacks by Viet Cong units. Troops could be and were moved quickly and efficiently into advance areas; with equal speed they could be supplied or lifted out of the area as it was deemed necessary.

Allied Support. By year's end, it was obvious that the United States had seized the military initiative in Vietnam. But this initiative could not have been accomplished without support from other nations as well. The Republic of (South) Korea in particular supported the effort with two of its best divisions. Similarly, Australia committed a military contingent which, though small in number, proved invaluable in the field (see AUSTRALIA). Toward the end of the year, the Philippines also contributed a force of 2,000 men (see PHILIPPINES, THE).

The continuing use of airpower in support of ground units in South Vietnam, as well as in bombing raids in North Vietnam, was generally considered to be having a telling impact on the war. Many military experts, however, questioned the effectiveness of the air raids. The flow of Viet Cong supplies from the north into the south seemed to continue despite the bombings. Although the Ho Chi Minh trail, which passes through Laos and Cambodia, had supposedly been put out of commission by the bombers, it still carried a substantial supply of material from the north, and it still served as a base for Viet Cong operations. In addition to the Ho Chi Minh trail, the Viet Cong were also using the direct route from north to south through the so-called demilitarized zone.

Battle Lines Shift. Through the combined efforts of the South Vietnamese and American forces, large-scale efforts by the Viet Cong in central Vietnam were apparently becoming too costly. Accordingly, the war began to shift out of the central plains during the year. It moved southward into the Mekong Delta, the heartland of South Vietnam, whose rice-rich paddies held the strategic key to the future control of the country.

It was in this delta area that a major thrust began to develop toward the end of the year. Although the Viet Cong initially enjoyed an advantageous position, it did not last long. By December, U.S. and South Vietnamese troops had again seized the initiative as they moved into the delta area and began pursuing the Viet Cong.

All of these military efforts, with their subsequent gains, were not equaled in the political arena, however. It was there that the war was not going too well for the South Vietnamese. In part, this was the result of the fact that the South Vietnamese government, headquartered in Saigon, had yet to enlist the loyalties and full support of the people of South Vietnam. The newly elected government of Premier Nguyen Cao Ky was still too untried to mean very much to millions of Vietnamese (see KY, NGUYEN CAO). Second, its Saigon-oriented policies, as well as its Roman Catholic emphasis, meant that it would have to change much before it could count on any degree of popular support.

Buddhist Dissension. The Ky government's most immediate problem was dissatisfaction within South Vietnam, particularly among the ever-active Buddhists and their adherents in central Vietnam. It was in the Buddhist stronghold of Hue and Da Nang that the government faced its strongest opposition. There, under the leadership of Thich Tri Quang, the Buddhists repeatedly demonstrated and rioted against the Saigon government. In some instances, they were supported militarily by various disaffected units of the South Vietnamese army. In April and again in May, the Buddhists attempted to force the resignation of the Ky government. While the attempts failed, the demonstrations did show results. Because of them, Ky was finally forced to take action toward a return to civil government.

In April, Premier Ky announced plans to hold a national election for a constituent assembly. The assembly would draw up a new constitution and decide on the type of nationally elected government that would replace Ky's ruling military junta. Although the Viet Cong threatened to take violent action against anyone who participated in the election, the government went ahead and, in September, the elections were held. Some 5,238 polling places remained open despite Communist threats. Of about 5,000,000 registered voters, more than 80 per cent voted. Some 117 candidates were elected, and at year's end the Ky government and the assembly were reportedly working toward the restoration of civil government in South Vietnam.

"Pacification" Program. During the year, as American troops assumed an increasingly larger share of the actual fighting, the South Vietnamese forces became more and more involved in what were called "pacification" programs for the nation. Under these programs, the troops were held responsible for the elimination of any Viet Cong from a specific area. They were also charged with such responsibilities as the compilation of intelligence information about the area. It was hoped their activities would stimulate local governments to open the channels of communication with Saigon.

If this program succeeded, a degree of loyalty to the central government might be attained. As an adjunct of this pacification policy, American aid–in the form of commodities, construction supplies, and health and educational assistance–was to be sent into each area. As a secondary benefit, it was hoped that if U.S. aid could thus go directly into the provinces where it was needed, less and less would

Grim-faced U.S. airmen, who were taken prisoner by the North Vietnamese, are marched through the streets of Hanoi by their captors.

fall into the hands of corrupt central government officials in Saigon and other port cities.

Concern Over Aid Diversion. Corruption, particularly as it affected the diversion of U.S. military and civilian aid, was beginning to cause grave concern in both Washington, D.C., and Saigon. The vast outpouring of American aid, together with huge expenditures by the U.S. military establishment and black marketeering of diverted supplies, were beginning to have a disastrous effect on the South Vietnamese economy.

Inflation in terms of skyrocketing prices on certain items made the situation even worse. Because of it, Vietnamese government officials, whose salaries were set at a government-fixed level, were tempted to indulge in additional corruption to keep up with the rising price levels. All attempts at reform were temporary at best, however.

The Ky government faced an incipient revolt in the fall, when South Vietnamese members of the cabinet began to question an imbalance between the posts they held as compared to the key positions that had been given to refugees from the north. As centuries-old animosities came out into the open, Ky was forced to reshuffle the cabinet. Key cabinet appointments were reassigned to the southerners. Temporarily, at least, the move seemed to satisfy the southerners. But the issue remained, as did the issue of Roman Catholicism versus Buddhism in government.

There were indications during the year that American efforts in Vietnam were largely in the hands of the U.S. military, rather than under the control of U.S. civilians. It was General William C. Westmoreland, rather than U.S. Ambassador Henry Cabot Lodge, who seemed to many to be playing the leading role in U.S.-South Vietnamese relations.

Debate Over U.S. Policy. It was this preponderance of American military influence which led to sharp debates in the United States over the Johnson administration's position in Vietnam. It was also the cause for dissatisfaction among an outspoken minority within the United States which frankly denounced U.S. participation in the war. This, of course, was echoed throughout a large portion of the world, and particularly by the Communists. There were indications that the Soviet Union was unhappy over the extent of Communist China's participation in the war and its refusal to let Russian supplies and influence move into North Vietnam. By the end of the year, it was clear that the Chinese Communists had moved a large number of men into North Vietnam, though the exact nature of their duties was not yet known.

U.S. Commander in Chief Lyndon B. Johnson shakes hands with American servicemen during his October visit to South Vietnam.

A platoon of battle-ready U.S. infantrymen opens fire on a nest of Viet Cong snipers holed in near a South Vietnamese village.

Johnson Tour. Growing criticism of U.S. participation in the war at home and abroad, unsuccessful U.S. peace overtures, and the repeated denunciations of American efforts by the Communists led U.S. President Lyndon B. Johnson to take a bold step. In October, he decided to go to Southeast Asia for a major conference with the nations most immediately involved in the struggle. On his tour, which included the conference in Manila, Johnson reaffirmed the United States' determination to stay in Southeast Asia until a peaceful and equitable solution to the Vietnamese problem could be found.

Although the year ended with a cease-fire on Christmas Day, the United States announced plans to send in more troops to South Vietnam as they were needed in the war effort.

Facts in Brief.

Vietnam (North). Population: 19,224,000. Government: President Ho Chi Minh, Premier Pham Van Dong. Monetary Unit: dong (2.94=U.S.$1). Foreign Trade: exports, $19,500,000; imports, $12,500,000. Principal Exports: agricultural products, minerals.

Vietnam (South). Population: 16,376,000. Government: Premier Nguyen Cao Ky. Monetary Unit: piaster (117.26=U.S.$1). Foreign Trade: exports, $35,300,000; imports, $356,400,000. Principal Exports: rice, rubber, tea. JOHN N. STALKER

Unsightly Bulge

VITAL STATISTICS. In 1966, there were fewer births, about the same number of marriages, and more deaths than in the year before. Estimates based on figures for the first 10 months of the year showed that the birth rate declined nearly 5 per cent, while the death rate increased 2 per cent. The rate and numbers of births in the United States have fallen steadily since 1960.

Heart disease continued to be the leading cause of death in 1966. Deaths due to bronchitis and related diseases, accidents, and homicides increased.

U.S. Vital Statistics

	1965*	1966*
Live births	3,812,000	3,645,000
Birth rate†	19.7	18.6
Infant deaths (under age 1)	94,900	86,300
Deaths	1,817,000	1,871,000
Death rate*	9.4	9.6
Marriages	1,768,000	1,825,000
Divorces	283,211	303,428
(38 reporting areas Jan.-Oct.)		

*12 months through October. †Per 1,000 population.
Source: U.S. Public Health Service

Among persons under 35 years of age, accidents (particularly motor vehicle accidents) continued to cause the greatest number of deaths. For the entire U.S. population, accidents ranked fourth among all causes of death.

VOCATIONAL EDUCATION. See EDUCATION.

VORSTER, BALTHAZAR JOHANNES (1915-), minister of justice of the Republic of South Africa since 1961, was named prime minister on Sept. 13, 1966. He was chosen at a caucus of Nationalist party members to succeed Hendrik F. Verwoerd, who had been assassinated a week earlier. See SOUTH AFRICA, REPUBLIC OF.

In assuming office, Vorster pledged to uphold the nation's policy of *apartheid* (strict separation of races). He is the principal author of many of the apartheid laws, and so the choice was expected to breed difficulties with both the British Commonwealth of Nations and Africa's new nations. On November 1, Vorster defied a United Nations decision to end South Africa's administration of the mandated territory of South West Africa.

Vorster was born Dec. 13, 1915, on a farm in Jamestown, Cape of Good Hope Province. He was the 13th of 14 children. He earned his B.A. and LL.B. degrees at the University of Stellenbosch, where he first became prominent in the Nationalist party. After graduation, he practiced law at Port Elizabeth until World War II. He was arrested in 1942 for joining a pro-Nazi organization and was held in a detention camp for two years. He then settled in Brakpan, resuming law practice. He was elected to parliament in 1953. His wife is the former Martini Malan. WALTER F. MORSE

WAR ON POVERTY. See POVERTY.

WASHINGTON, D.C. It was a frustrating year for the nation's capital. Last-minute maneuvers failed to get congressional action on self-government. Progress was halting in such vital areas as transit, freeways, housing, and urban renewal. Behind the scenes, however, the powerful National Capital Planning Commission (NCPC)–appointed by the White House–agreed on June 9 to the construction of major links in the city's network of interstate highways. By approving long-deferred projects, the NCPC also paved the way for congressional approval of millions of dollars of funds for a 25-mile subway system.

The commission's 1985 Plan, released in September, showed an already serious lack of housing growing even more intense. Partly due to this shortage, the commission gave its blessing to plans to build a large "city within the city" on the site vacated by the National Training School. But elsewhere, local groups were unable to persuade Congress to set aside deactivated Bolling Air Force Base as a site for needed public housing.

Precedent was established on November 23 in the groundbreaking for the small Sibley renewal project. The 2½-acre effort marked the first time that urban renewal and public housing were linked together in the nation's capital. DONALD W. LIEF

WATER AND FLOOD CONTROL. See CONSERVATION.

WEATHER. Global weather forecasting was enhanced in 1966 with the launching of three ESSA (Environmental Science Services Administration) satellites and Nimbus II, the first night-operating weather satellite. ESSA I was launched February 3. It was followed by ESSA II on February 28, and ESSA III on October 2. ESSA II was the first weather satellite to transmit pictures of the earth more than once per orbit. Once every six minutes it transmitted a cloud picture which could be received by any organization or individual willing to build a receiving station. Nimbus II, launched May 15, carried an infrared camera that obtained cloud pictures from the dark side of the earth.

In May, it was announced that American weather satellites have furnished over 2,600 storm warnings since the inception of the satellite program.

Balloon System. A new type of weather balloon, designed to drift indefinitely, was launched in March from New Zealand. The balloon circled the earth six times before radio contact was lost 74 days after launch. Nearly 50 similar balloons were sent aloft between March and August in the first major test of Project GHOST (Global Horizontal Sounding Technique). The tests are a joint venture of the National Center for Atmospheric Research (NCAR), ESSA, and the New Zealand Weather Service.

Still years from completion, the project is a plan to have space satellites gather weather data from

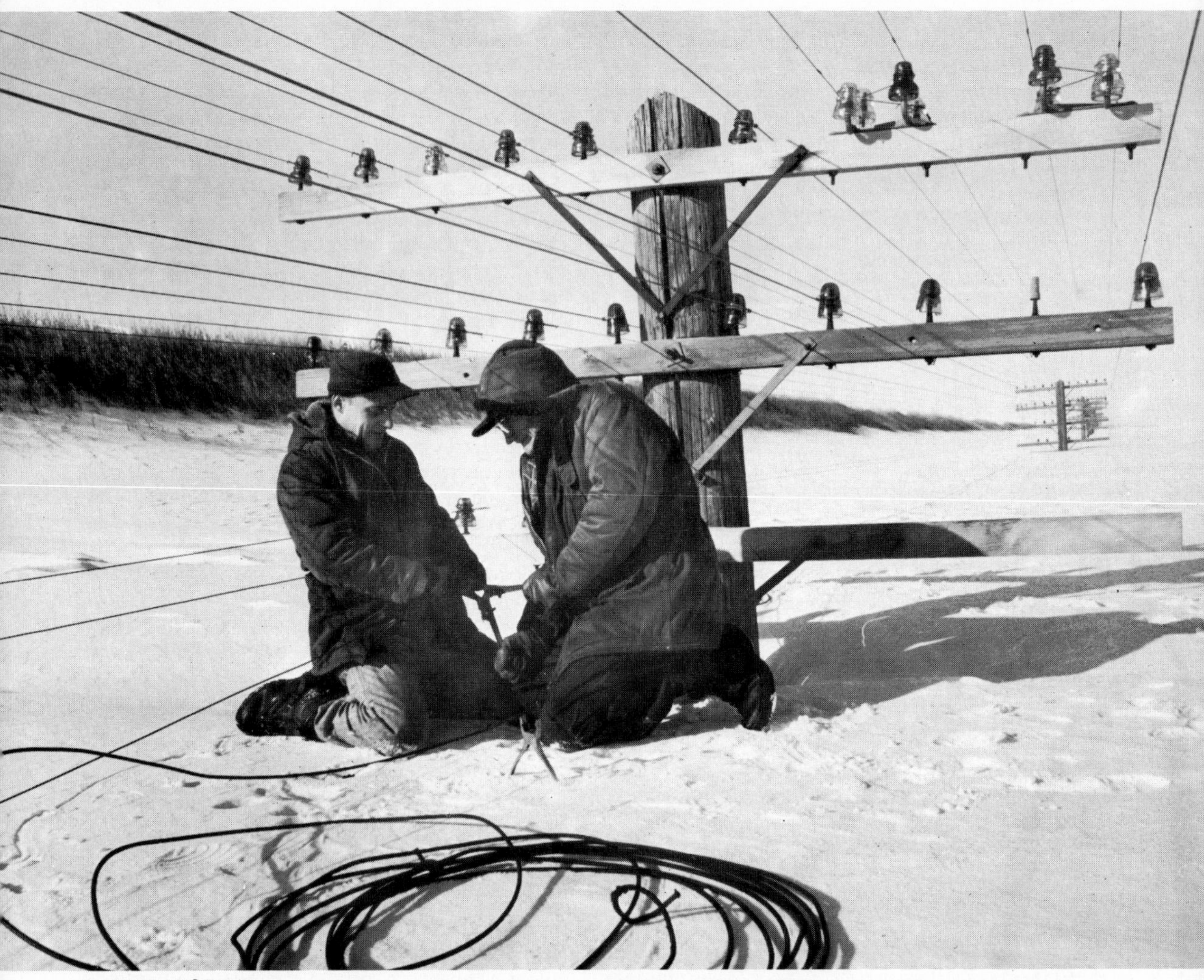

Fred Schnell, *Life* © Time Inc.
South Dakota telephone repairmen had no trouble reaching the wires after a Spring snowstorm raised the ground level by many feet.

thousands of globe-circling balloon-borne telemetry systems. The satellites would transmit the data to central receiving stations where giant computers would process it to provide long-range world weather forecasts. Plans were being made to launch suitable satellites in 1968 and 1969. The GHOST balloons are designed to float at predetermined altitudes. Their instrument packages record data such as air temperature, humidity, and atmospheric pressure. Wind direction and velocity are determined from the speed and direction of the balloons' drift.

Another project involving weather balloons was announced in June, and is a long-range cooperative program between France and the United States. The French National Center for Space Studies will develop and launch the balloons and payloads, as well as design, build, and test a satellite that will gather the information relayed by the balloons. The United States will train French personnel, provide a scout launching rocket, and launch the French rocket. There will be no exchange of funds.

Tornadoes. Man-made tornadoes, created for the first time in a laboratory, were studied at the Catholic University of America, Washington, D.C. Chieh-Chien Chang, head of the department of space sciences at the university, generated the tornadoes within a rotating screen cage, six feet in diameter and nine feet high. The rotation caused a column of air to whirl at high speed and form a hollow core. The whirlwinds created in the machine resembled an actual tornado closely enough to allow study of the destructive winds under controlled laboratory conditions.

Warming. Russian and Swedish meteorologists predicted that the earth's weather is approaching a heat peak, to be reached between the years 2400 and 2500, after which average temperatures will steadily decline. The scientists claimed that the world currently is warming much as it did in the centuries preceding A.D. 700. That early heat peak was followed by a period of falling temperatures, reaching a low in 1433. Evidence has been gathered from historical records and oceanographic studies to support a theory of a 900-year heat-cold cycle for the earth, though theories differ as to the reason for such a cycle.

Inez. The season's most destructive storm, Hurricane *Inez*, was spawned in the Caribbean in September and resulted in the deaths of over 220 persons during an 18-day rampage across Cuba, the southern Florida coast, and across the Gulf of Mexico to the central Mexican coast. See DISASTERS.

The U.S. Office of Emergency Planning, a section of the executive branch of the government, revealed in 1966 that hurricanes, floods, droughts, and tornadoes in the United States caused more disasters in 1964 and 1965 than in any previously recorded two-year period. During the period, 50 emergencies were declared.

JAMES A. PEARRE

WEAVER, ROBERT CLIFTON (1907-), a veteran government administrator, was appointed Secretary of the Department of Housing and Urban Development by President Lyndon B. Johnson on Jan. 13, 1966. He was the first man named to head the new department, established in 1965, which deals primarily with urban housing. He became the first Negro to serve in a Cabinet post. The 58-year-old Weaver had been administrator of the Housing and Home Finance Agency (HHFA) since 1961.

The new Secretary was born in Washington, D.C., on Dec. 29, 1907. He majored in economics at Harvard University and, after a year of teaching, returned to Harvard to take a Ph.D. degree in economics in 1934.

He went to Washington, D.C., in 1933 and has administered a succession of housing, education, and race relations programs for city, state, and federal government and private foundations. Before his appointment by President Kennedy to head the HHFA, he was vice-chairman of the Housing and Redevelopment Board of New York City. He has been active in promoting Negro equality and has written three books on the subject: *Negro Labor: A National Problem* (1946), *The Negro Ghetto* (1948), and *The Urban Complex* (1964).

Weaver married Ella V. Hiath in 1935. Their adopted son died in a firearms accident in 1962.

WEIGHT LIFTING. See SPORTS.

WEST INDIES, a group of Caribbean islands, added another name to its roster of independent nations in 1966. On November 20, at 12:01 A.M., Barbados became the newest nation to achieve independence in the island group. Like its predecessors –Jamaica and Trinidad and Tobago–it had been a former British colony. Like them, it remained a member of the British Commonwealth of Nations.

On November 30, the new Barbadian government headed by Prime Minister Errol Walton Barrow was formally installed. Shortly thereafter, it was announced that Sir Lionel Luckhoe would be the high commissioner for Barbados in London. On December 10, Barbados became the 122nd member of the United Nations. See UNITED NATIONS (UN).

The new nation immediately indicated that it would take an active interest in Latin American affairs rather than concentrate on its historic ties with Europe. Accordingly, the Barbadian government announced that it planned to apply for membership in the Organization of American States. By so doing, it would then become eligible for Alliance for Progress development funds with which to strengthen its economy.

The Bahamas, which had not yet gained independence, replaced its old 20 shilling pound sterling currency in May. The new decimal system had eight notes and nine coins based on a 100-cent dollar. At present rates, the Bahamian dollar was worth 98 cents in U.S. currency. See MONEY.

The Bahamas continued to depend on U.S. tourism for the larger part of its national income. In 1965, the last year for which comprehensive figures were available, U.S. tourists spent $53,000,000 in the islands and the figure for 1966 was expected to be considerably higher. Public gambling, meanwhile, became a political issue late in November when opposition party leader Lynden Pindling, a 36-year-old Negro graduate of the University of London, flew to London to ask for a Royal Commission investigation of gambling and government corruption in the Bahamas.

Jamaica, which had become independent in August, 1962, declared a state of emergency on October 3 in parts of western Kingston and neighboring St. Andrews. Both areas were the scenes of gun battles and bomb explosions in June and July. The wave of violence was described as political.

Trinidad and Tobago, which had won statehood in August, 1962, continued to face serious economic problems. Sugar, one of the nation's chief sources of income, had fallen on hard times because of a drop in world prices. During 1966, the industry was being sustained mainly because of Trinidad's membership in the Commonwealth and benefits from the relatively favorable prices of the Commonwealth sugar agreement. Oil, another important source of revenue, was falling behind in production. Even more serious was the prospect that the nation's oil reserves would be depleted in another decade. Consequently, unemployment was a serious problem. About 14 per cent of the total work force of about 350,000 was seeking jobs.

Facts in Brief.

Bahamas. Population: 130,721. Government: Governor Sir Ralph Grey; Premier Sir Roland Symonette. Monetary Unit: dollar (1.02 = U.S. $1). Foreign Trade: exports, $26,800,000; imports, $179,600,000. Principal Exports: salt, fish.

Barbados. Population: 251,000. Government: Governor-General Sir Lionel Luckhoe; Prime Minister Errol Walton Barrow. Monetary Unit: pound (1 = U.S. $2.80). Foreign Trade: exports, $3,528,000; imports, $18,363,690. Principal Exports: rice, flour, animal feeding stuffs, meat.

Jamaica. Population: 1,755,000. Government: Governor-General Sir Clifford C. Campbell; Prime Minister Forbes Burnham. Monetary Unit: pound (1 = U.S. $2.80). Foreign Trade: exports, $213,600,000; imports, $295,100,000. Principal Exports: bauxite, sugar, aluminum.

Trinidad and Tobago. Population: 1,015,000. Government: Governor-General Sir Solomon Hochoy; Prime Minister Eric Eustace Williams. Monetary Unit: dollar (1.71 = U.S. $1). Foreign Trade: exports, $401,800,000; imports, $474,400,000. Principal Exports: petroleum, sugar. PAUL TULLIER

WILDLIFE. See CONSERVATION.

YEMEN. The uneasy truce between republican and royalist forces, worked out in 1965 by United Arab Republic (UAR) President Gamal Abdel Nasser and Saudi Arabia's King Faisal, was generally maintained. The republicans' UAR expeditionary force of 70,000 troops pulled back and formed a strongly defended triangle around the cities of San'ā', Ta'izz, and Al Hudaydah. The royalists, were in nominal control of the rest of Yemen.

A power struggle among the republicans exploded in September with the resignation of Premier Hassan al-Amri and his cabinet. Three groups of young intellectuals—with ties to the Arab-Ba'ath party in Syria, the "Yemen first" group of al-Amri, and President Abdullah al-Salal's pro-Egyptian group—all battled for leadership. Then al-Salal returned from Cairo, UAR, after almost a year of medical treatment, and named himself premier. When al-Amri flew to Cairo with nine members of his cabinet to ask Nasser to remove al-Salal from office, they were arrested there.

Facts in Brief. Population: 5,075,000. Government: President and Premier Abdullah al-Salal. Monetary Unit: riyal (1.1 = U.S. $1). Foreign Trade: exports, $3,100,000; imports, $2,800,000. Principal Exports: coffee, hides and skins, cotton, fruit. WILLIAM SPENCER

See also MIDDLE EAST; SAUDI ARABIA; UNITED ARAB REPUBLIC (UAR).

YOUNG MEN'S CHRISTIAN ASSOCIATION (YMCA) in 1966 further implemented its policy of racial integration and eliminated all remaining segregation in YMCA facilities. Delegates to the 40th annual National Council meeting in Minneapolis, Minn., May 13 to 15, proposed the following:

- All YMCAs were urged to comply fully with the provisions of the Civil Rights Act of 1964, which forbids racial discrimination in places of public accommodation.
- All YMCAs were called upon to eliminate any remaining discrimination in membership, whether in program participation or on their boards, staffs, and committees. This goal was to be achieved by 1968, when the association's five-year plan for interracial advance ends.
- All YMCAs were asked to adopt a program of action to promote better understanding of true integration and interracial practices.

The council authorized an experimental program to provide special two-week training for staff members who have not completed the academic requirements for professional certification.

George E. Gullen, Jr., of Detroit, Mich., was elected president of the National Council. William J. Bullock of Kannapolis, N.C.; Henry B. Clark, Jr., of Honolulu, Hawaii; Frank E. Masland, III, of Carlisle, Pa.; and John N. Stauffer of Springfield, Ohio, were vice-presidents. JOSEPH P. ANDERSON

YOUNG WOMEN'S CHRISTIAN ASSOCIATION (YWCA) branches increased their efforts to reach economically and socially disadvantaged girls and women. During 1966, 175 associations participated in 350 War on Poverty projects. These ranged from helping with a community action program to the full-scale operation of one of the nation's first Job Corps Training Centers for women, in Los Angeles, Calif.

YWCA student members sought to provide equal rights and opportunities for minority groups. They used their spring vacations to help minorities in several communities with voter education and registration. In addition, several hundred students attended national training conferences to improve their tutorial skills at Chapel Hill, N.C., and Pittsburgh, Pa. They then worked with children living near college campuses.

A special commission, first authorized in 1964 for the study of the YWCA as a Christian movement, presented preliminary findings at four regional meetings in the spring of 1966. The commission's final recommendations will be presented to the national convention in Boston in April, 1967.

The international division of the YWCA's World Service Council announced that, as of June 1, 1966, they had received $375,000 for the international building fund. The money will be used to make low interest loans to YWCAs. JOSEPH P. ANDERSON

President Lyndon B. Johnson, with Mrs. Johnson seated behind him, welcomes delegates to a national youth conference on natural beauty.

YOUTH ORGANIZATIONS provided a wide variety of national and international activities to satisfy the interests of rapidly expanding memberships. A national event of unusual significance was the first National Youth Conference on Natural Beauty and Conservation which was held in Washington, D.C., from June 26 to 29. Sponsored by 10 youth organizations, it was attended by more than 500 young people from the 50 states, Canada, and Puerto Rico, representing a total membership of about 20,000,000.

The purpose of the conference was to explore steps youth might take in their home communities to promote natural beauty and conserve the nation's resources. Mrs. Lyndon B. Johnson spoke at the opening ceremony held on the White House lawn.

Boy Scouts of America presented their 19th annual "Report to the Nation" to President Lyndon B. Johnson in February. The visit of a Boy Scout contingent to Washington also was the occasion for celebrating the 50th anniversary of the signing of their Congressional Charter, which was granted Feb. 9, 1916.

The Boy Scouts Association of Great Britain was urged to make changes in its titles, uniforms, and programs. A study committee recommended that the word "boy" be dropped from the name and that divisions now called Senior Scouts and Rover Scouts become Venture Scouts. The short pants in the official uniforms, in the opinion of the committee, were childish and should be replaced by smartly tapered, long trousers. The committee also found that much of the program was outmoded and juvenile. It urged that the program be abandoned in favor of more sophisticated activities.

Boys' Clubs of America held their 60th annual convention in New York City from May 1 to 5. Delegates were informed that steady progress was being made toward the goal of "1,000 Boys' Clubs for 1,000,000 Deserving Boys." Early in 1966, there were 650 clubs serving 700,000 members. At the convention, board members and the professional staff joined in discussions of program and management concern. Boys' Clubs activities in public housing, and their involvement in the government's War on Poverty program received major attention.

J. Edgar Hoover, director of the Federal Bureau of Investigation, was awarded the Herbert Hoover Memorial Award for 1966. It was presented to Hoover by Peter Arroyo, 18, of Bridgeport, Conn., who was named "1966 Boy of the Year."

Camp Fire Girls enlarged the intensive action-research program which was started and is being carried on in three metropolitan areas–Boston, Detroit, and Washington, D.C. Camp Fire Girls councils in 12 additional areas agreed to cooperate with the Metropolitan Critical Areas Project to study how services could be provided to girls in low income communities.

A thousand Camp Fire Girls from 35 states, most of whom had never been out of the United States before, hailed the first Horizon Club Conference Afloat as a great success. The girls spent 20 days on a cruise to Colombia, Jamaica, and Puerto Rico.

Four-H Clubs reported a total membership of 2,250,000 in 96,000 clubs in all 50 states and Puerto Rico. Substantial membership gains were made in large cities and metropolitan areas, resulting in better communication between farm and city youth and a greater appreciation of what each can offer the 4-H program. The National 4-H Service Committee awarded 308 college scholarships and fellowships valued at $164,500. The 45th National 4-H Club Congress was held November 27 through December 1 in Chicago, Ill.

Future Farmers of America (FFA) widened its program and revised its membership requirements to better prepare members for farmer service occupations such as feed and grain sales and food processing. Delegates to the annual convention, held during October in Kansas City, Mo., voted down a proposal to allow girls to join the FFA. Richard Engelbrecht, 22, of Madison, N.Y., was named Star Farmer of America. Gary L. Swann, 17, of Jasper, N.Y., was elected president.

Girl Scouts of the United States of America completed the third year of their redesigned program which had been adopted in 1963. Under it, troops had been organized into four age groups: Brownie Girl Scouts (7 and 8), Junior Girl Scouts (9 through 11), Cadette Girl Scouts (12 through 14), and Senior Girl Scouts (15 through 17). A program was instituted to emphasize one continuing plan for all Girl Scouts. The new approach has resulted in larger troops, a wider age range within groups, and a greater variety of projects.

An outstanding event of 1966 was the All-States Encampment held in Nantahala National Forest in western North Carolina. The encampment was attended by 105 Girl Scouts from 39 states and 15 Girl Guides from Canada and the British West Indies. The encampment gave Senior Girl Scouts an opportunity to use their training in realistic trail situations and to assume leadership responsibilities.

Girls Clubs of America (GCA), Inc., began a five-year capital funds campaign with the goal of raising $2,000,000. The funds will be used to employ nine regional directors who will strengthen existing Girls Clubs and help to organize new units. Requests from citizen groups seeking to organize new Girls Clubs indicated a potential of 350 clubs. Mrs. John J. McCloy of New York City was named chairman of a national advisory committee for this project.

The 21st national conference was held in Chicago, Ill., from April 17 to 20. Mrs. J. H. Tyler McConnell of Wilmington, Del., was elected president. Harriet Williams, 17, of Norfolk, Va., was named "1966 Girl of the Year." JOSEPH P. ANDERSON

YUGOSLAVIA. The dismissal of Alexsandar Ranković, vice-president and party secretary, in July, marked a turning point in the conflict between conservative and progressive Communism in Yugoslavia. The move eliminated from the top leadership one of President Tito's closest colleagues and the man commonly regarded as most likely to succeed him.

Ranković, the organizer of the secret police, was blamed for the placing of listening devices in President Tito's residence, the discovery of which had touched off the crisis. Tito also charged him with conducting a struggle for supreme power while using the secret police as the base of his operations. The power of the security system became the main target of the initial attacks on Ranković. There followed an extensive purge of his supporters in the security apparatus, as well as in the diplomatic service and in the party.

The Ranković Crisis was closely linked with the far-reaching economic reforms adopted in 1965 and the planned democratization of the political system. On Feb. 25, 1966, Tito had openly referred to the conservative opposition to these measures within the party. In July, he charged Ranković with spearheading that opposition. Ranković's deposition opened the way toward a more vigorous pursual of economic reforms, and led to a decision, announced on October 4, to reorganize the League of Communists and modify its role in Yugoslav politics.

Under the reorganization program, the state administration was to function without direct intervention by the Yugoslav Communist party. The party itself was to remain the leading force in the political system, but was to be democratized. A Presidium, composed of 35 members, was made responsible for policymaking between sessions of the Central Committee. The once-powerful executive committee assumed a purely administrative role.

Step Forward. The measures represented a significant step forward in the liberalization of Yugoslavia's economic and political life. They did not signify, however, an abandonment of the one-party system. This was emphasized by the arrest of Mihajlo Mihajlov, a writer and former university lecturer, and his sentencing to one year in prison for seeking to establish an opposition magazine.

Yugoslavia, meanwhile, remained outside the Soviet bloc. Relations with the United States, while continuing relatively good, were marred somewhat by Yugoslavia's opposition to the war in Vietnam. On June 25, Yugoslavia re-established diplomatic ties with the Vatican.

Facts in Brief. Population: 19,800,000. Government: President Tito; Vice-President Koca Popović. Monetary Unit: dinar (12.5=U.S. $1). Foreign Trade: exports, $893,000,000; imports, $1,323,000,000. Principal Exports: bauxite, fuel and pulpwood, lumber, vegetables, fruit, meat. H. GORDON SKILLING

ZAMBIA. See AFRICA.

ZOOLOGY. Scientists urged that the Nimbus III weather satellite, to be launched in 1967, be assigned the added task of monitoring the migratory movements of animals throughout the world. In their proposal to the National Aeronautics and Space Administration (NASA), they suggested that radio transmitters, attached to whales, could be monitored by the satellite to provide valuable information on the migratory habits of various species.

Suggestions were also made for tracking elephants, polar bears, sea turtles, seals, and other migratory animals. NASA scientists already have a 26-pound transmitter that could be carried by large animals, but they hope to develop a much lighter instrument. The satellite would store the information beamed to it from the ground transmitters and release the data as it passed over receiving stations.

Whale Extinction. The world whale population continued to decline in 1966. Only 4,089 blue whale units were processed by whalers during the 1965-1966 season, even though the limit imposed by the International Whaling Commission was 4,500 units. The blue whale unit, the basis on which catches are calculated, may consist of one blue whale, two finback whales, two and a half humpback whales, or six sei whales.

The majority of whales killed in 1966 were sei whales because the finback and other whales have become scarce. The blue whale, according to some zoologists, has even been reduced in numbers below the level required for the species to survive. See CONSERVATION (Wildlife).

Reptile Skin. Reptiles have been found to lose water or "sweat" through their skins, according to P. J. Bentley and Knut Schmidt-Neilsen of Duke University. In a study of five species of reptiles, long thought to have skin impermeable to water, all were found to sweat, with the crocodile having the highest rate of water loss per unit area of hide. The study included a box turtle, a desert lizard, and several species of tropical lizards.

Compact Pigs. Though pigs are particularly suited for medical research due to their physiological similarity to human beings, they are not often used for research purposes because of their size and large appetites. Several institutions have successfully bred strains of pigs that grow to no more than 200 pounds. An eventual goal of one group is to produce a pig that grows no heavier than 60 pounds.

Cooperative Studies. Animal behavior under nearly natural conditions will be studied by the newly organized Institute for Research in Animal Behavior. The organization is a cooperative venture of the New York Zoological Society and Rockefeller University. Its members will conduct studies in the university's laboratories, at the New York Zoological Park and Aquarium, and at the Trinidad Station of the zoological society. JAMES A. PEARRE

See also INSECT.

ZOOS AND AQUARIUMS. Russian and British zoo officials tried to mate two giant pandas–Chi Chi, a female from the Regent Park Zoo in London, and An An, Moscow zoo's male, in 1966. The London panda was flown to Moscow in October for the historic meeting, but she took no interest in An An and kept him at arm's length as long as they were caged together. The British and Russian zoo officials finally had to admit defeat, at least for 1966. As Desmond Morris, curator of mammals at the London zoo said, "Chi Chi is far more interested in people than in male pandas."

The officials of the two zoos disagreed, however, as to which of the two pandas bore the main responsibility for the romantic failure. Morris put the blame squarely on Chi Chi. "She has become completely humanized," he said. But Igor Sosnovsky, director of the Moscow zoo, held that his panda was at fault. "We feel he could have been more forceful, and that might have brought her around," he said.

The failure left Communist China, the giant panda's homeland, as the only country to have bred giant pandas in captivity. The two born there–Ming Ming, in September, 1963, and Ling Ling, in 1965–were reportedly produced by means of artificial insemination.

The New York Bronx Zoo acquired a male takin in April. The takin is a "clumsily built" creature re-

A Milwaukee Zoo keeper swaps final hugs with a gorilla he helped raise. The animal's growth had made his embraces dangerous.

Chi Chi was flown to Russia from her home in the London Zoo in the hope of mating her with Moscow's panda, An An, but the attempt failed.

lated to the musk ox. Like the giant panda, it is a native of western China. Zoo officials hope that it can be bred at maturity with the zoo's female takin, Gracie. They are the only pair of takins known to be in captivity outside of China, according to Joseph A. Davis, Jr., curator of mammals.

Outstanding Births. Successful breeding of several rare species of animals and birds was accomplished in 1966. Two kiwis were hatched at Taranga Park Zoo in Sydney, Australia, the first born in captivity outside of their native habitat in New Zealand. Baby koala bears from Australia were born at the San Diego (Calif.) Zoological Garden. The Fort Worth Zoo in Texas succeeded in mating a pair of bald eagles, the only breeding pair in captivity.

Two orang-utans, which are rapidly becoming extinct in the wild state, were born, one at the St. Louis (Mo.) Zoological Garden and the other at the Philadelphia (Pa.) Zoological Garden. The first Adélie penguin chick to be hatched in captivity was born at the Milwaukee (Wis.) County Zoological Park on July 4. Two other penguin chicks, one a king penguin and the other a cross between an Adélie and a Gentoo, were also hatched during the summer at the St. Louis zoo.

Survival Centers. Many zoos are now setting up special areas for the breeding of animals threatened with extinction. There, the animals can be kept in environments conducive to the propagation of the species. The zoos often work with animals that cannot be imported because rare species are usually protected by countries in which they are found.

Zoo directors have expressed particular concern over two rapidly diminishing ape species. The mountain gorilla of East Africa is disappearing because its habitat is now overrun by cattle, which through overgrazing have changed the whole biological complex of the area. Orang-utans of Borneo and Sumatra are disappearing because of poachers who kill orang-utans to capture their young for zoos. In the hope of discouraging this practice, all members of the International Union of Zoo Directors have agreed not to buy orang-utans lacking proper registration papers.

New Exhibits. A new Los Angeles (Calif.) zoo was opened to the public on November 28. It included the animals from the old Griffith Park Zoo. New zoos were also opened at Abilene, Tex.; Aberdeen, Scotland; and Bremen, Germany.

The Gage Park Zoo in Topeka, Kans., opened a new mammal building. Other new buildings included: a children's zoo building at the Buffalo (N.Y.) Zoological Gardens; a bird exhibit hall at the San Diego Zoological Garden; a great ape house at Swope Park Zoo in Kansas City, Mo.; an aquarium at Nassau, Bahama Islands; and a Hall of Fishes at the Vancouver (British Columbia) Public Aquarium.

R. Marlin Perkins

Section Four

In its function of keeping all World Book owners up to date, The World Book Year Book herewith offers a significant new article from the 1967 edition of The World Book Encyclopedia. This article, chosen because of its timeliness and lasting value, should be indexed in The World Book Encyclopedia by means of The Year Book cross-reference tabs.

The World Book Supplement

A new and comprehensive article on Russia prepared by members of the Executive Committee of the Center for Russian Studies at the University of Michigan.

Burt Glinn, Magnum

Red Square in Moscow is the scene of a huge May Day parade every year. Communists set aside the May 1 and 2 holiday to honor working people. The marchers carry Russian flags past 400-year-old Saint Basil's Church. The Communists changed the building from a place of worship to a museum.

The six contributors of this article are all members of the Executive Committee of the Center for Russian Studies at the University of Michigan. These contributors are William B. Ballis, Professor of Political Science; Morris Bornstein, Professor of Economics; Deming Brown, Professor of Russian Literature; George Kish, Professor of Geography; William K. Medlin, Professor of Education; and Arthur P. Mendel, Professor of Russian History.

RUSSIA

Union of Soviet Socialist Republics

RUSSIA, the UNION OF SOVIET SOCIALIST REPUBLICS (U.S.S.R.), is the largest country in the world, and the most powerful Communist nation. Russia covers more than half of Europe and nearly two-fifths of Asia. It takes up more than a seventh of the world's total land area. Russia is larger than four continents—South America, Antarctica, Europe, and Australia—and is almost as large as all of North America. Only China and India have more people than Russia. Moscow, Russia's capital and largest city, is the fifth largest city in the world.

The official name of Russia is the *Union of Soviet Socialist Republics*. In the Russian language, this name is *Soyuz Sovetskikh Sotsialisticheskikh Respublik*. In the Russian alphabet, the initials of these words are C.C.C.P., and they appear on Russian postage stamps. Most people call the country *Russia* or the *Soviet Union*.

A thousand years ago, Russia was a small region in Europe. It grew to its present size by adding territory on all sides. As the country expanded, peoples of many different backgrounds came under Russian rule. These peoples have kept many of their customs and their own languages. As a result, "Russia is not a country, but a world," according to an old Russian saying.

For hundreds of years, Russia was ruled by *czars*, who had complete power over Russian life. The czars kept Russia cut off from the progress being made in Western Europe. By the early 1900's, many other countries had become industrialized, but Russia had little industry. Most Russians were poor, uneducated peasants. They farmed Russia's broad plains with the same kinds of hand tools that their ancestors had used. In spite of their harsh life, the peasants loved their giant land, which they called "Mother Russia." They expressed this love in beautiful and sad songs, and in folk dances and colorful festivals. Many educated Russians produced great works of art under the czars. Anton Chekhov, Fyodor Dostoevsky, and Leo Tolstoy wrote masterpieces of literature. Modest Mussorgsky and Peter Ilich Tchaikovsky composed music of lasting greatness.

In 1917, a revolution drove the czar from power. The *Bolsheviks* (later called *Communists*) seized the government several months later and set up a dictatorship. They brutally took over the factories, farms, and other means of production, and Russia became the first Communist nation. Its economy expanded rapidly. Today, Soviet industrial production ranks second only to that of the United States. Only the United States leads Russia in crop production.

The early Communists hoped to take over the industrialized Western nations by force. Today, Russia believes that Communism can triumph throughout the world without a major war. Russia expects to defeat the United States and other Western nations economically, politically, and scientifically in what is called the *Cold War*. See the COLD WAR and COMMUNISM articles in WORLD BOOK.

ZFA from Publix

Russia's *Sputnik I*, honored by this monument in Moscow, opened the space age in 1957. It was the first spacecraft to circle the earth.

FACTS IN BRIEF

Capital: Moscow.

Official Language: Russian.

Official Name: Union of Soviet Socialist Republics.

Form of Government: Communist dictatorship; 15 Union Republics. *Head of State*, Chairman of the Presidium of the Supreme Soviet of the U.S.S.R. *Head of Government*, Premier, or Chairman of the Council of Ministers (Cabinet).

Legislature: Supreme Soviet of the U.S.S.R., consisting of two houses—Soviet of the Union (767 deputies, 4-year terms); Soviet of Nationalities (750 deputies, 4-year terms).

Area: 8,649,500 square miles (2,151,000 square miles in Europe and 6,498,500 square miles in Asia). *Greatest Distances*, (east-west) 6,000 miles; (north-south) 3,200 miles. *Coastline*, 30,787 miles.

Elevation: *Highest*, Communism Peak, 24,590 feet above sea level. *Lowest*, Karagiye Depression, 433 feet below sea level.

Population: *1959 Census*, 208,826,650; distribution—48 per cent urban, 52 per cent rural. *1967 Estimate*, 235,300,000; density, 27 persons to the square mile. *1972 Estimate*, 250,100,000.

Chief Products: *Agriculture*, barley, beef and dairy cattle, corn, cotton, flax, milk, oats, potatoes, rye, sheep, sugar beets, tobacco, vegetables, wheat, wool. *Fishing*, cod, herring, salmon, sturgeon. *Manufacturing*, chemicals, electrical and electronic equipment, iron and steel, lumber, machinery, paper, petroleum products, processed foods, processed metals, textiles, transportation equipment. *Mining*, bauxite, coal, copper, gold, iron ore, lead, manganese, magnesium, natural gas, nickel, petroleum, platinum, salt, tungsten, zinc.

National Anthem: *Gosudarstveny Gimn Sovetskogo Soyusa* (National Anthem of the Soviet Union).

National Holiday: November 7 and 8, the dates of the Bolshevik Revolution of 1917.

National Motto: *Proletarii Vsekh Stran, Soyedinyaites!* (Workers of All Countries, Unite!)

Money: *Basic Unit*, ruble. One hundred kopecks equal one ruble. For the value of the ruble in dollars, see MONEY (table, Values). See also KOPECK; RUBLE.

Burt Glinn, Magnum

The Grand Kremlin Palace, *center,* in Moscow is the meeting place of the Supreme Soviet of the U.S.S.R., Russia's parliament. Fireworks light the sky every May Day.

RUSSIA/*Government*

Russia has a long constitution that gives all political power to the people and to their elected representatives. The constitution mentions the Communist party only once. However, Russia is completely controlled by the Communists. The men who run the Communist party run Russia. The government is like a glove, and the party is like a hand inside the glove. The glove moves only the way the hand does. The government simply accepts all Communist party decisions, puts them into laws and orders, and sees that they are obeyed. When a Russian votes, he or she has only one choice—the person selected by the party. A voter may cross out the name of the party's choice, but almost no one does.

Russia is made up of 15 *union republics*. Each republic, like the entire nation, is governed by a *soviet* (council). This political structure gives Russia its official name, the *Union of Soviet Socialist Republics* (U.S.S.R.). See the separate articles on the union republics listed in the *Russia Map Index*.

The Communist Party of the Soviet Union permits no other political party to oppose it. It has about $12\frac{1}{2}$ million members and candidates for membership. Thus, the men and women in the Communist party make up only about 5 per cent of Russia's population.

A Russian who wants to join the Communist party must be at least 18 years old. He or she must be recommended by three members of the *primary party organization* (the lowest party unit) that he wishes to join. The recommending members must have been party members for at least five years, and must have known the candidate for at least one year. Both the primary party organization and the party organization on the next higher level must approve the candidate. The candidate then must wait a year before he can be approved as a full member. This whole process permits only those who are most loyal to Communism to join the party.

The Communist party structure is like a pyramid. At the bottom of the pyramid are about 320,000 primary party organizations. They operate throughout Russia, wherever there are at least three Communists. These groups are set up in such places as factories, farms, government offices, and schools. They have great influence over local political and economic life. To a Russian, the man who heads the local party group is a person to be respected—and sometimes feared. Many of Russia's leaders worked their way to the top from positions in local party organizations.

Most primary party organizations have many members. If an organization has more than 15 members, it elects a *bureau* to conduct its work. If an organization

The Flag of Russia. The red stands for revolution; the hammer and sickle for united peasants and workers; and the star for the Communist party.

The Coat of Arms carries the motto, "Workers of All Countries, Unite!" The hammer and sickle represent the spread of Communism. The rising sun is a symbol of the dawning of the "new day" of Communism.

H. E. Harris & Co.

WORLD BOOK map

Russia, the World's Largest Country, is nearly three times as large as the United States, not counting Alaska and Hawaii. Russia extends about 6,000 miles across Europe and Asia.

has more than 150 members, its bureau elects a full-time *secretary* to head the organization. The secretary is released from his regular job and is paid for his party duties. The secretary and his staff make up the *secretariat* of the organization.

Just above the primary party organizations are the *rayon* (district) *party organizations*. The primary groups in each district elect representatives to a *district conference*, held every two years. This conference elects a *committee*, which, in turn, elects a bureau and a secretariat. The committee, bureau, and secretariat direct the district party between district conferences.

The district organizations operate under the *oblast* (region) *party organizations*. The district groups in each region elect representatives to a *regional conference*, which is also held every two years. The regional conference also elects a committee, which then chooses a bureau and a secretariat.

On the next party level, in 14 of the 15 union republics, is the *republic party organization*. Each republic organization is made up of representatives from lower party groups in the republic. The representatives meet in a *congress* at least every four years. The congress elects a *central committee*, which also selects a bureau and a secretariat. The Russian Soviet Federated Socialist Republic, the largest republic, has no separate party organization. Its party activities are managed by bodies of the national party organization.

The main organization at the top of the nationwide Communist party pyramid is the *All-Union Party Congress*. Under party rules, the congress must meet at least every four years. But it does not meet that regularly. The All-Union Party Congress consists of about 5,000 delegates from lower party organizations throughout Russia. It elects a Central Committee to handle its work between congresses. The Central Committee, which has about 350 regular and alternate members, meets at least every six months. It elects a *Politburo* (Political Bureau) and a *Secretariat* to direct its work between meetings. In actual practice, the party congress does not really "elect" the Central Committee, nor does the Central Committee really "elect" the Politburo and Secretariat. The Politburo and the Secretariat select their own members and those of the Central Committee. The Central Committee and the All-Union Party Congress simply approve these selections.

The Politburo of the Central Committee is the most powerful body in Russia. It establishes all important Soviet policies in national and foreign affairs. The Politburo has 11 regular members and 8 alternates. They meet in secret and never reveal their discussions or how they voted. Only their decisions are announced.

The Secretariat of the Central Committee manages the daily work of the Communist party. The Secretariat

The Palace of Congresses in Moscow is the meeting place of delegates from Communist party organizations in all parts of Russia. The white marble building was completed in 1961.

Kenneth Katzner

has 11 members, several of whom are also members of the Politburo. The *general secretary* of the Central Committee heads both the Secretariat and the Politburo. He is the most powerful person in the Soviet Union.

The Secretariat is aided by a staff of about 1,000 professional party secretaries called *apparatchiki*. They form a chain of command like that of an army, with the general secretary at the top. The secretaries at each level are selected by those above them in the party structure. They manage the work of all party organizations, and have wide control over Russian life.

Federal Government. The structure of the Soviet government, like that of the Russian Communist party, resembles a pyramid. Each government body is responsible to the one above it. At the top, the main body is a two-house federal parliament, the *Supreme Soviet of the U.S.S.R.* Almost all its members are Communists. The members are elected to four-year terms, and meet twice a year for a week or less. They pass without question all proposed laws, which come from the Communist party's leaders.

One house of parliament, the *Soviet of the Union*, has 767 members called *deputies*. Each deputy is elected from a district of about 300,000 residents. The other house, the *Soviet of Nationalities*, has 750 deputies. Each of the 15 union republics elects 32 deputies. Within the various union republics are 20 *autonomous* (self-governing) republics, 8 autonomous regions, and 10 *okrugs* (national areas). Each of these elects 11, 5, or 1 deputy to the Soviet of Nationalities.

In elections to the Supreme Soviet, there is only one candidate for each position. Several candidates are nominated in the voting districts, but Communist party officials make the final choice. Russian voters must be at least 18 years old.

The Supreme Soviet elects two important bodies, but their members are actually selected by the Communist party's leaders. These bodies are the *Presidium of the Supreme Soviet* and the *Council of Ministers*. The Presidium handles legislative matters between sessions of the Supreme Soviet. Its chairman is considered Russia's head of state, but he has little real power. He is assisted by 15 deputy chairmen (one from each union republic), a secretary, and 16 other members.

The powerful Council of Ministers, or cabinet, is the highest executive body of the Soviet government. Its members are among the highest-ranking Communist party leaders. The council chairman, often called *premier* or *prime minister*, is the actual head of the Soviet government. The dictators Joseph Stalin and Nikita S. Khrushchev held this position while they headed the Communist party. The council also includes 2 first deputy chairmen, 9 deputy chairmen, almost 50 department ministers, and nearly 30 committee chairmen.

Local Government. Each of the 15 union republics and the 20 autonomous republics has a constitution. Each also has a supreme soviet with a presidium, and a council of ministers. Members of the supreme soviets are elected to four-year terms. The lower levels of government, from the autonomous regions down to the smallest districts, have *soviets of working people's deputies*. The members of these soviets are elected to two-year terms. Most soviets elect *executive committees* to handle local work between legislative sessions.

Courts in the Soviet Union differ from those in the Western democracies. Western courts operate according to general ideas of justice. Court rulings in Russia, on the other hand, are based on policies of the Communist party. Soviet courts are under the *procurator-general*, Russia's chief legal officer. He is selected by Communist party leaders and appointed to a seven-year term by the Supreme Soviet of the U.S.S.R.

Russia's highest court is the *Supreme Court of the U.S.S.R.* Each republic also has a supreme court. All supreme court judges are elected by the supreme soviets to five-year terms. Below them, the judges of the *regional courts* are elected, also to five-year terms, by the regional soviets. The lowest courts are the *people's courts*. Local voters elect people's court judges to five-year terms.

The *Party Control Committee* sees that the rules of the Communist party are followed on all government and party levels. This committee is appointed by the national party's Central Committee. The *Committee on State Security*, an agency of the Council of Ministers, is the government's political police system. It has offices and agents throughout Russia.

Armed Forces of the Soviet Union are the largest in the world. Western military experts estimate that Russia has a total of more than 3 million men in its army, navy, and air force. Required military service begins at the age of 18 and lasts at least two years. See AIR FORCE (Russia); ARMY (The Russian Army); NAVY (The Russian Navy).

The 23rd All-Union Communist Party Congress met in 1966 in the main auditorium of the Palace of Congresses. Above the stage is a portrait of Lenin, the founder of Communist Russia.

Tass from Sovfoto

THE STRUCTURE OF POLITICAL POWER IN RUSSIA

The constitution of Russia provides that representatives elected by all the people shall run the government. However, there is only one candidate for each political office in Russia. In addition, the all-powerful Communist party selects each candidate. Thus, the Communist party has complete control over the government. The government simply passes all laws proposed by the party's leaders. The Communist party allows no other political party in Russia. Its power reaches to all levels of Russian life.

Communist Party of the Soviet Union

HEAD OF THE COMMUNIST PARTY

The general secretary of the Communist party's Central Committee heads its Politburo and Secretariat. He is the most powerful person in Russia.

POLITBURO OF THE CENTRAL COMMITTEE

The policy-making body of the Communist party is the Politburo of the Central Committee. It establishes economic programs, determines Russia's relations with other countries, and sets other important policies. The Politburo has 11 regular members. They meet in secret and reveal only their decisions.

SECRETARIAT OF THE CENTRAL COMMITTEE

The day-to-day work of the Communist party is managed by the Secretariat of the Central Committee. The group has 11 members. Several of them are also members of the Politburo. The Secretariat is aided at all levels of the Communist party by a staff of about 1,000 professional party secretaries.

CENTRAL COMMITTEE

The Central Committee of the Communist party handles Communist affairs between sessions of the All-Union Party Congress. The committee meets at least once every six months. It has about 350 regular and alternate members. The party's leaders select the members on the basis of their loyalty to them. The persons they select are then "elected" to the Central Committee by the All-Union Party Congress.

ALL-UNION PARTY CONGRESS

The rules of the Communist party grant supreme power in the party to the All-Union Party Congress. The congress consists of about 5,000 delegates from lower party organizations throughout Russia. It is actually controlled by the party's leaders, and simply approves their decisions. Under the party's rules, the All-Union Party Congress is supposed to meet every four years. But it does not meet that regularly.

Federal Government

PRESIDIUM OF THE SUPREME SOVIET

The Presidium handles legislation between sessions of the Supreme Soviet of the U.S.S.R., which meets twice a year. It has 33 members. The chairman is considered Russia's head of state.

SUPREME SOVIET OF THE U.S.S.R.

Russia's legislature is the Supreme Soviet of the U.S.S.R. It has two houses—the Soviet of the Union and the Soviet of Nationalities. Members of both houses are elected to four-year terms. They pass all laws proposed by the Communist party's leaders. The Supreme Soviet "elects" the members of its Presidium and the Council of Ministers after they are selected by party leaders.

SOVIET OF THE UNION

The Soviet of the Union consists of 767 members, who are called *deputies*. Each of the deputies represents a district of about 300,000 persons.

SOVIET OF NATIONALITIES

The Soviet of Nationalities has 750 deputies. Each of the 15 union republics elects 32 deputies. Various regions within the republics elect the rest.

PREMIER

The premier, or chairman of the Council of Ministers, heads the government of Russia. Joseph Stalin and Nikita S. Khrushchev each headed the government and the Communist party at the same time.

COUNCIL OF MINISTERS

The highest executive body of Russia's government is the Council of Ministers, or cabinet. It controls Russian economic and cultural life through various ministries and committees. It also handles Russia's relations with other countries. The Council of Ministers has about 90 members. They are among the highest-ranking officials of the Communist party.

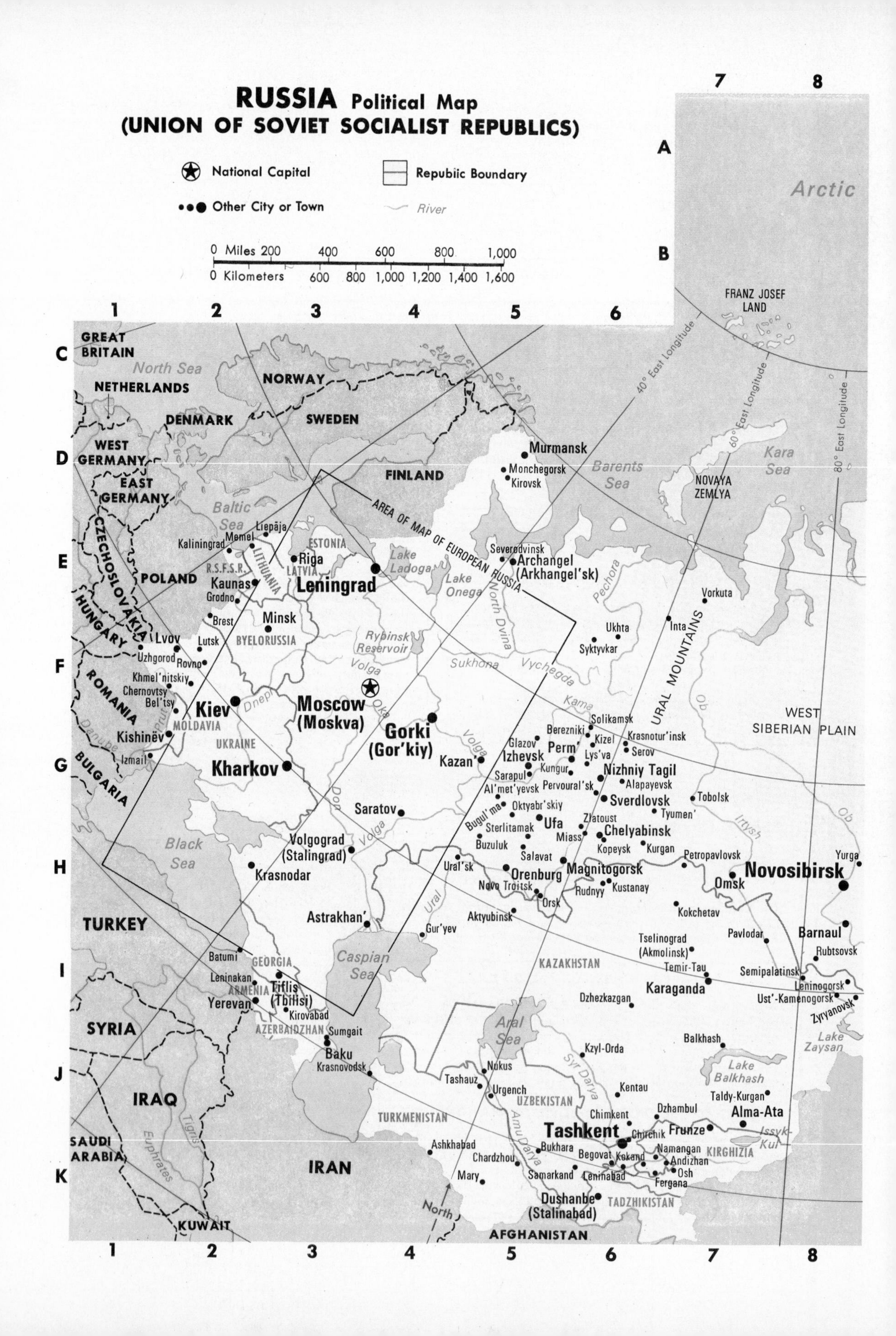
RUSSIA Political Map
(UNION OF SOVIET SOCIALIST REPUBLICS)
National Capital
Other City or Town
Repubiic Boundary
River
0 Miles 200 400 600 800 1,000
0 Kilometers 600 800 1,000 1,200 1,400 1,600
Arctic
FRANZ JOSEF LAND
40° East Longitude
60° East Longitude
80° East Longitude
GREAT BRITAIN
North Sea
NETHERLANDS
NORWAY
DENMARK
SWEDEN
WEST GERMANY
EAST GERMANY
FINLAND
Murmansk
Monchegorsk
Kirovsk
Barents Sea
Kara Sea
NOVAYA ZEMLYA
CZECHOSLOVAKIA
Baltic Sea
Liepāja
Memel
Kaliningrad
ESTONIA
Riga
LATVIA
LITHUANIA
R.S.F.S.R.
Kaunas
POLAND
Leningrad
Lake Ladoga
Lake Onega
AREA OF MAP OF EUROPEAN RUSSIA
Severodvinsk
Archangel (Arkhangel'sk)
Pechora
North Dvina
Vorkuta
Inta
URAL MOUNTAINS
HUNGARY
Grodno
Brest
Minsk
BYELORUSSIA
Rybinsk Reservoir
Ukhta
Syktyvkar
Lvov
Lutsk
Uzhgorod
Rovno
Sukhona
Vychegda
Khmel'nitskiy
Chernovtsy
Bel'tsy
ROMANIA
Kiev
Dnepr
Volga
Moscow (Moskva)
Oka
Gorki (Gor'kiy)
Kama
Ob
WEST SIBERIAN PLAIN
MOLDAVIA
Prut
Kishinёv
Danube
Izmail
UKRAINE
Solikamsk
Berezniki
Kizel
Krasnotur'insk
Glazov
Perm'
Lys'va
Serov
Izhevsk
BULGARIA
Kharkov
Kazan'
Kungur
Nizhniy Tagil
Sarapul
Al'met'yevsk
Pervoural'sk
Alapayevsk
Sverdlovsk
Tobolsk
Don
Saratov
Bugul'ma
Oktyabr'skiy
Ufa
Zlatoust
Tyumen'
Sterlitamak
Miass
Chelyabinsk
Irtysh
Volgograd (Stalingrad)
Buzuluk
Salavat
Kopeysk
Kurgan
Black Sea
Ural'sk
Orenburg
Magnitogorsk
Petropavlovsk
Novosibirsk
Yurga
Krasnodar
Novo Troitsk
Orsk
Rudnyy
Kustanay
Omsk
Kokchetav
TURKEY
Astrakhan'
Ural
Aktyubinsk
Gur'yev
Pavlodar
Barnaul
Rubtsovsk
Tselinograd (Akmolinsk)
Batumi
GEORGIA
Caspian Sea
KAZAKHSTAN
Temir-Tau
Semipalatinsk
Leninakan
Tiflis (Tbilisi)
ARMENIA
Karaganda
Leninogorsk
Yerevan
Kirovabad
Dzhezkazgan
Ust'-Kamenogorsk
Zyryanovsk
SYRIA
AZERBAIDZHAN
Sumgait
Aral Sea
Baku
Kzyl-Orda
Balkhash
Lake Zaysan
Krasnovodsk
Nukus
Syr Darya
Lake Balkhash
Tashauz
Urgench
Kentau
Taldy-Kurgan
IRAQ
UZBEKISTAN
Tigris
TURKMENISTAN
Amu Darya
Chimkent
Dzhambul
Alma-Ata
Tashkent
Chirchik
Frunze
Issyk-Kul
SAUDI ARABIA
Euphrates
Ashkhabad
Bukhara
Namangan
KIRGHIZIA
Chardzhou
Begovat
Kokand
Andizhan
IRAN
Samarkand
Leninabad
Osh
Mary
Fergana
North
Dushanbe (Stalinabad)
TADZHIKISTAN
KUWAIT
AFGHANISTAN
A
B
C
D
E
F
G
H
I
J
K
1 2 3 4 5 6 7 8

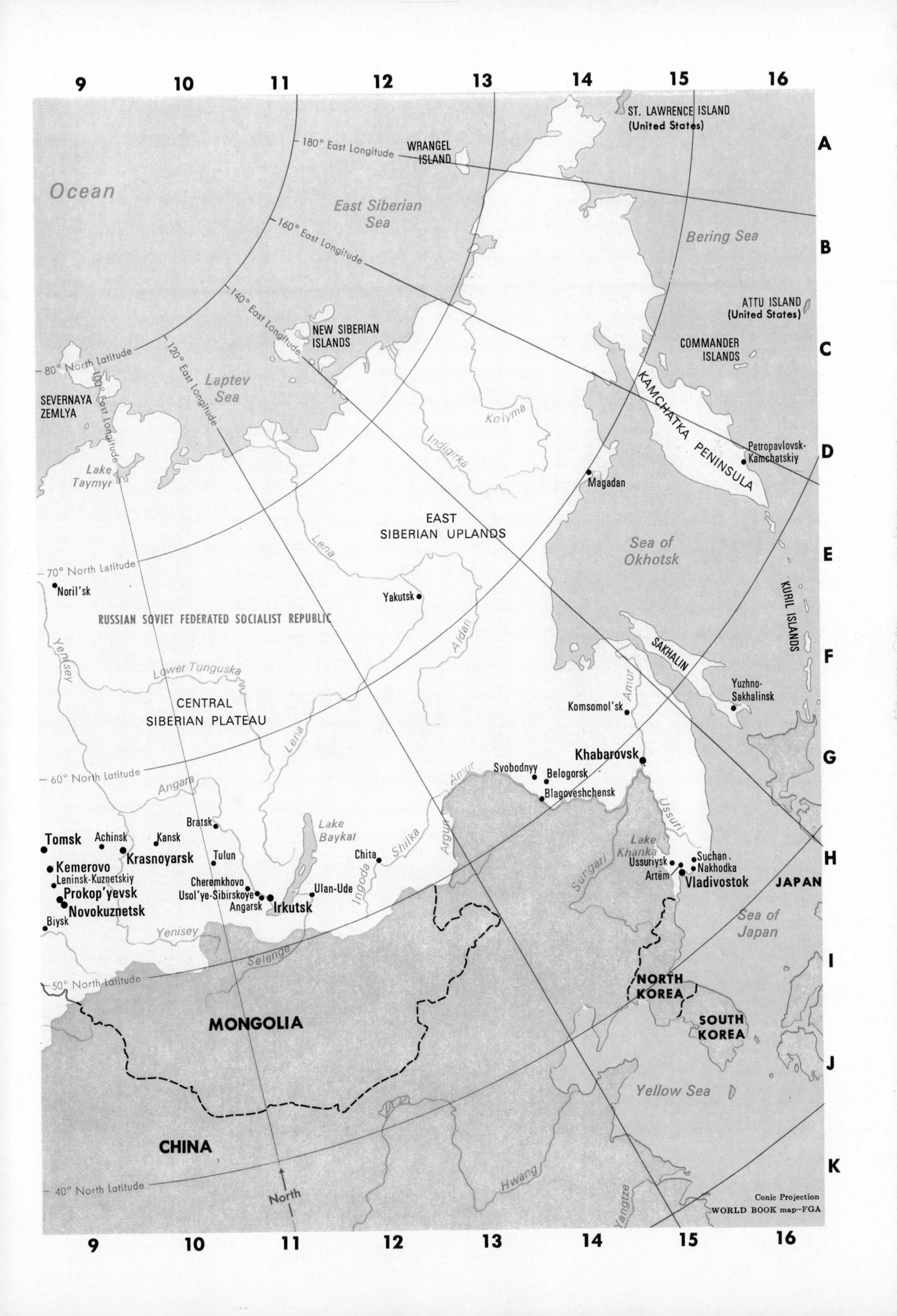

9
10
11
12
13
14
15
16
A
B
C
D
E
F
G
H
I
J
K
ST. LAWRENCE ISLAND
(United States)
180° East Longitude
WRANGEL ISLAND
Ocean
East Siberian Sea
160° East Longitude
Bering Sea
ATTU ISLAND
(United States)
140° East Longitude
NEW SIBERIAN ISLANDS
COMMANDER ISLANDS
80° North Latitude
120° East Longitude
100° East Longitude
Laptev Sea
SEVERNAYA ZEMLYA
KAMCHATKA PENINSULA
Kolyma
Indigirka
Lake Taymyr
Petropavlovsk-Kamchatskiy
Magadan
EAST SIBERIAN UPLANDS
Lena
Sea of Okhotsk
70° North Latitude
Noril'sk
Yakutsk
KURIL ISLANDS
RUSSIAN SOVIET FEDERATED SOCIALIST REPUBLIC
Aldan
Yenisey
Lower Tunguska
SAKHALIN
CENTRAL SIBERIAN PLATEAU
Amur
Yuzhno-Sakhalinsk
Komsomol'sk
Khabarovsk
60° North Latitude
Svobodnyy
Belogorsk
Blagoveshchensk
Angara
Ussuri
Bratsk
Lake Baykal
Lake Khanka
Tomsk
Achinsk
Kansk
Krasnoyarsk
Tulun
Chita
Shilka
Argun
Sungari
Suchan
Ussuriysk
Nakhodka
Artëm
Vladivostok
Kemerovo
Leninsk-Kuznetskiy
Prokop'yevsk
Novokuznetsk
Biysk
Cheremkhovo
Usol'ye-Sibirskoye
Angarsk
Irkutsk
Ulan-Ude
Ingoda
JAPAN
Sea of Japan
Yenisey
Selenge
50° North Latitude
NORTH KOREA
SOUTH KOREA
MONGOLIA
Yellow Sea
CHINA
40° North Latitude
North
Hwang
Yangtze
Conic Projection
WORLD BOOK map-FGA

RUSSIA MAP INDEX

(All places indexed A through K or I through 16 are on the two-page map of Russia. All places indexed L through W or 17 through 24 are on the one-page map of European Russia.)

Union Republics

Map Key	Name	Population	Area (Sq. Mi.)	Capital
I 2	Armenia	2,102,000	11,506	Yerevan
J 3	Azerbaidzhan	4,455,000	33,436	Baku
F 2	Byelorussia	8,482,000	80,155	Minsk
E 3	Estonia	1,265,000	17,413	Tallinn
I 3	Georgia	4,456,000	26,911	Tiflis
J 7	Kazakhstan	11,690,000	1,048,303	Alma-Ata
K 7	Kirghizia	2,542,000	76,641	Frunze
E 3	Latvia	2,229,000	24,595	Riga
E 2	Lithuania	2,926,000	25,174	Vilnius
G 2	Moldavia	3,274,000	13,012	Kishinëv
F 7	Russian Soviet Federated Socialist Republic			
F 7	(R.S.F.S.R.)	125,240,000	6,592,829	Moscow
K 6	Tadzhikistan	2,388,000	55,251	Dushanbe
K 4	Turkmenistan	1,835,000	188,456	Ashkhabad
G 2	Ukraine	44,900,000	232,047	Kiev
J 5	Uzbekistan	9,997,000	173,591	Tashkent

Each republic has a separate article in WORLD BOOK.

Population

Year	Population
1972 Estimate	250,100,000
1967	235,300,000
1959 Census	208,826,650
1939	170,557,093
1926	147,027,915
1917 Estimate	163,000,000
1913	165,713,200
1897	128,200,000

Cities and Towns

Name	Population	Map Key
Abakan*	68,000	H 9
Achinsk	62,000	H 9
Akmolinsk, see Tselinograd		
Aktyubinsk	122,000	H 5
Alapayevsk	50,000	G 6
Aleksin	52,000	P 20
Alma-Ata	610,000	J 7
Almalyk*	64,000	K 6
Al'met'yevsk	64,000	G 5
Andizhan	154,000	K 7
Angarsk	170,000	H 11
Angren*	68,000	K 6
Anzhero-Sudzhensk*	120,000	H 9
Archangel (Arkhangel'sk)	296,000	E 5
Armavir	129,000	U 21
Artëm	63,000	H 15
Artëmovsk*	73,000	G 3
Arzamas	51,000	P 22
Asbest*	71,000	G 6
Ashkhabad	219,000	K 4
Astrakhan'	332,000	U 23
Azov	50,000	T 20
Baku	725,000 ★1,128,000	J 3
Balakovo	65,000	R 23
Balashikha*	70,000	P 21
Balashov	69,000	R 22
Balkhash	70,000	J 7
Baranovichi	70,000	P 17
Barnaul	373,000	H 8
Bataysk	78,000	T 20
Batumi	94,000	I 2
Begovat	54,000	K 6
Belaya Tserkov'	81,000	R 18
Belgorod	98,000	R 20
Belogorsk	49,000	G 14
Beloretsk*	64,000	H 5
Belovo*	114,000	H 9
Bel'tsy	79,000	F 2
Bendery	53,000	T 17
Berdichev	59,000	R 17
Berdyansk*	79,000	G 2
Berezniki	125,000	G 6
Biysk	173,000	I 9
Blagoveshchensk	108,000	G 14
Bobruysk	113,000	Q 18
Bokovo-Antratsit*	54,000	T 20
Bor	48,000	P 23
Borisoglebsk	61,000	R 22
Borisov	69,000	P 18
Borovichi	48,000	N 20
Bratsk	100,000	H 10
Brest	85,000	F 2
Bryanka*	79,000	G 10
Bryansk	259,000	Q 19
Bugul'ma	68,000	G 5
Buguruslan*	47,000	H 5
Bukhara	92,000	K 5
Buzuluk	60,000	H 5
Chapayevsk	86,000	R 24
Chardzhou	80,000	K 5
Cheboksary	154,000	P 23
Chelyabinsk	790,000	H 6
Cheremkhovo	116,000	H 11
Cherepovets	144,000	N 21
Cherkassy	109,000	S 18
Cherkessk	51,000	V 21
Chernigov	119,000	Q 18
Chernogorsk*	58,000	H 9
Chernovtsy	154,000	F 2
Chimkent	192,000	J 6
Chirchik	89,000	K 6
Chistopol'*	59,000	G 5
Chita	194,000	H 12
Chusovoy*	64,000	G 6
Daugavpils	80,000	O 18
Derbent*	55,000	I 3
Dneprodzerzhinsk	214,000	S 19
Dnepropetrovsk	755,000	S 19
Dolgoprudnyy	46,000	P 21
Donetsk (Stalino)	794,000	T 20
Donetsk*	46,000	H 3
Drogobych*	50,000	F 1
Dushanbe (Stalinabad)	303,000	K 6
Dzerzhinsk	189,000	P 22
Dzerzhinsk*	48,000	G 3
Dzhambul	143,000	J 6
Dzhezkazgan	54,000	I 6
Elektrostal'	111,000	P 21
Engel's	114,000	R 23
Feodosiya	54,000	U 19
Fergana	87,000	K 6
Frunze	346,000	J 7
Gatchina	46,000	M 19
Glazov	65,000	G 5
Gomel'	208,000	Q 18
Gorki (Gor'kiy)	1,066,000	G 4
Gorlovka	333,000	S 20
Grodno	94,000	E 2
Groznyy	308,000	V 22
Gubakha*	45,000	G 6
Gukovo*	63,000	H 3
Gur'yev	93,000	I 4
Gus'-Khrustal'nyy*	60,000	F 4
Inta	49,000	F 7
Irbit*	48,000	G 6
Irkutsk	397,000	H 11
Ishimbay*	51,000	H 5
Ivano-Frankovsk*	80,000	F 2
Ivanovo	380,000	O 22
Izhevsk	341,000	G 5
Izmail	57,000	G 1
Jelgava	45,000	N 17
Kadiyevka	137,000	S 20
Kalinin	299,000	O 20
Kaliningrad (Königsberg)	247,000	E 2
Kaliningrad*	87,000	F 4
Kaluga	164,000	P 20
Kamenets-Podol'skiy*	48,000	F 2
Kamensk-Shakhtinskiy	66,000	T 21
Kamensk-Ural'skiy*	158,000	G 6
Kamyshin	70,000	S 23
Kansk	92,000	H 10
Karaganda	477,000	I 7
Karpinsk*	49,000	G 6
Kaunas	262,000	E 2
Kazan'	743,000	P 24
Kemerovo	343,000	H 9
Kentau	46,000	J 6
Kerch'	111,000	U 19
Khabarovsk	393,000	G 15
Kharkov (Khar'kov)	1,048,000	G 3
Khasavyurt	47,000	V 23
Kherson	200,000	T 18
Khimki	62,000	P 20
Khmel'nitskiy	78,000	F 2
Kiev	1,292,000	F 2
Kimry	47,000	O 21
Kineshma	92,000	O 22
Kirov	292,000	O 24
Kirovabad	160,000	I 3
Kirovakan*	66,000	I 3
Kirovograd	150,000	S 18
Kirovsk*	55,000	H 3
Kirovsk	47,000	D 5
Kiselëvsk*	140,000	H 9
Kishinëv	270,000	G 2
Kislovodsk	84,000	V 21
Kizel	59,000	G 6
Klaipėda, see Memel		
Klin	64,000	O 20
Klintsy	48,000	Q 19
Kohtla-Järve	62,000	M 18
Kokand	122,000	K 6
Kokchetav	69,000	H 7
Kolomna	129,000	P 21
Kommunarsk	151,000	S 20
Komsomol'sk	200,000	G 14
Königsberg, see Kaliningrad		
Konotop	58,000	R 19
Konstantinovka*	97,000	H 3
Kopeysk	169,000	H 6
Korkino*	88,000	H 7
Kostroma	198,000	O 22
Kotlas	58,000	M 23
Kovrov	110,000	P 22
Kramatorsk	132,000	S 20
Krasnoarmeyskaya	51,000	U 20
Krasnodar	377,000	U 20
Krasnodon*	66,000	H 3
Krasnogorsk*	48,000	F 15
Krasnokamsk*	56,000	G 6
Krasnotur'insk	64,000	G 6
Krasnovodsk	45,000	J 4
Krasnoyarsk	521,000	H 9
Krasnyy Luch	101,000	T 20
Kremenchug	115,000	S 19
Krivoy Rog	477,000	S 18
Kropotkin	60,000	U 21
Kulebaki	46,000	P 22
Kungur	69,000	G 6
Kurgan	191,000	H 6
Kursk	240,000	R 20
Kushva*	49,000	G 6
Kustanay	108,000	H 6
Kutaisi	149,000	W 21
Kuybyshev	928,000	Q 24
Kuznetsk	71,000	R 23
Kzyl-Orda	82,000	J 6
Labinsk	47,000	V 21
Leninabad	90,000	K 6
Leninakan	123,000	I 2
Leningrad	3,218,000 ★3,607,000	E 4
Leninogorsk	70,000	I 8
Leninsk-Kuznetskiy	142,000	H 9
Liepāja	81,000	E 3
Lipetsk	218,000	Q 21
Liski	45,000	R 21
Lugansk	323,000	S 20
Lutsk	72,000	F 2
Lvov (Lwów)	487,000	F 2
Lys'va	78,000	G 6
Lyubertsy	107,000	P 21
Magadan	76,000	D 14
Magnitogorsk	347,000	H 6
Makeyevka	393,000	T 20
Makhachkala	146,000	W 23
Margelan*	86,000	K 6
Mariupol, see Zhdanov		
Mary	56,000	K 5
Maykop	97,000	V 20
Melekess	67,000	Q 24
Melitopol'	109,000	T 19
Memel (Klaipėda)	115,000	E 2
Mezhdurechensk*	71,000	H 9
Miass	115,000	H 6
Michurinsk	88,000	Q 21
Mineral'nyye Vody	47,000	V 22
Minsk	688,000	P 17
Mogilëv	151,000	P 18
Monchegorsk	52,000	D 5
Moscow (Moskva)	6,427,000	F 4
Mukachëvo*	54,000	F 1
Murmansk	262,000	D 5
Murom	89,000	P 22
Mytishchi	111,000	P 21
Nakhodka	82,000	H 15
Nal'chik	108,000	V 22
Namangan	146,000	K 6
Nevinnomyssk	51,000	V 21
Nezhin	51,000	R 18
Nikolayev	272,000	T 18
Nikopol'	101,000	T 19
Nizhniy Tagil	367,000	G 6
Noginsk*	100,000	F 4
Noril'sk	121,000	E 9
Novgorod	82,000	N 19
Novocherkassk	110,000	T 21
Novokuybyshevsk*	91,000	H 4
Novokuznetsk	466,000	H 9
Novomoskovsk	122,000	Q 21
Novomoskovsk*	57,000	G 3
Novorossiysk	110,000	U 20
Novoshakhtinsk	109,000	T 21
Novosibirsk	1,013,000	H 8
Novo Troitsk	76,000	H 5
Nukus	48,000	J 5
Odessa	721,000	T 17
Oktyabr'skiy	75,000	G 5
Omsk	702,000	H 7
Ordzhonikidze	202,000	W 22
Orekhovo-Zuyevo	116,000	P 21
Orël	190,000	Q 20
Orenburg	300,000	H 5
Orsha	79,000	P 18
Orsk	226,000	H 5
Osh	98,000	K 7
Osinniki*	71,000	H 9
Panevėžys	54,000	O 17
Pavlodar	130,000	I 8
Pavlograd*	54,000	G 3
Pavlovo	58,000	P 22
Pavlovskiy Posad*	65,000	F 4
Penza	305,000	Q 23
Perm'	745,000	G 6
Pervomaysk	50,000	S 18
Pervomaysk*	46,000	G 4
Pervoural'sk	108,000	G 6
Petropavlovsk	156,000	H 7
Petropavlovsk-Kamchatskiy	110,000	D 16
Petrozavodsk	149,000	M 20
Pinsk	49,000	Q 17
Podol'sk	153,000	P 21
Polevskoy*	53,000	G 6
Polotsk	55,000	O 18
Poltava	163,000	S 19
Poti	45,000	W 21
Priluki	52,000	R 18
Prokop'yevsk	292,000	H 9
Pskov	105,000	N 18
Pyatigorsk	77,000	V 22
Ramenskoye*	51,000	F 4
Revda*	58,000	G 6
Riga (Rīga)	649,000	N 17
Rostov-on-Don	706,000	T 20
Roven'ki	59,000	S 21
Rovno	81,000	F 2
Rubezhnoye	47,000	S 20
Rubtsovsk	135,000	I 8
Rudnyy	75,000	H 6
Rustavi*	80,000	I 3
Ryazan'	275,000	P 21
Rybinsk	205,000	O 21
Rzhev	58,000	O 20
Salavat	82,000	H 5
Samarkand	226,000	K 6
Saran'*	54,000	I 7
Saransk	132,000	Q 23
Sarapul	85,000	G 5
Saratov	665,000	R 23
Semipalatinsk	191,000	I 8
Serov	104,000	G 6
Serpukhov	118,000	P 20
Sevastopol (Sevastopol')	184,000	U 18
Severodonetsk	60,000	S 20
Severodvinsk	108,000	E 5
Shadrinsk*	64,000	H 6
Shakhtërsk*	70,000	T 19
Shakhty	208,000	T 21
Shchëkino	52,000	Q 20
Shchëlkovo*	68,000	F 4
Shostka	47,000	Q 19
Shuya	69,000	O 22
Šiauliai*	73,000	E 2
Simferopol'	208,000	U 18
Slavyansk	106,000	S 20
Slavyansk-na-Kubani	49,000	U 20
Smela	49,000	S 18
Smolensk	177,000	P 19
Snezhnoye	71,000	T 20
Sochi	177,000	V 20
Sokol	50,000	N 22
Solikamsk	84,000	G 6
Stalingrad, see Volgograd		
Stalino, see Donetsk		
Stavropol'	162,000	U 21
Sterlitamak	145,000	H 5
Stupino	51,000	P 21
Suchan	50,000	H 15
Sukhumi	83,000	V 21
Sumgait	80,000	J 3
Sumy	123,000	R 19
Sverdlovsk	897,000	G 6
Sverdlovsk*	70,000	H 3
Svobodnyy	60,000	G 13
Syktyvkar	89,000	F 6
Syzran'	163,000	R 24
Taganrog	229,000	T 20
Taldy-Kurgan	47,000	J 8
Tallinn	322,000	M 18
Tambov	199,000	R 21
Tartu	82,000	N 18
Tashauz	53,000	J 5
Tashkent	1,073,000	K 6
Tavda*	50,000	G 6
Tbilisi, see Tiflis		
Temir-Tau	138,000	I 7
Ternopol'*	63,000	F 2
Tiflis (Tbilisi)	794,000	I 3
Tikhoretsk	55,000	U 21
Tiraspol'	82,000	S 17
Tobolsk (Tobol'sk)	44,000	G 7
Tolyatti	105,000	Q 24
Tomsk	292,000	H 9
Torez	92,000	T 20
Troitsk*	82,000	H 6
Tselinograd (Akmolinsk)	150,000	I 7
Tula	360,000	Q 20
Tulun	49,000	H 10
Tyumen'	191,000	G 6
Ufa	651,000	H 5
Ukhta	48,000	F 6
Ulan-Ude	209,000	H 11
Ul'yanovsk	256,000	Q 24
Uman'	54,000	S 17
Ural'sk	114,000	H 4
Urgench	58,000	J 5
Usol'ye-Sibirskoye	66,000	H 11
Ussuriysk	119,000	H 15
Ust'-Kamenogorsk	197,000	I 8
Uzhgorod	56,000	F 1
Uzlovaya	50,000	Q 21
Velikiye Luki	73,000	O 19
Vichuga	53,000	O 22
Vilnius	287,000	O 17
Vinnitsa	144,000	R 17
Vitebsk	181,000	P 18
Vladimir	188,000	P 21
Vladivostok	353,000	H 15
Volgograd (Stalingrad)	684,000	T 22
Vologda	156,000	N 22
Vol'sk	69,000	R 23
Volzhskiy	91,000	T 22
Vorkuta	62,000	E 7
Voronezh	558,000	R 21
Voskresensk	56,000	F 4
Votkinsk*	70,000	G 5
Vyborg	61,000	M 19
Vyshniy Volochëk	72,000	O 20
Yakutsk	86,000	E 12
Yalta	54,000	U 18
Yangi-Yul'*	52,000	K 6
Yaroslavl'	467,000	O 21
Yegor'yevsk	62,000	P 21
Yelets	91,000	Q 21
Yenakiyevo	93,000	T 20
Yerevan	611,000	I 2
Yessentuki	50,000	V 21
Yevpatoriya	64,000	U 18
Yeysk	64,000	T 20
Yoshkar-Ola	126,000	P 23
Yurga	53,000	H 8
Yuzhno-Sakhalinsk	88,000	G 16
Zagorsk	82,000	O 21
Zaporozh'ye	529,000	T 19
Zelënodol'sk	69,000	P 24
Zhdanov (Mariupol)	352,000	T 20
Zhigulevsk*	47,000	G 5
Zhitomir	124,000	R 17
Zhukovka	56,000	Q 19
Zlatoust	174,000	H 6
Zyryanovsk	56,000	I 8

★Population of metropolitan area, including suburbs.
*Does not appear on map; key gives general location.

Source: Official estimates (1964).

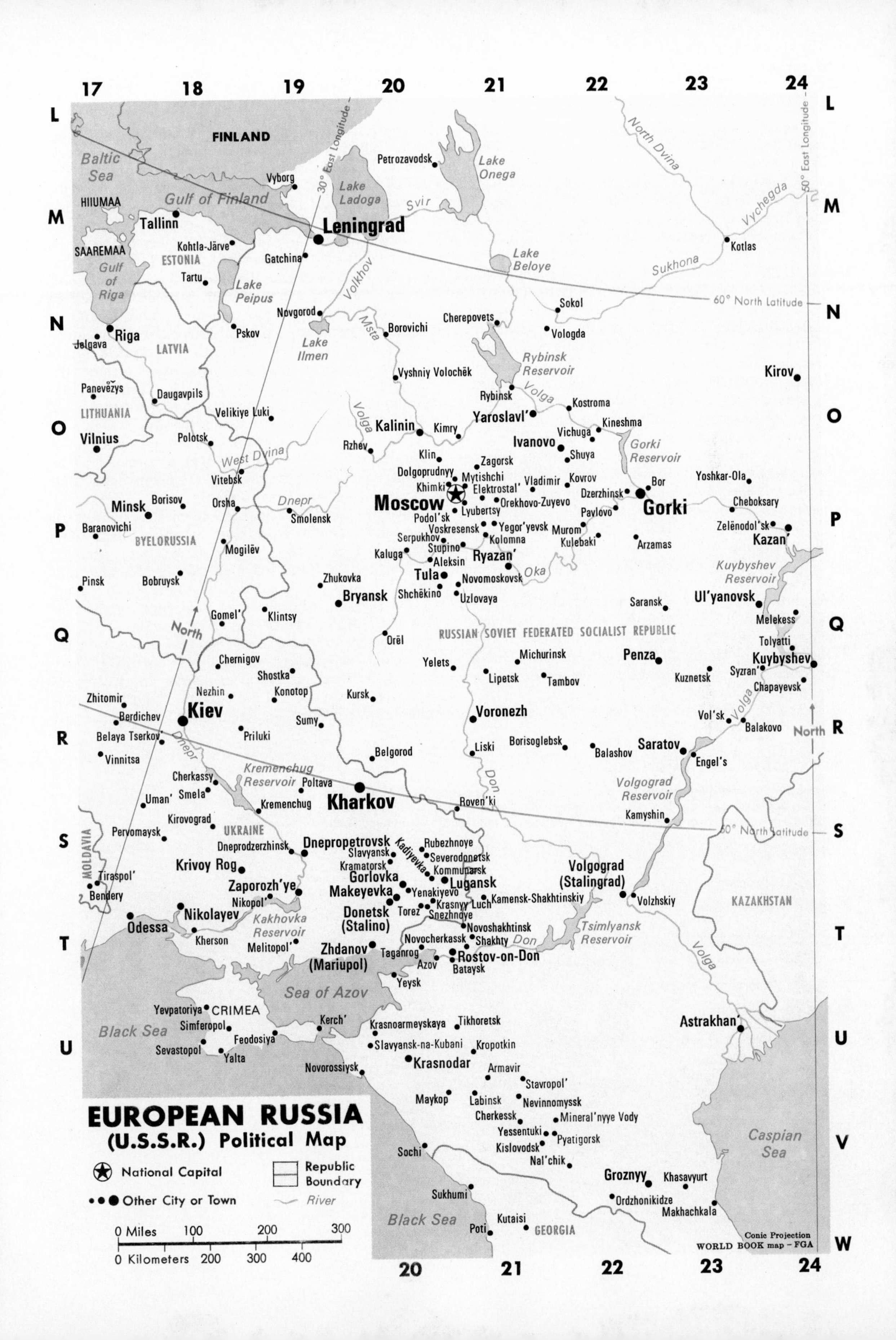
EUROPEAN RUSSIA
(U.S.S.R.) Political Map
National Capital
Other City or Town
Republic Boundary
River
0 Miles 100 200 300
0 Kilometers 200 300 400
Conic Projection
WORLD BOOK map - FGA
FINLAND
Baltic Sea
Gulf of Finland
HIIUMAA
SAAREMAA
Gulf of Riga
ESTONIA
LATVIA
LITHUANIA
BYELORUSSIA
UKRAINE
MOLDAVIA
CRIMEA
GEORGIA
KAZAKHSTAN
RUSSIAN SOVIET FEDERATED SOCIALIST REPUBLIC
Leningrad
Moscow
Kiev
Kharkov
Gorki
Tallinn
Riga
Vilnius
Minsk
Lake Ladoga
Lake Onega
Lake Peipus
Lake Ilmen
Lake Beloye
Rybinsk Reservoir
Gorki Reservoir
Kuybyshev Reservoir
Volgograd Reservoir
Kremenchug Reservoir
Kakhovka Reservoir
Tsimlyansk Reservoir
Sea of Azov
Black Sea
Caspian Sea
North Dvina
Vychegda
Sukhona
Svir
Volkhov
Msta
Volga
West Dvina
Dnepr
Oka
Don
30° East Longitude
50° East Longitude
60° North Latitude
50° North Latitude
North
Vyborg
Petrozavodsk
Kotlas
Kohtla-Järve
Gatchina
Tartu
Novgorod
Pskov
Jelgava
Borovichi
Cherepovets
Sokol
Vologda
Kirov
Panevėzys
Daugavpils
Vyshniy Volochëk
Rybinsk
Kostroma
Yaroslavl'
Velikiye Luki
Kalinin
Kimry
Kineshma
Vichuga
Ivanovo
Shuya
Polotsk
Rzhev
Klin
Zagorsk
Dolgoprudnyy
Mytishchi
Vladimir
Kovrov
Khimki
Elektrostal'
Dzerzhinsk
Bor
Yoshkar-Ola
Vitebsk
Borisov
Orsha
Smolensk
Lyubertsy
Orekhovo-Zuyevo
Pavlovo
Cheboksary
Podol'sk
Voskresensk
Yegor'yevsk
Murom
Zelënodol'sk
Kazan'
Baranovichi
Serpukhov
Kolomna
Kulebaki
Arzamas
Mogilëv
Stupino
Kaluga
Aleksin
Ryazan'
Tula
Novomoskovsk
Pinsk
Bobruysk
Zhukovka
Bryansk
Shchëkino
Uzlovaya
Saransk
Ul'yanovsk
Melekess
Gomel'
Klintsy
Orël
Tolyatti
Chernigov
Michurinsk
Penza
Kuybyshev
Yelets
Shostka
Lipetsk
Tambov
Kuznetsk
Syzran'
Chapayevsk
Nezhin
Konotop
Kursk
Zhitomir
Berdichev
Voronezh
Vol'sk
Balakovo
Sumy
Belaya Tserkov'
Priluki
Vinnitsa
Liski
Borisoglebsk
Balashov
Saratov
Engel's
Belgorod
Cherkassy
Poltava
Smela
Uman'
Kremenchug
Roven'ki
Kamyshin
Kirovograd
Pervomaysk
Dneprodzerzhinsk
Dnepropetrovsk
Rubezhnoye
Slavyansk
Severodonetsk
Kadiyevka
Kramatorsk
Kommunarsk
Krivoy Rog
Gorlovka
Lugansk
Volgograd
(Stalingrad)
Tiraspol'
Zaporozh'ye
Makeyevka
Yenakiyevo
Bendery
Nikopol'
Krasnyy Luch
Kamensk-Shakhtinskiy
Volzhskiy
Donetsk
(Stalino)
Torez
Snezhnoye
Nikolayev
Odessa
Novoshakhtinsk
Kherson
Novocherkassk
Shakhty
Melitopol'
Zhdanov
(Mariupol)
Taganrog
Rostov-on-Don
Azov
Bataysk
Yeysk
Yevpatoriya
Kerch'
Krasnoarmeyskaya
Tikhoretsk
Astrakhan'
Simferopol'
Feodosiya
Slavyansk-na-Kubani
Kropotkin
Sevastopol'
Yalta
Krasnodar
Novorossiysk
Armavir
Stavropol'
Maykop
Labinsk
Nevinnomyssk
Cherkessk
Mineral'nyye Vody
Yessentuki
Pyatigorsk
Kislovodsk
Sochi
Nal'chik
Groznyy
Khasavyurt
Sukhumi
Ordzhonikidze
Makhachkala
Kutaisi
Poti
17 18 19 20 21 22 23 24
L M N O P Q R S T U V W

The population of Russia is spread out unevenly across the country. About 75 per cent of the people live in European Russia, which covers about a fourth of the land. European Russia has an average of more than 80 persons to the square mile. Asian Russia averages fewer than 10 persons to the square mile.

Nationalities and Languages. Russia's people have many different backgrounds and speak many different languages. The Soviet census lists over 100 nationality groups in Russia. They are identified mainly by the languages they speak. Soviet republics are set up on the basis of various nationality groups and carry their names, such as *Ukrainian* Soviet Socialist Republic and *Latvian* Soviet Socialist Republic. Most nationality groups are of *Caucasoid* (white) stock. Others are of *Mongoloid* (yellow) stock, or are mixtures of the two races. See LANGUAGE (Language Families).

Slavic Nationality Groups make up more than three-fourths of the total population. They speak different, but closely related, Balto-Slavic languages. The ancestors of the Slavs established the original Russian state more than a thousand years ago.

The *Russians* are the largest Slavic group, though all Soviet peoples are generally called Russians. This group, once known as *Great Russians*, makes up about 55 per cent of the nation's population. The Russians live throughout the country, and hold most positions of leadership in the government and Communist party. Russian is the official language, and is taught in all Soviet schools. Almost all Soviet citizens speak Russian, as either their main language or their second one. See RUSSIAN LANGUAGE.

The *Ukrainians*, the second largest Slavic group, live in southern European Russia. The *Byelorussians*, sometimes called *White Russians*, are the third largest Slavic group. Most of them live in western European Russia. Closely related to the three major Slavic groups are the *Lithuanians* and *Latvians*—Baltic peoples—and the *Poles* of westernmost Russia.

Turkic Peoples rank second in number to the Slavs. Their languages are also closely related. Some Turkic peoples are Mongoloid. The largest Turkic groups live in Soviet Central Asia, a region between the Caspian Sea and China. The *Uzbeks* are the most numerous and the most advanced people of the region. Their ancestors were among the first settled farmers in the world. Other Turkic groups of Soviet Central Asia include the *Kazakhs*, *Kirghiz*, and *Turkmen*. The *Tuvinians* and *Yakuts* live in Siberia, a huge region that covers most of Asian Russia. The *Azerbaidzhani* live in the Caucasus Mountain region west of the Caspian Sea. The largest Turkic groups of European Russia live in the Volga River Valley. They are the *Bashkirs*, *Chuvash*, and *Tartars*, or *Tatars*. See TARTAR; TURK.

Other Groups. The *Finno-Ugric* peoples live in northern Russia, between the Baltic Sea and central Siberia. The largest of these groups include the *Estonians* near the Baltic Sea; the *Finns* and *Karelians* near Finland; and the *Mari*, *Mordovians*, and *Udmurts* of the Volga Valley.

The *Germans* are widely scattered over many parts of Russia. The ancestors of most of the Germans were settlers who arrived during the 1700's and 1800's. Yiddish-speaking *Jews*, listed as a nationality group by the Soviet census, live mainly in European Russia. The *Moldavians* live near Romania, and are closely related to the Romanians. Their language is much like Romanian, but it

POPULATION AND LANGUAGE

This map shows where the people of Russia live. Each dot represents about 65,000 people. The colors on the map show where the major languages are spoken. The regions in which these languages are spoken closely resemble the individual republics of Russia.

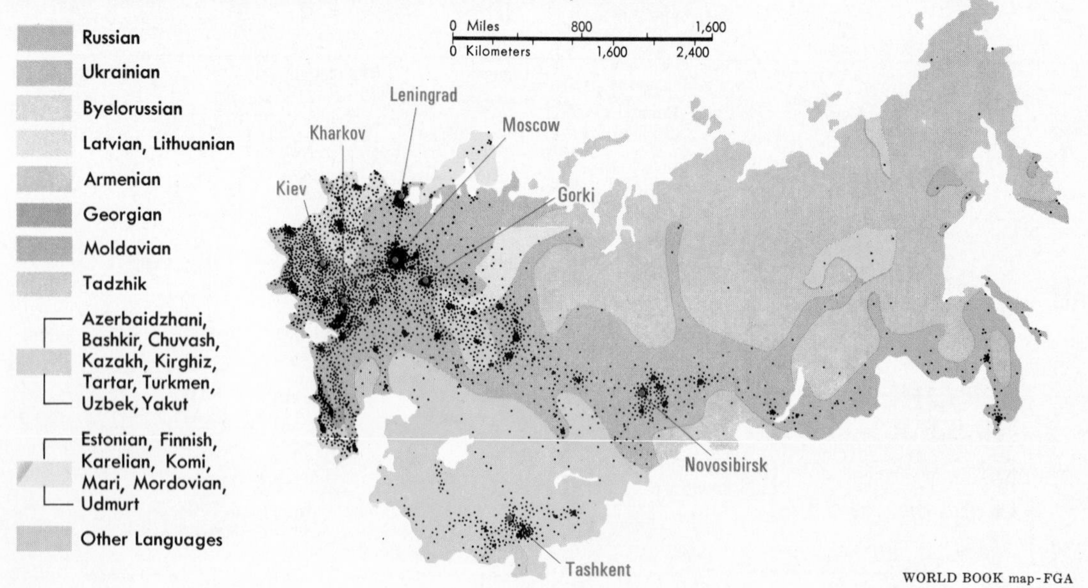

WORLD BOOK map-FGA

is written in the Russian *Cyrillic* alphabet (see ALPHABET [The Cyrillic Alphabet]).

The *Armenians* and *Georgians* are the major nationality groups of the Caucasus region. The *Tadzhiks*, whose language resembles Persian, live in the mountain valleys of Soviet Central Asia. Many small Siberian groups are related to American Indians and Eskimos.

Religion. The Russian Orthodox Church was the official Russian church before the Communists rose to power. The Communists were *atheists* (persons who believe there is no God). They looked on religion as an anti-Communist force, and called it the "opium of the people." The Communists destroyed many churches, made museums of others, and arrested or killed many church leaders who refused to follow Communism.

Religious worship survived in the Soviet Union, however, and the persecution gradually decreased. Many religious restrictions were dropped during the early 1940's, after church leaders supported Russia's war effort in World War II. These restrictions were brought back during the late 1950's. The government closed many churches and prohibited religious services outside officially recognized places of worship.

Today, the Communists do all they can to discourage religion through propaganda and education. However, many Russians worship in secret as well as in public. The Russian Orthodox Church probably has between 20 million and 45 million followers, more than any other church in Russia. Moslems are the second largest religious group in Russia. Other religious groups in the country include Buddhists, Evangelical Christian Baptists, Jews, Lutherans, Roman Catholics, and members of the Armenian Church.

A Leningrad Crowd hurries home from work in the second largest city in the Soviet Union. The population of Leningrad, like that of the entire country, consists mostly of Slavic people.

ZFA from Publix

Burt Glinn, Magnum

Ukrainian Woman wears government medals awarded for her high farm-production record.

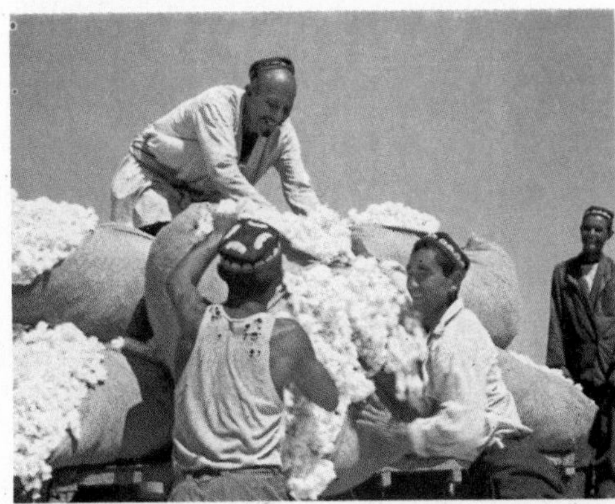

Howard Sochurek

Uzbek Cotton Workers belong to the largest Turkic group in Russia. The Uzbeks live in Soviet Central Asia.

Soviet Life

Siberian Yakut Woman, of the Mongoloid race, is a geologist. Women make up over half the workers in Russia.

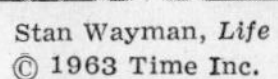

Stan Wayman, *Life* © 1963 Time Inc.

Estonian Girl wears one of her people's historic costumes in a parade. The Estonians are closely related to the Finns.

RUSSIA/*Way of Life*

The early Communists hoped to achieve a *classless society*—a society with neither rich nor poor people. The government took over all privately owned factories, farms, and other means of production. The Communist slogan was: "From each according to his ability, to each according to his needs." Everyone would serve the government as best he could, and no one would have any special rights.

The Communists have failed to achieve their goal of a classless society. The old classes that had special rights based on inherited rank and wealth have disappeared. However, new classes with special rights have appeared under the Soviet system. These groups include top officials of the Communist party and the government, and some professional persons, including artists, engineers, and scientists. They have automobiles, comfortable apartments and *dachas* (country homes), and other luxuries that most Russians do not have. For the great majority of Russians, living conditions are poor.

Personal Freedom. In the past, especially during the 1930's, the people of Russia lived under extreme terror. The secret police arrested millions of Russians suspected of anti-Communist views or activities. The victims were shot or sent to prison camps.

Today, the Russians live under greater freedom, though few dare criticize the government or the Communist party in front of a stranger. The government allows a limited amount of criticism to go unpunished. Also, many Russian writers whose views have been officially disapproved are widely popular with the people. But any Russian who opposes party policies too strongly may be expelled from his city, or even sent to a prison labor camp.

The government restricts the people's contacts with the Free World. It allows few Russians to travel outside the country. A person even needs official permission to move into a city or from one apartment to another. On the other hand, the government provides some important free benefits, including medical and hospital care. Higher education is provided for every student with a good record in schoolwork and behavior.

City Life. A little more than half the people of Russia live in cities and towns. Twenty-nine Russian cities have over 500,000 persons. Seven cities have more than a million persons. They are, in order of size, Moscow, Leningrad, Kiev, Tashkent, Gorki, Kharkov, and Novosibirsk. See the separate articles on the cities of Russia listed in the *Related Articles* at the end of this article.

Russian cities are so crowded that millions of families must share small, plain apartments with one or more other families. A family may wait for years to get its own apartment, which will probably have only one or two rooms.

Russian housewives have a special problem shopping for food and clothing. There is a shortage of meat, and

Gunvor Betting, P.I.P.

Sharing Tiny Apartments is a way of life for millions of Russian families. There is a severe housing shortage, and a family may wait years for its own apartment.

Soviet Life from Sovfoto

New Apartment Buildings are going up in Moscow and other Russian cities to help reduce the shortage of housing.

Novosti

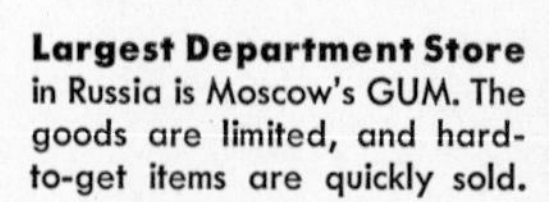

Largest Department Store in Russia is Moscow's GUM. The goods are limited, and hard-to-get items are quickly sold.

it is expensive. Clothing in the stores is plain and lacks variety. Shoppers often go from store to store looking for what they want, much of the time without finding it. They sometimes stand in line for hours before they can be waited on.

Village Life. Every year, about a million Russians leave the villages and move to the cities. Jobs are easier to find in the rural areas, but living conditions there are much worse than in the cities. In the villages, many Russians live in small log huts or in community barracks. Most of the families have no gas, plumbing, or running water, and many do not have electricity. There are fewer stores in the villages than in the cities, and they carry a smaller variety of goods. The quality of education that is provided in the villages is far below that of the cities.

Most Russians in the rural areas work on huge government-controlled farms. A Russian farmer is allowed to cultivate a small plot of land for himself, and to keep a few animals on it. He can sell his own dairy products, meat, and vegetables in the cities for private income.

Family Life. Many Russian mothers spend little time at home with their families. Over half of all Russian workers are women, partly because millions of Russian men were killed during World War II. Like the men, the women work six days a week and do every kind of work. They even lay bricks, dig ditches, and repair streets. About 75 per cent of Russia's doctors are women. In addition to working, a Russian mother must spend much time away from home to do the shopping.

The government operates about 60,000 nursery schools for children from $2\frac{1}{2}$ months to 3 years old. Each nursery cares for as many as 200 youngsters. The nurseries, as well as kindergartens for children up to 7 years old, help make it possible for Russian mothers to work. Most of the mothers bring in their children at 7:30 A.M. and call for them at 5:30 P.M.

Recreation. Russians are enthusiastic sports fans, and Soviet athletes have won the respect of the world for their skill. Sports training for Russian children begins in nursery school and kindergarten, and continues throughout school. There are also special sports camps and clubs for children and adults. Most factory and office workers take part in daily group exercises. The exercises are broadcast from Moscow twice a day.

Soccer, a form of football, is the most popular sport in Russia. Soccer teams are sponsored by trade unions and other groups. Beginning at the age of 12, children are selected and trained by the various teams. Other popular sports include basketball, hockey, ice skating, skiing, and track and field events. The government strongly encourages sports, and often sends athletic teams outside Russia to compete against teams of other nations. Chess is especially popular, and millions of Russians begin to play the game at an early age. Russian players often win international chess tournaments.

Novosti

Few Russian Villages have gas, plumbing, or running water. Most of the villages in the Soviet Union have no more than one paved street.

Howard Sochurek

Workers on a State Farm eat a noon meal of soup and bread. It was prepared in a field kitchen, *background*, and on an outdoor stove, *right rear*.

During the early 1900's, Russia was largely an underdeveloped country of poor, uneducated peasants. After the Communists seized control, they promoted education strongly. Great numbers of highly trained managers and workers were needed to build up the nation. Russian schools began expanding to meet this need.

Today, Russia has more than 50 million students, and nearly all the people can read and write. Russia is a mighty industrial nation partly because of its educational program. The schools stress science and technology, which includes industrial skills. Soviet achievements in these fields are among the highest in the world.

Russian students know that education is the surest road to success in their country. Students who earn high marks can look forward to important, highly paid careers. But students are graded on more than schoolwork. Their behavior and leadership in group activities in class and after school are also graded. Students who receive low marks in behavior may not be permitted to continue their education.

During the 1930's, Soviet law required children to attend school for four years. Today, eight years of school are required, from the age of 7 to 15. Russia has no private schools, and all education is free. Students buy their textbooks, which cost little. About three-fourths of the students in schools of higher education receive government allowances for their living expenses.

The same basic courses are given throughout Russia. The Communist party approves all educational programs and policies. Lower education is supervised by ministries of education in the union republics. Higher education is directed by the federal Ministry of Higher and Secondary Specialized Education. All schools stress Communist beliefs. Communism is presented as the best form of society, and other forms receive little attention.

In most schools, pupils are taught in the local language of the republic or region. All republics also have schools that teach in Russian. Parents decide which of these schools their children will attend. In schools that teach in a local language, children begin studying Rus-

Weston Kemp

Kindergarten Children learn folk dancing under a portrait of Lenin, *background*. The Russians see a picture of the founder of Communist Russia almost everywhere they turn.

Howard Sochurek

Young Pioneers, members of a group for Soviet children from 9 through 15 years old, do exercises on the grounds of an old Leningrad palace, their activities center.

American Broadcasting Company

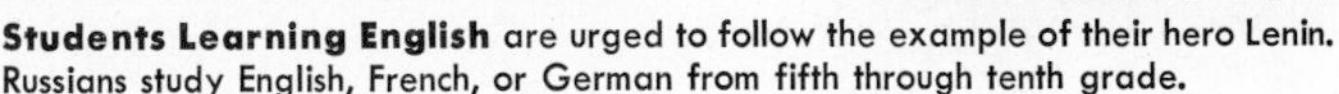
Students Learning English are urged to follow the example of their hero Lenin. Russians study English, French, or German from fifth through tenth grade.

Marc Riboud, Magnum

Student Uniforms are worn in many Russian schools. Classes meet six days a week.

sian in second grade. From fifth grade through tenth grade, pupils study English, French, or German.

Elementary Grades in Russia are the first four grades. Classes meet six days a week—about $4\frac{1}{2}$ hours daily Monday through Friday, and a shorter period on Saturday. The program includes arithmetic, art, language, music, physical education, and simple work skills. Nature study and Soviet history are started in fourth grade.

Intermediate Grades consist of fifth grade through eighth grade. Classes meet about 30 hours a week, and each subject is taught by a different teacher. Fifth-grade subjects include arithmetic, botany, geography, history, language, and shop work skills. Algebra, geometry, literature, physics, and zoology are taught in sixth grade. Chemistry is started in seventh grade. Eighth-grade courses include anatomy and physiology.

Secondary Grades are the ninth and tenth grades. About 60 per cent of the secondary program consists of mathematics, science, and work skills of various trades. These courses are designed to help meet the government's need for specialists in science and industry. Russian secondary schools also teach history, language, literature, physical education, and social studies. Graduates with high marks receive gold or silver medals. They are freed from required military service so they can continue their education.

Special Schools. After eighth grade, students may attend technical or trade schools. These schools train young people to be skilled technicians and workers in agriculture, engineering, industry, and other fields. Soviet law requires that jobs must be provided for graduates of these technical or trade schools. If a technician receives high marks and then works for three years, he may be quickly admitted to a higher technical institute.

The Soviet Union has many schools for gifted children who are selected by their teachers. These schools, beginning in first grade, stress the arts, foreign languages, or mathematics and physics. They also cover subjects in the general educational program.

Higher Education. Russia has about 700 specialized institutes and about 40 universities. Almost $3\frac{1}{2}$ million students attend these schools of higher education. From 85 to 90 per cent of them attend specialized institutes. The rest go to universities.

At the institutes, students are trained in agriculture, engineering, medicine, teaching, and other fields. More than two-fifths of the students specialize in engineering. University students are trained chiefly to be researchers, scholars, or teachers. Moscow State University is the oldest and largest university in Russia. It was established in 1755 and has more than 30,000 students.

Most programs in higher education take from 4 to $5\frac{1}{2}$ years of study. After completing their studies, students must work for three years at government-assigned jobs in their fields. Many are sent to underdeveloped areas of Russia, where specialists are needed. The students receive their diplomas after working one year.

After-School Activities are required of Russian children. These activities include crafts, folk dancing, music, sports, and cleaning and repairing the schools. The children also may join organizations supervised by the Communist party. Youngsters from 7 through 9 years old may join the *Little Octobrists*, a group named in honor of the October Revolution of 1917. This organization encourages children to be leaders in such activities as after-school duties, preparing for holiday ceremonies, and organizing plays. Children from 9 through 15 years old may join the *Young Pioneers*. The activities of this group include boat building, homemaking, music, painting, and radio operating.

The *Komsomol* (Young Communist League) is an organization for Russians from 15 through 28 years old. Students who do not join the Komsomol may have difficulty being admitted to schools of higher education. The organization is primarily a political movement to gain support and members for the Communist party. The Komsomol works with children's groups and helps spread Communist teachings. Most persons who join the party come from the Komsomol.

Young people also may work on projects at scientific and technical clubs. The clubs' equipment, staff members, and workrooms are provided by Soviet industries. Other clubs operate for young and adult Russians interested in acting, dancing, or music.

Libraries. The Soviet Union has about 400,000 libraries, more than any other country. About 135,000 of them are general libraries. Every city, town, and village has a general library. The rest of Russia's libraries are special libraries, operated by farms, industries, schools, unions, or other organizations. Russia's largest library, the Lenin State Library in Moscow, is one of the biggest in the world. It has about 22 million books and magazines. The M. E. Saltykov-Shchedrin State Public Library in Leningrad, the second largest in Russia, owns more than 14 million books. The Library of the Academy of Sciences of the U.S.S.R. in Leningrad has about 6 million volumes.

Museums. There are more than 900 museums in Russia. Every important city and town has at least one museum. The museums deal with the arts, history, and science. Many families spend their holidays visiting local museums, because Russia has a limited number of popular amusements. The State Historical Museum in Moscow is Russia's chief historical museum. Its displays cover Russian history from ancient times until the Revolution of 1917. The Museum of the Revolution, also in Moscow, has exhibits from the revolutionary period to the present time.

Sovfoto

Education Means Success in Russia. These students use a sign that reads: "Do not disturb! We are preparing for exams."

N. Granovsky, Sovfoto

Moscow State University, Russia's largest university, has over 30,000 students. Many of them live in its main building.

E. Kassin, Sovfoto

University Students enjoy a friend's guitar playing at a New Year's party. Although Communist leaders disapprove, young Russians like jazz and the latest Western dances.

RUSSIA / *Communication*

The Soviet government operates all communication activities in Russia, including broadcasting, motion-picture production, and publishing. They are controlled by various ministries and committees of the Council of Ministers. The Communist party checks all broadcasts and publications to make sure that they follow party policies. The party also publishes many books, magazines, and newspapers. Moscow is the communication center of the Soviet Union.

Russia has more than 400 radio stations, and there are about 20 radios to every 100 Russians. Many stations broadcast in local languages. The nation has over 90 main television stations, and about 75 TV stations that rebroadcast programs to distant areas. There are only about 3 television sets to every 100 Russians. Television programs consist mainly of movies, music, and sports.

In Russia, motion pictures are an important means of spreading Communist beliefs, as well as entertainment. In most of the movies, the hero or heroine is an eager worker for Communism. Films are produced in about 30 studios. The largest studio is Mosfilm in Moscow. The Soviet Union has about 90,500 movie theaters.

Thousands of newspapers are published in Russia, including those published by factories, farms, and government agencies. The newspapers are printed in more than 50 languages. Twenty-five major newspapers are sold throughout the country. *Izvestia* (News) of Moscow has a daily circulation of more than 8 million copies, more than any other paper in the world. *Izvestia* is the official newspaper of the Soviet government. *Pravda* (Truth), also of Moscow, is Russia's second largest paper. It has a daily circulation of about 7 million copies. *Pravda* is published by the Communist party.

Most of Russia's other major newspapers represent various activities of national life, including the armed forces and trade unions. *Tass* is the official Soviet news agency (see TASS).

Nearly 4,000 magazines are published in Russia. Every year, about 80,000 different books and pamphlets are published in Russia, probably more than in any other country. Russia's huge publishing industry, like the nation's other communication industries, is an important tool for spreading Communist beliefs.

Telephone and telegraph lines cross the huge country. There are about 7,200,000 telephones in the Soviet Union, or about 3 telephones to every 100 Russians.

Sovfoto

A Russian Cartoon from *Krokodil* (Crocodile), the official magazine of humor, pokes fun at village managers. The woman, *lower left*, says: "Good gracious! There must be a fire somewhere!" She is told: "Don't get panicky, Auntie! This is only our management watching how the field work is going."

Homer J. Smith

The Communist Party Newspaper, *Pravda* (Truth), has one of the world's largest circulations. *Pravda* sells about 7 million copies a day.

The Trinity by Andrew Rublev. State Tretyakov Gallery, Moscow

Religious Paintings called *icons* are outstanding examples of Russian art during the Middle Ages.

Act II, *The Cherry Orchard* by Anton Chekhov. Novosti

Masterpieces of Drama written by Anton Chekhov and other great Russian playwrights are presented by the famous Moscow Art Theater.

Novosti

Young Russian Poets such as Yevgeny Yevtushenko attract large audiences to their public readings.

Lenin State Museum (Constantine Manos, Magnum)

Soviet Art follows an official style called *socialist realism*. This painting shows Lenin with a group of Russian workers.

RUSSIA/*Arts*

Artists in Russia must present the ideas of Communism in their works. Artists' unions and the Communist party carefully control all artistic production. The Soviet government accepts only a simple art style that it calls *socialist realism*. This style stresses the goals and benefits of Soviet life, and ignores the faults. Works difficult to understand are officially discouraged, and artists who criticize Communism may be sent to prison labor camps. Many artists who work within the official restrictions receive large government salaries.

Architecture of old Russia is represented by churches with many-colored, onion-shaped domes. The most famous of these churches is 400-year-old Saint Basil's Church in Red Square in Moscow (see ARCHITECTURE [picture, Saint Basil's Church]). Until the 1950's, Soviet architects designed buildings in a highly decorative style known in the West as "wedding cake." Since then, the government has encouraged standard, simple designs to help speed its huge housing program.

Literature. The 1800's were years of great literary activity in Russia. Outstanding writers of the period included Anton Chekhov, Fyodor Dostoevsky, Alexander Pushkin, Leo Tolstoy, and Ivan Turgenev.

Since 1917, strict Communist controls have interfered greatly with literary production. Communist Russia has produced only a few great writers. They included Ilya Ehrenburg, Maxim Gorki, Boris Pasternak, and Mikhail Sholokhov. Pasternak and Sholokhov won the Nobel prize for literature. But the Communist party disapproved of Pasternak's views of Soviet life, and forced him to refuse the prize. During the 1960's, the popular poet Yevgeny Yevtushenko demanded

John G. Ross, Photo Researchers

Ballet Dancers of the Bolshoi Theater in Moscow are world famous for their skill and gracefulness.

Louis Renault, Photo Researchers

The Winter Palace in Leningrad, a home of the czars, represents the baroque style of architecture. The palace was built between 1754 and 1762.

Burt Glinn, Magnum

Music by Aram Khachaturian and other Soviet composers is often based on old folk songs of Russia.

Scene from *The Cranes Are Flying*, directed by Mikhail Kalatozov (Novosti)

Motion Pictures are an important means of spreading Communist beliefs in Russia. Most of the leading characters are eager workers for Communism.

more freedom from government control for writers, and was officially criticized several times. See RUSSIAN LITERATURE and the biographies of Russian writers listed in the *Related Articles* with that article.

Music. Mikhail Glinka, who wrote operas during the early 1800's, is considered the father of serious Russian music. Many of Russia's greatest composers wrote during the late 1800's. They included Modest Mussorgsky, Nicholas Rimsky-Korsakov, and Peter Ilich Tchaikovsky. The famous composers Sergei Rachmaninoff and Igor Stravinsky left Russia in the early 1900's. Well-known composers of Communist Russia include Aram Khachaturian, Sergei Prokofiev, and Dimitri Shostakovich. See the biographies of Russian composers listed in the *Related Articles* with the MUSIC article.

Painting. Early Russian artists painted large religious pictures on church walls, and also smaller religious pictures called *icons* (see ICON). By the mid-1800's, Moscow and St. Petersburg (now Leningrad) had busy art schools, and Russian artists were painting more varied subjects. The two most famous Russian-born painters, Marc Chagall and Wassily Kandinsky, left the country in the early 1900's.

Theater and Ballet in Russia have a long history of high quality. They still present skillful performances under Communism, but have adopted few new ideas. Several fine drama groups developed in Moscow during the late 1800's. The most famous, the Moscow Art Theater, still performs. Many experts consider the ballets of Moscow's Bolshoi Theater the highest achievement in Russian arts today. See BALLET (Russian Ballet); DRAMA (Continental Development and Influence).

RUSSIA/*The Land*

Russia is the largest country in the world. It covers more than 8½ million square miles, or over a seventh of all the land on earth. Russia spreads across northern Europe and Asia for about 6,000 miles, from the Baltic Sea to the Pacific Ocean.

Land Regions. Russia is a land of huge *steppes* (grassy plains), thick forests, high mountains, and rugged plateaus. The country has six main land regions: (1) the European Plain, (2) the Ural Mountains, (3) the Aral-Caspian Lowland, (4) the West Siberian Plain, (5) the Central Siberian Plateau, and (6) the East Siberian Uplands. See SIBERIA.

The European Plain is the home of about three-fourths of the Russian people. Most of the nation's industries and much of its richest soils are in this region. The plain is mostly flat to gently rolling, with some low hills. It averages about 600 feet above sea level. At the southern edge of the plain, the Caucasus Mountains rise more than 18,000 feet. The highest point in Europe, 18,481-foot Mount Elbrus, is in the Caucasus. The Caucasus mark the beginning of a series of high mountains that extends eastward along Russia's southern border to Lake Baykal in Siberia. See CAUCASUS MOUNTAINS.

The Ural Mountains form the boundary between European Russia and Siberia. These old, rounded mountains have been worn down by streams to an average height of only about 2,000 feet. Several peaks in the north and south rise above 5,000 feet. In the middle section, the most heavily populated part of the region, the range splits into a series of low ridges. The Urals are a storehouse of great mineral wealth, and have many industries. See URAL MOUNTAINS.

The Aral-Caspian Lowland, or *Soviet Central Asia*, has broad, sandy deserts and low, grassy plateaus. The deserts include the *Kara Kum* (Black Sands) and *Kyzyl Kum* (Red Sands). The Karagiye Depression, 433 feet below sea level, is the lowest point in the Soviet Union. It is on the Mangyshlak Peninsula, which extends into the Caspian Sea. The highest point in Russia, 24,590-foot Communism Peak, also is in the region. It rises in The Pamirs, a rugged mountain system along Russia's southern border. See PAMIRS, THE.

Land Regions of Russia

European Plain
Ural Mountains
West Siberian Plain
Central Siberian Plateau
East Siberian Uplands
Aral-Caspian Lowland

Physical Features

Feature	Key
Aldan Plateau	D 8
Altai Mts.	E 6
Amgun River	D 8
Amu Darya (River)	E 5
Amur River	D 8
Anadyr Range	C 10
Anadyr River	C 10
Angara River	D 7
Aral Sea	E 4
Arctic Ocean	A
Argun River	D 7
Atlantic Ocean	D 1
Ayon Island	B 10
Azov, Sea of	E 3
Baltic Sea	D 2
Barents Sea	B 3
Baykal Mts.	D 7
Belyy Island	B 5
Bennett Island	B 9
Bering Sea	D 10
Bering Strait	C 11
Black Sea	E 3
Cape Chelyuskin	B 7
Cape Kanin	C 4
Cape Lopatka	D 9
Cape Navarin	C 10
Cape Olyutorskiy	D 10
Cape Svyatoy	B 8
Cape Zhelaniya	B 5
Caspian Depression	E 4
Caspian Sea	F 4
Caucasus Mts.	E 4
Cherskiy Mts.	C 9
Commander Islands	D 10
Communism Peak	F 5
Crimea (Peninsula)	E 3
Dnepr River	D 3
Dnestr River	F 3
Don River	E 4
Donets Basin	E 3
Dzhugdzhur Mts.	D 8
East Siberian Sea	B 9
Faddeyev Island	B 9
Franz Josef Land	A 5
Gulf of Anadyr	C 11
Gulf of Shelekhov	D 9
Gydan Mts.	C 9
Irtysh River	D 5
Ishim River	D 5
Issyk-Kul (Lake)	E 5
Japan, Sea of	E 8
Kama River	C 4
Kamchatka Peninsula	D 9
Kara Kum (Desert)	E 4
Kara Kum Canal	F 5
Kara Sea	B 5
Karaganda Basin	E 5
Karagin Island	D 10
Karagiye Depression	E 4
Khanka Lake	E 8
Khatanga River	B 7
Klyuchevskaya (Volcano)	D 10
Kola Peninsula	C 3
Kolguyev Island	C 4
Kolyma River	C 9
Koryak Mts.	C 10
Kotelny Island	B 8
Kuril Islands	E 9
Kuril Strait	D 9
Kuybyshev Reservoir	D 4
Kuznetsk Basin	D 6
Kyzyl Kum (Desert)	E 5
Lake Balkhash	E 5
Lake Baykal	D 7
Lake Chany	D 5
Lake Chelkar Tengiz	E 5
Lake Ladoga	C 3
Lake Onega	C 3
Lake Peipus	D 3
Lake Tengiz	D 5
Laptev Sea	B 8
Lena River	C 8
Lenin Peak	E 5
Long Strait	B 10
Lower Tunguska River	C 6
Medvezhi Islands	B 10
Merv (Oasis)	F 5
Mezen River	C 4
Moscow-Volga Canal	D 3
Mt. Belukha	D 6
Mt. Chen	C 9
Mt. Elbrus	E 4
Mt. Karkaraly	E 5
Mt. Piramida	D 6
Mt. Polkan	D 6
Mt. Purpula	D 7
Mt. Sokhondo	D 7
Mt. Yamantau	D 4
Narodnaya (Mtn.)	C 5
Neman River	D 3
New Siberian Islands	B 9
Northern Dvina River	C 4
Novaya Sibir Island	B 9
Novaya Zemlya (Islands)	B 4
Ob River	C 5
Obskaya Guba (Bay)	B 5
Okhotsk, Sea of	D 9
Olenek River	C 7
Olekma River	D 8
Pamirs, The (Mts.)	F 5
Pechora River	C 4
Pur River	C 5
Queen Victoria Sea	A 2
Rybinsk Reservoir	D 3
Sakhalin (Isl.)	D 9
Sayan Mts.	D 6
Severnaya Zemlya (Islands)	B 6
Shantar Islands	D 8
Siberia (Region)	C 6
Sikhote-Alin Mts.	E 8
Snezhnyy Peak	D 7
Stanovoy Mts.	D 8
Syr Darya (River)	E 5
Taymyr Lake	B 7
Taymyr Peninsula	B 6
Taz River	C 6
Tien Shan (Mts.)	E 5
Tobol River	D 5
Turan Lowland	E 5
Ural Mts.	D 4
Ural River	E 4
Ussuri River	E 8
Ust-Urt Plateau	F 4
Valday Hills	D 3
Vaygach (Island)	C 4
Verkhoyansk Mts.	C 8
Vilyuy River	C 7
Volga-Baltic Waterway	C 3
Volga-Don Canal	E 4
Volga River	D 4
Volgograd Reservoir	D 4
White Sea	C 3
White Sea-Baltic Canal	C 3
Wrangel Island	B 11
Yablonovyy Mts.	D 7
Yamal Peninsula	B 5
Yana River	C 8
Yenisey River	C 6
Zaysan Nor (Lake)	E 6

Specially created for **World Book Encyclopedia** by Rand McNally and World Book editors

The West Siberian Plain is almost entirely flat. It lies north of the Altai Mountains, and is the largest level region in the world. The plain covers more than a million square miles, and in no place is more than 500 feet above sea level. This region is drained by the Ob River system, which flows northward into the Arctic Ocean. Drainage is poor, and much of the plain is marshy.

The Central Siberian Plateau has an average height of about 2,000 feet. The region slopes upward toward the south from coastal plains along the Arctic Ocean. The Sayan and Baykal mountains, which rise more than 11,000 feet, are along the southern edge of the plateau. The plateau has been deeply cut by streams, some of which flow through canyons. This region has a wide variety of rich mineral deposits.

The East Siberian Uplands are mainly a trackless wilderness of mountains and plateaus. The mountains rise as high as 10,000 feet. They form part of a series of ranges that curves along the eastern coast of Asia and continues in offshore islands. The Kamchatka Peninsula has about 25 active volcanoes. Snow-capped Klyuchevskaya, the highest, rises 15,584 feet.

Rivers and Lakes. Russia's longest river, the 2,683-mile Lena, is in Siberia. Other long rivers in Siberia include the Amur, Ob, and Yenisey. These rivers are frozen from seven to nine months a year. The Volga River is the longest river in Europe. It flows 2,290 miles from the Valday Hills, northwest of Moscow, to the Caspian Sea. Most of the Volga is frozen three months a year. Other important rivers of European Russia include the Dnepr, Don, Neman, and Northern and Western Dvina. Soviet Central Asia has few rivers.

The Caspian Sea, a salt lake 92 feet below sea level, is the largest inland body of water in the world. It covers 163,500 square miles in southern Russia between Europe and Asia. Lake Ladoga, which covers 6,835 square miles, is the largest lake entirely in Europe. Lake Baykal in Siberia, more than 5,315 feet deep, is the deepest fresh-water lake in the world. Other large lakes include the salty Aral Sea and Lake Balkhash, both in Soviet Central Asia. See the separate articles on the rivers, lakes, and other physical features of Russia listed in the *Related Articles* at the end of this article.

Burt Glinn, Magnum

The European Plain includes huge *steppes* (grassy plains) with some of the richest soils in the world. North of the steppes, forests cover much of this region.

Howard Sochurek

The Ural Mountains are rich in iron ore, petroleum, and other minerals. Their low valleys have long been used for travel between Europe and Siberia.

Burt Glinn, Magnum

The Aral-Caspian Lowland consists largely of sandy deserts where camel-riding Turkic herdsmen raise sheep. Much cotton is grown with irrigation.

The West Siberian Plain includes much of the forest zone that extends across northern Russia. This flat region becomes marshy toward the north.

Soviet Life from Sovfoto

Howard Sochurek

Pictorial Parade

Central Siberian Plateau is a cold region of thick forests and swampy Arctic plains. The people raise reindeer for food and transportation.

The East Siberian Uplands are a wild region of mountains and plateaus. An offshore chain of volcanoes forms the Kuril Islands in the Pacific Ocean.

RUSSIA/*Climate*

Russia is famous for its long, bitter winters, which have had a great influence on the nation's history. Napoleon and Adolf Hitler, both of whom set out to conquer Russia, were defeated partly by the icy winds that roar across the Russian plains. A large part of Russia lies north of the Arctic Circle. Snow covers more than half the country six months a year. Almost half the country has *permafrost* (permanently frozen soil) beneath the ground surface. Most of Russia's coastal waters, lakes, and rivers are frozen much of the year.

Northeastern Siberia is Russia's coldest region. January temperatures average below −50° F. there, and temperatures below −90° F. have been recorded. The region averages 60° F. in July, but sometimes has temperatures of nearly 100° F. This great range between temperature highs and lows—almost 200 degrees—is the widest in the world. Russia's summers are hot or warm, but short. Only the southern deserts have long summers. July temperatures there average about 90° F., and may rise above 120° F.

The heaviest rainfall in the Soviet Union occurs in the Caucasus region. There, some foothills get more than 100 inches of rain a year. Parts of western and central Siberia receive the heaviest snowfall, up to 4 feet a year.

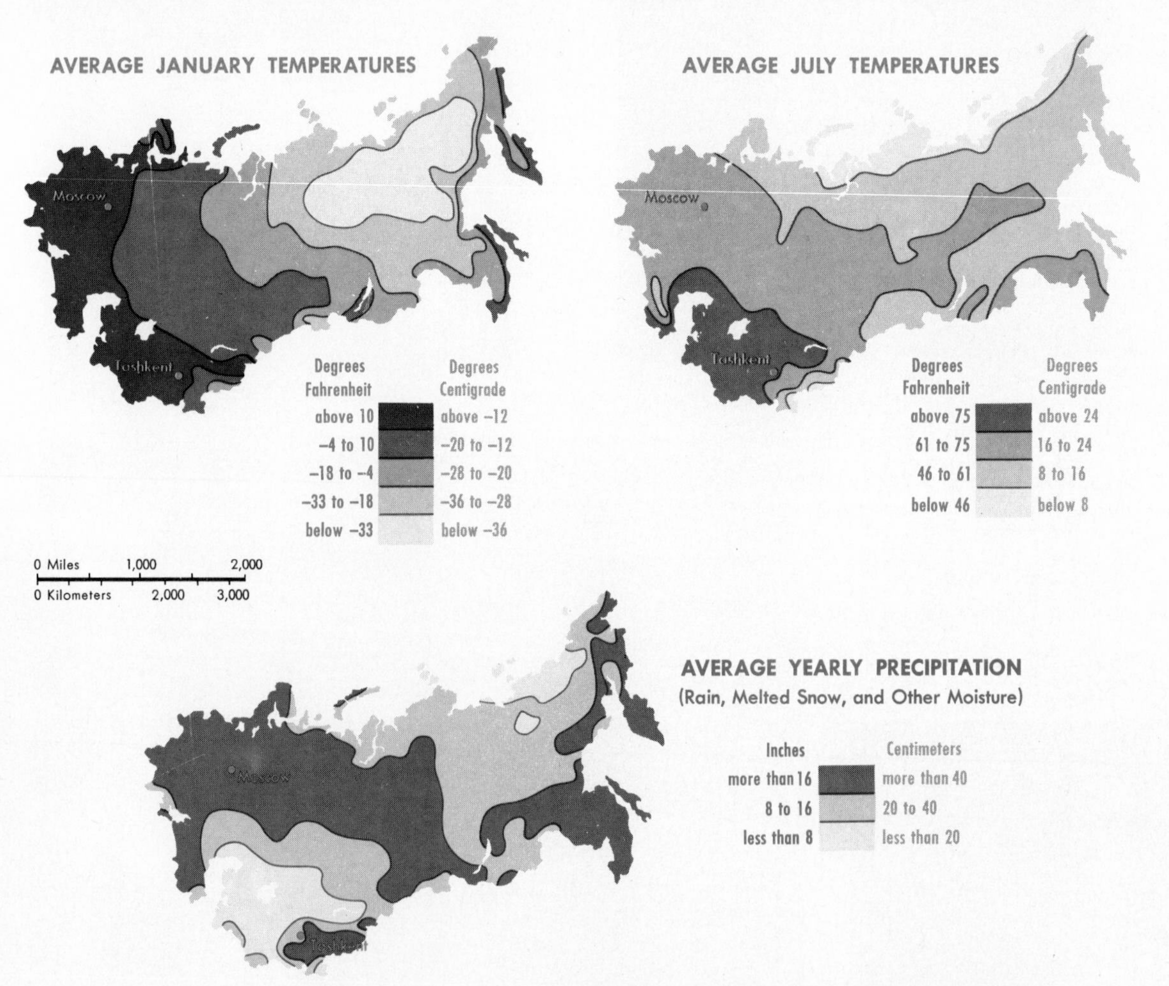

Sources: Meteorological Office, London; Ministry of Geology USSR, Moscow

MONTHLY WEATHER IN MOSCOW AND TASHKENT

	JAN	FEB	MAR	APR	MAY	JUNE	JULY	AUG	SEPT	OCT	NOV	DEC	Average of:
MOSCOW	21	23	32	47	65	73	76	72	61	46	31	23	High Temperatures
	9	10	17	31	44	51	55	52	43	34	23	13	Low Temperatures
	11	9	8	9	9	10	12	12	9	11	10	9	Days of Rain or Snow
TASHKENT	10	8	12	10	7	4	1	1	1	5	7	9	Days of Rain or Snow
	37	44	53	65	78	87	92	89	80	65	53	44	High Temperatures
	21	27	37	47	56	62	64	60	52	41	35	29	Low Temperatures

Temperatures are given in degrees Fahrenheit.

WORLD BOOK maps - FGA

Russia's total production ranks second only to that of the United States. Russia is the world's leading example of a socialist, centrally planned economy. The Soviet government owns the nation's banks, factories, land, mines, and transportation and communication systems. It plans and controls the production, distribution, and pricing of almost all goods. Since 1928, Russia's economy has expanded rapidly under a series of plans pushing industrialization. But improvements in living conditions have come slowly. The standard of living still remains far below that of the United States.

Russians work an average of about 40 hours a week. Their salaries are set by the government, and vary among different jobs and industries. For example, coal miners earn about twice as much as most factory workers. Since the mid-1950's, Russian workers have been free to quit their jobs. But a housing shortage discourages them from looking for work in other cities.

Natural Resources. The Soviet Union has some of the most fertile soils in the world. No other nation has so much farmland, so many mineral deposits or forests, or so many possible sources of hydroelectric power. Russia also has a variety of plant and animal life.

Soils. The steppes of Russia have the country's richest soils. These are *chernozem* soils—rich, black topsoils from 3 to 5 feet deep. Chernozem soils cover more than two-fifths of Russia's farmland. They lie in the *Black Earth Belt*, which extends from the western Ukraine to southwestern Siberia. The deserts of Soviet Central Asia lie south of the Black Earth Belt. When irrigated, the sandy desert soils can support plant life. The Caucasus region has rich yellow and red soils with large amounts of clay. North of the Black Earth Belt, soils are either poor or somewhat fertile. Spongy, swampy soils are found in the *tundra*, the low plains along the Arctic Ocean (see TUNDRA).

Minerals. Russia has great supplies of almost every

SOVIET GROSS NATIONAL PRODUCT

Total estimated gross national product (1964)—$293,000,000,000

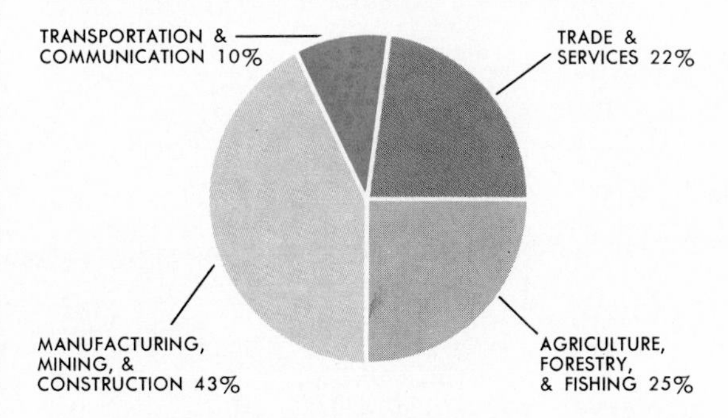

Source: *New Directions in the Soviet Economy*, Joint Economic Committee, U.S. Congress, 1966

EMPLOYMENT IN RUSSIA

Average yearly number of persons employed—97,541,000

Leading Occupations	Number of Employees
*Agriculture	35,354,000
Manufacturing & Mining	25,057,000
Transportation & Communication	7,718,000
Education	5,835,000
Construction	5,237,000
Trade	4,181,000
Public Health	3,933,000
Science	2,370,000
Housing & Communal Services	2,182,000
Administration	1,308,000
Public Dining	1,306,000

*Including about 27,000,000 collective farmers.
Source: *Current Economic Indicators for the U.S.S.R.*, Joint Economic Committee, U.S. Congress, 1965

Siberia, Russia's New Economic Frontier, has rich deposits of oil and other minerals. Trucks carry equipment to men who are developing areas that have long been frozen wilderness.

Soviet Life

FARM, MINERAL, AND FOREST PRODUCTS

This map shows where the leading farm, mineral, and forest products of Russia are produced. The map also shows the major manufacturing centers. Most of the cropland and all the major industrial centers are in European Russia.

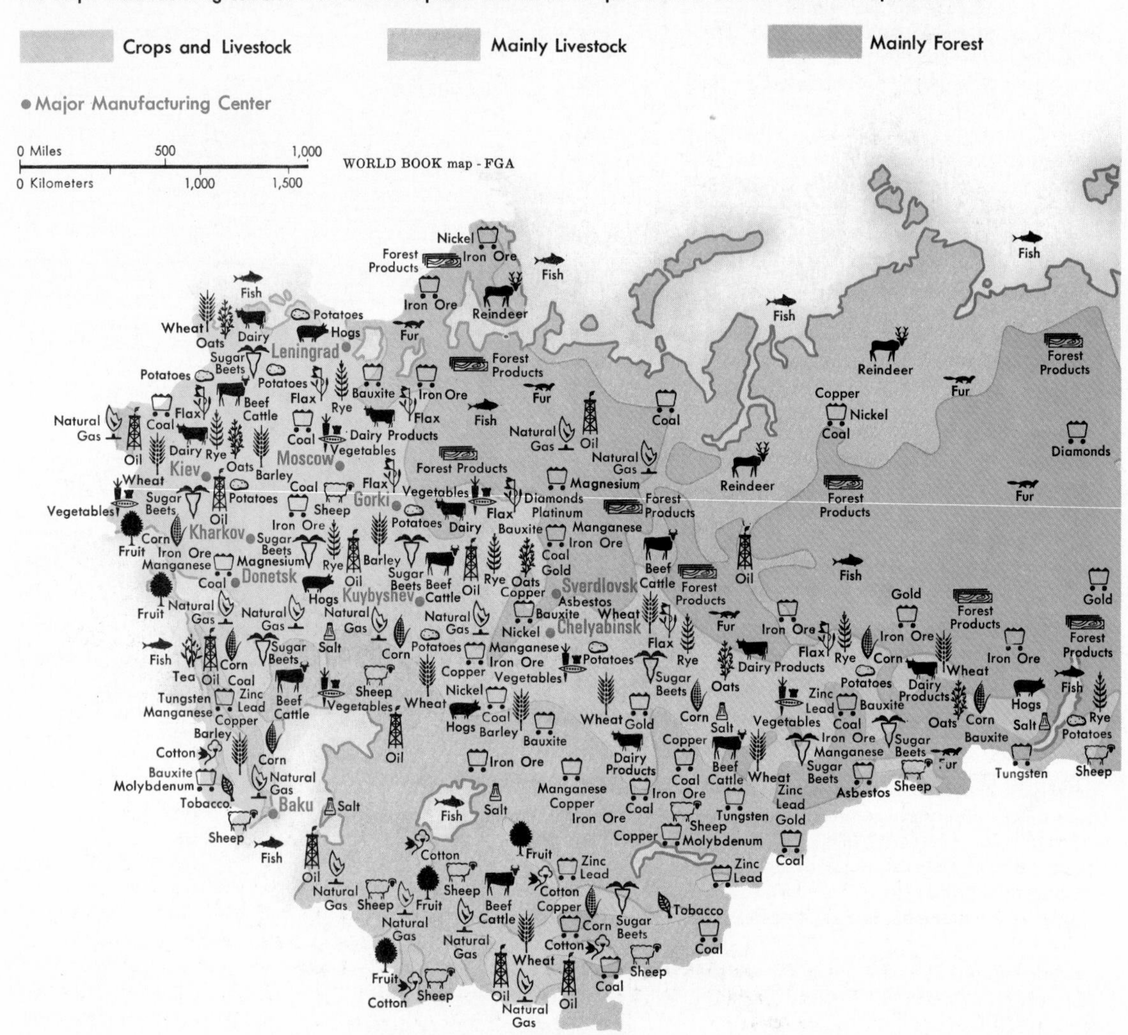

mineral needed for modern industry. Tin is the only important mineral not found in quantities large enough for Soviet needs. Russia has about a third of the world's coal deposits, and huge reserves of petroleum and natural gas. The eastern Ukraine and the Ural Mountains are great storehouses of iron ore. The world's largest deposits of manganese are in the republics of Georgia and the Ukraine. Chromium and nickel are found throughout the Urals. The republic of Kazakhstan has great deposits of copper, lead, and zinc.

Forests cover about a third of Russia's land. The country has about a fifth of the world's timber. A huge forest zone of cone-bearing trees extends more than 5,000 miles across northern Russia, from Finland to the Pacific Ocean. This northern forest consists of fir, larch, and pine trees. Between the forest and the almost treeless steppes is a mixed-forest zone of these cone-bearing trees and such trees as beeches, elms, lindens, maples, and oaks.

Plant Life of Russia's tundra consists of mosses, moss-like plants called *lichens*, and low shrubs. Some small, shrublike birches and willows also grow there. Large areas of the northern forest have marshes and peat bogs, especially in Siberia. The mixed-forest zone has some open grasslands. Long grasses once grew on the steppes, now Russia's major farming region.

Animal Life of the tundra includes reindeer and such small animals as the arctic fox, ermine, hare, and lemming. Huge flocks of waterfowl spend the summer along the Arctic coast. Many large animals roam the forests. They include the brown bear, deer, elk, lynx, and reindeer. Smaller forest animals include the beaver, rabbit, and squirrel. Antelope live in the eastern steppes. Antelope, bear, deer, hyenas, leopards, and tigers live in the deserts or mountains of Soviet Central Asia. Many kinds of fish are found in Russia's coastal waters, lakes, and rivers.

Manufacturing. During the 1920's, Russia was

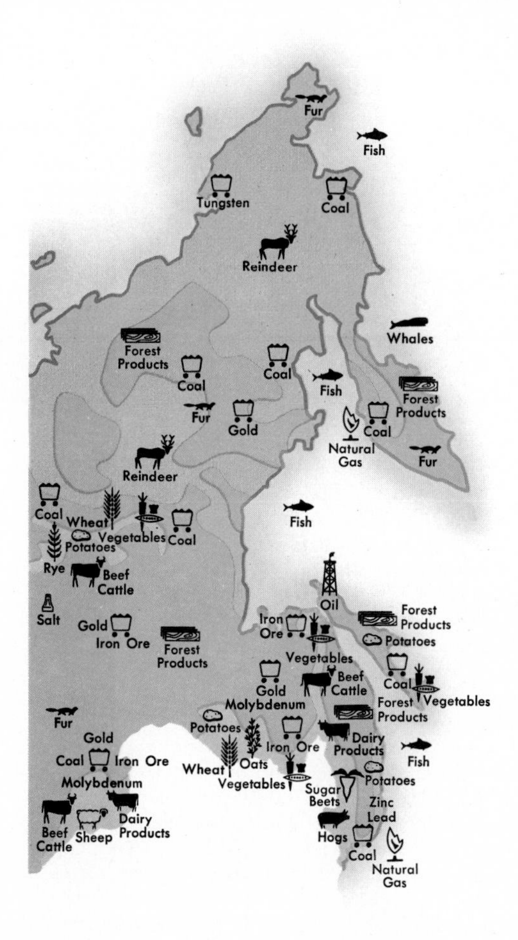

mainly a farming nation. Today, it is an industrial giant. Only the United States outranks Russia in the value of manufactured products.

In 1928, Russia's Communist leaders began the first of a series of *five-year plans* to promote industry. Each plan set up investment programs and production goals for a five-year period. At first, the government chiefly developed factories that produced heavy-industry products, including chemicals, construction materials, machine tools, and steel. As a result, heavy industry, especially steelmaking, expanded rapidly. But housing construction and the production of *consumer goods*, such as clothing, food, and household articles, lagged seriously. During the mid-1950's, the Soviet government began to increase somewhat the production of consumer goods. But the increase still fell far short of the people's needs.

Until 1965, the government took almost all the profits of the nation's factories. Government agencies told

Novosti

Wheat Is Russia's Chief Crop. The Soviet Union produces about 2 billion bushels a year, more than any other country.

factory managers which products to make, how many items of each to produce, and where to sell them. The quality of consumer goods was almost ignored. Many products were so poorly made and so unattractively styled that few people bought them. In 1965, the government began putting factories on a profit basis. Government agencies now set sales and profit goals for plant managers, instead of production goals. The managers base their production on what their customers want. The factories keep more of their profits to pay bonuses to the better workers and to improve production methods.

The Moscow area is Russia's leading manufacturing center. Its factories produce chiefly automobiles, buses, and trucks. Other products made in Moscow include chemicals, electrical and electronic equipment, processed foods, steel, and textiles. Ships are built and many kinds of industrial equipment are produced in the Leningrad area. The Ukraine is Russia's leading iron and steel region. It also produces a wide variety of machinery. Metal processing and machinery production are important in the Urals, and most Russian oil is refined in the Volga-Urals oil fields. Lumber and paper mills operate in many parts of Russia. Many new industries are being developed in Siberia to make use of the region's great mineral and hydroelectric resources.

Agriculture. Russia has more farmland than any other country. Its farmland covers more than $2\frac{1}{4}$ million square miles—over a fourth of all Russia. Only the United States produces more crops than the Soviet Union. But the United States has less than half as much farmland. Most U.S. farmland is more fertile. In addition, much Russian farmland lies near the Arctic Circle, where growing seasons are short, or in regions of light rainfall. American farmers receive higher prices for their products, have better equipment, and use more fertilizers. Many Russian government farm production plans are impractical and interfere with the farm managers'

Homer J. Smith

Automation in Russia is increasing. This electronic computer was set up to operate an electric power plant in Kharkov.

Sovfoto

Women Oil Field Workers check production figures on their way home after work. Women hold every kind of job in Russia.

job of making the best use of the land and workers.

More than half of Russia's farmland consists of about 9,000 *sovkhozy* (state farms). These farms average about 75,000 acres in size. The average size of U.S. farms is about 300 acres. Russia's state farms are operated like government factories, and the farmworkers receive wages. Less than half the nation's farmland consists of about 39,000 *kolkhozy* (collective farms), which are controlled by the government. These farms average about 15,000 acres in size. In general, more than 400 families live on a collective farm. The collective farmers are paid lower wages and a share of the production and profits. Families on state or collective farms are allowed to farm small plots of land for themselves. Farmers grow crops and raise animals on these plots. They can sell their products privately.

Barley, rye, and wheat are the main grain crops, and Russia leads all countries in their production. Wheat, the most important crop, is grown in the Ukraine, southwestern Siberia, and northern Kazakhstan. Barley is grown in many regions. Rye is produced in the less fertile, wetter parts of northwestern European Russia. The Soviet Union also leads all countries in the production of flax, potatoes, and sugar beets. Potatoes, the basic food of most of the people, are grown throughout most of Russia. Irrigated regions of Soviet Central Asia produce large crops of cotton. Farmers along the Black Sea coast grow tea plants. Tea is the national beverage. Other important crops in Russia include corn, fruits, oats, tobacco, and vegetables.

Livestock production is the weakest part of Russian agriculture. During the late 1920's and early 1930's, millions of Soviet farmers were forced to join collective farms. In protest, they killed great numbers of farm animals. Livestock production did not reach its earlier levels until the mid-1950's, and its growth since then has been slow. Today, Russians eat about half as much meat as Americans do.

Beef and dairy cattle and hogs are raised chiefly in the Ukraine and in some regions to the north. Sheep graze on the grasslands of Soviet Central Asia and other regions, and wool is an important product. Many farmers raise poultry on their private plots.

Mining. Russia leads all countries in the production of coal, iron ore, manganese, and the platinum-group metals. Russia's largest coal mines are in the Donets River Basin in the Ukraine, and in the Karaganda and Kuznetsk basins in Siberia. The eastern Ukraine and the Urals provide about 85 per cent of the Soviet Union's iron ore. Over 40 per cent of the world's manganese is produced near Nikopol' in the Ukraine, and near Chiatura in Georgia. Platinum is mined in the Urals and in northern Siberia.

The Soviet Union ranks second among all nations in the production of bauxite, copper, gold, lead, natural gas, nickel, petroleum, and tungsten. Bauxite, used in making aluminum, is mined north of Serov in western Siberia and in Kazakhstan. About 85 per cent of the country's natural gas comes from European Russia. Kazakhstan is the nation's leading producer of copper. About 70 per cent of the petroleum comes from the Volga-Urals region, and another 25 per cent comes from the Baku oil fields near the Caspian Sea. Other important minerals mined in Russia include asbestos, diamonds, magnesium, molybdenum, salt, and zinc.

Forest Products. Russia also leads all nations in lumbering. Most timber cut in Russia comes from the European section, which has about a fourth of the nation's forests. The high cost of transportation to the huge forests of Asian Russia has held back the development of forest industries there.

Fishing. In the Barents Sea and White Sea, Russian fishermen catch cod, haddock, herring, salmon, and other fishes. Sturgeon are caught in the Caspian Sea. Russia's famous black *caviar* is the salted eggs of sturgeon. Russian fishermen also fish in the Atlantic and Pacific oceans and in the Baltic and Black seas. They catch whales in the waters off Antarctica.

Electric Power. Only the United States produces more electric power than Russia. Fuel-burning plants generate more than four-fifths of Russia's power. Hydroelectric plants and a few nuclear power stations provide the rest. The Soviet Union has about an eighth of the world's undeveloped hydroelectric power. About four-fifths of Russia's undeveloped hydroelectric power is in the Asian section of the country. The world's largest hydroelectric station is near Bratsk, on the Angara River in south-central Siberia. Other huge hydroelectric plants are near Volgograd and Kuybyshev, both on the Volga River.

Foreign Trade plays only a small part in the Russian economy. Russia's enormous natural resources provide

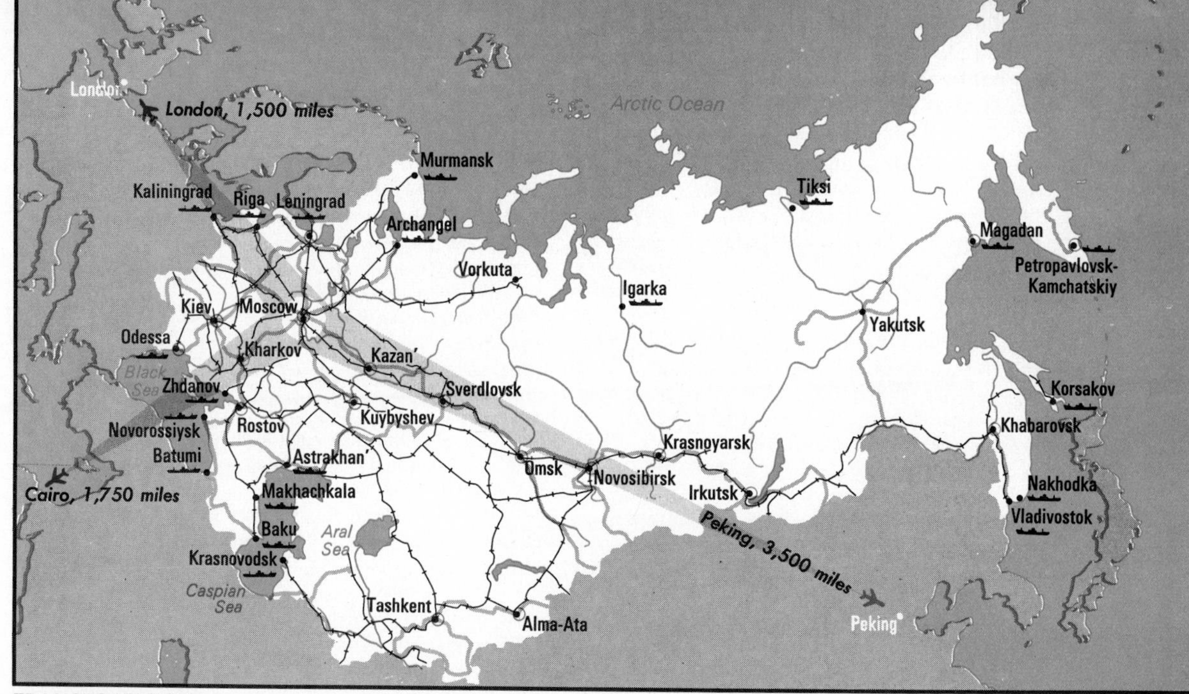

TRANSPORTATION

This map shows the major roads, rail lines, airports, seaports, and inland waterways of Russia. European Russia has large networks of rail lines and waterways. The rest of Russia depends chiefly on rail lines and air transportation to cover the great distances. Most of Siberia lacks any form of modern transportation. The Russians do not depend on roads so much as people do in North America.

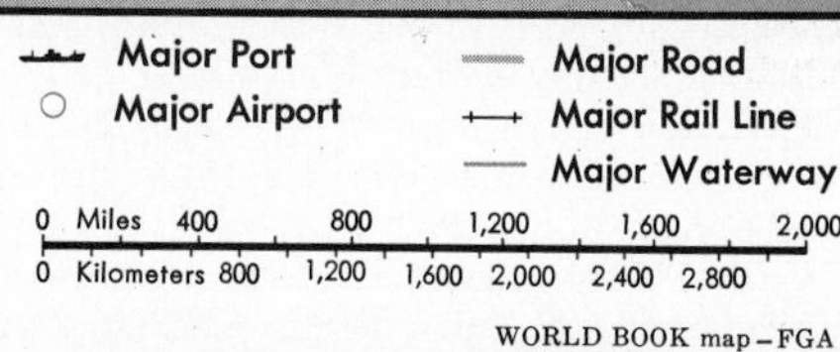

WORLD BOOK map–FGA

almost all the important raw materials that the nation needs. Also, the government does not want to become dependent on foreign markets or suppliers. Russia's major exports are iron and steel, lumber, machinery, and petroleum. Its main imports are industrial equipment and consumer goods.

About 70 per cent of Russia's foreign trade is with other Communist countries, especially those of Eastern Europe. This trade is set up largely by the Council for Mutual Economic Assistance (COMECON). COMECON is an economic planning organization made up of Russia and seven other Communist nations. Russian trade with the United States is limited by strict laws in both countries.

Transportation. Railroads carry about 80 per cent of Russia's freight and passenger traffic. Russia has about 80,000 miles of track, more than any other country except the United States. Eleven main rail lines extend from Moscow, Russia's transportation center, to all parts of the country. One line, the 5,600-mile Trans-Siberian Railroad, is the world's longest continuous railway. It connects Moscow with Vladivostok on the Pacific coast, and is Siberia's major railroad. The Trans-Siberian Express covers the distance in eight days. In Soviet Central Asia, railways extend from Tashkent to Moscow, Novosibirsk, and other cities.

There are only about 926,000 automobiles in Russia, compared with over 75,000,000 in the United States. Russia has about 200,000 miles of hard-surface highways, compared with about 2,700,000 miles in the United States. Trucks in Russia are used mainly for short trips, such as hauling freight to and from railroads.

Aeroflot, the national airline, is the largest public airline in the world. It connects all the major cities of the Soviet Union, and links Russia with about 50 countries. Aeroflot's 6,770-mile flight between Moscow and Havana, Cuba, is the longest nonstop airline route in the world. Russia's largest airport is at Domodedovo, near Moscow.

Novosti

Russia's Largest Airport opened in 1965 at Domodedovo, near Moscow. It can handle about 3,000 passengers an hour.

Inland waterways carry only about 5 per cent of Russia's freight traffic, because most of the rivers are frozen many months every year. Several canals link rivers and seas. The most important canals include the Volga-Don and the White Sea-Baltic. The Moscow Canal connects Moscow with the Volga River.

The harbors of most Russian seaports are also frozen much of the year. Some nearly ice-free ports are on the Black and Baltic seas. The long Arctic coast is icebound about nine months of the year. During the warmer months, ships sail along the Arctic coast from the ports of Murmansk and Archangel in Europe to ports in northern and far eastern Siberia.

RUSSIA / *History*

Russian history can be thought of as a long tug of war between *Eastern* (Asian) and *Western* (European) forces. Since ancient times, first one side and then the other gained power. Peoples and influences from the East and West changed Russian life many times. As a result, Russia has never been entirely an Eastern or a Western country.

This article traces the major developments of Russian history. To understand more fully who and what made Russia what it is today, read also the articles listed in the *Related Articles* at the end of this article.

Early Days. Beginning about 1000 B.C., the Cimmerians, a Balkan people, lived north of the Black Sea in what is now the southern Ukraine. They were defeated about 700 B.C. by the Scythians, an Iranian people from central Asia. The Scythians controlled the region until about 200 B.C. They fell to invading Sarmatians, another Iranian group. The Scythians and the Sarmatians lived in close contact with Greek colonies—later controlled by the Romans—along the northern coast of the Black Sea. They absorbed many Greek and Roman ways of life through trade, marriage, and other contacts. See CIMMERIAN; SCYTHIAN.

Germanic tribes from the West, called the Goths, conquered the region about A.D. 200. The Goths ruled until about 370, when they were defeated by the Huns, a warlike Asian people. The Huns' empire broke up after their leader, Attila, died in 453. The Avars, a tribe related to the Huns, began to rule the region in the mid-500's. The Khazars, another Asian people, won the southern Volga and northern Caucasus regions in the mid-600's. They became Jews, and established a busy trade with other peoples. See GOTH; HUN.

By the 800's, Slavic groups had established many towns in what is now European Russia. They had also

MIGRATIONS—700 B.C. TO A.D. 700

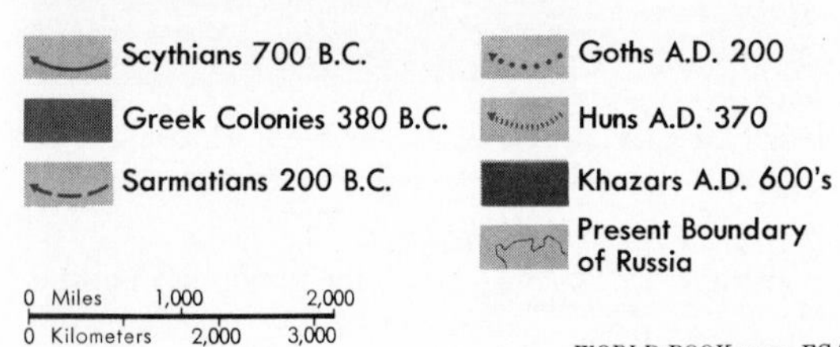

WORLD BOOK map - FGA

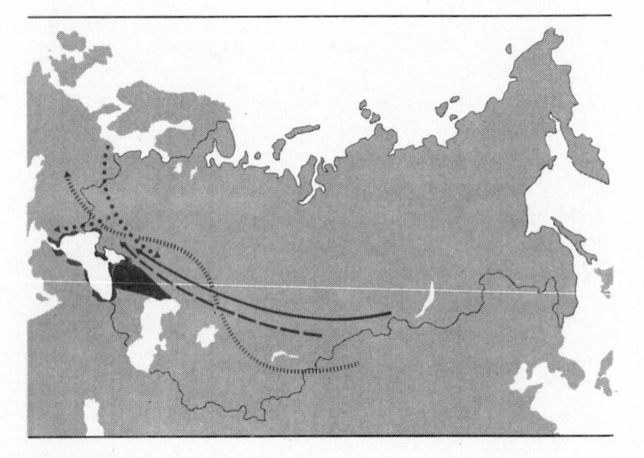

IMPORTANT DATES IN RUSSIA

A.D. 800's The first Russian state was established at Kiev.

c. 988 Vladimir I converted the Russians to Christianity.

1237-1240 The Mongols conquered Russia.

c. 1318 The Mongols appointed Prince Yuri of Moscow as the Russian grand prince.

1480 Ivan III broke Mongol control over Russia.

1547 Ivan IV became the first ruler to be crowned czar.

1604-1613 Russia was torn by civil war, invasion, and political confusion during the Time of Troubles.

1613 Michael Romanov became czar. He started the Romanov line of czars, which ruled until 1917.

1703 Peter I founded St. Petersburg and began building his capital there.

1773-1774 Russian troops crushed a peasant revolt.

1812 Napoleon invaded Russia, but was forced to retreat.

1825 The Decembrist revolt, led by discontented army officers, was put down.

1861 Alexander II freed the serfs.

1905 Japan defeated Russia in the Russo-Japanese War. A revolution forced Nicholas II to establish the *Duma* (parliament).

1914-1917 Russia fought Germany in World War I.

1917 A revolution overthrew Nicholas II in March. The Bolsheviks (Communists) seized power in November, and Lenin became dictator. Russia withdrew from World War I.

1918-1920 The Communists defeated their anti-Communist opponents in a civil war.

1922 The Union of Soviet Socialist Republics was established. Joseph Stalin became general secretary of the Communist party and began his rise to power as dictator.

1928 Stalin began the First Five-Year Plan to expand Russia's economy.

Mid-1930's Millions of Russians were shot or imprisoned during the Great Purge ordered by Stalin.

1941 German forces invaded Russia during World War II.

1942-1943 Russia defeated Germany in the Battle of Stalingrad, a major turning point in the war.

1945 Russian troops captured Berlin on May 2. Germany surrendered to the Allies on May 7.

Late 1940's Russia set up the Iron Curtain to cut off contacts between Communist and Western nations. The Cold War developed between East and West.

1953 Stalin died, and Nikita S. Khrushchev became head of the Communist party.

1956 Khrushchev announced a policy of peaceful coexistence with the West. This policy led to a bitter dispute with China over the basic methods of reaching the goals of Communism. Khrushchev also criticized Stalin's rule by terror, and Russian life became freer.

1957 Russia launched *Sputnik I*, the first spacecraft to circle the earth.

1958 Khrushchev became premier of Russia.

1961 Yuri A. Gagarin, a Russian air force officer, became the first man to orbit the earth.

1962 Russia set up missile bases in Cuba, and then removed them under United States pressure.

1964 High-ranking Communists forced Khrushchev to retire. He was replaced by Leonid I. Brezhnev as head of the Communist party, and Aleksei N. Kosygin as premier.

1965 Soviet factories were put on a profit basis.

1966 A Russian spacecraft made the first soft landing on the moon. Another reached the planet Venus, and a third went into orbit around the moon.

developed an active trade. No one knows where the Slavs came from. Some historians believe they came during the 400's from what is now Poland. Others think the Slavs were farmers in the Black Sea region under Scythian rule or earlier. See SLAV.

The earliest written Russian history dealing with the 800's is the *Primary Chronicle*, written in Kiev, probably in 1111. It says that quarreling Slavic groups in the town of Novgorod asked a Viking tribe to rule them and bring order to the land. The Vikings were called the *Varangian Russes*. Historians who accept the *Chronicle* as true believe Russia took its name from this tribe. According to the *Chronicle*, a group of related Varangian families headed by Rurik arrived in 862. Rurik settled in Novgorod, and the area became known as the "land of the Rus."

Many historians doubt that the Slavs of Novgorod invited the Vikings to rule them. They believe the Vikings invaded the region. Some historians claim the word *Rus*, from which Russia took its name, was the name of an early Slavic tribe in the Black Sea region. It is known, however, that the first Russian state was established during the 800's at Kiev, an important trading center on the Dnepr River. Whether it was developed by the Vikings is unclear.

The Kievan State. The *Primary Chronicle* states that Oleg, a Varangian, captured Kiev in 882 and ruled as its prince. During the 900's, the other Russian *principalities* (regions ruled by a prince) recognized Kiev's major importance. Kiev lay on the main trade route connecting the Baltic Sea with the Black Sea and the Byzantine Empire. In addition, Kiev's forces defended Russia against invading tribes from the south and east. The Kievan ruler came to be called *grand prince*, and ranked above the other Russian princes.

The Battle of Kulikovo in 1380 was the first Russian victory over the Mongol forces. It took place near the Don River.

Illustration from the Russian manuscript *Life of St. Sergius* of the 1500's. Lenin State Library, Moscow

Historical Pictures Service

About 988, Grand Prince Vladimir I became a Christian. He was baptized in the Eastern Orthodox branch of the Christian church, centered in the Byzantine capital of Constantinople (now Istanbul). The Russians were *pagans*, and worshiped idols representing the forces of nature. Vladimir made Christianity the state religion, and most Russians turned Christian. He later became a saint of the Russian Orthodox Church.

Several grand princes were strong rulers, but Kiev's power began to decrease after the mid-1000's. Other Russian princes grew in power, and they fought many destructive wars. In Novgorod and a few other towns with strong local governments, the princes were driven out. Badly weakened by civil wars and without strong central control, Kievan Russia fell to the huge *Tartar* (Mongol) armies that swept across Russia from the east during the 1200's (see TARTAR).

The Golden Horde. In 1237, Batu, a grandson of the conqueror Genghis Khan, led between 150,000 and 200,000 Mongol troops into Russia. These savage Asians destroyed one Russian town after another and killed the people. They destroyed Kiev in 1240. Russia then became part of the Mongol empire. It was included in a section of the empire called the *Golden Horde*. The capital of the Golden Horde was at Sarai, near what is now Volgograd. See MONGOL EMPIRE.

Batu forced the surviving Russian princes to pledge allegiance to the Golden Horde and to pay heavy taxes. From time to time, the Mongols left their capital and wiped out the people of various areas because of their disloyalty. The Mongols also appointed the Russian grand prince and forced many Russians to serve in their armies. But they interfered little with Russian life in general. The Mongols were chiefly interested in maintaining their power and collecting taxes.

THE GOLDEN HORDE—ABOUT 1300

Golden Horde

Other Parts of the Mongol Empire

Byzantine Empire

Present Boundary of Russia

0 Miles 1,000 2,000

0 Kilometers 2,000 3,000

WORLD BOOK map - FGA

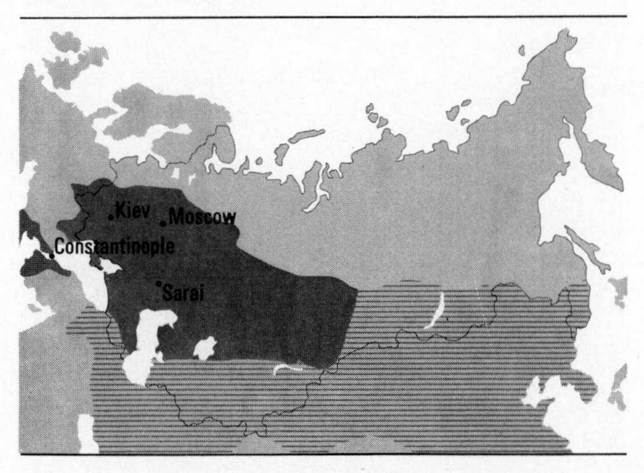

Illustration from *Voyages du Sr. Adam Olearius* (1633-1639) by Adam Olearius. The Newberry Library

The Bell Tower of Ivan the Great was built during the 1500's in the Kremlin, the walled central area of Moscow.

Peter the Great at Deptford, England by Daniel Maclise (Bettmann Archive)

Peter the Great learned Western ways on a trip through Europe in 1697 and 1698. The czar studied shipbuilding in England.

Catherine the Great saw apparently prosperous peasants during a trip through southern Russia in 1787. But the real peasants had been hidden, and her route falsely beautified.

Deceiving an Empress by R. Caton Woodville. *Illustrated London News*, April 15, 1905 (Mansell)

During the Mongol period, which ended in the late 1400's, the new ideas and reforming spirit of the Renaissance were dramatically changing Western Europe. But under Mongol control, Russia was cut off from these important Western influences. See RENAISSANCE.

The Rise of Moscow. During the early 1300's, Prince Yuri of Moscow married the sister of the Golden Horde's *khan* (ruler). Yuri was appointed the Russian grand prince about 1318. Mongol troops helped him put down threats to his leadership from other principalities. The Mongols also began letting the grand prince of Moscow collect taxes for them. This practice started with Ivan I (called the Moneybag) about 1330. Ivan kept some of the tax money. He bought much land and expanded his territory greatly. Other princes and *boyars* (high-ranking landowners) began to serve in Moscow's army and government. Ivan also persuaded the chief bishop of the Russian Orthodox Church to remain in Moscow. Until then, Kiev had been the spiritual center of Russia.

Moscow grew stronger and richer. But the Golden Horde grew weaker, chiefly because of struggles among the Mongols for leadership. In 1380, Grand Prince Dmitri defeated a Mongol force in the Battle of Kulikovo, near the Don River. The victory freed Moscow of Mongol control for a short period. The Mongols recaptured Moscow in 1382, but the belief that they could not be beaten had been destroyed.

During the late 1400's, Moscow became the most powerful Russian city. Ivan III (the Great) won control of Moscow's main rivals, Novgorod and Tver (now Kalinin), and great numbers of boyars entered his service. In 1480, Ivan made the final break from Mongol control by refusing to pay taxes to the Golden Horde. Mongol troops moved toward Moscow, but turned back to defend their capital from Russian attack.

Ivan the Terrible. After the rise of Moscow, its grand prince came to be called *czar*. In 1547, Ivan IV (the Terrible) became the first ruler to be crowned czar. Ivan made the czar's power over all Russia complete.

Ivan was brutal, extremely suspicious, and perhaps, at times, insane. He formed a special police force, and began a reign of terror in which he ordered the arrest and murder of hundreds of *aristocrats* (princes and boyars). He feared they were planning to kill him. Ivan gave his victims' estates as payment to the *service gentry* (landowners serving in the army and government). He also established strict rules concerning the number of warriors and horses each landowner had to supply to the army. Ivan burned many towns and villages, and killed church leaders who opposed him. In a fit of rage, Ivan even struck and killed his oldest son.

The number of service gentry increased rapidly. But their estates had no value unless the peasants remained on the land and farmed it. Ivan and later czars passed a series of laws that bound the peasants to the land as *serfs*. Serfdom became the economic basis of Russian power. The development of Russian serfdom differed sharply from changes occurring in Western Europe. There, during the Renaissance, the growth of trade led to both the use of money as royal payment and the disappearance of serfdom. See SERF.

Ivan fought Tartars at Astrakhan' and Kazan' to the southeast, and won their lands. Russian forces crossed the Ural Mountains and conquered western Siberia. Ivan also tried to win lands northwest to the Baltic Sea, but he was defeated by Lithuanian Polish, and Swedish armies. See IVAN.

The Time of Troubles developed because of a breakdown of the czar's power after Ivan's death. Theodore I, Ivan's second son, was a weak czar. His wife's brother, Boris Godunov, became the real ruler of Russia. Theodore's younger brother, Dmitri, was found dead in 1591, and Theodore died in 1598 without a male heir. The *Zemskii Sobor* (Land Council), a kind of parliament with little power, elected Boris czar. But a man believed to be Gregory Otrepiev, a former monk, posed as Dmitri. This *False Dmitri* claimed Dmitri had not died, and fled to Lithuania to avoid arrest. In 1604, he invaded Russia with Polish troops. The invaders were joined by large numbers of discontented Russians of all classes. This invasion marked the beginning of the Time of Troubles. Russia was torn by civil war, invasion, and political confusion until 1613.

False Dmitri became czar in 1605, but a group of boyars killed him the next year. Prince Basil Shuisky then became czar. In 1610, Polish invaders occupied Moscow. They ruled through a powerless council of boyars until 1612. Meanwhile, a new False Dmitri and a number of other pretenders to the throne won many followers. Peasant revolts swept through Russia. Landowners and frontier people called *Cossacks* fought each other, and sometimes joined together to fight powerful aristocrats (see COSSACK). The Polish control of Moscow led the Russians to unite their forces and drive out the invaders. They recaptured the capital in 1612.

The Early Romanovs. After the Poles were defeated, there was no one of royal birth to take the throne. In 1613, the Zemskii Sobor elected Michael Romanov czar. The Romanov czars ruled Russia for the next 300 years, until the February Revolution of 1917 ended czarist rule. See ROMANOV.

During the 1600's, Russia won much of the Ukraine and extended its control of Siberia eastward to the Pacific Ocean. During this same period, the Russian Orthodox Church made changes in religious texts and ceremonies. People called *Old Believers* objected to these changes and broke away from the church. This group still follows the old practices today.

Peter the Great. In 1682, a struggle for power resulted in the crowning of two half brothers—Peter I (the Great) and Ivan V—as co-czars. Both were children, and Ivan's sister Sophia ruled as *regent* until Peter's followers forced her to retire in 1689. Peter made close contact with the many Western Europeans living in Moscow, and absorbed much new information from them. He came into full power in 1696, when Ivan died.

Under Peter, Russia expanded its territory to the Baltic Sea in the Great Northern War with Sweden. In 1703, Peter founded St. Petersburg (now Leningrad) on the Baltic, and began building his capital there. After traveling throughout Europe, he introduced Western-type clothing, factories, and schools in Russia. Peter also strengthened the czar's power over the aristocrats, churchmen, and serfs. See PETER I, THE GREAT.

Catherine the Great. After Peter's death in 1725, a series of struggles for the throne took place. The service gentry and the leading noblemen were on opposite sides. Candidates for the throne who were supported by the service gentry won most of these struggles and rewarded their followers. The rulers increased the gentry's power over the serfs and local affairs. The gentry's enforced service to the state was gradually reduced, and was ended altogether in 1762.

Magnificent royal parties and other festivities, all in the latest Western fashion, took place during the 1700's. The arts were promoted, and many new schools were started, mainly for the upper classes. The Russian Imperial School of Ballet was founded, and Italian opera and chamber music were brought to Russia. It also became fashionable in Russia to repeat the newest Western ideas on freedom and social reform, especially during the rule of Empress Catherine II (the Great). In 1767, Catherine called a large legislative assembly to reform Russian laws, but it achieved nothing.

The great majority of Russians remained in extreme poverty and ignorance during this period. In 1773 and 1774, the peasants' discontent boiled over in a revolt led by Emelian Pugachev, a Cossack. The revolt swept through Russia from the Ural Mountains to the Volga River. It spread almost to Moscow before being crushed

CZARS AND EMPRESSES OF RUSSIA

Ruler	Reign	Ruler	Reign
*Ivan IV	1547-1584	Peter II	1727-1730
Theodore I	1584-1598	Anne	1730-1740
Boris Godunov	1598-1605	Ivan VI	1740-1741
Theodore II	1605	Elizabeth	1741-1762
False Dmitri	1605-1606	Peter III	1762
Basil Shuisky	1606-1610	*Catherine II	1762-1796
Michael		Paul	1796-1801
Romanov	1613-1645	*Alexander I	1801-1825
Alexis	1645-1676	*Nicholas I	1825-1855
Theodore III	1676-1682	*Alexander II	1855-1881
Ivan V	1682-1696	*Alexander III	1881-1894
*Peter I	1682-1725	*Nicholas II	1894-1917
*Catherine I	1725-1727		

*Has a separate article in WORLD BOOK.

EXPANSION OF RUSSIA—1360 TO 1917

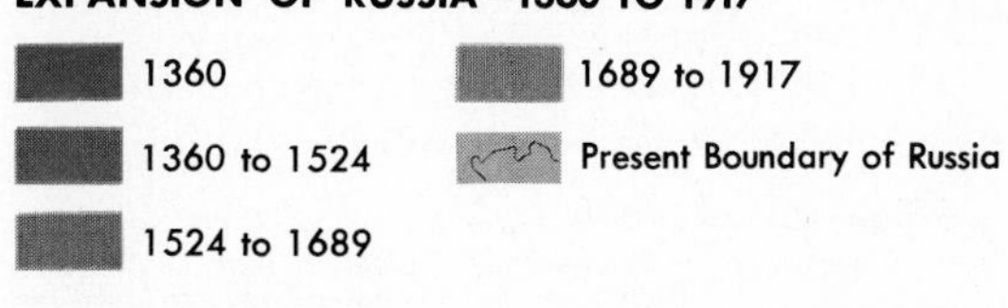

0 Miles 1,000 2,000
0 Kilometers 2,000 3,000

WORLD BOOK map-FGA

by government troops. In 1775, Catherine further tightened the landowners' control over the serfs.

Under Catherine, Russia rose to new importance as a major power. Russian armies won most of what is now the republic of Byelorussia from Poland. In wars against the Ottoman Empire (now Turkey), Russia gained the Crimea and other Turkish lands. Catherine died in 1796, and her son, Paul, became czar. See CATHERINE.

Alexander I. Paul's five-year rule ended with his murder in 1801. Alexander I, Paul's son, became czar and talked about freeing the serfs, building schools for all young Russians, and even giving up the throne and making Russia a republic. He established several reforms, such as freeing many political prisoners and spreading Western ways and ideas. But he did nothing to lessen the czar's total power or to end serfdom. Alexander knew that Russia's military strength and position as a major power depended on income provided by serfdom. Under his rule, Russia continued to win territory from the Persians, Swedes, and Turks.

In June, 1812, Napoleon led the Grand Army of France into Russia. Napoleon wanted to stop Russian trade with France's chief enemy, Great Britain, and to halt Russian expansion in the Balkan region. The French swept forward and reached Moscow in September, 1812. Most of the people had abandoned the city, and Napoleon entered without a struggle.

Soon afterward, fire destroyed most of Moscow. Historians believe the Russians themselves set the fire. After 35 days, the French left the city because they feared they might not survive the approaching bitter Russian winter. They began a disastrous retreat with little food and under continual attack by the Russians. Of the estimated 600,000 French troops in Russia, about 570,000 died or were captured. Russia then became a major force in the campaign by several European countries that defeated Napoleon. See NAPOLEON I (Disaster in Russia).

Although Alexander had begun some reforms, harsh rule continued in Russia. Beginning in 1816, many young aristocrats became *revolutionaries* (persons who seek to overthrow a government). They formed secret organizations, wrote constitutions for Russia, and prepared to revolt. Alexander died in 1825, and Nicholas I became czar. In December of that year, a group of revolutionaries took action. This group, later called the *Decembrists*, included about 30 army officers and 3,000 soldiers. They gathered in Senate Square in St. Petersburg, and government troops arrived to face them. After several hours, the Decembrists fired a few shots. Government cannons ended the revolt.

Napoleon Captured Moscow during his 1812 invasion, but a fire, believed set by the Russians, destroyed most of the city.

Return from Petrovsky Palace by V. V. Vereshchagin from Lenin State Library, Moscow

Nicholas I. The Decembrist revolt deeply impressed and frightened Nicholas. He removed aristocrats, whom he now distrusted, from government office, and replaced them with professional military men. He tightened his control over the press and education, reduced travel outside Russia, and prohibited organizations that might have political influence. Nicholas established six special government departments. These departments, which included a secret police system, handled important economic and political matters. Through the departments, Nicholas avoided the regular processes of Russian government and increased his power.

In spite of Nicholas' harsh rule, the period was one of outstanding achievement in Russian literature. Nikolai Gogol, Mikhail Lermontov, Alexander Pushkin, and others wrote their finest works. Fyodor Dostoevsky, Leo Tolstoy, and Ivan Turgenev began their careers. Many educated Russians began to debate the values of Westernized Russian life against those of old Russian life. The pro-Western group argued that Russia must learn from and catch up with the West economically and politically. The other group argued for the old Russian ways, including the czarist system, a strong church, and the quiet life of the Russian countryside.

Nicholas became known as the "policeman of Europe" because he sent troops to put down revolutions in Poland and Hungary. Nicholas also posed as the defender of the Eastern Orthodox Church, and fought two wars with the Moslem Ottoman Empire. In the war of 1828 and 1829, Russia gained much territory in the Balkan region. Russia also won the right to move merchant ships through the Turkish-controlled straits connecting the Black Sea with the Mediterranean Sea.

In 1853, the Crimean War broke out between Russia and the Ottoman Empire. Austria, Great Britain, France, and Sardinia came to the aid of the Turks. These countries objected to Russian expansion in the Balkans. Russia was defeated, and signed the Treaty of Paris in 1856. This treaty forced Russia to give up much of the territory it had taken earlier from the Turks. See CRIMEAN WAR; RUSSO-TURKISH WARS.

Expansion in Asia. After its defeat in the Crimean War, Russia began to expand in Asia. In the Far East, Russia won disputed territories from China. In 1858 and 1860, the Chinese signed treaties giving Russia lands north of the Amur River and east of the Ussuri River. By 1864, Russian forces defeated rebel tribes in the Caucasus. Central Asia was won during a series of military campaigns from 1865 to 1876. In 1867, Russia sold its Alaskan territory to the United States for $7,200,000 (see ALASKA [History]).

Alexander II. Nicholas I died in 1855, during the Crimean War. His son, Alexander II, became czar. Russia's defeat in the war taught Alexander a lesson. He realized that Russia had to catch up with the West to remain a major power. Alexander began a series of reforms to strengthen the economy and Russian life in general. In 1861, he freed the serfs and gave them land. He began developing railroads and organizing a banking system. Alexander promoted reforms in education, reduced controls on the press, and began a jury system and other reforms in the courts. He also established forms of self-government in the towns and villages.

But many young Russians believed that Alexander's reforms did not go far enough. Some revolutionary groups wanted to establish socialism in Russia. Others wanted a constitution and a republic. These groups formed a number of public and secret organizations. After a revolutionary tried to kill Alexander in 1866, the czar began to weaken many of his reforms. The revolutionaries then argued that Alexander had never been a sincere reformer at all. During the mid-1870's, a group of revolutionaries tried to get the peasants to revolt. They wanted to achieve either socialism or *anarchism* (absence of government) for Russia (see ANARCHISM). After this effort failed, a terrorist group called the *Will of the People* tried several times to kill the czar. Alexander then decided to set up a new program of reforms. But in 1881, he was killed by a terrorist's bomb in St. Petersburg.

Alexander III, Alexander's son, became czar and soon began a program of harsh rule. Alexander III limited the freedom of the press and of the universities, and sharply reduced the powers of local self-governments. He set up a special bank to help the aristocrats increase their property. He also appointed *land captains* from among the aristocrats, and gave them much political power over the peasants. Alexander started some programs to help the peasants and industrial workers. But their living and working conditions improved very little. See ALEXANDER (of Russia).

Nicholas II became Russia's next, and last, czar in 1894. The revolutionary movement had been quiet until the 1890's, when a series of bad harvests caused starvation among the peasants. In addition, as industrialization increased, discontent grew among the rising middle class and workers in the cities. Discontented Russians formed various political organizations of which three became important. (1) The *liberal constitutionalists* wanted to replace czarist rule with a Western type of parliamentary government. (2) The *social revolutionaries* tried to promote a peasant revolution. (3) The *Marxists* wanted to promote revolution among the city workers. The Marxists followed the socialist teachings of Karl Marx, a German social philosopher (see MARX, KARL).

In 1898, the Marxists established the Russian Social Democratic Labor party. It split into two groups in 1903—the *Bolsheviks* (members of the majority) and the *Mensheviks* (members of the minority). The Bolshevik leader was Vladimir I. Ulyanov, who used the name Lenin (see LENIN). The Bolsheviks wanted party membership limited to a small number of full-time revolutionaries who would lead the *proletariat* (workers). The Mensheviks wanted the party to have a wider membership and more democratic leadership.

Discontent among the Russian people grew after an economic depression began in 1899. The number of student protests, peasant revolts, and worker strikes increased. The unrest grew further after war broke out with Japan in 1904. Russia's expansion in the Far East had alarmed Japan. After a series of disputes, the Japanese attacked Russian ships at Port Arthur, a Chinese port leased by the Russians. The small but well-supplied Japanese forces won battles on land and sea, and defeated the Russians in 1905. See RUSSO-JAPANESE WAR.

The Revolution of 1905. On Jan. 22, 1905, thousands of unarmed workers marched to the czar's Winter Palace in St. Petersburg. The workers were on strike, and planned to ask Nicholas II for reforms. Government troops fired on the crowd and killed or wounded hundreds of marchers. After this *Bloody Sunday* slaughter, the revolutionary movement, led mainly by the liberal constitutionalists, gained much strength. More strikes broke out, and peasant and military groups revolted.

In October, 1905, a general strike paralyzed the country. Revolutionaries in St. Petersburg formed a *soviet* (council) called the Soviet of Workers' Deputies. Nicholas then agreed to establish an elected *Duma* (parliament), which could pass or reject all proposed laws. Many Russians were satisfied, but many others were not. The revolution continued, especially in Moscow, where the army crushed a serious uprising in December.

Each of the first two Dumas, which met in 1906 and 1907, was dissolved after meeting a few months. The Dumas could not work with Nicholas and his high-ranking officials, who refused to give up much power. Nicholas illegally changed the election law, and made the selection of Duma candidates less democratic. The peasants and workers were allowed far fewer representatives in the Duma, and the upper classes many more. The third and fourth Dumas cooperated with the czar. They lasted their full five-year terms, from 1907 to 1917. During this period, Russia made important advances in the arts, education, farming, and industry.

World War I. By the time World War I began in 1914, Europe was divided into two tense armed camps. On one side was the *Triple Entente* (triple agreement), consisting of Russia, France, and Great Britain. Russia and France had agreed in 1894 to defend each other against attack. France and Great Britain had signed the *Entente Cordiale* (friendly agreement) in 1904, and Russia had signed a similar agreement with Great Britain in 1907. The Triple Entente developed from these treaties. Opposing the Triple Entente was the *Triple Alliance*, formed in 1882 by Austria-Hungary, Germany, and Italy. See TRIPLE ENTENTE; TRIPLE ALLIANCE.

On Aug. 1, 1914, Germany declared war on Russia, a rival for influence in the Balkans. Soon afterward, Russia changed the German-sounding name of St. Petersburg to Petrograd. German troops crushed the Russians at Tannenberg, Germany. But the Russians defeated an Austrian army in the Battles of Lemberg in the Galicia region of Austria-Hungary.

In 1915, Austrian and German forces drove back the Russians. The next year, Russian troops attacked along a 70-mile front in Galicia. They advanced 60 miles and captured more than 400,000 prisoners. Russian troops moved into the Carpathian Mountains in 1917, but the Germans pushed them back. For the story of Russia in the war, see WORLD WAR I.

The February Revolution. During World War I, the Russian economy could not meet the needs of the soldiers and also those of the people at home. The railroads carried military supplies, and could not serve the cities. The people suffered severe shortages of food, fuel, and housing. Russian troops at the front were loyal, but the untrained soldiers behind the fighting lines became disloyal. They knew they would probably be sent to the front and be killed. The townspeople and these soldiers were tense and angry.

By the end of 1916, almost all educated Russians opposed the czar. Nicholas had removed many capable officials from high government offices, and replaced them with weak, unpopular men. He was accused of crippling the war effort by such acts. Many Russians blamed his actions on the influence of Grigori Y. Rasputin, adviser to the czar and the czarina. The royal couple believed that Rasputin was a holy man who was saving their sick son's life. In December, 1916, a group of noblemen murdered Rasputin. But the officials who supposedly had been appointed through his influence remained. See RASPUTIN, GRIGORI Y.

Early in March, 1917, the people revolted. (The month was February in the old Russian calendar, which was replaced in 1918.) In Petrograd, riots and strikes over shortages of bread and coal grew more violent. Troops were called in to halt the uprising, but they joined it instead. So did the aristocrats, who had turned against the czar. The people of Petrograd turned to the Duma for leadership. Nicholas ordered the Duma to dissolve itself, but the parliament ignored his command. The Duma established a *provisional* (temporary) government consisting of some Duma leaders and other public figures. Prince George Lvov became chairman of the Council of Ministers, or premier. Nicholas had lost all political support, and he gave up the throne on March 15. See NICHOLAS (of Russia).

A new Soviet of Workers' and Soldiers' Deputies was also formed in Petrograd in March. It was a kind of unofficial partner of the provisional government. Many similar soviets were set up throughout Russia. The soviets seriously weakened the government's ability to carry on the war. Many Russian army units refused to fight. In April, Lenin demanded "all power to the soviets," but the soviets were unwilling to take over the government then. In July, however, armed workers and soldiers tried to seize power in Petrograd. They failed. Lenin fled to Finland, and his followers escaped or were jailed. Later that month, Alexander F. Kerensky, a socialist, became premier.

The February Revolution of 1917 began in Petrograd (now Leningrad). The revolt ended czarist rule within a few days.

United Press Int.

The October Revolution. Many powerful Russians blamed Kerensky for failures in the war, and opposed his socialist views. General Lavr Kornilov, the army commander in chief, planned to seize power. Kerensky freed the imprisoned Bolsheviks, and let them arm the Petrograd workers against Kornilov. The general advanced on Petrograd in September, 1917, but his group broke up before reaching the capital. The Bolsheviks were free, however, and now the workers had guns.

Also in September, 1917, the Bolsheviks won a majority in the Petrograd soviet. Lenin returned from Finland in October and convinced the Bolsheviks that they should try to seize power. He hoped a revolution would set off other socialist revolts in Western countries. Lenin's most capable assistant, Leon Trotsky, helped him plan the take-over. On November 7 (October 25 in the old Russian calendar), the armed workers took over important points in Petrograd. Early that evening, the workers and Bolshevik-led soldiers and sailors attacked the Winter Palace, headquarters of the provisional government. They seized the palace, which was weakly defended by students from a military school, and arrested members of the government. After a bloodier struggle in Moscow, the Bolsheviks controlled that city by November 15.

The Bolsheviks formed a new Russian government, headed by Lenin. They spread Bolshevik rule from town to town through the local soviets. For a short time, Lenin let the peasants seize much farmland. He permitted workers to control the factories, and allowed them to play important roles in the local soviets. But the government soon tightened control, and forced the peasants to give the government most of their products. The government also took over Russian industries, and set up central management bureaus to control them. The Cheka, a secret police force, was established. Bolshevik rule became complete.

After the Bolsheviks seized the government, Russia withdrew from World War I and began peace talks with Germany. In March, 1918, Russia signed the Treaty of Brest-Litovsk with Germany. Under the treaty, Russia gave up large areas, mostly in the fertile western and southwestern regions. Much of this land was returned to Russia after Germany surrendered in November, 1918.

In 1918, the Bolsheviks moved the Russian capital back to Moscow. They also changed the name of their Russian Social Democratic Labor party to the Russian Communist Party (Bolsheviks). This name was later changed to the Communist Party of the Soviet Union. The Bolsheviks organized the Red Army, named for the color of the Communist flag. The Communists themselves were called *Reds*. See COMMUNISM.

Civil War. From 1918 to 1920, Russia was torn by war between the Communists and anti-Communists, who were called *Whites*. The peasants believed they would lose their lands to their old landlords if the Whites won, and supported the Reds. The Whites were aided by troops from France, Great Britain, Japan, the United States, and other countries that opposed the Communist government. But these nations provided little help, because they were unwilling to fight another war after

Novosti

Lenin, the first dictator of Communist Russia, led the Bolshevik takeover of the government in the October Revolution of 1917.

Sovfoto

Joseph Stalin, *third from right,* one of the cruelest rulers in world history, was dictator of Russia from 1929 to 1953.

World War I. The aid probably did the Communists more good than harm. It allowed them to claim they were defending Russia against invaders. The Whites were poorly organized, and the Reds defeated them.

The Red Army had less success against Polish invaders in 1920. The Polish government claimed that western parts of Byelorussia and of the Ukraine belonged to Poland. Polish troops, aided by the French, defeated the Russians. A treaty, signed in 1921, gave Poland much of the land it claimed.

The New Economic Policy. By 1921, seven years of war, revolution, civil war, and invasion had exhausted Russia. During the civil war alone, more than 20 million Russians had died in epidemics, in the fighting, or of starvation. Agricultural and industrial production had fallen disastrously. A million Russians, many of them skilled and educated, had left the country. The people's discontent broke out in new peasant uprisings, in workers' strikes, and in a sailors' revolt at the Kronstadt naval base near Petrograd.

In 1921, Lenin established the New Economic Policy (NEP) to strengthen the country. This program replaced many of the socialist measures started earlier. Small industries and retail trade were allowed to operate under their own control. The peasants no longer had to give most of their farm products to the government. They could sell freely to customers after paying a tax. The government kept control of heavy industry, the transportation and banking systems, and foreign trade. The economy recovered steadily under the NEP, though the Communists disliked its nonsocialist features.

Formation of the U.S.S.R. In December, 1922, the Communist government established the Union of Soviet Socialist Republics (U.S.S.R.). The union consisted of four *union republics*—the Russian Soviet Federated Socialist Republic (Russian Republic), Byelorussia, Transcaucasia, and the Ukraine. The first republic formed after the Bolshevik revolution, the Russian Republic, has always been the largest and most powerful one.

During the 1920's, three other union republics were established—Tadzhikistan, Turkmenistan, and Uzbekistan. In 1936, Transcaucasia was divided into Azerbaidzhan, Armenia, and Georgia. Kazakhstan and Kirghizia also became union republics in 1936. In 1940, during World War II, Russia gained the union republics of Estonia, Latvia, Lithuania, and Moldavia.

From Lenin to Stalin. Lenin became seriously ill in 1922. A struggle for power developed among members of the *Politburo* (Political Bureau), the policy-making body of the Communist party's Central Committee. Leon Trotsky ranked after Lenin in power. But the next two most important members of the Politburo—Lev Kamenev and Grigori Zinoviev—joined forces to oppose Trotsky. They chose Joseph Stalin to be their partner. Stalin had become general secretary of the party in 1922. See Stalin, Joseph.

After Lenin died in 1924, leading Communists held three different views on how far Russian socialism should go, and also on the need for world revolution. (1) Trotsky and his followers believed in immediately promoting both full socialism in Russia and world revolution. Kamenev and Zinoviev shared this view. (2) A group led by Nicholas Bukharin agreed with Trotsky that Russian socialism depended on world revolution. But Bukharin felt that Russia should continue Lenin's temporary program of weakened socialism because other countries were not ready for revolution. (3) Stalin and his followers agreed with Bukharin's economic policies at first. But they believed that Russian socialism could succeed without world revolution.

Stalin's power in the Communist party grew rapidly. As general secretary, he had the support of the local party secretaries, whose careers depended on his approval. Stalin built up this following carefully behind the scenes. Stalinist groups became stronger at the party *congresses* (meetings), which elected the top Communist bodies and approved Communist programs.

Stalin defeated his rivals one by one. Trotsky lost power in 1925. Stalin then joined the Bukharin group to expel Kamenev and Zinoviev, his former partners, from the party. At the 15th Communist Party Congress in December, 1927, Stalin won a sweeping victory. By then, Stalin, like Trotsky, urged full socialism. The congress adopted measures to begin Stalin's economic program the next year. In 1929, Stalin removed Bukharin and his followers from power. They signed a statement, ordered by Stalin, admitting that Stalin's economic views were correct and theirs were wrong. Stalin had become dictator of the Soviet Union.

Planned Economy. By the mid-1920's, Lenin's New Economic Policy had served its purpose. All factories and other means of production that had closed during the civil war were operating again. Russia's agricultural and industrial production had increased above pre-World War I levels. However, the prices of manufactured consumer goods were rising faster than the prices of farm products. As a result, the peasants held back their grain and other products.

Stalin then proposed the First Five-Year Plan. This socialist program had two major goals. First, the small peasant farms would be combined into large *kolkhozy* (collective farms) controlled by the government. Second, the production of such heavy-industry products as chemicals, construction materials, machine tools, and steel would be expanded rapidly. The 15th Communist Party Congress approved these goals, and the *Gosplan* (State Planning Commission) worked out the details. The First Five-Year Plan started in 1928, and the government began taking over private businesses.

Stalin forced the collective farmers to give most of their products to the government. These products were needed to supply raw materials to industry, to feed the people of the growing manufacturing centers, and to pay for imported machinery. The peasants opposed being forced to join collective farms, and destroyed much of their livestock and crops in protest. As punishment, Stalin sent several million peasant families to prison labor camps in Siberia and Soviet Central Asia during the early 1930's. Farm production lagged, but Soviet industries expanded rapidly.

The Great Purge. Many Russians opposed Stalin's policies during the mid-1930's. To crush this opposition, Stalin began a program of terror called the Great Purge. His secret police arrested millions of persons. Neighbors and even members of the same family spied on one another. Fear spread throughout Russia. Stalin eliminated all real or suspected threats to his power by having the prisoners shot or sent to labor camps. The victims included thousands of Communists. Some were party members Stalin had defeated during his rise to power. Many were old Bolsheviks who had been associated with Lenin. Others were officers of the Red Army.

Stalin staged "trials" at which arrested Communist leaders were forced to confess to "crimes against the people." Most of these *purge trials* took place from 1936 to 1938. Stalin replaced the party leaders he eliminated with young Stalinists he could trust. The secret police enforced strict loyalty to Stalin's policies on all levels of life. Stalin controlled everything that was published, taught, or publicly spoken.

Foreign Policy Before World War II. In 1919, Lenin had established the *Comintern* (Communist International) as part of the world Communist movement. Through this organization, Lenin hoped to control Communist parties in other countries and to promote world revolution. But he feared attack by the more powerful Western, non-Communist countries. Lenin became especially fearful after these nations aided the Whites during the Russian civil war. As a result, Soviet leaders put aside the movement for world revolution during the early and mid-1920's. They concentrated on developing friendly relations with other nations. Their immediate goals were to avoid attack and to strengthen Russia through foreign trade.

The First Five-Year Plan (1928-1932) expanded Russia's economy. These new tractors were supplied for farms near Moscow.
P.I.P.

During the late 1920's, Russia became more active in the world Communist movement. But soon Russia's fear of attack again became the major concern of Soviet foreign policy. Russia felt itself threatened by two events. First came the Japanese invasion of China in 1931. Second, and even more threatening to Russia, was the rise of Adolf Hitler in Germany. Hitler became dictator of Germany in 1933, and one of his major programs was to destroy Communism. This threat led the Soviet Union to sign many military and political agreements with the Western democracies. In 1934, Russia joined the League of Nations as further protection against invasion by Germany (see LEAGUE OF NATIONS). Soviet leaders also ordered Communists throughout the world to combine with political parties in other countries. These combined groups, called *popular fronts*, opposed the growing parties that supported Hitler.

But Russia still feared and suspected the Western democracies. Stalin felt that various agreements among the Western powers were attempts to strengthen Germany against Russia. In 1938, France, Germany, Great Britain, and Italy signed the Munich Agreement. This agreement forced Czechoslovakia to give much of its land to Germany. See MUNICH AGREEMENT.

German expansion in Europe continued, and war between Germany and the Western powers seemed likely. Probably to escape the war, Russia signed an agreement with Germany on Aug. 23, 1939. This agreement provided that neither nation would attack the other. The two countries agreed secretly that each could conquer various territories without interference from the other. Russia and Germany also agreed secretly to divide Poland between themselves.

World War II began when Hitler's troops invaded Poland from the west on Sept. 1, 1939. Two days later, France and Great Britain declared war on Germany. Russia invaded Poland from the east on Sept. 17, 1939. The Russians, claiming they had to "protect" their borders, soon occupied the region. Also to "protect" their borders, the Russians attacked Finland on November 30. In December, Russia was expelled from the League of Nations for this attack. Russia won much Finnish territory by March, 1940, when Finland surrendered. See RUSSO-FINNISH WARS.

In June, 1940, the Red Army moved into Bessarabia (then part of Romania) and the Baltic countries of Estonia, Latvia, and Lithuania. Russia had lost all these lands after World War I, and now took them back. In August, 1940, the three Baltic countries became separate republics of the U.S.S.R., and Bessarabia became part of the new Moldavian Soviet Socialist Republic.

On June 22, 1941, what the Russians had long feared

took place. A huge German force invaded Russia. The German attack pushed back the heavily outnumbered Red Army. German warplanes destroyed much of the Russian air force, and Hitler's tanks and troops drove deep into Soviet territory. In September, the Germans captured Kiev and attacked Leningrad (formerly Petrograd). By December, the Germans came close to Moscow. The attack on Leningrad lasted until January, 1944, when the Germans were finally driven off.

Great Britain and the other Western Allies welcomed Russia as a partner in the war against Germany. Britain, Canada, and the United States began shipping supplies to Russia. The United States joined the Allies in December, 1941, after the Japanese attack on Pearl Harbor. The supplies sent to Russia by the Allies included billions of dollars' worth of food, raw materials, planes, tanks, and trucks.

The Germans were not prepared for the bitter Russian winter. By early 1942, the Russians had driven them back from the Moscow area and some other battlegrounds. The five-month Battle of Stalingrad (now Volgograd), during the winter of 1942-1943, was a major turning point in the war. By the time the Germans surrendered, about 350,000 of their troops had been killed or captured. See STALINGRAD, BATTLE OF.

After the victory at Stalingrad, the Red Army advanced steadily across Eastern Europe and into eastern Germany. As the Russians swept across Eastern Europe, they freed many countries from German control, including Czechoslovakia, Hungary, Poland, and Romania. In April, 1945, Soviet troops began to attack Berlin. Red Army units joined forces with United States troops at Torgau on the Elbe River. Berlin fell to the Russians on May 2, and Germany surrendered to the Allies on May 7. The war in Europe was over.

More than 20 million Russian servicemen and servicewomen were killed or wounded in World War II. No other country suffered so many military casualties. In addition, millions of Russian civilians died, whole regions of Russia lay in ruins, and much of the Soviet economy was shattered.

In February, 1945, Stalin had met with President Franklin D. Roosevelt of the United States and Prime Minister Winston Churchill of Great Britain at Yalta in Russia. At this conference, Stalin promised to help in the war against Japan (see YALTA CONFERENCE). On August 6, the United States dropped on Japan the first atomic bomb used in warfare. Two days later, Russia declared war on Japan and invaded Japanese-held Manchuria and Korea. The Russians occupied Manchuria for eight months and took nearly a billion dollars' worth of industrial machinery from the region. Japan's surrender to the Allies on Sept. 2, 1945, marked the end of World War II. For the story of Russia in the war, see WORLD WAR II.

The Cold War. During World War II, Stalin had promised Roosevelt and Churchill to help promote freedom throughout the world. After the war, however, Russia cooperated with its Allies only in dividing Berlin and the rest of Germany into occupation zones. East-West relations in Germany soon became tense. Russia set up a Communist police state in its zone, and blocked Western efforts to unite Germany. See GERMANY (After World War II).

Red Army units remained in the Eastern European countries that they had freed from German control. The Red Army helped establish Communist governments in these nations. The Russians used terrorist methods, such as arresting anti-Communists, bringing them to "trial," and shooting them as "fascists."

The Communists in Eastern European countries formed what seemed to be *coalition* governments. In such governments, two or more political parties share power. But the Communists, supported by Russia, seized important government positions and held the real power. Their strength grew, and they did not permit free elections. By early 1948, Russia controlled seven countries in Eastern Europe. These *satellite* countries were Albania, Bulgaria, Czechoslovakia, Hungary, Poland, Romania, and Yugoslavia. Russia also controlled its East German occupation zone, which surrounded West Berlin. The Russians promised the Western powers freedom to move through East Germany to West Berlin. In June, 1948, however, the Russians blocked all land and water routes to West Berlin. The Western powers then flew food and other supplies to West Berlin daily. The Russians lifted the blockade in May, 1949. See BERLIN AIRLIFT.

Russia cut off nearly all contacts between its satellites and the West. The Soviet barriers against communication, trade, and travel came to be known as the *Iron Curtain*. Extreme distrust grew between East and West. An East-West struggle called the *Cold War* spread through Europe and many other regions of the world. For the story of this struggle, see the article on COLD WAR.

Soviet expansion forced the Western nations to act. In 1947, the United States sent military and economic aid to Greece and Turkey. This aid helped prevent Communists from making those countries Soviet satellites. In 1948, the United States began the Marshall Plan to provide aid to help rebuild war-torn European countries. Russia did not allow its satellites to receive the aid. The West also formed a military union called the North Atlantic Treaty Organization (NATO) for defense against possible Communist attack. See MARSHALL PLAN; NORTH ATLANTIC TREATY ORGANIZATION.

Russia, in turn, strengthened the Communist nations

The Battle of Stalingrad was a turning point in World War II. The Russians defeated attacking Germans in the five-month fight.

Pix from Publix

in the Cold War. In 1947, it established the *Cominform* (Communist Information Bureau) to spread Soviet policies in the satellites. In 1948, however, Yugoslavia broke away from Soviet control (see YUGOSLAVIA [History]). In 1949, Russia set up COMECON (Council for Mutual Economic Assistance) to bring the economies of the satellites under greater control. In 1955, the Warsaw Pact provided for military unity among Russia and its satellites (see WARSAW PACT).

From Stalin to Khrushchev. Russia's rapid industrialization continued after World War II under new five-year plans. Restrictions on the workers and peasants, which had been loosened somewhat during the war, again became severe. For example, workers could not quit or change their jobs without government permission. The collective farms were reorganized and made much larger. Stalin also began a new wave of political arrests and executions. Then, on March 5, 1953, Stalin died after a stroke.

No one man immediately replaced Stalin. A *collective leadership* made up of several men ruled the Soviet Union. For almost two years, Georgi M. Malenkov held the major leadership as premier, or chairman of the Council of Ministers. During this period, a struggle for power developed among Malenkov and other leading Communists. Nikita S. Khrushchev became head of the Communist party in September, 1953 (see KHRUSHCHEV, NIKITA S.). Also that year, Lavrenti P. Beria, chief of the secret police, was executed secretly on charges of plotting to seize power.

Khrushchev's strength increased steadily, and Malenkov was forced to resign in 1955. Nikolai A. Bulganin became premier, but Khrushchev held the real power. At a closed session of the 20th Communist Party Congress in 1956, Khrushchev bitterly criticized Stalin. He accused Stalin of murdering many innocent people and of faulty leadership.

RUSSIA IN WORLD WAR II

Territory Gained by Russia

Farthest Advance of German Forces

Farthest Advance of Russian Forces

Present Boundary of Russia

0 Miles 1,000 2,000

0 Kilometers 2,000 3,000

WORLD BOOK map-FGA

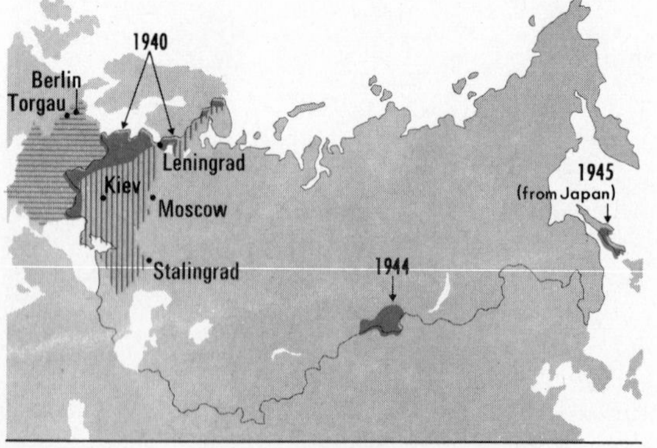

Khrushchev almost lost power in 1957. Following anti-Communist revolts in Hungary and Poland in 1956, Khrushchev's powerful rivals demanded that he resign. But he took the matter before the party's Central Committee, which included many of his followers. Through the committee, Khrushchev defeated his enemies and forced them to lose all positions of power. In 1958, Khrushchev became premier and also remained party leader.

To strengthen his position further, Khrushchev repeated his attacks on Stalin openly at the 22nd Communist Party Congress in 1961. Buildings, cities, and towns named for Stalin were renamed. Pictures and statues of Stalin were destroyed. The government removed Stalin's body from its place of honor in Lenin's tomb in Moscow, and buried it in a simple grave nearby.

Khrushchev's Policies differed greatly from Stalin's. The secret police did not spread terror, and the government allowed somewhat freer political discussion. The workweek was shortened to about 40 hours, and workers were allowed to quit or change their jobs. Khrushchev also tried to raise the nation's standard of living. Government industrial planning aimed for greater production of clothing, food, household appliances, and other consumer goods. But gains were slow.

Russia's relations with the West improved after Stalin's death. Unlike other Communist leaders, Khrushchev denied that war with the West was necessary for Communism to triumph throughout the world. In 1956, Khrushchev announced a policy of *peaceful coexistence*. He described this policy as avoiding war while competing with the West in the fields of science and economic development. Khrushchev loosened restrictions on communication, trade, and travel across the Iron Curtain. He made friendly visits to several Western countries, including the United States. But Russia still tried to expand its influence by encouraging revolts, riots, and strikes in non-Communist countries.

Communist China believed that war with the West was necessary, and strongly criticized Russia's "soft" policy. A bitter split developed between the two major Communist powers. Their dispute reached a climax at the 22nd Communist Party Congress in Moscow in 1961. The Chinese premier, Chou En-lai, suddenly left the congress and returned to China. Albania, a Russian satellite, supported China, and Russia ended relations with Albania.

Russia took an early lead over the United States in exploring space. Under Khrushchev, the Soviet Union spent huge sums to develop powerful launching rockets. On Oct. 4, 1957, Russia launched *Sputnik I*, the first spacecraft to circle the earth. This achievement marked the beginning of the space age. In 1961, Yuri A. Gagarin, a Russian air force officer, became the first man to orbit the earth. See SPACE TRAVEL (Steps in the Conquest of Space).

The Spy Plane and Cuba. Khrushchev and President Dwight D. Eisenhower of the United States scheduled a meeting in Paris in May, 1960, with British and French leaders. Shortly before the meeting began, the Russians shot down an American U-2 plane over Soviet territory. The pilot, Francis Gary Powers, confessed that he had been spying. Eisenhower admitted that U-2 planes had been taking photographs over Russia for four years. When the Paris meeting began, Khrushchev demanded that Eisenhower apologize. The President refused, and Khrushchev angrily left the conference. The meeting broke up the next day.

Another Cold War crisis occurred in October, 1962. The United States learned that Russia had built and equipped missile bases in Cuba. These bases could have launched atomic attacks against the United States or other parts of the Western Hemisphere. President John F. Kennedy ordered a naval blockade of Cuba to prevent more Russian missiles from reaching the island. He also demanded that Russia remove all the missiles and missile bases. Khrushchev met these demands. See CUBA (The Cuban Crisis).

Khrushchev's Fall from Power. In 1963, Russia, the United States, and Great Britain signed a treaty prohibiting all nuclear weapons tests except those conducted underground. Also in 1963, Russia and the United States set up a direct teletype connection called the *hot line* between Moscow and Washington, D.C. They hoped it would help prevent any misunderstanding from leading to war. In 1964, Russia, the United States, and Great Britain agreed to reduce their production of materials for nuclear weapons.

Although Khrushchev improved Russia's relations with the West, many of his other policies failed. His farm program collapsed, and in 1963 Russia had to buy more than 10 million tons of wheat from the West. Soviet industrialization slowed down. The economy also suffered because the people refused to buy many poorly made products. In addition, the split with China and Khrushchev's withdrawal of the missiles from Cuba drew sharp criticism from many Soviet leaders. On Oct. 15, 1964, pressure from high-ranking Communists forced Khrushchev to retire. He was replaced by Leonid I. Brezhnev as head of the Communist party, and Aleksei N. Kosygin as premier (see BREZHNEV, LEONID I.; KOSYGIN, ALEKSEI N.).

Russia Today is still the leading Communist power, but the Communist world is no longer united behind the Soviet Union. The bitter dispute with China has become a struggle for influence over other Communist nations and over newly independent countries, especially those in Africa. Albania's support of China's growing power in the Communist world continued into the late 1960's. Russia also is losing some control over its satellites, especially Czechoslovakia, Poland, and Romania. But these countries are far from making a complete break from Soviet control.

In 1965, Brezhnev and Kosygin reorganized Russia's economy. Factories were put on a profit basis. Government supervision of the factories was taken from regional agencies and given to federal bodies under the Council of Ministers. (For a discussion of these changes, see the *Manufacturing* section of this article.) A new five-year plan eliminated Khrushchev's impractical goals, such as producing more than the United States by 1970. New goals included increasing industrial production by half, the people's income by a third, and farm production by a fourth. This five-year plan, unlike earlier ones, placed almost as much importance on consumer goods as on heavy-industry products. It was approved by the 23rd Communist Party Congress in 1966.

During the mid-1960's, the Vietnam War endangered the improved Soviet-U.S. relations. American forces aided South Vietnamese troops against the Communists of North and South Vietnam. Russia sent the Communists surface-to-air missiles and other weapons. See VIETNAM WAR.

The fear of nuclear war has probably kept Russia from a major clash with the West. Soviet leaders appear to believe that Russia can win worldwide power by doing better than the West economically, politically, and scientifically. They hope Soviet advances will attract other nations to Russia's side in the Cold War.

In 1966, the Soviet Union played an important part in ending a war between India and Pakistan. The two nations had been at war over an old border dispute. Kosygin invited the leaders of both countries to Russia, and helped them reach a peace agreement.

Russian scientists scored three more firsts in space in 1966. A Soviet spacecraft made a soft landing on the moon. Another Russian spacecraft reached the planet Venus, and a third was put into orbit around the moon.

Also in 1966, Russia shocked much of the world by imprisoning two Russian writers who had criticized Soviet life. Their books had been published in Western countries. The writers, Andrei Sinyavsky and Yuli Daniel, were sentenced to long terms in a prison labor camp.

WILLIAM B. BALLIS, MORRIS BORNSTEIN, DEMING BROWN, GEORGE KISH, WILLIAM K. MEDLIN, and ARTHUR P. MENDEL

Weston Kemp

Soviet Spacemen are honored in a space exhibition near Moscow. The spacecraft on display is *Vostok I*, in which Yuri A. Gagarin, a Russian air force officer, became the first man to orbit the earth in 1961.

RUSSIA / *Study Aids*

Related Articles in World Book include:

Political and Military Leaders

Alexander (of Russia)
Beria, Lavrenti P.
Brezhnev, Leonid I.
Bulganin, Nikolai A.
Catherine
Furtseva, Ekaterina
Gromyko, Andrei A.
Ivan
Kaganovich, Lazar M.
Kalinin, Mikhail I.
Kerensky, Alexander F.
Khrushchev, Nikita S.
Konev, Ivan S.
Kosygin, Aleksei N.
Lenin
Litvinov, Maxim M.
Malenkov, Georgi M.
Mikoyan, Anastas
Molotov, Vyacheslav
Nicholas (of Russia)
Peter I, the Great
Plekhanov, Georgi V.
Rasputin, Grigori Y.
Rykov, Aleksei I.
Shepilov, Dmitri T.
Stalin, Joseph
Timoshenko, Semyon K.
Trotsky, Leon
Vishinsky, Andrei Y.
Vladimir I
Voroshilov, Kliment E.
Zhukov, Georgi K.

Cities

Archangel
Astrakhan
Baku
Dnepropetrovsk
Donetsk
Dushanbe
Gorki
Irkutsk
Kaliningrad
Kazan
Kharkov
Kiev
Kuybyshev
Leningrad
Lvov
Magnitogorsk
Minsk
Moscow
Murmansk
Novosibirsk
Odessa
Omsk
Rostov-on-Don
Samarkand
Saratov
Sevastopol
Smolensk
Sverdlovsk
Tashkent
Tiflis
Tobolsk
Vladivostok
Volgograd
Yalta
Yerevan

History

Berlin, Congress of
Bolshevik
Cold War
Crimean War
Czar
Duma
Genoa Conference
Hungary (History)
Mongol Empire
MVD
Paris, Treaties of
Poland (History)
Russo-Finnish Wars
Russo-Japanese War
Russo-Turkish Wars
Triple Entente
World War I
World War II

Physical Features

Alma River
Altai Mountains
Amu Darya
Amur River
Aral Sea
Azov, Sea of
Caspian Sea
Caucasus Mountains
Commander Islands
Dnepr River
Dneproges Dam
Dnestr River
Don River
Dvina River
Franz Josef Land
Irtysh River
Kamchatka Peninsula
Kara Kum
Kara Sea
Karelian Isthmus
Kuril Islands
Kyzyl Kum
Lake Balkhash
Lake Baykal
Lake Ilmen
Lake Ladoga
Lake Onega
Lake Peipus
Lena River
Merv
Mount Elbrus
Neman River
Neva River
Novaya Zemlya
Ob River
Oka River
Okhotsk, Sea of
Sakhalin
Severnaya Zemlya
Stanovoy Mountains
Syr Darya
Ural Mountains
Ural River
Volga River
White Sea
Wrangel Island
Yablonovyy Mountains
Yenisey River

Regions

Bessarabia
Bucovina
Caucasia
Crimea
Daghestan
Galicia
Karelia
Ruthenia
Siberia
Turkestan
Tuva

Union Republics

See the separate article on each union republic listed in the *Russia Map Index*.

Products and Industry

For Russia's rank among other countries in production, see the following articles:

Agriculture
Aluminum
Barley
Cattle
Cheese
Coal
Copper
Corn
Cotton
Electric Power
Fishing Industry
Flax
Forest and Forest Products
Gas (fuel)
Gold
Horse
Iron and Steel
Lead
Lumber
Manganese
Nickel
Oats
Paper
Petroleum
Platinum
Potato
Rubber
Rye
Salmon
Salt
Sheep
Ship and Shipping
Silver
Sugar
Sugar Beet
Tea
Tin
Tobacco
Tungsten
Vegetable
Wheat
Wine
Zinc

Other Related Articles

Clothing (color picture)
Communism
Cossack
Dancing (Ballet)
Eastern Orthodox Churches
Five-Year Plan
Flag (color picture, Historical Flags)
Government (Comparing Democracy and Communism)
Iron Curtain
Kremlin
Politburo
Ruble
Russian Language
Russian Literature
Slav
Soviet
Tass
Warsaw Pact

Outline

I. Government
II. People
- A. Nationalities and Languages
- B. Religion

III. Way of Life
- A. Personal Freedom
- B. City Life
- C. Village Life
- D. Family Life
- E. Recreation

IV. Education
- A. Elementary Grades
- B. Intermediate Grades
- C. Secondary Grades
- D. Special Schools
- E. Higher Education
- F. After-School Activities
- G. Libraries
- H. Museums

V. Communication
VI. Arts
- A. Architecture
- B. Literature
- C. Music
- D. Painting
- E. Theater and Ballet

VII. The Land
- A. Land Regions
- B. Rivers and Lakes

VIII. Climate
IX. Economy
- A. Natural Resources
- B. Manufacturing
- C. Agriculture
- D. Mining
- E. Forest Products
- F. Fishing
- G. Electric Power
- H. Foreign Trade
- I. Transportation

X. History

Questions

What is the longest nonstop airline route in the world?
What led to the Russian-Chinese dispute of the 1960's?
What Russian achievement started the space age?
What were some ways in which Russian life differed under Joseph Stalin and under Nikita S. Khrushchev?
How does the Komsomol serve Communism?
How did Soviet factory operations change in 1965?
Why does foreign trade play only a small part in the economy of Russia?
What is the largest inland body of water in the world?
Why is it so important for Russian schoolchildren to receive high marks in behavior?
Who planned the October Revolution of 1917?

Section Five

This section lists important words to be included in the 1967 edition of THE WORLD BOOK DICTIONARY. This dictionary, first published by Field Enterprises Educational Corporation in 1963, keeps abreast of our living language with a program of continuous editorial revision.

The Dictionary Supplement

The following supplement has been prepared under the direction of the editors of THE WORLD BOOK and Clarence L. Barnhart, editor in chief of THE WORLD BOOK DICTIONARY. It is presented as a service to owners of the dictionary and as an informative feature to subscribers of THE WORLD BOOK YEAR BOOK.

A

Ab·i·tur (äb′i tůr′), *n. German.* a final examination given to secondary school students, passage of which authorizes matriculation in a university.

ABM (no periods), antiballistic missile.

ab·sci·sin (ab sī′zin), *n.* a hormone that regulates abscission in cotton plants: *Abscisin is the first material known to promote leaf and fruit drop.* [< *abscis*(sion) + *-in*]

ac·e·tyl·cho·lin·es·ter·ase (as′ə təl kō′lə nes′tə rās, -kol′ə-), *n.* cholinesterase: *Acetylcholinesterase is an enzyme that inactivates acetylcholine* (Scientific American).

aer·o·train (ãr′ə trān′), *n.* a high-speed train that combines the air-cushion element of the hovercraft and the single-rail feature of the monorail: *The aerotrain* [will] *provide rapid transportation between cities that are too close for economic air travel* (Time).

à go-go (ə gō′gō), *Slang.* go-go: . . . *hostess à go-go of Arthur, Manhattan discothèque* (Time). [< French *à go-go*]

air·boat (ãr′bōt′), *n.* a small boat driven by an airplane propeller mounted on the boat and revolving in the air: *Skim through the Everglades in an airboat* (New Yorker).

Alaska Standard Time, the standard time in central Alaska, two hours behind Pacific Standard Time.

a·le·a·tor·ic (ā′li ə tôr′ik, -tor′-), *adj. Music.* consisting of random or chance elements: *Aleatoric music is that in which the instrumentalists have complete leeway . . . to finish the thoughts of the composer* (New York Times). [< Latin *āleātōrius* aleatory + English *-ic*]

all-up weight (ôl′up′), *Especially British.* the gross weight of an aircraft.

ANF (no periods) or **A.N.F.,** Atlantic Nuclear Force (a proposed military force equipped with nuclear weapons under the command of NATO): *The virtual eclipse of MLF leaves . . . ANF the outstanding proposal for solving the problem of organising NATO's nuclear forces* (Manchester Guardian Weekly).

An·glo·phone (ang′glə fōn), *n.* an English-speaking inhabitant of a bilingual or multilingual country: "*Quebec's Anglophones behave like the British in one of their African colonies*" (Harper's). [< French *anglophone* < *anglo-* Anglo- + *-phone* -phone]

an·ti-art (an′ti ärt′), *n.* any form of art that rejects standard artistic or aesthetic concepts, values, etc.; nonart: *It was not surprising that Miró . . . joined the anti-art iconoclasm of the Dadaists* (Observer).

an·ti·pov·er·ty (an′ti pov′ər ti), *adj.* designed to combat poverty; organized to help the poor, especially in depressed areas: *The new act authorizes the expenditure of $947 million . . . to be spent on antipoverty projects* (Observer). *-n.* an antipoverty program, campaign, or organization.

a·près-ski (à pre skē′), *adv., adj., n. French.* —*adv., adj.* after skiing: *après-ski wear.* —*n.* after skiing activity.

aq·ua·naut (ak′wə nôt), *n.* an underwater explorer: *The experiment proved that aquanauts could live and work for long periods of time hundreds of feet below the surface* (Time). [< *aqua* + *-naut,* as in *astronaut*]

ar·gy-bar·gy (är′gi bär′gi), *n. Informal.* noisy dispute; bickering, wrangling: . . . *constant interrogation, argy-bargy and palaver* (Punch). [reduplication and alteration of *argue*]

a·ri·bo·fla·vi·no·sis ā′rī bō flā′və-nō′sis), *n.* a condition caused by insufficient riboflavin in the diet.

B

balance of nature, a balanced condition existing in the animal and plant population of a region when relatively few changes occur in the environment.

bar chart, a chart or graph representing different quantities by bars of different lengths; bar graph.

be·low-the-line (bi lō′ᴛʜə līn′), *adj.* (in a financial statement) indicating an out-of-the-ordinary revenue or expense: *a below-the-line expenditure on aid.*

Ber·ing Standard Time (bir′ing, bãr′-), the standard time in the extreme western portion of Alaska, three hours behind Pacific Standard Time.

big bang theory, a theory which maintains that the universe originated in a cosmic explosion of hydrogen, which became condensed into the galaxies: *Quasi-stellar blue galaxies may . . . confirm the big bang theory of the origin of the universe* (Science News Letter).

black humor, a type of fictional writing characterized by bizarrely or morbidly humorous plots and descriptions: *Some writers, of course, take up black humor for just one novel* (Time).

bleep (blēp), *n.* a sharp, short sound issued as a signal; beep. *-v.i.* to emit such a sound: *One sits listening to . . . the bleeping of the satellites* (Punch). [imitative]

Blooms·bur·y (blümz′bėr i, -bri), *adj.* of or having to do with a literary and intellectual circle formed in the Bloomsbury section of London after World War I: *Real luster derived from England's . . . Bloomsbury group: Lytton Strachey, Virginia Woolf, John Maynard Keynes, E. M. Forster, Clive Bell* (Atlantic).

bludge (bluj), *Australian Slang. v.,* **bludged, bludg·ing,** *n. -v.i.* to avoid work or one's share of work. *-n.* an easy job.

blue galaxy, an extragalactic body brighter than a quasar: *Both the blue galaxies and the quasars* [are] *apparently stages in the . . . development of a normal galaxy, such as our own mature Milky Way* (New Yorker).

bon·kers (bong′kərz), *adj. British Slang.* crazy; mad.

C

camp (kamp), *adj., n., pl.* **camp.** *Slang. -adj.* given to or admiring things formerly considered trivial, unsophisticated, lowbrow, etc.: *You have camp taste if you can discuss authoritatively the early . . . comic books* (Saturday Night). *-n.* anything formerly (but no longer) considered trivial, unsophisticated, etc.: *Turn-of-the-century postcards are camp; so is . . . the 1933 movie King Kong* (Time).

car·nap·er (kär′nap ər), *n.* (in the Philippines) a person who steals a car or cars: *Carnapers . . . broke into his garage and drove off with a jeep* (Manila Chronicle). [< *car* + *-naper,* as in *kidnaper*]

catch-up (kach′up′), *adj.* helping to overtake or keep up with something: *There was catch-up buying following the strike* (New York Times). *Project Head Start provides catch-up preschool education* (Time).

cer·a·top·si·an (ser′ə top′si ən), *n.* any of a group of herbivorous dinosaurs of the Cretaceous period, including the triceratops. [< Greek *kéras, -ātos* horn + *ōps* face + -ian]

chan·son·nier (shäɴ sô nyā′), *n. French.* a songwriter or singer, especially of popular songs.

charmed circle, any very select or exclusive group: *No outsiders broke into the charmed circle of the annual Assembly* (Manchester Guardian Weekly).

chi·ack (chī′ək), *v.t. Australian Slang.* to jeer at; tease. [probably alteration of *cheek,* verb]

chu·kar (chə kär′), *n.* a gray and reddish-brown Asian partridge, common in southeastern Asia and Europe, and now a game bird in the Pacific Northwest.

cis·tron (sis′tron), *n.* the smallest unit of genetic material producing a phenotypic effect. [< *cis* + *-tron,* probably suggested by *electron*]

citizens band, *U.S.* a radio transmitting channel for general public use: *Component kits for citizens band radio* [are] *available at varying prices depending on the sets* (Science News Letter).

civil right·er (rī′tər), *U.S. Informal.* an advocate or champion of civil rights: *Civil righters were set to boycott schools in protest against de facto segregation* (Time).

co·don (kō′don), *n. Biology.* **1.** a sequence of three chemical units or bases in protein synthesis, represented in the genetic code by a three-letter code word: *Codon after codon in the messenger RNA . . . adds the attached appropriate amino acid in the right sequence to the growing protein molecule* (New Scientist). **2.** the three-letter code word: *Each of the 20 different amino acids . . . is represented by one or more three-letter words, or codons* (Scientific American).

COFO (no periods), Council of Federated Organizations (an association of the major civil-rights organizations in the United States, formed in 1964).

com·put·er·i·za·tion (kəm pū′tər ə zā′shən), *n.* the act or process of computerizing: *The government is able . . . to encourage computer use not only in its own offices and laboratories, but also by setting an example of the advantages of computerization* (New Scientist).

computer language, machine language: *When someone wishes to solve a problem, he defines the problem in computer language–a combination of letters, numbers, . . . and mathematical symbols* (Time).

con·scious·ness-ex·pand·ing (kon′shəs nis ek span′ding), *adj.* (of a psychodelic substance or drug) producing a mental state of extremely intensified awareness or perception: *consciousness-expanding chemicals.*

conspicuous consumption, the ostentatious use or display of wealth as a status symbol in society.

conversation pit, *U.S.* a sunken or recessed area in or near a living room for entertaining.

cop-out (kop′out′), *n. Slang.* **1.** a failure or loss: *It* [the play] *sounded like the worst possible cop-out* (Punch). **2.** a plea of guilty to the lesser of several charges: *One goal is to do away with the need for a lengthy trial by producing a fast guilty plea–a "cop-out"* (Time). **3.** an avoidance of something difficult or painful.

copying machine, any machine that makes copies of written, typed, printed, or drawn material quickly and cheaply, such as the duplicator, photocopier, etc.

Cré·di·tiste (krā dē tēst′), *n. French.* (in Canada) a member of the Quebec wing of the Social Credit Party.

cry·o·sur·ger·y (krī′ō sėr′jər i), *n.* surgery utilizing extremely low temperatures to destroy or remove diseased tissue; cryogenic surgery: *Cryosurgery has been used in such eye operations as retinal detachments, cataracts and glaucoma* (Science News Letter). [< Greek *krýos* cold + English *surgery*]

cu·bane (kū′bān), *n.* a hydrocarbon whose carbon atoms are joined in the shape of a cube: *The first successful synthesis of cubane . . . paved the way to an extensive study of the chemistry of boxlike molecular structures* (London Times). [< *cub*(e) + *-ane*]

Cui·se·naire rods (kwiz′ə nãr′), wooden rods of various related sizes and colors, used in teaching arithmetic: *Six-year-olds . . . do fractions with Cuisenaire rods* (Saturday Night). [< French *Cuisenaire,* a proper name]

CVA (no periods) or **C.V.A.** or **c.v.a.,** cerebrovascular accident.

D

day-care (dā′kãr′), *adj. U.S.* of or for the daytime care of preschool children: *Day-care centers are clearly needed for those mothers who want to work* (Harper's).

de·beak (dē bēk′), *v.t., v.i.* to remove the beak of a bird. [< *de-* + *beak*]

de·cou·page or **dé·cou·page** (dā′kü päzh′), *n.* **1.** a picture made by pasting paper cutouts together. **2.** the art of making such pictures. [< French *découpage* < *decouper* cut out]

de-es·ca·late (dē es′kə lāt), *v.t., v.i.,* **-lat·ed, -lat·ing.** to reverse growth or expansion; reduce or diminish something automatically: *They would certainly like to de-escalate the Vietnam conflict* (London Times).

de·ne·go·ti·ate (dē′ni gō′shi āt), *v.t.,* **-at·ed, -at·ing.** to negotiate the breaking of (an agreement): *The French took pains to denegotiate the accord* (New York Times).

de·vein (dē vān′), *v.t.* to remove the vein of (a shrimp) after shelling it: *Other fancy seafoods at Seabergh's are Peeled Deveined Shrimp and Cooked Alaskan King Crabmeat* (New York Times).

differential analyzer, an analogue computer used to solve differential equations.

dill (dil), *n. Australian Slang.* a simpleton; gull; a gullible person.

dirty word, 1. a coarse or obscene word. **2.** anything vile or contemptible; an evil: *The steel industry is still under the threat of nationalization and . . . profits are considered a dirty word by many* (London Times).

do-it-your·self·er (dü′it yər sel′fər), *n. Informal.* a handy person; person who does himself the work usually done by a handyman or professional: *Items come in aerosol cans for hobbyists and do-it-yourselfers* (Science News Letter).

domino theory, the political theory that if one country falls to an expansionist power, the next or neighboring countries will inevitably fall in turn: *The domino theory guided U.S. foreign policy . . . If Laos went, so, like a row of dominoes, would South Vietnam, Thailand and the rest of Southeast Asia* (Time).

dump·er (dum′pər), *n. Australian Informal.* in surfing, a large breaking wave.

dusty answer, a cold, unfeeling, or empty reaction or response: *He recalled many western attempts to get a genuine settlement but everyone . . . had been given a dusty answer* (London Times).

E

Early Bird, *Trademark.* an active communications satellite designed to relay microwave signals between North America and Europe: *Early Bird orbits the earth once every 24 hours, so it remains in one spot above the Atlantic Ocean at the Equator* (World Book Encyclopedia). Also called **Telstar.**

e·co·sphere (ē′kə sfir, ek′ə-), *n.* any region suitable for life; biosphere. [< *eco*(logical) + *sphere*]

educational park, *U.S.* a complex of public schools and colleges built in a large, parklike area within or on the outskirts of a city: *The Board of Education announced . . . that it would begin at once to establish two educational parks* (New York Times).

Einstein shift, a slight shift in the light spectrum of stars toward the red.

eld·er·care (el′dər kãr′), *n. U.S.* any program of medical care for persons over sixty-five years of age: *The association's own "eldercare" plan . . . seeks to subsidize with state and federal funds health insurance for poor persons aged over 65* (London Times).

ELDO (no periods), European Launcher Development Organization (a group of seven European countries engaged in a joint satellite development program).

ESRO (no periods), European Space Research Organization (a group of ten European countries engaged in joint space research).

ex·tra·ve·hic·u·lar (eks′trə vi hik′yə lər), *adj.* outside a vehicle in outer space; beyond an orbiting spacecraft: *Only by means of rendezvous, docking, and extravehicular activity can the astronauts venture onto the moon* (New York Times).

F

factory farming, a system of farming using many of the methods of a factory, especially in the processing of livestock: *Factory farming in the dairy industry is considered unlikely* (London Times).

fan·ta·size (fan′tə sīz), *v.,* **-sized, -siz·ing.** *–v.t.* to imagine; fancy: *For Genêt the theater is an instrument of the outcast's fantasized revenge* (Time). *–v.i.* to engage in fantastic speculation; daydream.

fit-up (fit′up′), *n. British.* **1.** a stage or other theatrical accessory fitted up for the occasion. **2.** a member of a traveling theatrical company using fit-ups.

flash distillation, a method of distilling salt water by heating it progressively in successive chambers of a distilling plant: *Flash distillation . . . is conceded to be the best method for converting sea water into fresh at present in operation* (London Times).

flip side, the reverse side of a phonograph record, especially the side with the less important or popular piece of recorded music: *"I'm Mad Again" . . . is the next-to-last number on the flip side of their first album* (New Yorker).

fran·glais or **Fran·glais** (fräng glā′), *n.* (usually in humorous use) French spoken with many English words and expressions: *Whatmough spoke eleven languages from Hittite to Franglais* (Time). *"Le forcing"* [*is*] *the Franglais term he uses for the overproduction of art works* (New Yorker). [< French *franglais;* blend of *français* French and *anglais* English]

PRONUNCIATION KEY: hat, āge, cãre, fär; let, ēqual, tėrm; it, īce; hot, ōpen, ôrder; oil, out; cup, pu̇t, rüle, ūse; child; long; thin; ᴛʜen; zh, measure; ə represents **a** in about, **e** in taken, **i** in pencil, **o** in lemon, **u** in circus.

free-float·ing (frē′flō′ting), *adj.* **1.** floating or moving without an attachment: *free-floating grass, a free-floating astronaut.* **2.** not established; unfounded; unproven: *a free-floating theory.* **3.** not bound or committed; independent.

front·lash (frunt′lash′), *n. U.S.* a reaction that offsets or reverses an unfavorable reaction: *The "frontlash" in support of President Johnson's civil rights stand had been far greater than the "backlash" of racial prejudice* (New York Times).

frug (früg), *n., v.,* **frugged, frugging.** *–n.* a rock'n'roll dance in which partners perform rhythmic movements of the hips, shoulders, and arms, usually without touching. *–v.i.* to dance the frug: *Nureyev . . . frugs as energetically as he does ballet leaps* (New York Times). [origin unknown] **–frug′ger,** *n.*

G

go-go (gō′gō), *adj. U.S. Slang.* of or having to do with a discothèque; characteristic of discothèques: *Go-go girls on little platforms did the Jerk* [a dance] (New York Times). *Youthful customers . . . buy the go-go clothes aimed at them* (Time). Also, **à go-go.** [probably reduplication of *go*]

good-oh or **good-o** (gu̇d′ō′), *interj. Australian Slang.* fine! excellent!

Group of Ten, a group comprising the major industrial and financial powers in the West: United States, Great Britain, France, West Germany, Italy, Japan, Canada, Belgium, Sweden, and Netherlands.

H

hang·tag (hang′tag′), *n.* a tag on a garment that identifies the fabric and tells how it should be treated: *Be sure you launder any wash-and-wear shirts as the hangtag directs* (Good Housekeeping).

heat of formation, the amount of heat released or absorbed in the formation of one mol of a compound from its constituent elements.

ho·lo·muu (hō′lō mü), *n. Hawaiian.* a fitted version of the muumuu.

Ho·mo hab·i·lis (hō′mō hab′ə-ləs), an extinct species of man whose fossil remains were discovered in the Olduvai Gorge, Tanganyika, in 1964: *Research on Homo habilis, a . . . species that lived in Africa almost two million years ago, will settle the dispute that this is an older human fossil than Telanthropus* (Science News Letter). [< Latin *homō habilis* skillful man]

hoʻo·ma·li·ma·li (hō′ō mä′lē mä′-lē), *n. Hawaiian.* flattery.

hu·i (hü′i), *n. Hawaiian.* **1.** a club; an association. **2.** a corporation.

hype (hīp), *v.t.,* **hyped, hyp·ing.** *Slang.* to stimulate artificially, as if with a hypodermic injection: *The Savannah Phillies . . . have been suffering lately at the gate, despite manful attempts to hype attendance with simulated Civil War battles* (New Yorker). [alteration of *hypo*]

hy·per·charge (hī′pər chärj′), *n. Nuclear Physics.* a physical property, analogous to the electric charge, assigned to strong interaction in the eightfold way theory of elementary particles: *Each . . . multiplet consists of several subgroups of particles having the same mass, hypercharge, and isotopic spin* (Science News Letter).

I

id·i·ot sa·vant (id′i ət sə vänt′; *French* ē dyō′ sà väɴ′), *Psychiatry.* a mentally retarded person who has a remarkable special skill: *Charles and George . . . two 24-year-old identical twins who cannot add two and two but can easily name the day, week and month as far ahead as 3500 A.D.* [*are*] *idiot savants* (Science News Letter). [< French *idiot savant* (literally) scholarly idiot]

im·mu·no·sup·pres·sive (i mū′-nō sə pres′iv), *adj.* suppressing immunity: *an immunosuppressive drug.*

i·mu (ē′mü), *n. Hawaiian.* a shallow pit used for cooking.

in·ter·cut (in′tər kut′), *v.t.,* **-cut, -cut·ting.** to interpose (a camera shot or scene) in a motion-picture sequence: *Scenes of old farmers and young boys . . . are intercut with shots of Franco's disciplined soldiers* (Time).

in·ter·val·ic (in′tər val′ik), *adj.* of or having to do with a musical interval or intervals: *I always compose as if it were in syllables, not with words. You might say I am an intervalic composer* (Igor Stravinsky).

J

jel·la·ba (jə lä′bə), *n.* djellaba: *. . . ordinary Muslim people of the country–men wearing the long woollen jellaba* (London Times).

jet setter, *U.S. Slang.* a member of café society: *After dusk, international jet setters in white dinner jackets brush shoulders . . . at the super-heated discothèque* (Time).

Job Corps, an agency of the U.S. government established in 1964 to provide training and work for unemployed youths between 16 and 21.

jump-cut (jump′kut′), *v.,* **-cut, -cut·ting,** *n.* —*v.i.* to intercut motion-picture shots or takes rapidly or abruptly: *He recklessly jump-cuts from scene to scene, using gimmicky transitions* (Time). *–n.* an act or instance of jump-cutting: *Were those jump-cuts for a purpose, or were they made necessary by the dubbing?* (Punch).

K

ka·ma·ai·na (kä′mä ī′nä), *n. Hawaiian.* a native-born or old resident of Hawaii.

Ken·ne·dy round (ken′ə di), a round of international trade and tariff negotiations aiming at a lowering of all tariffs, named after President John F. Kennedy, who sponsored the tariff-reducing Trade Expansion Act of 1962: *The main participants in the Kennedy round* [*met*] *at GATT headquarters* (London Times).

KGB (no periods) or **K.G.B.,** the official secret service agency of the Soviet Union, in charge of state security: *The author* [*Mr. Allen Dulles*] *goes into the interesting question of how the powerful Soviet central espionage agency, the KGB, recruits foreign agents* (Wall Street Journal). [< Russian *K*(*omissija*) *G*(*osudarstvennoj*) *B*(*ezopasnosti*) Commission of State Security]

kinetic art, 1. a form of abstract art concerned with the representation or suggestion of movement: *Kinetic art includes visual artifacts of three-dimensional or constructional type with mechanical motion . . . such as animated clockwork systems* (New Scientist). **2.** optical art: *Optical or kinetic art . . . takes in artists as diverse as Soto and Tingueley* (Manchester Guardian Weekly).

K-shell (kā′shel′), *n.* the innermost space, or lowest energy level occupied by the orbits of electrons around the nucleus of an atom.

L

la belle é·poque (lȧ bel′ ā pôk′), *French.* **1.** the period at the turn of the century: *The Ashenden series . . . are still unusually good spy stories, but now they seem overdressed, in the manner of la belle époque* (Saturday Night). **2.** (literally) the beautiful epoch.

la dol·ce vi·ta (lä dōl′chā vē′tä), *Italian.* the sweet life; dolce vita: *Existentialism . . . presents an escape from the morass of conformity, la dolce vita, boredom* (Harper's).

lash-up (lash′up′), *n.* anything put together hastily or offhand; an improvisation; makeshift: *This machine was somewhat of a lash-up of available equipment built on the chassis of a trailer fire-pump* (New Scientist).

lau·lau (lou′lou), *n. Hawaiian.* a dish of chopped taro leaves, meat, and fish wrapped in ti plane leaves and steamed.

lazy dog, *Slang.* a fragmentation bomb: *U.S. planes are dropping lazy dogs, which explode in the air and spray the ground with small, razor-sharp projectiles* (Time).

lov·at (luv′ət), *n.* a brownish-green color mixture often blended with other colors in fabrics. [< *Lovat*, a Scottish proper name]

lu·bra (lü′brə), *n. Australian.* a female aborigine; gin.

M

ma·ha·lo (mä hä′lō), *n. Hawaiian.* thanks.

Ma·phil·in·do (mä fi lin′dō), *n.* **1.** the plan or policy of uniting Malaysia, the Philippines, and Indonesia into a confederation. **2.** Malaysia, the Philippines, and Indonesia regarded as a geographical or political unit.

Medal of Freedom, Presidential Medal of Freedom.

men·e·hu·ne (men′ə hü′nə), *n., pl.* **-ne, -nes.** a legendary Polynesian dwarf or elf who worked only at night, building ponds, roads, etc. [< Hawaiian *menehune*]

Mer·cal·li scale (mer kä′li), a scale for measuring the intensity of an earthquake, ranging from 1 to 12. [< Giuseppe *Mercalli,* an Italian scientist]

mer·i·to·crat·ic (mer′ə tə krat′-ik), *adj.* **1.** having to do with a meritocracy: *a meritocratic society.* **2.** based solely upon intellectual achievement: *Higher education in Britain is in danger of becoming a "meritocratic treadmill"* (London Times).

mes·o·scaph or **mes·o·scaphe** (mes′ə skaf, -skāf; mē′sə-), *n.* an apparatus similar to the bathyscaph, used to explore the middle depths of the ocean: *The smooth-lined mesoscaph . . . may soon be scanning the Gulf Stream* (Science News Letter). [< Greek *mésos* middle + *skáphē* a bowl, tub]

mi·cro·dot (mī′krō dot′), *n.* a microphotograph in the shape of a dot, used in espionage: *A male Russian agent . . . gave Mintkenbaugh a 35-mm. camera, along with a quick course in developing microdots and hiding microfilm* (Time).

mill·age (mil′ij), *n.* a rate of taxation expressed in mills per dollar.

min·i (min′i), *adj., n., pl.* **min·is.** *British.* *-adj.* small for its kind; miniature (usually in compounds such as *minibus, mini-home*): *A waiter serves me with three mini-sandwiches* (Punch). *-n.* a mini-car: *You see him zipping by in the family mini* (London Times). [< *mini*(ature)]

moment of truth, the point in time when a harsh truth must be faced; a moment of direct confrontation with some unpleasant fact or circumstance: *It was a shaking moment of truth for the Government and for the British public, who suddenly received a lightning, unflattering imitation of exactly how solid a risk they looked to the neighbors* (New Yorker).

mul·ti·ver·si·ty (mul′tə vėr′sə ti), *n., pl.* **-ties.** a large educational institution comprising several universities and their related colleges and professional schools: *The Board of Governors, whether of a small liberal arts college or a multiversity, will need . . . persuasiveness if our universities are to grow and change* (Saturday Night). [< *multi-* + (uni)*versity*]

N

native companion (in Australia), brolga.

ne·o·nate (nē′ə nāt), *n.* a newborn baby. [< *neo-* + Latin *nātus* born, past participle of *nāscī* be born; see NATIVE]

New Realism, 1. neorealism, especially in literature: *New Realism . . . has been rated a "cult of squalidity" by some proper Britons* (Time). **2.** any form of neorealistic (as opposed to abstract) art, especially pop art: *The "New Realism" . . . takes as its subject matter the most banal objects and images of commercial culture* (New Yorker).

new town, a planned urban community where people can both live and work, designed especially to relieve the overcrowding of a nearby metropolis.

nob·bler (nob′lər), *n. Australian.* a glass of beer or hard liquor.

non·pro·lif·er·a·tion (non′prō-lif′ə rā′shən), *n.* the regulation of the spread of nuclear weapons among nations, especially by means of an agreement.

nuke (nük), *n. Slang.* **1.** an atomic nucleus: *Stage I involves the firing of an inner "nuke" . . . of U-235 or plutonium* (Bulletin of Atomic Scientists). **2.** a nuclear weapon: *The enemy's temptation to . . . use "nukes" against Taiwan would be discouraged* (Atlantic).

O

OEO (no periods) or **O.E.O.,** Office of Economic Opportunity (an antipoverty agency of the U.S. government, established in 1964).

on-board (on′bôrd′, -bōrd′; ôn′-), *adj.* on or within a vehicle; installed aboard: *The Gemini 5 rendezvous experiment will be the first to use an on-board computer linked with on-board radar* (New York Times).

op (op), *adj.* having to do with optical art: *op artists, an op show; . . . new op paintings and textile designs* (Scientific American). *-n.* optical art: *Opinions vary as to how influential op will be* (New York Times). [< *op* art]

op·to·e·lec·tron·ic (op′tō i lek′-tron′ik, -ē′lek-), *adj.* combining optical and electrical properties; using light and electricity to transmit signals: *an optoelectronic computer.* [< Greek *optós* seen + English *electronic*]

out·port (out′pôrt′, -pōrt′), *n.* **1.** an outlying port: *The union itself is expected to put pressure on the outports* (New York Times). **2.** (in Canada) an isolated fishing village, especially in Newfoundland.

P

par·a·quat (par′ə kwot), *n.* a herbicide activated by photosynthesis upon contact with weeds: *The plough could be replaced by the substance paraquat, which blasts anything green and growing* (Punch). [< *para-*[1] (def. 2) + *quat*(ernary), part of the formula]

pé·tanque (pā tänk′), *n. French.* a game somewhat resembling bowls: *Pétanque is . . . played normally within a span of fifteen to thirty-five feet* (New Yorker).

pi·li·ki·a (pē lē kē′ä), *n. Hawaiian.* trouble; bother.

plas·ti·queur (plas′ti kœr′), *n. French.* a person who throws plastic bombs: *Plastiqueurs have blown up two flats in the next street* (Punch).

plug·o·la (plə gō′lə), *n. U.S. Slang.* undercover payment for mentioning or displaying a product on another sponsor's radio or television program: *. . . the Congressional investigation into the plugola and payola radio scandals* (Harper's).

po-faced (pō′fāst′), *adj. British Informal.* poker-faced: *Several times . . . that rather po-faced aspect of his raises a smile* (Manchester Guardian Weekly).

pos·i·grade (poz′ə grād), *adj. Aerospace.* having positive acceleration; going or thrusting forward: *posigrade motion. The thrust of the small, posigrade rockets . . . gives the spacecraft a gentle separation push away from the booster* (John H. Glenn, Jr.).

Presidential Medal of Freedom, a decoration given by the United States to a civilian, or to a member of the armed forces of a friendly nation.

prime time, the peak hours of television viewing (in the United States, approximately 6 to 11 p.m.): *The network was . . . gambling on soap opera in prime time* (Time).

psy·chot·o·mi·met·ic (sī kot′ō-mi met′ik, -mī-), *adj.* producing a state akin to or symptomatic of psychosis: *They were conducting experiments with LSD and other psychotomimetic drugs* (Harper's). *-n.* a psychotomimetic drug or substance. [< *psychot*(ic) + connective *-o-* + *mimetic*]

R

R & B or **R and B** (no periods), rhythm and blues.

receiver general (in Massachusetts), an elected state official who collects assessments.

re·con (rē′kon), *n. Biology.* the smallest molecular unit of genetic material out of which the larger units, the muton and cistron, are built. [< *rec*(ombination) + *-on,* as in *muton*]

ref·fo (ref′ō), *n. Australian Slang.* a European refugee.

REM (no periods), rapid eye movement (a phenomenon occurring during sleep, thought to be a manifestation of dreaming).

re·strict·ee (ri strik′tē′, -strik′tē), *n.* a person who is restricted to a particular area, such as a ghetto.

re·stud·y (rē stud′i), *n., pl.* **-stud·ies,** *v.t.,* **-stud·ied, -stud·y·ing** *—n.* a new study. *-v.t.* to study anew.

re-up (rē up′), *v.i.,* **-upped, -up·ping.** *U.S. Slang.* to rejoin the army, navy, etc.; reënlist: *More cooks, truck drivers, and other practitioners of "soft skills" actually "re-up" . . . than the services need* (Newsweek).

S

screen pass, *Football.* a forward pass in which the offensive linemen form a protective screen in front of the receiver.

shick·er (shik′ər), *Australian Slang.* *adj.* drunk. *-n.* drunkard. [< Yiddish *shiker* < Hebrew *shikkūr*]

Si·las·tic (sə las′tik), *n. Trademark.* a silicone plastic much used in making artificial parts for damaged organs of the body: *Silastic was the material from which Dr. DeBakey made the artificial ventricle* (London Times).

PRONUNCIATION KEY: hat, āge, cãre, fär; let, ēqual, tėrm; it, īce; hot, ōpen, ôrder; oil, out; cup, pu̇t, rüle, ūse; child; long; thin; ᴛʜen; zh, measure; ə represents a in about, e in taken, i in pencil, o in lemon, u in circus.

silky oak, any of several Australian trees whose wood is used for ornament.

skate·board (skāt′bôrd′, -bōrd′), *n.* a narrow board resembling a surfboard, with roller-skate wheels attached to each end, used for skating. –**skate′board′er,** *n.*

skil·lion (skil′yən), *n. Australian.* a lean-to or shed.

skurf (skėrf), *v.i. Slang.* to ride on a skateboard: *Hundreds of vacationing teen-agers chanting "we want to skurf" wheeled to City Hall yesterday on their skateboards* (Toronto Globe and Mail). [blend of *skate* and *surf*] –**skurf′er,** *n.*

smoodge (smüj), *v.i. Australian.* **1.** to curry favor. **2.** to kiss.

SNCC (no periods) or **S.N.C.C.,** Student Nonviolent Coordinating Committee (an organization formed by Southern Negro students in 1960 to promote Negro civil rights in the South).

sonnet sequence, a series of sonnets by one poet usually having a single theme.

sool (sül), *v.t. Australian.* **1.** to incite (usually, a dog) to attack someone. **2.** to attack or snap at.

space race, the competition between the Soviet Union and the United States for first place in the exploration of outer space.

space·walk (spās′wôk′), *n.* the act of moving or floating while outside an orbiting spacecraft; extravehicular motion or activity.

splash·down (splash′doun′), *n.* the landing of a spacecraft in the ocean after reëntry.

spy·plane (spī′plān′), *n.* a high-altitude aircraft for secret reconnaissance of foreign defense installations by means of aerial photographs and tape recordings of radio and radar emissions.

squat·toc·ra·cy (skwo tok′rə si), *n. Australian.* squatters, especially the socially and politically important sheep ranchers.

stick·y·beak (stik′i bēk′), *n. Australian.* a prying person.

stride piano, *Jazz Slang.* ragtime piano playing consisting of single notes on the first and third beats of the bar and chords on the second and fourth beats. –**stride pianist.**

su·per·cold (sü′pər kōld′), *adj.* **1.** extremely cold: . . . *the eerie world that exists at supercold temperatures two or three degrees Fahrenheit* (Wall Street Journal). **2.** using extremely low temperatures; cryogenic: *Supercold surgery . . . known as cryosurgery, uses extreme cold to replace or supplement traditional methods of surgery in killing and removing diseased tissue* (World Book Year Book).

swing wing, *British.* variable-sweep wing: *When applied to aircraft the terms . . . variable sweep, polymorphism, and swing wings all refer basically to wing mobility* (London Times).

switched-on (swicht′on′), *adj. Slang.* smart; alert; up-to-date; modern: *Preceding the actual bridal gown, it might appeal to a very switched-on bride-to-be* (New York Times).

T

Tan·za·ni·an (tan zə nē′ən), *adj.* of or having to do with the republic of Tanzania (formed in 1964 by the union of Tanganyika and Zanzibar) or its people. –*n.* a native or inhabitant of Tanzania.

tape deck, the mechanical component of a tape recorder, used in high-fidelity systems, computers, etc.: *The simplest playback machine is the tape deck* (Harper's).

teach-in (tēch′in′), *n.* **1.** one of a series of informal, all-night sessions of lectures, debates, and seminars held in the mid-1960's by American college teachers and students to discuss, criticize, or protest against the prevailing American policy on Vietnam. **2.** any similar gathering or forum of teachers and students: *"Does Britain need the young?" was the theme of the discussion during a teach-in on community service . . . at Toynbee Hall, London* (London Times).

ther·o·pod (thir′ə pod), *adj.* of or belonging to a group of carnivorous dinosaurs that walked on their hind legs. –*n.* a theropod dinosaur. [< New Latin *Theropoda* the suborder name < Greek *thēr, thērós* wild beast + *poús, podós* foot]

third world, the world of neutral or nonaligned nations; the countries taking neither side in the cold war between Communist and Western nations.

tilt·me·ter (tilt′mē′tər), *n.* an instrument used by seismologists to detect and measure a tilt in the earth's surface. [< *tilt*[1] + *-meter*]

time-share (tīm′shãr′), *v.*, **-shared, -shar·ing.** –*v.i.* (of a computing system or program) to allocate divisions of the total operating time to two or more functions. –*v.t.* to share the operations of (a time-sharing computer or program).

trans·for·ma·tion·al (trans′fər mā′shə nəl), *adj. Linguistics.* having to do with or using transformations: *Transformational grammar* [assumes] *that language consists of irreducible kernel utterances, plus transformational laws, plus lexicon* (Harper's).

tu·tu (tü′tü), *n. Hawaiian.* grandma; grandpa.

U

UDI (no periods) or **U.D.I.,** the unilateral declaration of independence proclaimed by the British self-governing territory of Southern Rhodesia on November 11, 1965.

UNCTAD (no periods), United Nations Conference on Trade and Development.

unemployment compensation, *U.S.* payment under a system by which eligible workers are guaranteed a small weekly income during a limited period of involuntary unemployment.

unemployment insurance, *U.S.* a Federal insurance program, supported by employer-paid taxes, which provides income for a limited period of time to eligible workers who are involuntarily unemployed.

up·man·ship (up′mən ship), *n. Informal.* one-upmanship: *Upmanship is the art of being one-up on all the others* (London Times).

UV (no periods), **1.** ultrahigh vacuum. **2.** ultraviolet.

V

van·i·to·ry (van′ə tôr′i, -tōr′-), *n., pl.* **-ries. 1.** a bathroom fixture combining a washbasin and dressing table. **2. Vanitory.** a trademark for this fixture. [< *vani*(ty), def. 7 + (lava)*tory*]

-ville, *combining form. U.S. Slang.* in a state of; being in or from: *He's Despairville, see, . . . and he's fed up with humanity* (S.J. Perelman). *I just finished it* [a book] *and all I can say is like War and Peaceville* (Bruce Jay Friedman). [< *-ville,* place name suffix, as in *Nashville, Louisville*]

VISTA (no periods), Volunteers in Service to America (an antipoverty agency of the U.S. government, established in 1964 to send volunteers to work and help in depressed areas of the country).

W

wa·tu·si (wä tü′si), *n., v.,* **-sied, -si·ing.** –*n.* a dance in two-beat rhythm, marked by vigorous, jerky movements of the arms, head, etc. –*v.i.* to dance the watusi.

weird·o (wir′dō), *n. Slang.* a weirdie: *The weirdo in this melodrama* [is] *a young man who kidnaps a girl* (New York Times).

wet suit, a skin-tight rubber suit worn by skin divers, surfers, etc.: *In wintertime he will don a . . . wet suit and go right on surfing* (Peter Bart).

white backlash, a hostile reaction on the part of whites to Negro demands for racial equality: *The removal of* Little Black Sambo *from the schools provoked some local white backlash* (Canadian Forum).

wi·ki·wi·ki (wē′kē wē′kē), *adv. Hawaiian.* quickly.

wog (wog), *n. British Slang.* a native of one of the former British colonies, especially in the Middle East (used in an unfriendly way). [origin uncertain]

X

X-ray star, any of a group of stellar bodies that emit X rays, first observed in 1962: *The brighter of these "X-ray stars" came from a spot in the constellation Scorpius . . . The second X-ray star, only ⅛ as strong, is in the Crab Nebula* (Isaac Asimov).

Y

yé-yé (ye′ye′), *adj. Slang.* of or having to do with a style of teenage dress, such as above-the-knee skirts and ankle-high boots, associated with discothèques, rock'n'roll dancing, etc.: *yé-yé fashions, yé-yé girls.* [< French Slang *yé-yé* < English *yeah, yeah,* refrain used by rock'n'roll singing groups]

Z

zero grazing, *British.* zero pasture.

Section Six

How to Use the Index

This index covers the contents of all editions of THE WORLD BOOK YEAR BOOK from 1963 to 1967. It indexes subjects discussed in the first four sections of each edition, and lists the titles of all new or revised articles from THE WORLD BOOK ENCYCLOPEDIA appearing in the supplement section.

Each index entry is followed by the edition years (in italics) and the page numbers, as:

ADVERTISING, *67*-200, *66*-210, *65*-206, *64*-204, *63*-174

This means that information about advertising begins on the pages indicated for each of the editions.

An index entry that is the title of an article appearing in THE YEAR BOOK is printed in capital letters, as: **AUTOMOBILE.** An entry that is not an article title, but a subject discussed in an article of some other title is printed: **Tires.**

Index

The various "See" and "See also" cross references in the index list are to other entries within the index. Clue words or phrases are used when two or more references to the same subject appear in the same edition of THE YEAR BOOK. These make it easy to locate the material on the page, since they refer to an article title or article subsection in which the reference appears, as:

Air pollution: automobile *66*-236; botany, *67*-247; health, *64*-357; Houston, *67*-366; New York City, *67*-440; *Special Report*, *66*-165.

The indication "*il.*" means that the reference is to an illustration only. An index entry in capital letters followed by "*WBE*" refers to a new or revised WORLD BOOK ENCYCLOPEDIA article, which is printed in the supplement section, as:

RUSSIA: *WBE*, *67*-556

INDEX

A

B

F

G

H

N

O

Q

R

U

V

Acknowledgments

The publishers of the 1967 World Book Year Book gratefully acknowledge the courtesy of the following artists, photographers, publishers, institutions, agencies, and corporations for the illustrations in this volume. Credits should be read from left to right, top to bottom, on their respective pages. All entries marked with an asterisk (*) denote illustrations created exclusively for the World Book Year Book. All maps were created by the World Book Cartographic staff. All charts and diagrams were prepared by Murrie-White and Associates, Inc., Chicago, Ill., unless otherwise noted.

Preface

3 Neal Cochran*

Focus Reports

14 James Hill*
16 Pictorial Parade
18 United Press Int.
20 James Hill*
23-24 United Press Int.
26 James Hill*
28 Wide World
32 James Hill*
34 Wide World
35 A. W. Ambler, NAS
38 James Hill*
40 Wide World
42 United Press Int.
44 James Hill*
47-48 NASA
50 James Hill*
53 E. F. Hoppe*
54 Chicago Association of Commerce and Industry
56 James Hill*
58 United Press Int.
59 Wide World

Special Reports

62 Del Borer, World Book Encyclopedia Science Service, Inc.*
64 NASA
65-66 U.S. Navy
68-69 Globe Photos
71 Globe Photos/U.S. Navy
72-73 J. R. Eyerman
74 U.S. Navy
75 Globe Photos
76 J. R. Eyerman/Globe Photos
77-78 Globe Photos
79 Del Borer, World Book Encyclopedia Science Service, Inc.*
83-96 Paul Peck
97-106 Tor Eigeland*
107 Gioia Nalin*
108-112 Tor Eigeland*
113 Gioia Nalin*
114-116 Tor Eigeland*
118 Cornell Capa, Magnum*
120 Marvin Koner, Black Star/Wide World
122-123 Cornell Capa, Magnum*
124-125 Ko Saw Lwin*
126 Cornell Capa, Magnum*
129-139 E. F. Hoppe*
140-142 U.S. Food and Drug Administration
143-144 E. F. Hoppe*
147 Lee Balterman*
148-149 Fran Ortiz
150 United Press Int./Tony Triolo
152-153 Jay Leviton*
155 Jack Stager, Globe
156 Lee Balterman*
157 Lee Balterman*/*The Milwaukee Journal*
159 Tony Triolo
160 Wide World
162-175 George Roth*

Year on File

200 The Advertising Council
201 Wide World
202-203 Ted Grant
207 Eugene Anthony, *Newsweek*
209 Massey-Ferguson, Inc.
214 *EXPO 67*
216-217 United Press Int.
218 Wide World/William H. Mauldin
221 NASA
224-225 *The Illustrated London News*
226 *Sydney Morning Herald*
227 United Press Int.
229 Wide World
230 William H. Mauldin
231 Pictures of the Year: James Ogata, United Press Int.
232 The Boeing Company/*Newsweek*
239 Pictures of the Year: Warren Winterbottom, Wide World
241 United Press Int.
242 Ed Kelly*
246 Pictures of the Year: Bruce McKim, *The Seattle Times*
250 Keystone
253 Wide World
254-255 Kalium Chemicals Limited
257 Pictorial Parade
258 *EXPO 67*
262 Wide World
266-267 Wide World
268 Eastfoto
270 Wide World
271 Pictorial Parade
275 Pix from Publix/Norris McNamara from Nancy Palmer
276 William H. Mauldin
278 Sovfoto
280-281 Pictures of the Year: Stanley Tretick, © *Look* Magazine
285 Wide World
288-289 Edgar G. Mueller
290 U.S. Bureau of Reclamation
291 Billy Davis
295 Arnold Eagle
297 Wide World/Martha Holmes, *Life* © Time Inc./Wide World
298 Wide World/Wide World/Steve Shapiro, *Life* © Time Inc.

300 Wide World/Wide World/Wide World
301 Inge Morath, Magnum/Wide World/United Press Int.
302 United Press Int.
305 Pictures of the Year: Robert Kotalik, *Chicago Sun-Times*/Wide World
309 Terence Spencer, *Life* © Time Inc.
310 Pictures of the Year: Harry Koundakjian, Wide World
311 Kakuro Ikegami
314-315 The White House, Washington, D.C.
319 Wide World
323 United Press Int.
325 United Press Int./*Chicago Daily News*/ Larry Fried
327 Wide World
329 Radio Corporation of America
332-333 Hubert Le Campion, *Life* © Time Inc.
334 Max Koot, ABC Press Service
336 *EXPO 67*/George Leaven, *Time* Magazine © Time Inc.
337 *Chicago Sun-Times*
338 Henry Grossman, *Life* © Time Inc.
339 *The New York Times*
341 Bob Gomel, *Life* © Time Inc.
345 Elliott Erwitt, Magnum
348 Serge Gautier, L'Humanité
349 E. F. Hoppe*
353 Pictorial Parade
354 United Press Int.
357 Wide World
358 Pix from Publix
359 William H. Mauldin
361 United Press Int.
362 Wide World
364 United Press Int.
366 *Houston Chronicle*
369 Wide World/Pierre Boulat, *Time* Magazine © Time Inc.
370-371 Scheler, *Stern* Magazine
372 United Press Int.
373 Louis Kraar, *Time* Magazine © Time Inc.
375 Westinghouse Electric Corporation
376 Wide World
380-381 Pictorial Parade
382 Wide World
384 Wide World
385 Wide World/William H. Mauldin
388 United Press Int.
390 Phil MacMullan, *Newsweek*
396-397 Richard Avedon
398 Burt Glinn, Magnum
399 Bernard Gotfryd, *Newsweek*
406 *Chicago Tribune*/United Press Int.
408-409 United Press Int.
413 United Press Int.
415 Wide World
416 E. F. Hoppe*/*Chicago Sun-Times*
417 David Rubinger, *Life* © Time Inc.
419 United Press Int.
421 United Press Int.
423 United Press Int.
424-425 20th Century Fox Film Corporation
427 Ezra Stoller
428-429 Wide World
430 *The New York Times*
432 Lee B. Johnson, *Life* © Time Inc.
433 Wide World
434 *U.S. News & World Report*
436 William H. Mauldin
438 *U.S. News & World Report*
442 William H. Mauldin
443 Flip Schulke, *Life* © Time Inc.
445 Morton R. Engelberg, Office of Economic Opportunity/James Foote, Office of Economic Opportunity
446-447 *The Beanery* by Edward Kienholz, courtesy The Kliener Foundation, Beverly Hills, Calif.
448 Mr. and Mrs. Barnet Hodes Collection, Chicago, Ill./United Press Int.
451 Pictures of the Year: John Adams Orris, *The New York Times*
452 United Press Int.
453 Wide World
454 United Press Int.
455 United Press Int.
457 United Press Int.
459 Pictures of the Year: Tom Colburn, *Houston Chronicle*/Anscochrome of the Year: Mrs. Ann Zaiser/Newspaper National Snapshot Award: William T. Hubbard/Pictures of the Year: Larry Burrows, *Life* © Time Inc.
461 Elliott Erwitt, Magnum
463 Wide World
466-467 Pictures of the Year: Bruce Baumann, *The Sunday Courier and Press*, Evansville, Ind.
468-469 Pictures of the Year: Gordon Harding, *The Washington Star*
471 Wide World
473 World Council of Churches
475 Chicago Historical Society
477 Pictures of the Year: Bill Eppridge, *Life* © Time Inc.
481 Wide World
484 United Press Int.
487 Sovfoto
488 Sovfoto
490 Wide World
492 United Press Int.
494 *Chicago Daily News*
497 Pictorial Parade
498 Press Association
500-501 Wide World
500 Wide World
502-503 NASA
504 NASA
507 NASA
508 NASA/NASA
509 Wide World
510 Ed Greer
513 The Kentucky Company
515 Wide World
516 Wide World
518 CBS Television
520 Bill Bridges
521 United Press Int.
522-523 Mark Kauffman, *Life* © Time Inc.
524 United Press Int.
530 Wide World
532 Wide World
534 Pix from Publix
536 William H. Mauldin
541 U.S. Department of Defense
542 Pictures of the Year: Larry Burrows, *Life* © Time Inc.
543 Pix from Publix
544-545 Wide World
546 Pictures of the Year: John T. Wheeler, Wide World/William H. Mauldin
548 Fred Schnell, *Life* © Time Inc.
551 Girl Scouts of the U.S.A.
553 Wide World
554 Pictorial Parade

A Preview Of 1967

January

1-Dec. 31 Canadian Confederation Centennial.
1-Dec. 31 International Tourist Year.
1-Dec. 31 Johann Strauss Waltz Year (Austria).
1-31 March of Dimes.
United Cerebral Palsy Month.
1 New Year's Day.
1-8 Universal Week of Prayer.
6 Epiphany, Twelfth Day after Christmas.
10 90th Congress of U.S. Opens first session in Washington, D.C.
15 World Religion Day.
22-28 National Junior Achievement Week.
22-29 National YMCA Week.
29-Feb. 5 Youth Week.
30 Franklin D. Roosevelt Day (Ky., W.Va.).

February

1-28 American Heart Month.
American History Month.
American Music Month.
1 National Freedom Day.
2 Candlemas Day.
Ground-Hog Day.
5-11 National Children's Dental Health Week.
7 Shrove Tuesday: *Mardi Gras of the French; Pancake Day of the English;* and *Carnival of the Italians.*
7-13 Boy Scout Week.
8 Ash Wednesday.
9 Chinese New Year.
12 Abraham Lincoln's Birthday.
12-18 National Crime Prevention Week.
12-19 Negro History Week.
14 Saint Valentine's Day.
18-25 Future Farmers of America Week.
19-25 Catholic Book Week.
19-26 Brotherhood Week.
20-Mar. 26 Easter Seal Campaign.
22 George Washington's Birthday.

March

1-31 American Red Cross Month.
Children's Art Month.
1 Nebraska Centennial, admitted to Union as 37th state in 1867.
Saint David's Day, patron saint of Wales.
7 National Teachers Day.
12-18 Girl Scout Week.
17 Saint Patrick's Day.
19 Palm Sunday.
19-25 Camp Fire Girls Birthday Week.
National Wildlife Week.
21 First Day of Spring (2:37 A.M., E.S.T.).
24 Good Friday.
25 Annunciation Day.
Arturo Toscanini Centennial.
26 Easter Sunday.
Purim, Jewish Festival of Lots.
27-31 Catholic Library Association Conference, Cleveland, Ohio.
30 Alaska Purchase Centennial. U.S. and Russia signed Treaty of Cession in 1867.

April

1-30 Cancer Control Month.
Freedom Shrine Month.
National Hobby Month.
Teaching Career Month.
1 April Fools' Day.
2-8 National Boys' Club Week.
7 World Health Day.
9 Bataan Day (Philippines).
Sir Winston Churchill Day (U.S.).
13 Thomas Jefferson's Birthday.
14 Pan American Day.
16-22 National Garden Week.
National Library Week.
National YWCA Week.
23-29 Canada-U.S. Goodwill Week.
Youth Temperance Education Week.
24 Total Eclipse of Moon, visible from Pacific Ocean and eastern Asia.
25-May 2 Passover.
26 Confederate Memorial Day (Ala., Fla. Ga., and Miss.).
28-Oct. 27 Canadian Universal and International Exhibition of 1967 (Expo 67), Montreal.
30 Daylight Saving Begins in many U.S. communities.
Rogation Sunday.
Rural Life Sunday.

May

1 May Day.
Law Day.
Loyalty Day.
1-7 Mental Health Week.
4 Ascension Day.
6 Kentucky Derby, Louisville, Ky.
7-13 Be Kind to Animals Week.
National Hospital Week.
7-14 National Family Week.
National Music Week.
8 V-E Day.
9 Partial Eclipse of Sun, visible in U.S.
10 Confederate Memorial Day (N.C., S.C.).
14 Mother's Day.
Pentecost, or Whitsunday.
14-20 National Girls Club Week.
14-June 18 Multiple Sclerosis Hope Chest Campaign.
20 Armed Forces Day.
20-June 18 Music Festival, Vienna, Austria.
21 Trinity Sunday.
21-27 Girl Guard Anniversary Week.
21-28 National Salvation Army Week.
21-July 31 Opera Festival, Glyndebourne, England.
22 Victoria Day and Queen's Birthday, official celebration in Canada.
25-June 11 International Grieg Festival, Bergen, Norway.
27-Sept. 10 Alaska Centennial Exposition, Fairbanks.
30 Memorial (Decoration) Day.
Confederate Memorial Day (Va.).
500-Mile Speedway Race, Indianapolis.
31-June 14 Festival Casals, San Juan.

June

1 Kentucky 175th Anniversary, admitted to Union as 15th state in 1792.
3 Confederate Memorial Day (Ky., La., Tenn.).
Jefferson Davis' Birthday.
8-Oct. 15 Shakespearean Festival, Stratford, Ontario.
10 Queen Elizabeth II's Birthday, official celebration, London, England.
11 Children's Sunday.
12-18 National Little League Baseball Week.
14 Flag Day (U.S.).
14-15 Shabuot, Jewish Feast of Weeks.

January

Sun	Mon	Tue	Wed	Thu	Fri	Sat
1	2	3	4	5	6	7
8	9	10	11	12	13	14
15	16	17	18	19	20	21
22	23	24	25	26	27	28
29	30	31				

February

Sun	Mon	Tue	Wed	Thu	Fri	Sat
			1	2	3	4
5	6	7	8	9	10	11
12	13	14	15	16	17	18
19	20	21	22	23	24	25
26	27	28				

March

Sun	Mon	Tue	Wed	Thu	Fri	Sat
			1	2	3	4
5	6	7	8	9	10	11
12	13	14	15	16	17	18
19	20	21	22	23	24	25
26	27	28	29	30	31	

April

Sun	Mon	Tue	Wed	Thu	Fri	Sat
						1
2	3	4	5	6	7	8
9	10	11	12	13	14	15
16	17	18	19	20	21	22
23/30	24	25	26	27	28	29

May

Sun	Mon	Tue	Wed	Thu	Fri	Sat
	1	2	3	4	5	6
7	8	9	10	11	12	13
14	15	16	17	18	19	20
21	22	23	24	25	26	27
28	29	30	31			

June

Sun	Mon	Tue	Wed	Thu	Fri	Sat
				1	2	3
4	5	6	7	8	9	10
11	12	13	14	15	16	17
18	19	20	21	22	23	24
25	26	27	28	29	30	

A Preview Of 1967

July

Sun	Mon	Tue	Wed	Thu	Fri	Sat
						1
2	3	4	5	6	7	8
9	10	11	12	13	14	15
16	17	18	19	20	21	22
23/30	24/31	25	26	27	28	29

August

Sun	Mon	Tue	Wed	Thu	Fri	Sat
		1	2	3	4	5
6	7	8	9	10	11	12
13	14	15	16	17	18	19
20	21	22	23	24	25	26
27	28	29	30	31		

September

Sun	Mon	Tue	Wed	Thu	Fri	Sat
					1	2
3	4	5	6	7	8	9
10	11	12	13	14	15	16
17	18	19	20	21	22	23
24	25	26	27	28	29	30

October

Sun	Mon	Tue	Wed	Thu	Fri	Sat
1	2	3	4	5	6	7
8	9	10	11	12	13	14
15	16	17	18	19	20	21
22	23	24	25	26	27	28
29	30	31				

November

Sun	Mon	Tue	Wed	Thu	Fri	Sat
			1	2	3	4
5	6	7	8	9	10	11
12	13	14	15	16	17	18
19	20	21	22	23	24	25
26	27	28	29	30		

December

Sun	Mon	Tue	Wed	Thu	Fri	Sat
					1	2
3	4	5	6	7	8	9
10	11	12	13	14	15	16
17	18	19	20	21	22	23
24/31	25	26	27	28	29	30

17-July 1 Mozart Music Festival, Würzburg, West Germany.
18 Father's Day.
21 First Day of Summer (9:23 P.M., E.S.T.).
25-July 1 American Library Association Convention, San Francisco, Calif.
25-Aug. 20 National Music Camp, Interlochen, Mich.
26-July 8 All-England Lawn Tennis Championships, Wimbledon, England.
29 Feast of Saints Peter and Paul.

July

1-31 National Arts and Crafts Month.
1 Dominion Day (Canada).
1-Aug. 31 American Dance Festival, New London, Conn.
2-8 National Safe Boating Week.
4 Independence Day (U.S.).
American Philippine Friendship Day (Philippines).
4-9 International Musical Eisteddfod, Llangollen, Wales.
11 John Quincy Adams Bicentennial. Sixth President of the United States born in 1767.
12 Henry David Thoreau Sesquicentennial.
14 Bastille Day (France).
16-22 Captive Nations Week.
21-Aug. 24 Richard Wagner Festival, Bayreuth, West Germany.
22-Aug. 7 Pan American Games, Winnipeg, Manitoba.
22-Sept. 10 Oregon Shakespearean Festival, Ashland.
23-29 National Farm Safety Week.
26-Aug. 31 International Music and Drama Festival, Salzburg, Austria.

August

1-9 Boy Scouts of America Jamboree, Ottawa, Canada.
6 Feast of the Transfiguration.
10-12 World Judo Championships, Salt Lake City, Utah.
14 Atlantic Charter Day.
V-J Day (original).
15 Feast of the Assumption.
15-31 Royal Danish Ballet and Music Festival, Copenhagen, Denmark.
20-Sept. 9 International Festival of Music and Drama, Edinburgh, Scotland.
28-Sept. 3 World Water Ski Championships, Sherbrooke, Quebec.

September

1-30 Youth Month.
2 V-J Day (official).
4 Labor Day.
6-13 National Child Safety Week.
8-20 Opera, Concerts, Ballet, and Drama Festival, Stockholm, Sweden.
11-Dec. 15 Boy Scouts of America Fall Roundup.
12 America's Cup Yacht Race, Newport, R.I.
17 Citizenship Day.
Constitution Day.
17-30 American Youth Enrollment.
23 First Day of Autumn (12:38 P.M., E.S.T.).
Kiwanis Kids' Day.
24 National Gold Star Mothers Day.
24-30 Christian Education Week.
24-Oct. 1 National Sunday School Week.
29-Oct. 24 Synod of Roman Catholic Bishops, Rome, Italy.

October

1-31 National Science Youth Month.
1-7 National Employ the Physically Handicapped Week.
National 4-H Club Week.
2 Child Health Day.
2-15 Dublin Theatre Festival, Ireland.
5-6 Rosh Hashanah, Jewish New Year.
8-14 Fire Prevention Week.
National Y-Teen Roll Call Week.
9 Thanksgiving (Canada).
11-17 Roman Catholic World Congress of the Apostolate of the Laity, Rome, Italy.
12 Columbus Day, 475th anniversary of the discovery of America.
14 National Newspaper Carrier Boy Day.
14-15 Yom Kippur, Jewish Day of Atonement.
18 Total Eclipse of Moon, visible in U.S.
19 National Day of Prayer.
21 English Thanksgiving Day.
24 United Nations Day.
29 Daylight Saving Ends in many U.S. communities.
World Temperance Day.
29-Nov. 4 National Children's Book Week.
31 Halloween, or All Hallow's Eve.
Protestant Reformation 450th Anniversary.

November

1-30 March for Muscular Dystrophy Month.
1 All Saints' Day.
2 All-Souls' Day.
Total Eclipse of Sun, visible in South Atlantic Ocean near Antarctic Circle.
7 General Election Day (U.S.).
5-11 American Education Week.
11 Remembrance Day (Canada).
Veterans Day (U.S.).
12-18 YMCA-YWCA World Fellowship Week.
13-Dec. 31 Christmas Seal Campaign.
17-23 National Farm-City Week.
17-26 International Livestock Exposition, Chicago.
19-25 Latin America Week.
23 Thanksgiving Day (U.S.).
23-Dec. 25 World-Wide Bible Reading.
24-Dec. 24 Jewish Book Month.
26-Dec. 1 National 4-H Club Congress, Chicago.

December

2 Pan American Health Day.
3 First Sunday in Advent.
3-10 Universal Bible Week.
6 Feast of Saint Nicholas, patron saint of children and sailors.
7 Twenty-Sixth Anniversary of Pearl Harbor Attack by Japanese.
8 Feast of the Immaculate Conception.
10 Mississippi Sesquicentennial, admitted to Union as 20th state in 1817.
Nobel Prizes Presentations in Stockholm, Sweden, and Oslo, Norway
Second Sunday in Advent.
United Nations Human Rights Day.
15 Bill of Rights Day (U.S.).
17 Third Sunday in Advent.
22 First Day of Winter (8:17 A.M., E.S.T.).
24 Fourth Sunday in Advent.
25 Christmas Day.
Feast of the Nativity.
27-Jan. 2, 1968 Hanukkah, Jewish Feast of Lights.
31 New Year's Eve.